Anonymous

A New and Complete Pronouncing Bible Dictionary

containing more Scriptural words than any other work of the kind

Anonymous

A New and Complete Pronouncing Bible Dictionary
containing more Scriptural words than any other work of the kind

ISBN/EAN: 9783337100254

Printed in Europe, USA, Canada, Australia, Japan

Cover: Foto ©Lupo / pixelio.de

More available books at **www.hansebooks.com**

PRONOUNCING
BIBLE DICTIONARY,

CONTAINING

MORE SCRIPTURAL WORDS THAN ANY OTHER WORK OF THE KIND,

COMPILED FROM THE MOST AUTHENTIC SOURCES, DESIGNED TO PROMOTE A BETTER UNDERSTANDING OF THE

HOLY BIBLE,

ILLUSTRATED WITH NEARLY FOUR HUNDRED FINE ENGRAVINGS:

ALSO,

A COMPLETE CONCORDANCE

OF THE

OLD AND NEW TESTAMENTS.

PHILADELPHIA
WILLIAM W. HARDING,
630 CHESTNUT STREET.
1873.

Entered according to Act of Congress, in the year 1872, by WILLIAM W. HARDING, in the Office of the Librarian of Congress, at Washington.

PRONOUNCING
BIBLE DICTIONARY.

A

AAR'ON. Eldest son of Amram and Jochebed, brother of Moses and Miriam, of the tribe of Levi, and the first high priest of the Jews (Ex. i.). Born, B. C., 1574. His wife was Elizabeth, of the tribe of Judah, by whom he had four sons, Nadab, Abihu, Eleazer and Ithamar (vi.). Moses made him Priest and Prophet of Israel, and his assistant in

AARON'S TOMB, MOUNT HOR.

the great work of liberating the nation from Egypt (vi.). While Moses was engaged in the mount (forty days), Aaron made a calf of gold, in imitation of the Apis (bull) of Egypt (xxxii.). He was jealous of the power of Moses, and joined Miriam in murmurs against him; but when he saw his sister's leprosy he repented and begged forgiveness for both (Num. xii.). He also showed a want of faith in God at Meribah (xx.), and as a punishment was denied entrance into Canaan, and died at Mosera, on Mt. Hor, aged 123 (Ex. xx.). A tomb called Aaron's is shown on a summit of Mr. Hor.

AAR'ONITES. Priests, descendants of Aaron (1 Chr. xii. 27). An important family in David's time.

ĀB (*father*). Absalom, *makes peace*; Abner, *causes light*. ABBA, father, as used by Jesus (Mark

ABEL

xiv. 36), and Paul (Rom. viii. 15; Gal. iv. 6).—2. The name of the fifth (sacred) month, as used after the captivity.

ABAD'DON (*destruction*, or *the place of the dead*). ASMODEUS in the Apocrypha; APOLYON, Rev. ix. 11; Job xxvi. 6 (destruction).

ABADĪ'AS. Obadiah, son of Jehiel (1 Esd. viii. 35).

ABĀG'THA (*father or cause of fortune*). An officer of the presence before King Ahasuerus (Esth. i. 10).

ABĀ'NA (*perennial*). Amana. The main river of Damascus, now called Barada. It has several channels, and irrigates the whole city and suburbs. Rises in Anti-Lebanon, near Zebedany (Abila) and a tributary at Ain-Fijy), 23 miles N. W. of Damascus, and 2400 feet higher. It empties into the lake and marsh of Ateibeh, 15 miles E. of the city. See 2 K. v. 12.

AB'ARIM (*beyond*). A mountain range east of the Dead Sea and the Jordan. Nebo is its highest peak, and Pisgah is the top of Nebo. Average height 2000 to 4000 feet.

AB'BA. Father. The ancient Aramaic word. The peculiar term for the father-God used by Jesus.

AB'DA. Father of Adoniram (1 K. iv. 6).—2. Son of Shammua (Neh. xi. 17) called Obadiah in 1 Chr. ix. 16.

AB'DEEL. Father of Shelemiah (Jer. xxxvi. 26).

AB'DI. Ancestor of Ethan the singer (1 Chr. vi. 44).—2. Father of Kish (2 Chr. xxix. 12).—3. One of the sons of Elam (Ezr. x. 26).

ABDI'AS. Obadiah the prophet, in 2 Esd. i. 39.

AB'DIEL (*servant of God*), Abdallah in Arabic. Son of Guni (1 Chr. v. 15). The name is noted for its use by Milton in his Paradise Lost, for an angel,—"Among the faithless, faithful only he."

AB'DON (*servile*). BEDAN in 1 Sam. ii. 11. A judge of Israel.—2. Son of Shishak.—3. Eldest son of Jehiel, son of Gibeon.—4. Son of Micah, also called Achbor.—Had forty sons and thirty nephews.

ABED'NEGO (*servant of Nego*—that is, *Mercury the god*). The name given by the Chaldeans to Daniel's companion Azariah (Dan. i. 3).

A'BEL (*weakness, breath*). In Hebrew HEBEL.

1

Second son of Adam; killed by his brother Cain (Gen. iv).

A'BEL (*meadow*). Several places so named.—1. A'BEL-BETH-MAA'CHAH, or ABEL-MAIM; a strong city on the slope of Mt. Hermon, near the Jordan, where Joab besieged Sheba (2 Sam. xx. 14).—2. A'BEL-KERA-MIM (*of the vineyards*). Near Rabbath, and even now famous for its wines (Judg. xi. 33).—3. A'BEL-MEHO-LAH (*of dancing*). South of Bethshan near Jordan. The birth-place of Elisha

THE SO-CALLED TOMB OF ABSALOM.

(1 K. xix. 16), and noted for Gibeon's victory over Midian (Judg. vii. 22).—4. ABEL-MIZ-RAIM (*of the Egypts*). Near Hebron, where Joseph, his brethren, and the Egyptians mourned for Jacob (Gen. l. 11). Lost.—5. ABEL-SHITTIM (*of the acacias*). In Moab, near the head of the Dead Sea. The last camping ground of the Exodus (Num. xxxiii. 49). Acacia trees are now found wherever there is water in that region.

A'BEZ. Town in Issachar (Josh. xix. 20). Now Tubas, near Shunem.

A'BI (*father*). Abijah. Mother of King Hezekiah (2 K. xviii. 2).

ABI'AH (*Jehovah his father*). Son of Becher (1 Chr. vii. 8).—2. Wife of Hezron (1 Chr. ii. 24).—3. Son of Samuel, and a judge in Beersheba (1 Sam. viii. 2).—4. Mother of Hezekiah. Abi.—5. Son of Rehoboam (1 Chr. iii. 10).—6. Descendant of Eleazar. See ABIJAH.

ABI'ASAPH (*the gatherer*). Head of a family of Kohathites (Ex. vi. 24). Noted persons of this family were Samuel the prophet, and Elkanah his father, and Heman the singer. The family lived in Mount Ephraim (1 Sam. i).

ABI'ATHAR (*abundance*). The only son of Ahimelech the priest, who escaped Saul's massacre at Nod (1 Sam. xxii.), and who joined David in his flight, and was afterwards priest with Zadok in David's reign. "Solomon thrust out Abiathar from being priest unto the Lord," fulfilling the doom of Eli's house.

ABI'DAH (*wise*). Grandson of Abraham by Keturah (Gen xxv. 4; 1 Chr. i. 33).

AB'IDEN (*father of the judge*). Chief in Benjamin at the Exodus (Num. i. 2).

A'BIEL. Abi'el (*strong*). Father of Kish, grandfather of Saul and Abner.—2. One of David's 30 "mighty men."

ABIE'ZER (*helper*). Eldest son of Gilead (Josh. xvii. 2), formerly of the east of Jordan, later of Ophrah, a lost place, which was near the south border of Esdraelon. Gideon was of this family (Judg. vi. 31).—2. One of David's "mighty men." ABIEZRITES, the family title.

AB'IGAIL (*maker of joy*). Nabal's beautiful wife, who saved her husband from David's anger—Nabal having died ten days after, David made her his wife (1 Sam. xxvi. 14).—2. A sister of David, mother of Amasa.

ABIHA'IL (*mighty*). Father of Zuriel, chief of the Merari (Num. iii. 35).—2. Abishur's wife (1 Chr. ii. 29).—3. Son of Huri of Gad (1 Chr. v. 14).—4. Rehoboam's wife (2 Chr. xi. 18), a descendant of Eliab, David's elder brother.—5. Father of Esther, and uncle of Mordecai (Esth. ii. 15).

ABI'HU (*God is father*). Second son of Aaron by Elizabeth. He was consecrated, with his father and brothers, for the ministry. Abihu and his brother Nadab lost their lives for an error in the altar service, while intoxicated (?).

ABI'JAH (*father God.*) A son of Samuel, whose misconduct gave the Israelites the occasion to demand a change of government to a monarchy. (1 Sam. viii. 1).—2. Son and successor of Rehoboam (B. C. 958). He followed the idolatries of his father (1 K. xiv. 23).

ABI'LA, ABILE'NE (*grassy meadow*). On the E. slope of Mt. Hermon. Mentioned by Josephus (Ant. 14, 13, 3). The name is derived from Abel, the first martyr (by tradition). ABILA was the capital city of the district, under the Romans, and its ruins are now seen on the banks of the Barada ravine, 12 miles N. W. of Damascus. The district is well watered by the Abana, and by many other streams from Anti-Lebanon; is fertile and affords good pasture. When Luke wrote (iii. 1) the tetrarchy was divided between Lysanias and Philip. There is a coin bearing the name and title of Lysanias of Abilene.

ABRAHAM GIVING LOT HIS CHOICE OF COUNTRY.

ABIM'AEL (*father of Mael*). Of Joktan (Gen x. 28). A supposed trace of the name is in Mali, a town in Arabia (the Minæans).

ABIM'ELECH (*father-king*). A title of the kings of Philistia.—1. King of Gerar in the time of Abraham, B. C. 1898 (Gen. xx.). The kings of those days had the right (or power) of choosing the fairest unmarried women for themselves (Gen. xii. ; Esther ii. 3).—2. King of Gerar in Isaac's time, B.

C. 1804 (Gen. xxvi).—3. Son of Gideon, and king of Shechem (Judg. ix.). He was the first who attempted to make himself a king in Israel.

ABIN'ADAB (*princely*). A Levite of Kirjathaim, in whose house the ark "rested" for 20 years (1 Sam. vii. 1).—2. Second son of Jesse (1 Sam. xvi. 8).—3. Son of Saul, killed on Mt. Gilboa (1 Sam. xxxi. 2).—4. Father of one of Solomon's cabinet officers (1 K. iv. 11).

AB'INER. Hebrew form of ABNER.

ABIN'OAM (*gracious*). Barak's father (Judg. iv. 6).

ABI'RAM (*high*). Reubenite and conspirator. See KORAH—2. Eldest son of Hiel, who died because his father undertook to rebuild Jericho (1 K. xvi.; Josh. vi.).

ABISE'I. Son of Phinehas (2 Esd. i. 2).

AB'ISHAG (*cause of error*). The beautiful Shunemite wife of David in his old age.

ABISH'AI (*gift-maker*). Son of David's sister Zeruiah, brother of Joab, and one of David's chief and best officers.

ABISH'ALOM (*peaceful*). Father of Maachah, wife of Rehoboam and mother of Abijah (1 K. xv. 2). Same as Absalom.

ABISHU'A (*of happiness*). Son of Bela (1 Chr. viii. 4).—2. Son of Phinehas, father of Bukki (1 Chr. vi. 4). High-priest after Phinehas and before Eli. Josepos, in Josephus (Ant. 8, 1, 3).

AB'ISHUR (*upright*). Son of Shammai (1 Chr. ii. 28).

AB'ISUM. Son of Phinehas (1 Esd. viii. 2).

ABI'TAL (*protection*). Wife of David (2 Sam. iii. 4).

ABI'TUB (*goodness*). Son of Shaharaim by Hushim (1 Chr. viii. 2).

ABI'UD. Grandson of Zerubbabel by Shelomith (Matt. i. 13).

AB'NER (*light-maker*). Cousin of Saul and commander-in-chief of his army. After Saul's death, he made Ishbosheth, Saul's son, king, but betrayed him to David, and was killed by the friends of Asahel, *in blood revenge* (Num. xxv. 19). David mourned his untimely loss, following his bier.

ABOMINA'TION. Any thing or custom detested or disliked for religious reasons. The Egyptians would not eat with any foreign people, or eat any thing touched by them; and the Hebrews adopted a similar rule. The ABOMINATION OF DESOLATION (Matt. xxiv. 15; Dan. ix. 27), is a reference to an idol worship (of images) on or near the sacred altar on Moriah. See ANTIOCHUS EPIPHANES.

A'BRAHAM (*father of a multitude*). First named ABRAM (*of elevation*). His name was changed, and he received from God the PROMISE of the blessing to all nations in his posterity, when he was 99 years old. Son of TERAH, born in UR, "of the Chaldees," B. C. 1996; had two elder brothers, HARAN and NAHOR, and a half sister, SARAH, (Iscah), who was his wife and the mother of Isaac. The *spiritual* element in the life of Abraham is the chief topic in the Bible narrative, very few incidents of his natural life being recorded. He was

ABRAHAM'S OAK, NEAR HEBRON.

60 when his father's family left Ur and went to Haran (where Terah died, aged 215), and 75 when the promise was first made, when, as directed, he entered Canaan, and fixed his camp under a sacred oak near Shechem, where he built an altar and worshiped God, receiving a promise of the inheritance of the land by his descendants.

Abraham is the first recorded worshiper of the one true God. The promise made to him was two-fold—temporal and spiritual: that his descendants should be many and prosperous, and that by him all the families of the earth should be blessed. The promise has been fulfilled in both ways: his descendants, both Jews and Arabs, have been and are now countless, and the spiritual blessings, by the rapid distribution of the Bible through the world, are reaching all the "families."

Besides Sarah he had a wife named KETURAH, who bore him several sons; and also a *handmaid*, Hagar, whose son, Ishmael, was the head of a great family (see ISHMAEL).

Before Isaac was born, Lot, his nephew, was regarded as his heir, and lived with him. He built an

altar between Bethel and Hai. From here he went south "going and pulling up" his tent-pins, towards Beersheba, whence a famine drove him into Egypt.

Pharaoh hearing of the beauty of Sarai, according to the kingly privilege, took her into his family, but soon returned her to Abraham with presents— "a blessing" of cattle and servants, so that when Abram returned into Canaan he was much richer in cattle, silver and gold. Lot had been with him, and again they camped near Bethel.

Their cattle having increased to a great number, and contentions among their servants arising, Abram and Lot separated, one choosing the plains of Jericho and the other the hills of Judea. After this time the promise was again repeated; and Abram pitched his tent in the oak grove near Mamre, where he built another altar.

He is first called THE HEBREW on the rescue of his nephew Lot from Chedorlaomer; but his language is supposed to have been Chaldaic, rather than the Hebrew of the Old Testament.

and the destruction of the cities of the plain announced, Abraham discovered that he "had entertained angels unawares." He begged to save his nephew Lot and his family, and the next morning, when offering the daily sacrifice, as he saw the ascending smoke from the plain, he probably felt sure of Lot's safety.

During the next few months he practiced the same deception on the Abimelech of Gerar that he had 23 years before on the Pharoah of Egypt. The king was warned of his danger in a dream, and dismissed Sarah with presents.

Isaac was born B. C. 1896, and Ishmael (with his mother) was dismissed at the time Isaac was weaned (at 3 years), because Ishmael mocked at the child (probably offered pretended worship to the child of the promise).

Isaac was 25 when he was laid on the altar, and saved from burning by the angel's voice, Abraham's faith having proved true. His mother died at Hebron 12 years after, at the age of 127, and was

HEBRON.

At this time he could arm 318 of his *trained servants*, showing that his family must have been very large. The Bedawins of Syria are now exact representatives of the ancient patriarch, in their manner of living in tents, by keeping flocks, in habits and religion, and in being ready on the shortest notice to make a raid for defence or reprisal. At Mamre his faith was made stronger by having the promise once more repeated, and by the prophesy of the bondage in Egypt, with the deliverance.

Ishmael was born of Hagar when Abram was 85 years old, and Sarah 75, and was to have been considered a son of Sarai, but the childless woman could not restrain her envy and jealously of the favored mother Hagar. When Abram was 99 the promise was renewed, a distinction being made— of *temporal* blessings for Ishmael and *spiritual* for Isaac who was promised to Sarai. Abram's name was changed to Abraham and his wife's to Sarah, and the covenant of circumcision was renewed to all the family and servants.

A few days after he entertained "three men," who appeared at his tent door in the dress and manner of the natives. This is one of the most beautiful instances on record of ancient customs. The patriarch and his wife, with their own hands, prepared refreshments, and stood by while their guests ate. Travelers in Syria meet with such attentions now among Abraham's descendants. When the promise of a son to Sarah was renewed,

buried in Machpelah, which Abraham bought of the sons of Heth. This legal conveyance of land is the oldest on record.

Abraham sent Eliezer to renew family ties with his family in Haran, and get a wife for Isaac, when that beautiful and touching incident of "Rebekah at the Well" occurred. This brilliant picture includes all the requisites of a perfect marriage— the sanction of parents, favor of God, domestic habits of the wife, her beauty, modest consent, kindness, and her successful hold on her husband's love even while living in the same tent with her mother-in-law.

Abraham's descendants occupy the land from Egypt to the Euphrates, besides those that are "scattered and peeled" all over the world.

He died aged 175, and was buried in the cave of Machpelah by his sons Isaac and Ishmael. To this day he is called the "friend of God," and is reverenced alike, as the Father of the Faithful by Jew, Mohammedan and Christian.

ABRAHAM'S BOSOM. Meaning a place of peace, repose and happiness. See LORD'S SUPPER.

ABRO'NAH (*passage*). Station in the desert near Eziongeber.

ABRO'NAS. Torrent near Cilicia, perhaps NAHR-ABRAIM, the ancient Adonis. Arbonai in Judg. ii. 24.

AB'SALOM (*peacemaker*). Third son of David, only son of his mother, Maachah, daughter of Tal-

mai, king of Geshur, born at Hebron. He is described as a very handsome man, having a very heavy head of hair. Absalom killed his half-brother, Amnon, for an outrage on his sister Tamar, and fled for security to his grandfather, king Talmai, where he stayed 3 years. Joab, by the help of a talented woman of Tekoah, induced David to pardon Absalom and recall him, but kept him two years longer out of his presence. By the death of Amnon, and it may be of Chileab also, Absalom was the oldest son of the king living, and he was ambitious for the throne, plotted for the place of power, "stole the hearts of the people" by flatteries and promises, and proclaimed himself king at Hebron. His father, David, was obliged to fly to Mahanaim, and Absalom took possession of Jerusalem. The crafty Hushai, whom David sent to advise and assist Ahithophel in counseling Absalom, gained time for the true king, and the forces of Absalom were defeated in the wood of Ephraim, and Absalom himself, having entangled his hair in a tree, was killed by Joab, David's general, and buried under a heap of loose stones as a mark of contempt. David waited in the gate of Mahanaim for the news of the battle, and mourned bitterly when he knew his son was dead.

Absalom raised a pillar "in his lifetime," in the king's dale, but the pillar and its place have disappeared, leaving no trace. The monument called Absalom's tomb, in the Kidron valley, is a modern structure, nearly all cut from the solid rock, and on a side hill, not in a dale.

AB'SALON. Ambassador to Lysias (2 Macc. xi. 17.)

ABŪ BUS. Father of Ptolemeus, son-in-law of simon Maccabeus (1 Macc. xvi. 11).

AC'CAD. In Shinar, built by Nimrod. *Akkerkoof* (Arabic name) is 9 miles E. of the Tigris. A ruined brick mound 400 feet around, 125 high, cemented by bitumen, and divided into layers of 12 to 20 feet by reeds, and remains of canals, reservoirs, and other works, show the size and importance of the ancient city.

AC CHŌ. ACRE. (*hot sand?*). PTOLEMAIS. St.

ACRE—ANCIENT ACCHO OR PTOLEMAIS.

John D'Acre. Seaport 8 miles north of Carmel, by the bay of Acre. The ancient port is filling with sand, and large ships must land at Hepha, near Carmel. The plain of Acre is 6 miles wide, to the hills of Galilee, and is one of the most fertile in Palestine. It was given to Asher by Joshua, but never conquered (Judg. i.). Paul stayed here one day. Very few antiquities are to be found in the modern town, except such as have been used in rebuilding the walls and houses. Napoleon failed to capture Acre in 1799. During the crusades it was an important city, next to Jerusalem. It has been taken by many people; Egyptian who named it Ptolemais; Antiochus the Great; the Maccabees (?); Alexander Balas; Alexander Janneus failed, but Cleopatra succeeded; Tigranes; the Romans; Crusaders; Mohammedans; Ibrahim Pasha; and is now ruled by the Turks. Pop. 5000 to 10,000.

ACEL'DAMA (*field of blood*). Bought for the 30 pieces of silver that Judas received for betraying Jesus and returned. Potter's Field. On the steep south slope of Hinnom, opposite the Siloam pool. A few old olive trees grow near an old ruin called the house of Ananus. The hill side is full of rock-hewn tombs. Ship-loads of earth have been carried away from this spot as holy earth, and the Campo Santo (holy field) at Pisa is filled with it.

ACHA'IA. Province of Rome in Greece. Gallio was proconsul when Paul was there (Acts xviii. 12).

A'CHAN (*troubler*). Stoned at Jericho for stealing public property (Josh. vii.).

A'CHAR (*trouble*). Variation of Achan.

ACH'BOR (*mouse*). Father of Baal-hanan, king of Edom (Gen. xxxvi. 38).—2. Son of Michaiah, in Josiah's time (2 K. xxii. 12).

ACHIACH'ARUS. Keeper of the seal of Esarhaddon, king of Nineveh (Tobit i. 21). Nephew to Tobit, son of his brother Anael. Supposed to be the Hebrew for Mordecai.

ACHI'AS. Son of Phinees, high-priest (2 Esd. i. 2). AHIJAH?

A'CHIM. Son of Sadoc, father of Eliud. In Hebrew JACHIN (Gen. xlvi. 10; Mat. i. 14).

A'CHIOR (*fighter*). A general in the army of Holofernes (Judg. v.), after, a convert to Judaism (Judg. xiv.).

A'CHISH. King at Gath (Ps. xxxiv. Abimelech). David fled twice to him from Saul. (1 Sam. xxvii. 3-12, etc.)

ACHI'TOB. Ahitub, high-priest (1 Esd. viii. 2).

A'CHOR (*valley of trouble*). Near Jericho, in *Wady Kelt.* Where Achan was stoned.

ACH'SA. Daughter of Caleb (1 Chr. ii. 49).

ACH'SAH (*anklet*). Daughter of Caleb, given to his nephew, Othniel, in reward for leading the attack on Debir. The "upper and lower springs"

ACHMETHA.

that were given her as a dower, with the south land (Negeb), are located 6 miles S. W. of Hebron.

ACH'SHAPH (*incantation*). Royal city of Canaan (Josh. xi.). HEPHA on the bay of Acre.

ACH'ZIB. Judah in the Shefela.—2. In Asher, from which the Canaanites were not driven out. Ecdippa. Now *Es Zib*, 7 miles N. of Acre. After the return from captivity this was the most northern limit of Israel.

ACTS OF THE APOSTLES. The similarity of words and forms of sentences between the Acts and LUKE leads to the belief that Luke wrote both. The book repeats a part of Christ's history, especially the ascension and what attended that event, and the advent of the Holy Spirit at the Pentecost, with the wonderful success of their preaching. The Church in Jerusalem is then noticed; its persecutions, and the conversion of one of its most violent enemies (Paul); and then the narrative includes the efforts made to spread the Gospel by

EARTHEN LAMP. 1.

Peter and by Paul. The chief interest in the book, after the introduction, is the activity, success, sufferings and teachings of the great apostle. The book seems unfinished. The author was a companion of Paul, and a witness of most of the acts he records. His design was to show the co-operation of God in spreading Christianity, and to prove the perfect equality of right and privilege in the new Church of Gentile and Jew, and to give illustrations of the power and working of the religion of Jesus. Written after A. D. 63. The place is not known. Perhaps in fragments as they traveled or lived in different cities, finishing the work at Rome. See HISTORY OF THE BIBLE.

There are several spurious books called Acts; of Christ, of Paul, and others. See APOCRYPHA.

AD'AH (*beauty*). First wife of Lamech, mother of Jabal and Jubal.—2. Daughter of Elon the Hittite, one of the three wives of Esau, mother of Eliphaz, and so of the Edomites (Gen. xxxvi.). BASHEMATH in Gen. xxvi.

ADA'IAH (*adorned by Jehovah*). Maternal grandfather of Josiah (2 K. xxii. 1).—2. Gershonite, ancestor of Asaph (1 Ch. vi. 41). Iddo in v. 21.—3. Son of Shimhi, a Benjamite (1 Chr. viii. 21).—4. Son of Jeroham.—5. Of the descendants of Bani (Jedenus in Esd. ix. 30; Ezr. x. 29).—6. Son of another Bani—both 5 and 6 took foreign wives.—7. Of the line of Pharez.—8. Ancestor of Maaseiah (2 Chr. xxiii. 1).

ADA'LIA. Son of Haman (Esth. ix. 8).

AD'AM (*the man; or reddish tint*). The peculiar work of the 6th day of the creation, the crown of the whole fabric, was man, made in the divine image, he alone of all animals having a spiritual life. Adam was made male and female, and the two were placed in the garden Eden (EDEN), where proper food abounded. Some believe that a pair of each race were made, black, brown, red, yellow, white, and many others, because there are such great differences in complexion and figure among mankind.

The original state of man was one of activity and enjoyment. God assumed form and speech, and instructed His children how to dress and keep the garden, and exercised their faculties in naming the animals that He had made; and taught them something of the qualities and relations of vegetables, earths, the heavens, and external objects to which they were related.

The forming of the woman from a rib of Adam has been declared a poetic myth; but the lesson is just as surely taught, whether it is a fact or a fable, that woman stands in a peculiarly close relation to man. The "tree of the knowledge of good and evil," and the "tree of life," were tests of obedience, and as such might have been of any kind. The serpent is described as if it had been a special agent—perhaps one of those spirits that are believed to be superior to man, invisible to his eyes, good and bad, powerful, and always contending for his soul (2 Cor. ii. 11).

Woman was sentenced to endure the pains of child-bearing, and the humiliating dependance on a husband; and man to labor, with or without reward, and both to be subject to death (spiritual?). The sentence of the serpent is hard to interpret. The serpent is not CURSED literally, but rather blessed in having an extra means of protection in the dread of all other animals; he does not suffer by crawling on his belly because he is especially made to go in that way; and he does not eat dust. The denunciation of the serpent was symbolical, and is by some said to be the *first gospel promise.* "I will put enmity between thee and the woman, and between thy seed and her seed; he will attack thee on the head, and thou wilt attack him at the heel." The serpent was the spirit of lying and cruelty, as opposed to God, holy, good and wise.

It is probable that the first garments were made of the skins of animals, offered in sacrifice.

Cain was born the year after the expulsion; Abel a few years later, and Seth at least 130 years after Cain. Other sons and daughters were born to them of whose history nothing is recorded.

Adam's death at the age of 930 is stated, but that of Eve is not given.

AD'AM (*red earth*). City on the Jordan near Zarthan (Josh. iii. 16).

AD'AMAH. N. W. of the Sea of Galilee (Josh. ix. 36). Lost.

Probably the horned viper, the asp of Cleopatra, found in great numbers in the deserts. Arabia *Siffon*. It is extremely venomous, only 15 inches long, but fatal even in slight scratches.

AD'DI. Son of Cosam, father of Melchi (Luke iii. 28).—2. See ADNA (1 Esd. ix. 31).

ANCIENT EGYPTIAN FUNERAL PROCESSION.

AD'AMI. DAMIN.

A'DAR. Name after the captivity of the 6th month. The holy days in it were: 7th, a fast for the death of Moses; 9th, a fast for the memory of the School of Hillel; 13th, Fast of Esther, and for the death of Nicanor; 14th and 15th, the fast of Purim (Esther ix. 21).

AD'ASA. Ephraim near Beth-horon (Jos. Ant. xii. 10, 5 ; 1 Macc. vii. 40, 45).

AD'BEEL (*Sign of God*). Son of Ishmael (Gen. xxv. 13).

AD'DAN (*strong*). ADDON (Ezra ii. 59).

AD'DAR. Son of Bela (1 Ch. viii. 3). ARD in Num. xxvi. 40.

ADDER.

ADDER. There are four Hebrew names translated adder.—1. *Acshub*, in Ps. cxl. 3, quoted by Paul in Rom. iii. 13. The original (coiled and hiding) would apply to any kind of serpent.—2.

AD'DO. Grandfather of Zechariah (1 Esd. vi. 1). IDDO.

ADDUS. His sons returned with Zerubbabel (1 Esd. v. 34).—2. A priest removed for losing his family record (1 Esd. v. 38). Called Barzillai, in Ezra and Nehemiah, whose daughter Augia he married.

A'DER. Son of Beriah, of Aijalon (1 Chr. vii. 15). EDER.

ADIAB'ENE. The chief of the six provinces of Assyria, watered by the great and little Zab, which flow into the Tigris.

AD'IDA. In the Shefela, fortified by Simon Maccabeus against Tryphon.—2. Mentioned by Josephus near Jordan. HADID. ADITHAIM.

A'DIEL (*ornamented*). Prince in Simeon (1 Chr. iv. 36).—2. Priest (1 Chr. ix. 12).—3. Ancestor of Azmaveth (1 Chr. xxvii. 25).

A'DIN. 454 of his family returned with Zerubbabel (Ezr. ii. 15), and 51 with Ezra (viii. 16).

AD'INA (*pliant*). Son of Shiza, David's captain east of Jordan (1 Chr. xi. 42); next in rank to the "30 mighty men."

AD'INO, THE EZNITE. JASHOBEAM.

AD'INUS. JAMIN (1 Esd. ix. 48).

ADITHA'IM (*two shares of booty*). In the Shefela. HADID. (Josh xv. 36.)

AD'LAI. Ancestor of Shaphat, David's shepherd (1 Chr. xxvii. 29).

AD'MAH (*fort*). In the vale of Siddim, always with Zeboim (Gen. x.). It had a king (xiv.), and was destroyed with Sodom and Gomorrah.

ADMA'THA. One of the 7 princes of Persia.

AD'NA (*pleasure*). Returned with Ezra (x. 30),

MODERN EGYPTIAN FUNERAL PROCESSION.

Pethen, the cobra.—3. *Tsepha*, in Prov. xxiii. 32, adder; in Is. xi. 8; Je. viii. 17, cockatrice. The original means *to hiss*. In the Septuagint, basilisk—which is a fabulous serpent.—4. *Shephiphon*, only in Gen. xlix. 17, of Dan, "a serpent by the way."

and married a gentile wife.—2. Priest in Joiakim's reign (Neh. xii. 15).

AD'NAH (*pleasure*). A Manassite; deserted Saul for David (1 Chr. xii. 20).—2. General of 300,000 in Jehoshaphat's army (2 Chr. xvii. 14).

fürl, rude, pu=b; c, i, o, silent; c as s; ch as sh; e, ch as k; ḡ as j; ḡ as in get; s as z; x̱ as gz; ṇ as in linger, link; th as in thine.

A̍DŌ'NAI (*Lord*, *Master*). Hebrew word for Lord, God, and Lord of Hosts.

The Hebrews did not pronounce the sacred name J. A. H. which we now call Jehovah, and its true pronunciation is supposed to be lost; instead of doing so, they said ADONAI when J. A. H. occurred in the text.

ADŌ NI-BĒ'-ZEK (*lord of Bezek*). Canaanite king of Bezek, 17 miles E. of Shechem. He was head of the Canaanite and Perizzite bands, and was beaten and taken prisoner, maimed and died in Jerusalem, B. C. 1449 (Judg. i.).

ADŌNI'JĀH (*my lord is Jehovah*). Fourth son of David, born of Haggith at Hebron (2 Sam. iii.). After the death of Amnon and Absalom he made pretensions to the throne of David, supported by Joab and Abiathar, the high priest; but David caused Solomon to be proclaimed and crowned, and invested with authority. Adonijah was pardoned; but after David's death he renewed his attempt on the throne and was executed by Solomon's order (1 K.).

ADŌNI'RAM (*lord*, *high*). ADORAM. Chief of the tribute receivers in the reigns of David, Solomon and Rehoboam. He became hateful to the people and was stoned to death (1 K.).

ADŌNIZE'DEK (*lord of justice*). King of Jerusalem when Joshua entered Canaan. He joined with four Amorite kings to punish the Gibeonites for their league with Joshua. Being beaten by Joshua, they fled to a cave in Makkedah, where they were taken; had their necks trod upon as a sign of subjection, and were killed and buried in the cave (Josh. x.).

ADOP'TION. Placing as a son one who is not so by birth. Never done by the Hebrews. Paul alluded to the Roman custom (Gal. iv.), where the law gave the adopted son equal rights with a real son. Abraham did not adopt Hagar's son, nor Jacob the sons of the maids of Leah and Rachel, nor the sons of Joseph; Moses was not adopted by Pharaoh's daughter according to law, but as an exception.

ADŌRĀ'-IM. SHEFELA. Built by Rehoboam (2 Chr. xi.). *Dura*, a large village 5 ms. S. W. of Hebron, marks the site.

ADORĀ'TION. The acts and postures in worship are similar in all Oriental nations, and have come down to the present from remote antiquity unchanged. It is believed that the Hebrews in all their prayers used all the forms of posture and prostration that the modern Arabs have grouped into one prayer, which are nine positions. All of these are found on the monuments of Egypt and Assyria. Prayer is made standing, with the hands lifted or crossed or folded; this is the posture before kings or great men. The hands are also stretched forth as in supplication; one hand only is lifted in taking an oath (Gen. xiv.). Kneeling is a common mode (1 K. vii.; Ezra ix.; Dan. vi.; Luke xxii.); prostration of the body, resting on the knees and arms, the forehead touching the ground, and the whole body lying along, the face being down. The monuments show figures kneeling on one knee and smiting the breast; sitting on the heels, the hands being folded, is a very respectful attitude (1 Chr. xvii. 16; 1 K. xviii. 42). Among the Romans

PRIEST.

prostration was the peculiar act of adoration and worship (Acts x. 26), but Orientals do so in respect or reverence only. Kissing the head (1 Sam. x.),

ADORATION—MODERN EGYPTIAN.

the hand, the hem of the garment, or the earth near the object of respect, and kissing one's own hand (Job xxxi. 27; Hosea xiii. 2), to persons or idols. Holding the hand on the mouth as in kissing it is the highest act of respect and adoration.

A-DRAM'-MĒ-LECH (*fire king*). An idol worshiped by the colonists from Assyria in Samaria (2 Kings xvii. 31), by sacrificing children by fire. The idol represented the male power of the sun-god, ANAMMELECH, the female.

AD-RA-MYT'-TIUM (*named after Adramys, brother of Croesus, king of Lydia*). Seaport in Asia Minor, where the ship belonged in which Paul was wrecked. The gulf of the same name was opposite the island of Lesbos. Pop. 1500, with some commerce.

Ā-DRĪĀ. A'DRIAS. Sea named from Adria on the Po, Italy. At first the name was given to the upper end of the Gulf of Venice; afterwards to the whole gulf; and in Paul's time to the Mediterranean as bounded by Sicily, Italy, Greece and Africa (Acts xxvii. 27).

AD'-RI-EL (*God's flock*). Son of Barzillai, to whom Saul gave his daughter Merab, who had been promised to David (1 Sam. xvii. 19).

A-DUL'-LAM (*people's justice*). Judah, in the Shefela (Josh. xvi. 35). A place of great antiquity. Fortified by Rehoboam.

The CAVE OF ADULLAM is located 6 miles N. of Beit Jibrin, and now called Deir Dubban. There are many caves in this region. Some think the cave must have been nearer the Dead Sea, among the mountains, 6 miles S. W. of Bethlehem, in *Wady Khureitun*.

A-DUL'-TERY. Crime of a married woman with a man not her husband. Or of either man or woman who is bound, with any other person not their mate. Orientals do not include the man in the condemnation. ADULTERY in the O. T. means symbolically idolatry and apostasy from the Hebrew church. In the N. T. "an adulterous generation" (Matt. xii. 39), means a faithless and impious generation — who did not worship the true God, but did worship false gods.

ADUM'MIM (*red pass*). B E N J.— (Josh. xv. 7). On the road from Jericho to Jerusalem, in *Wady Kelt*. It was always noted for robbers, and was therefore selected for the locality of the parable of the Good Samaritan. (Luke x.) Eight miles E. of Jerusalem there are ruins of a convent and a khan, on opposite sides of the road.

ADORATION—ANCIENT EGYPTIAN.

AD'-VENT, THE SECOND. The second coming of Jesus Christ, often foretold by Jesus, and frequently mentioned by the apostles. This event has been looked for and expected in every age and every year since the ascension. Some hold that Christ reigns now, at the right hand of the Father, and must reign until all enemies are put under his feet. They hold that the judgment is now going on; the wicked are passing away; and that men become *consciously* the subjects of this judgment as they pass into the invisible world.

AD'VOCATE (*Greek* Paraclete). The name given to the Holy Spirit by Jesus (John xiv. 16); and to Jesus by John (1 John ii.).

Æ'NEAS. A paralytic healed by Peter (Acts ix. 33), at Lydda.

Æ'NON. Enon. (*Springs*). Near Salim, where John baptized (John iii. 22). Six miles S. of Bethshan, at Tell Redgah. A tomb near is called Shekh Salim. The brook in *Wady Chusneh* runs near, and many rivulets wind about in all directions. Here is "much water."

AG'ABUS (*locust*). One of the 70 disciples. Two prophesies of his are recorded, and their fulfilment (Acts xi. 27-30; xxi. 10). The famine through "all the world" was only through the world in Palestine—the Jews' world. It is mentioned by Josephus (xx. 2, 5), about A. D. 42, 14 years after Agabus met Paul at Cæsarea, and warned him of his sufferings at Jerusalem if he went up there.

MODERN EGYPTIAN HEAD DRESSES.

A'GAG (*burn*). A title of the king of the Amalekites, like Pharaoh of the Egyptians, Cæsar of the Romans, and Abimelech of the Philistines (Num. xxiv. 7; 1 Sam. xv. 8). AGAGITE for Amalekite in Esther iii. 1, 10; viii. 3, 5.

AG'A-PE (*Gr. agapē, to love*). The Church perpetuated the commemoration of the death of Jesus by certain symbols at meals; a custom most beautiful and most beneficial; for it was a supporter of love, a solace of poverty, a moderator of wealth, and a discipline of humility. Tertullian, speaking of the Agape does not mention the Eucharist as distinct from the meal. "The nature of our supper may be gathered from its name, the Greek term for love. However much it may cost us, it is real gain to incur such expense in the cause of piety; for we aid the poor by this refreshment; we do not sit down to it till we have first tasted of prayer to God; we eat to satisfy our hunger; we drink no more than benefits the temperate; we feast as those who recollect they are to spend the night in devotion; we converse as those who know that the Lord is an ear-witness. After water for washing hands, and lights have been brought in, every one is required to sing something in the praise of God, either from the Scriptures or from his own thoughts. By this means, if any one has indulged in excess, he is detected. The feast is closed with prayer." Pliny mentions this custom of the Christians, and says they eat common food (not such as was used for idol worship). Paul speaks of the abuse of this custom in 1 Cor. xi. 21; and, perhaps to avoid such abuse, the Eucharist was celebrated apart from any meal from about the year A. D. 150.

a, Plow. *b*, yoke. *f*, goad &c. *c*, points.

AG'ATE. Second precious stone in the high-priest's breastplate (SHEVO in Ex. xxviii. 19). In Is. liv. 12, and Ez. xxvii. 16, CADCOD, meaning a ruby. The same word is also translated chrysoprase and emerald. See PRECIOUS STONES.

AGE. Old age. Peculiar respect to old age is a general custom in the Orient, and has been from most remote times. The Scriptures record many instances of such respect and honor. The young rose and stood up in their presence (Lev. xix. 32); and even old men before one especially honored (Job xxix. 8). They were privileged to give the first words of counsel (Job xxxii.; Eccl. xxxii.); and old men, ELDERS, became a class, such as the FATHERS, and SENATORS in Rome, and were regarded as the depositaries of knowledge and experience (Job xv.). The attainment of old age was set forth as a blessing (Gen. xv.; Job v.), in prolonging the enjoyment of life, and a sign of peaceful times (Zech. viii.; Is. lxv.); a reward for piety, and a token of God's favor. Of all marks of respect, that to age is most willingly paid; because we may ourselves become aged, and receive such homage.

AGO'RA. A public place, broad street, marketplace, forum; where goods are sold, meetings held for debate, and trial, and to idle away the time. See AREOPAGUS.

PLOW, HOE.

AG'RICULTURE. The earliest records are of the best men engaged in this pursuit. Laws regulating its affairs formed the chief code of the Hebrews, and tended to produce an equality in interest, binding the son and elevating the slave to a com-

mon servitude. The earth was the Lord's, and all were tenants to him, payable in the rent of the Sabbatical year. The family possession was inherited, and if sold must be returned on the year of Jubilee to the original owner, and wealthy owners of many fields were denounced (Is. v. 8). IRRIGATION was always needed for the best results in Palestine—being neglected now, the soil is dry and sterile—although the rains of Canaan distinguished the country from the rainless Nile valley. There is in Palestine almost every variety of climate. Perpetual snow on Mt. Hermon and Mt. Lebanon; at Jericho, 60 or 80 miles distant, there is tropical heat, and snow is never seen. The hills of Bashan, Gilead, Galilee, Samaria, and Judea are the homes of forests, vines, fig-trees, and all kinds of fruit trees and vegetables; the plains produce bananas, oranges, lemons, besides all these, and frost is almost unknown. Palms formerly grew all over the country, as far north as Beirut and Baalbek. The greatest heat at Jerusalem is 90° (Fah.), and the cold 30°. Damascus is in a cooler latitude, and the record is 88° and 29°. The sky is almost cloudless for a large part of the year; the variations of sunshine and rain affecting only the autumn and winter months. The autumnal rains begin in the latter part of October, and gently continuing through November and December; and rain is rare after March, seldom or never so late as May. The ground is not often frozen in winter, snow lying during the night only; and in the plain of Jericho no snow or frost is ever seen, but there is on the hills around a spring-like temperature and air. The summer heat is oppressive, and fatal on exposure, but not on the higher hills, where heavy dews fall, and the nights are cool. The winter is the season of green fields and foliage, the summer heat destroying the grass. The HARVEST begins in the plain early in April; in Esdraelon in May, and on the hills in June.

The seasons were usually counted as two in the Scriptures, but we find six terms altogether (used by the Rabbins):—1. SEEDTIME, Oct. to Dec.; 2. WINTER, Dec. to Feb.; 3. COLD, Feb. to April; 4. HARVEST, April to June; 5. HEAT, June to Aug.; 6. SUMMER, Aug. to October.

The terraces, formed by stone walls along the hillsides, are a constant feature, and a necessity, in the hill country. On these narrow levels the vines, fruits and crops were raised, and frequent reference to fertilizers show a high state of culture, probably when the population was the greatest. Fences were not used, but watchmen guarded the ripening products, and the view was variegated by

PLOWING AND SOWING.

their different colors. The boundaries were marked by trees or piles of stones (Job xxiv.; Deut. xix. 14), and about gardens, orchards and vineyards there were walls (or hedges), having towers for watching and defense.

The monuments bear the sculptured figures of many implements, and pictures of the modes of using them in field and garden work. The PLOW is a kind of heavy hoe, used in the hand or drawn by animals or men (Job i. 14). It was made of a crooked root, shod with iron and fitted with one or two handles. The yoke was a straight or bent stick with rope or bent bows. The ox-goad was a pole six or eight feet, sharp at one end, and fitted with a spade at the other for clearing the plow, or for breaking clods (Is. xxvii. 24; Hosea x. 11; Job. xxxix. 10, where "harrow the valleys" should be "break the clods," as in the Hebrew). *Seed was sown* and hoed (harrowed) or plowed in, in drills or broadcast. Moses alluded in Deut. xi. 10 to the mode of sowing during the inundation, or by irrigation, in Egypt by using the foot (to open or stop the little rills of water). *Reaping* was of several modes: pulling up by the roots (as barley and doora are now in Egypt); and as wheat and barley do not grow very high (20 to 30 inches), it is pulled for convenience; by the sickle, at the ground, or just under the heads, as the straw may be wanted or not. Ears were carried in baskets; the whole stalk in sheaves (Gen. xxxvii. 7), and a cart is mentioned in Micah ii. 13. Camels or other animals are used to carry the produce. The poor were allowed to glean (Ruth ii. 7; Lev. xix. 9). *Threshing* was done on level places made in the

THRESHING AND WINNOWING.

field, called floors, about fifty feet across, circular. The grain was trodden out with cattle, arranged three or four abreast, and driven around, and the cattle were not to be muzzled (Deut. xxv. 4). Sticks and flails were used to thresh out small quantities (Ruth ii. 17; Is. xxviii. 27). Threshing machines were made of frames filled with sharp stones

or pieces of iron set in holes, or fitted with circular saws (Land and Book ii. 315), which were drawn over the grain (Is. xxviii. 27; xli. 15; Amos i. 3). *Winnowing* was done, and is now, by tossing the grain against the wind with a fork or fan (Matt. iii. 12; Jer. iv. 11), and then passing it through a sieve (Amos ix. 9). It was stored in granaries cut in the rock, built underground, or above (Jer. xli. 8).

A'GUR (*one of the assembly*). Author of the sayings in Prov. xxx. Native of Massa, East Arabia, and lived about B. C. 600. Some have supposed that this was an assumed name of Solomon, such as was "Koheleth," translated "preacher."

A'HAB (*father's brother*). Son of Omri, king of Israel, and reigned 22 years, B.C. 918 to B.C. 897. His wife was JEZEBEL, daughter of Ethbaal, king of Tyre, a woman of strong character, and an idolatress. She succeeded in introducing the worship of Baal into Israel, a temple being built at Samaria for the worship. Elijah, the prophet, pronounced the judgment of God on Ahab's house, and he died of wounds received in battle (see 1 Kings).—2. A false prophet, son of Kolaiah, who deceived the Jewish exiles in Babylon (Jer. xxix. 21).

AHAR'AH. Third son of Benjamin (1 Chr. viii. 1).

AHAR'HEL. The family (in Judah) traced its descent from Ashur, a posthumous son of Hezron, through Coz (1 Chr. iv. 8).

AHA'SAI. Priest; ancestor of Amashai (Neh. xi. 13).

AHAS'BAI (*refuge in God*). Father of Eliphelet (2 Sam. xxiii. 34).

AHASUE'RUS (*Achashverosh*). The title of the Persian king, and means *lion-king*. Four persons are mentioned by this title, who were, 1. ASTYAGES (Dan. ix.); 2. CAMBYSES (Ezra iv.); 3. The husband of Vashti and Esther, the same who was called XERXES by the Greeks; the marriage with Esther is assigned to his 7th year, in which he returned to Shushan from his disastrous expedition to Greece; 4. Mentioned in Tobit xiv. 15, who was Cyaxares I.

AHA'VA (*river*). River in Babylonia, on whose banks Ezra collected the Jewish exiles for the return to Jerusalem (Ezra viii. 15, 31). Hit.

A'HAZ (*possessor*). Son and successor of Jotham, and 11th king of Judah. Reigned 16 years, B.C. 741 to 729. He respected neither God, the law nor the prophets.

AHAZI'AH (*holden of Jehovah*). Son and successor of Ahab, and 8th king of Israel. B. C. 897 to 896.—2. Son of Jehoram, 6th king of Judah. B. C. 885.

AH'BAN (*brotherly*). Son of Abishur by Abihail (1 Chr. ii. 29).

A'HER (*another*). Ancestor of the Hushim (1 Chr. vii. 12).

A'HI (*brother*). Chief of a family in Gad, Gi-

PROFILE OF PALESTINE, N. TO S.

lead (1 Chr. v. 15).—2. A descendant of Shamer, of Asher (1 Chr. vii. 34). AHIJAH?

AHI'AH (*friend of God*). AHIJAH.

AHI'AM (*father's brother*). One of David's 30 heroes (2 Sam. xxiii. 33).

AHI'AN. Of Shemida, Manasseh (1 Chr. vii. 19).

AHI'EZER (*helper*). Chief in Dan, in the Exode (Num. i. 12).—2. Chief of a band of bowmen with David (1 Chr. xii. 3).

AHI'HUD (*brother of Jews*). Chief in Asher; one of Joshua's assistants in the allotment (Num. xxxiv. 27).—2. Chief in Benjamin (1 Chr. viii. 7).

AHI'JAH, or AHIAH (*friend of Jehovah*). Son of Ahitub; grandson of Phinehas (1 Sam. xiv. 3, 18). He was a priest at Shiloh, in care over the ark; giving oracles by the aid of the ark and the ephod. It is not known what caused the neglect of the ark in the latter day of Saul's reign. Saul's rash curse, Jonathan's danger, the failure to get an answer from the oracle, the peoples' rescue of Jonathan, led to coolness between the king and the high priest, which ended in a terrible revenge, after Ahimelech's favor to David. Ahimelech may have been Ahijah's brother.—2. Son of Bela. ACHIA (1 Chr. viii. 7).—3. Son of Jerahmeel.—4. One of David's 30 (1 Chr. xi. 36).—5. Levite in David's reign; treasurer in the temple (1 Chr. xxvi. 20).—6. AHIAT. Son of Shisha, an officer of Solomon (1 K. iv. 3).—7. AHIAS. Prophet in Shiloh (Shilonite), in the time of Solomon and Jeroboam (1 K. xiv. 2), who prophesied the breaking loose of the ten tribes from Solomon's kingdom in punishment for his idolatry (1 K. xi. 31-39); and the death of Abijah, the king's son, and at the same time the captivity of Israel (1 K. xiv. 6-16). See 2 Chr. ix. 29, for a reference to work by Ahijah, now lost.—8. Father of Baasha, king of Israel (of Issachar), (1 K. xv. 27).—9. A chief who signed the covenant with Nehemiah (Neh. x. 26).

PROFILE ACROSS—JAFFA TO MOAB.

AHI'KAM (*enemy's brother*). Son of Shaphan the scribe (2 K. xxii. 12). He has one of the delegates sent to Huldah, the prophetess, by the king. He protected Jeremiah, the prophet, after he was taken out of the pit (Jer. xxxix. 14).

AHI′LUD (*maker*). Father of Jehoshaphat the recorder (2 Sam. viii. 16).—2. Father of Baana (1 K. iv. 12).

A-HI-MA′-AZ (*choleric*). 1. Father of Saul's wife, Ahinoam.—2. Son and successor of Zadok, high priest, in David's reign.—3. Son-in-law of Solomon, and one of his 12 chief purveyors, or tax collectors; whose district was Naphtali.

AHI′MAN (*giver*). One of three famous giants. Anakim of Hebron (Num. xiii. 22).

AHIM′ELECH (*king's brother*). Great grandson

THOTHME'S RING.

of Eli, priest at Nob, who gave David some of the sacred bread from the presence-table, and the sword of Goliath, which had been in safe keeping there.

AHI′MOTH (*deathly*). Kohathite in David's reign (1 Chr. vi. 25).

AHIN′ADAB. One of 12 officers who gathered monthly supplies for Solomon's household at Mahanaim, in Manasseh (1 K. iv. 14).

AHI′O (*brotherly*). Son of Abinadab. Ahio went before and his brother behind the ark, when it was carried from their father's house (2 Sam. vi. 3).—2. Benjamite, a son of Beriah (1 Chr. viii 14).—3. Benjamite, son of Jehiel, founder of Gibeon (1 Chr. viii. 31).

AHI′RAM (*exalted brother*). Son of Benjamin; Ehi in Gen. xlvi. 21. AHI′RAMITES. Descendants of Ahiram.

AHIS′AMACH (*supporter*). Danite, father of Aholiab, architect on the tabernacle (Ex. xxxi. 6).

AHISH′AHAR (*morning dawn*). Son of Bilhan, grandson of Benjamin (1 Chr. vii. 10).

AHI′SHAR (*upright*). Controller of king Solomon's household. Always an office of great trust and influence in the east (1 K. iv. 6).

AHITH′OPHEL (*foolish*). A statesman of brilliant talents in David's time. His counsels were regarded as oracles (2 Sam. xvi.). When his counsels to Absalom were neglected for those of Hushai (whom David had sent), he went home and hanged himself at Giloh. The only suicide mentioned in the O. T., except those engaged in war.

AHITUB (*goodness*). Father of Ahimelech.—2. Son of Amariah, grandfather of Zadok, the high priest (1 Chr. vi. 7).

AH′LAB (*fertility*). City in Asher (Judg. i. 31). Gush Caleb in after times, and now El Jish, near Safed.

AH′LAI (*a wish*). Daughter to Sheshan, wife of Jarha an Egyptian slave (1 Chr. ii. 31, 35). Zabad, one of David's heroes descended from her (1 Chr. xi. 41), and Azariah, one of Joash's captains (2 Chr. xxiii. 1).

AHO′AH (*friend of God*). Son of Bela, of Benjamin (1 Chr. viii. 4). Ahoite in 2 Sam. xxiii. 9.

AHO′LAH (*her own tent*). AHOLI′BAH (*my tent in her*). Two fictitious names used by the prophet Ezekiel for Israel (Samaria) and Judah. Describing their neglect of the true worship of Jehovah, and their consequent disgrace and ruin.

AHO′LI-AB (*father's tent*). Skilful artizan of the tribe of Dan, who, with Bezaleel, constructed the Tabernacle.

AHU′MAI. Son of Jahath, Judah (1 Chr. iv. 2).

AHU ZAM. Ahuzzam. Son of Ashur, founder of Tekoa (1 Chr. iv. 6).

AHUZ′ZATH (*possession*). The "friend" or "favorite" who was with Abimelech II on his visit to Isaac (Gen. xxvi. 26). Some interpret the word ahuzzath to mean a company, or a retinue.

A-I (*heap of ruins*). Benj. (Gen. xii. 8). HAI, E. of Bethel. The second city taken by Joshua in Canaan. Eight miles N. of Jerusalem.—2. Burial place of Elon, in Zebulon (Judg. xii.).

A′IAH (*clamor*). Son of Zibeon. Ajah in Gen. xxxvi. 24 (1 Chr. i. 40).

A′IATH (Is. x. 28). AI. AI′JA.

AI′JALON (*gazelle place*). A city of the Kohathites (Josh. xxi. 24), in Dan. (xix. 42); fortified by Rehoboam (2 Chr. xi. 10). Celebrated in the poem on the battle of Joshua in the "Book of Jasher" (Josh. x. 12). Now Ain Yalo, 12 miles N. W. of Jerusalem.—2. City of Zebulun; birth-place of Elon, and his burial-place. JALUN, east of Acre.

AI′JELETH. AYELETH HAS-SHACHAR (*hind of the dawn*). Only in Ps. xxii. in the introduction, as the name of the tune in which that psalm might be chanted.

A′IN (*fountain*). En. Prefix to many names, as Engedi, Enrogel.—1. Num. xxxiv. 11, a source of the Jordan, or a town near.—2. City in Judah (Josh. xv. 32).

A′JALON (*stag*). Valley and town in Benj. noted in Joshua's exploits (Josh. x. 12). Several other towns of the same name, in Dan, Ephraim and Zebulun.

A′KAN (*keen-sighted*). Descendant of Esau (Gen. xxxvi. 27). Jakan in 1 Chr. i. 42.

AK′KUB (*insidious*). Descendant of Zerubbabel; one of the 7 sons of Elioenai (1 Chr. iii. 24). 2. Doorkeeper at the east-gate of the temple. His descendants are reported among the returned from Babylon (1 Chr. ix. 17). Dacobi in 1 Esd. v. 28.— 3. A Nethinim (Ezr. ii. 45). Acub in 1 Esd. v. 30.— 4. A Levite (Neh. viii. 7). Jacubus in 1 Esd. ix. 48.

AK-RAB′-BIM (*scorpions*). Maa′leh Akrab′bim, *scorpion pass*, in the mountains south of the Dead Sea.

AL′EMA. City in Gilead, large and strong (1 Macc. v. 26). BEER-ELIM?

ALABASTER VASES.

ALABAS′TER. So named from the town of Alabastron, in Middle Egypt, where there are quarries of this fine-grained, pink-colored gypsum. It is not clear, but is colored in stripes, much varied in width and tint—very near the tint of their finger-nails, including the crescent light place at the upper end of the nails. It was made into cups, boxes, etc. for holding perfumes, ointments, and other precious articles. Boxes for the same uses of any

substance—wood, glass, stone, metal—were also called alabasters (Matt. xxvi. 7; Mark xiv. 3; Luke vii. 37).

ALEXAN'DER (*men helper*). King of Macedon. Called the Great. Born at Pella B. C. 356, son of Philip and Olympias. Educated by the famous philosopher Aristotle. Alluded to in Daniel's prophesy. He destroyed the Persian empire and placed Greeks in power there; conquered Asia, Egypt, Syria, and founded the city of ALEXANDRIA (B. C. 332), which may be said to have been built on the ruins of Sidon and Tyre, for it grew rich and powerful on the Oriental trade which formerly fed those cities, and was then diverted from the Euphrates to the Red Sea route. Alexander's toleration of Oriental customs and religions, guaranteeing to all people (and especially the Jews, who were exempted from tax on the 7th year,) the free observance of their hereditary laws, showing the same respect to their gods as to the gods of Greece, thus combining and equalizing the West and the East, weakened all the nationalities of his empire, and tended to dissolve the old religions. The Greek and Hebrew learning of Alexandria greatly influenced the planting of Christianity there, as well as in Asia. He married Roxana and Parysatis, Eastern princesses, an example followed by 80 generals and 10,000 soldiers of his army, who married Oriental wives. Josephus gives an ac-

TETRADRACHM OF ALEXANDER THE GREAT. B. C. 350.

count of a visit of Alexander to Jerusalem, and his reception by the high priest, which has been called fabulous (Ant. xi. 8). He died at Babylon B. C. 323, only 32 years old, of intemperance.

ALEXAN'DER BĀLAS. A pretended son of Antiochus Epiphanes. He reigned four years over Syria (1 Macc. x. 11; Jos. Ant. xiii. 2).

ALEXAN'DER JANNÆUS. The first prince of the Maccabees, who called himself king.

ALEXAN'DER. Four persons so named in the Gospels.—1. Son of Simon the Cyrenean, who bore the cross part of the way (Mark xv.).—2. A powerful opponent of the apostles, related to the high priest (Acts iv. 6).—3. Son of Herod the Great and Marianne.—4. A Jew of Ephesus, who took part in the uproar in the temple of Diana, against Paul.—5. A coppersmith, excommunicated by Paul for errors.

ALEXAN'DRIA. Greek, Roman, and Christian capital of Egypt, founded by Alexander, B. C. 332, by the help of the same architect who rebuilt the Temple of Diana, at Ephesus. For centuries this was the largest city in the world. Pop. 600,000 (Diodorus). The lighthouse of its spacious port was famous in the world of commerce as the PHAROS, one of the 7 wonders. The great library is said to have had 700,000 volumes (Strabo), even after losing 400,000 by fire (B. C. 47), and was finally destroyed by the Saracens, A. D. 642.

ALEXANDRIA.

Among the learned men were Philo, a Jew (author of works which contain the best array of Hebrew Platonism—almost an imitation of Christian ethics), and Origen and Clement, Christians, whose writings have influenced and directed religious men in all Christian nations to the present. Ptolemy Philadelphus favored the translation from Hebrew into Greek of the Holy Scriptures (Old Testament), and the work was called the SEPTUAGINT, finished about B. C. 280. It is now the oldest known version, and is called the Codex Alexandrinus (Jos. c.; Apion ii. 4). See WRITING.

The Museum was the means of spreading a knowledge of Aristotle through the civilized world, and at one time it gathered 14,000 students from all the world. Modern astronomy arose there, under the direction of Eratosthenes, who taught the globe shape of the earth, its poles, axis, equator, arctic circles, equinoctial points, solstices, horizon, eclipses, and the distance of the sun. Callimachus (poet) wrote a treatise on birds; Apollonius one on mathematics and geometry, and invented a clock. Hipparchus was the great astronomer of the age, and discovered the precession of the equinoxes, gave methods of solving all triangles, and constructed tables of chords, tables of latitude and longitude, and a map of more than 1000 stars. The Almagest of Ptolemy (A. D. 138), was for 1500 years the highest authority on the phenomena and mechanism of the universe. The same author described the world from the Canaries to China.

These systems were supplanted by the discoveries of Newton of the law of gravitation, and of Columbus of the New World. There was a very extensive botanical and zoological garden, and a school for the study of Anatomy and dissection. The temples of Isis and Sarepis were among the finest ever built, and were partly

ALEXANDER BALAS.

used for scientific purposes, having the most perfect instruments for astronomical observations then known. They were destroyed by Bishop Theophilus A. D. 390. Present pop. about 60,000 from all nations.

AL'LON (*oak?*). **ELON**. Naphtali (Josh. xix. 33). Zaanannim, *loading tents*, near Kedesh (Judg. iv. 11).—2. ALLON-BAC'HUTH (*oak of weeping*), under which Rebekah's nurse, Deborah, was buried (Gen. xxxv. 8). Palm tree of Deborah in Judg. iv. 5, between Ramah and Bethel.

AL'MOND. Nut tree, larger than a peach tree; thrives from China to Spain, and on both sides of the Mediterranean, and nowhere better than in Syria. It is the earliest to blossom in spring (February), the pink-white blossoms appearing some weeks before the leaves.

ALMOND TREE AND BLOSSOMS.

ALMS. The Hebrews had no word for a free gift to the poor, such as alms, but used *righteousness* for such acts, as in Job xxix. 10-16; Prov. x. 2; Deut. xiv. 29; xxiii. 24, 25; xxiv. 19; xxvi. 12; Lev. xix. 9, 10; xxiii. 22; xxv. 5. The laws of Moses made ample provision against poverty, and if they had been strictly kept, in letter and spirit, there could not have been any destitution. The gospel recognizes the duty of alms-giving and enforces it, and this virtue was a peculiar mark of a Christian in the early age. This was not made a definite rule, but was left to the constraint of inward principle and feeling, "to prove the sincerity of their love." Encouragement of idle vagrancy was denounced as wrong, and such idlers were scorned (2 Thess. iii. 10-12). The Jews, since the destruction of Jerusalem, have regarded their poor as the people of God, and those who give to them are credited with as much virtue as if they kept all the commandments, and they teach that alms-giving atones for their sins. As Jesus sought the needy and the sick, and kindly ministered help and consolation, so it is his will that his Church shall show the same spirit towards the poor and afflicted.

AL'MUG. ALGUM. Fragrant sandal-wood, white and yellow, found in the mountains of Malabar. The trees are 9 to 12 inches through, 25 to 30 feet high. Its uses were for perfume, incense, beads, rosaries, fans, elegant boxes, and cabinets, and for musical instruments. Solomon used it for pillars in the houses he built, and for musical instruments (1 K. x. 12; 2 Chr. ix. 10).

AL'NATHAN. ELNATHAN (1 Esd. viii. 44; Ezr. viii. 16).

AL'OE. An ordoriferous, precious tree of Siam, where it is worth its weight in gold, and is used for perfuming garments and rooms, and as a medicine. It is not our gum aloes.

AL'PHÆUS (Alpheus, *exchange*). Father of the lesser James (Matt. x. 3). Called Cleopas in John xix. 25. Alphæus and Cleopas are synonymous in Hebrew and Greek.

ALPHABET. WRITING.

AL'TAR. The central point of religious worship, as a mount, table or structure of turf, wood, stone or metal, on which sacrifice was made to some deity. The first one mentioned in the Bible is that built by Noah. Moses restricted the building of altars to those for the temple service only; but the law was often broken (Lev. xvii.; Deut. xii.; Judg. vi.; 1 Sam. vii.; 2 Sam. xxiv.; 1 K. iii.). Moses directed two kinds to be made: 1. ALTAR OF BURNT-OFFERING, the table of the Lord (Ex. xxvii. 8), having horns to which the animal to be sacrificed might be bound (Ps. cviii. 27); and a ledge half way up, on which the priests could stand, which was fenced below with a net work of metal; —2. ALTAR OF INCENSE, the golden altar, Ex. xxxix. 38, (the other being the brazen) (Ex. xxxviii. 30). This was not strictly an altar, as no sacrifice was offered on it. Both had rings for carrying by poles.

ALTAS'CHITH (*destroy not*). In the introduction to Psalms lvii., lviii., lix., lxxv., indicating the melody to which the psalms were to be sung.

A'LUSH (*wild place*). Station in the Exodus, not identified (Num. xxxiii. 13).

AL'VAN (*thick*). Horite, son of Shobal (Gen. xxxvi. 23). ALIAN (1 Chr. i. 40).

A'MAD (*station*). In Asher, lost (Josh. xix. 26).

AMAD'ATHA. AMADATHUS. (Est. xii. 6; xvi. 10.) HAMMEDATHA.

A'MAL. Descendant of Ashur, son of Jacob (1 Chr. vii. 35).

AM'ALEK (*to lick up*). Son of Eliphaz, grandson of Esau, and a Shekh of Edom (Gen. xxxvi.).

AMAL'EKITES. An ancient nomadic race, found from Petræa to the Persian Gulf, and may have been descendants of the grandson of Esau. The mention of this country in Gen. xiv. 7, does not imply that they were a people at that early time, but that they were a people in that country when the history was written. They were doomed to extinction because they opposed the Hebrews; and they were fewer and weaker from age to age up to the last mention in David's time (1 Sam. xxvii.; xxx. 17), who destoyed their remnant.

A'MAN. HAMAN. (Tobit xiv. 10; Esth. x. 7, etc.).

AM'ANA. Mt. near the S. end of Anti-Lebanon, where the Abana rises (Cant. iv. 8).

AMARI'AH (*whom Jehovah promised*). 1. Father of Ahitub.—2. High priest in the reign of Jehoshaphat.—3. A Kohathite Levite.—4. Priest in Hezekiah's time.—5. Son of Bani (Ezr. x.).—6. Priest with Zerubbabel.—7. A descendent of Pharez.—8. Ancestor of Zephaniah the prophet.

AM'ASA (*burden*). Son of Ithra, by David's sister Abigail. Was general to Absalom, and was defeated by Joab, but pardoned by David, and appointed Joab's successor as general. Joab killed him treacherously (2 Sam.).

EARTHEN LAMP. 2.

AMA'SHAI. Son of Azareel, priest in the time of Nehemiah (xi. 13). Amashi also, correctly.

AMASI'AH (*whom God bears*). Son of Zichri, Jehoshaphat's general of 200,000 in Judah (2 Chr. xvii. 16).

A'MATH. HAMATH.

AMATHE'IS (1 Esd. ix. 29). ATHLAI.

AM'ATHIS (*the land of*). HAMATH. (1. Macc. xii. 25).

AMAZI'AH (*whom Jehovah strengthens*). Son of Joash and 8th king of Judah. Began to reign at 25, B.C. 838, and reigned 29 years. He was the first to hire men to fill his army. He conquered Edom and carried home the idols for worship, and so brought on his own ruin, and was killed by conspirators at Lachish.—2. Priest of the golden calf at Bethel, under Jeroboam II, in the time of the prophet Amos (vii. 10).

GLASS LAMP.

AMEDA'THA. (Esth. iii. 1) HAMMEDATHA.

A'MEN' (*truth*). Hebrew word, usually translated *verily;* or at the end of sentences not translated, but meaning *so be it.* In Rev. iii. 14 it is used as a name of the Lord, "the Amen, the faithful and true witness." It is used as a word of confirmation, binding a saying, or an oath (Num. v. 22; Deut. xxvii. 15; Neh v. 13; Ps. cvi. 48), and as a response or closing of a prayer (Matt. vi. 13; Rom. xi. 36).

AM'MI (*my people*). The name of Israel when they shall have been restored to God's favor (Hos. ii. 1).

AM'MIDOI. Returned with Zerubbabel (1 Esd. v. 20). Humtah in Josh. xv. 54. AMMIDIOI.

AM'MIEL (*people of my God*). Spy from Dan, in the Exodus (Num. xlii. 12).—2. Father of Machir of Lodebar (2 Sam. ix. 4).—3. Father of Bathshua, wife of David (1 Chr. iii. 5); ELIAM in 2 Sam. xi. 3. Son of Ahithophel.—4. Sixth son of Obed-edom (1 Chr. xxvi. 5), a doorkeeper of the temple.

AMMI'HUD (*people of Judah*). Father of Elishama; chief in the Exodus; an Ephraimite (Num. i. 10); ancestor of Joshua (1 Chr. vii. 26).—2. Simeonite chief in the allotment; father of Shemuel (Num. xxxiv. 20).—3. Father of Pedahel, chief in the allotment (ib. 28).—4. Father of Talmai, king of Geshur (2 Sam. xiii 37).—5. Descendant of Pharez (1 Chr. ix. 4).

AMMIN'ADAB (*bounteous people*). Son of Aram, father of Elizabeth, wife of Aaron; an ancestor of Jesus (Matt. i. 4).—2. Kohathite Levite in David's time.—3. One of the most noted charioteers of his day (Cant. vi. 12). If this last is read *ammi-nadib*, it will mean *my loyal people.*

AMMIN'ADIB. (Cant. vi. 12).

AMMISHAD'DAI (*people of the Almighty*). Father of Ahiezer, chief in Dan in the Exodus (Num. i. 12).

AMMIZ'ABAD (*people of the giver*). Son of Benaiah, and his father's lieutenant over the 3d division of David's army, in the 3d monthly course (1 Chr. xxvii. 6).

AM'MON (*son of my relative*). AMMONITES. Ben Ammi in Gen. xix. 38. Descended from Lot. The people occupied the territory afterwards given to Reuben and Gad, after driving out the Zamzummim (Deut. ii. 20). Jabbok was their border on the N. They were nomadic, restless and predatory, as the Moabites were settled, civilized and industrious. They opposed the march of Israel to Canaan, and although favored by Moses (Deut. ii. 9), yet they were hated and warred with always. They worshipped *Moloch*, also called *Milcom*, and *Malcham*. Saul was made king (the second time) on account of his relief of Jabesh from the Amalekites (1 Sam. xi.). Women of this people were in Solomon's house. The last mention of them is in 1 Macc. v. 6, 30-43.

AM'NON (*faithful*). Eldest son of David by Ahinoam, born at Hebron B.C. 1056. Killed by Absalom 1032.

A'MOK (*deep*). Priest; returned with Zerubbabel (Neh. xii. 7).

AM'OMUM. An aromatic plant growing in India, Armenia, Media, and Pontus, described by Pliny, but not identified in our day. In Rev. xviii. 13 of the Hebrew—not in the A. V. The oily extract was used for the hair; and the name given to any fine perfume.

A'MON (*builder*). Son of Manasseh, and king of Judah. An idolater, and reigned only two years, B. C. 644-2 (2 K. xxi.).

A'MON (*multitude*). Egyptian deity. The name is translated generally in the O. T., which confuses the meaning. In Jer. xlvi. 25 "multitude of No" should be "Amon of No." And in Nahum iii. 8 "populous No" means No-Amon. The Greeks called this god Jupiter Ammon. On the monuments the name is Amun-re—Amon the son. He was supposed to be in the form of man, and was the supreme god of Egypt—king of gods.

AMON.

AM'ORITE (*mountaineers*). On both sides of Jordan (Num. xxi.; Gen. xv. 16; Deut. i. 20). From Emor, 4th son of Canaan. Og and Sihon, their kings E. of Jordan, opposed Moses, but were beaten, and their land was given to Reuben, Manasseh, and Gad. This district was good pasture, and is now. Five Amorite kings on the W. of Jordan opposed Joshua, and were defeated. The Jebusites were a branch, who held Zion 400 years after Joshua, until David took it (2 Sam. v. 6). Solomon imposed a tribute on the remnant of the people (1 K. ix. 20).

A'MOS (*burden*). Prophet in the days of Isaiah and Hosea. Native of Tekoa, and was a dresser of sycamore (fig) trees. He prophesied at Bethel. His book is one of the finest in style, being full of pure language, vivid pictures, and often sublime thoughts; most of his imagery is taken from rural life. B. C. 780. See HISTORY.

A'MOZ (*strong*). Father of Isaiah.

AMPHIP'OLIS. Capital of a district in Macedonia (Acts xvii). On a height on the east bank of the river Strymon, 3 miles from the sea. The gold mines of Mt. Pangeus made the city famous.

Now *Newtown*. Xerxes sacrificed nine young men and maids, and several white horses, on the bank of the Strymon (Herod. vii. 113).

AMPLI'AS. Disciple at Rome, beloved of Paul in the Lord (Rom. xvi. 8).

AM'RAM (*high ones*). Son of Kohath, father of Moses and Aaron.

AM'RAPHEL (*keeper of the gods*). Hamite king of Shinar (Gen. xiv. 1, 9).

MODERN EGYPTIAN AMULET.

AM'ULET (*pendant*). Any object carried as a magical protection against evil or danger. Tickets with writing; stones and metal with pictures and writing. Moses tried to turn the practice to good use by directing his laws to be written on them (Ex. xiii. 9, 16; Deut. vi. 8; xi. 18). They are now very common in oriental countries, and not unknown in our own land. Jacob found some worn as earrings (Gen. xxxv.).

AM'ZI. Merarite; ancestor of Ethan the singer (1 Chr. vi. 46).—2. Ancestor of Adaiah, priest in Nehemiah's time (xi. 12).

A'NAB (*grapery*). Judah (Josh. xi. 21), from which Joshua expelled the Anakim. A tower marks the site near Maon (Rob. ii. 195).

A'NAH (*answer*). Son of Zibeon, father of Esau's wife, Aholibamah (Gen. xxxvi. 24). He discovered the hot springs of Callirohoe. He was a Horite, that is, a mountaineer. He is also called BEERI (fountains) the Hittite, in honor of his finding the springs.

ANAHA'RATH (*pass*). Place in Issachar (Josh. xix. 19). ARANEH, 2 miles E. of Jenin (Rob. ii. 316, 319. Hackett).

ANA'IAH (*whom God answers*). Who stood at Ezra's right hand during the reading of the law (Neh. viii. 4). ANANIAS in 1 Esd. ix. 43.

A'NAK. AN'AKIM (*neck-chain*). Name of a race of tall people, who lived at Hebron, and vicinity (Num. xiii. 33; Josh. xv. 14), descended from ARBA. They appear on the monuments of Egypt as tall and light colored, and are called Tamahulu, from the Hebrew Talmai.

ANAM'MELECH (*kingly image*). The Assyrian Moloch, in whose worship the people passed their children through the fire. This was the *female* power as ADRAMMELECH was the *male* power of the sun-god.

A'NAN (*cloud*). A chief who signed the covenant with Nehemiah (x. 26).

ANA'NI (*protected*). Seventh son of Elioenai, of the royal line of Judah (1 Chr. iii. 24).

ANANI'AH (*protected by Jah*). Priest; ancestor of Azariah; assisted in rebuilding the wall (Neh. iii. 23).

ANANIAH. Place between Nob and Hazor (Neh. xi. 32).

ANANI'AS. A disciple at Jerusalem who, with his wife, Sapphira, tried to impose on Peter and the brethren, and defile the house of God, died suddenly, and was buried at once (Acts v).—2. Made high priest (Acts xxiii.) about A. D. 477 by Herod, king of Chalcis (Ant. xx. 5, 2). He made himself great wealth out his office. Paul when before the Sanhedrin called him a white wall, and prophesied his ruin, which came in a time of trouble, and he fell by an assassin (Wars ii. 17; vi. 69). —3. Disciple at Damascus, who was directed (by the Lord) to go to Saul and lay hands on him, to ordain him to the ministry (Acts ix. 10–17). Tradition makes him bishop of Damascus, and a martyr.

ANAN'IEL. Forefather of Tobit (i. 1). HANANEEL.

A'NATH (*answer*). Father of Shamgar (Judg. ii. 31).

ANATH'EMA (*suspended*). When said of things given to God, it is pronounced anathema (Luke xxi. 5). It was also the religious curse of the Hebrews. It means also *devoted*—any person or thing devoted to God. Paul means *devoted* where he says *accursed*, in Rom. ix. 3. Those Jews *devoted* themselves to the work of killing Paul (Acts xxiii. 12). *Anathema maranatha* (*the Lord comes*), means that the curse (as well as a blessing) has its operation in Christ's kingdom, and rises to its highest power at his coming, and he will surely come to bless as well as to curse (1 Cor. xvi. 22). It was used as the church censure, or final excommunication, and it is so used now, of those who are excluded from the company of the believers.

AN'ATHOTH (*echoes*). Ben., near Nob and Hazor (Neh. xi. 32). *Anata*, 3½ ms. N. E. of Jerusalem, where there are remains of walls and buildings in the midst of orchards of figs and olives. The quarries still supply Jerusalem.

JEWISH HIGH PRIEST.

ANDREW (*strong man*). Brother of Peter, and native of Bethsaida in Galilee (John i. 44). He was first a disciple of John the Baptist, but followed Jesus on John's testimony, and informed his brother Peter of what he had found—that Jesus was the Christ (verses 35, 36, 41). He did not leave his business of fishing until some time after (Mark i. 14). He was present at the feeding of the 5000 at Jerusalem, when the Greek Jews wished to see Jesus (John vi. 8); and, with others, on Olivet, asked privately of Jesus what he meant by his strange words about destroying and rebuilding the temple. Of his after-life and death nothing is recorded. Tradition says he preached in Scythia, or Achaia, and was crucified on a cross, now called St. Andrew's, which is of a peculiar shape, and still bears his name. The early writers mention the "Acts of Andrew," and the "Gospel of St. Andrew," but they were rejected, and are lost.

ANDRŌ'NICUS (*man conqueror*). Fellow-prisoner of Paul, and his kinsman, and a disciple before Paul's conversion. The allusion in Romans xvi. 7 probably has reference to some part of Paul's history, now lost.

A'NEM (*two springs*). In Issachar (1 Chr. vi. 37). ENGANNIN.

by Quirinus), and then deposed by Valerius Gratus. Father-in-law to Caiaphas, who was high priest when Jesus was crucified (John xviii.; Acts iv. 6). The office of high priest was judicial, in addition to the temple service, and Annas for a long period held this honored place, his term having been 20 years. Five of his sons succeeded each other to

ANTIOCH IN SYRIA.

A'NER (*boy*). A Canaanite sheikh who joined Abram, Eshcol and Mamre in pursuit of Chedorlaomer (Gen. xiv).—2. Town of the Levites in Manasseh (1 Chr. vi. 70).

AN'ETHOTHITE, THE. Resident of ANATHOTH. ANTOTHITE (2 Sam. xxiii. 27).

ANGAREU'O (*compel*). From the Tartar language, meaning forced service (as a mounted courier) without pay (Matt. v. 41; Mark xv. 21).

AN'GEL (*messenger*). Whatever God employs to do his will. In Ps. civ. 4 (quoted in Heb. i. 7), the wind (spirit) is His angel. Haggai was called the Lord's angel (i. 13), as was John the Baptist by Malachi (iii. 1). Israel was God's angel, sent to enlighten the world (Is. xlii. 19), as well as the priests (Mal. ii. 7), meaning the priests as a body. Jesus spoke of *angels of God*, who were neither married nor given in marriage, but were *spirits*, not in the flesh, but above, more free, more powerful, more wise (Matt. xxii. 30; xxvi. 53; Gen. xvi. 7; Heb. xii. 22). There are angels of light (of heaven), and angels of darkness, "that kept not their first estate." Isaiah speaks of the *angel of the presence* (lxiii. 9), and Moses of the angel that went before Israel (Ex. xxiii. 21), who has the whole world as his heritage (Rev. viii. 3), and who is believed to be the Lord Jesus, whom the Father sent to reveal Him to men.

ANK'LET. Ornament of gold, silver, brass iron or glass, for the ankles, worn in ancient and modern days in the East by women. Isaiah (iii. 16) says they made a tinkling with the feet; that is, the women tinkled them together when they walked in a mincing way. A string of little bells is worn by some Arab girls.

AN'NA. Prophetess of the tribe of Asher, daughter of Phanuel. She was 84 when in the temple, as mentioned by Luke (ii. 36), she recognized the Messiah.

AN'NAS. High priest for 15 years (appointed

the same office, and then his son-in-law; and in all these changes he had exercised the highest judicial authority. He might have been a member of the Sanhedrin, and possibly was its president or vice-president.

ANNUN'CIĀTION. This word means the announcement of the selection of the Virgin Mary as the favored mother of Jesus. About the year 800 the church decreed (council of Trullo) a day for celebrating the event.

ANNU'US. Error in 1 Esd. viii. 48; "with him" in A. V. Ezra viii. 19.

ANOINT. Anointing. Use of oil on the head or any object to be honored. Jacob poured oil on his stone pillow at Bethel, consecrating it to God.

ANOINTING.

Guests were honored by having their hair oiled. The monuments have pictures of the act. It was a common custom among the Hebrews, and is often referred to in the O. T. (Ps. xxiii. 5; xlv. 7; Prov. xxi. 7; xxvii. 9). To omit the use of this per-

fumed oil was a sign of grief and mourning (Dan. x. 3; Is. lxi. 3). It was also used as a medicine (Is. i. 6; Mark vi. 13; James v, 14). Kings were called "the anointed of the gods," and both kings and priests were confirmed in their office by the anointing of oil, both in Egypt and Palestine. Anointing the eyes denoted a spiritual recovery of sight—knowledge of divine truth. The Holy Spirit descended on the head of Jesus, like a spiritual

ANTIOCH IN PISIDIA.

anointing, a divine confirmation of his office of Messiah.

The bodies of the dead were also anointed, or embalmed, with spiced oil. See PERFUMES.

A'NOS. Son of Bani (1 Esdr. ix. 34). VANIAH.

ANT. The Hebrew word for this insect was *namal, cut off* (Gen. xvii. 11). The males and females have four wings, which soon fall off. The workers are wingless. They feed on vegetables, animals and insects. They will rob a granary in a few days, or even hours. Solomon alluded to the ant as an instance of the use of *proper seasons* for collecting provisions (Prov. vi. 6).

ANTI'AM (*sighing of the people*). Son of Shemidah, Manasseh (1 Chr. vii. 19).

AN'TI-CHRIST (*against Christ*). Unbelievers, heretics, and persecutors (1 John ii. 18, 22). Some understand this term to mean all men (or an organized body), who oppose Christ, and whom he will overcome or destroy (Rev. xi. 13, 17).

AN'TIOCH in Syria. On the Orontes, 30 miles from the sea, 300 from Jerusalem. Founded by Seleucus Nicator (*conqueror*), B. C. 300, and named in honor of his father, Antiochus. It was the capital of the Greek and Roman governors of Syria for nearly 1000 years. Its suburb Daphne was famous for its sanctuary to Apollo and Diana (2 Macc. iv. 33); the sacred grove extending its cool shades and brooks of water for ten miles around. It was a sensual paradise, where pleasure, under the disguise of religion, dissolved the firmness of manly virtue. The first GENTILE CHURCH was founded here by Paul, and the disciples were here first called CHRISTIANS in derision by the pagans (Acts xi. 21–26). Ignatius who suffered martyrdom under Trajan, at Rome, was bishop of Antioch 40 years. In the time of Chrysostom (born here A. D. 344), the pop. was 200,000, one half being Christians. The city had a street colonnade from end to end, built by Antiochus Epiphanes, and paved with granite by Antoninus Pius; most sumptuous marble baths, built by Caligula, Trajan and Hadrian; a marble palace of Diocletian, and was the finest and largest city in Western Asia. It lost greatly in wealth and population in several earthquakes: one in A. D. 526, destroying 250,000 people, at the time of the festival of the Ascension,

when many strangers were gathered; and in 1822 one-fourth of the city and people, about 5000. It was of great importance during the Crusades, and is often mentioned for its sieges, battles, and the brilliant exploits of both Christian and Moslem in and about its walls. Am. Prot. missionaries began to preach there in 1856. Pop. now about 20,000. Ar. name *Antakia*. Ruins of aqueducts, marble pavements, columns, and other evidences of its ancient splendor are often found buried under rubbish.

AN'TIOCH in Pisidia. Founded by the same king (who built 10 or 15 others of the same name), and peopled them by hired immigrants from Magnesia on the Mæander. On the S. side of Mt. Paroreia, on the boundary between Pisidia and Phrygia, overlooking a broad plain. Recent discoveries of ancient inscriptions prove the site correct. There are ruins of several churches, temples, a theatre, and an aqueduct of which 21 arches are now entire. The ancient city was often visited by Paul (Acts), with Barnabas, Silas, and Timothy who was a native of this district.

ANTIOCHIA (2 Macc. iv. 33), for Antioch.

ANTIO'CHIANS. Partizans of A. Epiphanes, or Jason (2 Macc. iv. 9). "Sinful men" in Doway.

ANTI'OCHIS. In the family of A. Epiphanes (2 Macc. iv. 30).

ANTI'OCHUS (*who lasts out*). There are several of this family name. 1.' ANTIOCHUS II. THEOS (*the god*). Son of A. Soter (*savior*.) He succeeded his father B. C. 261. He was the "king of the north" of Daniel (xi.), who joined "the king of the south" (Ptolemy) by marrying his daughter Berenice.—2. ANTIOCHUS III, THE GREAT, succeeded his brother Seleucus Keraunus (*thunderer*), who was poisoned after ruling 3 years), and was the first really strong man since Seleucus, who founded the family and empire in Syria. He was only 15 when he began to rule, and his great rival, Ptolemy IV, Philopator (*father loving*), of Egypt, was crowned only two years later. Ptolemy began his reign by murdering nearly all of his relations, including his mother and father. Antiochus did no violence to his friends, but planned how to in-

TETRADRACHM OF ANTIOCHUS IV EPIPHANES.

crease the wealth and power of his people, and passed his whole life in war. One part of his policy was to put a great trust in the Jews as a people, and especially as soldiers (Ant. xii. 3, 4). At one time he moved 2000 families of Jews from Mesopotamia to Lydia and Phrygia for garrison service. He increased the honors and privileges of the Jews in Palestine, when he became master there, and they were very near to the actual enjoyment of social and religious liberty. He is also mentioned by Daniel (xi. 41), as one who should stand "in the glorious land which by his hand was

to be consumed." His own daughter, Cleopatra, whom he gave to Ptolemy Epiphanes as a wife, opposed him in favor of her husband. Hannibal influenced him to war against Rome, and he was beaten finally at Magnesia in Lydia, B. C. 190. He lost his life B. C. 187, in an attempt to plunder the temple of Belus in Elymais.—3. ANTIOCHUS IV EPIPHANES (*illustrious*), youngest son of A. the Great, succeeded to his brother Seleucus Philopator, who reigned 10 years, chiefly as "a raiser of taxes" (Dan. xi. 20). Epiphanes gained the kingdom *by flatteries* (s. 21), that is, by a system of lavish bribery. These and other acts caused the Greeks to call him Epimanes (*crazy*), a very sharp and sarcastic pun on his title. He wished to plun-

ANTIOCHUS TRYPHON.

der the Jewish temple, because he needed money, and to do this it was his policy to make the Jews hateful, and destroy their nationality. But he raised up the Maccabees who, after many years of war and suffering, delivered their people (B. C. 143), as is recorded on the coins of that period (MONEY). He was a type of Antichrist, so made by his want of respect to God and religion, and the disregard of every higher feeling among men. He worshiped the Roman war-god, whose forts were his temples.—4. ANTIOCHUS V EUPATOR (*of noble descent*), succeeded his father A. IV, B. C. 164, while a child, and was under the guardian Lysias, and they were killed by Demetrius Soter, when the rule fell to Antiochus VI, son of Alexander Balas and Cleopatra, who while a child was under the care of Tryphon, B. C. 145, who contended for the throne against Demetrius Nicator. Tryphon, by treachery and success in war, gained supreme power, killed Antiochus, and assumed the throne. The coins bear his head as Antiochus and Trypho, and on some the title of Theos is added. The books of Daniel and the Maccabees give a large space to the life and deeds and bad character of this king.—5. ANTIOCHUS VII SIDETES (*from Side in Pamphylia*). Called also EUSEBES (*pious*). This was the last king of the Seleucid family, who ruled B. C. 141-128. There were some who assumed the name Antioch as a title until the Romans made Syria a province, B. C. 63.

ANTOTHI'JAH (*Jah's answers*). Son of Shashak (1 Chr. viii. 24).

ANTIPAT'RIS (*against father*). Built by Herod the Great, on the edge of Sharon, now *Kefer Saba*, 12 ms. N. E. of Joppa. Capharsaba in Josephus. Dr. Eli Smith found and identified the place while on a journey expressly to follow Paul's night march from Jerusalem to Cæsarea (Acts xxiii. 31). There are remains of the Roman road, which led by Gophna.

ANTO'NIA. Fort built by Herod on the N. W. corner of the temple site, and named after his friend. JERUSALEM.

A'NUB (*bound*). Son of Coz, of Judah (1 Chr. iv. 8).

A'NUS. A Levite (1 Esd. ix. 48). BANI?

APA'ME. Of Darius' family; daughter of Bartacus (1 Esd. iv. 29).

APE. Brought by Solomon's ships (1 K. x. 22) from India or Malabar, where they are now found, called KAPI (Heb. KOPH). They were prized as curiosities then as now.

APEL'LES (*Apollo's gift*). A disciple saluted by Paul (Rom. xvi. 10). Tradition says he was bishop of Smyrna.

APHARSACH'ITES. Persians transplanted into Samaria (Ezr. iv. 9). Fars—Persia.

APHEK (*firmness* or *strength*). 1. Issachar (Josh. xii. 18; xv. 53). APHAKAH.—2. Asher (Josh. xix. 30; Judg. i. 31). APHIK. (Josh. xiii. 4). W. of Baalbek 15 ms., on the E. slope of Lebanon. AFKA. A temple to Venus made this city famous.—3. Where the Philistines encamped before the battle in which the sons of Eli were killed and the Ark was taken (1 Sam. ix. 1). In the mountains N. W. of Jerusalem.—4. The site of another battle, where Saul was killed (1 Sam. xxix. 1), near Shunem, or Jezreel.—5. Aphik, now called Fik, E. of the sea of Galilee 6 ms.; the site of several battles with the Syrians (1 K. xx. 26; 2 K. xiii. 17). Ben Hadad was defeated here; and Joash at the word of Elisha drew a bow at a venture, and afterwards gained several battles over the Syrians. The houses occupy a crescent-shaped cliff, at the base of which are three fine fountains, which send a stream into the lake below the hill on which Gamala stood.

APOC'RYPHA (*hidden*). The name of a certain class of books, offered as genuine, but not received as of divine origin, and of equal authority with the other books of the Bible. These are, as they stand in the A. V.:

1. Esdras, 1 and 2.
2. Tobit.
3. Judith.
4. Addition to Esther.
5. Wisdom of Solomon.
6. Wisdom of Jesus, Son of Sirach.
7. Baruch, and Jeremiah's Epistle.
8. The Song of the Three Holy Children.
9. The History of Susanna.
10. Bel and the Dragon.
11. Prayer of Manasseh.
12. Maccabees, 1 and 2, and the Book of Enoch, accepted in Abyssinia.

APE.

Besides these there are a number that never were admitted to a position among the Sacred writings, such as, The Assumption of Moses, Testament of the Twelve Patriarchs, and many others attributed to Abraham, Eldad, Modad, etc.

The original meaning of apochrypha was *hidden*, but it is now used to mean *spurious*.

The real value of these books is in their being specimens of Jewish literature, and books of their history, throwing light on their religion and theological opinions, although more or less colored by fancy or fable. They are assigned to a period dating since 300 B. C., the latest, Esdras, dating about 30 B. C., or even later. The books themselves do not assert the use of the prophetic gift.

but do say that this gift had departed from Israel (1 Macc. ix. 27), but it was hoped that prophets would again appear (iv. 46; xiv. 41). The style and power of the writing is inferior, and especially so is the poetry, excepting only the Song of the Three Children, which may be the reproduction of some ancient sacred service. There are many blunders and anachronisms in their historical allu-

BEDAWIN.

sions. The books of the New Testament era that have been regarded as doubtful are, 2d Ep. of St. Peter; Ep. of St. James; Ep. of St. Jude; 2d and 3d Eps. of St. John; the Apocalypse, and the Ep. to the Hebrews. Those condemned as spurious: Acts of Paul; Shepherd of Hermas; Revelation of Peter; Ep. of Barnabas, and Instructions of the Apostles. Those denounced as impious are, Gospels of Peter, Thomas, Matthias, and the Acts of Andrew, John, and the other apostles.

Some of these books were read in the churches for instruction, but not for a rule and guide. The Westminster Confession says, "The books called Apochrypha, not being of divine inspiration, are no part of the canon of Scripture, and therefore are of no authority in the Church of God, nor to be any otherwise approved, or made use of, than other human writings." See HISTORY OF THE BOOKS.

APOLLŌ'NIA (*from Apollo*). Macedonia. Visited by Paul and Silas (Acts xvii. 1; Pliny iv. 10, 17).

APOL'LOS (Apollonius). Jew from Alexandria, who had some errors corrected by Aquila and Priscilla at Ephesus, and afterwards preached in Achaia and in Corinth (Acts xviii. 27), seconding the work of Paul, whom he very much resembled in his teaching, character and attainments. He is mentioned as bishop of Corinth.

APOS'TLE (*sent forth*). The Jews so called those who carried about letters from their rulers. There were but few who had this honor, and to whom Jesus entrusted the organization of his Church. There were twelve originally whom he ordained, that they should be with him; and he gave them power over unclean spirits, and to heal all manner of diseases; commissioning them to preach the kingdom of God (Mark iii.; Matt. x.; Luke vi.), saying, "As the Father hath sent me, so send I you." It seems to have been essential to this high office, 1. That they should have seen the Lord, and have been eye and ear witnesses of what they testified to the world (John. xv. 27; Acts i. 21). Paul claims equal authority from having seen Jesus in a vision (1 Cor. ix. 1; xv. 8).—2. Called and chosen by the Lord himself (Acts i. 24).—3. Infallible inspiration (John xvi. 13; 1 Cor. ii. 10), because it was their office to explain the O. T., and to set forth the New (Luke xxiv. 27).—4. The power of working miracles (Mark xvi. 20; Acts ii. 43).—5. To these were added the power to settle points of faith, and determine all controversies. Jesus is once called "the apostle of our profession" (Heb. iii. 1). THE APOSTLE'S CREED is not of their own making, but contains their doctrine as set forth by Christian men in later times. THE APOSTOLIC AGE dates from the day of Pentecost, and is usually divided into two periods, before and after the destruction of Jerusalem A. D. 70, the latter period ending at the death of John A. D. 99. There was not a revelation of the Lord's commands and the duties they involved complete as final at one time, but rather a progressive illumination—a peculiar succession and combination of events—from the first call to be apostles, the day of pentecost, the visions at Cæsarea and Joppa, the conversion and call of Paul—by which the five heralds of the Gospel were instructed, and enabled to teach its free and comprehensive spirit. The first Christian church was composed of Jews only, and they observed the Mosaic ritual strictly, and were continually in the temple (Luke xxiv. 53; Acts ii. 46; iii. 1); and the Jews spoke of them as the SECT of the Nazarenes, as the Pharisees and Sadducees and Essenes were sects within the Jewish church (Acts xxiv. 5; xxviii. 22; xv. 5; xxvi. 5; v. 17). A community of goods was required at first, but was soon abandoned. The Greeks (and other Gentiles) were admitted and elevated the tone of the society, and increased its power for diffusion, for the Gentiles so outnumbered the Jews at Antioch as to require a new name—which was given by their scorners—Christian. Shortly before the destruction of Jerusalem the members of the church found a refuge in Pella, east of Jordan, away from the power of the Sanhedrin, which held its sessions at Jamnia on the Great Sea, and this ended the connection of the new church with the old—Moses was to be thereafter second to Jesus in authority, and from that time an enmity grew up between

ASSYRIAN ARMLET.

them which has not yet been healed—and can never be (2 Cor. iii). The second period is almost a blank, since there is no account of any of the apostles except John, and with his death the age closes. Since then the church has been left to the guidance of man only, assisted by the invisible spirit, towards its spiritual maturity.

APOTHECARIES. Hananiah, one of the rebuild-

ers of the wall, was a perfumer, or maker of ointment (Neh. iii. 8).

APPA'IM (*nostrils*). Son of Nadab, of Judah (1 Chr. ii. 30).

APPHI'A. Disciple (Philemon 2); member of Philemon's household. Appii in Acts xxviii. 15.

AP'PHUS. Surname of Jonathan Maccabeus (1 Macc. ii. 5).

AP'PII-FO'RUM (*market place of Appius*). On the Appian bay, between Naples and Rome, 43 ms. from Rome. Appius Claudius, who built the famous road from Rome to Brundusium, had a statue in his honor here (Acts xxviii. 15).

AQ'UILA (*eagle*). Jew at Corinth, tent maker and friend of Paul (Acts xviii. 2). He and his wife Priscilla had been banished from Rome with all Jews, by Claudius. They became zealous promoters of the cause, as Paul says "helpers in Christ Jesus," "who have for my life laid down their own necks" (Rom. xvi. 3, 4). The Greek church honor Aquila as a bishop, on July 12. The Romans call him bishop of Heraclea, and the festival of Aquila and Priscilla is on July 8.

AR. Capital of Moab, on the Arnon (Num. xxi. 15–28). The place is still called Rabba, and is 17 miles E. of the Dead Sea, 10 S. of the Arnon, and its ruins occupy a low hill overlooking a plain, where are found the remains of two Roman temples and some water-tanks. It was burnt by King Sihon (Is. xv. 1). Rabbath Moab.

A'RA (*lion*). Son of Jether, of Asher (1 Chr. vii. 38).

AR'AB. Judah. (Josh. xv. 52). Near Hebron. Lost.

AR'ABAH (*waste—sterile*). The valley of depression from Mt. Hermon to the Red Sea at Ezion Geber (Akabah). (Deu. i. 1; Job xxiv. 5; Is. xxxiii. 9). Now restricted to the valley from the Sea of Galilee to the S. end of the Dead Sea, and called El Ghor. It is 150 miles long by 1 to 10 or 12 miles wide. ARBOTH, the plural of Arabah was the name given to the plain of Jericho (Josh. v. 10; Num. xxii. 1; 2 Sam. xv. 28). The region is called KIKKAR in Gen. xiii. 10. From the Dead Sea to Akabah the Arabs name the valley *Wady el Arabah*. The desert of TIH bounds the A. on the west, by long walls of limestone, 1500 to 1800 feet above its floor. The mts. of Edom form the E. wall, and are of granite, basalt, and porphyry, 2,000 to 2,300 ft. in elevation, and covered with vegetation. Mt. Hor, the highest peak, is 5,000 ft. above the sea. A line of chalk cliffs, 150 ft. high, 6 ms. S. of the Dead Sea, running E. and W., divides the A. from El Ghor. W. EL JEIB is the principal water-course—flowing only in winter. The A. is a desert of sand, gravel, low hills, and cut by numberless water-courses. The sirocco blows almost constantly. There are a very few shrubs and plants, as rushes, tamarinds, oleanders, anemones, lilies, and palms. The water-shed is 40 ms. N. of Akabah, from which the water flows both N. and S. The pass up out of the A. near Akabah, upon the plateau of Tih, is now used by pilgrims on the route from Suez to Mecca, and is called NUKB, the pass. From this plateau to 1000 ft. above it is another pass, on the route from Mt. Hor to Hebron, called *es Sufah*, where Israel was repulsed by Canaan (Deut. i. 44; Num. xiv. 43–45). On the E. side *Wady Ithm* leads through the mts.

near Akabah, where there are remains of a Roman road, leading to the country E. of the Dead Sea, over the same route traversed by the Exodus, when Edom was compassed (Num. xxi. 4).

ARA'BIA (*east country*). E. of Palestine, including all the descendants from Ishmael and Keturah (Gen. x. 30; xxix. 1; Judg. vi. 3.) Sons of the East (Num. xxiii. 7; 2 Chr. ix. 14). Sons of Kedem (s. xxi. 13). "Forest in A." (Ex. xii. 38; Neh. xiii. 3; 1 K. x. 15), "Mixed multitude" are Arabians. Now called by the Arabs BILAD EL ARAB—country of the Arba. Bedawin are people of the open country, not living in towns. Extends from the Euphrates and the Persian Gulf to Egypt and the Red Sea; and from the Indian Ocean to the Mediterranean, or Great Sea. The ancients divided it into ARABIA FELIX, A. DESERTA, and A. PETRÆA. The modern divisions are the Peninsula of Sinai, Arabia, and North A. (See Sinai, Edom, Petra, Mt. Hor, Arabah, Syria, Aram.) The original settlers were the sons of Shem and Ham

MT. ARARAT, ARMENIA.

(Gen. x. 21, 15). There are many ruins in Arabia of a more ancient people than any known to history—(Marib, Sana, Reydan, Riam, Inen, Rien).

There are many allusions in the Bible to the Arabs; and the manners and customs of the modern people are a help to the interpretation of those texts that refer to the ancients, and especially in Job. The Bedawin constantly remind us of the accounts of the patriarchs, or later Israelites. Respect to age (Lev. xix. 32); deference to superiors (2 K. v. 13); engravings on signets of sentences having the name of God (Ex. xxxix. 30; John iii. 33). As a pledge, the ring is given (Gen. xli. 42); they wear an inkhorn in the girdle (Ezek. ix. 2, 3, 11). Many of the most obscure passages are explained by a knowledge of the present customs.

The people have in all ages been active, enterprising, restless; ambitious in commerce, conquest, and religion.

The country of A. was never conquered.

ARA'BIANS (2 Chr. xvii. 11). Nomades, east and south of Palestine, a part being descended from Keturah. The Sheikh (*king*) was called Aretas (2 Macc. v. 8).

A'RAD (*wild ass*). Son of Beriah, a Benjamite (1 Chr. viii. 15).

A'RAD. S. of Judah (Num. xxi. 1; King of A., Josh. xii. 14; Judg. i. 16). Tell Arad, 20 ms. S. of Hebron. (R.)

AR'ADUS. ARVAN (*wandering*). Phoenicia (Ezek. xxvii. 8; Gen. x. 18). An island 3 ms. from the

coast, near the river Eleutherus, Nahr el Kebir; and opposite to it is the site of Antaradus, now called Ruad (1 Macc. xv. 23). The island was settled by fugitives from Sidon. High and rocky, about a mile in extent, near Tripoli.

A'RAH (*traveler*). Son of Ulla, of Asher (1 Chr. vii. 39).—2. 775 of the "sons of Arah" returned with Zerubbabel (Ezr. ii. 5). Ares (1 Esd. v. 10).

A'RAM (*height*). N. E. of Palestine. Called also Syria— which see (Gen. xxxi. 18; xxxiii. 18). 1. A. *Dammesek*, Syria of Damascus (2 Sam. viii. 5, 6).—2. A. Naharaim (*two rivers*), the country of Abraham (Gen. xxv. 20).—3. Padan A., Aram at the foot of the mountains.—4. A. Zobah (2 Sam. x. 6, 8).—5. A. Beth Rehob.—6. A. Maachah (1 Chr. xxi. 6). Geshur (2 Sam. xv. 8; 1 K. xi. 25). Aram was a son of Shem, and his brethren were Elam, Asshur, Arphaxad. Aram is also Assyria (2 K. xviii. 26; Is. xxxvi. 11; Jer. xxxv. 11; 2 K. xvi. 6).— 2. Aram, of whose family was Elihu who visited Job (xxxii. 2).

A'RAMITESS. Woman of Aram (1 Chr. vii. 14).

ARAM-NAHARAIM. Mesopotamia. (Plain of Damascus?)

A'RAM ZOBAH. Aram and Zobah (Ps. lx.).

A'RAN (*wild goat*). A Horite (Gen. xxxvi. 28).

AR'ARAT (*holy land*). A mountainous district, or lofty plateau, nearly 5000 ft. above the sea, between the Black and Caspian seas, where rise the Euphrates and Tigris, which flow into the Persian Gulf; the Araxes and Cyrus, into the Caspian; and the Acampsis, into the Black Sea. The range of Mt. Taurus begins at the N. E. end of the Great Sea, near Antioch in Syria, runs N. E., meeting the range of Abus, from the head of Persian Gulf running N. W., at the Mt. Ararat, which is 17,750 feet high. It is alluded to in Scripture as—1. *Ararat* (Gen. viii. 4), the land on which the Ark rested; and where the sons of Sennacherib fled after killing their father (2 K. xix. 37).—2. *Minni* (Jer. li. 27). Josephus says there is a great mountain in Armenia called Baris (Ant. i. 3, 6).—3. *Togarmah.* In Gen. x. 3, this is the name of the youngest son of Gomer. Ezek. (xxxviii. 6) says, "the house of Togarmah of the north." Tyre traded in horses with Togarmah (Ezek. xxvii. 14).

AR'ARATH. ARARAT (Tobit i. 21).

ARAU'NAH (*Jah is strong*). The Jebusite who sold his threshing-floor to David for a place for an altar to God (2 Sam. xxiv.). He was one of the royal family of the Jebusites (2 Sam. xxiv. 23). David bought the whole hill Moriah for 600 shekels of gold, and the threshing-floor and oxen for 50 shekels (1 Chr. xxi. 25).

AR'BA. See HEBRON.

AR'BA (*hero-baal*). Ancestor of the Anakim— named Hebron Kirjath-arba (city of Arba). Josh. xiv. 15; xv. 13). Arbah in Gen. xxxv. 27.

AR'BATHITE. Resident in the Arabah, the Jordan valley (2 Sam. xxiii. 31).

ARBAT'TIS. Error for Acrabattine; or meaning *Ard el Butihah* in Galilee (1 Macc. v. 23).

ARBE'LA (1 Macc. ix. 2), Arabella, near Maisaloth. Beth Arbel, or what is now called *Irbil*, a few miles W. of Magdala. (Hos. x. 14.)

AR'BITE THE. Resident of Arab (2 Sam. xxiii.

35). Paarai, the Arbite, one of David's guard; Naarai, the son of Ezbai in 1 Chr. xi. 37.

ARBO'NAI (Judg. ii. 14, Mambre). See ABRONAS.

ARCHELA'US (*leading the people*). Son of Herod by Malthace, a Samaritan, brought up at Rome. Appointed by Augustus Ethnarch after his father's death. Banished to and died in Gaul at Vienne. He had a bad reputation (Matt. ii. 22) for cruelty and oppression.

THE AREOPAGUS, OR MAR'S HILL, AND ACROPOLIS.

AR'CHEVITES. People from Erech(?) living in Samaria (Ezr. iv. 9).

ARCHIP'PUS (*driver of horses*). Disciple in Colosse, "our fellow soldier" (Philemon 2). He is supposed to have been a teacher, one of the 70 sent out, as well as deacon, in Colossæ and Laodicea, and to have suffered as a martyr at Chonæ.

ARCHITE. Hushai, the Archite in 2 Sam. xv. 32. No town of Arca is known in Palestine; the one north of Tripoli is in Phœnicia. Josh. (xvi. 2) has "the borders of Archi" near Bethel and Luz.

ARCTU'RUS. Heb. ASH, AYISH, in Job ix. 9; xxxviii. 32. The Arabians name the cluster of four stars in the body of the "Great Bear" *en nash*, and those in the tail *el Benat*, the daughters.

ARD (*descent*). Son of Benjamin, the youngest (Gen. xlvi. 21).—2. Son of Bela (Num. xxvi. 40). Addar in 1 Chr. viii. 3. Ardites, from him.

AR'DATH. The field in 2 Esd. ix. 26, meaning that all Palestine was but a field or waste (Arboth?) to the Jews.

AR'DON (*fugitive*). Son of Caleb by Azubah (1 Chr. ii. 18).

ARE'LI (*hero's son*). ARIEL. Son of Gad (Gen. xlvi. 16). Arelites (Num. xxvi. 17).

AREOP'AGUS (*hill of Ares*). Mars Hill. Athens. A rocky height opposite the west end of the Acropolis, used from the earliest times as a place of assembly for the honorable men who had held the office of Archon. On this hill Paul stood, in the midst of these august men, when he said, "Whom ye ignorantly worship, Him declare I unto you." Dionysius, the Areopagite (Acts xvii. 23–34). "In the market daily." The AGORA, or market, was a public place, surrounded on three sides by the architectural glories of Athens. It may be described thus: To the northeast was the Acropolis, a rocky height 150 feet above the street below, crowned with the *Parthenon* and other temples; north the *Areopagus*; west the Pnyx (pulpit); and south the *Museum*, with other buildings. (See plan of Athens.)

At the time of Paul's visit, Athens was a magnificent city, ornamented in every quarter with memorials sacred to religion and patriotism, show-

ing the highest achievements in art. The famed Academy had its groves of plane and olive trees, retired walks and cooling fountains, altars and statues and temples, near which was the house of Plato, the great teacher.

The Acropolis had clustered on its summit memorials and monuments of religion and art, such as were never seen on an equal space. Pericles had adorned it with a flight of steps and a Propylæa, with five entrances and two flanking temples of Pentelican marble, where were placed the equestrian statues of the Roman emperors Augustus and Agrippa, the temple of the Wingless Victory; a picture-gallery; and there still stands the ruin of the unequaled Parthenon, which was then adorned with the masterpieces of the sculptor Phidias.

The Erechtheium, containing the holy olive-tree, sacred to Minerva, the holy salt-spring, and other sacred things. A colossal bronze statue of Pallas Promachus, by Phidias, stood near, the plume of whose lofty helmet was visible from the sea between Sunium and Athens.

Pausanias gives an account of a great number of statues on the Acropolis, so that we wonder how there could be any space left for the people.

It is no wonder, however, that Paul, with his natural genius and vast experience, should have been inspired by the surroundings. (See Life of Paul.)

AREOP′AGITE. A member of the council at Athens (Acts xvii. 34). DIONYSIUS.

AR′ETAS (*graver*). Title of the kings of Arabia, as Ptolemy of Egypt, and Augustus of Rome.—1. In the time of Antiochus Epiphanes, B. C. 170 (2 Macc. v. 8).—2. Father-in-law of Herod Antipas, whose Ethnarch ruled in Damascus when Paul escaped in a basket (2 Cor. xi. 32).

ARE′US. King of the Lacedemonians, whose letter to the high-priest Onias is given in 1 Macc. xii. 20–23; about 300 B. C.

AR′GOB (*stony*). Manasseh, east of Jordan, in Bashan. Had sixty fortified cities (Deut. iii. 4, 13, 14; 1 K. iv. 13), called *Trachonitis*, a translation of the Hebrew name. The Samaritans called it *Rigobaah*=*stony*. The Arabs named it *Mujeb*=*stony*, and it is now *El Lejah*. It lies fifteen miles south of Damascus, is triangular, twenty-two miles from north to south, and fourteen from east to west. The region is elevated above the surrounding country, and is very rocky, like an ocean of basaltic rocks and boulders; thickly studded with deserted cities and villages, in all of which the houses are solidly built and of remote antiquity. A Roman road runs through the district, probably leading from Damascus to Bosra. *Kenath* and *Edrei* are on the border, to the southwest. The *Hauran* presents the utmost contrast to the Lejah, in being a country of the richest agricultural soil, in rolling downs, from the Sea of Galilee to the desert, far beyond the Lejah.

AR′GOB. The two princes, Argob and Ariel, were killed with Pekahiah, in the palace at Samaria, by Pekah.

ARIARA′THES. Mithridates, king of Cappadocia, B. C. 163–130.

ARIDAI. Son of Haman (Esth. ix. 8).

ARIDA′THA. Son of Haman (Esth. ix. 8).

ARI′EH. ARJEH (*the lion*). See ARGOB. ARIEL.

Ā′RIEL (*lion of God*). Poetical name of Jerusalem (Is. xxix. 1, 2, 7).

Ā′RIEL (*lion of God*). Chief under Ezra (viii. 16), in his caravan. One of the Gileadite chiefs killed by Pekah. See ARGOB. The same word occurs in 2 Sam. xxiii. 20, where it is rendered "two lion-like men"—and might be "two sons of Ariel." 2. Isaiah (xxix. 1) so names Jerusalem.—Lion of God, or hearth of God; the same word in Ezekiel (xliii. 15) translated altar, means *hearth of God*.

ARIMATHE′A. A city of Judea (Luke xxiii. 51). King Demetrius writes (1 Macc. xi. 34): "We have ratified unto them the borders of Judea, with the three governments of Aphereum, Lydda, and Ramathaim, that are added unto Judea from the country of Samaria." Joseph of Arimathea (Matt. xxvii. 57; Mark xv. 43; John xix. 38). The place has been identified as the village of Renthieh, ten miles east of Joppa, on the road from Lydda to Antipatris, but this is doubted on the authority of Josephus. See RAMLEH.

Ā′RIOCH (*lion-like*). 1. King of Ellasar (Gen. xiv.1).—2. Captain of the guard (Dan. ii. 14).—3. King of the Elymæans. In Judith i. 6, Erioch king of the Eliceans; in DOWAY, Deioces, king in Media.

ARI′SAI. Son of Haman (Esth. ix. 9).

ARISTAR′CHUS (*excellent ruler*). A Thessalonian, companion of Paul; with him at Ephesus (Acts xix.), and on the voyage, and at Rome, a fellow-prisoner and laborer (Col. iv. 10; Philem. 24). Tradition makes him bishop of Apamea.

ARISTOBU′LUS (*best advised*). 1. Jewish priest in Egypt in the reign of Ptolemy VI, B. C. 165. Judas Maccabeus addressed him as a counsellor of the king (2 Macc. i. 10). He wrote and dedicated to Ptolemy an allegorical exposition of the Pentateuch. Eusebius and Clement of Alexandria preserve fragments of his works.—2. A resident at Rome, whose household is the subject of a salutation in Rom. xvi. 10.—3. Son and successor of John Hyrcanus.—4. Second son of Alexander Jannæus.—5. Grandson of No. 3, and the last of the Maccabeans; murdered by the designs of Herod, B. C. 34.—6. Son of Herod the Great by Marianne.

ARITH′METIC (*numbering*). The Hebrews were not a scientific, but a religious and practical people; but it must be in ferred from what they did, in certain trades and arts, that they had the needed skill, and reckoning by numbers was not an exception. For figures, after the captivity, they used their letters, as is seen on the Samaritan coins; and this may have been their earliest custom also.

EGYPTIAN ARK.

ARK. A word adopted from the Egyptian. A chest. The word for Noah's ark is TEBAH, the same as used for that of Moses (Gen. vi.; viii.; Ex. ii). ARK OF THE COVENANT. An oblong chest of acacia wood, gilded, 45 inches long, 27 wide, and 27 deep (Ex. xv. 10; Num. vii. 9.) It was to contain (or by its side), the book of the law, the covenant, and perhaps also the pot of manna, and Aaron's rod (Heb. ix. 4). When Solomon's temple was dedicated the ark contained only the "two tables" of stone (1 K. viii. 9). It was to be kept in the most holy place, excluding all idols, and itself be the centre of regard, as denoting the presence of God, on the Mercy Seat, which was on the lid, overshadowed by two images with wings. Jeremiah predicted (iii. 16), that it should be finally abandoned as a sacred object. It "rested" at Shiloh until the superstitious warriors took it into battle and lost it to the Philistines. Not long after its recovery it was placed in the temple. It is believed to have been burnt when the Babylonians destroyed Solomon's temple.

NOAH'S ARK. The form and size cannot be learned from the text. The figures are given as 300 cubits long, 50 wide, and 30 high. The cubit was of several kinds, 18, 19, and 21 inches in length. The present opinion (among some), is that the Deluge was a local inundation, extending only far enough to destroy the human race, which is supposed to have dwelt in the valley of the Euphrates and Tigris. The form of the ark may be seen in that of the great rafts on those rivers, which have a flat-roofed cabin on them, like a rude house. The Apameans had a tradition that the ark rested near their city, in Phrygia, of which the coin here shown, dating from A. D. 150, is a memorial, now in Paris.

BRACELETS AND ARMLETS.

ĂR'KITE. Canaanite people living at Arka, under Mt. Lebanon on the sea (Gen. x. 17). Alexander Severus was born there, and it was then named Cæsarea Lebani. The ruins are on a hill looking over a fine plain, the sea, and mts.

ARMAGED'DON. A name for the plain of Jezreel. ESDRAELON. Mount Megiddo (Rev. xvi. 16). There is a symbolical meaning attached to this name and place which it is impossible to explain in this limited space. It may be interesting to recount the several great battles fought on the plain, which have given it a solemn importance in history. The great victory of Barak over the Canaanites (Judg. iv., v.), and of Gideon over the Midianites (Judg. vii); and two great disasters—the death of Saul (1 Sam. xxi. 8) in the invasion of the Philistines, and the death of Josiah in the invasion of the Egyptians (2 K. xxiii. 29). See JEZREEL.

ARMĒ'NIA. ARARAT. Christianity was established here in the 4th century. The whole number of the Armenians is about two millions. They have a rich convent on Zion (See Jerusalem). The ARMENIAN VERSION of the Bible was made in A. D. 410 by (the patriarch Isaac and) Miesrob, aided by his pupils Joannes Ecclensis and Josephus Palnensis, from the Syriac. It was afterwards corrected from the Greek, and was finished in the year 431.

ĂRM'LETS. Ornaments worn by men, as bracelets are by women.

ARMS. ARMOR. Offensive. 1. Club, mace, bar, hammer, or maul (shevet-barzel, Ps. ii. 9). At first of wood, then of metal.—2. Throw-stick (maphitz) figured on the monuments, and called by Arabs lissan. The Australian boomerang is an instance.—3. Dirk or sword, of flint, a deer's horn (chereb, now used in the East), of wood as now in Nubia, or of metal. The sword is carried in a belt or slung (girded, 1 Sam. xvii. 39).—4. Spear (romach), a short blade of a deer's horn straightened, or of metal, on a pole of wood. The horn of the oryx is about 40 inches long. Some were very heavy (chanith, 1 Sam. xvii. 7).—5. Javelin (ridon), a light spear for throwing, a dart (shelach, 1 Sam. xii. 22). SHEBET, baton, or sceptre, with which Joab killed Absalom, (2 Sam. xviii. 14).—6. Bow (kesheth), and arrow (hitz), of a reed, branch, rib of palm, wood and horn, ivory, iron or brass. There were cases for the bow and for the arrows.—7. Sling (kela), for throwing stones; of plaited thongs. Stones were cast 400 feet and lead bullets 600. Balista were strong bows or springs rigged to throw stones (1 Chr. xii. 2).—8. Ram (car), a loaded car with a heavy pole shod with iron, sometimes shaped like a ram's head. Some were large towers on wheels, holding soldiers. Defensive. 1. Shield (tsinnah), buckler, (magen) roundel, (purnus) target, (shelet), made of wood, or wickerwork, covered with hide, bordered with metal; kings and chiefs had them made of gold, silver or brass.—2. HELMET (koba); of rushes, osiers, skins, wood, cloth (turban), and metal.—3. ARMOR for the body; of leather, iron, brass. Shown on the monuments, covering the breast, or breast and back, or the whole body, with separate pieces for the arms and legs (Goliath wore them). Armor was also placed on the horse.

ĂR'MY. The Hebrews began, continued, and ended their national life in war. The law of Moses enrolled in the army every male from 20 to 50 years (Num. i. 3; 2 Chr. xxv. 5; Ant. iii. 12, 14), except the Levites. The divisions were 10, 50, 100, 1000, with proper officers (1 Macc. iii. 56; Num. xxxi. 14; 1 Sam. viii. 12). Messengers with trumpets summoned to the camp (Judg. iii. 27). The head of the nation was leader, as Moses, until the time of David, when the office of "captain of the host" was made distinct from that of king. Foot soldiers were the only kind at first used (Num. xi. 21), even while the Canaanites had chariots of iron (Judg. i. 19). David introduced horses and chariots contrary to the divine direction (Deut. xvii. 16), and was followed by his successors. The soldiers had to provide their own arms and food (1 Sam. xvii. 17), until a STANDING ARMY was made by the kings (1 Sam. viii. 11, 12; xiii. 2; 1 Macc. xiv. 32). David had 600 chosen men (2 Sam. xv. 18), "mighty men," perhaps his body guard (1 K. xiv. 28). A division served in each month, changing through the year. Foreigners were admitted to the service, and even advanced to high places (1 Sam. xv. 19; Ant. xiii. 13, 5).

HEAVY ARMED WARRIOR.

ĂR'NA. Forefather of Ezra (2 Esd. i. 2).
ĂR'NAN (active). Son of Rephaiah (1 Chr. iii. 21, "sons of").

MAP OF ENVIRONS OF JERUSALEM.

AR'NON (*swift—noisy*). River forming the boundary between Moab and Ammon, east of the Dead Sea (Num. xxi.; Judg. xi.). Fords of Arnon (Is. xvi. 2). Near the Dead Sea the stream is eighty-two feet wide, four feet deep, and flows between almost perpendicular walls of red, brown, and yellow sandstone. Now the Wady Mojeb. (Josh. xiii. 9), "Aroer that is upon the bank of the river Arnon, and the city that is in the midst of the river." There is a ruin at the junction of the Lejum with the Arnon, name not known.

A'ROD (*wild ass*). Son of Gad (Num. xxvi. 17). ARODI (Gen. xlvi. 17). ARODITES.

AR'OER (*ruins*). Name of several places east of Jordan. 1. On the Arnon, north bank, ten miles from the Dead Sea, now in ruins. A Roman road connected it with cities north and south (Deut. ii. 36; iii. 12; iv. 48; Josh. xii. 2; xiii. 9; Judg. xi. 26; 2 K. x. 33; 1 Chr. v. 8).—2. Gad, facing Rabbah (Num. xxxii. 34; Josh. xiii. 25). Ayra, six miles east from the Jordan, two miles north of W. Sheriah.—3. The cities of Aroer (Is. xvii. 2). Supposed to be in Bashan.—4. Judah (1 Sam. xxx. 28). Ararah, on the road from Gaza to Petra, eleven miles southwest of Beer-sheba (Rob).

AR'OERITE. Hothan, father of two of David's captains (1 Chr. xi. 44).

A'ROM. 32 sons of Arom returned with Zorobabel (1 Esd. v. 16). ASOM? HASOM in Ezr. ii. 19.

COIN OF APAMEA.

ARPHAX'AD (*region of the Chasdim*). Third son of Shem, born B. C. 1658, and lived 438 years (Gen. x. 22; xi. 12—). Arrapachitis, in N. Assyria, was the original home of the Chaldeans.—2. King of the Medes (Deioces) who founded Ecbatana. Another account says he was Astyages, their last king.

ARSA'CES (*prince of the noble*). Title of the kings of Parthia and Media. Mithridates I took Demetrius II, of Syria, prisoner B. C. 139 (1 Macc. xiv. 2), and treated him with respect, giving him his daughter in marriage. Persians now call their king SHAH.

AR'SARETH. Region beyond the Euphrates (2 Esd. xiii. 45).

ARTAXERX'ES (*great king*). *Artachshast*. 1. One who hindered the rebuilding of the temple (Ezr. iv. 7), from his time to that of Darius. He is believed to be the Magian imposter Smerdis, B. C. 521). —2. Artaxerxes Longimanus in whose 7th year Ezra led the second colony of exiles back to Judea (c. 7). He was son of Xerxes who was defeated in Greece.—3. Who allowed Nehemiah, in the 20th year of his reign, to go to Jerusalem on civil business, and to remain in office there 12 years, B. C. 425. Some think that 2 and 3 were the same person.

AR'TEMAS. Companion to Paul (Tit. iii. 12). Bishop of Lystra?

AR'TEMIS. DIANA (Acts xix. 24).

ART L'LERY. Bows and arrows, slings, etc., in 1 Sam. xx. 40.

AR'UBOTH. Commissariat district of Solomon (1 K. iv. 10). Probably Shefelah.

ARU'MAH. Near Shechem. Residence of Abimelech (Judg. ix. 41).

AR'VAD (*wandering*). Phœnicia. On the island of Ruad, and on the mainland. Lately examined by Renan (Phœnicia, Paris, 1862). The island is a steep rock on every side, and has ruins of walls, some still very high (Strabo).

ARVADI TES. Descendents of Arvad, son of Canaan (Gen. x. 18). They lived on the island, and mainland (above) and were described as a colony of Sidon, and as noted mariners (Ez. xxvii. 8; Strabo 16, p. 754), and had a king of their own (1 Macc. xv. 23).

AR'ZA (*earth*). King Elah's prefect at Tirzah (1 K. xvi. 9). In the Targum, Jonathan, "idol of Beth-Arza."

A'SA (*physician*). Son of Abijah, grandson of Rehoboam, and 3d king of Judah, from B. C. 955 to 914, 41 years. "He walked in the steps of his ancestor David" (1 K. xv. 11).

ASADI'AS. HASADIAH (Baruch i. 1; 1 Chr. iii. 20).

AS'AEL. Ancestor of Tobit (i. 1). JAHZEEL?

AS'AHEL (*made by God*). Son of David's sister Zeruiah, brother to Joab and Abishai. Noted as a swift runner, and so lost his life (2 Sam. ii. 18).

ASAHI'AH (*God-made*). One of Josiah's messengers sent to Huldah the prophetess, to inquire about the newly found book of the law of Moses (2 K. xxii. 12). ASAIAH.

ASA'IAH (*God-made*). Chief in Hezekiah's reign (1 Chr. iv. 36).—2. Levite in David's reign (ib. vi. 30).—3. First-born of the Shilonite (ib. ix. 5).

AS'ANA (1 Esd. v. 31). ASNAH in Ezr. ii. 50.

A'SAPH (*choir leader*). Levite, son of Barachias (1 Chr. vi. 39), and David's choir leader. The "sons of Asaph" succeeded him as leaders (1 Chr. xxv.; 2 Chr. xx. 14). Eleven of the Ps. have his name in their titles (Ps. lxxiii.-lxxxiii.).—2. Recorder to king Hezekiah.—3. Keeper of the royal forest under Artaxerxes (Neh. ii. 8).

BATTERING RAM.

ASA'REEL (*God-bound*). Son of Jehaleleel (1 Chr. iv. 16).

ASARE'LAH. Son of Asaph, instrumental musician (1 Chr. xxv. 2).

ASBAZ'ARETH (1 Esd. x. 69). ESARHADDON. See ASBAZZARETH.

ASE'AS (1 Esd. ix. 32). ISHIJAH?
ASEBEBI'A. Levite in 1 Esd. viii. 47. SHEREBIAH?
ASEBI'A. HASHABIAH.
ASE'NATH (*worshiper of Neith*). Daughter of Potipherah, priest of On, Joseph's wife.
A'SER (Tobit i. 2). City in Galilee. HAZOR? (Luke ii. 36; Rev. vii. 6). ASHER.
ASE'RER (1 Esd. v. 32). SISERA?
A'SHAN. Ai Ghuweir, in Simeon (Josh. xv. 42; xix. 7).

goddess (2 K. xxi. 7; xxiii. 6). Grove in A. V. Perhaps a head or bust on a straight pillar.
ASH'IMA (*goat with short hair*). A god of the Hamathites, in Samaria, brought from Assyria (2 K. xvii. 30). The Mendesian god of Egypt was a goat (as the Greek Pan), and the Phœnician Esmun.
ASH'KELON. One of the five cities of the Lords of the Philistines (Josh. xiii. 3; 1 Sam. vi. 17). Samson retired to A. as to a remote place (Judg. xiv. 19). Since the crucifixion it has been more noted than before. There was a temple and sacred

ASHDOD.

ASHBE'A (*I adjure*). Eshba in the Targum of Joseph. It is not known whether this means a house or a place.
ASH'BEL (*God's charge*). Son of Benjamin (Gen. xlvi. 21).
ASHDOD. AZO'TUS. Eighteen miles south of Joppa, in Philistia. On an elevation above the plain, was strongly fortified, and was one of the seats of the worship of the god Dagon (1 Sam. v. 5; Josh. xv. 47). The birthplace of Herod the Great, who adorned it with baths. It was on the high road to Egypt, and besieged by the Assyrian Tartan, B. C. 716 (Is. xx. 1). Psammetichus besieged it for 29 years, B. C. 630 (Jer. xxv. 20). Philip was found at Azotus (Acts viii. 40; Neh. xiii. 23, 24). It was noted during the Crusades. Now called Usdud. The modern village is built among the ruins of the ancient city, and is embowered in groves, tall sycamores, and hedged with cactus, while the sand drifting with the wind is creeping up to the very doors, two miles from the sea, and burying every green thing.
ASH'DOTH-PIS'GAH (*to pour forth*). Springs E. of the Dead Sea (Deut. iii. 17; Josh. xii. 3; xiii. 20; Num. xxi. 15). Ravine on the E. slope of Pisgah.
ASHER (*happy*). The eighth son of Jacob, by Zilpah, Leah's handmaid (Gen. xxx. 13). The names of one of the 12 tribes. The boundaries are extremely difficult to trace, but were N. of Carmel, on the Great Sea (Josh. xix. 24-31). It contained some of the richest soil in Palestine, and minerals. Anna, who lived in the temple, watching for the coming of Christ, was of this tribe.
ASHE'RAH (*straight*). Idol of the Phœnician

lake to Derceto, the Syrian Venus. It was celebrated for its groves of cypress, figs, olives, pomegranates, vines, and for henna, which grew best here of any place, except only Canopus, and also for the peculiar onions called shallot. Richard I of England, during the Crusades, fortified and held his court at A. The Muslim called it the Bride of Syria. The ancient city was enclosed in a natural wall of hills forming an amphitheatre on the shore of the sea, and on the top of this ridge was the wall, which was very high, thick, and built of small stones and old columns of granite and marble. The modern village Askulan, is very beautiful in its groves, orchards, and shade-trees (Gen. xx. 2). Gerar is supposed to be A. by the Samaritans.
ASH'KENAZ. One of the sons of Gomer, son of Japhet. The tribe or nation was located in or near Armenia, Ararat, Minni (Jer. li. 27). The name is a compound, As-kenz = As-race. Probably the origin of ASIA.
ASH'NAH. Judah. Two cities. 1. 9 ms. W. of Jerusalem, near Zanoah (Josh. xv. 33). 2. S. W. of Jer. 16 ms., near Nezib (Josh. xv. 43).
ASH'PENAZ (*horse-nose*). Chief of the eunuchs in Assyria (Dan. i. 3).
AS'PHAR, THE POOL OF. Jonathan and Simon encamped in the vicinity of this pool before the battle with Bacchides (1 Macc. ix. 33; Jos. Ant. xiii. 1, § 2). Is it lake Asphaltitis?
ASH'RIEL. Son of Manasseh (1 Chr. vii. 14). ASRIEL?
ASH TERATHI'TE. Resident in Ashtaroth (1 Chr. xi. 44). Uzzia was one.
ASH'TORETH. ASHTAROTH (*star*). BASHAN.

ASHUR 27 ASTRONOMY

The seat of the idolatry of the goddess Ashtaroth, or Astarte. *Tell Ashareh*, a mound 70 feet high, at one time occupied by a village or buildings. A fine spring issues near some ruins at the base. Following the Samaritan Pentateuch, which reads Afinit Karnaim, instead of Ashtaroth Karnaim, the site of the temple and city of Astarte, is looked for on the S. W. slope of Jebel Hauran, 8 miles N. E. from Bozrah at a place called *El Afineh*.—2. *A. Karnaim* (*of the two horns*). Now supposed to be Es Sunamein, 25 miles S. of Damascus on the pilgrim route to Mecca. *Sunamein=two idols*.

ASH'UR (*hero*). Son of Hezron; "father" (chief) of Tekoa (1 Chr. ii. 24).

ASH'URITES. In the list of Ishbosheth (2 Sam. ii. 9). House of Asher, meaning the whole of Galilee (Judg. i. 32).

COIN OF LAODICEA—STRUCK BY THE ASIARCH.

ASH'VATH. Son of Japhlet, of Asher (1 Chr. vii. 33).

A'SIA (*orient*). Found only in 1 Macc. viii. 6, and the N. T. Now Asia Minor.—2. The country of the king of Pergamos, Mysia, Lydia, Phrygia. 3. Name claimed by the kings of Antioch, now Cilicia (1 Macc. xii. 39). Chief town, Ephesus (Acts ii. 9).

ASIAR'CHÆ. Chief of Asia in Acts xix. 31. A religious office in Asia (Minor), under the Romans, annual, and subject to the proconsul. There are coins of several cities which show by their inscriptions that this office was a great honor. Their duties were the control of the public GAMES and SPECTACLES in the theatres (which were at their own expense?). Philip was the Asiarch when Polycarp was killed at Smyrna. Only wealthy men could have it. Each city sent one person annually to the council, ten were chosen from the whole number, one was made president, or Asiarch. Others think the ten were all Asiarchs.

ASIHI'AS. Son of Phorosh, or Parosh (1 Esd. ix. 26).

A'SIEL (*God-made*.) Ancestor of Jehu of Hezekiah's reign (1 Chr. iv. 35).—2. One of the five writers employed by Esd. on the law and history (2 Esd. xiv. 24).

ASI'PHA (1 Esd. v. 29). HASUPHA.

ASMODE'US (*to destroy*). "King of the demons." (Tobit. iii, 8, etc.)

ASNAP'PER (*general*). "The great and noble" officer who settled the Assyrians in Samaria (Ex. iv. 10).

A'SOM (1 Esd. ix. 33). HASHUM.

ASP. Cobra of Egypt. See ADDER.

ASPAL'ATHUS. A sweet perfume (Ecclus. xxiv. 15).

ASPA'THA. Son of Haman (Esth. ix. 7).

AS'PHAR, THE POOL. In the wilderness of Thecoe (1 Macc. ix. 33). ASPHALTITIS?

ASPHAR'ASUS. MISPERETH (1 Esd. v. 8).

AS'RIEL (*vow of God*). Son of Gilead (Num. xxvi. 31). ASRIELITES.

ASSAHI'AS (1 Esd. i. 9). HASHABIAH. ASSHIA.

ASSAL'IMOTH (1 Esd. viii. 36). SHELOMITH?

ASSANI'AS (1 Esd. viii. 54). HASHABIAH?

ASSARE'MŌTH (1 Macc. iv. 15). Margin. GAZERA?

AS'SHUR. Son of Shem. Named Assyria.

ASSHU'RIM. From Dedan, grandson of Abraham (Gen. xxv. 3). Ashur in Ezr. xxvii. 23.

ASSIDÆ'ANS (*pious*). A sect who upheld the doctrine of the unity of God, and opposed Grecian manners and idolatries (1 Macc. vii. 13). The name afterwards denoted a life of austerity and religious exercises, in the hope of hastening the coming of the Messiah, and of making an atonement for their own and others' sins. (There is a sect of the name of Assidians now in Poland).

AS SIR (*captive*). Son of Korah (Ex. vi. 24).—2. Son of Ebiasaph (1 Chr. vi. 23). 3. Son of Jeconiah (1 Chr. iii. 17). Jeconiah, the captive?

AS'SOS. Seaport in Mysia, on a peninsula in the Ægean Sea (Acts xx. 13). The ruins are very extensive, and give a more perfect idea of an entire ancient Greek city than any other known site. Paul met Luke and others here after walking from Troas.

ASSYR'IA. Country on the Tigris (Gen. ii. 14), the capital of which was Nineveh (x. 11): named from *Asshur*, the Son of Shem, who was deified and worshiped as their chief god by the Assyrians: 500 ms. N. E. to S. W. and 350 to 100 ms. wide. Divided from Armenia by a high range of mountains. Its northern part is mountainous, the middle hilly, with fertile plains, and the southern is the great plain of *Mesopotamia* (*midst of rivers*)—the district now called *El Jezira*. This plain is 250 miles long, divided by the rocky ridge, *Sinjar*—a limestone range, sparsely wooded, and of a golden color, with purple lines of shade at a distance. 80 ms. N. of the Sinjar the plain extends to the hilly region, and was once densely populated, but is now a wilderness. The mounds are the only relics of antiquity, and these contain (in those of Nineveh, and others recently partly explored by Layard), proofs of their greatness, in sculptures, inscriptions, and remnants of architecture. The first king of A. who oppressed Israel was Chushan-Rishathaim, B. C. 1400 (Judg. iii. 8). Art and architecture, civil and religious institutions, were in a very advanced state. They used the arch, tunnels, drains, the level, and roller; engraved on gems; enamelled, inlaid, and plated with metals; made glass, optical instruments, ivory, bronze, and precious metal ornaments. The prophesies against A. are those of Nahum, B. C. 645; Zephaniah ii., B. C. 608; and Ezekiel xxxi. B. C. 584.

ASSYRIAN KING.

ASSYR'IANS. In Heb. ASSHUR (Is. x. 5., etc.).

ASTAR'TE. ASHTORETH.

ASTATH (1 Esd. viii. 38). AZGAD?

ASTRON'OMY (*star-naming*). The knowledge of this science by the Hebrews was very limited, as may be judged from their writings; but they in no case oppose scientific fact or truth. Some special

knowledge was needed for the temple service. Worship of the stars was denounced with other idolatries (Job xxxviii. 32; K. xxiii. 5. MAZZAROTH. 2. Signs of the Zodiac. MAZZALOTH—planets). The Chaldeans and Egyptians were more cultivated in this and other sciences, and used them in their religious systems.

ASSYRIAN KING PUTTING OUT THE EYES OF HIS CAPTIVES.

ASY'LUM (*inviolable refuge*). The earliest recorded was the temple of pity at Athens, or perhaps one made by Cadmus at Thebes, Greece. Christians adopted the pagan custom and made their churches asylums, and this is still the case in Italy. Moses set apart 6 cities of refuge in the Holy Land. (CITIES OF REFUGE). He also made the "horns of the altar" an asylum; which privilege afterwards attached to the temple and its courts (1 Macc. x. 43).

ASYN'CRITUS. Disciple at Rome (Rom. xvi. 14).

A'TAD (*thorn*). Threshing-floor on the W. of Jordan, near Hebron, (Gen. l. 10–11). ABEL-MIZRAIM.

AT'ARAH (*crown*). Wife of Jerahmeel, mother of Onam (1 Chr. ii. 26).

AT'AROTH (*crowns*). 1. A. Beth Joab, Judah (1 Chr. ii. 54).—2. A. Addar, Eph. (Josh. xvi. 2), 6 ms. N. W. of Bethel.—3. A. Shophan-Gad (Num. xxxii. 34), S. of Heshban, near Jebel Atarus.—4. A. Reuben (Num. xxx. 3).

A'TER (*dumb*). Gate-keepers in the temple (Ezr. ii. 42). Sons of Jatal (1 Esd. v. 28).—2. 98 sons of Ater returned with Zerubbabel (Num. viii. 21).

ATERE'ZIAS (1 Esd. v. 15). See ATER 2.

ATHARI'AS (1 Esd. v. 40). Correctly "the Tirshatha."

ATHENO'BIUS. Envoy by Antiochus Sidetes to Simon (1 Macc. xv. 28).

ATH'ENS. Capital of Greece, founded by Cecrops, B. C. 1556. Visited by Paul (Acts xvii.; 1 Thess. iii.). He founded a church. The people were lovers of music, painting, sculpture, architecture, and oratory, and took part in politics. The fine arts, history, and philosophy were a part of the education of all freemen. The plan shows the position of the Agora (*market-place*), between the four hills. Pausanius says the Athenians surpassed all others in attention to the gods; and their city was crowded with temples, altars, statues, and other sacred works. Paul said they were "too religious." See AREOPAGUS.

ATH'LAI. ATHALIAH. Error in Ezr. x. 28.

ATIPHA (1 Esd. v. 32). HATIPHA?

ATONE'MENT (*at-one-ment*). Satisfaction for sin by which forgiveness is had. When Jacob sent a present to his brother Esau, he said, "I will cover his face, so that he shall forgive my offence, I will make atonement before him, I will placate him" (Gen. xxxii. 21). In Ps. xvi. 14, "a wise man will pacify it" (the wrath of the king). Only once in the N. T., in Rom. v. 11, where it means reconciling. THE DAY OF ATONEMENT was a great feast of the Jews, on the 10th of Tisri, and was held as a day of rest, a kind of Sabbath of Sabbaths, the only day in the year when the whole people fasted. The service was peculiar. The high-priest, clothed in white linen, without ornaments, took a young bull and a ram for himself and his house, and two goats as a sin-offering, and a ram as a burnt offering for the people. The goats were selected by lot, one for Jehovah and one for Azazel in the wilderness (*that is to be sent away surely*). The blood of the victims was taken into the most holy place and sprinkled upon and before the mercy-seat. The scape-goat, to be sent away, was brought forth and the high-priest confessed over his head his sins and those of the people, and he was sent into the wilderness by a trusty man. The bullock and the goat were not eaten, but entirely burnt. This was a symbol of the great truths of the redemptory system by means of propitiation, and it is understood as a type of the vicarious intercession of Jesus Christ.

AT'TAI (*timely*). Grandson of Sheshan, son of Ahlai and Jarha, the Egyptian slave (1 Chr. ii. 35). 2. One of David's "lion-faced" warriors (1 Chr. xli. 11).—3. Second son of Rehoboam by Maachah, daughter of Absalom (2 Chr. xi. 20).

ATTAL'IA. Maritime city in Pamphylia, named from Attalus Philadelphus, king of Pergamos. (Acts xiv. 25). Now Adalia, whose ruins witness its former greatness. Pop. 8000.

ATTHARA'TES (1 Esd. ix. 49). Error for "the Tirshatha" in Neh. viii. 9.

AU'GIA. Daughter of Barzillai (1 Esd. v. 38).

AUGUS'TUS (*venerable*). Title of the Roman Emperors. First assumed by Caius Julius Cæsar Octavianus (nephew of the great Julius Cæsar), when at the battle of Actium he became sole ruler of the empire, B. C. 29. Born B. C. 63, died A. D. 14, aged 76. He gained his great power by gradually uniting in himself all the principal state offices. Tiberius was associated with him in the empire long before his death. He was truly venerable and worthy of regard, for he used his absolute power with great moderation and prudence.

PLAN OF ATHENS.

AUGUSTUS' BAND (Acts xxvii. 1). Independent guard of the governor.

AURA'NUS. Leader of a riot in Jerusalem (2 Macc. iv. 40).

AUTE'AS. Levite (1 Esd. ix. 48). HODIJAH?

A'VA (*overturning*). In Assyria; AHAVA—IVAH (2 K. xvii).

ā, ē, ī, ō, ū, ȳ, long; ă, ĕ, ĭ, ŏ, ŭ, ў, short; câre, fär, låst, fạll, whạt; thêre, veil, têrm; pîque, fîrm; dône, fôr, do, wolf, food, foot;

AV'ARAN (*killer of the royal elephant*). (1 Macc. vi. 43-46). Title of honor given to Eleazar, brother of Judas Maccabeus.

A'VEN (*nothing*). 1. Plain of AVEN, perhaps the Bukaa, of Baalbek (Amos i. 5).—2. High places of AVEN (Hos. x. 8), BETHEL.—3. In Ezr. xxx. 17, AVEN—ON, HELIOPOLIS in Egypt.

A'VIM, (*ruins*). AVITES. 1. Inhabitants of Ava. (2 K. xvii).—2. Town in Benj., ruins-town (Josh. xviii. 23). It is supposed, from Joshua, xiii. 3, that the country of the Avim was taken from them by the Philistines; called Hazerim in Deut. ii. 23.

A'VITH. Chief city of Hadad, king of Edom, (Gen. xxxvi. 35). Jebel Ghoweythe, N. E. of Kerak.

AXES.

AX. The Hebrew words are KARDOM, or GARZEN, the softer form, for a heavy ax with a long handle. MAATZAD, a carving knife (Is. xliv. 12), and also a file for wood or iron (Jer. x. 3); CHEREB, a longer knife, or sword; CASH SHIL (Ps. lxxiv. 6), a carpenter's hatchet; MAGZERAH, ax or clever; MAPPETS, a maul or battle-ax. In some the ax is fastened to the handle with a thong or strip of leather, wound around a great many times; in others there is a hole or eye through the head. See KNIFE, HOE.

AZ'AEL (1 Esd. ix. 14). ASAHEL. AZAE'LUS

A'ZAL. ATZAL (Zech. xiv. 5). The limit of the Mt. of Olives in a poetical passage of Zechariah.

AZALIAH (*God-spared*). Father of Shothan, the scribe (2 K. xxii. 3).

AZANIAH (*God hears*). Father of Jeshua, the Levite (Neh. x. 9).

AZA'PHION. SOPHERETH ? (1 Esd. v. 33).

AZAR'AEL. AZA'REEL (*God helps*). Korhite, with David at Ziklag (1 Chr. xii. 6).—2. Levite musician in David's time (1 Chr. xxv. 18); Uzziel in xxv. 4.—3. Son of Jehoram, of Dan (1 Chr. xxvii. 22).—4. Son of Bani (Ezr. x. 41). Esril in 1 Esd. ix. 34. —5. Father of Amashai, priest in Jerusalem (Neh. xi. 13).

AZARIAS (1 Esd. ix. 21). Uzziah in Ezr. x. 21. Several errors in the Apocrypha of this name, the correct form being found in Ezra and Nehemiah, Azariah. AZARIAS, the angel Raphael (Tobit v. 12).

A'ZAZ (*strong*). Father of Bela (1 Chr. v. 8). REUBENITE.

AZA'ZEL. Scape-goat in Lev. xvi. 8. See ATONEMENT.

AZAZIAH (*God strengthens*). Musician in David's choir (1 Chr. xv. 21). Harpist.—2. Father of Hosea, prince in Ephraim (1 Chr. xxvii. 26).—3. Treasurer of tithes in Hezekiah's time (2 Chr. xxxi. 13).

AZBAZ'ARETH. ESAR-HADDON (1 Esd. v. 69).

AZ'BUK. Father of Nehemiah, prince of Beth-zur (Neh. iii. 16).

A'ZEKAH. In the plain of Judah, having "daughters," suburbs (Josh. 10). *Tell Zakariya?*

A'ZEL. Descendant of Saul (1 Chr. viii. 37). ASEL.

A'ZEM (*bone*). EZEM.

AZEPHURITH. ARSIPHURITH (1 Esd. v. 16);— Jorah, in Ezr. ii. 18, and Hariph in Neh. vii. 24; combined by an error of the scribe.

AZE'TAS. Family that returned (1 Esd. v. 15); not in Ezra and Nehemiah.

AZ'GAD. Family of 1222 returned with Ezra (ii. 12); and 110 in his second caravan (viii. 12). Sadas in 1 Esd. v. 13, and 3222. Astath in 1 Esd. viii. 38.

AZI'A. Porter in the temple (1 Esd. v. 31). UZZA.

AZI'EI (2 Esd. i. 2). Ancestor of Esdras. AZARIAH. EZARIAH. EZIAH.

A'ZIEL. JAAZIEL.

AZI'ZA (*strong*). Of the family of Zattu (Ezr. x. 27). SARDEUS (1 Esd. ix. 28).

AZMA'VETH (*strong as death*). One of David's "valiant men" of Bahurim (2 Sam. xxiii. 31).—2. Descendant of Mephibosheth (1 Chr. viii. 36).—3. Father of Jeziel and Pelet, Benjamite slingers and archers who joined David at Ziklag (1 Chr. xii. 3). 4. Overseer of the royal treasures in David's reign.

AZMA'VETH. City in Benj. now Hizmeh, S. E. of Er-Ram (Ramah). The sons of the singers settled there (Neh. xii. 29).

AZ'MON. S. border of Palestine, near Hazar-addar (Num. xxxiv. 5). Now ASEI'MEH, west of Kedesh.

AZ'NOTH TABOR (*ears of Tabor*). W. in Naphtali, near Dio Cæsarea (*Eusebius*).

A'ZOR. Son of Eliakim in the genealogy of Jesus (Matt. i. 13).

AZO'TUS. ASHDOD.

AZOTUS, MOUNT. Battle-field in which Judas Maccabeus was killed (1 Macc. ix. 15). Hill on which Ashdod was built?

AZ'RIEL (*God's help*). Patriarch in Manasseh (1 Chr. v. 24).—2. Ancestor of Jerimoth, chief in Naphtali (1 Chr. xxvii. 19). Uzziel in the lxx.— 3. Father of Serriah (Jer. xxxvi. 26).

AZ'RIKAM (*help against an enemy*). Son of Neariah, of Judah (1 Chr. iii. 23).—2. Son of Azel (1 Chr. viii. 38).—3. Ancestor of Shemaiah (1 Chr. ix. 14).—4. Prefect in the palace of Ahaz, in Pekah's invasion (2 Chr. xxviii. 7).

AZU'BAH. Wife of Caleb (1 Chr. ii. 18).—2. Mother of Jehoshaphat (1 K. xxii. 42).

COIN OF HADRIAN AUGUSTUS.

A'ZUR. AZ'ZUR. Father of Hananiah, the false prophet (Jer. xxviii. 1.)—2. Father of Jaazaniah (Ezr. xi. 1).

AZU'RAN (1 Esd. v. 15). Azzur in Neh. x. 17.

AZ'ZAH (*strong*) (Deut. ii. 23, etc.). Correct name of Gaza.

AZ'ZAN (*sharp*). Father of Paltiel, of Issachar, a prince (Num. xxxiv. 26).

AZ'ZUR (*helper*.) Signer of the marriage covenant (Neh. x. 17). AZUR.

B

BĀ'AL (*sun* or *lord*). The supreme male god of the Phœnicians, as Ashtoreth was the supreme female goddess. The worship has been practiced from the most ancient times, and was adopted by the Jews, and carried on with great pomp and ceremony in special temples adorned with his images. The several names by which he was known were—1. BAAL-BE'RITH (*covenant*), at Shechem (Judg. viii. 33).—2. BAAL-ZE'BUB (*of the fly*), at Ekron.—3. BAAL-HA'NAN (*gracious*). BAAL-PE'OR (see Smith's Dictionary). The name was given to many places.

1. Simeon (1 Chr. iv. 33). Baalath Beer.
2. **BĀ'ALAH**. Kirjath Jearim, Judah, 7 miles W. of Jerusalem (Josh. xv. 9).—3. Town of the same name in Dan (Josh. xix. 44).
3. **B. BĒER** (*B. of the well*, or *holy well*), south Judah, and given to Simeon. Other sacred wells in this region were called Beer-lahai-roi (*of the vision of God*), and Beersheba (*of the oath*).
4. **B. GAD** (*fortune*). The most northern point of Joshua's victories (xi. 17 ; xii. 7). Supposed to have been a Phœnician sanctuary. Robinson thought it was the same as Banias, which has been a sanctuary of the god Pan from a remote age.
5. **B. HĀ'MON** (*of multitude*). Where Solomon had a vineyard (Cant. viii. 11). May have been not far north of Samaria (Judith viii. 3).
6. **B. HĀ'ZOR** (*village*). Where Absalom had a sheep-farm, and where Amnon was murdered (2 Sam. xiii. 23).
7. **MT. BĀ'AL HERMON**. Mt. Hermon.
8. **B. MĒ'ON**. BETH-BAAL-MEON. BETH-MEON (1 Chr. v. 8). 9 miles from Heshbon, near the mountain of the hot springs, and reputed to be the native place of Elisha.

OCTAGON TEMPLE, BAALBEK.

10. **B. PĒR'AZIM** (*destructions*). Scene of David's victory over the Philistines (2 Sam. v. 20; 1 Chr. xiv. 11).
11. **B. SHAL'ISHA** (*third idol*). Not far from Gilgal, Sharon (2 K. iv. 42).
12. **B. TĀ'MAR** (*of the palm*). Benjamin, near Gibeah (Judg. xx. 33). The palm-tree of Deborah is supposed to be meant by some. Lost.
13. **B. ZĒ'PHON**. Near the crossing-place of the Red Sea in the Exodus. Lost.

BA'ALAH. BAAL.
BA'ALATH. BAAL.
BA'ALE, of Judah. BAAL.
BA'ALIM. BAAL.
BA'ALIS. King of the Bene-Ammon (Jer. xl. 14).
BA'ANA. Son of Ahilud (1 K. iv. 12).
BA'ANAH. 1. Son of Rimmon (2 Sam. iv.).—2. Fathers of Heleb (2 Sam. xxiii. 29).—3. Cor-

GREAT STONE IN THE QUARRY AT BAALBEK.

rectly Baana, Son of the Cushai (1 K. iv. 16).—4. Returned with Zerubbabel (Ezr. ii. 2).

BA'ARA. Wife of Shaharaim.

BAASEI'AH. A Gershonite, ancestor of Asaph (1 Chr. vi. 40).

BAASHA (*bad*). The first king of the second line which reigned over the ten tribes. He was an idolater—worshiped the calves, and compelled the people to break off intercourse with Jerusalem.

BĀ'ALBEK (*city of the sun*). BAAL GAD (Josh. xi. 17; xii. 7), in Cœle-Syria, the valley of Lebanon, under Mt. Hermon. The ruins are the most important and remarkable in the whole country ; the site pleasantly located on the lowest slopes of Anti-Lebanon, at the opening of a small valley into the plain El Bukaa. A small stream, divided into many rills for irrigation, waters the fertile soil.

The city was not regular in plan, and heaps of ruins scattered over a space of two miles indicate its size. The chief attractions are the three temples. 1. The Great Temple, whose ruins are very grand and picturesque, but seems to have been left unfinished. The Great Gate is ornamented with every device that could be used in the most florid Corinthian style. Ears of grain, vine-leaves and grapes, with little figures of genii, or elves half-hid among them, and many choice touches of scroll-work, attract the eye and gratify the taste. Only 6 columns of the peristyle of this temple are now standing (75 ft. high, 7 ft. thick, the pediment 120 ft. above the ground), besides two courts and a portico. These are on an artificial platform, which is elevated 30 feet, and has vaults underneath. The three great stones forming a part

of the wall of this platform measure (1) 64 ft., (2) 63 ft. 8 in., (3) 63 ft. Thickness, 13 feet. The large stone left in the quarry is 69 ft. long, 17 ft. wide, and 14 ft. thick. 2. The Octagon Temple is Ionic and Corinthian in style, circular inside and outside, having niches which are seen each between two columns. Carved wreaths ornament the space above each. This has been used as a Christian church, but is now ruinous. 3. The Temple of the Sun, also Corinthian, is the most beautiful work there. The great work of Wood and Dawkins contains drawings and plans of every object of interest at Baalbek, and also at Palmyra.

BA′ASHA (*lays waste*). Son of Ahijah, 3d king of Israel, for 24 years. B. C. 953 to 930.

BA′BEL, BAB′YLON (*gate of God*). Capital of the Plain of Shinar (Gen. x. 10). Built B. C. 2600 (ver. 25), on both sides of the river Euphrates: a vast square, 56 miles in circuit. About 5 miles above *Hillah*, on the E. bank of the river, are a great many artificial mounds of enormous size, in three groups: 1. Babil, or Mujellibe (*overturned*), a high pile of unbaked bricks; 2. The palace or *Kasr*; and 3. The mound on which the modern tomb of *Amram ibn Ali* stands. In a line with the Amram mound, on both sides of the river, are the ruins of a great palace, the bricks of which bear the name of Nergal-Sharezer (Neriglissar), who was the chief magician (Rab-mag) and officer of Nebuchadnezzar (Jer. xxxix. 3). Similar mounds, but smaller, are scattered over the country on both sides of the river, one of which, 6 miles S. W. of Hillah is called *Birs Nimrud*, which some say is the tower of Babel. Inscriptions found here, of the date of Nebuchadnezzar, mark the site of Borsippa, outside of Babylon. A broad and deep moat, kept full of water, surrounded one wall of the ancient city, outside of which was another wall 200 royal cubits high and 50 thick. (*Pliny* says 200, *Strabo* 75, and *Rawlinson* 60 to 70 feet). Scarcely a trace of these walls can be found now, except it may be a few mounds which are supposed to mark the sites of some of the gates. Ctesias says there were 250 towers on the walls. The houses were generally built of bricks made of the river mud, sundried, or burnt in kilns, cemented with bitumen, and were three and four stories high.

The streets were straight, and crossed each other at right angles, the cross streets having gates of bronze at the river. Ctesias mentions a bridge of stone 3,000 feet long and 30 feet wide, connecting two palaces on opposite sides of the river. There were 3 walls around the royal palace on the Eastern side, the second or middle wall being 300 ft. high and the towers 420 ft., and 4½ miles in circuit, made of colored brick, representing hunting scenes, with figures of Ninus and Semiramis. A tunnel under the river also connected the two palaces (Jer. li. 58, 53; l. 15). There were a hundred gates of bronze with posts and lintels of the same. The banks of the river had quays, whose ruins still exist, and on the bricks was written in arrow-head characters the name of the last king. The most imposing ruin examined by Layard is called *Birs Nimrud*, and was found to be in seven stories, with a chamber on the top, each story smaller, forming an oblique pyramid with a square base. It was called the *Temple of the Seven Spheres*, and is not the Tower of Babel of the Scriptures, which is not yet identified. The stories were colored, and were, beginning at the lower—1st, 272 ft. square, 26 ft. high, colored black; 2d, 230 sq. 26 h., orange; 3d, 188 sq. 26 h., red; 4th, 146 sq. 15 h., golden color; 5th, 104 sq. 15 h., yellow; 6th, 62 sq. 15 h., blue; 7th, 20 sq. 15 h., silver color; and the ark nearly covering the entire upper platform and 15 feet high, color not given: making, in all, 153 feet above the platform, which was three feet above the plain. The empire lasted 1300 yrs. (Jer. xxv. 12, 14). It is now a desolation, the great city has become heaps (ii. 37), the land a wilderness for wild beasts, and even the Arabs refuse to pitch the tent, and the shepherd to fold sheep there (Is. xiii. 19–22).

BA′BI (1 Esd. viii. 37). BEBAI.

BĀ′CA (*weeping*). The valley (Ps. lxxxiv. 6). Located in Hinnom (2 Sam. v. 23). A valley of the same name is now found in Sinai. (*Burck.*).

BACCHI′DES (*son of Bacchus*). Friend of Antiochus Epiphanes, and governor of Mesopotamia; after Judas Maccabeus fell he reëstablished the power of the Syrian faction in Judæa. B. C. 161–158.

BACCHU′RUS. A holy singer who married a foreign wife (1 Esd. ix. 24).

BAC′CHUS. Greek *Dionysus*. (2 Macc. vi. 7; xiv. 33). A god of special abhorence to the Jews. He

VIEW OF BABIL.

was the god of wine, and of general festivity and jollity, and his rites sanctioned the most frantic excesses of revelry and excitement. Nicanor threatened to build a temple to Bacchus on the site of the temple of Solomon.

BACE′NOR. Captain under Judas Maccabæus (2 Macc. xii. 35).

BACH′RITES. Family of Becher, son of Ephraim.

BADG′ER (Heb. *Tachash*). The antelope. Tachaitze of Eastern Africa, bluish slaty-gray in color. Sculptured in Egypt.

BA′GO. BIGVAI.

BAGO′AS. EUNUCH (Judith xii. 11).

BA′GOI (1 Esd. v. 14). BIGVAI.

BAHARU'MITE, THE. BAHURIM.

BAHU'RIM (*young men's village*). Near the Jerusalem-Jericho road; where in the *Wady Ruwaby*, there are some ruins.

BALA'AM (*stranger*). Son of Beor, and a prophet (Num. xxii. 5). This strange man worshiped Jehovah, and at the same time knew and practiced the forbidden arts of divination. His prophesies are distinguished for dignity, compression, vividness, and fulness of imagery: there is scarcely any work equal to them in the later prophets (Rev. ii. 14).

BA'LAC (Rev. ii. 14). BALAK.

BAL'ADAN, MERODACH–BALADAN.

BA'LAH (Josh. xix. 3). BAAL.

BA'LAK (*empty*). Son of Zippor, king of Moab, who hired Balaam to curse the Israelites (Num. xxii. 24).

BAL'AMO. BAAL. (Judith. viii. 3).

BALAS'AMUS (1 Esd. ix. 43).

BALDNESS, is natural and artificial. The artificial is caused by shaving the head, in token of mourning for the dead (Jer. xvi. 6), which Moses forbade to the Jews because it was a heathen custom. Baldness was ridiculed (2 K. ii. 23), perhaps on suspicion of leprosy. A bald man was declared unfit for the priestly office (Lev. xxi. 20).

BALM. TSORI.

BALNU'US (Esd. ix. 31). BINNUI.

BALTHA'SAR. (Bar. i. 11-12). BELSHAZZAR.

BA'MAH (*High-place*) (Ezr. xx. 29). Jehovah gave this name to every place of idolatrous worship.

BA'MOTH. Station in the Exodus (Num. xxi. 19.)

BA'MOTH-BA'AL. BAAL. High-place in Moab (Josh. xiii. 17).

BAN (1 Esd. v. 37). TOBIAH.

BANAI'AS (1 Esd. ix. 35). BENAIAH.

BA'NI. 1. Gadite; one of David's 30 (2 Sam. xxiii. 36).—2. A Levite (1 Chr. vi. 46).—3. Father of Imri (1 Chr. ix. 4). 4. Children of Bani, returned with Zerubbabel (Ezr. ii. 10–5. An Israelite—son of Bani (Ezr. x. 38).—6. A Levite (Neh. iii. 17). 7. A Levite [ANUS] (Neh. viii. 7).—8. Another Levite (Neh. ix. 4).—9. Levite—son of Asaph (Neh. xi. 22).

BA'NID (1 Esd. viii. 36). Lost out of Ezr. viii. 10.

BANNAI'A (1 Esd. ix. 33). SABAD in Ezra

BAN'NUS (1 Esd. ix. 34). BANI or BINNUI.

BAN'QUET. Entertainment furnished at the expense of one man; usually towards the close of the day, between 5 and 6, and called supper. On grand occasions the invitations were given out some days before, and on the day appointed a servant was sent to announce that the time had arrived, and the guest was expected (Matt. xxii. 8; Luke xiv. 17). After accepting the invitation, to neglect to attend was no less than an insult. When all who had been invited had arrived the master of the house shut the door (Luke xiii. 24). The first act of welcome was washing the feet and anointing the hair with perfumed oil; and among the wealthy, on great days, a handsome cloak was furnished to each guest, to be worn during the festivity (Ecc. ix. 8; Rev. iii. 4).

BAN'UAS. Returned from captivity (1 Esd. v. 26).

BAPTISM. Washing before prayer or sacrifice was a custom among all ancient nations, as a sign of spiritual purity in the physical cleanness, and baptism was instituted as an initiatory rite of his religion by the Lord Jesus Christ. To be baptized for Moses (1 Cor. x. 2) means to become subject to the law of Moses; to be baptized for Christ, shows an intention to become a true follower of Christ. John baptized with water unto repentance—not causing repentance but as a sign of it. Perhaps only a sign of their willingness to enrol themselves among John's followers. Jesus himself did not baptize with water, but with the Spirit, and Christian baptism was only instituted after the resurrection, when the Lord gave the commission to his apostles "to go into all the world and preach the gospel to every creature." There are different views of Baptism. 1. That it is a direct instrument of grace, when applied by a properly qualified person; infusing into the soul positive moral goodness; or, as some believe, giving only the *capacity*

KASR, RUIN OF ANCIENT PALACE.

to receive goodness, which if rightly used will lead to salvation; while others again see that the good will only be enjoyed by those who are predestined to salvation.—2. It is a seal of grace, divine blessings being thereby confirmed to the soul.—3. Some hold that it is only a sign of initiation into Church membership.—4. Or a token of regeneration, to be received only by those who give evidence of being really regenerated.—5. A symbol of purification. The *mode* of baptism differs; and there is practiced immersion and affusion or sprinkling. The Marcionites, and the Gnostics baptized the dead (1 Cor. xv. 29), by proxy, some one answering for the dead, while the water was applied to the dead body; and parents were baptized for their children, from a mistaken reading of the words of Paul. He meant "If the dead rise not at all, what benefit do they expect who baptize vicariously for the dead?"

BARAB'BAS (*son of Abba*). One who had forfeited his life for sedition and murder (Mark xv. 7). The Armenian Version reads "Whom will ye that I shall deliver unto you, Jesus Barabbas, or Jesus that is called Christ?"

BAR'ACHEL. Father of Elihu, a Buzite (Job xxxii. 2-6).

BARACHI'AS (Matt. xxiii. 25). ZACHARIAS.

BA'RAK (*lightning*). Son of Abinoam of Kedesh, Naphtali (Judg. iv. 6). Summoned by Deborah to fight against Jabin and Sisera.

BARBA'RIAN. Any nation but the Greek, was the Greek definition. The term meant to the Greeks what Gentile did to the Jews—any people but Jews. The Egyptians had a similar term; and the oriental nations all had, and have now some term for distinction between their own and other people.

BARHU'MITE. BAHURIM. AZMAVETH.

BARI'AH. Son of Shemaiah, of Judah (1 Chr. iii. 22).

BAR-JE'SUS. ELYMAS.

BAR-JO'NA. PETER.

BARKOS. A Nethinim returned with Zerubbabel (Ezr. ii. 53).

BAR'LEY. Used, by the poor only, for bread, mixing it with wheat, beans, lentils, millet, etc., and as fodder for horses (Judg. vii. 13; 2 K. iv. 42; Ezr. iv. 9; 1 K. iv. 28). The barley harvest is in March and April, earlier than the wheat harvest by three weeks.

Barley bread is a sign of poverty, and is little esteemed (Ezr. xiii. 19). Its value was one-third that of wheat (Rev. vi. 6).

BARN. Ten different Hebrew and Greek words are translated barn. Barns, as we know them, for storing hay, grain, etc., are unknown in the East. Rooms, or pits (granaries) are often made underground or cut into the solid rock. It is the custom to keep animals, produce, grain, and all kinds of goods, in the lower story of the dwelling. Poor people often sleep in the same room with their cattle.

BAR'NABAS (*exhorter*). Joses, a Levite of Cyprus, an early disciple and companion of Paul, was called Barnabas—son of eloquence—because of his ready oratory (Acts. iv. 36). He was the first to recognize Paul's sincerity, and introduce him to the church in Jerusalem (ix. 27). Being honored with the mission to Antioch, he sought for Saul (Paul) in Tarsus as a helper, and they worked together a year. Barnabas's sister's son, Mark, was the Evangelist. He is not counted as an apostle (see APOSTLE), although Luke so speaks of him in Acts xiv. 14; and they were equally honored by the church until after the quarrel and separation of Barnabas from Paul. After that Barnabas is lost sight of. The Epistle called by his name is believed to be spurious, because it has in it errors in the Jewish history and worship, and very feeble grasp of divine truth, unworthy of a Levite and a disciple. It is assigned to the 2d century A. D. by Alford.

BARO'DIS. Servant of Solomon, returned with Zerubbabel (1 Esd. v. 34).

BARSABAS. See JOSEPH and JUDAS.

BAR'TACUS. Father of Apame. "The admirable" was probably an official title belonging to his rank (1 Esd. iv. 29).

BARTHOL'OMEW (*son of Talmai*). One of the 12. The same as Nathanael. Born at Cana. Philip had some difficulty in bringing him to regard Jesus as the Christ. He was one of the 7 to whom Jesus appeared after the resurrection at the lake of Tiberias, and a witness of the ascension. Tradition only gives any account of him after that time, when he is supposed to have gone as a preacher into "the East" (India). A spurious gospel bears his name.

BARTIME'US (*son of Timai*), a blind beggar of Jericho (Mark x. 46).

BA'RUCH (*blessed*). 1. Friend and amanuensis of Jeremiah (Jer. xxxii. 12). See HISTORY OF THE BOOKS.—2. Son of Zabbai (Neh. iii. 20).—3. Son of Col-hozeh (Neh. xi. 5).

BARZILLA'I. A wealthy Gileadite who was hospitable to David when he fled from Absalom (2 Sam. xvii. 27); but declined David's invitation to reside at court, because of his great age.—2. Whose son married Saul's daughter Michal.

BAS'ALOTH. BAZLITH. (1 Esd. v. 31).

BAS CAMA. Gilead, where Tryphon killed Jonathan Maccabeus, whose bones were afterwards

ORIENTAL BANQUET.

removed to Modin by Simon (1 Macc. xiii. 23-25). Lost.

BA'SHAN, (*soft, rich soil, or basalt soil*). Land of Bashan. E. of Jordan, N. of Jabbok; from the border of Gilead to Hermon, and from the Jordan to Salcah (Josh. xii. 4, 5; Deut. iii. 10-14). At Edrei, Og, king of B., was defeated, and the land given to the half-tribe of Manasseh, with half of Gilead. It was famous for its oaks (Is. ii. 13; Zech. xi. 12), and cattle; and now the granary of Damascus. Modern travelers speak of its delightful forests, of its flocks and herds, and grain fields. Argob, with its 60 cities, was in Bashan.

BA'SHAN-HA'VOTH-JA'IR. Name given to Argob after its conquest by Jair (Deut. iii. 14.)

BASH'EMATH (*fragrant*). Daughter of Ishmael, Esau's 3d wife (Gen. xxxvi. 3). MAHALATH (xxviii. 9).—2. Daughter of Elon the Hittite, and wife of Esau (Gen. xxvi. 34).

BA'SIN. The translation of four Hebrew words, and one Greek word. The forms of some kinds have been preserved on the monuments, and are given in the article WASHING THE HANDS AND FEET.

EGYPTIAN BASKETS.

BAS'KET. Five Hebrew words are translated basket. The form of the bread-basket is shown in the cut. They were made of grass, or willow twigs.

BAS'MATH. Daughter of Solomon (1 K. iv. 4), wife of Ahimaaz, one of the king's officers.

BAS'SA. Bezai. (1 Esd. v. 16).

BA'STAI. Besai. (1. Esd. v. 31).

BAS'TARD (Heb. *mamzer*). A child born to those who marry within the limited degrees of relationship, as two of the same family; or a Jew and a gentile.

BAT. Among the animals forbidden to be eaten (Lev. xi. 20). The peculiar habitation of bats, in the dark recesses of rocky caves, and their nocturnal habits, give great force to the prophesy that the idols shall be cast to the bats and the moles. Baruch shows (among other images) that the idols are no gods because bats sit on their heads, with birds and cats.

BATHING. Baptism. In Palestine, Syria and Egypt, bathing is a luxury as well as a necessity, and is now a religious ceremony, as in ancient times.

BATH-RABBIM. Gate of the ancient city of Heshbon. The two pools were near this gate; were likened to the eyes of Shelomith's beloved (Cant. vii. 4).

BATHSHE'BA (*promised—sworn*). A daughter of Eliam, wife of Uriah, and grand-daughter of Ahitophel, the statesman. Mother of Solomon. There are recorded instances of her vigorous understanding and kindness of heart.

BATH'SHUA. Daughter of the oath.

BATH ZACHĀRI'AS (*house of Z.*). Now *Beit Sakarich*. 8 ms. N. of Beit Sur.

BAVAI. Ruler of Keilah (Neh. iii. 18).

BAY-TREE. A native—not an exotic (Ps. xxxvii. 35). Grows near Antioch.

BAZ'LITH (*stripping*). "Children of B." returned with Zerubbabel (Neh. vii. 54).

BDELLIUM. The gum of a tree that grew in the land of India and Arabia—used in sacrifice and as a perfume and flavor for wine. The word may mean pearls (Gen. ii. 12; Num. xi. 7).

BEALI'AH. A Benjamite who went over to David at Ziklag (1 Chr. xii. 5).

BE'ALOTH. A town in the extreme South of Judah (Josh. xv. 24).

BE'AN, CHILDREN OF. Beon. (1 Macc. v. 4), probably Bedouins.

BEANS. A native of Palestine, Syria and Asia Minor. (2 Sam. xvii. 28). Blossoms from January to March. Planted in November; gathered in February. Both the green pod and ripe beans, boiled with oil and garlic, are commonly used by persons of all classes. There are several kinds, some of which are fed to horses.

BEARDS.

BEAR. The Hebrew name (*dob*) is still in use for the bear in the East, which is found on Mts. Hermon, Lebanon, and other parts of the country; and naturalists have shown that it is a species peculiar to Syria.

BEARD. The beard in the East is a badge of manhood and a mark of freedom. The Egyptians shaved it off and wore a false beard of plaited hair, in style and length to suit their rank. The Hebrews were distinct from both their Egyptian and Assyrian neighbors, as may be shown on the monuments, where captives are drawn in their proper costume and feature. It was a shame to lose the hair or beard (Is. i. 6), and also a sign of mourning. It was carefully dressed and oiled (Ps. cxxxiii), and a full, long beard was, and is, a highly coveted ornament.

BE'BAI. 1,623 sons of Bebai returned with Zerubbabel (Ezr. ii. 11); 28 more with Ezra; 4 took foreign wives (Ezr. x. 28).—2. Father of Zechariah.—3. Bebai—Chobai (Judg. xv. 4).

BE'CHER (*first-born—young camel*). 1. Second son of Benjamin (Gen. xlvi. 21).—2. Son of Ephraim (Num. xxvi. 35).

SYRIAN BEAR.

BECHO'RATH. Son of Aphiah—grandson of Be'cher (Sam. ix. 1.)

BEC'TILETH, THE PLAIN OF (*house of slaughter*) between Nineveh and Cilicia (Judg. ii. 2). Bactiali was a plain 21 miles from Antioch. (Peutinger tables).

BED. 1. A mat of grass, reeds, straw, hemp, or one or more cloths.—2. A quilt or mattress, filled with cotton, wool, grass, or straw. The pillow for the head is a frame of wood, a stone, or a stuffed bag, or sheep-skin. The bed was laid on the *divan* (platform 6 to 8 feet wide, and 8 to 15 inches high, on one or more sides of a room). *Bedsteads*, or movable frames (1 Sam. xix. 15; bier, 2 Sam. iii. 31), were used, perhaps, only, by the wealthy. Some were made of palm-sticks, and others of iron (Deut. iii. 11). Sculptures in Asia Minor show many elegant shapes of bedsteads, and couches. The *canopy* (Judith xvi. 23) was, and is still used in the East, for display, and for protection against light, dust and insects (Esth. i. 6; Ps. vii. 16). The people seldom or never change their dress on going to bed; only taking off the outer garment (see Dress), excepting in hot weather.

BE'DAD (*separation, part*). Father of Hadad, king of Edom (1 Chr. i. 46).

BE'DAN (*son of Dan—servile*), judge of Israel. (1 Sam. xii. 11).

BE-DEI'AH. Son of Bani (Ezr. x. 35).

BEE (*děbôrâh*). Palestine abounded in bees, for it was a land "flowing with milk and honey"

(Deut. xxxii. 13). The banded bee of Palestine is not found in this country. So plentiful was wild honey that it was exported. It was eaten mixed with butter. There is a vegetable substance called honey which is a thick juice of grapes.

BEELI'ADA (*known by Baal*). Son of David; born in Jerusalem (1 Chr. xiv. 7).

BEEL'SARUS. BIL-SHAN (1 Esd. v. 8).

BEELTETH'MUS (*chancelor*). Officer of Artaxerxes in Palestine (1 Esd. ii. 16-25.)

BEEL'ZEBUB (*fly-god*). BEEL'ZEBUL (*lord of dirt*). *House-god*, and *dung-god*, by some. A belief that demons possessed persons, led to a belief in a *prince* of demons, who was supposed to rule over them.

BĒ'ER (*well*). 1. A well dug by the "princes" beyond Arnon, near one of the last stations of the Exode, and celebrated in poetry (Num. xxi. 16, 18). —2. Jotham, son of Gideon, fled to this place (Judg. ix. 21). Site lost.

BĒ'E-RA (*well*). Son of Zophah (1 Chr. vii. 37).

BĒ'ER-AH (*well*). Prince of the Reubenites (1 Chr. v. 6.)

Isaac's servants also "digged" a well (xxvi. 32). Two principal wells and five smaller ones are on the N. bank of Wady Seba on the edge of the desert. One is 12½ ft. diameter, 44½ ft. to the water (*Rob.*, Apr. 12). The other is 5 ft. diam. and 42 ft. to the water. Watering-troughs of stone lie around the wells, and among the grass are crocuses and lilies. The 5 lesser wells are at some distance from the 2 larger. The ruins of a town are on the hills N. of the wells. It is very frequently mentioned as one of the boundaries of all Israel: From Dan to Beer-sheba. The Arab name is Bir es Seba', Well of the Lion.

BEESHTE'RAH. MAN. (Josh. xxi. 27). ASHTAROTH.

BEE'TLE. LOCUST.

BEEVES. BULL; OX.

BEGGAR. ALMS; POOR.

BEGOTTEN. Jesus Christ, the Son of God (John i. 14, 18; Rev. i. 5).

BEHEADING. PUNISHMENTS.

BEHE'MOTH (*excellences*). Mentioned only in Job xl. 15-24. It is not certain which is meant, the elephant or the hippopotamus (river horse).

EGYPTIAN HUNTING HIPPOPOTAMUS.

BĒER-ELIM (*well of heroes*). BEER 1 (Is. xv. 8).

BĒ'ER-I (*illustrious*). 1. Father of Esau's wife. (Gen. xxvi. 34).—2. Father of Hosea (Hos. i. 1).

BĒ'ER-LAHĀ'I-ROI (*well of the living and seeing God*). Between Kadesh and Bered, wilderness of Shur (Gen. xvi. 14; xxiv. 62; xxv. 11). Located by Ritter 25 ms. S. E. of Beersheba, at Moyle, Beit Hagar.

BEĒ'ROTH (*wells*). One of the 4 cities of the Hivites; the other 3 being Gibeon, Chephirah, and Kirjath Jearim (Josh. ix. 17; xviii. 25, 26, 28). 10 ms. N. of Jerusalem, on the Shechem road, the customary resting-place of travelers (*Rob*).—Bene Jaakan. Edom, a station (Deut. x. 6).

BĒER'SHEBA (*well of swearing or well of seven*). S. border of Judah. Dug by Abraham (Gen. xxi. 31). The compact of Abraham and Abimelech was ratified by setting apart 7 ewe-lambs (sheba, seven).

Both answer the description, but the elephant comes much nearer to all the points required.

BE'KAH (*part-half*). WEIGHTS AND MEASURES.

BE'LEMUS (1 Esd. ii. 16). BISHLAM.

BEL. The national god of the Babylonians (Is. xlvi. 1; Jer. l. 2) Zeus Bel is the male, and Hera the female of the same deity. Writers are divided as to whether Bel (Baal) was the sun or the planet Jupiter: if the sun, then Ashtoreth was the moon goddess.

BEL AND DRAG'ON. DANIEL, ADDITIONS TO.

BĒLA. Son of Beor, king of Edom; capital Dinhabah.—2. Eldest son of Benjamin.—3. Son of Ahaz. BELAH—Bela 3.

BE'LAITES. Descendants of Bela 3.

BELI'AL, SON OF. Good-for-nothing—worthless fellow.

BEL-TE-SHAZ'ZAR. Name given to Daniel (Dan. i. 7). Correctly BEL-SHAT-ZAR (*favored by Bel*).

färl, rude, push; c, i, o, silent; ç as s; çh as sh; e, ch as k; ġ as j; ġ as in get; ṣ as z; x as gz; ṇ as in linger, link; th as in thine.

BELLS. Large bells were not used in ancient times, nor are they in use now. Small hand bells were used by the Greeks, Romans and Jews. The high priest wore round the hem of his dress seventy-two gold bells, which were placed alternately with pomegranates. The little girls of Cairo wear strings of them round their feet. They were sometimes attached to the harness of horses and camels.

BEL'LOWS. The ancients used two kinds, according to the monuments, ingeniously contrived to be worked by the feet (Jer. vi. 29).

BLACK SLAVE.

BEL'MA-IM. BELMEN. Place S. of Dothaim (Judg. vii. 3).

BEL'MEN. ABEL-MAIM. Place in Samaria (Judg. iv. 4). ABEL-MEHOLAH.

BE'LIEVE. Faith in the Lord Jesus Christ (Acts xiii. 35).

BE'LIEV'ERS. Christians (Acts v. 14).

BELSHAZZAR (*Bel's prince*). The last king of Babylon. A mysterious writing appearing on the wall during a great feast, and his magicians not being able to read it, Daniel was called, and explained its meaning. He died the same night (Dan. v.).

BEN (*son*). A Levite—a porter of the ark (1 Chr. xv. 18).

BEN-A-BIN'A-DAB. Son of Abinadab (1 K. iv. 11).

BENA'IAH (*god-built*). 1. Son of Jehoiada, of Kabzeel, a Levite (2 Sam. xxiii. 20-23).—2. One of David's 30 valiant men ; an Ephraimite. Seven others of this name, but none very noted.

BEN-AM'MI (*son of my kindred*). Son of the younger daughter of Lot (Gen. xix. 38).

BENCH'ES. Hatches, or "thy deck" (Ez. xvi. 15 ff).

BEN-DE'KAR (*Lance-bearer*). Son of Dekar (1 K. iv. 9).

BE'NE-BE'RAK (*sons of lightning*). City of the tribe of Dan (Josh. xix. 45).

BEN-E-FAC'TOR (*a doer of good*). Title of honor (Luke xxii. 25).

BENEJAAKAN. Tribe descended from Jaakan (AKAN), a Horite chief (Gen. xxxvi.), and who owned wells where Israel encamped in the Exode (Num. xxxiii. 31).

BENEKEDEM (*people of the East*). Kedem was the name for the whole country E. of Palestine, far or near. They lived (as now) in tents, kept flocks and herds, and were always ready for robbing expeditions.

BEN-GE'BER. Son of Geber (1 K. iv. 13).

BENHA'DAD (*son of Adad, a god of Syria*). 1. King of Syria, who was hired by Asa, king of Judah, to invade Israel (1 K. xv. 18). Supposed to be the same as Hadad, the Edomite, who rebelled against Solomon (1 K. xi.).—2. King of Syria, son of the former, and always at war with Ahab (1 K. xxi. 30). He consulted he prophet Elisha, by means of Hazael, and was smothered by him soon after, B. C. 884 (2 K. viii.).—3. A king of Syria, son of Hazael (2 K. xiii.).

BEN-HA'IL (*warrior*). A prince Jehoshaphat sent to teach in Judah (2 Chr. xvii. 7).

BEN-HA'NAN (*son of one gracious*). Son of Shimon (1 Chr. iv. 20).

BEN-HE'SED (*son of Hesed*), (1 K. iv. 10).

BEN'-HUR (*son of Hur*), (1 K. iv. 8).

BE-NI'NU (*our son*). A Levite, who sealed the covenant with Nehemiah (Neh. x. 13).

BEN'JAMIN (*fortune*). Named Benoni by his dying mother. Youngest son of Jacob, second of Rachel, born near Bethlehem ; his father's favorite, next to Joseph, and the mark of special honors from him. He had the affection of his brothers, and received their favors as a matter of course, and was not very positive, but a quiet, gentle spirit. He had ten sons and grand-sons at the migration into Egypt (Gen. xlvi.). He made no special history for himself. The *tribe* was always of least consequence. At the Exodus there were 35,400 of full age, and at the passage over Jordan 45,600. There were 26 cities in their portion (see map). The tribe was almost destroyed for violating the rights of hospitality (Judg. xix. 20), 600 only escaping to the rock Rimmon (see RIMMON and SHILOH). The first deliverer of Israel (from Moab) in the time of the judges, was Ehud, a Benjamite. The first king of Israel was Saul, a Benjamite ; and Saul (Paul), the apostle, was also of this tribe.

BEN'JAMIN, GATE OF. In Jerusalem.

BEN'JA-MITE. Decendant of Benjamin (Judg. iii. 15).

BE'NO (*his son*). A Levite, son of Merari (1 Chr. xxiv. 26, 27).

BENO'NI (*son of my sorrow*). Name given by Rachel to her son (Gen. xxxv. 18).

BEN-ZO'HETH (*son of Zoheth*). Decendant of Judah (1 Chr. iv. 20).

BE'ON. Place E. of Jordan (Num. xxxii. 3). (Compare verse 38).

BE'OR (*torch or lamp*). 1. Father of Bela. Edomite king (Gen. xxxvi. 32).—2. Father of Balaam.

BE'RA (*son of evil*). King of Sodom (Gen. xiv. 2).

BERA'CHAH (*blessing*). 6 miles S. of Bethlehem, 1 mile E. of the Hebron road, now called *Bereikut* (2 Chr. xx. 26).

BER-A-CHI'AH. A Levite (1 Chr. vi. 39). BERECHIAH.

BE-RAI'AH or **BER-A-I'AH** (*Jehovah created*). Son of Shimhi. A Benjamite chief (1 Chr. viii. 21).

BERE'A. Macedonia (Acts xvii. 10). Visited by Paul and Silas, Paul's companion. Sopater of Berea (xx. 4 ; Rom. xvi. 21). Sosipater. Now called Verria, on the E. slope of Olympus, well watered, and commanding a fine view of the plains of Axius

and Haliacmon; 15,000 population. The ruins are Greek, Roman, and Byzantine.—2. A name of Aleppo.—3. Judea, near Jerusalem (1 Macc. iv. 4; Jos. Ant. xi. § 1). Jerome says certain persons lived in this city who had, and used St. Matthew's Hebrew Gospel.

BER-E-CHI'AH (*God blessed*).—1. Son of Zerubbabel (1 Chr. iii. 20).—2. Father of Meshullam 13 (Neh. iii. 4, 30).—3. A Levite (1 Chr. ix. 16).—4. A doorkeeper for the Ark (1 Chr. xv. 23).—5. A chief in Ephraim (2 Chr. xxxviii. 12).—6. Father of Asaph (1 Chr. xv. 17).—7. Father of Zechariah. (Zech. i. 1, 7).

BE'RED. In the wilderness, near Kadesh (Gen. xvi. 14). Located at Elusa, Khulasa (Ar.), 12 ms. S. of Beersheba, where there is a well. Supposed to be Shur, and also Gerar.

BERE'ITES. Descendants of Beriah 1.

BERE-NI'CE (*gift*). Eldest daughter of Herod Agrippa. 1. Married to her uncle Herod, king of Chalcis, and was after his death wife of Polemon, king of Cilicia. She was also with Vespasian and Titus (Ant. xix. 5, 1; xx. 7, 2, 3).

BE'RI. BEERI. Son of Zophah (1 Chr. vii. 36).

BE-RI'AH (*in evil, or a gift*).—1. Son of Asher (Gen. xlvi. 17), descended from the Bereites.—2. Son of Ephraim (1 Chr. vii. 20, 23).—3. A Benjamite (1 Chr. viii. 13, 16).—4. A Gershonite Levite, son of Shimre (1 Chr. xxiii. 10, 11).

BE'RITES (*well*). People visited by Joab in his search after Sheba (2 Sam. xx. 14).

BE'RITH (*The God*) (Judg. ix. 46).

BE-RO'DACH—BAL'A-DAN. MERODACH (2 K. xx. 12).

BE'ROTH (1 Esd. v. 19). BEEROTH.

BERÔTHÂH. BERO'THAI; BERY'TUS; BEI'RUT (*bu-root*). Chief seaport in North Palestine (Syria) (2 Sam. viii. 8; Ezr. xlvii. 16). A city of the Phœnicians, named after Baal Berith (*god of wells*). Van de Velde proposes for the Scripture place *Tell el Byruth*, between Tadmor and Hamoth. See PHŒNICIA.

BEROTH'ITE, THE (1 Chr. xi. 39), from Beroth or Beeroth.

BERRIES. Fruit of the olive-tree (Is. xvii. 6; Jas. iii. 12).

BER'YL. See PRECIOUS STONE.

BER-ZE'LUS (1 Esd. v. 38). BARZILLAI 1.

BE'SAI (*victory?*) Returned with Zerubbabel (Ezr. ii. 49).

BES-O-DE'IAH. Father of Meshullam—(*Intimate of Jehovah*) (Neh. iii. 16).

BE SOM. A broom or brush of twigs (Is. xiv. 23).

BE SOR (*cool*), THE BROOK. Judah (1 Sam. xxx. 9). A winter torrent, rising south of Hebron, and reaching the sea a few miles S. of Gaza.

BESTEAD' (Is. viii. 21). Distressed.

BE STOW'. To give or confer (Ex. xxxii. 29).

BE'-TAH (*trust, confidence*). City of Hadadezer king of Zobah (2 Sam. viii. 8). TIBHATH (Gen. xxii. 24).

BETA'NE. BETHANIN of Eusebius, two miles from Terebinth, or Oak of Abraham, and four from Hebron. This has been variously identified with Betharath, Bethainun (Beth-anoth) and Betaneh, or Estabana, in Syria.

BE'TEN (*belly*). A city on the border of Asher (Josh. xix. 25), 8 miles E. of Ptolemais.

BETH. House of any kind. TENT. HANGINGS. FAMILY. TEMPLE.—AB'ARA (*house of the ford*), where John was baptizing (John i. 28). The oldest MSS. read BETHANY. It was beyond Jordan, and nearly opposite Jericho.—A'NATH. Naph. Fenced city (Josh. xix. 38; Judg. i. 33). Site lost. —A'NOTH. Judah (Josh. v. 59). Beit ainun, near Halhul, and Beit Sur. (*Rob.*) 3 ms. N. of Hebron.

BETH'ANY (*house of dates*). One of the most interesting places in Palestine. The residence of Lazarus, who was raised from the dead; the frequent resting-place of Jesus; the home of Mary and Martha, and of Simon, the leper; and from whence the triumphal entry began; and near this place was the scene of the Ascension. On the Mt. of Olives (Mark xi. 1; Luke xix. 29); 15 furlongs off (John xi. 18); on the road to Jericho (Luke xix. 1, 29), and near it was Bethphage. It is now called El Azariyeh, the city of Lazarus. Is in a hollow, surrounded with olives, almonds, pomegranates, oaks, and carobs. The buildings are ruinous and wretched. The house of Lazarus is pointed out as a square tower, very ancient; and his tomb, a cave in the rock, descended by 26 steps.

BETH-AR'ABAH (*house of the desert*). One of the six cities of Judah in the Arabah—sunk valley of the Jordan (Josh. xv. 6, 61; xviii. 22).

BETH-ARAM. Gad, E. of Jordan (Josh. xiii. 27, xxxii. 36). Site located two miles E. of Jordan in W. Seir. *Livias. Tell Ihurun*.

OLIVES.

BETH-ARBEL (Hos. x. 14). Site lost. Supposed to refer to Judg. viii.

BETH-AVEN (*house of naught*). Benj. E. of Bethel (Josh. vii. 2).

BETH-AZ'MAVETH. Benj. (Neh. vii. 28). On the hills S. E. of Jeba.

BETH-BAAL-MEON. Reuben, on the downs E. of Jordan (Josh. xiii. 17). Baal Meon (Num. xxxiii. 38). The name is still given to a ruin of large size, two miles S. W. of Hesban (*Burck.*) in W. Zurka Main, where there are remains of a Roman road.

BETH-BA'RAH (*house of the ford*) (Judg. vii. 24). Gideon's victory was near Bethshean, and the fords were probably the outlets of the brooks coming down from the mountains of Ephraim. The place where Jacob crossed on his return from Mesopotamia, and at which Jephtha slew the Ephraimites. Located by Van de Velde on the Jordan, at the ford on the Nablus-Es—Salt road.

BETH-BA'SI. In the Jordan valley, not far from Jericho (1 Macc. ix. 62, 64; Jos. Ant. xiii. 1, § 5).

BETH-BIR'EI. Simeon (1 Chr. iv. 31), near Beersheba.

BETH'-CAR (*house of lambs*). West of Mizpeh (1 Sam. vii. 11; Jos. Ant. vi. 2, § 2).

BETH-DA'GON (*house of Dagon*).—1. In the Shefelah, Judah (Josh. xv. 41). Site supposed to be found at Beit dejan, between Lydda and Jaffa (*Rob*).—2. Asher, near the coast (xix. 27).—3. Beit dejan, about 5 ms. S. E. of Nablus, Shechem.

BETH-DIBLA-THA'IM (*house of the double cake*). Moab (Jer. xlviii. 22).

BETH-EDEN (*house of pleasantness*) (Amos i. 5.)

BETH-E'-KED (*shearing house*).

BETH-EL (*house of God*). Ten miles north of Jerusalem, to the right of the Shechem road, where Jacob saw the ladder in his dream (Gen. xxviii. 19). The name of the city was originally Luz. Another account is, that Jacob set up a stone to mark the spot where God spake with him (Gen. xxxv. 14, 15; Hosea xii. 4, 5). In Abram's time it was called Bethel (xii. 8). Jeroboam, the king, set up a golden calf at Bethel (1 K. xiii). Jehu continued the worship of the calf. It was near Bethel that the event of the bears and Elisha and the forty-two children took place. It was a royal residence (Amos vii. 13). There were winter-houses and summer-houses and houses of ivory at B. (iii. 14, 15; 2 K. xxvii. 28). Josiah destroyed it. The worship of God and of idols went on side by side for many years (Amos v. 14, 22). Was a strong place in later times (1 Macc. ix. 50). It is not mentioned in the N. T. Josephus relates its capture by Vespasian (Wars iv. 9, § 9). The ruins cover four or five acres: on a low hill between two valleys, which run into es Suweinit (*Rob*).—2. Judah (Josh. xii. 16; 1 Sam. xxx. 27). Chesil, Bethul. HILL, the BETHELITE, the rebuilder of Jericho (1 K. xvi. 34.)

BETH'-EL-ITE. Hiel, the Bethelite, re-built Jericho (1 K xvi. 34).

BETHE'MEK (*house of the valley*). Asher, on the border of Jiphthah-el. 'Amkah, 8 miles N. E. of Akka (*Rob*).

BE'THER. Mountains of (Cant. ii. 17). Lost.

BETHES'DA (*house of mercy* or *place of flowing water*). A pool at Jerusalem, near the sheep-gate, or "market," with five porches, extensive enough to accommodate a large number of sick and infirm people, who resorted there for relief (John v. 2). Supposed to be the great excavation near St. Stephen's gate, now called Bethesda. The porches and water are gone, and all around it are ruins, but it is very large, cemented as if for holding water, and there might have been buildings on its east and north sides anciently. See JERUSALEM.

SECTION OF POOL.

BETHE'ZEL (*fixed*). Philistia (Micah i. 11).

BETH'GADER (*wall*). Geder (Josh. xii. 13).

BETH'GA-MUL (*house of the weaned*, or *camel*). Moab, in the plains. Um-el Jemail, a few miles south of Busrah, in the Hauran (*Rob*.).

BETH-HAC CEREM (*house of the vine*). New Tekoa (Jer. vi. 1; Neh. iii. 14). See KARIM.

BETH-HAG'GAN (*garden-house*).

BETH-HE'RAN. East of Jordan, at the mouth of Wady Seil. Now Tell Haran-Livias. Built by the Gadites (Num. xxxii. 36; Josh. xiii. 27).

BETH-HOG'LAH (*house of partridge*). On the border of Judah (Josh. xv. 6) and Benjamin, near Jericho. A great spring and ruin in the Jericho plain is now called Ain Hajla (*Rob*.).

BETH-HO'RON (*house of caverns*). Two cities, on the Jerusalem-Jaffa upper road, built by Sherah, a woman of Ephraim, on the boundary between Ephraim and Benjamin (Josh. xvi. 3, 5; xviii. 13, 14; xxi. 22). Two of the most memorable victories

INN. CARAVANSERAI.

of the Jews occurred here—Joshua over the five Amorite kings, when the sun and moon stood still at his command (Josh. x.), and that of Judas Maccabeus over the forces of Syria, under Seron (1 Macc. iii. 13-24). The Roman army, under Cestius Gallus, was defeated here in the reign of Nero, with a loss of 5,680 men (Jos. Wars, ii. § 8).

BETH-JESH'IMOTH (*house of the wastes*). East of Jordan, in the deserts of Moab (Num. xxxiii. 49). Was one of the cities which were "the glory of the country" (Ez. xxv. 9). Beth Jisimoth is now half a mile east of the Jordan, and a mile north of the Dead Sea.

BETH-LEB'AOTH (*house of lionesses*). Simeon (Josh. xix. 6; 1 Chr. iv. 31). BETHBIREI.

BETH'LEHEM (*house of bread*). Four and a half miles south of Jerusalem. One of the most ancient cities in Palestine. Called EPHRATH (*fruitful*) (Gen. xxxv. 16; xlviii 7). The residence of Boaz and Ruth, the birthplace of David, and the residence of Saul. Rehoboam fortified it (2 Chr. xi. 16). The INN OF CHIMHAM was a halting place for those who would "go to enter into Egypt" (Jer. xli. 17); which was probably the same inn in which Jesus was born (Matt. ii. 1, 5; Luke ii. 4, 5). Called also B. JUDAH and CITY OF DAVID. Justin Martyr (A. D. 150) speaks of our Lord's birth as having taken place "in a certain cave very close to the village." The village is not again mentioned after the birth of Jesus, in the Scripture. The Emperor Hadrian planted a grove of Adonis over the cave, which stood 180 years (A. D. 135-315). The Empress Helena, after clearing away this grove, built a church on the spot, which has been continued, with additions, making it "a half church and half fort," until the present day.

The modern town is built on the low hill behind the convent (or church), facing the east. The hill is an offshoot of the main ridge, and ends in a little valley or narrow plain. The village is walled in, and is triangular. The plain east of the ridge is that on which tradition says the angels appeared to the shepherds, and it is called the Shepherds' Field (Arabic, *Beit Sahur*—house of Sahur). As the plains were always, anciently, cultivated, it is probable that the shepherds would have been found on the hill, where they now may be found, with their flocks.

A church containing the monuments of the three shepherds is mentioned by an early writer (Arcul-

fus), as standing in the midst of the fields and terraced gardens. Jerome lived here, in a cell which is now pointed out, next to the great church, where he wrote most of his commentaries, and compiled the Latin Vulgate, the best ancient version of the Scriptures, A. D. 385-420. The present town has about 3,000 people, nearly all Christians, who are makers of crucifixes, beads, models of the holy places, and other articles for sale to pilgrims.—2. Zebulon, 7 ms. W. of Nazareth (Josh. xix. 15). Birthplace of Ibzan, the judge (Judg. xii. 8).

BETH'LEHEMITE. One from Bethlehem (1 Sam. xvi. 1, 18; 2 Sam. xxi. 19).

BETH-MA'ACHAH. See ABEL.

BETH-MAR'CABOTH (*house of chariots*). HAZAR-SUZIM, MADMANNAH (Josh. xix. 5). Of Simeon in Judah, extreme S. A station on the way to Egypt, where Solomon's chariots were kept (1 K. ix. 19; 2 Chr. viii. 6). Post-station.

BETH-ME'ON. House of habitation (Jer. xlviii. 23).

BETH-MILLO (*wall-house*). Near Shechem (Judg. ix. 20, 46-49). Perhaps a part of the fortification of Shechem.—2. A fort or tower on Zion (2 K. xii. 20). MILLO (2 Sam. v. 9).

BETH-NIM'RAH (*house of pure water*). E. of Jordan, N. of Beth-aram, in the Jordan valley, opposite Jericho; a fenced city (Num. xxxii. 36; Josh. xiii. 27; Is. xv. 6; Jer. xlviii. 34). Eusebius mentions it as a large place. A group of ruins 2 m. E. of the Jordan are now called Nimrin or Wady Shoaib. Supposed to be the Bethabara of John i. 28; Matt. iii. 5; Mark i. 5.

BETH-O'RON. BETH-HORON (Judg. iv. 4).

BETH-PA'LET (*house of flight*). Judah (Josh. xv. 27; Neh. xi. 26). Near Moladah and Beersheba. Lost. PALTITE (2 Sam. xxiii. 26).

BETH-PAZ'ZEZ. ISSA. (Josh. xix. 21). Lost.

BETH-PE'OR. E. of Jordan, opposite Jericho, 6 m. N. of Libias; a place dedicated to Baal (Josh. xiii. 20). It is supposed that Moses was buried in this ravine (Deut. iii. 29, iv. 46, xxxiv. 6). Beth is used for Baal.

BETH-PHA'GE (*house of figs*). On the Mt. of Olives near the Jericho road (Matt. xxi. 1; Mark xi. 1; Luke xix. 29). Probably W. of Bethany (Matt. xxi. 19). The locality of the miracle of the withered fig-tree.

BETH-PHE'LET (Neh. xi. 26).

BETH-RA'PHA (*house of the giant*). Judah (1 Chr. iv. 12). Lost.

BETH-RE'HOB (*house of room*). Naph. Near Dan Laish (Judg. xviii. 28). A little kingdom of Aram (2 Sam. x. 6). Now called Hunin, and was one of the strongest forts in the North P., and commanded the plain of Huleh. Its beveled masonry marks its Phoenician origin (Rob. iii. 371).

BETHSA'IDA (*house of fish*). Two places on the Sea of Galilee. 1. B. of Galilee (John xii. 21). The city of Andrew, Peter and Philip (John i. 44). In the land of Gennesaret.—2. B. on the E. of Jordan, raised to importance by Philip the Tetrarch, and named Julias, after the daughter of the emperor (Jos. A. xviii. 2, § 1). The 5,000 were fed near this place (Luke ix. 10; John vi. 3-10; Mark vi. 39; Matt. xiv. 19). A blind man was healed here (Mark viii. 22-26). About two miles N. of the lake, and half a mile E. of the Jordan, is a long hill called Tell Julias, now covered with extensive ruins (Rob. ii. 413).

JULIAS.

BETHLEHEM EPHRATAH.

BETHSA'MOS. BETH-AZMAVETH.

BETH-SAN. BETH-SHEAN. (1 Macc. v. 52; xii. 40, 41).

BETH-SHAN. BETH-SHEAN (1 Sam. xxxi. 10, 12).

BETH-SHE'AN. BETHSMAN (*house of rest*). Town of Manasseh in Issachar (1 Chr. vii. 29; Josh. xvii. 11). In the Ghor, 18 ms. S. of the lake of Galilee, 4 ms. W. of the Jordan. Called Scythopolis, from the Scythians, B. C. 631 (2 Macc. xii. 29; Judith iii. 10; Col. iii. 11). The corpses of Saul and his sons were fastened on its walls by the Philistines (1 Sam. xxxi. 10, 12). Three or four large brooks run near, and Ain Jalud, one of these, was the fountain which was near Jezreel, referred to in 1 Sam. xxix. 1. The ruins of Beisan now cover about 3 ms. in circuit, among which is a tower of Phoenician origin. The ruins are on several hills, high, steep, between whose black,

rocky bases the four brooks run. The highest hill is nearly 200 feet high, and overlooks the Jordan for many miles N. and S. It must have been a city of temples (Rob. iii. 328; 1 Chr. i. 10). Josephus names it as the chief city of the Decapolis (Jos. Wars, iii. 9, 7).

BETH-SHÉ'MESH (*house of the sun*). Several places of this name. 1. Judah, near Kirjath Jearim (Josh. xv. 10; 1 Sam. v. 13). The ark was sent here by the Philistines from Ekron (1 Sam. vi. 9-12, 18). Now *Ain Shems*.—2. Issachar (Josh. xix. 22).—3. A fenced city of Naphtali (Josh. xix. 38).—4. An idolatrous temple in Egypt (Jer. xliii. 13). AVEN. ON.

BETH-SHITTAH (*house of the acacia*). In the N. of Palestine, to which the Midianites fled before Gideon (Judg. vii. 22). In the valley of the Jordan (Rob. ii. 356).

BETH-TAP'PUAH (*house of the citron*). Judah, near Hebron (Josh. xv. 53; 1 Chr. ii. 43). Now called Teffuh, and surrounded by olive groves, vines and fig-trees.

BETH'SUA. BETH-ZUR (1 Macc. iv. 29, 61; vi. 7, 26, 31, 49-59; ix. 52).

BETHU'EL (1 Chr. iv. 30). BETHUL. Simeon (Josh. xix. 4).

BETHU'LIA. S. of the Plain of Esdraelon, near Dothan, in which the chief events of the book of Judith occurred (Rob. ii. 313). The Frank Mountain was called Bethulia in the middle ages. Safed was also called by the name of the lost city.

BETH-ZACH-ARI'AS. BATHZACHARIAS.

BETH'ZUR (*house of rock*). Judah (Josh. xv. 58). Josephus says it was the strongest fortress in Judea. Built by Rehoboam, or fortified by him, and built by the people of Maon (1 Chr. ii. 42, 45). In the days of Jerome this was considered as the place of the baptism of the eunuch by Philip. Robinson finds it in Beit Sur, 4 ms. N. of Hebron, near the Jerusalem road.

BE-TOLI-US (Esd. v. 21). BETHEL 1.

BET-O-MES'-THAM and **BETOMASTHEM**. Lost.

BETROTHING. See MARRIAGE.

BETO'NIM (*pistachio nuts*). Gad (Josh. xiii. 26; Gen. xliii. 11).

BEU'LAH (*married*) (Is. lxii. 4). The name which the land of Israel is to bear when it is married.

JESUS CHRIST, KING OF KINGS.

BÉZEK (*lightning*). Two places.—1. ADONI-BEZEK (*lord of B*). Judah (Judg. i. 5).—2. Where Saul mustered his army (1 Sam. xi. 8). Supposed to have been in the Jordan valley, between Shechem and Bethshean (Jos. Ant. vi. 5, § 3). Lost.

BÉZER (*gold or silver ore*). A city of refuge in Reuben. In the wilderness (Deut. iv. 43; Josh. xx. 8). E. of Jericho (xxi. 36; 1 Chr. vi. 78). Bosor in Maccabees. East of the Dead Sea. Site lost. Supposed to have been near Um er Russas.

BEZETH. Part of the Mt. of Olives (1 Macc. vii. 19; Jos. Ant. 10, § 2). Lost. (Judg. iv. 6, xv. 4). BEZETHA?

BE-ZAI. BESAI. Returned with Zerubbabel (Neh. vii. 23; x. 18).

BEZ'ALUL (*in the shadow of God*). Of Judah, son of Uri (1 Chr. ii. 20).

BI'ATAS (1 Esd. ix. 48). PELAIAH 2.

BIBLE. See History of the Books.

BICH'RI, (*first-born—youthful*). Ancestor of Sheba (2 Sam. xx. 1, etc.).

BID'KAR (*stabber*). Jehu's captain (2 K. ix. 25).

BIER. BURIAL 2.

BIG'THA (*garden—gardener*, or *given by fortune*). ABAGTHA, one of the seven princes of Ahasuerus' court (Esth. i. 10).

BIG'THAN and **BIG'THA-NA**. BIGTHA, fellow-conspirator with Teresh (Esth. ii. 21).

BIG'VAI or **BIG'VA-I**, (*husbandman*). 2056 children came home from captivity with Zerubbabel (Ezr. ii. 14).

EARTHEN LAMP, 3.

BIK'ATH. A'VEN (Amos. i. 5). AVEN 1.

BIL'DAD (*son of contention*). The second of Job's three friends (Job. ii. 11, etc.).

BIL'EAM. BALAAM. Manasseh, near Megiddo (1 Chr. vi. 70).

BIL'GAH (*cheerfulness*). 1. A priest in David's time (1 Chr. xxiv. 14).—2. A priest who returned from Babylon with Zerubbabel (Neh. xii. 5, 18).— 3. BILGAI.

BIL'HAH. Simeon. BAALAH. BALAH. (1 Chr. iv. 29).

BIL'GAI or **BIL'GA-I**. BILGAH, a priest who sealed the covenant with Nehemiah (Neh. x. 8). BILGAH 2.

BIL'HAN (*modest*). 1. A Benjamite (1 Chr. iv. 29).—2. Son of Ezer (Gen. xxxvi. 27; 1 Chr. i. 42).

BIL'SHAN (*eloquent*). Companion of Zerubbabel (Ezr. ii. 2).

BIM'HAL (*circumcised*). Son of Japhet (1 Chr. vii. 33).

BIN'EA (*fountain—gushing forth*). Son of Moza. Descendant of Saul (1 Chr. viii. 37, ix. 43).

BIN'NU-I (*a building*). 1. Levite—father of Noadiah (Ezr. viii. 33).—2. Son of Pahath-Moab (Ezr. x. 30).—3. Son of Bani (Ezr. x. 38).—4. Bani (Neh. vii. 15).—5. Levite—son of Henadad (Neh. iii. 24, x. 9).

BIRTHDAY. Birthday feasts were common (Job i. 4), and martyrs and heroes were honored on that day. It was the king's day (Matt. xiv. 6), and kept holy, without work.

BIRTHRIGHT. The privilege of the firstborn son to a double share of the inheritance (Elisha asked for a double share of Elijah's spirit). Great respect was (and is) paid to him as the expected successor of his father as head of the family. He is supposed to have been a kind of priest of the family, but there is no allusion to this in Scripture. Reuben lost his birthright, which was given to Joseph, whose two sons enjoyed it, one share each. There was a sacredness in the title, as is seen in the "first-begotten," as applied to the Messiah, and to the Jewish people as the chosen of God.

THE SHEPHERD'S FIELD, BETHLEHEM.

BIR'ZAVITH (*olive source*). In the line of Asher (1 Chr. vii. 31); probably a place. Lost. MALCHIEL?

BISH'LAM (*son of peace*). Officer in Persia at the time of the return from captivity (Ezra iv. 7). Belemus in 1 Esd. ii. 16.

BISH'OP (*overseer*). An old title of the Romans adopted in the early church for its officers who were charged with its superintendence. Originally the same as *elder*. Both deacons and elders were preachers as well as overseers. In Paul's time the two titles had already become descriptive of different duties required of the different officers. The church elected them, and the apostles confirmed them by laying on their hands (sometimes also the hands of the presbytery—ELDERS), (2 Tim. i. 6; 1 Tim. iv. 14). They were to lead blameless lives, be the husband of one wife; have a spiritual care over the flocks (1 Peter v. 2); teach in private and public; visit the sick (James v. 14), receive and entertain strangers (1 Tim. i. 2). Bishops succeeded to the authority of the apostles.

BI-THI'AH (*worshiper—daughter of Jehovah*). Wife of Mered of Judah, and daughter of a Pharaoh (1 Chr. iv. 18).

BITH'RON (*the broken-up place*). A district in the Jordan valley, E. of the river (2 Sam. ii. 29). Not determined.

BITHYN'IA. Province in Asia Minor, on the Black Sea (Acts xvi. 7). Paul was not suffered to visit B., but the gospel was preached there (1 Peter i. 1). The country is mountainous and well watered.

BIT'TER. BITTER HERBS. A *bitter* day (Amos viii. 10). A *bitter* and hasty nation (Acts viii. 23). Simon at Samaria being in the gall of *bitterness*. The passover was eaten with *bitter herbs* (Ex. xii. 8).

BIT'TERN (Heb. *kippod*). The Hebrew word is translated both hedgehog and bittern. The Arabic name of hedgehog is *kunfod*. Is. xxxiv. 7, &c., corrected would read, "The pelican and hedgehog" instead of "cormorant and bittern." (See Wood's Bible Animals). Others refer to porcupine as offering all the required points (Imp. Bible Dict., p. 227).

BITU'MEN. SLIME.

BIZJOTH'JAH (*contempt of Jehovah*). Judah, near Beersheba (Josh. xv. 28). *Deir el Belah*, on the coast 10 ms. from Gaza? *Beeaty*, 15 ms. S. of Gaza?

BIZ'THA. The second of the seven eunuchs of king Ahasuerus (Esth. i. 10).

BLACK. COLORS.

BLAINS (*to boil up*). Violent ulcerous inflammations, the sixth plague of Egypt (Ex. ix. 9, 10). In Deut. xxviii. 27, 35, called the botch of Egypt.

BLAS'PHEMY (*speaking evil of God*). This crime was punished with death (by stoning) by the Jews, and both Jesus and Stephen were condemned on a charge of breaking the law. The *Blasphemy against the Holy Ghost* (Matt. xii. 31) has never been determined, unless it was the saying that the miracles of Jesus were the work of Satan.

BLAST'ING A scorching of grain by the E. wind (Deut. xxviii. 22; Gen. xli. 6, ff.).

BLAS'TUS (*a bud, sprout*). The chamberlain of Herod Agrippa I. An officer of great influence with the people of Tyre and Sidon when they aimed at a reconciliation with the king (Acts xii. 20).

BLEM'ISH. All priests and animals for sacrifice were required to be without blemish or bodily defect (Lev. xxi. 17, 86). Jesus Christ is compared to "a lamb without blemish" (1 Pet. ii. 13).

BLESSING. Favors or benefits specially given by God. Men bless God by thankfully acknowledging his goodness and excellence. The same acts and returns among men have the same name.

BLINDING. PUNISHMENTS.

BLIND'NESS. Is very common in the East from many causes (Matt. ix. 27, ff., xi. 5, xii. 22, xx. 30 ff). "Opening the eyes of the blind" is mentioned as a peculiar attribute of the Messiah (Is. xxix. 18). Blindness was wilfully inflicted as a punishment (Judg. xvi. 21). See cut on p. 16.

BLOOD. Among the Hebrews called the life (Lev. xvii. 11-14). In sacrifices the blood was caught and disposed of in a prescribed manner (Lev. iv.). Murder was held to curse the place where it was done (a superstition still strong in nearly every country (Gen iv. 10).

The Jewish people from the time of Noah were forbidden to eat blood (Gen. ix. 4), when at the same time animal food was permitted, because the blood was specially offered to God in sacrifice (Lev. xvii. 11). Since animal sacrifices have been

BITTERN.

abolished by the one great sacrifice of Jesus, blood is eaten by Christians. THE AVENGER OF BLOOD is the nearest relative (to the fifth degree) to any person who has been murdered, whose duty it is to avenge the death (Gen. ix. 5). A money payment is often accepted for a life in the East. The 6 Cities of Refuge were appointed as a refuge for any who accidentally killed another [not for murderers, for whom there was no refuge or pardon]. The "blood-revenge" has, more than any other custom or power, prevented the tribes of Arabia from exterminating each other.

BLOT. Blame, or blameworthiness (Job xxxi. 7; Prov. ix. 7).

BLUE. COLORS.

BOANER'GES (*sons of thunder—loud voiced?*). Names given to the two zealous sons of James and John (Mark. iii. 17).

BOAR. SWINE.

BOAT. SHIP.

BO'AZ (*agile*). Married Ruth as directed by the law (Deut. xxv. 5). He was a pure and high-

BOC'CAS (1 Esd. viii. 2). BUKKI.

BOCH'ERU (*youth or first-born*). Son of Azel (1 Chr. viii. 38).

BO'CHIM (*the weepers*). W. of Jordan, N. of Gilgal (Judg. ii. 1, 5).

BO'HAN. A stone set up on the border of Benjamin and Judah, between Betharabah and Bethhoglah on the E., and Adummim and Enshemesh on the W. (Josh. xv. 6; xviii. 17).

and Love are expressed by this word when we speak of *bosom* friends; it was well known to the ancients (Luke xvi. 20).

BO'SOR. E. of Jordan, in Gilead (1 Macc. v. 26, 36).

BŌSŌ'RA. Gilead. A strong city taken by Judas Maccabæus; probably the same as Bozrah (1 Macc. v. 26, 28).

BOSS. ARMS.

BOTCH. BLAINS. MEDICINE.

BOT TLE. One Greek and four Hebrew words are

BOZRAH.

BOIL. MEDICINE.

BOLLED (*formed into seed-vessels*). The flax was bolled (Ex. ix. 31).

BOLSTER. BED.

BOND. Bondage. See SLAVERY.

BON'NET. HEAD-DRESS.

BOOK. WRITING.

BOOTHS. Huts made of branches of trees or other very perishable materials.

BOTTLES.

BOOTY. See SPOIL.

BO'OZ. BOAZ (1 Matt. i. 5; Luke iii. 32).

BO'RITH (2 Esd. 1, 2). BUKKI.

BOR'ROW. LOAN.

BOS'CATH (*stony*). BOZKATH (2 K. xxii. 1).

BO'SOM. Abraham's bosom. DRESS. Intimacy

translated bottle (*chemeth, nebel, bakbuk, nod* and *onkos.*) Bottles are of skins, or of earth or glass. Skins of goats and kids are used for the smaller, and of the ox for the larger. These skin bottles are mentioned by Homer, Herodotus and Virgil, and are now used in Spain and all over the Orient. Earthen and glass bottles were also used, and are often mentioned.

BOWELS. In the Bible meaning the seat of the feelings as we now use heart; also mercy and compassion (Gen. xliii. 30).

BOWING. ADORATION.

BOWL. CUPS.

BOX. ALABASTER; VIAL.

BOX-TREE. This elegant shrub, or small tree, is twice named by Isaiah for its beauty (Is. xli. 19, lx. 13; 2 Esd. xiv. 24). It is thought that the word ivory ought to be translated box-wood in Ezr. xxvii. 6. Box is still used for combs, and by the carver and the turner. It is the best material for blocks for the wood-engraver.

BŌ'ZEZ (*shining.—Teeth of the cliff*). The rock on the N. of the pass by which Jonathan entered the Philistine camp (1 Sam xiv. 4, 5). In the Wady Suweinit, near Michmash.

BOZ'KATH. Judah, in the Shefelah (Josh. xv. 39; 2 K. xxii. 1). The native place of King Josiah.

BŌZ'RAH (*enclosure; sheepfold*). Chief city in Edom (Gen. xxxvi. 33). The modern name is Buscirch—*little Busrch* (Rob., ii. 167). It is still a strong fort on a hill-top among the mts., about 25 ms. S. E. of the Dead Sea, half way to Petra (Is. xxxiv. 6, lxiii. 1; Jer. xlix. 13, 22; Amos i. 12; Mic. ii. 12). It is the centre of a pastoral region.—

2. In the plain country—the land of Mishor—(Jer. xlviii. 24). E. of the Dead Sea and Lower Jordan are high table-lands, called Belka, where there are three ruins, named Um-el-Jemal (Beth-gamul), Kureiyeh (Kerioth), and Busrah (Bozrah), in the N. E. section, which is a rich district near the Hauran. The walls of Bozrah were 4 ms. in extent, and they did not include the suburbs. Temples, churches, mosques, and a beautiful theatre, are all in ruins; only a strong castle is left entire.

BRACELET. Armlet, wristlet. Ornament worn around the arm, above or below the elbow.

BRAMBLES. Thorns.

BRANCH. Limb of a tree—figuratively a person related to another, or to a family—as Jesus to the line of David (Is. iv. 2; xi. 1; Jer. xxiii. 5; xxxiii. 15; Zech. iii. 8, vi. 12)—Christians to Christ.

BRI´DLE. Bridles were in the lips of captives, as seen in the Assyrian sculptures. The prisoners are all fettered and have in the under lip a ring to which is attached a cord held by the king (Is. xxxvii. 29; 2 K. xix. 28). See page 28.

BRI´ER. Thorns.

BRIG´AN-DINE. Arms.

BROID´ERED. "Broidered Hair" (1 Tim. ii. 9).

BROTH or SOUP (Judg. vi. 19, 20; Is. lxv. 4). Food.

BRIM´STONE. Sulphur. Found on the shore of the Dead Sea. See Geology.

BROOK. See River.

BROTH´ER. 1. Kinsman, brother, nephew, cousin.—2. Of the same tribe.—3. Of the same people.—4. An ally in war.—5. Any friend (Job. vi. 15).

BRICK-MAKING IN EGYPT.

BRASS. The Hebrews did not mix copper and zinc, as we do, to make brass, but used the copper pure, or mixed tin with it, forming *bronze;* of which metal are nearly all the antique coins not gold and silver.

BRA´VERY. In Is. iii. 18, beauty, splendor.

BRAY. To make a noise like an ass (Job vi. 5, etc.) or to break in pieces (Prov. xxviii. 22).

BRA´ZEN SEA. Sea, molten.

BRA´ZEN SERPENT. Serpent, Brazen.

BREACHES (Judg. v. 17), a rent, notch. House, War.

BREAD (Hebrew *lehem,* or *lechem*). First mentioned in Gen. xviii. 6. Bread was a term for the whole meal; as meal (ground grain) is for all that is eaten at any time. The best was made of wheat, ground and sifted, leavened and baked. Poorer kinds were made of barley, rye, beans, and lentiles. The bread was kneaded with the hands or with the feet (as shown on the monuments), in a trough, and if unleavened baked thin and quickly, as now by the Bedawins. There were private and public ovens (Jer. xxxvii. 21; Neh. iii. 11). Hot, smooth stones are used for baking now. The objectionable passage in Ez. iv. 12 is explained when we know that dried dung of all kinds, in the East where there is no wood, is used for burning. Ephraim is a cake not turned (Hosea vii. 8). The baking-pan was used (Lev. ii. 5; 2 Sam. xiii. 9), and the frying-pan.

BREAST-PLATE. See Arms.

BREECHES. Under-drawers (Ex. xxviii. 42).

BRETHREN. Brothers.

BRIBE. Bribery of magistrates was forbidden (Ex. xxiii. 8; Deut. xvi. 19), and when Samuel's sons took bribes, and perverted justice, the people asked for a king (1 Sam. viii.).

BRICK. Made of clay, clay and sand, mud with straw, burnt in kilns, or dried in the sun. They were sometimes colored or painted in patterns. Houses of sundried bricks had layers of reeds or straw at intervals. David made the prisoners work in brick-kilns (2 Sam. xii. 31). Bitumen, mud, and and a very hard cement, were used to join the bricks.

BRIDE and BRIDEGROOM. Marriage.

BRIDGE. The only mention of a bridge is in 2 Macc. xii. 13. The Romans made the first bridges in Syria and Palestine.

—6. One in the same office (1 K. ix. 13).—7. Fellow man (Luke xix. 17).—8. One of a similar character (Job xxx. 29).—9. Disciples (Matt. xxv. 40).—10. Of the same faith (Amos i. 9; Acts ix. 30). A term meaning similarity, as "brother of dragons," in Job xxx. 29. See James for brethren of the Lord.

BROWN. Colors.

BRUIT. News or Rumor (Jer. x. 22).

BUBAS´TIS. Pi-beseth.

BUCK´LER. See Arms and Armour.

BUFFET. To smite, to maltreat (Matt. xxvi. 67).

BUILDING. Architecture.

BUK´KI (*mouth of God*). Fifth in the line of high priests after Aaron. Son of Abishua (1 Chr. vi. 5). Boceas in Esdras viii. 2.—2. One of Joshua's assistants in the allotment. Of the tribe of Dan (Num. xxxiv. 22).

BUK-KI´AH (*hasting from Jehovah*). A Levite. Son of Heman. Musician in the temple (1 Chr. xxv. 4, 13).

BUL (*rain*). Eighth month. Climate.

BULL. Bullock. Cattle.

BUL-RUSH. Reed.

BUL´WORKS. Fenced City.

BOTTLES.

BU´NAH. Son of Jerahmeel, of Pharez and Judah (1 Chr. ii. 25).

BUN´NI (*built*). A Levite (Neh. ix. 4).—2. A chief (x. 15).—3. Ancestor of Shemaiah (xi. 15).

BUR´IAL. The custom was to bury in tombs or graves, and there were no exceptions, not even criminals (Deut. xxi. 23). The tombs cut in the rocks of Palestine and Egypt have been found to be depositories of much valuable information on the manners and customs of antiquity. Sepulchres for families were cut near the residence, in a gar-

den, or by the road, long before they were expected to be needed. Only kings and prophets were buried in towns (1 K. ii. 10; 2 K. x. 35; 1 Sam. xxv. 1). Rachel's tomb was a monument erected on the spot where she died. It was a misfortune and a dishonor to fail of burial in the family tomb (1 K. xiii. 22); and an honor to a person or family to wish to be buried with them (Ruth i. 17); or to give one a place in a sepulchre (Gen. xxiii. 6; Luke xxiii. 50). It was the custom to wash them with lime ("white"), each year (Matt xxiii. 27). Spices were used to prepare the body for the grave (2 Chr. xvi. 14; John xix. 40), which were omitted as a mark of popular dishonor (2 Chr. xxi. 19). Burning was very rare, and only recorded of Saul and his sons. The next of kin presided over the whole offices, but there were public buriers (Ez. xxxix. 12; Acts v. vi. 10). The body was wrapped in its usual dress, and with bandages. Coffins were rarely used. A stone sarcophagus was used for a great person—king, etc. The dead were carried on a bier, by the relatives or hired persons, or by any who wished to honor the dead or the relatives. The desire was to be buried in the native place, as Jacob and Joseph wished to be carried to Canaan, because of a superstition that only those buried in the Promised Land would rise in the resurrection.

BURN'ING. BURIAL.
BURN'ING-AGUE (Lev. xxvi. 16). FEVER.
BURNT'-OFFERING. TEMPLE.
BUSH. MOSES.
BUSH'EL. MEASURES.
BUT'LER. Cup-bearer.
BUT'TER. The term usually means *curdled milk*, curds, milk, and cheese. Butter (churned cream) is made by shaking a skin of cream, or milk, and when formed, melting, and pouring into skin bottles, or earthern jars. It is more like oil than our butter.
BUY'ING. AGRICULTURE.
BUZ.—1. 2d son of Nahor and Milcah (Gen. xxii. 21). Elihu, the Buzite (Job xxxii. 2, 6), was of this family (of Aram) which settled in Arabia (Jer. xxv. 23).

BU'ZI. Buzite, father of Ezekiel (Ez. i.).
BUZ'ITE. Descendant of Buzi (Job xxxii. 2, 6).
BY. Sometimes meaning *against* (1 Cor. iv. 4).
BYB'LUS. GEBAL. The Greeks changed the name of Gebal to Byblus, and the Septuagint uses that name in 1 K. v. 18, etc. In mythology this was the birth-place of Adonis, and contained the principal temple and sanctuary of that god. Byblus had a fleet of war vessels in the time of Alexander. For many centuries it was a place of importance, and in Christian times had a bishop.

C

CAB. WEIGHTS AND MEASURES.
CAB'BON. Judah, in the Shefelah (Josh. xv. 40).
CA'BUL (*little*). 1. Asher (Josh. xix. 27; Jos. vi. § 43, 45). Modern site, 8 ms. E. of Acre.—2. Region in Galilee given by king Solomon to Hiram, king of Tyre, which "pleased him not" (1 K. ix. 12, 13; Jos. Ant. viii. 5, § 3).
CAD'DIS. Eldest brother of Judas Maccabæus (Macc. ii. 2).
CÆSARE'A. On the shore of the Great Sea, N.

CÆSAREA PALESTINA.

W. of Jerusalem 70 ms., and 35 N. of Joppa, on the ancient road from Tyre to Egypt (Jos. Wars, i. 21, § 5). The political capital of Palestine, and a very important city in the time of the apostles (Acts viii. 40; ix. 30; x. 1. 24; xi. 11; xii. 19; xviii. 22; xxi. 8, 16; xxiii. 23, 33; xxv. 1, 4, 6, 13). In Strabo's time there was at this place Strato's Tower, and a landing-place; and Herod the Great, at immense cost, built an artificial breakwater and founded a city, B. C. 22. The sea-wall was built of very large blocks of stone, 50 feet long, and extended into water of 120 feet depth, enclosing several acres, on which a large fleet could safely ride (Jos. Ant. xv. 9). Named, in honor of Augustus, C. Sebaste (Jos. Ant. xvi. 5, § 1). Sometimes called C. Palestina, and C. Stratonis. Called Sebaste on coins. The residence of Philip, one of the 7 deacons of the early church, and the home of the historian Eusebius; the scene of some of Ori-

gen's labors and the birthplace of Procopius. Was noted in the time of the Crusades. Is now utterly desolate.

It was at Cæsarea that Origen (A. D. 185–204), a man of great natural ability, collated the text of the Septuagint, Hebrew and other Greek versions, making a page of six columns, each version in its proper column, thus forming what was called the *Hexapla—Six-ply* version of the Scriptures, which is the most important contribution to biblical literature in ancient times. Of some books he gave eight versions.

CÆSARE'A PHILIP'PI. PANEAS (*Pan*). At the S. W. foot of Mt. Hermon, on a broad terrace overlooking the Huleh plain; behind the mountain range rises in rugged bold peaks, wooded and capped with snow. Groves of evergreens, oaks and olives, hawthorns, myrtles, oleanders, and beautifully carpeted with grass. One of the chief sources of the Jordan is in a cave near the castle, and pours out an abundance of water, spreading fertility in its course. Named by Philip in honor of Tiberius Cæsar and himself. Agrippa II named it Neronias, after Nero. Titus exhibited gladiators there (Jos. Wars vii. 2, § 1). On the coins it is C. Paneas. Its most ancient name is now only known at the spot. The castle (Subeibeh) is of Phœnician work, and one of the largest in the land. Supposed to be Baal Gad (Josh. xi. 17). The charge to Peter was given here by Jesus (Matt. xvi. 18), and near it was probably the scene of the Transfiguration (xvii. 1, 2).

CAIA'PHAS (*rock, or depression*). Joseph Caiaphas, high-priest of the Jews, under Tiberius at the crucifixion—appointed by Valerius Gratus, A. D. 25, holding it till removed by Marcellus, A. D. 37. His long term indicates unusual power and fitness. Son-in-law of Annas. He pronounced judgment that Jesus was guilty of blasphemy (Matt. xxvi. 57–66), and uttered a prophesy of Jesus without being conscious of it.

CAIN (*acquisition*). The first-born of the Adamic race. Son of Adam and Eve (Gen. iv. 1). Eve said, "I have got a man, by the help of Jehovah." It is supposed that he worked in the field, and that his brother Abel kept the flocks. After the murder of Abel (through envy and jealousy) he went into the land of Nod (*wandering land*); saw a sign from heaven, and was assured that no attempt would be permitted against his life; he married *Save*, and built the city of Enoch. Society was thoroughly organized in his time, and we find such names as Zillah (*shadow*), Naamah (*pleasant*), and Adah (*ornamented*); and Jabal living in tents; Jubal making musical instruments; Tubal Cain in the shop of the smith; Lamech composing poetry; while history and genealogy were carefully preserved.—2. CAIN. A place in Judah, in the mts., near Zanoah and Gibeah (Josh. xv. 57).

CAI'NAN (*possessor*). Son of Enos. Great-grandson of Adam. Father of Mahalaleel. Died aged 910 (Gen. v. 9; Luke iii. 37).—2. Son of Arphaxad and father of Sala. The name is supposed to have been *added* to the genealogy for some reason by the scribes or some compiler.

CA'LAH (*old age*). One of the most ancient cities of Assyria, built by Asshur (Gen. x. 11). HALAH (2 K. xvii. 6). Shalmaneser carried Israel captive to this city. The Nimrud ruin, which has yielded vast quantities of Assyrian remains, is believed to be the ancient Calah, once capital of the empire.

CAL'COL (*sustenance*). Son or descendant of Zerah (1 Chr. ii. 6).

CALD'RON. A pot or kettle (2 Chr. xxxv. 13).

CA'LEB (*dog*). The only one besides Joshua, of all those who left Egypt, who was permitted to enter Canaan. Son of Jephunneh, the Kenezite (Josh. xiv. 14), not a Hebrew, but so adopted, and the city of Hebron was given to him as his portion.—2. Son of Hezron—Pharez—Judah—and father of Hur; his wives were Azubah, Jerioth and Ephrath, Ephah and Maachah.—3. Son of Hur.—4. CALEB EPHRATA. BETHLEHEM.

CALF. Image for worship made at Sinai in imitation of the Apis (Mnevis?) of Egypt, from the jewelry borrowed of the Egyptians (Ex. xxxii. 2). Not solid gold, but of wood, gilded or plated with gold (as the emblem of Osiris—Apis—was made). Moses burnt the image as an allegorical act (Job xv. 16; Hos. viii. 56; x. 6). Another was set up at Bethel, and one at Dan.

CAL'NE (*fort of Ann*). Calno, Calnah, Canneh, Assyria, on the E. bank of the Tigris, opposite Seleucia (Gen. x. 10), Ctesiphon, 200 ms. below Nineveh, 20 below Bagdad, 6 N. of Babel. *Tauk Keara* is its present name, and the ruins are very interesting.

CALIS'THENES. Burnt by the Jews (2 Macc. viii. 33).

CAL'PHI Father of Judas (1 Macc. xi. 70).

CALVARY (*a bare skull*). GOLGOTHA. Place of the crucifixion of Jesus. Wm. C. Prime this year found a wall in Jerusalem which he thinks is the long-lost second wall of Josephus, running south of the so-called Church of the Holy Sepulchre, and so far proves the claim that the true site of calvary, and the sepulchre are known and in that church (Matt. xxvii. 33; Mark xv. 22; Luke xxiii. 33; John xix. 17).

GROUP OF CAMELS.

CAM'EL (Heb. *gamal*). Mentioned in Gen. xii. 16; Ex. ix. 3, as abundant (2 Chr. xiv. 15). Used as a means of traveling, especially across the desert (1 K. x. 2), both for riding and for burdens; and also used in war. The coarse hair (shed in the spring) was made into tent-cloth, and heavy cloaks for rough weather, and used in the desert or open country (Matt. iii. 4); and the fine hair into the delicate "camel's hair shawls." Its meat was forbidden as food or sacrifice, because it does not divide the hoof. Many trinkets and ornaments are hung on the neck and sides of favorite camels (Judg. viii. 21, 26). Its foot is provided with pads under the two toes which do not easily sink in the sand; its nostrils can be closed against the dust or fine sand, or hot wind; its sharp, long teeth are exactly adapted to cut off the prickly shrubs of the desert; its hump is almost pure fat, which can be absorbed on a long journey, where food is scanty; and its stomach has several extra water-bags, holding many days supply. The desert would be uninhabitable without the camel (and the palm-tree). Camel's milk is a luxury much esteemed in the East. The swiftness of the dromedary (*swift-camel*) is proverbial, 900 miles in 8 days having been done.

CA'MON (*full of grain*). GILEAD? (Ant. 5, 7, 6). Where Jair was buried (Judg. x. 5). Lost. CYAMON.

CAM'PHIRE. Camphor (Cant. i. 14; iv. 13). Hebrew *kopher*, Greek *kupros*, Arabic *alcana*.

Lawsonia mermis, a privet, with clusters of delicate little lilac blossoms, and exquisite in perfume. The ladies wear them in their bosoms as a boquet. The dried leaves are mixed with citron juice and used to stain the nails and palms with a yellowish brown (rust-color), very much liked (and is compelled by fashion), in the East. In Persia men also dye the nails. The hair is colored also, by adding indigo, black. Deut. xxi. 12, should read "adorn her nails" instead of "pare her nails."

CA'NA (*the nest*). Galilee (John ii. 1). 7 ms. N. of Nazareth. Scene of the first miracle of Christ, turning water into wine; and another, healing the son of a nobleman (iv. 46–54). The native place of Nathanael, Bartholomew. Now called Kana el Jelil, and in ruins, occupying a beautiful side-hill overlooking the plain of Buttauf. (Robinson ii. 346–9, iii. 108). Howard Crosby, D.D (*Life of Jesus*), decides in favor of Kefr Kenna, 4 ms. N. E. of Nazareth. The text is equally explained by either place.

CA'NAAN (*bowed down*). 4th son of Ham (Gen. x. 6), progenitor of the Phœnicians. The word is also translated "traffickers" (Is. xxiii. 8), "merchant" (11), "the land of traffic" (Ezr. xvii. 4), "merchant people" (Zeph. i. 11), and in scorn by Hosea (xii. 7), "he is a merchant; the balances of deceit are in his hand," speaking of degenerate Israel. Ham, the younger son of Noah, behaved with indecent levity towards his father, becoming a shame and reproach to him in his old age, and so Ham was punished in his youngest son, for indecent levity, shameless profligacy, and insufferable abominations, have poisoned the whole line, taking the shape and plea of religion, the most hateful being worshiped as the most holy. Mt. Lebanon is now the harbor of the most revolting types of idolatry, the relics of antiquity.

CA'NAAN (*lower country*). That is, lower than Gilead. The ancient name of the country between the Jordan and the Great Sea, extending from Hamath on the N. to the desert below Beersheba on the S. (Gen. xii. 5; xiii. 12; Zeph. ii. 5; 1s. xix. 18; Judg. iii. 1; Ex. xv. 15). In Matt. xv. 22, the name is applied to Philistia and Phœnicia, the low lands.

CANDLESTICK.

CA'NAANITE. Simeon the Zealot (Cannaanite—from the Syriac *kannean*, of which the Greek is *zelotes*).

CA'NAANITE. Dwellers in the land—lowland—as lower than Gilead. And again, dwellers in the lower lands of the plains by the sea; and in the Jordan valley (Num. xiii. 29; Gen. x. 18–20).—2. Any people in the land not Hebrew (Gen. xii. 6; Num. xxi. 3).

CAN'DACE (Greek, *kandake*). Title of the queens of Meroe, whose capital was Napata. A prime minister from this court was converted by Philip, on his way back from Jerusalem to Ethiopia (Acts viii. 27). Queens of this country were sculptured on the ancient monuments, mentioned by Herodotus (Nitocris, ii. 100), Pliny (vi. 35), Strabo (xvii. 820), Dio Cassius (liv. 5), and Eusebius.

CAN'DLE. LAMP.

CANDLESTICK. LAMPSTAND. The only light of the tabernacle, and afterwards of the temple, was that of the 7 lamps on the golden stand; or *ten*, according to 1 K. vii. 49, and *one* in 1 Macc. i. 23; iv. 49; Wars vii. 5. The only ancient figure we have of this is the sculpture on the Arch of Titus at Rome.

CANE (*reed, grass*). A sweet-scented vernal grass, much valued for its perfume (Is. xliii. 24; calamus (*reed*) in Cant. iv. 14. There is no notice of the sugar-cane.

CANKERWORM. LOCUST.

QUEEN CANDACE.

CA'NON (*rule*). The authoritative standard of religion and morals, composed only of divinely inspired writings, which have been added from the time of Moses to that of John. In making the selection of the books, the four conditions were kept in view: 1. Divine authority; 2. Entire and incorrupt work as made by the writer; 3. The whole complete as a rule, and guide; and 4. Therefore needing no further addition. The Holy Bible is then the only and supreme standard of religious truth and duty. The evidences are: The decision of the Church in council; the concurrent testimony of ancient Jewish and Christian writers; and the internal evidence of the books themselves. Inquiring, we wish to know—1. Were the books written by their reputed authors? 2. Were the writers believed to be divinely inspired by their cotemporaries? and 3. Have the books been kept as they were written, unchanged? In Exodus and the earlier books of the Old Testament, the term used for the Sacred Writings is *The Law*, or the Book of the Covenant (Ex. xxiv. 7). After the return from the captivity (about 400 B. C.) they are called recitations, or the words read or recited (Neh. viii. 8). They were also called *The Books* in Ecclesiasticus. Josephus, Philo, and the writers of the New Testament call them *Sacred Writings, Sacred Letters*, and *Scriptures* (Matt. xxi. 42, xxii. 29; John v. 39; Acts viii. 32, 35; Rom. xvi. 26; 2 Pet. i. 20); and Paul, twice, Holy Scriptures (Rom. i. 2; 2 Tim. iii. 15). After the New Testament was written, Jerome (A. D. 400) called them the Sacred Books (following 2 Macc. ii. 13), the name *Bible* being first

CANON 47 CANON

applied by Chrysostom A. D. 400, adding the title *Divine*, or, as we now write it, *Holy Bible*. The word *Bible* is Greek, and means *book*. The sacred book of Mohammed is called *Koroun—the book* (i. e., the thing to be read). The word *Scriptures* is Latin, and means writings. The Bible is divided into the Old and New Testaments (2 Cor. iii. 14), and according to the *Canon* (*Kanon*, Gr., *rule*, meaning *The Catalogue of the Sacred Books*), consisting of 39 books in the Old and 27 in the New Testament. The Roman church adds 10 other books (or parts). The Old Testament collection was completed by Ezra, having been begun by the ancient patriarchs, continued by Moses (Deut. xxxi. 9), by Joshua (xxiv. 26), by Samuel (1 Sam. x. 25), by David, Solomon, and others; and his arrangement has been preserved up to the present time. It was divided into three classes of writings: the *Law* (*Thorah*), the *Prophets* (*Nebiim*), and the *Psalms* (*Chethubim*), (Luke xxiv. 4). Josephus names the same divisions (c. Apion i. 8). The first canon on record is that of Laodicea in Phrygia,

A. D. 365, which fixed the names and order and number of the books very much as we find them now. The Council of Hippo in 393, of Carthage in 419, in which Augustine (Bishop of Hippo), had great influence, held (A. D. 397) that the entire canon of Scripture is comprised in these books—Genesis, Exodus, Leviticus, Numbers, Deuteronomy, Joshua, Judges, 1 small book of Ruth, ** the 4 books of the Kingdoms, and 2 of the Remains. These are the historical books: Job, Tobit, Esther, Judith, 2 books of Maccabees, and 2 books of Ezra. Next are the prophets; 1 book of the Psalms of David, 3 of Solomon—viz., Proverbs, Canticles, and Ecclesiastes. The 2 books Wisdom and Ecclesiasticus are called Solomon's only because they resemble his writings, and they were written by Jesus, the son of Sirach, which are to be reckoned among the prophetical books. The rest are the prophets, 12 of them being reckoned together as one book; and after these the four prophets of large volumes—Isaiah, Jeremiah, Daniel and Ezekiel. The New Testament was the same as now received.

BOOKS OF THE OLD TESTAMENT, WRITTEN IN HEBREW.

NAME.	CHAP.	WRITTEN BY	B. C.	YEARS.	REMARKS.
1. Genesis,	50	Unknown,		2278	
2. Exodus,	40	Moses,	1491	145	These five are called Pentateuch, Greek for *five* books.
3. Leviticus,	27	Moses,	to		
4. Numbers,	36	Moses,		38	
5. Deuteronomy,	34	Moses,	1450		
6. Joshua,	24	Joshua,	1433	17	
7. Judges,	21	Several,	721–562	299 (430)	
8. Ruth,	4	Unknown,			Written long after the events narrated.
9. 1 Samuel,	31			72	
10. 2 Samuel,	24	Compiled by Jeremiah,	550	40	
11. 1 Kings,	22			(427	
12. 2 Kings,	25			+26)	
13. 1 Chronicles,	29	Compiled by Daniel and Ezra.	580	2969	
14. 2 Chronicles,	36		450	500	
15. Ezra,	10	Daniel, Nehemiah, Haggai, Ezra.	430	79	
16. Nehemiah,	13	Nehemiah,	440	36	
17. Esther,	10	Unknown,	425?		
18. Job,	42	Unknown,			
19. Psalms,	150	Compiled by Ezra or by Simon.	450 300		Written by David 73; Asaph 12; Korah 11; Heman 1 (78th); Ethan (89th); Solomon (72d, 127th); Moses (90th); and others.
20. Proverbs,	31	Compiled by Solomon,	1000		
21. Ecclesiastes,	12	Unknown,	400?		
22. Song of Songs,	8	Unknown,	900?		
23. Isaiah,	66	Isaiah,	700		Dr. Stanley urges that there were two prophets named Isaiah and two Zechariahs.
24. Jeremiah,	52	Jeremiah,	550		
25. Lamentations,	5	Jeremiah,	550		
26. Ezekiel,	48	Ezekiel,	525		
27. Daniel,	12	Daniel,	525		
28. Hosea,	14	Hosea,	750		The age of prophesy is chiefly included between 800 and 400, B. C. Several prophets, as Shemaiah, Ahijah, Elijah and Elisha, left no writings.
29. Joel,	3	Joel,	700		
30. Amos,	9	Amos,	780		
31. Obadiah,	1	Obadiah,	?		
32. Jonah,	4	Jonah,	800		
33. Micah,	7	Micah,	725		
34. Nahum,	3	Nahum,	725		
35. Habakkuk,	3	Habakkuk,	550		
36. Zephaniah,	3	Zephaniah,	600		
37. Haggai,	2	Haggai,	500		
38. Zechariah,	14	Zechariah,	500		
39. Malachi,	4	Malachi,	420		

BOOKS OF THE APOCRYPHA, OF THE OLD TESTAMENT AGE, IN THE ORDER GIVEN IN THE AUTHORIZED VERSION.

1. 1 and 2 Esdras; 2. Tobit; 3. Judith; 4. Esther; **5.** Wisdom of Solomon; 6. Wisdom of Jesus, son of Sirach—Ecclesiasticus; 7. Baruch; 8. Song of **the** Three Holy Children; 9. History of Susanna; 10. Bel and the Dragon; 11. Prayer of Manasseh; 12. 1 and 2 Maccabees. The Book of Enoch is accepted by the Abyssinians. There have been also included in the Apocrypha—3 and 4 Esdras, the Book of Elias the Prophet; 3, 4 and 5 Maccabees (now received by the Greek Church); the Ascension of Isaiah; the Assumption of Moses, and others.

BOOKS OF THE NEW TESTAMENT, WRITTEN IN GREEK.

NAME.	CHAP.	WRITTEN BY	A. D.	REMARKS.
1. Matthew,	28	Matthew,	50–60	Palestine, Aramaic and Greek.
2. Mark,	16	Mark,	63–70	At Rome, directed by Peter.
3. Luke,	24	Luke,	58–60	Cæsarea, when Paul was there.
4. John,	21	John,	78	Ephesus.
5. Acts,	28	Luke,	63	
6. Romans,	16	Paul,	58	Corinth.
7. 1 Corinthians,	16	"	57	Ephesus.
8. 2 Corinthians,	13	"	58	Philippi.
9. Galatians,	6	"	54	Ephesus.
10. Ephesians,	6	"	62	Rome.
11. Philippians,	4	"	62	Rome.
12. Colossians,	4	"	62	Rome.
13. 1 Thessalonians,	5	"	53	Corinth.
14. 2 Thessalonians,	3	"	53	Corinth.
15. 1 Timothy,	6	"	67	Macedonia.
16. 2 Timothy,	4	"	68	Rome.
17. Titus,	3	"	67	Ephesus.
18. Philemon,	1	"	62	Rome.
19. Hebrews,	13	"	58	Corinth, in Hebrew and Greek.
20. James,	5	James,	47–62	Brother of the Lord.
21. 1 Peter,	5	Peter,	60–67	Babylon.
22. 2 Peter,	3	"		
23. 1 John,	5	John,	78	Ephesus.
24. 2 John,	1	"	78	} Addressed to individuals.
25. 3 John,	1	"	78	
26. Jude,	1	Judas,	60–67	Brother of James (Luke vi. 16.)
27. Revelation,	22	John,	80–99	In Patmos.

APOCRYPAL BOOKS OF THE NEW TESTAMENT AGE.

EUSEBIUS, in his list of the sacred books, makes a distinction against certain ones which were doubtful or heretical, and which were: 1. The doubtful—Acts of St. Paul, Shepherd of Hermas, Apocalypse of Peter, Epistle of Barnabas, Doctrine of the Apostles, Gospel to the Hebrews. 2. The heretical—Gospels of Peter, Thomas, Matthias, and others; the Acts of Andrew, John, Epistle of Clement, and others. The oldest version in any language of which there is a record, is the *Septuagint*, written in Greek, at Alexandria, Egypt, B. C. 286–286. The oldest known copy of this version is written on thin vellum, contains the whole Bible, and is dated in the 5th century; now in the British Museum, and is called the *Codex Alexandrinus*.

Κ ἐτι ἐπτλη θυνθη ϹΑΝΟΙ ΘΛΙΒΟΝ
ΤΕϹΜΕ
ΠΟΛΛΟΙ ΕΠΑΝΕϹΤΗϹΑΝ ΕΠ ΕΜΕ.

Codex Alexandrinus. 5th century. (Ps. iii. 2).

The *Codex Vaticanus* is a manuscript in the Vatican Library, Rome; contains the whole Bible, except a few lost leaves, and belongs to the 4th century.

ΜΙϹΘΟϹΟΥΛΟΓΙΖΕΤΑΙ
ΚΑΤΑΧΑΡΙΝΑΛΛΑΚΑΤΑ

Codex Vaticanus. 4th C. (Rom. iv. 4).

The *Codex Sinaiticus* was found in the Convent on Mount Sinai. It belongs to the 6th century, but

ΚΑΙΟΜΟΛΟΓΟΥΜΕ
ΝΩϹΜΕΓΑΕϹΤΙΝ

C. Sinaiticus. 6th C. (1 Tim. iii. 16).

is a copy of one of an earlier date. Besides the O. and N. T., it has the Gospel and Epistles of Barnabas and the Epistle of Hermas.

Fragments of the Gospel are contained in a palimpsest MS. in a library at Wolfenbuttel, Ger-

many, where the ancient Greek letters have been scraped off, and a modern text written over them.

ϵⲨⲂⲁⲉⲨⲁⲥⲁⲉⲟⲓⲥⲉⲓⲡⲡⲉⲛⲁⲧ
ⲧⲟⲓⲥ ⲡⲁⲣⲁⲛⲟⲓⲥⲧⲟⲩⲧⲟ

This specimen is from a copy in the library of Trinity College, Dublin, a palimpsest, and belongs to the 6th century. It is dated A. D. 200 (about), and shows a very neat and clear text, as well as all the others. The oldest Hebrew MS. known is dated A. D. 489; is a roll, and was found in the Karaite Synagogue in the Crimea. The specimen given here is from a Pentateuch written on a roll of leather, preserved in Odessa, originally brought from Derbend, in Daghestan. It was "corrected" in 580, and therefore probably written some time before.

ⲈⲜⲎⲀⲐⲈⲚⲀⲈ
From a copy of the Book of Genesis in Greek, written for Origen, A.D. 185-255.

חָשׁוּב לְבָאֲבוֹת עָלַי

Ancient Hebrew MS. A.D. 580. (Mal. iv. 6.).

As a specimen of the ancient Hebrew letter used about the time that Paul was a pupil of Gamaliel, here is a copy from a gravestone in the Crimea, of the year A. D. 6. This style of letter is like that on the coins of the Maccabees, B. C. 139, and other coins down to A. D. 130, given in the chapter on *Coins*. We have records of Origen's work, in which he placed side-by-side six different versions of each book of the Bible, thus forming the most valuable contribution to the critical study of the Scriptures known to scholars; but no specimen of his MS. is extant. The oldest known MSS. in our own, or the Anglo-Saxon language, is the Durham Bible, dated A. D. 688. The oldest *printed* Hebrew Bible (Old Testament) was issued at Soncino, Italy, A. D. 1487, in folio. The Complutensian Polyglott was published at the expense of Cardinal Ximenes in 1514-1522, in 6 vols. folio, and sold at 6½ ducats. The Hebrew Vulgate, and Greek texts of the O. T. (with a Latin translation of the Greek), were printed in three parallel columns; the Targums of Onkelos, with a Latin translation in two columns below. The oldest known version in the Latin language is the *Vulgate* (current text), which was the work of Jerome, A. D. 385-420, while he lived at Bethlehem. Tertullian (160-245) mentions a Latin version, but there is nothing known of any belonging to his age. The first book

זאת ציון בוק
בן יצחק בהוה
עת ישועת יש
אל שנת תשב
שנים לגלותנו

(On a gravestone at Simpheropol, Crimea.)
"This is the grave Buki, son of Isaac, the priest; may his rest be in Paradise! (Died) at the time of the deliverance of Israel, in the year 702 of our captivity." (*i. e.* A. D. 6).

printed was the Bible, in Latin; and the splendid pages of the Mazarin Vulgate, printed by Gutenburg and Fust in 1455, at Mainz, are not surpassed at this day as specimens of typography.

A.D. 688. *quadraguua duaru* from *abaabrahain usque-* Anglo Saxon. "Durham Bible."

CANOPY. Curtain over a bed (Judith x. 21). See HISTORY OF THE BOOKS.

CANTICLES. Song of Solomon.

CA-PER'NA-UM (*village of Nahum*). On the N. W. shore of the Lake of Galilee. The scene of many of the works of Christ. Not mentioned in the O. T. or the Apocrypha. Site now located at Tell Hum, where there are ruins of a magnificent synagogue, with beautiful specimens of columns, some of which are double; cornices and massive walls; and a great extent of ruins, half a mile long by a quarter wide. The home of Jesus after leaving Nazareth on being rejected (Mat. ii. 1). Here Matthew was chosen (ix. 10). Simon, Peter and Andrew belonged here (i. 29). (For the miracles wrought here, see LIFE OF CHRIST). The son of the nobleman was healed here by words spoken at Cana. The woes denounced against this city and others near it have been so literally fulfilled that even their sites cannot be determined (*Stanly*, S. & P., ch. x.; *Rob.* ii. 403–4, iii. 344–358). Mentioned by Josephus (Wars, iii. 10 § 8). *Wilson*, Lands of the Bible (ii. 139, 149). The Palestine Exploration has this last year added new facts to the evidence in favor of Tell Hum being the true site. (The Recovery of Jerusalem, p. 265, &c.)

ASSYRIAN KITCHEN.

CA'PHAR. A village (1 Chr. xxvii. 25).

CA'PHAR-SAL-A'MA. A place where a battle was fought between Judas and Nicanor (1 Macc. vii. 31).

CAPHEN'ATHA. A place on the E. of Jerusalem (1 Macc. xii. 37).

CAPH'TOR. CHETE. CAPHTORIM. Mentioned three times as the origin of the Philistines (Deut. ii. 23; Jer. xlvii. 4; Amos ix. 7). By some supposed to be an ancient name of a part of Egypt, KEFT-HOR in hieroglyphics.

CAPPADO'CIA. Asia Minor (Acts ii. 9; 1 Peter i. 1; Jos. Ant. xii. 3, § 4). The road from Palestine passed through the famous Cilician Gates, which led through Mt. Taurus. It is an elevated table-land divided by chains of mountains, well watered but scantily wooded. Mazaca, afterward called Cæsarea, was the Roman capital, and at the base of Mt. Argæus, the highest in Asia Minor. The people were mixed, Scythian and Persian.

CAP'TAIN. Some times a civil and at others a military chief is meant. The Lord is called the captain of his people's salvation (Heb. ii. 10).

CAPTIVITY. The Hebrews reckon four captivities: Babylonian, Median, Grecian and Roman. The expatriation of the people belongs to two periods only—the first and second captivity. In the first—the Babylonish—the best of the nation were carried to Assyria. They were not slaves, but were free under their own civil laws (they would not obey the divine law of ceremonies away from the temple, and it is thought that the custom of building synagogues in every city arose during the captivity), and were ruled by their own elders (Ez. xiv. 1; xx. 1), and held slaves themselves (Tobit viii. 18); while some filled high offices at the court, as Mordecai and Daniel. This event occupied, from beginning to end, 150 years, ending B.C. 588. Judah was carried away captive by Nebuchadnezzar about a hundred years after the first deportation of Israel (Jer. lii). The decree of Cyrus granting the return of the Jews, was dated B.C. 536. A part of the people, under Zerubbabel, returned B.C. 535; and more under Ezra B.C. 458; and of others, under Nehemiah, B.C. 445. The return thus extending over a period of 145 years. (See Nehemiah, Ezra, Haggai and Zechariah.) The number of those who remained in Assyria was about six times those who returned to Jerusalem, and they were known in the time of Christ as the DISPERSED (John vii. 35; James i. 1). Besides those who remained in Assyria, there were many Jews who fled into Egypt (Zech. x. 6-10), and into Arabia, settling in Yemen (Sheba). After this time the TEN TRIBES were lost to history. It is supposed that they intermarried with each other and with the people among whom they lived, and so became lost as distinct tribes, or even as a people. During and after the captivity the Jews laid aside their prejudices, forgot their peculiar tribal pride, and became one nation (Is. xi. 13; Ez. xxxvii. 22); and since that time no one of them is able to trace his lineage to any particular tribe, but may reasonably claim to have the blood of the whole twelve mingled in his veins. So Paul seems to have felt (Acts xxvi. 7) when pleading before Agrippa.

CARBUNCLE (Is. liv. 12). PRECIOUS STONES.

CARCAS. One of the seven princes of Ahasuerus (Esth. i. 10).

CARCHE'MISH (*fort of Chemosh*). Assyria (Is, x. 9). By Euphrates (Jer. xlvi. 2; 2 Chr. xxv. 20). Assyrian inscriptions discovered in modern times show it to have been a chief city of the Hittites, from B.C. 1100 to B.C. 850, who were masters of Syria. Taken by Pharaoh Necho, B.C. 608, and 3 yrs. after by Nebuchadnezzar.

CA'RIA. S. W. in Asia Minor.

CARMA'NIANS. People of Carmania, north of the Persian Gulf (2 Esd. xv. 30).

CARE'AH. Father of Johanan (2 K. xxv. 23).

CAR'MEL (*park—fruitful field*). A mountain range branching off to the north-west from the mountains of Samaria, 15 miles long, 2 to 4 wide, and 600 to 1800 feet high, ending in a steep cape far out into the Great Sea, dividing the plain of

Acre from Sharon (Josh. xii. 22, xix. 26; Jer. xlvi. 18). The plain of Esdraelon lies east, and the river Kishon washes its north side. No part of Palestine equals it in picturesque beauty and variety of scenery, the luxuriance of its herbage, and the brilliance and variety and abundance of its flowers (Is. xxxv. 2; Cant. vii. 5). There are many deep ravines, which abound in partridges, quails, woodcock, hares, jackals, wolves, hyenas, and wild-boars; and it is said, anciently also lions and bears. There are many caves in the vicinity of the convent, which were once occupied by hermits; and one of these is said to be the one referred to in 1 K. xviii. 4; and also see Amos ix. 3. The chief incident in its history is Elijah's sacrifice, the site of which is now located at el Mukrakah (*the burning—the sacrifice*), on a rock terrace, Tell el Kusis (*hill of the priests*), at the east end; from which was seen the whole of the plain of Esdraelon, the river Kishon, Gilboah with Jezreel at its base, Jezebel's temple and Ahab's palace in full view, the sea being hid by the hill to the west, up which the servant could climb in a few minutes and see the sea in its entire expanse (1 K. xviii. 30; 2 K. iv. 23). Pythagoras visited it, and Vespasian, the emperor, came to consult the oracle of Carmel. Elijah was sitting on the mountain when the "fifties" were sent by Ahaziah to take him prisoner for stopping his messengers to Baal at Ekron, and two bands were consumed by fire from heaven (2 K. i. 9-15). After the ascent of Elijah, Elisha went to reside on Carmel for a time (2 K. ii. 25), and was here when the woman from Shunem found him, and told him of her son's death (iv. 25). Called now Jebel Mar Elias. The convent was built A. D. 1830, over ancient ruins, and is famous for having been founded by St. Louis of France, and its name given to the Barefoot Carmelite Friars.—2. Judah, 6 miles southeast of Hebron. City of Nabal (1 Sam. xxv. 2), and of Abigail, David's favorite wife (xxvii. 3), where Saul set up a "place" after his victory over Amalek (xxv. 12), and Uzziah had vineyards (2 Chr. xxvi. 10). It is mentioned by Jerome and Eusebius as having a Roman garrison; and in the history of the Crusades, A. D. 1172. The heaps of ruins now called Kurmul, lie around the sloping sides of an oval valley, the head of which is shut in by rocky ridges. The castle (*Kusr el Birkeh*) had walls 10 feet thick of beveled stones, 60 feet long, 40 wide, and 30 high. Near it was a round tower, and there are the remains of several churches, one of which was 150 by 50 feet. There is a fine reservoir of sweet water supplied from springs near (*Van de Velde*).

CAR'MELITE. Of Carmel in the mountains of Judah (1 Chr. xi. 37).

CARMELITESS. Woman of Carmel in Judah (1 Sam. xxvii. 3).

CARMI. (*a vine-dresser*).—1. Father of Achan (Josh. xii. 1, 18).—2. 4th son of Reuben (Gen. xlvi. 9).

LOCUST.

CAR MITES. Of Reuben (Num. xxvi. 6).

CARNAIM. In the land of Galaad, Gilead. Ashteroth Karnaim.

CARPENTER. Since wood was always too scarce and precious in Palestine for any use besides for doors, windows, etc., and for decorations, the carpenter was probably a carver of such finishing as is now seen in the best rooms of the East.

CAR'PUS. A disciple at Troas with whom Paul left his cloak (2 Tim. iv. 13), books and parchments. He is mentioned as bishop of Berytus in Thrace by Hippolytus.

CARRIAGE. This word means baggage in the A. V.

CAR'SHENA. One of the seven princes (Esth. i. 14).

CART.

CART. Wagon. Were open or covered (Num. vii. 3), and used to carry persons and burdens (Gen. xlv. 19; 1 Sam. vi. 7), or produce (Amos ii. 13). There were no roads, and the only ones now in use have been lately made, from Joppa to Jerusalem, and from Beirut to Damascus.

CAR'VING. Carving and engraving have always been much used for the decoration of houses, furniture, arms, jewelry, etc. The occupation of Joseph was that of a carver and not a carpenter, as wood has always been too scarce and expensive to use in the framework of houses.

CASIPH'IA. Place between Babylon and Jerusalem (Ezr. viii. 17).

CAS LEU (1 Macc. i. 54).

CAS'LU'HIM. Mizraite people (Gen. x. 14). In Upper Egypt. Bochart thinks they were the Colchians of the Greeks.

CAS'PHON (1 Macc. v. 36).

CAS'PHOR. Fortified city in the land of Galaad (1 Macc. v. 26). The Jews took refuge there from the Ammonites.

CAS PIS. A strong, fortified city. Was taken by Judas Maccabaeus (2 Macc. xii. 13, 16).

CAS SIA. One of the principal spices in the composition of the "oil of holy ointment" (Exr. xxx. 24); a choice perfume. Also, an article among the precious merchandise of Tyre (Ezr. xxxvii. 19).

CAS TOR and **POL'LUX** (*sons of Jupiter*), (Acts xxviii. 11). Name of the vessel in which Paul sailed from Malta to Rome; derived from the name of the two stars called "the twins," the fabled sons of Jupiter and Leda.

CATS (Bar. vi. 22). The cat was a favorite of the Egyptians, and is found embalmed among their mummies.

CAT'-ER-PIL-LAR. See LOCUST.

CÁTHUA. GIDDEL (1 Esd. v. 30).

CAUL. A head-dress, made in checker-work; long, like a scarf; worn by women for ornament.

CAUSE'-WAY. Raised path (1 Chr. xxvi. 16, 18).

CAVE. Mentioned in the early history as often useful to men. There are a great number in the limestone region of Palestine and Syria, many of which have been cut out larger for shelter or defence. Several Hebrew words are used to denote caves, holes and fissures, and many places were named from noted caves, and some people, as the Horites (caveites), were so named from their dwellings. The great cave near Aleppo will hold 3000 horse-soldiers. Maundrell described a large system of caves, containing 200 rooms, near Sidon. Lot is the first who is recorded as living in a cave. The cave of Machpelah is the first mentioned as a

burial-place. Other noted caves were Makkedah (five kings taken in by Joshua); Adullam (where David cut Saul's skirt off); and in Josephus, the famous robber-caves of Arbela, near Gennesaret.

CEDAR (Heb. erez; Ar. auz, *the larch*). There are eleven groves of cedars on the Lebanon mountains, which have been visited by travelers recently. One, near the highest peak, 6000 feet above the sea, N. E. of Beirut, and long famous for its 400 ancient trees of immense size, standing near the summits, which are covered with perpetual snow; the second, near Deir El Kamr. The six largest of this northern group measured, in 1868, 48, 40, 38, 33½, 30, 29¾ feet; and a third, near Ain Zehalteh, on the Beirut-Damascus stage road, lately found. Dr. Robert Morris recently brought several camel loads of cones from these trees for distribution among Sunday-School scholars. The references to cedar-wood in the Scripture do not always mean the cedar of Lebanon—as, for instance, when at Sinai (Lev. xii. 6). The word erez means also pine, cypress, fir and juniper. Rev. Henry H. Jessup, an American missionary in Syria, thinks the whole range of Lebanon, from 3000 to 7000 feet altitude, was at one time covered with cedar groves.

CE'DRON. Near Jamnia and Azotus; fortified by Antiochus Sidetes.—2. Kidron, the torrent E. of Jerusalem, which see.

CEI'LAN (1 Esd. v. 15). Azetas.

CEILING. The ceilings of the principal apartments in Eastern houses are the parts on which the chief care is expended in adorning. The Jews bestowed much care on these parts in their houses (Jer. xxii. 14; Hag. i. 4).

CEN'CHREÆ. Harbor of Corinth, on the Saronic Gulf, east, whence Paul sailed for Ephesus (Acts xviii. 18). There was a church here, of which Phœbe was a member (Rom. xvi. 1), and Lucius its first bishop, appointed by Paul. There was a temple at the end of each mole, and a statue of Neptune on a rock between, as may be seen on an ancient coin of Corinth.

CENDEBE'US, correctly Cendebæ'us. One of Antiochus' generals in Palestine (1 Macc. xv. 38, ff).

GOAT OF SINAI

CENSER. A small portable vessel of metal, fitted to contain burning coals (2 Chr. xxvi. 18; Luke i. 9).

CENSUS. See Population.

CENTU'RION. Captain of 100. Century. A Roman military officer. Cornelius, a centurion, was one of the first disciples. Several others are mentioned.

CE'RAS (1 Esd. v. 29). Keros.

CE'TAB (1 Esd. v. 30).

CHA'BRIS. Son of Gothoniel (Judith vi. 15; viii. 10; x. 6).

CHA'DIAS (1 Esd. v. 20). Ammidoi.

CHAFF (Is. v. 24; xxxiii. 11). The carrying away of chaff by the wind in Scripture is used as a symbol of the destruction of the wicked (Is. xvii. 13).

CHAIN. Chains were in use by the ancients; they were made of precious metal for ornaments, and were worn alike by men and women—of iron for other purposes. The gold chain given to Joseph (Gen. xli. 42), and the one promised to Daniel (Dan. v. 7), were the first mentioned.

CHALCE-DO-NY. Precious Stones.

CHAL'COL (1 K. iv. 31).

CHALK (Is. xxvii. 9). Limestone.

CHAL'DÆA, Chaldea, Casdim (*Khaldi in Armenian, the moon*). Babylonia—the whole, or sometimes the southern part (Dan. v. 30, ix. 1; Gen. xi. 28). Haran died in Ur of Casdim (Ezek. i. 3). The whole of Mesopotamia occupied by Chaldeans. The Chaldeans were one out of many Cushite tribes peopling Babylonia. Hence came Sabeans to afflict Job (i. 15-17). Recently discovered inscriptions on ancient works show that there were two languages in use: one a Semitic, for civil purposes, and another a Cushite, for learned and religious purposes (Dan. i. 4; v. 11). The Chaldeans were priests, magicians or astronomers—the depositaries of learning and science. The plains were formerly irrigated by canals led from the river, spread over the country like a network. Groves of palm-trees, pleasant gardens, fields of grain and vineyards, proved the richness of the soil, and supported a dense population. It is now a waste of drifting dust and sand, with heaps of bricks and rubbish (Is. xiv. 23; Jer. l. 38). The chief cities were Accad, Babel, Borsippa, Calneh, Cutha, Erech, Sippara and Teredon. Herodotus mentions a vast number of cities, and the mounds over all the country prove his statements true.

CHAMBERS OF IMAGERY. Used by Ezekiel (viii. 12) in denouncing the idolatrous corruptions of the kingdom of Judah, or that part which imitated the Egyptians in painting on the walls of a chamber pictures of idols, &c., for worship. (See *Wilkinson's Manners and Customs of the Ancient Egyptians*.) Every man has a chamber in his own mind filled with his idols—his dearest objects of regard.

CHAM'BER-ING (Rom. xiii. 13).

CHAM'BER-LAIN. Erastus, "the chamberlain." An officer who had charge of a king's lodgings and wardrobe (2 K. xxiii. 11).

CHAME'LEON (Heb. ko-ach, *strength*). There are two lizards, each of which has been proposed as the animal meant. Lizards are very plentiful in Palestine and Egypt. 1. The chameleon is noted for its strong grasp, by which it sustains its position for a long time on twigs and branches. The normal color is black or slaty, but can be changed in an instant to many other tones, as green, yellow, spotted, which changes seem to be independent of the will of the animal.—2. The Nile Monitor is sometimes called the land crocodile, being about 6 feet in length. It eats the eggs and young of the crocodile.

CHAM'OIS. A specie of wild goat found in Arabia (Deut. xiv. 5).

CHAM-PAIGN (*a plain*) (Deut. xi. 30).

CHA'NAAN (Judg. v. 39, 10).

CHA'NAANITE (Judg. v. 16).

CHAN'CEL-LOR (Ezr. iv. 8, 9, 17).

CHAN'EL-BONE (Job xxxi. 22). The bone of the arm above the elbow.

CHAN'GERS (Judg. ii. 15). Money Changers.

CHANGERS OF MONEY. A class who made a business, in accommodating the temple worshipers at the annual feasts of the Jews, by exchanging the money of those who came from foreign countries for the half-shekel which was the lawful tribute to the treasury. They probably crept gradually nearer the temple until they occupied the corners and passages of the sacred courts. From these Jesus drove them, because no trading was lawful there, and certainly not dishonest, sharp practices, which had made God's house a "den of thieves."

CHAN-NU-NE'US. Merari (1 Esd. viii. 48).

CHA'NOCH. Enoch (Gen. iv. 17).

CHAP'EL (*a holy place, sanctuary*). Idol's temple (1 Macc. i. 47). Bethel was crowded with altars (Amos iii. 14).

CHAP'ITER. The upper part of a pillar (Ex. xxxviii. 17).

CHAP'MEN. Traders (2 Chr. ix. 14). Foot-peddlers.

CHARAATH'ALAR (1 Esd. v. 36).

CHAR'A-CA. A place E. of Jordan (2 Macc. xii. 17). Lost.

CHAR'A-SHIM, THE VALLEY OF. A place settled by Joab 2 (1 Chr. iv. 14), and reinhabited by Benjamites after the captivity (Neh. xi. 35).

CHAR'CHAMIS (1 Esd. i. 25). Carchemish.

CHAR'CHEMIS (2 Chr. xxxv. 20).

CHAR'CUS (1 Esd. v. 32). Barkos.

CHA'RE-A. Harsha (1 Esd. v. 32).

CHAR'GER. (Heb. Agartal). Basin in Ezra i. 9, that is, a tank for catching the blood from the victims on the altar.—2. Kearah, deep dishes (Num. vii. 13).—3. Pinax, a tray, or server, of wood inlaid, or of metal (such as is now used for the common table), (Matt. xiv. 8).

CHARIOT. Heb. *merkabah*, and *rekeb*, and *agaloth* for war-chariots, or wagons or carts. The Egyptian monuments present paintings of several kinds of chariots, all of two wheels only, differing chiefly in the ornaments. The king's was different only in being more richly ornamented, and as having the king alone—as a sign that to him belonged the entire glory of the victory. In the Assyrian sculptures are some 4-wheeled carriages. Three persons usually ride in them—the king, his umbrella-bearer, and the charioteer. The Persian chariots were heavier than those of Egypt or Assyria.

CHARITY. Greek *agape*, which is properly love (1 Cor. viii. 1, 13; Luke xi. 42; Rom. v. 5, 8.) Agape.

CHAR'MIS. Son of Melchiel; one of the three rulers of Bethulia (Judg. vi. 15).

CHAR'RAN. Haran (Acts vii. 2, 4).

CHASTE-BA (1 Esd. v. 31).

CHA'VAH (Gen. iii. 20). Eve.

CHE'BAR (*great river*). Chaldea (Ez. i. 3). Some of the Jews were located here during the captivity (Ez. i. 1, 3, iii. 15; 2 K. xxiv. 15). Habor. This was the largest artificial canal of Babylonia, and was cut by the Jewish captives.

CHE'DORLA'OMER (Gen. 14). King of Elam, perhaps a part of Persia and Media. His marauding excursion, aided by four other kings, was brought to an abrupt and disastrous end by Abraham.

CHEESE. There is no Hebrew word for cheese. The three words translated cheese are: 1. *gebinah*, curdled milk (Job x. 10); 2. *charitse hechalab*, slices of curds (1 Sam. xvii. 18); 3. *shephoth bakar*, curd rubbed fine—of kine (2 Sam. xvii. 20). Cheese now in use in the East is in small round cakes (4 inches), white, very salt, and hard. The Bedawins coagulate buttermilk, dry it, and grind to powder.

CHEL'LAL. Son of Pahath-moab (Ezr. x. 30).

CHELCI'AS. 1. Of Baruch (Bar. i. 1).—2. Highpriest (Bar. i. 7)—3. Father of Susanna (Sus. ii. 29, 63).

CHEL'LIANS (Judg. ii. 23). Chellus.

CHEL'LUH (*strong*). Son of Bani (Ezr. x. 35).

CHEL'LUS. Place west of Jordan (Jud. i. 9).

CHE'LOD (corrupted text in Jud. i. 6).

CHE'LUB (*basket*). 1. Father of Mehir, of Judah

CHARIOT.

(1 Chr. iv. 11).—2. Father of Ezri, David's officer (xxvii. 26).

CHE-LU'BAI. Caleb, son of Hezron (1 Chr. ii. 9).

CHEM'ARIM (*idol-priests*). An ascetic; one who goes about dressed in black (Zeph. i. 4). Idolatrous priests in 2 K. xxiii. 5. Priests of false worship (Hos. x. 5).

CHE'MOSH (*subduer*). The national god of the Moabites (1 K. xi. 7; Jer. xlviii. 7), who were called the people of Chemosh (Num. xxi. 29). Also of the Ammonites, though Moloch was afterwards their god (Jer. xlix). Moloch and Chemosh may mean the same god, who might have been also called Baal Peor. Traces of the same worship are found at Babylon, Tyre, and it was introduced among the Hebrews by Solomon, who built a high place on the Mt. of Offense, so named for that act. The Arabs worshiped a black stone as his emblem—as a black stone in the Kaaba at Mecca is an emblem now worshiped by all Mohammedans. This idol represented some of the planets: perhaps Saturn.

CHE'NA-AN (Gen. ix. 18). Canaan.

CHE-NA'ANAH. Son of Bilhan, a Benjamite (1 Chr. vii. 10).—2. Father of Zedekiah (1 K. xxii. 11, 24).

CHENA'NI. A Levite (Neh. ix. 4).

CHENANI'AH. Chief of the Levites (1 Chr. xv. 22, 27).

CHE'PHAR-HAAMMO'NAI (*village of the Ammonites*); a city of Benjamin (Josh. xviii. 24).

CHEPH'IRAH (*the village*). Benjamin (Josh. ix. 17). East of Yalo, two miles. Kefir (Rob. iii. 146). The Gibeonites of this place (and also Kirjath Jearim and Beeroth) played the trick on Joshua mentioned in Josh. ix. 3, which led him to make a treaty with them.

CHE'RAN. Son of Dishon (Gen. xxxvi. 26).

CHE'REAS. Brothers of Timotheus; governor of Gazara where he was slain by the Jews (2 Macc. x. 32, 37).

CHER'ETHIM. Cher'ethims; pl. of Cherethites (Ez. xxv. 16).

CHERETHI'TES and PELETHITES. Body-guard

of David. No other king had one, that is recorded, but they had runners. Their captain was Benaiah the son of Jehoiadah (2 Sam. viii. 18). Under Solomon, Benaiah was made general instead of were *round about* the throne. They are especially called *living creatures* (Ezekiel and John), and so full of eyes, the peculiar sign of life. The cherubim were designed as symbols of faith and hope to

ENTRANCE OF PALACE AT KOUYUNJIK.

Joab. The names are of Philistine origin, and the men may have been partly of Philistine and partly of Hebrew (refugee) origin, attached to David in his adversity, and rewarded by him in his prosperity.

CHE'RITH. The brook Cherith, in a valley now called Kelt, running by Jericho to the Jordan (1 K. xvii. 3, 5; Jos. Ant. viii. 13, § 2). Some have supposed that it must be looked for on the east of Jordan.

CHER'UB (*mystic figure on the ark*). Cherubim, plural. A keeper, warder or guard of the Deity. Josephus said no one in his day could even conjecture the shape of the cherubim that Solomon made for the Holy of Holies (Ant. viii. 3, 3). They were of wood, gilded, and 15 feet high (1 K. vi. 23). Ezekiel describes them as having each four faces and four wings; but he gives only two faces (or it may be but one) to those in the temple on the walls. The cherubim of Rev. iv. 7, 8, are living creatures, with one body, four faces full of eyes, and six wings. The fourfold combination was of man, lion, ox, and eagle. Monstrous combinations of this kind are figured and sculptured both in Assyria and Egypt. These combined forms are symbolical of united powers; the lion of strength, royal majesty; the ox of patient industry; wings of swiftness, quickness, and the human head the intelligence to guide all these for one purpose; and

SPHINX.

thus showing that the divine government is sustained by intelligence, power, patience, and speed. They were servants of God, and they were ministers of vengeance (Ez. x. 7; Rev. xv. 7), and attendants of the heavenly king, praising and extolling the wonders of his grace (Rev. v. 11), and thus always nearest to God, "*in the midst of the throne*" (Rev. iv. 4-6), while others as angels and elders.

man, pointing to the possibility of man attaining to the highest and holiest places. (See EGYPT for picture of the Sphinx, and NINEVEH for winged figures.)

CHE'SALON (*flank*). Judah (Josh. xv. 10). Now Kesla, 7 ms. W. of Jerusalem.

CHE'SED (*increase*). Son of Nahor (Gen. xx. 22).

CHE'SIL. Simeon (Josh. xv. 30). Near the desert, 8.

CHEST (Heb. ARON and GENAZIM). Meaning Ark of the Covenant, Joseph's coffin, and the contribution box in the temple. Treasuries in Esther iii. 9.

CHESTNUT TREE. In the A. V. (Gen. xxx. 37; Ez. xxxi. 8) the translation of the Heb. ARON, the plane tree. In Ecclus xxiv. 14, wisdom is a plane tree by the water.

CHESUL'LOTH (*loins*). Issa. Between Jezreel and Shunem (Josh. xix. 18). Iksal? Chisloth Tabor?

CHET'TIM. CHITTIM (1 Macc. i. 1).

CHE'ZIB (*false*). Birthplace of Shelah (Gen. xxxviii. 5). AIN KUSSABEH. A fountain and ruins 10 ms. S. W. of Beit Jibrin.

CHI'DON (*javelin*). Near Kirjath Jearim (1 Chr. xiii. 9; 2 Sam. vi.). An accident happened here to the ark while on its way to Jerusalem.

CHICKENS (2 Esd. i. 30; Matt. xxiii. 37). HEN.

CHILD. CHILDREN. Were regarded as God's gifts. Parents were bound to teach them their own faith and fit them to occupy the place of true members of the covenant (Gen. xviii. 19; Deut. vi. 7; xi. 19), and required of children a kind of sacred reverence, sanctioned in the Decalogue; the parent standing to his children as God does to the parent. At five the child was placed under the father's special care, and at twelve the son was called *the son of the law*. Very severe laws regulated the conduct of the child and punished misconduct (Lev. xix. 3; Ex. xxi. 15, 17; Deut. xxvii. 16), in the father as well as the son (Deut. xxi. 21). Property descended to the sons in equal shares, the oldest having a double portion, no wills being necessary. The child might be sold for a debt of the parent (2 K. iv. 1; Is. i. 1; Neh. v. 5), until the year of jubilee. The word child also means a person noted for certain qualities, as "children of the world"— selfish; "children of light" having religion; "child of song," a good singer.

CHIL'ION (*sickly*). Son of Elimelech. An Ephrathite (Ruth i. 2-5, iv. 9).

CHIL'MAD. On the Euphrates; mentioned by Xenophon (Anab. i. 5, 10). Had traffic with Tyre (Ez. xxvii. 23).

CHIM'HAM (*longing*). Son of Barzillai—returned with David (2 Sam. xix. 37, 38, 40; Jer. xli. 17). See BETHLEHEM.

CHIN'NERETH. Naph. Fortified city (Josh. xix. 35). Lost. It is a question which was named first, the lake or the city. Gennesar is a proper change of the same name. (See GENNESARETH.)

CHI'OS. Island in the Ægean Sea, 5 ms. from the shore of Asia Minor, 32 ms. long, 8 to 18 ms. wide (Acts xx. xxi.)

CHIS'LON (*confidence—hope*). Father of Elidad, the prince of Benjamin (Num. xxxiv. 21).

CHIS'LOTH-TA'BOR (*loins—flanks*). West end of Mt. Tabor (Josh. xix. 12). Iksal?

CHIT'TIM, KITTIM (*maritime*). Josephus says it was Cyprus. Mentioned many times (Gen. x. 4; 1 Chr. i. 7; Num. xxiv. 24). Fleets from Tyre sailed there (Is. xxiii. 1, 12; Jer. ii. 10). Cedar or box-wood was got there (Ez. xxvii. 6). Some suppose the name means all the islands settled by the Phœnicians, as Crete, the Cyclades, &c.

CHLO'E (*verdant—short*). A disciple mentioned by Paul (1 Cor. i. 11).

CHO'BA. Ephraim (Judg. iv. 4). **CHO'BAI** (xv. 4, 5). Hobah?

CHORA'SHAN (*smoking furnace*). Visited or haunted by David (1 Sam. xxx. 30). May be the ASHAN of Simeon, S. of Hebron (Josh. xv. 42).

CHORA'ZIN. One of the cities in which the mighty works of our Lord were done (Matt. xi. 21; Luke x. 13), 2 ms. from Capernaum. Supposed to be Kerazeh, a small Arab village 3 ms. inland from Tell Hum. The woes pronounced upon this city have come to pass. Its site even is doubtful.

CHOZE'BA. CHEZIB. ACHZIB (1 Chr. iv. 22).

CHRIST. Title of Jesus as the Messiah. See JESUS.

CHRISTIAN. Followers of the highest and best known divine laws as taught by Jesus Christ. The name Christian was given to the disciples of Jesus at Antioch by the Greeks in derision, in the reign of Claudius. They were before that called Nazarenes and Galileans.

COIN OF CYPRUS.

CHRŎNOL'OGY. The chronology of the Bible is that of the Jews and their ancestors, from the earliest records to the end of the writing of the New Testament. Since the Bible is not a complete history of the whole time it represents, nor of the whole world, it must not be expected to have a continuous chronology. Designed alterations by bad men and careless copying have changed many points, and have made it necessary to exercise the greatest care in determining and correcting the errors. The Jews were not a mathematical people, or scientific in any respect, and computed the year by observation only. The Egyptians and Chaldees were far in advance of the Hebrews in science, and attained to a high standard of mathematical knowledge and chronological computation. The observation of the moon was the basis of the year's reckoning. Messengers were stationed on the heights around Jerusalem, on the 30th day of the month, to announce the appearance of the new moon, who reported to the Sanhedrin. This custom, among the Jews, was older than Moses, as appears in the regulation of it in Num. xxviii. 11. The year was made of twelve moons; and every fourth or fifth year a month was added at the end of the year, after the month Adar, called Veadar, Second Adar. The sacred year began with the month Nisan, in which Moses brought Israel out of Egypt (Ex. xii. 2; Esth. iii. 7). The civil year began as now, with the month Tishri, which was supposed to be the month of the creation.

CHART OF MONTHS, FEASTS, ETC.

Modern	Sacred No.	Months	Civil No.	Festivals
April,	1,	Nisan or Abib,	7,	Passover, 15.
May,	2,	Iyar-Zif,	8,	2d Passover, 14.
June,	3,	Sivan,	9,	Pentecost, 6.
July,	4,	Tammuz,	10,	4th mo., 17.
August,	5,	Ab,	11,	Temple taken by Chaldees, 9.
September,	6,	Elul,	12,	Nehemiah dedicated the walls, 7. Wood-offerings, 21.
October,	7,	Tishri,	1,	Trumpets, 1. Atonement, 10. Tabernacles, 15.
November,	8,	Marchesvan,	2,	Fast, 19.
December,	9,	Chislev,	3,	Dedication, 25.
January,	10,	Tebeth,	4,	Feast of 10th mo., 8. Siege of Jerusalem, 10.
February,	11,	Shebet,	5,	Beginning of year of trees, 15.
March,	12,	Adar,	6,	2d Temple, 3; Purim, 14, 15.

The year was also dated from the king's reign, as in Esther, Chronicles, Kings, etc.; from the building of King Solomon's temple; and from the beginning of the Babylonish captivity. The week was of seven days, ending with the Sabbath. The Egyptians and Greeks divided the month into periods of ten days, called decades. The day was divided into night and day: thus, in Gen. i. 5, "the evening and the morning were the first day." The evening began at sunset, the morning at sunrise. There were four divisions of the day in common use—evening, morning, double light (noon), and half night (midnight). The night was divided into watches, the first and the second. A middle watch is mentioned once in Judg. vii. 19; and the morning watch in Ex. xiv. 24, and 1 Sam. xi. 11. Four night-watches were adopted from the Romans in later times (Mark viii. 35). The day and the night were divided into 12 hours each (Dan. iv. 19, 33). The Egyptians divided the day and night into hours from about 1200 B. C. The division into 24 hours was unknown before the fourth century B. C. The most common usage was to divide the day by the position of the sun, as the Arabs do now. The length of the day was longer in summer than in winter, and the hour longer in propor-

tion. There were many contrivances for measuring time, such as dials, gnomons and clepsydræ, which had long been known by other nations. The day was divided into four parts only for the Temple service (Acts ii. 15; iii. 1; x. 9). The Sabbath (a day of *rest*), at the end of the week, was kept up by the patriarchs, and continued by the law of Moses, as a memorial of the deliverance from Egypt (Deut. v.), and was a day of joy and rejoicing. The morning and evening sacrifice in the Temple were doubled, the shew-bread changed for fresh, the law was publicly read and expounded; and this custom, simple at first, finally developed into the grand ceremonials of the Synagogue, especially under Ezra, after the return from Babylon. The resurrection of our Lord Jesus, the Christ, occurred on the FIRST day of the week (John xx.), and several of his appearances to his friends and disciples happening on that day also, the day of Pentecost in that year fell on that day, when the miraculous gift of tongues prepared the apostles for their peculiar work among all nations; therefore it was adopted as the day for stated meetings of the believers, and called the Lord's day. The seventh day, the seventh month, the seventh year, and the YEAR OF JUBILEE (the 49th or 50th), were sacred, and had their festivals and privileges. The seventh month contained the FEAST OF TRUMPETS, the DAY OF ATONEMENT and the FEAST OF TABERNACLES (which was the most joyful of all the Hebrew festivals), and the opening of the New Year. On the seventh year the land was to rest (Ex. xxiii. 10), in which no field was to be tilled nor vineyard dressed, nor even grain gathered that had sowed itself, nor grapes plucked. All debts were released. The Sabbatical year completed the Sabbatical scale. It began on the seventh month, and was marked by high and holy occupation, connected with sacred reflection, and was completed in the YEAR OF JUBILEE. It is quite certain that the year of jubilee was the 49th. It was to begin on the tenth day of the seventh month, at the sound of a horn (trumpet) all through the land (Lev. xxv.). The laws respecting this year were: 1. Rest for the soil; 2. Restoration of land to its original owner; 3. Freedom to all slaves, whether by poverty or other causes. A notable instance of the release from debt is recorded in Nehemiah v., after the captivity, when the people were rebuilding the walls. There were several eras used in reckoning, by writers, and as national customs. 1. The Exodus (1 K. vi. 1; Num. xxxiii. 38), counting from the first starting out of Egypt.—2. The foundation of King Solomon's Temple.—3. The captivity of Jehoiachin (Ezek. i. 2; xxix. 1; 2 K. xxv. 27; Jer. lii. 31).—4. The return from the captivity of Babylon (Ez. iii. 1, 8).—5. The era of the Seleucidæ.—6. The year of liberation under Simon Maccabæus, marked by coins (1 Macc. xiii. 41). And the years of the reign of each king in his own time, reckoned from the beginning of the new year next after his accession. The original records are so few, and so indefinite, that it is difficult to fix on the precise date of any event, either in the Old or the New Testament. The Bible does not give a connected chronology from Adam down, nor from Noah, nor even from Abraham; nor is there any apparent purpose or system of dates that we can find. At one time it was expected that a better acquaintance with the originals would disclose a perfect system of chronology, giving periods, years, months, and even days; but such close study has unexpectedly shown us that the Bible treats of men and character, and God's dealing with man, and of certain distinct and separate periods of time only as were occupied in the passing events recorded. The people of the East, and the Arabs of the desert in particular, have never been mathematical, founding their chronology on astronomy; but have from

the first regulated their calendar by observation only. Since they did not have the exact machinery of our modern clocks for determining the precise times of the sun's, moon's or stars' rising and setting, eclipses, &c. (which are the foundation of our most exact calculations), they never could have had more than a moderate degree of accuracy in their observations. The new moon would be expected on a certain day, and the precise moment of its appearance would depend on the place of observation, on a hill or in a valley, and the careful watch and good eyesight of the sentinel. The true figures of the original Hebrew chronology are very obscure in many instances, because there are three different versions—the Hebrew, the Samaritan and the Septuagint—each of which gives a different series of figures for the ages of the patriarchs, as shown in the following

TABLE OF THE AGES OF THE PATRIARCHS.

Date B.C.	Name.	Age of each when the next was born			Whole life of each.		
		Heb.	Sam.	Sept.	He.	Sa.	Sep
4004	Adam	130	130	230	930	930	930
3874	Seth	105	105	205	912	912	912
3769	Enos	90	90	190	905	905	905
3679	Cainan	70	70	170	910	910	910
3609	Mahalaleel	65	65	165	895	895	895
3544	Jared	162	62	162	962	962	847
3382	Enoch	65	65	165	365	365	365
3317	Methuselah	187	67	187	969	720	969
3130	Lamech	182	53	188	777	653	753
2948	Noah	502	502	502	950	950	950
2446	Shem	100	100	100	600	600	600
2348	FLOOD	1656	1307	2262			
2346	Arphaxad	35	135	135	438	438	535
	Cainan			130			460
2311	Salah	30	130	130	433	433	460
2281	Eber	34	134	134	464	404	404
2247	Peleg	30	130	130	239	239	339
2217	Reu	32	132	132	239	239	339
2185	Serug	30	130	130	230	230	330
2155	Nahor	29	79	79	148	148	208
2126	Terah	130	70	70	205	145	205
1996	Abraham	100					
1896	Isaac	60					
1836	Jacob	91					
1726	Joseph						

1. Here is a continuous chronology from Adam to Joseph, subject to only three questions: 1. Are the numbers given in either version of the text genuine? If so, which is correct? 2. What was Terah's age at the birth of Abraham? 3. When did the 430 years (of the period from the Promise to the Exodus) begin? A synopsis of the debates on these points may be found in Smith and Kitto. The accuracy of the *original Hebrew* is not doubted; but the alterations cannot be pointed out, so as to harmonize the three records in the Hebrew, the Septuagint, and the Samaritan. The Hebrew text, as interpreted by Ussher, is adopted here for convenience.

2. From the call of Abraham to the Exodus, 430 years; estimated as follows;

Abraham to Jacob	85
Levi's age	137
Kohath's age	133
Amram's age	137
Moses at Exodus	80
Abraham to Isaac	25
Isaac to Jacob	60
Joseph entered Egypt	130
Joseph lived after	71
Oppression after Joseph.	
572	Moses at Exodus . . 80

B.C. 1921 − 430 = 1491.

CAPERNAUM.

From the number 572 we may take the average years of each before the birth of the next, making a sum of 142, and this will leave 430. To the 366 we may add the years of oppression (Ex. i. 8-22) after Joseph died, say 64, and this gives the number required. Joshua's ancestry, from Ephraim, is given in 1 Chr. vii. 23-27; and if their ages were equal to their brethren of the other tribes mentioned, 430 years is not too long a period.

The specimen of ancient Egyptian papyrus preserved in the Bibliotheque at Paris, and published in *fac-simile* (pl. V in the Astor Library), gives independent and disinterested evidence on the question of the long life of Jacob and others of this age. At the close of the essay (on morals) the writer says: " I have become an elder on the earth; I have traversed 110 years of life by the gift of the king and the approval of the elders, fulfilling my duty toward the king in the place of favor." The inscriptions at Memphis corroborate this account, and show that the writer *Ptah-hotp*, was eldest son of *Assa*, 5th king of the 15th dynasty (B. C. 1960-1660), whose father's age must have been at least 150. Manetho also verifies the same point. The increase of the Jews in Egypt was from *seventy families* to about *three millions*.

From Exodus to the Foundation of King Solomon's Temple, 480 years (1 K. vi. 1).

		Ussher.	B. C.	Poole.	Josephus.	Crosby.	Miner.	Hales.	B. C.
Exodus to Joshua,		40	1491	40	40	40	40	40	1648
Joshua and Elders,		6.4m	1451	13	25	37	17	26	1608
			1438	32				27	1553
First Servitude, Othniel, 1st Judge,	Mesopotamian,	40	1398	430	18	390	Book of Judges,	8	1526
					40			40	1518
Second Servitude, Ehud and Shamgar,	Moabite,	80	1323		81	317		18	1478
								80	1460
Third Servitude, Deborah and Barak,	Canaanite,	40	1265		20			20	1426
					40			40	1406
Fourth Servitude, Gideon,	Midianite,	40	1245		7			7	1368
					40			40	1359
Abimelech,		9.2m			3			3	1319
Tola,		48	1232		23			23	1316
Jair,			1210		22			22	1293
Fifth Servitude, Jephthah,	Ammon,	6	1188		18			18	1271
					6			6	1253
Ibzan,			1182		7			7	1247
Elon,		25	1175		10			10	1240
Abdon,			1165					8	1230
Sixth Servitude, Samson,	Philistia,	40			40	1 Es. vii.		40	1222
Interim,					20	Samson, Samuel, and Eli, cotempo- raries,		Eli xxx. 2 Sam. x.	
									1182
Eli,			1157		40		Book of 1 Sam.	20	1152
Seventh Servitude, Samuel and Saul, 18, Saul, 22,	Anarchy,	40	1095	40	12		72	Samuel.	1142
				40	18	40	2 Sam.	12	1123
				40	2	32	40	40	1110
David,		40	1014	40	40	40		40	1070
Solomon,		3		3	3	3		3	1030
		478½		638	592	580	740	621	
Solomon's Temple (foundation B. C.),			1012			1006	1012		1027
Destruction,		424	588						
Return from captivity,		145	536						
Under Zerubbabel,			535						
" Ezra,			458						
" Nehemiah,			445						

B. C.
443. Walls of Jerusalem rebuilt by Nehemiah. Herodotus reads his history at Athens. The age of Phidias (sculptor), Euripides (poet) Pericles in Greece. Military tribunes in Rome.
425. Xerxes II, king of Persia (Darius II, 424). Thucydides (historian). His book ends B. C. 410, and Xenophon's begins).
414. Amyrtæus, king of Egypt, revolts from Persia. The Athenians being alarmed by an eclipse, are defeated before Syracuse, Sicily. —413. Archelaus, king of Macedon. The 400 rule in Athens.
404. Artaxerxes II, king of Persia.—401. Xenophon and the 10,000 retreat. Socrates dies.
383. Mithridates, king of Pontus. Bithynia made a kingdom. Plato (philosopher). Aristæus (mathematician).
368. A *celestial globe* brought from Egypt to Greece.
366. Joshua slain by Johanan in the temple of Jerusalem.—361. Darius Ochus king of Persia.
360. Cappadocia made a kingdom. Tachos king of Egypt. Philip II, king of Macedon. Demosthenes.
356. Temple of Diana burnt at Ephesus. Alexander born.
349. Darius Ochus takes Egypt and robs the temples. Aristotle (tutor to Alexander, 343). —345. 12 cities in Italy buried by an earthquake.—336. Eclipses first calculated by Calippus of Athens.
330. Alexander conquers Persia. He enters Jerusalem. Seeing the high priest, Jaddua, in his sacred robes, he respects him, and offers sacrifice to Jehovah.—323. Alexander died at Babylon.
100,000 Jews carried into Egypt by Ptolemy. Onias I, high priest.—312. Seleucus Nicator, king of Syria.
311. Judæa subject to Antigonus. Appian Way made.
301. Judæa under the Ptolemies. Euclid, mathematician in Alexandria. Chinese wall built.
284. Colossus of Rhodes. Sect of Sadducees. The Pharos (first light-house) at Alexandria.

267. Ptolemy makes a canal from the Nile to the Red Sea. Silver money coined. Parthia.
248. Onias II, high priest.—246. Ptolemy Euergetes conquers Syria.—237. Simon II, high priest.
241. Attalus I, king of Pergamus. Archimedes, mathematician.
203. Judæa conquered by Antiochus. Onias III, high priest.—200. Jesus, son of Sirach (Ecclesiasticus). First mention of the Sanhedrin (70 rulers).
187. Syria a Roman province.—175. Jason, high priest. The temple plundered by Antiochus Epiphanes, and dedicated to Jupiter Olympus (168). See head on page 11.
165. Judas Maccabæus expels the Syrians and purifies the temple. Rise of the Pharisees.
161. First treaty with the Romans.—146. Carthage destroyed.
135. End of the Apocrypha. Antiochus IV, (Sidetes) besieged Jerusalem.
130. John Hyrcanus delivers Judæa from the Syrians, and reduces Samaria and Idumæa.
107. Aristobulus, king of Judæa.—116. Ptolemy Lathyrus, king of Egypt.—107. Alexander I, king of Egypt.
105. Alexander Jannæus at war with Egypt. Libraries of Athens sent to Rome by Sylla (86).
92. Tigranes, king of Armenia. See portrait in COINS.
79. Alexandra, widow of Jannæus, governs Judæa. Pompey in Africa. Julius Cæsar.
70. Hyrcanus II, high priest, deposed by his brother Aristobulus. They appeal to Pompey, who conquers Judæa and Syria, and makes them Roman provinces.—63. Antiochus XII, the last of the race of the Seleucidæ.
53. The temple plundered by Crassus (proconsul of Syria). Augustus born.—31. Cæsar passes the Rubicon.
48. Antipater of Idumæa. Calphurnius Bibulus, governor of Syria. Battle of Pharsalia.
45. Cæsar reformed the calendar, using solar years instead of lunar. Gives the Jews privileges.
44. Cæsar assassinated.—42. Battle of Philippi.
40. Herod the Great marries Mariamne, granddaughter of Hyrcanus, and is made king by the Romans (at Rome, with Pagan sacrifices).—30. Mariamne, and all the Sanhedrin but Pollio and Sameas, killed by Herod.
37. Romans assist Herod by taking Jerusalem. Antigonus, last Asmonean, killed at Antioch.
30. The Roman Republic becomes a monarchy. Antony and Cleopatra in Egypt.
27. Battle of Actium. The title of Augustus (Venerable) created and given to Cæsar Octavius.
20. Augustus (nephew of Julius Cæsar) visited Judæa and enlarged Herod's kingdom, by Paneas, where Herod built a temple in honor of Augustus (Cæsarea Philippi), ordering heathen games to be celebrated every fifth year. Herod built a temple at Samaria and called the city Sebaste (Venerable). He began to rebuild the temple, which was finished in the reign of Herod Agrippa II, A. D. 65.
15. Augustus (Germanicus) assumes the title of Pontifex Maximus (Pope).—11. Germany conquered by the Romans.
5. Varrus, gov. of Syria; Cyrenius (Quirinius) of Judæa. Cymbeline, king of Britain. Dionysius of Halicarnassus, historian. Herod robs the tomb of David.
1. Jesus the Christ born in Bethlehem. Flight into Egypt. Herod dies; his son Archelaus succeeds as Ethnarch. Herod Antipas tetrarch of Galilee. (For events in the life of Jesus and of Paul, see BIOGRAPHY).

A. D.
14. Tiberius, emperor.—19. Jews banished from Rome. Herod builds the city of Tiberias.
25. Pontius Pilate, gov. of Judæa.—26. John the Baptist's ministry begins. Thrace becomes a Roman province.—27. Jesus baptized.
30. Crucifixion Friday, April 7th (Nisan 15th). Philo, a Jew of Alexandria. Seneca.
37. Apion of Alexandria (grammarian). See Josephus. Caligula emperor.—40. First Christians at Antioch, Syria.
41. Herod's persecution.—52. Council of Apostles at Jerusalem.
48. Population of Rome, 1,200,000.

CHRYS'OLITE, CHRYS'OPRASE, CHRYSO'PRASUS. See PRECIOUS STONES.

CHUB. A country or people associated with Egypt. Lud, Phut and others in Ez. xxx. 5.

CHUN (to stand up). A city of Hadadezer (1 Chr. xviii. 8). BEROTHAI in 2 Sam. viii. 8.

CHURCH (called). The Lord's faithful people. The Lord's house, where his people gather. A church is any number of souls, called and united in one vow, in one place, for divine worship, where the pure word is preached, and the sacraments duly administered, and godly living, after his law, as given by the head of the church, the Lord Jesus Christ. The church in Galatia means all the societies or churches in that country.

CHU'SHAN or **CUSHAN-RISHATHAIM** (Ethiopian of wickedness). King of Mesopotamia, who oppressed the Israelites 8 years. Probably a sheikh, not a king.

CHU'SI (Judg. vii. 18). A place near Ekrebel.

CHUZA (seer). Steward of Herod Antipas (Luke viii. 3).

CILIC'IA (Cilix, son of Agenor). (Herodotus vii. 91). Asia Minor, southeast on the sea. Separated from Pamphylia, W., Lycaonia and Cappadocia, N., and Syria E., by lofty mountains. Chief rivers are Calycadnus, Cydnus, and Sarus. Fertile and populous. Tarsus was its capital. Josephus supposed it was the Tarshish of Gen. x. 4 (Ant. i. 6, § 1.) Native land of Paul the Apostle. The high road between Syria and the West. The Roman general Pompey destroyed the pirates and robbers of Cilicia.

CASTOR AND POLLUX.

CI'MAH (cluster), (Job. ix. 9).

CIN'NAMON. A native of Ceylon and other islands of the Indian Ocean. It was one of the principal spices in the precious ointment used in the Tabernacle, and highly valued for its perfume (Ex. xxx. 23; Prov. vii. 17).

CIN'NEROTH. NAPHTALI (1 K. xv. 20). CHINNEROTH.

CIRA'MA (1 Esd. v. 20). Ramah in Ezr. ii. 26.

CIRCUMCIS'ION (cutting around). The cutting off of the foreskin of man, first practised by Abraham by divine command, as a token of a covenant between God and man. It was a very ancient custom founded on (supposed) sanitary laws, by the Egyptians and Ethiopians, and the practise is widespread in modern days; the Abyssinian Christians holding to the rite strictly. The Egyptian priests were required to observe this rite, and it was only strictly binding on those who entered the

priesthood. So it became the badge of a religion that made undue account of outward distinctions, and merely natural virtues. The Hebrews were to practice it because they were to be *a nation of priests* (Ex. xix. 6), and it was to signify spiritual purity, being so considered by the leading men, implying a call to a holy life and purity of heart. The time was the 8th day after birth; among other people at full age—20 years. Foreigners on adoption into the Hebrew nation were required to submit to it.

CIS. Kish (Acts xiii. 21).

CI'SAI (Esth. xi. 2). Kish.

CIS TERN. A dug place, for the water of a spring, or from rain. Some were built up of stone and cement, and the best were cut in the solid rock. The largest are called pools, such as Solomon's, the Royal Cistern, Bethesda, etc. (See Jerusalem.) A wheel is used to pass the rope over for drawing up the water, alluded to in Eccl. xii. 6. Keeping to one's own sources of pleasure, and not meddling with the property of others, is taught in the Proverbs (v. 15), by the figure of the cistern. Idolatry is compared to broken cisterns (Jer. ii. 3).

CIT TIMS. Chittim (1 Macc. viii. 5).

CITIZEN. Among Romans, etc., a member of the state, or of a city. Among the Hebrews a member of the nation at large. Paul was an instance of one born to the rights of a Roman citizen, which protected and benefited him on three occasions (Acts vi. 37; xxii. 25; xxv. 11). The Roman law made two classes of citizens—the first entitled to hold office and vote, and carry on public and private business—the second to enjoy only the protection of the laws as a free man. The sacred law was the basis of the civil among the Jews, and citizenship was acquired by complying with the terms of the covenant, and lost by certain transgressions. Christians are counted as citizens of the celestial state.

CIT Y. Any inhabited place, large or small.

CLAU'DA. An island S. W. of Crete (Acts xxvii. 16). Now Gozzo.

CLAU'DIA. A British maiden; wife of Pudens, daughter of King Cogidubnus, an ally of Rome and a disciple (2 Tim. iv. 21).

CLAU'DIUS. 5th emperor of Rome, A. D. 41 to 54. Tiberius Claudius Nero Germanicus. He succeeded Caligula. The famine mentioned in Acts xi. 28, happened in his reign; and he banished all Jews from Rome (xvii. 2). His head is on the coin of Cyprus. Agrippina, his fourth wife, poisoned him.

CAMEL AND HODAJ.

CLAY. A beautiful symbol of the divine power over the destinies of man was derived from the potter's use of clay, as he produced such elegant and useful forms from such a crude material (Is. lxiv. 8; Rom. ix. 21). "It is turned as clay to the seal" (Job xxxviii. 14), refers to the use of clay in stopping up doors in tombs or granaries, and the use of a seal engraved with a private design on the soft surface, leaving its impression as a protection against intrusion. Bricks were stamped also as may be seen on the numberless specimens from the ruins. Locks on the storehouses in the East are now further secured by the clay, stamped with a seal.

EGYPTIAN DRESS.

CLEAN and **UNCLEAN.** Terms of frequent occurrence in the Bible, concerning the rites and usages of the Abrahamic covenant, having both a natural and a symbolical meaning. It is mentioned as in use at the sacrifice made by Noah and it is probable that it was then an ancient distinction. Animals, birds, beasts and reptiles were pronounced good for food without distinction (Gen. ix. 3). It then has no foundation in the laws of diet or health. The line was fixed by man between the wild, obnoxious, poison-fanged animals, filthy in habit and suggestive of evil, and the tame, docile creatures, more cleanly in their habits and more akin to the better instincts of mankind. The Egyptians sacrificed dogs, cats, crocodiles, etc., and held them as sacred. Moses, to separate his people from those pagans, confined sacrifices to animals from the flock and herd, sheep, goats and cattle, and to the dove species among birds; while, for food, a larger limit was allowed, but in the same time, the animals allowed being those that chew the cud and divide the hoof, among wild animals only the deer species, and of birds, a few were prohibited by name, and the rest allowed; and of fishes those that had both fins and scales; and of insects, locusts and grasshoppers. The unclean were called *abominations*, and were to work a *spiritual defilement* if eaten. The clean and unclean animals had a counterpart in the soul, and the restrictions laid on the appetite became a bit and bridle to the soul. This law was abolished by the Lord in a vision to Peter at Joppa. There were other laws relating to ceremonial impurity, touching certain animals, dead bodies, diseased persons,

the intercourse between man and wife, and the office of the mother. Particulars in Leviticus.

CLEAVE. To adhere to; "clave to" (Ruth i. 14); to divide; separated (Acts ii. 2).

CLEFT. (Deut. xiv. 6; Cant. ii. 14, etc.).

CLEMENT. Mentioned by Paul in Phil. iv. 3, with much esteem and honor, as his fellow laborer at Philippi, whose name (with the others) was in the book of life. He is said to have been bishop of Rome (Pope Clemens Romanus, the third from Peter), and wrote a letter to the Corinthians very much esteemed by the ancients and read publicly in the churches. It is in the Alexandrian MS. copy of the Scriptures as Codex A.

CLEO'PAS. One of the two disciples that saw Jesus on the way to Emmaus.

CLEOPAT'RA. Daughter of Antiochus III (the Great), and the name of several queens of Egypt. 1. Wife of Ptolemy V, called Epiphanes, B. C. 193; 2. Wife of Ptolemy VI, Philometer (Esth. xi. 1); 3. Wife of Alexander Balas, B. C. 150, daughter of No. 2; afterwards given by her father to Demetrius Nicator (1 Macc. xi. 12); also wife of Antiochus VII, Sidetes, B. C. 125, who killed Demetrius. She murdered her son Seleucus, and died by a poison she had prepared for her second son, A. VIII.

CLEOPHAS ALPHEUS (John. xxix. 25).

CLIFF, anciently called CLIFT (Is. xxxii. 14). A steep rock split off by violence.

WOMAN RIDING.

CLIMATE. There is no country in the world which has such a variety of climate and temperature, within the same limits, as Palestine. On Mts. Hermon and Lebanon there is perpetual snow; and at Jericho, only 60 or 80 miles, there is tropical heat. The hills of Bashan, Gilead, Galilee, Samaria, and Judæa, are the home of forests, vines, fig-trees, and all kinds of fruits and vegetables; and the plains produce bananas, oranges, etc. From Jerusalem to Jericho, in a direct line, is about 15 miles. At one place snow and ice sometimes are seen in the winter, but at the other frost is never known. Frost is also unknown in the plains of Sharon and Philistia. The temperature at Engedi is as high as that of Thebes, in Egypt. Palms grow as far north as Beirut, and bear fruit also at Damascus in sheltered positions. The greatest heat on the hills of Judæa, Hebron, and Jerusalem, is seldom above 90° Fahrenheit, and the cold only once so low as 28° in five years (*Barclay*.).

Damascus is cooler, the highest being 88°, and the lowest 29°.

TABLE OF MEAN MONTHLY TEMPERATURE RAINFALL, PRODUCTS, ETC.

Months	Jerusalem			
	Degrees	Rainfall Inches	Rainy Days	Relief
Jan.	49.4	13	47	58
Feb.	54.4	16	53	61
Mar.	55.7	8	55	62
Apr.	61.4	2	57	63
May	73.8	1	73	72
June	75.2		78	75
July	79.1		86	82
Aug.	79.3		81	82
Sept	77.		79	80
Oct.	74.2	2	72	80
Nov.	63.8	2	62	66
Dec.	54.5	12	45	54
Annual	66.5	56	67	69

Highest in Judea 90°, shade at noon; lowest 28°, night. Damascus 88°, noon; 29°, night; winter. On Lebanon, Shumlan, highest 82°, in August. In Gennesaret, 450 ft. above the sea, from March 17 to April 5, average, 63°, and 73° from 8 A. M. to 8 P. M. In May 78°, and day only 83°. Dead Sea shore, 42°; average, night 47°, day 67° in Jan. In April 105°, in the shade. The Arabs leave for the high lands in the hot months, June to Sept.

Beersheba, Feb., night 31°, noon 72°; in summer 65° night, and 90° day, highest range.

Nablus is sheltered and warmer than Jerusalem; and Nazareth also.

January.—Last sowing of wheat and barley. Last roasting ears of corn (the 3d crop of the year!). Trees in leaf. Almond blossoms, apricot, peach, plum, beans. Winter figs still on the trees. Cauliflowers, cabbages, oranges, lemons, limes, citrons. Mandrake in bloom; wormwood also. New leaves on the olive-trees. Fire is needed in the house. Many flowers.

February.—Barley may be sown. Beans, onions, carrots, beets, radishes, etc. Oranges, etc. Apple trees in bloom. Flowers in the fields abundant.

March.—Beans and peas in the market. Trees in full leaf. Barley ripe at Jericho. Fig tree blossoms while the winter fig is still on. First clusters of grapes. Pear trees, apple, palm, and buckthorn in bloom. Sage, thyme, mint, etc. Carob pods ripe. Celery. Rue, parsley, hyssop, leeks, onions, garlic, etc. Flowers carpet the fields.

April.—Barley and wheat harvest. Sugar-cane set. Beans, etc., lettuce, cucumbers; lavender, rosemary, mulberries. Oleander blossoms; also rose of Sharon. Great variety of flowers. Early ears of corn. Apricots.

May.—Harvest in the plains and on the hills. Almonds, apples, mandrakes, and many vegetables. Grass begins to wither for want of rain. Melons of all kinds, onions, cucumbers, tomatoes, potatoes, corn. Walnuts, blackberries, sycamore and mulberry figs.

June.—Threshing grain. Figs, cherries, plums cedar-berries, olives, almonds, quinces, plantain fruit, bananas, grapes, liquorice plant, dandelion, egg-plant, doum palm dates. Henna (for dyeing the nails) and roses gathered.

July.—Pears, nectarines, peaches, grapes, melons, potatoes, tomatoes, egg-plant, Indian figs, prickly pear (cactus fruit), gourds. Millet, doura, linseed, tobacco, grapes.

August.—All fruits and vegetables before named, and also citrons, pomegranates. Olives now perfect. Grapes. The fruit month.

September.—Every fruit and vegetable still in market. Cotton and hemp mature. Millet, doura, maize, lentils, chick-peas, lupines, beans, fenngreek, fennel, castor-oil plant. Grapes.

October.—Sesame (for lamp oil) ripe. Wheat and barley may be sown. Vegetables planted. Olives yield the last berries. Pomegranates, pis-

tachio nuts. Lettuce, radishes, and other garden sauce. Cotton mature. Fig leaves fall. Plowing.

November.—Principal sowing of wheat and barley. Trees lose their leaves. Early dates. Very few olives. Grapes. Plowing.

December.—Grass abundant. Wheat and barley may still be sown, and pulse also. Sugar cane, cauliflowers, cabbage, radishes, lettuce, lentils. Plowing.

This calendar is mainly true of Jerusalem and the hill country. Some weeks allowance must be made for the higher temperature of the Jordan valley, and the plains by the Mediterranean sea.

RAIN. The average rain-fall at Jerusalem for the year is 56; in very wet seasons it has gone higher, 85, 44—66 average. The average in London is only 25, in the highlands of England 60, in New York, 62, and the highest in the lake country 65. There is a wet and a dry season. In the wet, the winter, the rains fall in two series of showers, called the early (*yoreh*) and the latter rain (*malkosh*), with occasional lighter showers between, and many clear sunny days. The loss of rain is sure to affect the harvest, and a total want of rain would destroy all crops (Amos iv. 7). From April to November there is scarcely ever a cloud. The dews are heavy often like a small shower. Chilly nights, succeeding hot days have always been a constant feature in the East (Gen. xxxi. 40). The different climate of Jericho has been often noticed. Josephus says, and it is true now, that linen clothing can be worn at Jericho when there is snow in the hills around Jerusalem. The plains along the sea shore are but little hotter than the hills. Beirut is much hotter the year round than Jerusalem. In the desert are found the greatest extremes of heat and cold. In winter the heat will be greater than our summer in the day, and the night colder than our average winter. The winds are very regular in their season and effects. West or S. W. wind invariably brings rain in winter (Luke xii. 54). The North wind is cool, but rare. The South wind is always hot (55; Job xxxvii. 17). The East wind is very rare in the winter, and blowing on the desert in summer, is dry and hot (Ez. xvii. 10; Hos. xiii. 15). In the Jordan valley there is an under and an upper current. The under current blows down the valley in winter and up in summer. There are no East and West winds in the Arabah.

CLOUD. See CLIMATE. Pillar of a cloud. The peculiar sign and symbol of the Lord's presence with his ancient people, during the exodus (Ex. xiii. 21), as of a cloud by day and of fire by night. It disappeared (or is not mentioned) from the passage of the river Jordan until the dedication of Solomon's temple (2 Chr. v. 13), and then only as a momentary sign for that occasion. The figurative use of the cloud has reference to the peculiar climate. "A cloud of the latter rain" (Prov. xvi. 15) means the gladdening influence of the king's countenance when well favored toward his subjects. The commanding the clouds to rain not was a sign of desolation (Is. v. 6; Deut. xi. 17). Dark clouds were emblems of gloom and sadness (Joel ii. 2). Swift wind-driven clouds, with lightning, were an emblem of Jehovah (Ps. civ. 3). Their height expressed loftiness (Ps. lvii. 10).

CLOUTED (Josh. ix. 5). Mended. Spotted.

CLOUTS (Jer. xxxviii. 11, 12). Cast-off rags or torn clothes.

CNI'DUS. Caria, S. W., in Asia Minor (Acts xxvii. 7). Passed by Paul. Celebrated for the worship of the goddess Venus (Strabo xiv. 955).

COACHES (Is. lxvi. 20).

COAL (PEHHAM—*black*, and GAHHELETH—*burning*). There are veins of coal in Mt. Lebanon, a few miles from Beirut, and it is probable that the Hebrews and Phoenicians knew and used it. But charcoal must have been specially meant in Psalm cxx. 4, in coals of juniper; and only charcoal was used in the censer at the temple service.

COAST. border, bound (Ex. x. 4; xiv. 19).

COCK. Domestic poultry are not mentioned in the O. T., unless in Is. xxii. 17, 18. The compassion of the Lord towards Jerusalem is compared to the tender care of a hen over her chickens (Matt. xxii. 37; Luke xiii. 34). The cock-crowing of Matt. xiii. 35, refers to a certain hour of the night, just before dawn, and the special signal given at that hour to Peter (Matt. xxvi. 34, 74). They are on the monuments in Assyria but not in Egypt; also on the Etruscan pottery of great antiquity (Mrs. Gray's *Etruria*), and on the coins of Greeks and Romans. The ancient Britons kept them, but did not think it right to eat them (Cæsar's Wars, 5).

COFFER. A box hanging from the side of a cart (1 Sam. vi. 8, 11, 15; Ezr. vi. 2). "In a coffer."

COLHŌZEH (*all-seeing*). A man of Judah (Neh. iii. 11, 5).

CO'LIUS (1 Esd. ix. 23) KELAIAH.

COLLARS (Judg. viii. 26). EAR-RINGS.

COL'LEGE (2 K. xxii. 14; and *second* in Zeph. i. 10). Where Huldah the prophetess lived "in the lower (or *second*) part of the city" (Neh. xi. 9).

COL'LOPS OF FAT (Job xv. 27). Slices of fat.

COL'ONY. Philippi, in Macedonia, is so called (Acts xvi. 12). A body of citizens sent out to found a new state for themselves, under the same laws and rights.

COL'ORS. There are about twenty different words, meaning color, in the O. T.; but only white, black, red, yellow or green are distinctly named. In the N. T. there are seven words meaning color. 1. *Leben*, white (Lebanon, white mts). Milk is leben, and so is manna, snow, horses, clothing, the moon, the pale face, and white hair. It was the symbol of joy, of innocence, purity; the clothing of angels, saints, and of Jesus.—2. *Shahor*, black: as hair, complexion of the sick, horses, mourners' robes, clouded sky, night, turbid brook; and as opposed to white, the symbol of evil.—3. *Adom*, red

ASSYRIAN GALLEY.

(Adam). Blood, pottage of lentiles, a horse, wine, complexion, leprous spot, a grape-vine; and the symbol of bloodshed.—4. *Argaman*, purple. Made at Tyre, from a shell-fish. The color was only a drop in the throat of each animal. It was purple, violet, or blue, according to the fixing. Some say the violet (or blue) was had from a different shell-fish, and called—5. *Tekeleth*, blue. The deep blue

of the sky, violet, and sometimes as black; the ribands and fringes of the Hebrew dress (Num. xv. 38), tapestries of Persia (robes of perfection in Ez. xxiii. 12).—6. *Shani*, shine (as scarlet); *tolaath*, worm scarlet (our word vermillon means *worm color*). Lips, in Cant. iv. 3, fire; scarlet robes were luxuries, and appropriate for a warrior's cloak (Na. ii. 3). The vermillion of the ancients was like our Venitian-red—dull red—such as is seen on the monuments, where it has preserved its tint for many ages.

chief word), with many definitions, in alphabetical order, with a reference to the place where each may be found. They are useful for comparing passages bearing on the same subject, which may explain each other, and for finding the place where any particular text or subject is located. So, in a few minutes, all the texts on the subject of the Lord's Supper may be found and read. The first work of the kind was made by Antony of Padua (born A. D. 1195, died 1231). Cruden's is the best now in use.

COLOSSE.

COLOS'SE, COLOSSÆ. On the Lycus, a branch of the Mæander, in Phrygia, near Laodicea (Col. ii. 1; iv. 13). Pliny (Nat. Hist. v. 41) describes it as a celebrated city in Paul's time. Paul founded a church here, on his third tour. The ruins of the ancient city are near the modern village of Chonas.

COM'FORTER. A name given to the Holy Spirit (2 Sam. x. 3).

COM'MERCE (trade, Heb. REKEL, traffic). The first record of bargain and sale is of Abraham's purchase of the burial-place for Sarah of Ephron, at Hebron, for 400 shekels weight (as sovereigns are weighed at the Bank of England) of silver. Job throws much light on the commerce, manufactures and science of his age. He mentions gold, iron, brass (copper or bronze), lead, crystal, jewels, weaving, merchants, gold from Ophir, topazes from Ethiopia, building of swift ships, writing in books, engraving on plates of metal and stone, and fine seal or gem engraving; fishing with hooks, nets, spears; harp, organ, and names of stars. The history of Sidon and Tyre is a record of commercial affairs; and that of the building of King Solomon's Temple is also. Foreigners were the principal traders before the Captivity, but after that, and especially after the destruction of Jerusalem by Titus, the Jews have been an entire people of traffic.

COM'PEL (Mark xv. 21). To press into service.

CONANI'AH (*whom Jehovah hath sent*). Chief of the Levites in time of Josiah (2 Chr. xxxv. 9).

CON'CIS'ION (*cutting off*). A term of contempt for outward circumcision (Phil. iii. 2).

CON-COR'DANCE. A book which gives the names of persons, places and things (and ideas by their

CON'CU-BINE. A wife of second rank, where more than one wife was allowed. Her condition was assured and provided for by Moses. She was either 1. A Hebrew girl bought; 2. A captive taken in war from the Gentiles; 3. A foreign slave bought; 4. Or a Canaanite woman, bond or free. She could not be sold, but might be sent away free.

CON'DUIT (French, aqueduct), (2 K. xviii. 17). The largest mentioned is from Solomon's Pool to the Temple site.

CO'NEY (Heb. SHAPHAN, *rabbit*). The Syrian Hyrax. Its habits are very much like the rabbit, only it is a little larger. Its teeth and hoofs (instead of claws on each toe), are like those of the rhinoceros (Lev. xi. 5; Deut. xiv. 7; Ps. civ. 18; Prov. xxx. 26).

CONFEC'TION (*a compound*), (Ex. xxx. 35).

CON-GRE-GĀ'-TION (*edah*). The Hebrew people collected as a holy community, held by religious bonds (for political ends). Circumcision and full age (20), were the requisites for membership, which might be forfeited for certain faults (Deut. xxiii. 1-8). During the Exodus the whole nation could gather from their tents, but when they occupied the country on both sides of Jordan, it became a necessity to appoint representatives, who are called, in Num. i. 16, persons "wont to be called to the Congregation"; and, in xvi. 2, they are styled "chiefs of the Congregation, who are called to the Convention"; and, in Ex. xxxviii. 25, their name is, "those deputed to the assembly" (numbered in A. V.). Besides these, the heads of families (patriarchs—sheikhs now), and a fourth class, the judges of cities, magistrates (cadi, now). They

met at the door of the tabernacle, or in some other noted places, as Shechem by Joshua; Mizpeh by the Levite (Judg. xx. i.); Gilgal by Samuel. In the Exodus the sound of the trumpet called the assembly together (Num. x. 2-4), but in Canaan messengers were used of necessity. It did not have legislative powers, for the law of Moses was supreme, but by-laws could be made. They could not lay taxes. The divine law was submitted to the assembly for acceptance or rejection (Ex. xix. 3-9, xxiv. 3). Chiefs were confirmed in their office (or rejected) by this body (Num. xxvii. 19; 1 Sam. xi. 15, 2 Sam. v. etc.). The assembly could arrest the execution of the king's sentence, as Jonathan was "rescued" (2 Sam. xiv. 44, 45), by the action of the Elders. Peace and war with foreign powers were considered in it (Josh. ix. 15, 18). It was the high court of appeal, and had control of death-penalties. After Jeroboam's usurpation, it was called the C. of Jerusalem (2 Chr. xxx. 2), or of Judah (v. 25). It finally was reduced to the 72 members of the Sanhedrin.

money, in great quantities, is often found buried, dated many centuries back. See MONEY.

CORAL (*lofty*). Coral is mentioned only twice in Scripture (Job xxviii. 18; Ez. xxvii. 16). It often occurs in ancient Egyptian jewelry. The coral which is described as being brought from Syria was probably that of the Red Sea where coral abounds.

CORBAN (*a sacred gift*). A present devoted to God or to his temple (Matt. xxiii. 18). The Jews were reproved by Christ for cruelty to their parents in making a *corban* of what should have been theirs (Mark ii. 7).

CORIANDER. An aromatic plant found in Egypt, Persia and India, mentioned twice in Scripture (Ex. xvi. 31; Num. xi. 7)

CORD. The word cord means line, band, rope, thread, string, etc. It is made of various materials according to its uses. Strips of camel hide are still used by the Bedawins. The finer sorts were made of flax (Is. xix. 9); others of the fibre of the date palm, and of reeds and rushes. The tent

CORINTH.

CONI'AH. JEHOIACHIN (Jer. xxii. 24).

CONONI'AH. A Levite; ruler of the offerings in Hezekiah's time (2 Chr. xxxi. 12, 13).

CONSCIENCE. Internal knowledge; moral faculty which judges between right and wrong (John viii. 9.)

CONVER-SA'-TION. The whole tenor of one's life, acts, and thoughts.

COOKING. MEALS.

CON-VO-CA'TION. The religious gathering on the Sabbath and the great feast-days.

COOS. **COS**. Island at the E. entrance to the Archipelago, and between Miletus and Rhodes, and the peninsulas on which are Halicarnassus and Cnidus (Acts xxi. 1) 21 ms. long, N. E. to S. W., and 6 ms. wide. Was an important island in Jewish history from early times (1 Macc. xv. 23; Jos. Ant. xiv. 7 § 2). Stanchio.

COPPER. (Heb. NEHOSHETH). Copper was and is now used more extensively in the East than any other metal. There is no certain mention of iron in the Scriptures, and all kinds of instruments, weapons and tools must have been made of copper or bronze, which is a mixture of copper and tin. Wherever brass, iron and steel are mentioned copper was the metal meant in the original. Copper

being an image of the human body, the cords which held it represented the principle of life (Job iv. 21). For leading or binding animals (Ps. xviii. 27). For bow-strings made of catgut (Ps. xi. 2). A line of inheritance (Josh. xvii. 14; xix. 9).

CORINTH'. On the isthmus that joins Peloponnesus to Greece. The rock, Acrocorinthos, south of the city, stood 2,000 feet above the sea, on the broad top of which there was once a town. The Acropolis of Athens can be seen from it, 45 miles (Liv. xlv. 28). It has two harbors: CENCHREA (now Kenkries), on the Saronic gulf, 7½ ms. distant, east; and LECHAEUM, on the Gulph of Lepanto, 1½ ms. west (Strabo viii. 6). Corinth was the natural capital of Greece, and was the commercial centre. Eminent for painting, sculpture, and works in metal and pottery. Famous for a temple to Venus of great wealth and splendor, the most ancient in Greece. Was the military centre during the Achaian league. Destroyed by the Romans, B. C. 146, and after 100 years of desolation the new city visited by Paul was built by Julius Caesar, and peopled with freedmen from Rome (Pausanias—Strabo). Paul lived here eighteen months, and became acquainted with Aquila and Priscilla. The Posidonium, the sanctuary of Neptune was the scene of the Isthmian games, which

were celebrated, every other year, and gave Paul some of his most striking imagery. It was N. E. of the city, near the harbor of Schœnas, now Kalamaki, on the Saronic gulf (1 Cor. ix. 24, 26). The foot-races were run in the stadium; the boxing held in the theatre; and the victor's wreaths were made from the pines that grew near.

CRANE.

CORINTH'IANS. The people of Corinth. For Paul's epistles to, see PAUL.

COR'MO-RANT. The cormorant (Heb. SHALAK, Lev. xi. 17; Deut. xiv. 17); and Pelican (Heb. KAATH, Ps. cii. 6). Common in Syria, among the rocks on the coasts.

CORN. A term for all kinds of grain. The grains and loaves of Indian corn (maize), were found under the head of an Egyptian mummy, and it is supposed to be mentioned by Homer and Theophrastus. The offering in Lev. ii. 14, was of green corn, roasted, which was eaten with oil, etc. (ver. 15). The "seven ears of corn" on one stalk is possible, and has been noticed (N. Y. *Evening Post*, Aug. 26, 1863) lately in this country and is in accord with the proper character of maize, but not of wheat, and we may so understand the dream interpreted by Joseph.

COR-NE'LIUS. A Roman centurion, commander of 100 (Acts x. 1). He seems to have worshiped the true God before his conversion (x. 2), and not the pagan deities. He was the first Gentile convert, and was received by Peter.

CORNER. The Levitical law gave a portion of the field called a "corner" to the poor, and the right to carry off what was left, also the gleanings of the trees and the vines (Lev. xix. 9). See also RUTH. GLEANING.

COR'NER STONE. A stone of size and importance in the corner of a building, uniting two walls. This is laid with ceremonies in large buildings. Christ is the corner stone of our salvation (Eph. ii. 20; 1 Pet. ii. 6; Matt. xxi. 42).

CORNET. MUSICAL INSTRUMENTS.
CORRUP'TION, MOUNT OF (2 K. iii. 13.) MT. OF OLIVES.
CO'SAM (*a diviner*). Son of Elmodam, in the line of Joseph (Luke iii. 28).
COTES. Enclosures for sheep (2 Chr. xxxii. 28).
COTTAGE (*house*), (Is xxiv. 20). A tent or shelter made of boughs.
COTTON (Heb. KARPAS; Sans., *karpasum*; Arabic, *karfas*); mentioned in Esther i. 6, as *green* hangings. "Hanging curtains of calico, in stripes, and padded, are used, in India, as a substitute for doors." In the king of Delhi's palace there is a roof supported by beautiful pillars, between which hangs striped and padded curtains, easily rolled up or removed. Some of the passages where *fine linen* is said, in our version, *cotton* was probably the article meant in the original.
COUL'TER (1 Sam. xiii. 20, 21). "Plowshare."
COUN'CIL. An assembly of people, rulers, priests or apostles. See SANHEDRIN.
COURT (Heb. CHATSER). An inclosed space, or yard, belonging to a house.
COU'THA. A servant of the temple (1 Esd. v. 32).
COV'ENANT (Heb. BERITH). Contracts between men, and between God and men. Various rites were used: joining hands (Ez. xvii. 18); by an oath (Gen. xxi. 31); by a heap of stones; (ib. xxxi. 46); by a feast (ib. xxvi. 30); by sacrificing victims, dividing the parts, and both parties to the covenant walking between the parts of the sacrifice (xv. 8–17); and, more common and above all others, eating salt (Num. xviii. 19; Lev. ii. 13).

The covenants between God and men were also ratified by signs. By the sacrifice, when a symbol of deity, a smoking furnace and a burning lamp, passed between the parts (Gen. xv. 17); by the 12 loaves on the table of shew-bread (Lev. xxiv. 6–8); and the crucifixion of the Christ (Heb. ix. 15, xiii. 20; Is. lv. 3).

COZ (*thorn*). A man of Judah, also a Levite. (1 Chr. iv. 8, xxiv. 10).
COZBI, (*false*). A Midianite woman, daughter of Zur (Num. xxv. 15, 18).
CRACK'NELS. Hard, brittle cakes (1 K. xiv. 3).
CRAFTS'MAN. A mechanic (Deut. xxvii. 15). CHARASHIM.
CRANE (Heb. AGUR). Is a wader, migratory, utters a twittering cry, and goes in vast flocks (Is. xxxviii. 14; Jer. viii. 7).
CRE-A'TION. The origin of all things, material and living, in the world, and this heavens around it (Gen. i; Ps. cxlviii. 5). When rightly understood God's works and His Word are in harmony. The Mosaic account in Genesis opens with a notice of the work of God in the original creation of the world and the heavens, in the vastly remote past,

and passes at once to the final preparation of the earth for man's occupation, which has extended through six (geological) periods of unknown extent, which are called days. It is supposed by the geologist that the first formations were rocks, either in water by deposit, or both water and fire. There are traces of living things in the rocks, called *fossils*, and they are without eyes; perhaps because there was no light—for light was made after the heavier materials. Both vegetables and animals appear at the same time. These oldest rocks are called the CAMBRIAN, and are 5 miles thick.

The next in the series is the SILURIAN, of sediment, whose thickness is 6 miles. Fossils are very numerous, and of low types, having no animal with vertebræ (back-bone), except a few fishes on the very top. Vegetation first appears in this place. There was light, and there were *eyes* in the living things. The firmament (expanse) divided the waters above (clouds) from the waters below (the ocean).

The third in the series is the OLD RED SANDSTONE, which marks the time when the great mountain ranges of the world were lifted into their present position. Sedimentary, and two miles thick, and having fossils of animals found in the other two, and of vertebrates. Dry land appeared, grass, herbs and trees. No land animals.

The fourth was the CARBONIFEROUS (coal bearing), in which we find coal, minerals, limestone. Coal is made of wood, and the fossil wood found in the coal series does not show the *rings* which we now find in all wood as marks of the yearly growth, which is evidence of dense fogs and very pale light. The lifting of the fogs towards the end of this period, letting the sunshine on the earth, is described by Moses as the events of the fourth day. The fossil remains in these rocks are the same at the equator and everywhere, indicating a uniform heat all over the earth. Animal life on land is first seen: insects, such as beetles, scorpions, and reptiles—such as frogs.

The fifth series was the PERMIAN, which has remains of a higher order of vegetation and of animals, such as the *saurians* (lizards), and birds, whose fossils are in the NEW RED SANDSTONE of this series.

The TRIAS and OOLITE show fossils of more advanced orders, both vegetable and animal. Palm, pine, cypress, insects, and three kinds of lizards, called by Moses "the moving creature that hath life"—a better translation of the original being "the reptile that hath the breath of life"—and also great sea monsters (called *whales* in Genesis). The fossils of these animals exist in such amazing numbers as to give the name *age of reptiles* to this day, which was the fifth in the account of Moses.

ARK.

The next was the CHALK, which has but few remains, while the Tertiary, which followed, is full of mammals, such as cattle, beasts and creeping things, which mark the progress of the sixth day, which ended on the creation of man.

There are no fossil remains of man among all the vast number of living things in all the series. And there are no animals now living on the earth whose origin cannot be traced in the fossil remains of similar races living on the earth before man was placed here.

The discovery of flint implements (hatchets, spears, arrow-heads and wedges) in the gravel quarries of Abbeville and Amiens, France, does not carry back the history of man into the age of the extinct species of elephant, whose bones were found in the same deposit, because no human bones were found there.

The truth of the Mosaic account is thus peculiarly shown in the records of the rocks.

The account is true as it would appear if shown to a man in a vision, every item agreeing with the optical appearances.

CART.

It may be that there was a race of men living on the earth before the birth of Adam; and if so, the passages which seem to imply other races besides Adam's would have an explanation. The several species of men, with their distinct languages, indicate more than one origin.

The most skeptical scientist of the present day admits that the breath of life was breathed into at least one original form—if not three or four—and that is the whole question. God did create a living being, or several; and since the most careful examination shows that species and groups of animals were from the first—in the oldest rocks, and in all of them—distinct, as distinct as they are now, and so may have been created each by itself, "after its own kind." The history of the past is proved true by the discoveries of the present. However short the account, the *order* of the events is correct, according to science.

CRES'CENS (*growing*), (2 Tim. iv. 10). One of the seventy disciples. An assistant of Paul.

CRETE. CANDIA. S. of the Archipelago; 160 ms. long from E. to W., and 6 to 35 ms. wide. Homer says it had 100 cities (Iliad ii. 649; Virgil, Æ. iii. 106). Minos, the great legislator, was a native. Very mountainous, but full of fruitful valleys. There was a very early connection with the Jews (1 Sam. xxx. 14; 2 Sam. viii. 18; Ez. xxv. 16; Zeph. ii. 5; 1 Macc. x. 67, xv. 23; Jos. Ant. xvii. 12, § 1). Cretans were at the feast of Pentecost at Jerusalem (Acts ii. 11). Visited by Paul (see Life).

CRETES (Acts ii. 11), CRETANS (Tit. i. 12). People of Crete.

CRIB (Job xxxix. 9), (*to fodder*). Feeding-box for animals, made of small stones and mortar, or cut from a single stone.

CRISP'ING-PINS (Is. iii. 22).

CRIS'PUS (*curled?*). Ruler of the Jewish synagogue (Acts xviii. 8).

CROC'ODILE (Heb. LEVIATHAN). The Jewish translations of Job xli. give crocodile for leviathan, and the description is very poetical as well as true. Herodotus says the Egyptians paid divine honors to this reptile, keeping a tame one, whose ears were hung with rings and fore-paws circled with bracelets; and when he died they embalmed his body. The worship began in the fear of man for the most terrible animal in the river Nile.

CROSS. An upright stake, with one or more cross-pieces, on which persons were suspended for punishment. It was an emblem of pain, guilt and ignominy, but has been adopted by Christians as the most glorious badge of a servant and follower of the Christ, who was crucified on it. Constantine was the first emperor who adopted it as an ensign, whose coins bear its form, with monograms of Christ or of Constantine. The image was added to the cross, forming the crucifix, in the 6th century. The term *cross* was used for self-denial by Jesus and others (Matt. xvi. 24). See cut, p. 22.

CROWNS.

CROWN. Originally the band or ribbon about the head or hair of a king or a priest. The ornamented cap differed in style in every country, as is shown on the sculptures and coins. A wreath of leaves crowned the winners in the Grecian games. The final inheritance of the saints is figured as *a crown of righteousness* (2 Tim. iv. 8.). The figures are of crowns from Egypt: 1. Upper E.; 2. Lower E.; 3. Upper and Lower united; 4. Assyria; 5. Assyria (Sardanapalus 3d.); 6. Assyrian (Sennacherib); 7. Tigranes (Syria); 8. At Persepolis; 9. Crown of leaves, Roman coin of Galba. The Roman soldiers crowned Jesus with a wreath of thorn twigs, made from what is now called Christ's thorn (*zizyphus*), and by the Arabs *nubk*, the jujube tree. It is very abundant, and forms dense thorny hedges (growing or laid in rows two or three feet high). through which no large animal can pass.

CRUCIFIX'ION. Putting a person to death on a cross was a very common practice in ancient days, as hanging is now. Jesus was condemned to the cross by the Sanhedrin for blasphemy, and by Pilate for sedition against Cæsar. The scarlet robe, crown of thorns, and other insults were the inventions of those engaged in the execution, and were peculiar to his case. Whipping was a part of the punishment, but in the case of Jesus was not the legal act, being applied before sentence. The sufferer was to carry his cross, or a part of it. The clothes were perquisites to the guards. A cup of stupefying liquor was often given in mercy, just before the hands and feet were nailed. The body was often left to waste away naturally on the cross, or be eaten by birds and beasts, by the Romans, but they allowed the Jews to bury their dead on account of the law of Moses (Deut. xxi. 22, 23). Constantine abolished crucifixion.

CRUSE (Heb. TSAPPAHATH, *a flask*). A small vessel for holding water and other liquids (1 Sam. xxvi. 11, 12, 16), still used in the East.

GATE AT SIDON.

CRYS'TAL. Three Hebrew words, 1. ZEKUKITH, 2. GABISH, and 3. KERACH, are translated crystal. 1. is, no doubt, the word for glass; 2. means (like) clear ice; and 3. means ice or frost. "Clear as crystal," is a figure in Ez. i. 22; Rev. iv. 6; xxi. 11, etc.

CUCK'OO (Heb. SHACHAPH), (Lev. xi.; Deut. xiv.). The Arabs think its note sounds like *yakoob*, and so call it Jacob's bird. It migrates, and winters in Palestine. Tristram suggests the shore petrel as the bird of the Hebrew text.

CU'-CUM-BER (Heb. KISHUIM, heavy, hard to digest). Grown only in the fertile land which is overflowed by the Nile, and is esteemed the coolest and most pleasant fruit in the East (Is. i. 8).

CUM'BER. Overload, harass (Luke x. 40).

CUM'BRANCE. Burden (Deut. i. 12).

CUM'MIN (Heb. KAMMON). An umbelliferous plant (fennel), bearing aromatic seeds, like anise, coriander, dill and caraway. Used as a styptic after circumcision. Cultivated for export (Is. xxviii. 25; Matt. xxiii. 23).

CUN'NING. Skilful, expert as a workman (Gen. xxv. 27).

CUP OF THE PTOLEMIES.

CUP (Heb. 1. COS, 2. KESAOTH, 3. GEBIA; Greek, *poterion*). The designs were imitated from those of Egypt and Assyria, Phœnicia, etc., as shown by

the Scriptures and specimens from antiquity. They were of metal, earthenware, wood, etc. The "sea" or "laver" of Solomon's temple was called a cup, and was of brass (bronze?), and highly ornamented with sculptured lilies.

EGYPTIAN CUPS.

Nos. 1, 2, 3, From paintings at Thebes, Egypt. 4. Porcelain. 5. Green earthenware. 6. Coarse pottery. 7. Wood. 8. Arragonite. 9. Earthen. Bronze cups (and other vessels) are often found in the ancient tombs. A kind of stone was wrought into jugs and bottles, vases and cups at Alabastron, in Upper Egypt, now called *alabaster*. Matt. xxvi. 7, should read alabaster *vase*, not *box*. The "Cup of the Ptolemies" is a work of the time of Nero, 5 inches high, of a single sardonyx, set in a base. See SIDON and ALABASTER.

ASSYRIAN CUPS.

1. Lion head, Khorsabad. 2. Lion-head with handle. 3. From Khorsabad, all of bronze. 4. Red pottery, Nimroud. 5. Painted cup, Karamles. 6, 7. Bronze, Nimroud. The workmanship is excellent, and they are often ornamented with jewels, and embossed with sculptures of animals, or groups of men and animals. Cups of brass and silver are now in use all over the East; generally decorated with some sentence in Arabic of a mystical sense. See BOTTLES and BOWLS.

The office of CUP-BEARER is of great antiquity, being mentioned at the courts of the Pharaoh, the Assyrian, Persian, and Jewish kings. RABSHAKEH of 2 K. xviii. 17, should read *chief cup-bearer*, as in Luther's bible, (*der Erzschenke*). The cup is used as a figure: of a man's lot (Ps. xi. 6, etc.); of a nation's great riches (Jer. li. 7); as a contrast in "cup of God," true worship, and "cup of devils" idolatry (Ps. lxxv. 8; Is. li. 17, 22); signifying afflictions (Matt. xx. 22, xxvi. 39); of salvation (Ps. cxvi. 13), and of blessing (Luke xxii. 17; 1 Cor. x. 16).

CURTAIN (Heb. TERIAH). Made of linen goats' hair, silk, and cotton; used for beds, partitions in tents, and for doors in houses. Heaven compared to a curtain (Ps. civ. 2; Is. xl. 22). The curtains of the tabernacle were embroidered with many colors, in figures on fine linen. Curtains of Solomon (Caut. i. 5).

CUSH. Son of Ham (Gen. x. 6). Country in Africa, Ethiopia (Ez. xxxix. 10; 2 Chr. xii. 3). Tirhakah, king of C. (Is. xxxvii. 9). Modern name Kesh. Geez. People were black (Jer. xiii. 23).

CUSHITE. "Ethiopian" (Num. xii. 1).

CUTH AH. CUTH. In Asia, Shalmaneser transplanted people from here to Samaria during the Jews' captivity (2 K. xvii. 24, 30). Mixing with the Jews of the 10 tribes they became the Samaritans, and were called Cutheans (Jos. Ant. ix. 14, § 3, xi. 8, § 6, xii. 5, § 5). Between Tigris and Euphrates rivers.

CUTTINGS IN THE FLESH. Mutilations of the body, practised by the Heathens in mourning for the dead (Jer. xvi. 6, 7, xli. 5); prohibited to the Jews (Lev. xix. 28).

CY A-MON (*beans*). *Tell Kaimon* on the E. slope of Mt. Carmel (Judith, vii. 3; Chelmon in *Douay* V). Burial place of Jair.

CYM BAL and CYM BALS. MUSICAL INSTRUMENTS.

CY PRUS. Island off the coast of Phoenicia and Cilicia, 148 miles long, 40 wide, and irregular. (see map). The highest mountain is Olympus, 7,000 feet. Gold, silver, and copper are mined. Its cities were, Salamis, Citium (now Larneka), and Paphos (now Baffa), and many others. Alexander got 120 ships there for his siege of Tyre. It was the birth-place of Barnabas (Acts iv. 36), and was visited by Barnabas and Paul (Acts xiii). The Pagans worshiped Astarte (Venus), in a licentious manner. Barnabas and Mark (Acts xv). Cyprians, the people, in 2 Macc. iv. 29.

CY RENE. Lybia, Africa. Founded B.C. 632, by Greeks. Built on a table-land 1800 ft. above the sea, in a region of great beauty and fertility, 500 ms. W. of Alexandria. The Pentapolis of Cyrenaica were Cyrene, Apollonia, Ptolemais, Arsinoe, and Berenice (Strabo, xvii.). After Alexander the Great's death Jews were settled there with many privileges. In the time of Christ the Cyreneans had a synagogue in Jerusalem (Acts vi. 9; Philo). Simon, who bore the cross, was from C. (Matt. xxvii., etc.). Lucius of C. was with Paul and Barnabas (xiii. 1). Lucius and Mark are named as bishops of the church at C. Arabic name *Ghrenna*.

CYRE'NIUS (Latin). Publius Sulpicus Quirinus was governor of Syria twice; before A. D. 1 (B. C. 4); and again, the second time, A. D. 6. Died A. D. 21 (Luke ii. 2).

CY'RUS. The Persian name for the sun (Heb. KORESH), and the same as the Egyptian name *Phrah*. Thus, Cyrus is a title for the king, as Pharoah, Augustus, etc. The Bible mentions only the one who conquered Babylon, unless the Cyrus, the Persian, of Daniel, was the uncle of Cyrus, who issued the decree permitting the return of the captive Jews to Judæa. It is impossible to separate the history of Cyrus from the fables connected with it, and now more than when Herodotus found the same difficulty, only a century after the events.

The work of a resident historian, Ctesias, in the court of Persia, about fifty years later than Herodotus, has been lost, except a few extracts by Photius, and that of Xenophon, are both historical romances.

That he became supreme king of Persia, and conquered Babylon, is undoubted. The turning of the course of the river Euphrates and capture of Babylon during a great feast, are also facts.

Daniel's Darius, the Mede, is the Astyages of history, and was a viceroy of the Cyrus who first ruled over Babylon.

It is supposed that the Persian religion, which is almost purely a monotheism, prepared Cyrus to

sympathize with the Jews, and that Daniel's explanation of the prophecies, that he had been helping to fulfil, unknown to himself, concluded him to issue the decree for the Jews' return to their native land and temple.

A tomb of Cyrus is shown at Parsargadæ near Persepolis.

D

DAB'AREH (Josh. xxi. 28). DABERATH.

DAB BA-SHETH (*hump* of a camel). Town on a hill. ZEBULON.

DAB ERATH. Is. Lev. (Josh. xxi. 28). Now Deburich, W. of Mt. Tabor. Beautifully situated on a rocky platform, with Tabor behind and the broad plain of Esdraelon in front. Boundary of Zebulon (Josh. xix. 12).

DAB'RIA. One of 5 scribes employed by Esdras (2 Esd. xiv. 24).

DĀCŌ BI (1 Esd. v. 28). AKKUB.

DAD'DEUS. SADDEUS (1 Esd. viii. 45). IDDO.

DAGON—FROM A GEM.

DĀ'GON (Heb. DAG, *little fish, dear*). The type of the god of the Philistines. His temples were at Gaza and Ashdod (Judg. xvi. 21; 1 Sam. v. 5). Traces of the worship are left in the names Cephar-dagon and Beth-dagon. Sanconiatho says the name is derived from dagon, grain, and it was the god of agriculture; but this origin does not agree so well with the *idea*, which was *to multiply, increase*, as fish do by millions. This god was known in Assyria, and is sculptured there, as shown in the large cut. Miss Fanny Corbeaux ("*The Re-*

DAGON, THE FISH GOD.

a woman's face, and fishbody. Atergatis, Argatis, Arathis, and Argata, are different forms of Derceto.

DĀI'SAN (1 Esd. v. 31). Error for REZIN.

DALĀ'IAH (*Jehovah delivers*). Son of Elioenai, of Judah (1 Chr. iii. 24).

DALE (Gen. xiv. 17); valley.

DĀLMANŪ'THA. On the shore of the Sea of Galilee; visited by Jesus (Mark. viii. 10). Near Magdala. Possibly it is the same as Zalmon, near Tiberias, now called Ain el Barideh (*the cold fountain*), where are fine fountains and the ruins of a city (Rob. ii. 396).

DALMĀTIA. Illyricum. On the E. shore of the Adriatic Sea, N. W. of Greece. Visited by Paul (Rom. xv. 19), and Titus (2 Tim. iv. 10) during Paul's imprisonment in Rome.

DAL'PHON. Son of HAMAN (Esth. ix. 7).

DĀ'MA. Capital of the Ledja. See TRACHONITIS.

DAMASCUS.

phoim") shows that the Chaldean Oannes, the Philistine Dagon, and Egyptian On, are identical. DERCETO was the female (as Dagon was the male), and was worshiped at Ashkelon. She had

DAM'ARIS (*heifer*). A disciple in Athens (Acts xvii. 34), and (perhaps) the wife of Dionysius the Areopagite. Correctly, DAMALIS.

DĀMAS'CUS. On the E. of Anti-Lebanon, 2,200

feet above the sea, in a fertile plain near the desert. The oldest city known to history. It is cut through by the Barada river, which divides into many branches, and together with the Helbon on the N. and the Awaj on the S., fertilizes a region 30 ms. in extent, which being favored by the finest climate, produces almost every valuable product of forest, field and garden. First mentioned in Gen. xiv. 15 and in Gen. xv. 2, as the city of Abraham's steward. For 800 yrs., from Abraham to David, the Scriptures are silent on Damascus. David put a garrison in D. (1 K. xi. 23; 2 Sam. viii. 6; Jos. Ant. ii. 5, § 2). During Asa's reign Benhadad pillaged cities in Naphtali (1 K. xv. 19, 20). After this it is mentioned many times. Naaman, the leper, who was cured by Elisha the prophet, was of D. (2 K. v. 1). The Assyrian king, Tiglath Pile'ser, took the city and carried captive the people to Kir (2 K. xvi. 7–9). Isaiah's prophesy (xvii. 3; Amos i. 4, 5). Jeremiah described it, B. C. 600: "D. is waxed feeble, and turneth herself to flee, and fear hath seized on her" (xlix. 24). At the time of the Apostle Paul the city was under Roman rule, and Aretas, the Arabian, king (2 Cor. xi. 22; Jos. Ant. xvi. 11, § 9). Has now 150,000 people; Christians 15,000; Jews, 6,000

The fine fabrics of D. were celebrated as early as 800 B. C. (Amos iii. 12). The damask silk and sword-blades are still famous. Certain localities are pointed out as having a historical connection with Paul's time. The "street called straight" is now the street of Bazaars; there is a "house of Judas;" the house of Ananias; the scene of the conversion, which is an open green spot surrounded with trees, now used as a Christian burial-ground; the place where Paul was let down by the wall in a basket; and also several spots connected with the history of the prophet Elisha. The old city stands on the S. bank of the principal river, surrounded by a ruinous wall of ancient Roman foundations, and a patchwork of all the succeeding ages. The city is splendid, when viewed at a distance, but the houses are rudely built; the narrow streets, paved with big rough stones, or not at all, partly roofed across with mats, or withered branches; the bazaars are covered ways with a few stalls on both sides, each trade having its own quarter. Although rough and rude on the street, yet the interior of the private houses is neat, paved, with fountain and fruit-trees, with grateful shade, and the rooms opening from the court decorated with carving, gilding, and all that wealth and taste can provide. Modern name ESH SHAUM.

DAMASCENES. Inhabitants of Damascus (2 Cor. xi. 32).

DAMNATION (*condemnation*), (Mark xvi. 16).

DA'MON. Near Shefa Amer. E. of Acre.

DAN (*judge*). Fifth son of Jacob. First son of Bilhah, Rachel's maid (Gen. xxx. 6.) One of the twelve tribes. The last to receive its portion, and the least portion, but among the most fertile in the land.—2. The city originally called LAISH. LESHEM (Josh. xix. 47). They were idolaters from the beginning (Gen. xiv. 14; Deut. xxxiv. 1; Judg. xviii). The worship was continued by Jeroboam (1 K. xii, 29, 30; Amos viii. 14). "From Dan to Beersheba," was the common form of speaking of the extent of Palestine (Judg. xx. 1; 1 Sam. iii. 20, etc.). Tell el Kadi (*judge's mound*) is the modern name, and is a long, steep hill, covered with ruins, from the base of which flows one of the largest fountains in the world (Rob. 390).

DANCE (Heb. MACHOL), to move or leap in a circle, twist or turn around, as the dancing Dervishes now do in the East. The sacred song and dance always go together (Ex. xv. 20); words, and music and motion, aiding each other in expressing the joy or sorrow of the soul (Judg. xi. 34; Eccl. iii. 4). The Romans also danced in their worship; so, also, the Egyptians.

In the modern Oriental dance a woman leads off, and goes through a number of graceful and artistic attitudes, and then all the others of the party follow her in every motion. The two companies of dancers are called by an error *armies* in Cant. vi. 13.

DAN'IEL (*God's Judge*). 1. David's son (1 Chr. iii. 1).—2. A Levite (Ezra viii. 2).—3. A celebrated prophet in the Chaldean and Persian period, and a (princely) descendant of Judah. He was taken with other captives (Ananiah, Mishael, and Azariah) to Babylon, B. C. 607, at the age of 12 to 16, educated thoroughly and made a cup-bearer at the court, when he was given a new name Belshatzar (*favorite of B. l*). He kept the Jewish law of clean and unclean meat (Dan. i. 8, 16), and was constant and faithful in his devotions to God. After three years service he interpreted a dream (v. 17) on the occasion of the king's decree against the magi, and for this service was made "ruler" and "chief governor" over the province and magistrates of Babylon. He interpreted Nebuchadnezzar's second dream, and the handwriting on the wall, thus introducing the knowledge of the true God, and alluding to the profane use (and consequent insult to God) of the holy vessels of the temple, as one of the crowning sins of the king and his people, which were the means of ending the nation's life, by the conquest of the Medes and Persians (v. 10, 28), while he lived at Susa, and after he had been removed from office, when he was again placed in one of the highest offices of trust and honor. During an interval in which no event in Daniel's life is recorded, his three companions were delivered from a fiery furnace.

Darius made him first of the three presidents of the empire. Having exercised the rites of his religious faith, contrary to law, he was thrown to the lions, but was delivered alive (vi. 10, 23). He was in favor with the king in the third year of Cyrus, and saw his last vision on the banks of the Tigris (B. C. 534), when the prophesy of the 70 weeks was delivered to him (ch. ix.). He died at the age of over 90, at Susa, where there was a monument to his memory in the 12th century, described by Benjamin of Tudela.

DANJA'AN (Ps. ii. 26). LAISH.

DAN'NAH. Town in Judah (Josh. xv. 49), S. W. of Hebron. Lost.

DANCE OF PRIESTS—EGYPTIAN.

DAPH'NE. A grove and sanctuary sacred to Apollo, 5 miles S. W. of Antioch, Syria, founded by Seleucus Nicator. See ANTIOCH. The right of asylum—where criminals could shelter themselves from justice, because it was thought to be sacrilege to take any one away by force—was an honor attached to this place (2 Macc. iv. 33). The sacred right was often violated, especially when a good man sought safety from the wicked, as in the case of Onias. Now called *Beit el Maa—house of water* (Jos. Wars, i. 12, § 5).

DA'RA. DARDA. Son of Mahol; a wise man, in

Solomon's age (1 K. iv. 31). Son of Zerach (1 Chr. ii. 6). Sirach or Esrachite?

DAR'IC. Gold coin of Persia, current in Palestine after the captivity (Ezr. ii. 69; viii. 27; Neh. vii. 70, etc.). The darics that have been found among the ruins are thick pieces of pure gold, stamped, as in the engraving. The gold pieces found at Sardis are of older date, and were made by Cræsus. The name daric may be derived from "DARA," the Persian name for king, or from "Darius, the king." Plutarch mentions silver daries. See MONEY.

DARIC.

DA-RI'US (in Heb. DARJAVESH). The Assyrian title lord-king—Dara, lord; shah, king. 1. The first mentioned is DARIUS, THE MEDE (Dan. v. 31, etc.), called also Cyax'ares (B. C. 538). The gold coin was named Daric—that is, king's money.—2. DA-RIUS, SON OF HYS-TAS-PES (Vashtaspa), made king B. C. 521. He conquered Babylon, Scythia, Libya, Thrace, Macedonia and some of the islands in the Ægean sea, but the Greeks defeated him at Marathon (B. C. 190). Died B. C. 485 (Ezr. iv. 7.).—3. DARIUS, THE PERSIAN. Darius II, Nothus, king of Persia, B. C. 424-404. Perhaps DARIUS CODOMANUS (Neh. xii. 22).

DARK'NESS. Opposite of light, absence of light (Gen. i. 2). Three times mentioned in the Bible. In Genesis, at the creation; at the Exodus, as one of the plagues of Egypt, and at the crucifixion. Used as a figure of adversity and misery (Job xviii. 6; Ps. cvii. 10). "Works of darkness," heathen rites and ceremonies (Eph. v. 11), "outer darkness," shut out of heaven (which is glorious with light).

FRUIT OF DATE PALM.

DAR'KON. Children of Darkon were among the servants of Solomon, who returned from the captivity (Ezr. ii. 56).

DARLING. My only one (Ps. xxii. 20).

DA'ROM (south), (Deut. xxxiii. 23). Naphtali was to possess the sea and Darom. Jerome and others so name Philistia and the plain toward Egypt.

DA'RON (south). Fort built by the Crusaders at Deir el Belah (convent of dates), near Gaza, on ancient ruins).

DATES. Fruit of the palm tree, called clusters in Caut. vii. 7, and honey in 2 Chr. xxxi. 5, dates in the margin. In many parts of Arabia the staple product and the main source of landed wealth, is the date-palm, of which there are many species. The ripening season is August and September. The fruit is a substitute for the bread of other countries. To cut down the date trees is a great achievement in war—and the absence of those trees from Palestine indicates a long period of wars in Egypt. To plant the palm on new ground is a sign of prosperity—as now in Egypt. The Arabs believe the tree is a blessing granted only to them, and denied to all other people. Mohammed taught, "Honor the date tree, she is your mother." There are 139 varieties, 70 of which are well known, each of which has its peculiar name. Some six kinds are superior. El Shelebi, the best, are two inches long, with small stones. The value in Arabia is about three cents a pound.

DATH'AN (fountain). Chief in Reuben, who joined Korah in rebellion against Moses and Aaron.

DATH'EMA. Fort in Gilead (1 Macc. v. 9), near Mizpeh.

DAUGH'TER. 1. Female offspring; of the wife; or adopted; or of a sister; or of a cousin (Ruth iii. 18; Gen. xxxiv. 17); or a grand-daughter.—2. The female inhabitants of a place, or those who hold the faith of a certain place, as "daughters of Zion" (Is. iii. 16), "daughters of the Philistines," "daughters of Jerusalem," "daughters of Aaron" (Num. xxv. 1; 2 Sam. i. 20; Luke i. 5). Cities were named or spoken of under female names, and were said to have daughters, suburbs or villages near. A vine had daughters (branches, in Gen. xlix. 22). Sarah was the daughter of 90 years—that is, she was 90 years old.

DAVID (beloved). SYNOPSIS OF HIS LIFE. Born at Bethlehem in Judah, B. C. 1084. His father, Jesse; his mother's name not recorded (1 Sam. xvi. 10, 17, 35). Had 7 elder brothers—Eliab, Abinadab, Shammah, Nethaneel, Raddai, Ozem, and Elihu; and two sisters—Zeruiah, and Abigail.

He watched the flocks in the field, and in their defense killed a lion and a bear. He was short, light, "comely," had red hair and blue eyes; was strong, and swift of foot; valiant and prudent.

At a yearly family feast he was anointed king by Samuel "from the sheep-cote" (2 Sam. vii. 8). He went to carry food to his three brothers in Saul's army, and was introduced to the king as valiant and brave. He killed Goliath with a stone from a sling. The sword and armor of the giant were first taken to his tent in Bethlehem, afterwards to Nob, and laid up in the Tabernacle (Ps. viii. 19, 29). Saul takes David into his service as a minstrel. Jonathan, his friend. Women sing his praise as superior to Saul. Saul jealous; seeks twice to kill David. Being afraid of David he made him captain of 1,000. David behaved wisely, and all Israel and Judah loved him. Merab is offered to David as a wife as a reward for his service against Goliath, the Philistine. But Saul gave Merab to Adriel. Michal, Saul's daughter, loved David, and Saul offered her to David for a price, and David paid double the price, for he killed 200 Philistines. He paid twice for his wife, killed Goliath and the 200. He is made armor-bearer and captain of the body guard, with a place at the king's table. Saul seeks to kill him; sets men to watch for him; Michal assists his escape. Goes to Ramah to Samuel (Ps. lix). Michal is given to Phaltiel. Secret meeting with Jonathan. The sign of the arrow. David flies. Saul tries to kill him at Ramah. David eats consecrated bread, and gets Goliath's sword at Nob (Ps. lii); against

Doeg, who informed against David and killed the priests. David goes to Abimelech (Achish), and feigning madness, escapes (Ps. xxxiv. 56). In the cave of Adullam. Joined by his family beside outlaws, debtors, etc. The incident of the water at Bethlehem (1 Chr. xi. 17). Moves to Herodium or to Masada. Takes his parents to the king of Moab; (they are never mentioned again). Nahash, of Ammon, treats him kindly. Gadites swim the Jordan at its flood and join him. God influences a move to the forest of Hareth. Amasai, a Benjamite, joins him. Relieves Keilah, where sins. Reigned in Hebron 7½ years. David crowned (3d time) king of all Israel (Ps. lxxviii., lxx.). Constitutional law. Festival 3 days; the tribes send produce, fruits, etc., to the feast, and contingents to the army, which was "like the host of God" (1 Chr. xii. 22). Joab (his nephew) commander; Issacharites his counselors. Jehoiada and Zadok join him. (Ps. xxvii.). Jebus taken. Joab made commander-in-chief. Royal residence in the City of David—Zion. His wives were increased by hostages from surrounding princes. Two attacks by Philistines repulsed; their idols burned.

DAVID'S TOMB, MOUNT ZION.

Abiathar the priest joins him with an ephod. His troop is now 600. Saul appears; David flies to Ziph.

Twice the Ziphites betray him to Saul, who hunts him "like a partridge" with 3,000 men (Ps. liv.), in the wilderness of Maon. Sees Saul two or three times, once at the cliff of divisions, again in a cave near Engedi, when he cuts off his skirt, and then in a fortified camp, when David carried off by night the water-jar and spear from Saul's bedside.

Twice Saul repented, and said he was reconciled to David. Psalms of this date liv., lvii., lxiii., cxlii. Nabal and Abigail; marries Ahinoam, and Abigail. David again goes to Achish, with his troop. Achish gives him Ziklag. Benjamite archers join him. Studies the Philistines' art of war. Attacks the Bedawins to deceive Achish. Philistine nobles suspicious, and cause him to be sent back from the army. Saul and Jonathan killed on Gilboa. Manassites join David. Amalekites plunder Ziklag. Abiathar prophesies victory, and David recovers the spoil from the Amalekites. Makes a present to many friends, whose places "he was wont to haunt." Makes a law of division of the spoils (1 Sam. xxx.). News of the battle on Gilboa: kills the messenger. Laments for Saul and Jonathan. David anointed king at Hebron (30 years old). Thanked the men of Jabesh-Gilead for burying Saul. Ishbosheth, king in Mahanaim. David the only king west of Jordan. War between the two sections. Abner kills Asahel, David's nephew; Abner quarrels with Ishbosheth, and comes to David. Michal restored to David. Abner and Ishbosheth murdered. David executes the two assassins. Hiram of Tyre an ally; sends cedar-wood for David's palace.

The ark removed from Kirjath Jearim—Obed Edom. The new Tabernacle on Zion; the old left standing at Gibeon. The great assembly on Zion. Musical art developed. Zadok and Abiathar. Nathan the prophet. David, as a priest and minstrel, in the procession. He blesses the people from the new Tabernacle on Zion (Ps. xv. xxiv., xxix., xxx., lxviii., ci., cxxxii.): "The Lord of Hosts, he is the King of Glory" (Ps. xxiv., x.). Michal reproaches him, and is rebuked. God's house designed. Prophesy by Nathan of a Messiah (2 Sam. vii. 12-17). David organizes a court and camp. Mephibosheth cared for, in memory of Jonathan. Hanun, son of Nahash, abuses David's messengers. Ammon and Syria beaten. Joab commander-in-chief (1 Chr. xi. 6): 12 divisions of 24,000 men, one for each month, all infantry, without cavalry. Chain armor in use. Benaiah captain of David's body-guard, the Cherethites and Pelethites—Ittai. The band of 600 continued as Gibborim, heroes; Abishai, David's nephew, captain. Social and moral institutions formed. Ahithophel and Jonathan, Hushai, Shera the scribe, Jehoshaphat, and Adoram, councillors. Gad the seer and Nathan the prophet advisers. Abiathar and Zadok high priests; the musicians, under Asaph, Heman, and the Levites, guardians of the gates and treasures. The Philistines, Moabites, Syrians, Edomites (Ps. lx.), and Ammonites, subdued. Rabbah taken. David wears the gold crown of Milcom (Ps. xxi. 3, lxxxix. 39). Uriah murdered. Nathan's rebuke (Ps. xxii. 51), "Thou art the man." Bathsheba taken. David fasts for his sick child. The child dies: "I

shall go to him, but he shall not return to me." Solomon, "the peaceful," born, (Ps. xx. 21). Educated by Nathan the prophet. His daughter Tamar outraged; his eldest son Amnon murdered. Absalom fled to Geshur. The artifice of Joab and the widow of Tekoa, to restore Absalom. Absalom waits two years to see his father; burning Joab's field, is brought to the king. Absalom plots—rebels: David a wanderer again. Leaves the city; a vast multitude go with him. Ittai the faithful, Zadok and Abiathar with the ark, which David sent back. Hushai, "the friend", sent to watch Ahithophel (grandfather of Bathsheba), who was untrue.

Absalom arrives from Hebron. At Bahurim, Ziba's deceit—Shimei's curses. David rested in the Jordan valley, near the ford (Ps. iii. 145). They cross the Jordan to Mahanaim (Ps. xlii.) against Ahithophel (iv., lxix., cix.). Barzillai, Shobi, and Machir his friends. Ahithophel kills himself. Joab, Abishai, and Ittai, were there. Amasa, David's nephew, was with Absalom. Battle in the forest of Ephraim. Absalom killed by Joab. David waiting in the gate. The two messengers, Ahimaaz, and Cushi. David vows to supersede Joab by Amasa. The return to Jerusalem. Shimei forgiven. Mephibosheth partly reinstated; Barzillai rewarded in his son Chimham. Judah and Israel are reconciled.

Sheba's rebellion. David's ten women shut up. Amasa sent to assemble the militia. The forces sent after Sheba. Joab killed Amasa. Sheba's head cast out of Abel. Adoram over the tribute; Jehoshaphat, recorder; Sheva, scribe; Zadok and Abiathar, priests; and Ira, a chief ruler.

A famine of three years on account of the Gibeonites' murder by Saul. David delivered 7 sons of Saul to be hanged, as an atonement. The bones of Saul and Jonathan buried in Zelah. David grows faint in the fight with the Philistines. Ishbibenob, the giant, thought to kill David. Abishai kills the giant. Psalm of thanksgiving (2 Sam. xxii.).

EGYPTIAN DOOR.

David numbered the people unlawfully, in pride. Joab and the captains opposed it. Gad, the prophet, warns of 3 calamities; David would not choose, and the 3 days' pestilence killed 70,000, and was stayed at the threshing-floor of Ornan. David bought the site for a sanctuary, and it is now marked by an ancient church—the Dome of the Rock (see JERUSALEM). David renews his resolve to build a house for the Lord, and gathers materials. Charges Solomon with the solemn duty (1 Chr. xxii.).

The young Abishag. Adonijah's rebellion. Joab and Abiathar helped (Ps. xcii. 2). By David's order Solomon is anointed king at Gihon. Adonijah pardoned by Solomon. David's last song (2 Sam. xxiii. 1–7). David's last words (1 K. ii. 1–9) describe the perfect ruler fearing God. Died at the age of 70. Buried "between Siloah and the guard-house." Reigned in Jerusalem 33 years (Neh. iii. 16). The site of his tomb is lost.

DAVID'S FAMILY.—1. Michal (no children, 2 Sam. vi.). 2. Ahinoam—son Amnon (1 Chr. iii. 1). 3. Abigail—son Daniel (ib.) Maachah—son Absalom, 3 sons died. Tamar (2 Sam. xiii.). 5. Haggith—son Adonijah (2 Sam. iii.). 6. Abital—son Shephatiah (1 Chr. iii.). 7. Eglah—son Ithream. Sons whose mothers are not named: Ibhar, Elishua, Eliphelet, Nogah, Nepheg, Japhia, Elishama, Eliada, Eliphalet and Jerimoth (1 Chr. xiv. 7; 2 Chr. xi. 18). 8. Bathsheba—sons: one died—Shammua, Shobab, Nathan and Jedidjah or Shelomoh = Solomon (2 Sam. xii. 25). The children of the 10 concubines, and their mothers, are not named. There is no reason to suppose he had more than eight wives. The text of 2 Sam. v. 13, probably refers to Michal, Bathsheba and the 10 women whom he took at Jerusalem.

David was a soldier, shepherd, poet, prophet, priest, statesman and king, a romantic friend, chivalrous leader, devoted father. He represents the Jewish people at the point of the change from the laity writers of their older system to the higher civilization of the newer, and was a type of the Messiah, who is called the Son of David.

David as king is almost above reproach; his private life only proved him a man. Next to Abraham's. David's is the most dearly cherished name of all the ancient patriarchs. The Psalms, whether his own or others' writings, have been the source of consolation and instruction far beyond any other of the holy scriptures, and are the only expressions of devotion that have been equally used by all branches of the Christian church and by the Jews.

It is now thought that the saying that David was a man after God's own heart meant only that he was chosen, while Saul was rejected—and his excellence as a king justified the choice.

The noble qualities of his soul, his sublime piety, which was the habit of his life, his intense struggle against fiery passions, and his mournful remorse over occasional sins, far outweighed his faults.

Because he passed through temptation, passion and humiliation, we are instructed and comforted; and through the divine psalms which he wrote we are provided with language for our times of distress and trouble.

DAY. See CHRONOLOGY.

DAY'S JOURNEY. SABBATH. See MEASURES.

DAYS'MAN. Arbitrator; one to appeal to (Job. ix. 33).

DAVID, CITY OF. Zion in Jerusalem, and also Bethlehem.

DEACON. Assistant, helper. Christ is called a deacon (A. V. minister, Rom. xv. 8). The Apostles appointed officers and made rules as circumstances required. The 7 deacons appointed to care for the widows (serving tables), had special duties which passed away with the occasion. But there was then a difference made between the ministers of spiritual and of material things. They also assisted at the communion by carrying the food and drink to the members. They received the contributions; cared for the sacred vessels; read the gospel sometimes, and baptized. They were to be grave, venerable, of good report in life, sincere, truthful, temperate, not using their office for profit, keeping the faith in a pure conscience, husband of one wife, ruling their children and house well (1 Tim. iii.; Acts vi.).

DEA'CONESS (Rom. vi.). The records show that they were useful in the early centuries—a service which was afterwards absorbed into the nunneries.

DEAD SEA. This name is first met in history, about 200 years after Christ. In the O. T. it is called the Salt Sea, sea of the Plain. See SALT SEA.

DEATH. 1. Natural death; end of the life of the body. 2. Spiritual death; insensible to holiness; alienation from God (Matt. viii. 22; Eph. ii.; Rom. vi. 21). The poetic expressions are "return to dust" (Gen. iii. 19); "removal from the body" (Job x. 21); "asleep" (Jer. li. 39; John xi. 11); "losing the breath" (Ps. civ. 29); the soul laying off its clothing" (2 Cor. v. 3); "to depart" (Phil. i. 23); "for a great trial" (2 Cor. i. 10). GATES OF DEATH (Job xxxviii. 17); doors of the shadow. Some believe that we should be able to live forever if we did not break God's law. But the Bible is a spiritual book and not a treatise on Natural History.

DEB'IR (*oracle*). 1. Ancient royal city of Canaan (Josh. x. 33). Kirjath-Sepher (*book city*). Now Dibeh, 6 ms. S. W. of Hebron, where there is a fine spring and aqueduct.—2. Judah near the valley of Achor. Wady Daborat the N. W corner of the Dead Sea (Josh. xv. 7).—3. Boundary of Gad, near Mahanaim. Lo-debar (Josh. xiii. 26.—4. A king of Eglon, hanged by Joshua (x. 3).

DEB'ORA. Mother of Tobeil, the father of Tobit, (Tobit i. 8).

DEB'ORAH (*bee*). 1. Rebekah's nurse (Gen. xxxv. 8). Buried under an oak called Allon-bachuth.—2. A prophetess, wife of Lapidoth who lived near a palm tree between Ramah and Bethel (Judg. iv. 4). She composed a song (ch. v.) in memory of the victory over Sisera (by Barak and Deborah) which, for poetic beauty, is much valued, and gives her the title of prophetess (singer).

DEBT'OR. The strict law of inheritance, of Moses, provided against commercial speculation and debts, by requiring all landed property and slaves to be freed on the year of jubilee (7th) (Lev. xxv. 39). No debtor could be sent to prison, or whipped, or oppressed unfairly, except by breaking the law. In Egypt the creditor could send the debtor to prison, and seize his family tomb and prevent burials there. The Roman laws were very severe against the debtor, and hard on slaves (made by debt). Bankers and sureties in the commercial sense were unknown (Prov. xxii. 26). No interest could be lawfully taken from a poor person, but relief was to be given without price, laws being made to prevent evading this rule (Ex. xxii. 25; Lev. xxv. 35, etc.). Nehemiah corrected such abuses (Neh. v.), and Jesus approved of the law of Moses, although in the later times the custom of usury had become popular, and usurers had their tables in the courts of the Temple. Loans could be secured by pledges, under certain rules: 1. The cloak, which was used day and night by the poor, must be returned at sundown. A bedstead (a luxury) might be taken (Ex. xxii.); no widow's garments, or a millstone, could be taken (Deut. xxiv. 6, 17). The creditor could not enter a house for his pledge but must wait outside (Deut. xxiv. 10). Debtors held as slaves must be released at the jubilee, and might be redeemed for a price. Foreign slaves were not released (Lev. xxv. 44). A year was allowed to redeem houses sold for debt. The Romans superseded the law of the jubilee year, and the debtor could be held *in prison* until the last farthing was paid (Matt. v. 26).

DEC'ALOGUE (*ten words*). TEN COMMANDMENTS (Ex. xx). The basis of all laws. The *number ten* was regarded as perfect or complete, therefore the TEN GREAT WORDS were the perfect law of God (Ps. xix. 7) given on Sinai. They were cut on two tables of stone, and kept for several centuries in the ark, in the very centre of the holy place, as a symbol of the centre of the whole system. The *two* tables indicate a division of the law, into duties towards God, and duties toward our neighbor (Matt. xx. 37-39). Some critics point out more than 20 decalogues in the laws of Moses. See LEVITICUS in the HISTORY.

SYRIANS.

DECAP'OLIS (*ten cities*). Mentioned three times in the N. T. (Matt. iv. 25; Mark v. 20, vii. 31), and many times in Josephus and other ancient writers. Soon after the Romans conquered Palestine they rebuilt and colonized ten cities, and gave them especial privileges. The list of the names of these ten cities is given differently by various writers. Pliny names Scythopolis, Hippos, Gadara, Pella, Philadelphia, Gerasa, Don Canatha, Damascus, and Raphana. Ptolemy includes Capitolias; and an inscription in Palmyra makes Abila one. The name was probably given to a large district in Christ's time. Damascus is the only one of the ten cities left, all the others being in ruins.

DE'DAN (*low country*). 1. Son of Raamah, grandson of Cush (Gen. x. 7). An island on the shore of the Persian Gulf is called *Dadan*, and another *Sheba*.—2. A son of Jokshan, grandson of Abraham by Keturah (Gen. xxv. 3). In each case the brother is named Sheba, and both tribes may have intermarried and occupied the same country. "The travelling companies of Dedanim" of Is. xxi. 13, are caravans. They traded with Tyre (Ez. xxvi. 15, 20) in ivory, ebony and fine dry goods (precious cloths).

DEDICA'TION, FEAST OF THE. Instituted in memory of the purification of the temple by Judas Maccabæus after driving out the Syrians (B. C. 164), (1 Macc. iv. 52; Jer. x. 22). It lasted 8 days—Dec. 25 (CHISLEV) to Jer. 3. Carrying branches of trees and singing, especially the Hallelujah song, every day.

DEEP, THE. Abyss. Bottomless pit in A. V. (Luke viii. 31; Rev. ix. 1, 2, 11; xx. 1, 3; 2 Cor. xi. 25). In Rev. x. 6, 7, "ascend into heaven," "descend into the deep," the place of the dead. This does not include Hades, which is supposed to include the deep, which is, then, only a part of the great unknown place of the dead,

DEGREE. 1 Tim. iii. 13, should read: "For they who well served as deacons obtain for themselves a good degree, and much confidence in faith in Christ Jesus." That is, in spiritual matters.

DEGREES, THE SONG OF (*stairs* or *steps*), is a title of 15 Psalms by different authors. Pilgrim songs, sung by the people as they went up to Jerusalem (Ex. xxxiv. 24; 1 K. xii. 27; Ezr. vii. 9; Ps. cxxii. 4). 5 were written by David (4) and Solomon (1), and the other 10 after the return from Captivity. See Ps. cxx. to cxxxiv. See PSALMS in the HISTORY.

DEHA'VITES (*villagers*), (Ezr. iv. 9). Planted in Samaria by Assyria. Dahi (Herodotus i. 125), in Persia; and Daci, in Europe (Dacia).

DE'KAR. An officer of Solomon's in Judah (1 K. iv. 9).

DELOS.

DELAI'AH (*Jehovah's freedman*). 1. Priest in David's time, leader of the 23d course (1 Chr. xxiv. 18).—2. Children of D. returned from Captivity (Ezr. ii. 60).—3. Son of Mehetabel (Neh. vi. 10).—4. Son of Shemaiah, in Jehoikim's time (Jer. xxxvi. 12).

DELI'LAH (*drooping, languishing*). Samson's love; lived in the valley of Sorek, Philistia. She was a wily seducer, who loved the bribes, and not her honor or her lover's safety, and captivated only to destroy. Her bribe was large—5,500 pieces of silver—shekels ($2,750), equal to $3,000 as to our standard of wages. See MONEY.

DEL'UGE. Flood (Heb. HAMMABAL, the fulness of waters), from *gâlal*, a river (fulness). Deluge is used instead of flood.

The belief in a deluge of greater or less extent is of very ancient date, in all nations who have kept records, or have traditions. It is very often noticed in the Bible, as a fact from which a great lesson is to be learned (Matt. xxiv. 38), and its history is given in Gen. vi. viii. The account next in value to this is that of the Greeks (Ovid)—the flood of Deucalion and Pyrrha. The Hindus (Sir Wm. Jones, *Asiatic Res.* iii. 116) also have an account, which, with the Greek, agrees with that in Genesis in many points. The Chinese legend is not very parallel, but agrees in a few items. The Parsee account says the flood washed away all the wickedness which Ah'ri-man (the Evil One) had brought about. The Chaldee (Jos. Ap. i. 19), (that Noa saved Sem, Japet, and Chem. The Assyrian is (Eusebius, *Ev. Prep.* c. ix.) similar. The Scandinavian, Mexican, Peruvian, and others, have each a story to tell, of a great flood, and a few persons saved.

The Scripture account is, the God sent the deluge as a punishment for sin, destroying all flesh but such as he directed Noah to place in the ark.

The time occupied was 358 days, 7 days less than our year, or 1 year and 10 days by the Jews' calendar. The present majority opinion is, that the subject has a *moral* rather than a *physical* character. That mankind had not spread beyond the valley of the Euphrates and Tigris, and Syria; and that the deluge only extended far enough to be universal as to *mankind*. There has been no evidence yet brought to light, such as human bones, or teeth, proving any great destruction of life in this, or any other region, which can be dated to the time of the deluge. The *size of the ark* is a great argument against the deluge being so universal as to cover the whole globe. There are now known 1700 species of animals, about 1000 of which are *clean*, of whom 7 of each species were to be kept; 6000 species of birds, 1000 of reptiles, and 550,000 of insects; and the entire space in the ark—547 by 91 feet (21 ins. to the cubit) 3 stories high—is 150,000 sq. ft. too small, by many times, for standing-room, besides food and storage. And how could 8 persons attend to so many animals daily? Many animals, some in the polar regions, others in the tropics, cannot bear a change of climate, even if they could be carried so far from their homes. Peculiar species belong to each quarter of the globe, whose ancestors have left their record in the ancient rocks, fossilized, showing an unbroken succession. It was also impossible to lay up provision for the wild beasts. Seeds and plants must have perished by so long a soaking in water, and fresh-water fish also, if covered by the salt ocean several months. The notion of a universal deluge is at variance with the light of reason. Geological records (in the rocks, etc.) show the record of many floods in the past history of the earth. Vast extents of the earth's surface have been raised or depressed in modern times (in Chili 100,000 sq. ms., 2 ft. high), and the work of sinking is now going on in Holland. The temple of Jupiter, near Naples, shows that it has been sunk, with the island on which it stands, under the waters of the Bay of Baiæ, until it had its hight, by the holes halfway up the marble columns, all round the temple on a water-line that were bored by a shell-fish that lives under water only. Those who suppose the deluge related only to the ancestors of the Hebrews, and had no reference to any other races, are answered by a denial of the remote antiquity of Egypt and Assyria. The evidences of the antiquity of Egypt and Assyria are far more convincing than any yet offered for the deluge. Only by limiting the deluge to a small part of the earth's surface can the account of Moses be made to harmonize with science.

DELUS (G. *delos, visible*). The smallest of the Cyclades, islands in the Grecian Archipelago, the chief seat of the worship of Apollo and his sister Diana (1 Macc. xv. 23). The island was said to have suddenly appeared anciently, as several others have in our time. It was the center of an extensive commerce B. C. 146.

DE'MAS, DEMETRIUS or DEMARCHUS. Companion to Paul (Philemon 24; Col. iv. 14; 2 Tim. iv. 10). One of Keble's grandest hymns is founded on the association of Demas and Luke with Paul in his earlier trials, and of the desertion of Demas after.

DE-MĒ'TRI-US (*rotary of Demeter, Ceres*). Maker of silver shrines of Artemis at Ephesus (Acts xix. 24). They were small models of the great statue of Diana. He made an adroit speech against Paul, exciting their religious and selfish feelings against the new sect, which aimed to spoil the business of shrine-making.—2. Another Demetrius is commended by John as having a character so purely Christian as to carry its own testimony with it (3 John 12).—3. DEMETRIUS SOTER, king of Syria, son of Seleucus IV. (See SYRIA and ANTIOCHUS).—4. D. NICATOR, son of No. 3, who was excluded by Alexander Balas from the throne until B. C. 146. He first treated the Jews well, but afterwards so badly that they took sides with Antiochus Theos. Killed at Tyre, B. C. 126.

DĒ'MON (Gr. *daimon, god*). At first the Supreme, then a god, and later, to spirits believed to be between gods and men; a kind of messenger, who became tutelary deities of men and cities; and finally the notion of *evil* demons the latest form. Some believed they were the spirits of evil men after death. It was used to denote fortune, chance, fate. In the Hebrew it is used for a pestilence (Ps. xci. 6), idols (xcvi. 5; Lev. xix. 4), devils (Deut. xxxii. 17), God (troop in A. V.), the goddess of fortune (Is. lxv. 11), satyrs (Is. xiii. 21; xxxiv. 14). The Hebrews meant evil spirits. In the N. T. they are spiritual, evil, at enmity with God, having power to work evil to man with disease and sin, positively and actively wicked. Called devils in 1 Cor. x. 20; 1 Tim. iv. 1; Rev. ix. 20. The modern notion is that there is but one devil (Lardner), although demons are innumerable (Dr. Campbell). The devil, the old serpent, the adversary, satan, prince of the power of the air, etc., are one. God and his angels are opposed to the devil and his angels, the demons.

The angels are sent forth from God's presence to minister on earth to the heirs of salvation; it is the spirit of God which gives his people that character of life-giving and blessed fruits by which they are known; on the contrary, the devil and his demon agency are discovered in the strong delusions and grievous oppressions which men have suffered and do suffer from their power.

DE-MŌ'NI-ACS. Men subject to the power of demons, and who are deaf, dumb, blind, epileptic, frenzied, hypochondriac, imbecile, and suffer ills both of body and mind. Demons cannot be known to our senses, nor their powers distinguished from natural causes; and the few words about them in the scripture do not help to a clear idea of them. Some suppose that the demoniacs were madmen—under the influence of melancholia or mania—in neither case using reason. There are accounts of some who were maniacs and others lunatics. Some also ascribe every form of disease, bodily or mental, to demons. Jesus said the casting out of demons was a part of his work, and by this work he brought the kingdom of God to us (Lev. xiii. 32; Matt. xii. 28).

DEM'OPHŌN. Syrian general, under Antiochus V. (2 Macc. xii. 2).

DENĀ'RIUS. Penny. 12 to 15 cents. See MONEY.

DEP'UTY. Proconsul (Acts xiii. 7, etc.).

DER'BE. Lycaonia, on the road from Tarsus to Iconium (Acts xiv. 6), which passes through the famous CILICIAN GATES, and where the pass opens upon the plains of Lycaonia, the city of Derbe stood. Gaius belonged here (Acts xx. 14).

DESCRY To reconnoitre (Judg. i. 23).

DES'ERT. Four words of the Hebrew text are translated desert, and they are: 1. ARABAH. The Ghor—the Jordan valley; Jericho at the S., and Bethshean at the N. (Ezek. xlvii. 8; Is. xxxv. 1, 6, xl. 3, xli. 19, etc.; Jer. ii. 6, v. 6, etc.).—2. MIDBAR. Pasture grounds, or the wilderness of the wanderings, where the Israelites had flocks and herds with them during the whole of the passage from Egypt to Canaan (Ex. iii. 1, v. 3, x. 26, xii. 38, xix. 2; Num. xi. 22, xxxii. 21, xxx. 15).—3. CHARBAH. Waste places, dryness, desolation (Ps. cii. 6; Is. xlviii. 21); W. of Sinai (Ez. xiii. 4; Job iii. 14).—4. JESHIMON. Waste places on each side of the Dead Sea. Usually translated Beth Jeshimon (Num. xxi. 20; 1 Sam. xxiii. 19). Is more expressive of utter desolation than any of the others (Deut. xxxii. 10).

DEMETRIUS I.

DES'SAU. Judah (2 Macc. xiv. 16.) Nicanor's army encamped there. Supposed to be Adasa.

DEŪ'EL (*El knows*). Father of Eliasaph (Num. i. 14). REUEL.

DEU-TER-Ŏ'NO-MY (Gr. *second law*). Fifth book of the Pentateuch. Named in Hebrew ELLEH HADDEVARIM, *these are the words*. See HISTORY.

DEV'IL (Gr. *Diabolos, slanderer, false accuser*). Called SATAN (*to lie in wait, oppose*) by the Hebrews, and *Shetan* by the Arabs. This character expresses the antagonistic, malicious, and perverse nature of the enemy of God and man. See DEMON. It is not believed (by all) that he is an independent, self-existent spirit of evil, though some do so believe, with the Manicheans. He is also called Dragon, Evil One, Angel of the Bottomless Pit, Prince of this World, the God of this World, Prince of the Power of the Air, Apollyon, Abaddon, Belial, Beelzebub. The word Satan is used also to mean an adversary. Hadad the Edomite was an adversary (Heb. SATAN) to Solomon (1 K. xi. 14); David is suspected of being an adversary (satan in 1 Sam. xxix. 4) to the Philistines; the angel of the Lord was a satan (adversary) to Balaam (Num. xxii. 22); a wicked man is a satan in Ps. cix. 6. The wicked wives are adversaries (satans, diabolous; the Hebrew Satan is the Greek Diabolos) in 1 Tim. iii. 1; false accusers, 2 Tim. iii. 3, and Titus ii. 3; and Jesus said one of the 12 was a devil (diabolos, Satan), an adversary. The Hebrew marks, by the article, a difference between a satan, an adversary, and the Satan, a person, the chief. In Zech. iii. 1, 2, it is the Satan, and also in Job 1st and 2d chapters, and 1 Chr. xxi. 1; Matt. iv. 1–11; Luke viii. 12; John viii. 44; Acts xiii. 10; Eph. vi. 11; 1 Pet. v. 8; 1 John iii. 8; Rev. xii. 9.

DEMETRIUS II.

It is said that the Devil is spiritual, but not spirit—not eternal. He works by deceiving, producing or keeping in ignorance, misunderstanding, evil thoughts, unholy desires, pride, anger, revenge, discontent and repining; and besides these moral, he works in physical ways, producing disease (Job ii. 7; Luke xiii. 6; Acts x. 38), which is sometimes used as a divine chastisement (1 Tim. i. 20). As

God is the only supreme self-existence, and Satan is not eternal nor in accord with God, but an adversary, he will be overcome, when he has served the will of God, and will go down into the abyss, with death and hell, into utter and final annihilation (Rev. xx. 2, 10, 14).

HEAD-DRESSES.

DEVŌ′TIONS. Objects of worship—temples, images, altars, etc. Paul meant *objects* of devotion in Acts xvii. 23.

DEW.—The dew falls copiously in Palestine, at night, in spring and autumn, but very little in the summer—May to August. It falls some weeks before, and also after the rains, and so shortens the dry season. It is used as a figure of God's goodness in Hos. xiv. 5, "I will be as the dew unto Israel;" and in Job, of his prosperity (xxix. 19), "the dew lay all night on my branch;" in Ps. cx. 3, of freshness and energy, 'dew of his youth" (Christ); of eloquent speech, "distilling like the dew" (Deut. xxxii. 2); of brotherly love, as the "dew of Hermon" (Ps. cxxxiii. 3); and as a sign of calamity, if wanting, in 2 Sam, i. 21, indicating barrenness.

DĪ′-A-DEM (*bound around*). Crown. Only four passages have this, and they might be read, "fillet," "mitre," "tiara," or "turban," the original meaning *rolled together*, or around, like the modern Eastern head-dress (Is. iii. 23). The diadem as worn by kings, as a badge of absolute power, was a band about two inches wide, made of silk, ornamented with gold, tied behind, as in No. 7. The ends of the ribbon are frequently shown on the coins. Gibbon describes one as "a broad white fillet, set with pearls" like No. 5. Nos. 1, 2 and 3 are Egyptian; 4, 5, 6, Assyrian; 7, from a coin of Tigranes, king of Syria; 8, sculpture at Persepolis; 9, Roman, civic, of leaves, from a coin. See page 36.

DIVAN.

DĪ′-AL. (Heb. MAALOTH, *degrees*). The earliest mention of the sun-dial is among the Babylonians, 540 B. C. Herodotus says the Greeks adopted it from them, as also the division of the day into 12 parts, being introduced to Greece by the astronomer Berosus, the Chaldean. The first notice of "the hour" is by Daniel (iii. 6). The degrees of Ahaz (2 K. xx. 11), cannot be explained. It may have reference to a dial with degrees (lines numbered). This might have been a present from Tiglath Pileser, the ally of Ahaz, and made in Babylon.

DĪ′-A-MOND (Heb. YAHALOM, *precious stone*, and SHAMER, *sharp point*). The hardest and most precious of all the gems. One was in the sacred breast-plate of the high priest, though some say that (*yahalom*) was an onyx. Ezekiel speaks of making his forehead hard as a diamond (SHAMIR, adamant in A. V. Ez. iii. 9), and Jeremiah of an iron pen pointed with a diamond (Jer. xvii. 1), and Zechariah, of hearts as hard as an adamant stone (vii. 12). The same word *shamir* is Hebrew for brier.

DIAN′A, Latin. (Greek, ARTEMIS). The twin sister of Apollo, the sun-god. She is the moon goddess. The Assyrians named them Adrammelech and Anammelech. Diana was called the goddess of hunting, chastity, marriage, and nocturnal incantations. In Palestine the name was ASHTORETH. The services were performed by women (*melissai*), and eunuchs (*megabisoi*), with a high priest (*essene*). The great temple at Ephesus, and grove at Daphne were the most noted shrines of this worship. The image at Ephesus was said to have fallen out of heaven complete! The great temple was 425 by 220 feet, and had 127 columns of marble, each 60 feet high. See EPHESUS.

DIANA.

DIB′LAIM. Mother of Hosea's symbolical wife Gomer (Hos. i. 3).

DIB′LATH. By some supposed to be the same as RIBLAH. By others it is located in Moab, where it is applied to a district in which was Almon-Diblathaim (Num. xxxiii. 46), and Beth D. (Jer. xlviii. 22). S. E. of Heshbon.

DĪ′BON. E. border of Moab, 3 ms. N. of Arnon river (Num. xxxiv. 45). Rebuilt by the Gadites. Dibon-Gad (xxxii. 34). In Reuben (Josh. xiii. 9, 17). The ruins are still called *Dibon*, and are extensive. Dimon (Is. xv. 9).—2. Judah. DIMONAH (Neh. xi. 25).

DIB′RI. Father of Shelomith, who had married an Egyptian, and her son having "blasphemed the name" was stoned (Lev. xxiv. 11).

DID′YMUS (*twin*). The apostle Thomas (John xi. 16).

DIK′LAH (*palm-tree*). There is a district in Arabia, extending along the Red Sea, from Edom to Medina, called *Dakalah*, from its fruitful palmgroves. Another district is Yemen, now called *Minœi*, also fruitful in palms, is thought to be the the real location; where there is a tribe of Arabs *Daklai*. (Burckhardt). (Gen. x. 27, 31; 1 Chr. i. 21).

DIL′EAN (*place of cucumbers*). Judah (Josh. xv. 38). Lost. Possibly Tima, near Ekron.

DIL′LY. Hauran, 6 ms. W. of Edrea, on the edge of a large marsh; the aqueduct for conveying water to Gadara begins here.

DĪ′MAS. Village on E. slope of Hermon; on Damascus—Beirut road.

DIM′NAH. Zeb. (Josh. xxi. 35; Lev.) Damon, near Accho.

DI′MON, WATERS OF. Streams E. of the Dead Sea. Moab (Is. xv. 9). DIBON.

DIMO′NAH. Judah. S., near the desert (Josh. xv. 22).

DIM′REH. V. 8 ms. S. of Askulan, on the W. Esneil.

DI′NAH (*acquitted*). Dau. of Jacob by Leah. Her history is a short tragedy (Gen. xxxiv.). Her two full brothers took her part against Shechem, and for their deceit and cruelty were condemned by Jacob on his death-bed. Among all the tribes

of the East, to this day, any wrong to a sister must be avenged by her brothers or father, or the whole family is disgraced. She may have gone with Jacob into Egypt (xlvi. 15), but she is not mentioned again, nor is her death recorded.

DĪ NAITES. Cuthæan colonists who were placed in Samaria (Ezr. iv. 9).

DINHĀ BAH (*present*) (Gen. xxxvi. 32). Capital city and birthplace of Bela, son of Beor, king of Edom. 8 ms. from Ar. toward the river Arnon. —7 ms. from Heshbon, on Mt. Peor (Eusebius). DANABA was a bishop's see in Palmyrene, Syria (Zosimus iii. 27).

DIONYSIA. Feast of Bacchus (2 Macc. vi. 7).

DIONYS'IUS, THE AREOPAGITE. (Acts xvii. 34). Dionysus or Bacchus. He was a member of the supreme court of the Areopagus, and one of the few converts of Paul at Athens. A. D. 420, a writer called Pseudo-Dionysius wrote a book in the name of the disciple, which was believed to be genuine for a long time, but is now condemned.

DIONY SUS. BACCHUS (3 Macc. ii. 29).

DIOCÆSAREA. SEPPHORIS.

THE KING, CHIEF OFFICERS, AND GODS OF ASSYRIA DIVINING WITH A CUP.

DIOT REPHES (*Jove-nurtured*). A disciple who resisted the apostle John, in Asia-Minor.

DIR WEH. Ruin and fountain E. of Beth-Zur, 4 ms. N. of Hebron.

DISCIPLE. Believer. Member of the Church of Christ.

DISCOV ER. To uncover. "The voice of the Lord—discovereth the forests," that is, the lightning strips off the bark and branches (Ps. xxix. 9).

DIS CUS. A quoit of iron, copper, or stone, for throwing in play, in the gymnasium. Jason introduced Greek games into Jerusalem in the time of Antiochus Epiphanes, which the priests indulged in to the neglect of their duties (2 Macc. iv. 14).

DISH (Heb. SEPHEL, TSALLACHATH, and KERAH, and Greek *trublion*). Bowl, charger. See MEALS, CUPS.

DI SHAN. Youngest son of Seir the mountaineer (Horite). (1 Chr. i. 38). DISHON (Gen. xxxvi. 21).—2. Son of Anah, and grandson of Seir (1 Chr. i. 41).

DISSOLVE. To explain (Dan. v. 16).

DISPER SION, THE JEWS OF THE. Those who remained in Babylonia after the return from captivity were called the "dispersed, or "of the dispersion," or in Heb. "stripped naked." "Removed" in Deut. xxviii. 25; Jer. xxxiv. 17. This included the 12 tribes. The Jewish *faith* succeeded to the *kingdom* of David at the return of the remnant, and faithful Jews everywhere contributed the half-shekel to the temple services (Jos. Ant, xviii. 9, 1). Three sections of the dispersion are noticed in history, of Babylon, of Syria, and of Egypt. The Greek conquests extended the limits of the dispersed, by securing greater liberties to the Jews. See ANTIOCHUS, THE GREAT. The African dispersion centred at Alexandria, the best fruit of which is the Septuagint. After the rise of the Jews, in Trajan's time, they were nearly exterminated and the remnant driven into Europe. Those in Rome followed Pompey after his victories in the East. They were banished from the city under Claudius, because they "were continually raising disturbances, Chrestus being their leader" (Suetonius, c. 25). Probably on account of their opposition to the preaching of Christ by Paul and others. The dispersion influenced the spread of the gospel, because the apostles and preachers followed the Jews into "all the world" (Acts ii.).

DIS TAFF. SPINNING. (Prov. xxxi. 19).

DI VES. A Greek word meaning *rich*, which Jesus used in the parable of Lazurus and the "rich" man (Luke xvi. 19). It has since Chaucer's time (see Sompnoure's Tale, "Lazar and Dives") been used in theological literature as a proper name.

DIVINA TION (Heb. KESEM, *to divide*) Imitation of prophesy; the art of pretending to foretell future events, from the appearance of cards, dice, liquids in a vial, or sediment in a cup (Gen. xliv. 4) which had magical writing on it, or engraving on it; of the earth, sea, and sky; the entrails of animals; the flight of birds; of graves; in dreams; (Num. xii. 6). ("good dreams are one of the great parts of prophesy."—*Koran*) by talismans, images, oracles; by arrows (see Assyrian sculptures, where the king holds divining arrows, or a rod); and also by magic arts. Plato calls it science without reason. It was taught that the gods gave signs of future events, all through the universe, and that men of observation and study could read those signs. Moses condemned the whole system (Deut. xviii. 10-12), and those who practiced it as impious impostors. The desire to know the future was proper, and would be gratified by God's own *prophet*, who should speak as he was inspired. This superstition is found among all people, at this day, and is even now practiced under the name of clairvoyants, second-sight, trance-mediums, seventh daughter or son, by cards, water, rods, palm, etc. The result of such practices is the same in all ages, a certain loss of judgment, of purity, and piety, and is as hateful now as ever (1 Sam. xv. 23). The divination by lot seems to be an exception, and is said to be divine (Prov. xvi. 33), and with the Hebrews was conducted solemnly and with religious preparations (Josh. vii. 13), as in the case of Achan and of the division of the Promised Land (Num. xxvi. 55), the election of Saul as king (1 Sam. x. 20), and the chosing of Matthias to the vacant apostleship (Acts i. 26). Many appearances are recorded as of the direct work of God, as the serpent rod of Moses; leprous hand; burning bush; plagues; cloud; Aaron's budding rod; the dew of Gideon, etc., and also visions (Num. xii. 6). See Cup on p. 37.

SHEKEL.

DIVORCE. The law of Moses is found in Deut. xxiv. 1-4, and xxii. 19, 29. The original words are *some uncleanness* (Heb. ERVATH DABAR), and are very loosely explained by the Jewish doctors, so that many causes for divorce were admitted. One school (Shammai) limited it to a moral cause, and another (Hillel) included many others; as a bad breath, snoring, a running sore, and burning the

food when cooking. When Jesus was appealed to (Matt. v. 31), with a view to entangle him in their disputes, he said, The practice allowed by the Mosaic law of divorcing a wife without crime on her part, and on the ground of dislike or disgust, is opposed to the original, divine idea of marriage; according to which a man and his wife are joined together by God, to be one flesh, and are not to be put asunder by man. He who puts away his wife by a bill of divorce without her crime, causes her to commit adultery by placing it within her power to marry another man. The party who permits the divorce is criminal in marrying again. The mere exchange of a piece of writing will not dissolve the spiritual bond. Unless the union is dissolved by crime, any who unite with either party are criminal.

The apostle Paul allowed (1 Cor. viii.) *separation* of a believer from an *unbeliever*, but not to marry another, but to seek reconciliation and reunion. In the Roman church a marriage with an unbeliever may be annulled by the believer, who may marry another. Some Protestants follow the same custom, and also in case of desertion. See MARRIAGE.

DIZ'AHAB (*place of gold*). On the Red Sea, now Dohab (Deut. i. 1).

DOCTOR. Teacher (Luke ii. 46). SCRIBE.

DO'CUS (*small fort*). Near Jericho (1 Macc. xvi. 15). Built by Ptolemens, son of Abubus, in which he entertained and murdered his father-in-law, Simon Maccabeus and his two sons (Ant. xiii. 8). Dagon, ruins near Ain Duk, are supposed to mark the site (Rob. II. 309).

ANCIENT RINGS.

DO DAI (*loving*). An Ahohite, captain of the course of the army (24,000), who served in the 2d month (1 Chr. xxxii. 4). Dodo? Brother of Jesse?

DODA'NIM. Descendants of the 4th son of Javan (Gen. x. 4). Rodanim. The island of Rhodes and the river Rhone are relics of the name.

DODA'VAH (*love of Jah*). Father of Eliezer, who denounced Jehoshaphat's alliance with Ahaziah (2 Chr. xx. 37).

DO'DO (*God his friend*). 1. Of Bethlehem, father of Elhanan, one of David's noted 30 captains (1 Chr. xi. 26).—2. Dodai, the 2d in chief command of David's army (2 Sam. xxiii. 9, 24; 1 Chr. xi. 12). 3. Of Issachar, forefather of Tola, the judge (Judg. x. 1).

DO'EG (*fearful*). Chief of Saul's herdsmen (1 Sam. xxii. 9). He obeyed king Saul, and killed the priests of Nob (85, and their families also). He was a proselyte to the Jewish faith, attending there to fulfil a vow?

DOG (Heb. KELEB, *seizer*; Ar. *kelb*). From most ancient times the humble friend and servant of man. Sculptured on the monuments of Assyria and Egypt. Mentioned as shepherd dogs by Job (xxx. 1); Moses as property (Deut. xxiii. 18), and Solomon (Eccles. ix. 4). The vile rulers of Israel were compared to dogs by Isaiah (lvi. 10, 11). The dog is almost ownerless in the East, and runs, half-wild, in the streets; never caressed, or made pets of, and seldom admitted to a house or tent. They eat anything that comes in their way, and also each other, if a dog strays from his proper district. Jezebel's fate (2 K. ix.) might be repeated any day or night in any city of the East. Byron writes in his Siege of Corinth:

"He saw the lean dogs, beneath the wall,
Hold o'er the dead their carnival;
Gorging and growling o'er carcass and limb,
They were too busy to bark at him."

David wrote of Saul's hired assassins lying in wait to kill him: "They return at evening: they make a noise like a dog, and go round about the city. Let them wander up and down for meat, and grudge if they be not satisfied" (Ps. lix. 6). He also speaks of them in Ps. xxii. 16, 20. The caravans to Mecca have many dogs, going from Egypt, Syria and Persia. The dog was held to be unclean, and was despised, and is now, the name being a term of reproach, commonly applied to Christians by the Mohammedans.

STONE DOOR.

DOOR. (Heb. SHAAR, *to divide, gate*; PETHAH, *entering*; SAPH, *threshold*; DALETH, *to hang down as a curtain, a door*; TERA, PULE, PULON, *gate*). The door had a threshold, side posts and lintel in houses, and was an opening in the side of a tent. The door is generally of wood, and sometimes of cedar, handsomely carved, and also a cloth for inside use. In the Hauran are now to be seen doors of stone, turning on hinges of stone, dating from antiquity. Doors and doorways in the East are generally small and mean in appearance compared with ours, or with the interior to which they open.

MODERN EGYPTIAN DOOR.

The gates of cities are built strong for defense, with towers and chambers (2 Sam. xviii. 24), and rooms inside for public assembly, for hearing the news, buying or selling, or judicial affairs. In Assyrian cities they were similar; and in the temples were highly ornamented with sculpture and colors. The doorway in the engraving from the ruins of the palace (or temple) at Koyunjik (a part of Nineveh), shows the magnificent style of sculpture, in the use of ideal figures combining men, and animals, and birds. (See cut on page 54.)

The principal doorways in the palaces were guarded by symbolic bulls, or winged gods. Images

of the gods were hidden in the walls and floor as a kind of protection.

The Egyptian temple was a kind of fort, with massive walls, and a gate with strong, high towers. The doors had double leaves, often plated with metal. They were provided with locks and bars of metal.

The gates of Babylon are said to have been of bronze (brass). On the doors of Egypt in our day, there are sentences from the holy book, following the ancient custom (Deut. vi. 9; Is. liv. 12; Rev. xxi. 21; Lane, Mod. Egyptians, Wilkinson). Petitions were presented to the king at the gate; and the gate was sometimes made a place of sanctuary—a refuge for criminals.

The doors of Solomon's Temple are described as being very valuable, richly carved, and overlaid with gold (1 K. vi. 31, etc). Those of the holy place were double. The Beautiful Gate of Herod's Temple is said to have been of Corinthian brass (bronze), (Jos. Wars, v. 5, § 3), and required twenty men to move it.

The gates of precious stones of Revelations and Isaiah were suggested to the writers by the stone doors of the Hauran, which are often several inches thick, of fine hard basalt, beautifully carved.

To open, or lift up as a curtain, a door to a coming guest, was and is an especial honor, as alluded to in Ps. xxiv. 7.

"I would rather be a door-keeper in the house of my God than dwell in the tents of wickedness" (Ps. lxxxiv. 10), may be better understood as meaning "I would rather lay at the door of the house of my God (like Lazarus), than have a home in their tents."

DOPH'KAH (*cattle driving*). Station of the Exodus (Num. xxxiii. 12). See WILDERNESS.

DOR (*habitation*). Royal city of the Canaanites (Josh. xvii. 11; 1 K. iv. 11). On the Great Sea, 14 miles S. of Carmel, 7 ms. N. of Caesarea. Its king was defeated with others near the waters of Merom (Judg. i. 27), in Manasseh, but the ancient people were never expelled. Solomon made them pay tribute. This was the most southern city built by the Phœnicians. The ruins are on a hill and extend half a mile, the most conspicuous being an old tower, which is a landmark, called Tantura (*the hora*).

DO RA (1 Macc. xv. 11). Dor.

DOR'CAS. See TABITHA.

DŌRYM ENES. Father of Ptolemy (1 Macc. iii. 38). He fought against Antiochus the Great (Polybius, v. 61).

DŌSITH'EUS. 1. Captain under Judas Maccabæus against Timotheus (2 Macc. xii. 19).—2. A horseman of Bacenor's band (2 Macc. xii. 35).—3. Son of Drimlus, an apostate Jew at Raphia (3 Macc. i. 3).—4. "Said he was a priest and Levite," messenger to carry the translation of Esther to Egypt (Esther xi. 1, Doway). Another mentioned by Josephus (c. Apion ii. 5).

DO THAN. Dothaim (*two wells*). 14 ms. N. of Shechem (Gen. xxxvii. 17). Joseph was sold by his brethren here to the Egyptians (ib. 25). Elisha, the prophet, lived at D. when Benhadad thought to capture him (2 K. vi. 8-23). Tell Dothan is now at the S. end of a rich plain, separated by slight hills from Esdraëlon, and the ruins are on a very large hill; with a fine spring at its foot. The massive ancient Jewish or Roman pavement is to be seen in the road that runs near, from Beisan to Egypt.

DO TO WIT. To make known. Not used. (2 Cor. viii. 1).

DOVE (Heb. YONAH). Two species are mentioned in the law—turtle-dove and pigeon. Both were to be offered in burnt offering (Deut. i. 14). It is a symbol of peace, and the most exalted of animals, as symbolizing the Holy Spirit, and the meekness, purity and splendor of righteousness. Two ancient relics show its use as a national ensign—one on a Phœnician coin, where the dove, with rays about its head and wings closed, stands on a globe; and the other, a sculpture in the Hauran, where the dove's wings are spread, also stands on a globe, the rays behind terminating in stars. Carrier pigeons are figured in Egypt. A dove has carried a letter from Babylon to Aleppo in two days. The DOVE'S DUNG of 2 K. vi. 2, has been explained as chick-peas or the roots of the *ornithogalum umbellatum*, or the Star of Bethlehem, used now by the poor. Pigeon cotes are common all over the East, usually made of coarse stone jars piled into a kind of house, by itself or on a roof.

DRACH'MA. See MONEY.

DRAG'ON (Heb. TANNIM, dragons). A mammal, living in the desert (Is. xiii. 22), crying like a child (Job xxx. 29); probably the jackal, which has a mournful howl. Another (Heb. TANNIN) was a great sea monster. Used as a metaphor of the Pharaoh (Is. li. 9; Ez. xxix. 3), where it means the crocodile (see Jer. li. 34). The word is also used as a metaphor for the devil in Rev. xii.

DREAM. We know that God needs no rest, and

DOVE.

is as active when we sleep as when we wake, and therefore we may suppose that divine influences fashion our dreams, as well as direct our waking thoughts. It is supposed that God appeared to Moses, Abraham, Jacob and Joseph, in dreams. So the Greeks believed (Homer, Il. i. 63). Moses promised such visitations (Num. xii. 6); Peter (Acts 10), and Paul (2 Cor. xii. 1), had such dreams. Jeremiah condemns those who pretended to have revelations in dreams (xxiii. 25), and in visions, etc. xxvii. 9), and Ezekiel also (xiii. 2-9). The modern imitators of Spiritism pretend to a divine converse—perhaps deluding themselves—believing that the wild fancies of their trances are the work of the divine mind.

DRESS. Oriental dress has preserved a peculiar uniformity in all ages, from Abraham to the modern Bedawin. The monument at Behistun exhibits the antiquity of the costume, which can be compared with that of figures of modern Syrians and Egyptians. The dress for men and women differed but very little; many articles being worn by both in common, varied only by the manner of putting them on. Men wore the shawl over the head and shoulders, or over the shoulders, while the women used it around the waist.

The *drawers* are scant or full, gathered around the waist, and show, when on, as in the figure of Bedawin, p. 20, and of the woman in street costume. They are fastened just below the knee by garters.

YELEK, GOWN.

The *skirt* reaches to, or falls a little below the knees, and is worn outside of the drawers generally, as in the picture of Syrians, p. 73. When dressed in the drawers and shirt only, a person was said to be naked (Mark xiv. 51). They also wear a vest, like ours, buttoned up to the chin. The buttons are sewed on the edge of the garment, and passed through a loop, never using a buttonhole.

The *coat* has sleeves to the wrist, or longer, and skirts to the knees or ankles.

Over the coat is worn the *girdle* (Acts xxi. 11), which is two or three yards long and about half a yard wide, and is made of any material, from a strip of leather or a rope, to the finest silk, with embroidery. The coat, when cut off at the hips, is sometimes embroidered very highly. The same garment is worn by women, and is called Yeick. This is the robe of ceremony for both sexes, referred to in 1 K. v. 5, and 2 Chr. ix. 4, and (the long skirt) the present that Jehu gave the prophets of Baal (2 K. x. 22).

CLOAK.

The *cloak* (ABBA, LEBUSH) is a large square bag, open on one side, with holes at the upper corners for the hands, and a band around the neck. Goat's or camel's hair is used in the desert (Matt. iii. 4) as worn by John the Baptist. Joseph's coat of (many) colors was of this pattern; and such rich garments are common among the wealthy, being made of silk or wool, and richly embroidered. The same garment is called a *burnous* when it has a hood, as worn in Algeria. The *hyk* is a square shawl, folded cornerwise, and worn as is the cut of Egyptians. Bedawins use a cloth woven with thread of silver or gold, called *Abul*. The head is covered first with a white cotton cap (*libdeh*), over which is worn the *terbush* (see HEAD-DRESS), a red woolen cap, generally with a blue tassel. Around the tarbush a narrow shawl (three or more yards long) is wound, forming the turban. Women cover themselves with a thin cloak and a veil, leaving only the eyes (or only one eye) visible, as in the figure (Oriental street costume). The ancient

TUNIC. CAFTAN. COAT.

Jewesses did not vail their faces, but covered the hair only. Women wear the hair long, braided, curled, etc., and decorated with jewels and coins. Men generally shave the head (2 Sam. xiv. 26). The ancient Jews probably wore the hair as low as the ears or neck, and, as Josephus says of the body-guard of Solomon, used powder (Ant. viii. 7, 3). In mourning the head was shaved (Is. xxii. 12, etc.).

EGYPTIANS.

There are many ornaments in use for the hair, head, ears, nose, and neck, not very much different from those in use here; except the nose-ring. The eyebrows and lashes are frequently colored.

The feet are loosely covered, and are seldom deformed as ours are by tight shoes. The inner slippers are very soft, and only worn in the house; the over-shoes and boot being worn out doors, and always left at the door. Stockings and leggings for cold weather are in common use.

SANDALS.

Sandals are still used in the house, but could never have been in common use out doors, because of the many thorns and briers. The *kubcobs* are high wooden stilts, used in the bath, or on wet floors. SANDALS.

Jos. Ant. iii. 7, § 7: "The vestments of the high priest, being made of linen, signified the earth; the blue denoted the sky, being like lightning in its pomegranates; and in the noise of the bells, resembling thunder. And for the Ephod, it showed that God had made the universe of four elements; and as for the gold interwoven, I suppose it related to the splendor by which all things are enlightened. He also appointed the breast-plate to be placed in the middle of the ephod, to resemble the earth, for that has the very middle place. And the girdle which encompassed the high priest round, signified the ocean, for that goes round about and includes the universe. * * * * And for the turban, which was of a blue color, it seems to me to mean heaven, for how otherwise could the name of God be inscribed upon it?"

Exodus xxviii.: "And these are the garments which they shall make—the breast-plate, and the ephod, and the robe, and the coat of checker-work, the turban, and the girdle;" all of which were peculiar to and worn only by the high priest.

In this description the under-garments are not mentioned. In verse 42, linen drawers are directed to be worn, and it may be presumed that the other undergarments worn by the upper classes were used by the priests.

Breastplate (v. 4, 15). This was embroidered, in two halves sewed together, the front to receive the 12 stones, and the back to shield the studs; and besides, so as to fit the chest better, because the stuff was thick and stiff from embroidery, and the fine wires of gold worked into the design. The making of the wires is described in xxxix. 3. In it were set four rows of engraved stones, bearing the names of the twelve tribes of Israel. Each stone was set in a rim of gold, like a cameo (or breast-pin), with a button or stud at the back, which was put through a button-hole in the breast-plate. Putting the twelve stones into their places was a solemn service, showing the presence of the twelve tribes before the altar of Jehovah, and they were called LIGHTS and PERFECTIONS—(Urim and Thummim). It was two spans high, and one wide.

Two cord-like chains of gold wire were fastened to the upper corners of the breast-plate by two rings of gold (v. 14), which were attached to the engraved stones on the shoulders, one to each stone. Two gold rings on the lower corners of the breastplate were opposite two rings in the girdle; and a blue cord tied the rings together and kept the breast-plate in its place (v. 26, 27, 28).

The other garments were peculiar only in color and ornament, their pattern being similar to those already described.

SANDALS.

DRINK (Heb. SHECAR, *any intoxicating beverage*). Strong drink was made from several fruits besides grapes: as pomegranates (Cant. viii. 2), figs, apples, dates, carob fruit, and from grain: as wheat, barley, millet, and from honey. A fine wine is made by putting raisins in water and burying the jars in the ground until after fermentation.

DROM'EDARY (Heb. BECHER, BICRAM, RECESH, RAMMAC). See CAMEL. The A. V. translates in error RECESH in 1 K. iv. 28, and Esth. viii. 10, 14, dromedaries, when the original means swift horses; also RAMMAC in Esther viii. 10, 14, mules instead of mares.

ORIENTAL STREET COSTUME.

DROPPING, A CONTINUAL (Prov. xxvii. 15). Drops of rain in a wintry day drive a man out of his house; in the same manner also does an abusive woman (Lam. xx.). See HOUSE.

DRUSIL'LA (feminine of Lat. *Drusus*). Daughter of Herod Agrippa I, and Cypros (Acts xii. 1). She was betrothed to Antiochus Epiphanes, but on his refusing to become a Jew she was married to Azizus, king of Emesa. She afterwards left her husband for Felix (ib. xxiv. 24). She, with her son, perished in an eruption of Mt. Vesuvius.

DUKE. Translation of the Heb. ALLUPH, which means patriarch, head of a family, or, in Arabic, *sheikh*, chief, leader.

DUL'CIMER (Heb. or Chal. SUMPHONYAH). Musical instrument mentioned by Daniel (iii. 5, 15). The modern dulcimer is a box, strung with about 50 wires—the longest 36 inches, the shortest 18—played with two small hammers, held in the hands. MUSICAL INSTRUMENTS.

DU'MAH (*silence*). Son of Ishmael, founder of a tribe of Ishmaelites. The DISTRICT was in the N. of Arabia, near Edom (Gen. xxv. 15; Is. xxi. 11), where there is now a city called *Doomah el*

Jeodel, 240 miles E. of Petra, in a circular valley, surrounded by very fine gardens and orchards. An ancient castle, of massive masonry, is in ruins. Another DUMAH is in Judah, 17 miles from Eleutheropolis, 6 miles S. W. of Hebron.

DUMB. Unable to speak (Ex. iv. 11). See MIRACLES.

GRIFFON-VULTURE.

DUNG (Heb. GILALA). Used both for manure and for fuel. Its use as manure is very much the same as with us. For fuel it is carefully dried. Many poor people spread cow dung on the outside of their houses to dry for fuel (Ezr. iv. 12.) See Deut. xxiii. 12. The word was omitted in writing, as in 2 K. x. 27, where *draught-house* is substituted. One of the gates of Jerusalem was named Dunggate (Neh. iii. 13, Dung Port). Public execration or insult was shown by using his house as a "draught-house."

DUNG-GATE. JERUSALEM.

DUN GEON. PRISON.

DU RA (Heb. CIRCLE). Where Nebuchadnezzar set up an image (Dan. iii. 1). Oppert found the pedestal of a colossal image in a plain called Dowair, S. E. of Babylon, where he thinks the plain of Dura was.

DUST. An image of what is low, mean and impure. Abraham calls himself but dust and ashes (Gen. xviii. 27). In times of grief and mourning the custom in the East is to sit in the dust, and to sprinkle it over the head. To throw dust on one is to show contempt (as Shimei to David, 2 Sam. xvi. 13), and the Jews to Paul (Acts xxii. 23). Shaking the dust off the feet was to leave it as a testimony to the great wickedness of the persons who had offended. To lick the dust is to be prostrated or subdued; to put the mouth in the dust is to show great humility. To return to the dust is a term for death. The dust of the desert sometimes is carried by whirlwinds to great distances, land falling, covers a caravan or the fertile land, leaving desolation in its track.

E

EAGLE (Heb. NESHER; Ar. *niser, to tear with the beak*). Eagles are found in all parts of the world, and there are several species in Palestine. 1. Imperial. 2. Short-toed. 3. Golden. 4. Spotted. 5. White-tailed. 6. Bonelli's eagle. 7. Gier eagle, or Egyptian vulture, and others. The NESHER is not an eagle, but a Griffon-vulture, which is found in all hot countries of the old world. It measures nearly five feet; eight feet extent of wing. The allusion in Matthew (xxiv. 28), "wheresoever the carcase is, there will the eagles be gathered together," refers to vultures, because eagles do not gather more than two or three, while vultures assemble in large flocks. Its bare head is alluded to in Micah i. 16. Job mentions its strong eye-sight and wing (xxxix. 27-30). "The cliffs are perforated with caves at all lights, wholly inaccessible to man, the secure resting place of hundreds of noble griffons." (*Tristram, Land of Israel.*) This gorge was the one Josephus describes near Arbela as inhabited by robbers, who were dislodged with great labor and hard fighting. The god NISROCH, specially worshiped by Sennacherib, the Assyrian, was a vulture-headed figure, with wings. Ezekiel and John use this vulture as one of the heads in their symbolic figure (Ez. x. 14; Rev. iv. 6). Its longevity is alluded to in Ps. cii. 5. "Thy youth is renewed like the eagle's," (NESHER). One was kept in Vienna 104 years. They are always in sight in the East, every day in the year. Its care for its young is twice used as an example of God's fatherly care (Deut. xxxii. 11; Ex. xix. 4).

The gier eagle (Lev. xi. 18), called in Hebrew and Arabic RACHMAH, and is the modern Pharaoh's Hen, or Egyptian Vulture. It is migratory in Palestine, and ranges from Asia Minor to the Cape of Good Hope. The DAYAH is probably a kite (Lev. xi. 14), of which four kinds are known in Palestine. (See KITE.)

The golden eagle lives in pairs only, and requires a wide range of country, five pairs occupying as much as twenty miles. It is smaller than the Griffon, and not so strong.

The short-toed eagle is strong, heavy, and handsome, about two feet long, dark brown, and marked with black spots. There are twice as many of these as of all the other eagles put together in Palestine.

E ANES (1 Esd. ix. 21). HARIM, MASSEIAH and ELIJAH.

EAR (*to plow*) (Deut. xxi. 4; Is. xxx. 24.)

EAR'NEST. (Heb. ARABON), a pledge, security (Gen. xxxviii. 17, 18, 20. Prov. xvii. 18).

EAR RINGS (Heb. NEZEM). Ear-rings were made of gold, silver, brass or bronze, and glass, and in a great variety of forms, and varying in size from half an inch to three inches across. The nose ring is peculiar to the East, and is mentioned in Genesis (xxiv. 47), where Abraham's servant gave one to Rebekah. Except the nose ring men wear nearly all of these ornaments among oriental nations, and have from remote antiquity, as appears on the monuments in Egypt and Assyria. Rings were especially used for purposes of superstition and idolatry. The ring of ABRAXAS is an instance of superstitious use, as adopted by Christian Gnostics, and the museums of Europe and America furnish a great many other curious

NOSE-RING.

specimens of similar designs. Rings, coins and medals are hung in strings around the neck, by the sides of the face, and across the forehead sewed to the edge of the tarbush (see HEAD DRESS). Some ear-rings in the East are very large; two or even three inches across, and are loaded with pearls, precious stones, or glass.

EAR-RINGS.

EARTH (Heb. ERETZ, Gr. *ge*). Land and water, the whole visible surface of the globe. The Hebrew writers often used the term as we now use it, if meaning a local and limited space (James v. 17; Lev. iv. 25). and especially in the account of the crucifixion, where the darkness may have been over all the land of Israel, but probably not over all the globe (Matt. xxvii. 45; Luke xxiii. 44).

EARTH'QUAKES. Earthquakes have been frequent in all ages in Palestine, and their ravages may be traced at Aleppo (1616, 1812). Antioch (1737), Laodicea, Beirut, Sidon, Tyre, Safed, and Tiberias (1837). One is mentioned in the time of King Uzziah (Zech. xiv. 5); another in 31 B. C., when a great part of Jerusalem was destroyed and 10,000 persons killed. Josephus speaks of one about the time of the crucifixion (Ant. ix. 10, 4), when a large rock fell from Olivet.

EAST (Heb. KEDEM) (*before or in front*). By the east was often meant sun-rise. The Jews used to designate the lands lying east and north-east of Palestine (Gen. xxv. 6).

EAS'TER (Acts xii. 4). PASSOVER.

EAST'GATE (Neh. iii. 29). A gate of Jerusalem.

EATING. MEALS.

E'BAL. Mt. N. of Shechem (Deut. xi. 29). Moses charged the Israelites to put the blessing upon Mt. Gerizim, and the curse on Mt. Ebal. Both mts. are now terraced and cultivated, from bottom to top, by fine gardens. Ebal is 2700 feet high; Gerizim 2000 above the sea, and about 1000 above Shechem. The valley is about 600 ft. wide.

E'BED (Heb. *servant*).—1. Father of Gaal (Judg. ix. 26, xxviii. 30, xxxi. 35).—2. Son of Jonathan (Ezr. viii. 6); Obeth in 1 Esd.

LOCUST.

E BEDME'LECH. Ethiopian eunuch of Zedekiah, who released the prophet Jeremiah from prison, and was therefore saved when Jerusalem was taken (Jer. xxxviii. 7, ff).

E'BEH (Heb. EBEH)—*reed, bulrushes, papyrus* (Job. ix. 26). Boats or skiffs made of papyrus—light and swift.

EBEN-EZEL (*stone of departure*). (1 Sam. xx. 19).

EBEN-E'ZER (*stone of help*). Set up by Samuel between Mizpeh and Shem (1 Sam. vii. 12). Site lost.

EBER (*beyond*), HEBER.—1. Son of Salah, great-grandson of Shem; from whom the Hebrews were named.—2. Son of Elpaal, a Benjamite (1 Chr. viii. 12).—3. A priest of Amok under Joiakim (Neh. xii. 20).

EBI ASAPH (Heb. ABIASAPH). A Levite (1 Chr. vi. 23). The prophet Samuel and Heman the singer descended from him. ASAPH.

EBONY. True Ebony is a native of the coast of Malabar and of Ceylon. The tree is large, the stem nine feet in circumference, and shoots up, before it branches, to 29 ft. in height; the branches are stiff, irregular and numerous. This elegant plant furnishes valuable materials for inlaying; its fine-grained wood being sometimes black, gray, or green.

EBRO'NAH. Near Ezion-geber.

E-CA'NUS. One of the five swift scribes who assisted Esdras (2 Esd. xiv. 24) ASIEL 2.

ECBATA'NA. ACHMETHA (Ezr. vi. 2). Two cities of this name.—1. Capital of N. Media. Atropatene of Strabo. The 7-walled town of Herodotus, and said to have been the capital of Cyrus. Where the roll was found which proved to Darius that Cyrus had really made a decree allowing the Jews to rebuild their temple. Ruins the most massive and antique, now called Takht-i-Suleiman, are on a conical hill 150 ft. above the plain, enclosing 2400 by 1200 ft. An artificial lake, 300 ft. across, is filled with clear, sweet water. The walls of the Temple were colored 7 tints—black, white, orange, blue, scarlet, silver and gold, in the order of the days dedicated to the planets. Was an important city as late as the 13th century, called Gaza, Gazaca, Cauzaca, by Greeks and Romans, and Shiz by Orientals.—2. The southern city, capital of Greater Media, is now called Hamadan, and is one of the great cities of Persia, with 20,000 inhabitants. Was the summer residence of the Persian kings from Darius downward. Was occupied by Alexander. The Jews say it was the residence of Ahasuerus, and show the tombs of Esther and Mordecai near it. See cut on page 6.

EAR-RINGS.

ECCLESIAS'TICUS. See HISTORY OF THE BOOKS.

ECLIPSE OF THE SUN. Supposed to be alluded to in Amos viii. 8, 9; Mic. iii. 6; Zech. xiv. 6; Jer. xv. 9.

ED (Heb. *witness*), (Josh. xxii. 34).

E'DAR (*flock-tower*). Where Jacob first pitched his tent after the death of Rachel (Gen. xxxv. 21). Near Bethlehem. Eder? There is a Jewish tradition that the Messiah is to be born there.

EDDIAS (1 Esd. ix. 26). JEZIAH.

EDEN (*garden of God*). The idea of a paradise of purity and happiness is found in all nations and in every religion. The location of the garden is lost.

Dr. Robinson proposed as the site of Eden the ruin called Jusieh el Kadimeh, in the valley of the Orontes, 30 ms. N. of Baalbek, 3 ms. S. E. of Riblah. A fortress in it was 396 ft. sq., having towers at the corners. Houses and streets are

traced among the ruins over a space of 2½ ms. Much material has been carried away to build a new town of Jusieh, 1 m. N. W., toward Ribiah. Ptolemy, Strabo and Pliny mention Paradisus in this same district. It is now dreary and barren, and water is found only in cisterns.—2. Beit-Jenn (*the house of Paradise*), S. W. of Damascus, on the E. slope of Hermon, near Mejdel, on a branch of the Pharpar.—3. Ez. xxiv. 23. In Assyria, with Haran, Canneh and Sheba, trading with Tyre. Supposed to be Aden.—4. Beth E. A country residence of the kings of Damascus (Amos i. 5). Near the cedars of Lebanon is a village of Ehden, but it is not identified with any historical event.

SIGNET RING OF SUPHIS.

ED'NA (Heb. *pleasure*). Wife of Raguel (Tob. vii. 2; viii. 14, 16).

E'DOM. IDUMEA (Mark iii. 8). The name of Esau (Gen. xxv. 29–34). The country settled by Esau's descendants. The ruddy hue of the mountains may have given the name Edom, which is *red* in the original. The ancient name was Mt. Seir. Seir means rugged. On the E. side of W. Arabah, from Elath on the S. to Moab on the N., at the brook Zered (Deut. ii. 13, 14, 18), about 100 ms. long by 20 ms. wide. The whole country is wild, rugged, and full of deep glens, but is also very fertile on the terraces; while the desert on each side is barren. The people dwelt amid the rocky hights, in caves and houses perched on dizzy crags, like eagles in their nests, living by their swords (Gen. xxvii. 40; Jer. xlix. 16); yet, as Isaac promised, this land possessed "the fatness of the earth, and of the dew of heaven" (Gen. xxvii. 39). The ancient capital was Bozrah. Sela (*Petra*) was the stronghold, and Ezion-geber its seaport, where Solomon built a fleet (2 Sam. viii. 14; 1 K. ix. 26). The crusaders built a fortress 12 ms. N. of Petra, on Mons. Regalis, now a ruin, called Shobek. The people were always idolaters (2 Chr. xxv. 14; Jos. Ant. xv. 17, § 9). The rock temples and dwellings of Edom were cut in a soft rock; were large, airy, well lighted and dry, and a safe protection against robbers.

E'DOMITES. Descendants of Edom (Gen. xxxvi. 1, ff.). See EDOM.

E'DREI. Bashan, one of its two capitals, the residence of Og (Deut. i. 1). In Manasseh (Josh. xiii. 12, 31). Two modern places claim this ancient name—(1) Edhra, at the S. W. angle of the Lejah, and (2) Dera, in the open plain of the Hauran, 14 ms. S. of the former. The ruins of Edhra are extensive and important above any other of the region; on a rocky projection from the Lejah, 3 ms. in circuit, raised 30 feet above the plain, which is wide and of unequalled fertility. The walls, roofs and doors are of a dark stone. There were many public buildings.—2. Naphtali, 3 ms. S. of Kedesh (Josh. xix. 37).

EDUCATION. The Jews were strictly charged in the law to educate their children (Deut. iv. 9), but probably only in moral and religious discipline. The exceptions were those who were intended for priestly or civil

EGYPTIAN KING. RHAMSES IV.

office, as in the cases of Moses, Paul, Ezra, Daniel. There were schools of prophets (singers?), one of which, kept by Samuel, David attended. The sect of Essenes instructed children.

EG'LAH (Heb. *a heifer*). Wife of David at Hebron (2 Sam. iii. 5; 1 Chr. iii. 3). See DAVID.

ECLA'IM (2 *pounds*). (Is. xv. 8). Moab. Lost.

EGLON. Judah, in the Shefelah (Josh. xv. 39; x. 3–5). Now Ajlan, a shapeless mass of ruins, 10 ms. S. W. of Beit Jibrin, on the road to Gaza, from which it is 13 ms. Name of a very fat king of Philistia (Judg. iii. 14).

SIGNET OF THOTHMES III.

EGYPT. It would be interesting and valuable if we could give here a full account of all the monuments which confirm scripture, found in Egypt; but as that would fill a large volume, we must admit only a few illustrations, referring the student to the larger works.

Concerning Abraham, we find that the account of his visit to Egypt is confirmed by many facts which may be compared with the history, laws and customs of the country as found in Wilkinson, Lane, and other writers. The principal points illustrated by evidence derived from Egypt are: 1. That Egypt was then a rich, powerful, and civilized nation. 2. The lower part, or Delta, was dry. 3. Its kings were called Pharaoh. 4. Slavery was an institution. 5. There was a famine in Canaan and an abundance in Egypt. 6. Abraham's wife, Sarah, was fair and did not wear a veil. 7. Pharaoh wished to place Sarah in his harem. 8. Abraham was well received as a shepherd. 9. He had sheep, oxen, asses, men and maid servants, and camels. 10. Abraham accepted Pharaoh's gifts because he dared not refuse them, for the custom of the time then, as well as now, makes the refusal of a present an insult.

Joseph was sold to the Ishmaelites for a household servant; was bought by Potiphar, an officer of Pharaoh; made an overseer in the king's house; was tempted by Potiphar's wife; thrown in prison; interpreted the king's dream; was elevated to office; was invested with a ring and robes of office, a gold chain; had his name changed to an Egyptian one; and was married to Asenath, daughter to a priest of On.

KING OF JUDAH.

The ring of Suphis, here engraved, was found on a mummy in the necropolis of Sakkara, near Memphis, is of pure gold, massive, and is now in the Abbott Egyptian Museum of the Historical Society, New York. The mummy was entirely

cased in pure gold, every limb, even to the fingers' ends, being wrapped separately, and the whole was inscribed with hieroglyphics. Joseph was embalmed and put in a coffin (Gen. 1. 26). The mummy cased in gold is of the age of Thothmes III, the Pharaoh who reigned in the time of Joseph, whose signet was found attached to a chain of gold, around his neck. The seal turns on a swivel, and so has two tablets, which are engraved. The whole is of very pure gold. Pharaoh made Joseph a ruler over all the land of Egypt, and called him ZAPHNATH-PAANEAH (*preserver of the world*) (Gen. xli. 37–45.) The seal bears the name of Pharaoh, and also the title "Paaneah." (These, with the chain, are now in the Leyden Museum.) "He made him to ride in the second chariot" (v. 43).

MERCHANT OF CAIRO CARRYING HIS KEYS.

"Now there arose up a new king over Egypt, which knew not Joseph," and there was a period of bondage in which the Jews were held until the time of Moses and the Exodus.

The monuments show us the taskmaster and his men, the several kinds of work, punishment by the bastinado, etc.

The picture on p. 43, is in the tomb of Roschere, at Thebes. Rosellini (See his great work on Egypt, in the Astor Library) says: "Of the laborers, some are bringing clay in vessels; some mingling the straw with it; others taking the bricks out of the moulds and arranging them in order for burning; others carrying away the burnt bricks: all are different from the three overseers at the right-hand end of the picture (a fourth is sitting), in com-

the skill requisite to make a golden image of a calf, such as they made in Sinai?" As proof that they had, we offer the pictures on the monuments, showing men actually at work at the furnaces, "the refiner's fire," weighing, etc. The "calf" they made was an image of the Egyptian god Apis, which was a live bull, kept at Memphis; and they had probably, while slaves, made many images of him for use in all parts of the country.

Selections might be made showing workers in nearly every industry known in the East, but the student will be better satisfied with the larger works; and we have given enough here to point the argument, that the scriptures are true.

Long after the Exodus, "Shishak, king of Egypt, came up against Jerusalem" (2 Chr. xii. 2), and on one of the walls in a temple at Karnac there is a picture of 63 prisoners, each one representing a city, tribe, or nation, and among them is a "king of the country of Judah." The names of Beth-horon, Megiddo, Mahanaim, and other cities in Palestine, are there, on shields. There are 84 names of persons or places of Canaan on the monuments at Abu Simbel, Thebes, and other ruins in Egypt, written in hieroglyphics. (See SHISHAK.) The word mizraim (*the two Egypts*) in the Hebrew Scriptures is translated Egypt in many passages (Ez. xxix. 10, etc.). Misr is *red mud* in Arabic. The name on the monuments is KEM (black). Upper E. extended from the cataracts to Memphis, and was called THEBAIS; and Lower E. from Memphis to the sea called the DELTA. Upper E. was also called PATHROS (Is. xi. 11). Land of Ham (Ps. cv. 23). The sign for Upper E. was a bent reed, and for Lower E. a bee (Is. vii. 18).

E'HI (Heb. *connection*), a Benjamite chief (Gen. xlvi. 21). AHIRAM.

E'HUD (Heb. *union, powerful*). 1. Son of Bilhan (Zech. vii. 10, viii. 6).—2. Son of Gera, tribe of Benjamin (Judg. iii. 15, ff), the second Judge of the Israelites (B. C. 1336), called a deliverer.

E'KER (Heb. *transplanted*). Descendant of Judah (1 Chr. ii. 27).

PYRAMIDS AND SPHINX.

plexion, physiognomy and beard. The original is in colors and the figures are very large.

The inscription at the top is translated, "Captives brought by his majesty to build the temple of the great God."

The question has been asked, "Had the Jews

EK'REBEL (Judg. vii. 18), AKRABEH A village 7 miles S. E. of Nablûs.

EK'RON (Heb. *eradication*). A royal city in the north of Philistia (Josh. xiii. 3), now AKIR, built on the accumulated rubbish of past ages. The deity worshiped was Baal-zebub. Ekron was the last

EK'RONITES. People of Ekron (Josh. xiii. 3).

E'LAH (valley of Terebinth). Where David slew Goliath (1 Sam. xvii. 2, 19; xxi. 9).

E'LAH (*strength*), (Heb. TEREBINTH or *oak*).—1. Son of Baasha, king of Israel (1 K. xvi. 8–14).—2. Father of Hoshea (2 K. xv. 30).

EL'AH. Duke of Edom (Gen. xxxvi. 41).—2. Father of Shimei (1 K. iv. 18).—3. Son of Caleb (1 Chr. iv. 15).—4. Son of Uzzi, a Benjamite chief (1 Chr. iv. 8).

EL'AHDAH (Heb. ELADA). (*whom God adorns*). A descendant of Ephraim (1 Chr. vii. 20).

E'LAM. Oldest son of Shem (Gen. x. 22). The country peopled by his descendants was along the Ulai, and its capital was Shushan, one of the most powerful and magnificent cities of antiquity. The name is found in the ancient inscriptions. Called also Nuvaki. Extended from the Persian Gulf to Assyria on the N., to the Zagron mts. on the E., and the Tigris on the W. In the time of Abram, the king of Elam was one of the most powerful in Asia (Jer. xlix. 34–39). The people were idolaters, and their images are found in the ruins. Elamites were at the Pentecostal feast (Acts ii. 9).

E'LAMITES. They were the original inhabitants of ELAM (Gen. x. 22; Ezr. iv. 9).

E'LASAH (*God-created*). ELASA. 1. A priest of Pashur (Ezr. x. 22).—2. Son of Shaphan. Sent on a mission by king Zedekiah to Babylon. (Jer. xxxi. 3).

E'LATH. Idumæa, on the E. gulf of the Red Sea. First named in Deut. ii. 8; and the reference in 1 K. ix. 26, shows that E. was more ancient than Ezion-gaber. King Solomon built a navy here. A fort is kept garrisoned here now, called Akaba, for the benefit of the pilgrims to Mecca.

EL'BETH'EL (*God of Bethel*). The place where God appeared to Jacob when he was fleeing from Esau (Gen. xxxv. 7).

EL'CIA. HILKIAM (Judg. viii. 1).

EL'DA-AH (Heb. *whom God called*) (Gen. xxv. 4). Son of Midian.

EL'DAD (*whom God loves*) and MEDAD. Two of the seventy Elders who had the gift of prophesy (Num. xi. 16, 26).

EL'DER (Heb. ZAKEN, Gr. *presbyter*). An old man. A title of honor and respect given to persons in authority (Gen. xxiv. 2; l. 7), as stewards or as master workmen. The elder was a political officer among the Hebrews, Moabites, Midianites and Egyptians (Num. xxii. 7). The office is the keystone of the political system among the modern Syrians, who use the name SHEIKH, which means *old man*, for the chief or head of the tribe. Moses adopted the idea and regulated its use by laws (Ex. iii. 16; iv. 29). Their authority was almost unlimited, within the law and customs (Josh. ix. 18). They became judges or magistrates in Canaan, in the local towns, sitting in the gates (Deut. xix. 12). They are called the Senate in 1 Macc. xii. 6. See SYNAGOGUE. The office of elder in the Christian church was adopted from the Jewish custom.

E'LEAD (*whom God applauds*). A descendant of Ephraim (1 Chr. vii. 21). SHUTHELAH.

ELE'ALEH (*God's light*). E. of Jordan, on the plateau of Moab, 1 m. N. E. of Heshbon, on the summit of a conical hill. Was once strongly fortified; and there are ruins of walls, cisterns, etc. Rebuilt by Reuben (Num. xxxii. 37).

ELEA'SA. Near Azotus (1 Macc. ix. 15).

ELE'ASAH (Heb. ELASAH.) 1. Son of Helez of Judah (1 Chr. ii. 39).—2. Son of Rapha (1 Chr. viii. 37, ix. 43).

ELEA'ZAR (Heb. *whom God helps*). 1. Son of Aaron (Lev. x. 1, ff). Eleazar was chief over the Levites (Num. iii. 32).—2. Son of Abinadab (1 Sam. vii. 1).—3. Son of Dodo the Ahohite; one of the three chiefs of David's army (2 Sam. xxiii. 9, ff).—4. A Levite, son of Mohli (1 Chr. xxiii. 21, 22).—5. A priest (Neh. xii. 42).—6. A descendant of Parosh; an Israelite (Ezr. x. 25).—7. Son of Phinehas (Ezr viii. 33).—8. Elizzer (1 Esd. viii. 43).—9. Avaran (1 Macc. ii. 5).—10. A distinguished scribe of great age, who was a martyr in the time of Antiochus Epiphanes (2 Macc. vi. 18, 31).—11. Father of Jason (1 Macc. viii. 18).—12. Son of Eliud (Matt. i. 15).

ELECT (*chosen, selected*). Election. The designation of persons to office (Acts ix. 15); of people or nations to the enjoyment of peculiar privileges (Deut. vii. 6-8) and of a definite number of persons to eternal life (2 Thess. ii. 13). This subject belongs to the mysteries of God and cannot be so clearly stated as to leave no uncertainty in the mind. The position is: that God does and will save a number of persons, and He does this according to a plan which he formed before the world was made; and he has never, and never will change that plan (Eph. i. 4; 2 Tim. i. 9); their election is of free grace and love, and not for any good in the person (Eph. i. 5); the redemption of Christ is included in the great plan. This plan enters into our destiny as a controlling element; as, it may be said by analogy, the patriotic determination of Washington resulted in the independence of our country; and the plans of a father determines where his family shall reside, the college his son shall attend, and the studies he shall pursue.

EL-ELOHE-ISRAEL (*Almighty, God of Israel*). Name of the altar that Jacob built facing Shechem (Gen. xxxiii. 19, 20).

ELEPH (or). Benj. (Josh. xviii. 18).

ELEPHANTS (Heb. SHEN-HABBIM). Elephants were used in warfare (1 Macc. i. 17, iii. 31). See IVORY.

ELEUTHEROP'OLIS. On the E. border of the plain of Philistia, at the foot of the hills of Judæa, in S. Palestine, 25 ms. S. W. from Jerusalem. Not mentioned in Scripture, but was an important city

WORKING IN METALS.

in the early Christian ages, when its name was Betogabra, *House of Bread*. Eusebius mentions it as the seat of a bishop, and reckons distances to other cities from it as a centre. The ruins are still shown of a fine chapel, and of a fort built by the Crusaders, 200 ft. square, in the 12th cent. Now Beit Jibrin, having 50 or more houses. The great attractions here are the caverns, or houses cut in the solid rocks. Rooms 100 feet or more in length, with smooth and ornamented walls, and lofty, arched roofs; some 40 to 70 ft. by 60 ft. high; most

WORKING IN METALS.

of them lighted by openings in the roof, and connected by doorways. Jerome says they were built by Idumæans.

ELEU'THERUS. River in Syria (1 Macc. xi. 7, xii. 30). Strabo says it divided Syria from Phœnicia. Now the Nahr el Kebir, *Great River*; rising in Lebanon, passing through the entrance to Hamath (Num. xxxiv. 8), emptying into the Great Sea 18 miles N. of Tripolis.

ELHA'NAN (*God-endowed*). 1. A great warrior in David's time (2 Sam. xxiii. 24). Son of Dodo, one of David's thirty men.—2. Son of Jair (or Jaor).

ELI (*high*). A high-priest descended from Aaron (1 K. ii. 27; 2 Sam. viii. 17).

E'LI LA'MA (*my God*) **SABACH'THANI**—*wherefore hast thou forsaken me!*—words uttered by Christ on the cross (Matt. xxvii. 46; Ps. xxii.).

ELI'AB (*God is father*). 1. Son of Helon (Num. i. 9).—2. Son of Phallu (Num. xxvi. 8, 9).—3. One of David's brothers, son of Jesse (1 Chr. ii. 13).—4. A Levite, porter and musician (1 Chr. xv. 18, 20).—5. A Gadite leader in David's time (1 Chr. xii. 9).—6. Son of Nohath (1 Chr. vi. 27).—7. Son of Nathanael (Judg. viii. 1).

ELI'ADA (*whom God knows or cares for*). 1. Son of David (2 Sam. v. 16).—2. A Benjamite who led 200,000 men to the army of Jehoshaphat (2 Chr. xvii. 17).

ELI'ADAH (Heb. ELIADA). Father of Rezon (1 K. xi. 23). **ELI'ADAS** (1 Esd. ix. 28)—ELIOENAI.

ELI'AH (Heb. ELIJAH). 1. Son of Jeroham (1 Chr. viii. 29).—2. Son of Elam (Ezr. x. 26).

ELI'ABA (*whom God hides*). One of David's thirty men (2 Sam. xxiii. 32).

ELI'AKIM (*whom God has set up*). 1. Son of Hilkiah I (2 K. xviii. 26, 37); he was a prefect in the king's house (Is. xxii. 20).—2. The original name of Jehoiakim, king of Judah (2 K. xxii. 34).—3. A priest who assisted at the dedication of the new wall of Jerusalem (Neh. xii. 41).—4. Son of Abiud, and father of Azor (Matt. i. 13).—5. Son of Melea (Luke iii. 30, 31).

ELIAM. ELIAB (*God's people*). 1. Father of Bathsheba (2 Sam. i. 3).—2. Son of Ahithophel (2 Sam. xxiii. 34).

ELIAS. See ELIJAH.

ELI'ASAPH (*whom God has added*). 1. Son of Deuel (Num. i. 14).—2. Son of Lael (Num. iii. 24).

ELI'ASHIB (*God restores*). 1. A priest in David's time (1 Chr. xxiv. 12).—2. Son of Elioenai (iii. 24).—3. High-priest at Jerusalem (Neh. iii. 1, 20, 21).—4. A singer (Ezr. x. 24).—5. Son of Zattu (x. 27).—6. Son of Bani (x. 36).

ELI'ATHAH (*God comes*). Son of Heman (1 Chr. xxv. 4, 27).

ELI'DAD. Son of Chislon; a prince who assisted in the division of the land of Canaan (Num. xxxiv. 21).

E'LIEL (*God is strength*). A common name among the Hebrews, but nothing of any note is known of any one bearing it (1 Chr. viii. 20; ii. 46).

ELIE'NAI. Son of Shimhi (1 Chr. viii. 20). Elioenai, a chief.

ELIE'ZER (*God helps*). 1. Steward of Abraham's

WILLOW BOAT.

house (Gen. xv. 5).—2. Son of Moses and Zipporah (Ex. xviii. 4).—3. Son of Becher (1 Chr. vii. 8).—4. Priest in David's reign (xxv. 24).—5. Son of Zichri (xxvii. 16).—6. Son of Dodavah (2 Chr. xx. 37).—7. A chief Israelite—a learned assistant to Ezra (Ezr. viii. 16).—8, 9, 10. Priests (Ezr. x. 18, 23, 31).—11. Son of Jorim (Luke iii. 29).

ELIHOE'NAI. Son of Zerahiah, who, with 200 men, returned from the captivity with Ezra (Ezr. viii. 4).

CARMEL.

ELIHO'REPH (*God rewards*). Son of Shisha, scribe of Solomon.

ELI'HU (*Jehovah*). 1. Son of Barachel (Gen. xxii. 21).—2. Son of Tohu (1 Sam. i. 1).—3 (1 Chr. xxvii. 18). "Of the brethren of David."—4. Captain of the thousands of Manasseh (1 Chr. xii. 20). A Levite (1 Chr. xxvi. 7).

ELI'JAH (Heb. ELI'AHU, *God-Jah, El-Jehovah*). On his first appearance he is simply denominated "Elijah the Tishbite, of the inhabitants of Gilead" (1 K. xvii. 1). It is supposed that Thisbe, in Galilee, was the birth-place of Elijah, but there is no proof. Such points were left in doubt that he might be known and thought of simply as *the great prophet reformer*. In this light alone he appears in the sacred history. His one grand object was to awaken Israel to the conviction that Jehovah, *Jehovah alone is God*. The period of Israelitish history at which Elijah appeared was one that emphatically called for the living exhibition of this great truth. It was that period of Ahab's apostasy, when, through the influence and example of his wife Jezebel he formally introduced the worship of other gods into Israel. In the language of the sacred historian, "It seemed a light thing for him to walk in the sins of Jeroboam, the son of Nebat; he took the daughter of Ethbaal to wife, and served Baal, and worshiped him. He reared up an altar for Baal in the house of Baal, in Samaria" (1 K. xvi. 31). He did not rest, like his predecessors, with the corrupt worship of Jehovah under the form of a calf, but brought in the worship of the Tyrian Baal, with its usual accompaniment of the Asherah pollutions—the rites of the Syrian Venus. Hence he enters on the work assigned him as the special servant of Jehovah, and in his name announces what shall absolutely come to pass, confident that there is no power in heaven or earth capable of reversing the word. "And Elijah said unto Ahab, As Jehovah, God of Israel liveth, before whom I stand,

there shall not be dew nor rain these years, but according to my word" (1 K. xvii. 1). After the utterance of a word by which the genial influences of heaven were to be laid under arrest for a series of years, it became necessary that a hiding place should be provided for Elijah, that he might escape from the violence of those in high places, and from the importunities of others, who might try to prevail upon his pity. Such a hiding-place was found for him to the east —beyond the limits of the kingdom of Israel—beside the brook Cherith, that flowed into the Jordan. There he found not only water from the brook, but also supplies of bread and flesh, morning and evening, ministered at God's command by ravens. The brook Cherith, however, in course of time dried up, and another place of refuge had to be provided for the prophet. This was found in the house of a poor widow, with an only son—and she not in the land of Israel, but at Zarephath (Sarepta), in the territory of Zidon, the native region of the infamous Jezebel (1 K. xvii. 9). Brought by divine direction to the place and to the woman, he found her near the gate of the city, gathering a few sticks to prepare her last meal, that she and her son might thereafter die. In the confidence of faith he bids her go and bake the bread as she intended, but in the first instance to bring a portion of it, with a little water, to him, demanding such faith from her as he himself exercised toward God. And he added, as the ground for her belief and his own demand, "For thus saith Jehovah, God of Israel, the barrel of meal shall not waste, neither shall the cruse of oil fail till the day that Jehovah sendeth rain on the earth." On the occasion of a severe illness befalling her son, she said to Elijah in a petulant tone, "What have I to do with thee, O thou man of God? Art thou come unto me to call my sin to remembrance, and to slay my son?"

Josephus does not understand that the child died. Jewish tradition says that this boy afterwards became a servant to the prophet, and also the prophet Jonah.

This seems to imply that she looked upon him as the occasion of her calamity, and that it would have been better for her had she not known him. However she graciously overlooked what might be wrong in it; as it was, the calamity proved a heavy trial to Elijah, and with holy freedom he laid it before God, and said, " O Jehovah, my God, hast thou also brought evil upon the widow with whom I sojourn, by slaying her son? I pray thee, let this child's soul come into him again." The child began to breathe, and presently was delivered alive to his mother. She said, "Now, by this I know that thou art a man of God, and the word of Jehovah in thy mouth is truth."

It was in the third year of Elijah's sojourn with the widow, that the Lord came to him, announcing the near prospect of rain, and bid him go and show himself to Ahab (1 K. xviii. 1). Returning to King Ahab, he procured the great assembly at Mount Carmel, where God "answered by fire," and the prophets of Baal were destroyed. (See CARMEL.) Now the long terrible drought was broken, and a plentiful rain descended at the prophet's prayer. He fled from the fury of Jezebel, first to Beersheba where he left his servant (Jonah), and went on alone into the wilderness (of Sinai.—Dr. Crosby), where he wished for death. "It is enough, Lord, let me die, for I am not better than my fathers." (The oratorio of Elijah, by Mendelssohn, is a beautiful and effective commentary on this part of the prophet's life.) Here the prophet saw the Lord pass by, in answer to his complaint. The wind rent the mountains, and brake in pieces the rocks of Sinai; then an earthquake; and after that a fire, burning in the constant blaze of lightning. These were symbols of the angry frame of mind that the prophet had. Then, after a profound stillness, there came a small voice, soft and gentle. This was Jehovah's method of winning men—not by exhibitions of terrible power. The persecutions of Ahab and Jezebel, the slaughter of Baal's priests, had nothing of God in them; but he was to be found as truly worshiped by the few who had not bowed the knee to Baal. These commands were given him:—To return to the wilderness of Damascus, and at a proper time anoint Hazael, king of Syria, Jehu, king of Israel, and Elisha as his successor. Elisha was appointed by having Elijah's cloak (of coarse camel hair, or wool) cast on him, when, from that time "He poured water on the hands of Elijah," that is, served him daily. Six years after he denounces Ahab and Jezebel for their crime against Naboth, in taking his vineyard. He foretells the death of Ahaziah, the king. The warning letter to Jehoram is by a later hand, of the same school. Two bands of guards having been sent by Ahab to arrest him, he calls down fire from heaven on their heads. Soon after that he crossed the Jordan with Elisha "on dry ground," and was separated from him by fire and carried away by a wind "into heaven." Elisha asked for the first born's double portion, as the eldest follower of Elijah. His whole life as a prophet was one of trial and conflict. The Jews, in the time of Jesus, expected Elijah to reappear, and Jesus alludes to the belief (Matt. xi. 14), explaining the fulfilment as in John the Baptist. Elijah (Elias in Greek) became a name for any or all true prophets, as David for the king, Abraham or Israel for the Hebrews.

ELIM (*trees*). Had twelve fountains (not wells), and a palm grove, being a kind of desert paradise (Ex. xv. 27). *Wady Ghurundel* has now several fine fountains, supplying a perennial stream, and has more trees, shrubs, and bushes than any other spot in the desert. Here the plain ends and the mountain begins.

ELIM'ELECH (*God is King*). The Bethlehemite husband of Noomi; the father of Mahlon and Chilion. See RUTH in the HISTORY OF THE BOOKS.

MULBERRY.

ELIOË'NAI (*eyes turned to El-God*).—1. Benjamite, and head of a family (1 Chr. vii. 8).—2 Simeonite, and head of a family (1 Chr. iv. 36).—3. Korhite Levite, and doorkeeper in the Temple of Solomon (1 Chr. xxvi. 3). Two before, and two others after the captivity, were not noted.

EL'IPHAL (*judged by El*). Son of Ur (1 Chr. xi. 35).

ELIPH'ALET. Son of David, the last of 13, born in Jerusalem (2 Sam. v. 16).—2. One of David's 30 heroes.—3. A Benjamite. ELIPHELET.

EL'IPHAZ, or **ELIPHAZ** (*God for strength*). 1. Son of Esau, and father of Teman (Gen. xxxvi. 10).—2. Chief of the three friends of Job, called the Temanite (Job. ii. 11). See JOB in the HISTORY OF THE BOOKS.

ELIPH'ELET (*God distinguishes*).—1. Son of David (1 Chr. iii. 6). ELPALET.—2 ELIPHALET 1. —3. Son of AHASBAI (2 Sam. xxiii. 34). ELIPHAL in 1 Chr. xi.—4. Son of Eshek, and of Saul through Jonathan (1 Chr. viii. 39).—5. One of the Bene-Adonikam who returned with Ezra (Ezr. viii. 13).— 6. One of the Bene-Hashum in Ezra's time (Ezr. x. 33).

TORTOISE.

ELIS'ABETH (*fulness of God*).—1. Wife of Zacharias, and mother of John the Baptist (Luke i. 5, 42), and cousin to Mary, the mother of Jesus.— 2. The wife of Aaron (Ex. vi. 23).

ELISEUS. The name of Elisha in the Apocrypha and the N. T. (Luke iv. 27).

ELI'SHA (*God for salvation*). Son of Shaphat, and a native of Abel-Meholah, where Elijah found him, whose pupil and successor he was from B. C. 903 to 838 (1 K. xix. 16). He was with Elijah when he divided the Jordan, and was carried away by a whirlwind and chariot of fire. Elijah's mission was to show that El was the God of Israel—Elisha to show that God should also be the salvation of his people. Beneficent working and kindly blessing were Elisha's chief work. His first act was to heal the bitter waters of Jericho. Following this were: the anathema on the young lads who mocked at God's prophet; refusing to prophesy for Jehoram the son of Ahab, "the son of a murderer," he did so to Jehoshaphat, giving them counsel which secured victory; he multiplied the widow's pot of oil; restored the Shunemite's son; cured the poisoned pottage; he multiplies a scant supply (twenty barley loaves and some roasted corn) to enough for 100 men; cured Naaman's leprosy; Gehazi lies, and is cursed with leprosy, restored the ax lost in the Jordan; showed a host of spiritual warriors to his servant, and struck blind the whole Syrian army, but he saved them from destruction by the Jews, caused the king to feed and send them away; he predicts plenty and the death of the king; the king restores her land to the Shunemite; predicts the death of king Ben-hadad, and the succession of Hazael; anoints Jehu king over Israel; the incident of the smiting with the bundles of arrows. Even after death he restored the dead to life. Elisha is seen to resemble Christ in his miracles, and in his loving, gentle character. He had no successor. The Greek church honors Elisha as a saint, on June 14.

ELISHA (*firm bond*). Son of Javan (Gen. x. 4), who named the "Isles of Elisha," which traded with Tyre (Ez. xxvii. 7). ELAS is from the same source. HELLAS, ancient Greece.

ELISHA'MA (*God hears*). Prince in Ephraim (Num. i. 10).—2. Son of David (2 Sam. v. 16).— 3. Son of David, also called ELISHUA (1 Chr. iii. 6).—4. Of Judah, son of Jekamiah (1 Chr. ii. 41), and father of Nethaniah, grandfather of Ishmael of the Captivity (2 K. xxv. 25); ELISHAMAM in some editions.—5. Scribe to Jehoiakim (Jer. xxxvi. 12).—7. Priest to Jehoshaphat, and sent to teach (2 Chr. xvii. 8).

ELISH'APHAT (*God judges*). Captain of "hundreds," in the service of Jehoiada (2 Chr. xxiii. 1).

ELISH'EBA (*God of the oath*). Daughter of Amminadab, of Judah, wife of Aaron; same as Elisabeth (Ex. vi. 23; Num. i. 7). Her marriage to Aaron united the royal and priestly tribes, Judah and Levi.

ELISHU'A (*Ei is salvation*). David's son, born at Jerusalem (2 Sam. v. 15). ELISHAMA in 1 Chr. iii. 6).

ELIU. Ancestor of Judith (viii. 1), of Simeon.

ELI'UD (*Jews' God*). Son of Achim (Matt. i. 15). From Abina.

ELIZAPHAN (*God protects*).—1. Son of Uzziel, a Levite (Ex. vi. 22). The family are mentioned in the times of David and Hezekiah. ELZAPHAN. 2. Son of Parnach, appointed by Moses, from Zebulon, to assist in dividing the land (Num. xxxiv. 25).

ELI'ZUR (*God the rock*). Son of Shedeur, of Reuben (Num. i. 5).

ELKA'NAH (*El creates*). Son of Korah (Ex. vi. 24). Several generations of Korah's sons are given in 1 Chr. vi. 22, etc.—2. Son of Joel, in the same line as 1 (vi. 25, 36).—3. Another, in the line of Ahimoth, or Mahath (vi. 26, 35).—4. A Kohathite Levite, in the line of Heman. Son of Jeroham, and father of Samuel the prophet (1 Sam. i. 1, etc). He lived in Mt. Ephraim, or Ramah, and attended yearly meeting for worship and sacrifice at Shiloh. He was rich enough to give three bullocks when Samuel was presented at the house of the Lord.—5. A Levite living in Netopha (ix. 16).—6. Doorkeeper in David's time, for the Ark (xv. 23).—7. Joined David at Ziklag (xii. 6).—8. The second in command in the house of Ahaz, killed by Zichri (2 Chr. xxviii. 7).

BULBUL.

ELKOSH' (*El's power*). Birthplace of Nahum (i. 1). There is a place so named in Assyria (34 ms. N. of Mosul), and modern Jews and the resident Chaldean Christians show a tomb of Nahum there. Jerome says the place was in Galilee, where there is now a traditional tomb of the prophet at *kefr tanchum*, near Tiberias.

ELKOSH'ITE. From Elkosh.

EL'LASAR (Gen. xiv. 1). THELASAR TELASSAR. The country and kingdom of Arioch in the days of Abraham.

ELM. Error for *oak* (Heb. ALAH), in Hos. iv. 13.

ELMŌ'DAM. Son of Er, in Joseph's line (Luke iii. 28). Almodad in Gen. x. 26.

ELNĀ'AM (*Et his delight*). Father of Jeribai and Joshaviah, two of David's guard (1 Chr. xi. 46).

ELNĀ'THAN (*whom Et gave*). Maternal grandfather of Jehoiachin (2 K. xxiv. 8).—2. Three Levites of this name in Ezra's time (Ezr. viii. 16). In 1 Esd. viii. 44, etc., the names are ALNATHAN and EUNATAN. Elnathan was sent by the king into Egypt to bring back the fugitive Urijah (Jer. xxvi. 20); and he was present at the burning of Jeremiah's roll, protesting against the act. See JEHOIAKIM.

ELŌ HIM. A plural word in Hebrew, meaning the true God. See GOD.

ELŌ I. When applied to heathen idols, it means gods. My God (Mark xv. 34).

E LON (Heb. ALLON, *an oak*). 1. Father of Esau's wife Adah, a Hittite (Gen. xxvi. 34).—2. Founder of the Elonites (Gen. xlvi. 14).—3. Judge for ten years (Judg. xii. 11); from the tribe of Zebulon. E'LON (*oak*). Dan (Josh. xix. 43). Same place as E'LON-BETH-HANAN (*oak of the house of grace*). Dan (1 K. iv. 9). Lost.

EL'PAAL (*Et, his reward*). Son of Hushim, a Benjamite, and founder of a family (1 Chr. viii. 12).

ELPĀ'RAN. Terebinth of Paran (Gen. xiv. 6).

EL'TEKEH (*Et fearing*). Place in Dan (Josh. xix. 44). Levitical.

ELTEKON (*God its foundation*). In Judah, 4 miles from Hebron (Josh. xv. 59). Lost.

ELTŌ LAD (*El's kindred*). In Judah, near Beersheba (Josh xv. 30). Wilton thinks it was in *Wady Lussan*, 60 miles S. of Gaza. Rowland places it in *Wady Selud*, 10 miles S. E. of Gaza.

ELUL. Name of the sixth Hebrew month.

ELU'ZAI (*God my praise*). Soldier who joined David at Ziklag (1 Chr. xii. 5).

ELYMĀ'IS. ELAM. City in Persia, containing a very rich temple, in which were many trophies deposited by Alexander the Great (1 Macc. vi. 1). Antiochus Epiphanes failed to capture it (Ant. xii. 9, § 1). In Tobit, ii. 10, Elymais is the name of a province.

ELYÆ'MANS. Elamites (Judith i. 6). See ELAM.

EL'YMAS (Ar. *wise*). Arabic name of Barjesus (Acts xiii. 6), the sorcerer. The Orientals called fortune-tellers by their true names, sorcerers, imposters.

EL'ZABAD (*given by El*). Warrior from Gad, who joined David in the wilderness (1 Chr. xii. 12).—2. A Korhite Levite, son of Shemaiah (1 Chr. xxvi. 7), a doorkeeper in the Temple.

MUMMY.

EL'ZAPHAN (*protected by El*). Cousin to Moses, and son of Uzziel (Ex. vi. 22). He was one of the two bearers of Nadab and Abihu (Lev. x. 4). ELIZAPHAN.

EMBALMING (*em-bá-ming*). Preserving by spices, gums, etc., dead bodies from decay. Two instances are mentioned in the O. T.: Jacob's and Joseph's bodies (Gen. l. 2, 26). The soft parts of the interior were removed, and spices, gums, etc., filled in their stead, and the whole was then steeped for 70 days in natron (petroleum or asphaltum), after which the body was carefully wrapped in strips of linen, dipped in gum, and delivered to the friends, who put it in the coffin, which was of wood carved and painted, or of stone, sculptured. The whole art was carefully guarded by strict laws. The body could only be cut by an authorized person, with a stone knife (see KNIFE). Embalming was not practiced by the Hebrews. Asa was laid in a bed of spices (2 Chr. xvi. 14), and Jesus had a hundred pound weight of spices placed in the tomb (John xix. 39, 40).

The Egyptians practiced the art because of their belief in the doctrine of transmigration of souls. (See Pettigrew's *Hist. of Eg. Mummies*).

EMBROIDERY (Heb. ROKEN), (Ex. xxxv. 35). Needlework. Two kinds of extra fine cloth was made, one by the *raken* of various colors and figures, called *riknuah*, and the other by the *chosheb* (*cunning workmen*), into which gold or other metallic threads are woven, besides the usual colors, both of which were made in the loom. The needle was used where the figure was wanted on one side only of the cloth. Wilkinson says that "Many of the Egyptian stuffs presented various patterns, worked in colors by the loom, independent of those produced by the dyeing or the printing process, and so richly composed that they vied with the cloths embroidered by the needle." The art was known in Assyria also, as the sculptures show. Ezekiel mentions embroidered work as the production of Egypt and Assyria, imported by way of Tyre (Ez. xxvii. 7, 23, 24). See DRESS.

EMBROIDERED RUFF.

EM'ERALD (Heb. NOPEK). A precious stone in the 2d row in the breastplate of the high-priest (Ex. xxviii. 18).

EM'ERODS. Some kind of tumors which afflicted the Philistines, because of their want of respect for the ark of the covenant (1 Sam. v. 6).

E'MIM (Heb. *terrors*). Moabite name for a race of giants or strong men, on the east of the Dead Sea (Gen. xiv. 5; Deut. ii. 10).

EMMAN'UEL. IMMANUEL (Matt. i. 23).

EMMĀ'US. Now called Kuriet El Enab, 7¼ ms. west of Jerusalem. Josephus mentions it (Wars vii. 6, 9). Jerome mistook Nicopolis, the present Amwas, for this place, a proof of how early some scripture localities of the N. T. times were lost.— 2. In the plain of Philistia; fortified by Bacchides (Ant. xiii. 1, 3; Macc. ix. 50). Destroyed A. D. 4, by the Romans. Rebuilt A. D. 220, and called Nicopolis.—3. A village on the shore of the Sea of Galilee, S. of Tiberias, the same as Hammath (*hot baths*).

EM'MOR. See HAMOR (Acts vii. 16).

EN. AIN Hebrew for *fountain*. The word means *an eye*. See AIN.

ENĀ JIM. ENAM. An open place (Gen. xxxviii. 14, 21), in the gate of Enam.

E'NAM (*double spring*). Judah, in the Shefelah (Josh. xv. 34). The residence of Tamar. (Gen. xxxviii. 14).

Ē NAN (*having eyes or fountains*). Ahiram Ben Enan was a chief of the tribe of Naphtali, at Sinai (Num. i. 15).

ENCAMPMENT (Heb. MAHANEH). The camp of the Lord's host, with the Lord himself symbolically resident among them. The whole camp was a sacred place, and all impurities both actual and ceremonial must go outside of its limits (Deut. xxiii. 14). Criminals were also executed outside, as also of the cities. It was managed and guarded in a military style, with sentinels, etc. See WILDERNESS OF THE WANDERING. The modern Bedawins now camp in any fit place, near water, if possible. The Sheikh marks his place by his spear standing in front of his tent. The walled cities were fortified camps.

above the level plain; the water is sweet and warm (81° Fahr.). Ruins of the ancient city are scattered tered over the hills and plain. The soil is rich and fertile, and the variety of trees even now produced gives evidence of its ancient fruitfulness. The vineyards mentioned in Cant. i. 14, are still represented by fine vines. Its history is 4000 years, but may be told in a few words. The Amorites dwelt here (Gen. xiv. 7; 2 Chr. xx. 2). David cut off the skirt of Saul's robe in a cave at E. (1 Sam. xxiv. 1-4). The early Israelites of Palestine, the Essenes, had their chief seat at Engedi, and not far from there is the convent of Mar Saba (Saint Saba), in the gorge of Kidron.

		EAST.		
FIRST DIVISION.		JUDAH.		186,400.
	ISSACHAR. 54,400.	JUDAH, 74,600.	ZEBULON. 57,400.	
	NAPHTALI, 53,400.	MOSES. Priests. AARON	SIMEON. 59,300.	
NORTH. DAN.	DAN, 62,700.	MERARITES, 3,200. Court of the Tabernacle. KOHATHITES, 2,750.	REUBEN, 46,500.	SOUTH. REUBEN.
FOURTH DIVISION.	ASHER, 41,500.	GERSHONITES, 2,650.	GAD, 45,650.	SECOND DIVISION.
	BENJAMIN, 35,400.	EPHRAIM, 40,500.	MANASSEH, 32,200.	
THIRD DIVISION.		EPHRAIM. WEST.		108,100.

ENCHANTMENTS. Several Hebrew words are so translated.—1. LATIM (Ex. vii. 11); secret arts.—2. CESHAPHIM (2 K. ix. 22); witchcrafts, sorceries, in Isaiah xlvii. 9, meaning muttered spells.—3. LAHASH (Eccl. x. 11); ear-rings, amulets in Is. iii. 20. Used in the charming of serpents.—4. NAHASH (Num. xxiii. 23), augury, omen.—5. HEBER, spell. See MAGIC, DIVINATION.

EN'DOR (spring of Dor). In Issacher, but belonging to Manasseh (Josh. xvii. 11). The great victory over Sisera and Jabin (Ps. lxxxiii. 9, 10). Saul visited the witch (1 Sam. xxviii. 7). Now a little village at the N. of Jebel Duhy, Little Hermon. The rocks around are full of caves.

ENE'AS. A paralytic healed by Peter at Lydda (Acts ix. 33, 34).

ENEGLA'IM (spring of two heifers). On the shore of the Dead Sea. Lost. (Ez. xlvii. 10).

ENGANNIM (spring of gardens). Judah, in the Shefelah near Zanoah (Josh. xv. 34).—2. Issachar (Josh. xix. 21; Lev. xxi. 29). Now Jenin, at the head of the plain of Esdraelon (Jos. Ant. xx. 6, § 1). The spring and orchards are still famous.

ENGE'DI (spring of the kid). In the wilderness of Judah, on the W. shore of the Dead Sea (Josh. xv. 62). HAZEZON TAMAR (the pruning of the palms) was its original name, from its palm-groves (2 Chr. xx. 2; Eccl xxiv. 14; Jos. Ant. ix. 1, § 2). A rich plain half a mile square, gently sloping up from the water to the base of the mts., watered by a fountain a mile from the sea, up a ravine 400 ft

EN'GINE. In military affairs, machines for throwing things, first mentioned of Uzziah's time (2 Chr. xxvi. 15). They were: 1. balista, cross-bows, for arrows or stones, and catapulta, the same, much larger,—2. the battering ram (see cut on page 25), for breaking walls (Ez. iv. 2).

ENGRA'VER (harash, in Ex. xxviii. 11, etc.).

SPHINX.

Any worker in wood, stone, or metal. The work was cutting names or devices on rings or seals; as on the high-priest's dress, breast-plate, etc. The art was known among all ancient nations, as evidences from the ruins prove. Many beautiful specimens of engravings on rings, etc., are preserved in the museums of Europe and in the Abbott Egyptian Museum, New York.

ENHAD'DAH (*swift spring*). In Issachar, near ENGANNIM (Josh. xix. 21).

ENHAKKO'RE (*spring of the crier*). The spring which came forth in answer to the call of Samson (Judg. xv. 19). See LEHI.

ENHA'ZOR (*spring of the village*). Naph., a fenced city, near Kedesh (Josh. xix. 37). Lost.

ENGEDI.

ENMISH'PAT (*spring of judgment*), (Gen. xiv. 7). KADESH.

E'NOCH. HENOC (*teacher*). Eldest son of Cain, who named his city after himself (Gen. iv. 17).—2. The son of Jared, and father of Methuselah, the seventh from Adam (Jude, 14). Enoch was a type of perfected humanity, "a man raised to heaven by pleasing God, while angels fell to earth by transgression." Some have thought Enoch was the

ROMAN STANDARDS.

god of the new year, because he lived 365 years, and did not die. The phrase "walked with God," is also used of Noah (Gen. vi. 9), and of Abraham (xvii. 1), and of others, as well as of people, and means a spiritual, upright life. The Greek and Latin fathers used the instances of Enoch and Elijah as evidences of the possibility of a resurrection and a future life. He is supposed to be one of the two witnesses alluded to in Rev. xi. 3. He is called Edris (*the learned*) in the Koran, and is credited with inventing the art of writing and the sciences of arithmetic and astronomy. See HISTORY OF THE BOOKS for the Book of Enoch.—3. Third son of Midian (1 Chr. i. 33, Henoch).—4. Son of Reuben (Gen. xlvi. 9, Hanoch), from whom came the Hanochites (Num. xxvi. 5).—5. In 2 Esd. vi. 49, 51, Enoch is found in the Latin and English versions, and Behemoth in the Æthiopic.

E'NON (John iii. 23). AENON.

E'NOS (Heb. ENOSH, *man*). Son of Seth (Gen. iv. 26). Enosh (1 Chr. i. 1).

ENRIM'MON. Reinhabited after the return from the Bab. Cap. (Neh. xi. 29). Probably Ain and Rimmon (Josh. xv. 32).

EN-ROGEL (*fuller's fountain*). Spring near Jerusalem, at the junction of the valleys of Jehoshaphat and Hinnom (Josh. xv. 7; xviii. 16). Jonathan and Ahimaaz hid here (2 Sam. xvii. 17). Adonijah held a feast here, by the stone Zoheleth; his first and last attempt on the crown (1 K. i. 9). Josephus (Ant. vii. 14, § 4; ix. 10, § 4) mentions the royal gardens. The well is 125 feet deep, walled up square with large stones, and arched over. It overflows underground most of the time, over the top only a little while in the rainy season. "It is a singular work of ancient enterprise" (Thomson, *Land and Book*, ii. 528).

ENSHE'MESH (*spring of the sun*). Landmark on the N. of Judah (Josh. xv. 7). The only spring now known east of the Mt. of Olives is the Well of the Apostles, so called because it is supposed that Christ and his apostles rested there often, about a mile east of Bethany. The sun shines on the spring all day long.

EN'SIGN. STANDARD. Several Hebrew words are so rendered: NES, an elevated signal, not a military standard, having on it a device, emblem or inscrip-

tion, as "Jehovah nissi" (Ex. xii. 15); the pole on which the brazen serpent was lifted is so called (Num. xxi. 8), which was an ensign of deliverance. DEGEL was the standard given to each of the four divisions (see ENCAMPMENT) of the Israelite host in the Wilderness (Num. i. 52). The Egyptia banners had on them sacred emblems—

EGYPTIAN STANDARDS.

as a beast, an animal, a bird, or the king's name. The Hebrew banners are described by the Rabbis as follows: Judah, a lion; Reuben, a man; Ephraim, an ox; Dan, an eagle. It is more probable that each tribe and each company in a tribe had a particular ensign for its own use—as a figure or inscription. The Romans made images on their standards of certain gods and of deified men, which they worshiped. The Assyrian standards were very similar to those represented here as Egyptian and Roman.

ENSUE'. In 1 Pet. iii. 11, ensue means to follow after and overtake—a meaning now obsolete.

ENTAP'PUAH (*citron-spring*). Boundary of Manasseh, near Shechem (Josh. xvii. 7). TAP-PUAH.

ENTRE'AT. INTREAT. TREAT. To be entreated means in Scripture to be persuaded, as in 1 Chr. v. 20; Is. xix. 22, etc.

EPŒN'ETUS. EPENETUS (*praised*). Disciple at Rome, mentioned in Rom. xvi. 5, as the first fruit of Asia unto Christ. Tradition says he was first bishop of Carthage.

EP'APHRAS (*lovely*). Paul's assistant at Colossæ (Col. i. 7), of which he was a native, and very kind to Paul, who was in prison in Rome.

EPAPHRODI'TUS (*favored by Venus*). A disciple at Philippi, who was sent to Paul at Rome with contributions (Phil. ii. 25). He preached in North Greece and Macedonia.

E'PHAH (*darkness*). Son of Midian (Gen. xxv. 4; Is. xl. 6, 7). There is a town in Arabia, near Bilbeys, called Gheyfer (jä-fĕr), which is supposed to be Ephah.—2. Woman in Caleb's family, in the line of Judah (1 Chr. ii. 46).—3. Son of Jahdai, in the same line (ib. 47).—4. See MEASURES.

E'PHAI (*weary*). OPHAI (*languid*). Of Netophah, whose sons were officers left in Judah during the Captivity (Jer. xl. 8). Killed with Gedaliah by Ishmael (xli. 3—compare xl. 13). Ishmael 6.

E'PHER (*calf*). Son of Midian (Gen. xxv. 4). The Arabs have a town named Ghifr (*jiffer*, a calf), but trace to Amalek and Ishmael, and not to Midian.—2. Son of Ezra, of Judah, in Caleb's line (1 Chr. iv. 17).—3. Chief in Manasseh, E. of Jordan (1 Chr. v. 24).

E'PHES-DAM'MIM (*end of blood*). Between Socoh and Azekah, where the Philistines encamped the evening before David slew Goliath (1 Sam. xvii. 1). PAS-DAMMIM (1 Chr. xi. 13).

EPHE'SIAN. Trophimus, the Ephesian (Acts xxi. 29).

EPHE'SIANS. Citizens of Ephesus, who worshiped Diana (Acts xix. 28, etc.). The Epistle to the Ephesians is described in the HISTORY OF THE BOOKS.

EPH'ESUS. About the middle of the W. of Asia Minor, opposite the Island of Samos. The capital of Asia, whose province under the Romans included only the W. part of the peninsula. Built partly on hills and partly on the plain. The climate was excellent. The country around the city was very fertile, and its position most convenient for trafile with other regions of the Levant. In the time of Augustus it was the great metropolis of this section of Asia Minor. Paul's journeys indicate the facilities for travel by sea and land.

The harbor was elaborately constructed, and at its head stood the famous temple of Diana. The first temple was burnt on the night Alexander the Great was born; the second, which stood in Paul's time, was built by the contributions of all Asia: 425 feet long by 220 wide, with 127 marble columns, each 60 feet high. Built in the Ionic order, perfected here first. The magnificence of this great temple was a proverb throughout the world. Here the people held an "uproar" against Paul for two hours (Acts xix. 23. See PAUL). Public games were held in the month of May, which was

SITE OF EPHESUS.

sacred to Diana, and Paul was probably there at that time (1 Cor. xvi. 8). Plutarch mentions the charms and amulets which were made and sold here, and accounts of faith in their value reach as far down as the 6th century. The coins of E. have many allusions to the Diana worship. Josephus says the Jews were numerous there. Disciples of

John the Baptist were found here after the ascension of Christ (Acts xviii. 25; xix. 3). Paul established a church here, of which Timothy was at one time the head. It is supposed that St. John the Divine wrote his Gospel and Epistles here; the Apocalypse being written on Patmos. E. was one of the *seven churches*, and is named first; and its attempts to conquer E. were ever made, and Shalmaneser only succeeded through the internal divisions of the kingdom of Samaria (721 B.C. See SHECHEM; SAMARIA).—2. A city on a hill N. E. of Jerusalem, 10 ms. See OPHRAH.—3. A forest E. of Jordan, near Mahanaim, where Absalom was caught by his hair in a tree and killed, when fighting against his father David, the king (2 Sam. xviii. 6).

THEATRE AT EPHESUS.

E'PHRAIN. EPHRON (2 Chr. xiii. 19). Supposed to be Ophrah.

E'PHRAIM, THE GATE OF. See JERUSALEM.

E'PHRAIM, MOUNT, means the whole hill country of the district between Jordan and the plain of Sharon.

E'PHRAIM, THE WOOD OF. EPHRAIM 3.

E'PHRAIMITE. Ephrathite (Judg. xii. 5), of E.

EPH'RATAH, EPH'RATH. The ancient name of Bethlehem. Ephralites, cities of Bethlehem-Judah (Ruth i. 2). The second wife of Caleb, the son of Hezron, mother of Hur, and grandmother of Caleb the spy, was named Ephrath (1 Chr. ii. 19), Ephratah in verse 50. Caleb-ephratah in verse 24.

"candlestick" has been removed surely, for all is desolation now where the city once stood. The fine columns have been carried to other cities, chiefly Constantinople and Italy. Ruins cover the hills and a swamp the plain. There is a tradition that the mother of Jesus was buried here, and also Timothy and St. John.

There is now a railroad from Smyrna to Aidin, with a station near the ruins of Ephesus, called Aysaluk (á-sa-look, *city of the moon*). The whole district covered by the ancient city and suburbs are now desolate. The map was copied from one constructed on the spot by Prof. Eddy, 1870. See LIFE OF PAUL, of JOHN, DIANA.

EPH'LAL (*judgment*). Son of Zabad (1 Chr. ii. 37), in the tribe of Judah.

EPH'OD (*girdled on*). Part of the high-priest's dress—the peculiar badge of his office.

E'PHOD (*oracle-giving*). Father of Hanniel, chief in Manasseh (Num. xxxiv. 23).

E'PHRAIM (*double fruitfulness*). Second son of Joseph by his wife Asenath. Blessed by Jacob above his elder brother, Manasseh (Gen. xlviii.). Joshua, the son of Nun, was of E. The portion of E. in Canaan was 55 ms. from E. to W. and 70 ms. from N. to S. in extent; elevated, hilly, and having the plain of Sharon, a narrow strip, on the W., Esdraelon on the N., and the Jordan valley on the E., in the centre of the country, the whole called Mt. E. (1 Sam. i. 1, vii. 17; 2 Chr. xiii., xv. 8). It had the "precious things of the earth, and the fulness thereof," as blessed by Moses. The finest and most fruitful of all the land. Afterward called Samaria. Its wealth and importance were increased by the presence of the Ark of the Covenant and the Tabernacle at Shiloh within its borders. The people were jealous, and at enmity with the tribe of Judah from the time of David. Very few

E'PHRON (*fawn*). Son of Zohar (Heb. ZOCHAR) a Hittite, who sold the field to Abraham (Gen. xxiii. 8, etc.).

E'PHRON. E. of Jordan, a strong city between Carnaim and Bethshan (1 Macc. v. 46-52; 2 Macc. xvi. 27). Lost.

E'PHRON, MOUNT, Cities of, were landmarks (Josh. xv. 9). Said to be Ain Lifta (Nephtoah), and Kuriet el Enab (Kirjath-Jearim).

EPICU'REANS. Disciples and followers of the philosopher Epicurus (lived B. C. 342-271), who taught at Athens. He tried to find in philosophy a practical guide to happiness. True pleasure, and not absolute truth, was his aim. He endeavored to remove superstitious fears, and made the study

EPHRAIM.

of physics (nature) useful for the good of mankind. Epicurus was a follower of Diogenes Laërtius. His system had degenerated into mere materialism at the time when Paul was at Athens (Acts xvii. 18). The Stoics were their opponents; who were named from a portico (Greek *stoa*) in which the philos-

opher Zeno taught, at Athens, a system of ethics based on *pride*, as Christianity is on humility. This school taught the Fatherhood of God, the common bonds of mankind, and the sovereignty of the soul. Christianity was a practical union of the two schools of Epicureans and Stoics. The same ideas among the Jews produced the sect of Sadducees. The teaching of the Hebrew patriarchs and prophets was independent of any system of philosophy, and it is curious that Greek philosophy arose just after the Hebrew prophets closed their oracles, Malachi being cotemporary with Socrates.

EPIPH'ANES. ANTIOCHUS EPIPHANES (1 Macc. i. x.)

EP IPHI. The 11th month of the Egyptian year, the third of the "season of waters," inundation. Named from the goddess Apapt. The Hebrews derived from this their name Abib, the 1st sacred, and the 7th civil month in their calendar.

EPIS'TLES. See HISTORY OF THE BOOKS.

E'QUAL. Means to make equal in Lam. ii. 13.

ER (*watchful*). First-born of Judah, son of Bath-Shuah, a Canaanite. He married Tamar, who became mother of Pharez and Zarah by Judah. He probably sinned by idolatry (prompted by his wife ?) (Gen. xxxviii. 3-7).—2. In the line of Judah, son of Shelah (1 Chr. iv. 21).—3. Son of Jose, a cotemporary with king Uzziah (Luke iii. 28).

E'RA. CHRONOLOGY. The Era of Jesus Christ is dated four years too late, and was fixed by the Abbot Dionysius Exiguus, in the 6th century, so that the true date would be now not 1871 but 1875.

E'RAN. Son of Shuthelah, and ancestor of the Eranites.

E RANITES. Descendants of Eran (Num. xxvi. 36).

ERASTUS (*beloved*). Chamberlain of Corinth, and a disciple (Rom. xvi. 23). He was with Paul on some of his journeys (Acts xix. 23), and probably settled at Corinth (2 Tim. iv. 20).—2. A deacon in the church at Ephesus. Supposed to be different from No. 1.

E'RECH. Land of Shinar. Built by Nimrod (Gen. x. 10). Now Irak, 43 ms. E. of Babylon. The place seems to have been the metropolis of the Assyrian kings, mounds and the remains of bricks and coffins being found through a wide district. People from this city were transplanted to Samaria by Asnapper (Ezr. iv. 9). See *Rawlinson's Five Great Monarchies*.

E RES. Hebrew word for a species of pine. See CEDAR.

E RI (*watching*.) HERI, HER. Son of Gad (Gen. xlvi. 16).

E RITES. Branch of the tribe of Gad, from Eri (Num. xxvi. 16).

ESA'IAS. The Greek form of the Hebrew Isaiah (ISAIAHU), (Matt. iii. 3, etc).

E'SAR-HAD'DON (*fire-given*). King of Assyria, son of Sennacherib (2 K. xix. 37). He first appears in history B.C. 680, as king, after his father's murder (Is. xxxvii. 38). The monuments exhibit him as one of the most powerful of the Assyrian kings, conquering all Asia, from the Persian Gulf to the mountains in Armenia, and the Mediterranean Sea. He is the only Assyrian king who dwelt (a part of the time) at Babylon, where bricks are found bearing his name. It is while living there (B. C. 680-667), that Manasseh, king of Judah, was brought before him at Babylon (2 Chr. xxxiii. 11). He proved his great clemency by restoring Manasseh to his throne in Jerusalem, and by giving territory on the Persian Gulf to a son of Merodach-Baladan, whom he had conquered, and who submitted to him and became a refugee at his court. He was a builder of great works, such as his palace at Babylon, and three others, in different cities, for himself and his son; and one inscription mentions thirty temples in Assyria and Mesopotamia. These works were ornamented highly with silver and gold. The palace at Nimroud is the best preserved of any. Mr. Layard found its plan to agree quite closely with that of Solomon's palace (1 K. vii. 1-12), but much larger, the great

PLAN OF TEMPLES.

hall being 220 by 100 feet, and the porch 160 by 60. The sculptures were winged bulls, sphinxes and slabs, most of which were almost destroyed by fire. It is believed that Phœnician and Greek artists were employed as assistants on these works. His son, Asshur-banipal, succeeded him (SARDANAPALUS).

ESAU (Heb. ESAV, *hairy*). Oldest son of Isaac, twin of Jacob. The bitter enmity of the two brothers, and the strife between the two nations derived from them, were foreshadowed even in the womb (Gen. xxv. 22 to 27). Esau was a robust, active, real Bedawy, "son of the desert," and was loved for his wild, roaming disposition, but his brother Jacob was more crafty, and, succeeding in buying his birthright for a dinner ("mess of pottage," verse 34), Esau attempted to get from his blind father the blessing be-

longing to the first-born, and which he had sold to Jacob, but Jacob again was too crafty for his brother, and succeeded in deceiving Isaac, and received the blessing. From this time he was called Edom (*red*), which was given to the country that he afterwards lived in. At the age of 40 he married, against the will of his parents, two Canaanite women. Jacob was sent to Padan-aram, out of the way of Esau, who took another wife, Mahalath, his cousin, daughter of Ishmael (xxviii. 8, 9). He then went to Mt. Seir, where he was living when Jacob returned from Padan-aram, and had become rich and powerful. The brothers met on the east of Jordan, when Jacob again acted in a double-faced way, and parted to meet again only at the side of their dead father, twenty years after, at Machpelah. From this time he lived in Mt. Seir, but nothing is recorded of his later history. See EDOM, EDOMITES.

ESCHEW. To flee from, as used in Job i. 1, 8, ii. 3; 1 Pet. iii. 11. Obsolete.

GOLDEN EAGLE.

ESDRAE'LON. The Greek name of Jezreel (Judith iii. 9), the Great Plain of Josephus, the valley of Megiddo. It is very rich in soil, lying on a volcanic basalt, but there is not an inhabited village in its whole extent, which is triangular, 18, 15, by 12 miles, on the three sides. See Map. It is noted for the number and importance of the battles fought on its surface. "Warriors from every nation have pitched their tent in the plain of Esdraelon." The names Deborah, Barak, Gideon, Josiah, Holofernes, Vespasian, the Crusaders, Saracens, Turks, and French, give a hint of the events which have made the valley memorable.

ES'DRAS. The form of Ezra in the Apocrypha. —2. The books of Esdras. See the HISTORY OF THE BOOKS.

E'SEK (*strife*). Well dug in the valley in Gerar (Gen. xxvi. 20) by the herdsmen of Isaac.

ESHBA'AL (*baal's man*). ISHBOSHETH? Fourth son of Saul (1 Chr. viii. 33).

ESH'BAN (*wise hero*). HESHBON. A Horite, son of Dishon (Gen. xxxvi. 26).

ESH'COL (*cluster*). Valley N. W. of Hebron, visited by the spies who were sent by Moses from Kadesh Barnea, from which place they brought away a huge cluster of grapes, so remarkable as to name it the valley of the cluster (Num. xiii. 24). The valley was named from Eshcol, the brother of Mamre, the Amorite, in Abraham's time (Gen. xiv. 13, 24).

ESH'EAN. Judah, near Hebron (Josh. xv. 52). Lost.

E'SHEK. A Benjamite, descendant of Saul, founder of a noted family of archers (1 Chr. viii. 39).

ESH'KALONITES. Citizens of Ashkelon (Josh. xiii. 3).

ESH'TAOL. Judah, in the Shefelah, allotted to Dan. The residence, during his youth, of Samson; and here he was buried (Judg. xiii. 25; xvi. 31). Some of the Danites who were sent to look for a new home in the N. were from E. (xviii. 2, 8, 11). Lost. In the time of Jerome it was said to lie between Azotus and Ascalon, and named Astho; and another, named Esthaul, 10 miles N. of Eleutheropolis, probably near the present Yeshua.

ESH'TAULITES. Among the citizens of Kirjath-Jearim (1 Chr. ii. 53).

ESHTEMO'A (*women of note*). Judah, in the mountains (Josh. xv. 50; 1 Chr. vi. 57). Frequented by David (1 Sam. xxx. 28). Now Semua, 7 ms. S. of Hebron. Founded by the descendants of the Egyptian wife of Mered (1 Chr. iv. 17).—2. Name of a person in 1 Chr. iv. 19, as a Maachathite.

ESH'TON (*uxorious*). In the line of Judah (1 Chr. iv. 11).

ES'LI. Son of Naggai, father of Naum (Luke iii. 25).

ESO'RA. Perhaps Hazor or Zorah. Fortified by the Jews on the approach of Holofernes (Jud. iv. 4). Possibly Bethhoron.

ESPOU'SAL. MARRIAGE.

ES'ROM. In the genealogy of Jesus (Matt. i. 8; Luke iii. 33). HEZRON.

ESSE'NES. Josephus says they combined the ascetic virtues of the Pythagoreans and Stoics with a spiritual knowledge of the Divine Law, and arose about 200 B. C. Their chief city was Engedi (Pliny). The name is supposed to mean *silent, mysterious* or *pious* (Dr. Ginsburg). The origin of the party was rather in a certain tendency of religious thought among all classes towards an ideal purity. Special doctrines had for their object a life of absolute purity and divine communion. Next to God, Moses was honored; the Sabbath was carefully kept; food was eaten only when prepared by their own members, and never cooked on the Sabbath; and they practiced self-denial, temperance, and agriculture. Slavery, war, and commerce were forbidden. They were very regular in their devotions; before sunrise they began their prayer and praise; said grace before and after meals; ate from only one kind of food at a meal; disallowed oaths, holding truth to be sacred; held all things in common. Their system was a compound of mystical and ceremonial elements. The applicant for membership was obliged to live a year outside of the order, but keeping its rules (?), having received as badges an ax, a white apron, and a white dress. One year more he would share in the ablutions but not in the meals. After two more years he was admitted to full membership, solemnly binding himself to piety to God, justice to men, to hate the wicked, assist the righteous, injure

no one, speak the truth, avoid robbery and theft, and keep the rules and secrets of the society. Some of their rules were: 1. To bathe, if touched by a stranger, or a lower grade of their own order, and before and after meals, and other natural acts; not to spit in an assembly, and if so not on the *right side;* the social meal was a sacrament. 1. Baptisms produced bodily purity, which led to 2. celibacy, and 3, spiritual purity, and 4, to a meek and lowly spirit, banishing all anger and malice, thus reaching 5, holiness, arriving at 6, a state wherein he is a Holy Temple for the Holy Spirit, and could prophesy, and advancing to 7, could perform miraculous cures, raising the dead, attaining finally to the lofty state of Elias, the forerunner of the Messiah, and no longer subject to death.

Jesus alludes to the Essenes in Matt. v. 34, "swear not at all," and in xix. 12, "who abstain from marriage for the kingdom of heaven's sake," and Paul in 1 Cor. vii., which is hardly intelligible without a knowledge of the tenets of the Essenes, and by James in v. 12, and the first church held all things in common as they did (Acts iv. 32–34). Their number was never larger than 4000. See Josephus and Eusebius. They disappeared after the destruction of Jerusalem, and are not heard of again, although various orders of monks follow more or less strictly their rules and practices.

ES'THER (*the planet* VENUS, ASTER, ASTARTE, ASHTORETH, meaning *good fortune*). The Persian form of the Hebrew name HADASSAH (*a myrtle*). She was daughter of Abihail, son of Shimei, a Benjamite, cousin of Mordecai. Her parents did not return from captivity, but died, leaving her in care of her relative (cousin?) Mordecai. The Persian king having divorced his queen, Vashti (*a beauty*), for contempt, the royal choice fell on Esther, after passing many others by. In this position she delivered her people, who were still very numerous, from a threatened calamity, which was the origin of the yearly feast of Purim. See HISTORY OF THE Books, Esther and Apocrypha.

E'TAM (*place of wild beasts*). Simeon (1 Chr. iv. 32).—2. Judah; fortified and garrisoned by Rehoboam (2 Chr. xi. 6). Near Bethlehem and Tekoah.

E'TAM (*the rock*). To which Samson retired after his slaughter of the Philistines (Judg. xv. 8, 11). Probably in the valley of Urtas.

ETER'NAL (Heb. OLAM, *hidden, time long past,* and of future *to the end*).

ETER'NITY (Heb. AD), only once, in Is. lvii. 15, meaning duration in time.

E'THAN (*limit of the sea*). Station in the Exodus, near the Red Sea, east.

E'THAN (*firmness*) 1. The Ezrahite, son of Mahol, a wise man, only excelled by Solomon (1 K.iv. 31; Ps. lxxxix).—2. Son of Kish, a Levite in David's time (1 Chr. vi. 44). Played cymbals with Heman and Asaph (xv. 17, 19).—3. Levite ancestor of Asaph, the singer (1 Chr. vi. 42).

ETH'ANIM. MONTH.

ETH'BAAL (*with Baal*). A king of Sidon, father of Jezebel (1 K. xvi. 31). Josephus said he was king of Tyre and Sidon. Menander says that Ithobalus, a priest of Astarte, killed Pheles and usurped the throne, reigning 32 years, B. C. 940–908.

E'THER (*abundance*). Judah, in the Shefelah (Josh xv. 42), in Simeon. Now Attarah near Gaza.

ETHIO'PIA (*burnt*). The country called in Hebrew CUSH. S. of Egypt, from Syene (Ez. xxix. 10). Lybian desert W., Abyssinian highland E. and S. The Hebrews traded with E. (Is. xlv. 14) in ebony, ivory, frankincense, gold and precious stones (Job xxviii. 19; Jos. Ant. viii. 6, § 5). Settled by a Hamitic race (Gen. x. 6), dark (Jer. xiii. 23), men of stature (Is. xviii. 2), and fine-looking (xxxviii. 7). The Sabeans were the most noted tribe. There are ruins of many temples in E. built during the reigns of the Hyksos kings of Egypt. Queen Candace is mentioned in Acts viii. 27.

The official title of the queen was CANDACE, and there was a line of queens who governed the country about the time of Christ, who successfully resisted even the Romans.

ETHIOPIANS.

ETHIO'PIAN (Heb. CUSHITE). Black man (Jer. xiii. 23). Zereh (2 Chr. xiv. 9) and Ebed-melech (Jer. xxxviii. 7, etc.), were Ethiopians.

ETHIO'PIAN WOMAN. Wife of Moses. A CUSHITE (Num. xii. 1). She is also said to be a Midianite, and so supposed to be a second wife.

ETHIO'PIANS. In several passages meaning CUSHITES.

ETHIO'PIC LANGUAGE. See LANGUAGE.

ETHIO'PIC VERSION. See HISTORY OF THE Books, page 4.

ETH'NAN (*gift*). Son of Hela, the wife of Ashur (1 Chr. iv. 7).

ETH'NI (*giving*). Ancestor of Asaph (1 Chr. vi. 41).

EUBU'LUS (*prudent*). Disciple at Rome (2 Tim. iv. 21).

EUER'GETES (*benefactor*). Title of honor among the Greeks. Two of the Ptolemies were so honored—Ptolemy III and VII.

EUME'NES (*friendly*). Eumenes II, king of Pergamus, succeeded his father, Attalus I, B. C. 197. He served the Romans against the Greeks in the battle of Magnesia (B. C. 190), for which he was rewarded with the provinces of Mysia, Lydia, Ionia, Phrygia, Lycaonia and Thracian Chersonese. Died probably B. C. 159 (1 Macc. viii. 8).

EU'NICE (*victorious*). Mother of Timothy (2 Tim. i. 5); a disciple of pure faith (Acts xvi. 1).

EU'NUCH (Heb. SARUS). Officer, chamberlain. The word indicates the incapacity which certain mutilation produces—a practice contrary to the law in Deut. xxiii. 1. The origin of the custom is ascribed to Queen Semiramis, but is probably as old as Eastern despotism itself, which delights in servants who excite no jealousy. It is supposed that the prophet Daniel and his companions were so treated, because it was so prophesied (2 K. xx. 17). The ETHIOPIAN EUNUCH was probably an officer of the queen, perhaps a Jew.

INK BOTTLE.

EUŌ'DIA. EUŌ'DIAS (*good journey*). Disciple, a woman of Philippi (Phil. iv. 2).

EUPHRĀ'TES (*the good river*). Now called Frat. Called in Scripture *the river*. The largest, longest, and most important river in W. Asia. Rises in the mts. of Armenia, near Erzeroum and Mt. Ararat. Of two branches: one is called Frat, and Black River (*Kara su*), and is 400 ms. long; the other, Murad Chai (*chief*), 270 ms. long; and both unite at Kebban Meden, in a stream 360 ft. wide, and from this point to the Persian Gulf it is 1,000 ms., making in all nearly 1,800 ms., 1,200 of which is navigable for steamers. Nebuchadnezzar dug canals to carry the water of the annual inundation across the wide plains of Chaldea. Herodotus describes the river and its traffic (i. 185). First mentioned in Gen. xv. 18, in the description of the promised land (Deut. i. 7, xi. 24; Josh i. 4). Fulfilled partially by Reuben (1 Chr. v. 9), and completely by David (Ps. cxxxvii. 1).

EUPŎL'EMUS (*good warrior*). Son of John the son of Accos, Koz (Neh. iii. 4, etc.). Envoy sent to Rome by Judas, about B. C. 161 (1 Macc. viii. 17). He was a well known historian, mentioned by Eusebius and Josephus.

EUROC'LYDON. Name of a wind from a certain quarter (Acts xxvii. 14). See PAUL.

EUTY'CHUS (*fortunate*). The youth who was resuscitated by Paul after having fallen out of a window at Troas (Acts xx. 9).

EVAN'GELIST (*publisher of glad tidings*). An order of men in the Christian Church. They were not attached to any particular locality, but worked wherever there was a field, by preaching or writing. Philip (Acts xxi. 8), and Timothy (2 Tim. iv. 5), and the four, Matthew, Mark, Luke, John are examples.

EVE (Heb. CHAVVAH, *living*). Name of the first woman. It is the feminine form of the noun which means life. There are two accounts of her creation 21 to 25, give the account of Eve's formation out of the rib of Adam. The story—or two stories—may mean simply that God holds both man and woman equal in duty and accountability, and one in nature and origin. Eve is not mentioned after the birth of Seth, and her death is not recorded.

E'VENING. CHRONOLOGY.

EV'ER, AND FOREV'ER. Eternal. Eternity. The whole period.

E'VI (*desire*.) Prince of Midian (Num. xxxi. 8).

EV'IDENCE. In Jer. xxxii. 10, etc., means bill of sale, in the prophet's petition; purchase of a field. This symbolic act meant that though desolation must come, God's promise was sure, and houses, fields and vineyards should again be possessed in Palestine by the Hebrews.

EVIL MERO'DACH (*Merodak's fool*). Son and successor of Nebuchadnezzar, B. C. 561; murdered and succeeded by Neriglissar, B. C. 559. Joachin was kindly treated by him (2 K. xxv. 27). The historian Berosus says that his change of policy from severe to mild caused his death by the violent men of his party.

EVIL-SPIRIT. Devil. DEMON.

EXCELLENCY OF CARMEL (Is. xxxv. 2). See CARMEL.

EX'CELLENT. Surpassing (Dan. ii. 31). Excellent glory (2 Peter i. 17). "Most excellent" was a title of rank and honor given to Theophilus (Luke i. 3), and to Felix (Acts xxiii. 23; xxiv. 3); and to Festus (Acts xxvi. 25).

EXCHAN'GERS. Money changers (Matt. xxv. 27).

EXCOMMUNICĀ'TION. Putting one out of church society. The Jews had three modes: 1. For twenty-four minor offenses an offender was under NIDDUI. Keeping a fierce dog, swearing, etc., were instances. The penalty was to abstain

WRITTEN VALLEY. WADY MOKATTEB.

in Genesis. 1. Gen. i 27: "So God created man in his own image, in the image of God created he him; male and female created he them;" 2. ii. 18: "And the Lord God said 'It is not good that the man should be alone,'" (his creation is noticed in verse 7), "'I will make him a help meet for him.'" Then, in verses 19 and 20, is the account of the creation of the beasts, and that among them there was not found a help meet for Adam. Verses from the use of the bath, the razor, wine, etc., and to keep at 6 feet (4 cubits) distance from every one. He could not worship in the temple in the usual manner, and this lasted 30 days.—2. The second was CHEREM. He could not teach or be taught to work for or buy any object not intended for food. —3. The SHAMMATHA, an entire cutting off from the congregation. Moses did not make this law, but the natural right of societies for self-preserva-

tion gave rise to it. The cases in Num. xvi. (of Korah, etc.), Judg. v. 23 (Meroz), Ezr. vii. 26; x. 8; Ex. xxx. 33, and Lev. xiii. 46; xvii. 4, are precedents. One instance is recorded in the N. T., John ix., of the young man who confessed that Jesus was the Christ. The fear of the result prevented some from such a confession (xii. 42). The blessing in Luke vi. 22, refers to the three forms of this law. The excommunication founded by Jesus was to be executed only after due trial, and a settled contempt for the church in refusing to atone for a trespass which the person has committed (Matt. xviii. 15-18). The final act of exclusion was to be done only after two warnings. Paul commanded the same (1 Tim. i. 20; 1 Cor. v. 11 Tit. iii. 10), and frequently used the power. Restoration was possible, and is urged in 2 Cor. ii. 6. The censure of the church was not to include enmity, curses, and persecution, as among some sects, but rather to look upon the excluded "as a heathen and a publican," that may be brought in again. It is a spiritual penalty, not physical, separating from the communion of the church, aiming to benefit the person and the church, by excluding heresy, immorality, and only put in force by the authority of the church at large (by a vote?) and the sanction of the highest officer, whose sentence was declared in the congregation to which the offender belonged; and that penitence is a condition of restoration, which is to be as public as the exclusion.

EXECUTIONER (Heb. TABBACH, *slaughter*). The duties were both those of an executioner and of the leader of the body-guard of the king, as in Egypt (Gen. xxxvii. 36), whose official residence was the prison. It was a post of high dignity. The Septuagint says Potiphar was *chief-cook*.

EXILE. CAPTIVITY.

EXODUS (*going out*). For the book, see HISTORY OF THE BOOKS. The date of the Exodus of the Hebrews from Egypt, led by Moses, is fixed by different writers: as Poole, B. C. 1652, Hales, 1648, Usher, 1491, Bunsen, 1320. The patriarchal institution ended and the era of the Law began at the Exodus—the family had become a nation. The departure was begun at Raamses (Rameses) in the early morning of the 15th of Nisan, which was from that time called the first month. Three stages brought them to the Red Sea, where they were overtaken by Pharaoh and delivered by Moses, as celebrated in the songs of Moses and Miriam (Ex. xv.).

The great difficulty in tracing the route of the Israelites from Egypt to Canaan has called out a large number of travelers in our day, who have minutely examined the district (or a part of it, omitting the region of the 38 years wandering, because there are no records from which to form a base of exploration), and from their researches it is "possible by the internal evidence of the country itself to lay down not indeed the actual route of the Israelites in every stage, but in almost all cases, and in some cases the very spots themselves."

The question of the passage of the Red Sea is referred to MIRACLES.

ETHAM was a district on both sides of the N. end of the Red Sea. The place of crossing might have been anywhere between Suez and Jebel Atakah, which is a steep, high promontory standing out into very deep water.

SHUR (*wall*) is a name for the whole desert from Suez to Beersheba, N. of the plain Er Ramleh, also called PARAN. The first water found was at MARAH (*bitter*), and the rest at ELIM (*stags*,) where there were twelve fountains, and a kind of desert paradise, among a grove of palm trees. *Wady Ghurundel* has several fine fountains, a perennial stream, and more trees, shrubs and bushes than any other place in the desert. Here the mountain district begins. The next camp was by the Red Sea, where, in a wild and lonely plain, there is a sublime view of Sinai's granite peaks on one side, and the blue sea on the other.

The WILDERNESS OF SIN is a continuation of

MAP OF SINAI.

this valley on the south, widening into the broadest plain in the whole region. Here they first murmured, and the quails were sent in answer to their cry, and the first fall of manna. DOPHKA and ALUSH were probably in the same plain. REPHIDIM (*supports*) is located in Wady esh Sheikh, the most spacious valley in this region, and the most fertile. Here the people found no water to drink, and Moses brought water out of a rock (Ex. xvii. 5, 6). The Amalekites attacked the people, and were routed. Jethro, Moses' father-in-law, visited him here and counseled him. They next pitched in the plain of *Rahah* (*rest*, Ex. xix.) in front of SINAI. *Jebel Musa* (Mount Moses), the Sinai of recent tradition, is in the midst of a group of mountains, and is 7,000 feet high. Katerin is 8,700, and Om Shomer is 9,300 feet high. On the summit of Jebel Musa is a platform nearly 100 feet across, partly covered with ruins, a chapel at the east end, and a small mosque. *Ras es Sufsafeh* (peak of the willow) is the Sinai of many scholars, because from it the plain can be seen, and every other requirement of the text answered, and every incident illustrated by the features of the

surrounding district. They stayed almost a year at Sinai. While Moses was on the mount, receiving the two tables, Aaron (his brother) made a calf of gold, probably in imitation of the Egyptians. Aaron's sons offered strange fire (Lev. x.), and were destroyed, and the second passover was held.

On leaving Sinai a certain order of march and of camping was adopted (Num. x.), and Hobab was engaged as a guide, to be unto them "instead of eyes" (ver. 31), as is the custom now in crossing the desert. From Sinai to Kadesh the route cannot be clearly laid down. After three days they pitched in Paran, at a place afterwards called TABERAH (*burning*, Num. xi. 3). Quails were sent here (ver. 31), the people suffered from a plague after eating them, and the place was named a second time KIBROTH-HATTAAVAH (*graves of lust*, ver. 33). The next station, HAZEROTH, has been identified with *Ain Hudherah*, a little fountain in a wild, dreary waste, among naked hills, 40 miles from Sinai. The place was noted for the foolish rebellion of Miriam and Aaron (xii.). The fountain of *El Ain*, north of *Hudherah*, is the most important watering-place in the district. The next station that can be located is EZION-GEBER, at the head of the Gulf of Akabah. Between this station and Kadesh, in the *Arabah*, there were many stations, and, as appears from the two accounts in Num. xxxiii. and in Deut. ii. 8, x. 6, they wandered up and down the valley several times.

KADESH (*holy*), next to Sinai, was the most important of all the resting-places in the wilderness. From here the twelve spies were sent into the promised land, and from Kadesh the rebellious people were turned back into the wilderness by the way of the Red Sea (Deut. i. 40) to wander for 38 years. And when they attempted to go up (by the pass Es Sufah) against the command of the Lord, they were defeated at Hormah with disgrace and slaughter (Num. xiv. 40).

Of the "great and terrible wilderness" of the wandering not one station is recorded, nor even a hint of its locality, and the only events noticed are (besides the ceremonial law) the execution of the man who gathered sticks on the Sabbath day (Num. xv.), the rebellion of Korah (xvi.), and (either during that time or soon after) the writing of the ninetieth Psalm by Moses. The great desert from Akabah to Gaza, is now called Et Tyh (the wandering), and it may be the very region; but having no names to locate or compare, there is nothing left us but conjecture.

HOUSE IN DAMASCUS.

They visited Kadesh a second time, where Miriam, the sister of Moses, died and was buried (Num. xx. 1). Moses brought water out of the rock, and the people and their beasts drank. Their flocks had survived through 38 years. Then they sent messengers to the king of Edom, asking permission to pass through his country, and making the fairest proposals, but they were denied their request (xx. 14).

They then left Kadesh and moved to Mt. Hor, where their first high-priest, Aaron, died and was buried, and Eleazar his son was invested with the "holy garments" and the office of his father. See AARON.

The next place that is identified is the pass through the east wall of the Arabah, up into the Arabian desert—*Wady Ithm*—by the way of the Red Sea (to compass the land of Edom, xxi. 4). Here the fiery serpents were sent, killing many; and the brazen serpent was set up, which became a type of the greater salvation. IJE ABARIM was reached, and then the willow brook (ZERED), and soon also the ARNON, and they were out of the desert. Sihon, king of the Amorites, opposed their advance, and Israel smote him, and possessed his land from the Arnon to the Jabbok. They next conquered Og, the king of BASHAN. His "giant cities" are still standing, deserted but not ruined, all over the vast plain of the *Hauran*. The king of *Moab* sent the prophet Baalam to curse Israel as they were encamped in the plains of Moab, and he blessed them, but laid a snare which caught them, and caused the loss of thousands of lives (xxxi. 16).

INTERIOR OF HOUSE.

Moses numbered the people in the plain of Moab, and found 601,730 men above the age of 20 (being only 1820 less than the number at Sinai, 39 years before), and of all these only three were among those who came out of Egypt, all the rest having fallen in the desert (Num. xiv. 29), leaving only Moses, Caleb and Joshua. After looking at the land from the hights of Nebo, Moses died, and was buried (by the Lord), "but no man knoweth of his sepulchre" (Deut. xxxiv. 6). With his death the wanderings ended.

EX'ORCISM. The formal ejection of evil spirits from persons or places. Those who do this are called EXORCISTS. This pretense is usually accompanied with incantations and magical arts of various kinds, and was common to all nations of antiquity (Jos. Ant. viii. 2, 5, Wars, vii. 6, 3). Jesus implied that such a power did exist, and might be used after peculiar preparation (Matt. xii. 27; Luke ix. 49). There was an order of Exorcists in the Christian church in the 3d century, which led to a great increase of superstition, fraud, and imposture. Some introduced forms of exorcism into baptism, saying, "as the soul before baptism is in bondage to the devil, so at baptism it should be formally released from the evil spirit." The priest was instructed to breathe three times on the face of the subject, and say, Depart from him, foul spirit—give place to the Holy Spirit, the Paraclete. Then another breathing on the face, with the words, Receive the Holy Spirit. The order still is in the Roman ritual. It was originally practiced by the Lutherans, but it is now disused. John wrote his Gospel in Asia, where medical science was advanced, and he seems to have known that the diseases attributed to demons were merely natural

EXPIATION

diseases, for he nowhere mentions possessions of evil spirits, except as being spoken of by Jews, whom he is reporting.

EXPIA'TION. Sacrifice. DAY OF ATONEMENT.

EYE (Heb. AYIN). Used as a symbol of many objects and ideas. Among the Hebrews a few uses were: 1. A *fountain*, or *spring* (AIN). 2. Color (Num. xi. 7; Prov. xxiii. 31). 3. Face; as in eye to eye (face to face), (Num. xiv. 14). 4. Look, as in Cant. iv. 9. 5. "In the eyes," means in his presence, or in his judgment (Gen. xix. 8, xxix. 20; 2 Sam. x. 3). 6. "To set eyes on one," is to look with favor (Job xxiv. 23), and also to express anger (Amos ix. 8). 7. Evil eye (Matt. xx. 15); wanton eyes, etc. In Zech. iv. 10, God's angels are "his eyes," and in Persia the ministers of state are "the king's eyes." In the East servants watch the hands of their master, receiving orders and directions by motion of the hand. PAINTING THE EYES is an ancient practice among Orientals, and referred to in 2 K. ix. 30, where Jezebel is spoken of as "painting her eyes," not "face," in Jer. iv. 30, where "rending the face," means "painting the eyes," and by Ezekiel in xxiii. 40. Lane says, of painting eyes: "Their charming effect is much hightened by the concealment of the other features (however pleasing they may be) and is rendered still more striking by a practice, universal among the females of the higher and middle classes, and very common among those of the lower orders, which is, blackening the edge of the eyelids, both above and below the eyes, with a black powder called *kohl*. The paint is made by burning a resin and catching the smoke on glass or any hard substance. Almond shells also make good black smoke. The black is moistened with rose-water. The ancient sculptures show the antiquity of the practice.

EZ. Hebrew word for she-goat, and in some passages also he-goat.

ESBA'I (*shining*). Father of Naarai, one of David's chiefs (1 Chr. xi. 37).

EZ'BON (*working*). 1. Son of Gad (Gen. xlvi. 16); OZNI.—2. Son of Bela (1 Chr. vii. 7).

EZE'KIEL. (Heb. YEHEZKEL, *God will strengthen*). One of the four greater prophets. Son of Buzi, a priest, and carefully educated. We know that he was in captivity because his prophesy is dated on the banks of the river Chebar, in the 5th year of Jehoiachin's captivity. Josephus gives other particulars. His age is not known. It is supposed, from several concurring allusions in his writings, that he was twenty-five when carried to Assyria a captive, and thirty at the time he wrote his first prophesy. He was energetic, earnest, spiritually minded. He prophesied twenty years, B. C. 595-575, ending with the 14th year after the last deportation from Judæa. The first 8 years were cotemporary with Jeremiah. See HISTORY OF THE BOOKS, for the BOOK OF EZEKIEL.

E'ZEL. (1 Sam. xx. 19). Where David parted from Jonathan.

E'ZEM. Simeon (1 Chr. iv. 29; Josh. xix. 3).

E'ZER (*treasure*). 1. Horite duke, in the line of Seir (Gen. xxxvi. 21; 1 Chr. i. 42; Ezar in 38).—2. Father of Hushah, in the line of Judah (1 Chr. iv. 4).—3. Son of Ephraim (ib. vii. 2).—4. Gadite, who joined David (ib. xii. 9).—5. Levite, who repaired the wall under Nehemiah (Neh. iii. 19).—6. Priest, assisting Nehemiah (xii. 42).

E'ZION-GE'BER (*giant's backbone*). At the head of the eastern arm of the Red Sea. Now Akabah (Num. xxxiii. 35; Deut. ii. 8; 1 K. ix. 26, xxii. 48; 2 Chr. viii. 17). Station of the Exodus. Port for Solomon's fleet. Jehoshaphat's fleet was broken here (2 Chr. xx. 37).

EZ'NITE (Heb. EZNI). Adine, the Eznite; also called Josheb-bassebet, the Tachmonite (2 Sam. xxiii. 8).

EZRA (*help*). 1. In the line of Judah (1 Chr. iv. 17).—2. The famous Scribe and Priest (Esdras in the Apocrypha), son of Seraiah 7 and descendant of Hilkiah 2, high priest in Josiah's reign (Ezra vii. 1). His history is given partly in Ezra vii. to x. and in Nehemiah vii., xii. 26, 36. His narrative includes 80 years, during which period, in Persia there were Cyrus, Cambyses, Smerdis, Darius Hystaspis, Xerxes and Artaxerxes Longimanus. The last named gave Ezra men, money and letters of power, and permission to return and rebuild the house at Jerusalem.

He collected and revised the books of the O. T. Tradition says he died at Babylon (or Zamzumu on the Tigris), aged 120. A tomb is shown as his, 20 ms. above the junction of the Euphrates and Tigris.

The works credited to him are: 1. Founding the

PEREGRINE FALCON.

Great Synagogue; 2. Forming the Canon of the O. T.; 3. Introduction and use of the Chaldee instead of the Old Hebrew letters; 4. Authorship of Chronicles, Ezra, Nehemiah, and Esther. Some

also add Ezekiel and Daniel; 5. Institution of Synagogues.—3. Another Ezra was head of one of the 22 courses of priests which returned with Zerubbabel and Joshua.—4. One who assisted at the dedication of the wall (Neh. xii. 33) For Book of Ezra, see HISTORY OF THE BOOKS.

FALLOW-DEER.

EZ'RAHITE (*of Ezra*, or *of Zerah*). A title of Ethan (1 K. iv. 31). There is no reason to believe that the Ethan and Heman, authors or singers, mentioned in the titles of the Psalms, are the same as those in 1 Kings. The two passages, in Chronicles and Kings have become mixed. There was no Heman an Ezrahite.

EZ'RI (*Jehovah's help*). Son of Chelub, over David's farmers (1 Chr. xxvii. 26).

F

FA'BLE. The deliberate choice of statements known to be inventions, which are intended to teach general truth. The Mythus is an unconscious evolution of traditional thought or fancy. The parable assumes that what is related might have been true, and deals with matters of human life, using the acts of men to figure those of a higher order of being. The fable draws its materials from the brute creation and inanimate nature, attributing the qualities of humanity to brutes, trees, &c.

The fable of Jotham about the trees of Shechem is the oldest extant (B. C. 1209), and as beautiful as any made since (Judg. ix. 8–15). The fable in Ezekiel xvii. 1–10, brings before us the lower forms of creation as representatives of human characters and destinies. The great Lokman, the Arabian writer of fables, lived about the time of David (B. C. 1025), Hesiod and Æsop of the Greeks are still later (B. C. 550). The fable exhibits relations between man and man, the parable those between man and God. The fables and inventions alluded to in 1 Tim. iv. 7; Titus, i. 14; 2 Pet. i. 16, were false and weak, probably, and unfit for instruction.

FACE. The most peculiarly indicative part of the human figure. The face is the presence; to stand before the face is to stand in the presence. The face is also the favor—as the prince's face, or favor. To turn away the face is to deny a favor. And the *face of the Lord* means His presence. "No one can see the face of God and live," but Jacob did see it, as he says so, and lived (Gen. xxxii. 30.) Jacob first mentions God's face, at Peniel. God's grace or favor is indicated in such passages as "seeking face," "lift on us the light of thy face," "pour out thine heart like water before the face of the Lord" (Lam ii. 19).

FAIR HA'VENS. Harbor on the south side of Crete, east of Cape Matala, and near Lasea (Acts xxvii. 8). Visited by Paul on his voyage to Rome, A. D. 60. (Gr. *Kaloi Limenes*).

FAIRS (Heb. IZEBONIM). Only in Ezekiel xxvii., where it is found seven times, once translated wares in verse 33. The word means *exchange*, and the sense of the chapter is much improved by this rendering.

FAITH (Heb. EMUN, *faith;* EMUNAH, *faithful;* Greek *elpis; faith* or *hope; pistis, one belief*). Faith is the assent of the mind to the truth of God's revealed will. There are two kinds: 1. *Historical*, which assents to the statements about the life and works of Jesus and the apostles, as historical truths. 2. *Evangelical*, or *saving faith*, is an assent to the truth of revelation, and an entire trust and confidence in God's character, and Christ's teachings, with an unreserved surrender of the will. Jesus Christ is then received into the heart as the Saviour, Prophet, Priest, and King, to be loved and obeyed. This is instrumentally a means of salvation, an essential grace, and a mainspring of Christian life.

FALLOW-DEER (Heb. YACHMUR). Permitted as food by the law, and supplied to Solomon's table (Deut. xiv. 5; 1 K. iv. 23). Two kinds of deer were known to the Hebrews in Palestine. Jacob refers to one in his blessing on Naphtali. Its beauty, speed and agility are frequently used by the poets and prophets. The opening of the xlii. psalm is as beautiful as familiar:

"As the hart pants after the water-brooks,
So does my soul pant for thee, O God."

This was written by David when Saul was hunting him from one place to another like a deer or "a partridge." Figures of deer are sculptured on the ancient monuments in Egypt. The bubale is classed among cattle in the East, and is found from Gibraltar to the Persian Gulf, living in small herds. The fallow-deer is quite rare, a few living around Mt. Tabor, and Lebanon, and is not found in Arabia, but Persia and Armenia are its peculiar home.

FAL'LOW-GROUND. Land that has been left to rest untilled a year or more. Figuratively, backsliding, unfruitful in spiritual things (Hosea x. 12).

FAMIL'IAR-SPIRIT. DIVINATION. MAGIC.

FAM'INE. A scarcety of food. Several are noticed: Gen. xii. 10; xxvi. 1, xlii; Ruth i. 1; 2 K. vi. 25; Acts xi. 27. The most noted is that of seven years in Egypt, by which the whole people were reduced to dependence on the king, when Joseph was prime minister. Famine results from want of rain, visits of locusts and other insects. Amos predicted a spiritual famine (viii. 11).

FAN. 1. A hand machine, like a flat basket, for winnowing grain (Is. xxx. 24).—2. A large fork with a long handle, with which the grain is thrown up against the wind (Jer. xv. 7; Matt. iii. 12).

FAR'THING (Gr. *quadrans, one fourth of the as, or assarion*). Equal to two lepta (mites), about ¾ of a cent. The specimens now extant are very neatly and artistically made, of copper or bronze, except that, like all ancient coin, the edge is unfinished.

ASSARION.

FAST. There is no word in the Pentateuch which means *to fast*. It was a voluntary, not a legal, act. This was probably a silent protest against the tendency to asceticism, so prevalent in the East. The vow of the Nazarite was voluntary, and only included wine and things related to it in origin, and the cases where it was necessary were few. Once a year, at the yearly atonement, the people were called to do what became, after a while, a fast in common terms (Lev. xvi. 29; Acts xxvii. 9), but there is no rule against eating or drinking, while there is against work—it was to be "a Sabbath of rest." Isaiah notices that when the spiritual element declined the ceremonial increased, and fasts became popular as an easy means of atonement (Is. lviii. 5). The true fast is to have a serious and heartfelt sorrow for sin, with earnest strivings to be delivered from it, as Isaiah says. Holiness and mourning are always, in the Hebrew mind, contrasts—opposite states of feeling. The public fast anciently among the Hebrews as well as among the modern Arabs, was a total abstinence from food for twenty-four hours, beginning at sunset. The forty days fast of Moses, Elijah and Jesus were miraculous. Jesus did not institute a fast, except the life-long fast of his disciples, after his death, intimated in Luke v. 34, 35, and directed those who did fast to conceal the fact by washing and dressing as usual, so as not to appear to fast before men and not really fast before God (Matt. vi. 17). The mere fast is no essential part of the gospel plan, although it was practiced by the apostles (1 Cor. vii. 5; Acts xiii. 2, etc.). The real fast is *the sacrifice of the personal will*, which is meant by the term *afflicting the soul* (Is. lviii. 5).

FAT. The fat, as being the choice part of animals, and especially sacred to the Lord, was always to be burned in sacrifice, even when other parts were to be eaten. The fat and the blood were not to be eaten (Lev. iii. 16, 17; vii. 23-27). The term *fat* was applied to the best and most excellent of all things, as the fat of the earth, of the wheat, of the oil, the vine, and even the fat of the mighty. The burning of it in the sacrifice is typical of the offering of what was best and loftiest in Christ's pure humanity. In him alone was there anything strictly good to offer. The offering of his followers is only acceptable through the working of his grace in their hearts (Ps. xii. 1).—2. Fat, for vat, in wine fat.

FATHER. 1. Male parent.—2. Any male ancessor, as Father Abraham.—3. Any man in the position of a father, as Joseph to Pharaoh.—4. The inventor or teacher of an art was called its father, and the father of those who practiced it. "Jubal was the father of all such as handle the harp or organ," that is, he was a teacher of music, if not its inventor; and "Jabal, the father of such as dwell in tents" (Gen. iv. 20, 21).—5. The builder or founder of a city, as Salma, the father of Bethlehem (1 Chr. ii. 51).—6. Any one who makes a thing or produces it, or tells a story, or recites a poem, is called the father of such a thing or poem. The authority of the father was sanctioned by the law of Moses, as standing between God and man. His blessing conferred special benefits, and his curse special injury. His sins affected his children, but they were not liable to punishment for them. The command to honor the parents was the only one to which a promise was attached, in the decalogue, while disrespect and filial insubordination were the worst of crimes.

The principle of respect to age and authority, so universal in the East, is derived from the patriarchal spirit, which still prevails outside of the walled cities, especially among the Arabs.

FATHOM. See MEASURES.

FAT'LING. Fat beast. In good condition.

FANCHION. Falchion, a short crooked sword (Judith xiii. 6; xvi. 9). Cimeter.

FEASTS. See FESTIVALS.

FEET. See WASHING FEET, SANDALS.

FE'LIX. Claudius Antonius Felix was the Roman governor (procurator) of Judæa, from A. D. 53 to 60. He was originally a slave and was freed by the Emperor Claudius. His brother Pallas was also freed by the Emperor's mother Antonia, and deservedly had great influence with Claudius. Felix is said to have ruled Judæa in a mean, cruel, and profligate manner. Under the pretense of destroying robbers he crucified hundreds of good and patriotic Jews. He had trouble with false Messiahs also, followers of a "certain Egyptian magician." He married Drusilla, a Jewess, sister of the younger Agrippa; whom he enticed from her second husband Azizus. He kept Paul in prison two years, hoping that his friends would buy his liberty with a heavy bribe (see PAUL). Felix being recalled to Rome, was succeeded by Festus, and being charged with crimes by citizens of Cæsarea, would have been condemned to death but for the influence in his favor of his brother Pallas.

GATE OF NICEA, BITHYNIA

FELLER. Who cuts trees down, for timber or wood (Is. xiv. 8).

FENCED CITIES (Heb. MIBZAR, *cut off, separate*). The difference between a city and a village in the Bible is the wall around the city. The village had a watch-tower only. Sometimes the houses are built close together around a space, forming a wall, the entrance having a gate. Jerusalem, as described by Josephus, had three walls on some sides, with towers and battlements. Some of the cities in Assyria were surrounded with very wide and high walls, with a ditch outside for water, and a palisade in the middle of the ditch. These are found drawn in the sculptures.

FER'RET (Heb. ANAKAH, *sighs* or *groans*). Formerly translated shrew-mouse, but now the Gecko, of which there are several in Palestine. It is also called the Fan-foot. It is a lizard, with padded feet, and can move up and down walls like a fly, without noise, except what it makes with its voice, which sounds like its name—geck-o. They are red,

SIEGE OF JERUSALEM.

brown, green, or bright blue, and all studded with clear white spots over the back and flanks.

FER'RY-BOAT (Heb. ABARAH). Perhaps a raft (2 Sam. xix. 18).

FESTIVALS. The law plainly intended stated and regular meetings for worship, at shorter or longer intervals. No rule was made for any particular form of gathering, but each community was left to direct its own affairs. When synagogues were built, after the Captivity, the service was made more uniform. These gatherings were intended to be holy (Is. i. 13; Ps. lxxxi. 3, etc.). They were sacred seasons—feasts of the soul.

1. THE WEEKLY SABBATH (Heb. SHABBATH, *a day of rest*). The 7th day of the week (Gen. ii. 3), was established by law (Ex. xvi. 23, 29), to be kept by the whole people (Ex. xxv. 25). Isaiah utters solemn warning against profaning, and promises blessings for the due observance of it (Is. lviii. 13). The Scribes and Pharisees invented many strict rules, which hedged about the day and bound the people hand and foot, so that Jesus found it necessary to repeat the saying that "the Sabbath was made for man, and not man for the Sabbath." It was the key-note to a system consisting of 7th day, 7th week, 7th month, 7th year, and year of jubilee, which was at the end of 7 times 7 years. Each of these periods had its sacred day. It was lawful and customary for the priests to light fires, bake the shew-bread, and do other needed work about the Temple. "There was no Sabbath in holy things."

2. PASSOVER OR FEAST OF UNLEAVENED BREAD. It was kept in the 14th day of the first month, "between the two evenings"—that is, late in the evening is the Lord's Passover. On the next day, the 15th, is the feast of the unleavened bread, continuing 7 days (Lev. xxiii. 5). The lamb sacrificed for the passover must be of the first year, and without blemish (1 Cor. v. 7). The flesh of the paschal lamb was eaten to show the actual fellowship which the partakers of the feast held with God as the result of the atoning sacrifice.

THE PASSOVER was the annual national birthday festival, and was held in the first month when the ears of grain were forming. The lamb was roasted (not boiled), not a bone broken, and was entirely eaten, the persons standing, with loins girt, a staff in hand, shoes on, ready for a journey, in memory of the Exodus. The Pharisees excused the custom of reclining at the table in their day, by saying that it was a sign of the rest that the Lord had granted his people. The bitter herbs eaten with the lamb were reminders of the bondage in Egypt, and of the anxiety and trouble mingled with blessings in life, an emblem of the crucifixion of nature. Leavened bread was not to be eaten for a week—unleavened bread was "the bread of affliction," "for they came out of Egypt in haste." Leaven is a species of corruption—against which Jesus warned his disciples as in the peculiar errors of the Pharisees (Matt. xvi. 6). The feast also pointed to the future—to the sacrifice of the Paschal Lamb (Luke xxii. 15, 16).

THE FEAST OF WEEKS (Greek name PENTECOST.) The presentation of the first ripe ears of barley. It was also the feast of *first-fruits* and of *harvest*. The offering was made by the priest waving two loaves, made of the best of the crop, of fine wheat flour, leavened and baked, but not put on the altar (where no leaven could be placed), (Deut. xxvi. 2). This feast was in memory of the giving of the Law. It was the end of the harvest, as the second day of the Passover was the first, and it was the end of the Week of Weeks—seven times seven days. Canaan was in a peculiar sense God's land, and as He manifests his care in providing, He should be honored by those who are partakers of his bounty. In spiritual matters it was also the harvest season—the end of Christ's personal ministry on earth.

THE FEAST OF TRUMPETS, OR NEW MOON. The year was reckoned by the moon, twelve or more moons making a year (see CHRONOLOGY). Besides the usual offerings (Num. xxii. 11-15), there was a blowing of trumpets, as sung in Ps. lxxxi. 3. It occurred on the first of the 7th month, near our October. The voice of God and the voice of the trumpet on Mt. Sinai were heard together (Ex. xix. 16-19). It was a symbol of the mighty voice of God. The first was the *sacred month*, and was therefore placed *seventh* in the calendar. Four days were sabbaths, the 10th was the Day of Atonement, the 15th was the Feast of Tabernacles.

THE FEAST OF THE DAY OF ATONEMENT (see ATONEMENT). It was the occasion above all others, on which the ideas of sin and atonement rose to their highest potency in the ritual of the old covenant, exhibiting those ideas in their clearest light, how one ordained from among men, for the purpose of drawing near to God, mediates in behalf of his fellow men in things pertaining to sin and salvation.

THE FEAST OF TABERNACLES, the last of the appointed festivals under the old covenant, beginning on the 15th of the 7th month, and lasting seven days. The real name is *booths*, and was celebrated "in the end of the year, when they had gathered in their labors out of the field" (Ex. xxiii. 16). The crops and the vintage are supposed to be ended, and this was practically the end of the year. The booths were temporary and slight structures of sticks and leaves (Neh. viii. 16). Its object was to keep in memory the sojourn in the wilderness, a sort of perpetual renewing of their religious youth, when the covenant of the Law was first given. There was the same sin-offering for each day, and double the other offerings, two rams and fourteen lambs each day, and thirteen bullocks on the first day, one less each day, ending with seven on the seventh day.

After the Captivity, and in later times, there was

A FOUNTAIN NEAR HESHBON, EAST OF JORDAN.

the Feast of the DEDICATION, in memory of the fresh consecration of the temple after it had been profaned by Antiochus Epiphanes (1 Macc. iv. 52 -59), B. C. 164 (John x. 22). It was held beginning on the 15th day of the 9th month (December) and lasted eight days. The modern Jews light one light on the first day, two on the next, etc. (8 on the last), making it a "Feast of Lights" (Ant. xii. 7, 7). Business and jollity going on as usual.

The FEAST OF PURIM is kept on the 14th and 15th of the 12th month, Adar (March). See BOOK OF ESTHER in the HISTORY.

FEASTS OF CHARITY or LOVE FEAST. See AGAPE.

FES'TUS PORCIUS. The successor of Felix as governor of Judæa, A. D. 60. His term was short, for he died in a little while (A. D. 62). He was superior to Felix, and would have set Paul at liberty, if he had understood the case, which Paul seeing, he appealed to Cæsar (Acts xxiv. 27). He gave the apostle a hearing in the presence of Agrippa and Berênice, and was astonished at his preaching, but supposed it came from a heated imagination aided by the peculiar dreamy speculations of the East. He got into a quarrel with the priests at Jerusalem by building a dining room in the governor's house, which overlooked the temple courts, when the priests built a high wall, cutting off the view. The emperor afterward sustained the priests (Ant. xx. 8). He was a good man and governor, but indifferent to religion.

FET'TERS. Chains to confine the feet, made of bronze or iron (Judg. xvi. 21; brass, iron in Ps. cv. 15).

FE'VER (Heb. KADDACHATH). Burning ague in Lev. xxvi. 21. DALLEKETH is translated inflammation in Deut. xxviii. 22, and CHARCHUR, extreme burnings. Greek *puretos*, fever in Matt. viii. 15, etc. Malignant fevers are still met with in Palestine, near water, in the spring and autumn, especially about the Sea of Galilee (*Land and Book*, i. 547).

FIELD (Heb. SADEH). A field which is not fenced; an open field (Num. xxii. 23, 24). Separate plots were marked by stones (Deut. xix. 14), which might be removed (Job. xiv. 2); and it was necessary to watch the flocks and herds day and night to prevent trespass. FULLER'S FIELD, POTTER'S FIELD.

FIG (Heb. TEENAH; Arab. *tin, the ficus carica tree*; Gr. *suké*, fig-tree; *suka* (sycamore) figs. Three kinds are cultivated: 1. The early fig (Heb. BOKKORE, *early fig*; BICCURAH, *first ripe*), ripe in June, green in color.—2. The summer fig (KERMOUS), ripe in August, is sweet and the best, purple in color; and the green fig (*pag*) which remains on the tree all winter. (*Beth-phage*, place of figs). DEBELAH, cake of figs in 1 Sam. xxx. 12. It is still used in the East as the most convenient and the best poultice (2 K. xx. 7; Is. xxxviii. 21). It is one of the few plants which grow wild all over the country. The fig tree puts forth its earliest fruit buds before its leaves, and the foliage forms a very dense shade. "To sit every man under his vine and under his fig tree," indicates in the East the fullest idea of peace, security and prosperity. Jeremiah (as well as several other prophets) uses the fig through all of his books as an emblem of good or evil, and particularly in chap. xxiv. Jesus made frequent use of the tree or its fruit as an emblem or a means of instruction, especially in the case of the barren fig tree, as a lesson against deceit. It grows best near a fountain or stream. The sycamore fig grows to a large size in Palestine and Egypt—sometimes 50 feet in circumference—and is evergreen. The fruit is purple, smaller than the other kinds, sweetish, and not so valuable. They ripen from November to June. The wood is used for many purposes, as it is almost the only large tree in Egypt.

FILE (Heb. PETSIRSAH). In 1 Sam. xiii. 21, translated file. The word means notched.

FIN'GER (Heb. ETSABA). The priest sprinkled with his forefinger (Lev. iv. 6). A certain gesture of the finger indicated contempt (Is. lviii. 9). The FINGER OF GOD, is his power (Ex. viii. 19).

FIR (Heb. BEROSH, BEROTH, *to cut up into boards*). Pine, cypress, juniper, or various evergreen trees. Found in the mountains. The timber was supplied to King Solomon by Hiram for the temple, for the floors and doors. It was used for musical instruments (2 Sam. vi. 5). The tree is next in size to the cedar. It is used by the poets and prophets among their figures.

SYCAMORE FIG.

FIRE (Heb. ESH). The symbol of Jehovah's presence, and first kindled by the Lord (Lev. vi. 9; 2 Chr. vii. 1). Sacred fire could only be had from the altar, and the crime of Nadab and Abihu was in using "strange fire" from some other source. No fire could be kindled on the Sabbath, except by the priests for holy purposes. Fire for cooking is made with sticks, grass and dried dung. To set fire to a grain field is a capital offense. Any damage by a careless fire must be made good (Ex. xxii. 6).

Fire was used to burn certain criminals and prisoners, and in some cases to destroy an enemy's city, and in the art of metallurgy. Fire was a symbol of fierce passion, calamities etc., and an emblem of healing spiritually (Mal. iii. 2). A baptism by fire.

FIRE-PAN (Heb. MACHTAH). Snuff-dish, or some utensil used about the altar.

FIRKIN (John ii. 6; Greek *metretes*). The firkin is a larger vessel than the one meant in the text.

FIR'MAMENT (Heb. RAKIA). The expanse; the sky over our heads. On the second day the expanse was made; on the fourth, *in the expanse* was made the sun, moon and stars.

FIRST-BORN (Heb. BECHOR). See BIRTHRIGHT. The religious bearing was the most important. Christ is the first born of all creation (Col. i. 16, 18), and the first born from the dead.

FIRST-FRUITS (BICCURIM). Among fruits what the first-born is among men and beasts. The first or best of the oil, of the wine, of the wheat, of all the harvest, was sacred to the Lord, to be given in a quantity, according to the will and inclination of each person. The faithful priest reaped a rich reward from the holy zeal that he instilled into the hearts of his people. The doctors limited the gifts to the 60th part as the least that would be accepted. In the later times the Jews turned the gifts into money. This custom was not peculiar to Israel. The first-fruits were often sent to Jerusalem from foreign countries.

PAPYRUS.

FISH (Heb. DAG, DAGAH; Gr. *icthus*). No particular kind of fish is mentioned by name in the Bible; but there are frequent references to fish generally. It is a little remarkable that the apostles, who were professed fishermen, did not designate by name any kinds of fish, saleable or unsaleable, and especially the one bearing the tribute-money. It would have been interesting to know the name of the fish, as well as that of the coin. Even the law of Moses does not mention names (as among animals), but character only, as fins and scales for pure or clean, that might be eaten. Solomon's treatise on fishes (1 K. iv. 33), is lost. The Greek furnishes 400 names for varieties of fishes, but the Hebrew has not one. Jacob knew how rapidly they increase, for he alludes to this fact in his blessings (Gen. xlviii. 16), "multitude," etc., meaning in the original "as fishes do increase." Fish were eaten from the earliest times (Num. xi. 22), and one of the gates of Jerusalem was called Fish Gate. In Egypt, the monuments show many pictures of fish and fishing. The historians speak of the vast quantities of fish taken, from which the royal revenue was derived for the queen's special use, for jewelry, perfumery, etc., of $350,000 a year. The Assyrian sculptures also show men fishing. The Egyptians also dried and salted fish, as shown in the sculptures.

FITCHES (Heb. KETZACH). "The fitches are beaten out with a staff," (Is. xxviii. 27). The fennel-flower, a coarse kind of pea, hard, but nutritious. In the great famine in England in 1555 wild fitches saved many people from starving. It grows all over Europe and Asia. The "fitches" in Ezekiel's symbolized bread (iv. 9), was spelt (Heb. KUSSEMETH), a grain something like wheat.

FLAG (Heb. SUPH, and ACHU). The ark of Moses was floated among the flags (Ex. ii. 3), SUPH. Isaiah predicts that the reeds and flags shall wither (xix. 6) in Egypt: "Can the flag grow without water?" (ACHU, Job. viii. 11). It is rendered meadow or marsh in Gen. xli. 2, 18. Any waterplant would answer the case. The Edible Rush, and Flowering Rush grow both in Egypt and Palestine. The name of the Red Sea is Yam Suph.

FLAG'ON (Heb. ASHISHAH). In 2 Sam. vi. 19; Cant. ii. 15, and Hosea iii. 1, it is a cake of raisins. —2. (Heb. NEBEL). In Is. xxii. 24 is a bottle of skin or pottery.

FLAX (Heb. PISHTAH, *peeled*). Very few plants are so beautiful and so useful as the slender flax, with its tall, taper leaves, large purple flowers, and its strong fibre from which the most delicate lawn or coarsest canvas is made. The holy garments of Aaron, and the curtains of the tabernacle were partly of linen. Its whiteness, in linen, was a symbol of purity. The ancient sculptures represent the manufacture of linen (Prov. xxxi. 13).

FLEA (Heb. PAROSH). "The king of the fleas holds his court in Tiberias," now as ever in old times. Frequent change of linen is the only means of keeping clear of them in the East. They almost disappear in the heat of summer. They swarm on travelers, when scarcely touching natives. They are said to produce a healthy irritation in the skin. David says: "After whom is the king of Israel come out? * * * after one flea?" (1 Sam. xxiv. 14, xxvi. 20).

FLESH (BASAR). All that is of flesh and blood (Gen. vi. 13); and the human race (Luke iii. 6, etc.). The weakness, and frailty of man is also flesh (Rom. iv. 1). Flesh is also the antipathy to spirit (viii. 1).

FLIES FLY (Heb. ZEBUB, AROB). Common house-flies swarm in great numbers in the East. The peculiar gray fly (Ar. *thebub*) which comes with the rise of the Nile is productive of disease in both man and animals. The *arob* was the fly, or swarm of insects of one of the plagues in Egypt. Flies in the East are very persistent in settling on persons, never quitting until dark, and are the means of carrying diseases from one to another. The Philistines had a god, Baal-zebub, whose special duty it was to take care of flies. Judging from their number they are well cared for. The "ointment (perfume) of the apothecary" (Eccles. x. 1) was attractive to flies, and their dead bodies spoiled its odor, and so would little follies spoil the reputation of a wise man. The man is the perfume, his little folly the dead fly, his disgrace the bad odor.

FLINT (CHALLAMISH). Used in Deut. viii. 15; and Psalms cxiv. 8, in reference to God's bringing water and oil out of the naturally barren rocks for the sake of his people. In Is. i. 7, it is a metaphor of the firmness of the prophet in resisting his enemies, as also in Ez. iii. 9.

FLOOD. DELUGE.

FLOOR. PAVEMENT.

FLOUR. BREAD.

FLOWERS. Flowering plants and shrubs are found in great numbers and variety all over Palestine, except in the highest regions of the moun-

tains, and in the shifting sands of the desert, 2500 have been named and classified, 500 of which are well known in Europe. The most abundant families of plants are Leguminous, pod-bearing, such as peas, beans, pulse; the Astragalus and the Acacia. A vast number of thistles, centauries, and other like plants, cover the richest plains and the stony hills. Many sweet flowering shrubs, such as marjoram, thyme, lavender, calaminth, sage, and others similar. A vast number and variety of weeds, mustard being the king of all. Fennel, Bupleurum, and Eryngium form dense rows of foliage and flowers along the border of woods, and in damp hollows. Soap plant is conspicuous, and the Boragineæ, annual weeds, besides which are the Echiums, Anchusas, and other fine species. Scrophularia, Veronica, Linaria and Verbascum (mulleins) are very abundant. Grasses are very numerous, many species bearing silky plumes of flowers of great beauty and grace. The variety and beauty of the family of lilies is no where exceeded. The lily springs up everywhere, and the Amaryllids are of great size, beauty, and variety. Fritillarias and squills are in abundance, and bear pretty flowers. Violets and geraniums are very numerous and finely colored. Roses are a subject of profitable cultivation for attar, and a valley near Jerusalem is called the Valley of Roses (Wady el Werd). The Narcissus is very beautiful, abundant and in several varieties, and is believed to be the flower alluded to by the poet in Cant. ii. 1, and the prophet in Is. xxxv. 1. Several other Amaryllids are found in great numbers, and almost the most showy plants in the field. Iris, crocus, and gladiolus grow very large and showy. Broom, ivy, dog-rose, elder, honeysuckle, berberry, hawthorn, and jasmine are found in Lebanon and Anti-Lebanon, at and above 4000 feet elevation. Rhododendrons, primrose, and a great variety of plants, from 5000 to 7000, and some kinds are found even up to the limits of the snow line; at 8000 Vicia forms tufts of pale blue, at 9000 there are Arenaria, Arabis, Drabas, Festuca, and Potentilla, while the little Noœa and the Oxyria grows on the very summit of Khodib, 10,200 feet high. From the sands of the desert to the snows of the mountain summits there are flowers of many varieties, blooming in every month of the year.

FLUTE (Chaldee, *mashrokitha*). Made of one or more pipes. Pipe in 1 K. i. 49. One of the simplest and oldest of musical instruments. Used at banquets (Is. v. 12), at public worship (Dan. iii. 5, etc.), marriages, funerals, and by pilgrims on the way to the yearly meeting.

FLUX. Dysentery of a very severe kind in the East, attended with fever (Acts xxviii. 8). The Oriental custom of wearing a bandage around the bowels is a preventive of bowel disorder by protecting against the sudden changes from hot to cold which always follows sundown. When bloody the dysentery is less dangerous. King Jehoram had a chronic dysentery, with *prolapsus ani* (2 Chr. xxi. 15).

FOOD. Some kind of prohibition in what may be eaten or may not has been known from the earliest times. The human race can eat "every herb bearing seed," and "every tree in which is the fruit of a tree" (Gen. i. 29), and also "every moving thing that liveth," but flesh with the life thereof, which is the blood, was prohibited (Gen. ix. 3, 4). And other rules made distinctions of clean and unclean among animals, fowls and fishes, for food. (See CLEAN.) The climate influences the diet all over the world. Animal food is not needed, and cannot be used, during the greater part of the year, nor can it be kept in a healthy state for any length of time in the hot season. The sacrificial feasts occurring at long intervals when animal food was eaten, were very acceptable, on account of the abstinence preceding them. Bread is the chief food besides fruit and vegetables. Rice is much used. (BREAD.) Neither eggs nor fowls are mentioned among gifts of first-fruits, although they are largely used now in the East. Almost every known fruit and vegetable can be had, in plenty and of good quality. Milk, cheese, butter (melted as oil), oil of olives, and honey, or molasses from grapes (dibs) can be found everywhere. Condiments of many kinds are in common use; and much use is made of aromatic herbs in cookery. Nuts cooked with meat adds delicacy to the flavor. Highly seasoned food, with spices, salt, onions, garlic, lemons, pomegranates, and verjuice, makes a savory dish. Cracked wheat is boiled with meat. "Killing, cooking, and eating in rapid succession is a very old custom" (*Land and Book*, ii. 162). The Arabs have many caustic terms of contempt for the man who neglects to honor a guest with a "sacrifice" of a lamb, kid, or calf, as required by the laws of hospitality. (See MEALS, WINE, WATER). Milk and honey, and oil with honey, or butter with honey, are choice dishes, eaten with bread, usually for breakfast.

FOOL. Used of moral more than of intellectual deficiencies, of one who does not fear God, and acts without regard to His law (Ps. xiv. 1).

FOOT. (See WASHING FEET). The foot was used as a symbol of many ideas. Such phrases as "slipping of the foot," "stumbling," and "from head to foot," need no explanation. "To be under the feet," means subject to a king, or as a servant to the master (Ps. viii. 6; Heb. ii. 8); derived from the symbolical act of a conqueror who placed his foot on the neck of his subdued enemies in token of triumph (Josh. x. 24), as may be seen in the sculptures on the ancient monuments. To be at any one's feet meant service or pupilage (Judg. iv. 10), and Paul actually sat at the feet of Gamaliel (who sat on a raised seat), as was the custom then (Acts xxii. 3). "Lameness of feet" is affliction or calamity (Ps. xxxv. 15). To set one's foot in a place is to take possession (Deut. i. 36). To water with the foot is to turn the little rills easily (this was a mark of the superiority of Palestine to Egypt, because rain and brooks were there instead of the Nile and the artificial canals); (xl. 10.) To walk with a straight foot "uprightly" in Gal. ii. 14. Naked feet (out of doors) was poverty or mourning

FITCHES.

(Ez. xxiv. 17). Uncovering the feet, or taking off the overshoe in the East, is equivalent to taking off the hat with us. Uncovering the feet was a part of the act of adoration (Ex. iii. 4), as Moses before the burning bush. "How beautiful on the mountains are the feet of him who brings glad tidings" (Is. lii. 7).

The Hebrews were modest in their writings, and used the word foot for certain parts and actions

which could not be named. "Hair of the foot," "water of the foot," "between the feet" (Deut. xxviii. 57), "he covereth his feet" (Judg. iii. 24 for "dismisses the refuse of nature.")

FOOT'MEN (Heb. RAGLI). 1. Soldiers; not horsemen.—2. (Heb. ROOTZ.) Swift runners (1 Sam. viii. 11; xxii. 17). Paul refers to them (1 Cor. ix. 24). Elijah ran before Ahab as a footman.

FORDS. Places for crossing a river by wading. See JORDAN.

FOUN'DER (Judg. xvii. 4; Jer. vi. 29). METALS.

FOUN'TAIN (Heb. AYIN, to flow; MAYAN, a gushing; BOR, a cistern; MABBUA, to bubble out; MAKOR, to dig). These several words are translated fountain, but only one, AYIN, really means a spring of water. The springs of Palestine are remarkable for their great number, and some of them for their immense volume. Water there is fertility and life, and the whole land is full of great fountains, such as those of the Dog River; of the River of Beirut;

GADARA.

Damur; Owely; Zahrany; Litany at Baalbek; Zahleh; Ainjar, and Mushgarah; Ras el Ain at Tyre; Kabery and Naamany near Acre; of the Kishon at Janin, Lejjun, and Wady Kusaby; Zerka near Cæsarea; Aujeh at Antipatris, and the Ras in Sharon. And so we might go all through Palestine, on both sides of the Jordan. Some are hot, as at Tiberias, Gadara, and Callirrhoë; others are intermittent as the Fuarr, the source of the Sabbatic River, and the Menbej, east of Beit Jenn, Mt. Hermon (Land and Book, i. 405). The fountain at Nazareth has a traditional antiquity and importance. Wealthy men in the East build handsome structures over fountains for their preservation, and the benefit of residents and travelers.

FORE'HEAD (Ez. ix. 4). It was (and is now in India) the custom in the East to mark or color the forehead, to distinguish the holy from the profane (Rev. xiii. 16), the devotees of certain idols, and also slaves. "Jewels for the forehead" (Ez. xvi. 12), means nose-rings, or, it may be, strings of coins.

FOREST (Heb. YAAR, abundance, forest; CHORESH, thick wood; PARDES, orchard). Since the historical era, Palestine has had few forests, the trees being mostly fruit or ornamental. The highlands were probably once well wooded. Several forests are mentioned: of Lebanon, which must have been one of great extent (see CEDAR, FIR); of Hareth; of Carmel; of Ephraim, etc. There are now extensive forests in Persia, of oak, terebinth (Is. ii. 13; Ez. xxvii. 6). "The house of the forest of Lebanon" was built of cedar and fir from Lebanon, with many pillars like a forest, in Jerusalem (1 K. vii. 2). The forest supplies the poets and prophets with many fine figures.

FORKS (1 Sam. xiii. 21). Hay-forks with three or more prongs; used, also, in winnowing grain.

FORNICA'TION. ADULTERY.

FORTIFICA'TION. FENCED CITIES (Micah vii. 12).

FOR'TRESS (2 Sam. xxii. 2; Ps. xviii. 2; Is. xxv. 12). FENCED CITIES.

FORTUNA'TUS. Disciple at Ephesus, native of Corinth (1 Cor. xvi. 17). He is also mentioned in Clement's Epistle.

FOUNDA'TION, GATE OF THE (2 Chr. xxiii. 5). JERUSALEM.

FOUNTAIN-GATE. JERUSALEM (Neh. xii. 37).

FOWL (Heb. BARBURIM (1 K. iv. 23) fatted fowl). Barn-door fowl, or geese. The Egyptian paintings represent catching, keeping, feeding, killing, salting, cooking, and eating of fowl.

FOX (Heb. SHUAL, to dig through). The Arab name for jackal is shikal, but a little different from the Hebrew SHUAL, and it is evident from the habits of the animal referred to that the jackal is meant. They are plenty now in Palestine, and are night-prowlers, lying concealed in the day-time, in caves, holes, or among the ruins. They go in packs of hundreds. They eat any carcase of either animal or man (Ps. lxiii. 9, 10). The Orientals never spare pain in men or animals, and Samson, who was revengeful and unscrupulous, tied a firebrand between two jackals and sent them into the dry wheat-fields of the Philistines, destroying vast

fields probably. (See FIRE.) Jackals are very fond of grapes (Matt. viii. 20; Luke ix. 58).

FRANK'INCENSE (Heb. LEBONAH). Resin of the *Boswellia tree*, which grows 40 feet high in India and Arabia Felix. It has a balsamic smell, and burns with a white flame and fragrant odor. Its burning was symbolical of the holiness of Jehovah (1 Chr. ix. 29) and of prayer (Ps. cxli. 2; Luke i. 10; Rev. viii. 3).

FRAY (Deut. xxviii. 26, etc.). To terrify. Not used now.

FREEDOM. CITIZEN. SLAVE.

FREE-WILL OFFERING (Lev. xxii. 18). Free gifts. SACRIFICE.

FRET (Lev. xiii. 55). A plague spot in a leprous garment.

FRINGES (Heb. ZITZITH, *flourish*). Bobs, tassels or fringes (Num. xv. 38). They are shown on many ancient figures. ASSYRIA; DRESS; EMBROIDERY.

FROG (Heb. ZEPHARDEA, *marsh-leaper*). Mentioned but three or four times in the Bible (always of the plague), but very common in Palestine and Egypt (Ex. viii. 2–14; Ps. lxxviii. 45; cv. 30; Wisdom xix. 10). It is believed that the frogs of the plague were the edible variety. Their noise is heard from one end of the land to the other (L. & B. i. 368). In Egypt they were regarded as a type of the Creator (Ptah).

FRONT'LET (Heb. TOTAPHOTH). Something bound on the forehead, "between the eyes," and as a sign or token in the hand (a ring?). Originally the meaning of the law or direction was to keep in memory, as in Prov. vi. 21: "Bind them on the heart, and tie them on the neck." But after the return from captivity the Jews made the law literal, and wrote it out (Ex. xiii. 2–10, 11–16; Deut. vi. 5–9; xi. 13–21) on bits of parchment, called Phylacteries, which were put in little cases of leather (metal in our day), and tied on the forehead and left arm. The ribbon for tying them was colored purple by the Pharisees, and made showy and broad (Mark vii. 3, 4), and were worn by all Jews except Karaites, women and slaves. The Rabbis made many rules about their uses. They were not worn on the Sabbath, because the Sabbath was itself a sign; the person reading them in the morning must stand; in the evening he may sit; the color of the thread might be changed to red in times of persecution; both hands must be used in writing them; the parchment must not have a hole in it; only one blot or error was permitted; a person wearing them must keep six feet off from a cemetery—and many others. They were a means of religious vanity, hypocrisy and display, and were so denounced by Jesus. The Rabbis said (by a kind of pious fraud) that God wore them, arguing from Is. xlix. 16; lxii. 8; Deut. xxxiii. 2. They were a kind of amulet, such as the modern Arabs use. AMULET.

FROST (Heb. HANAMAL, *hail-stones*, Ps. lxxviii. 47); KERACH, *ice* (Gen. xxxi. 40); KEPHOR, *hoar-frost* (Ex. xvi. 40). There is a great difference between the temperature of the day and night in the East. CLIMATE.

FRUIT (Heb. PERI, *fruit in general*; KAYITS, *summer fruits*). Their great variety and excellence would fill a volume.

FRYING-PAN. BREAD.

FUEL. DUNG.

FULLER. Business of cleaning and whitening cloth. It was carried on outside the city of Jerusalem, where was the *Fuller's Field*, mentioned three times in the Bible (2 K. viii. 17; Is. vii. 3; xxxvi. 2), so close, that one speaking in the field could be heard by one standing on the city wall. Perhaps near the pool of Gihon, or it might have been at En Rogel. Rabshakeh and his great host must have come on the north side.

FUNERAL. BURIAL. See cuts on pages 7 and 110.

FURLONG. The stadium; Roman, 201 $\frac{1}{15}$ yards; English, 220 yards (Luke xxiv. 13).

FURNACE. Several kinds are mentioned: 1. TANNER, *oven* (Gen. xv. 17); KIBSHAN, *lime-kiln* (Gen. xix. 28); KUR, *furnace for smelting metals*; ATTUN, *furnace* (Dan. iii. 6); Gr. *kaminos*, *baker's oven* (Matt. xiii. 42).

FRINGE.

FUR'NITURE (Heb. KELI, *apparatus*, Ex. xxxi. 7). The furniture of Eastern dwellings is very simple. Many articles deemed necessary with us would find no place there.—2. Heb. KAR, *a camel's saddle and its canopy* (Gen. xxxi. 34).

G

GA'AL (*loathing*). Son of Ebed (Judg. ix). A brigand who was ready to sell his services to the highest bidder.

GA'ASH (*earthquake*). Mount Gaash on the north side of which was Timnathheres, the city given to Joshua at his request (Josh. xix. 49, 50), and where he resided and was buried (Josh. xxiv. 30; Judg. ii. 9). Lost.

GA'BA. GEBA.

GAB'AEL (*God's highest*). 1. Descendant of Tobit (Tob. i. 1).—2. A poor Jew (Tob. i. 17), to whom Tobit lent money.

GABBAI (*tax-gatherer*). An important person in the family of Benjamin (Neh. xi. 8).

GAB'BATHA. Pavement (John xix. 13). Outside the Prætorium (judgment hall), where Pilate delivered Jesus to death. The *bema* was an elevated pavement, the usual place of justice.

GABDES. GABA (1 Esd. v. 20).

GA'BRIAS (*man of Jehovah*, Tob. i. 14). Brother of Gabael.

GABRIEL (*man of God*). Angel (Dan. viii. 16; Luke i. 19). In Jewish and Christian traditions the archangel of God.

GAD (*troop*). Jacob's seventh son, first-born of Zilpah, Leah's maid; brother to Asher (Gen. xxx. 11–13; xlvi. 16, 18). The country given to the

EGYPTIAN FULLER.

tribe was the centre of the east of Jordan (Deut. iii. 12), from Heshbon to Mahanaim. On the east was Aroer, that faces Rabbah (Josh. xiii. 25); west was Jordan (v. 27), and including the Arabah, from the Jabbok to the Sea of Chinnereth. The most beautiful district in Syria. It is a high range of purple-tinted mountains, cut down by deep ra-

vines, partially clothed with forests of oak, terebinths, sycamores, ilex, beech, fig, and evergreen shrubs. The climate is fine and soil fertile, affording the best pasturage. At one time the tribe possessed the land as far east as Salcah (1 Chr. v. 11, 16). Jephthah was a Gadite of Mizpah (Judg. xi. 34). Carried into captivity, and its cities inhabited by Ammonites (1 Chr. v. 26; Jer. xlix. 1).

COFFINS.

GAD'ARA. Five miles southeast of the Sea of Galilee, three miles from the river Hieromax. There were warm springs near the river, called Amatha. Josephus says it was a Greek city, and the capital of Peræa (Jos. B. J. iv. 7, § 3; Mark v. 1; Luke viii. 26-37). Here the Lord healed the demoniacs (Matt. viii. 28-34; Mark v. 1-21; Luke viii. 26-40). The most interesting ruins at Gadara are the tombs, which are very numerous in the cliffs around the city, cut in the solid rock, being rooms ten to twenty feet square, and some larger, with small recesses out of them for bodies, the doors being stone, turning on stone hinges. The space over which the ruins are scattered is about two miles, on a narrow, high ridge, sloping east, anciently walled all around. There was a straight street from end to end, with a colonade on each side, and two very large theatres, now in ruins. Not a house or a column is standing.

GADARENES'. People of Gadara.

GAD'DI (*fortunate*). Son of Susi (Num. xiii. 11).

GAD'DIEL (*fortune of God*). A Zebulonite spy.

GA'DI. A Gadite. Father of King Menahem (2 K. xv. 14, 17).

GADITES. Of the tribe of Gad.

GA'HAM (*swarthy*). Son of Nahor, brother of Abraham (Gen. xvii. 24), son of Reumah.

GA'HAR (*hiding-place*). Ancestor of Nethinim (Ezr. ii. 47).

GA'IUS. A common Roman name.

GAL'AAD (1 Macc. v. 9, 56; Jud. i. 8).

GA'LAL (*worthy*). 1. A Levite (1 Chr. ix. 15). —2. Son of Jeduthun (ix. 16; Neh. xi. 17).

GAL'ATIA (*country of the Galli, Asia*). Used in two senses.—1. Some suppose France (Gaul) is meant in 2 Tim. iv. 10, and 1 Macc. viii. 2. France (Gaul) may have been the origin of the people who invaded Greece and Asia Minor in the 4th century, B. C., and were first checked by Antiochus, who was called Soter (*saviour*) for the success, and were finally subdued by the Roman Manlius, B. C. 189, when they gathered into a district in the central region of Asia Minor. Visited twice by Paul (Acts xviii. 23). The Epistle to the Galatians was written after the second visit.

GALA'TIANS (1 Macc. viii. 2; 2 Macc. viii. 20; Gal iii. 1). People of any race, or Jews, or Gauls from France, living in Galatia. For Epistle to the Galatians, see HISTORY OF THE BOOKS.

GAL'BANUM (HELBENAH). A perfume used in the preparation of the sacred incense (Ex. xxx. 34). Resinous, yellow-brown, but it is not known from what plant or tree it is derived.

GAL'EED (*heap of witness*). The name which Jacob gave to the heap which he and Laban made on Mount Gilead (Gen. xxxi. 47, 48, xxiii. 25). JEGAR-SAHADUTHA.

GALGALA (1 Macc. ix. 2). MAGDALA?

GALILE'AN. Native of Galilee (Mark xiv. 70).

GALILEE (GALIL, *a circle*). At first applied to a small district about Kedesh, on the N. W. shore of the Sea of Galilee (Is. ix. 1). Afterward, during the Roman rule, the name of the whole country north of the Kishon river and Mount Gilboa, to the Leontes and Hermon, from the Jordan to the sea (Josephus Life, 12, Wars, iii.). Divided into Upper, as far as the N. W. angle of the Sea of Galilee, and Lower, as far south as Ginea (Jenin), including the great plain of Esdraelon. The hills are now wooded, with gentle slopes, and are fruitful of all that man uses, and luxuriant in flowers of every variety (Deut. xxxiii. 18; Gen. xlix. 20). The chief towns were Capernaum, Kedesh, Bethsaida, Tiberias, Nazareth, Cana, besides many other smaller, the ruins of which are scattered over nearly every hill-top or hill-side. Here was the scene of the greater part of the works and life of Jesus, which are the subject of the first three Gospels almost wholly. THE SEA OF GALILEE, GENNESARET.

GALL (Heb. MERERAH, *bitter;* ROSH, *poison-hemlock*, or *poppies*). Gall means the bitter nature of the drink offered Jesus (Matt. xxvii. 34).

GAL'LERY (Heb. RAHIT, *ceiling;* rafters in Cant. i. 17; RAMAT, *braided*, in Gen. xxx. 28, gutters; ATTIK, *pillar* for the support of a house, Ez. xli. 15).

GAL'LEY. SHIP.

GAL'LIM (*heaps*). Twice mentioned (1 Sam. xxv. 44; Is. x. 30). It was probably near Dan, Laish, but is lost.

GAL'LIO, JUNIUS ANNÆUS. Elder brother of the philosopher Seneca, who dedicated to him his treatise *De Vita Beta*, and in another work describes him as a man universally loved, and who especially abhorred flattery. He was the proconsul of Achaia, and by his prudent course much assisted Paul (Acts xviii. 12-17). He was a victim to Nero's cruelty.

GAMA'LA (*camel*). Built on a hill, near the middle of the E. shore of the Sea of Galilee. Described by Josephus as an important town.

GAMA'LIEL (*benefit of God*). 1. Son of Padahzur (Num. i. 10, ii. 20), head of the tribe of Manasseh, in the Exodus.—2. A Pharisee, and a celebrated doctor (Acts v. 34; xxii. 3); a Rabbi, teacher of Paul. He was grandson of the famous Hillel, and son of Rabbi Simeon, and president of the Sanhedrin during the time of Tiberius, Caligula, and Claudius. He lived 18 years after the destruction of Jerusalem.

GAMES. The ancient (and modern) Orientals are represented as very fond of games of many kinds, private and public, frequently mentioned in Scripture. The sculptures and paintings of antiquity exhibit these in every variety. Job alludes

to one in xli. 5, and Jeremiah in xxx. 19, and Jesus, in Matt. xi. 16. Music, dancing, and song were always enjoyed on festive occasions (Ps. xxx. 11; Luke xv. 25). Armed men jousted (2 Sam. ii. 14); they played with single-stick; with the cestus; wrestled; quoits; at leaping; running; and all Grecian games. The rewards in the Grecian games were of several kinds: A chaplet of wild olive; palm branches; and the honors freely given him by his friends and fellow-citizens, of sacrifices to the gods, and poems in his praise, exemption from public service, and a pension. There were four more celebrated: Olympic, Pythian, Nemean, and Isthmian, among the Greeks, in which the most eminent men contended for the prizes, which fact made them a fitting illustration of the Christian life. Temperance in eating and drinking was the rule, and severe exercise at stated times. The Romans added brutality and cruelty, and men were required to fight each other, and wild beasts also. Paul witnessed the games, in various cities where he preached, and is the only one in the N. T. who makes use of them as illustrations of the strife for good against evil in the theatre of life.

GAM'MADINE (Ez. xxvii. 11). Hired soldiers. Mercenaries.

GA'MUL (*weaned*). A priest (1 Chr. xxiv. 17), leader of the 22d course.

GAR. "Sons of Gar," servants of Solomon (1 Esd. v. 34).

GAR'DEN (Heb. GAN, GINNAH; Gr. *keros*). The garden was essential in Egypt. They made constant and general use of fruits and flowers at the table, which required careful cultivation. Their residences were surrounded with gardens, laid out with skilful care, with ornamental beds of curious devices, arbors of trellis-work, basins and rills of water with fish, and paved walks. The Israelites remembered the gardens when they were in the desert, and did not neglect them when in Palestine. Everywhere we find traces of such cultivation: in terraces, cisterns for water, springs cared for, and names of places compounded with Gan or Gen (Engannim, Gennesaret). The garden was often away from the village or house a half a mile perhaps, in some favored spot for water and good soil. The summer-house was decorated with handsome designs and showy colors. It was a place of retirement (John xxviii. 1), and also of merry-making (Is. li. 3). They were inclosed with walls, hedges, and had watch-towers; and even the poorest a booth to shelter the watchman (Is. i. 8; Mark xii. 1; Job. xxvii. 18). A family tomb was sometimes built in the garden (2 K. xxi. 18, 26; John xix. 41, 42).

GARDEN-HOUSE. Place where king Ahaziah II fled from Jehu (2 K. xix. 27); the modern Jenin (Engannim).

GA'REB, THE ITHRITE. A hero of David's army, from Jattir (2 Sam. xxiii. 38).

GA'REB, THE HILL. Near Jerusalem (Jer. xxxi. 39). Now occupied by the new and fine buildings of the Russian mission.

GAR'LIC (SHUM). A vegetable, something like the onion, found in Egypt (Num. xi. 5). The Egyptians have always made use of it as a stimulant, for it quickens the circulation.

GAR'MITE (*bony*), (1 Chr. iv. 9). Keilah, from Gerem.

GARNER. BARN.

GAR'RISON (Heb. MAZZAH, *garrison;* NEZIB, *a garrison,* or also *a column* (1 Sam. xiii. 3); MAZZEBAH, *a pillar* (Ez. xxvi. 11); Gr. *phoureo, to keep watch* (2 Cor. xi. 32). The garrison at Jerusalem was a citadel, or the tower of Antonia (Acts xxi. 34, 37). Another, in Damascus, was used to prevent Paul's escape.

GA'TAM (*burnt valley*). Fourth son of Eliphaz

(Gen. xxxvi. 11); head of an Edomite tribe. *Jith ma* is a modern town in Arabia.

GATE (Heb. SHAAR, *gate;* PETHAR, *entry;* SAPH, *threshold, door-post;* DELETH, *door, two leaved gate;* Chal. *tera, gate, door;* Gr. *thura, pule, pulon*). An entrance into a camp, a house, a tent, a temple, a city, etc. "To possess the gate," was a term meaning power and wealth (Gen. xxii. 17). It was the place of assembly (Prov. i. 21) for social (Ps. lxix. 12) and legal purposes (Ruth iv. 1). Daniel sat in the gate of the king of Babylon (iv. 49); for attracting the notice of the king (Esth. ii. 19), and for marketing (2 K. vii. 1). The gate was spoken of as meaning the city (Gen. xiv. 60; Ps. lxxxvii. 2) or the people of the city (2 Sam. xv. 2). There was (and is) generally an open place both outside and inside the gate. In such a one the king of Ai was buried (Josh. viii. 29), and Jeremiah the prophet was set in the stocks (Jer. xx. 2).

GATE.

The Assyrian palaces furnish many illustrations of Scripture, and especially in the architecture, paintings and sculptures of the gates. They were lofty, magnificent, built for the ages, guarded by symbolic figures, never used inside of buildings, who present to the visitor the fir-cone, a symbol of life. In the floor of the door-way are usually found concealed curious, small images of baked clay, with animal heads on human (or lion) bodies and bull's legs and tail, which were the guardian divinities of the gate (TERAPHIM, Arabic *tarf*, boundary).

RUINED GRANARY. GATH.

GATH (*wine-press*). One of the five royal cities of Philistia. The residence of the Anakim giants (Josh. xi. 22). The ark was carried there by the Philistines (1 Sam. v.). David was in danger of his life at Gath, and saved by a ruse of madness (ib. xxi. 10-15). Many of the people were attached to David all his life (2 Sam. vi. 10, xv. 18). The site has been lost for ages, and is now located by Robinson at Deir Dubban; by Thomson at Beit Jibrin; and by Porter at Tell es Safieh.

GATH-HE'PHER (*wine-press of the well*). Zebulon, near Japhia (Josh. xix. 13). Gittah-hepher. Benjamin of Tudela says that in his time (A. D. 1140) the tomb of Jonah was shown on a hill near Sepphoris.

GATH-RIM'MON. Dan, in the plain (Josh. xxi. 24). Lost.—2. Manasseh, west of Jordan (ib. 25). Probably Bethshan.

GA'ZA (*strong*). Az'ZAH (*desert*). The last town in the southwest of Palestine, on the coast toward Egypt. On the high road between Egypt and Syria. Mentioned in Genesis (x. 19), one of

the oldest cities in the world (Gen. x. 17), and is a town now. Joshua could not subdue it (x. 41). Held by Judah a short time (Judg. i. 18; iii; xii. 1). Samson carried off its gates (xvi. 1-31). Gaza is mentioned in the inscriptions at Nineveh (*Layard*, p. 144). The Ethiopian was baptized by Philip on the way to Gaza. There are deep wells of good water, orchards of varieties of fruit, and palm trees and olive groves. Settled by Avim or Ilivites, who were driven out by the Caphtorim from Egypt. Became one of the five royal Philistine cities, the last home of the giant Anakim (Josh. xi. 22). Taken by Alexander the Great, who was wounded there (Arrian ii. 26). A church was established there early, but idolatry was only abandoned publicly when the last eight temples were destoyed, A. D. 406. Taken by the Saracens A. D. 634. The Crusaders built a fort in 1152. The ancient harbor is covered by the sands. Now called Guzzeh.

7). A district S. of Moab, from W. el Ahsy S. to Shobek, near W. Shaweir. The cities were Arindela, Buzrah, Shobek, Tophel, and others smaller.—2. A very ancient city on a spur of Lebanon, close to the shore, anciently having a fine harbor, which is now choked up with sand and ruins of buildings, quays, etc. The castle is one of the best specimens of ancient masonry, having stones 20 feet long and beveled. The columns and walls, and their great extent especially, prove the splendor and importance of the city (Ez. xxvii. 9; Joshua xiii. 5). Workers in stone from G. were employed on Solomon's temple (1 K. v. 18—*stone-squarers* being a translation of Giblites—people of Gebal). Jebail.

GE'BER (*a man*). 1. Son of Geber (1 K. iv. 13). —2. Son of Uri (iv. 19).

GE'BIM (*ditches*). Village N. of Jerusalem, near Anathoth (2 K. iii. 16; Is. x. 31). Now *El Isawiyeh*.

GEDALI'AH (*Jehovah made him great*). 1. Son

GAZA.

of Ahikam (Jer. xl. 5), the secretary of King Josiah. He was appointed the executive officer of Nebuchadnezzar, after the Captivity, and was popular for his piety and gentleness, but was murdered soon after his appointment by Baalis and Ishmael. 2. A Levite, one of the musicians of Jehovah (1 Chr. xxv. 3, 9).—3. A priest (Ezr. x. 18).—4. Son of Pashur (Jer. xxxviii. 1).—5. Grandfather of Zephaniah (Zeph. i. 1).

GAZ'ARA. Near Azotus, Philistia (1 Macc. xiv. 34; Strabo xvi. 2). A very strong hold (2 Macc. x. 32). Supposed the same as Gazer—Gezer of 2 Sam. v. 25. Taken by Pharaoh, father-in-law to Solomon. 1 K. ix. 16; Josh. x. 33, xxi. 12. xvi. 3 point to a site between Bethhoron the nether and the sea, probably at the foot of the hills in the border of the Shefelah. There may have been two cities of the same name. Neither is located.

GAZ'ATHITES. People of Gaza (Josh. xiii. 3).

GA'ZER (2 Sam. v. 25). GEZER.

GA'ZEZ (*shearer*). 1. Son of Caleb.—2. Son of Haran (1 Chr. ii. 46).

GA'ZITES (Judg. xvi. 2). GAZA.

GAZ'ZAM (*devouring*). Ancestor of Nethinim (Exr. ii. 48).

GEBA (*the hill*). Benjamin (Josh. xxi. 17; 1 Chr. vi. 60). Was held by the Philistines (1 Sam. xiii. 3), who were expelled by Jonathan (1 Sam. xiv. 5). Isaiah (x. 28) describes the march of the Assyrians, and their halt at Geba.—2. (Judith iii. 10), where Holofernes is said to have encamped.

GE'BAL (*a line*, or *mountain ridge*). (Ps. lxxxiii.

GED'DUR (1 Esd. v. 30). GAHAR.

GED'EON. GIDEON. 1. Ancestor of Judith (Jud. xiii. 1).—2. Gideon (Heb. xi. 32). Greek form of the Hebrew Gideon.

GE'DER. Judah, extreme S. (Josh. xii. 13). Lost.

GED'ERAH (*sheepcote*). Judah, in the Shefelah (Josh. xv. 36). Lost.

GEDERASHITE. The natives of Gederah (1 Chr. xii. 4).

GEDERITE. Inhabitants of Geder (1 Chr. xxvii. 28).

GED'EROTH (*sheep-cotes*), GEDEROTHAIM (*two sheepcotes*), Lost.

GE'DOR. Judah, in the Mts. (Josh. xv. 58).

near Hebron, or half-way to Bethlehem. The modern name is Jedur.—2. Benj. (1 Chr. xii. 7).—3. (1 Chr. iv. 39). A place from whence Simeon expelled the Hamites, dwellers in tents, and the Maonites. Probably on the way to Petra. Lost.

GEHA'ZI (*valley of vision*). Servant of Elisha. An unfaithful messenger of the good Shunammite (2 K. iv., v.).

GEHEN'NA. The Greek name of Hinnom.

GELIL'OTH (*to roll or wind as a river*). Benj., near Adummim, the same as Gilgal (Josh. xviii. 17).

GEMAL'LE (*camel-driver*). Father of Ammiel. A spy (Num. xiii. 12).

GEMARI'AH (*Jehovah has made perfect*). 1. Son of Shophan, a noble of Judah, who had a chamber in the house of the Lord (Jer. xxxvi.).—2. Son of Hilkiah (xxix.).

GEMS. PRECIOUS STONES.

GENEAL'OGY. The Orientals are peculiar in keeping genealogies of their families, and also of horses and camels. They made them the means of proving titles to property and offices. No list is so long or complete as that of Jesus.

GEN'ERAL (1 Chr. xxvii. 34). ARMY.

GENERATION (Heb. DOR, *a period of time*). Now about thirty years. The Hebrews had no fixed limit. One term is mentioned as 86 years (Gen. xv. 16), another 130 (v. 3), and one 500 years (v. 32). Its average was 30 to 40, probably, as now.

GEN'ESIS. HISTORY OF THE BOOKS.

GENNES'ARET, SEA OF (*the garden*). The Sea of Tiberias; the Sea of Chinnereth; the Sea of Galilee (Num. xxxiv. 11; Josh. xii. 3). Named from a town of the same name (Josh. xix. 35), which is lost, if it is not the site between Tiberias and the hot baths (Josh. xi. 2; Deut. iii. 17). Most of the life of Jesus was passed near this lake. Capernaum was on its shore, "His own city" (Matt. iv. 13). He called his first disciples from among its fishermen (Luke v.). Near it were spoken many of his parables, the Sermon on the Mount, and a number of the miracles were performed. There were 9 cities on its shores, and many others near. It is about 13 ms. long and 6 ms. wide, and the surface is 700 feet below the level of the ocean. The water is, in some places, 250 feet deep. The E. shore is 2,000 feet high, bare of trees, and cut down by deep ravines, quite flat and uniform on the summits. The W. banks are similar, but not so regular in hight, and being opened for the plain of G. The whole basin has a scathed, volcanic look. The climate is quite tropical. Palms and all kinds of trees and vegetables grow luxuriantly, and indigo is cultivated. The beach is pebbly everywhere, and is covered by small, twisted shells, purplish grey. Only one of the 9 cities now remains, Tiberias, almost in ruins, and even the sites of the others are disputed and in doubt.

GENNI'US (*high-born*). Father of Apollonius IV (2 Macc. xii. 2).

GENTILES (Heb. GOYIM, *foreigners, not Jews;* Gr. *ethnos, people; hellene, Greeks*). Any people not Hebrews, and who do not worship Jehovah.

GENUBATH (*theft*). Son of Hadad 4, a member of Pharaoh's court (1 K. xi. 20).

GE'ON. GIHON. One of the four rivers of Paradise (Gen. ii. 13). Perhaps only used as a poetic figure (Eccl. xxiv. 27).

GERA (*a grain*). Descendant of Benjamin (Gen. xlvi. 21). Son of Bela (1 Chr. viii. 3).

GE'RAH (*berry*). WEIGHTS AND MEASURES.

GE'RAR. A very ancient city S. of Gaza (Gen. x. 19; xx. 1; xxvi. 1). Near Kedesh in Shur; peopled by pastoral Philistines. Isaac was born there (xxi. 2, 3), and found it a very fertile land (xxvi. 12), and grew so rich that the Philistines envied him (14).

GER'ASA. In Matt. viii. 28, mistaken for Gadarenes. On the E. border of Peraea (Jos. Wars iii. 3, § 3), in the Mts. of Gilead, 20 ms. E. of the Jordan, 25 N. of Rabbath Ammon, Philadelphia. It was once one of the proudest cities of Syria, as its abundant ruins testify. The Saracens have never occupied it. Built in a narrow valley, on both the sloping sides, 5 miles from the Jabbok. Through it a small creek winds, fringed with many trees and shrubs. There was a colonnade from end to end of the city, with a circular forum at one end. Hundreds of columns are still standing.

It was one of the cities of the Decapolis, but is not mentioned by name in the Bible. The present people are active and prosperous.

GERGESENES. People of Gergesa on the E. of the Sea of Galilee (Matt. viii. 28). GADARENES.

GERIZ'IM (*desert or shorn*). S. of Shechem. The law was given on Mt. Sinai, and the blessing and cursing on the two mountains Ebal and Gerizim. (See EBAL). Jotham stood on G. when he denounced Abimelech (Judg. ix.). When Alexander took Palestine he gave Sanballat (the Persian governor under Darius) permission to build a temple on Mt. G.; and Manasseh, brother of Jaddua the high priest at Jerusalem, was made high priest at Shechem. about 420 B. C. This temple was destroyed by the Jews, 129 B. C. The ruins are still shown. The Samaritans worship here yet, without temple or altar. The view from the summit is one of the finest in Palestine, commanding the deep blue of the Great Sea, snowy Mt. Hermon, purple Gilead and Moab, and the lovely green valley of Mokhna at its foot.

GER'IZITES (*dwelling in a desert land*). GERZITES.

GERRHE'NIANS, THE (2 Macc. xiii. 24). Inhabitants of Gerar.

FIG.

GER'SHOM. 1. Son of Moses (Ex. ii. 22, xviii. 3).—2. Son of Levi (1 Chr. vi. 16, 17, 20).—3. A member of the family of Phinehas (Ezr. viii. 2. GERSON.

GER'SHON (*expulsion*). Son of Levi (Gen. xlvi. 11).

GERSHO'NITES, THE. Descendants of Gershom (1 Chr. xxvi. 21). They had charge of the coverings, curtains, hangings, cords, etc., of the Tabernacle, and of transporting them.

GER'SON (1 Esd. viii. 29). Error for Gershon.

GER'ZITES (*dwelling in a desert*), people who occupied the land S. of Palestine and Egypt (1 Sam. xxvii. 8).

GE'SEM. Goshen. (Jud. i. 9).

GE'SHAM (*filthy*). Son of Jahdai (1 Chr. ii. 47).

GES'HEM (*carcase*). An Arabian (Neh. ii. 19, vi. 2). An inveterate enemy of the Jews in the time of Nehemiah.

GETHSEMANE.

GESH'UR (*bridge*). N.E. in Bashan (Deut. iii. 14). David married Maachah, the daughter of Talmai, king of G. (2 Sam. iii. 3), mother of Absalom. Joab found Absalom in this place (2 Sam. xiii. 37, xv. 8). It is supposed to be the district now called El Lejah.

GESHURI and **GESHURITES.** People of Geshur (Deut. iii. 14).—2. Ancient tribe, in the desert between Arabia and Philistia (Josh. xiii. 2).

GETH'ER (*fear*). Son of Aram (Gen. x. 23).

GETHSEM'ANE (*oil-press garden—wine-press*, oaths, *wine*). "A small farm." In the Kidron valley, on the lower slope of Olivet, 850 feet from St. Stephen's Gate, and 800 feet from the closed Gate, at the angle between the direct road up Olivet and that leading to the right around the hill (both leading to Bethany). Tradition only locates the "garden" (John xviii. 1) here; the "place" (Matt. xxvi. 36; Mark xiv. 32) was "over the brook Kidron, on Olivet somewhere, perhaps nearer Bethany on the road to the right; or rather away from any road. From the days of Eusebius, Jerome, and Adamnanus, some such place has been spoken of as "a place of prayer for the faithful" (Jerome), and having a church built on it. The place might have been selected by the Empress Helena (as many others were), to represent that mentioned in the Gospels. It is now walled in, enclosing eight very old olive-trees, and ornamented with beds of flowers. One of the trees is 25 feet in girth. The city walls and the top of the dome on the Great Mosque are in plain view. The Turks have pleasure-grounds, or gardens, further up the valley, where they resort to enjoy the cool shade of the olive-trees, some of which are quite as large as those in "Gethsemane." The antiquity of these trees is argued from the tax of one medina for each tree, which rate was fixed for trees that stood at the time of the conquest; all those planted since being taxed one-half their produce (Chateaubriand). This would carry the date back to A. D. 634, when Omar took Jerusalem; or, if the tax was decreed after the Turks took the city, to A. D. 1087. Pilgrims pay the guide for showing this place, with others at the Holy City.

GEU'EL (*God's majesty*). Son of Machi; a spy (Num. xiii. 15).

GEZ'ER. City of Canaan, not far from Bethhoron, the west limit of the tribe of Ephraim, (1 Chr. vii. 28). Horam, king of Gezer, came up to help Lachish, and was killed by Joshua (x. 33). David smote the Philistines from Geba to Gezer (2 Sam. v. 25). Site lost.

GEZ'RITES. Inhabitants of Gezer (1 Sam. xxvii. 8).

GHOST (*Spirit*). Holy Spirit.

GI'AH (*breaking forth*) (2 Sam. ii. 24). To distinguish the position of the hill Ammah.

GIANTS. (Heb. NEPHILIM, REPHAIM). Persons of great strength. The Nephilim were living in Canaan at the time of the Exodus (Num. xiii. 33). The sons of Anak were afterwards identified with the same race, living at Hebron. The Rephaim were a tribe living in Canaan, Og being a king of the branch on the east of Jordan (Deut. iii. 11). The same name was in later times given to any large and strong people. The Emim and Zamzummim were also of the giants (ii. 10, 20). These merely strong men gave way before the skilful, and disappear from the history of the cultivated people. Goliath and his brother are the last mentioned.

GIB'BAR (*hero*). 95 of this family returned with Zerubbabel (Ezr. ii. 20). Gibeon in Neh. vii.

GIB'BETHON (*hill*). Town in Dan (Josh. xix. 44). Levitical.

GIBEAH (*rounded—a hill*). 1. G. OF SAUL (1 Sam. xv. 34). The native place of Saul (1 Sam. x. 26; 2 Sam. xxi. 6), where he was a farmer. He made it his capital (xxii. 6). Seven of his descendants were hanged by the Amorites (Is. x. 29). The site is pointed out, four miles north of Jerusalem, at Tuleil el Ful (*little hill of beans*, where there is an ancient ruin on the top of a conical hill.—2. G. OF JUDAH (Josh. xv. 57). Jeba, in Wady Musurr, near Hebron.—3. G. IN BENJAMIN (Josh. xviii. 28), near to Kirjath Jearim, where the Ark of God was kept for a while (2 Sam. vi. 3), in the time of Saul.—4. G. OF PHINEAS (Josh. xxiv. 33). Where Eleazar, son of Aaron, was buried, in Mt. Ephraim, 12 miles north of Jerusalem, near a glen of the same name.—5. G. OF BENJAMIN (Judg. xix., xx.). A city, having a square, and 700 "chosen men," near Bethel; mentioned during the Philistine wars of Saul and Jonathan (1 Sam. xiii., xiv.). *Jeba* in the *Wady Suweinit*.—6. G. IN THE FIELD (Judg. xx. 31). On one of the highways leading from Gibeah of Benjamin. Lost.—7. Several other places are also called Gibeah. 1. (Josh. v. 3), called afterward Gilgal.—2. The hill of Moreh (Judg. vii. 1).—3. *Gibeath-ha-Elohim*, the hill of God (1 Sam. x. 5). Lost.—4. G. of *Hachilah* (1 Sam.

xxiii. 19, xxvi. 1).—5. *G. of Ammah* (2 Sam. ii. 24).—6. *G. of Gareb* (Jer. xxxi. 39).

GIB'EATH (Josh. xviii. 28). **GIB'EATHITE** (1 Chr. xii. 3).

GIBEON (*belonging to a hill*). (Josh. ix. 3-15). One of the 4 cities of the Hivites, the people who made a league with Joshua by an artifice, and so escaped the fate of Jericho and Ai. It was in Benjamin (xviii. 25). TULEIL EL FUL (*hill of beans*). The contest of the two parties of 12, of David and of Ishbosheth, was by the pool of Gibeon. Joab killed Amasa (2 Sam. xx. 10) at the great stone in Gibeon; and Joab himself fled to Gibeon for sanctuary, when condemned by Solomon, and was killed by Benaiah (1 K. ii. 34).

GIB'EONITES (Josh. ix. 17). Hivites who played a trick on Joshua, saving their lives, but accepting a life of servitude (v. 23, 27). Saul attempted their destruction (2 Sam. xxi.), and his sons were "crucified" to appease them.

GIB'LITES. Natives of Gebal (Josh. xiii. 5). The "land of the Giblites" was, among the Promised Land, to be governed by Joshua. They were noted as ship-carpenters in Solomon's time, and as stone-masons. Their chief city, Byblus, was the seat of the worship of Adonis (Ez. viii. 14).

GIDDAL'TI (*I have made great*). Son of Heman (1 Chr. xxv. 4).

GID'DEM (*giant*). 1. Children of G., returned with Zerubbabel (Ezr. ii. 47).—2. Children of G. were "servants of Solomon" (Ezr. ii. 56).

GIDEON (*destroyer*), also, JERUBBAAL (*striver against Baal*). The 5th Judge. He destroyed the Midianite host, with the "300 men that lapped" (Judg. viii. 10).

GIDEO'NI (*cutting down*). Father of Abidan (Num. i. 11).

GI'DOM. Near Rimmon (Josh. xx. 45).

GIFT. This is a formal business in the East. You are compelled by custom to accept and to return a gift from any person, or take the consequences of an insult by refusing. There are 15 names for gift: MINHAH, is a gift from one to a superior (Judg. iii. 15); MASOTH, from a king or any superior (Esth. ii. 18); NISSETH, is similar (2 Sam. xiv. 42); BERACHAH (*blessing*), complimentary; SHOCHAD, bribe; MATTAN, MATTANAH, present (Gen. xxv. 6); METTATH, false gift (Prov. xxv. 14); Greek *doma*, gift (Matt. vii. 11); *dorea*, *dorema*, *doron*, gift or offering; *anathema*, devoted; *charisma*, gift; *charis*, grace; and several others. It was no less an insult to neglect to give a present when custom led one to expect such a mark of respect (1 Sam. x. 27).

GI'HON. The second river of Paradise (Gen. ii. 13).—2. Near Jerusalem, where Solomon was anointed and proclaimed king (1 K. i. 33, 38, 45). The waters of Gihon were "stopped" by Hezekiah; that is, were conducted "straight down to the west side of the city of David" (2 Chr. xxxii. 30). See JERUSALEM.

GIL'ALAI (*heavy*). The son of a priest at the consecration of the wall of Jerusalem (Neh. xii. 36).

GIL'BOA (*bubbling fountain*). A mountain range between the plain of Esdraelon and the Jordan, near which is the city of Jezreel (1 Sam. xxviii. 4; xxix. 1). Mentioned only in connection with the death of Saul and Jonathan (xxxi. 1; 2 Sam. i. 6, xxi. 12; 1 Chr. x. 1, 8). The fountain from which it was named is at its northern base, and was called the well of Harod (Judg. vii. 1), and the spring of Jezreel (1 Sam. xxix. 1). The modern name is *Jebel Fukuah*, and it is 600 feet high above the plain, and there is on its highest summit a village and ruin called *Gelbus* by Eusebius, and *Wezar* by the Arabs.

GIL'EAD (*rugged*), **MOUNT, THE LAND OF** (Gen. xxxi. 21). First known in Jacob's time. It next appears when the Israelites were on the march from Egypt, as divided in two sections and governed by Og and Sihon. It is rich in pastures and forests, well watered, and the great number of ruins bear witness of a former numerous population. It was occupied by Reuben and Gad. The whole extent, from Rabbath Ammon to the Hieromax, is one broad, elevated region or mountain (Deut. iii. 12). The same elevation is called Bashan, north of that river. The Lord showed Moses, from the top of Pisgah, all the land of Gilead unto Dan. Probably a popular phrase, as was "from Dan to Beersheba" (Josh. xx. 8). The Gadites are supposed to have imitated the habits of the people they displaced, which are now preserved by the Bedawins in the same district. Thus Jephthah appears like an Arab sheikh of our day (Judg. xi.); and some of David's captains were trained there (1 Chr. xii. 8, 15). RAMOTH GILEAD was its chief city (1 K. xxii. 4). Gilead first fell before the Assyrians (2 K. xv. 29). It was an asylum for refugees (2 Sam. ii. 8), David fleeing there from Absalom. It is now known south of the Jabbok as *Jebel Jilad*, and north of that river as *Jebel Ajlun*, and the capital is *Es Salt*, on the site of the ancient Ramoth Gilead. The whole country is like a fine park. Graceful hills, rich vales, luxuriant herbage, bright wild-flowers, noble forests, wooded heights, and winding glens clothed with tangled shrubbery, open glades and flat meadows of richest green, all so strongly in contrast with the general barren aspect of Western Palestine.

GIL'EADITE, THE (Judg. x. 3). A branch of the tribe of Manasseh.

BALM OF GILEAD.

GIL'GAL (*circle*), (Josh. iv. 19). Near Jericho; the first encampment of the Israelites in Palestine, where they set up twelve stones as a memorial of the passage of the Jordan. An ancient city (Deut. xi. 30). It was for centuries the great place of the nation's assembly (ix. 6, x. 6, 43). The Tabernacle was pitched here until it was removed to Shiloh (xviii. 1). It was visited by Samuel and Saul and David (1 Sam. x. 8, xi. 14, xiii. 4, xv. 12, xix. 15). There was a high place there for idola-

ters (Hos. iv. 15; Amos iv. 4, v. 5). As prophetical, the place is utterly desolate. It is impossible now to find where the city was. It was probably not far from Jericho.—2. A royal city of the Canaanites, near Dor (Josh. xii. 23). *Jiljuleh* (?) 4 miles south of Antipatris.—3. G. IN THE MOUNTAINS (2 K. ii. 1), *Jiljilia*, 6 miles north of Bethel.

GI'LOH (Josh. xv. 51). Judah. Native place of Ahithophel (2 Sam. xv. 12). Lost.

GI'LONITE (2 Sam. xv. 12).

GIM'ZO (2 Chr. xxviii. 18). Judah, near Dan. Jimzu, a large village on a hill, well shaded with trees, 3 miles S. W. of Lydda, where the two roads from Jerusalem (by the Beth-horons and by the Wady Suleiman, which parted at Gibeon) join and go on to Jaffa. There are some large underground granaries here.

GIN. A trap for birds and beasts (Is. viii. 14; Amos iii. 5).

GI'NATH (*protection*). Father of Tibni (1 K. xvi. 21, 22). He disputed the throne with OMRI.

GIN'NETHO. A priest who returned with Zerubbabel (Neh. xii. 4).

GIN'NETHON (*gardener*). A priest (Neh. x. 6).

GIR'DLE (Heb. HAGOR, EZOR, MEZAH, ABNET; Gr. *zone*). DRESS.

GIR'GASHITES, THE (Gen. x. 16, xv. 21). The descendants of the fifth son of Canaan, who settled on the east of the Sea of Galilee. Called Gergesenes in Matt. viii. 28.

GIS'PA (*caress*). An overseer of Nethinim (Neh. xi. 21).

GIT'TAHHEPHER—GATH-HEPHER. (Josh. xix. 13).

GIT'TAIM (*two wine-presses*). (2 Sam. iv. 3). A place built by the Gibeonites after they had been expelled from Beeroth (Josh. ix. 17). Inhabited by Benjamites, after the return from captivity.

GIT'TITES. People of Gath. 600 men who went with David from Gath (2 Sam. xv. 18, 19).

GIT'TITH. A musical instrument. (Ps. viii., lxxvi., iv.).

GI'ZONITE (*pass, ford*) (1 Chr. xi. 34). Gouni. Guni.

GLASS BLOWERS.

GLASS. So many specimens of ancient glass vessels have been found lately, there is no longer any doubt as to the remote antiquity of the manufacture of glass. It was practiced in Egypt, where the ancient paintings represent men at work over the furnaces, and in the laboratory blowing vessels of glass, at least 1400 B. C. Images, beads, cups, vases, bottles, even coffins, and a great variety of useful and ornamental articles, were made of this material, which are now shown in the Museums at New York and in Europe. The emperor Hadrian was presented by an Egyptian priest with some glass vases, so rare and excellent as to be reserved for unusual occasions of display. Clear glass was not valued, but colored, every variety of tone and tint were sought after. The allusions to glass in the Bible are never to a transparent substance, but to a shining, brilliant, colored mass (Rev. iv. 4). But two colorless, transparent drinking cups were bought by Nero, at a great price. Glass was not used in windows; a thin stone, mica, or talc being used until long after our era. Mirrors (looking-glasses in Ex. xxxviii. 8) were made of metal, not of glass. (MIRROR). The Egyptians (and other ancients) practiced the art of grinding, engraving, and inlaying it with gold enamel, and of working elaborate designs in colors (as an image of a duck with the feathers imitated in form and color) in the midst of masses of clear glass. Precious stones were very successfully imitated by colored glass.

GLEAN'ING. CORNER. The poor had rights of gleaning fruit and grain-fields.

GLEDE (RAAH). *Kite*. Probably the buzzard. (Deut. xiv. 13).

GLORY. The heart, soul, intelligence, feeling, will, and so the glory of a man as a living, rational being. Of God, it is the manifestation of the divine attributes and perfections, or such a visible effulgence of light as indicates these (Ex. xxxii. 18; John i. 14). The chief end of the Christian is, to live "to the glory of God." "Give God the glory," is to confess the truth (Josh. viii. 19; John ix. 24). "My glory" is my soul, in Ps. xvi. 9, xxx. 12, etc.

GLOSS. Explanation. A glossary is a collection of notes intended to illustrate or explain the text. Many words in the Scriptures and the Gospels were obscure to the common people, and needed to be explained, in a theological, historical, geographical, or biographical, allegorical and mystical manner. Some glosses were written in the margin (marginal notes), or between the lines in a smaller letter. These were sometimes transferred into the body of the text by ignorant or careless copyists, a few instances being pointed out. Only the most competent scholars can detect these errors. The great exegetical thesaurus of the middle ages was collected by Walafrid Strabo from Augustine, Ambrose, Jerome, Gregory, Isidore, Beda, Alcuin, Rhabanus Maurus, and his own writings.

GNAT (NAT, Greek *konops*). *Mosquito*. One of the smallest of insects (Matt. xxiii. 24). The bite in the East often produces sores, with fever. Sleeping on high ground, away from water or trees, is one way of avoiding them.

GOAD (Heb. MALMAD, *a pole* (Judg. iii. 31); DORBAN, *the spike point* (1 Sam. xiii. 12). AGRICULTURE.

GOAT (AKKO, YEELIM, AZELAH, *wild goat*, ATTUD, ZAFIR, SAIR, *hairy*, *he-goat* (Greek *satyr*), EZ, *she-goat*, or *goat*, TAISH, GEDI, *kid*, Gr. *eriphion* (Matt. xxv. 33). Goats are an important part of pastoral wealth in the East. Neither Abraham or Job had them, unless they were included in the "flocks." Jacob tended them (ATTUDIM, he-goats, is rendered *rams* in Gen. xxxi. 10, 12). The goat was used in sacrifice as the type of the Christ, and the paschal-lamb could be from the sheep or the goats (Ex. xii. 5), as also the burnt-offering (Lev. i. 10), the peace-offering (iii. 12), the sin-offering (iv. 23), and the trespass-offering (ver. 6); the scape-goat (see ATONEMENT) was a peculiar type of Christ as the sin-bearer (xvi.). The flesh of the kid is excellent; of the old goat not very palatable. An old Karaite gloss says: "The idolaters seethed a kid in its mother's milk, and sprinkled the broth on their trees, gardens, etc., and Moses therefore condemned the practice." Goat's milk is very valuable (Prov. xxvii. 26, 27), and is milked at the door of customers every morning. The skin is used for bottles. The hair for cloth, for cloaks, or

GEM. FLORENCE.

tents (Cant. i. 5; Ex. xxxvi. 14), or pillows (1 Sam. xix. 13). The Angora goat has the longest and best hair for cloth. The long-eared Syrian goat is peculiar to Syria. (The ears are sometimes 2 ft. long). A delicate grey wool under the long hair is the valued stuff for cloth, only three ounces being had from each goat, but of extreme fineness. The goat was a symbol of Macedonia. It is used often by the prophets, poets, and evangelists, as a symbol or type.

GOAT, SCAPE. ATONEMENT.

GO'ATH (*to low*, as a cow). Goath, (*heifer's pool*). (Jer. xxxi. 39). Near the hill Gareb.

GOB (*pit*). (2 Sam. xxi. 18, 19). The scene of two battles between David's soldiers and the Philistines. GEZER, in 1 Chr. xx. 4.

GOB'LET (Heb. AGGAN). A vessel for wine or other liquid (Cant. vii. 2). BASIN, CUP.

GODLINESS, MYSTERY OF (1 Tim. iii. 16). Jesus, the Christ.

GOD-SPEED (2 John 10, 11). Good speed.

GOG (*mountain*). 1. Son of Shemaiah, of Reuben (1 Chr. v. 4).—2. MAGOG.—3. In the Septuagint of Num. xiv. 9, Gog is instead of Agag. Gog, as used by Ezekiel (xxxviii. xxxix), means the head or chief of Magog; and also John (Rev. xx. 8–10), making Gog and Magog persons.

GO'LAN (Deut. iv. 43). A Levitical city of Bashan in Manasseh (Josh. xxi. 27). One of the cities of refuge (xx. 8). The site is lost. The city is not mentioned after the time of Joshua in the Scriptures, but the city and the district of the same name is often mentioned by Josephus. Gamala (*El Husn*), on the east shore of the Sea of Galilee, was in the district (B. J. iv. i. 1). Its principal cities were Golan, Hippos, Gamala, Julias or Bethsaida, Seleucia, and Sogane (Josephus), and about 121 others, nearly all of which are unknown. The country is high (2500 feet), flat, and fertile, well watered, with good pasture. This is the MISHOR of 1 K. xx. 23, 25, where the Syrians were defeated near Aphek (now called *Fik*). The low, rounded hills, called *Tells*, extending south from Hermon for about 20 miles, are partly covered with forests or groves of oak and terebinth. The wandering Bedawins (*Anazeh*) visit the *Jaulan* every year in May, with their flocks and herds.

GOLD (Heb. ZAHAB; Gr. *chrusion, chrusos*). Gold has been known from the earliest times, and seems to have been very abundant among the ancients. It was a representative of wealth, and much used for ornaments and for the decoration and utensils of public buildings. Coined money of gold is not mentioned very early. See MONEY.

GOLDSMITH. Alluded to in Prov. xvii. 3; Is. xlvi. 6; Judg. xvii. 4; Neh. iii. 8, etc.

GOL'GOTHA (*a skull*), (Matt. xxvii. 33, etc.). Where Jesus was crucified, outside of the city gate (Heb. xiii. 12), but near the city (John xix. 20), and a road leading from the country, where there were passers-by (Matt. xxvii. 39); and there was a garden or orchard at the place (Mark xv. 46). The place is not mentioned again until A. D. 335, when a church was built to honor the spot.

The city at that time had a wall about Zion, and another about Acra. Beyond these, to the north, the *suburbs* were enclosed by another wall by Agrippa. This seems to leave no place for the site on that side, and therefore denies the claim of the present Church of the Holy Sepulchre, in the centre of the modern city. Another theory places the site on Mt. Moriah, where now stands the great mosque called the Dome of the Rock, which is claimed to be the real church built by Constantine. There is a cave in a rock under this building, which is claimed to be the tomb; and also that it was Araunah's threshing-floor. Another theory is, that the site was not far from St. Stephen's gate.

Wm. C. Prime has discovered (1871) a wall which he thinks is a part of the ancient 2d wall so long in question, and found it in the right position and direction to exclude the Holy Sepulchre Church, and so arguing for that as the site which was accepted by Constantine (or Helena) as the true one. JERUSALEM.

GOLI'ATH (*exile*) A giant of Gath, who defied the armies of Israel, "morning and evening for forty days," and whose defeat (1 Sam. xvii.) threw such glory around the youthful career of David.

GO'MER (Gen. x. 2, 3; Ezek. xxxviii. 6). Eldest son of Japheth. Progenitor of the Cimmerians, whose traces are found in the Cimmerian Bosporus, C. Isthmus, Mt. Cimmerian, Cimmeria, and the C. walls (Herodotus, iv. 12, 45, 100), and also in the modern name Crimea. The Cymri of Wales, Cambria, and Cumberland in England are assigned to the same origin.

GOAT.

GOMOR'RAH (*submersion*). One of the 5 cities of the plain or vale of Siddim, whose kings joined battle against four kings (Chedorlaomer and his allies, Gen. xiv. 2–8), when Abram came to the rescue. Four of them were destroyed, leaving only Zoar or Bela, which was spared at Lot's request (xix. 23–29). Their fate is alluded to by the prophets as a warning to Israel (Deut. xxix. 23; Is. xiii. 19); to Edom (Jer. xlix. 18; l. 40), to Moab (Zeph. ii. 9); and again to Israel by Amos (iv. 11); and by Peter (2 Pet. ii. 6); and by Jude (verses 4–7), as a warning to those who should "deny Christ."

The site of these cities is a question that it has been impossible to solve. They were said to be in the vale of Siddim, which *became* (is) the Salt Sea (Gen. xiv. 3), or sea of the plain (Josh. xii. 3). Josephus says the region was not submerged (B. J. iv. 8, 4), but remained visible, and parched. It is now known that the Dead Sea was a lake from the creation, being a natural formation which has been undisturbed, not even by a volcano, and the water being very deep (500 to 2,300 feet), leaves no place for sites of cities; and although the south bog (below Lisan) is shallow (3 to 12 feet), its bed has been elevated by the rivers which flow north from the Arabah. Not one of the cities has ever been found, except it may be Zoar. GOMORRHA in the Apocrypha.

GO'PHER (*pitch*). A hard, strong tree, from the wood of which Noah's ark was made (Gen. vi. 14). Cypress or pine.

GOR'GIAS. General of Antiochus Epiphanes (1 Macc. iii. 38).

GORTY'NA. In Crete (1 Macc. xv. 23). It was the capital of the Island under the Romans. The famous Cretan labyrinth was here, the ruins of which are found at the foot of Mt. Ida. Paul may have preached here, while his vessel was at Fair Havens, where "much time" was spent (Acts xxvii. 9).

GO'SHEN. That part of Egypt, east of the Delta, near the way of the land of the Philistines (Ex. xiii. 17), where there was pasture-land, suited to the habits of Joseph's brethren. The only limits that can be indicated from the ancient accounts are the present *Wady El Tumeylat*, and the desert lakes, *Temsah* and *Bitter Lakes*. This region is still very productive wherever it is watered, either from the Nile or from wells (Gen. xiv. 10; xlvi. 28, xlvii. 27, l. 8; Ex. viii. 22, ix. 26). The plagues of Egypt did not effect this land. The soil is capable of tillage to an indefinite extent.

GOS'PELS. Good news. See HISTORY.

SHORT-TOED EAGLE.

GOTHO'NIEL. Othniel, father of Chabris (Judith vi. 15).

GOURD (Heb. KIKAYON; Jonah iv. 6-10). Perhaps the castor-oil plant, which grows like a tree in the East. Some think it was a pumpkin, which grows very large and rapid. The PAKKUOTH (2 K. iv. 39) was a poisonous fruit, gathered by the pupils of Elisha. Thought to be the colocynth. Knops in 1 K. vii. 24.

GOVERNOR (Heb. ALLUPH). A sheikh (Zech. ix. 7); duke in some places.—2. ROKEK, cadi, a justice (Judg. v. 9).—3. MEHOKEK (v. 14).—4. MOSHEL, pasha, judge (Gen. xlv. 26; ruler in Josh. xii. 2).—5. NAGID.—6. NASI.—7. PECHAM.—8. PAKIA.—9. SHALLIT.—10. SAR.—11. SEGAN.—12. Gr. *ethnarches*, ruler.—13. *hegemon*, leader.—14. *oikonomos*, steward.—15. *architriklinos*, ruler of the feast (Eccl. xxxii).

GOZAN (*quarry*), (1 Chr. v. 26). The Gauzanites of Ptolemy, watered by the Habor, in Assyria, where the Israelites were carried captive. Mygdonia.

GRACE (*favor*). (Heb. CHEN; Gr. *charis*.) Kindness towards mankind shown by the Lord Jesus (John i. 14, 16, etc.).

GRASS. (Heb. HATZIO; *herbage*). (1 K. xviii. 5); DASHA, first-shoots, in Jer. i. 11; YEREK, green (Num. xxii.4); ESEB, *herbs* (Gen. i. 30). Gr. *chortos* (Matt. vi. 30); blade in Mark iv. 28.

GRASSHOPPER. LOCUST.

GRAY'HOUND. GREY-HOUND. Alluded to in Prov. xxx. 31, as one of "four things which are comely in going." Some prefer "horse," and others "cock."

GRE'CIAN. Believing Greeks from Greece (Acts vi. 1, etc.). Also such Jews as had been born in other lands, as well as in Palestine, but who had been educated abroad.

GREECE (Greek *Hellas*; Heb. JAVAN). Greece included the four provinces of Macedonia, Epirus, Achaia (Hellas) and Peloponnesus (Morea). Generally only Hellas and Peloponnesus are meant. The grand features are mountain and sea, which exerted a strong influence on the character of the people, as appears in their poetry, religion, and history. The climate is very temperate, the air salubrious, and the soil fertile. Its history extends back to B. C. 776, in authentic records, and beyond that in traditions and myths, such as that of Ægialus, who founded Sicyon B. C. 2089, and of Uranus, who settled there B. C. 2012. The Greeks said they received from Asia Minor, Phœnicia, and Egypt letters and laws, and certain tenets in religion. The Egyptian Inachus founded Argos B. C. 1856, and Cecrops led a colony 300 years earlier to Attica, carrying with him the worship of the goddess Neith (Athena). The Phœnician Cadmus founded Thebes in Bœotia, and taught the Greeks letters. (See MOABITE STONE.) The Phrygian Pelops took possession of the south, B. C. 1283, naming it after himself. The famous expedition of Jason and the Argonauts in search of the golden fleece, is dated B. C. 1263, and the siege of Troy, 1193. From the First Olympiad, B. C. 776, to B. C. 300, Greece was a leader power in politics and religion. It is chiefly from Alexander's time down, that the Bible has to do with Greece. First known to the Jews in the slave-market of Tyre, where the prophet Joel charges the Tyrians with selling Hebrew children to the Grecians (Joel iii. 6), B. C. 800; and Ezekiel says, "traded the persons of men and vessels of brass in thy market" (Ez. xxvii. 13). Greek slaves were highly valued in all the East (Bochart i., c. iii. 175). Daniel mentions Greece (viii. 21, etc.) in his sketch of Alexander and his successors. Alexander visited Jerusalem, and respected its religion (Ant. xi. 8, 3). The Lacedæmonians sent an embassy and a letter to the Jews, B. C. 300 (Ant. xii. 4, 10), when king Areus claims kinship for his people with the Jews. Paul visited Greece (Acts xx. 2), staying there three months. The Greeks, and their language, were so influential in Paul's time that the name Greek stands in the N. T. as Gentile does in the O. T. Their influence on the spread of the Gospel by a peculiar preparation of the mind for the Gospel teachings was very great, in quickening thought and destroying indifference to religion. (See GOSPELS in the HISTORY). The arts of war, and the fine-arts of peace were carried to a great perfection. Their Asiatic empire spread their institutions, and filled half of Asia Minor with temples, theatres, aqueducts, and well-built cities. The Church did not flourish in Athens, but was more eminent in Corinth.

GREEK. Educated in the religion and language of Greece. Barbarian was any one who was not a Greek.

GREEK VERSIONS OF THE O. T. See HISTORY, p. iv.

GRINDING. MILL.

GROVE (Heb. ASHERAH, *an image worshiped in the grove*), (2 K. viii. 6). A wood dedicated to idolatry. The sacred symbolic tree of Assyria refers to the same idea. The Hebrew word ELON also means grove (translated oak of Mamre, in Gen. xiii. 18, and of Moreh, in xii. 6, etc.). The grove took the place of the church building in the ancient heathen religions, where altars were erected to the gods. Pliny says trees were the first temples. Afterwards the temples were built in the groves. The Temple of Solomon had figures of trees on its interior walls for ornaments. The mosque which stands on its site now has olive, palm and cedar trees growing around it. Tree-worship was widespread, and is not yet passed away. The Buddhists of India venerate the banian (fig tree). The Etrurians worshiped a palm, the Druids and Celts an oak.

GUARD (Heb. 1. TABBACH, *a cook*, afterwards *an executioner*), (Gen. xxxvii. 36).—2. RAZ, *a runner* (2 Sam. xv. 1). They also carried dispatches. "Guard-chamber" (1 K. xiv. 28).—3. MISHMERETH, *watching* (Neh. iv. 9). "Which goeth at thy bidding," in 1 Sam. xxii. 14, should be "captain of the body-guard."

GUD'GODAH (*thunder*), (Deut. x. 7). HAGIDGAD.

GUEST. HOSPITALITY. Guest-chamber. HOUSE.

GUILTY. Bound by his oath (Matt. xxiii. 1). Deserving death (Num. xxxv. 31).

GUL'LOTH (Josh. xv. 19). Springs, upper and lower, added by Caleb to his daughter Achsah's dower. They were near Debir, but cannot now be identified. Possibly *Ain Nunkar*, and *Dewir Ban*, east of Hebron.

GU'NI (*colored*). 1. Son of Naphtali (Gen. xlvi. 24).—2. Descendants of Gael (1 Chr. v. 15), father of Abdiel.

GU'NITES, THE. Sons of Naphtali (Num. xxvi. 48).

GUR (*ascent*). Where Ahaziah was wounded (2 K. ix. 27) at Ibleam, between Jezreel and Bethhaggan (*garden-house*), which is now said to be Jenin. The pass may be the very steep place on the road from Jezreel to the plain of Esdraelon, near Megiddo.

GUR'BA'AL (*ascent of Baal*), (2 Chr. xxvi. 7). "And God helped him (Uzziah) against the Arabians that dwelt in Gur-baal." Supposed to mean Gerar.

GUTTER (correctly, *a water-course*). 2 Sam. v. 6, should read "but the blind and the lame will turn these away;" and verse 8, "Any one that smites a Jebusite, and gets to the water-course."

H

HAAHASH'TARI (Heb. *the Ahashtarite messenger*). Father (builder) of Tekoa (1 Chr. iv. 6).

HABA'IAH (*Jehovah protects*), (Ezr. ii. 61; Neh. vii. 63). Sons of Chobaijah were among the returned from captivity.

HABAK'KUK. See HISTORY OF THE BOOKS.

HABAZINI'AH (*light of Jah.*) Ancestor of Jaazaniah (Jer. xxxv. 3).

HABERGEON. A coat of mail covering the neck and breast. See ARMS.

HABOR (1 Chr. v. 26). A river and district in Assyria, where Tiglath Pileser placed some of the Jews of the tribes of Reuben and Gad, during the First Captivity; and where, 17 years after, Shalmaneser, his successor, settled captives from Samaria and Israel (2 K. xvii. 6, xxviii. 11). The Khabur (name of a river) is found in an Assyrian inscription of the date of 909 B. C.

HACHILI'AH (*Jehovah enlivens*). Father of Nehemiah (Neh. i. 1, x. 1).

HACHI'LAH, THE HILL (1 Sam. xxiii. 13, 19). On the S. of Jeshimon (the barren district), near Ziph, in a forest, where David and his 600 men hid from Saul, and David in the night took away Saul's spear and bottle of water from his couch, and showed them to Abner, the captain of Saul's guard, next morning from the opposite bank of the ravine (xxvi. 5-20). See DAVID.

HACHMO'NI (*wise*). Son of and *The Hachmonite* (1 Chr. xxvii. 32, xi. 11). Head of a large family. TACHMONITE.

HADAD, CHADAD (*mighty*). 1. Son of Ishmael (Gen. xxv. 15).—2. A king of Edom (Gen. xxxvi. 35).—3. The last king of Edom at Pai (1 Chr. i.

COIN OF VESPASIAN.

50).—4. Member of the royal house of Edom (1 K. xi. 14). He married the sister-in-law of the Pharaoh of Egypt. After David died, he attempted to recover his lost dominion from Solomon.

HADAD'EZER (*Hadad is his help*) (2 Sam. viii. 3, 12). HADAREZER.

HA'DAD RIM'MON (both words are names of Syrian idols). The city was a stronghold before Abraham's time. Here king Josiah "went against" Pharaoh Necho, was wounded, and died at Jerusalem (2 K. xxiii. 29; 2 Chr. xxxv. 20-23). Mentioned by the prophet Zechariah (xii. 11). Four or five miles south of *Lejjun* is a ruin on a hill, which (*Rumana*) is supposed to be the ancient site.

HA'DAR (*chamber*). Hadad, in 1 Chr. i. 30. Eighth son of Ishmael. The Mt. Hadad on the borders of the Syrian desert north of El Medineh, is supposed to mark the locality of this branch of Ishmael's family.

HA'DAREZER. Son of Rehob (2 Sam. viii. 3). King of ZOBAH (1 Chr. xviii. 3, ff). David captured from him 1000 "shields of gold" besides other great spoil.

HAD'ASHAH (*new*), (Josh. xv. 37). Judah, in the Shefelah. Adasa (1 Macc. vii. 40), where Nicanor was killed by Judas Maccabæus. Lost.

HADAS'SAH (*myrtle*), (Esth. ii. 7).

HADAT'TAH (*new*), (Josh. xv. 25). Judah, between Beersheba and Kedesh. Hazor-Hadattah; New Hazor.

HADES, HELL (*covered*) Heb. SHEOL, (*hollow*). The unseen world, the state (and condition) of the dead, both good and bad; Greek *gehenna*, from the Hebrew GE-HINNOM, the valley of Hinnom (Josh. xv. 8). This place became infamous because of the sacrifice of infants there by Manasseh, to the

god Moloch (2 Chr. xxxii. 6), at a spot called Topheth (Is. xxx. 33), and a type of torment in the spirit world. The Jews held a belief in a condition of the souls after death, in SHEOL, in reward or in punishment, and this they thought was in the bowels of the earth. Hades was the place (or condition) where the soul of Jesus went, and it was not Hell in the modern sense of that term—the place of the damned—but rather Abraham's bosom, or Paradise. There will be no fire, or brimstone, or gnawing worm, in hell, any more than thrones of gold, crowns of precious stones, gates,

HEAD DRESSES.

streets, rivers, etc., in heaven; these are only ideas of certain conditions of character in each case (Matt. xxiii. 15; Luke xii. 47, 48). The duration, so far as each soul is concerned is limited, and spiritual evil, sin and death and hell will be destroyed (Rev. xx.), but as the human race will be perpetual, always renewing by birth, always ending by death, so will hades be eternal; so long as there are living men to die there will be an underworld to receive the dead.

HA'DID (*sharp*), (Ez. ii. 33; Neh. vii. 37, xi. 34). Three ms. from Lydda, 10 ms. from Joppa (1 Macc. xii. 38). Alexander was defeated here by Aretas (Ant. xiii. 15, 2), and Vespasian made it an outpost during his siege of Jerusalem. ADIDA. ADITHAIM.

HAD'LAI (*resting*). Father of Amasa 2 (2 Chr. xxviii. 12).

HĀD'ORAM. Fifth son of Joktan (Gen. x. 27; 1 Chr. i. 21). Probably located, with Joktan's other descendants, in South Arabia, but not yet identified. The Adramitæ, and Hadramaut have been suggested, but rejected on philological grounds.

HĀ'DRACH (Zech. ix. 1). A district somewhere in the vicinity of Damascus. Lost.

HĀ'GAB (*locust*). Ancestor of Nethinim who returned with Zerubbabel (Ezr. ii. 46).

HAG'ABA. Ancestor of Nethinim who came with Zerubbabel (Neh. vii. 48). HAGABAH (Ezr. ii. 45).

HA'GAR (*stranger*). An Egyptian slave (Gen. xii. 16, xvi. 1), presented to Abraham by Pharaoh. Mother of Ishmael. The Hagarites settled in Paran (Gen. xxi. 21; Gal. iv. 22). They are mentioned in 1 Chr. xi. 38, where Mibhar, a Hagarite, is one of David's captains. Jaziz, a Hagarite, had charge of David's flocks, and an Ishmaelite of his camels, because they had experience in the care of such animals (1 Chr. xxvii. 31). The HAGARITES occupied the country south of Palestine, from the sea to the Euphrates, as the Bedawins do now.

Hejer is the capital of a district in the province of El Bahreyn, in N. Arabia, near the Persian Gulf.

HAG'GAI (*festive*). The 9th in order of the minor prophets, who returned with Zerubbabel from captivity. See HISTORY OF THE BOOKS.

HAG'GERI. Descendant of Hagar. Mibhar, son of Haggeri, was an officer of David's guard (1 Chr. xi. 38).

HAG'GI. Son of Gad (Gen. xlvi. 16). Haggites (Num. xxvi. 15).

HAGGI'AH (*festival of Jah*). A Levite (1 Chr. 30).

HAG'GITH (*festive*). Mother of Adonijah (2 Sam. iii. 4).

HAIL. Was one of the plagues of Egypt. Hail is more common than snow in the hill country of Palestine (Ps. cxlviii. 8). God smote the Amorites with "hail-stones" (Josh. x. 11). RAIN.

HAIR. The Egyptians were very uniform in their habits of dressing the hair. Herodotus says that they let their hair and beard grow only in mourning. The priests, who were to be clean to the highest possible degree, had to shave their whole bodies every third day. Other men shaved the head only—or the beard also. The women wore their hair natural, but braided, and dressed with strings of silk with ornaments. The Assyrian men wore the hair combed and curled, falling quite low about the neck; wearing the whiskers curled also. Among the Greeks and Romans, the fashion of wearing the hair passed through many changes. One style is shown on p. 76. The Hebrews cut the men's hair quite short, almost to the ears (Ez. xliv. 20), and to keep the beard a proper length by trimming it, but not to shave either head or beard. The NAZARITE was an exception, who let both hair and beard grow uncut or uncombed.

HAK'KATAN (*little*). Father of Johanan, who was a chief, and returned with Ezra from Babylon (Ezr. viii. 12).

HAK'KOZ (*thorn*). A priest in the service of David (1 Chr. xxiv. 10).

HAKU'PHA (*bent*). Ancestor of Nethinim; came from Babylon with Zerubbabel (Ezr. ii. 51).

HA'LAH (2 K. xvii. 6). In Assyria, where Tiglath Pileser planted some of the captive Jews. Now called Kalah, an ancient ruin on the side of the upper Khabur.

HEAD DRESS.

HA'LAK, THE MOUNT (*the smooth, bald mountain*). (Josh. xi. 17, xii. 7). The south limit of Joshua's conquests near Mt. Seir. The name of the east end of Akrabbim.

HAL'HUL (Josh. xv. 58). Judah. Four miles north of Hebron, on the top of a hill, is a ruin, and at its foot is a village bearing the ancient name.

HA'LI (Josh. xix. 25). On the border of Asher. May be Alia, 5 ms. N. E. of Acre.

HALICARNAS'SUS (1 Macc. xv. 25). In Caria, on the Ceramian gulf. The birth-place of Herod-

GETHSEMANE.

HALL. Court of the high-priest's house (Luke xxii. 55; in Matt. xxvii. 27, and Mark xv. 16). Hall, in John xviii. 28. "judgment-hall." A covered space, surrounded by rooms opening into it; or, perhaps, a large audience chamber. The court of a dwelling-house is not covered.

HALLELU'JAH (*praise ye Jah*). Praise ye the Lord. Allelula in Rev. xix. 1–6; Ps. cxiii.–cxviii., were called *hallel* (praise), and were used on special occasions.

HALLO'HESH (*enchanter*). A chief, who signed the covenant with Nehemiah (Neh. x. 24).

HALO'HESH. Son of Halohesh, ruler of half of Jerusalem (Neh. iii. 12).

HAM (*warm*), (Egyptian *chen, dark*). One of the sons of Noah (Gen. vi. 10), perhaps the third, if Japheth was the elder brother (x. 21). Settled in Africa (Ps. lxxviii. 51, cv. 23, cvi. 22), and also sent many branches into Asia (Canaanites). There is no ancient name so well preserved and located. Ham is identified with JUPITER AMMON, and also ZEUS, because both words are derived from a root meaning hot, fervent, or sunburnt. For the last 3000 years the world has been mainly indebted for its advancement to the Semitic races; but before this period the descendants of Ham—Egypt and Babylon—led the way as the pioneers in art, literature and science. Mankind at the present day lies under infinite obligations to the genius and industry of those early ages, more especially for alphabetic writing, weaving cloth, architecture, astronomy, plastic art, sculpture, navigation and agriculture. The art of painting is also represented, and music indirectly, by drawings of instruments.

THE SONS AND GRANDSONS OF HAM, AND THEIR LOCATION.

HAM.			
CUSH.	Seba,		Meroe, in Egypt.
	Havilah,		Abyssinia.
	Sabtah,		S. W. coast Red Sea.
	Raamah,	Sheba, Dedan.	Arabia, Persia.
	Sabtechah,		Ethiopia.
MIZRAIM.	Nimrod (Belus),		Shinar. Chaldæa.
	Ludim,		West, in Africa.
	Anamim,		Marcotis.
	Lehabim,		Libyans.
	Naphtuhim,		Memphis.
	Pathrusim,		Thebes. Pathros.
	Casluhim,		Arabia Petræa.
	Caphtorim,		Damietta.
PHUT.			Lybians.
CANAAN.	Sidon,		Sidon and Tyre.
	Heth,		Hittites.
	Jebusites,		Jerusalem.
	Amorites,		Judæa.
	Girgasite,		Gergesenes.
	Hivite,		Shechem.
	Arkite,		Arke.
	Sinite,		Sinnas.
	Arvadite,		Island of Arvad.
	Zemarite,		Sumrah (ruin).
	Hamathite,		Hamath.

HA'MAN (*magnificent*). Prime minister of King Ahasuerus (Esth. iii. 1). After he failed in his conspiracy he was hanged on the same gallows he had made for Mordecai. He is called a Macedonian in Esther xvi. 10 (Apoc.).

HAMATH (*to defend*). The principal city of North Syria and capital of a district of the same name (Gen. x. 18). In the centre of the Orontes valley. Toi, king of Hamath, paid tribute to David (2. Sam. viii.). Hamath was conquered by Solomon (2 Chr. viii. 3). Alexander took it and changed its name to Epiphania, in honor of Antiochus Epiphanes. It has now 30,000 people, is a well-built city, in a narrow and rich valley. Four bridges span the rapid river. The chief trade is in silk, woollen, and cotton. "The entrance to Hamath," so often used as a landmark in the O. T. (*Land and Book* i. 354), and Tristram (*Land of Israel*, 621), the entrance into the valley as you look north from Baalbek.

HAMATHZOBAH (*fortress of Zobah*), (2 Chr. viii. 3).

HAMATHITE (*from Hamath*). A family descended from Canaan (Gen. x. 18).

SHEKEL.

HAM'MATH (*warm baths*). One of the fenced cities of Naphtali (Josh. xix. 35). Josephus mentions a city called Ammaus (*warm water*), one mile from Tiberias, on the shore of the Sea of Galilee. Ibrahim Pacha built spacious baths over these four warm springs. The water is 144° Fahr., very salt and bitter, with a strong, sulphurous odor. There are ancient ruins for a mile or more around.

HAMMEDA'THA (*double*). Father of Haman (Esth. iii. 1, 10).

HAM'MELECH (Jer. xxxvi. 26; xxxviii. 6). Hebrew term for "the king."

HAM'MER. 1. A tool used by the gold-beaters (Is. xli. 7). Carpenter (Jer. xxiii. 29).—2. A tool for hollowing (1 K. vi. 7); a weapon of war (Prov. xxv. 18). See ARMS. The Maccabees were so named from Hammer (MACBEH).

HAMMOL'EKETH (*the queen*). Daughter of Machir (1 Chr. vii. 17, 18).

HAM'MON (*hot*). In Asher (Josh. xix. 28). *Hamul*, near Zidon.—2. Levitical, in Naphtali (1 Chr. vi. 76); the same as HAMMOTH DOR, (Josh. xxi. 32). Levitical city in Naph. HAMMATH.

HAMO'NAH (*multitude*). A city in which the people of Gog will be buried (Ez. xxxix. 16).

HA'MONGOG, THE VALLEY OF (*Gog's multitude*). Name to be given to a glen on the east of the sea (Ez. xxxix. 11, 15).

HA'MOR (*a he-ass*). Father of Shechem (Gen. xxxiii. 19).

HAM'UEL (*God's wrath*). Son of Mishma (1 Chr. iv. 26).

HA'MUL (*pillared*). Son of Pharez, son of Judah by Tamar (Gen. xlvi. 12).

HA'MULITES. The descendants of Hamul of Judah (Num. xxvi. 21).

HAMU'TAL (*dew's brother*). Daughter of Jeremiah (2 K. xxiii. 31).

HAN'AMEEL (*safety*). Son of Shallum (Jer. xxxii. 7–9, 12, 44).

HA'NAN (*merciful*). A chief of Benjamin (1 Chr. viii. 23). There are eight others of this name, but none famous.

HAN'ANEEL, THE TOWER OF. In the wall of Jerusalem (Neh. iii. 1). Between the sheep-gate and the fish-gate, on the N. E. corner of the city.

HANA'NI. 1. Son of Heman (1 Chr. xxv. 4, 25).—2. A seer (B. C. 941), king of Judah (2 Chr. xvi. 7).—3. A priest (Ezr. x. 20).—4. Brother of

Nehemiah (Neh. i. 2). Governor of Jerusalem B. C. 445 (vii. 2).—5. A priest (xii. 36).

HANANI'AH (*Jah is kind*). 1. Son of Heman (1 Chr. xxv. 4, v. 23).—2. Captain in King Uzziah's army (2 Chr. xxvi. 11).—3. Father of Zedekiah (Jer. xxxvi. 12).—4. Son of Azur, a false prophet (Jer. xxvii. xxviii.). He opposed Jeremiah in predicting a return from Babylon in 2 years, when the time had been fixed at 70.—5. Grandfather of Irijah (Jer. xxxvii. 13).—6. Head of a Benjamite house (1 Chr. viii. 24).—7. Shadrach, of the house of David (Dan. i. 3, 6, 7, 11).—8. Son of Zerubbabel (1 Chr. iii. 19).—9. Son of Bebai (Ezr. x. 28).—10. A priest (Neh. iii. 8)—11. Head of Jeremiah's priestly course (xii. 12).—12. Steward of the palace at Jerusalem vii. 2, 3).—13. A chief who signed the covenant with Nehemiah (x. 23).

HAND (YAD, *power, agency*). Laying on of hands, sign of authority, or of a blessing conferred (Num. xxvii. 18). Sitting at the right hand of power, man of my right hand.

HAN'DICRAFT. Special workmen were among the great benefactors of ancient times, and were honored as the chief favorites. God is honored for his "handiwork" (Ps. viii. 3; xix. 1; Gen. ii. 2; Job xxxiv. 19). Several men are honored in the O. T. for their work, as Tubal-Cain, Jabal, Jubal, and Bezaleel. The Hebrews were more agricultural than scientific or artistic, and invented little, yet their skill is recorded in the cases of the tabernacle and the temple. Among the metal workers were goldsmiths, silversmiths, coppersmiths, and ironworkers, whose work is often mentioned. The tools noticed are forceps (tongs, in Is. vi. 6), hammer, anvil, bellows. The carpenters (woodcarvers) were skilful (Is. xli. 7). Their implements were the rule (chalk-pencil), measuring-incl, compasses, plane or smoothing instrument, saw, hatchet, knife, awl, nail, hone, drill, mallet, chisel, etc. There were boat-builders also. Spinners, weavers, fullers, dyers, tent-makers, embroiderers. Tanning and dressing leather. Masons, bakers, butchers, cheese-makers, shoemakers, barbers, are mentioned in the Bible, and drawn on the monuments engaged in their proper avocations.

HAN'NIEL (*grace of God*). Son of Ephod. A prince (Num. xxxiv. 23).

HA'NOCH (*initiated*). ENOCH and HENOCH. 1. Children of Midian (Gen. xxv. 4).—2. Son of Reuben (Gen. xlvi. 9).

SILVERSMITHS.

HA'NOCHITES, THE. Descendants of Hanoch (Num. xxvi. 5).

HA'NUN (*favored*). 1. Son of Nahash (2 Sam. x. 1, 2).—2. A man who repaired the wall of Jerusalem (Neh. iii. 13).—3. Son of Zalaph, who also assisted in the repairs (iii. 30).

HAPH'RAIM (*two pits*), (Josh. xix. 19). Issa. Six miles E. of Lejjun, two W. of Shunem; now called El Fuleh.

HA'RA (*mountain land*), (1 Chr. v. 26). Province in Assyria, where some of the Jews of the tribe of Reuben and Gad were carried captive.

HAR'ADAH. Station in the wandering (Num. xxxiii. 24). Lost.

HA'RAN (Gen. ix. 31). Terah and his family (including Abraham) came to Haran and dwelt there; where Terah died. Called Padan Aram (plain of Aram). Aram Naharaim (A. of the two rivers). In 2 K. xix. 12, it is connected with Gozan, Mesopotamia, taken by the Assyrians. Ezekiel groups it with Canneh, Eden, and other cities in Assyria (xxvii. 23). Harran (of the Arabs) stands on the banks of the small river *Belik*, a branch of the Euphrates. From it a number of roads radiate to the great fords of the Tigris and Euphrates. Being in the route of the trade between Central and Western Asia it attracted Terah, and explains the allusion of the prophet Ezekiel. There is a *Harran el Awamid* 10 ms. east of Damascus, on the shore of the lake Ateibeh, between "the two rivers" Abana and Pharpar. In 1861 Dr. Beke made a journey to Palestine especially to follow the route of Laban and Jacob from Haran, and walked over the ground in about

BOAT-BUILDING.

HANDKERCHIEF (*napkin, apron*), (Luke xix. 20). Larger and longer than ours, and of stronger cloth, fit for various uses, as a girdle or turban.

HA'NES. In Egypt (Is. xxx. 4). ANASIEH on the W. branch of the Nile. Perhaps Tahpanhes.

HANGINGS. (Heb. MASACH, *curtain*, Ex. xxvi. 10). KELAIM, *tapestry* (xxvii. 9).

HAN'IEL. Son of Ulla (1 Chr. vii. 39).

HAN'NAH (*grace*). Wife of Elkanah, and mother of Samuel (1 Sam. i. 2.).

HAN'NATHON (*graceful*). Zebulon (Josh. xix. 14). Lost.

5 days, which agrees with the Bible narrative. The flocks, herds, and little children could not have been driven across the desert, 300 miles, 25 days without water. The route in the Hauran is well watered, and has good pasture all the way.

HAR'ARITE (*mountain*). One of David's men. 1. Father of Shammah (2 Sam. xxiii. 11).—2. Shammah, the Hararite (xxiii. 33.)—3. Sharar (xxiii. 33); father of Ahiam.

HARBONA (*ass-driver*). A eunuch in the service of King Ahasuerus (Esth. i. 10). Harbonah in Esth. vii. 9.

HARE (ARNEBETH). Unclean under the law, "because he cheweth the cud but divideth not the hoof." It is of the squirrel kind, and does not chew the cud, but moves the jaw as though it did. There are two kinds in Palestine, the Syrian and Egyptian, and are very plentiful in some parts, and afford good returns to the hunter. There are no rabbits.

HAR'EL (*the mountain of*), (Ez. xliii. 15).

HA'REPH (*early-born*). Son of Caleb, and father of Beth-gader (1 Chr. ii. 51).

HA'RETH, THE FOREST OF (1 Sam. xxii. 5). Forest in Judah, to which David fled after leaving the cave of Adullam. See DAVID.

HARHAI'AH (*dry*). Father of Uzziel 6 (Neh. iii. 8).

HAR'HAS (*poverty*). Ancestor of Shallum (2 K. xxii. 14).

HAR'HUR (*inflammation*). The sons of Harhur returned with Zerubbabel (Ezr. ii. 51).

HA'RIEL. HADID (Ezr. ii. 33).

HA'RIM (*flat-nosed*). 1. A priest in the house of God (1 Chr. xxiv. 8).—2. 1,017 "children of Harim," returned from captivity (Ezr. ii. 39).—3.—4. Families of the children of Harim, 320 in number, who came from the Captivity (Ezr. ii. 32). REHUM.

HA'RIPH (*autumnal rain*.) 112 "children of Hariph," who returned with Zerubbabel (Neh. vii. 24). People who sealed the covenant (x. 19).

HAR'LOT (ZONAH, NOCHRIYAH, KEDHISHA, *set apart for a sacred use*). They had a certain way of wearing their dress, and sometimes sat in a public place (Prov. vii. 10; Gen. xxxviii. 14), and might have been foreign women, not Hebrews. They sung in the streets (Is. xxiii. 16; Eccles. ix. 4). Some had houses (1 K. iii. 16). Jephthah's mother was a harlot, or "strange woman" (Judg. xi. 2). Gods were anciently, and are now actually worshiped in brothels (see Herodotus). This licentious worship was found at Baal-Peor, and among the Samaritans who came from Assyria (2 K. xvii. 30). The law of Moses was very strong against the practice, not even allowing the money earned by such a trade to come into the treasury (Lev. xix. 29), and made very severe laws in some cases (xxi. 9), which were sometimes carried out (Gen. xxxviii. 24), and neglected at others (Micah i. 7), as in the case of Samaria.

HAR'NEPHER (*panting*). Son of Zophah (1 Chr. vii. 36).

HAR'NESS (*armor*), (1 K. xx. 11). See HORSE.

HAR'NESSED (Josh. i. 14, iv. 12). Armed men.

HA ROD, THE WELL OF. Correctly, the fountain (Judg. vi. 33). The fountain by which Gideon pitched, having the Hill of Moreh on the north, in the valley of Jezreel (vii. 1). Now called *Ain Jalud*, at the foot of Mount Gilboa. It is a very large spring, and is visited constantly by a great number of flocks and herds (Judg. vi. 5).

HA'RODITE (*from Harod*). Descendants of David's strong men (2 Sam. xxiii. 25).

HA'ROEH (*the seer*). Son of Shobal (1 Chr. ii. 52).

HA RORITE, THE. One of David's guard (1 Chr. xi. 27).

HARO SHETH OF THE GENTILES (Judg. iv. 2). In the north of Palestine, the home of Sisera. *Tell Harothieh* is an immense double hill, covered with the ruins of old walls and buildings, commanding a narrow pass where the Kishon flows close to the foot of Carmel. Barak and Deborah chased Sisera and his scattered host as far as this pass, after their terrible defeat and slaughter along the plain of Esdraelon. (*Thomson, Land and Book*).

HARP (Heb. KINNOR; Gr. *kithara*). A stringed instrument of music. Josephus says it had 10 strings, and was played with a plectrum; others say it had 24 or 47 (1 Sam. xvi. 23, xviii. 10).

HARROW (1 Chr. xx. 3). See AGRICULTURE.

HAR'SHA (*worker*). Ancestor of Nethinim, who returned with Zerubbabel (Ezr. ii. 52).

HART. A clean animal (Deut. xii. 15). Permitted by the law for food. See FALLOW-DEER.

HA'RUM (*exalted*). Father of Aharhel (1 Chr. iv. 8).

HARU'MAPH (*snub-nosed*). Father of Jedaiah 2 (Neh. iii. 10).

HARU'PHITE (*strong*). A Korhite, who joined David at Ziklag (1 Chr. xii. 5).

HA'RUZ (*active*). Father of Meshullemeth (2 K. xxi. 19).

HAR'VEST. AGRICULTURE.

HASHADI'AH (*whom Jah loves*). A descendant of Judah (1 Chr. iii. 20).

HASENU'AH (*bristling*). A Benjaminite (1 Chr. ix. 7).

HASHABI'AH (*Jah regards*). Son of Amaziah

SARCOPHAGUS.

(1 Chr. v. 45). There are 13 of this name, but none of them were noted.

HASHAB'NAH. Chief of the people who signed the covenant with Nehemiah (Neh. x. 25).

HASHABNI'AH. 1. Father of Hattush 2 (Neh. iii. 10).—2. A Levite (ix. 5).

HASHBAD'ANA (*thoughtful judge*). One who stood with Ezra when he read the law to the people of Jerusalem (Neh. viii. 4).

HA'SHEM (*fat*). The sons of Hashim were among David's strong men (1 Chr. xi. 34). Joshen.

HASHMAN'NIM (*opulent nobles*). (Ps. lxviii. 31).

HASHMO'NAH (*fatness*). (Num. xxxiii. 29). Near Mt. Hor. HESHMON(?)

HA'SHUB. HASSHUB. 1. Son of Pahath-moab (Neh. iii. 11).—2. Another, who assisted in the repairs of the Jerusalem wall (iii. 23).—3. One of the heads of the people who signed the covenant (x. 23).—4. A Levite (xi. 15).

HASHU'BAH (*esteemed*). Part of the family of Zerubbabel (1 Chr. iii. 20). HASADIAH.

HA'SHUM (*rich*). 1. 1,023 "children of Hashum," returned with Zerubbabel (Ezr. ii. 19; x.

33).—2. One who stood on Ezra's left, when he read the law to the people (viii. 4).

HASHU'PHA. Ancestor of Nethinim (Neh. vii. 46).

HAS'RAH. Harhas (2 Chr. xxxiv. 22).

HASSENA'AH (*thorny*). "Sons of Hassenaah" rebuilt the fish-gate in the wall of Jerusalem (Neh. iii. 3).

HASU'PHA (*stripped*). Ancestor of Nethinim (Ezr. ii. 43).

HA'TACH (*verity*). Eunuch in Ahasuerus' court (Esth. iv. 5, 6 9, 10).

HA'THATH (*terror*). Son of Othniel (1 Chr. iv. 13).

HAT'IPHA (*captive*). Ancestor of Nethinim (Ezr. ii. 54).

HAT'ITA (*exploring*). Ancestor of the gate-keepers who returned with Zerubbabel (Ezr. ii. 42).

ARABIAN HAWK.

HAT'TEL (*wavering*). Ancestor of the "children of Solomon's servants," who returned with Zerubbabel (Ezr. ii. 57).

HATSIHAMMENU'CHOTH (*midst of resting-places*).

HAT'TUSH (*assembled*). 1. Son of Shechaniah (1 Chr. iii. 22; Ezr. viii. 2).—2. A priest (Neh. x. 4, xii. 2).—3. Son of Hashabniah (Neh. iii. 10).

HAU'RAN. Part of the district of Bashan. Ezekiel (xlvii. 16, 18) probably meant a region including the Lejah, Batanæa in the mountains (where the oaks of Bashan still grow around the ruins of ancient cities), and what is now Hauran. The Hauran is a vast fertile plain, the "granary of Damascus." Not a rock or stone encumbers its soil. More than a hundred ruined cities are found—though only deserted, not ruined; for the houses are quite perfect and habitable still, being built of stone, even to the doors and window-shutters, hinges and all, and roofs—of fine solid stone. Some of the dates are before our era, and it is quite probable that these cities are the very same that Moses described (Deut. iii. 5).—*Porter's Five Years in Damascus.*

HAVI'LAH (*sand*). 1. Son of Cush (Gen. x. 7); and, 2. A son of Joktan (x. 29).—1. On the Red Sea, in Arabia, between Mecca and Sanaa. It is a fertile region, abounding in fruit, gum and myrrh; mountainous, well watered, and has a numerous population. The people were called by Eratosthenes (in Strabo), Chaulanitæ—2. A district southeast of Sanaa. A third district of the same name is sought for in answer to Gen. ii. 11, which was compassed by one of the rivers of Eden. In Gen. xxv. 18, it is stated that the tribes of Ishmael dwelt from "Havilah unto Shur;" and this seems to call for a locality on the Persian Gulf or the Euphrates.

HA'VOTH JA'IR (Num. xxxii. 41). Jair took a number of small towns in Gilead, in the mountain district south of the Hieromax, and named them "Jair's villages." A descendant of his, of the same name, was a judge of Israel, and lived here in 30 cities (Judg. x. 3, 4.) Bashan-havoth-jair were among the 60 cities of Argob (Deut. iii. 14, etc.).

HAWK (NEZ; Arabic *nez*). In Job xxxix. 26 "does the nez fly by thy wisdom?" It was migratory, as are 10 or 12 kinds now. The *sak'r* is used to catch partridges, grouse, quail, herons, hares and gazelles.

HAY (CHATZIR, Gr. *herba;* Prov. xxvii. 25; Is. xv. 6). The modern Orientals do not make hay for such uses as we do, but the ancients mowed grass, and used the dried hay (Ps. lxxii. 6) for burning, or perhaps for feeding (Ps. xxvii. 2).

HA'ZAEL (*El is seeing*). A king of Damascus, B. C. 886-840 (see ELISHA). The Assyrian inscriptions furnish some accounts of wars in Syria in his day, which are also mentioned in Scripture. Hazael fulfilled a prophecy of Elisha in ravaging Gilead, etc. (2 K. x. 32, 33).

HA'ZAEL, THE HOUSE OF (Amos i. 4). Damascus, or Hazael's palace, or perhaps his family.

HAZAI'AH (*Jah beholds*). Son of Judah (Neh. xi. 5).

HAZ'AR AD'DAR (*walled space for a camp, named Addar*). (Num. xxxiv. 4). A south boundary of the promised land, near Kadesh-Barnea. There are walled-in places all over this district, but without names known to history.

HAZARMAVETH. Third son of Joktan (Gen. x. 26). Located in the south of Arabia, on the Indian Ocean. Now called *Hadramaut.* Capital city Shibam. Chief ports Mirbat, Zafari (SEPHAR), Kisheem. The native name of a person is *Hadramee*—very similar to their name in ancient history, Adramite. The country is well cultivated, and exports frankincense, myrrh, aloes (from Socotra), gum arabic, and dragon's blood. North of Hadramaut, the Great Red Desert of Arabia, called

DAMNA (*red sand*), extends to Nejed and the Persian Gulf, occupying a third of the whole peninsula.

HA'ZEL (Gen. xxx. 37). (Heb. LUZ.) The hazel or the wild almond tree, the cultivated being named SHAKED. The Heb. for hazel is EGOZ.

HAZELELPO'NI (*shade upon me*). Sister of the sons of Etam (1 Chr. iv. 3). The Zelelpo'nite.

HA'ZER (*enclosed, as a court-yard or camp*). These walls are found in many parts of Palestine and Arabia. Sometimes they are roofed in with a tent and become a dwelling for a short time (Is. xxxviii. 12) by shepherds. The name is used with others for several places: 1. *H. addar* (which see). 2. *H. enan* (*village of springs*). The north boundary of the promised land (Num. xxxiv. 9), the N. E. corner (ver. 10). *Kuryetein* (village of fountains), 40 ms. east of Riblah, and 60 north of Damascus. It is a large place, and has the only fountains in the region. There are ruined columns, probably of the city called by the Greeks Coradæa. 3. *H. gaddah* (Josh. xv. 27). In the south of Judah, between Moladah and Beersheba, now *Jer' rah*. 4. *H. shual* (1 Chr. iv. 28). A city near the last named, now called *Saawh*. Both of these places are in ruins, on low hills. 5. *H. hatticon* (Ez. xlvii. 16). On the boundary in Hauran. Lost. 6. *H. Susah* (*horse village*). (Josh. xix. 5). Allotted to Simeon, near Ziklag. 7. *H. susim* (*village of horses*). Probably the same as the last. 8. *Hazeroth*. Station in the wilderness on the route from Sinai to Ezion-geber. See WANDERINGS.

HAZERE. 4 ms. W. of Bint Jebeil, has extensive ruins, and the right location (*Land and Book*, i. 439).—2. (Josh. xix. 37). 10 ms. S. W. of Safed, Hazur, near El Mughar.

HAZE ROTH (Num. xi. 35). A place 25 ms. N. of Sinai.

HAZEZON TAMAR (*palm forest*). ENGEDI.

HA'ZIEL (*vision of God*). A Levite (1 Chr. xxiii. 9).

HA'ZIRIM. Hazer (Deut. ii. 3). Villages.

HA'ZO (Gen. xxii. 22). Azon of Nahor, settled on the Euphrates, in Chazene (Strabo).

COIN OF SARDIS.

HA'ZOR (Josh. xi. 1-12). An ancient, royal city, fortified, near Lake Merom. "The head of all those kingdoms," i. e., the chief city in North Canaan. Taken by Joshua, and given to Naphtali. In after-times, a king Jabin, of Hazor, held the Israelites in subjection 20 years. Jabin's army, including 600 chariots of iron, led by Sisera (perhaps intending to conquer all Palestine), were routed by Barak and Deborah (Judg. iv.). Fortified by Solomon (1 K. ix. 15.) Referred to by Josephus, and in Macc. xi. 67.—2. (Josh. xv. 23). Judah, south. Lost.—3. (Neh. xi. 33. Benjamin, after the Captivity. Tell Azur. 5 ms. N. E. of Bethel.—4. (Jer. xlix. 28). Some noted camping-ground of the Arabs. Lost. There are two or three Hazors named in Josh. xv. 23-25; one of them a *new* village (Hadattah); and one changed to Hezron. There were also BAAL HAZOR and EN HAZOR.

HEAD (Heb. ROSH, Gr. *kephale*). Used for the top of anything, as the summit of a mountain, top of a tree.

HEAD-DRESS. The head-dress is a very important matter in the hot climate of the East, besides its use "for glory and for beauty" (Ex. xxviii. 40). There are several names of different articles used by different persons, or at various times. 1. ZANIPH, (*to roll or wind*) worn by nobles (Job xxix. 14), and ladies (Is. iii. 23), and kings (Ixii. 3; *mitre* in Zech. iii. 5), was a turban, intended for display. 2. PEER, modern name tarbush (or kaook) the red cap. The Bedawin head-dress (*keffieh*) is formed by folding a square cloth across from the corners, and tying it on the head, so as to have one (double) corner behind and one on each side of the neck. The Assyrian was probably made of bright and mingled colors (Ez. xxiii. 15). See cuts on pps. 9, 76 and 120.

EGYPTIAN HEAD-DRESS.

HEART (Heb. LEB, Gr. *kardia*). The supposed seat of the intellect, soul, etc. (Judg. xvi. 17).

HEARTH (Heb. AH, ACH, MOKED, KIYOR). A floor of stones on which a fire is made. Used for the whole house. Jehoiakim's was probably a brazier of charcoal (Jer. xxxvi. 23).

HEATH (AROER, ARAR). A shrub used in thatch, for brooms, beds, etc., probably juniper or savin (Jer. xvii. 6, xlviii. 6).

HEATHEN (GOI, GOYIM). All nations have a term for distinguishing other people from their own. The Hebrews were very particular in this matter, because they were forbidden to marry out of their own nation, or even to mingle in society with them. The heathen were worshipers of false gods. After the Greeks came into power their name meant the same as heathen (Greek *hēthen*), and is the same or similar to "uncircumcised." Goyim also meant wicked as opposed to the righteous Jews.

HEAVEN. 1. RAKIA, *firmament, expanse*.—2. SHAMAYIM, *the high*, the heavens (and earth). Always plural in the Hebrew of the O. T.—3. MAROM (*mountain*), *hight, high region*; SHAHAKIM, *expanse, skies*.—4. ARABAH (*the desert*), *the heaven*; AHIPHIM (*distilling*), *clouds*; Greek, *ouranos* (*air*), *heaven*; *hupsos* (*hight*), *on high; another* (*from above*) heaven. The "third heaven" of Paul, in 2 Cor. xii. 2, is explained from the Jewish way of naming three parts in heaven, as: 1. The place of clouds in the air; 2. The place of the sun, moon and stars; 3. The place of God and his angels. Heavens and earth meant the entire universe. Once heaven, earth, and under the earth (Phil. ii. 10).

HE'BER (*society*). 1. Grandson of Asher (Gen. xlvi. 17).—2. Father of Socho, of Judah (1 Chr. iv. 18).—3. Gadite (v. 13).—4. Son of Elpaal, a Benjamite (viii. 17).—5. Son of Shashak (xxii.).—6. Husband of Jael, a Kenite (Judg. iv. 11-17).—7. The patriarch Eber (Luke iii. 35). Hebo-rites (Num. xxvi. 45).

HEBREW. This name was first used of Abraham in Gen. xiv. 13. Four sources have been offered: 1. From Abram; 2. From ABAR; 3. From EBER (*country beyond*); and 4. From EBER, the patriarch (this would have been IBRI). Hebrew of the Hebrews; a pure-minded Jew.

HEBREWS, EPISTLE TO THE. See HISTORY OF THE BOOKS.

HE'BRON (*the friend*). Third son of Kohath, who was second son of Levi (Ex. vi. 18). The clan is

mentioned in the time of David (1 Chr. xv. 9, xxiii. 19), as of the sons of Levi, who only ought to carry the ark of God; and also mighty men of valor of Jazer, in Gilead (xxvi. 31), who were officers in David's government; and another branch held the same rank on the west side of Jordan. There was a Hebron among the sons of Caleb. The CITY OF HEBRON is one of the most ancient, built 7 years before Zoan (Num. xiii. 22), and even older than Damascus (Gen. xii. 18). See cut of Hebron on page 4. Its original name was Arba, or Kirjath Arba (city of Arba), from Arba, the father of Anak (xxxiii. 2; Josh. xiv. 15, xv. 13). It was also called MAMRE (Gen. xxiii. 19, xxxv. 27). The ancient city was in a valley, and its pools help fix its site and identity (2 Sam. iv. 12). Many years of the lifetime of Abraham, Isaac and Jacob were spent here, where they were all buried; and from Hebron Jacob and his family set out for Egypt, by way of Beersheba. The city was given to Caleb by Joshua, who drove out the Anakim. One of the CITIES OF REFUGE. It was David's royal residence for 7 years and a half; where most of his sons were born; and here he was crowned king over all Israel (2 Sam. ii.), when David changed the royal residence to Jerusalem. Fortified by Rehoboam. It was occupied after the Captivity; but fell into the hands of the Edomites, from whom it was recovered by Judas Maccabæus (1 Macc. v. 65). It was called Hebron or Castle of Abraham during the Crusades. The modern town is called Khulil (*the friend* "of God"), by the Arabs, and lies on the eastern and southern side of a beautiful valley. The houses are all of stone, well built, having flat roofs with many domes. The streets are only a few feet wide, and the bazaars are covered either by awnings or arches. Glass is the only manufacture; lamps, and the bracelets and rings worn by women. The court in which the mosque over the tombs of the patriarchs is built is surrounded by an extensive and lofty wall, formed of large stones, strengthened by square buttresses, the greatest antiquity in Hebron, and probably the same as that seen and described by Josephus (Ant. i. 14; B. J. iv. 9, 7).

MELON.

The only other antiquities are the two cisterns for rain-water (pools). The one close to the south gate of the city is 133 feet square, 22 feet deep, and built of hewn limestone, with steps at each corner, down to the water. The other pool at the north end of the town is 85 by 55 feet, and 19 feet deep. The surrounding country is productive, and the many ruins show a once dense population and high state of cultivation. Population 5000.—2. In Asher (Josh. xix. 28). ABDON?

HE'BRONITES, THE. Descendants of Hebron, son of Kohath (Num. iii. 27).

HEDGE (GADER, GEDER, *a stone wall*, or other fence; MESUKAH, *hedge of thorns or cactus*). Besides stones, walls are made of sun-dried mud, (especially in Egypt); and the *nubk* thorn tree makes an impassable hedge, as well as the cactus.

HE'GAI or **HEG'AI.** *Eunuch* (prime-minister) of the court of Ahasuerus (Esth. ii. 8–15).

HE'GE. HEGAI (Esth. ii. 3). Aja or Aga in Sanscrit. Name of a modern Turkish officer.

HEIFER (AGLAH, *the young of kine*). They worked with other cattle, in treading out grain (Hosea x. 11), and in plowing (Judg. xiv. 18). Egypt was "a fair heifer" (Jer. xlv. 20), in allusion to the bull Apis worshiped there. Several names are made from it, as Eglah, En-eglaim, and Parah (*young mother cow*). Heifers are used at the plow now as anciently.

THE ORDINANCE OF THE RED HEIFER (Num. xix.), is a very peculiar item in the ancient religion, concerning cleansing rather than atonement. It was intended to cleanse from the ceremonial defilement which followed from touching a dead body, or a bone of a dead man, or entering a house where there was a person dead. Purification in the usual way required 7 days of time. A son of the high priest sprinkled the blood of a red heifer before the tabernacle (temple, not on the altar), and the carcase was to be burned entire, outside of the camp, in a clean place (with a bit of cedar wood, and of scarlet cloth), reserving nothing; the ashes were to be kept for use. Mixed with fresh water they were sprinkled on the unclean, on the third, and on the seventh day, with a bunch of hyssop. After changing his clothes and bathing he was clean. His house or tent was also to be sprinkled, with all its furniture, etc.

HE'LAH (*rust*). Wife of Ashur (1 Chr. iv. 5).

HE'LAM. On the west bank of the Euphrates, where David met and defeated the army of Hadarezer (2 Sam. x. 16). Alamatha of Ptolemy.

HEL'BAH (Judg. i. 31). Asher, not far from Sidon.

HEL'BON (Ezek. xxvii. 18). "In the wine of Helbon." A village 10 miles north of Damascus, in a wild and beautiful glen, which is clothed in vineyards. There are many ruins of temples, some with Greek inscriptions, and many other marks of ancient wealth.

HEL'DAI (*long-lived*). 1. Captain for the temple-service (1 Chr. xxvii. 15).—2. An Israelite (Zech. vi. 10).

HE'LEB (*fat*). Son of Baanah (2 Sam. xxiii. 29). Heled.

HE'LED (*strength*), (1 Chr. xi. 30). HELDAI 1.

HE'LEK (*possession*). Son of Gilead (Num. xxvi. 30).

HE'LEKITES, THE. Family from Helek (Num. xxvi. 30).

HE'LEM (*stroke*). 1. A descendant of Asher (1 Chr. vii. 35). Hotham?—2. (*strength*), (Neh. vi. 14). HELDAI 2.

HE'LEPH (Josh. xix. 33.) Where the north boundary of Naphtali began. *Beit Lif*, east of Ras Abyad and west of Kades.

HE'LEZ (*loin*). 1. One of David's guard (2 Sam. xxxii. 26; xxvii. 10).—2. Son of Azariah (fi. 39).

HE'LI, ELI. 1. Father of Joseph, the husband of the Virgin Mary (Luke iii. 23).—2. (2 Esd. i. 2; Ezr. vii. 2, 3).

HELIODŌ'RUS (*given by the sun*). The treasurer of Seleucus Philopator (2 Macc. iii. ff). He was appointed to carry away the private treasures in the Temple at Jerusalem, but fell down speechless and was restored by the high priest Onias.

HEL'KAI (*Joh, his portion*). A priest (Neh. xii. 15).

HEL'KATH (Josh. xix. 25). Boundary of Asher. Lost. Ikkrith? Hukkok in 1 Chronicles vi. 75.

HEL'KATH HAZZURIM (2 Sam. ii. 16). Near

the pool of Gibeon, where 12 of Joab's men and 12 of Abner's killed each other and brought on a general battle.

HELL. HADES.

HELLENIST. GRECIAN.

HEL'MET. ARMS.

HELPS (Gr. *antilepsis*). Care of the poor and sick, by the deacons and deaconesses, by a gift of the spirit. "From time to time God raises up heroes of Christian charity, angels of mercy, for the benefit of humanity."

HE'LON (*strong*). Father of Eliab, prince of Zebulon (Num. i. 9., ii. 7).

HEM OF THE GARMENT. The Jews attached a symbolical importance to the hem or fringe, because of the regulation in Num. xv. 38. See FRINGE.

HE'MAM. HOMAM. Son of Lotan (Gen. xxxvi. 22).

HEMAN (*faithful*). 1. Son of Zerah (1 Chr. ii. 6).—2. Son of Joel, a Levite and musician (1 Chr. vi. 33), to whom the vocal and instrumental music of the temple service, in the reign of David, was committed (xv. 16-22). He was also connected with the family of Zerah, the Ezrahite, and his name is in the title to Ps. lxxxviii.

HE'MATH. HAMATH (Amos vi. 14).

HE'MATH. HAMMATH. A person or place named as the origin of the Kenites (1 Chr. ii. 55), and the house of Rechab.

HEM'DAN (Gen. xxxvi. 26). East of Akaba there is an Arab tribe of the name of Hamran.

HEMLOCK (LAANAH and ROSH, *gall*).

HEN (*grace*). Son of Zephaniah (Neh. vi. 14). TOBIJAH 2.

HEN (Gr. *ornis*, *fowl*), (Matt. xxiii. 37; Luke xiii. 34), also (2 Esd. i. 30). Nowhere noticed besides in these passages, but were always kept as now, in every village or farm house.

HE'NA (2 K. xix. 13). Some ancient ruins, called Ana, are found on the Euphrates, near Mosaib. (Sippara).

HEN'ADAD (*favor of Hadad*). A chief Levite who helped rebuild the temple (Ezr. iii. 9; Neh. iii. 18, 24).

HE'NOCH. 1. Enoch 2 (1 Chr. i. 3).—2. Hanoch 1 (i. 33).

HE'PHER (Josh. vii. 17). West of Jordan, as was also the land of Hepher. Lost.

HE'PHER (*a well*). 1. Son of Gilead (Num. xxvi. 32).—2. Son of Ashur (1 Chr. iv. 6.)—3. One of David's men (xii. 36).

HEPHERITES. The family of Hepher (Num. xxvi. 32).

HEPH'ZIBAH (*my delight in her*). 1. Name given to the new Jerusalem (Is. lxiii. 4).—2. Queen to Hezekiah and mother of Manasseh (2 K. xxi. 1).

HE'RA. HERCULES.

HER'ALD (Chal. *karoza*). An officer (Dan. iii. 4).

HERBS. Bitter herbs. FOOD.

HER'CULES (*Hera's glory*). The national god of Tyre, called MELKART (*king of the city*). The worship extended to all colonies of Tyre, especially to Carthage. This was the Baal also. The Greeks make him the most famous hero of their famous history, remarkable for his great strength (SAMSON), and especially for 12 "labors" which were connected with the health and safety of men. Hera was the Greek name of Juno, who was the guardian deity of married women. In Assyria she was *Astarte*, "Queen of Heaven;" and as such is sculptured at Hierapolis, in Asia Minor.

HERA.

HERD. Herdman. The herd was one of the chief sources of wealth, and the ox the most precious, next to the horse and mule. The herd yielded the most esteemed sacrifice. Its supply for sustenance was most important, in flesh, milk, butter and cheese. The cattle were broken to service in the third year, after which they were rarely killed. The ox eats grass and browses on foliage also. The harvest is gathered and threshed by the help of cattle. Pharaoh made some of Joseph's brothers overseers of herds, and David's herdsmen were among the chief officers of his court.

HE'RES (*the sun*), (Is. xix. 18)—Irhaheres, for *Mount Heres*. See Judg. i. 35. IRSHEMESH.

HE'RESH. A Levite (1 Chr. ix. 15).

HER'MAS. HERMES. A disciple of Rome (Rom. xvi. 14). Tradition says he was the author of "The Shepherd of Hermas."

HERMES. One of the seventy disciples, afterward Bishop of Dalmatia (Rom. xvi. 14).

HERMOG'ENES (2 Tim. i. 15). A disciple who deserted Paul without cause.

HER'MON (*nose of mountain*). The highest peak of Anti-Lebanon, on or beyond the north border of the land (Josh. xi. 17; Deut. xxxiv. 1; 1 Sam. iii. 20). The Amorites called it *Shenir* (*to shine, as a coat of mail*); the Sidonians, *Sirion* (*to glitter*); also called *Sion* (*elevated*); and now by the Arabs *Jebel esh Sheikh* (*chief mountain*), and *Jebel eth Thelj* (*snowy mountain*). Its head is crowned with perpetual snow; and when the whole lowland country is burnt by the summer sun, long lines of snow streak down the sides of Hermon, like the white locks of an old man about his shoulders. There are three summits, about a quarter of a mile from each other in a triangular position, and 10,000 feet high. They are visible (at a distance as one peak) from every part of Palestine north of Shiloh, from the Jordan valley near the Dead Sea, and from the Moab mountains as far south as Nebo. Its rivers are Jordan, Abana, Pharpar, Orontes, and Leontes. It was the religious centre of pagan Syria, and the temples of Baal gave it a name. The ruins of these temples are now found on many of its lower shoulders, as at Rakleh, Sed Dan, Bustra, Mutaleih, Kefr Kuk, Burkush, Aiba, Hibariyeh, Tilthatha, Ain Hersha, Asheir, Bekkeh, Munseh, and Paneas. At Rakleh there is a god's face, 40 inches in diameter, surrounded by a wreath, all well cut in bold relief, and set in the wall of the temple, which is a ruin, and one of a circle of temples all around, facing the summit of Hermon. The temple at Asheir is on an elevated platform (which is ornamented with a frieze and cornice), 126 by 69 feet, and itself 89 by 40 feet, and 54 feet high. In the Ionic style, with cup and ball ornaments. On the very highest peak are the foundations of a circular wall of large stones, enclosing hewn stones (some beveled), in heaps, disclosing the plan of a small temple (Deut. xii. 2; 2 K. xvii. 10). The central peak is a bald cone of gray limestone, 2,000 feet higher than the surrounding ridges. These lower ridges are thinly clothed with

HERMONITES, THE. "The Hermons" (Ps. xlii. 6).

HERMONS (Ps. xlii. 6). The three summits of Hermon.

HEROD FAMILY, TABLE OF THE.

Father.	Son.	Mother.
	1. Antipater, governor of Idumea.	
	2. Antipater. See Josephus.	
2. Antipater,	3. Phasael.	
2. Antipater,	4. HEROD (the king in Matt. iii).	
"	5. Joseph,	Cypros, an Arabian.
"	6. Pheroras,	
"	7. Salome,	" "
3. Phasael,	8. Phasael.	
4. Herod,	9. Antipater,	Doris.
"	10. Aristobulus,	Mariamne, g. d. of Hyrcanus.
"	11. Alexander,	" "
"	12. Salampio,	" "
"	13. Cypros,	" "
"	14. Herod,	Mariamne, daugh. of Simon.
"	15. Antipas,	Malthae, a Samaritan.
"	16. Archelaus,	
"	17. Olympias,	
"	18. Herod,	Cleopatra.
"	19. Philip,	"
"	20. Phasael,	Pallas.
"	21. Roxana,	Phædra.
"	22. Salome,	Elpis.
"	Two wives, no name or children.	
5. Joseph,	23. Joseph.	
7. Costabarus,	24. Berenice.	
"	25. Herod.	
10. Aristobulus,	26. Aristobulus,	24. Berenice.
"	27. Agrippa,	"
"	28. Herodias,	"
11. Alexander,	29. Alexander,	16. D. Archelaus.
"	30. Tigranes,	"
14. Herod,	31. Salome,	28. Herodias.
23. Joseph,	32. Mariamne,	17. Olympias.
8. Phasael,	33. Cypros,	12. Salampio.
25. Herod,	34. Aristobulus,	32. Mariamne.
26. Aristobulus,	35. Jotape,	Jotape.
27. Agrippa,	36. Agrippa, K.,	33. Cypros.
"	37. Drusus,	"
"	38. Berenice,	"
"	39. Mariamne,	"
"	40. Drusilla,	"
29. Alexander,	41. Tigranes.	
34. Aristobulus,	42. Herod,	31. Salome.
"	43. Agrippa,	"
"	44. Aristobulus,	"
Felix,	45. Agrippa,	40. Drusilla.
Tigranes,	46. Alexander.	

Josephus says the Herods were Edomites (xiv. 15 § 2), but Nicolaus of Damascus, a historian of the times, says they returned from exile with other Jews (a story invented to please Herod). Antipater (1.) gained power, first in Idumea, and then by fomenting the divisions between Hyrcanus, the high priest and his brother Aristobulus. He also came into power in Judæa, although Hyrcanus was nominal ruler. Herod (4.) the Great was only 15 years (20?) when he began to rule, and soon won a popular enthusiasm by good measures of public safety and quiet. Being summoned before the Sanhedrin, he appeared robed in purple, with a strong guard of soldiers, and was not sentenced. Not long after receiving favor from Sextus, president of Syria, and Cassius, he punished Ma-

HEROD COIN.

lichus his father's murderer. He was made governor of Judæa jointly with his brother Phasael, B. C. 41. Antigonus being driven out of Judæa, joined the Parthians and got possession of Judæa, 40 B. C., Herod flying to Rome, while Phasael killed himself. Octavius Cæsar confirmed Herod in his office and Herod returned to Judæa, where he tried to gain the favor of the Jews by rebuilding and ornamenting the temple (commenced B. C. 24), and restoring such cities as Cæsarea, Antipatris, Sebaste (Samaria), and others, besides public buildings in Damascus, Tripoli, Ptolemais, Tyre, Sidon, Askelon and Antioch (a large open space, paved with marble, having a cloister), and also frequent public games and feasts, all at his own expense. He also made costly presents to Cæsar and Agrippa. He is said to have destroyed the genealogies of the Jewish priestly families. These deeds were prompted by the ambition to connect his name with the prosperity of his country, like Solomon's. The close of his career was stained with many cruel and barbarous crimes. His wives and children plotted against each other. (He had ten wives, two of whom were his own nieces.) Three of his sons (9, 10, 11) he had killed, with the mother of two (10, 11). In the midst of these family troubles, and of seditions in the city, he was seized with a terrible disorder in the bowels,

HEROD COIN.

and tried to kill himself, after giving orders for a magnificent funeral. He attempted to destroy the infant Jesus by killing all the children in Bethlehem (about 12), to get rid of an object of jealousy, for Jesus was spoken of as born king of the Jews. He died B. C. 4. He maintained peace at home and abroad by his vigor and timely generosity, and conciliated the good-will of the Romans. Many coins of his reign are still extant. (See MONEY.)

HEROD ANTIPAS (15) had been destined as his father's successor, but was appointed "tetrarch of Galilee and Peræa." He first married a daughter of Aretas (king of Arabia Petræa), and afterwards Herodias, his half-brother "Herod-Philip's" wife. This Herodias caused the death of John the Baptist. Aretas, in revenge for the slight put on his daughter, invaded Herod's territory and defeated him. He went to Rome, at the suggestion of Herodias, to ask for the title of a king, but being there opposed by the friends of Agrippa, he was banished to Lugdunum, A. D. 39, where he died, his wife being with him. It was to this Herod that Jesus was sent for examination by Pilate. He built Tiberias, and restored Sepphoris, and Betharem in Peræa, naming it Julias after the emperor's wife.

ARCHELAUS (16). The kingdom which had been once intended for his brother Antipas, was left to Archelaus, who was educated in Rome, and Augustus confirmed the choice, giving him Idumea, Judæa, Samaria, Cæserea, Joppa, and Jerusalem, with the title of Ethnarch. He broke the Mosaic law by marrying his brother's widow, Glaphyra; was denounced by his subjects, appealed to Cæsar, and was banished to Vienne, in Gaul, where he died (A. D. 39).

HEROD PHILIP I (14). His mother was daughter of the high-priest Simon. He married Herodias, sister of Agrippa I, and their daughter was Salome (31). Herodias left him for his half-brother Antipas (Matt. xiv. 3). He was excluded from all share in his father's possessions because of his mother's treachery, and lived a private life.

HEROD PHILIP II (19). He was brought up at Rome, and after his father's death was appointed governor (tetrarch) of Batanæa, Trachonitis, Auranitis, and Jamnia, which he ruled with justice

MOUNT HERMON.

and moderation, without taking part in the intrigues of the rest of his family. He rebuilt Paneas, and named it Cæsarea Philippi, and raised Bethsaida beyond Jordan to a city, naming it Julias after the daughter of the emperor, and died there (A. D. 31). He married Salome (31), but left no children.

HEROD AGRIPPA I (26).—Was educated at Rome with Claudius and Drusus, where Tiberius imprisoned him for an unguarded speech. Caius Caligula, the succeeding emperor, liberated him, and made him tetrarch of Galilee and Peræa (Lysanias). Herod Antipas and Herodias tried in vain to have him deposed, but he defeated their plans by a counter-charge of treason with the Parthians. Agrippa rendered important service to Claudius, and had his dominions enlarged by Samaria and Judæa, so that they equaled in extent those of Herod the Great. He was a strict keeper of the law, and was respected by the Jews. It is supposed that it was to increase their favor that he put to death James the Less, and put Peter in prison (Acts xii). In the fourth year of his reign over Judæa (A. D. 44), he attended some games in honor of the emperor. Appearing in a robe ornamented with silver embroidery, his flatterers saluted him as a god, when he was seized with a sudden illness, and died in five days (eaten of worms).

HEAD OF TITUS. COIN OF HEROD AGRIPPA II.

HEROD AGRIPPA II (36). He was educated at Rome, and was only 17 at his father's death. His first appointment was the kingdom of Chalcis, and afterwards the tetrarchies of Philip and Lysanias, with the title of king (Acts xxv). Nero added several cities. He built many splendid public buildings in Jerusalem and Berytus. Juvenal in his satires notices his relation to his sister Berenice. He died at Rome in the 3d year of Trajan, A. D. 100, the last of the Herods.

HERODIANS. Formed a party very keenly opposed to the claims of Jesus, who favored the Herod family and watched its interests. They "watched him, and sent forth spies, which should feign themselves just men, that they might take hold of his words, so that they might deliver him unto the power and authority of the governor" (Luke xx. 20). Herodias, daughter of Aristobulus, son of Herod the Great (4), and wife first of Herod Philip, and then, contrary to the law of Moses, of Herod Antipas, who had a wife, the daughter of the king of Arabia (Aretas). John the Baptist reproved her, and she in revenge caused his death (Matt. xiv. 8) at Machærus. She went with her husband Antipas into exile (see HEROD ANTIPAS), at a place now called St. Bertrand de Comminges, in France, near Spain, on the Garonne river, anciently Lugdunum Converarum, at the foot of the Pyrenees.

HERODION. A relative of Paul at Rome (Rom. xvi. 11). Tradition says he was bishop of Tarsus, or of Patræa.

HERON (ANAPHAH). An unclean bird (Lev. xi. 19; Deut. xiv. 18). There are several species "after its kind" in Palestine, one of which is called the White Ibis, which are found in immense flocks about the Huleh lake and marsh. The flesh is excellent.

HE SED (favor). Commissary for Solomon in the Aruboth (1 K. iv. 10).

HESH'BON (Num. xxi. 26). Capital city of Sihon, king of the Amorites, on the western border of the Mishor (Josh. xiii. 17), and on the boundary between Reuben and Gad. The ruins are 20 miles east of Jordan, opposite the north end of the Dead Sea, on an insulated hill, scattering over a space more than a mile in circuit, with not a single edifice entire. Many cisterns are whole, and a large reservoir near the base of a hill recalls the text in Cant. vii. 4, "Thine eyes are like the fishpools of Heshbon." The view from the summit is very extensive over the great undulating plateau, embracing the ruins of a great number of cities, whose names resemble those of the Scriptures. (See Tristram's Land of Israel).

HESH'MON (Josh xv. 27). On the south border of Palestine. Lost. Azmon? (Num. xxxiv. 4).

HES'RON (enclosed). Son of Reuben (Num. xxvi. 6). HEZRON. HEBRONITES.

HETH (terror). CHETH. Ancestor of the Hittites, son of Canaan (Gen. x.) In Abraham's time they were called Bene Cheth, sons of Cheth. The name CHAT is found on the Egyptian monuments for Palestine.

HETH'LON (stronghold). On the N. border of Palestine (Ez. xlvii. 15), at the north end of Lebanon.

HEZ EKI. A Benjamite, son of Elpaal (1 Chr. viii. 17). HEZEKIAH.

HEZEKI'AH (HIZEKIYAH, strength of Jah). 12th king of Judah, son of the idolator Ahaz. Made king at 25 (or 20), B. C. 726. He destroyed the images and the instruments of idol worship, even the image of the brazen serpent, which had been preserved in his time as a precious relic of the wilderness, and repaired the temple and its furniture. He then held a solemn assembly, and after that a feast of the Passover, to which a great many came, and others sent gifts, and the seven days were fully honored, so much so that another seven days were added "with gladness" (2 Chr. xxx. 23). He refused submission and tribute to the king of Assyria, which brought the Assyrian army to Samaria in the fourth year of his reign, and in the

HERON, OR WHITE IBIS.

14th year the assault on Judæa was made (2 K. xviii. 13), when Hezekiah made peace, being compelled to rob the temple to pay the tax. A strong confirmation of the leading facts in the Bible narrative has lately been discovered at Nineveh, sculptured in stone, with the names of Hezekiah and others familiar, which leave no doubt in the matter. Sennacherib insisted on an unconditional surrender, in the most offensive manner. Hezekiah humbled himself before God, and being assured by Isaiah of the favor of Jehovah, he called his army together and prayed for help, which came

as a plague upon the hosts of the Assyrians (2 K. xix. 35). Sennacherib was killed soon after his return home, in the house of his idol, by two of his sons. Hezekiah only lived a year longer, dying in his 54th year. He was one of the best kings of both Israel and Judah.—2. Son of Neariah, in the royal line of Judah (1 Chr. iii. 23).—3. Hizkiah in Zeph. i. 1.

HE'ZION (*vision*). King of Aram, father of Tabrimon (1 K. xv. 18).

HE'ZOR (*swine*). 1. A priest (1 Chr. xxiv. 15). —2. Head of the layman who signed the covenant (Neh. x. 20).

HEZ'RAI (*enclosed*). One of David's strong men (2 Sam. xxiii. 35.) Hezro (1 Chr. xi. 37).

HEZ'RON. HEZRAI. 1. Son of Reuben (Gen. xlvi. 9).—2. Son of Pharez(2 Gen. xlvi. 12).—3. Hazor (Josh. xv. 25).

HEZRONITES, THE. 1. Descendants of Hezron (Num. xxvi. 6).—2. Part of the tribe of Judah. Son of Pharez (xxvi. 31).

EAR-RINGS.

HID'DAI (*mighty*). One of David's guard (2 Sam. xxiii. 30). HURAI.

HID'DEKEL (Gen. ii. 14). One of the rivers of Eden—the 3d, "flowing *toward* the E. of Assyria." Daniel saw one of his poetic visions near its banks (Dan. x. 4). The Aramean name of the river Tigris is *Diyla*—Arabic, *Diklah*; and the Hebrew name seems to be compounded of the ancient name with the prefix for active, HIDDEKEL or HIDDEKEL. Pliny writes it Diglito, "an arrow;" Josephus, Diglath, "swift" (Ant. i. 1, 3), all of which refer to the great swiftness of its current. (See TIGRIS).

HI'EL. JEHIEL (*El is animation*). Native of Bethel (1 K. xvi. 34; Josh. vi. 26).

HIERAP'OLIS (Col. iv. 13). Five miles north of Laodicea. There are mineral springs, whose waters form stalactites, which gave it an ancient celebrity (Strabo xiii. 629) A great number of sepulchres are found in its vicinity. The ruins show its ancient greatness, and traces are still distinct of a temple of Apollo, a theatre (316 feet), a gymnasium (400 feet sq.), and three Christian churches (one 300 feet).

HIERON'YMUS (*hallowed*). A general of Syria (2 Macc. xii. 2).

HIGGAI'ON (Ps. ix. 17). Meditation. Soft music. A direction for singing.

HIGH PLACES (*bāmoth*). From the top of Hermon to the crest of the low hills, all over the land, there are evidences that they were used for religious rites, both in idolatrous and in pure worship. The temple on Moriah was intended to supersede all other high places, and no other worship was allowed, except on special occasions.

HIGH PRIEST. The office of the (COHEN, *priest*) high priest was legal, theological and historical. The legal included all the law of Moses alluding to it, as the substitute for the first-born. He alone was consecrated by the anointing oil, the underpriests being sprinkled only (Ps. cxxxiii.). His dress was symbolical. (See DRESS). He alone could enter the Holy of Holies, which he did but once a year (DAY OF ATONEMENT) clothed in pure white. The accidental man-slayer was safe in the City of Refuge during his life-time, and at his death could return to his friends. He could not follow a funeral, nor disfigure himself by mourning. There was an assistant, called

SAGAN (second priest), who could act in his stead (Luke iii. 2). The elders or Sanhedrin appointed him before the monarchy. No one could hold the office who was blemished, or was under 20 years (2 Chr. xxxi. 17), and it ended only at death, although one could be, or was deposed for ill-conduct. Theologically he was a type of Jesus the Christ. Historically his office concerns the history of the Jews for 1370 years, including nearly 80 different persons, from Aaron to Phannias. See pages 8, 16.

HIGHWAY. Roads or paths were used in ancient times, but the Romans made the first paved ways, traces of which still remain.

HI'LEN (1 Chr. vi. 58). Judah. Levitical.

HILKI'AH (*Joh's portion*). Son of Shallum, ancestor of Ezra the scribe (Ezr. vii. 1). Josiah effected the great reformation in his time, when the book of the law of Moses (see DEUTERONOMY in History of the Books) was found in the temple, where it had been hidden for centuries. Six others of this name were of little note.

HILL (GIBEAH, *knoll;* HAR *mountain;* MAALEH, *height, ascent;* Gr. *bounos, mount; hooreine, mountain*).

HIL'LEL (*praise*), Judge of Israel, father of Abdon (Judg. xii. 13-15).

HIN. WEIGHTS AND MEASURES.

HIND (Heb. AYYALAH, AYYELETH). Female stag. (HART). (Gen. xlix. 21). See FALLOW DEER.

HINGE (POTH, TSIR). Stone hinges are peculiar to Palestine and Assyria. See DOOR.

HIN'NOM, THE VALLEY OF (Josh. xviii. 16). On the S. and W. of Mt. Zion. The origin of the name is unknown (Jer. vii. 31). An idol of bronze of great size was set up in the valley, facing Olivet, where children were sacrificed in the fire, which seems to have been kindled inside the idol. Josiah abolished the worship, and strewed human bones over the place, making it unclean, and thus prevented the renewal of worship there (2 K. xxiii. 10). These inhuman practices gave the place a horrible character, and caused its name to be detested and used as a figure for a place of torment.

HIPPOPOT'AMUS (*river horse*). BEHEMOTH. See p. 35.

EAR-RINGS.

HI'RAH (*noble birth*). The friend of Judah (Gen. xxxviii. 1, 12).

HIRAM or HURAM (*high-minded*). 1. King of Tyre (2 Sam. v. 11; 1 Chr. xiv. 1). He built a palace for David (1 K. v. 1), also a temple for Solomon (1 K. vi. 1)—2. An artificer (vii. 13, 40, 45).

HIRCA'NUS. Son of Tobias (2 Macc. iii. 11).

HITTITES. Children of Heth. See HAM. The name is found in the Egyptian hieroglyphics, where are also found the names of their gods, Ashtoreth and others.

HI'VITES. Of the sons of Canaan. See HAM. They lived under Hermon, in the land of Mizpeh (Josh. xi. 3), and in Lebanon as far as Hamath (Judg. iii. 3). Jacob bought a small field of Hamor, the Hivite, at Shalem near Shechem (Gen xxxiii. 18, xxxiv. 2). Esau married Aholibamah, a Hivite. The Hivites of Gibeon made a treaty with Joshua by a deceit (Josh. ix. 3); and for this act they were condemned to the temple service. AVIM.

HIZKI'AH. HEZEKIAH. Ancestor of Zephaniah (Zeph. i. 1).

HIZKI'JAH (Neh. x. 17). "Ater of Hizkijah."

HO'BAB (*beloved*). The father-in-law of Moses,

or, more probably, his brother-in-law (Num. x. 29 -32). He was an experienced sheikh, and valuable as a guide. See Exodus.

HO'BAH (*hidden*; Gen. xiv. 15). Where Abraham's pursuit of the kings he defeated at Dan ended, north of Damascus. Three miles north-east of Damascus is a village called Jobar, where there is a synagogue dedicated to Elijah; and another village, Buzeh, near, in which there is a very ancient sanctuary of Abraham. Both places are offered as the site of Hobah.

HOD (*splendor*). Son of Zophah (1 Chr. vii. 37), of Asher.

HODA'IAH (*praise ye Jah*). Son of Elioenai (1 Chr. iii. 24).

HODAVI'AH. HODAIAH. 1. A man of Manasseh (1 Chr. v. 24).—2. Son of Hassenuah (1 Chr. ix. 7).—3. A Levite (Ezr. ii. 40). HODEVAH.

HO'DESH (*new moon*). Wife of Shaharaim (1 Chr. viii. 9).

HODE'VAH (Neh. vii. 4, 3). HODAIAH.

HODI'AH. Wife of Ezra (1 Chr. iv. 19).

HODI'JAH (*splendor of Jehovah*). 1. A Levite (Neh. viii. 7).—2. A Levite (x. 13).—3. Layman (x. 18).

HOG'LAH (*partridge*). Daughter of Zelophehad (Num. xxvi. 33). Heir.

HO'HAM (*Joh impels*). Canaanite. King of Hebron (Josh. x. 3).

HOLD. Place held by a garrison (Judg. ix., 46, 49).

HOLM-TREE. A species of oak. (History of Susanna, 58 v).

HOLOFER'NES (*symbolical*), (Jud. ii. 4). King over the Assyrians.

HO'LON (*abode*), (Josh. xv. 51). Judah, between Goshen and Giloh. Lost.—2. In Moab, in the Mishnor. HILEN. Lost.

HOLY CHILDREN, THE SONG OF THE THREE. See HISTORY OF THE BOOKS.

HOMAM (*extermination*), (1 Chr. i. 39). Homaima, a ruin south of Petra, half-way to Ailath, on the ancient Roman road. The native city of the Abassides (Rob., B. R., ii. 572).

HO'MER (*a heap*). WEIGHTS AND MEASURES.

HON'EY (DEBASH, YAAR, NOPHET). The product of bees, of sweet gum bearing trees, of dates, of grapes, and other vegetables or fruit. Butter and honey mingled are eaten with bread in the morning.

HOOD. DRESS. HEAD DRESS.

HOOK, Hooks. Fishing hooks (HACCAH, Am. iv. 2): ring for the nose (CHOACH, Job xli. 2). (See page 28, for ring in the lips of prisoners). Hooks in the pillars of the tabernacle (VAVIM, Ex. xxvi. 32); pruning-hook (MAZMERAH, Is. ii. 4); pot-hook for a cook (MAZLEG, 1 Sam. ii. 13); butcher's hooks (SHEPHATTAYIM, Ez. xl. 43).

HOPH'NI (*fighter*), and PHIN'EAS. Two sons of Eli, priests at Shiloh.

HOR, MOUNT (HAR, *mountain*), (Num. xx. 23). On the edge of Edom, not far from Kadesh and Zalmonah. Aaron was buried here (22–29). The ascent is very steep and difficult—rocky; and on its summit is a rude building called Aaron's tomb. (See page 1.) Juniper grows almost to the top. The view from the summit is very extensive in every direction: on the north the passes of Akrabbim, where the Jews were defeated, and the mountains around the Dead Sea; on the east, the rugged range of Edom (with the Deir, or convent of Petra, in sight), red, bare, and desolate; southward,

the wide downs of Mt. Seir; and westward the Arabah, with its hundred water-courses; and above it the great white wilderness, fading into the hot and trembling distance. 5,000 feet high.

HO'RAM (*height*). King of Gezer (Josh. x. 33).

HO'REB (*dried up*). SINAI. EXODUS.

HO'REM (Josh. xix. 38). Naphtali. Hurah, a ruin on a low tell in Wady Ain, west of and near Merom.

HORHAGID'GAD. GUDGODAH. (Num. xxxiii. 32).

HO'RI (*lives in caverns*). 1. Son of Lotan (Gen. xxxvi. 22).—2. (Gen. xxxvi. 30) "Hori."—3. Father of Shaphet (Num. xiii. 5).

HORITE. HORITES. Inhabitants of Mount Seir. (Gen. xiv. 6).

HORMAH (*destruction, cursed*), (Judg. i. 17). Zephath. City of a king, in the south of Palestine (Josh. xii. 14). El Sufa, S. E. of the Dead Sea. See EXODUS.

HORN (KEREN). Horns on cattle; often used as weapons—for which see ARMS—and for trumpets for calling workmen to dinner, the soldiers to the field, and for announcing religious ceremonies. Used also for bottles. The elephant's tusks were called horns (from their shape), as also trumpets of metal. The summit of a hill was a horn, as also the corners of the altar for burnt-offerings. The modern

EGYPTIAN PRIESTS.

Druses wear a horn on the head for ornament, but it was not an ancient custom of the Hebrews. In poetry the horn is strength, and also a nation, or a king, or a god.

HORNET (ZIRAH). A winged insect, used as a figure by the poets and prophets (Ex. xxiii. 27, 28; Deut. vii. 20; Josh. xxiv. 11, 12) of a persistent warrior. There are four kinds in Palestine, all different from the European varieties. ZOREAH, hornet-town.

HORONA'IM (*two caverns*), (Is. xv. 5; Jer. xlviii. 3, 5). Near Zoar, Luhith, Shurim, on a declivity, beside a noted road. Lost.

HOR'ONITE, or **HO'RONITE.** One from Horonaim. Sanballat (Neh. ii. 10).

HORSE (SUS). Not mentioned among Abraham's cattle, but first as coming from Egypt (Gen. xlvii. 17). The horse is almost exclusively used in war in Scripture, and is so sculptured on the monuments both of Egypt and Assyria. Job gives a most elegant description of a war-horse in ch. xxxix. 19–25. "An horse is a vain thing for safety" (Ps. xxxiii. 17), said the poet and the prophet also (Deut. xvii. 16). Solomon disobeyed the letter and spirit of the prohibition not to multiply horses, and his successors also. Horses are used as symbols by the prophets, as in Zech. i. 8, "a man riding on a red horse;" and he also mentions speckled (or bay) and white horses. John, in Rev. vi., saw four horses go forth: white, red, black and livid (green), indicating the spiritual condition of the nations. White horses are an emblem of triumph and power. Successful generals rode in triumph on white horses (Rev. xix. 11-15).

HORSE-LEECH (ALUKAH). Very common in all

the stagnant waters and in the running brooks, clinging to stones. Used as a figure in Prov. xxx. 15.

HO'SAH (*refuge*), (Josh. xix. 29). Asher, not far from Tyre.—2. A Levite (1 Chr. xxvi. 10, 38).

HO'SAI (*seer*), (2 Chr. xxxiii. 19). CHOZAI.

HŌSAN'NA (*save now*). Ps. cxviii. was sung on joyful occasions, such as the feast of Tabernacles. Verses 25 and 26 were sung with loud acclamation. "Hosanna to the Son of David" in Matt. xxi. 9.

HOSE'A (*salvation*). A prophet, called of God, with Amos, to declare his word to Israel. See HISTORY OF THE BOOKS.

HOSHA'IAH (*Jah helps*). A leader of the princes of Judah to the wall of Jerusalem (Neh. xii. 32). —2. Father of Azariah (Jer. xlii. 1).

LION.

HOSH'AMA (*Jah hears*). A son of king Jeconiah (1 Chr. iii. 18).

HOSHE'A (*safety*). Hosea I, son of Nur (Deut. xxxii. 44). OSHEA, the prophet.—2. The last king of Israel (Is. vii. 16). Shalmanezer, king of Assyria, besieged and ended the kingdom of Israel B. C. 721 (2 K. xvii).—3. Son of Azaziah (1 Chr. xxvii. 30), and ruler of Ephraim.—4. One of the people who signed the covenant (Neh. x. 23).

HOSPITAL'ITY. One of the chief virtues among the Orientals, and it is most highly esteemed on the desert, being less needed and less valued in the towns. The ancient Egyptians limited their practice to their own people, having a superstitious dread of all foreigners. The O. T. is full of allusions to the rites and the divine commands for their practice, and instances of the national belief of the Hebrews in their value. The laws of Moses give many directions for special cases, as with the stranger, "for ye were strangers in the land of Egypt" (Lev. xix. 34), the poor, and the traveler. To break the law was a very great offense, as in the case of Benjamin at Gibeah (Judg. xiii 15, xix. 17-21). The good Samaritan stands for all ages as an example of Christian hospitality. The account of Abraham entertaining the three angels is a perfect picture of how a modern Bedawin sheikh would treat a traveler in our day. (See ABRAHAM). Oriental respect for the covenant of salt (and bread) is a part of the law of hospitality. To taste another's salt is to make yourself his friend for the time. In every village there is a *mensil*, inn, for the use of travelers, where they are supplied with food by certain families near it. No money is paid, but presents may be made equivalent to the value of the articles used.

HOSTAGES (2 K. xiv. 14; 2 Chr. xxv. 24).

HOTHAM (*a seal*). Son of Heber (1 Chr. vii. 32). HELEM 1.

HO'THAN. HOTHAM. Father of Shama (1 Chr. xi. 44).

HO'THIR (*superior*). Son of Heman (1 Chr. xxv. 4, 28).

HOUR. See CHRONOLOGY, p. 31.

HOUSE (BETH, *to pass the night*). A dwelling for man or cattle. House, tent, palace, tomb, tabernacle, temple; heaven; family. The houses of the rich are made of stone with two or more stories arched over the rooms and passage-ways, with fine stair-ways, supplied with wide galleries or verandahs, and open places for light and air, generally built around two or three sides of a court, in which is a fountain or pool of water. The wall next to the street is usually blank, with a small door, and a window or two, high up, and latticed. (See WINDOW). The door often has an inscription, seldom the name of the resident. The poor live in houses of mud, sun-dried, usually of one story, roofed with mud laid on poles which are covered with grass or palm-leaves. In the rainy season the rain leaks through (see DROPPING), if not prevented by rolling the mud with a stone roller. When of two storys the lower is for the use of animals and for storage. In hot countries people sleep on the roofs under tents of cloth, or booths of branches. The cool of the evening is also passed on the roof, when proclamation is made by the public crier of any command of the ruler, or news of any public kind. It is also a place for prayer. Some roofs have vines so trained as to form a shelter from the sun or neighbors. The space is found useful for drying grain, fruit, and clothing from the wash. Stairways lead from the roof to the ground in the court without passing into the house. It is quite usual to build pigeon-houses of bottles on the battlements, and sparrows build their own nests in any corner or hole, even plugging up the chimneys (Ps. lxxxiv., cii. 7), and are caught in great numbers, being almost worthless (Matt. x. 29.) Very large houses, convents, and inns, have several courts, connected by passages. South of Nablus (Shechem) the roof is supplied with domes for lighting and enlarging the rooms below. The upper room or chamber is the choice place, given only to strangers or friends of distinction. The sculptures in Egypt and Assyria present houses of more than one story. The guest room, or divan, is provided with seats all around the room, except by the doors, like wide, low sofas; no chairs are used. The Romans and Greeks used chairs and reclining seats or sofas around the table at banquets. (See p. 33). The walls are often ornamented with carvings of wood, and sometimes painted in beautiful patterns. (See CARPENTER). The furniture is much more simple than ours, and less expensive, except in the houses of the rich. (See CORNERSTONE, BRICK, ROOF).

HUK'KOK (*incision*), (Josh. xix. 34). On the south border of Asher and Naphtali. *Yakuk*, in the Wady el Amud. An ancient Jewish tradition locates the tomb of Habakkuk here (Benj. of Tudela, ii. 421).

HUL (*region*), (Gen. x. 23). Second son of Aram, grandson of Shem. The plain or valley of the Jordan north of Lake Merom is called Ard el Huleh, and the lake's most ancient name is Huleh, and it is still so called by the Arabs.

HUL'DAH (*weasel*), a prophetess (2 K. xxii. 14; 2 Chr. xxxiv. 22), whose husband, Shallum, was master of the wardrobe to king Josiah (2 K. xxii.

14). Huldah was famous as an oracle when Jeremiah was a boy in the school at Anathoth.

HUMTAH (*lizards*), (Josh. xv. 54). Judah, in the hill country.

HUNTING. The Hebrews were not given to hunting, except for the protection of their fields or families from wild beasts. The names of many places indicate that wild game was plentiful, even to a degree of danger. Thomson (*Land and Book*) says it is still plenty in some places, especially in Galilee.

HU'PHAM (*coast-man*). Son of Benjamin (Num. xxvi. 39). HUPPIM.

HU'PHAMITES. Descendants of Hupham (Num. xxvi. 39).

HUP'PAH (*covering*) A priest (1 Chr. xxiv. 13), of the 13th course.

HUP'PIM (*screen*). A Benjamite (1 Chr. vii. 12).

HUR. A man with Moses and Aaron in the battle with Amalek (Ex. xvii. 10); husband of Miriam.—2. Son of Hur (Ex. xxxi. 2).—3. One of the 5 kings of Midian (Num. xxxi. 8).—4. Father of Rephaiah (Neh. iii. 9).—5. Son of Hur; an officer for Solomon (1 K. iv. 8).

HU'RAI (*noble*). One of David's guard (1 Chr. xi. 32). HIDDAI.

HURAM (*high-born*). 1. Son of Bela (1 Chr. xiii. 5).—2. King of Tyre (1 Chr. xiv. 1).—3. Hiram, the artificer (ii. 13). He was called Ab (father), a title of respect, used now in the East, and the origin of the title of the Bishop of Rome (*pope*, father).

HU'RI. Father of Abihail (1 Chr. v. 14).

HU'SHAH (*haste*), (1 Chr. iv. 4) A town built by Ezer.

CAROB FRUIT.

HU'SHAI (*hasting*). An Archite (2 Sam. xv. 32 ff.). A friend of David (xv. 37). Probably the father of Baanah 3. (1 K. iv. 16).

HU'SHAM (*haste*). King of Edom (Gen. xxxvi. 34, 35).

HU'SHATHITES. One from Husha. Two of David's guard. 1. Sibbechai (Hittite?), (2 Sam. xxi. 18).—2. Mebunnai (2 Sam. xxiii. 27).

HU'SHIM. 1. Children of Dan (Gen. xlvi. 23).—2. A Benjamite (1 Chr. vii. 12).—3. One of the wives of Shaharaim (viii. 8).

HUSKS (Gr. *keratia*). The fruit of the carob tree, which is very common in the East, and the Greek islands, where it is in great request for fattening hogs. It has a sweetish pulp when tender. The ripe pods (10 inches long) are dry and have seeds like beans. See HONEY. The leaves are like our ash, but dark and glossy. It blossoms in February and the pods are ripe in May.

HUZ. Nahor's elder son (Gen. xxii. 21) "And Buz his brother." There is a district of Kaseem, in Arabia, which some suppose to be the land of Uz (Job i. 1). See Palgrave's *Journey in Arabia*.

HUZ'ZAB (*fixed*). Queen of Nineveh? (Nah. ii. 7). Country of Zab, that is, the river.

HYDAS'PES. A river (Judith i. 6), in connection with the Euphrates and Tigris. Choaspes of Susiana.

HY'ENA. Not mentioned by name in the O. T. as translated, but meant in the original by the word ZEBUA (Ar. *dubba*), which is rendered *streaked bird* in Jer. xii. 9 (Hyena in the Sept.). Valley of Zeboim (hyenas in 1 Sam. xiii. 18). It is still found in numbers, ready to attack wounded, dying, or dead animals, eating all, even the very bones, its jaws being most powerful. Their flesh is not eaten, having a bad odor.

HYMENE'US One of the earliest Gnostics, who argued that the resurrection was passed already (1 Tim. i. 20; 2 Tim. ii. 17, 18).

HYMN. "In psalms, and hymns, and spiritual songs." The Greek word *Unmos*, or *humnos*, means a song (in praise of Deity), as a part of worship, and there are several collections of such as were used in ancient times, written by Callimachus, Orpheus, Homer, Linus, Sappho, and others. Jesus and his disciples sang a hymn before going out, on the eve of the last supper (Matt. xxvi. 30). The words used are supposed to have been Ps. cxv; cxviii, called the Hallel. Paul and Silas sang hymns in prison at Philippi (Acts xvi. 25; Gr. *humnoun*, praises); and Paul commends their use in his epistles (Eph. v. 19; Col. iii. 16). The hymn differs from the psalm in thought and composition. The different meters were adopted from the Greek models.

HYSSOP (EZOB; Gr. *hussopos*). The Arabic *zufa* is a plant growing on a slender square stem, free from thorns, or spreading branches, ending in a cluster of leaves, having a pleasant aromatic odor, growing on the walls in Palestine. No plant in the East is better fitted for purposes of sprinkling. Its leaves are often eaten (like summer savory) with bread.

HYSSOP.

I

I AM, and **I AM THAT I AM**. JAH.

IB'HAR (*chosen*). Son of David (2 Sam. v. 15).

IB'LEAM. Bil'eam (1 Chr. vi. 70; Josh. xvii. 11). Given to Manasseh, but in Asher. Jelama, north of Jenin, is perhaps the site. Ahaziah was wounded here by Jehu's soldiers (2 K. ix. 27).

IBNEI'AH (*Jah will build*). Son of Jehoram (1 Chr. ix. 8).

IBNI'JAH. IBNEIAH. A Benjamite (1 Chr. ix. 8).

IB'RI. HEBREW. A Levite (1 Chr. xxiv. 27).

IB'ZAN (*of tin*). A native of Bethlehem. Judge of Israel for seven years (Judg. xii. 8, 10). He had thirty sons and thirty daughters. BOAZ.

ICE. FROST. Ice is very rare in the plains and hills, and only familiar on the highest mountains.

ICHABOD (*wo, or departed glory*). Son of Phinehas (1 Sam. iv. 21). So named by his mother, who died at hearing of the loss of the Ark of God, her husband, and father-in-law, at the battle of Aphek.

ICO'NIUM (Acts xiii. 51). Konieh, a large city; is on a table-land, a fertile plain, near a semicircle of snow-capped mountains in Asia Minor. This level district was Lycaonia, of which Cicero says it was the capital. It was on the route leading from Ephesus to Tarsus, Antioch, and the Euphrates. Here Paul was stoned, and left for dead (xiv. 19). The city is built out of the ruins of the ancient structures, and pieces of marble columns, capitals, and carved cornices appear everywhere in the masonry. It is now quite large, the residence of a pasha, surrounded with beautiful groves and gardens, well watered, and the resort of pilgrims who visit a saint's tomb. In the middle ages it was the capital of the Seljukian Sultans, and is called the cradle of the Ottoman empire. The traditional story of Paul and Thecla is located here. (See Conybeare and Howson's Life of Paul.)

ID'ALAH (Josh. xix. 15). Zebulon. Semunîyeh, 3 ms. S. of Beit-lahur, was near it.

ID'BASH (*honeyed*). Son of "the father of Elam," (1 Chr. iv. 3).

ID'DO (*timely*). 1. Father of Ahinadab (1 K. iv. 14).—2. Descendant of Gershom, son of Levi (1 Chr. vi. 21). ADAIAH.—3. Son of Zechariah (xxvii. 21). —4. YEDOI, (*born on a festival*). A seer who had a "vision" which concerned Jeroboam and alluded to Solomon (2 Chr. ix. 29). He wrote a history and a genealogy, which are lost, but are probably preserved in part in "Chronicles."—5. Son of Id'do (Ezr. v. 1).—6. A chief; one of the Nethinim (Ezr. viii. 17, 20).

IDOL. There are 21 Hebrew words for idols or images for worship. 1. AVEN, *nought* (Bethel, house of God, Bethaven, house of vanity), nothing, iniquity; 2. ELIL, *no god*, as contrasted with ELOHIM, *God;* 3. EMAH, *terror*; 4. MIPHLETSETH, *horror* (Phallus, the productive power of nature and the nature-goddess Ashera; Priapus); 5. BOSHETH, *shameful;* 6. GILLULIM, *filthy gods;* 7. SHIKKUZ, *impurity;* 8. SEMEL, *likeness;* 9. ZELEM, *shadow;* 10. TEMUNAH, *model;* 11. ATSAB, *shape;* 12. EZAB, *fashion;* 13. OTSEB, *figure;* 14. ZIR, *a shape;* 15. MAZZEBAH, *statue;* 16. CHAMMANIM, *sun-images;* 17. MASCHITH, *device;* 18. TERAPHIM, *idols* (see TERAPHIM); 19. PESEL, *carved image;* 20. PESILIM, *graven images* (quarries, in Judg. iii. 19, 26); 21. NESEC, *molten image;* MASSEKAH, *shaped in a mould*. These various terms are obscure, because very little material has come down to us from antiquity which fixes the form of these images. Jeremiah described in a sarcastic way how these so-called gods were made, but he did not give an idea of the particular shape. All of these terms expressed worthlessness and vanity, contempt and abhorrence.

IDOLATRY (TERAPHIM; Gr. *idolatreia*). The worship of deity made visible, whether of true or false ideas, in images, pictures, stars, fire, or ideal statements, as shown in business pursuits or in pleasure, or for honor, where self is preferred above the honor and glory of God. Nearly three in four of all the human race are open idolaters; and if judged by the strict moral sense of the term, very many of the other fourth worship self rather than God (Col. iii. 5). By the Jewish law the idolater was to be stoned to death, and a city given up to it was to be wholly destroyed, with all it contained (Deut. xiii. 12, xvii. 2). The laws of Moses imply that idolatry was known to him, and the paintings and sculptures of Egypt prove its existence there before the time of Moses, but the earliest mention in the Bible is in the incident of Rachel stealing her father's teraphim (images in Gen. xxxi. 19), by which he was guided, as some who consult the clairvoyant or other "fortune-tellers" of our day (a species of idolatry very prevalent among the ignorant and superstitious). The story of Micah and his images shows how widespread the custom was in the age succeeding Joshua and the elders. Solomon did much to encourage idolatry of many kinds, which were brought into the country by his foreign wives (1 K. xi. 7; 2 K. xxiii. 13).

ICONIUM.

It has been a question whether the Hebrews did not so lapse into idolatry as to lose all knowledge of the true God. They lost the true sound of his name, for which we now substitute Jehovah. They may have only mingled foreign rites with the true worship, as many pagan ideas are now adopted into some branches of the Christian Church. We know that the Hebrews worshiped the sun (Baal), moon (Astarte, Diana), the stars (Ashtoreth, Mazzaloth in Job), planets Chiun or Remphan (Saturn, Acts vii. 40–43), and made representations of celestial bodies or ideas, in human form, for worship, as of the sun, moon and stars (Hera, Diana, see

HERA, Cybele, Apollo, Adonis (Tammuz, in 2 K. xxi. 3), Venus, etc.); of KEN, in Egypt, and MYLITTA, in Nineveh; and also images of beasts, as the ox (Ps. cvi. 20); Aaron's and Jeroboam's bull-calf; and of a goat (Ashima); fly (Beelzebub); a cock (Nergal); and fish (Dagon); the dog (Nibhaz); the mule and peacock (Adrammelech); the horse and pheasant (Anammelech). The Assyrians (Samaritans also) had a system of ancestor-worship (Asshur and others), and also a lower nature-worship, including the elements, trees, etc. The scape-goat of the Day of Atonement is a recognition of the existence of Satan (Typhon in Egyptian system), but was not a worship of that being, for only sins were sent to Azazel, nothing choice or precious.

The Christian Church now holds that God has sanctioned but one image, which was made by himself, for man's worship, which is the intelligent, rational, holy nature of man, which appears in all completeness and perfection in Jesus the Christ, and is reflected in his followers as they have more or less received the spirit of the gospel. "God is a spirit, and they that worship him must worship in spirit and in truth" (John iv. 24).

IDUME´A. Greek form of EDOM.
IDUME´ANS. EDOMITES. People of Idumea (2 Macc. x. 15, 16).
I´GAL (*El will avenge*). 1. A spy, son of Joseph (Num. xiii. 7).—2. One of David's men, son of Nathan (2 Sam. xxiii. 36; Joel 8).
IGDALI´AH (*Jah will make great*). Father of Hanan (Jer. xxxv. 4).
I´GEAL—IGAL. Son of Shemaiah (1 Chr. iii. 22).
I´IM (*ruins*). Ije Abarim (Num. xxxiii. 45), Lost.—2. Judah, south; near Beersheba (Josh. xv. 28). Lost. AZEM?
I´IM. JIM (Is. xlii. 22). BEAST.
IJE-AB´ARIM (*heaps, or ruins of Abarim*), (Num. xxi. 11). This region, east of the Dead Sea, is still unexplored by any Christian traveler in our day, and therefore it is impossible to say whether the stations of the Israelites can be located or not.
I´JON (*ruin*), (1 K. xv. 20; 2 K. xv. 29). In the N. Jordan valley, now called Tell Dibbin. The hill is a favorable site for a city, overlooking the whole plain of Merj Aiyun, and on the road leading from the coast into the interior.
IK´KESH (*perverse*). Father of Ira (2 Sam. xxiii. 26).
I´LAI (*supreme*). An Ahohite (1 Chr. xi. 29). ZALMON.
ILLYR´ICUM (Rom. xv. 19). Paul preached the gospel of Christ "from Jerusalem round about unto Illyricum." A country on the east shore of the Adriatic Sea, north of Epirus. Illyricum was at one time one of the four great divisions of the Roman empire, and included the whole country between the Adriatic, the Danube, the Black Sea, and Macedonia (Gibbon, c. i).
IM´LA (*full*). Father of Micaiah (2 Chr. xviii. 7, 8). Im'lah in 1 K. xxii. 8, 9.
IMMAN´UEL (*with us El, or God with us*). The name of the child (prophetic) which was to be given to the house of David (Is. vii. 14). Isaiah bids Ahaz ask a sign of Jehovah, which he, with pretended humility, refused to do, when this sign of a child by a virgin (virgin is a young woman), was given, and, as some think, the prophesy was fulfilled within a few years, and others look on the child as a type of Jesus the Christ, as seems to be the meaning in Matt. i. 23.
IM´MER (*talkative*). 1. Head of a family of priests (1 Chr. ix. 12; Ezr. ii. 37, x. 20).—2. A place in Babylonia (Ezr. ii. 59; Neh. vii. 61).
IMMORTAL´ITY (Gr. *athanasia*, deathless, not mortal). The Christian believes that the human soul will never die. Some hold the doctrine that only those who believe on Christ will be blessed with immortality, while those who deny him will die (Rom. ii. 7; 2 Tim. i. 10). The same Greek word is also rendered incorruption in 1 Cor. xv. 42, etc., and sincerity in Eph. vi. 24, etc.
IM´NA (*whom God keeps back*). Son of Helem (1 Chr. vii. 55).
IM´NAH (*good fortune*) (JIMNA, JIMNAH). 1. First born of Asher (1 Chr. vii. 30).—2. Father of Kore (2 Chr. xxxi. 14).

BROAD-TAIL SHEEP.

IMPUTE´ (*to reckon to one what does not belong to him*). (Heb. HASHAB Lev. vii. 18; Ps. xxxii. 2); and rendered "to think" in Gen. l. 20; and "to count" in Lev. xxv. 27, etc., "to reckon," "to esteem," "to devise," and "to imagine," in other places.—SUM, in 1 Sam. xxii. 15; "to put" in Gen. ii. 8; "to make" in xxi. 13.—3. Greek *ellegeo* in Rom. v. 13; "to put on account" in Philemon 18. —4. *logizomai*, in Rom. iv. 6, etc.; "to reason" in Mark xi. 31; and by several other terms.
IM´RAH (*refractory*). A chief of Asher (1 Chr. vii. 36).
IM´RI (*eloquent*). 1. A man of the family of Pharez (1 Chr. ix. 4).—2. Father of Zaccur 4 (Neh. iii. 2).
IN´CENSE (Heb. KETORAH, LEBONAH; Gr. *thumiana*). A compound of sweet-smelling gums used in acts of worship, and forbidden in private life (Ex. xxx. 27). The mixture is said to have been equal parts of stacte, onycha, frankincense, galbanum. The altar of incense was placed in front of the veil, from which on the great Day of Atonement the high-priest could raise a cloud of perfume which covered the mercy-seat (entered within and filled the holy of holies). It was a type of Christian prayer.
IN´DIA (Esth. i. 1, viii. 9). The extent of the kingdom of Ahasuerus was from India to Ethiopia, 127 provinces. Acts ii. 9, instead of Judea read India. The country around the river Indus, now the Punjaub, which Herodotus describes as part of Darius' empire (iii. 98). At a later period it was conquered by Alexander. The name is found in the inscriptions at Persepolis (1 Macc. viii. 8). Modern India, or Hindostan, is more extensive than the ancient. The articles obtained by Solomon from the East were Indian, such as horns of ivory, ebony, broidered work and rich apparel, sandal-wood, apes, peacocks, and tin.
IN´GATHERING, FEAST OF (Ex. xxiii. 16). TABERNACLES, FEAST OF.
INN (Heb. MALON). A lodging-place for the night. Only a room is to be had, the traveler must supply himself with furniture, bed, etc. They were built generally two stories high, and near water. One is mentioned in the history of Joseph (Gen. xlii. 27), and by Moses in his day (Ex. iv. 24), by Jeremiah; the habitation (inn) of Chimham

(xli. 17), and the same by Luke, where Jesus was born (ii. 7). The Good Samaritan is said to have left money (in our standard about $2.50) to pay charges at the inn (Luke xxii). The inn is usually built around a yard, having a well or fountain, and entered by a gate which can be closed against intruders at night. The baggage and animals occupy the lower rooms and the people the upper and better chambers. When the upper rooms were full of crowds at feast times, the late comers would be obliged to take a lower room, among the animals ("in the manger").

INSPIRA'TION (from the Latin, *in-breathing*). The supernatural influence of God's spirit on the human mind, by which prophets, apostles, and other sacred writers were qualified to record divine truth without error. Others hold that is only a divine impression on the mind, by which the understanding is informed. "All Scripture is given by inspiration of God" (2 Tim. iii. 16).

I'RAD. ARAD? JARED. Son of Enoch (Gen. iv. 18).

I'RAM (*duke, sheikh*), (Gen. xxxvi. 43). Where Iram was is not known. Probably either in or near Edom, if not an original component of Idumea.

IRHA'HERES (*the city of the sun*). The sacred city Heliopolis (its Greek name), or On, in Egypt (Is. xix. 18). Beth Shemesh, in Jer. xliii. 13. (See ON).

I'RI. IRAM. 1. Son of Bela (1 Chr. vii. 7). IR.—2. URIAH.—3. (1 Esd. viii. 62).

IRI'JAH (*founded*). Son of Shelemiah (Jer. xxxvii. 13, 14).

IR'NAHASH (*serpent city*). BETHLEHEM? (1 Chr. iv. 12). NAHASH.

I'RON (Josh. xix. 38). Naphtali. Sarun.

I'RON (Heb. BARZEL; Chal *parzlah*. The references are many to iron, and as early as the time of Tubal-Cain (Gen. iv. 22). A furnace of iron is taken as the image of the bondage in Egypt (Deut. iv. 28). Iron knives (or steel) are drawn on the monuments in Egypt. The remains of ancient Nineveh furnish articles of iron coated with bronze, which has preserved them. Tin melts at 470°, copper, silver and gold at 1800°, and cast iron at 3000°, while malleable iron requires a higher degree, but furnaces of clay, fed with charcoal and supplied with a blast of air from two skin-bellows, are used successfully in the East.

IR'PEEL (*restored by God*), (Josh. xviii. 27). Benjamin. Lost.

IR'SHEMESH (*mount of the sun*), (Josh. xix. 41). Danite city. MOUNT HERES, BETHSHEMESH?

I'RU (IRAM?). Son of CALEB (1 Chr. iv. 15).

I'SAAC (Heb. YIZHAK, *laughing*). Born at Gerar, B. C. 1896, of Sarah (who was 90) and Abraham (who was 100), in fulfilment of a divine promise (Gen. xxi. 17; Gal. iv. 29). When three years old,

EAGLE. LAMMERGEIER.

INSTANT. INSTANTLY (Luke xii. 4; xxiii. 23). Pressing, at once.

INTERCES'SION. Prayer for (or against) others (Jer. vii. 16; Rom. xi. 2).

INTERPRETATION (*explanation*). Making known clearly.

IO'NIA. That part of the coast of Asia Minor which is between Doris and Æolis. Ionia was celebrated for its 13 cities and its islands. The chief cities were Ephesus, Smyrna, Samos, Chios and Miletus (Jos. Ant. xvi. 2, 3). India in 1 Macc. viii. 8.

IPHEDEI'AH (*Jah sets free*). Son of Shashak (1 Chr. viii. 25).

IR (*city*). Int (1 Chr. vii. 12).

I'RA (*wakeful*). 1. "The JAIRITE," one of David's officers (2 Sam. xx. 26).—2. "The ITHRITE," one of David's guard (xxiii. 38; 1 Chr. xi. 40).—3. Son of Ikkesh, captain of the 6th monthly course (2 Sam. xxiii. 26).

at the feast made on the day he was weaned, he was mocked by Ishmael with pretended homage (as the child of the promise and type of the Messiah) which so offended his mother that his half-brother and his mother Hagar were sent away (Heb. xi. 17; James ii. 20). At maturity he almost fell a victim to his father's faith on the altar as a burnt-offering. He was married at the age of 40 to his beautiful cousin Rebekah, but was tormented with jealous fear (as his father was) that some powerful chief would carry her off for her beauty. In his old age he was deceived by his wife and her favorite son Jacob, who got from him the patriarchal blessing which belonged to Esau by birth-right. At the age of 60 his two sons, Esau and Jacob were born. In his 75th year he and his brother Ishmael buried their father Abraham, who died at Mamre, in the cave of Machpelah, beside Isaac's mother, Sarah. He lived in tents, and mostly in the south-country (Negeb), where seve-

ral places are mentioned as his residence for a time. When his father died he was at Beer-lahai-roi, from which the famine drove him to Gerar, where Abimelech put him in fear of losing his wife, when he practised the same deception that his father did in the same place a few years before. The Philistines envied his prosperity, and jealous of his increasing power (and disliking his religion?), tried to drive him out by filling up his wells; but he dug new ones. One of those which he was permitted to use in peace, quite a distance from Gerar, he named Rehoboth (*room*, i. e., *room enough at last*). The promise to Abraham was repeated to Isaac at Beersheba, where he sunk a well as a memorial, and built an altar. The well remains, but the altar has disappeared. He made peace with Abimelech there also, and dug another well as a memorial (well of the oath). His first great grief was the undutiful conduct of his son Esau in marrying two young Canaanite women. His eyesight failed many years before his death; but he lived to enjoy the return to him at Hebron of Jacob, with his large family and great wealth in flocks and herds. He died at the age of 180, and was buried beside his father, in the cave of Machpelah, by his sons Esau and Jacob. His character is very severely criticised, especially for the denial of his wife at Gerar, and so exposing her to danger; and in allowing Jacob to enjoy the fruit of his deception. He was a gentle and dutiful son, and a faithful and constant husband of one wife.

ISA'IAH (*Jah is helper*). See HISTORY OF THE BOOKS.

ISCAH (*she looks forth*). Niece of Abraham, daughter of Haran, and sister of Milcah and Lot. A Jewish tradition identifies her with Sarah. Abraham said she was the daughter of his father, but not of his mother (Gen. xx. 12). She might have been a grandchild, or any degree of descent (see DAUGHTER).

ISH'BAH (*praising*). In the line of Judah, father of Eshtemoa (1 Chr. iv. 17).

ISH'BAK (*leaving*). Son of Abraham and Keturah (Gen. xxv. 2), progenitor of a tribe in N. Arabia, called *Sabak* or *Sibak*, an extensive and fertile tract in Nejed, inhabited by the Beni Temeem. Shobek is the name of a ruined castle on a hill 12 ms. N. of Petra, which was a stronghold of the Crusaders, and called by them Mons Regalis.

ISH'BIBENOB (*his seat at Nob*). Son of Rapha, a Philistine giant, killed by Abishai (2 Sam. xxi. 16).

ISHBO'SHETH (*of shame*). Youngest of Saul's 4 sons, and his legal successor. His name was originally Esh'baal. He was 40 years old when he began to reign, and reigned two years at Mahanaim, while Abner was contending with David's generals (2 Sam. iii. 10). He fell a victim to revenge for some crime of his father, but David punished the murderers.

ISH'I (*saving*). 1. A descendant of Judah, son of Appaim (1 Chr. ii. 31).—2. Son of Zoheth (iv. 20).—3. Head of a family of Simeon (iv. 42).—4. A chief of Manasseh E. of Jordan (v. 24).

ISH'I (*my husband*), (Hos. ii. 16). Symbolical name.

ISHI'AH (*whom Jah lends*). The last one of Izrahiah's five sons, a chief in David's time (1 Chr. vii. 3).

ISHI'JAH. ISHIAH. One of the sons of Harim (Ezr. x. 31).

ISH'MA (*waste*). A descendant of Etam (1 Chr. iv. 3), in the line of Judah.

ISH'MAEL (*whom God hears*). Son of Abraham and Hagar (Gen. xvi. 15, 16). First-born of the patriarch. Born at Mamre, but was sent into the wilderness south of Beersheba, Paran, when he was 16 years old. He had a wife from Egypt (xxi. 21), who was mother of his 12 sons, besides a daughter. Esau married his daughter. His sons were Nebajoth, Kedar, Abdeel, Mibsam, Mishma, Dumah, Massa, Hadar, Tema, Jetur, Naphish, and Kedema. The Arabic historians divide the Arabs into two races: 1. Pure Arabs, descendants of Joktan; and 2. Mixed Arabs, descendants of Ishmael. Like the sons of Isaac his brother, or rather Jacob, Ishmael's sons were founders of tribes, some of which are known in history by their names; and "they dwelt from Havilah unto Shur that is before Egypt" (Gen. xxv. 18). Their language is spoken all over Arabia, with very few exceptions, and is the same in all rules and idioms now as in most ancient times; and the poetical, or rhyming, and the current language, are one and the same, with a different arrangement of words only. The prophecy, "He shall be a wild ass of a man, his hand against every man, and every man's hand against him," is now and ever has been true;

TYRE.

and also the other saying, Ishmael "shall dwell in the presence of all his brethren," for they have always been free. The desert is called in Arabic, Bedu, and the genuine Arab calls himself Bedawee (*desert-man*), Bedawin (*desert-men*). 4000 years have not changed their disposition, manners, habits, occupation, government, or dress.

ISHMAI'AH (*Jah hears*). Son of Obadiah (1 Chr. xxvii. 19).

ISH'MEELITE (1 Chr. ii. 17), and Ishmelites (Gen. xxxvii. 25, 27, 28). Descendants of Ishmael.

ISH'MERAI (*Jehovah keeps*). A Benjamite (1 Chr. viii. 18).

I'SHOD (*man of glory*). Son of Hammoleketh (1 Chr. vii. 18).

ISH'PAN (*bald*). A Benjamite (1 Chr. viii. 22).

ISH'TOB (2 Sam. x. 6, 8). A small kingdom on the east of Jordan, in Aram.

ISH'UAH (*even*). Son of Asher (Gen. xlvi. 17).
ISH'UAI. (ISHUAH.) Son of Asher (1 Chr. vii. 30).

ISH'UI. (ISHUAL.) Son of Saul (1 Sam. xiv. 49), by Ahinoam.

ISLE (Heb. IYIM; Greek *nesion, nesos, a habitable place*). Dry land (Is. xlii. 15); islands, coasts of the sea, or land in the sea, which were far away, and to be reached by crossing the sea (Ps. lxxii. 10).

ISHMACHI'AH (*Jah upholds*). An overseer of offerings under King Hezekiah (2 Chr xxxi. 13).

ISHMAI'AH or ISMAIAH. A chief (1 Chr. xii. 4).

IS'PAH. ISHPAN. A Benjamite chief (1 Chr. viii. 16).

IS'RAEL (*soldier of God*). The name given to Jacob at the time he wrestled with the angel at Peniel.—2. It was also used as the name of the Hebrew nation.—3. The north kingdom, not including Judah.

KINGS OF ISRAEL.	REIGN	B.C.	KINGS OF JUDAH.	REIGN	QUEENS IN JUDAH.
1 Jeroboam	22	975	Rehoboam	7	Naamah.
		957	Abijah	3	Michaiah.
			Asa	41	Maachah.
2 Nadab	2	954			
3 Baasha	24	953			
4 Elah	2	930			
5 Zimri	0	929			
6 Omri	12	929			
7 Ahab	22	918			
		914	Jehoshaphat	25	Azubah.
8 Ahaziah	2	898			
9 Jehoram	12	896			
		892	Jehoram	8	
		885	Ahaziah	1	Athaliah.
10 Jehu	28	884	Athaliah	6	
		878	Jehoash	40	Zibiah.
11 Jehoahaz	17	856			
12 Jehoash	16	841			
		839	Amaziah	29	Jehoaddan.
13 Jeroboam II	41	825			
		810	Uzziah	52	Jecholiah.
Interregnum.	11				
14 Zachariah	0	773			
15 Shallum	0	772			
16 Menahem	10	772			
17 Pekahiah	2	761			
18 Pekah	20	759			
		758	Jotham	16	Jerusha.
		742	Ahaz	16	
2d Interregnum.	9				
19 Hoshea	9	730			
			Hezekiah	29	Abi.
Samaria taken		721			
		698	Manasseh	55	Hephzibah.
		643	Amon	2	Meshullemeth.
		641	Josiah	31	Jedidah.
		610	Jehoahaz	0	Hamutal.
		610	Jehoiakim	11	Zebudah.
		599	Jehoiachin	0	Nehushta.
		599	Zedekiah	11	Hamutal.
		588	Jerusalem destroyed.		

ISRAEL, KINGDOM OF. The ten tribes which were divided to Jeroboam by the prophet Abijah of Shiloh (1 K. xi. 31, 35), leaving Judah alone to the house of David; Benjamin, Simeon, and Dan joining Judah afterward. SHECHEM was the first capital (1 K. xii. 25); TIRZAH the second (xiv. 17); and SAMARIA the third. Jezreel was occasionally a royal residence. The holy cities were Dan (Paneas) and Bethel. The population was at one time over 3 millions, if the number in the armies is correct as given in 2 Chr. xiii. 3. The area of the whole country, in the time of Solomon, occupied by the twelve tribes, was 12,810 sq. ms., of which 9,375 belonged to Israel and 3,435 to Judah. New Hampshire has about 9,000 sq. ms. Ephraim and Judah had always been rivals, and were nearly matched in numbers from the first, and the two largest of the twelve. For three, or perhaps, nearly four centuries, the ark was in the territory of Ephraim, at Shiloh, until the time of Eli. But when the theocracy was superseded by the kingdom, Saul, the king, was a Benjamite, and Solomon, the son of David, of Judah; but Jeroboam, the leader of the revolt, was an Ephraimite, and, before Solomon's death was accused of treason, and fled to Egypt. The burdensome taxes of Solomon's reign probably hastened, if it did not cause the revolt of the ten tribes; and the death of Solomon was the notice for Jeroboam's return, and the establishment of the new kingdom of Israel, B. C. 975. This was the most important event, and the greatest misfortune, since Joshua crossed the Jordan. Some of the mistakes which were fatal were : The driving out of the Levites from their possessions, for they carried with them their sacred character and powerful support of the king; the alliance with the kings of Egypt and Damascus; the marriage of Ahab with Jezebel, of Phœnicia. The want of a system of union among the tribes composing the kingdom, and the presence of a large number of slaves, were other elements of weakness. The Philistines took some towns; Damascus took its chances for plunder and revenge; Edom and Moab rescued themselves; and Assyria, after many visits to the once rich and prosperous country, finally carried away the gleanings of so many years of religious decline, moral debasement, national degradation, anarchy, bloodshed, and deportation.

IS'RAELITE. Descendant of ISRAEL. HEBREW. JEW (2 Sam. xvii. 25).

IS'SACHAR (*hire*), (Gen. xxx. 17), (Heb. ISASCAH). Ninth son of Jacob and fifth son of Leah. He is not mentioned again as a person—his name only, as the name of a tribe. In the order of march in the desert, Issachar's place was on the east of the tabernacle, with Judah and Zebulon. Only the tribes of Judah and Dan outnumbered them at the passage of the Jordan, Issachar having 64,300 fighting men. (For location, see map of the Twelve Tribes). Its location and boundaries are recorded in Josh. xix. 17-23. Its land was and is now the richest in Palestine. Esdraelon, the plain (called Jezreel, the seed-plot of God, on account of its rich soil), Mt. Tabor, and Gilboa were in its border, and the river Kishon ran through it. Jacob blessed Issachar in the image of "a strongboned beast, couching down between two hedgerows," which is a picture of contented ease and quiet. When David took the census, near the close of his reign, Issachar had 87,000, of whom 36,000 were mercenary "bands." Shalmaneser carried the tribe captive to Assyria. It was not known as a tribe after the return. We are left to suppose that the tribe fell into idolatry, because there is nothing recorded in favor of its religious history.—2. The seventh son of Obed Edom (1 Chr. xxvi. 5).

ISSHI'AH (*Jah lends*). ISHIAH. JESIAH. 1. Descendant of Moses (1 Chr. xxiv. 21).—2. A Levite (xxiv. 25). JESIAH 2.

IS'SUE, RUNNING. The law for males is in Lev. xv. 1-15; that for females in verses 19-31. It is supposed that the disease intended in men (gonorrhœa) arose from over-use or impure connection; and that in woman, the natural monthly purification of nature.

IS'UAH. ISHUAH. Son of Asher (1 Chr. vii. 30). ISUI (Gen. xlvi. 17).

ITAL'IAN (*from Italy*), (Acts x. 1).

IT'ALY. In the time of Paul the whole peninsula south of the Alps was included under this name (Acts x. 1). The ITALIAN BAND were soldiers recruited in Italy. Rome was the capital of the Roman Empire. The church was planted in Italy very early, since the Epistle to the Romans was written only about 25 years after the crucifixion, when a large number of Jews must have been there. From that day to this it has been the seat of civil and religious power, with many fortunes of revolution and persecution, the church always profiting, in all ages, so far as increasing in influence and power.

ITCH (SEARS). A disease inflicted on the Israelites as a punishment (Deut. xxviii. 27). MEDICINE.

I'THAI or ITH'AI. (ITTAI.) Son of Ribai (1 Chr. xi. 31).

ITH'AMAR. Youngest son of Aaron (Ex. vi. 23). After the death of Nadab and Abihu, he and Eleazar were appointed to their places in the priestly office (Ex. xxviii. 1). The high priesthood passed into Ithamar's line by Eli.

ITH'IEL (*God with me*). 1. Son of Jesaiah (Neh. xi. 7).—2. Ithiel and Ucal, to whom Agur delivered his lecture (Prov. xxxi. 1).

ITH'MAH (*orphanage*). One of David's guard (1 Chr. xi. 46).

ITH'NAN (*given*). A town in the south of Judah (Josh. xv. 23).

ITHRA. JETHER. An Israelite (2 Sam. xvii. 25). Father of AMASA.

ITHRAN. JETHER. 1. Son of DISHON (Gen. xxxi. 26).—2. A descendant of Asher (1 Chr. vii. 37).

ITH'REAM (*residue of the people*). Son of David (2 Sam. iii. 5; 1 Chr. iii. 3), born in Bethlehem.

ITH'RITE, THE. Descendant of Jether. Two of David's guard (2 Sam. xxiii. 38) were Ithrites.

IT'TAH KAZIN (*people of a judge*), (Josh. xix. 13). Boundary of Zebulon. Lost.

IT'TAI, the Gittite. Native of Gath; a Philistine in David's army, in the revolution of Absalom; commander of the 600 who were with David in his wanderings. He seems to have had equal command afterwards with Joab and Abishai, at Mahanaim (2 Sam. xviii. 2). Tradition says Ittai took the crown from the head of the idol Milcom. —2. Son of Ribai, one of David's guard. Ithai in 1 Chr. xi.

ITURÆ'A (*from Jetur, the son of Ishmael*). (Gen. xxv. 15). N. E. of Palestine, along the base of Hermon (Luke iii. 1). Philip was "tetrarch of Ituræa and the region of Trachonitis." Now Jedur. It is table-land, with conical hills at intervals, well watered, rich soil, and excellent pasture. The rock is basalt, and the houses are built of it. Its ancient cities are deserted, but standing. Bedawins still pitch their tents there.

I'VAH (2 K. xviii. 34). Hit, on the Euphrates. Ahava of Ezra (viii. 15). The ancient city was dedicated to Iva, the god of air. Shalmaneser brought people from it to Samaria, who carried their gods with them, according to custom among all ancient people.

IVORY (SHEN, *a tooth*). The tusks of the elephant are called teeth, and also horns (Ez. xxvii. 15). Solomon made use of it (Ps. xlv. 8), and had a throne of ivory (1 K. v. 18), overlaid (inlaid) with gold. The tusk of the African elephant sometimes weighs 120 pounds, and measures 10 feet long. There are many beautiful relics of carved ivory that were found in the ruins of Nineveh, and from Egypt, of figures on boxes, and various toilet ornaments—works of art of a high order.

I'VY (*Hedereh helix*). A creeping plant, sacred to Bacchus (2 Macc. vi. 7). It grows wild in Palestine.

IZ EHAR. IZHAR. (Num. iii. 19).

IZ EHARITES, THE. The Izharites (Num. iii. 27).

IZ'HAR (*anointed with oil*). Son of Kohath (Ex. vi. 18, 21; Num. iii. 19).

IZ'HARITES. Descendants of Izhar (1 Chr. xxiv. 22).

IZRAHI'AH (*Jah brings forth*). Son of Uzzi (1 Chr. vii. 3).

IZ'RAHITE, THE. Descendant of Zerah (1 Chr. xxvii. 8).

IZ'RI. Descendant of Jezer. A Levite (1 Chr. xxv. 11—in verse 3, ZERI).

J

There is no distinction in the Hebrew between j and i. The proper sound is that of y when placed before a vowel, as Jah, yäh; Jonah, yõnah.

JA'AKAN (*intelligent*). The Israelites encamped around the wells of the tribe " of the sons" (*Bene*) Jaakan (Deut. x. 6). Tayibeh (*Rob.*).

JA'AKOBAH (1 Chr. iv. 36). JACOB. Simeonite chief.

JA'ALA (*wild goat*). Sons of his were among the returned from captivity (Neh. vii. 58).

JA'ALAH (Ezra ii. 56). JAALA. Jeelin in Esdras.

JA'ALAM (*God hides*). Son of Aholibamah, wife of Esau (Gen. xxxvi. 5), and a sheikh in Edom. He was a phylarch (duke in Genesis).

JA'ANAI (*answers*). Chief in Gad (1 Chr. v. 12).

ASSYRIAN STANDARDS. SEE ENSIGN.

JA'ARE-ORE'GIM (*hair, the weaver?*). The Targum says. "And David, the son of Jesse, weaver of the veils of the house of the sanctuary, who was of Bethlehem, slew Goliath the Gittite." In 1 Chr. xx. 5, the account is "Elhanan, the son of Jair, slew Lahmi, the brother of Goliath," etc. JAIR.

JA'ASAU (*made by Jah*). A son of Bani, who had to put away his Gentile wife (Ezr. x. 37).

JA'ASIEL (*made by El*). Judge in Benjamin in David's time (1 Chr. xxvii. 21).

JAAZANI'AH (*Jah hears*), (Heb. YA'AZANYA'HU) Captain under Johanan (2 K. xxv. 3). Son of Hoshaiah (xlii. 1), the Maachathite (Jer. xl. 8).— 2. Son of Shaphan (Ez. viii. 11), leader of seventy elders, seen by Ezekiel worshiping idols.—3. Son of Azur, a chief, subject of Ezekiel's prophecy (Ez. xi. 1).—4. A Rechabite (Jer. xxxv. 3).

JA'AZER (*Jah helps*) Amorite town, E. of Jordan in Gilead (Num. xxxii. 1). Rebuilt by Gad, and assigned to the Levites (Merarites, v. 35).

Famous for its vineyards (Is. xvi. 8, 9). The land of Jazer; *Seir*, west of Ammon, north of Heshbon.

JAAZI′AH (*Jah consoles*). 3d son of Merari, the Levite (1 Chr. xxiv. 26).

JAA′ZIEL (*El consoles*). Musician in David's time (1 Chr. xv. 18). AZIEL.

JA′BAL (*stream*). Son of Lamech, "father" of dwellers in tents and graziers (Gen. iv. 20).

JAB′BOK (*flowing*). River in Gilead, falling into the Jordan about mid-way between the Sea of Tiberias and the Dead Sea (Josh. xii. 2). The border of the Ammon was strong (Num. xxi. 24), the river running in a defile, deep, narrow and wild, fringed by willows, cane, and oleanders, evergreen oak, pine and arbutus. *Wady Zurka.* Some think it was the Hieromax, *Wady Yarmuk.*

JAB′NEH. JABNEEL.

JA′CHAN (*afflicted*). A chief in Gad (1 Chr. v. 13).

JA′CHAN (*he will establish*). Name of one of the pillars in the porch of Solomon's temple (1 K. vii. 21).

JA′CHIN. 1. 4th son of Simeon (Gen. lxvi. 10). Jachinites (Num. xxvi. 12).—2. Head of the 21st course of priests (1 Chr. ix. 10); some of this course returned from captivity (Neh. xi. 10).

JA′CHINITES. Family founded by Jachin.

JA′CINTH (Gr. *yacinth*). 1. A dark purple flower. — 2. PRECIOUS STONES.

JA′COB (*supplanter*). Esau and Jacob were twins, sons of Rebekah, wife of Isaac, born B. C. 1836, at the well Lahai-roi. Jacob was the favorite of his mother, and was a shepherd. He bought the birthright of his elder brother Esau (at an unfair price in his brother's distress) and got the

APE, WANDEROO.

JA′BESH (*dry*). 1. Father of Shallum, 15th king of Israel (2 K. xv. 10).—2. Short form of

JA′BESH GIL′EAD. Jabesh, in Gilead, the largest city in the half-tribe of Manasseh, 6 miles from Pella, now called *Ed Deir*, on *Wady Yabis*. It did not send its contingent against Benjamin (Judg. xxi. 8), and was punished by the destruction of all its people but 400 young women, who were given to the Benjamites for wives. Nahash attacked it (1 Sam. xi.), but Saul came to the rescue. When the bodies of Saul and his sons hung on the walls of Bethshan, the valiant men of Jabesh Gilead made a raid at night and carried them off, and buried them honorably (1 Sam. xxxi. 11–13).

JA′BEZ (*causes sorrow*). 1. Town in Judah, where the Kenite scribes resided (1 Chr. ii. 55).—2. In the minute genealogy of Judah (iv. 9, 10) Jabez was more honorable than his brethren, who are not recorded.

JA′BIN (*intelligent*). King of N. Canaan, at Hazor, who headed a most powerful army against Joshua (xi. 1–4), and was surprised and defeated near the waters of Merom (7). Joshua afterwards burnt Jabin's city.—2. King of Hazor, in the time of the Judges, who lived in the same city of Hazor (rebuilt), raised an army against Israel, and was defeated, etc. Some have thought that the two accounts were of one event, or of two victories over one Jabin: one by Joshua and another by Barak, but it is more probable that there were two kings of that name, as recorded, and there were 150 years between the two kings.

JAB′NEEL (*El builds*). In Judah, near the sea,

patriarchal blessing from his father by a stratagem, in which he was aided by his mother. This blessing was material only, and did not include the spiritual promises. His quiet life ended when, at the age of 78 he was obliged to leave home, and was sent to Padan-Aram to find a wife among his mother's relatives. On the way there he had the dream of the ladder reaching from earth to heaven, at Bethel. Isaac had repeated his blessing when he left home, with the addition of the spiritual promises made to Abraham, and they were confirmed in the dream at Bethel. (Jacob seems to have thought only of *a local God who lived at Bethel*, with whom he was disposed to make a bargain for service on conditions). The beautiful incident of the meeting of Jacob with Rebekah at the well exhibits the pure and simple habits of the time, and the courtesy and kindness so native to those who follow the shepherd's life. Laban drove a very hard and shrewd bargain with Jacob, compelling him to serve 14 years for Rachel and marry Leah besides, but this was repaid by Jacob in his sharp practice in making himself rich in "much cattle," by skilful management. At the age of nearly 100 he returned to Canaan, and on the way his name was changed from Jacob to Israel (God's soldier) at Peniel, where he met his brother Esau, who was then a kind of Bedawin wanderer, such as now roam over the same district, although Esau appeared to be much the better man of the two.

The images (gods) that Rachel stole from her father's house, were small figures of certain designs, (TERAPHIM), such as are often found

buried among the ruins in Palestine, and were used in Pagan worship. The value put on them by Laban shows how little real knowledge he had of the true God. Jacob stayed awhile at Shechem, where he buried under a sacred tree the stolen images; and also at Bethel where he built an altar. While on the way to Hebron, where his father was, his son Benjamin was born, and the mother, Rachel, died and was buried near Bethlehem, where a tomb preserves her memory to this day.

Esau and Jacob met again at Hebron, when they buried their father Isaac.

Soon after this Joseph was sold into Egypt.

Jacob was living at Hebron with his eleven sons, when a famine brought about the migration to Egypt (see JOSEPH), where he was assigned a home in the pasture land of Goshen, by the Pharaoh, and where he died, aged 130 (147). His body was borne to the cave of Machpelah, and laid in the tomb with those of Abraham, Sarah and Isaac. The blessing that Jacob gave his sons was a proof that his faith in God's promise was strong—had increased—and that his idea of the true God had become clearer and more elevated. It is full of fine thoughts, poetic language, and abounds in the most beautiful images.

JA'DAU. IDDO. A son of Nebo, who married a Gentile (Ezr. x. 43).

JAD'DUA (*known*). 1. A layman, who signed the covenant with Nehemiah (x. 21).—2. Son(?) and successor of Jonathan, high-priest, the last whose name is recorded in the O. T. Josephus relates of him a ceremonious reception of Alexander (Ant. xi. 8, § 7).

JA'DON (*judge*). The Meronothite who assisted in repairing the wall of Jerusalem (Neh. iii. 7).—2. A man of God, from Judah, who withstood Jeroboam at Bethel, as said by Josephus, in error for Iddo (2 Chr. ix. 29).

JA'EL (*climber, Ibex*). Wife of Heber (of the family of Hobab), the Kenite, a sheikh of a Bedawin tribe, who had pitched his tent under an oak, called on that account "oak of the wanderers" (plain of Zaanaim in Judg. iv. 11), near Kedesh-Naphtali (HEBER, ELON). When his army was routed, Sisera fled in another direction, away from the flying host, and sought safety in the woman's private tent, where he would have been safe, under Jael's cloak, if the woman herself had not betrayed him, which she did do, killing him with one of the tent-pins. God's judgment on Sisera was celebrated in the song of Deborah, but not

JACOB'S WELL.—SHECHEM.

JACOB'S WELL. Is in a low spur of Mt. Gerizim, at the mouth of the valley of Shechem. "Formerly there was a square hole opening into a carefully built vaulted chamber, 10 ft. sq., in the floor of which was the true mouth of the well. Now a part of the vault has fallen in, and completely covered up the mouth, so that it looks like a shallow pit." The well is 9 feet diameter, circular, cut through limestone rock nearly 100 feet deep. It sometimes has water in it, but is often quite dry. There was a small church over it in the 4th century, and to the south-west there are a few shapeless ruins still left.

JA'DA (*skilful*). Son of Onam by Atarah (1 Chr. ii. 28).

Jael's treacherous and violent method.—2. A judge of Israel (Judg. v. 6).

JA'GUR (*lodging-place*). Town in the south of Judah (Josh. xv. 21). KINAH.

JAH (*yah*). The shorter form of Jehovah. Used in forming such names as Eli-jah, Isa-jah, Jerem-jah (Jeremiah). GOD (German *Gött*). The Hebrew names are: 1. EL, *might*, as EL-SHADDAI, *God almighty* (Gen. xiv.); EL-ELOHIM, *God mightier than all gods, God of gods;* EL-BETH-EL, *the place of the mighty God;* also in compounds, as AREZE-EL, *the cedars of God,* that is tall and strong; and peculiarly in poetry.—2. ELOAH, *strong;* ELOHIM, the plural. ELOAH is used only in poetry, and ELOHIM in both poetry and prose.

The plural is used in Hebrew to enlarge and intensify the idea expressed by the singular. ELOHIM is not *the gods*, but is the strongest of all strong beings, the fullness of divine perfections, the sum of all the powers of all imaginable gods. There is nothing in this name either for against the idea of a trinity. That belongs to the New Testament age. The unity of God was guarded with the utmost jealousy against idolatrous polytheists (Deut. vi. 4, xxxii. 39; Is. xlv. 6). The word was often used for the heathen gods and other ideas of divinity (Ps. viii. 6, xcvii. 7), as angels; and also to the rulers and judges of Israel (Ex. xxii. 9, 28), and God (Elohim) is said to judge among the rulers (Elohim in Ps. lxxxii. 1). All true sons of Israel were called sons of God (Elohim, John x. 35). The Cainites claimed to be "sons of God" in distinction from the Sethites, who took the more humble name of "sons of Adam," or "sons of the Man" (Gen. vi. 4). The peculiar name of God in relation to the covenant, is—3. JEHOVAH; but in reading the Scriptures the Jews always pronounced the word ADONAI, which is *Lord*. The vowel points now in use were not invented for centuries after the Hebrew ceased to be a living language, so that the true pronounciation of the name Jehovah was lost, and the word was written YHVH, and pronounced Adonai or Elohim. The vowel points of Adonai (ADONAI) were placed in Jehovah (JAHOVAH), but this is not found in the old copies, and not older than about 1500 A. D. Diodorus Siculus gives the Greek IAO for the Hebrew JHVH. The meaning of Jehovah is *underived existence*, HE IS, or I AM BECAUSE I AM, the God of Abraham, of grace, and truth, and love; self-existence, eternity. Elohim is God *in nature*, Jehovah is God *in grace*. (The temple of Isis, at Sais, had this inscription: "I am all that has been, that is, and that will be," meaning Isis, the universal mother.) The word Jehovah is supposed to mean YAMU, *joy;* VAH, *pain*—the God of good and evil. See HISTORY, page xlv. In Greek, the word is—4. THEOS, any deity, idol, or the true God (Matt. i. 23), and Satan (God of this world).—5. KURIOS, Lord in Matt. i. 20; and in the Septuagint as the translation of Jehovah; also of a man, a lord.

JA'HATH (*union*). 1. Son of Libni (1 Chr. vi. 20). Ancestor of Asaph.—2. Head of a family in the line of Gershom (1 Chr. xxiii. 10).—3. In the line of Judah (1 Chr. iv. 2).—4. A Levite, son of Shelomoth (xxiv. 2).—5. Merarite Levite in Josiah's time (xxxiv. 12); an overseer of repairs in the temple.

JA'HAZ. JAHA'ZA (Josh. xiii. 18). JAHA'ZAH. JAH'ZAH (Num. xxi. 23). A place where the battle was fought between the Israelites and Sihon, king of the Amorites. Jeremiah mentions it (xlviii. 21) as in Moab. Not yet identified.

JAHAZI'AH (*seen by Jah*). Son of Tikvah, and assistant to Ezra (x. 15). Ezechias in Esdras.

JAHA'ZIEL (*seen by El, that is, made strong*). 1. Deserted Saul for David at Ziklag (1 Chr. xii. 4). —2. Priest in David's time, who blew the trumpet at ceremonials (1 Chr. xvi. 6).—3. 3d son of Hebron, a Levite. The family is mentioned in David's time (1 Chr. xxii. 19).—4. Levite of the sons of Asaph who prophesied the destruction of the army that was coming to attack Jerusalem (2 Chr. xx. 14).—5. A son of Jehaziel returned from captivity as chief of the Bene-Shecariah (Ezr. viii. 5). Zattu (for Shecariah) in 1 Esdras viii. 32 (Bene Zathoe). JEZELUS.

JAH'DAI (*led by Jah*). In Caleb's line, father of 6 sons (1 Chr. ii. 47).

JAH'DIEL (*made joyful by El*). Chief in Manasseh, E. of Jordan (1 Chr. v. 24).

JAH'DO (*united*). Son of Buz, a Gadite (1 Chr. v. 11).

JAH'LEEL (*hope in El*). 3d son of Zebulon (Gen. xlvi. 14). JAHLEELITES (Num. xxvi. 26).

JAH'MAI (*Jah guards*). Chief in the house of Tola, Issachar (1 Chr. vii. 2).

JAH'ZAH (*threshing-floor*). JAHAZ (1 Chr. vi. 78).

JAH'ZEEL (*El divides*). 1st son of Naphtali (Gen. xlvi. 24). Jahzeelites (Num. xxvi. 48). Jahziel in 1 Chr. vii. 13. JAHZEEL.

JAH'ZERAH (*led back by Jah*). Priest of the family of Immer (1 Chr. ix. 12).

JA'IR (*splendid*). 1. Descended from both Judah and Manasseh. Leader in the conquest of Bashan, B. C. 1451. See HAVOTH-JAIR.—2. 8th judge of Israel, B. C. 1210, a Gileadite. Buried in Camon. —3. 2 Sam. xxi. 19.

BOAT OF THE NILE.

JAIRITE, IRA, THE (2 Sam. xx. 26). (Pasha?)

JAI'RUS (Gr. for the Heb. JAIR). Ruler in a synagogue in Galilee, whose daughter Jesus restored to life and health (Luke viii. 14).

JA'KAN. JAAKAN. Akan.

JA'KEH (*pious*). Father of Agur (Prov. xxx. 1). Supposed by some to be a name for David, father of Solomon, but without evidence.

JA'KIM (*lifted by Jah*). Chief of the 12th course of priests in David's reign (1 Chr. xxiv. 12). JACHIN?—2. One of the Bene Shimhi (1 Chr. viii. 19).

JA'LON (*abiding*). A son of Ezra, in the line of Judah (1 Chr. iv. 17).

JAM'BRI, children of (i. e. some of the tribe) attacked the Maccabees, and suffered reprisals (1 Macc. ix. 36). Amorites?

JAMES. Three persons are mentioned by this name in the N. T. The original form of the name in Hebrew is Jacob, and is so called now by the church in the East; St. Jacob (*Mar Yacoob*). The name has passed through several changes, through many languages. It was in Greek, Iakobos; Latin, Jacobus; Italian, Iacomo, or Giacomo, and Jacopo; Spanish, Iago (Diego), and Xayme, or Jayme (*Jayme*); French, Jacques, and Jame, which is in English James. (See Robertson's *Becket*, p. 139).

The modern derivatives are framed on the original form, as Jacobin, and Jacobite.

1. JAMES, THE SON OF ZEBEDEE. He first appears as a fisherman, A. D. 27, when he, with his brother John, was called by Jesus to be his disciple (Mark i. 20). His father owned a boat (ship) and employed help. On another occasion he, his brother John, with Simon and Andrew, were directed by Jesus, and caught a very large number of fish at one haul, which was explained by the

Great Teacher to mean that they all should become successful fishers of men. James was numbered with the 12, among the first 4. He was always selected for any special duty. He was present at the raising of Jairus' daughter (Mark i. 29); one of the three on the Mt. of Transfiguration (Matt. xvii. 1); one of the 4 who heard the sermon on the last days (Mark xiii. 3); and one of 3 in Gethsemane (Matt. xxvi. 37). He joined his brother John in the request that fire should be called down on the Samaritans (Luke ix. 54); and in the ambitious request, with their mother, to sit nearest to Christ in his kingdom (Matt. xx. 20). These requests were refused with indignation by Jesus, and they were named Boanerges (Mark ii. 17). They were at the Feast of Pentecost. He was a man of very resolute purpose and determined action, and was given a high position among the apostles (Acts xii. 2); and he is the only one of the 12 whose death is recorded, which took place about 40 years after the crucifixion.

2. JAMES THE LORD'S BROTHER. The children of Joseph and Mary were Jesus, James, Joses, Jude (Judas), Simon, and three daughters whose names are not given (Matt. xiii. 55, 56; Gal. i. 19, ii. 9, 12). His brethren did not believe in Jesus as the Christ at the first (John vii. 5), and some of them not until a few days before the Day of Pentecost (1 Cor. xv. 7). James occupied a prominent position among the apostles, and was surnamed "the Just." James and Peter seem to have been in authority on equal terms when Paul was admitted to the fellowship of the apostles on the word of Barnabas (Acts ix. 27; Gal. i. 18), and after that time he acts as the president of the council in Jerusalem (Acts xii. 17, xv. 13), whose decrees he delivered formally, a position recognized and recorded by Paul (Gal. ii. 9), and honored by a formal visit of ceremony in the presence of all the presbyters (Acts xxi. 18). He is believed to have been appointed Bishop of Jerusalem by Jesus in a vision, as is reported by Epiphanius and others of the early historians of the Church, only that Eusebius says the appointment was by the apostles. Hegesippus, a Jewish disciple in the 2d century, gives the most minute and interesting account, in which he is described as the brother of Jesus, holy from the womb, drinking neither wine nor spirits, nor eating animal food, and wearing both his hair and whiskers without shaving (but with trimming), and he avoided the use of perfumes and ceremonious bathing, and wore only linen clothes. He was a very constant attendant on the services in the temple, and prayed "on his knees" for the salvation of the people, so that he was looked upon as the "bulwark of the church," and it is said that "all who became believers believed through James." This same authority relates that he was thrown from the gable of the temple to the ground, and then stoned to death, shortly before the siege of Jerusalem. See the HISTORY for the EPISTLE OF JAMES. The question of the relation of James to Jesus is referred to the article MARY.

3. JAMES THE SON OF ALPHÆUS (Clopas), and Mary (John xix. 25), one of the apostles (Matt. x. 3; Mark iii. 18, etc.), (Matt. xxvii. 56; Mark xv. 40), and is also called James the Less. He had a brother named Joses, and a sister Salome. The occurrence of the same name in the mother and children of two families does not argue a relation, rather the contrary, and it is not likely that these were relatives of Jesus. See MARY.

JA'MIN (*right hand*). Son of Simeon, founder of the Jaminites (Gen. xlvi. 10).—2. Son of Ram of Hezron in Judah (1 Chr. ii. 27).—3. Reader under Ezra (Neh. viii. 7).

JAM'LECH (*Jah makes the king*). Chief in Simeon in the time of Hezekiah (1 Chr. iv. 34, 41).

JAM'NIA for JABNEEL in the Apocrypha.

JANGLING (Gr. *mataiologia*). Babbling, idle talk. "Jangling is whan a man spekith to moche biforn folk, and clappith as a mille, and taketh no keep what he saith." (Chaucer. *Person's Tale*).

JAN'NA. Father of Melchi in the line of Jesus. JOHN?

JAN'NES and JAM'BRES. The two Egyptian magicians who imitated Moses. Their names were given by Paul only (2 Tim. iii. 8, 9). The origin of the names is obscure. James may be Greek for the Egyptian AAN (Ian), two kings having that name (meaning *call-y*), one of which lived before Joseph. It is supposed that Paul found the names in some history (or tradition), now lost.

JANO'AH (*quiet*). In Naphtali, taken by Tiglath-Pileser (2 K. xv. 29). Janohah in Eusebius and Jerome.

JANO'HAH (*into rest*). On the N. boundary of Egypt (12 ms. E. of Neapolis—*Eusebius*). YANUN is in that locality (Van de Velde, ii. 303), in a valley which slopes toward the Jordan, a small village among extensive ancient ruins. *Khirbet Yanun*, N. E. of Yanun, may be the more ancient (Rob. 297).

JA'NUM (*slumber*). Judah in the mts., near Hebron (Josh. xv. 53). Ja'nus.

JA'PHETH (*extent*). Second son of Noah (Gen. x. 2, 6). YAPHAH (*fair*) may be the root-word, in allusion to the light complexion of the people of the Japhetic races who occupied the Isles of Greece (shores and islands), coasts of the Great Sea, and Asia Minor, Asia and Europe.

JAPHI'A (*fair*). Zebulon's boundary ran from Daberath to Japhia, and Gath-hepher (Josh. xix. 12). YAFA is two miles S. of Nazareth. A tradition says Zebedee was born here, and therefore the Latins call it San Giacomo (St. James).

JAPHI'A (*shining*). 1. King of Lachish (Josh. x. 3).—2. Son of David, born in Jerusalem. Nephia in the Peshito. See DAVID.

JAPH'LET. In the line of Asher, through Beriah (1 Chr. vii. 32).

JAPH'LETI. Boundary of the Japhletite on the S. of Ephraim (Josh. xvi. 3). Probably an ancient Canaanite tribe.

JA'PHO (*beauty*). JOPPA. (Josh. xix. 46).

JA'RAH (*honey*). Son of Micah (1 Chr. ix. 42). Jehoadah in ch. viii. 36.

COIN OF CORINTH.

JA'REB (*hostile*). A king of Assyria (Hos. v. 13; x. 6). The title of "avenger" (YAREB), was assumed by him, as "defender of the faith" was by Henry VIII.

JA'RED (*low ground*). A patriarch, son of Mahalaleel, father of Enoch (Gen. v. 15).

JARESI'AH (*Jah nourishes*). Chief in Benjamin (1 Chr. viii. 27).

JAR'HA. Egyptian servant of Sheshan, husband of his daughter Ahlai (1 Chr. ii. 34).

JA'RIB (*adhering*). 1. Jachin in Gen. xlvi.; Ex. vi.; Num. xxvi.—2, Chief with Ezra (Ezr. viii. 16).—3. A priest, son of Jozadak (x. 18).—4. Joarib.

JAR'MUTH (*hill*). In the Shefelah near Socoh (Josh. xv. 35). Its king, *Piram*, was routed (with

the 5 kings) at Beth-horon by Joshua (Josh. x. 3, 25). *Jarmuth*, about 9 miles N. E. of Beit Jibrin. —2. City in Issa. (Josh. xix. 17). Remeth in verse 21, and in 1 Chr. vi. 73, Ramoth.

JARO'AH (*moon*). Chief in Gad (1 Chr. v. 14).

JA'SHEN (*sleeping*). Sons of J. were in David's guard (2 Sam. xxiii. 32). Sons of Hashem in 1 Chr. xi. 34.

JA'SHER, THE BOOK OF (*book of the upright*). A book of heroic poetry and history mentioned in two places in the O. T. (Josh. x. 13, and 2 Sam. i. 18), and probably a book of songs and eulogies of distinguished men in Israel. The Vulgate has "the book of the just one;" the Septuagint, "the book of the upright one;" the Syriac, "the book of praises," or "psalms." There is an English forgery of 1751 (Bristol, 1829). The original was probably published first in the time of Joshua, and again in David's reign with additions. A scheme was started for gathering the supposed fragments of this work from the various books of the O. T. The supposed plan of the work is that it was written to supply a popular demand in Solomon's time, and its object was to show that God made man upright, but carnal wisdom led him away from the law (spiritual wisdom), when the Hebrews were chosen to keep the law; David was made (perpetual) king for his religious integrity. The compiler named is the prophet Nathan, and it contained the pith, or marrow of the religious system of the Hebrews. This is only a conjecture.

LAMP STAND.

JASHO'BEAM (*return*). Son of Zabdiel (1 Chr. xxvii. 2), a Korhite (xii. 6), or a Hachmonite (xi. 11). He slew 800 at one time (2 Sam. xxiii. 8). Chief in David's guard, over the 1st monthly course of 24,000 men.

JA'SHUB (*who returns*). 1. 3d son of Issachar (1 Chr. vii. 1). Job in Gen. xlvi.—2. son of Bani (Ezr. x. 29).

JASH'UBI-LE'HEM (*returns to bread*). Son of Judah by Bathshua (1 Chr. iv. 22). It may also be the name of a place—Chozeba, Chezib, or Achzib. The Targum (or Chronicles) says Chozeba is Elimelech; Joash and Saraph are Mahlon and Chilion, who had the dominion in Moab from marrying the two girls; Jashubi-Lehem is Noomi and Ruth who returned (*jashub*, *return*) to Beth-lehem (*lehem*, *bread*), after the famine. A poem derived from the book of Ruth.

JA'SHUBITES. Family of Jashub (Num. xxvi. 24).

JA'SIEL (*made by El*). One of David's guard (1 Chr. xi. 47). A Mesobaite.

JA'SON. Greek form of the name Jesus; Hebrew, Joshua.—1. Son of Eleazer, sent by Judas Macc. to treat with the Romans, B. C. 161 (1 Macc. viii. 17). —2. Father of Antipater, an envoy to Rome (1 Macc. xii. 16), perhaps the same as No. 1.—3. Of Cyrene, a Jewish author of "Five Books of the War of Jewish Liberation," from which the 2d book of Maccabees was compiled. (See MACCABEES in the HISTORY).—4. Jason the high-priest, 2d son of Simon 2, and brother of Onias 3. He got his office by fraud, and attempted to Hellenize the Jews by building a gymnasium on the Greek model in Jerusalem, which even the priests attended to the neglect of their duties (2 Macc. iv. 9), and by sending a deputation to the games in honor of Hercules at Tyre. Menelaus supplanted him by fraud and a bribe.—5. The Thessalonian who entertained Paul and Silas, for which the Jewish mob attacked him (Acts xvii. 5). He was a companion of Paul (Rom. xvi. 21). SECUNDUS? (Acts xx. 4).

JAS'PER (YASHEFEH). PRECIOUS STONES.

JATH'NIEL (*whom El gives*). Door-keeper in the temple (1 Chr. xxvi. 2). Of the family of Meshelemiah.

JAT'TIR (*eminent*). Judah in the mts. (Josh. xv. 48). David sent a part of the spoils of Ziklag to this place (1 Sam. xxx. 27). 12 ms. S. of Hebron is Attir, in ruins, on a hill.

JA'VAN. 4th son of Japheth, father (settler) of Elisha, Tarshish, Kittim, and Dodanim. The Hebrew name of Greece. In the Cuneatic it is *Yavnu*. Homer says that early settlers of Greece were *Iaones* (Iliad xiii. 685).—2. The Javan of Ez. xxvii. 19 is an error for UZAL in Arabia (*Yemen*).

JA'ZER. JAAZER.

JA'ZIZ (*shining*). A Hagarite shepherd in David's employ (1 Chr. xxvii. 31). Perhaps stationed in the country of his ancestors, east of Jordan (verses 19-22).

JE'ARIM, MOUNT. Chesalon (*Keslu*), is on a steep ridge, between *Wady Ghurab* and *Wady Ismail*, 7. ms W. of Jerusalem.

JEAT'ERAI (*following one*). Son of Zerah, a Levite (1 Chr. vi. 21). Ethni?

JEBERECHI'AH (*Jah blesses*). Father of Zechariah, in Ahaz's time (Is. viii. 2). Berechia?

JE'BUS (*trodden down*). JERUSALEM. JEBUSI.

JEB'USITE. Third son of Canaan (Gen. x. 16). First mentioned in the account of the spies (Num. xiii. 29). Jabin's army contained men from the Amorites, Hittites, Perizzites and Jebusites (Josh. xi. 3). The king was killed at Bethhoron (x. 1, 5, xii. 10); a part of it was taken and burned by Judah (Judg. i. 21), but the citadel held out for 300 years, until David's time (2 Sam. v. 6). Araunah, the Jebusite, is made immortal by his dealing with David. The remnant of the tribe was made tributary to Solomon (1 K. ix. 20), and are heard of as late as the captivity (Ezr. ix. 1).

JECAMI'AH (*Jah assembles the people*). Son of Neri, of the line of Nathan and of Jesus (Luke iii. 27).

JECHOLI'AH (*Jah is mighty*). Wife of Amaziah, king of Judah (2 K. xv. 2). Jecoliah in Chr. She was a native of Jerusalem.

JECHONI'AS. Greek form of Jechoni'ah.

JECONI'AH (*Jah builds*). Jehoiachin, the last but one of the kings of Judah.

JEDA'IAH (*Jah knows*). Head of the 2d course of priests (1 Chr. xxiv. 7). Some of this course returned from captivity (Ezr. ii. 36), and there were two priestly families (Neh. xii. 6, etc.).—2. A priest in the time of Joshua, the high-priest (Zech. vi. 10).

JEDA′IAH (*Jah's praise*). The Hebrew differs in these two names, but it is not easy to show the difference in English letters. 1. Ancestor of Ziza, of Simeon (1 Chr. iv. 37).—2. Son of Harumaph, who assisted in rebuilding the wall (Neh. iii. 10).

JEDI′AEL (*El knows*). Chief in Benjamin (1 Chr. vii. 6), whose family, with its branches, numbered 17,200 fighting men in David's time.—2. Son of Meshelemiah, a Levite, a doorkeeper in the temple (1 Chr. xxvi.).—3. Son of Shimri, of David's guard (1 Chr. xii. 45).—4. A "head" of 1000, who joined David near Ziklag (1 Chr. xii. 20).

JEDI′DAH (*only one*). Queen of Amon, mother of Josiah (2 K. xxii. 1). She was a native of Bozkath.

JEHEZ′EKEL (*El makes strong*). Priest in charge of the 20th course (1 Chr. xxiv. 16).

JEHI′AH (*Jah lives*). Door-keeper with Obed-edom for the ark (1 Chr. xv. 24).

JEHI′EL (*El lives*). 1. A Levite assistant in the temple (1 Chr. xv. 18).—2. Son of Jehoshaphat (2 Chr. xxi. 2).—3. Ruler in the temple in Josiah's time (xxxv. 8).—4. Levite, head of Laadan's sons (1 Chr. xxiii. 8).—5. Son of Hachmoni, in David's guard (xxvii. 32). Jerome says Jehiel was David's son Chileab (Daniel), and Achamoni David himself.—6. Levite in the time of Hezekiah (2 Chr. xxix. 14).—7. A Levite and an overseer of the sacrifices (xxxi. 13).—8. Father of Obadiah, who returned from captivity at the head of 218 sons of

DOME OF THE ROCK, JERUSALEM.

Joab (Ezr. viii. 9).—9. Father of Shekaniah, who assisted Ezra (x. 2).—10. Another of the same family who had to part with his Gentile wife (Ezr. x. 26).—11. A priest of the sons of Harim, who also put away his wife (x. 21).

JEHI′EL (different from the last in the Hebrew). Father of Gibeon in the line of Saul the king (1 Chr. ix. 35).—2. Son of Hotham the Aroerite, in David's guard (1 Chr. xi. 44).

JEHIE′LI. The Bene-Jehieli were treasurers of the temple (1 Chr. xxvi. 21).

JEHIZKI′AH (*Jah strengthens*). Son of Shallum, Chief in Ephraim in the time of Ahaz. He saved a large number of captives, and had them clothed, fed, tended, and returned to Jericho (2 Chr. xxviii. 12).

JEHO′ADAH (*Jah adorns*). Great-grandson of Merib-baal, in the time of Saul (1 Chr. viii. 36).

JEHOAD′DAN of Jerusalem, Josiah's queen, and mother of Amaziah of Judah (2 K. xiv. 2).

JEHO′AHAZ (*Jah holds*). Son and successor of Jehu, who reigned 17 years, B. C. 856-840, in Samaria (2 K. xiii. 1-9).—2. Shallum, 4th son of Josiah, whom he succeeded as king of Judah, being chosen over his elder brother, B. C. 610, but after a short reign he was deposed (2 K. xxiii. 32; Jer. xxii. 10), by Pharaoh Necho, taken to Riblah, put in chains, and taken to Egypt, where he died. The people lamented for him, and he was the first

JEDIDI′AH (*Jah's darling*). The name given to Solomon by the prophet Nathan. David named him Shelomoh, *peaceful*.

JEDU′THUN (*praising*). One of the conductors of the temple music in the time of David (1 Chr. xv. 17; xxiii. 6). The three were ETHAN, the son of Kushaiah, the Merarite; HEMAN, the Kohathite; and ASAPH, the Gershonite. He played on cymbals in the procession, when the ark was brought to Zion, but he was appointed to duty at Gibeon (Ps. cl. 5). His name is in the titles of several psalms (xxxix.; lxii.; lxxvii.), as choir leader.

JE′EZER (Num. xxvi. 20). ABIEZER. JEEZERITES.

JE′GAR-SAHADU′THA (*witness heap*). Name in Aramaic of the pillar, or heap of stones set up by Laban and Jacob. There are two accounts of the same heap (Gen. xxxi. 47), Jacob naming it Galeed.

JEHALE′LEEL (*who praises El*). Four sons of his are named in Judah's line (1 Chr. iv. 16).

JEHALE′LEL (*who praises El*). Father of Azariah who assisted in restoring the temple in Hezekiah's time (2 Chr. xxix. 12).

JEHDE′IAH (*Jah makes joyful*). Descendant of Gershom, in David's time (1 Chr. xxiv. 20). Shubael was head of the house in xxvi. 24.—2. A Meronothite who took care of David's she-asses (xxvii. 30).

king of Judah who died in exile.—3. Youngest son of king Jehoram. His name as king of Judah was Ahaziah.

JEHO'ASH (*Jah's gift*). Joash, 8th king of Judah.—2. 13th king of Israel.

JEHOHA'NAN (*Jah's gift*). Johanan (John). 1. Levite and doorkeeper in the tabernacle (1 Chr. xxvi. 3).—2. Chief of Judah, general of 280,000 under Jehoshaphat (2 Chr. xvii. 15). Father of Ishmael, a captain of 100 (xxiii. 1).—3. A Bene-Bebai who was parted from his Gentile wife (Ezr. x. 28). —5. A priest under Joiakim, h.-p. (Neh. xii. 13), after the captivity.—6. Priest and musician at the dedication of the wall (Neh. xii. 42).

JEHOI'ACHIN (*appointed by Jah*). Jeconiah, Coniah, Jeconias, Joiakim and Joacim. Son of Jehiakim and Nehushta, and 19th king of Judah, reigning 3 mos. 10 days. He was 18 years old (2 K. xxiv. 8), or 8 (2 Chr. xxxvi. 9), and was carried captive by Nebuchadnezzar, in revenge for the alliance that his father had made with Egypt. The best of the people, the sacred vessels of the temple, and all the treasure of the people, were taken to Babylon, leaving a poor and feeble remnant. Jehoiachin was kept a close prisoner nearly all the rest of his life, 36 years, when Evil-Merodach liberated him. (See EVIL-MERODACH.) He was the last of Solomon's line, as predicted by Jeremiah (xxii. 30), the succession passing over to Nathan's line.

EARTHEN LAMP. NO. 4.

JEHOI'ADA (*Jah favors*). 1. Father of Benaiah, David's general (2 Sam. viii. 18). He was also chief-priest, and leader of 3,700 Aaronites who joined David at Hebron (1 Chr. xii. 27).—2. Son of Benaiah, who succeeded Ahithophel as counselor to David—unless there is an error in position and Benaiah is meant.—3. High-priest at the time of Athaliah's usurpation, and in Joash's reign, B. C. 884-878. He succeeded Amariah. Married Jehosheba, daughter of king Jehoram, and sister of king Ahaziah (2 Chr. xxii. 11). He stole Joash when Athaliah killed all the other royal line of Judah, and hid him 6 years in the Temple, finally placing him on the throne.—4. 2d priest (sagan) to Seraiah the h.-p., and was deposed for friendship to the prophet Jeremiah (Jer. xxix. 25-29).—5. Son of Paseah, who repaired the Old Gate at Jerusalem (Neh. iii. 6).

JEHOI'AKIM (*Jah appoints*). 19th king of Judah (B. C. 609-598), 25 years old at his accession. He was first named Eliakim, and was the son of Josiah and Zebudah, but Pharaoh Necho changed his name when he made him king in his brother Jehoahaz's stead (2 K. xxiii. 33), who died in Egypt, in captivity (v. 34), and he also collected a heavy fine ($200,000) from Judah for Josiah's part with Babylon against Egypt. The battle at Carchemish ended the rule of Egypt in Palestine for that time, and Nebuchadnezzar besieged and took Jerusalem, and carried some of the royal family to Babylon as hostages, among whom were Daniel and his three companions. The prophets Jeremiah and Ezekiel warned the king and people of the results of their idolatries, but instead of repenting they burned Jeremiah's prophecy, put him in prison, and drove Urijah the prophet into Egypt, where he was killed, and his corpse treated in a barbarous manner (Jer. xxvi. 21-23; xxxvi.). According to the warnings of Ezekiel (xvii.) and Jeremiah (ii. xxvii.), enemies attacked them on all sides (2 K. xxiv. 7); the king lost his life, and was buried without honor (Jer. xxii. 18, 19). The king of Babylon came in a few weeks after his death and carried his son and all the best men and their families and treasures to Babylon. This act of the king in burning Jeremiah's book was the first recorded attack on the liberty of the public press, and it did not succeed ; the second edition was enlarged and improved (Jer. xxxvi. 32).

JEHOI'ARIB (*Jah a defender*). Head of the 1st course of priests in David's reign (1 Chr. xxiv. 7). His descendants were among the returned captives (Neh. xi. 10).

JEHO'NADAB (*Jah incites*). The son of Rechab (a Kenite), who assisted Jehu in his reforms, and in the destruction of the Baal worshipers (2 K. x. 15). Jeremiah holds up to the people the obedience of the Rechabites (pilgrims) who kept the law of abstinence from wine, and that to live only in tents, in contrast to the general disregard of the law of Moses (Jer. xxxv.), and prophesies an immortality of the house of Rechab. There is no historical trace of them after the Jewish nation went to pieces, and it is supposed that they became disciples of Jesus.

JEHON'ATHAN (*Jah's gift*). JONATHAN. 1. Son of Uzziah, steward to David (1 Chr. xxvii. 25).— 2. A Levite instructor of the people (2 Chr. xvii. 8).—3. A priest after the return from captivity (Neh. xii. 18).

JEHO'RAM (*Jah has exalted*). JORAM. 1. Son of Ahab, king of Israel, and successor to his brother Ahaziah, B. C. 896. His reign was noted for the lives of the two great prophets Elijah and Elisha. He was killed by an arrow from Jehu's bow in Naboth's vineyard (1 K. xxi. 21). He was the last of the line of Omri.—2. Eldest son of Jehoshaphat, succeeding as king of Judah at the age of 32, reigning 8 years, B. C. 893-885. He murdered his brothers, and (by the help of his wife Athaliah, the daughter of Ahab) revived the Baal worship (see ELIJAH). The latter part of his reign was a series of calamities to the nation, and death to his family, himself dying of a painful malady, not regretted, and being buried without honor.—3. A priest sent to teach the law to the people (2 Chr. xvii. 8).

JEHOSHAB'EATH (*Jah's worshiper*). Jehosheba the wife of Jehoiada, the high priest.

JEHOSHA'PHAT (*Jah is judge*). 1. Son of Asa and Azubah; succeeded to the throne of Judah at the age of 35, and reigned 25 years, B. C. 914-889 (1 K. xv. 24; 2 K. viii. 16; 2 Chr. xvii., xxi.). "The Lord was with Jehoshaphat, because he walked in the first ways of his father David, and sought not unto Baalim; but sought to the Jehovah God of his father." * * "He took away the high-places and groves out of Judah" (2 Chr. xvii. 6; 1 K. xxii. 43). He sent out teachers among the people to instruct them in the law, set up just judges in the walled cities, forming a supreme court in Jerusalem, for references and appeals. He built castles and store-cities, and aimed to restore commerce in the Red Sea. The army was reformed in five sections; and the Arabians, Philistines, and Edomites were laid under tribute. He was saved from a very great danger by his trust in God (2 Chr. xx.; Ps. lxxxiii., xli., xlvii., xlviii.). He made a friendly alliance with the idolatrous kingdom of Israel, and to secure peace married his son Jehoram to Athaliah, the daughter of Ahab. He was saved by a miracle with his army in the

desert (2 K. iii.), at the request of a prophet of Jehovah. The mutual relations between prophet and king in this reign is a sign of the high attainments which the king had made in the divine life. He was prudent enough to appoint his successor (Jehoram, 2 Chr. xxi. 3) in his life-time, as David had done to Solomon.—2. Son of Ahilud, a historian in David's reign (2 Sam. viii. 16) Such officers were attached to all eastern courts (Esther vi. 1).—3. A priest who blew a trumpet before the ark, on its way from the house of Obed-edom to Zion.—4. Son of Paruah, one of 12 commissaries (1 K. iv. 17). His district was Issachar.—5. Son of Nimshi, father of king Jehu (2 K. ix. 2).

JEHOSH'APHAT, VALLEY OF (*valley where Jah judges*), (Joel iii. 12). The valley between Scopus and Olivet and Jerusalem, so named after the greatest king after Solomon (2 Chr. xx.). The nations are to assemble for judgment, where Christ will appear the second time (Acts i. 11). Kidron. The Mohammedans point out a stone in the east wall of the temple area, near the S. end, from which a bridge will be stretched across the valley to Mt. Moriah, over which all souls must pass—the just in safety, the wicked falling off into Gehenna. This valley has been used as a burial-ground from the days of Josiah (2 K. xxiii. 6); and both Jews and Mohammedans look on the place as a most sacred resting-place; but the modern name cannot be traced beyond the 4th century A. D. Joel's prophecy was a poetical and symbolical figure, intended to teach that God is always present with and defending his faithful children. See JERUSALEM.

JEHOSH'EBA (*oath to Jah*). Daughter to Jehoram, king of Judah, but her mother is not mentioned. She married Jehoiada, the high-priest, being the only woman of Aaron's line who married into a royal family. She assisted her husband in preserving the young Joash (see JEHOIADA), (2 K. xi. 2).

JEHOSH'UA (*his help is Jah*). JOSHUA. (Num. xiii. 16).

JEHO'VAH. See JAH.

JEHO'VAH-JI'REH (*Jah will see*). The place where Abraham was about to sacrifice Isaac. Lost. (Gen. xxii. 14).

JEHO'VAH-NIS'SI (*Jah my banner*). Place of an altar built by Moses in memory of a victory over the Amalekites, on Horeb (Ex. xvii. 15).

JEHO'VAH-SHA'LOM (*Jah is peace*). Place of an altar built by Gideon in Ophrah, in memory of the salutation of the angel, "Peace be unto thee" (Judg. vi. 24).

JEHO'VAH-SHAM'MAH (*Jah is there*). The name of the city in Ezekiel's vision (Ez. xl., xlviii.).

JEHO'VAH-TSID'KENU (*Jah our righteousness*, in Jer. xxiii. 6). Supposed to be one of the titles of the Messiah. It was the prophetic name of a king to be raised up (a branch of David), who will reign and prosper, executing judgment and justice, Also, it is to be the name of the Jerusalem of the future, as the city of the great king (xxxiii. 16).

JEHOZ'ABAD (*gifted by Jah*). JOZABAD. There were several of this name: 1. The murderer of Joash (2 K. xii. 21), whose mother was a Moabitess.—2. A general of 180,000 in Jehoshaphat's army, a Benjamite (2 Chr. xvii. 18).—3. A porter or door-keeper of the south gate of the temple (1 Chr. xxvi. 4; Neh. xii. 25).

JEHOZ'ADAK (*Jah makes just*). JOZADAK. Son of Seraiah, the last high-priest before the captivity (2 K. xxv. 18), who was carried into captivity, and died there, but left a son Jeshua, who returned and revived the office (Ezr. iii. 2). JOZEDEC in the Greek, and in Haggai and in Zechariah.

JE'HU (*Jah is he*). 1. First in the 5th dynasty in Israel (see ISRAEL). He was the son of Jehoshaphat (2 K. ix. 2). His grandfather was Nimshi, who was better known than his father. Twenty years before he began to reign he was divinely singled out as the king of Israel by Elijah, and he was anointed by a servant of Elisha, when he was a general in the army, fighting against Hazael, king of Syria, at Ramoth-Gilead (vrs. 4-10). He carried out the directions of the prophecy to the very letter, and also destroyed the Baal (and Astarte) worshipers, their temple and images, but did not entirely purify the national worship, and therefore his line went to destruction in the 4th generation (2 K. xxix. 30; Hos. i. 4).—2. Son of Hanani, a prophet of Judah, whose prophesy was directed against Israel. He also wrote a life of Jehoshaphat (2 Chr. xvi. 7; xx. 34; 1 K. xvi. 1).—3. Man of the house of Hezron, in Judah (1 Chr. ii. 38).—4. Chief in Simeon (iv. 35).—5. "Jehu, the Anthothite," joined David at Ziklag (xii. 3).

SHIP.

JEHUB'BAH (*will be hidden*). Son of Shomer of Asher (1 Chr. vii. 34).

JEHU'CAL (*potent*). Son of Shelemiah (Jucal), "prince of the king" (Jer. xxxvii. 3, xxxviii. 1).

JE'HUD (*praise*). City in Dan (Josh. xix. 45). El Yehudiyeh, near Lydd, 7 miles east of Jaffa (Rob.).

JE'HUDI (*Jews*). Son of Nethaniah, sent to bring Baruch with Jeremiah's denunciation to be read to the king (Jer. xxxvi. 14, 21, 23).

JEHUDI'JAH (*Jewess*). Correctly Hajehudijah, a wife of Mered, sister of Naham (1 Chr. iv. 18). Hodijah in verse 19.

JE'HUSH (*collecting*). Son of Eshek in the line of Saul (1 Chr. viii. 39).

JEI'EL (*El's treasure*). There are eight of this name, but none are famous.

JEKAB'ZEEL (*El collects*). Kabzeel was so named after the return from captivity (Neh. ix. 25).

JEKAME'AM (*assembler*). Levite in David's time, in the line of Hebron (1 Chr. xxiii. 19).

JEKAMI'AH (*Jah collects*). Son of Shallum (in Ahab's time). Another person is called Jekamiah in 1 Chr. ii. 41.

JEHU'THIEL (*piety*). Son of Mered (see JERUDIJAH), who built Zanoah.

JEMI'MA (*dove*). Job's eldest daughter after his recovery (Job xlii. 14). JEMAMA is a name of a province in the centre of Arabia, said to have been named after an ancient queen of the Arabians.

JEM'INI (*right hand*). A Benjamite (1 Sam. ix. 1).

JEM'NAAN. JABNEEL. JAMNIA. (Judith ii. 28).

JEM'UEL (*El's day*). Son of Simeon (Gen. xlvi. 10).

JEPTHAE for **JEPHTHAH**, in Heb. xi. 32.

JEPH'THAM (Heb. YIFTAH, *he will open*, Judg.

xxii). Son of Gilead and a concubine. Driven out of the family by the other children, he went to Tob, where he became a leader of a band of marauders, ready for any service but not of robbery. Samuel names him among those who were raised up by God for his people (1 Sam. xii. 11), and Paul mentions his special faith (Heb. xi. 32). The Elders of Israel not finding any one offering to lead against the Ammonites, who had been masters for 18 years, appealed to Jephthah, who solemnly accepted the position. He tried to secure the aid of Ephraim, but in vain, and also to reason with the king of Ammon; and then after making a rash vow he completely overthrew the enemy, taking 20 cities; when having punished the Ephraimites, he held his office for 6 years. The story of his daughter's sacrifice by his vow has been variously understood. Josephus says she was made a burnt-offering, but modern scholars have inclined to the notion that she was devoted to perpetual virginity, and the sacred service of God in the temple. The story of Iphigenia (doomed as a sacrifice to Diana, and made a priestess in her temple) has been cited as a parallel example of the spirit of the Greeks in that age. The vow was that the first person that came out of his house to meet him should be the Lord's, that is, should be devoted to the Lord; if a man he should serve as a priest's servant: if a woman she should be devoted to the sacred duties of religion as a holy virgin (Judg. xi. 39), a companion to the women of the Gibeonites.

PISTACHIO.

Human sacrifice was contrary to the Hebrew idea of true worship of God, and is specially rebuked in the story of Abraham and Isaac. The idea of *sacrifice* is just as strongly brought out in the perpetual virginity of the young woman who, in common with all the daughters of Israel, might hope to become a mother, or the mother even of the Messiah. Besides, burnt-offerings must in all cases be males; and again, the vow to offer some animal would have been a small matter, unworthy of the important occasion. It is quite reasonable to suppose that Jephthah thought of his daughter when he made the vow, for he was a husband of one wife, and had but one child, who was his only hope of posterity, thus making it a real sacrifice. The Levites also were *devoted* in this same sense to the service of God, made dependent, sacred to the Lord, and *offered as an offering*. Samuel was also devoted to the Lord.

JEPHUN'NEH (*for whom a way is made*). The father of Caleb, a Kenezite of Edom.—2. Eldest son of Jether, in Asher (1 Chr. vii. 38).

JE'RAH (*new moon*). 4th Son of Joktan (Gen. x. 26). *Yerakh* in Yemen, and (more probable) the Alilœi (*the moon people*) of Herodotus; not those who are named from Mohammed's relative, Bene-Hilâl, living near the Red Sea, south, near Zafari. There is also a locality called El-Latt (*lah*), meaning the rock where a peculiar worship was offered (to the serpent?); a species of fetishism.

JERAH'MEEL (*El's mercy*). 1. Eldest son of Hezron (1 Chr. ii. 9).—2. A Levite of the family of Kish (xxiv. 29).—3. Son of Hammelech, or the king, the keeper of Jeremiah and Baruch in prison (Jer. xxxvi. 26).

JERAH'MEELITES. From No. 1 (1 Sam. xxvii. 10), lived in the S. of Judah.

JE'RED (*descent*). JARED. Son of Mahalaleel, father of Enoch (1 Chr. i. 2).—2. Builder of Gedor, in Judah (iv. 18).

JEREMAI (*living in the heights*). Son of Hashum (Ezr. x. 33).

JEREMI'AH (*Jah throws*). 1. The great Hebrew prophet. (See HISTORY OF THE BOOKS). Seven others of the same name.—2. Jeremiah of Libnah, father of Hamutal, wife of Josiah (2 K. xxiii. 31).—3, 4, 5, in David's army (1 Chr. xii. 4, 10, 13).—6. A hero in Manasseh, beyond Jordan (v. 24).—7. Priest of high rank, and head of the 3d course (Neh. x. 2-8), which assisted in the dedication of the wall of Jerusalem (xii. 34).—8. Father of Jaazaniah, the Rechabite (Jer. xxxv. 3).

JEREMIAH, LAMENTATIONS OF. See HISTORY OF THE BOOKS.

JEREMI'AS. Greek form of Jeremiah. JEREMAI.

JER'EMOTH (*hights*). 1. Chief of the House of Beriah, of Benjamin (1 Chr. viii. 14), who lived in Jerusalem.—2. A Levite, son of Mushi (xxiii. 23).—3. Son of Heman, head of the 13th choir of musicians (1 Chr. xxv. 22). Jerimoth in v. 4.—4. Son of Elam.—5. Son of Zattu, who complied with Ezra's reform in putting away his Gentile wives, and sacrificed for each (Ezr. x. 26, 27).—6. Ramoth in the Hebrew in verse 29.

JEREMY. The short English form of Jeremiah. JEREMY, THE EPISTLE OF. See Baruch in the HISTORY.

JERI'AH (*built by Jah*). A Levite chief of the House of Hebron (1 Chr. xxiii. 19). JERIJAH.

JER'IBAI (*Jah defends*). Son of Elnaan, in David's guard (1 Chr. xi. 46).

JER'ICHO (*city of the moon*; and another, *a fragant place*). (Num. xxii. 1). In the Jordan valley, 8 miles from the Dead Sea and 6 from the Jordan. When the Jews crossed the Jordan, Jericho was a large and strong city, whose origin is not recorded. Since it is not mentioned in Gen. xiii., when Abraham and Lot looked over the plain, it must have been built after that time. It was anciently surrounded by palm-trees, of which there were many kinds (Deut. xxxiv. 3; Jos. B. J., 8, § 3), thickly dotted about in pleasure gardens; besides balsam, figs, rose-plants, cypress, and many others. Josephus says, "It will not be easy to light on any climate in the habitable earth that can well be compared to it." It was the first city W. of the Jordan taken by the Israelites. Joshua cursed the city (Josh. vi. 26), and the curse was fulfilled in the person of Hiel the Bethelite (1 K. xvi. 34).

The Roman general Pompey camped there one night, and Gabinius made it one of the five cities of assembly. Under Herod the Great it rose to some importance; was full of treasure of all kinds

and had valuable revenues. Antony gave it to Cleopatra. Herod built a fort there, which he named Cyprus, in honor of his mother; and a tower, Phasaelis. He also built a new town higher up the plain, which he also called Phasaelis. Norman McLeod thinks the modern village marks the site of Gilgal (*Eastward*, p. 198).

Near Jericho was a copious spring, which was healed by Elisha (2 K. ii. 19-21), and is now called *Ain es Sultan*. It is about a mile and a half from the modern village of Er Riha.

There are extensive ruins, rubbish and foundations, in several places, on both sides the Wady Kelt (Brook Cherith) and at the Ain es Sultan, marking ancient sites—the most ancient at the fountain. The city of the New Testament was on the banks of the Wady Kelt, on the direct route from Peraea to Jerusalem. It was visited several times by Jesus. Approaching it he cured one blind man (Luke xviii. 35), and leaving it he cured another (Mark x. 46). In the house of Zaccheus (probably in a garden in the suburbs) he related the parable of the Ten Pounds.

Vespasian made it the head of a toparchy. It was destroyed during the siege of Jerusalem. It revived under Saracen rule, and in the time of the Crusades was one of the most fertile regions in Palestine.

The Latins have a tradition that Jesus was baptized in the Jordan, opposite Jericho, and the Greeks point to another place, not far off. Both places are visited by great numbers of pilgrims, especially at Easter. Many bottles and cans of the water of the Jordan are carried away as mementoes of the place.

daughter Mahalath was a wife of Rehoboam, her cousin, Abihail, being another (2 Chr. xi. 18).—8. A Levite, custodian of offerings, under Azariah the high-priest (xxi. 13).

JERI'OTH (*curtains*). Wife of Caleb (the ancient), (1 Chr. ii. 18). The Vulgate says she was Caleb's daughter by his first wife.

JEROBO'AM (Heb. YARAB'AM, *many people*). The founder of the Kingdom of Israel, an Ephraimite, the son of Nebat by Zeruah, a widow, (1 K. xi. 26). He was obliged to fly to Egypt for plotting against Solomon, when a young man, even after Solomon had given him an office of honor and profit (ver. 28). He found an asylum and a kind reception in Egypt, from the Pharaoh Shishak (Sesonchis), successor of the father-in-law of Solomon, who had also received kindly Hadad another enemy of Solomon. On the death of Solomon, and on the request of his friends, Rehoboam hastened to fulfil Ahijah's prophesy in forming a kingdom out of the 10 tribes, being chosen king B. C. 975. He made haste to change the religion of his people, in order to more certainly separate them from Jerusalem, and set up the calf-worship at Bethel (*Bethaven*), and Dan, and changed the time of holding the feasts. His hand was paralyzed because he attempted to arrest the prophet from Judah who predicted the overthrow of his idolatry, but was restored sound on the prayer of the same prophet. His political policy also was unsound, and did not perpetuate itself. He warred with Judah all his days, and died after a reign of 22 years.

JEROBO'AM II. Son of Joash, of the dynasty of Jehu, 13th king of Israel (B. C. 825). Corrup-

ROBINSON'S ARCH, JERUSALEM.

JER'ICHO, PLAINS OF. The wide valley of the Jordan around Jericho, about 8 or 10 miles across (2 K. xxv. 5; Jer. xxxix. 5).

JERI'EL (*founded by El*). Chief in the house of Tola, of Issachar (1 Chr. vii. 2).

JER'IMOTH (*hights*). 1. Son of Bela (1 Chr. vii. 7).—2. A hero who joined David at Ziklag (1 Chr. xii. 5).—3. A son of Becher (1 Chr. vii. 8).—4. Son of Musha, chief of a family of Merailes (xxiv. 30).—5. Son of Heman, head of the 15th choir of musicians (xxv. 4, 22).—6. Son of Azriel, of Naphtali (xxvii. 19). Princes in ver. 22.—7. Son of David, and of a concubine, whose

tions of all kinds, political and religious, were notorious, and were condemned by the prophet Amos (vii.) He reigned 41 years, and extended his father's conquests, taking Hamath, Damascus, the Hauran, Gilead, Ammon and Moab, and advanced his kingdom to its highest point of prosperity. These successes had been predicted by Jonah (2 K. xiv. 25-28). Amos was falsely reported by Jeroboam's high-priest at Bethel as having said that the king should die by the sword, but Amos meant (vii. 9-17) the *house* of Jeroboam, which was the recognized idea in the N. T. times (John viii. 52; Mark xiv. 57; Acts vi. 13). Ps. xiv. may

JERO'HAM (*one beloved*). 1. Father of Elkanah, and about the same age as Eli (1 Chr. vi. 27).—2. A Benjamite, and founder of a family (viii. 27).—3. Father of Ibneiah (ix. 8).—4. Leader of the 16th course of priests (i. 12).—5. Sons of Jeroham of Gedor joined David at Ziklag (xii. 7).—6. Father of Azareel, chief, in David's time, of Dan (xxvii. 22.)—7. Father of Azariah, a captain of hundreds, who aided in the matter of the young king Joash (2 Chr. xxiii. 1).

JERUSALEM — refer to Jeroboam. He was buried in state with his ancestors.

kingdom (Ez. v. 5); leaving Hebron, where he had reigned 7½ years. The seat of the religion had been before this at Shechem, Shiloh, Gibeah, Nob, and Gibeon. Zion was now called the CITY OF DAVID, and was soon enlarged by walls, strengthened by towers, and beautified by a palace for the king, built by the mechanics of Hiram, king of Tyre. After the ark, which had rested at Kirjath-Jearim 20 years after Eli's death, was brought to Zion, David assumed the duties of priest as well as king, offering burnt-offerings and peace-offerings under a new tent in the citadel of

SECTION AT JERUSALEM, SHOWING FILLING ABOVE THE ANCIENT LEVEL.

JERUBBA'AL (*Baal pleads*). Surname of Gideon, because he threw down an altar of Baal (Judg. vi. 32), and when the Abiezites complained to his father he replied, let Baal plead (his own cause).

JERUBBE'SHETH (*with whom the idol contends*). That is *shemeth* (the idol) a shameful thing. Same as Jerubbaal, and a name of Gideon.

JERU'EL (*founded by El*), THE WILDERNESS OF (2 Chr. xx. 16). Between Tekoa and Engedi, near Berachah, now Bereikut. There was a watch-tower (ver. 24), from which the enemy was seen, and reported to Jehoshaphat. The forces of Moab and Ammon were at the end of the brook (*wady*) facing the wilderness of Jeruel.

JERU'SALEM (*foundation of peace*). First mentioned in Gen. xiv. 18, by the name of Salem, whose king was Melchizedek (who is said by the Rabbis to be the patriarch Shem). The name Shalaim (Ps. lxxvi. 2) means two cities, and is applied to the cities or quarters on (modern) Zion and in

Zion. The ark was only removed from here to the Temple of Solomon. David's royal gardens were in the valley at En Rogel. David and most of his successors were buried in the citadel, but there are no traces of their tombs. (See p. 71.) The sepulchres of David were in or near Ophel (Neh. iii. 16, xii. 37). The three great works of Solomon were the Temple, with its east wall and cloister, the Palace, and wall of Jerusalem (Josephus). Also a palace for his Egyptian wife; which was not on Zion (1 K. vii. 8, ix. 24; 2 Chr. viii. 11). "All of these were costly stones, * * sawed with saws," just such stone as is now found in the great quarry under the city, north of the Temple area, which may be sawed almost as easy as chalk; the buildings probably required for residences by the thousand women of Solomon's house, who were of several nations and of different religions; the colleges for the several priests (very much such a state of things as is now found in the city, except that the

SECTION EAST AND WEST, SHOWING KIDRON VALLEY

the Tyropœon valley. At the conquest of Canaan the name of its king was Adoni-zedek (*lord of justice*), (Josh. x. l. 3), almost the same as Melchizedek (*king of righteousness*). Joshua speaks of the city as "The Jebusite" (xv. 8), after the name of its occupiers. In the time of the Judges the name was JEBUS (xix. 10, 11). Judah could not, and Benjamin did not drive out the Jebusites (Josh. xv. 63; Judg. i. 21), and the city only became the capital of the nation after about 450 years from the time of Joshua, when David made it his royal residence, and the sanctuary, near the centre of his

various sects support themselves independently of each other); the 1400 chariots, and 12,000 riding-horses requiring stables; and besides all these, "all that he desired to build in Jerusalem and in Lebanon," shows the activity of his reign. And we are compelled to notice that he also built shrines for Ashtoreth, Chemosh, and Milcom, heathen divinities, on the site now occupied by the village of Siloam, on that part of Olivet called the Mt. of Corruption (1 K. xi.; 2 K. xxiii); which Josiah destroyed, together with an image of Molech in Hinnom, 360 years after.

The first relic that we have in our day of the time of Solomon is a part of the foundation wall of the Temple platform, lately uncovered, an outline sketch of which is in the margin. These are the kind of stones that were "sawed," now very much harder, after long exposure.

The Son of Sirach (and also Tacitus) speaks of a "sea" of waters that was under the Temple, and this was recently brought to light by *Robinson* and *Barclay*, (City of the Great King, 526). It is 736 feet in circuit, 42 in depth, and capable of holding two million gallons.

The columns were once covered with metal, but are now bare, or plastered stone. The rain from the mosque of Aksa and other buildings is drained into it. No fountain has been discovered.

Under the S. E. corner of the Temple area are approach from Zion to the temple enclosure. Solomon's aqueduct from the Pools above Etham passes over this arch, and under the street above. This arch has at one time been used as a cistern. The rock was found on sinking a shaft 51 feet 6 inches below the floor. Below this room there were found vaults, tanks, etc., and a secret passage east and west, probably connecting the Temple with Zion.

The extent of the filling up above the original rock can be seen from the plan, where the debris is 85 feet deep at the S. W. corner of the Haram wall. The "chippings" of the stones and absence of any pieces of pottery, etc., show that this dirt, close to the wall, has never been disturbed since Hiram's builders put it there. The spring of "Robinson's Arch" is seen in its place; and the stones composing the arch were found by Lieut.

PLAN OF JERUSALEM.

many columns, arched over, supporting the platform above at its upper end, resting on the uneven surface of the original hill. The piers or columns are from 3 to 8 feet in diameter, from 5 to 23 feet apart, and there are 15 rows; and opening into this place, which is called Solomon's stables, is a triple gate, under the Aksa mosque. West of these, under the actual temple site, now under the Aksa mosque, is another series of piers and vaults, which seems to have been built up from more ancient materials. Besides the citadel, now called David's tower, there are scarcely any very ancient remains in the city that have not been thrown down and built up again several times.

"Wilson's" arch is one of a series forming an Warren buried under 40 feet of rubbish; one stone having broken through the roof of an aqueduct, lay on the rocky bottom at the depth of 63 feet.

This plan is of the city as it now is; with a few signs indicating ancient works, sites of ancient walls, churches, towers, and other structures in different ages; as many as could be laid down without confusing the work.

The city is small, but there is scarcely a place of any note, not even Nineveh or Babylon, that has been, to modern scholars, such a profound puzzle. The descriptions of Josephus are minute, his knowledge being exact and complete; and the hills on which the city stands are so marked and distinct from each other, that it seems almost mar-

fûrl, rüde, pŭsh; c, i, o, silent; ç as s; çh as sh; e, ch as k; ġ as j; ġ as in get; ṣ as z; x̱ as gz; ṇ as in linger, liṇk; tḥ as in thine.

velous that there could have been any difficulty, until we are reminded of the fact that during the middle ages, and especially during the Crusades, it

ST. STEPHEN'S GATE.

was regarded as a peculiarly sacred city, and as such must needs have every event that is mentioned in the Bible as having happened in or near it located and honored with some monument, costly and showy in proportion to the importance of the event so honored.

els inside the edifice. To describe these various "stations" would require a volume, and it has been already done completely by Bartlett (*Walks about Jerusalem; Jerusalem Revisited*); Barclay (*City of the Great King*); Thomson (*Land and Book*); in *Smith's Dictionary of the Bible;* Kitto's *Cyclopædia;* by Tristram, and others. The numbers on the plan of the church indicate:—1. The entrance. 2. Chapel of the Angel; a small model of a church, 10 ft. wide and 20 ft. high, standing under the great dome, built of marble, and containing The Holy Sepulchre (3). 4. Is the "centre of the world," according to the Greeks (based on Ez. v. 5). 5. Latin church. 6. 49 steps of solid rock lead down to the Chapel of the "Finding of the Cross." 7. Calvary; to which there is an ascent of marble steps from near 1. Although it is no proof of the truth of the traditions which locate the "stations" in this church, yet De Vogue and others (Sandys) give us a great mass of historical evidence that there has been a Church of the Holy Sepulchre for many ages in the city. The oldest engraved *seal of the city* is that here given, dated A. D. 1150; and there seems to have been a small church inside the larger one at that time, as there is now. The next one, dated 1162–'72, gives the Tower of David and the Temple, besides the Sepulchre; which would favor the opinion of Fergusson, in *Smith's Dict.* (article Jerusalem), that Moriah, Zion, the City of David, and the Holy Sepulchre were all on the same hill, now called the Haram. The history is continued in the seal of Baldwin IV, 1174, with the inscription "Tower of David;" and also by many others, which may be seen in De Vogue's work. The plan of the church of those ancient

CHURCH OF THE HOLY SEPULCHRE.

One of the most extensive of these monuments is the Church of the Holy Sepulchre, a collection of buildings in a vast mass, without order, 350 ft. long by 280 wide, including 70 sacred localities, presided over by 17 different sects in separate chap-

times is very much like that of the present day. That in Sandys, of 200 yrs. ago, is almost identical. The Knights of St. John, the ruins of whose hospital are in the next block south of the Sepulchre Church, have left a seal of their order, which gives

WAY TO JERICHO.

a hint of their objects and duties also. Jerusalem is now a sort of collection of churches and hospitals, with a great many vacant places strewed with ruins. Pilate's house, where Jesus was judged, is located at the N. W. corner of the Haram area, and it probably stood on the site of the Citadel of David. The Crusaders respected the Dome of the Rock, and held sacred service in it, but used the Aksa mosque for a stable, despising it as a work of Jews, the Temple of Solomon. It was so only in location, for El Aksa was built by the Mohammedans in the seventh century, on the site of the Temple of Solomon, whom they reverence among the prophets, as well as David, and also Jesus, the son of David.

PLAN OF THE CHURCH OF THE HOLY SEPULCHRE.

The twelve columns around the centre (with four square piers at equal intervals) are of porphyry, and have gilded capitals; the canopy is of crimson silk. The outside of this church is eight-sided, of marble, covered in the upper part with the finest glazed tiles, in colors, to the top of the dome, which is finished with a spire and bronze crescent. The piece of native rock, the top of which shows white in the picture, is 60 feet long by 55 feet wide, and 12 feet high above the floor at the highest point, and is hollowed out underneath—forming a large room, which is believed by many to have been the real sepulchre of Jesus, now very much enlarged.

The Temple has so entirely disappeared, that "not one stone is left on another." And, besides, its very location is still a matter of guesses and speculation. Several churches, a pagan temple, and other buildings, have occupied the platform for ages, and have disappeared, leaving very few traces.

The first mention of a street in the city is in 2 Chr. xxix. 4, where Hezekiah gathered the priests and Levites into the East street and his soldiers in the street of the City of David (xxxii. 5, 6). The Bakers' street is mentioned as that from

HOLY SEPULCHRE, A. D. 1150.

which the prophet Jeremiah was to receive his daily allowance while he was in prison (Jer. xxxvii. 21). The Cheesemongers' street of Josephus is supposed to have been in the Tyropœon valley.

The circuit of the outer wall in the time of Christ was about four miles. Josephus says (Wars, v. 4) there were many towers 30 feet square (some larger), and solid for a hight of 30 feet. Above the base there were rooms for the soldiers; and over these again rooms and cisterns for water. There were on the third wall 90 towers, 300 feet apart; 40 on the middle wall, and on the old wall 60. Psephinus, the most northern, was on high ground, N. W. of the city, was 105 feet high, and eight-sided. From its top could be seen the Jordan and the Dead Sea eastward, and the Great Sea westward. The tower Hippicus was named by Herod after his friend; and Phaselus after his (Herod's) brother, and it was 135 feet high; finished inside and outside "like a royal palace." Another was named after Mariamne, Herod's queen. It was 75 feet high, and equally splendid. The Castle of Antonia, at the N. W. corner of the Temple area, was built by John Hyrcanus. Pilate's judgment-hall was in this castle, which was probably on the site of David's citadel (John xviii. 28, xix. 9). The towers of Meah and Hananeel are also mentioned in Neh. iii. 1; Jer. xxi. 38.

The ancient plans located St. Stephen's Gate on the north side of the city, at what is now called Damascus Gate. The view shows a few of the tombs and gravestones, of which there are thousands in this valley of Jehoshaphat. The lions on each side of the gateway may date from the Crusades.

The water supply of the city has been remarkable in all ages for being sufficient in times of extreme drought, siege and famine. Hezekiah "stopped" some sources, which have remained hidden to the present; and it can only be supposed

CAVITAS. REGIS REGUM OMNIUM.
HOLY SEP. TOWER OF DAVID. TEMPLE.
Amorium I. 1102–1137.

that they were north of the city (2 Chr. xxxii. 4, etc.). Nearly every house has its cistern, or several, large or small. But the one pool of all others was Bethesda, which was near the Sheep-gate.

The masonry is of large blocks of stone, 18 to 20 inches square (A). (See cut on page 38, SECTION OF POOL). The joints are hollowed out, and blocks 16 inches deep inserted half their length (B); the spaces between these blocks being filled by others 8 inches deep. Over these is a coarse plaster with gravel (D); and the inside finish is a thick coat of cement.

The identity of this pool with that mentioned in the Gospel has been the source of many and long arguments, but the conclusion that it is the real Bethesda seems to be gaining in favor.

Siloam is supplied by an underground passage from the Virgin Fountain, 1700 ft. long. Recent explorations have discovered a water supply of the Virgin Fountain

TURRIS DAVID.
Baldwin IV, 1174–1185. A. D.

from a vault in the side of Ophel above it, shown in the plan and section here given. From this and many other recent discoveries it appears that Jeru-

salem is undermined with a series of water-courses, which are frequently alluded to by Josephus and other ancient writers.

In all the accounts of the sieges of the city we read of the besiegers suffering from thirst, but of the besieged from hunger only, since there never was a scarcity of water inside of the walls.

HOSPITALIS JERUSALEM.
Knights of St. John.

The proof of the connection, by an underground passage, of the Fountain of the Virgin with the Pool of Siloam was obtained, with great labor and peril and imminent risk of life by Lieut. Warren, Sergeant Birtles and an Arab laborer. They were obliged to crawl along on their backs, carrying instruments, books and pencil, a lighted candle in the mouth, and in a stream of dirty water 12 inches deep, in a passage which was sometimes only 16 to 20 inches high. The passage is about 1700 feet between the two pools, crooked, and occupied the party about four hours in its exploration.

in this valley, seen by Sir John Maundeville as late as 1322: the *waters of Gihon* were called "the brook that flowed through the land," and was brought straight down to the west side of the City of David (2 Chr. xxxii. 30). Solomon was anointed king at the lower *fountain* of Gihon (1 K. i. 33–45), which was located somewhere between Acra, Bezetha, and Moriah, and not in Hinnom, as now stated (*Barclay*); the Gihon valley would then commence north of the Damascus Gate, and end in the Tyropœon: *Siloam; En Rogel; Motza* (*spring-head*), Ain el Durrage (?), S. E. of En Rogel; *Dragon's Well* (in Hinnom, not far from the Jaffa Gate, the ancient Valley Gate); *Aqueduct of Pilate,* "whereby he brought water from a distance of 400 furlongs" (Josephus, Wars, ii. ix. 4); the *Stone Aqueduct* described by Aristeus; *Solomon's Pools* at Etham, and the aqueduct from them to the city, giving off a branch to the *Great Pool,* now Lower Gihon. Barclay thinks Herod brought the water from Etham by a more direct route than Solomon, and supplied the Upper Gihon Pool, the *Serpent's Pool* of Josephus. *Pool of Hezekiah,* built by Herod; a very large Pool near the Fish Gate (near St. Ann Church, Brocardus, in 1283; *Lacus Quidam,* not located; *The Pool that was made* somewhere in the Tyropœon, of which there are no traces; *Ditch* between Zion and Ophel—bears all the marks of having been an ancient pool; a large Pool (100 feet around, near the Absalom Pillar; the Well of Flagellation and two large tanks near Damascus Gate; the "Sea" under the Temple site, into which there are eight well-holes, from

VIEW OF JERUSALEM.

Abundance of water was required in the Jewish public worship, a part of which was a ceremonial of ablution. The many sources of supply and the means of storing it for use during the dry season, sieges, and times of drought, may be seen in the following list of fountains, pools, etc.

The brook *Kidron.* There was "a little river"

the platform above; 43 well-mouths in the Haram area lead down to wells or reservoirs; Well of the Healing, in Valley street; the Pilgrim Pool, near the Herod Gate; Helena's Cistern, in the Coptic convent; Cotton Megara Pool; Lady Mary Pool, near the St. Stephen Gate; Bath of Tiberius, on Zion, near the English Cemetery; several very

large pools, or tanks, within a mile radius of the city, more or less in ruins; and the great number of cisterns, before mentioned, under private houses, into which rain-water is conducted.

WILSON'S ARCH UNDER THE TYROPŒON VALLEY.

A picture of a siege of the city was found sculptured on a slab in the ruins of Khorsabad (see cut on page 104), in the "Retiring Chamber" of the palace, and is a concise and interesting record. At that time, it seems that the brook Kidron was full of water, and there was a plenty of olive trees on the hills about the city. There are now but a very few trees near the walls, the most interesting being those in the Garden of Gethsemane. Titus cut down all the trees around Jerusalem, and his tenth legion was camped on Olivet, building their part of the wall surrounding the city, along the bottom of the valley of Kidron. The Turks have pleasure-grounds, or gardens, farther up the valley (half a mile or so), where they resort to enjoy the cool shade of the olive-trees, some of which are quite as large as those in Gethsemane, and, it may be, as old. The antiquity of those in Gethsemane is argued from the fax, which is fixed by the Turks at *one medina* for each tree, which rate dates from before or at the time of their conquest; all those planted since everywhere in the empire being taxed one-half their produce. This would carry the date back to A. D. 634, when Omar took Jerusalem; or to the time when the Turks took it, A. D. 1087.

There are no level streets, and the passenger is always ascending or descending, over rough and uncared-for ways. The houses are built on heaps of rubbish, which have been gathering for ages. The foundations for the Church of St. James (English) rest on piers, built up from the rock through 40 to 50 feet of debris. The streets are often very narrow, the widest being only eight to ten feet. The houses are often built across the street on arches; and the custom of shading them with awnings of mats or boards, suspended by ropes, makes them dark and cool, which is very grateful in that hot climate. Only two or three streets have a name, except such as are being adopted lately by the Franks, generally those used by the Crusaders. The materials used for building is the native limestone, generally broken into squares, not hewn, or sawn, except by the most wealthy. In many walls may be found fragments of ancient structures, such as cornices, columns, capitals, and mutilated sculptures, built in as raw material.

Timber is only brought from other countries, and therefore very costly, and is only used for window-frames and doors, but not for floors or roofs. The windows are always small, and, if large enough to admit a thief, are barred with iron, and give the houses a jail-like appearance. Window-glass is only found in the houses of the rich. Only one door opens on the street, and there are no windows in the lower story opening on the street, secluding the houses, but making dismal streets. The interior of the rooms is pleasing, because of the arches and domes required in forming the upper stories and roof. The floors are frequently laid with colored stones, arranged in most beautiful patterns.

The principal trade is in beads, crosses, incense, crucifixes, pilgrim-shells, staffs, pressed flowers, and other keepsakes (besides relics, which are made in great quantities), with the thousands of pilgrims and other travellers, who visit the country every year. Soap-making, and weaving of coarse cotton cloth, are almost the only active manufactures in the city.

A vast number live professedly on charity. There are separate bazaars, frequented by the different people: By the Jews, in the street near their great synagogue, on the east slope of Mount Zion; by the Turks, in David, Damascus, and Temple streets; by the Arabs, in Via Dolorosa (El Wad), near the St. Ann church; and by the Christians, in Patriarch street. The Cotton Bazaar was once a very grand structure, but it is now abandoned to rubbish, and only used as a passage-way to the Haram area.

This short account of the "Holy City" would be still more incomplete without some brief notice of Solomon's Temple, and its successors.

Whatever we know about them is to be found in the First Book of Kings, in Jeremiah, in Ezekiel (who saw the first temple in a vision, ch. xl.), in Josephus, in Aristeas; and after these, the modern books of Williams, Robinson, Barclay, and Paine, in our language; and of those in foreign, the best is the German of Dr. Neumann, of Gotha (*Die Stiftshütte*). Mr. Paine's plan is copied here, because of its simplicity, and seeming fidelity to the original, as critically and clearly interpreted by the

INTERIOR OF THE DOME OF THE ROCK.

author (*Solomon's Temple*—T. O. Paine). Of the temple of Zerubbabel there is a very short account in Ezra, and in Hecatæus, quoted by Josephus. The size was a third larger than Solomon's, but its ornamentation was less showy. The size

of either was less than the average of our churches in the country villages. Josephus is almost the only authority for all we know about the Temple of Herod, which was the one seen by Jesus. There is not a word in the New Testament about its appearance, nor even its location. But it is supposed that while the figures of Josephus are correct as to the ground-plan, his figures of the elevation are twice the real hight (Ant. xv. 11, 3).

The bridge

Capital from Herod's temple

PLAN OF SOLOMON'S TEMPLE.

on which Titus stood at the siege and destruction of the city (described by Josephus), had fallen long ago, but its remains have been discovered by Robinson and Lt. Warren, and minute accounts published. The view engraved here shows the spring of the arch which rested against the temple wall (BR., in the plan of Herod's Temple). The bridge was 51 ft. wide, and extended across the valley to Zion, 350 ft.; probably resting on 5 or 6 arches (see p. 149). One of the stones, shown in the cut, is 21 ft. long, and another 29, by nearly 6 wide.

The famous "Wailing-place" of the Jews (where they go to bewail the desolation of Zion) is a few rods north of this place.

"The past of Jerusalem is overflowing with thought. But the future is equally impressive. These ruins are not always to remain. The future Temple, and the restored Israel, when "Jerusalem shall be the throne of the Lord to all nations," claim the most earnest thought. The day when "the feet" of the Lord "shall stand on the Mount of Olives, which is over against Jerusalem toward the east," is full of importance; and whether we look back or forward, we have to speak of Zion as "the joy of the whole earth," for "salvation is of the Jews." The present missionary work in Jerusalem is deeply interesting. * * But surely there is no spot on earth like Jerusalem."—(Dr. Tyng).

JERU'SHA (*possessed*). Daughter of Zadok, queen of Uzziah (2 K. xv. 33). In Chronicles the name is JERUSHAH (2 Chr. xxvii. 1).

JESAI'AH (Heb. ISAIAH). 1. Son of Hananiah, grand-son of Zerubbabel (1 Chr. iii. 21).—2. A Benjamite whose descendants were chosen by lot to reside in Jerusalem after the return from captivity (Neh. xi. 7).

JESHA'IAH (*Jah's salvation*). Son of Jeduthun, choir-leader in the temple, of the 8th division (1 Chr. xxv. 3).—2. A Levite, eldest son of Rehabiah, in the line of Amram (xxvi. 25).—3. Son of Athaliah and chief of the sons of Elam, who returned with Ezra (viii. 7).—4. A Merarite who returned with Ezra (viii. 19).

JESHA'NAH (*ancient*). Taken by Abijah from Jeroboam (2 Chr. xiii. 19). A place of importance in Benjamin, and now *Ain Sinia*, a well-watered village with vineyards, fruit-trees and gardens (Rob. iii. 80), 3 miles N. of Bethel.

JESHARE'LAH (*upright* towards El). Son of Asaph, chief of the 7th choir (1 Chr. xxv. 14). ASARELAH.

JESHEBE'AB (*father's abode*). Head of the 14th course of priests (1 Chr. xxiv. 13).

JE'SHER (*upright*). Son of Caleb by Azubah (1 Chr. ii. 18). JETHER.

JESH'IMON (*desert*). A more desolate region or place than a MIDBAR (*wilderness*), and applied to the plain and hillsides at the N. end and on the W. side of the Dead Sea. It consists of a level plain of nitrous earth, into which the feet sink several inches as into ashes, and hills of chalky limestone, without herbage, except a few alkaline plants and the usual fringe of the Jordan river. The Hill of Hachilah (*dark red cone*) may have been *Sebbeh*, (Masada), so well described by Josephus, as Metsadoth (strong-holds in 1 Sam. xxiii. 19), and the word CHORESH (Heb. for wood in verse 19) means a thicket, dense and thorny, such as is found along the shore there now.

JESHI'SHAI (*son of the old man*). Ancestor of the Gadites in Gilead (1 Chr. v. 14).

JESH'UA (*Jah saves*). JOSHUA or JEHOSHUA. 1. Joshua the son of Nun (Neh. viii. 17).—2. A priest in David's time, head of the 9th course (Ezr. ii. 36).—3. A Levite in the reign of Hezekiah (2 Chr. xxxi. 15).—4. Son of Jehozadak, the first high-priest after the return from captivity. His family succeeded for 14 times, down to Onias (Ezr. ii. 2; Neh. vii. 7). He took a leading part in the rebuilding of the Temple, and restoration of the nation. He was a man of earnest piety, patri-

otism, and **courage**. After a disuse for 50 years he restored the daily sacrifice on a new altar.—5. Head of a Levitical house, who returned from captivity (Ezr. ii. 40).—6. A branch of the family of Pahath-Moab, of Judah (Neh. x. 14).

JESH'UA. *Yeshua*, S. near Moladah, occupied after the return from captivity (Neh. xi. 26).

JESH'URUN. Symbolical name for Israel in Deut. xxxii. 15, etc., meaning *most upright, or to be blessed*, in an endearing sense also, as little one, or dear one, therefore *good little people*.

JESI'AH (*Jah lends*). A Korhite, a hero with David at Ziklag (1 Chr. xii. 6).—2. Son of Uzziel (xxiii. 20). Jeshiah (error) in xxiv. 25.

JESIM'IEL (*whom El places*). A Simeonite, of Shimei's family (1 Chr. iv. 36).

JES'SE (YISHAI, *manly*). Son of Obed, father of David. His name is never mentioned again, not even when David took his parents to Nahash in Moab for security from Saul (1 Sam. xxii. 3). He was grandson of Boaz, one of the wealthy ones in that favored place. His wife's name is not mentioned. Tradition says that the king of Moab killed both Jesse and his wife, with their attendants.

JES'UI (Heb. ISHUAI). Son of Asher. The Jesuites were numbered in the plains of Moab (Num. xxvi. 44).

JE'SUS (Gr. and Latin form of the Heb. Joshua, or Jehoshua, *the help of Jah*, or *Saviour*). 1. The father of SIRACH, and grandfather of—2. The SON OF SIRACH (Eccles. i. 27), author of the Book of ECCLESIASTICUS, or the WISDOM OF JESUS, THE SON OF SIRACH. See HISTORY OF THE BOOKS. He was also known as Ben Sira, a writer of proverbs which closely resemble those in Wisdom.

2. **JE'SUS**, called JUS'TUS (*the just*). A disciple Paul at Rome (Col. iv. 11). Tradition makes him Bishop of Eleutheropolis.

3. **JESUS CHRIST.** The name Jesus means Saviour, and was a common name, derived from the ancient Hebrew Jehoshua.

The title CHRIST means anointed, consecrated, sacred, and is used only for the MESSIAH, who came in fulfilment of prophesy.

The prophets, from the time of Moses, hold up to view an illustrious person who was to appear, and should belong to the highest order of being, since the name of the Eternal One is His; and he should also be called Wonderful, Counselor, the Mighty God, the Everlasting Father; that he should assume human nature and be born of a virgin of the family of David (Is. xi. 1), in Bethlehem of Judæa, (Mic. v. 2), and his mission should be the salvation of his people and all mankind (Is. xlix. 6); that He should be despised and rejected of his people; be cut off, but not for himself; be wounded for men's transgressions, bruised for their iniquities; by His stripes men should be healed (Is. liii.); the Lord should lay on Him the iniquity of men; He should make his soul an offering for sin; and should be exalted and made very high; should see of the travail of his soul and be satisfied, and by his knowledge justify many; and Jehovah say to Him, "Sit thou at my right hand, until I make thine enemies thy footstool" (Ps. cx. 1); to Him should be given dominion, glory, and a kingdom, and all people should serve Him,—an everlasting dominion which shall not pass away (Dan. vii. 13, 14): all of which has been completely fulfilled in Jesus, the son of Mary of Nazareth, who was divinely appointed to be the Messiah, from everlasting, before the foundations of the world (Prov. viii. 23; 1 Pet. i. 20; Luke ii.).

Jesus was born in Bethlehem, and our era is dated from the event, which was, at this time of writing, 1870 (4) years ago. The very day, and even the very year, has been indefinite, but is not far from the one adopted. Joseph and Mary were espoused and had gone up from Nazareth to answer to the census-roll ordered by Augustus, for taxation; and they came to Bethlehem because they were of the house of David. The event was announced by an angel to some shepherds who were watching their flocks by night in the field near the village; and the heavenly host, who were with the angel, praised God, saying, "Glory to God in the highest, and on earth peace, good-will toward men" (Luke ii. 14).

The coming of Christ was an event of general expectation, and the Gentiles were next to the shepherd Jews in rendering homage to Him, in the visit of the Wise Men from the East, who brought offerings and rich presents (Matt. ii. 1).

Herod the king, who is described as a cruel tyrant, having been made jealous of the wonderful child, who was born King of the Jews, ordered that all the children (about 12) in Bethlehem from two years old and under should be killed; and Jesus was saved only by Joseph hurrying him and his mother away to Egypt, where it is supposed that they stayed about a year.

On the way from Egypt the family avoided Bethlehem and returned to Nazareth.

When he was twelve years old, his parents took him with them to attend the annual feast of the Passover, when he was one day found in the Temple, questioning and answering the Jewish priests, and displaying astonishing wisdom (Luke ii. 47).

The account of his childhood and youth, and even maturity, up to "about thirty years of age," besides the incident in the Temple, is given in two grand sentences by Luke, indicative of the increase and development of the human powers, the spiritual being perfect from the beginning: "And the child grew, and waxed strong in spirit, filled with wisdom, and the grace of God was upon him. And Jesus increased in wisdom and stature, and in favor with God and man" (ii. 40, 52).

The modesty and brevity of the Gospels on this part of the life of Jesus, is one great evidence of its truth, as compared with tales of fiction, wherein the hero is perfected in minute and wonderful details.

PLAN OF HEROD'S TEMPLE.

Joseph (the reputed father of Jesus, and so called by his mother Mary, ii. 48), is not again mentioned in the Scriptures after this event. Whether he lived to witness the wonderful events and profit by the teaching of the Saviour, does not appear.

The question of the family of Jesus, as to whether his mother Mary had any other children besides him, is unsettled, although Matthew distinctly mentions four brothers, besides sisters. Some have held that these were brothers and sisters-in-law, children of Joseph by a former wife, and others, that they were the children of the sister of Jesus' mother, who was also named Mary, and was the

wife of Clopas; this would have them to be cousins of Jesus. See MARY.

The person, the life, and the work of Jesus are the subject of the whole New Testament, (and, in prophecy, of the Old), and, as a whole, are the *historical* and *doctrinal* foundation of Christianity.

His life may be studied in several sections by students, as here arranged:

1. Birth, including the appearances to Zechariah, Elizabeth, Mary, and Joseph, and the birth of John the Baptist.

2. The witnesses of the Messiah—the Shepherds, the Magi and Herod.

3. Preparation and baptism.

4. Fasting, temptation and public manifestation in Galilee, Judæa and Samaria.

5. His offered proof of his divinity in his miracles, may be classed in two groups:

(1). Of Love. { In raising the dead. Curing mental disease. Healing the body.

(2). Of Power. { In creating; destroying; overcoming men's wills.

6. The instruction in his discourses and parables.

7. Incidents showing the effect of his contact with various persons.

8. The scene of his ministry, of which details are given in the GEOGRAPHY.

Matthew, Mark and Luke's records are mainly of the events in Galilee, never mentioning his visits to Jerusalem until the time near the crucifixion, and only implying such visits and teaching by his lamentations, and the visits of the scribes, etc., besides the intimacy with the family at Bethany. John records a few acts in Galilee, and gives all the rest of his book to the events in Judæa—nearly one-half being about the last three months; and seven chapters (one-third), on the last few days. Neither writer attempted a complete chronology, but aimed at a general picture of the life. See GOSPELS, in the HISTORY OF THE BOOKS.

9. The duration of the ministry cannot be determined exactly. Those who interpret the prophesy of Isaiah literally, limit it to one year (Is. lxi. 2). But John mentions *six feasts*, at five of which Jesus was present. 1. (ii. 13), soon after his baptism; 2. (v. 1), a feast when he went up to Jerusalem; 3. (vi. 4), and another, from which he stayed away, in Galilee; 4. (vii. 2), the feast of Tabernacles, to which he went privately; 5. (x. 22), the feast of the dedication; 6. (xii. xiii), and the last, the Passover, at which he was crucified—extending through three years.

10. And, while on this subject of time, it may be valuable to consider, by the help of the map, tracing each movement as closely as possible, the amount of labor, traveling—mainly on foot (or on animals)—that must be compressed into a single year, if the short period is chosen.

The date of the birth of Jesus, and the month and the day, have each been the subject of much debate, without any definite settlement. The various opinions have ranged through four years of time, and have suggested nearly every month in the year. Tischendorf and Wieseler say that Jesus could hardly have been born before the first of January, A. U. C. 750; and suggest February as the latest date probable. Gresswell says that April 5 or 6 must be the day of his birth (A. U. C. 750). Dr. Robinson supposes it could not have been later than in the autumn of A. U. C. 749; while it may have occurred one or two years earlier; Lardner fixes the time about the middle of August or the middle of November, A. U. C. 748 or 749; Winer, Ideler and others say 747; Dr. Wordsworth says in the spring of 749 (B. C. 5); Clement of Alexandria says some placed the day on April 20, and others on May 20; the 25th of December as the day dates from the traditions of the 4th century.

HARMONY OF EVENTS FROM THE FOUR GOSPELS.

	Matthew.	Mark.	Luke.	John.
Genealogy,	i. 1-17		iii. 23-38	
Angel appeared to Elizabeth, Yuttah,			i. 5	
Angel appeared to Mary, Nazareth,			i. 26	
Mary visits Elizabeth, Yuttah,			i. 39	
Jesus born, Bethlehem,	i. 18-25		ii. 1	
Shepherds watch, Bethlehem,			ii. 8	
Circumcision, Bethlehem,			ii. 21	
Presentation, Jerusalem,			ii. 22	
Visit of Wise Men, Bethlehem,	ii. 1			
Flight into Egypt,	ii. 13			
Jesus with the Doctors,			ii. 39	
			ii. 40	
Baptism of Jesus the Christ,	iii. 13	i. 9	iii. 21	i. 32
Temptation, Quarantana,	iv. 1	i. 12	iv. 1	
Andrew and Peter follow him,				i. 37
Nathanael's witness,				i. 49
Water made wine, Cana,				ii. 1
Cleanses the temple, 1st passover,				ii. 12
Nicodemus, Jerusalem,				ii. 23
Jesus and John baptizing, Enon,				iii. 22
Woman of Samaria, Shechem,				iv. 1
Nazareth, Nobleman's son healed,				iv. 46
Draught of fishes, Capernaum,			v. 6	
Four apostles called, Capernaum,	iv. 13	i. 16	v. 1	
Demoniac healed, Capernaum,		i. 21	iv. 31	
Simon's wife's mother healed, Capernaum,	vii. 14	i. 29	iv. 38	
Circuit in Galilee,	iv. 23	i. 35	iv. 42	
Leper healed, Galilee,	viii. 1	i. 40	v. 12	
Stills the storm, Galilee,	viii. 18	iv. 35	viii. 22	
Land of the Gadarenes,	viii. 28	v. 1	viii. 26	
Jairus' daughter raised, Capernaum,	ix. 18	v. 21	viii. 41	
Woman healed, Capernaum,	ix. 27			
Blind man, Demoniac, Capernaum,	ix. 1	ii. 1	v. 17	
Paralytic, Capernaum,				

	Matthew.	Mark.	Luke.	John.
Matthew called, Capernaum,	ix. 9	ii. 13	v. 27	
Second Passover, Jerusalem,				v. 1
Pool of Bethesda, Jerusalem,				v. 2
Plucking grain on the Sabbath,	xii. 1	ii. 23	vi. 1	
Withered hand healed, Samaria,	xii. 9	iii. 1	vi. 6	
Jesus by the sea, Capernaum. The twelve chosen,	x. 24	iii. 13	vi. 12	
Sermon on the mount, Hattin,	v. 1		vi. 17	
Centurion's servant healed, Capernaum,	viii. 5		vii. 1	iv. 6
Widow's son raised, Nain,			vii. 11	
Messengers from John,	xi. 2		vii. 18	
Woe to the cities of Galilee,	xi. 20			
Jesus' feet anointed, Capernaum,			vii. 06	
The two debtors,			vii. 41	
Second circuit in Galilee,			viii. 1	
Parable of the sower, Capernaum,	xii. 1	iv. 1	viii. 4	
" Candle under a bushel,		iv. 21	viii. 16	
" Sower,		iv. 26		
" Wheat and tares,	xiii. 24		xiii. 18	
" of grain of mustard-seed,	xiii. 31	iv. 30	xiii. 20	
" of the leaven,	xiii. 33			
Wheat and tares explained,	xiii. 36			
The treasure, pearl and net,	xiii. 44			
His mother and brethren,	xii. 46	iii. 31	viii. 19	
Reception at Nazareth,	xiii. 53	vi. 1		
Third circuit in Galilee,	ix. 35	vi. 6		
Twelve sent out, Capernaum,	x.	vi. 7	ix. 1	
Herod's opinion Jesus (Tiberias),	xiv. 1	iv. 14	ix. 7	
Death of John the Baptist,	xiv. 3	vi. 17		
Third passover,			vi. 4	
5000 fed near Bethsaida,	xiv. 13	vi. 30	ix. 10	vi. 1
Walks on the sea of Galilee,	xiv. 22	vi. 45		vi. 16
Miracles in Gennesaret,	xiv. 34	vi. 53		
Bread of life,				vi. 22
Washen hands, Capernaum,	xv. 1	vii. 1		
Syrophœnician woman, coast,	xv. 21	vii. 24		
Miracles of healing in Galilee	xv. 29	vii. 31		
4000 fed in Decapolis,	xv. 32	viii. 1		
The sign from heaven, Magdala,	xvi. 1	viii. 10		
Leaven of the Pharisees,	xvi. 12	viii. 14		
Blind man healed, Bethsaida,		viii. 22		
Peter's profession near Cæsarea,	xvi. 13	viii. 27	ix. 18	vi. 66
His passion foretold,	xvi. 20	viii. 30	ix. 21	
Transfiguration on Mt. Hermon,	xvii. 1	ix. 2	ix. 28	
Of Elijah,	xvii. 10	ix. 11		
Lunatic healed,	xvii. 14	ix. 14	ix. 37	
His passion foretold in Galilee,	xvii. 22	ix. 30	ix. 43	
Fish caught with the tribute, Capernaum,	xvii. 24			
The little child, Capernaum,	xviii. 1	ix. 33	ix. 46	
One casting out devils,		ix. 38	ix. 49	
Offenses,	xviii. 6	ix. 42	xvii. 2	
The lost sheep,	xviii. 10		xv. 1	
Forgiveness of injuries,	xviii. 15			
Binding and loosing. Forgiveness,	xviii. 18			
Parable unmerciful servant,	xviii. 21			
Salted with fire,		ix. 49		
Journey to Jerusalem,			ix. 51	vii. 1
Fire from heaven, Samaria,			ix. 52	
Foxes have holes, birds have nests, etc.,	viii. 19		ix. 57	
The seventy sent out, Capernaum,			x. 1	
Feast of Tabernacles, Jerusalem,				vii. 11
Woman taken in adultery, Jerusalem,				viii. 1
Dispute with the Pharisees, Jerusalem,				viii. 12
The man born blind healed, Jerusalem,				ix. 1
The good shepherd, Jerusalem,				x. 1
The seventy return, Jerusalem,			x. 17	
The good Samaritan, Jerusalem,			x. 25	
Mary and Martha, Bethany,			x. 38	
The Lord's Prayer,	vi. 9		xi. 1	
Prayer effectual,	vii. 7		xi. 5	
"By Beelzebub," Jerusalem,	xii. 22	iii. 20	xi. 14	
The unclean spirit, Jerusalem,	xii. 43		xi. 24	
The sign of Jonah, Jerusalem,	xii. 38		xi. 29	
The light of the body,	v. 15 / vi. 22		xi. 33	
The Pharisees,		ii. 3	xi. 37	
What to fear,			xii. 1	
Master, speak to my brother,	x. 26		xii. 13	

	Matthew.	Mark.	Luke.	John.
Covetousness. Watchfulness,	vi. 25		xii. 16	
Galileans that perished,			xiii. 1	
Woman healed on the Sabbath, Perea,			xiii. 10	
The grain of mustard-seed, Perea,	xiii. 31	iv.	xiii. 18	
The leaven, Perea,	xiii. 33		xiii. 20	
Toward Jerusalem, Perea,			xiii. 22	
Are there few? Bethany,			xiii. 23	
Warning against Herod,			xiii. 31	
O Jerusalem! Jerusalem!	xxiii. 37		xiii. 34	
Dropsy healed on the Sabbath,			xiv. 1	
Chief rooms. Great supper,	xxii. 1		xiv. 7	
Following Christ with the cross,	x. 37		xiv. 25	
Parables—Lost sheep, Piece of money, Prodigal Son,			xv.	
Unjust steward, Rich man and Lazarus,			xvi.	
Offenses,	xviii. 6		xvii. 1	
Faith and merit,	xvii. 20		xvii. 5	
Ten lepers healed, Samaria,			xvii. 11	
How the kingdom cometh, Perea,			xvii. 20	
Parable of unjust judge, Perea,			xviii. 1	
Parable of Pharisee and Publican, Perea,			xviii. 9	
Of divorce, Perea,	xix. 1	x. 1		
Infants brought to Jesus, Perea,	xix. 13	x. 13	xviii. 15	
Rich young man inquiring, Perea,	xix. 16	x. 17	xviii. 18	
Promises to the disciples, Perea,	xix. 27	x. 28	xviii. 28	
Laborers in the vineyard, Perea,	xx. 16			
His death foretold the third time, Perea,	xx. 17	x. 32	xviii. 31	
Request of James and John, Perea,	xx. 20	x. 35		
Heals two blind men, Jericho,	xx. 29	x. 46	xviii. 35	
Zaccheus. Parable of ten talents, Jericho,	xxv. 14		xix. 11	
Feast of Dedication, Jerusalem,				x. 22
Beyond Jordan, Bethabara,				xi. 1
A. D. Raising Lazarus, Bethany,				xi. 45
29 Meeting of the Sanhedrin, Caiaphas,				xi. 54
Apr. Jesus in Ephraim,				xii. 3
" 1. Mary anoints his feet, Bethany,	xxvi. 6	xiv. 3	vii. 36	xii. 12
" 2. Triumphal entry into Jerusalem,	xxi. 1	xi. 1	xix. 29	ii. 13
2d cleansing of the temple,	xxi. 12	xi. 15	xix. 45	
" 3. The barren fig-tree, Olivet,	xxi. 17	xi. 11		
Fig-tree withered, between Bethany and the city,		xi. 19		
" 4. Pray and forgive,	vi. 14	xi. 24		
By what authority—parable of the two sons,	xxi. 23	xi. 27	xx. 1	
Parable of the wicked husbandman,	xxi. 28			
	xxi. 33			
Parable of the wedding garment,	xxii. 1	xii. 1	xx. 9	
The tribute money,	xxii. 15	xii. 13	xx. 16	
The state of the risen,	xxii. 23	xii. 18	xx. 20	
The great commandment,	xxii. 34	xii. 28	xx. 27	
David's son and David's Lord,	xxii. 41	xii. 35	xx. 41	
Against the Pharisees,	xxiii. 1	xii. 38	xx. 45	
The widow's mite,		xii. 41	xxi. 1	
Christ's second coming,	xxiv. 1	xiii. 1	xxi. 5	
Parable of ten virgins,	xxv. 1			
Parable of five talents,	xxv. 14		xix. 11	
The Last Judgment,	xxv. 31			
Greeks ask to see Jesus. The voice,				xii. 20
John's reflections on the Jews' unbelief,				xii. 36
His crucifixion foretold,	xxvi. 2			xii. 32
The priests, scribes and elders conspire,	xxvi. 3	xiv. 1	xxii. 1	
" 5. Judas Iscariot,	xxvi. 14	xiv. 10	xxii. 3	
" 6. Pascal supper, last passover,	xxvi. 17	xiv. 12	xxii. 7	xiii. 1
Disciples' feet washed,				xiii. 5
The disciples contend,			xxii. 24	
The Lord's Supper,	xxvi. 26	xiv. 22	xxii. 19	
Peter's fall foretold,	xxvi. 30	xiv. 26	xxii. 31	xiii. 36
Last discourse. Departure—Comforter,				xiv. 1
Vine and branches. Abiding in love,				xv. 1
Work of Comforter,				xvi.
Prayer of Jesus Christ,				xvii. 1
" 7. Gethsemane, on Olivet,	xxvi. 36	xiv. 32	xxii. 40	xviii. 1
The betrayal, Gethsemane,	xxvi. 47	xiv. 43	xxii. 47	xviii. 2
Malchus' wounded ear healed,	xxvi. 51	xiv. 47	xxii. 50	xviii. 10
Before Annas. Hill of Evil Counsel,	xxvi. 57	xiv. 53	xxii. 54	xviii. 12
Peter's denial,	xxvi. 69	xiv. 66	xxii. 56	xviii. 17
Jesus before the Sanhedrin, Jerusalem,	xxvi. 59	xiv. 55	xxii. 63	xviii. 19
Before Pilate, Jerusalem,	xxvii. 1	xv. 1	xxiii. 1	xviii. 28

WILSON'S ARCH RECENTLY DISCOVERED AT JERUSALEM.

	Matthew.	Mark.	Luke.	John.
Judas dies,	xxvii. 3			
Jesus before Herod silent,			xxiii. 4	
Accused and condemned,	xxvii. 15	xv. 6	xxiii. 13	xviii. 29
Mocked by soldiers,	xxvii. 27	xv. 16	xxiii. 36	xix. 3
Crowned with thorns,	xxvii. 29	xv. 17		xix. 2
The crucifixion, Calvary,	xxvii. 35	xv. 24	xxiii. 33	xix. 18
The veil rent—Darkness,	xxvii. 51	xv. 38	xxiii. 45	
The body buried by Joseph,	xxvii. 57	xv. 43	xxiii. 50	xix. 38
" 8. The sepulchre guarded,	xxvii. 62			
" 9. The Resurrection,	xxviii. 1		xxiv. 1	xx. 1
Appearance of Emmaus,		xvi. 1	xxiv. 13	
Appearance of Jerusalem,		xvi. 12	xxiv. 13	
Appearance Sea of Tiberias—Charge to Peter,		xvi. 14	xxiv. 36	xx. 19
Appearance on a mount in Galilee—(Paul),	xxviii. 16			xxi. 1
Appearance in Jerusalem—(Peter in Acts),				
Ascension, Olivet,		xvi. 19	xxiv. 50	
Unrecorded works,				xxi. 25

The life of Jesus combined in a three-fold character the offices of prophet, priest and king. His prophesies pointed both to the manner and the time of the mission and work of redemption; and, as John said, were really clear light shining; his priestly office was shown in his vicarious atonement for the sins of men; and his kingly office appears in his royal power of subduing all men to his will for the good of his people. To his church he was also prophet, priest, and king above all others who had held either of those offices. He first said, "No one hath seen God at any time, the only begotten Son, who is in the bosom of the Father, he hath declared him" (John iii. 16). Jesus founded a system of ethics, revised and over-ruled all the old systems of morals, and so purified the system that it will stand for all the coming ages without changing. This was done among those men who thought they were learned and wise, and that they needed only to extent Phariseeism or Essenism to perfect the moral system of mankind, when Jesus showed them that such ascetic notions were born in the desert and would die there. An obscure Galilean wood carver readily and surely did what so many eminent men had failed to accomplish—he laid the foundations of a universal religion—on a perfect morality, showing how the divine and human elements can be made to appear in harmonious action in every soul. He is therefore superior to all the prophets who preceded him.

The priestly element was almost peculiar in Judaism. The Pharisees enlarged upon the hint of Moses and declared the whole people to be a nation of priests; but that the sacrifices and oblations (while so many fell short of the ceremonial purity) had to be offered by a mediating priesthood, and by them alone, as having immediate access to God, and only acceptable through them, while it was held to be blasphemy to attempt to change the institutes of Moses (Acts vi. 11, 14,) even although the prophets had so distinctly said, something higher and purer was needed, and would be given from above, being brought by the Messiah, the great spiritual king, successor of David (Ps. civ). The sufferings and glory, struggle with temptation and sin, ransom paid, and atonement made, whereby the guilt of iniquity was to be forever atoned, and sacrifice and oblation cease, and a new temple consecrated (Zech. vi. 12), in every heart, was the burden Jesus bore in his character and office of the great high-priest (Heb. x.). The necessity for his work was not seen until after it had been done, and he was gone from among men. His priesthood was more perfect than any before him.

The Jews had expected a temporal king, a King of Zion, as announced in the letter of the prophets, the spiritual meaning being overlooked. The angel said to Mary that the throne of his father David should be given to him; the Eastern Magi inquired after him, and did obedience to him as King of the Jews (Luke i. 32). Herod struck at the infant as at a pretender to his throne; John announced him as coming to set up the Kingdom of Heaven; and even when he declared before Pilate the spiritual nature of his kingdom, the Jews failed to see what sort of a King he was. However feeble and powerless he may have seemed then as a king before Pilate, and when wearing the crown of thorns and the purple robe, succeeding history has proved his actual power among men, above and beyond all other kings, moving and controlling their hearts and minds, and this power is extending throughout the world, not by force or violence, but as gently and surely as the light of the sun. As a king he is more winning, powerful, more enduring, and more holy and good than any who have reigned before him.

GOAT OF AOUDAD.

Christians in all ages have wished for some picture or figure of Jesus, which should represent the Saviour of the Man of Sorrows, and a great number of attempts have been made to represent one or the other of those phases of the great character: some with an expression of calm serenity and dignity, without grief; and others with the crown of thorns, purple robe, and face of sorrowful aspect. Except a few crude outlines, painted on the walls of sepulchres, (as in the Catacombs under Rome), or on tablets, or rude engravings of the early ages, no work of this kind, claiming excellence, can be

dated earlier than Leonardo da Vinci's or Raphael's time, who have made the most acceptable works, from which nearly all others have been imitated; and even theirs were reproductions of the traditionary likeness, fashioned after the Greek model of the young hero-god Apollo, or the Egyptian Serapis. The story that Pilate had a likeness engraved on an emerald is a fable, and the likeness in question is a copy from Raphael's cartoon of the Miraculous Draught of Fishes. The likeness, the actual birth-place, the several places of his residence, of his crucifixion, and of the sepulchre have one and all been lost beyond all hope of authentic recovery. We know that he was born in Bethlehem, raised in Nazareth, began his work in Cana and Capernaum, was crucified and buried near Jerusalem, but the exact places have, perhaps by divine intention, been purposely forgotten.

QUARRY CAVE UNDER JERUSALEM.

JE'THER (*excellence*). 1. Jethro, father-in-law to Moses (Ex. iv. 18), who is also called Hobab (Num. x. 31).—2. Gideon's eldest son (Judg. viii. 20).—3. Father of Amasa, general of Absalom's army. ITHRA (2 Sam. xvii. 25). He was an Ishmaelite, or a Hebrew living among Ishmaelites. He married Abigail, David's sister (probably in the land of Moab).—4. Son of Jada (1 Chr. ii. 32). 5. Son of Ezra, in the line of Judah (1 Chr. iv. 17).—Ezra and Amram being one, this Jether may be Aaron, as some suggest.—6. Chief in Asher, father of Jephunneh (1 Chr. vii. 38).

JE'THETH (*a tent-pin*). A duke in Edom (Gen. xxxvi. 40). There is a place called *El Wetideh* in Nejed (in the *Dahna*, sandy desert), and an *El Wetid* range of mountains, which may preserve the name of the ancient family, for Wetedeh is stable, firm, as a tent-pin.

JETH'LAH (*hanging*). In Dan, near Ajalon (Josh. xix. 42). Lost.

JE'THRO (*superiority*). JETHER. Father-in-law of Moses (Ex. iv. 18, xviii. 1), and also called Hobab (Num. x. 31; Judg. iv. 11). Reuel (Raguel) was the head of the family into which Moses married (Ex. ii. 18), but was probably his wife's grandfather, for Hobab was his son (Num. x. 29). He became a convert to the worship of Jehovah, and sacrificed (Ex. xviii. 12).

JE'TUR (*comp*). Son of Ishmael (Gen. xxv. 15). ITUREA.

JEU'EL (*El's treasure*). Chief in Judah, of the sons of Zerah, at the first occupation of Jerusalem (1 Chr. ix. 6).—2. A son of Adonikam, returned from captivity (1 Esd. viii. 39).

JE'USH (*Jah hastens*). 1. Son of Esau by Aholibamah (Gen. xxxvi. 5).—2. Benjamite chief, son of Bilhan (1 Chr. vii. 10).—3. Levite of the house of Shimei (xxiii. 10).—4. Son of king Rehoboam and Abihail (2 Chr. xi. 18).

JE'UZ (*Jah counsels*). Benjamite chief (1 Chr. viii. 10). Born in Moab, son of Shaharaim and Hodesh.

JEW. Short form of JEHUDI (*people of Judah*). First mentioned in 2 K. xvi. 6, when the king of Syria drives the (Jehudim) Jews from Elath. Jeremiah frequently uses it, perhaps because the tribe of Judah was very numerously represented in the captivity. In the N. T. the Jews are spoken of as the determined opponents of the gospel.

The history of the Jews, as a people, may be divided into three eras: 1. From Abraham (or Heber) to the close of the collection of the Laws, originally oral, then written, B. C. 536;—2, ending A. D. 600.—and 3. From then to the present. The chief interest to the Bible student is found in the history before A. D. 70, since which time the affairs of this people have had but little value in the world, as compared to them during the ages before. The influence of foreign people and native powers may be distinctly traced from age to age: of Persia, in organization, order, and the ritual; of Greece, by liberty and speculation; of the Asmonean leaders, in independent thinking and faith; of the Herods, the separation of the church and state, with the falling to pieces of the Jewish Church in favor of its successor, the Church of Jesus Christ.

JEW'ESS. Born a Hebrew, of any tribe (Acts xvi. 1), as the mother of Timothy, and Drusilla the wife of Felix (xxiv. 24). See HEROD.

JEW'ISH. Paul warns Titus (1. 14) against Jewish fables. See FABLE.

JEW'RY. Judah, Judæa (Dan. v. 13; Luke xxiii. 5; John vii. 1).

JEWS' LANGUAGE. Jewishly (2 K. xviii. 26).

JEZANI'AH. JAAZANI'AH. AZARIAH.

JEZ'EBEL (*chaste*). Wife of king Ahab, mother of Athaliah, queen of Judah, and Ahaziah and Joram, kings of Israel. She was daughter of Ethbaal, king of the Zidonians, who had proved himself a powerful and wise king. Jezebel brought her religion with her, and transplanted it into the willing hearts of the Hebrews (1 K. xvi. 31), and the king of Israel and his people adopted formally the worship of the Phœnician gods. Elijah, Carmel, Naboth, Jehu, and Jezreel, are names that recal the main points in her history, which may be read in those articles.

Jezebel is charged with sorcery in the O. T. (2 K. ix. 22), and in the New (Rev. ii. 20), where her name is used as the symbol of a wife given over to unholy practices. As human nature is the same from age to age, so do persons enact the same deeds over and again.

JE'ZER (*image*). Son of Naphtali (Num. xxvi. 49). Jezerites.

JEZI'AH (*Jah sprinkles*). Of the family of Parosh; married a Gentile wife (Ezr. x. 25).

JEZI'EL (*El's assembly*). Benjamite with David at Ziklag (1 Chr. xii. 3).

JEZLI'AH (*Jah preserves*). Benjamite, son of Elpaal (1 Chr. viii. 18).

JEZO'AR (*whiteness*). Son of Helah, wife of Asher (1 Chr. iv. 7).

JEZRAHI'AH. A Levite, chief chorister at the dedication of the wall (Neh. xii. 42).

JEZRE'EL (*El has planted*). Founder of Etam

(1 Chr. iv. 3). "These are the families of the father of Etam."

JEZ REEL (*what God plants*). At the west foot of Mt. Gilboa, on a hill overlooking the great plain of Jezreel (Esdraelon, Judith iv. 5). The hill is rocky and steep on the N. E. side, and about 100 ft. high. Carmel can be seen to the west, and the Jordan valley to the east. There was a temple here to Astarte, with 400 priests, supported by Jezebel; Ahab's palace (ivory house, 1 K. xxiii. 39); a watch-tower (2 K. ix. 17), which may be also the tower in Jezreel near which Pharaoh encamped when Josiah "went against him" and was wounded (xxiii. 29). The spring of Harod is about 1 m. E. where the story of Gideon's night adventure with lamps and pitchers is located, and also the defeat and death of Saul and Jonathan. To this city Elijah ran before Ahab from Carmel, 12 ms.; here Naboth was murdered, that Ahab might have his vineyard; and the "house of Ahab" (the whole family) were killed; and Jezebel was thrown from a window and eaten by dogs in the same field that was taken from Naboth. There are about a dozen poor houses and a ruined tower in the modern village, which is called Zerin.—2. A town in Judah, near Carmel (Josh. xv. 56). Here David took Ahinoam the Jezreelitess for his first wife (1 Sam. xxvii. 3).—3. Eldest son of the prophet Hosea (i. 4).

JIB SAM (*pleasant*). Son of Tola, of Issachar (1 Chr. vii. 2).

JID LAPH (*tearful*). Son of Nahor (Gen. xxii. 22).

JIM'NA. Jimnah, eldest son of Asher (Num. xxvi. 44). IMNAH.

JIMNI TES. Descendants of Jimna.

JIPH TAH (*freed*). Judah, in the Shefelah (Josh. xv. 43). Lost.

JIPH'THAH-EL (*El opens*), **THE GORGE OF.** Jotapata (the same city) was besieged by Vespasian, held out, and stood a long time (B. J. iii. 7). Now Jefat, 12 ms. N. W. of Nazareth. The valley (*gorge*) of Abilin extends from near Jefat to the plain of Acre. It is inclosed with steep, wooded hills.

JO'AB (*Jah his father*). Son of Zeruiah, David's sister. He and his brothers Abishai and Asahel cast their lot with David (1 Sam. xxii. 3), and their history runs close to his. Joab's native power and and martial deeds made him the most famous of the three brothers, and he was ambitious and crafty, jealous and revengeful, as is shown in his history as "captain of the host." Joab earned at Jebus his title of commander-in-chief. The duel between 12 young heroes on each side, between the forces of Joab and Abner, took place at the pool of GIBEON, and brought on a general battle, which turned in favor of Joab and David's forces. Abner quarreled with Ishbosheth and went over to David, when Joab killed him, treacherously pretending it was "in blood-revenge" for his brother Asahel, whom Abner had killed. David dared not punish Joab, because he and his two brothers were so useful to him in the army. In the war against Hanun, Joab made a speech which is justly noticed as a perfect model of military address: "Be of good courage, and let us play the men for our people and for the cities of our God, and the Lord do as seemeth him good," (2 Sam. x. 12). It was in the second year of this war that Uriah was murdered by David, by the help of Joab. He also, at the close of the siege, sent for David, and gave him his share of the spoil, generously waiving his own right.

Joab was very kind and generous to Absalom in restoring him to his father's favor, after his flight from killing his brother Amnon, but was equally ready to kill Absalom when in rebellion against David, especially since Absalom preferred Amasa as his commander. Joab met at the great stone in Gibeon, his cousin Amasa, who had been appointed commander-in-chief over him, and treacherously murdered him as he did Abner. David prayed often to be released from such a terrible man. He opposed David's desire to number the people with true religious fervor (2 Sam. xxiv. 3). In the last days of David, Joab joined Adonijah in rebellion to the king, but Solomon was proclaimed, and executed his father's injunction, even taking Joab from the sacred sanctuary of the altar (Ex. xxi. 14), and killing him by the hand of Benaiah.—2. Son of Seraiah, of Kenaz (1 Chr. iv. 11).—3. Sheikh of a family which outnumbered any other in the return from captivity (Ezr. ii. 6).

JO'ACHAZ. JEHOAHAZ. The son of Josiah (Matt. i. 11).

JO'ACHIM. 1. JEHOIAKIM, JOACIM.—2. A high-priest in the time of Baruch, at Jerusalem (Bar. i. 7).

JO'ACIM. 1. JEHOIAKIM.—2. JEHOIACHIM (1 Esd. i. 43).—3. Joiakim, the son of Jeshua (v. 5).—4. High-priest in Jerusalem (Judith iv. 6, 14).—5. Husband of Susanna. See HISTORY OF THE BOOKS.

JOADA'MUS. GEDALIAH.

JO'AH (*Jeh is helper*). 1. Son of Asaph, historian to Hezekiah. Commissioned to treat with the Assyrian general Rab-shakeh (Is. xxxvi. 3).—2. Son of Zimmah (1 Chr. vi. 21), brother of Ethan (ver. 42).—3. Son of Obed-edom (xxvi. 4), doorkeeper.—4. Father of Eden, assisted in Hezekiah's reformation (2 Chr. xxix. 12).—5. Son of Joahaz, a recorder or historian to Josiah (xxxiv. 8).

JO'AHA (*Jah sustains*). Father of Joah.—3. Jo'anan. Johanan, son of Eliashib.

JOAN'NA (*Jah's gift*). Son of Rhesa (Luke iii. 27). Hananiah in 1 Chr. iii. 19?

JOAN'NA (*Jah's gift*). Wife of Chuza, Herod's steward, contributed to the support of Jesus, and brought spices to put into the tomb where his body was laid (Luke viii. 3, xxiv. 10). Joan.

JOAN'NAN. Jehohanan, surnamed Caddis, eldest brother of Judas Maccabæus (1 Macc. ii. 2).

JO'ASH. JEHOASH (*Jah gave*). Father of Gideon, a wealthy man of the Abiezrites, who permitted the worship of Idols, but also defended his son for destroying them (Judg. vi.).—2. Son of Ahaziah and 8th king of Judah. The only child of Ahaziah who escaped the massacre by Athaliah, being saved by a pious aunt and kept in the temple 6 years (2 Chr. xxii. 11). Athaliah counseled the murder of all Jehoram's relatives as a security against rebellion or conspiracy (2 Chr. xxi. 4, 6), and also advised her son Ahaziah (xxii. 10), until his death, when she reigned 6 years, until Joash was brought out. Pure religion was restored (except that some high places were not destroyed), sacrifice and contributions restored the temple. After 23 years, Jehoiada, the high-priest, died; Joash had evil counselors and revived the worship of Baal and Ashtaroth, and being rebuked by a son of Jehoiada, Zechariah, he caused him to be stoned in the court of the temple (Matt. xxiii. 35). After an invasion by Hazael, king of Syria, who carried off a great sum in treasure, Joash was murdered in his bed by servants. The prophets Elisha and Joel lived in this age. He reigned 40 years, from B. C. 878 to 838. His name is omitted in Matthew's genealogy.—3. Son and successor of Jehoahaz on the throne of Israel, B. C. 840–825 (2 K. xiv. 1; comp. xiii. 1 with xiii. 10). The kingdom was in a very reduced condition from the inroads of Hazael, and Joash, either from pity or policy, visited the pro-

LION WEIGHT.

phet Elisha just before the prophet's death, receiving from him a promise of success against the king of Syria, when the incident of the arrows occurred (2 K. xiii. 14-19). He gained victories over Syria, and also over Judah, and carried off immense treasures from Jerusalem, and threw down 600 feet of the walls.—4. Several others of this name are only known in the lists.

JŌ'ATHAM. Jotham, son of Uzziah (Matt. i. 9).

JOAZAB'DUS. Jozabad, the Levite.

JŌB (Heb. YOB, *convert*). 3d son of Issachar (Gen. xlvi. 13). Jashub in 1 Chr. vii. 1.

JŌB (Heb. IYOB, *afflicted*). The hero of the BOOK OF JOB; see HISTORY.

JŌ'BAB (YOBAB, *howling*). Son of Jokhan (Gen. x. 29). The etymology points to a district or locality which is a *howling desert*, and may be anywhere in the desert region of Arabia, S.—2. King of Edom (Gen. xxxvi. 33), in the line of Esau, son of Zerah of Bozrah. The Septuagint identifies this king with Job, the suffering patriarch.—3. King of Madon, routed by Joshua at Merom (Josh. xi. 1).—4. Chief in Benjamin.

JOCH'EBED (Heb. YOKEBED, *Jah's glory*). The aunt and wife of Amram, and mother of Moses and Aaron (Ex. vi. 20). The Sept. says "cousin" instead of aunt.

instead of Joel, *Vashni* is given as a name; the word vashni (VESHENI) means "and the second." The word may also mean (VESHNI) *Jah is strong*, as Joel is sometimes rendered, and so be used as a substitute.—4. Chief in Simeon (1 Chr. iv. 35).—5. Son of Hanoch, in the line of Carmi, in Reuben (1 Chr. v. 4).—6. Chief in Gad (v. 12).—7. Son of Izrahiah, in Issachar, general of a division of 36,000 (1 Chr. vii. 3). Son of Uzzi, according to the Syriac. Seven others of this name were not very noted, except as leaders and officers about the temple.

JŌE'LAH (*Jah helps*). Son of Jeroham of Gedor, with David at Ziklag.

JŌE'ZER (*Jah's help*). With David among the Philistines (1 Chr. xii. 6).

JOG'BEHAH (*elevated*). Built and fortified by the tribe of Gad (Num. xxxii. 35). Mentioned with Jaazer and Beth Nimram, and now called *Jebeiha*, 4 ms. N. of *Amman* (Burck. Rob.).—2. In the account of Gideon's pursuit of the Midianites (Judg. viii. 11). Gideon's route can be traced to *Nowa* (KARKOR). The village of *Jubieh*, near *Tell Jubieh*, a few miles N. E. of *Fik*, is the ancient Jogbehah.

JOG'LI (*exiled*). Father of Bukki, chief in Dan (Num. xxxiv. 22).

JŌ'HA (*Jah revives*). Son of Beriah, a Benjamite (1 Chr. viii. 16).—2. One of David's guard, a Tizite, son of Shimri (xi. 45).

JOHA'NAN (*Jah's gift*). JEHOHANAN. 1. Son of Azariah in the line of Zadok (1 Chr. vi. 9), high-priest in Rehoboam's reign.—2. Son of Elioenai, in the line of Zerubbabel (1 Chr. iii. 24).—3. Son of Kareah, captain in the siege of Jerusalem, and one of the first to submit to the Chaldean governor. He arrested the murderers of this governor. (Jer. xl. xli. 11). He, with others, passed a night at the Khan of Chimham (see BETHLEHEM), and settled in Egypt (2 K. xxv. 23). 8 others of this name were but little known.

JOHAN'NES (1 Esd. ix. 29). Jehohanan in Ezr. x. 28.

JOHN. Short form of Jehohanan (*Jah's gift*). 1. Father of Mattathias, of the Maccabees (1 Macc. ii. 1).—2. Eldest son of Mattathias; Caddis (ii. 2; ix. 36).—3. Father of Eupolemus, Envoy to Rome (viii. 17).—4. Son of Simon (xiii. 53).—5. Envoy to Lysias (2 Macc. xi. 17).—6. One of the high-priest's family who sat in judgment, with Annas and Caiaphas, on the Apostles Peter and John (Acts iv. 6). Rabbi Johanan ben Zaccai, president of the Great Synagogue at Jamnia.—7. Surname of Mark (Acts xii. 12).

8. JOHN, THE APOSTLE. Was a native of Bethsaida, on the Sea of Galilee, the son of Zebedee and Salome. He was acquainted with the character of Jesus as the Messiah before the call to be an apostle. In company with his brother James, and

JŌ'DA. Judah the Levite in 1 Esd. v. 58 (Ezr. iii. 19); Hodaviah (ii. 40); Hodevah (Neh. vii. 43); Hodijah (x. 10); Sudias (1 Esd. v. 26).

JŌ'ED (*Jah is witness*). Son of Pedaiah, a Benjamite (Neh. xi. 7).

JŌ'EL (*Jah is El*). The prophet. See HISTORY OF THE BOOKS.—2. In 1 Chr. vi. 36 an error for Shaul of ver. 24.—3. Eldest son of Samuel, the prophet (1 Sam. viii. 2), and father of Heman, the singer. He and his brother Abiah were judges in Beersheba, and disgraced their office by corruption, bribes, and perverted judgment. A singular error of some copyist has occurred in 1 Chr. vi. 28, where

LANNER FALCON.

Peter he was specially favored by Jesus on several occasions: at the Transfiguration; the restoring of Jairus' daughter; in the garden Gethsemane; and (including Andrew) at the discourse on the fall of Jerusalem. He was mistaken, with the others of the twelve, in his idea of the temporal mission of the Messiah; and with James joined his mother in the ambitious request for places of dignity and honor. He and James were called Boanerges, for their zeal. John was called also the DIVINE and the REVELATOR, from his writings. His family could not have been poor, because they kept servants, and contributed to the support of Jesus; and he received Mary into his home at Jerusalem, after the crucifixion. He also enjoyed social privileges, and the acquaintance of the high-priest.

Jesus loved John, who was the youngest of the twelve. Twice he showed himself to him as the Lord, by a miracle touching his own occupation, that he could understand without doubt. He was probably more intimate with him than any other, as the leaning on his bosom at the supper would indicate. After the ascension Paul found him living in Jerusalem, where he was a pillar in the church; and he was yet there when Paul was in Ephesus, A. D. 58. After Paul left Ephesus, John was sent there, about A. D. 65. From there he was exiled to Patmos, where he wrote the Apocalypse, about A. D. 96. (*Patmos and 7 Churches*). Polycrates (A. D. 200) calls him a martyr, but does not record either the time, place, or manner of his death. His epistles give evidence of a large diocese, requiring many journeys of pastoral visitation. Jerome states his age at 100, and Suidas at 120. He is described as a mild man, affectionate almost to effeminacy; but as a true Oriental, sometimes firing up as in the case of the Samaritans, when they rejected Jesus. See HISTORY OF THE BOOKS for the GOSPEL, EPISTLES and the REVELATION.

JOI'AKIM. From Jehoiakim. High-priest, son of Jeshua (Neh. xii. 10).

JOI'ARIB. From Jehoi'arib. 1. Three of this name, but little known.

JOK'DEAM (*by the people*). City in Judah, near Hebron (Josh. xv. 56).

JŌ'KIM. JOIAKIM. Son of Shelah son of Judah (1 Chr. iv. 22).

JOK'MEAM (Kitzaim in Josh. xxi. 22). In the Jordan Valley, near the east end of Esdraelon (1 K. iv. 12).

JOK'NEAM (*had by the people*). City in Zebulon (Josh. xxi. 34). *Tell Kaimon* near the east end of Carmel.

JOK'SHAN (*fowler*). Son of Abraham and Keturah (Gen. xxv. 2), whose sons were Sheba and Dedan. The Arabs have a Yokshan in their literature, but there is no trace of connection with the son of Abraham.

JOK'TAN (*made small*). Son of Eber (Gen. x. 25), father of the Joktanite Arabs in the S. of Arabia. Their dwelling was from Mesha to Sephar, a mount of the East (v. 30). The ancestor of the southern Arabs was KAHTAN, who is said to be the same as Joktan. The Jewish tradition may have been adopted by the Mohammedans. There is undisputed evidence of the settlement of Joktan's sons in that region, who founded a great kingdom which existed for ages before our era, and was renowned in the world of classical antiquity.

JOK THEEL (*subdued by El*). City in the Shefelah of Judah (Josh. xv. 38), near Lachish, now *Keitulaneh*.—2. The cliff *Selah*, the stronghold of the Edomites (2 K. xiv. 7; 2 Chr. xxv. 11-13).

JŌNA. JOHANAN or JONAH. BAR-JONA (PETER).

JON'ADAB. JEHONADAB. 1. Son of Shimeah, nephew of David (2 Sam. xiii. 3). He was "very subtle," and a friend of his cousin Amnon, heir to the throne, and gave him the fatal advice concerning his sister Tamar, and he knew of Absalom's purpose to kill Amnon (verse 32).

JŌ'NAH (YONAH, dove). Son of Amittai, of Gath-hepher, in Zebulon. See JONAH, in the HISTORY OF THE BOOKS.

JŌ'NAN. Son of Eliakim (Luke iii. 30). JOHN.

JŌ'NAS. Greek for Jonah.

EARTHEN LAMP. No. 5.

JON'ATHAN (*Jah gave*). JEHONATHAN. 1. Eldest son of Saul the king. He is first mentioned at the age of 30, when his father was made king (1 Sam. xiii. 2). He was married, and had one son, Mephibosheth (if no more), born about 5 years before his death (2 Sam. ii. 8, iv. 4). He was the heir to the throne. His courage was shown in the night exploit at Michmash, and his strength and skill in the use of the bow and spear (i. 22). He was a friend to David, and stood between him and his father as a peacemaker. The story of the friendship of David and Jonathan is one of the most pathetic in history. The people knew his value and sustained the elders in saving his life when in danger from Saul's foolish vow. He nobly yielded his own expectations of the kingdom to David, whom he believed to have been divinely selected. He perished with his father on Gilboa (1 Sam. xxxi.). David sung a eulogy over their graves that is unmatched for pathos and elevation (2 Sam. i. 18). Jonathan's son Mephibosheth was cared for by David in his own family.—2. A Levite, son of Gershom, who after the death of Joshua, impiously served as a priest, first to Micah, and then to the Danites in Dan Laish (Judg. xvii. 18).—3. Son of Abiathar the priest, who took an active part in Absalom's revolt, aiding David as a spy (2 Sam. xv. 36, xvii. 17); and also in the revolt of Adonijah (1 K. i. 42).—4. A soldier, son of Shimeah, and nephew to David, who killed a gigantic Philistine of Gath (2 Sam. xxi. 20).—5. Uncle to David, "a counselor, a wise man, and a scribe," (1 Chr. xxvi. 32). The word דוד, *uncle*, means any near relation, or even a friend (Is. v. 1).—6. Son of Jashen, a hero (2 Sam. xxiii. 32), who may be the one called the son of Shage, the Hararite (1 Chr. xi. 34). Nine others of this name are mentioned, one of whom owned the house in which Jeremiah was in prison (Jer. xxxvii. 15).

JŌ'NATH-E'LEM-RECHŌ'KIM. The name of a musical instrument which produced soft, mellow sounds, and found only in the title of Ps. lvi., as a direction to the choir leader.

JOP'PA (YAFA, *beauty*). In Dan on the seashore, a seaport in Solomon's time (Josh. xix. 46; 2 Chr. ii. 16). The cedar for the two temples, Solomon's and Zerubbabel's, and the palaces of David and Solomon was landed here (Ezr. iii. 7). Jonah embarked here when trying to escape from the unpleasant mission to Nineveh. During the wars of the Maccabees it was a stronghold (1 Macc. x. 75). Peter's "vision of tolerance" was on a house-top in this city (Acts x. 9-18). A Christian bishop resided here until the Saracens took the place. Pilgrims from all lands have landed here for many ages to go up to Jerusalem.

It was taken and retaken many times during the crusades. Saladin destroyed and Richard (Lionheart) rebuilt the fortifications. In the 13th century there was not a house entire on the site. It has now 5,000 people, 3 convents, Greek, Latin, and Armenian, and several mosques. The bazaars are interesting and antique. The city is on a hill, close to the sea, and is surrounded by miles of orchards—orange, lemon and many other fruits, besides gardens, which are scarcely surpassed.

The poet Ovid located here the beautiful myth of Andromeda and the sea-monster, a poetical allusion to the rocky barriers of the port, which to this day make approach to Joppa impossible by sea in a storm.

JŌ′RAH (*watering*). Ancestor of a family of 112 who returned from captivity (Ezr. ii. 18). Hariph in Neh. vii. 24.

JŌ′RAI (*Jah teaches*). A Gadite (1 Chr. v. 13).

JŌ′RAM. JEHORAM.

RINGS.

JŌR′DAN (*the descender*). Heb. YARDEN; Ar. El Urdon, descender, and Esh Sheriah, the watering-place. The largest river in Palestine. Rises in Mt. Hermon and empties into the Dead Sea. The sources are in the south, west and north-west slopes of Hermon, whose melting snows supply the fountains, some of which are so copious that each one of three forms a full stream at once. These three are: the Hasbany, the most northern, longest and muddiest; the Leddan (Ar. Eleh-Dan), the largest but shortest; and the Baniasy (of Paneas), the clearest.

There are, also, a fountain and stream from Ijon; one from Belat, 3 miles N. W. of the Huleh lake, another from Ain Mellalieh one mile N. W.; all of which are perennial, and large enough, each one, to turn a mill. About a mile S. of Hasbaiya the fountain of Shiba, 5 miles up the slope of Hermon, sends a stream north of the hill on which stands the Pagan temple of Hibbariyeh in ruins; another stream from the same direction is the Lasany, and flows into the Jordan at El Gujar, after coursing around the ruined castle of Bostra. These streams flow in deep, rocky channels, several feet below the general level of the country. The slopes of Hermon are "alive with streams" which supply the Jordan. The Hasbany, Leddan, and Baniasy unite in the Huleh marsh, pass S. into the lake Huleh, and flowing west from its S. angle, tumbles down a rocky ravine, with cliffs on each side, full of rapids, sinking 700 feet in 9 miles, to the Sea of Galilee.

From the S. of this sea the Jordan flows in a channel 100 feet wide, rocky, winding, *always descending;* falling over about forty cascades and rapids, sinking 600 feet in 60 miles, in a straight line, but making nearly 200 by its windings, to the Dead Sea, where it is a shallow stream. 360 feet wide, and deep in the rainy, or shallow in the dry season. The surface is there 1300 feet below the ocean. (SEA).

The tributaries below Genessaret on the east are the Yarmuk (Jabbok?), 5 ms. S. of the sea, 120 feet wide and 4 deep; and the Jabbok, which has two outlets into the Jordan, about midway between the two seas.

There are many winter torrents, dry in summer, and several fountains, as at Pella, Wâ′dy Shê′riah, Nim′rin, on the east; and on the west, Bethshan (from the well of Harod), Nâ′lim, Wâ′dy Fe′râh (from Mokhna), Wâ′dy Fasâ′il, Wa′dy Nemâirah,

Wâ′dy Kelt, and the Fountain of Elisha at Jericho, besides many small and nameless fountains and streams on both sides.

This section is the only part referred to in the Bible.

Nearly the whole course is below the ocean level.
Fountain at Hasbaiya 1700 feet above.
" " Paneas 1147 " "
" " Dan 350 " "
Lake Huleh 100 " "
Sea of Galilee 650 " below.
Dead Sea 1312 " "

JORDAN VALLEY (ARABAH) is a long, narrow plain, N. to S., bordered by steep and nearly parallel ridges; Gilead on the east, rising 3,000 to 5,000 ft., and Samaria, on the W., rising from 2,000 to 3,000; and is about 6 ms. wide in the northern part, widening to 10 or 12 at Jericho. The sides are not regular, but are broken by ridges, or spurs, from the mountains, which run out into the plain at several places, indicated on the map, as at Bethshan, and SURTABEH (Zarthan). See GEOLOGY in PALESTINE. The surface is not level, but lifted into low hills and ridges. The map shows the course of the river through the Ghor as very winding. The upper Jordan, above the lake and marsh Huleh, is fordable in many places, the brooks being shallow, with stony beds. In the rainy season they often overflow, and are then impassable for a few days at a time. S. of the lake Huleh there is more water, and the fords are fewer. Just north of the Sea of Galilee, near Bethsaida Julias, there is a ford over sand-bars in the dry season. The road from Damascus into Galilee passes over a bridge about 2 ms. S. of the Huleh, called Jacob's Daughters (after a mythical race, said to live in oak trees), 1/4 a m. S. of the Sea of Galilee there is a Roman bridge, in ruins, and a ford called SEMAKH. The bridge Mejamia is Saracenic, 5 ms. farther S., but there is no ford.

There is no mention of a bridge over the Jordan in the Scriptures, and the Mejamia is the only one now in use, S. of the Sea of Galilee. Opposite Bethshan the river is fordable in the dry season. Near Succoth, just N. of Wady Yabesh (Jabesh), there is an island with sand-bars on each side, forming a ford in summer. This is probably the Bethabara of Judges vii. 24. S. from this place to the mouth of the Jabbok there are several fords at low water. 10 ms. S. of the Jabbok is the ford on the Shechem Es Salt road, and traces of a Roman bridge. There is a ford both above and below the pilgrim's bathing-place, opposite Jericho. The upper one, called El Mashraa, is the supposed one crossed by Joshua.

The banks of the river are fringed with trees, flowering shrubs, cane and reeds; oleanders, hollyhocks, purple thistles, marigolds, anemones, willows, tamarisk, cedar, arbutus, aspen, and ghurrab; where beasts and birds in great numbers find shelter.

JŌ′RIM. Son of Matthat (Luke iii. 29).

JOR′KOAM (*people spreading*). City near Hebron (1 Chr. ii. 44).

JOSA′BAD. Soldier with David at Ziklag (1 Chr. xii. 4).

JOS′APHAT for Jehoshaphat in Matt. i. 8.

JŌ′SE. Son of Eliezer (Luke iii. 29).

JOS′EDEC. JEHOZADAK.

JŌ′SEPH (*he will increase*). The son of Jacob by Rachel, was born in Haran, (near Damascus?) B. C. 1726. Of his youth, up to the age of 17, we know nothing; but at that age he had so excited the envy and hate of his brothers, by simply receiving his father's gifts and attentions, and by telling his ominous dreams, and also by his acts of filial fidelity, that his brothers, prompted by Judah, sold him for a slave at Shechem, for 20 shekels of silver, to a band of Ishmaelites, who took him to

Egypt (Gen. xxx. xxxvii.). Reuben had intended to rescue Joseph, and had him cast into a dry pit, from which he might be taken afterward; but he was too late. His coat (of many colors) was a long tunic with sleeves, striped or embroidered. (See DRESS.) The brothers dipped this in a kid's blood, and sent it to Jacob, who was deceived by the trick, and believed Joseph had been killed by some wild beast.

The merchants sold him to Potiphar (chief of the executioners), a native of Egypt, and an officer of the Pharaoh (B. C. 1709), in the reign of Thothmes III, whose ring is engraved on page ? (Gen. xxxix.).

In Potiphar's house he prospered, rising to the highest position of honor and confidence. Being tempted by his master's wife, and honorably denying her request, he was falsely accused by her, and thrown into prison. Here he again prospered, and was advanced to the charge of all the other prisoners (Ps. cv. 17-18).

While in the prison, two other prisoners, a butler and a baker, dreamed dreams which Joseph interpreted (Gen. xl.). These accounts are interesting, because they agree with the manners of the ancient Egyptians, as recorded on their monuments (Anc. Egypt ii. 152).

Joseph begged the butler, when he should be restored to favor, as he showed from his dream, to think of him, and speak of him to the Pharaoh; but he did not do so (Gen. xl. 13-16, 23), until the Pharaoh dreamed two prophetic dreams, which found in Joseph a successful interpreter, on the recommendation of the butler (xl.). He was then released, after two years' confinement. The dreams foreboded the approach of a seven years' famine; and on consultation with his advisers, Joseph was chosen by the Pharaoh to exercise full power over all Egypt, except the throne, as one whose wisdom was of divine origin, in token of which he put his ring on Joseph's hand, invested him with royal garments, and gave him a new name, Taphnath-paaneah (saviour of the world); and gave him for a wife Asenath, daughter of Potipherah, a priest of On.

He was now thirty years old. His two sons, Manasseh and Ephraim, were born during the seven years of plenty. His wisdom appeared when the famine was known to extend to "all lands" i. e. bordering on Egypt, and their people came to buy corn in Egypt (xli. 56-57). Among others, the ten brothers of Joseph came also, and he recognized them; but they did not know him, for he had probably adopted the dress and speech of Egypt, and, besides, the boy of seventeen that they sold for a slave was now a man over thirty, and a governor.

Joseph severely tried and punished his brothers by calling them spies, putting them in prison for three days, and detaining one (Simeon) while the others returned with corn to Canaan, with orders to bring Benjamin down to Egypt. But even while pretending this severity his good heart caused him to weep; it may be as much from joy at seeing them, as from anxiety about Benjamin and his father.

As soon as Benjamin came his manner changed—with difficulty only could he act longer in a false character, and he gave orders to prepare for them to dine with him at noon (hiding himself to weep in his room). The account of the dinner agrees exactly with the monuments as to the customs of the Egyptians, which were also adopted by the Jews. Joseph was served by himself—his brethren by themselves, and the Egyptians also apart by themselves; and when each one was seated in order, according to his birthright, Simeon being released and with them, they wondered that any one should know their ages.

Joseph wished to try how far his brothers would be faithful to his father, and laid a plan to trap them and detain Benjamin by putting a cup in Benjamin's sack. On being arrested when a little way out of the city, and brought back before Joseph, with Benjamin as the detected criminal, Judah showed the deepest regard for his aged father's feelings, and offered himself a ransom, that Benjamin might return to him. This, in the Scripture, is one of the most touching passages in the whole course of literature (Gen. xliv. 18-34).

Joseph could bear it no longer, but made himself known to his brothers, and then his first question was, "Is my father alive?" and he hastens to relieve them of anxiety and fear, by showing them that it was God's providence that sent him to Egypt to prepare the way for their salvation from death by famine (xlv. xlvi.).

Pharaoh gave Joseph leave, and ordered him to bring his father and his household into Egypt; and accordingly they were brought and settled in Goshen, where Joseph met his father, honored him by presenting him before the king, and sustained him and his through the remaining years of famine (xlvii. 12).

Joseph's prudence and policy made Pharaoh absolute master and owner of all Egypt, except the priest's land, by the sale of the stores which had been laid up during the years of plenty. This is the greatest social revolution recorded in history—the reduction of an entire nation to slavery or dependence by famine (13-26).

Jacob died, and Joseph had his body embalmed and carried to the cave of Machpelah (l. 13).

Joseph's brothers feared him after his father's death, and coming near, begged his forgiveness, when he made the noble reply: "Fear not; I will nourish you and your little ones."

He lived to the age of 110 years, and saw Ephraim's children to the third generation; and Manasseh's also were brought up on his knees.

When he died, they embalmed his body, and put it in a coffin in Egypt. (B. C. 1616.)

He had reminded them of God's promise to bring them again into Canaan, and required them to carry his bones with them when they went. So they carried the body in the desert for forty years, and laid it in its final resting-place at Shechem (Josh. xxiv. 32).

Joseph is above all others the purest character known to history, (always excepting Jesus). Unlike David, Solomon, and any other, he left only good reports of his heart and hands. His trials, resistance to temptation, degradation, exaltation, saving his people, and confounding his enemies, mark him as a type of the Christ.

JŌ'SEPH. The son of Heli, the husband of Mary, and the legal father of Jesus (Matt. i.). The first fact we learn of him is his descent from David. He is then mentioned as the betrothed husband of Mary.

This custom of espousal was the beginning of marriage, and was made by the parents if the parties were under age. It was a public and formal proceeding, confirmed by oaths, and presents to the bride (Gen. xxiv. 22, 53). Twelve months were allowed to pass before the marriage ceremony; and the betrothal could only be broken off by a bill of divorce. Mary was the daughter and heir of Joseph's uncle, Jacob.

The age at which marriage was legal was 18; but probably, then as now, in Palestine, many married much younger—from 12 years upward; so if this was a first marriage, with Joseph as well as Mary, they were most probably under 20 years, and it may be that Mary was only 15 to 18. During the twelve months after the betrothal, Joseph was grieved at the discovery that Mary was with

child, and intended to divorce her as privately as possible; but being reconciled by divine instruction in a dream, he accepted her as his wife. Mary bore several children to Joseph, two of whom became believers after the crucifixion, and James was the first Christian bishop of Jerusalem. We have also the names of Joseph, Simon, and Jude. Of the daughters no names are given (Matt. i. 18, 24, 25, xxvi. 56, xiii. 55, 56).

Joseph was an artisan of some kind (the original Greek word meaning *smith*, or maker of articles out of any material); and it is probable that he was a carver of wood for interior decoration (a carpenter), and that his son Jesus was taught the same trade. All handicraft were held in honor, and they were learned and followed by the sons of the best men.

The decree of Augustus Cæsar, taxing all the people, required them to appear for that purpose at their proper places, according to their tribes; so Joseph and Mary were at Bethlehem (if they did not reside there) when Jesus was born. At the proper age for presenting the child in the temple, Joseph went with the child and his mother, and heard Simeon's and Anna's prophetic words. He was also present when the magi visited the child; and being warned in a dream, "took the young child and his mother at night and departed into Egypt." On his return, after Herod's death, "he turned aside" and dwelt at Nazareth.

When Jesus was 12 years old, they went up to Jerusalem, to the annual feast of the Passover, and the incident of the child among the doctors occurred.

Joseph is not mentioned again in the gospels after this time.

It is supposed that he died before the crucifixion, from the words of Jesus when on the cross, recommending his mother to the care of the beloved disciple (John xix. 26). The question of his neighbors at Nazareth, as recorded by Mark, seems to indicate that he was then dead. See MARY.

COIN OF ANTIOCHUS III.

JOSEPH 3, of Issachar, one of the spies (Num. xiii. 7).—4. One who had married a Gentile wife (Ezr. x. 42).—5. Four of the ancestors of Jesus had this name (Luke iii. 23, 24, 26, 30).—6. Of Arimathea. All we know of him is that he had some wealth, and was a member of the Sanhedrin, a secret disciple of Jesus, and that he appeared for a time, taught one great lesson, and was heard of no more. He was looking and waiting for the Messiah; did not consent to the judgment against Jesus, and begged for his body, that it might be properly buried. A tradition says he went to England, and settled there, near Glastonbury.

JOSEPH, called **BARSA'BAS** (*son of the old man, or wisdom*). Nominated but not chosen to fill a vacancy in the 12 (Acts i. 23). Also called Justus. The fact that he was nominated to be an apostle shows that he had seen Jesus, heard and believed, and had been with the others, perhaps constantly. Eusebius says he was one of the 70.

JO'SES (*Jesus, or Joseph*). 1. Son of Eliezer (Luke iii. 29).—2. Brother of Jesus (Matt. xiii. 55).—3. Joses Barnabas (Acts iv. 36).

JOSE'PHUS (Greek-Latin form of Joseph). FLAVIUS JOSEPHUS is the ancient historian, whose works were composed from materials found in the Scripture, the Apocrypha, the Targums, and in Jewish traditions. It is believed that he intended to tell the truth so far as he knew, except when the Jewish people, or the Roman power were to be flattered, when his text was colored for that purpose. This may be the reason why he so carefully omitted any account of Jesus and his teachings, which must have caused a great commotion in the Jewish church, if considered only in the light of a new sect—the Nazarenes. Recent explorations confirm his statements in matters of history, except in minute figures, in which exaggeration seems to have been sometimes the design.

JO'SHAH (JOSHAVIAH, *Jah lets dwell*). Chief in Simeon. Son of Amaziah (1 Chr. iv. 34).

JOSHA'PHAT (JEHOSHAPHAT), the Mithnite, a hero in David's guard (1 Chr. xi. 43).

JOSHAVI'AH (*Jah lets dwell*). Son of Elnaam, one of David's guard (1 Chr. xi. 46).

JOSHBEKA'SHAH (*Jah sits firm*). Son of Heman, leader of the 16th choir (1 Chr. xxv. 4).

JOSHEBBAS'SEBET (*the people turn to Jah*). The Ethnite (in the margin of 2 Sam. xxiii. 9).

JOSH'UA ((*Jah his help*). (The same in the Hebrew as the original of Jesus). The son of Nun, and successor of Moses as leader of the people. His name was first Oshea (Num. xiii. 8), and in the N. T. he is called Jesus (Acts vii. 45; Heb. iv. 8). He was of the tribe of Ephraim (1 Chr. vii. 27). He is first mentioned in Ex. xvii., at the time of the attack of the Amalekites, but in such a manner as to convey that he was well known before; and Moses at that time indicated him as his successor by giving him a new name (or title), Jehoshua (*salvation*). He was one of the 12 spies (Num. xiii. 16). He opposed Aaron's calf-worship, and he with Caleb were the only two souls excepted from the judgment of wandering and dying without seeing Canaan, and was specially selected even when Moses was rejected at the waters of Meribah-Kadesh. He did not originate, his office and work being completion—leading the people into the Land of Promise, dividing and occupying Canaan, and destroying their enemies. His personal and official life is without a blemish, except the hasty treaty with the Gibeonites. The people of Israel under Joshua were nearest to the original conception of a united, obedient, willing, company of children serving a father. But he was not perfect; since he did not occupy all the land, nor prevent the bitter quarrels which divided the people after his day. He received his commission (or had it confirmed), in the same manner as Paul did, in a vision (Josh. v. 13-15), from the Lord Jesus (when he was 84). He was a type of Jesus the Christ, as was also Jeshua, the high-priest, in the second redemption of the nation (Zech. iii.). See BOOK OF JOSHUA in the HISTORY OF THE BOOKS, and TIMNATH SERAH. He died at the age of 110.

JOSH'UA. JESHUA. The son of Josedech, who was carried away by Nebuchadnezzar (1 Chr. vi. 15), and high-priest after the return from Babylon.

There are several other persons of this name, of whom very little is known.

JOSI'AH (YOSHIAHU, *Jah heals*). 1. Son of Amon, and 15th king of Judah, from B. C. 641 to 610, reigning 31 yrs., from 8 yrs. old. His history is given in 2 K. xxii., xxiv.; 2 Chr. xxxiv., xxxv., and Jeremiah i. to xii. In his day the Temple was repaired and the BOOK OF THE LAW was found (see HISTORY OF THE BOOKS). He was wounded in a battle against Pharaoh Necho, and died near Jerusalem, where he was buried with great display.—2. Son of Zephaniah (Zech. vi. 9).

JOSIBI'AH (*Jah makes to dwell*). Father of Jehu (1 Chr. iv. 35).

JOPPA.

JOSIPHI'AH (*Jah increase him*). Ancestor of Shelomith, who returned with Ezra (viii. 10).

JOT (Heb. YOD, *the hand*). The smallest letter in the Hebrew alphabet. Used as a symbol of the least. Jot or tittle (Matt. v. 28); not even the finishing touch.

JOT'BAH (*goodness*). Native town of Haruz and his daughter Meshullemeth (2 K. xxi. 19). *El Taiyibeh* (see OPHRAH). Arabic, *Et Tayib, good*. There are three sites so named. 1. S. of Hebron; 2. W. of Hebron; 3. N. of Jerusalem.

JOT BATH. JOTBA'THAH (*goodly*). *Wady el Aithah*, in the desert, N. W. of Akabah.

JŌ THAM (*Jah is upright*). 1. Son of Gideon (Judg. ix. 5). His parable of the bramble is the oldest of its kind. He lived at Beer.—2. Son of king Uzziah, succeeding him to the throne of Judah B. C. 158, at the age of 25, and reigning 16 years (2 K. xv.; 2 Chr. xxvii.).—3. Son of Jahdai, in Judah's line (1 Chr. ii. 47).

JOZ'ABAD. JEHOZABAD. There were seven of this name, without special note.

JOZ'ACHAR (*Jah remembers*). Son of Shimeath (2 K. xii. 2). Zabad in 2 Chr. xxiv. 26.

JU'BAL (*music*). Son of Lamech, by Adah (Gen. iv. 21); a teacher, and perhaps inventor of musical instruments, both for string and wind.

JU'BILEE (YOBEL, *rushing sound*). See CHRONOLOGY, p. 56. The year of Jubilee was the 49th, so as to count full 7's, and no more. If on the 50th, the count by 7's would be interrupted.

JU'DA (*Judas*). Son of Joseph, father of Simeon (Luke iii. 30).—2. Son of Joanna (Hananiah), (iii. 26). Abiud in Matt. i. 13.—3. Brother of Jesus (Mark vi. 3).—4. JUDAH.—5. Juda, for the land of Judah in Matt. ii. 6, etc.

JUDÆ'A. Latin form of Judea.

JU'DAH (YEHUDAH, *praise Jah*). The Jew or Hebrew. JUDA. JUDAH. 1. Fourth son of Jacob, by Leah. His brothers were Reuben, Simeon, Levi (Judah), Issachar, Zebulon. He was a leader in family matters from his youth up, and more is known of him than of any other except Joseph. Reuben advised the brothers to throw Joseph into the pit, and Judah proposed the sale to the traders, both acting honorably to themselves, wishing to save the life of Joseph (Gen. xxvii. 26). See JOSEPH for Judah's conduct in Egypt (Gen. xliv. 14, 16-34). Judah went before Jacob into Egypt (xlvi.). Jacob honors Judah first in his blessings (xlix. 8-10). He had 5 sons, 3 by a Canaanite, the daughter of Shuah—ER, ONAN and SHELAH—and 2 by the widow of Er (TAMAR), Pharez and Zerah. (See 12 TRIBES). The boundaries of Judah are more carefully noted than any of the others (Josh. xv. 20-63). The district was about 45 miles N. to S., and nearly 50 wide E. to W. See PALESTINE, GEOLOGY, CLIMATE, KINGDOM OF JUDAH.—2. A Levite ancestor of Kadmiel (Ezr. iii. 9).—3. A Levite, who had a Gentile wife (x. 23).—4. A Benjamite, son of Senuah (xi. 9).—5. Assisted in dedicating the wall (xii. 34).

JU'DAH, KINGDOM OF. The kingdom actually began with the revolt of the 10 tribes, but was really a continuation of the kingdom of Saul and David. The kingdom was an original element in the system that Moses projected, and the first elections, of Saul, David and Solomon, were divinely directed. See list of kings in ISRAEL. Rehoboam, Solomon's son and successor, lost the ten tribes, and also suffered from the Pharaoh SHISHAK, who robbed the temple (2 Chr. xii.).

Jehoshaphat was the greatest king after David, and increased the power and wealth of his people. His ships being destroyed in a storm, his scheme for commerce was given up.

A grave error was committed in a marriage with the house of Ahab, Jehoram taking Athaliah for a wife, who introduced her mother Jezebel's image-worship.

The treasures of the temple or of the king were several times carried away from Judah. All the vast hoards of David and Solomon were lost by Rehoboam to Shishak (1 K. xiv. 26); Benhadad took from Asa the savings of 40 years. Jehoash sent to Hazael all that Jehoshaphat, Jehoram, Ahaziah, and himself had dedicated, besides his private wealth (2 K. xii. 18); Jehoash of Israel took from Amaziah all the treasures (xiv. 11-14); Ahaz surrendered to Tiglath Pileser (xvi. 8); Hezekiah to Sennacherib 300 talents of silver, and 30 of gold (xviii. 14-16); in the days of Josiah (or after he was killed) the Pharaoh could only collect 100 talents of silver, and 1 talent of gold, by taxation, there being no treasure in the temple, and (perhaps a mistake) Nebuchadnezzar carried off all the treasures of the temple, with the very vessels that Solomon had made (xxiv. 13), 5400 in number (Ezra i. 11). The royal line was twice almost destroyed, by Jehu, and by Athaliah. The real cause of decay in this power was the contest between the Church and the State; the priest grew stronger as the king was weaker. Faction grew bold and fierce, and bloodshed was common (Ez. xxii.). The nation grew wealthy, luxurious, superstitions, idolatrous, with only a formal show of true religion. The king appointed the high-priest, but did not dare to depose one. The high-priests gained more honor than the kings—especially it was a great honor to trace to Zadok the priest. But the nation could not be saved even by a pure high-priesthood. Society was corrupt, and full of contention, and unable to defend itself against Egypt and Babylon. The kingdom lasted 487 yrs.; 387 after Israel seceded, and 133 after Israel's captivity.

SPHINX.

JU'DAS (Greek-Latin form of Judah). 1. In 1 Esd. ix. 23.—2. 3d son of Mattathias, the Maccabæus (1 Macc. ii. 4, etc.).—Son of Calphi (xi. 70).—4. A Jew in Jerusalem (2 Macc. i. 10).—5. Son of Simon, and brother of John Hyrcanus (1 Macc. xvi. 2).—6. The patriarch Judah, in Matt. i. 2, 3.—7. A man in Damascus, who lodged Paul (Saul) after his conversion (Acts ix. 11).—8. BAR'SABAS a leading member of the Church at Jerusalem (Acts xv. 22), a prophet (v. 32), chosen with Silas to go with Barnabas and Saul to Antioch as delegates on the Gentile convert question (v. 27).—9. Of Galilee, the leader of a revolt in the time of Quirinus (A. D. 6), mentioned by Gamaliel in his speech before the Sanhedrin (Acts v. 37). He was a religious enthusiast, whose motto was, "We have no Lord or Master but God." See Jos. xviii. 1, § 1.

JU'DAS ISCAR'IOT (from KERIOTH, his native place). Son of Simon (John vi. 71). His early life is not recorded. He was awarded the unhappy notoriety of betraying Jesus, his Lord and Master. He must have been a useful man among the 12, because he was appointed their steward (John xii. 6). Jesus knew his character from the first (vi. 64); but no one else even suspected him up to the very last day, when Peter and John were only made to know by a private sign from the Master who was the betrayer (xiii. 26). He got from the high-priest

30 shekels, the price of a slave, but returned the money when repentance overtook him, after the crucifixion. His tender heart and quick conscience appears in the fact that he killed himself rather than live with the feeling of remorse for his crime.

Some have thought that he believed that Jesus would be able to free himself from the priests, and stand higher than ever for the trial; others think that he as well as the rest believed Jesus was delaying the opening of his temporal kingdom, and that he would only force him to declare his power and majesty by bringing him face to face with his enemies. While these theories are only possibly true in a slight degree, the love of money was beyond question a motive. The other 11 were weak, perplexed, vascillating, faint-hearted, but Judas was active and speculative, in the trying moment, his religion is only a servant to his worldly interest, and he perhaps discovered that the spiritual kingdom would not pay. This is why he was dishonest in his stewardship (John xii. 4), and grudged the value of the perfume that Mary honored Jesus with at Bethany. His presence among the 12 is explained in "The presence of such a false friend in the company of his disciples was needed to complete the circle of Christ's trials and temptations." David in the Psalms describes such a character, whose words were smooth as butter; whose actions were drawn swords; who ate his meat, and lifted his heel against him.

It seems probable that Judas did not stay to the Lord's Supper.

JUDAS. JUDE. A disciple, writer of the Epistle (see HISTORY OF THE BOOKS). He was "brother of James" (Jude 1), "the Lord's brother" (Gal. i. 19; ii. 9, 12; Matt. xiii. 55; Mark vi. 3). He was not an apostle, for he did not believe on Jesus as the Christ until after the crucifixion (John vii. 5). Only one question of his to Jesus is all that is recorded of him (John xiv. 22). Eusebius (History iii. 20, 32), says the Lord's relatives were feared by the Emperor Domitian, and were known as late as the end of Trajan's reign.

JUDÆA. JUDE'A (Jewish). The Roman name of the territory of Judah or the southern of the three divisions, Galilee, Samaria, Judea. (See the Map). Jewry in John vii. 1, and Dan. v. 13. Judea also in Ezra v. 8, on the return from the captivity. The chief interest in Judea is in Jerusalem and it's vicinity, although there are many names of cities all over its territory, connected with interesting persons and events.

HEAD OF JUPITER.

JUDÆA, THE WILDERNESS OF. Was along the W. shore of the Dead Sea.

JUDG'ES (SHOPETIM). Patriarchal seniors who administered justice, usually the chief or head of a tribe (Sheikh). Moses introduced the system on the advice of his father-in-law, Jethro (Ex. xviii). There were two distinct orders of judges. 1. The leader, or chief of the whole nation, instead of or before the kings were elected.—2. The elder princes or chiefs of families. A list of judges over all Israel is given in CHRONOLOGY, page 57. For BOOK OF JUDGES see HISTORY OF THE BOOKS.

JUDG'MENT. Judicial decision. Sentence of a judge. The Day of Judgment (Matt. x. 5; xi. 22), the great day (Jude 6), last day (John xi. 24), in which Christ will judge the world (Acts xvii. 31; John v. 22), in righteousness (Matt. xxv. 31-46; 2 Cor. v. 10; Rev. xx.). See ADVENT. Some believe that resurrection follows immediately after death, and that judgment is already pronounced on ourselves by our lives, the Christ only carrying out the sentence, so that the world may continue without end, and souls go to their final account, the judgment never ending. See HADES. Others hold that the resurrection is reserved to the end of the world, when there will be no more souls born, and all the dead from the beginning will be raised at one time. It seems more probable that the spirit world, heaven, is entered at once by the blessed soul, recognizing friends, relatives, the ancient worthies, Jesus and God the Father. See RESURRECTION.

JUDG'MENT HALL (Gr. praetorium), (John xviii. 28). This has been located in Pilate's house, and in Herod's palace, and in the Castle Antonia. There was another hall at Caesarea (Jos. Ant. xv. 9, § 6).

JU'DITH (YEHUDITH, Jewess). 1. Wife of Esau, dau. of Beeri; also called Aholibama (Gen. xxvi. 34, xxxvi. 2).—2. Judith the heroine of the BOOK OF JUDITH; see HISTORY.

JU'LIA (feminine of Julius). A disciple at Rome, wife(?) of Philologus (Rom. xvi. 15).

JU'LIUS. Centurion of the "Augustus Band," who conducted Paul to Rome from Caesarea, and used him courteously (Acts xxvii. 1, 3).

JU'NIA. A disciple at Rome (Rom. xvi. 7).

JU'NIPER (ROTHEM). A white-blossomed broom, found in Spain, Barbary, Syria, and the desert of Sinai, and called Spanish broom, in Arabic Ethem. The bush is the largest in the desert, and gives shade from the sun, wind, and rain, and the Bedawins make charcoal from the twigs (illustrating Ps. cxx. 4). Job speaks of eating rothem roots (xxx. 4), as a picture of abject poverty and want. Elijah slept under a broom bush (Kob. i. 203).

JU'PITER (Gr. Zeus, Latin Jupiter, Diumpater, heaven-father). The son of Saturn and Ops, brother and husband of Juno, father and king of gods and men, and supreme ruler of the universe, in the Greek and Roman mythology. Jupiter Tonans, the thunderer; fulminator, the lightning-wielder; Pluvius, the rain-giver. See PAUL. The worship of Jupiter was general in all Greek countries, and was once attempted on Mt. Moriah, in the temple, by order of ANTIOCHUS EPIPHANES. See MACCABEES.

JU'SHAB-HE'SED (loving kindness is returned). Son of Zerubbabel (1 Chr. iii. 20).

JUSTIFICA'TION (Gr. dikaio). Used in the Bible to mean passing sentence or giving a decision (Deut. xxv. 1; Prov. xvii. 15; Is. v. 22; Ps. cxliii. 2). It is opposed by condemn (Gr. katakrino), in Rom. viii. 33, 34. By the deeds of the law there shall no flesh be justified in God's sight (iii. 20). It is a judicial act of God, by which the sinner is declared innocent, as if he had never sinned, not because of works, but of Christ's righteousness; the means by which it is apprehended is faith. Justified by faith and through faith (iii. 28, iv. 5; Gal. ii. 16, iii. 8).

JUS'TIFY. The faith that justifies is a working living faith, and must so prove itself whenever occasion demands.

JUS'TUS (just). 1. Surname of Joseph Barsabas (Acts i. 23).—2. A disciple at Corinth (xviii. 7).—3. Surname of Jesus, a friend of Paul (Col. iv. 11).

JUT'TAH (YUTAH, inclined). An ancient city of Judah, allotted to the priests (Josh. xv. 55). The residence of Zacharias, a priest, the father of John the Baptist. It is now a large village, five miles south of Hebron. (See Luke i.). It is found on the Egyptian monuments as toh-n-nu, a fort of the Anakim, near Hebron. Called "a city of Juda" in Luke i. 39.

KAB'ZEEL (*gathered by El*). Judah in the S. E. (Josh. xv. 21). The native place of Benaiah, one of David's "mighty men" (2 Sam. xxiii. 20; 1 Chr. xi. 22). Jekabzeel in Neh. xi. 25, where it is one of the places occupied after the return from captivity. It was probably a shepherd settlement (so many of which are known), its name being derived from "the gathering of the flocks."

KABBALAH. Reception; doctrine received orally. The teachings are: 1. God is above everything; even above being and thinking. Therefore it cannot be said truly that he has either a will, desire, thought, action—language, because these belong to finite man. He cannot be comprehended by the intellect, nor described with words. He is in a peculiar sense without life, for He cannot die, and He in a certain sense does not exist, because that which is incomprehensible does not exist to us. He therefore made known some properties of His existence to us.

The will to create implies limit, therefore the imperfect world, limited and finite, is no work of the infinite; but since there cannot be any accident or chance where infinite wisdom resides, the world (and universe) must have been indirectly created by the 10 intelligences (SEFIROTH), which emanate from the One original emanation, the infinite intelligence (EN SUF). These 10 powers have bodies, the one original emanation (not created) has a form also. They are divided into 3 groups; which operate on the 3 worlds, of intellect, of souls, and of matter.

All human souls are pre-existent in the world of *sefiroth*, and must live the life of probation on the earth. If its life is pure it rises to the sphere of the *sefiroth*; but if it sins, it will have to live over and over again until it becomes pure. (Some say the limit is to 3 trials). The souls that have lived have the first right to new-born bodies, and so there are many waiting even for the first chance, and Messiah cannot be born until all others have been born, at the end of days. This is a hermeneutical (explaining Scripture) system, invented to satisfy those Jews who did not agree with the descriptions of heaven by the prophets.

THE ENDLESS.

```
           1
        CROWN.
       |       |
INTELLIGENCE.  WISDOM.
      3           2
      |           |
   JUSTICE.     LOVE.
      5           4
       |       |
        BEAUTY.
           6
       |       |
  SPLENDOR.  FIRMNESS.
      8           7
       |       |
      FOUNDATION.
           9
           |
       KINGDOM.
          10
```

KADES (Judith, i. 9). Summoned to aid him by Nebuchadnezzar. Kadesh Naphtali (Josh. xv. 23).

RADES. Greek form of *Kadesh* (Judg. i. 9).

KA'DESH, K. BARNEA, KADESH, EL MISH-pat (*spring of judgment*), which is Kadesh (Gen. xiv. 7). The most northern place reached by the Israelites in their direct road to Canaan. Located at Ain el Weibeh, on the western side of the Arabah, N. W. of Petra, where there is the most copious fountain and the most important watering-place in that valley. There are no ruins of any "city" (v. 16), nor of the tomb of Miriam (Jerome, Onom.). See EXODUS.

KAD'MIEL (*one stands before El*). A Levite who returned with Zerubbabel (Ezr. ii. 40, iii. 9; Neh. vii. 43).

WASHING HANDS BEFORE MEALS.

KAD'MONITES, THE. Children of the East (Gen. xv. 19).

KA'IN. CAIN (Num. xxiv. 22).

KAL'LAI (*swift messenger of Jehovah?*) A priest (Neh. xii. 20).

KA'NAH (*reed*) (Josh. xix. 28). Asher. Seven miles S. E. of Tyre; a village of 300 families. A mile north of it is the ancient site (Ein el Awainid, *mother of columns*), with ruins, some of which are colossal—foundations, oil-presses, cisterns, and posts of houses, and great numbers of columns (L. and B. 238). AIN KANAH, five miles S. E. of Sidon, is also claimed as the true site.

KA'NAH, THE RIVER. Boundary between Ephraim and Manasseh, flowing into the Mediterranean two miles S. of Cæsarea (Josh. xvi. 8, xvii. 9), now called *Nar Ahkar*.

KA'REAH (*bald-head*). Father of Johanan and Jonathan (Jer. xl. 8), called CAREAH.

KAR'KAA (*flat*). On the boundary, next to Azmon, on the south side of Judah (Josh. xv. 3). Lost.

KAR'KOR (*level place*). Where Zeba and Zalmunna felt "secure" with their host, and Gideon smote them (Judg. viii. 10, 11). Somewhere on the level Mishor, but not identified.

KAR'TAH (*city*). (Josh. xxi. 34). In Zebulon. Lost.

KAR'TAN (*two towns*). Naphtali (Josh. xxi. 32). Kirjathaim?

KATT'ATH (*small*). Zebulon (Josh. xix. 15). Lost.

KE'DAR (*black*). Second son of Ishmael (Gen. xxv. 13). Settled his tribe in the N. W. of Medina, in Arabia, bordering Palestine. The glory of the sons of Kedar is mentioned by Isaiah (xxi. 13-17), their villages (xlii. 11), and their princes by Ezekiel (xxvii. 21), who supplied Tyre with sheep and goats; and in Canticles (i. 5) their tents are noticed as "black, but comely." Mohammed traces his lineage to Abraham through the celebrated Koreish tribe, which sprang from Kedar. The Arabs in the Hejaz are called Beni Harb (*men of war*), and are Ishmaelites as of old, from their beginning. Palgrave says their language is as pure now as when the Koran was written (A. D. 610), having

remained unchanged more than 1200 years; a fine proof of the permanency of Eastern institutions.

KEDE'MAH (*eastward*). Son of Ishmael (Gen. xxv. 15).

KED'EMOTH (*beginnings*). Reuben, east of the Dead Sea, near the Arnon (Deut. ii. 26). Name of a city and a wilderness (*i. e.* the pasture-land) near it. Lost. This district has not been explored.

KE'DESH (*sanctuary*). 1. Kedesh in Galilee, one of the Cities of Refuge. A fortified city in Naphtali (Josh. xix. 37). The residence of Barak (Judg. iv. 6), where he and Deborah assembled their army. The tree of Zaanaim, under which was pitched the tent in which Sisera was killed, was in the vicinity. It was captured by Tiglath Pileser, with other towns, and its people removed to Assyria (2 K. xv.). The tomb of Barak was shown in the 12th century (*Benjamin of Tudela*). The site is beautiful. A little green plain among the mountains, with a border of wooded hills, and well watered. The ruins on a rounded *tell*, which was once fortified, and the broken columns and handsome capitals, sarcophagi, and heaps of hewn stones, show its former grandeur.—2. In Issachar (Josh. xxi. 28 has Kishon, and 1 Chr. vi. 72, Kedesh).—3. South, in Judah (Josh. xv. 23). Kadesh Barnea ?

KE'DRON. KIDRON.

KEHE'LATHAH (*assembly*). (Num. xxxiii. 22). Between Sinai and Kadesh. Lost.

Now called *Kenawat*, and beautifully situated on the west slope of the Hauran, in the midst of oak groves. The ruins extend a mile and a half long by half a mile wide, and consist of temples, palaces, theatres, towers, churches (of the early Christians), and many private houses with doors and roofs of stone. A colossal head of Ashtoreth, found by Porter, shows that this goddess was worshiped there.

KE'NAZ (*hunting*). One of the "dukes" (sheikhs) of Edom (Gen. xxxvi. 15; 1 Chr. i. 53). Caleb and Othniel were of this race. The modern tribes of the *Aaneh*, the most powerful of all the Bedawins in Arabia, cover the desert from the Euphrates to Syria, and from Aleppo to Nejed. Their army numbers 90,000 camel-riders and 10,000 horsemen.

KE'NEZITE (Gen. xv. 19.) An ancient tribe of unknown origin, inhabiting the land promised to Abraham, east of Palestine.

KE'NITE (*smith*). A tribe much mentioned, but whose origin is not recorded. They may have been a branch of Midian, for Jethro is a Kenite, and lived in Midian when first known by Moses. The RECHABITES are the most noted of this people. Jael, who killed Sisera, was a Kenite (Judg. iv. 11).

KEN'IZZITES (*hunter*). (Gen. xv. 19). Lost.

KE'RENHAP'PUCH (*paint-horn*). Daughter of Job (Job. xlii. 14). Horn of plenty. See EYES.

AIN KAREM.

KEI'LAH (*fort*). Judah, in the Shefelah (Josh. xv. 41). David rescued it from the Philistines in harvest-time (1 Sam. xxiii. 1). It was then fortified (ver. 7). After the return from Babylon the people of Keilah assisted Nehemiah in rebuilding the walls of Jerusalem (Neh. iii. 17, 18). The tomb of the prophet Habakkuk was said to be here, by Josephus and Jerome. The site is located N. W. of Hebron about ten miles; on a projecting cliff on the right bank of Wady el Feranj, where there is a large ruined castle called *Kilah*.

KEI'LAH, THE GARMITE. Descendant of Caleb (1 Chr. iv. 19).

KELAI'AH (*assembly*). KELITA (Ezr. x. 23).

KEL'ITA (*dwarf*). A Levite who returned with Ezra (Ezr. x. 23). KELAIAH.

KEM'UEL (*assembly of El?*). 1. A son of Nahor (Gen. xxii. 21).—2. Son of Shiptan, appointed by Moses to assist in dividing the land of Canaan (Num. xxxiv. 24).—3. Father of Hashabiah (1 Chr. xxvii. 17).

KE'NAN. CAINAN. Son of Enos (1 Chr. i. 2; Gen. v. 9).

KE'NATH (*possession*). A strong city of Bashan, or rather Argob. Taken by Nobah, who changed its name to Nobah (Num. xxxii. 42). One of 60 cities, all fenced, with high walls, gates, and bars, taken by Jair in Argob (Deut. iii. 3, etc.). Gideon went up by Nobah after Zeba and Zalmunna.

KER'CHIEFS (Ez. xiii. 18, 21). DRESS.

KE'RIOTH (*cities*). (Josh. xv. 25). Judah, south. Kuryetein (*two cities*), 15 miles S. of Hebron. The town from which Judas Iscariot was named.—2. A town in Moab, mentioned with Dibon, Bozrah and others (Jer. xlviii. 24). Now Kureiyeh, six miles east of Busrah, on the west slope of the Hauran. There are many ruined columns; and a cistern having a stone roof supported on a triple row of columns, under which are benches, rising like a theatre. A Greek inscription on one of the benches dates the cistern A. D. 286. The houses had walls four to eight feet thick, of solid basalt, with roofs of slabs of stone reaching across from wall to wall. In Amos ii. 2, Kirioth means the "cities of Moab."

KE'ROS (*weaver's comb*). A Nethinim, who returned with Zerubbabel (Ezr. ii. 44).

KET'TLE (*dud*). A vessel used for sacrifices or cooking (1 Sam. ii. 14).

KETU'RAH (*incense*). Wife of Abraham (Gen. xxv. 1). See ABRAHAM. The sons of Keturah were Zimran, Jokshan, Medan, Midian, Ishbak and Shuah. Keturah herself is lost to history.

KEY (*mafteah*). Keys are sometimes very large in the East, two feet or more long (see page 46). It is a symbol of authority (Is. xxii. 22, etc.).

KEZI'A (*cassia*). Daughter of Job (Job xlii. 14).

KĒ ZIZ, THE VALLEY OF (*destruction*). A city of Benjamin, named Emekkeziz, and mistranslated in Josh. xvii. 21. Near Jericho. Lost.

KIB ROTH HATTA'AVAH (*graves of lust*). Station of the wandering.

KIBZĀ'IM (*two heaps*). In Ephraim (Josh. xxi. 22). JOKMEAM.

KID. Young goat. MILK.

KID'RON (*turbid*). In the original Hebrew it is always called a dry water-course or wady (*nachal*. See RIVER). East of the walls of Jerusalem, at the foot of Olivet (2 Sam. xv. 23; John xviii. 1). Now called the Valley of Jehoshaphat. It is in most places narrow, with steep, naked banks, and only a few strips of cultivable land. The Tyropœon joins it at the Pool of Siloam, and the Hinnom at En Rogel, all three forming what is now called the Wady en Nar (*fire*), leading to Mar Saba and the Dead Sea. The whole valley is filled with tombs and graves. The most ardent desire of every dying Jew (or Mohammedan) of Palestine is to be buried there. Dr. Barclay mentions a fountain in the north end of the valley, flowing in winter several hundred yards, and sinking out of sight, probably running under ground, being covered many feet deep by rubbish, as proved by recent digging through the accumulation, near the temple area (see JERUSALEM), and heard murmuring at En Rogel, and also two miles down the valley, where water was found in midsummer. William of Tyre and Brocardus heard the subterranean waters in their day. Where the path from St. Stephen's Gate crosses the valley there is a bridge, with one arch 17 feet high, near which are the church and tomb of the Virgin and the garden of Gethsemane. Another bridge, on a single arch, crosses near the Absalom tomb. The temple area wall is here 150 feet above the bottom of the valley.

KILN. KIL. Brick.

KI'NAH (*lamentation*). Judah, next to Edom (Josh. xv. 22). Lost.

KIN'DRED. Relatives.

KING (MELECH; Gr. *basileus*). A title applied to men. Sometimes it is used of men who were only leaders or rulers of one city, as the king of Sodom, etc. This form of government seems to be native to the East. The will of one man rather than the union of many. The true king of Israel, as designed by Moses, was God; and that form of government is called a theocracy (Gr. *theos*, god). Moses saw that a visible king would be wanted, and provided for such a state (Deut. xvii. 14-20), The king was to be anointed with oil (1 Sam. x. 1), and was called, therefore, "the Lord's anointed." This was an ancient Egyptian custom. ANOINTING.

KINGDOM OF GOD. The divine kingdom of Jesus the Christ. Matthew only says "kingdom of the heavens" for the state of things to be expected at the coming of the Messiah, as soon as converted sinners become citizens of the heavenly kingdom (Rev. i. 6). For BOOK OF KINGS, see HISTORY.

KING'S DALE (Gen. xiv. 17; 2 Sam. xviii. 18). (SHAVEH, *level place*). The Plain of Rephaim. Absalom's pillar, a name given to a modern structure (of the later Roman age in style), is a mistake, for his pillar was reared up in a plain of broad valley (*Emek*. See PLAIN). See cut of Absalom's Tomb, page 1.

KIR (*a wall*). Where the people of Damascus were carried by the king of Assyria (2 K. xvi. 9). Elam and Kir are mentioned together by Isaiah (xxii. 6). The river Cyrus, flowing from the Caucasus to the Caspian Sea, still bears its ancient name, *Kur*. But it is not yet known where the city or district was located. *Kerend* is offered, and also *Curna*, both cities in Media. Elam (which see) was near the Persian Gulf, and Kir may have been a variant name for Kish, the eastern Ethiopia.

KIR HA'RESH, KIR HAR'ASETH, KIR HAR'E-SETH, KIR HE'RES (*brick fort*) and **KIR MŌ'AB** (2 K. iii. 25; Is. xvi. 7; Jer. xlviii. 31, 36). One of the chief fortified cities of Moab (built of brick —*heres*). When Joram, king of Israel, invaded Moab, Kir was the only city not taken, and this was saved by the sacrifice by the king of Moab of his eldest son, on the wall (2 K. iii. 27). *Kerak* (the modern name) stands on the top of a rocky hill, about 10 miles from the Dead Sea, and 3,000 feet above its level. It was at one time strongly fortified, on the top of a high hill, surrounded on all sides by a deep valley, and again enclosed by mountains higher than the town, from which hights the slingers threw stones into the city, as mentioned in 2 K. iii. 25. The entrances to the ancient city were only two, and tunnelled through the solid rock for a hundred feet, on the north and south. On the western side stands the citadel, a strong building, built by the Crusaders, containing a chapel, on the walls of which are some rude paintings. On clear days Bethlehem and Jerusalem may be seen from here.

MOABITE STONE.

Rev. Mr. Klein (of the Palestine Exploration) in 1868 found a Semitic monument in Moab, on which there is an inscription (translated by Mr. Deutsch, of the British Museum), giving an account of many cities named in the Bible, which king Mesha built, among which is *Karkha* (Kerak). This is the oldest monument in the Phœnician language that is known. It adds to our knowledge of that day. In 2 K. i. 1, is a mention of a rebellion of Moab, which was put down by Israel and Judah. This stone gives particulars, not in the Bible, of the acts of the king of Moab; his conquest of cities; rebuilding others; his religious wars; and that he believed himself divinely guided by the god Chemosh.

Almost the whole of the Greek alphabet is found on this stone, such as is in use now, and identical with the Phœnician, even including those letters which were supposed to have been added during the Trojan war; and also the Greek letter upsilon, which was supposed to have been added later. The most ancient letters are here shown to be the most simple—mere outlines.

KIR'IAH (*town*). Kerioth, Kartah, Kartan,

Kiriathaim (Ez. xxv. 9). In Moab. One of the "glories of the country," named among the denunciations of Jeremiah (xlviii. 1. 23).

KIR'JATH (Josh. xviii. 28). In Benjamin. Lost.—2. KIRJATHAIM, KIRIATHAIM (*double city*). Reuben, a little south of Heshbon (Num. xxxii. 37). It was a large Christian village in the time of Eusebius and Jerome. *Kureiyat* is a ruin near *Jebel Attarus*, south of Wady Zurka Main, south of which is a level plateau called *el Koura* (*plain*), which may be the Plain of Moab. It is one of the oldest of Bible cities (Gen. xiv. 5). It was on the "Plain" (shaveh) Kiriathaim that the Emims were smitten by the eastern kings who plundered Sodom.—3. A town of Naphtali (1 Chr. vi. 76). Kartan.—4. KIRJATH ARBA. Hebron. It is supposed that Hebron was the ancient name, the Canaanites calling it Kirjath Arba on their taking possession, when the Israelites restored the ancient name. A tradition says the city was called Arba, or *four*, because Adam, Abraham, Isaac, and Jacob were buried there. But Joshua says *Arba* was a great *man* (xiv. 15).—5. KIRJATH BAAL (*Baal's city*). (Josh. xv. 60, xviii. 14). Kirjath Jearim.—6. KIRJATH HUZOTH. Where Balaam was conducted by Balak to offer sacrifice (Num. xxii. 39). Kureiyat.—7. KIRJATH JEARIM (*city of forests*), (Josh. ix. 17). One of the 4 cities of the Gibeonites, who tricked Joshua. Also Kirjath Arim, peopled after after the Captivity (Ezr. ii. 25). A boundary (Josh. xv. 9). The ark remained here 20 years after it was brought from Bethshemesh, until it was removed by David to Jerusalem (1 Sam. vii.). Now *Kuryet el Enab* (*city of grapes*).

The Danites pitched "behind Kirjath Jearim" on the eve of their expedition to Laish, and the name Mahaneh Dan (camp of Dan) remained for a long time after they left (Judg. viii. 12). EMMAUS, where Jesus appeared after his resurrection (Mark xvi. 12; Luke xxiv. 13-35), is located here by recent scholars. The exploits of a noted robber sheikh who lived here has given it the name of Abu Gosh (father of lies) village. There are a few houses around an old convent (Minorite), and a Latin church, one of the most solidly built in Palestine.—8. KIRJATH SANNAH (*city of palms*), (Josh. xv. 49). KIRJATH SEPHER (*city of the book*). Judah. Called also Debir.

KNIVES.

KISH (*a bow?* see ARMS, i. 3). Father of Saul 2 (1 Sam. x. 21).—2. Son of Jehiel (1 Chr. viii. 30; ix. 35).—3. Great-grandfather of Mordecai (Esth. ii. 5).—4. Levite (1 Chr. xxiii. 21).

KISH'I (KUSHAIAH). A Merarite, ancestor of Ethan (1 Chr. vi. 44). KISH 4.

KISH'ION (*hard*). Issachar, in Estraëlon (Josh. xix. 20). Kedesh (1 Chr. vi. 72).

KISH'ON, THE RIVER (Judg. iv. 7). Drains Esdraelon and neighboring hills, being fed by the large spring of water at Daberath (*Deburieh*) at the N. W. foot of Mt. Tabor, and by another large fountain at En Gannim (*Jenin*), which is its most remote source; and also by the waters of Megiddo (a spring at *Leijun*), running along the north base of Carmel. After receiving many small tributaries from the hills on each side, it enters the plain of Acre by the narrow pass between Harosheth (*Tell Harothith*) and Carmel, just below which it receives Wady Malik, with the drainage from the plain of Zebulon (*Battauf*), as far as Mt. Kurn Hattin, Araba, and Jabel Kaukab, near Cana. Below this point it is fed by the very copious fountains (*Saadiyeh*) three miles S. E. of Hepha (*Caiffa*), and others from under Carmel (Shaw), when it empties into the Bay of Acre near Caiffa, the last few miles only being a river with water the year round, flowing between banks of loamy soil fifteen feet high, with a stream 50 to 75 feet across. The whole system of tributaries above Harosheth are dry wadys through the summer or dry season. There are many historical associations belonging to this river, referred to in other places. See Armageddon. (*Land and Book*, c. xxix).

KI SON. KISH'ON (Ps. lxxxiii. 9).

KISS (NASHAK; Gr. *phileo*). The kiss is used to denote: 1. on the lips, affection; 2. on the cheek, respect, or salutation; 3. a symbol of charity in the early Church (Rom. xvi. 6; 1 Cor. xvi. 20; 2 Cor. xiii. 12, etc.); 4. on the beard, respect to age or authority; 5. on the forehead, condescension; 6. on the back, or palm, of the hand, submission; as also to kiss the feet; 7. on the ground near, a mark of respect; 8. to kiss the hand to an idol, worship (1 K. xix. 18; Hos. xiii. 2).

KITE (AYAH, vulture, in Job xxviii. 7). See page 124 for cut. A bird of prey (Lev. xi. 14; Deut. xiv. 13). The word AYAH was probably the name of the species, and is well translated kite.

KITH'LISH (Josh. xv. 40). Judah, in the Shefelah, near Eglon. Lost.

KIT'RON (Judg. i. 30). The Canaanites were not driven out, but remained as tributaries. Lost.

KIT'TIM (Gen. x. 4; 1 Chr. i. 7). CHITTIM.

KNIFE (CHEREB), (Josh. v. 2), sword; MAAK'ELETH (Judg. xix. 29) table-knife; MACHALAPHIM (Ezr. i. 9) slaughter-knives; SAKKIN, knife (Prov. xxiii. 2). The most ancient historians mention knives of stone and of iron. The Easterns make little use of the knife at the table. Jeremiah speaks of a pen-knife (xxxvi. 23). The razor was used to shave the head of the Nazarite (Num. vi. 5, etc.), and the bodies of priests in Egypt (Herodotus ii. 36).

KNOP (CAPTOR, crown, Ex. xxv. 31). Imitation of the blossom of an almond tree; and a small gourd or cucumber (PEKAIM, cucumbers, in 1 K. vi. 18; vii. 24). See FRINGE, on page 109. Fringes, tassels and borders were symbolical in the dress of the high priest and of the Jews generally.

KO'A (Ez. xxiii. 23). Lost.

KO HATH (*assembly*). Son of Levi (Gen. xlvi. 11). KLHATH. He died aged 133 (Ex. vi. 18). Moses and Aaron were of his line. The posterity of Kohath in the Exodus numbered 8600 males, 2750 being over 30. They (except Aaron and his sons) bore the ark and its furniture (Num. iii. 31).

KO HATHITES. Descendants of KOHATH (Num. iii. 27, 30).

KOLI'AH (*voice of Jah*). 1. A Benjamite (Neh. xi. 7).—2. Father of Ahab (Jer. xxix. 21).

KOPH (*back of the head*), (Ps. cxix.). WRITING.

KO'RAH (*bald*). 1. Son of Esau (Gen. xxxvi. 5, 14, 18), one of the "dukes" of Edom.—2. Another duke, son of Esau (xxxvi. 16).—3. Son of Hebron (1 Chr. ii. 43).—4. Son of Izhar, a Levite, and ringleader of a rebellion against Moses and Aaron; the only person of note in it. His sons were not guilty, and escaped his doom. Samuel the prophet

was of this family (1 Chr. vi. 22.). Ten psalms bear their names in the titles, as choristers in the temple.

KŌ'RAHITE (1 Chr. ix. 19, 31). Kōr'hite, or Kō'rathite, descendant of Korah.

KO'RAHITES, THE. Descendants of Korah 4 (Num. xxvi. 58). KORAHITE.

KŌ'RE (*partridge*). 1. A Korahite, ancestor of Shallum (1 Chr. ix. 19, xxvi. 1).—2. Son of Imnah, an overseer of offerings (2 Chr. xxxi. 14).—3. (1. Chr. xxvi. 19). "Sons of Kore."

KOR'HITES, THE. Descendants of Korah 4 (Ex. vi. 24). KORAHITE.

KOZ (*thorn*). ACCOZ, COZ, HAKKOZ (Ezr. ii. 61).

KUSHAI'AH (*rainbow*). KISH, father of Ethan (1 Chr. xv. 17).

L

LA'ADAH (*order*). Son of Shelah (1 Chr. iv. 21).

LA'ADAN (*put in order*). 1. Ancestor of Joshua (1 Chr. vii. 26).—2. Son of Gershon; Libni (xxiii. 7, 9; xxxi. 21).

LA'BAN (*white*). (Deut. i. 1). Libnah? (Num. xxxiii. 20). Ptolemy mentions an *Auara*; the Peutinger tables a *Hauarra*; and the Arabs have a place called *Ain Howara*—all of which mean *white*, and may refer to the same locality.

LA'BAN (*white*). Son of Bethuel, brother of Rebekah, father of Leah and Rachel.

LAB'ANA. LEBANA (1 Esd. v. 29).

LACE (*thread, cord*), (Ex. xxviii. 28, 37).

LACEDEMO'NIANS. Inhabitants of Sparta (1 Macc. xii. 2, 5, 6, 20, 21).

way to Egypt, and required all his power (2 Chr. xxxii. 9). This siege has been found pictured on one of the chambers of the palace at Koyunjik, under the name Lakhisha.

The inscription sculptured with the picture is translated: "Sennacherib, the mighty king, king of the country of Assyria, sitting on the throne of judgment before the city of Lakhisha. I give permission for its slaughter." There are several pictures, one of which gives a plan of a circular city with double walls and many towers. The expedition moved on to Egypt, and on its return Lachish was a second time besieged, at the same time that the great host of the Assyrians were slain by a miracle on the plain north of Jerusalem (Is. xxxvii. 36). It was rebuilt, and suffered a siege by Nebuchadnezzar (Jer. xxxiv. 1-7). The Jews occupied it after the return from Babylon.

LACU'NUS. Son of Addi (1 Esd. ix. 31). CHEBAL.

LADDER OF TYRE. A high mountain, 10 ms. north of Acre, which stands out into the deep sea without a beach, and is only passed by a zigzag road cut in its face. The cape 6 ms. further north is passed by a similar way, which was built by Alexander. Simon was made governor of the country from the Ladder of Tyre to the borders of Egypt (1 Macc. xi. 59). Now called *Ras en Nakhura* (the excavated cape), and there is a small village of the same name on the hight.

LA'EL (*of God*). Father of Eliasaph (Num. iii. 24).

LA'HAD (*oppression*). Son of Jahath (1 Chr. iv. 2).

LAHA'IROI, THE WELL (*the well where God was seen by one who still lives*). Where Hagar took refuge from her imperious mistress, in the desert, between Kadesh and Bered, in the way to Shur (Gen. xvi. 14). It was afterward a favorite camping-ground of Isaac (xxiv. 62; xxv. 11).

SIEGE OF LACHISH.

LA'CHISH (*obstinate*). An ancient royal Amorite city (Josh. x. 3), whose king, Japhia, joined the alliance with Adonizedec, king of Jerusalem, to smite Gibeon for making a treaty with Joshua. The allied kings were defeated at Beth-horon, and were hanged at Makkedah (v. 26). The city was taken on the second day. Dr. Robinson found the site on a rocky hill, having but few ruins, 11 miles S. W. of *Beit Jibrin*, only two miles W. of Egion. Lachish was fortified by Rehoboam, after the separation of the kingdom of Israel (2 Chr. xi. 9). Amaziah fled to it as a secure place (2 K. xiv. 19). It is supposed that the city was not taken, because it is said, in 2 Kings xix. 8, that "Sennacherib had departed from Lachish," and, in 2 Chr. xxxii. 1, that he had "thought to win" the fenced cities of Judah. It was taken by Sennacherib when on his

LAH'MAM (*place of contest*). In the Shefelah (Josh. xv. 40). Lahmas?

LAH'MI (*Bethlehemite*). Brother of Goliath (1 Chr. xx. 5).

LA'ISH (*strong, lion*). An ancient Phœnician city, occupied by a colony of Sidonians, in the valley between Hermon and Lebanon, at one of the great fountains of the Jordan. Its ancient name was *Leshem* (Josh. xix. 47), and it was an ancient sanctuary.

The LAISH of Isaiah x. 30 was near Jerusalem. Another (Laisa) is mentioned, where Judas encamped, in 1 Macc. ix. 5.

LA'ISH. Father of Phaltiel (1 Sam. xxv. 44).

LA'KUM (*to stop up a way*). In Naphtali (Josh. xix. 33). Perhaps near the bridge of the "Daughters of Jacob."

LAMB (Chal. *Immer*), Heb. 1. KEBES, (Ez. vi. 9), a male, and KIBSAH, female of the first year.—2. TALEH (1 Sam. vii. 9), the young of any animal, especially a sucking lamb.—3. KAR (2 K. iii. 4), a fat ram.—4. TSON (Ex. xii. 26), flock of lambs.—5. SEH (ib. 3), the individuals of the flock.—6. Greek *Amnos* (John i. 29, 36; Acts viii. 32; 1 Pet. i. 19), a lamb, and, figuratively, of Christ as the lamb for sacrifice.—7. Gr. *Aren* (Luke x. 3), *Arnion*, little lamb. See PASSOVER.

LA'MECH (*powerful*). 1. A descendant of Cain (Gen. iv. 18, 24). He is the only one except Enoch whose history is sketched with a few particulars, before the flood, and is the first recorded polygamist, having two wives, Adah and Zillah. His daughter was Naamah. His sons were Jabal, Jubal, and Tubal Cain. Josephus says he had 77 sons. The earliest recorded poem in the Bible is by him, supposed to have been an exultation over the invention of the sword.—2. Father of Noah (Gen. v. 29).

LA'MED (*ox-goad*). Twelfth letter of the Hebrew alphabet (Ps. cxix.). WRITING.

LAMENTATIONS OF JEREMIAH, THE. See HISTORY OF THE BOOKS.

EARTHEN LAMP. NO. 6.

LAMP. NER, *light*, (Ex. xxv. 37; 1 K. vii. 49, etc.). The lamp used in the tabernacle, and the ten in the temple. The ancient lamps were rude in design, small, and were supplied with olive oil, and trimmed with a wick of flax. Many specimens have been found lately in Palestine, among ancient ruins. See cuts on pages 6, 14, 15, 40, etc.

There are several other names for lamp. 1. IYER; 2. LAPPID, *torch* (Judg. vii. 16, 20); 3. Gr. *lampas, a light* (Acts xx. 8). The lamp was carried in marriage processions (Matt. xxv.), and the Mohammedans use very ornamental and showy patterns in their ceremonies. The wick now used is generally of cotton twisted around a straw. Gideon's lamps might have been of similar make to the modern paper or cloth lanterns. The cloth is waxed, and stretched over a wire frame or rings, and is contrived so as to close up in a small space when not in use. The small size of the lamp made it necessary to carry a little jug of oil, or to have the lamp filled if a whole evening was passed away from home. The lantern is a protection against the wild dogs of the streets, who are sure to attack any one in the dark.

LAN'CET (1 K. xviii. 28). ARMS.

LAN'TERN (*light*), (John xviii. 3).

LAODICE'A (Rev. i. 11, iii. 14; Col. iv. 13, 15). There were four of the same name: 1. In Phrygia, near Hierapolis;—2. In the east of Phrygia; —3. On the coast of Syria, the port of Aleppo; —4. East of Lebanon. The first is the only one mentioned in Scripture, as one of the SEVEN CHURCHES (which see).

LAODICE'A. An ancient city on the Lycus, in the valley of the Meander, forty miles east of Ephesus. Its site was on seven hills, which were drained by two brooks, the Asopus and Caprus. The ruins are of a stadium, in very complete preservation, three theatres (one of which was 450 feet in diameter), bridges, aqueducts, and a gymnasium, which testify to its ancient wealth and importance. Its original name was Diospolis, (the city of Jupiter), which was changed to Rhoas, under which title it became the largest city in Phrygia (Pliny). Antiochus II gave it the name of his wife, Laodike.

It became the seat of an archbishop, and in its cathedral church were gathered several councils; in one of which, a system of supplying the villages or small societies in the interior with church services by itinerating presbyters, was adopted (somewhat similar to the Methodist plan now in use), under the direction of the bishop of Laodicea. Here was also adopted a rule "that Christians should not Judaize by resting on the seventh day, but to work on it as usual, and rest on the Lord's day as far as possible, like Christians."

The city was utterly destroyed A. D. 1230, since when it has lain in shapeless ruins, only visited for its marble and other materials.

The aqueduct (which supplied the city, and is now almost perfect), which conveyed water *down* one hill, across the plain, and *up* another, in *stone pipes*, proves the Romans to have been acquainted with the hydrostatic law of water finding its level. The stone pipes have a diameter of two feet, and are fitted into each other at the ends, and the calcareous deposit from the water has incrusted them, forming almost a continuous pipe without a visible joint.

The seats in the stadium have letters and numbers, their owner's or the keeper's marks.

A recent visitor found a number of workmen sawing up the richly sculptured entablature of the ancient theatre, having been busy there for six years, cutting up the marble. Near them was a colossal statue, sawn into several pieces. In this manner, have disappeared, during the past twenty years, two agate pillars, 18 inches in diameter; a great number of composite richly sculptured columns, adorned with busts and heads in relief, and vases with wreaths of leaves and fruits, and statues and busts and architectural ornaments without number.

Colossæ is about ten miles east from Laodicea, near the village of Chonas, but is without any interesting ruins, although it was an important city in the time of the expedition of Xerxes. Hierapolis (which see in the Geography) has lately afforded a fine proof of the truth of an account of Strabo (xiii. iv. 14), who speaks of a deadly vapor (carbonic acid gas?) which killed any animal that approached the place. The experiment was tried by Svoboda recently on two fowls, and resulted fatally to both in a few seconds.

LAODICE'ANS. People of Laodicea (Col. iv. 16; Rev. iii. 14).

LAP'IDOTH (*torches*). Husband of Deborah (Judg. iv. 4).

LAP'WING (Lev. xi. 19). An unclean bird. Its feathers are long and very beautiful. The hoopoe (Solomon's bird with the golden crown) is supposed by some to be the one. The Sadducees supposed it was the common hen (DUKIFATH), and others that it was the cock of the woods. There are many legends about the hoopoe, one of which is that a vast flock flew over King Solomon's head, while on a desert journey, shadowing him from the sun, in reward for which he gave them a crown of golden feathers.

LASÆ'A (Acts xxvii. 8). City in Crete, identified in 1856 by Rev. G. Brown, 5 miles inland from Fair Havens. A Venetian MS. of the 16th century describes Lapsea, with a temple in ruins, and other remains in the harbor. This city is one proof of the accuracy of Luke's account, even in minute details. 16 miles east of Gortyna.

LA'SHA (*fissure*). Southeast in Palestine, the limit of the country (Gen. x. 19). Callirhoë answers to the text in its position and character. Herod built a residence there; and recently there have been found on the site tiles, pottery and coins. En English? See MACHAERUS.

LAS THENES (*strength*). An officer of nobility (1 Macc. xi. 31, 32; xiii. 4).

LATCH ET. The fastening used to hold the sandal on the foot (Luke iii. 16).

LAT IN (John xix. 20; Luke xxiii. 38). The language of the Romans.

LAT TICE. A window (Judg. v. 28; Prov. vii. 6). 1. ESHNAB, casement in Prov. vii. 6; the word means *to be cool*, and we understand the use of the term for the latticed windows, in which water-jars are set to cool, and air is admitted also to the room. —2. HARAKKIM, *a net-work before a window* (Cant. ii. 9). Orientals are very jealous of observation by neighbors, and screen their windows by carved work, lattices of wood, coarse mats, or open work of bricks.—3. SEBAKAH, *net-work;* the same word is used for a net in Job xviii. 8, and also for the ornamental net-work on the columns before Solomon's Temple (1 K. vii. 18).

term law is used for the Old Testament as a whole in John x. 34, etc.

The Law of Moses depended on the Abrahamic covenant, which concerned the temporal promises, which were conditional on the keeping of the spiritual laws. Its principles were universal, but it had special rules for the Jews also. There were several kinds of laws: 1. Civil; 2. Criminal; 3. Judicial; 4. Constitutional; 5. Ecclesiastical; and 6. Ceremonial.

1. CIVIL.—Of the authority of a father over his family; of husband and wife (the wife was *nothing* without the husband, not even recognized as a person (Num. xxx. 6-15). The degrees of relation in the matter of marriage; of divorce; of slave-wives; slander against a wife; the vicious before marriage to be put to death; the Levirate marriage; master and slave; master's power limited; no one could kill a slave or maim one; the slave free at the year of jubilee, except foreign slaves, who were perpetual; fugitive slaves from foreign nations were not given up; protection and kindness to foreigners (strangers) was a sacred duty, as they had very few rights under the law.

THE LAWS OF LAND AND PROPERTY.—All land was God's alone, and men were only tenants (Lev.

LAODICEA.

LAUGH (Job ix. 23; 2 K. xix. 21; Ps. lxxx. 6), LAAG; TASHAK in Gen. xvii. 17, to mock; SACHAK (Ps. ii. 4), to play, to make sport; SEROK, laughter in several passages, and derision in others; Gr. *Gelos;* in James iv. 9, laughter; *katagelao,* to laugh to scorn (Matt. ix. 24, etc.).

LAVER (KIYOR). A vessel containing water for washing hands and feet before offering sacrifice, and standing between the altar and the tabernacle (Ex. xxx. 19).

The form is not given, and can only be supposed to have been round, and to have had a movable stand, perhaps on wheels for convenience in moving. In the temple, besides the SEA, there were ten lavers, all of brass, on bases (1 K. vii. 27, 39), 5 on the north and 5 on the south side. They contained each 160 gallons of water used for washing the sacrifices for burnt-offerings (2 Chr. iv. 6). They are particularly described in Josephus viii. 3, § 6.

LAW (TORAH). The Mosaic Law. A guide in the way of moral conduct. Greek *nomos.* The

xxv. 23); all sold land returned to the original owner at the jubilee; houses were sold to be redeemed in a year, or not at all; the Levitical houses redeemable at all times; lands or houses sanctified were redeemable at prices according to the time before the jubilee; if devoted by the owner, to sacred purposes, and not redeemed at the jubilee, then they were a perpetual property of the priests. INHERITANCE descended to 1. sons, 2. daughters, 3. brothers, 4. uncles on father's side, 5. on mother's side, 6. other relatives.

LAW OF DEBT.—All debts between Israelites to be released on the year of jubilee; interest for loans of money not to be taken; pledges not to be insolently exacted (Deut. xxiv. 19, 20).

TAXATION.—The poll-tax for the support of the temple service was ½ shekel each year; spoil taken in war was halved, and 1-500 of one, and 1-50 of the other paid to the temple treasury; tithes of all farm produce 1-10; a second tithe for feasts and charity, 1-60 of first fruits of corn, wine, and oil;

firstlings of clean beasts; the redemption money for man 5 shekels, and for unclean beasts ½ shekel, to be given to the priests.

POOR.—They had a right to the gleaning of the fields; and to eat fruit, or grapes, etc., on the spot, but not to carry away; wages to be paid day by day; the priests reckoned as poor; the price of all devoted things was fixed for redemption; for a man 50 shekels, a woman 30, a boy 20, a girl 10.

2. CRIMINAL.—Offenses against God: Idolatry; witchcraft and false prophesy; divination; magic; blasphemy; Sabbath breaking (punishment in all these cases, death by stoning).

Offenses against man: Cursing, smiting, or disobedience to parents and to the judges (penalty, death by stoning); murder to be punished without reprieve, or satisfaction in money; death by negligence, or of a slave by whipping; accidental murder or killing must be avenged by the next of kin, but could be avoided by fleeing to one of the Cities of Refuge; where the murderer was not known the elders of the nearest city must disavow and sacrifice·retaliation and damages for assault.

SECTION OF PYRAMID.

ADULTERY was to be punished by death to both offenders; rape of a married woman, of betrothed maid, by death to the offender; seduction of a young woman to be compensated by marriage, with a dowry of 50 shekels, without privilege of divorce; or, if she choose, a full dowry without marriage; unlawful marriages punished in various ways (Lev. xx.).

Theft, double or four-fold retribution; a nightrobber could be killed; trespass or injury to things lent to be made good; perversion of justice strictly forbidden; kidnapping punished with death; false-witness, slander, by law of retaliation.

JUDICIAL LAWS. Judges were appointed, and were usually Levites; their sentence was final, and it was a capital offense to reject their judgment; two witnesses were required in capital matters; whipping must be limited so as not to leave marks. The KING set aside by his laws much of the law of Moses, and its scheme of officers, even deposing the high-priest (1 Sam. xxii. 17). 70 elders were appointed by the king with a religious sanction, forming the Sanhedrin (see SANHEDRIN), of priests, scribes, and elders (2 Chr. xix. 8-11). The king's power was limited by the law, and he was directly forbidden to be despotic (Deut. xvii. 14-20). He could tax 1-10; compel service; declare war.

The chiefs of each tribe or family acted for that tribe or family (Josh. xi. 15); and in some reigns controlled both the king and the priests (Jer. xxvi. 10).

The king's revenue was raised from the tenth, from confiscation of criminal's land (1 K. xxi. 15); the bound service of foreigners; his flocks and herds; tributes from foreign kings; commerce (in Solomon's time, 1 K. x. 22).

RELIGIOUS. There were laws for sacrifices, on many occasions; as the various offerings on the altar (where the fire must never be left to go out), for priests, women, lepers, the Day of Atonement and Festivals.

THE LAW OF HOLINESS (which resulted from the union with God through sacrifice), was shown in the dedication of the first-born, and the offering of all first-fruits (Ex. xiii. 2, etc.; Deut. xxvi.); the distinction of clean and unclean food; the rules for purification; against maiming; unnatural marriages; and the laws regulating the orders of priests, holy places and things, and also the times of holding services; as the Sabbath, the Sabbatical year (7th), the year of Jubilee; passover; feast of weeks (Pentecost); of tabernacles; of trumpets; and Day of Atonement.

The law is purely theocratic—derived from God, and not from man, and depended on the faith of the nation, the belief in God as the head of the Jewish people.

LAW YER (Gr. *nomikos*). Scribe was the official title, and lawyer meant one learned in the law (Matt. xxii. 35; Luke x. 25; Tit. iii. 13).

LAZ'ARUS (ancient ELEAZAR, *God is his helper*). 1. Lazarus of Bethany, brother of Martha and Mary (John xi. 1).—2. Lazarus in the parable of the rich man and Lazarus (Luke xvi. 19-31). This is the only instance of a proper name in any of the parables.

It is supposed that "Simon the leper" was the father of Lazarus and the two sisters Martha and Mary, and that when the leprosy had made Simon an outcast, his children managed the house, and the daughters especially, since it is they who gave the feast when Jesus was there (Luke x. 38; John xii. 2), and was perfumed with the costly spikenard by Mary. The family were moderately wealthy, as appears in their having a house that could accommodate a large party, in their giving a feast, having so expensive a perfume (300 pence, that is the price of 300 days wages), and a family tomb cut in the rock. Simon may have been a Pharisee, as would seem from their friendly acquaintance with the Nicodemus branch of that sect in Jerusalem, and the ready use of their creed by Martha (John xi. 24). Simon may have been sent to Galilee with others to watch Jesus as a teacher of a new sect in the church, and partly through reverence, and also in the line of his duty he took him to his house. His disease might have been developed afterwards, and he have been removed, either by death or by the seclusion required by the law for a leper, when his daughters continued the hospitality their father began. This explains why Lazarus was a young man of some importance in his circle, had many acquaintances and friends, and perhaps held the position of an *archôn* (ruler in the village). His description agrees with this in its details, the salutation of Jesus as the "Good Master" (Mark x. 17), his respectful attitude, and his quick and earnest inquiry after the most important truth. The answer of Jesus to him was the same as that to his sister (to him "One thing thou lackest;" to her "One thing is needful"). Jesus is said by Mark to have loved him, which term is only applied to John and the sisters of Lazarus (John xi. 5). The craving for truth and holiness in Lazarus was that which Jesus loved. Martha was apparently occupied and contented with outward activity, and the teachings of the Pharisees, not suspecting the great truth that eternal life is even now present to the faithful. Lazarus hesitates between his old faith which he had "kept from his youth up" and the new light, and in this condition he is struck down by the fever, which does its work quickly in the East.

The words and conduct of Jesus show the deep concern of the friend and the restoration especially

the affectionate work of the Great Teacher, who brought truth home to many hearts by one lesson.

The sisters believed that he would have healed him of his sickness if he had been there at the time (John xi. 21), and their want of faith even after the loss of their brother brings tears of sympathy mingled with indignation to his eyes. The raising of Lazarus cannot be told in more fitting words than are used by John (xi.), who writes as an eye witness, and one who saw also with a spiritual eye. A tradition states that the first question Lazarus asked after being raised was whether he should die again, and when told he must go the way of all men, it touched him with a deep sadness, and he never smiled again. What he saw during his four days' sleep was never made known, nor whether he was even conscious.

Lazarus was naturally made the subject of the spite of the Scribes and Pharisees for his part in the seeming assistance that he gave to Jesus, whose works were denounced by them as imposture and the work of the devil, or Beelzebub (Matt. ix. 34, x. 25; Mark iii. 22, etc.).

There is an explanation of the remark of Judas at the feast which is, that he, with others, had expected at this feast a distribution of large sums to the poor, and therefore the perfume used on one of themselves was "waste" because it lessened the amount expected to be distributed.

Nothing is recorded of Lazarus after the feast.

The whole story of Lazarus, so full of beauty and simplicity, sympathy and truthfulness, is above criticism, and the work of a man who, in his old age and ripe faith was a witness in this account that Jesus was "the resurrection and the life."

LEAD (OPHRETH; Gr. *molibdos*). Was known very early to the ancient Hebrews, being found in Sinai and Egypt (Ez. xxvii. 13). It was used for weights (Ex. xv. 10; Eccles. xxii. 14). Oxide of lead was used to glaze pottery then as now.

LEAF (ALEH, *to grow up*; TEREF, *to pluck off*; ZELAIM, *two-leaved doors*), (DELETH). Leaves of a book or roll.

LE'AH (*wearied*). Daughter of Laban, 1st wife of Jacob, mother of Reuben, Simeon, Levi, Judah, Issachar, Zebulon, Dinah. She had but little share of her husband's love, and she suffered the pain of witnessing Dinah's dishonor at Shechem, with the terrible retribution that followed. She lived longer than Rachel, and died in the Negeb, and was buried in the cave of Machpelah.

LEAS'ING (*falsehood*), (Ps. iv. 2; v. 6). Lies, in Ps. xl. 4; lviii. 3.

LEATH'ER (2 K. i. 8; Matt. iii. 4). There are very few notices of leather, unless the word skin means leather in use, as in Lev. xi. 32; xiii. 48; Num. xxxi. 20, etc. TANNER.

LEAVEN (SEOR, *fermentation*). There was also besides fermented (KAMEZ), sharpened (MAZZOTH) bread, unleavened (Ex. xii. 7). Leaven was strictly forbidden in all sacrifices, as typical of corruption or decay. Jesus uses leaven as a figure in describing the peculiar corruption of ideas of the Scribes and Pharisees. The pagans also avoided it in their offerings to their gods. It is also used as a figure for the gospel for its secretly penetrating and diffusive power (1 Cor. v. 6).

LEB'ANA (*white*). A Nethinim, who returned with Zerubbabel (Neh. vii. 48).

LEB'ANAH. LEBANA (Ez. ii. 45).

LEBANON (*white*). The white mountain of Palestine, on the north of the country given to the Israelites (Deut. i. 7; xi. 24; Josh. i. 4). There are two ranges, Lebanon on the west, and Anti-Lebanon on the east, almost parallel, extending from near Tyre to Hamath, about 110 miles. See GEOLOGY and HERMON.

The valley of Lebanon is alluded to in the description of the extent of the land taken by Joshua (xi. 17). It is 5 to 8 miles wide, the whole length of the Lebanon, and watered by the two rivers Leontes and Orontes. The original name was Bukaa (*the valley*), which was changed to Cœlo-Syria (*hollow Syria*), by the Romans, and is now restored by the Arabs. Lebanon toward the sun-rising, was the name for Anti-Lebanon in Joshua xiii. 5. (The best description is in *Porter's Damascus*).

Lebanon, from the Leontes to the Eleutherus, has an average elevation of 6,000 to 8,000 feet, with two higher groups of peaks—Sunnin, 8,500, and Makhmel (Khodib)—10,051 (10,200 by one authority). The view of Lebanon from the sea is exceedingly grand. The wavy top is covered with snow during winter and spring, and the two highest peaks capped with ice on the sultriest days of summer. Cultivation, chiefly by terraces, extends to a height of 6,000 feet. Little fields and gardens are often seen on high places, difficult of approach, where it would seem that the eagles only could have planted the seed. Fig trees and vines cling to steep rocks and narrow ledges; long rows of mulberry trees fringe the winding terraces, and olive orchards fill the ravines. Hundreds of villages and convents cling like swallows' nests to the steep cliffs. The mountain seems to be built of thousands of terrace walls, rising like steps from the sea to the snow. Seen from below, the rocky

ANCIENT STONE. TYRE.

walls alone appear, divided by many deep and wild ravines. Looking down upon the terraces from a height, the vegetation is seen everywhere clothing the slopes with a great variety of tints from fields of grain, gardens of vegetables, vineyards, and different fruit and forest trees. One of the most striking and beautiful scenes in the world is from the upper slopes of Lebanon, where far away, over and beyond some deep, dark glen, clothed with dense foliage, the broad and bright Mediterranean reposes under a cloudless sky. The beauties of Lebanon were noticed by the poets and prophets of Israel (Cant. iv. 11; Hosea xiv. 5, 6, 7). The coolness of its snows and waters was appreciated by Jeremiah in contrast to the heats of summer in the lower lands (Jer. xviii. 14). The finest view of Lebanon from the east is at Baalbek, where the snowy crests extend north and south as far as the eye can see. The view from the range of Anti-Lebanon is more grand and extensive, but less picturesque, because more distant.

The glory of Lebanon was its cedar, pine and oak forests, which were used in Solomon's Temple and his other grand edifices, for temples and palaces, in Rome and Assyria, and in ship-building (1 K. vi.; 2 Sam. v. 11; Ezr. iii. 7; Is. xiv. 8; Ez.

xxvii. 4-6; Jos. Wars v. 5, 2; Pliny xiii. 11; Layard 356). There are two groups of cedars now standing as witnesses of past grandeur. One is in a basin formed by the highest summits of Lebanon, which rise in a semi-circle around the head waters of the Kadisha, 6,172 feet above the sea. The other is on the slope of Kenisch, near the new stage-coach road from Beirut to Damascus, from which our sketch was taken. The rivers are not very large nor long, but are among the most famous in the world's history. Beginning at the north, the Eleutheras (*Nahr el Kebir*) rises in the plain of Emesa, flows around the north end of Lebanon, and falls into the sea between Arvad and Tripolis. The *Kadisha* (*sacred river*), now *Nahr Abu Aly*, rises near the cedars under the highest summits of Lebanon, and flows through a gorge of surpassing grandeur, to the sea, at Tripolis. The perpendicular walls of rock at one place are 1000 feet high. The *Nahr Ibrahim*, the classic Adonis (the scene of the romantic story of Venus and Adonis. Adonis being killed by a boar, his blood now annually colors the water of the river, which runs red to the sea). Ezekiel mentions Adonis under the name Tammuz (viii. 14). It rises near the ancient Apheka, where there is a ruined temple of Venus, and falls into the sea near Gebel. The Lycus (*Nahr el Kelb*, Dog river) rises on Sunnin and empties into St. George's Bay, a few miles north of Beirut. At its mouth are the famous sculptured rocks on the side of the pass, where the armies of Assyria, Egypt, Greece, Rome and France have left records of their deeds. Pliny mentions the Magoras, which is probably the *Nahr Beirut*. The Tamyras or Damuras of Strabo rises near Deir el Kamar, the modern capital of Lebanon, and reaches the sea about ten miles south of Beirut.

The Bostrenus (*Nahr el Awaly*) is a small stream, 6 miles further south.

The Leontes (see SYRIA), in the lower part, rushes through a wild chasm, the banks of which are a thousand feet or more high, almost perpendicular, and are spanned at one place by a natural bridge 60 feet long and 100 feet above the stream. All of these are on the western slope; and there are none on the eastern, except those in the valley of Lebanon, the Orontes and the Leontes. The rivers of Anti-Lebanon are the Abana, *Barada* (the golden-flowing stream), which rises in the beautiful little plain of Zebedany, flows along the western side of the ridge, and then down through a wild gorge into the plain of Damascus, where it divides into several channels, and is lost in the

TEMPLE.

marsh and lake east of that city. The Pharpar (*Nahr Awej*) rises high up on the eastern side of Hermon, flows across the Hauran, and is also lost in a marsh and lake south of the former. The Helbon waters the fertile glen of Helbon.

It is supposed that the Maronites in Lebanon are descendants of the ancient Syrians, but there is no direct evidence. The Druses are Arabs. No other country has such a mixture of many races, holding to their ancient religions, more or less idolatrous. There are very few remains of ancient temples on Lebanon, while Hermon is crowded with them. The American Mission has a station at Abeih, a few miles S. E. of Beirut, not far from *Deir el Kamar*. Young men, and also young women, of every class and of every faith, are seeking education for its uses in commerce and benefits in social and private life; and the Syrian college, lately established in Beirut, will complete the work.

LEB'AOTH (*lioness*). Judah in the south (Josh. xv. 32). Given to Simeon out of Judah's lot. Beth Lebaoth (*place of lions*). The place may have been invested by wild beasts, and therefore so named.

LEBBÆ'US (*courageous*), (Matt. x. 3). THADDEUS.

LEBO'NAH (*frankincense*). Three miles west of Shiloh, now *El Lubban*. The village stands on the slope of a hill bordering the wady Lubban, and its houses have a gray and antique appearance. In the cliffs above are caves and sepulchres, witnesses of a former importance (Judg. xxi. 19).

LE'CAH (*journey*), (1 Chr. iv. 21). A town built by Er. Lost.

LEEKS (CHAZIR, *grass*). There are several plants offered in explanation of the 20 allusions in the O. T. to "leeks." The *trigonella* grows in gardens in Egypt, and is eaten in large quantities in the fall, as greens are with us. The seeds are also eaten boiled. Radishes, onions, garlic (and leeks) were supplied to the workmen who built the pyramids. The priests were not permitted to eat any of these, as Plutarch explains.

LEES (SHEMER, *preservation*). Wine was left standing on the lees to give it color and body (Is. xxv. 6). The wine undisturbed was thick, and before it was used it was necessary to strain off the lees.

LE'GION (Matt. xxvi. 53; Luke viii. 30). A portion of the Roman army, about 6,000 infantry.

LEHA'BIM (Gen. x. 13). Mizraim's third son, perhaps the ancestor of the Lubim, allies of the Egyptians, mentioned in the inscriptions on their monuments at Medinet Habu (dated 1250 B. C.); and also of the Libyans. Jeremiah noticed them in the 6th century B. C., and Daniel still later. They are located on the African coast, west of Egypt, as far as and beyond Cyrene. The great Arab tribe, the Beni Ali, now extends from Egypt to the Atlantic, and illustrates the probable extent of the ancient Lubim and their accessions. There has been from the earliest times a constant stream of colonization flowing along the coast of Africa, north of the Great Desert, from the Nile to the Straits of Gibraltar, from different nations and people. The Phœnicians and Greeks drove the Lubim into the desert and the mountains, where they still remain.

LE'HI. The place where Samson slew a thousand men with a jaw-bone (Judg. xv. 9-19). L'ehi is the Hebrew word for *jaw-bone*, but the name of the place was Ramath-lehi (v. 17). It was on the border of Judah and Philistin. The spring of Enhakkore was known in Jerome's time, near Morasthi, the prophet Micah's birth-place, east of Eleutheropolis. Now Lost.

LE'MECH. LAMECH 2 (Gen. v. 25).

LEM'UEL (*devoted*), (Prov. xxxi. 1-9).

LEN'TILES (ADASHIM). A bean-like plant much esteemed in the East as an article of food. There are several kinds (Gen. xxv. 34; Ez. iv. 9). They were used in making bread in times of scarcity. The present Arabic name (ADAS) is the same as the Hebrew. Red pottage is made of the red lentile, and is a very palatable dish, called ADOM in Gen. xxv. 30. The poor in Egypt now use it because it is cheaper than wheat. There is a tradition that Esau sold his birthright at Hebron,

and in memory of **this the Arab monks (dervishes)** distribute daily a **supply of lentile soup to the** poor, and strangers.

LEOPARD (NAMER; *spotted*). Mentioned in 7 passages. The word was compounded into several of towns **as Beth-nimrah, Nimrah, Nimrim** (Leopard-town, **etc.**), (Is. xi. 6; Jer. v. 6, etc.).

Habakkuk compares the Chaldæan horses to the swift leopard (i. 8), and Daniel alludes to the "winged leopard," as **a** type or figure **of** the rapid conquests of Alexander. The hills of Palestine were frequented **by** the leopard in ancient times, as may be inferred from Cant. iv. 8., and **it is now found in** the mountains of Hermon **and** Lebanon, and sometimes in the gorges near Jerusalem, especially the lower Kidron, where it retreats into caves from the heat of the sun.

The Cheetah may be included in this **description,** as it was used by the ancient Egyptians in hunting, and so sculptured on the monuments. Their skins were worn by the priests during **their re**ligious ceremonies, and are so worn by the **modern** dervishes.

LEPER (ZARUA; leprosy, ZARAATH; **Gr.** *lepra, lepros*). Supposed to be the peculiar scourge **of** an offended deity. The white variety was more common (if there is more than one) covering the entire body, or the most of it, and was called **the** leprosy of Moses. This was the "clean" kind. The symptoms were first a swelling, a scab **or bald**ness, and a shiny spot. The hair changed **to a white or** yellowish-white over the swelling. Sometimes raw flesh ("proud flesh") appeared in the sore. It often disappeared after going so far. **If it went** farther it became "unclean." While **disease was** active **and** spreading it was unclean, **but when it** had spread all over the body, and **could go** no farther, the person became clean again. **The** object of the disease seems to have been to create a nameless horror, and dread of contagion. It is **not** known whether it was propagated by contagion. Some passages mean any disease that spreads in the skin (Lev. xiii., xiv.). The modern Elephantiasis (*Barbadoes leg, swelled leg*) is not the leprosy of the Hebrews, although sometimes called "black leprosy." The leprosy of garments and of walls has caused many ingenious explanations. One of walls is that of a fungus growth on the wall producing spots; another of the nitrous efflorescence in red spots.

LE SHEM (*glancing*—the stone *jacinth*). The city Laish (Josh. xix. 47; Rev. xxi. 20).

LE THECH (*pouring*). **A measure for grain** (Hos. iii. 2) WEIGHTS **AND MEASURES.**

LET TUS. HATTUSH (1 Esd. viii. 29).

LETU SHIM. Second son of Dedan (Gen. xxv. 3), who founded a tribe **in Arabia called by** Ptolemy *Allumæoti* (Heb. LEUMMIM). There was **a** city called Luma in Arabia Deserta.

LEUM'MIM (*nations*). Sons of Dedan (Gen. xxv. 3).

LE VI (*to adhere*). Third son of Leah, wife of Jacob. Born in Mesopotamia, B. C. 1750 (Gen. xxix. 34). When Dinah went **out** to see the young **women** of Shechem, as Josephus says, at an annual festival **of** nature-worship, such as that mentioned in Numbers **xxv.** 2, of the people in Moab, she was taken by Shechem as a wife; which was resented as an insult by her brothers, Jacob, Simeon, and Levi, who executed their revenge on the city in a fearful manner (Gen. xxxiv.), destroying the whole city for the error of one man. This is an early instance of a blood feud, which are so common in the East now. Levi plotted with others against Joseph. He went into Egypt with his three sons, Gershon, Kohath, and Merari, and as one of the eldest, was presented to Pharaoh. The descendants of Levi, among whom were Moses and Aaron, were made the ministers of religion and the representatives of the national faith; Jacob prophesied that Levi should be scattered among his brothers, which was fulfilled in the distribution of the tribe among the 48 Levitical cities, which were scattered throughout the whole country. The tribe displaced the earlier priesthood of the first-born as representatives **of** the holiness of the people.

LENTILES.

Their first enumeration gave 22,000, which was nearly equal to the number of the first-born males of all the other tribes, which was 22,263—reckoning from one month old upward. The 273 were redeemed by 5 shekels each, being paid to Aaron. They guarded the ark, and were reckoned separately as the host (of the Lord), and were not counted in the army. Their special duties were the daily sacrifice, and the work about the tabernacle (and Temple), in a certain appointed order (Num. iii., iv., vii.).

A table of the family will show the division of the tribe into the three seperate brances according to their functions (Ex. vi. 16-25).

Father			4 Merari	12 Mushi.
Levi	1	Levi.	7 Amram	13 Moses.
"	2	**GERSHON**.	"	14 Aaron.
"	3	**KOHATH**.	8 Izhar	15 Korah.
"	4	**MERARI**.	"	16 Nepheg.
2 Gershon	5	Libni.	"	17 Zithri.
"	6	Shimei.	10 Uzziel	18 Mishael.
3 Kohath	7	Amram.	"	19 Elzaphar.
"	8	Izhar.	"	20 Zithri.
"	9	Hebron.	14 Aaron	21 Eleazar.
"	10	Uzziel.	"	22 Ithamar.
4 Merari	11	Mahali.		

The Levitical order proceeded from the people, and were **not a** privileged class (Ex. xxviii.); nor was the monarchy designed to be so (Deut. xvii. 14-20), and the people always took part in the coronation of the king and the installation of the high-priest (1 Chr. xxix. 22; 1 Macc. xiv. 35) They did not cultivate land or work at trades, but were to receive a tenth as tithes from the people; a part of which was again divided to the priests (Num. xviii. 21, etc.). Their duty was to instruct the people in the law, and to enable them to spread this knowledge through the land. 48 cities were assigned for residences to them, **6 of** which were cities of refuge, and 13 were for the priests, distributed as follows: KOHATHITES—Priests: Judah and Simeon 9; Benjamin 4. Not priests: Ephraim 4; Dan 4; half Manasseh (west) 2. GERSHONITES—Half Manasseh (east) 2; Issachar 4; Asher 4; Naphtali 3. MERARITES—Zebulon 4; Reuben; Gad 4. Each **of** these cities was to have a suburb

for pasture-ground, for the Levites' cattle (Num. xxxv. 4, 5). Saul massacred the priests at Nob, slew the Gibeonites in their service, and assumed the priestly office; but David reorganized and restored them to their proper service. The CHORAL SERVICE is first mentioned in David's time (1 Chr. xv. 16, and minutely in ch. xxv.). Ethan (1 Chr. 19), one of the singers, was a man of great talent (1 K. iv. 31), and author of the 89th Psalm. The tribe was divided into 12 orders or courses, to serve each one month in rotation. The porters served only a week, but the four chief porters lived in the temple court (1 Chr. ix. 27). Psalm cxxxiv. was a song of the night-watchmen around the temple. The Levites appear as SCRIBES first in 2 Chr. xxxiv. 13, under Josiah. The books of Chronicles were probably compiled by scribes, under the direction of Daniel and Ezra. The age at which service was to be required was originally 30 years, but was reduced to 20 in the tribe of Solomon (1 Chr. xxiii. 24–27). Ezekiel records the idolatry of the Levites in chs. xliv. and xlviii. Psalm cxxxvii. is a mournful and touching record of the Levites' experience in captivity. The priests, Levites, singers, and porters who returned from Babylon were (it seems from Ezr. ii. 36–42) a very small "remnant" (iii. 8). None of the Levites came to the first meeting of preparation for the return (viii. 15). Their service and residence were established as of old, and they joined in the last great song of praise which is recorded (Neh. ix. 6–38). From this time down we have scarcely any account in the Old, and but a very few notices of them in the N. T. (as in Luke x. 32; John i. 19, etc.). They were also dispersed among the Gentiles, with the other tribes (Acts iv. 36).

The religious system established by custom from Abraham's time was changed when Aaron was made the high-priest. The eldest son of each house inherited the priestly office, and performed the duties (Ex. xxiv. 15), and this idea led to that other that Israel was a nation of priests. The great change was made when the entire tribe of Levi was set aside as a priestly caste—an order—as witnesses and guardians of the national worship. The Levites took the place of the first-born in the nation which were numbered, being 22,273, the Levites being 22,000, counting all from a month old upward, and the difference was balanced by paying for each one of the odd number the price of a victim vowed in sacrifice. The tabernacle was a sign of the presence of God among the people, and the Levites were the royal guard of this invisible king. They were not included in the armies, although called the Lord's Host. The Kohathites held the highest offices, guarding and bearing the sacred vessels, including the ark, after these had been covered with the dark-blue cloth by the priests. The Gershonites bore the tent-cloths, curtains, etc., and the Merarites carried the boards, bars, and pillars, using oxen and carts. They purified them selves by a ceremonious washing and sprinkling, and were solemnly consecrated by the people (Num. viii. 10).

CROWN.

LEVI′ATHAN (LIVYATHAN, *an animal wreathed*). The crocodile.

Described as living in the sea (or river), and probably a term including several kinds of monsters of the deep (Ps. civ. 26), and also serpents, Job iii. 8 has *mourning* for leviathan. The practice of enchantment is referred to, which was similar to the modern snake-charming. The description in Job xli. is of the crocodile (so in the version of T. J. Conant), and also in Ps. lxxiv. 14. The Arabic name is *Timsah*, which is given to the lake near Suez, through which the Suez canal runs. The word is translated dragon in Ezekiel (xxx. 3). The leviathan of Is. xxvii. 1 (NACHASH, *serpent*), is used as a type of Egypt, and the crocodile was an emblem of that country. The python (satan) was worshiped by the Egyptians as well as the crocodile.

LEV′IRATE (*husband's brother*). The law by which a younger brother married the widow of the elder brother, and raised children in his name.

LE′VIS. Corruption of "the Levite" in Ezr. x. 13.

LIB′ANUS. LEBANON (1 Esd. iv. 48, v. 55).

LIB′ERTINES (Acts vi. 9). Two explanations of this difficult text are offered: 1. People or disciples from Libertum near Cyrene, Africa.—2. That the Libertines were Jews who had been made prisoners in various wars, reduced to slavery, and afterward liberated, converted, and received into the synagogues with disciples from other cities (Jos. Ant. xviii. 3, § 5).

LIB′NAH (*whiteness*). Station in the desert (Num. xxxiii. 20), between Sinai and Kadesh, near Rissah, perhaps on the Red Sea. Laban Deut. i. 1).—2. A city in the S. W. of Palestine, taken by Joshua next after Makkedah, on the day that "the sun stood still." Sennacherib besieged it (2 K. xix. 8). The great destruction of his army, when 185,000 died in one night (Is. xxxvii. 8–36; 2 K. xix. 8), took place either here (where Rabshakeh, his general, joined him with the force that had camped at Jerusalem), or, according to Josephus and Herodotus, at Pelusium (Ant. x. 1, 4). King Zedekiah's mother was of this place (Jer. lii. 1). A little village called El Menshieh, 5 ms. W. of Eleutheropolis, on the direct road between Makkedah and Eglon, with a few ruins which are evidences of its former strength, marks the site of the ancient Libnah.

LIB′NI (*white*). 1. Son of Gershom (Ex. vi. 17).—2. Son of Mahli (vi. 29).

LIB′NITES, THE. Descendants of LIBNI.

LIB′YA (Acts ii. 10). Libya about Cyrene. LUBIM.

LIB′YANS. People of LIBYA (Jer. xlvi. 9).

LICE (KINNIM). Only in Ex. viii. 16–18, and Ps. cv. 31; both references applying to the plague in Egypt. It is urged by some that the original means gnats and not lice: 1. Because the Greek *knips* (*knipes*) may mean that insect.—2. Plant-lice may have been meant, and an Arabic word (*kaml*, a louse) is referred to in proof, when describing "a thistle black with plant-lice," which is often seen in Egypt. The Egyptians were very scrupulous on the subject of purity, and especially avoided lice and all vermin. The plague of lice was therefore especially obnoxious to them.

LIEUTENANTS. The official title of one who governed the Persian empire (Esth. iii. 12, viii. 9).

LIFE (HAY, or CHAY), living thing (Gen. i. 20); NEPHESH, soul (xii. 5; Ps. xi. 1); mind (xxiii. 8); person (xiv. 21); heart (Ex. xxiii. 9); Greek *bios*, present life (Luke viii. 14); *zoe*, (Matt. vii. 14); *zao*, to live; *pneuma*, spirit, ghost (Rev. xiii. 19); *psuche*, soul (Matt. ii. 20). Life and to live used of the existence of men and animals, and of the enjoyment of what makes life valuable, as happiness (Ps. xvi. 11), and the favor of God (Rom. vi. 4). The true life is immortality in blessedness and glory, and it is believed by some that Jesus taught that such a life was only to be won by a pure life of faith and deeds, believing on him who is the Lord of Life (Matt. xix. 16, 17, 29; Rom. ii. 7, v. 17, vi. 17.

LIGHT (OR; Gr. *phos*). The element light; that which enables us to see. Also, figuratively, the

LI'GURE (LESHEM). PRECIOUS STONES.

LIK'HI (*learned*). Son of Shemida (1 Chr. vii. 19).

LIL'Y (SHU-SHAH, SHOSHAN-NAH; Gr. *Krinon*). There is a great difference of opinion on this question as to what flower was meant by the Hebrews, or by Jesus, which appears in our translation as the lily. Dr. Thomson, (*Land and Book*, i. 394.) says, "The Huleh lily is very large, and the three inner petals meet above and form a gorgeous canopy, such as art never approached, and king never sat under, even in his utmost glory.

LILIES.

Nothing can be in higher contrast than the luxuriant, velvety softness of this lily, and the crabbed, tangled hedge of thorns about it."

The Phœnician architects ornamented the temple with lily work, probably imitating the use of the lotus in Egypt about the columns, and the rim of the brazen sea. These ideas are wrought into visible shape in T. O. Paine's *Temple of Solomon*.

LIME. Limestone is the common rock of Palestine (Deut. xxvii. 2, 4). Lime-kilns are frequent, and where limestone is not easily accessible, as in Asia Minor, the Turks are in the habit of breaking up the marble columns, capitals, handsomely carved entablatures, and even statues of the gods, to be burnt into lime.

LINEN. Heb. 1. SHESH, fine linen (Gen. xli. 42); 2. BAD, linen used for the under clothes of the priests (Ex. xxviii. 42; Lev. vi. 10); 3. BUTS, fine linen, perhaps from the Greek *Bussos* (2 Chr. v. 12), of which the vail of the temple was made (iii. 14), and Mordecai was arrayed (colored purple), and the rich man arrayed in the parable (Luke xvi. 19); 4. ETUN, made of fine flax (Prov. vii. 16); 5. MIKVE, linen yarn (1 K. x. 28); 6. SADIN, linen garments (Judg. xiv. 12); 7. Gr. *sindon*.

Egypt, from the most ancient time, was celebrated for its fine linen, which was used for the sacred garments of the priests, for mummy wrappers, and to write upon. Some specimens may be seen in the Abbot Egyptian Museum, in New York (Hist. So. Building, on 2d Ave., near 9th st.).

LIN'TEL. The upper framework of a door (1 K. vi. 31) correctly "upper door-post" (Ex. xii. 7). Heb. AYIL, post (Ez. xl., xli.). Some say that nyil meant a wall along an entrance way which could be divided into panels; 2. KAFTAR, knop (Amos ix. 1; Zeph. ii. 14); 3. MASHKOF (upper door-post in Ex. xii. 22). Aben Ezra translates mashkof by window, because it means "to look, as from the window over the door upon any one below. See WINDOW.

LI'NUS (*flax*). A disciple at Rome (2 Tim. iv. 21).

The first bishop of Rome after the apostles was Linus (A. D. 68-80), and no lofty pre-eminence was attached to the office at that time, as appears from the simple mention of his name among others. He is said to have written an account of the dispute between Peter and Simon Magus.

LI'ON. There are no lions now in Palestine, but they abound in the deserts, and the swamps of the Euphrates. There are several names of places compounded of the name of lion which show that the animal was known there anciently, as Leboath, Laish (Josh. xv. 32; Judg. xvii. 7).

These seven names for lion, indicating different ages: 1. GUR, or GOR, a cub (Gen. xlix. 9); 2. KEFIR, a young lion (Judg. xiv. 5); 3. ARI, ARYEH, full grown lion (Gen. xlix. 9); 4. SHAKHAL, (*the roarer*) large, strong lion (Job iv. 10); 5. SHAKHAZ, in full vigor (xviii. 8); 6. LABI, or LEBBIYA, an old lion (Gen. xlix. 9), (Coptic, *labui*, lioness); 7. LAISH, old, decrepit, feeble (Job iv. 11).

The lion of Palestine was probably the African, which was shorter and rounder, and had less mane than the Asiatic variety. Sometimes a "multitude of shepherds" turned out to hunt the lion (Is. xxxi. 4), and a few instances are recorded of a single person attacking him (1 Sam. xvii. 34), or perhaps two or more (Amos iii. 12). The Arabs now dig a pit for the lion, covering it slightly, and decoying him with some small animal, as a kid.

The kings kept lions for amusement (Ez. xix. 9), and for hunting in Assyria (Anc. Egyptians iii. 17), as represented on the monuments (Layard, *Nin. and Bab.* 138). Poets and other writers made much use of the lion for his strength (Judg. xiv. 18), courage (Prov. xxviii. 1), and ferocity (Gen. xlix. 9); qualities which were attributed to brave, or other noted men. The lion's roar is given by four Hebrew words: 1. SHAAG, thunder (Judg. xiv. 5), his roar when hunting; 2. NAHAM, the cry when the prey is seized (Is. v. 29); 3. HAJAH, growl of defiance; 4. NAAR, the yelp of young lions (Jer. li. 38). Besides these there are terms for other qualities and acts; as RABATS, crouching (Ez. xix. 2); SHACHAT, lying in wait in a den; ARAB, secret watching for prey; RAMAS, creeping in a stealthy manner (Ps. civ. 20); ZINNEK, the spring upon the prey (Deut. xxxiii. 22). The lion was used in poetry and in sculpture as a symbol of majesty and power, as in the Assyrian compound figures. In Egypt it was worshiped at Leontopolis. It was the emblem of the tribe of Judah, and is mentioned as a symbol by John in Revelation v. 5. Solomon's throne was ornamented with lions, as also the brazen laver (1 K. vii. 29, 36).

LITTER. A couch or sedan chair, borne by men, between mules or on camels, now in use by

LITTER.

the Egyptians (Num. vii. 3; Is. lxvi. 20). They are shown in use on the ancient sculptures and paintings.

LIVER. Internal organ of the body (Prov. vii. 23).

LIZ'ARD (Heb. LETAAH). The fan-foot lizard is reddish brown, spotted with white, and lives on

insects and worms. It is named from its note which sounds like "Gecko." They lay small, round eggs. Their feet cling to the wall like a fly's, and they run around the house without noise, always at night.

LOAM'MI (*not my people*). Second (symbolical) son of Hosea (Hos. i. 9).

LOAN. The law of Moses required the rich to lend to the poor without interest, only taking security against loss. Foreigners were not included in this rule. The practice of usury was always discreditable among the Hebrews (Prov. vi. 1, 4, xi. 15, xxii. 18, etc.), and Nehemiah restrained its exercise (v. 1, 13). The MONEY CHANGERS of the Temple were useful to the worshipers from a distance, and especially from foreign countries, in changing their money to the only lawful coin, the half-shekel, the annual temple dues from each person; but their presence in the temple itself was illegal and a desecration of the holy place. Their proper place was among business men, on the street with the merchants.

LOCK. The common wooden lock of the East is a clumsy wooden bolt kept in place by a few loose pins which may be lifted by a key with pegs fitted to match (see KEY). Bolts and locks were used (Judg. iii. 23; Cant. v. 5; Neh. iii. 3).

LOCUST.

LO'CUST. Heb. ARBEH (*multitude*) locust in Ex. x. 4, and many other passages; CHAGAB (*locust* generally) grasshopper in Num. xiii. 33, and others; CHARGOL, (*locust*) grasshopper; beetle in Lev. xi. 22; SALAM (*bald locust*) locust in Lev. xi. 22; GAZAM (*palmer-worm*); GOB (*great grasshopper*) in Nahum iii. 17; Is. xxiii. 4; CHANAMAL (*hail or frost?*) locust in Ps. lxxviii. 47; YELEK (*rough*) cankerworm in Nahum iii. 15; caterpillar in Ps. cv. 34; CHASIL (*caterpillar*); ZELAZAL, locust in Deut. xxviii. 42. The clouds of locusts sometimes obscure the sun, and they are very destructive, eating every green thing in their way. See cuts on pages 51, 83.

Their great voracity is alluded to in Ex. x. 12; Joel i. 4; and several other passages, and they are compared to horses in Joel ii. 4, 5, and in Rev. ix. 7, 9, where the noise they make in flying (like a heavy shower of rain) is also noticed, and their irresistable progress. Sometimes they enter the houses and eat the wood work. They do not travel in the night. Some kinds of birds eat them (Starling, Ar. smurmur); and they are eaten by men also, after being roasted, fried or stewed, mixed with flour and ground or pounded fine, and by boiling in water. Vast quantities are drowned in the sea, being carried into it by the wind. They generally die in a day or two. The children catch some kinds, as they do handsome butterflies, for their beauty, being marked with many colors, streaked and spotted. The women often put the eggs of the locust (chargol) into their ears as a cure for, or a preventive of, ear-aches.

LOD. Built by Shamer (1 Chr. viii. 12). Always connected with Ono. It is called Lydda in the Acts (ix. 32), where Peter healed Æneas of palsy. One of the murderers of Julius Cæsar (Cassius Longinus) was stationed in Palestine, and sold the whole people of Lydda into slavery (Ant. xiv. 11, 2); and Antony restored them. Cestius Gallus burnt it, and Vespasian, some time after, colonized it. The Romans gave it a new name, Diospolis (on the coins of Septimus Severus), and it became a seat of Jewish learning, and a large and wealthy town. It was the seat of a bishopric at an early date. Tradition connects the birth of St. George with the ruins of a church in the town, once a splendid structure, built by Justinian (Rob. ii. 244). There are about 1000 people now in the place, which is called by its ancient name, as near as an Arab can speak it (Lud).

LODE'BAR (*without pasture*). The native place Machir ben Ammiel, in whose house Mephibosheth found a home, after his father's death, on the E. of Jordan (2 Sam. xvii. 27, ix. 4, 5). This same Machir was one of the first to supply the wants of David when he fled from Absalom. It was near Mahanaim. Lost.

LODGE. (Is. i. 8). COTTAGE. Shelter made of boughs.

LODGE, to. To "tarry all night" (Gen. xix. 2; Judg. xix. 10; Matt. xxi. 17). HOSPITALITY. INN.

LOINS. The lower region of the back, the seat of strength (Gen. xxxv. 11, xxxvii. 34). Figuratively the source of progeny.

LO'IS (*better*). Grandmother of TIMOTHY, (2 Tim. i. 5, iii. 15).

LORD. See JAH.

LORD'S DAY, THE. (Greek, *He kuriakō hēmera*, in Rev. i. 10). The first day of the week, the weekly festival in memory of the resurrection of the Lord on that day. Some of the "fathers of the early Church" understand it to mean Easter day.

The first day of the week was chosen for the weekly meetings and feasts by those who "preached Jesus and the Resurrection." The appearance to the disciples, apostles, and others, were all on the Lord's day, and the custom of assembling on that day was adopted without a recorded exception in all the Churches. Besides the evidence of the early fathers there is that of Pliny in his letter to Trajan, from Pontus, "The Christians were accustomed to meet together on a stated day, before it was light, and sing hymns to Christ or God, and to bind themselves by a sacrament, and after separating they met again to take a general meal. Justin Martyr calls it Sunday, saying the exercises were prayer, the celebration of the Holy Eucharist, and the collection of alms, because it was the first day on which God dispelled the darkness, and because Jesus Christ rose from the dead on it." This is not the SABBATH, for that was the 7th day, and was a day of rest and a "Holy day" to Jehovah (Is. lviii. 13), and the two are carefully separated in character and intention. The Lord's day was to be a day of joy, cheerfulness, and of relaxation, and of religious meetings, no work being formally forbidden or rest commanded, and the law of Moses in the 4th commandment is nowhere in the Gospels applied to the day.

Some deny any religious character or obligation to the day; others held it to be an institution of the Church only, without divine sanction; and a third opinion is that it is a continuation under the new order of spiritual things, of the original Sabbath, and the 4th commandment applies equally to the Lord's day.

CEDARS OF LEBANON.

The first legal act affecting the day that is recorded is that of Constantine, A. D. 321, "Let all judges and city people, and the business of all arts, rest on the venerable Day of the Sun. Yet let those in the country freely and without restraint attend to the cultivation of the fields, since it frequently happens that not more fitly on any day may corn be planted in furrows, or vines in the trenches, lest through the moment's opportunity the benefit granted by heavenly foresight be lost."

Constantine had a nation of many kinds of people with many kinds of religion, and he so framed the laws in favor of his new faith as to do as little violence as possible to the old institutions. This law was acceptable to the Christians who could keep it with joy, and not burdensome to the Pagans, who could feel no interest in it. He certainly did not honor the day, but rather accepted the honor that it brought to him as a convert to the new faith.

The Council of Nice, A. D. 325, notices the day incidentally as already an old institution, and makes some rules concerning the posture of worshipers.

LORD'S PRAYER, THE. The name (not in the Scriptures) of the prayer spoken by Jesus as a model to his disciples, given in Matt. vi. 9–13; Luke xi. 2–4.

LORD'S SUPPER, (Gr. *kuriakon deipnon*, 1 Cor. xi. 20). The great central act of Christian worship, described by Paul (verses 23–26), as having been instituted on the night of the betrayal, as a continuation or a substitute for the Passover (Matt. xxvi. 19, etc.). See AGAPE.

The Paschal Feast was kept, not precisely as Moses directed (Ex. xii.), but in this manner: The members of the company met in the evening, reclined on couches (John xiii. 23, etc.), the head of the company or house asking a blessing "for the day and for the wine," over a cup, of which he and all the others tasted. Then all present washed their hands. Then the table was set out with the Paschal lamb, unleavened bread, bitter herbs and sauce of dates, figs, raisins and vinegar (HAROSETH), the herbs being dipped into the sauce and eaten, by the leader first. After this the dishes were changed and the cup of wine was again blessed and passed around. Then the real supper began with the solemn introductory words and a thanksgiving, with the psalms cxiii., cxiv., after which the hands were again washed. Then the leader broke a loaf of bread and gave thanks, dipping a piece with the bitter herbs into the sauce (*sop* in A. V.), and eating it, followed by all the company. The lamb was then eaten, with bread and herbs, after which the third cup of wine, called "the cup of blessing," was passed around. A fourth cup (of the Hallel) was passed around during the chanting of psalms cxv., cxviii. The fifth cup was passed during the chanting of the GREAT HALLEL (Ps. cxx.–cxxxviii.).

The Lord's Supper was to take the place of this feast, and the bread and wine instead of being memorials of the deliverance from Egypt, were to be memorials of the Lord and Master. The Paschal feast was annual, but no rule was given for the new supper, which was left to be settled by inclination and custom.

The unleavened bread broken was a memorial of his broken body; the wine of his blood (see Matt. xiii. 38, 39; Gen. xli. 26; Dan. vii. 17), which was the New Testament (Jer. xxxi. 31), symbolical of the new covenant. The custom was well observed from the beginning (Acts ii. 42). Some even suppose that the blessing of the bread and wine occurred at every meal, and at least one a day, each assembly around a table being known as the church of such a place, the materials being paid for out of the common fund.

The bread was such as was commonly used, for they did **not** propose to continue the obligation of the Passover in using unleavened bread; the wine, as is the general custom in the East, was mixed with water. A part of the ceremony was "a holy kiss" (1 Cor. xvi. 20).

The original supper of "fellowship" passed by degrees into the "communion" service, as taking the place of the feast of charity, which had been abused by selfish souls. The new rule given by Paul separated the idea of

BRONZE LOCK, FULL-SIZE, FOUND AT JERUSALEM.

a full meal from the celebration of the Lord's Supper, or the Eucharist, and instead of daily it was to be only on the Lord's Day, and also the time was changed from evening to the morning (Acts xx. 11).

The practice of Paul himself seems to have joined the Feast of Charity and the Eucharist, especially shown on board the ship in the storm (xxvii. 35).

LORUHA'MAH (*the uncompassionated*). Daughter of HOSEA (Hos. i. 6). ROHAMAH.

LOT. Son of Haran, nephew of Abraham (Gen. xi. 27), born in Ur of the Chaldees, and settled in Canaan. He took refuge in Egypt with Abram during the famine (xii. 4, xiii. 1), and returned with him into the south of Palestine. He chose the Arabah for his pasture-land, leaving Abram on the hills of Benjamin and Judah. When the four kings captured him, he was rescued by his uncle (xiv.). Lot had probably entered into the cities, adopted some of their customs, and gathered other property besides cattle and tents (v. 12), including women (servants). The last scene in his life is recorded in connection with the destruction of the cities of the plain, when there appears in contrast with some of the darkest traits of human nature in the people of the cities, the pleasant habits and customs of Lot's wandering life; the chivalrous hospitality—washing feet, unleavened bread, the ready feast, such as we read of on the hills of Hebron among Abram's tents, and was referred to by Paul in the beautiful passage, "Be not forgetful to entertain strangers, for thereby some have entertained angels unawares" (Heb. xiii. 2). The traveler now meets with these traits among the Bedawin, which are almost identical with those of their ancestors of that early age. Where Zoar was, or in what mountain Lot dwelt, has not been determined (see ZOAR). The story of Lot's wife, and especially the strange conclusion, might have been passed by as a mystery, but for the use of it as an example in one of the discourses of Jesus (Luke xvii. 31, 32), where he says, "In that day he that is in the field let him not return back: remember Lot's wife" (who did). The author of the Book of Wisdom (x. 7), and Josephus (Ant. i. 11, 4), seem to have believed in an actual monument of salt; and many travelers from their day to this have seen and described pillars of salt which they accepted as Lot's wife. See GEOLOGY for salt-mountain of Sodom.

Ammon and Moab were the children of Lot (Deut. ii. 9, 19), and as such were exempted from conquest by Moses. (See Ps. lxxxiii.) The Arabs have traditions of Lot (Koran, ch. vii., xi.), in which he is described as a preacher sent to the cities of the plain, which they call Lot's cities. The Dead Sea is also called the Sea of Lot (Bahr Loot).

LO'TAN (*covering*). Son of Seir (Gen. xxxvi. 20).

LOVE (Heb. AHABA, Gr. *agape*). Natural affection. Also spiritual affection for holy things (Rom. xiii. 10; 1 John. iv. 7, etc.), which is a fruit of the Spirit, opposed to all evil, and only satisfied with a likeness to Jesus Christ and God.

LOVE-FEAST. See AGAPE.

LOW COUN'TRY (2 Chr. xxvi. 10). PLAIN. Arabah?

LO'ZON. Ancestors of Solomon's servants, who returned with Zerubbabel (1 Esd. v. 33). DARKON.

LU'BIM (*people of a dry land*). LEHABIM. In Shishak's army (2 Chr. xii. 3). Mentioned by the prophets (Nahum iii. 9; Dan. xi. 43), and on the Egyptian monuments, where they are called LEBU, who contended with Egypt in war, and were subdued about 1250, B. C. They are painted as a Shemitic race, fair and strong. Perhaps the same as the LEHABIM. They occupied the shores of the Great Sea, and the Desert inland, west of Egypt. The Kabyles and Berbers of that district may be descendants, as they are the successors of the Lubim (Libyans).

LU'CAS. LUKE. Companion of Paul at Rome (Col. iv. 14).

LU'CIFER (*light bearing*). Son of the morning, morning star (Is. xiv. 12), a symbol of the king of Babylon. Since the time of Jerome it is a name for Satan. See DEMON, DEVIL.

LU'CIUS (*born in the day-time*). 1. A Roman consul (1 Macc. xv. 10), and uncertain whether 1. L. Furius, B. C. 136; 2. L. Cæcilius Metellus Calvus, B. C. 142; or 3. L. Calpurnius Piso, B. C. 139, who is probably the one referred to. —2. A kinsman of Paul (Rom. xvi. 21), afterwards bishop of Cenchræa.—3. Lucius of Cyrene, was probably at the Feast of Pentecost, if not one of the 70, and also one of the "men of Cyrene," who preached in Antioch (Acts xi. 20). Different traditions make him bishop of Cenchræa, Cyrene and Laodicea in Syria.

LU'CRE. That which is gained unworthily (1 Sam. viii. 3; 1 Tim. iii. 8).

LUKE (Gr. *Loukas*; Latin *Lucas*, *born at daylight*). A common name among Romans. A Gentile born at Antioch in Syria, educated a physician, and an artist (Nicephorus ii. 43). Some have supposed him one of the 70, and also one of the two who saw Jesus at Emmaus, but without good reason. He first appears historically at Troas with Paul, going with him into Macedonia (Acts xvi. 9, 10), and writing his history after that as an eye witness. See GOSPEL and ACTS in the HISTORY.

It is supposed that he died a martyr between A. D. 75 and 100, but no locality is given.

LU'NATIC (*moon-struck*), (Matt. iv. 24, xvii. 15). Disease of the body and mind. MADNESS.

LUST. Desire (Ps. lxxviii. 18, 30), inordinate and sensual (Rom. i. 27).

LUZ. LUZAM (*almond-tree*). An ancient city of Canaan, named Bethel by Jacob (Gen. xxviii. 19).

It is likely that the place of Jacob's pillar, or the El-Beth-el sanctuary (xxxv. 6, xlviii. 3), and of Jeroboam's idolatry (1 K. xii. 29), were not *in*, but *south* of the city of Luz (Josh. xvi. 1, 2, xviii. 13). —2. One of the men of Luz was allowed by the house of Joseph to escape, when the city was destroyed, and he went into the land of the Hittites, where he built another Luz. Probably on the Orontes river (Porter).

LYCAO'NIA (*Lucus*, a wolf, *wolf-country*). An undulating plain, 20 miles by 13, among the mountains in Asia Minor, north of Cilicia.

Iconium (its capital), Derbe, and Lystra were there, and visited by Paul. The speech of this district was a corrupt form of Greek (Acts xiv. 11). It was a Roman colony, and had a good road. The streams are brackish, and there are several small salt-lakes; but flocks find good pasture.

LY'CIA (LI'KEA). A province and peninsula southwest in Asia Minor, opposite the island of Rhodes; mountainous and well watered with small creeks.

Bellerophon, one of its ancient kings, is celebrated in Greek mythology. The Romans took it from Antiochus the Great, after the battle of Magnesia (B. C. 190). There are many ruined cities in this region, described in the excellent works of Fellows, Spratt, and Forbes, full of architecture, sculpture, and inscriptions of the ancients. It is mentioned in 1 Macc. xv. 23, during its golden period, just after its emancipation from the rule of the island Rhodes. Paul visited two of its cities, Patara and Myra.

LYDDA.

LYD'DA. Greek form of Lod. The first historical notice of this city, since Christ, is the signature of Ætius Lyddensis to the acts of the Council of Nicæa (A. D. 325); after which it is frequently mentioned, especially during the Crusades. The Arabs have a tradition that the final contest between Christ and Antichrist will be at Lydda. (Sale's *Koran*, c. 43, note).

LUD. Fourth son of Shem (Gen. x. 22), from whom descended the Lydians; who first settled north of Palestine, and afterward in Asia Minor. The name is found on the Egyptian monuments of the 13th, 14th and 15th centuries B. C. as a powerful people called Luden. (See LYDIA).

LU'DIM (Gen. x. 13). Allies of the Egyptians (2 Chr. xii. 3, xvi. 8; Nahum iii. 9). Probably the same people as the Lehabim.

LU'HITH, THE ASCENT OF (Is. xv. 5; Jer. xlviii. 5). A famous pass somewhere in Moab, not yet identified.

LYD'IA (*from king Lydus*). A province in Asia Minor, on the Sea, south of Mysia, and north of Caria. Taken by the Romans from Antiochus the Great, after the battle of Magnesia, B. C. 190, and given to the king of Pergamus, Eumenes II (1

LYDIA (*from Lydia!*). The first convert in Europe, by Paul, and his hostess at Phillippi (Acts xvi. 14, 15, 40). She was a Jewess and was found by Paul attending Jewish Sabbath worship by the side of a stream. She was by occupation a traveling dealer in dyed goods and dyes, and belonged in Thyatira, which was noted for such products. The mention of the conversion of her household indicates some wealth and importance, whether as head of a family or only of hired servants. Her character as a Christian woman is shown in her acceptance of the Gospel, her urgent hospitality, and continued friendship for Paul and Silas when they were persecuted. Her death is not recorded.

LYDIANS. People of Lydia (Jer. xlvi. 9).

LYSANIAS (*ending sorrow*). Tetrarch of Abilene, in the 15th year of Tiberius, when Herod Antipas was tetrarch of Galilee, and Herod Philip was tetrarch of Ituræa and Trachonitis.

Josephus mentions a Lysanias who ruled in that district, near Lebanon, in the time of Antony and Cleopatra, 60 years before the one mentioned by Luke, and also another of the time Caligula and Claudius, 20 years after Luke's reference. The name may have been a common one to several rulers; and the last one mentioned by Josephus the one referred to by Luke.

LYSIAS (*relaxing*). 1. A nobleman who was intrusted with the government of Syria, B. C. 166 (1 Macc. iii. 32.)—2. Claudius Lysias, a military tribune who commanded Roman troops at Jerusalem under Felix.

He rescued Paul from the mob of Jews, and afterwards sent him to Cæsarea, under a guard. Since he bought his freedom, and bore a Greek name, it is supposed that he was a Greek by birth (Acts xxi. 31–40, etc.).

LYSIMACHUS (*ending strife*). 1. Son of Ptolemæus (Esth. xi. 1).—2. Brother of Menelaus, the high-priest, and his deputy at the court of Antiochus (2 Macc. iv. 29–42). He was killed by a mob, B. C. 170, on account of his tyranny and sacrilege.

LYSTRA. In Lycaonia. Where divine honors, after the Greek manner, were offered to Paul, and where he was at once stoned. It was the home of Paul's companion, Timothy. The extensive ruins of *Bin bir Kilissi* (one thousand and one churches) lie along the eastern declivity of the Karadagh (black mountain), where are to be seen the remains of about 40 churches, some 25 of which are quite entire (*Hamilton*, Asia Minor).

M

MA'ACAH. 1. Mother of Absalom (2 Sam. iii. 3).—2. Daughter of Nahor (Gen. xxii. 24).—3. Father of Achish, king of Gath (1 K. ii. 39).—4. Grand-daughter of Abishalom (1 K. xv. 2, 10, 13). —5. Second wife of Caleb, mother of five of his children (1 Chr. ii. 48).—6. Daughter of Talmai and mother of Absalom (iii. 2).—7. Wife of Jehiel (1 Chr. vii. 29, ix. 35).—8. Wife of Machir (1 Chr. vii. 15, 16).—9. Father of Hanan (xi. 43).—9. Father of Shephatiah (xxvii. 16).

MA'ACAH (*oppression*). MAACHAH. A small kingdom on the N. E. of Palestine, near Argob (Deut. iii. 14), and Bashan (Josh. xiii. 5), founded by a son of Nahor, Abraham's brother (Gen. xxii. 24). The people were not expelled, but mingled with the Jews. Eliphelet, of this nation, was one of David's 30 captains (2 Sam. xxiii. 34), and Jaazaniah was a captain in the army of Israel at the time of the Captivity.

MAACH'ATHI, MAACHATHITES, THE. People of Maachah (Deut. iii. 14).

MA'ADAI. Son of Bani (Ezr. x. 34).

MAADI'AH (*ornament of Jehovah*). A priest who returned from captivity (Neh. xii. 5).

MA'AI or **MAA'I** (*compassion*). Son of a priest at the dedication of the wall of Jerusalem (Neh. xii. 36).

MA'ALEH-ACRAB'-BIM. See AKRABBIM.

MA'ANI. BANI 4 (1 Esd. ix. 34).

MA'ARATH (*a bare place*). In the hill country of Judah (Josh. xv. 59).

TRYPHON.

MAASEI'AH (*work of Jehovah*). 20 persons of this name, but none very famous. 1. A descendant of Jeshua (Ezr. x. 18).—2. A priest (21).—3. Another priest (22).—4. A descendant of Pahath-Moab (30).—5. Father of Azariah (Neh. iii. 23).—6. An assistant of Ezra (viii. 4).—7. A Levite (viii. 7).—8. A chief (x. 25).—9. Son of Baruch (xi. 5.)—10. Ancestor of Sallu (xi. 7).—11. Ten priests who assisted Ezra (xii. 41, 42).—12. Father of Zephaniah (Jer. xxi. 1, xxix, 25).—13. Father of Zedekiah (xix. 21).—14. A porter of the temple (1 Chr. xv. 18, 20).—15. Son of Adaiah (2 Chr. xxiii. 1).—16. An officer of high rank (xxvi. 11).—17. The "king's son" (2 Chr. xxviii. 7).—18. Governor of Jerusalem (xxxiv. 8).—19. Son of Shallum (Jer. xxxv. 4).—20. A priest (Jer. xxxii. 12).

MA'ASAI. A priest who returned from captivity and lived in Jerusalem (1 Chr. ix. 12). AMASHAI.

MAASI'AS. MAASEIAH 20 (Bar. i. 1).

MA'ATH. Son of Mattathias (Luke iii. 26).

MA'AZ (*anger*). Son of Ram (1 Chr. ii. 27).

MAAZI'AH (*consolation of Jah*). 1. A priest (1 Chr. xxiv. 18).—2. A priest who signed the covenant (Neh. x. 8).

MAB'DAI. BENAIAH 8 (1 Esd. ix. 34).

MABNAD'EBAI (Ezr. x. 40). MACHNADEBAI.

MAC'ALON (1 Esd. v. 21). MICHMASH.

MAC'CABEES. See HISTORY OF THE BOOKS.

THE FAMILY OF THE MACCABEES.

ASMONÆANS.

	1 Chasmon.
	2 Johanan.
	3 Simeon.
	4 Mattathias.
4 Mattathias.	5 Johanan
"	6 Simon.
"	7 Judas.
"	8 Eleazar.
"	9 Jonathan.
6 Simon.	10 Judas.
"	11 Johannes Hyrcanus I.
"	12 Mattathias.
"	13 Daughter, m. Ptolemæus.
11 J. Hyrcanus.	14 Aristobulus I, m. Salome.
"	15 Antigonus.
"	16 Jannæus Alexander.
"	17 Son, 18 Son.
16 J. Alexander.	18 Hyrcanus II.
"	19 Aristobulus II.
19 Aristobulus II.	20 Antigonus.
"	21 Antigonus.
20 Alexander.	22 Mariamne, m. Herod (Gt.)
"	23 Aristobulus.

MACEDO'NIA. The country N. of Thessaly and the Ægean Sea, S. of the Balkan mts., extending to Thrace on the E., and to Illyria on the W. There are two great plains, one watered by the Axius, which empties into the Thermaic gulf near Thessalonica, and the other by the Strymon, which flows by Philippi and Amphipolis into the Ægean Sea. Mt. Athos is a peninsula between these two plains. Philip and Alexander ruled here, and the Romans conquered it from Perseus (B.C. 168.) In the N.T. times a proconsul of one district resided at Thessalonica, ruling over Macedonia, Thessaly, and a tract along the Adriatic (Acts xvi. 9, 10, 12, xix. 21, etc.). In the Apocrypha there are some notices of this country. Haman is called a Macedonian (Esth. xvi. 10). The Maccabees mention Alexander, son of Philip (1 Macc. i. 1), who came out of the land of the Chettiim and smote Darius, king of the Persians and Medes. This was the first part of Europe that received the Gospel, by the labor of Paul and his companions (Acts xvi. 9), who first preached to a small congregation of women (v. 13), on the banks of the Strymon near Philippi; and the first convert was a woman, LYDIA.

MACEDO'NIAN. From MACEDONIA (Esth. xvi. 10, 14). See HISTORY OF THE BOOKS.

MACH'BANAI (*thick one*). Soldier of David at Ziklag (1 Chr. xii. 13).

MACHBE'NAH (*a mantle*). A town built by Shevah. Lost. (1 Chr. ii. 49).

MA'CHI (*diminution*). Father of Geuel (Num. xiii. 15).

MACHIR (*sold*). 1. Son of Manasseh (1 Chr. vii. 14). His children were caressed by Joseph (Gen. l. 21).—2. Son of Ammiel, a chief on the E. side of Jordan (2 Sam. ix. 4, 5).

MA'CHIRITES, THE. People of Machir (Num. xxvi. 29).

MACHMAD'EBAI (*gift of the noble*). Son of Bani (Ezr. x. 40).

LYSIMACHUS.

MACH'PELAH. The district in which was the field of Ephron the Hittite, containing the cave which was bought by Abraham, and became the burial-place of Abraham himself, Sarah, Isaac, Rebekah, Leah and Jacob. This cave and the field around it was the only spot which belonged to Abraham in the country. The Haram at Hebron (see view of Hebron) is said to stand over this cave. It is a massive stone structure, in the ancient style, of dark gray stone, 200 ft. long, 115 wide, and 50 high. Some of the stones are 12 to 20 ft. long, by 4 to 5 thick, with beveled edges, like the temple wall at Jerusalem, and must be as old as Solomon's time.

There are shown inside of this building, which is now called a mosque, several small monuments, standing on the floor, each enclosed in a shrine, with iron railings. The first on the right as you enter is that of Abraham; on the left that of Sarah, each guarded by a silver gate. Isaac and Rebekah are also honored, each with a separate chapel; and also Jacob and Leah, opposite the entrance. The cave is under the floor, is in two rooms, and most strictly guarded from intrusion. The best description is given by Stanley (*Jewish Church*, etc.). This is almost the only spot on earth which attracts all who profess the simple creed "I believe in God." And this is only the grave of an old shepherd, who lived under a tent there 4,000 years ago, whose only title was "The Friend," which is now the Arab name of Hebron, *Al Khulil*.

MA'CRON (*long head*). Son of Dorymenes (1 Macc. iii. 38), governor of Cyprus (2 Macc. x. 12).

MAD'AI (Gen. x. 2). Third son of Japheth, from whom descended the Medes. See 2 K. xvii. 6; Dan. xi. 1; Esth. i. 3, in all of which passages the same original word is found, although differently translated in each.

MADI'ABUN. The son of Madiabun assisted at the Temple dedication (1 Esd. v. 58).

MA'DIAN. MIDIAN (Judg. ii. 26).

MADMAN'NAH (*dunghill*). South in Judah, not far from Gaza (Josh. xv. 21, 31). Beth Marcaboth?

MAD'MEN (Jer. xlviii. 2). Included in the curse of Moab. Near Heshbon.

MADME'NAH (Is. x. 31). A small village between Anathoth and Nob. The prophet said Madmenah *flies* (before the Assyrian).

MAD'NESS (SHAGA, *to be stirred* or *excited*), (1 Sam. xxi. 13); HALEL, *to flash out*, as light or sound (Prov. xxvi. 18); MAINOMAI or *mania* (John x. 20). Among Oriental nations madmen were looked upon with reverence, as possessed of a sacred character. LUNATICS.

MA'DON. City of Canaan before the conquest, whose king, Jobab, was killed at the waters of Merom by Joshua (xi. 1-9). Somewhere in the north.

MAE'LUS (1 Esd. ix. 26). MIAMIN.

MAG'BISH (*freezing*). One hundred and fifty-six of the children of Magbish returned from captivity (Ezr. ii. 30). In Benjamin. Lost.

MAG'DALA (*tower*). In most of the MSS. the name is MAGADAN. Christ came into the limits of Magdala after the miracle of feeding the 4,000 on the other side of the lake (Matt. xv. 89). Now called *El Mejdel*, on the west shore of the Sea of Galilee, close to the water, about three miles north of Tiberias, at the southeast corner of the plain of Gennesaret. There was a watch-tower here that guarded the entrance to the plain. Here was the home of Mary Magdalene. Dalmanutha in Mark viii. 10.

MAGDALE'NE, MARY OF. MAGDALA (Mark xvi. 9).

MAG'DIEL (*praise of El*). A Duke of Edom (Gen. xxxvi. 43).

MA'GED (1 Macc. v. 36).

MA'GI (Heb. CHARTUMIM; Gr. *Magoi*). Wise men, magicians, imagians. They are credited all over the East with certain secret learning which in remote antiquity distinguished Egypt and Chaldæa. Among the Jews they were considered a sort of *sacred scribes*, skilled in divining, and interpreting the hidden meaning of certain passages of the Scriptures. In Egypt and Chaldæa they seem to have been the sole interpreters of secret things, the past and the future, but in Palestine they never ranked with the prophets, unless among the idolatrous people. The Books of Exodus and Daniel show their eminent position and influence, and pretense to occult knowledge. Some among them were probably free from superstition; men of sound minds, and finding in their books sounder views of the Divine government of the world than the great body of their associates were capable of understanding. The exiled Jews carried to such as these the welcome knowledge of the true Jehovah. Of this class were the three who, as "wise men from the East," came to see him who was born king of the Jews.

The Gospel narrative is simple and direct. They were guided by a star, in which they saw the sign of the expected Messiah, which was then the "hope of all nations." As magianism was then the chief religion of the kingdom of Parthia, it is supposed they came from that country, or it may be from Eastern Chaldæa. Their dress and appearance commanded respect at Jerusalem, and their presents also indicated persons of no ordinary rank. (The presents do not seem to have raised Joseph and Mary above their condition of poverty.) In the apocryphal book of Seth it is said that this "star" was a circle of light with a figure of a child and a **cross** over its head inside. The general opinion **now** is that it was a meteoric substance, divinely guided. The office of the star ended at the "manger," for the magi **were sent** back by a dream (Matt. ii. 12).

The number of the magi **was** not stated, but has been since fixed by the Roman Church as three, with the names Gaspar, Melchoir, Balthasar, **and** the title of kings, whose relics are shown in Cologne, where they are honored as saints, and have a gorgeous monument. Ps. lxxii. 10 is the foundation for this invention; "The kings of Tarshish and of the isles shall bring presents, the kings **of** Sheba and Saba shall offer gifts." There is also a legend that they were converted by the apostle Thomas. The number three was supposed from the gifts being three, gold, frankincense, and myrrh. "The gold was a symbol of a king; the myrrh of the bitterness of the Passion, and the preparation of the tomb; the frankincense was offered in adoration of the divinity of the Son of God."

The Greek Church makes the occasion magnificent and important. The magi arrive with a grand escort of 1000, who were part of an army of 7000 who rested on the East bank of Euphrates. They came on the expedition in obedience to a prophecy of Zoroaster, who said that in the latter days there should be a Mighty One, a Redeemer, and that a star should announce his coming. Twelve of the holiest priests had kept watch for this star for many ages, on the Mount of Victory. When the star appeared it was in the form of an infant with a cross, and a voice bade them to follow it to Judea, which they did, traveling two years, during all of which time their provisions and water were supplied by a miracle. The gifts were the identical ones that Abraham gave to the sons of Keturah, the Queen of Sheba returned to Solomon, and which had found their way back East again. The other fanciful legends would fill a volume.

MAGIC. Wonder-working, in some way beyond the ordinary powers of man. This is only a pretense, and has nothing to do with Natural Philosophy. The belief in magic as a reality is very wide-spread in the East, and is simply an undue exercise of certain mental faculties, which take the place of religion in undeveloped persons. Some races in Africa have no higher conception of God and religion than the supposed magical powers of the air, minerals, etc., and worship by incantations. Even the Shemites were not exempt, as appears in the notices of Laban's images, but with them it took a kind of second rank to the true religion, being considered unlawful, but still very valuable as an aid to men in various selfish desires (Gen. xxxi. 19, 30, 32-35). This is the first notice of that superstition which in after time worked so much mischief in the Hebrew community. The name TERAPHIM has been derived from Egypt, TEN, a shape, figure, or rather, in Coptic, *to change figure*.

The next instance in the history of the magician is in the account of Moses before Pharaoh. There is a little doubt as to the intention of the writer, whether he means to represent that the Egyptians were natural philosophers or practicers of magic arts (supernatural magic). They had notice of what Moses was to do, and had time to prepare an imitation, but in no case did they undo what the Hebrew workers did; for they did not restore the purity of the river Nile water, nor drive away the frogs, lice, and locusts, but they did increase the evil in each case, or appeared to do so. The Pharaoh did not expect anything more of them. When the last plague came, which they could not imitate, nor dare to increase, they acknowledged the "finger of God." The Egyptian magicians counted Moses and Aaron as members of their own profession, possessed **of a** little **more** of the secret knowledge, or of some strange **device** unknown to them, and the Pharaoh seems to **have** thought the same, until the miracle of the **boils** appeared, which seems to have convinced him. When the plague of boils attacked the magicians they disappeared. They could **not** imitate that, **nor** dare to increase it in themselves.

COIN OF MACEDONIA.

Some writers accept the theory that magic is an imitation of the Divine sign-work,—miracle—but the work of the Satan, or his inferior demons. The original Hebrew account of the work before Pharaoh says "the revealers (magicians) did so with their fumigations."

The tricks of the magicians in the case of Pharaoh were paralleled by that of Artabanus, who caused the wine in the cup of Xerxes to change from white to red, which he interpreted to mean that the gods were displeased with the expedition (the displeased one was Artabanus.)

The NACHASHISM (enchantment, or serpent-divining) of Balaam is the next point in this history. But it appears that this prophet knew the true Jehovah, and consulted him instead of the "evil demons."

All through the history of the Jews, as recorded in the Scriptures, in both the Old and New Testaments, the belief in the actual power of evil spirits is recognized, and called into use in many cases. The same superstition is still very powerful among the poorly informed, and leads to consulting fortune-tellers, clairvoyants, and other professors of "black art." Pliny's Natural History is full of curious fables on this topic, and these fables were the only storehouse of the so-called wisdom of the magicians. The Roman Church has perpetuated this belief and practice in its miracle fables, such as in the life of Gregory of Neo Cæsarea, the Thaumaturgist (wonder-worker), and the "Our Lady of Lourdes," besides many other books of "Lives of Saints." (See DEMON.)

The notion of the "Elixir of Life" arose from the belief that Adam would have lived forever if he could have eaten from time to time of the fruit of the tree of life; but that being excluded from the garden, he died; and therefore if the true composition of the fruit can be discovered and used by men, it will restore youth from time to time, and so make man immortal. The "philosopher's stone" is the same notion applied to minerals, which are to be purified by contact with a pure substance, which changes all metals into gold—the purest known metal. The early Christian did not dispute the theory, but denied the possibility of discovering the true "Elixir" or the true "Stone."

The immediate mischief of this "black art" is in promising power, pleasure, riches, wisdom, without the necessary sacrifice of study and labor.

The Easterns now make Solomon a sort of king of magicians, ruling them with a certain "seal" (a six-pointed star—made of two triangles), and credit all manner of wonderful deeds. (See SOLOMON.)

Paul met this "imposition and crime" as it deserved on several occasions, the most noted that was recorded being at Ephesus, when so many of the books of magic were burned (Acts xix. 19), estimated at the value of $85,000.

There is no evidence in the Scriptures that any real results were ever produced by these magicians; it was all trick, effect on the imagination and fancy, based on the known superstition and false instruction of the dupes.

The Greek and Roman magicians were of the same character, and it is probable that all nations and tribes have a set of impostors of a like kind, descending from the magician to the serpent-charmers, fetish-men, clairvoyants, and medicine men of the Indians.

MAGNIFICAL (1 Chr. xxii. 5). Grand, splendid.

MA'GOG. Second son of Japheth (Gen. x. 2), and founder of a race (Rev. xx. 8), the great Scythian tribe, now called Russian. Ezekiel places the nation in the north (xxxix. 2), near Togarmah, and the maritime regions of Europe (v. 6). They had cavalry and used bows. In the 7th century B. C. they were a formidable power, felt through the whole of Western Asia. They took Sardis (B. C. 629), and overran the country as far as Egypt, where they were turned back by a bribe given by Psammetichus, and took Ascalon.

MA'GOR-MIS'SABIB (*terror on every side*). Name given to Pashur by Jeremiah (Jer. xx. 3). The same words are found in other passages, but not as a name (vi. 25, xx. 10, xlvi. 5; xlix. 29; Lam. ii. 22; Ps. xxxi. 13).

MAGPI'ASH (*moth-killer*). A chief who signed the covenant (Neh. x. 20). Magabish in Ezra ii. 30.

MA'HALAH (*sickness*). One of the children of Hammoleketh (1 Chr. vii. 18).

MAHALA'LEEL (*praise of God*). 1. Son of Cainan (Gen. v. 12, 13, 15, 17).—2. Descendant of Perez, son of Judah (Neh. xi. 4).

MA'HALATH (*a lyre*). 1. Daughter of Ishmael (Gen. xxviii. 9).—2. First wife of King Rehoboam (2 Chr. xi. 18).—3. Mahalath, a stringed instrument like the kithara, (harp), and used in the sacred chant (Ps. liii. title; Gen. iv. 21). —4. Mahalath Lean'noth, the beginning of a song (Ps. lxxxviii. 1).

MA'HALI (Ex. vi. 19). MAHLI (*sick, infirm*).

MAHANA'IM (*two camps*). 18 ms. E. of Jordan, and 10 N. of Jerash, now Birket Manneh (Tristram). Here Jacob divided his people and flocks into two bands, through fear of Esau. At the conquest it was a city on the border of the two tribes, Gad and Manasseh, but given to Gad (Josh. xiii. 26, 30, xxi. 38). Abner selected it as the capital of the kingdom of Ishbosheth, crowning him, there king over all Israel (2 Sam. ii. 8, 9). David took refuge there when Absalom rebelled, and sat between the two gates of the walled city when the news of

COLUMN AT PERSEPOLIS.

the death of his son was brought to him (2 Sam. xvii. 24, xviii. 24, 33), and retired to the chamber over the gate to weep for him. It was the seat of an officer of Solomon, and is alluded to in Cant. vi. 13—"Two armies"—Mahanaim. The name is found on the monuments in Egypt, at Karnak. See EGYPT.

MAHA'NEHDAN (*camp of Dan*). Behind Kirjath Jearim (Judg. xviii. 12, see 22-26). Where the Danites camped just before setting out for their northern home.

MA'HARAI (*impetuous*). General of the tenth division in David's army, numbering twenty-four thousand (1 Chr. xxvii. 13).

MA'HATH (*grasping*). 1. Son of Amasai (1 Chr. vi. 35). AHIMOTH.—2. A Kohathite who had charge of the tithes in the reign of Hezekiah (2 Chr. xxix. 12).

MA'HAVITE, THE. One of David's strong men (1 Chr. xi. 46).

MAHA'ZIOTH (*visions*). Son of Heman, chief of the twenty-third choir of musicians (1 Chr. xxv. 4, 30).

MA'HER-SHA'LAL-HASH'BAZ. The name was given by divine direction and means that Damascus and Samaria now soon to be plundered by the king of Assyria (Is. viii. 1-4).

MAH'LAH (*disease*). Daughter of Zelophehad (Num. xxvii. 1-11).

MAH'LI (*sickly*). 1. Son of Merari (Num. iii. 20).—2. Son of Mushi (1 Chr. vi. 47).

MAH'LITES, THE. Descendants of MAHLI (Num. iii. 33; xxvi. 58).

MAH'LON (*sickly*). First husband of RUTH. Son of Elimelech (Ruth i. 2, 5; iv. 9, 10).

MA'HOL (musical instrument, Ps. cl. 4). Teacher of ETHAN, HEMAN, CHALCOL and DARDA, musicians, and famous for wisdom next to Solomon (1 K. iv. 31).

MAIA'NEAS (1 Esd. ix. 48).

MA'KAZ (*end*, 1 K. iv. 9). In Dan.

MA'KED (1 Macc. v. 26). A strong and great city in Gilead. Where Judas Maccabeus delivered the Jews from the Ammonites. Lost.

MAK'HELOTH (*assemblies*). Desert camp (Num. xxxiii. 25).

MAK'KEDAH (*shepherd camp*). An ancient royal city of Canaan taken by Joshua after the defeat of the allied kings at Gibeon (Josh. x. 28, xii. 16). This stronghold was the first one taken in this region. El Kledidh, in Wady es Sumt. There are many caves in this part of the country, but no one has been identified as *the cave*.

MAK'TESH (*mortar*). A quarter, or part of Jerusalem (Zeph. i. 11). The merchants and mechanics gathered their shops in and around the Tyropœon valley. The Bazaar is now in the same ancient place.

MAL'ACHI. HISTORY OF THE BOOKS.

MAL'CHAM. 1. Son of Shaharaim (1 Chr. viii. 9).—2. An idol invested with honors by its worshipers (Zeph. i. 5).

MAL'CHIA (*Jah's king*). 1. Son of Levi (1 Chr. vi. 40).—2. Son of Parosh (Ezr. x. 25).—3. Son of Harim (x. 31).—4. Son of Rechab, ruler of the circuit of Beth-haccerem (Neh. iii. 14).—5. Son of Zephaniah, who assisted in rebuilding the wall of Jerusalem (Neh. iii. 31).—6. A priest who stood with Ezra when he read the Law to the people (viii. 4).—7. Father of Pashur (xi. 12).—8. Son of Hammelech (2 Chr. xxvii. 7).

MAL'CHIEL (*God's king*). Son of Beriah (Gen. xlvi. 17). Founder of Birzavith (1 Chr. vii. 31).

MALCHIELITES. The descendants of Malchiel (Num. xxvi. 45).

MALCHI'JAH. 1. A priest, father of Pashur (1

Chr. ix. 12).—2. Chief of the fifth of the twenty-four courses by David (xxiv. 9).—3. A layman (Ezr. x. 25).—4. Descendant of Harim (Neh. iii. 11).—5. A priest who sealed the covenant (x. 3). —6. A priest who assisted in the dedication of the wall of Jerusalem (xii. 42).

MALCHI RAM (*king of altitude*). Son of Jeconiah (1 Chr. iii. 18).

MAL CHISHU'A (*king of help*). Son of Saul (1 Sam. xiv. 49).

MAL'CHUS. Servant of the high-priest maimed by Peter and restored by Jesus (John xviii. 10; Luke xxii. 51).

MALE LEEL. Son of Cainan (Luke iii. 37).

MAL'LOS (*a lock of wool*), (2 Macc. iv. 30). A city of Cilicia, 20 ms. from Tarsus, at the mouth of the river Pyramus.

MALLO THI (*fulness*). Pupil of Heman and leader of the nineteenth choir (1 Chr. xxv. 4, 26).

MAL LOWS (MALLUAH). The leaves and pods used as a pot-herb, eaten in Arabia and Palestine (Job. xxx. 4).

MAL'LUCH (*reigning*). 1. Ancestor of Ethan (1 Chr. vi. 44).—2. Son of Bani (Ezr. x. 29).—3. Descendant of Harim (32).—4. A priest (Neh. x. 4). —5. A chief who signed the covenant (x. 27).—6. A priest who returned from captivity (xii. 2).

MAMA'IAS (1 Esd. viii. 44).

MAM'MON (*riches*), (Matt. vi. 24).

MAM RE (*fruitfulness*). An ancient Amorite in alliance with Abram (Gen. xiv. 13-24); his name was given to the site on which HEBRON was built (xxiii. 17, 19).

MAM RE. Faces Machpelah (Gen. xxiii. 17, etc). One of Abraham's favorite camping-grounds. In its grove he had a sanctuary, which he called his Bethel (house of God). Here Abraham entertained the 3 angels, and Isaac was promised. The name has not been preserved in any locality.

MAM'UCHUS (1 Esd. ix. 30).

MAN. Four Hebrew words are rendered man: 1. ADAM, ruddy, like Edom.—2. ISH, a man; ENESH, a woman.—3. GEBER, to be strong.—4. METHIM, (mortal) men (as in Methusael, Methuselah). The Adam (HA-ADAM, *the man*) was the person created in the image of God. The term red in the Eastern languages means many different tints or tones of red; as a red horse or camel, and, when used of a man, means "fair." Some explain the word as derived from *adamah*, earth, because he was made from the dust or earth. The word Enoch (*strong*, or *nobleman*) is a compound of the word ISH. The variant Enoch is only apparent in orthography, the meaning being the same.

MAN'AEN. Teacher in the church at Antioch (Acts xiii. 1). Josephus says he was in high repute among the Essenes for wisdom and piety. He foretold to Herod the Great that he was to attain royal honors.

MAN'AHATH (*offering*). MAN'AHETHITES. A place called Manocho in a list of eleven towns given in the Septuagint, but omitted in the A. V., as not far from Bethlehem.

MAN'AHATH. Son of Shobal (Gen. xxxvi. 23).

MANASSE'AS. Son of Pahath-Moab (1 Esd. ix. 31; Ezr. x. 30).

MANASSEH. There is no reason given for depriving Manasseh of his birthright, as there was in the case of his grand-uncle Esau. On leaving Egypt at the Exode this was the least of the twelve tribes, numbering at Sinai only 32,200, but at the census, just before the crossing of the Jordan, they had increased to 52,700 men over 20 years old, at which Manasseh is honored with a first mention before Ephraim. The division of the tribe is one of the singular facts in the history of the Israelites, and seems to be at variance with the national feeling and laws. Some of this tribe were warriors, and made extensive conquests: as Machir, who took Gilead and Bashan; Jair, who took 60 cities in Argob; and Nobah, who captured Kenath and its vicinity, a tract of country the most difficult in the whole land, being full of fortified cities, and in the possession of Og and Sihon. (See HAURAN, BASHAN, HESHBON, ARGOB, KENATH, NOBAH, etc.).

The lot of the half-tribe west of the Jordan was small, lying along the north border of Ephraim, but since the boundary is so slightly recorded it is very difficult to follow it. The line is drawn from the river Kanah (supposing that river to have been just south of Cæsarea), to a place on the Jordan "before Shechem" (Josh. xvii. 7, 9, 11; Jos. Ant. v. i. 22). See IBON, IBLEAM, ENDOR, TAANACH, and MEGIDDO). There is no account of this tribe separate from Ephraim, and it is likely that the two neighbors were spoken of as one people (2 Chr. xxxi. 1, xxxiv. 6, 9).

MANAS'SES. 1. (1 Esd. ix. 33).—2. King of Judah (Matt. i. 10). See HISTORY OF THE BOOKS.— 3. Son of Joseph (Rev. vii. 6).—4. Husband of Judith (Jud. viii. 2, 7). See BOOK OF JUDITH.

MANASS'ITES, THE. Members of the tribe of Manasseh (Deut. iv. 43).

MANDRAKE.

MAN'DRAKES (Cant. vii. 13). The mandrake is now called ATROPA MANDRAGORA. The odor or flavor of the plant is a matter of opinion. They have a delightful smell, and the taste is agreeable, though not to every body. The Orientals especially value strongly smelling things, that to more delicate senses are unpleasing. The fruit was ripe as the time of wheat harvest. From a rude resemblance of old roots of the mandrake to the human form, some strange superstitious notions have arisen concerning it (Jos. Wars, vii. 6, § 3). The leaves are dark-green, the flowers white, with veins of purple, and the fruit orange, and the size of nutmegs.

MAN'GER (Gr. *phatne*). The feeding-place for animals, or a trough made of mortar or cut out of single stones. See INN.

MA'NI (1 Esd. ix. 30).

MAN'LIUS, TITUS (*born early in the morning*). Ambassador of the Romans (2 Macc. xi. 34–38).

MAN'NA (Heb. MAN). A month after leaving Egypt the people were in want of food, and murmured against their leaders, when the quails were sent in the evening and the manna appeared in the morning, after the "dew was gone up." It was a small round thing, like hoar-frost or corrianderseed, and the people said "what is this?" (MANHU). Moses answered that it was the bread that

SARCOPHAGUS AT SIDON.

the Lord had given them to eat (Ex. xvi. 1–3, 11–15). Its flavor was like wafers of flour-bread and honey. The gummy drops which form on the leaves of the tamarisk are of a similar sweetish substance, as also the tarfa gum, and several other articles called manna in Arabia; but the true manna was none of these, and probably a distinct thing made for the occasion. Its similarity to other things offers no explanation of its character. It came without notice, and as abruptly discontinued. Botanists have tried to explain the thing by references to many articles, as esculent lichen, which is eaten in Northern Africa. It is a species of moss. Some have considered the miracle as multiplying the natural supplies of the desert as that of the loaves and fishes was at Bethsaida, increasing five loaves and two fishes.

MANO'AH (*rest*). Father of SAMSON (Judg. xiii. 2).

MAN-SLAYER. Not an intentional murderer. Death by a blow in a quarrel (Num. xxxv. 22). Death by a stone thrown at random (xxii. 23). In these and like cases the man-slayer could escape to a CITY OF REFUGE. An animal, not known to be vicious, causing death to a person was put to death; but if it was known to be vicious, the owner was liable to be fined or put to death (Ex. xxi. 28, 31). A thief taken at night might lawfully be put to death; but if the sun had risen, killing him was regarded as MURDER (Ex. xxii. 23).

MAN'TLE (Heb. SEMICHAH). See CLOAK in DRESS.

MA'OCH (*breast-band*). Father of ACHISH. King of Gath (1 Sam. xxvii. 2).

MA'ON. In the mts. of Judah (Josh. xv. 55), near Juttah. It was in the wilderness near this place (bleak and hilly pasture-lands) that David hid himself from Saul. Main 7 ms. S. E. of Hebron (*Rob.*). On a conical hill, 200 ft. high, are ruins of foundations of hewn stone, a square enclosure, towers, and cisterns. The people use the caves near for dwellings, as of old.

MA'ONITES (Judg. x. 12). An ancient and powerful nomad tribe, allied to the Phœnicians, first settled with the Amalekites in the vale of Sodom, and afterward migrated eastward into Arabia. They named Maon in Judah, Beth-Maon in Moab, and Maan in Edom, 15 ms. E. of Petra. This last is now an important pilgrim station, on the caravan route to Mecca. A castle and other antiquities mark its ancient strength. Mehunim (2 Chr. xxvi. 7). Among the descendants of Caleb, the son of Shammai, the builder of Beth-zur (1 Chr. ii. 45).

MA'RA (*bitter*). The name given to NOOMI at Bethlehem (Ruth i. 20).

MA'RAH (*bitter*). Well, on the route of the Exodus. See EXODUS.

MAR'ALAH (*trembling*). On the border of Zebulon (Josh. xix. 11). 4 ms. S. W. of Nazareth, the little village of Malul stands on a hill, and contains the ruins of a temple and other antiquities.

MARANATH'A (*our lord cometh*), (1 Cor. xvi. 22). See ANATHEMA.

MAR'BLE. Called by Josephus white stone, quarried from under Jerusalem (Esth. i. 6).

The vast excavation under the N. E. section of Jerusalem, so long lost, was discovered a few years ago by Dr. J. T. Barclay, author of "The City of the Great King," and since that time has been visited by many travelers. It is entered from outside of the wall of the city, east of the Damascus Gate. A guide is necessary to avoid getting lost, there are so many chambers running into each other for nearly 800 feet from the entrance. There is water in the cave, but it is limy and bitter. On the walls are carved crosses, Hebrew letters, and other marks, showing that the place has been known since the crucifixion.

The chalky limestone of Palestine is full of caves, many of which are noted. (See ADULLAM).

The white stone of this quarry is nearly as soft as chalk, and is easily cut out with a saw. The cream-colored is also streaked with orange-tawney and other similar tints, in coarse and fine, wavy lines; is much harder than the white, and is called dolomite.

The marble columns of Tyre, Cæsarea, Joppa and other ruins, were probably imported, as there are no quarries of such hard, fine, white marble known in the country.

MAR'CUS (*a large hammer*). Both a first and a surname (Col. iv. 10).

MARDOCHI'US. MORDECAI. 1. Uncle of Esther (Esth. x. 1).—2. (1 Esd. v. 8).

MARE'SHAH (*head-town*). 1. A city of Judah (Josh. xv. 44). Hebron was founded by Mareshah (1 Chr. ii. 42). It was one of the cities fortified by Rehoboam (2 Chr. xi. 8). It was the native place of Eliezer, who prophesied the destruction of Jehoshaphat's fleet at Ezion Geber.— 2. Father of Hebron (1 Chr. ii. 42).—3. Mareshah, grandson of SHELAH (1 Chr. iv. 21),

MAR'IMOTH. A priest (2 Esd. i. 2).

MAR'ISA (2 Macc. xii. 35).

MARK. HISTORY OF THE BOOK.

MAR'KET (MAARAB). An open place, where people came for business or to converse (Ez. xxvii. 13, 17).

The market-place was a resort for news and

social chat (Matt. xi. 16; Luke vii. 32). There justice was administered, especially if it was at a gate. They were generally open places just inside the gate, although there were other localities for certain occupations, as Bakers' street (Jer. xxxvii. 21), and many others mentioned by Josephus. They were probably covered by a roof, forming a piazza.

MAR'MOTH. A priest (1 Esd. viii. 62).

MA'ROTH (*bitterness*). Mentioned by the prophet Micah (i. 12), and probably near Jerusalem.

MARRIAGE. Instituted in the garden of Eden (Gen. i. 27, 28; ii. 18, 24). The Saviour advocated the divine character of marriage apart from civil laws. He opposed divorces except for one cause (Matt. v. 32, xix. 3, 6, 9), and all breaches of the marriage vow (Matt. v. 28). Betrothal preceded the marriage rite and was a binding engagement (Matt. i. 18-25). Groomsman referred to as "the friend of the bridegroom" in John iii. 29. A procession formed part of the ceremony, and took place at night accompanied by young unmarried women bearing lamps (Matt. xxv.).

The modern Jews make a solemn contract before witnesses, in writing, which is signed. The ceremony consists of the bride standing in her best garments, and jewelry (borrowed if necessary), under a canopy, beside the bridegroom, where the contract is read to them by a Rabbi, and their hands are joined in the presence of witnesses. A glass of wine is tasted by both, when the glass is broken by the bridegroom, and a ring is given to the bride, of plain gold. In nearly all cases in the East a dower is given for the wife, which belongs to her. Some few parents (as the Circassians) take the dower as a price paid for the daughter. The Mohammedan custom is to pay the bride two-thirds of the dower, reserving the other part until her death or divorce. The Hebrews called the husband lord (BAAL). The first wife was the only one recognized by the civil law, but all others were valid in the Church (2 Chr. xxiv. 3, 2 Sam. xii. 8), where (in the law of Moses) the second, or other wife, was called maid-servant (Ex. xxi. 7). The rich often married poor relatives to give them support and protection. The strongest motive for a plurality of wives was the great desire for many children, and the fact that many women are barren (1 Sam. i. 2). The Talmudists limited the number to four, except in the case of the king who could have eighteen. Polygamy was only prohibited by an imperial edict of Honorius, A. D. 400.

Just before the Christian era the idea arose that marriage affected the intellectual and spiritual nature. Up to that time the Hebrews taught it as a duty, but then it was urged that its effect was to lessen man's holiness, the teaching of the Essenes, an ascetic order of celibates (Jos. Wars, ii. 8; 2, 13). The Therapeutæ and Gnostics adopted the same idea, from whom the Christians copied it, forming monastic orders (a monk is a living insult to woman), in direct opposition to the instruction of Jesus and his apostles, who recognized the duty and holiness of the state, and enjoined respect to its laws. In the case of a widow it was regarded as a sign of holiness to remain a widow, in the latter time only, for it is expressly charged upon a brother to raise up children to a deceased brother (Gen. xxxviii. 8,) by his widow (by Moses, Matt. xxii. 23). The same custom (Levirate marriage, from Levir, a brother-in-law,) was and is held among other people, as in the case of the Ossetes in Georgia (Asia), and Arabia, with some changes, which include the privilege of the father of the deceased husband to claim the widow for a wife if the brother refuses. (Perhaps in consequence of Judah's example).

The laws regulating legal marriage were very strict, and were of two kinds, 1. when between two Hebrews, and 2. when a Hebrew married a Gentile. (1). The first restriction was based on ideas of health and propriety among relatives (Lev. xviii. 6-18), both of blood kin, and by marriage, because the husband and wife were "one flesh" (Matt. xix. 5). Surprising exceptions were made in the cases of the daughter and the niece; a man might marry his daughter and his niece; but the mother could not marry a son or a nephew. An heiress could not marry out of her tribe (out of policy, in keeping the land in the original owner's tribe). The high-priest must only marry a young unmarried woman, a Hebrew, never a widow, or one divorced, or a Gentile. No person physically defective could marry. The apostle restricted church officers to one wife, and prohibited a second marriage during the life-time of the first, even after divorce. The wife could divorce her husband for some causes. There was no rule in regard to age, except that early marriage is commended (Prov. ii. 17; v. 18; Is. lxii. 5). The age at which marriage may be consummated is from 12 (or even 10), upwards, in a woman; and was limited to 13 in a man. The usual age varies from 16 to 18. The first marriage (of virgins) is usually on a Wednesday; a second, as of a widow, etc., on Thursday.

The wife is almost always chosen for a man by his parents, if living, or by his guardian, or a friend, or relations (Gen. xxiv.). The son could request such favors (xxiv. 4); but if the son broke this custom the parents had "a grief of mind" (xxvi. 35). The maid's consent was asked in some cases (but not as a rule), after her father's decision. A friend sometimes did the whole business of selecting the bride for the bridegroom; and in modern days the bridegroom seldom sees the face of his wife until the actual moment of marriage, or until after the ceremony. The espousal was legal and binding, confirmed by oaths, a feast, sometimes a ring to the "bride," and exchange of presents, or at least presents to the bride. A year passed between betrothal and marriage in the case of a first marriage of the woman, a few weeks or days if a second. The custom of a settlement of property on the wife came into use after the Captivity.

VINE.

The bridegroom wore a new dress, if able, and a crown of gold, silver, roses, myrtle or olive.

The bride's dress, among the wealthy, was a magnificent display of fine clothes and curious traditions. Both parties perfumed themselves. The bride took a bath (Ruth iii. 3; Eph. v. 26) in a formal manner, accompanied by her relatives and friends (Ez. xxiii. 40). After putting on her finest garments, around her waist was wound a peculiar girdle (KISHURIM, the attire, Jer. iii. 32); and over her head was thrown the veil or long shawl (Gen. xxiv. 25), covering the whole figure; while on her head was set a crown ornamented with jewels, or a chaplet of leaves and flowers (KALLAH, chaplet, also bride). A pair of ornamented slippers were a gift from the husband before marriage. The moderns carry the presents to the bride in procession through the street, with bands of music, instrumental and vocal, nearly every one carrying a lantern; arriving at the bride's house, she is es-

corted to the bridegroom's house, where the marriage-feast is held. The very wealthy prolong the feast several days, furnishing garments for each guest, to be worn only during the time. Amusements of many kinds are in order.

There were three kinds of legal marriage: 1. By written contract; 2. By payment of a sum of money (or an equivalent) before witnesses; and 3. By force—as a man compelling a woman to submit to him, or by seduction.

The wife's rights were food, raiment (including house), and conjugal privileges (Ex. xxi. 10). Her duties were as extensive as the entire household, as shown in Prov. xxxi.

Marriage is used as a type in both the Old and New Testaments of true religious union with God in many beautiful passages.

MAR'S HILL. AREOPAGUS.

MAR'SENA (*worthy man*). A prince of Persia (Esth. i. 14).

MARTHA. Daughter of Simon the leper, and sister of LAZARUS and MARY of BETHANY. She was the elder sister, the head and manager of the household. She was present at the supper at Bethany (John xii. 2).

Luke calls their residence Martha's house, because there was no reason for mentioning anyone else of the family at that time, and she was the subject of the record then writing. When Jesus first visited the house (Luke x. 38-42), Martha hastens to provide the repast, while Mary was attracted by the teaching of the master, when Martha complained of Mary's neglect of the work to be done, forgetting the *one* thing needful (the thirst for spiritual waters?).

Martha character appears again in the same light at the time of the sickness, death and resurrection of Lazarus. She hastened out of the village to meet the coming Saviour, while Mary sat still in the house and awaited his coming (John xi. 20, 22). Her anxiety clouded her perception of the true meaning of the words of Jesus, "He shall rise again," supposing that he referred only to the general belief in the resurrection beyond the grave. When she learned the truth she made a confession of faith in him as "The resurrection and life," and acknowledged his power and goodness, although a moment before she had objected to rolling away the stone from the door of the tomb, supposing the body of Lazarus to be decayed.

She is mentioned once more after that, again serving at the table where Jesus, several disciples, and Lazarus, were dining, but then she also bathed the feet of the beloved Master with tears, and perfumed him with a very expensive unguent (xii. 1, 2). Her character is clearly drawn by both Luke and John, as a pattern of domestic care and fidelity, and sisterly friendship. Her death is not recorded.

MAR TYR (Gr. *martus*). "Witnesses" in Matt. xviii. 16. Simply witness. Witnesses of the gospel, suffering persecution, became *martyrs* in the modern sense.

MAS'ALOTH (*terraces*). Near Arbela: the great caverns in the Wady al Hamam (*pigeon valley*), which were fortified by Josephus (Josephus, Life, 37). Kulaat Ibn Maan. Herod drove a band of robbers out of them by letting soldiers down the face of the cliff to the mouth of the caves in large boxes.

MAS'CHIL. A musical term denoting a melody requiring great skill in execution (Ps. xxxii., xlii.).

MASH (Gen. x. 23). 4th son of Aram; settled in Mesopotamia. Mt. Masius (between the Euphrates and the Tigris, in the N.), and the river Masche flowing at its base, preserve the name. A prince of Masou was taken by Rameses II on the Orontes, at Kedesh.

MASH EL. City of Asher (1 Chr. vi. 74). Misheal (Josh. xix. 26).

MASI'AS. Servant of Solomon (1 Esd. v. 34).

MAS'MAN (1 Esd. viii. 43).

MAS PHA (1 Macc. iii. 46). Massepha, or Mizpeh?—2. A city taken by Judas Maccabæus, E. of Jordan (1 Macc. v. 35). It may be the same as Mizpeh of Gilead, or Mizpeh of Moab.

MASRE KAH (*vineyard*). Native city of Samlah, king of Edom (Gen. xxxvi. 36). The region called Jebal, N. of Edom, is now famous for its vineyards (owned by the Refaya tribe), and this place may have been located there, as Eusebius and Jerome say.

MAS'SA (*burden*). Son of Ishmael (Gen. xxv. 14).

MAS'SAH (*temptation*). In the Sinai desert (Ex. xvii. 2, 7). REPHIDIM. (See WANDERING.)

MAS SIAS (1 Esd. ix. 22).

MAS'TICH-TREE. The gum is used to strengthen the teeth and gums. It was prized by the ancients on this account, and for its medicinal properties. It is used in the preparation of spirits, as a sweetmeat, and in varnishes. The trees are very wide, and circular, 10 or 12 ft. high, and are found on the shores of the Mediterranean.

MATHANI'AS. A descendant of Pahath-Moab (1 Esd. ix. 31).

MATHU SALA. Son of Enoch (Luke iii. 37).

MA'TRED (*propelling*). Daughter of Mezahab (Gen. xxxvi. 39).

MA'TRI (*rain of Jah*). Family of Benjamin (1 Sam. x. 21).

MAT'TAN (*a gift*). 1. Priest of Baal (2 K. xi. 18).—2. Father of Shephatiah (Jer. xxxviii. 1).

MAT'TANAH (*gift*.) Station S. E. of the Dead Sea (Num. xxi. 18).

MATTANI'AH (*gift of Jah*). 1. Original name of ZEDEKIAH, king of Judah (1 K. xxiv. 17).—2. Son of Asaph (1 Chr. ix. 15). He was leader of a Temple-choir (xi. 17).—3. A descendant of Asaph (2 Chr. xx. 14).—4. Son of Elam (Ezr. x. 26).—5. Son of Zattu (27).—6. Descendant of Pahath-Moab (30).—7. Son of Bani (37).—8. Father of Zaccur (Neh. xiii. 13).—9. Pupil of Heman (1 Chr. xxv. 4, 16).—10. Descendant of Asaph, who assisted in the purification of the Temple (2 Chr. xxix. 13).

MAT TATHA. Son of Zathan (Luke iii. 31).

MAT TATHAH. A descendant of Hashum (Ezr. x. 33).

MATTATHI'AS. 1. An assistant to Ezra (1 Esd. ix. 43).—2. Father of MACCABEES (1 Macc. ii. 1).—3. Son of Absalom (xi. 70; xiii. 11).—4. Son of Simon Maccabæus (xvi. 14).—5. Nicanor's envoy

(2 Macc. xiv. 19).—6. Son of Amos (Luke iii. 25).
—7. Son of Semei (26).

MAT'TENAI. 1. Of the family of Hashum (Ezr. xi. 33).—2. Descendant of Bani (37).—3. A priest (Neh. xii. 19).

MAT'THAN. Son of Eleazar (Matt. i. 15).

MAT THANI'AS. Descendant of Elam (1 Esd. ix. 27).

MAT'THAT. 1. Son of Levi (Luke iii. 24).—2. Son of Levi (29).

MATTHE'LAS (1 Esd. ix. 19).

MATTHEW (Mattathias, *the gift of Jehovah*). Is only mentioned at the time of his call to be an apostle, when he was in "the receipt of custom," (Matt. ix. 9). Mark gives him another name—Levi, the son of Alphæus (Mark ii. 14; iii. 18) who has been supposed to have been the same as the Alphæus the father of James the Less, but without reason. On his call he gave a feast by way of a farewell to his friends, to which Jesus was invited (Luke v. 27). His humility is seen in his styling himself "the publican" (Matt. x. 3). He was with the other apostles after the resurrection (Acts i. 13). After this there is no record of him or his acts. It is not known how or where he died. There is a tradition that he lived in Jerusalem 15 years after the crucifixion, and that he became a martyr in Persia. See HISTORY OF THE BOOKS for the GOSPEL.

MATTHI'AS. 1. MATTATHAH (1 Esd. ix. 33).—2. An apostle chosen to succeed Judas (Acts i. 26). Tradition says he preached in Cappadocia.

MATTITHI'AH (*gift*). 1. First born of Shallum (1 Chr. ix. 31).—2. A musician of David's choir (1 Chr. xvi. 5).—3. Of the family of Zebo (Ezr. x. 43).—4. A priest who assisted Ezra (viii. 4).—5. Son, or pupil of Jeduthun, leader of the 14th Temple choir (1 Chr. xxv. 3, 21).

MAT'TOCK (CHEREB). A single-headed pick-axe. The Egyptian hoe was of wood, and answered for hoe, spade and pick (1 Sam. xiii. 20, 21). See cut on page 6.

MAUL (MEPHITS). A heavy, war-like instrument (Prov. xxv. 18). See ARMS.

MAUZ ZIM (*forts*). Layard (*Nin.* ii. 456) after describing Hera, the Assyrian Venus, as "standing erect on a lion, and crowned with a tower or mural coronet, which, we learn from Lucian, was peculiar to the Semetic figure of the goddess," adds, "May she be connected with the 'El Maozem,' the deity presiding over bulwarks and fortresses, the 'god of forces' of Dan. xi. 38." See cut, page 70.

MAZITI'AS (1 Esd. ix. 35).

MAZ ZAROTH. See ASTRONOMY.

MEAD'OW (Heb. ACHU), (Gen. xli. 2, 18). Translated meadow. Rendered *cave* in the Peshito-Syriac.

ME'AH (*a hundred*). The tower of Meah was on the city wall north of the sheep-gate, when rebuilt by Nehemiah (iii. 1, xii. 39). Located by some at the N. W. corner of the Temple area, where the fortress of Antonia was afterwards built, and now called Pilate's house. Porter locates it at the N. E. corner of the Harem area, where there are massive foundations.

MEALS. The Jews generally eat their dinner before noon, and their supper after sundown. The chief meal of the Jews was in the evening; of the Egyptians it was at noon. The early Hebrews sat or squatted round a low table upon which the meal was served, but in later times couches were used to recline upon before the tables. The guests were ranged in order of rank side by side (Gen. xliii. 33), resting upon the left elbow, the right arm being free—this posture explains the text "leaning on Jesus's bosom (John xiii. 23, xxi. 20). The dishes, as they are to this day, were generally stews of rice, beans, and burgul (cracked wheat), with soups or sauces. The meats were so cooked that when served they fell to pieces. Knives and forks were not used at the table, but spoons, and generally thin slices of bread, were doubled up and dipped into the dishes, all eating from the same dish. These pieces of bread also served the purpose of napkins. It was after this manner that Judas eat of the sauce or *sop* at the Last Supper (John xiii. 26). Washing of the hands, from being a necessity, was elevated to a form and ceremony.

MEA'NI (1 Esd. v. 31).

MEA'RAH (*cave*). Boundary of the unconquered land near Zidon (Josh. xiii. 4). Half way between Tyre and Sidon are ruins called *Adlun*, and in the cliffs near are many caves and grottos (*Rob.*). William of Tyre mentions a fortified cave near Sidon, occupied by the Crusaders.

MEAT. LEHEM, *bread* (1 Sam. xx. 24); TEREF, *spoil* (Ps. cxi. 5); Gr. *bromos* and *brosis* (Matt. iii. 4; Acts xxvii. 33; Heb. v. 12). Anything that may be eaten. This word was never used for flesh-meat, unless it was included in a general sense, as we now say food.

MEAT-OFFERING. See SACRIFICE.

MEBUN'NAI (*strong one*). One of David's guard (2 Sam. xxiii. 27). Called SIBBECHAI (xxi. 18; 1 Chr. xx. 4).

MECHE'RATHITE, THE. "The Maachathite (2 Sam. xxiii. 34).

MED'ABA. Greek form of Medeba (1 Macc. ix. 36).

ME'DAN (*strife*). Son of Abraham by Keturah (Gen. xxv. 2). Traces of this people are supposed to be found in the village of Madan, on the Euphrates, and the city Maadan in Hejaz, Arabia. Maadan, *mines*.

ME'DEBA (*quiet waters*). In Moab (Num. xxi. 30). Name of the Mishor south of Heshbon (Josh. xiii. 9, 16). The Ammonites were defeated here by Joab, David's general (1 Chr. xix.). Not recorded as possessed by Reuben, and was probably only tributary. It was a strong fortress in the

AT DINNER.

time of the Maccabees (1 Macc. ix. 35; Ant. xiii. i. 4, 9, 1). Ptolemy locates a Medeba between Bostra and Petra. Eusebius and Jerome mention a Christian village east of Medeba. It was a noted bishopric of the patriarchate of Bitira Arabiæ, and so named in the acts of the Council of Chalcedon (A. D. 451). A large tank, columns, and extensive foundations, on a rocky hill 4 miles S. E. of Heshbon, on the Roman road, mark the site.

MEDES. Media (Gen. x. 2, Madia; 2 K. xvii. 6, Medes; Esth. i. 3, Media; Dan xi. 1, Mede). 3d

son of Japhet, and founder of a great race. 1500 years of their history is a blank, from their first mention to the time when Isaiah threatened to stir them up against Babylon (xiii. 7, B. C. 72). Berosus (Chaldæan historian) says that the Medes conquered Babylonia B. C. 2458. This date may be very much too ancient, for the word Mede is first found on the Assyrian monuments at the date of B. C. 880 (Rawlinson); but there is no doubt that both Cushite and Semitic races occupied Mesopotamia together from a very early date. They were called Arians in the time of which Herodotus writes; and traces of them are found from Hindustan to Thrace. It is supposed that the race had its origin on the banks of the Indus, from whence its people found their way into Persia, Media, Greece, etc.

In Media, Sargon, Sennacherib, and Esar-haddon reigned from B. C. 720 to B. C. 660, over a country which before that time had been ruled by a great many sheikhs (chiefs of families or tribes). About the middle of the 7th century B. C., Cyaxares (the Mede) led a fresh immigration of Arians into Media, and is called the first king of Media by Diodorus. In his reign the three kingdoms, Media, Lydia, and Babylon, were united by treaty and marriages. The empire extended from the Halys river to the Caspian gates, 1500 miles long, and from the Euphrates and the Persian Gulf to the Black and Caspian Seas, 450 miles wide. It lasted only 75 years.

The Persians, led by Cyrus, conquered Media and terminated the kingdom, B. C. 558.

One of the tribes of Media, the Budii, are mentioned in the Scripture by the name of Phut (Ez. xxvii. 10), whose soldiers were in the army of Tyre, together with Persians and others.

VICTORY.

The ancient religion was a belief in two nearly equal divinities of opposite principles, Ormazd the good, and Ahriman the evil—both self-existent and irresistible, and both always contending with each other. Ormazd was worshiped; and also the sun, moon, and stars, and respect paid to genii. The fire-worship of Armenia was more or less blended with this system. Magism consisted of the worship of the elements, chiefly fire. Altars on mountaintops were kept continually burning, and sacrifices were frequent. The priesthood formed a distinct class, and professed ability to interpret dreams, explain visions, and to divine future events.

The captive Israelites were placed in certain cities of the Medes by the king of Assyria (2 K. xvii. 6, etc.). Both Isaiah and Jeremiah prophesied the part which the Medes were to take in destroying Babylon (Jer. li. 11, 28). Daniel interpreted the writing on the wall as the sign of the coming conquest by the Medes and Persians (xi. 25-28). Ezra mentions the palace of Achmetha, where the decree of Cyrus was found (vi. 2, 5), which the monuments prove to have been the residence of Cyrus at that time. See ECBATANA.

In the Apocrypha, Media is the chief scene of the book of Tobit, and a large part of that of Judith.

ME′DIAN. Citizen of MEDIA (Dan. ix. 1).

MEDIATOR (*interpreter*). Moses was the Mediator between Jehovah and the Israelites (Gal. iii. 19, 20). Jesus Christ is the one Mediator between God and men (1 Tim. ii. 5).

MED′ICINE. The Egyptian physicians (barbers?) were skilled, and perhaps also educated, if we may believe the Greeks, before the Exodus. The first mention of a physician was of the "servants of Joseph" who embalmed his father (Gen. l. 2); they were probably regular attendants on the royal house. Specialists are mentioned by Herodotus (ii. 84), 'each physician is for one kind of sickness, such as for the eyes, teeth, head, stomach, etc. The practice of medicine was largely superstitious. The medicines mostly used were salves, balms, (Jer. viii. 22), plasters or poultices (2 K. xx. 7); bathing (2 K. v. 10), oils, and mineral baths. Charms and amulets were used by the Jews, also charming by the hand, as in 2 K. v. 11. Knowledge of anatomy is suggested in Job x. 11, and also shown in monumental figures. Physicians received public salaries, and their office was held in high esteem. The Jews at a later period, overcame much of their abhorrence of uncleanness, and of their reverence for human remains, in the pursuit of medical knowledge. Alexandria became the centre for medical study. (See ALEXANDRIA.) Luke is referred to as "the beloved physician," and his medical education was probably Greek.

MEE′DA (1 Esd. v. 32).

MEEK. Heb. ANAV, *oppressed, afflicted, humble*. Applied to those who rather suffer wrong than do wrong, and therefore enjoy God's favor (Num. xii. 3). The word translated meek in Num. xii. 3, in reference to Moses, means "disinterested."

MEGIDDO (*place of troops*). An ancient royal city of the Canaanites, on the south border of the plain of Esdraelon, commanding a pass leading from the plain to the Samarian hills (Josh. xii. 21). In the territory of Issachar, but belonging to Manasseh. The people were not driven out, but paid tribute (Judg. i. 27, 28). It is made famous in the song of victory of Deborah, when Barak defeated Sisera (Judg. iv. 13, etc.). One of Solomon's officers was placed here, and some important works built (1 K. ix. 15). Ahaziah fled here from Jehu, and died (2 K. ix. 27). The "good king" Josiah "went against" Pharaoh Necho, as an ally of the king of Assyria, was wounded here, and died at Jerusalem (2 Chr. xxxv. 22-24). From this event the name of the place became a poetical synonym for terrible conflict and grief; as in the Revelation (xvi. 16. See also Zech. xii. 11; 2 Chr. xxxv. 25). El Lejjun. Waters of Megiddo. See KISHON.

MEGID′DON (Zech. xii. 11). PLAIN OF.

MEHETA′BEEL. Ancestor of Shemaiah (Neh. vi. 10).

MEHET′ABEL (*El benefits*). Daughter of Matred (Gen. xxxvi. 39).

MEHI′DA (*junction*). Ancestor of Nethinim, returned from captivity (Ex. ii. 52; Neh. vii. 54).

ME′HIR (*price*). Son of Chelub (1 Chr. iv. 11).

ME′HOLATHITE, THE. (1 Sam. xviii. 19). See ABEL MEHOLAH. This place was called Meadow of the Whirlpool, and was near some rapid or whirlpool in the river Jordan.

MEHU′JAEL (*smitten by El*). Son of Irad, and fourth in descent from Cain (Gen. iv. 18).

MEHU′MAN (*faithful*). A chamberlain of Ahasuerus (Esth. i. 10).

MEHU′NIMS. Maonites. (See MAON.) Josephus speaks of a city built by king Uzziah on the Red Sea to overawe the Arabs, who adjoined Egypt (Ant. ix. 10, 3). Probably near or in the valley of Gerar. One of the three friends of Job was Sophar, king of the Minæans, who is also called Zophar the Naamathite. (See NAAMAH.) This people were located by Strabo and Ptolemy in the S. W. corner of Arabia, in Hadramaut. There is a Minyay S. E. of Gaza, a station on the road to Sinai, mentioned in the Christian records of the 6th century with some distinction. *Main*, a ruin south of Heshbon (BAAL MEON), is another relic of the tribe. Some of them returned from captivity with Zerubbabel (Ezr. ii. 50).

MEJARKON (*yellow waters*). In Dan (Josh. xix. 46), near Joppa. Torrent?

MEKO′NAH (*a place*). A city of some size, having suburbs, in the south, near Ziklag; occupied after the return from captivity (Neh. xi. 28).

MELATIAH (*Jah delivers*). A Gibeonite who assisted in building the wall (Neh. iii. 7).

MEL′CHI (*my king*). 1. Son of Jamri (Luke iii. 24).—2. Son of Addi (iii. 21).

MELCHI′AH. Father of Pashur (Jer. xxi. 1).

MELCHI′AS. 1. MALCHIAH 2 (1 Esd. ix. 26).

MEL′CHIEL. Son of Melchiel, governor of Bethulia (Judg. vi. 15).

MELCHIS′EDEC (Heb. v., vi., vii.).

MEL′CHISHU′A. Son of Saul (1 Sam. xiv. 49; xxxi. 2).

MELCHIZ′EDEK (*king of righteousness*). He lived in the time of Abraham, worshiped God, and was "a priest of the most high God," perhaps a first-born, and a patriarch or elder in the city of Salem (Gen. xiv.). He received Abraham's homage and presents or tithes, and gave him a blessing, and gave bread and wine to his tired and hungry army.

Some have thought that the bread and wine were sacrificial, and that Melchizedek was a type of Christ. Others have strangely imagined that it was an appearance of Christ himself in the disguise of the priest.

He really was both a king and a priest—and so far typical of the spiritual king and priest, Jesus the Christ.

The "order of Melchizedek" (Ps. cx. 4) means "likeness in official dignity," being both king and priest. The object of the Hebrews was to show that Christ was the king and priest of the new dispensation, and it was objected that he was not of the tribe of Levi, and his father was not a high-priest (Ex. xxix. 29, 30), nor even any priest, and his mother fell short of the requirements of the law (Lev. xxi. 13, 14). His descent must have been preserved in the records, and have been pure from stains on both father and mother's side; and he was to become a priest by education and high-priest by consecration (Ex. xxix. 9) with the holy oil, while wearing the holy garments of Aaron; and he must hand over his office to a successor before his death. Jesus did not carry out this Levitical idea, and was not therefore a priest after that order. Paul, in his letter to the Hebrews, discusses the question very freely and clearly. See SALEM.

MEL′COM (Heb. MALCAM), (Jer. xlix. 1, 3).

ME LEA (*full*). Son of Menan (Luke iii. 31).

ME′LECH (*king*). Son of Micah (1 Chr. viii. 35, ix. 41).

MEL′ICU (Neh. xii. 14). MALLUCH.

MEL′ITA. MALTA. A small island, 20 by 12 miles in extent, and 60 miles south of Sicily, where Paul was wrecked when on his way to Rome (Acts xxvii. xxviii.). The island is full of mementoes of Paul, who is its tutelary saint. The bay where the shipwreck occurred is called St. Paul's, and is a deep inlet on the north side of the island, 5 miles from the port of Malta, and is one mile wide and

PAUL'S BAY, MALTA.

two miles long, inland, having the small island Salmonetta on the western side of the entrance. The whole island is a barren rock, but has been made fertile to some extent by great labor. The Phœnicians colonized it, from whom the Greeks took it about 736 B. C.; and in turn the Carthaginians became its masters in the Second Punic War, 528 B. C., and the Romans in 242 B. C., whose officer, Publius, governed it when Paul was there. Its history since then has been full of changes in its masters, in which we read of Vandals, Greeks (A. D. 553), Arabs, Normans (A. D. 1090), Germans (1530, by whom it was given to the Knights of St. John, of Jerusalem), the French (1798), and finally the English, who hold it now. The Anglican Bishop of Gibraltar resides there. The island is a station for several lines of steamers and submarine telegraph cables. The island of Meleda, in the Adriatic Sea, on the coast of Dalmatia, 125 miles southeast of Venice, was once supposed to be the one on which Paul was wrecked; but a more careful examination of all the facts, and of the course of the prevailing winds, and position of the islands and places mentioned, both before and after the shipwreck, have determined the question in favor of Malta. The "barbarous people" of Acts xxviii. 2, were simply not Greeks. The Greeks called every nation or tribe barbarians who did not speak the Greek language.

MEL′ONS (Heb. ABATICHIM). Melons are extensively cultivated in the East, and used as a common article of diet; here we make a luxury of them. Thomson says "Nothing could be regretted in the burning desert more than these delicious (water) melons, whose exuberant juice is so refreshing to the thirsty pilgrim," (Num. xi. 5).

MEL'IZAR (Heb. MELZAR, *steward*), (Dan. i., ii. 16).

MEM (Heb. MEYM). The thirteenth letter of the Hebrew alphabet (Ps. cxix.).

MEM'MIUS, QUIN'TUS. A common first name among the Romans (2 Macc. xi. 34).

MEMPHIS (*the abode of the good one*). In Hebrew MOPH or NOPH (Hosea ix. 6). The ancient Egyptian name was Men-nefru, the *pyramid city*. On the west bank of the Nile, just south of the junction of the three branches, Canopic, Sebennytic and Pelusiac. It was built on a district which was reclaimed by Menes from a marsh, by turning the Nile into a new channel, east of the ancient one which ran close to the Libyan mountains; and in a position which commanded both the Delta and Upper Egypt. Of all the temples, palaces, walls, and houses which the ancient historians describe, not one stone is left on another—the pyramids only remaining. The necropolis in the vicinity witnesses the ancient importance of the city. The principal pyramid field extends along the west bank of the Nile for about 15 miles; and the whole district, including many ruins and small pyramids, for nearly 60 miles. There are from 40 to 60 pyramids, according to the count of various travelers, who include more or less large and small pyramids and ruins of supposed pyramids. The Hebrew prophets distinctly predicted the fall of Memphis (Is. xix. 13; Jer. ii. 16, xlvi. 14, 19; Ez. xxx. 16), the latest about 525 B. C., 50 years before the invasion of Cambyses, and their words seem to have been fulfilled to the very letter. Only one of all its multitude of images and idols now remains, fallen, broken, half buried in sand and mud (the statue of Rameses II, the finest known work of Egyptian sculpture). There is a vast collection of antiquities from Egypt in the Abbott Museum, New York, where may be seen a countless number of relics of the past, of cloth, papyrus, wood, stone and metal, with works of art from Memphis and other localities throughout Egypt. The pyramids stand on a rocky shelf of the desert, 150 feet above the Nile basin.

The Great Pyramid was 480 feet high, and built of stone quarried near, and (the finest) across the river, at Toura. The surface was smooth, when complete, being finished with polished marble, or with a hard cement. This is now taken off, leaving the surface in rude steps, 3 to 6 feet high, varied by the thickness of the layers of stone. The interior walls were also polished, and are now. The king's chamber is of red granite, and contains the lower part of a porphyry sarcophagus, the lid having been removed. Cambyses nearly destroyed the city, B. C. 470, and the rise of Alexandria into importance completed its overthrow.

MEMU'CAN (*in authority*). A privy council of the king (Esth. i. 14, 16, 21). They were "wise men who knew the times" (skilled in the planets, according to Aben Ezra) and appeared to have formed a council of state, interpreting the laws.

PETRA. EDOM.

MEN'AHEM (*consoler*). Son of Gadi, king of Israel from B. C. 772 to 761. He continued the idolatrous calf-worship of Jeroboam. The cotemporary prophets Hosea and Amos devoted their lives and talents to attempts at reform of the Church in Israel, but without success. Their books are a picture of society in their time, poetically expressed, but certainly not flattering to either king or people.

ME'NAN. Son of Mattatha (Luke iii. 31).

ME'NES. MENA, (*numbered*). The first word in the mysterious writing on the wall in Belshazzar's palace, interpreted by Daniel (v. 25-28).

MENELA'US. A high-priest, appointed to the office from Antiochus Epiphanes by a bribe, B. C. 172 (2 Macc. iv. 23-25).

MENES'THEUS (*one who abides*). The father of APOLLONIUS (2 Macc. iv. 21).

MENI (*destiny*). An object of idolatrous worship, the moon goddess, LUNA (Is. xv. 11).

MEN-STEALERS were put to death (Ex. xxi. 16).

MENU'CHA (*place of rest*), (Jer. li. 59). SERAIAH II.

MENU'CHAH (*without noise or tumult*). With ease in Judg. xx. 43.

MENU'CHITES (1 Chr. ii. 52).

MEON'ENIM, THE PLAIN OF. Correctly, The OAK of Meonenim (*the enchanters*); (Judg. ix. 37). There were five noted trees near Shechem. 1. The oak of Moreh (not *plain*, as in Gen. xii. 6) where Abram built his first altar in the Promised Land.—2. Jacob took from his family all the strange gods, and ear-rings, and hid them under an oak at Shechem (xxxv. 4).—3. The oak under which Joshua set up the stone-witness (Josh. xxiv. 26).—4. The oak of the pillar (not *plain*, as in Judg. ix. 6), under which Abimelech was made king—5. The oak of the enchanters, where Gaal, son of Ebed, saw the soldiers of Abimelech coming, as he stood in the gate of Shechem (Judg. ix. 37). Jacob and Joshua may have chosen the same tree, and the words used by the two men are almost identical in form and spirit. Probably, also, the holy place and the crowning of the king were under the same tree: altogether making four references to the same sacred oak. These sacred trees were found all over the land, and this one may have been connected with the shrine of Baal Berith in its vicinity (Judg. viii. 33, ix. 46).

MEON'OTHAI (*my dwellings*). Son of OTHNIEL (1 Chr. iv. 14).

MEPHA'ATH (*sightly*). Moabite city in Reuben, near Heshbon (Josh. xiii. 18; Jer. xlviii. 21), given to the Merarite Levites. The Romans had a garrison here in the time of Eusebius. Lost.

MEPHIB'OSHETH (*shame-destroyer*, or *image-breaker*). The name is given in Chr. as Merib-baal—Baal and Bosheth being synonymous. (See IDOL.) 1. Son of Saul by Rizpah (2 Sam. xxi. 8). He was crucified, with six others by the Gibeonites (as an offering to the god of Famine?), and hung on the cross for five months. Their bones were buried by David in the cave of Kish, at Zelah, when the famine, which had continued for three years, ended.—2. Son of Jonathan, Saul's son. His life was full of trial and suffering. He was but an infant of 5 yrs. when his father and grandfather were killed on Mt. Gilboa, living at Gibeah, when he was dropped from the arms of his nurse, both of his feet being permanently injured (2 Sam. iv. 4). He was taken to Lodebar, where he was cared for by Machir, the sheikh.

ME'RAB (*increase*). Eldest daughter of king Saul (1 Sam. xiv. 49). She was betrothed to David (xviii. 17), but married Adriel, to whom she bore five sons (2 Sam. xxi. 8). See DAVID.

MERA'IAH (*rebellion*). A priest of the family of Seraiah (Neh. xii. 12).

MERA'IOTH (*rebellions*). 1. He was the immediate predecessor of Eli in the office of HIGH PRIEST (1 Chr. ix. 11).—2. Another priest in the time of Joiakim (Neh. xii. 15).

ME'RAN. A place mentioned with Theman as famous for its merchants and wise men (Baruch iii. 23). In Arabia, but not identified. MIDIAN?

MERA'RI (*sorrowful*). Third son of Levi, head of the great division. For their position and duties in the service, see LEVI. The history of the family is traced from Exodus to after the Captivity.—2. Father of Judith (Jud. viii. 1).

MERA'RI (*unhappy*). Head of the 3d division of the tribe of Levi. The Merarites carried the boards, bars, pillars, sockets, pins, and cords of the Tabernacle, by the help of oxen and carts (Num. iii. 20, etc.). In the division of the land they had 12 cities, in Reuben, Gad, and Zebulon (Josh. xxi. 7). They furnished a third part of the musicians, and a third of the doorkeepers. They are frequently mentioned in the history until the return from captivity (Ezr. viii. 18). The family and its anches may be seen in the table:

GENEALOGY OF MERARI.

LEVI.

1 Merari.	1 Merari.
2 Mushi.	2 Mushi.
"	3 Mahli.
"	4 Eder.
"	5 Jerimoth.
3 Mahli.	6 Libni.
6 Libni.	7 Shimei.
"	8 Uzza.
"	9 Shimei.
"	10 Haggiah.
"	11 Asariah.
3 Mahli.	12 Abihael.
11 Abihail.	13 Zuriel.
3 Mahli.	14 Shamer.
13 Shamer.	15 Bani.
	16 Amzi.
	17 Hilkiah.
16 Hilkiah.	18 Amaziah.
17 Amaziah.	19 Hashabiah.
16 Hilkiah.	20 Jeriuthum?
18 Hashabiah.	21 Malluch.
20 Malluch.	22 Abdi.
21 Hashabiah.	23 Jaaziah or Jaaziel.
22 JaaziahorJaaziel.	24 Shoham.
" "	25 Zaccur, or Zechariah.
" "	26 Ibri or Abdi.
21 Abdi.	27 Eleazar.
	28 Kishi, Kish, or Kashaiah.
19 Jeduthun?	29 Hosah.
"	30 Obed-Edom.
"	31 Galal, or Gedaliah.
"	32 Zeri or Izri.
"	33 Jeshaiah.
"	34 Hashabiah.
"	35 Mattithiah.
27 Kishi.	36 Jerameel.
	37 Ethan, or Jeduthan.
28 Hasah.	38 Simri.
"	39 Hilkiah.
"	40 Tabaliah.
"	41 Zecariah.
34 Hashabiah.	42 Azriham.
42 Azrikam.	43 Hasshub.
43 Hushub.	44 Hashabiah.
"	45 Shemaiah.
	46 Hashabiah.
	47 Jeshaiah.
	48 Sherebiah.

MERATHA'IM (*bitter affliction*). A name given by Jeremiah to Babylon (l. 21).

MERCU'RIUS. In Greek and Roman mythology, the son of JUPITER and Maia (Acts xiv. 12).

MER'CY (Heb. CHESED). In the Scriptures it is a development of benevolence, a feeling of kindness or compassion toward the needy and helpless, and an attribute of God toward mankind (Ex. xx. 6).

MER'CY-SEAT (Heb. KAPPŌRETH). The lid of the Ark of the Covenant. See ARK.

ME RED (*rebellion*). Son of Ezra (1 Chr. iv. 17). He took for a wife BITHIAH a daughter of Pharaoh. Perhaps a poetical or Kenite name of Moses. Others say of Caleb instead.

MER'EMOTH (*hights*). Son of Uriah, of the family of Hakkoz (Ezr. viii. 33), and appointed a register of gifts and treasure in the Temple. He worked on the repairs of the wall (Neh. iii. 4, 21).—2. Layman, son of Bani (Ezr. x. 36).—3. Family of priests who signed the covenant (Neh. x. 5). Mentioned a century before in ch. xii. 3.

ME'RES (*worthy*). Counselor to Ahasuerus (Esth. i. 14).

MER'IBAH (*strife*). A fountain in the desert of Sin, which flowed at the command of Moses (Ex. xii. 1–7). The place was called Massah (*temptation*), and Meribah (*chiding*).—2. Another fountain of the same character was near Kadesh (Num. xx. 13; Deut. xxxiii. 8). This is also called the Waters of Meribah (Ps. lxxxi. 7, cvi. 32). It was here that Moses sinned in impatience and assumption of power, for which offense he was not permitted to cross over Jordan (Num. xx. 12).

MERIBBA'AL (*against Baal*). MEPHIBOSHETH.

MERO'DACH (*bold*). The Babylonian Bel, a gilded image of which was worshiped at Babylon. The planet Jupiter.

MERO'DACH BAL'A-DAN. BALADAN. Berodach is an error. Reigned twice over Babylon, B. C. 721 to 709, and in 702 six months.

The Assyrian inscriptions give his name distinctly, and have records of both reigns. Sargon deposed him the first time, and Sennacherib the second, appointing Belib in his place. There is no certainty of the date of the embassy sent by him to Hezekiah, king of Judah (2 Chr. xxxii. 31), but it was probably between B. C. 721 and 709. If the real object of the league was to effect a political union for strength against Assyria, of Babylon, Judæa, and Egypt, then the business failed, for Sargon seized Babylon and Ashdod.

GRIFFIN.

ME'ROM, THE WATERS OF (Josh. xi. 5, 7). Where Jabin, king of Hazor, and his allies were defeated by Joshua. The lake El Huleh or Samochonitis (Jos. Ant. v. 5, 1). This lake lies in the south end of a marshy plain, between the foot of Hermon and the hills of Galilee, which is 15 miles long by 5 wide; the lake being triangular and 3 to 5 miles across, according to the dry or wet season. It is 120 feet above the ocean. Several streams (see JORDAN) unite in the marsh, form the Jordan, and flow through the lake. The plain on each side of the lake is of rich soil, and is cultivated by the Bedawin Arabs from Lebanon and merchants of Damascus,—a repetition of life 3,000 years ago, as recorded in Judges xviii. The

modern is really the most ancient name, being derived from Hu¹, the second son of Aram (Gen. x. 23). A district near Hannah is named after him, and also the town Huleh, near the castle of Hunin. The large spring on the west bank of the plain, Ain Mellahah, which pours out a brook 50 feet wide, once gave its name to the lake, Melcha (*William of Tyre*).

MERO'NOTHITE, THE. Native of Meronoth (1 Chr. xxvii. 30).

ME'ROZ (*asylum*), (Judg. v. 23). Whose people refused to help Deborah and Barak against Sisera. *El Murussus*, north of Bethshan 4 miles (*Rob.* ii. 356).

ME'RUTH (1 Esd. v. 24). A corruption of IMMER.

COIN OF TARSUS.

MES'ECH. The sixth son of Japheth (Gen. x. 2), and founder of a nation (Ps. cxx. v.), which traded with Tyre (Ez. xxvii. 13), and was ruined with Egypt (xxxii. 26), and a neighbor of Gog and Magog (xxxviii. 2). Herodotus speaks of the Moschi and Tibarini in Persia (iii. 94), who formed a part of the army of Xerxes; and these are the Meshech and Tubal of the Scriptures. They were settled in the mountains of Caucasus, and in north Armenia; and their descendants to-day follow the customs mentioned by Ezekiel, and sell their daughters for wives and for slaves (to the Turks). The name is written *Muskai* on the Assyrian monuments and *Mashoush* on the Egyptian, of the time of the third Rameses (*Wilkinson*). They are the *Muskovs* of Russia (*Rawlinson*).

ME'SHA. The Joktanites dwelt from Mesha unto Mt. Sephar (Gen. x. 30). The mountain range of Zames (Mesha) runs from near the Persian Gulf S. W., nearly across Arabia. There is a mount Zafara on the Indian Ocean. Here is now, and has been from remote times, the country of the *Beni Kahtan* (Joktanite Arabs), inhabiting Yemen, Hadramaut and Oman, separated from the Ishmaelites by the Nejed mountain range.

ME'SHA (*safety*). 1. King of MOAB (2 K. iii. 4), who revolted from the 10 tribes after the death of Ahab, against whom Jehoshaphat and Jehoram led their armies. He was a great sheep-breeder. A monument erected by him is mentioned in the article KIR HARESH, with an engraving of "THE MOABITE STONE," on page 173.—2. Son of Caleb, who founded Ziph (1 Chr. ii. 42).—3. (*retreat*). Son of Shaharaim (1 Chr. viii. 9).

ME'SHACH (*ram*). The name given to MISHAEL 3, companion of Daniel (Dan. i. 4). It was a name of the sun-god of the Chaldæans.

ME'SHECH (*drawing out*). 1. Son of Japheth (Gen. x. 2), and of the race in connection with Tubal, Magog and other northern nations.—2. MASH (1 Chr. i. 17).

MESHELEMI'AH (*whom Jah repays as a friend*). Son of Kore, a porter in the house of Jehovah (1 Chr. ix. 21). Shelemiah in 1 Chr. xxvi. 1.

MESHEZ'ABEEL (*delivered*). 1. Ancestor of MESHULLAM 13 (Neh. iii. iv.).—2. A family who sealed the covenant (x. 21).—3. Father of Pethahiah (xi. 24).

MESHIL'LEMITH. Son of Immer, a priest (Neh. xi. 13).

MESHIL'LEMOTH (*requital*). 1. A chief under Pekah, ancestor of Berechiah (2 Chr. xxviii. 12). —2. MESHILLEMITH (Neh. xi. 13).

MESHO'BAB (*returned*). A prince in Hezekiah's reign (1 Chr. iv. 34).

MESHUL'LAM (*friend*). 1. Ancestor of Shaphan (2 K. xvii. 3).—2. Son of Zerubbabel (1 Chr. iii. 19).—3. A Gadite chief in the time of Jotham (v. 13).—4. A Benjamite chief (viii. 17).—5. Son of Hodaviah, and father of Sallu (ix. 7; Neh. xi. 7).—6. Son of Shephathiah (1 Chr. ix. 8).—7. Father of Hilkiah (ix. 11).—8. A priest and son of MESHUL'LEMITH (1 Chr. ix. 12).—9. Overseer of the workmen in rebuilding the Temple (2 Chr. xxxiv. 12).—10. A chief sent by Ezra to Iddo (Ezr. viii. 16).—11. A chief who assisted Jonathan and Jahaziah in examining the marriages which the people had contracted with foreign wives (x. 15).—12. Descendant of Bani (x. 29). —13. Son of Berechiah (Neh. iii. 4, 30, vi. 18).—14. Son of Besodeiah; he assisted in restoring the gate of Jerusalem (iii. 6).—15. One who stood with Ezra when he read the law (viii. 4).—16. A priest who sealed the covenant (x. 7).—17. One who sealed the covenant (20).—18. A priest (xii. 13) —19. Another priest.—20. A porter (25).—21 A prince who assisted at the dedication of the wall (xii. 33).

MESHUL'LEMETH (*friend*). Daughter of Haruz, wife of Manasseh (2 K. xxi. 19).

MESO'BAITZ (MEZOBAYAH, *gath-ring-place of Jah*). A title of JASIEL (1 Chr. xi. 47).

MESOPOTA'MIA (*between the rivers*). Between the Tigris and Euphrates, 700 miles long by 20 to 250 wide. The Aram Naharaim (in the Hebrew) of Gen. xxiv. 10, and Padan Aram of xxv. 20. It is a plain, but is crossed by the Sinjar hills east to west, near its centre, not far from Mosul. The nomade tribes are the only people, and they are driven to the hills in the hot season, when the pastures become dry, dusty and parched, except near the streams. (See Assyria.) It is becoming the belief among scholars that the Mesopotamia (the city of Nahor) of Terah and Haran of Abraham were near Damascus (*Dr. Beke*), where Bethuel and Laban lived, and Abraham sent a servant to fetch Rebekah to be Isaac's wife; and a hundred years after that Jacob earned his two wives in 21 years. It was also the residence of Balaam (Deut. xxiii. 4). All of these references may apply to the region around Damascus, between the rivers Pharpar and Abana.

MESSI'AH. CHRIST. The anointed (as a king). The word is found in the original Hebrew many times, in all of which it is translated anointed, except in Daniel ix. 25, 26. The ceremony of ANOINTING was intended to mark what God had set apart for his own purposes. It was His royal stamp, which was to be applied to the high priest (Ex. xxviii. 41), the offerings, the tabernacle, table, ark, candlestick, altar of incense, laver and vessels attached to them, "to sanctify them, and they shall be most holy; whatsoever toucheth them shall be holy."

Samuel anointed Saul and David (three times), while Absalom was anointed by the rebels. The ceremony was performed by the prophets or the priests.

The prophetic use of the title was historic among the Hebrews, and well known to Herod, who was affected by the idea, although he doubted the truth of the divine claim to a belief and hope for the Messiah. The Messiah was to be a son of David (the great king), by the covenant (Ps. lxxxix.) who is described as "the mighty God, the Father of Ages, the Prince of Peace" (Is. ix. 6). See JESUS, page 157. Some expected a temporal king, a literal king, like David. In their view "Son of

David" meant one who inherited his wisdom and kingly power, who should make the Jews as great a people as ever, or even greater.

In view, also, of the spiritual darkness and ignorance of their oppressors, and all of their neighbors—as judged by their standard—there seemed to be a real need of a deliverer, not only for Israel, but for "all nations." The true Messiah was to be an instrument by whom God's great purpose to man was to be carried out by a sacrificial work. The idea of a Messiah is as old as the history of the Hebrew race, being found, or rather alluded to, in the oldest writings, before the time of Moses, and especially in the blessing of Jacob, and in the psalms of David, and the prophecies of Isaiah, Daniel, etc. The expectation of a "golden age" was common among the ancient nations, to which the Jews added the particular personage, the Messiah, who was to reign in that good time; and this is still kept up by the modern Jews, who pray, at every meal, "Merciful God, make us worthy of seeing the days of the Messiah."

Historians give accounts of about 30 different pretended Messiahs, since the destruction of Jerusalem by Titus (Matt. xxiv. 24; Mark xiii. 22); which are so many proofs of the real Messiah, who foretold them.

METALS. The earliest record of the production and manufacture of metals is in the reference to Tubal Cain, a Cainite, the son of Lamech (Gen. iv. 22). The first mention of metal as money is in Gen. xxiii. 16. The gold and silver possessed by the Jews was of vast amount even allowing for over statements (1 Chr. xxii. 14, xxix. 4). The trade in metals was mostly held by the Phoenicians (Ez. xvii. 7). Metals were also supplied worked in thin plates (Jer. x. 9). The holy vessels used in the Temple were mostly gold (Ezr. v. 14). Tin is mentioned among the spoils of the Midianites (Num. xxxi. 22), and lead in Ez. xv. 10. In the earliest times copper (NECOSHETH) and bronze were used for many purposes in the place of iron introduced at a later period. The passage in Job xxviii. 2, "Molten out of stone," refers to the smelting of copper ore. In Jer. vi. 28, the word copper is used as a term of vileness (by its comparison with silver and gold). It is also used as a term of strength (Ps. cvii. 16; Jer. i. 18, xv. 20). The word brass is frequently used for copper. The art of coating with brass (?) and silver was known to the Hebrews (Ex. xxxviii. 2, and Prov. xxvi. 23). The working of copper into weapons and utensils (Num. xvii. 4); of castings in 1 K. vii. 45, and of gilding (Is. xl. 19). Iron (Barzel) found in the hills of Palestine as well as copper. Probably steel was known to the Hebrews, but this word appearing in 2 Sam. xxii. 35; Job xx. 24; Ps. xviii. 34; Jer. xv. 12, might be translated *brass*, or more correctly, *copper*. Arms were made of bronze (2 Sam. xxi. 16; Job xx. 24; Ps. xviii. 34), and armor in 1 Sam. xvii. 5, 6, 38. See MONEY.

METE RUS. Sons of Meterus returned from captivity (1 Esd. v. 17).

ME THEGAM'MAH (*bridle of the mother city*). A place David took from the Philistines (2 Sam. viii. 1).

METHU'SAEL (*man of God*). Son of Mehujael, and father of LAMECH 1 (Gen. iv. 18).

METHU'SELAH (*man of offspring*). Son of Enoch (Gen. v. 25-27). He lived 969 years, longer than any other PATRIARCH, and died the year of the flood.

MEU'NIM (Neh. vii. 52).

MEU'ZAL (Ez. xxvii. 19).

MEZA'HAB (*water*). Father of Matred (Gen. xxxvi. 39).

MI'AMIN (*from the right hand*). 1. A layman (Ezr. x. 25).—2. A priest who returned from captivity (Neh. xii. 5).

MIB'HAR (*choice*). Son of Haggeri, one of David's men (1 Chr. xi. 38).

MIB'SAM (*sweet odor*). 1. Son of Ishmael (Gen. xxv. 13).—2. Son of Simeon (1 Chr. iv. 25).

MIB'ZAR (*fort*). A duke of Edom (1 Chr. i. 53).

MI'CHA. 1. Son of Mephibosheth (2 Sam. ix. 12). —2. A Levite who signed the covenant (Neh. x. 11).—3. Father of Mattaniah (xi. 17, 22).—Father of Ozias, governor of Bethulia (Jud. vi. 15). See MICAH, in HISTORY OF THE BOOKS.

MI'CHAEL (*like God*). 1. Father of Sethur (Num. xiii. 13).—Son of Abihail (1 Chr. v. 13).—3. A Gadite ancestor of Abihail (ver. 11).—4. Ancestor of Asaph (vi. 40).—5. One of the chief men of Issachar (vii. 3).—6. Of the sons of Beriah (viii. 16). —7. A captain who joined David (xii. 20).—8. Ancestor of Omri (xxvii. 18).—9. Son of Jehoshaphat (2 Chr. xxi. 2, 4).—10. Ancestor of Zebadiah (Ezr. viii. 8).

MI'CHAH. Eldest son of Uzziel (1 Chr. xxiv. 24).

MI'CHAIAH (*like Jah*). 1. Father of Achbor, of high rank in the time of Josiah (2 K. xxii. 12).—2. Son of Zaccur (Neh. xii. 35).—3. A priest at the dedication of the wall of Jerusalem (xii. 41).—4. Daughter of Uriel (2 Chr. xiii. 2).—5. A prince sent to teach in Judah (xvii. 7).—6. Son of Gemariah (Jer. xxxvi. 11-14).

MI'CHAL (*who like El?*). The youngest daughter of Saul, espoused to David. Saul had intended to make her a party to his designs, but was foiled by her devotion to David. This was especially illustrated in the incident in 1 Sam. xix. 11-17, by which she assisted the escape of David. Saul afterwards canceled the marriage, but a reunion followed through the mission of Abner (2 Sam. iii. 12-21). Through her conduct on meeting David, after his return from celebrating the entry of the ark into Jerusalem, she was punished with the curse of barrenness (2 Sam. vi. 16-23). Thus it was that the races of Saul and David were not united.

MICHE'AS. The prophet Micah 7 (2 Esd. i. 39).
MICH'MAS (Ezr. ii. 27). MICHMASH.

COIN OF TROAS.

MICH'MASH (*something hidden*). In Benjamin. A pass celebrated by the exploit of Jonathan, Saul's son (1 Sam. xiii., xiv. 4, 16). Jonathan Maccabeus also resided there (1 Macc. ix. 73), on account of the military strength of the pass (Ant. xiii. 1, 6). *Mukhmas*, in the *Wady Es Suweinit*, has ruins of many foundations of hewn stones, columns, cisterns, etc., indicating a once strong place, perhaps a city devoted to the heathen deity Chemosh (the two names being similar). The two rocks (see BOZEZ and SENEH), may still be seen; one on each side of the narrow and precipitous valley (*Rob.*). Isaiah, in speaking of the invasion of Judah by Sennacherib, says he laid up his carriages at Michmash (x. 28), which agrees with the character of the place, it being too steep for wheels.

MICH METHAH (*hiding-place*). Boundary of Ephraim and Manasseh, west of Jordan, facing Shechem (Josh. xvii. 7).—2. Between Ephraim and Benjamin (xvi. 6), toward the Great Sea.

MICH'RI (*price of Jah*). Ancestor of Elah, a chief after the Captivity (1 Chr. ix. 8).

MICH'TAM. A musical term applied to three Psalms (xvi., lvi., lx.).

MID'DIN (*measures*). Judah, in the wilderness. Um el Bedun, S. W. of the Dead Sea? (Velde).

MID'IAN (*strife*). Fourth son of Abraham by Keturah, and founder of a nation (Gen. xxv. 2; Num. xxii.), the rulers of Northern Arabia for a long time; inhabiting the peninsula of Sinai, where Moses fled after killing the Egyptian (Ex. ii. 15), and the country east of Edom and Palestine (xxxvii. 28). They were a snare to the Israelites, and Moses denounced their mischief-making (Num. xxv. 15, 17). Gideon's night-attack with trumpets, and lamps in pitchers, was on a host of Midianites in the valley of Jezreel (Judg. vi. to viii.). They were nomadic, pastoral, wealthy, and delighted in plunder, exactly as their descendants the Bedawins do now. There is no mention of this great nation, which has had an existence for 30 centuries, in any other book but the Bible, unless the accounts of the Arabs of the city of Medyen (the ruins of which are shown on the Akabah Gulf) refer to a city of this people. There is a tradition in the *Marasid*, and a history of the people in *El Makhrezi*, that this is the city visited by Moses, and they point out a well at which he watered his flocks. They are also mentioned in the Koran (vii., xi.). It is conjectured that Jethro, who is called a priest of Midian, was of the Kenites, who were a branch of this people, and who remained friendly to the Israelites when the main body of the Midianites made war, and incurred the Divine vengeance.

MID'IANITE. One from MIDIAN (Gen. xxxvii. 28, 36).

MID'IANITISH. Belonging to MIDIAN (Num. xxv. 6 ff).

MID'RIFF. CAUL (Ex. xxix. 13).

MID'WIFE. Childbirth in the East, on account of open-air living, is usually easy. The office of midwife, when necessary, is performed by relatives, and sometimes by a professional. Two or three days before the time of delivery, the midwife carried to the house a chair, of peculiar form, upon which the patient is seated during birth (Ex. i. 16). CHILD. The modern Egyptian practice explains that alluded to in Exodus. See MEDICINE.

MIG'DAL E'DAR. Translated "O tower of the flock," in Micah iv. 8. A poetic name of Zion, because of its strength and watchfulness over Israel (Jer. xiii. 17).

TIMBREL.

MIG'DAL EL (*tower of God*). A fenced city in Naphtali (Josh. xix. 38). A place is mentioned in the Wady Kerkerah, 8 ms. E. of Nakura, called Mujeidel. But it is supposed Magdala is referred to in the text.

MIG'DAL GAD (*tower of God*). Judah, in the Shefelah (Josh. xv. 37), near Lachish and Eglon. El Mejdel. 2 ms. E. of Askalan, is a large and fine village, in the midst of groves, orchards, and cultivated fields. Large hewn stones, columns, etc., indicate an antiquity of importance; probably of a city devoted to the worship of the heathen deity Gad, as Baal Gad was, under Mt. Hermon.

MIG'DOL (*tower*). 1. A place between which and the Red Sea the Israelites were directed to camp on leaving Egypt (Ex. xiv. 2).—2. A boundary town mentioned by Jeremiah and Ezekiel, on the N. as Syene was on the S. of Egypt. Hecatæus of Miletus places Magdolo 12 ms. S. of Pelusium.

MIG'RON (*precipice*). Near Saul's city (1 Sam. xiv. 2), where there was a pomegranate tree, under which Saul and the remnant of his host "tarried" while Jonathan went on his famous exploit against the Philistines. Isaiah (x. 28) names it in the list of places passed by Sennacherib, on the S. side of the Wady Suweinit. Whether it was a rock or a town is not known.

MIJ'AMIN. 1. Chief of the 6th course of priests (1 Chr. xxiv. 9).—2. A priest who signed the covenant with Nehemiah (Neh. x. 7).

MIK'LOTH (*staves*). 1. Son of Jehiel (1 Chr. viii. 32).—2. A leader of the 2d division of David's army (xxvii. 4).

MIKNEI'AH (*possession of Jah*). One of the gatekeepers of the Ark (1 Chr. xv. 18, 21).

MIL'ALAI (*eloquent*). A priest who assisted at the wall of Jerusalem (Neh. xii. 36).

MIL'CAH (*queen*). 1. Daughter of Haran (Gen. xi. 29).—2. Fourth daughter of Zelophehad (Num. xxvi. 33).

MIL'COM (*little Molech*). The abomination of the children of Ammon (1 K. xi. 7).

MIL DEW (*pale*). Blasting and turning yellow from disease (Deut. xxviii. 22).

MILE. The Roman measure of a mile was equal to 1618 English yards. (The English is 1760 yds.). "To go a mile" (Matt. v. 41). The Jewish mile was of two kinds, long or short, according to the length of pace. The Roman measurement was ultimately introduced into Palestine.

MILE TUS. Seaport and the ancient capital of Ionia, Asia Minor, 36 ms. S. of Ephesus. The presbyters of the Church of Ephesus met Paul at this place on his return from his third missionary journey (Acts xx. 6). Several men of renown were born here—Democritus (460 B. C.), Anaximenes (504), Hecatæus, Anaximander (611), Thales (639), and Timotheus. There were four harbors, one of which would hold a fleet. The oracle of its famous temple of Apollo was consulted as late as the 4th century. Christian bishops of Miletus were present at several councils from the 5th to the 8th centuries. It is now a ruin called Melas, near the mouth of the river Meander. The sea has receded from the site several miles.

MILK. There are two Hebrew terms for milk, one (CHALEB), meaning *fresh milk*, the other (CHEMAH) *curdled*. Both are frequently used in Scripture; fresh milk is figuratively used to mean abundance (Gen. xlix. 12; Ez. xxv. 4; Joel iii. 18, etc.). It is often mentioned with honey, as a "land flowing with milk and honey," applied to describe Egypt as well as Palestine (Num. xvi. 13). As a term of simplicity it occurs in 1 Cor. iii. 2; Heb. v. 12, 13; 1. Pet. ii. 3; Is. lv. 1). The milk was from goats, cows, sheep and camels (Prov. xxvii. 27; Deut. xxxii. 14). "Thirty milch camels" were given by Jacob to Esau (Gen. xxxii. 15). The word butter used in the A. V. generally means curdled milk (Gen. xviii. 8; Judg. v. 25). The meaning in Deut. xxxii. 14 and Prov. xxx. 33 is butter. The plan of preparation of butter by the Hebrews was probably the same as that now in use in the East. The milk, mixed with a little sour milk, is heated over a slow fire, in a copper pan. The separated milk is put into a goat-skin, which is tied to a stake or tent pole, and shaken until the butter comes. The water is pressed from this butter and it is put into another skin. After two days the butter is returned to the fire, wheat, boiled with leaven, being added—the whole is boiled and then skimmed, the butter remaining on the top, foreign matter being precipitated, *buryoul* or wheat and leaven. See CHEESE.

MILL (RECHAIM, *the two mill-stones*, Ex. xi. 5); also in the preparation of manna for food in Num. xi. 8. The ordinary mill was a household machine of two stones two feet in diameter and six inches thick, the lower one hollowed out a little, and the upper fitted to it, and turned from right to left around by a wooden handle. This is the work of women or slaves. Captives (as Samson) were often forced to grind (Judg. xvi. 21); but more generally women were thus employed, as in Ex xi. 5 and Matt. xxiv. 41. The use of the mill in each household was incessant, so that when the mill was not working it was a sign of desolation (Jer. xxv. 10; Rev. xviii. 22; Eccles. xii. 3, 4). So necessary to the daily subsistence was the use of the mill that there was a law against pledging either of the stones (Deut. xxiv. 6). In the East, to this day, these hand-mills are seen worked by two women. There are mills on nearly every running stream, with the most primitive machinery, where the wheels are fitted with wooden pins for cogs. Other mills are turned by animals. Millstone is used figuratively, as in Matt. xviii. 6; Job xli. 24; Mark ix. 24; Luke xvii. 2. See MORTAR.

MIL'LET (DOCHAN). Mentioned only in Ez. iv. 9. There was the "common millet" (*Panicum Miliaceum*), and the "Turkish millet." It was probably the latter. Millet produced a bread of inferior quality.

MIL'LO (*fulness*). An ancient Jebusite name of a part of the citadel of Jerusalem (2 Sam. v. 9). Solomon raised a levy to build or enlarge this work (and others, 1 K. ix. 15). Hezekiah repaired Millo, *the City of David* (2 Chr. xxxii. 5). The HOUSE OF MILLO was a chief clan of Shechem (Judg. ix. 6, 20). King Joash was murdered by his slaves at "the house of Millo that goeth down to Silla" (2 K. xii. 20), which is supposed to have been the place mentioned first.

MI'NA (Luke xix. 13).

MIN'CING (Heb. TAPOF). Short, quick step; refers to an affectation of gait (Is. iii. 16).

MINES. MINING. (See METALS). The ancients were skilful miners, and their operations are alluded to by Job (xxviii. 1-11). Evidences remain of Egyptian copper mining in the Sinai desert. Palestine produced iron and copper. The Phœnicians brought tin from Spain, and possibly Cornwall, in England. There were lead mines bordering the coast of the Red Sea. Iron mining is referred to in Deut. iv. 20. See cut, p. 122. SILVERSMITH.

MIN'GLED PEOPLE (Heb. HAEREB). Mixed population (Jer. xxv. 20; Ez. xxx. 5). Rulers over mingled tribes (1 K. x. 15) and mercenaries.

MIN'IAMIN. 1. A Levite (2 Chr. xxxi. 15).—2. A priest (Neh. xii. 17).—3. A priest at the dedication of the wall (xii. 41).

MINNI (*division*). Armenia (Jer. li. 27). The Minnai of the Assyrian inscriptions were located near lake *Urumiëh*. (See ARMENIA).

MIN'ISTER (Heb. MESHARETH). One who serves another; the term to distinguish from master; Solomon's servants and ministers (1 K. x. 5). "Moses rose up and his *minister* Joshua" (Ex. xxiv. 13). He who *administers* an office. "God's ministers" (Rom. xiii. 4, 6). "Ministers of Christ" (1 Cor. iv. 1). "Christ came not to be ministered unto, but to minister." Minister "of the circumcision" (Rom. xv. 8).

MIN'NITH (*given*). A town east of Jordan (Judg. xi. 33), celebrated for its wheat (Ez. xxvii. 17), which was exported at Tyre. *Menjah*, a ruin, 4 ms. N. E. of Heshbon (*Vetle*).

MIN'STREL. In the A. V. the word minstrel only occurs twice in 2 K. iii. 15. "But now bring me a minstrel;" and in Matt. xix. 23, "When Jesus saw the minstrel." The Hebrew in the first text means a player upon a stringed instrument, as David was (1 Sam. xvi. 23; also 1 Sam. x. 5). In Matthew minstrel means pipe-player. Pipe-playing was used by professional mourners. See MUSIC and MUSICAL INSTRUMENTS.

MINT (Gr. *heduosmon*). One of those herbs, the tithe of which the Jews were most exact in paying. Mint was used by the Greeks and Romans in medicine and cookery. The horse-mint (*Mentha sylvestris*) is common in Syria. Mint is only mentioned in Matt. xxiii. 23, and Luke xi. 42, as a tithe. Probably the horse-mint (*Mentha sylvestris*).

COIN OF PERSEUS.

MIPH'KAD, THE GATE (*number*). A gate of Jerusalem in the time of Nehemiah (iii. 31); perhaps in the City of David.

MIRACLES. Two Hebrew words, OTH, sign, and MOPETH, wonder, (plural NIFLAOTH, wonders), and three Greek words, *terata*, wonders; *semeia*, signs; *dunameis*, powers, mighty works, are translated miracles. None of these words imply supernatural power, or religious purpose, because those points are always left to be inferred from the simple narrative of the event, for many wonderful events are recorded which were not supernatural, as in the case of Isaiah who walked naked and barefoot for three years, for a sign (Is. xx. 3). Natural and common events may be used for signs, and do indicate the miracle if they were predicted.

The meaning of miracle in our day is a work or sign that is above and beyond nature. A miracle may be defined as a violation of a law of nature by a particular volition of the Deity, or by the interposition of some visible agent. This is not quite correct, for the miracle is the result of a new power, or new law, which produces effects not included in our ordinary experience. It is simply one law operating on another so far as to neutralize it, and produce unexpected results.

In the case of healing sickness, the word, or touch, or gesture, is the prediction of the cure, and the supernatural is seen in the prediction, or seeing before time what will come to pass. The prediction and the fulfilment may occur near together, or at a great length of time apart, and two sets of independent witnesses depose to the prediction and the fulfilment, leaving no room for doubt or fraud.

Viewed as mere wonderful events for man's astonishment miracles are highly improbable occurrences, but considered as signs of a moral and religious revelation, and witnesses or evidences of the commission of the teachers of religion to instruct and inform mankind, they are no longer improbable, but are signs of the presence of God in action.

The prediction of an eclipse appears supernatural to the ignorant savage who is not aware that the laws of the motions of the heavenly bodies are known and can be calculated precisely; to the scholar it is no wonder, for he can either compute the exact time for himself, or can understand by what means another can do it. The means are natural, the foreknowledge is also within the province of nature. If we could be elevated to a spiritual plane where we should be able to see the powers which move and control the human frame, we should be able to see how Peter cured the lame

man, or Jesus healed the blind, and should no longer wonder, for we should recognize the source of the power as God himself manifested in Jesus. We should only recognize the source, not see the means, except that we should see the result, and the agent, for God cannot be seen and followed by us.

The miracles of Jesus were a necessary part of his mission, and formed an integral part of his teaching, and were therefore more than mere signs or specimens of the presence of God, and more than mere proofs of a divine commission. The life and teaching of Jesus form one column or set of columns, and his miracles another, on which rest the roof and dome of the church.

The mission of the Christ was to teach and redeem mankind; to tell them what to believe, and how to be saved, and to be himself the author of their salvation, the worker of a new creation. The Christ was God in the flesh, and Christianity is God in action, made known, or communicated to man, so that we are partakers of the divine nature, through faith in Christ.

The miracles of the Old Testament are nearly all found in two groups, being almost wholly absent from other periods in the track of the Jewish history; and Moses and Elijah are the two central figures, who are the impersonations of the law and the prophets. One of the evidences of the truth of the Bible history is that there are no miracles ascribed to many of the prominent characters, not even such as David, Solomon, or Abraham. The period of over 400 years from Malachi to Christ are without any authentic record of a miracle.

The Old Testament miracles are nearly all of power, and were wrought for the destruction of the enemies of the Hebrew Church or the preservation of its members. A few were works of mercy also, as of Elijah's restoration of the widow's son.

The miracles of Christ were both of power and love. (See JESUS.) The miracle attested by eye witnesses and the teaching of Christ were the foundation of the Christian religion, which still remains the belief of a large part of the enlightened sections of the world.

Miracles ceased when the Christian Church was established. The ecclesiastical miracles of the ages since the Apostles are totally different in purpose and kind from those recorded in the Scriptures, and very closely resemble the legendary inventions with which Pagans in all ages have amused or astonished and imposed on mankind. The accounts of the miracles are always simple and direct, without attempt to explain, or even a notice of the wonderful character of the event. The reports of modern "miracles" are so minute as to suggest the novel or fable.

MIR'IAM (*bitter*). Sister of Moses, who it is supposed watched her infant brother when he was exposed in the Nile (Ex. ii. 4). Upon the flight of the Israelites from Egypt, Miriam is called prophetess (Ex. xv. 20), where she celebrates the passage of the Red Sea with music. The arrival of Zipporah, Moses' Ethiopian wife, excited the enmity of Miriam, who incited Aaron to sedition (Num. xii.); for this conduct Miriam was stricken with leprosy, and was recovered by the intercession of Moses. She died in the 1st month of the 40th year after the Exodus, at Kadesh-Barnea (Num. xx. 1). See EXODUS, HISTORY OF THE BOOKS.

MIR'MA (*deceit*). Son of Shaharaim (1 Chr. viii. 10).

MIR'ROR (Heb. MARAH, REI). Mirrors were of polished metal. The Israelitish women probably brought Egyptian-made mirrors out of Egypt. These were given to make the "laver of brass and the foot of it" for the Temple (Ex. xxxviii. 8). Figuratively mentioned in Job xxxvii. 18.

MIS'AEL. 1. MISHAEL 2 (1 Esd. ix. 44).—2.

MISHAEL 3. (SONG OF THE THREE HOLY CHILDREN.)

MIS'GAB (*lofty fort*). City of Moab (Jer. xlviii. 1). Mizpeh (1 Sam. xxiii. 3).

MISH'AEL (*who is what God is*). 1. Son of Uzziel (Ex. vi. 22). He assisted in removing the bodies of Nadab and Abihu from the sanctuary (Lev. x. 4, 5).—2. One who stood with Ezra (Neh. viii. 4).—3. Companion of Daniel (Dan. i. 6, 7, 11, 19).

MI'SHAL (Josh. xxi. 30).

MI'SHAM (*swift-going*). Son of Elpaal (1 Chr. viii. 12).

MISHEAL (*entreaty*). A city of Asher (Josh. xix. 26).

MISH'MA (*hearing*). 1. Son of Ishmael (Gen. xxv. 14).—2. Son of Simeon (1 Chr. iv. 25).

MISHMAN'NAH (*fatness*). A Gadite, who joined David at Ziklag (1 Chr. xii. 10).

MISH'RAITES (*slippery place*). People from Mishra (1 Chr. ii. 53).

MIS'PERETH (*number*). One who returned from captivity (Neh. vii. 7).

MIS'REPHOTHMAIM (*burnings of waters*). Near Sidon (Josh. xi. 8); not conquered at Joshua's death (xiii. 6). Zarephath. Sarepta.

MIST (Heb. ED). Vapor rising from the earth, and forming clouds (Gen. ii. 6).

MITE (Gr. *lepton*). See MONEY.

MITH'CAH (*sweetness*). Desert station. Lost. (Num. xxxiii. 28).

MITH'NITE, THE (*extension*). The native place of JOSHAPHAT (1 Chr. xi. 43).

MITH'REDATH (*given by Mithra*). 1. Treasurer of Cyrus (Ez. i. 8).—2. An officer at Samaria (Ezr. iv. 7).

MITHRIDA'TES. 1. MITHRIDATH 1 (1 Esd. ii. 11).—2. MITHREDATH 2 (ii. 16).

MITYLE'NE. Chief town in Lesbos (Acts xx. 14, 15). The Romans called it "the beautiful," from its fine buildings. It was a free city in Paul's time. It is a city now, and gives its name to the whole island.

MIXED MULTITUDE (*a medley of people*). Mentioned as amongst the Israelites in their journey from Rameses to Succoth (Ex. xii. 38). See Num. xi. 4. In the return from the Babylonish Captivity, *mixed multitude* refers to Arabians (Neh. xii. 4), which is probably the meaning in the other references.

MIZ'AR, THE HILL(*little*). From which the Psalmist uttered the pathetic appeal recorded in Ps. xlii. E. of Jordan. Lost. (Not Little Hermon).

MIZPAH, MIZPEH, (*watch-tower*, or *look-out*). 6 places of this name: 1. Mispah (also Galeed), where Jacob and Laban set up a memorial stone-heap (Gen. xxxi. 45), saying, The Lord watch between us. Mizpah was the Hebrew form of the ancient name of the place. N. of Mahanaim, on some hill-top. Jebel Osha, near Es Salt? The top is broad and flat—a fine place for an assembly—and on the N. slope is a ruin, called Jilad (Gilead). (Grove, in *Smith's Dict.*).—2. THE LAND OF MIZPAH. The Hivites of this land helped Jabin against the Israelites (Josh. xi. 3).—3. THE VALLEY OF MIZPEH. Where Joshua chased Jabin and his multitude (ver. 8). Cœle-Syria, or Bukaa? Perhaps the reference is to the Hauran, "eastward" from the waters of Merom.—4 (Ib. xv. 38). In the Shefelah. Tell es Safieh (Velde).—5. A city of Benjamin (Ib. xviii. 26), on Neby Samwil, 4 ms. N. W. of Jerusalem. Here the whole nation assembled to avenge the Levite (Judg. xx.); and to sacrifice before attacking the Philistines by order of

Samuel (1 Sam. vii.); and again to elect Saul king (x.); the city of Gibeon was about 4 m. N. of the hill; and perhaps on this very high place Solomon offered sacrifice, and was endowed with wisdom (1 K. iii. 4). It was fortified by Asa, who took the materials from Ramah, 5 ms. N. E. Gedaliah, Nebuchadnezzar's governor, lived here when he was killed by the fanatic Ishmael (Jer. xl. 7, 8). After the destruction of the Temple it was held as a holy place, where sacrifice was made (xli. 5) in a house of the Lord. This character continued as late as the time of the Maccabees (1 Macc. iii. 46). There is a village and a mosque (formerly a church) on the summit of *Nebý Samwil*. The hill rises steeply 600 ft. above the plain, and commands a very extensive view, especially E., as far as Kerak, in Moab, and W. to the Mediterranean.—6. MIZPEH or MOAB (1 Sam. xxii. 3). Where David sought an asylum for his father and mother, with the king of Moab (among the relatives of Ruth?).

MIZ'RAIM (*the two Egypts*). EGYPT (Gen. x. 6). This name (not of a man but of a country) represents a centre from which colonies went out from the remotest antiquity. Egypt is now called *Misr* in Arabic. See EGYPT.

MIZ'ZAH (*fear*). Son of Reuel (Gen. xxxvi. 13, 17).

KNA'SON (*remembering*). An old disciple, a resident of Jerusalem, and a native of Cyprus (Acts iv. 36, xxi. 16).

MO'AB (*from father*). Son of Lot, and founder of a tribe, located E. of the Dead Sea (Gen. xix. 37), in the district once occupied by the Emims (Gen. xiv. 5; Deut. ii. 11). Zoar, the city of this tribe, was most probably N. E. of the Dead Sea, from which the Amorites drove them, and which was given to Reuben. The whole region is undulating, without any high ridges or sudden hills, except near the Dead Sea and Jordan, is covered with sites of ruined towns, on every hill or other convenient place, and its soil is rich. The country must, when prosperous, have presented a scene of plenty and happiness scarcely equalled. The Roman roads have not entirely disappeared, on which there are still milestones of the time of Trajan, Marcus Aurelius, **and** Severus, with the numbers yet readable. The argument in favor of the truth of prophesy receives great strength from the consideration of the past and present condition of Moab, especially when it is known that the prophets spoke at the time of its greatest prosperity (Is. xv., xvi., xxv., B. C. 720; Jer. xlviii., B. C. 600), 12 yrs. before the invasion of Nebuchadnezzar (xxvii. 3); and the country was promised to the Arabs of the east (Bedawins), who now occupy it (Ez. xxv. 8-11). Sanballat, the Moabite (Horonite), was **a** chief among those who laughed the Jews to scorn, after their return from captivity, and when they attempted to rebuild the walls of Jerusalem (Neh. ii. 19). Manasseh, a son of Joiada, the high-priest, married his daughter (xiii. 28), and became high-priest of the Samaritans in the temple built by his father-in-law on Mt. Gerizim (Josephus). The Moabites probably had a national record of events, from which the account of Balak and Balaam (Num. xxii.-xxiv.) was borrowed. Of Mesha, a king of Moab, an interesting relic has this [1870] year been found by the Palestine Exploration (see KIR HARESH).

MO'ABITE. Descendant of MOAB (Deut. ii. 9).

MO'ABITESS. A female of MOAB (Ruth i. 22).

MOADI'AH (*festival of Jah*). One who returned from captivity (Neh. xii. 17).

MOCH'MUR (*foaming*). Probably the Wady Ahmur.

MO'DIN. The native city of the Maccabees, who were of the race of the priests (1 Macc. ii. 1, xlii. 25), where their ancestral sepulchre was located (Jos. Ant. xiii. 6, 6; 1 Macc. xiii. 27-30, ii. 70; ix. 19). Here the resistance to Antioch was begun by Mattathias; and here the Jewish armies encamped on the eve of two of their most noted victories—that of Simon over Cendebæus (1 Macc. xvi. 4), and that of Judas over Eupator (2 Macc. xiii. 14). The site of Modin is located at Latrun, on the road from Jerusalem to Ramleh, 12 miles from the former, where there are ancient remains of importance (*Rob.*).

MO'ETH. Son of Sabban (Ezr. viii. 33).

MO'LADAH. South, in Judah (Josh. xv. 26); given to Simeon. Reoccupied after the Captivity (Neh. xi. 26). Herod retired to a tower in Malatha of Idumæa (Josephus). *El Milh* is a ruin of great extent, with two large wells, and is on the regular road from Petra to Hebron.

MOLE (TINSHEMETH). Mentioned in Lev. xi. 18, as the name of a bird (*swan*) or in Lev. xi. 30, as *mole*—amongst "creeping things" that are unclean. Probably a *chameleon* on a general allusion. In Is. ii. 20 it is more likely to mean **a** mole (CHEPOR PEROTH).

MOLECH (MELEK, *king*). The chief god of the Phoenicians—mentioned as the god of the Ammonites. Probably known to the Israelites before the time of Solomon. Human sacrifices (infants) were offered up to this idol, the victims being slowly burnt to death in the arms of the idol, which were of metal, hollow, and could be heated on the inside. Manasseh sacrificed his son to Molech. Solomon erected an altar to this god on one of the summits of Mount Olivet (see JERUSALEM, p. 83), described in 1 Kings xi. 7. This idol worship being continued, both there and in Tophet, until Josiah abolished it and defiled the altars (2 Kings xxiii. 10, 13). His son Jehoahaz revived this worship (2 Kings xxiii. 32). Molech was worshiped by the Phoenician colonies, as at Carthage, where there were at one time sacrificed 200 boys, believing this would relieve the city from a siege. See PHŒNICIA.

MO'LI. Son of Merari (1 Esd. viii. 47).

MO'LID (*begetter*). Son of Abishur (1 Chr. ii. 29).

MO'LOCH (Amos v. 26; Acts vii. 43). MOLECH.

MOM'DIS. Son of Bani (1 Esd. ix. 34).

WEIGHING MONEY.

MON'EY. The most ancient notices of money refer to certain weights of precious metals, but not to coins. The first mention of wealth in the Bible is of the wealth of Abraham when he left Egypt to return to Canaan; and of the 1000 pieces of silver that the Abimelech gave Abraham for Sarah's use (Gen. xlii. 2, xx. 16), unless Job lived before his time, when the "kesitah and ring of gold," which each of his friends gave him after his recovery, would belong to an earlier age.

Abraham bought the cave of Machpelah and weighed to Ephron 400 shekels of silver, current with the merchant (xxiii. 6). Jacob paid 100 kesitahs for a field at Shalem; Achan stole 200 shekels of silver, and a tongue of gold weighing 50 shekels (Josh. vii.).

Jewels in the East have in all ages been a convenient and recognized means of keeping property, the precious metals being always weighed, as in the case of the presents to Rebekah (Gen. xxiv. 22). Egyptian (and perhaps also other) money was made into rings, for convenience, as when the sons of Jacob carried bundles of money of certain weight to Egypt to buy corn (xliii. 35, xliii. 21). The Midianites were "spoiled" of jewels of gold, chains and bracelets, rings, ear-rings, and tablets, of 16,750 shekels' weight.

Jehoiada "took a chest, and bored a hole in the lid of it, and set it beside the altar, on the right side, and the priests put therein all the money" (2 K. xii. 9.) This is the first mention of a contribution box, 850 B. C. These small pieces *may* have been coins.

Saul's servants said that they had only the fourth part of a shekel to give the prophet, and it seems to have been customary to give more (1 Sam. ix. 8). A half-shekel was the yearly temple dues (Ex. xxx. 13, 15).

HALF-SHEKEL.

The credit for making the first coins, is given to the Lydians, Asia Minor, by Herodotus (i. 94), which were of gold; and to Phidra of Argos, in the island of Ægina, 860 B. C., of silver, by the Parian chronicle (a series of inscriptions, or records, on marble, dated 260 B. C.).

The earliest coins used in Palestine were Persian, and called Daric (*king's money*, from Darius), 450 B. C. (Ezr. ii. 69; Neh. vii. 70; 1 Chr. xxix. 7). (See cut on page 70). The stater (*standard*) was another Persian coin, of silver and of gold, and also the siglos (Greek for *shekel?*).

There are still to be found in the museums of Paris, Gotha, London, and in some private collections, coins of Sardis (see cut on page 125), Scythopolis (Bethshan), Joppa, Tarsus, Sycamina, Ascalon, Ephesus, Philadelphia, and several other cities of Palestine, of the date of Alexander, 350 B. C.

Antiochus VII, 139 B. C. granted the privilege of coining money among the Jews to Simon Maccabæus, and the various pieces are dated "In the first, or second, year of Simon (see cut on page 121), benefactor of the Jews, High-Priest" (1 Macc. xiii. 34, 42; Ant. xiii. 6). The date was always given in letters. (See NUMBER). Some coins have "etlmarch." There are some shekels with the inscription SHEKEL HAKODESH, shekel of the Sanctuary, that is the Temple.

Eleazar, son of Simon, struck coins both of silver and bronze (see cut on page 77). Jehonathan, high-priest, struck coins, B. C. 105-78, of which some are still extant.

The money of Herod is less interesting, because of its Greek character, and being of bronze only. The farthing of the New Testament was the smallest of Herod's coins, unless the mite was smaller. The text in Mark xii. 42, is explained, "she threw in two *leptra*, (mites) which is a quadrans " (farthing), (see page 193), as though we should say two mills, which are a quarter of a cent (nearly). Such very small coins are often found buried, with others, among the ancient ruins of Palestine. The modern Arabs also use small pieces which look very much like fish scales, in size and thickness.

The coin which Peter found in the mouth of the fish, was probably the stater, or tetradrachm, the only Greek silver coin in use at that time, equal in value to the shekel, which was not then coined, or in use, unless for Temple dues (see pages 13 and 18 for cuts of tetradrachma). The tribute money (Matt. xxii. 15-21) bore the head of a Cæsar, Tiberius or some earlier one, and was a day's wages of a soldier, and such as was paid the laborers in the vineyard (Matt. xviii. 28, xx. 2, 9, 13, xxii. 19; Mark vi. 37, xii. 15, xiv. 5; Luke vii. 41, x. 35, xx. 24; John vi. 7, xii. 15; Rev. vi. 6).

The piece of money paid Judas is represented by the tetradrachm of Antiochus III (cut on page 168), which was equal to the shekel. As there were money-changers in the Temple, who changed Gentile coins for the Temple money (shekel of the sanctuary), the thirty pieces may have been Jewish shekels of Simon or Eleazar (pages 77, 121).

The last coins struck by the Jews are those of Barkokab, A. D. 130. (This is doubted by some numismatists).

The Romans struck several coins and medals in memory of the fall of Jerusalem, one of which is given on page 78. Herod Agrippa also gives a head of Titus, when Emperor, on one of his coins. The Aretas who ruled Damascus when Paul was there struck coins, one of which is now well known. The coin of Ephesus bears a model of the temple of Diana, and a head of Nero.

There is a curious medal with a head of Christ on a cross, which was found at Urfa, Syria (by Rev. G. B. Nutting, missionary, who loaned it to me), and is engraved on page 40. It is very ancient, but cannot be dated, except that it is probably later than the time of Constantine.

A coin if genuine is often the very best evidence concerning ancient persons and places, which cannot be denied or explained away. Even if they were forged, in some age near the true date, they have still a value according to their antiquity. It is often found that ancient records are confirmed by coins, as for instance in the case of the port of Cenchreæa, where the coin of Corinth explains the text. See page 143.

The frequent allusions to burying money and treasure was confirmed as true records a few years ago by the discovery of some earthen jars in a garden at Sidon, containing nearly 8000 pieces of gold, the coinage of Philip of Macedon, and Alexander, his son. There were no banks or places of secure deposit, and the only safety was in burying money or treasure in some secret place, as alluded to in Prov. ii. 4; and also in Jer. xli. 8, where the treasures hid were produced.

MONTH (HODESH or CHODESH, YERAH or YERACH). The Hebrew months were divided into twenty-nine and thirty days alternately. The period of New Moon marked the first day called New Moon day or New Month. (See CHRONOLOGY). The months were numbered, as first, second; and also named in the calendar (Gen. vii. 11; 2 Kings xxv. 3; Esth. viii. 9). The Hebrew month does not run even with ours, being regulated by the moon, and having about 29 days, while ours has an arbitrary number given it, varying from 28 to 31 days.

MONUMENT (Is. lxv. 4). Various terms used, as *preserved* in Is. xlix. 6; *hōld'n* (xlviii. 6); *besi'ged* (i. 8, and Ez. vi. 12). It is a general reference to retired places.

MOON. Three names of the moon were used by the Hebrews: YARCAH, *paleness;* LEBONAH, *white;* and HODESH (*renewing*) *new moon*. The hodesh moon was the means of reckoning the months and fixing the feasts, etc. In the account of the festivals it appears that the authorities set a watch on the hills about Jerusalem, who looked for the new

moon, and when it was seen they were to report to the Sanhedrin. (See NEW MOON). The new moon regulated the month, and if any cloud or other cause prevented the discovery, the month would vary by a day.

The names of the moon in the account of the creation were framed on its light-giving property and color.

It is (and was anciently) a common superstition in Palestine that the moon has a powerful effect on both animal and vegetable life. That sleeping in the open air, exposed to the light of the moon, produces serious ills, blindness (Ps. cxxi. 6), etc. That as dew fell most abundantly on clear cool nights, the moon was the cause of its falling; and also the cause of all fertility.

The moon was worshiped (as also the sun) as a power, and was personified, several moon-goddesses being recorded. Some nations directly addressed the moon itself in their ceremonies, as the Pelasgians, Carthaginians, Teutons, Celts and others made images of women in certain drapery and attitude, called by the Armenians, Anaitis; by the Phœnicians, Astarte (Job xxxi. 26; 2 K. xxiii. 13; Jer vii. 18; viii. 2; xix. 13; xliv. 17-19). Queen of heaven; Syrians, Ashtoreth; Babylonians, Sin; Egyptians, Isis or Neith; Greeks, Artemis; Romans, Diana. The Chaldæans called the moon (and the woman-image) Queen of Heaven. See cut on page 127.

The worship was very widely known and practiced, and was specially denounced by Moses (Deut. iv. 19; xvii. 3), but in spite of his laws it was introduced with other idolatries by Manasseh, B. C. 694. Josiah reformed the Church in his day, but not permanently (2 K. xxiii. 5). The moon was worshiped as the power to which women were peculiarly subject; and women offered incense, drink-offerings and cakes, and by the kissing of the hand towards the bright orb.

MOR DECAI (*little man*), (Esth. ii. iii. iv. v.). He was the guardian of Esther, who was selected to succeed Vashti as queen of Ahasuerus, king of Persia, her Jewish descent remaining unknown to the king. Mordecai, who was an officer at the court, became informed of a plot against the king's life; this he communicated to Esther, who warned the king; this service, however, was, at the time, unrewarded. Haman at this time rose into favor and the highest office in court; he was an Agagite, and to him Mordecai showed no reverence. The anger of Haman was excited, and he obtained the king's order for the immediate massacre of all Jews throughout the kingdom. Esther becoming informed, through Mordecai, of this decree, hastened, uncalled for, to the king's presence, and with boldness pleaded the cause of the Jews. This, together with the memory of Mordecai's previous service, recalled by the reading of the records, determined the king to counteract the effect of the order (which by the Persian law could not be recalled), and by giving the Jews facilities for defense. Mordecai was promoted to the highest position, and Haman was ordered to be executed upon the gibbet he had prepared for Mordecai. Mordecai used his influence to the service of the Jews with wisdom and goodness. See ESTHER in the HISTORY OF THE BOOKS.

MO REH (*a teacher*). THE OAK OF MOREH (not plain), was the first halting-place of Abram in Canaan (Gen. xii. 6), and was near Shechem. (Land of Moriah?) The field which Jacob bought probably included this sacred grove. The name Mortha is found on some ancient coins as a title of Neopolis—Shechem. Josephus has a Mamortha, or Mabortha, which he says was a local name (B. J. v. 8, 1). THE HILL OF MOREH. At the base of this hill the Midianites encamped on the night when Gideon attacked them with his 300 (Judg.

vii. 1). Now called Little Hermon or *Jabel ed Duhy.*

MORESHETH **GATH** (*possession of the winepress*), (Micah i. 14). In the Shefelah, near Lachish. The prophet Micah was a native of a Moresheth, but whether this is the one is not certain.

PENNY.

MORI'AH. Found only in two passages—Gen. xxii. 2, and 2 Chr. iii. 1. 1. THE LAND OF MORIAH (Gen. xxii. 2) was more than two days' journey from Gerar, where Abram then lived (Beersheba being mentioned just before and just after the event of the journey), and probably in the same region with the oak of Moreh, Shechem.— 2. MOUNT MORIAH would in that case be Mt. Gerizim, according to the tradition of the Samaritans; but it is said, in 2 Chr. iii. 1, that Solomon began to build the house of the Lord at Jerusalem, in Mount Moriah. There must have been two mountains of that name, or the one at Jerusalem is the only one. This mount, then, has witnessed the offered sacrifice of Isaac, the vision of God's judgment and mercy, the presence of His Temple and worship, and the crucifixion.

MOR TAR (MEDOKAH). Mill or mortar, in which grain was pounded for domestic use (Num. xi. 8). The Arabs use the same simple machine now. They were made of stone or hard wood. (See MILL). The mortar for olives (KUTTASH) was made expressly for that use, of a heavy stone roller or wheel, which rolled around in a circular trough or tub, of stone also, moved by a long handle of wood. This squeezed or bruised the pulp, but did not crush the pits.

MO'SERAH (*bond*). Station in the Arabah, near Mt. Hor (Deut. x. 6). Moseroth (*bonds*), in Num. xxxiii. 30. *Wady Mousa* is supposed to be a remnant of the name Moserah. Aaron died while the people were encamped here.

MO'SES (MOSHEH, *drawn out of the water*). The son of Amram and Jochebed, of the tribe of Levi. Aaron was his brother, and Miriam his sister. He was saved from the Pharaoh's decree, of death to all male infants born to the Hebrews, by being laid in an ark (boat) of papyrus (A. V. bulrushes), and left among the reeds near the Nile bank, where the daughter of the Pharaoh was in the habit of bathing, where she found and drew him out of the water. He was educated as an Egyptian in the priest's college at Heliopolis, and was probably initiated into the sacred order of the priests (Acts vii. 22), and named Osarsiph, or Tisithen (Strabo, Ant. ii. 9, 7). It is probable, also, that he became acquainted in that seat of learning with Greek, Chaldæan, and Assyrian literature.

The great importance of selecting proper nurses may be learned from the history of Moses, whose mother, a Hebrew woman, nursed him, although he was brought up by the Egyptians; and when he became of age he chose the religion and people of his own race, although he was offered a place in the Pharaoh's family as an adopted son.

He became the champion of his people from the first, and showed his compassion for their sufferings by killing one of the task-masters who was abusing a Hebrew. Pharaoh would have punished him with death for the murder, if he had not fled into Arabia, where "sat down by a well" in the land of Midian, where his first act was to defend the

daughters of Reuel (Jethro), a priest of Midian, against their oppressors, the shepherds. (See MIDIAN). He became a shepherd in the service of Jethro, and married Zipporah, his daughter, by whom he had two sons, Gershom and Eliezer. During the seclusion of his shepherd life, in the valley of Shoayb (or Hobab), he received a divine commission to deliver his people Israel from the Egyptian bondage, and at the same time the divine name Jehovah (Heb. YEHEVEH = self-existence), which was explained to him, and a confirmation of his mission in the three miracles of the burning bush, the serpent rod, and the leprous hand. Supported by his brother Aaron, sustained in a wonderful way by the miracles of the ten plagues, the last of which was the most terrible, in the death of the first-born in all Egypt, Moses led out the Israelites to the E. side of the Red Sea, blessed with liberty, and a large tribute from their late oppressors.

On this occasion Moses wrote his first recorded poem (Ex. xv.). His sister Miriam also sang a song, the title, or subject only, of which is known.

Moses was at this time 80 years old. His life during the next 40 years is a part of the history of the Israelites, inseparable, and for 38 years entirely unknown. He died at the age of 120, and was not careful of his memory, leaving no monument of stone to mark his grave, which is unknown (Deut. xxiv.).

Moses is the only character to which Jesus compares himself, as a revealer of a new name of God, and the founder of a new religious faith, as a lawgiver, and as a prophet; and they both were misunderstood in their office as peacemakers; and the death of Moses suggests the ascension of Jesus (John v. 46; Heb. iii. xii.).

DOOR OF A TOMB.

The laws framed by Moses have influenced and even controlled the larger part of civilized mankind since his time; and the religion which he found scattered in traditions and shaped into a beautiful system still holds millions to its faith; while its successor, Christianity, claims present hold of a large part of mankind, and promises a universal sway in the future.

Besides the song on the passage of the Red Sea, Moses wrote others, of which only fragments have been preserved.

1. A war-song against Amalek (Ex. xvii. 16).

"As the hand is on the throne of Jehovah,
So will Jehovah war with Amalek
From generation to generation."

2. On the revelries at the calf-worship at Sinai (Ex. xxxii. 18):

"Not the voice of them that shout for mastery,
Nor the voice of them that cry for being overcome,
But the noise of them that sing, do I hear."

3. The songs recorded (and lost) in the Book of the Wars of the Lord, and the fragment of the Song at the Well, in Moab.

4. The Song of Moses in Deut. xxxii. was probably written in Moab.

5. The Blessing on the Twelve Tribes, which contains a concise statement of the characteristics of the different tribes.

6. The 90th Psalm (if not also some others following), is a sublime view of the eternity of God, which he describes as more enduring than the "everlasting" mountains.

Moses is called a prophet by one of the later prophets.

The word translated *meek*, in Num. xii. 3, means *disinterested*, which describes Moses better. He always forgot himself when the good of his people was to be served. Gave up his position in Pharaoh's house; avenged his people's wrongs; desired Aaron to take the lead; wished all were gifted as he was; preferred that his name be blotted out to save his people, when he was offered the promise of Abraham; not his sons, but Aaron's, were raised to the honor of priests, nor even to leaders, for after his death the leadership passed to Joshua, of another tribe; and although he earned the title of the father of his people, yet they were never called the children of Moses but of Abraham.

MOSOL'LAM (1 Esd. ix. 14). MESHULLAM.

MOSOL'LAMON (1 Esd. viii. 44).

MOTE (*a twig* or *mote*). The emblem of lesser faults (Matt. vii. 3–5).

MOTH (Heb. ASH; Gr. *sēs*). A destructive insect. Nearly every instance where this insect is mentioned it is in reference to its destroying garments (Job. xiii. 28).

MOTHER (Heb. EM; Gr. *mētēr*). The mother was honored and esteemed in the Hebrew system, and far above the station given her in any other system of the age (1 K. ii. 19; Ex. xx. 12; Lev. xix. 3; Deut. v. 16; Prov. x. 1, xv. 20, xvii. 25, xxix. 15, xxxi. 30). See WOMEN.

MOULD'Y (Heb. MIKKUDIM), (Josh. ix. 5, 12).

MOUNTAIN. The Hebrew words are, HAR, HARER, or HARAR, and the Chaldee, *tur*; which are translated mount, mountain, and hill. The various parts of a mountain were described by the names of parts of the human body: 1. Head (ROSH, Gen. viii. 5), meaning tops or summits.—2. Ears (AZNOTH, Josh. xix. 34); projections or spurs. Uzzen Sherah.—3. Shoulder (KATHEF, Deut. xxxiii. 12), meaning side or slope.—4. Side (ZAD, 1 Sam. xxiii. 26).—5. Loins (KISLOTH, Josh. xix. 12); Ha-Cesulloth (*loin-village*).—6. Rib (ZELA, 2 Sam. xvi. 13).—7. Back (SHEKEM), the origin of the name Shechem, which is on the back of Gerizim.—8. Thigh (JARKAH, Judg. xix. 1, 18).—9. In Chaldee *tur* is mountain, and this is borrowed in the modern name of Olivet, Jebel et Tur.

MOUNTAIN OF THE AMMONITES (Deut. i. 19, 20). On the plateau of Et Tyh, from Jebel Araif en-Nakah to Jebel el Mukrah, but also extended in lower ranges as far as Hebron.

MOURN'ING. There are a great many allusions to mourning in the Bible. Its customs include: beating the breast and body; weeping and screaming in an excessive manner; wearing dark-colored garments; songs and shouts of lamentation; funeral feasts; hired mourners; the disuse of perfumes, oil, and fine food, and the use of ashes, and coarse food and clothes. The time of mourning lasted from 7 to 30 days. Outward expression of sorrow for the dead, and also signs of repentance. The earliest notice is in Job (i. 20), who, on hearing of the calamities to his children, "arose, rent his mantle, shaved his head, and fell down upon the ground, and worshiped," uttering words of submission, and sitting down in the ashes. 7 days and nights the mournful rites were prolonged, with the use of sack-cloth and dust. On his recovery the friends held a kind of congratulatory mourning over him for his past sufferings (xlii. 11). The next instance is of Abraham, who wept for Sarah (B. C. 1871), in words which indicate a formal mourning (Gen.

xxiii. 2). The time usually given was 7 days as for Saul, in 1 Sam. xxxi. 13. The oak under which Deborah, the nurse of Rebekah, was buried was called Allan-bakuth, oak of weeping. The instances of mourning and weeping are very many in the Scriptures, in all the ages. The Egyptians decreed a mourning for a king of 72 days (Herodotus), and the people tore their garments, closed the temples, forbid sacrifices, and held no festivities, but instead they wandered through the streets, throwing dust on their heads, singing a funeral dirge. Ornaments were left off (Ex. xxxiii. 4; Joel ii. 16); but the Jews were forbidden to cut their flesh, as the pagans did (1 K. xviii. 28; Lev. xix. 28), or to shave the eyebrows or hair. The priests were denied all outward signs of grief (Lev. x. 6, xxi. 1, 4, 11), and the Nazarite also (Num. vi. 7). The mourning ordered by David for Abner was in form, with all the required rites, ceremonies, and processions. David also wrote an elegy and lamentation for Abner (2 Sam. iii. 31, 35). Elegies were very often composed for the dead (Ez. xxvi. 1–18, xxvii. 1–36; Amos v. 1, etc.). The customs did not change until the days of Christ, when "many of the Jews came to comfort Martha and Mary" (John xi. 19); "much people" were with the widow of Nain (Luke vii. 12). Mourning apparel is mentioned in 2 Sam. xiv. 2; ashes were put on the head, and oil was denied. The head was shaved. Mourning women were hired, and the custom is still in use. The monuments in Egypt show all these customs in actual practice. It was the custom, also, to give food to the mourners at funerals. The cries and songs used are peculiarly mournful and affecting. Idolatrous mourning (for Tammuz) was prohibited (Ez. viii. 14). The most singular custom of wailing every week, at the wall of the Temple in Jerusalem, has been kept up for ages, by those Jews who still look for the Christ, and hope for the deliverance of Zion.

MOUSE (AKBAR, *field-ravager*). An unclean animal (Lev. xi. 29), forbidden as food. Five golden mice were made for a trespass offering (1 Sam. vi. 4, 5). It is not known what they were, and some think jerboas answer the meaning of the original.

MOUTH (PEH). Is used in the Scriptures both literally of men and beasts (Gen. viii. 11).

MOW'ING. The heat of the climate in Palestine is so great it soon dries up the herbage so that hay-making is not in use (Amos vii. 1). Grass and green grain were cut for immediate use (Ps. cxxix. 7; Amos vii. 1).

MO'ZAH (*spring-head*). Benjamin (Josh. xviii. 26), near Cephirah, the modern Kefir.—2. Son of Zimri, and in the line of Saul—Mephibosheth—Micah (1 Chr. ix. 42).

MUF'FLERS (*veils*). A female ornament (Is. xii. 19).

MUL'BERRY TREES (BACA, BEKAIM). It is not certain that mulberry trees are meant in 2 Sam. v. 23, 24; 1 Chr. xiv. 14. Some think it was a species of poplar. See cut on p. 88.

MULE (PERED, *mule*; REKESH, *dromedary*; and YEMIM, *warm springs*; are all translated mule. First mentioned in David's time, when horses became common, and they appear to have become favorites all at once, being mentioned in hundreds (Neh. vii. 68). The king's sons rode on mules. The law forbid the Jews from raising mules, and they either imported them or broke the law (Lev. xix. 19). Yemim, warm springs, were found by Anah (and not mules as in Gen. xxxvi. 24), east of the Dead Sea, now called Machærus or Callirrhoe.

MUP'PIN (*sorrow*). A descendant of Rachel (Gen. xlvi. 21).

MURDER. Was an outrage on the likeness of God in man, and also a damage to society in the loss of a member. There was to be no reprieve of the murderer, for money, as the pagans allowed. The accidental man-slayer might escape to the City of Refuge.

The custom of blood-revenge is very ancient, and Moses regulated it by certain restrictions, which protected the accidental homicide, but punished the wilful criminal. Bloodshed, even in war, was polluting (Num. xxxv. 33; Deut. xxi. 1; 1 Chr. xxviii. 3). Some of the ancients held that an attempt to murder was equally criminal as an actual murder. Child murder, parricide, poisoning, are not included among other particular things mentioned in the law (Ex. xxi.).

If an animal, known to be unruly and violent, caused the death of a person by the neglect of its owner or keeper, both the animal and its owner were destroyed.

The question of guilt was to be determined by the judges, but the execution of the sentence was the duty and privilege of the next of kin to the sufferer originally, but was directed by the king and his officers in later times. At least two witnesses were required on a capital offense.

Private revenge caused many assassinations in some ages, several instances of which are recorded in 1 K. xv. 27; xvi. 9, 10; 2 K. viii. 15; x. 7; xi. 1, 16; and there are many others.

Burglars, if taken in the act, before day light (or sunrise), could be killed, but not after sunrise.

MULBERRY.

MUR'RAIN (DEBER). A plague among cattle.

MU'SHI (*forsaken*). Son of MERARI (Ex. vi. 19).

MU'SHITES. Descendants of Mushi (Num. iii. 33).

MUSIC. The first record of music is in Gen. iv. 21, referring to Jubal (brother of Tubal-Cain) as the father (teacher?) of musicians upon the harp and organ; probably the lyre and the Pandean pipes. Music was used socially from an early date, as in Gen. xxxi. 27, both as an accompaniment to song and dance. Music was an especial employment of women, and, at a later period, "foreign girls" visited Palestine as musicians (Is. xxiii. 16). David was an accomplished musician, and gave much attention to its cultivation, and introduction into the Temple worship (1 Chr. xxv. 1). It is probable that in this service were female choirs (Ezr. ii. 65). The prophets were great cultivators of music, and it was an important branch of the instruction in the schools of the prophets.

From the time of Abraham, the Israelites were essentially a musical people, as the Arabs are to this day, living in the same country, exhibiting their musical nature in their constant habit of singing. The Egyptians were practical musicians, and introduced music upon all festive occasions. During the Israelitish bondage, the Hebrews, naturally musical, became acquainted with the musical instruments of the Egyptians, which they carried with them across the desert into Canaan, and their use has been recorded in every succeeding age. In the titles of the Psalms both tunes and musical terms appear. See MUSICAL INSTRUMENTS. We have no records of any tunes used by the ancient Hebrews, and can only suppose that they had a system of musical notation. The most eminent composers of music (especially sacred music) in our age are Hebrews.

```
ΕΝΑΡΧΗΜΝΟΛΟΓΟΣΚΑΙΟΛΟΓΟΣ
ΤΙΡΟΣΤΟΝΘΝΚΑΙΘΣΗΝΟΛΟΓΟΣ·
ΟΥΤΟΣΗΝΕΝΑΡΧΗΠΡΟΣΤΟΝΘΝ
ΠΑΝΤΑΔΙΑΥΤΟΥΕΓΕΝΕΤΟΙΚΑΙΧω
ΡΕΙΣΑΥΤΟΥΕΓΕΝΕΤΟΟΥΔΕΝ·
ΟΓΕΓΟΝΕΝΕΝΑΥΤωΖωΗΗΝ
ΚΑΙΗΖωΗΗΝΤΟΦωΣΤωΝΑΝωΝ
ΚΑΙΤΟΦωΣΕΝΤΗΣΚΟΤΙΑΦΑΙ·
ΝΕΙΚΑΙΗΣΚΟΤΙΑΑΥΤΟΟΥΚΑΤΕ
ΛΑΒΕΝ·
```

CODEX ALEXANDRINUS.—John I. 1.

MUSICAL INSTRUMENTS. There were three kinds in use. 1. Stringed, (harp, viol, sackbut). 2. Wind, (trumpet, horn, cornet, pipe, flute, organ, dulcimer). 3. Of percussion, (bells, cymbals, timbrel). See cut. p. 202.

The cornet (SHOFAR) was made of the horn of a ram or wild goat, or ox. Its use was for signals, as for the jubilee (Lev. xxv. 9), new year, and muster for war (Jer. iv. 5), and for giving alarm by the sentinels on the approach of an enemy (Ez. xxxiii. iv.). KEREN was a horn of any kind. Two silver trumpets were ordered by Moses, for calling the assembly together; for the signal to march in the wilderness, and for the muster for war, and for festivals (Num. x. 10). YOBEL was probably the name of a distinct style of horn or trumpet (Ex. xix. 13), called ram's horn in Job vi. 5, 6. The modern cornet is not a successor of the ancient in tone and effect, being of brass and much more harsh and noisy.

The horn (KEREN) was probably the primitive trumpet, being a horn of an ox, ram, or goat, with a mouth piece, or simple open end. The same word is used for the horn which held the oil used in consecration or anointing the king, priests or sacrifices (1 Sam. xvi. 1, etc.). The word KEREN meant also to shine, and is so used in the account of Moses at Sinai, where, instead of horns, it was more likely to have been light reflected from his face.

The pipe (CHALIL) or flute (1 K. i. 40), was an instrument bor d o ut, as of wood. The form of the flute was very much the same in all ancient countries. We know what the Greek flute was, both single and double, and may guess at the Hebrew very closely. The flute is very much improved in modern days by keys, especially in the Bœhm variety, which is really the ancient instrument improved by modern keys. The bore is the same size throughout, differing from the common flute, which is very large at the mouth end, tapering towards the other. The small sizes are called fife and piccolo. The flute was used in mourning, for its soft, sad tones (Matt. ix. 23), and in the Temple choirs (Ps. lxxxvii. 7, "pipers"). They were made of reeds also for the altar service because of their softer tones.

The flute (MASHROKUTHA, *the hisser*), was made of one, two, or several pipes, and was not the organ. The dervishes use the flute in their sacred dances.

The organ (UGGAB, *the blower*), a general term for all musical instruments that are blown (Gen. iv. 21; Job xxi. 12, xxxi. 31; Ps. cl. 4). Supposed to be the same as the Pandean pipe, which was the favorite with the shepherds in Homer's age.

The dulcimer (SUMPONIAH), an Assyrian instrument (Dan. iii. 5, 15); a triangular chest, with 50 wires (18 to 36 inches), played with two small hammers.

There are several words rendered musical instruments about which there are doubts; as DAHAVAN, 2d wife (Dan. vi. 8); MINNIM, *stringed instruments* (Ps. cl. 4; xlv. 8); NEBEL ASOR, *ten stringed psaltery* (Ps. xxxiii. 2, cxliv. 9); SHIDDAH *palanquin* (Eccl. ii. 8); SHALISHIM, *triangle*, or *cymbals* (1 Sam. xviii. 6).

MUSTARD, (*sinapis nigra*). Is found abundantly in Palestine both in a wild and cultivated state. The mustard plant grows to a very large size on the banks of the Jordan. In comparison with any other "garden herb" it would be a "tree."

MUTH-LAB BEN. Occurs in the title of Ps. ix. Muthlabben either referred to the instrument or the tune to which the Psalm was to be sung.

MYN'DUS. Between Miletus and Halicarnassus, the residence of Jews for convenience in trade (1 Macc. xv. 23). Mentioned by Herodotus and Strabo for its ships and harbor. There is an ancient pier and other ruins at the site.

MY'RA. In Lycia, where Paul changed vessels on the way to Rome (Acts xxvii. 5). The city was on a hill, at the foot of which flowed a navigable stream, with a good harbor at its mouth (Pliny). There are ruins of various periods of its history; ornamented tombs, with inscriptions in the Lycian character; a very large theatre, of the Greek age; and a Byzantine church.

MYRRH (MOR). One of the ingredients in the "oil of holy ointment," and used as a perfume (Prov. vii. 17). It was one of the gifts brought to the infant Jesus (Matt. ii. 11). Myrrh was used for EMBALMING (John xix. 39).

The tree which produces the myrrh of commerce (*Balsamodendron myrrha*), has a hard wood and bark, with a strong odor. The gum is at first soft, like thick turpentine, hardening on exposure.

LOT (Gen. xxxvii. 25, xliii. 11), is also rendered myrrh, and is believed to refer to the odorous gum of the *cistus creticus*, ladanum. It is used as a stimulant in medicine, and also as a perfume.

MYRTLE-TREE (Heb. HADAS). It is a shrub or tree common in Southern Europe, North Africa and Syria. Its berries are used as a substitute for spices. The Jews use it in their adornments at the Feast of Tabernacles (Neh. viii. 15).

MY'SIA. Province in the N. W. of Asia Minor, west of Bithynia, north of Æolis, or Lydia. It was celebrated for its corn and wine. Paul passed through it on his first journey (Acts xvi. 7, 8). Assos and Adramyttium were in Mysia, but Troas was independent.

MYSTERY (Gr. *mustērion*). One initiated. Truths hidden from the natural sense and from the merely natural reason (1 Cor. xiii. 2). The New Testament idea is a hidden truth to the natural sense, but seen by the spiritual sense, as

N

NA'AM (*grace*). A Son of Caleb.

NA'AMAH (*pleasing*). 1. Daughter of Lamech, by Zillah.—2. Wife of Solomon and mother of king Rehoboam; she was an Ammonite.

NA'AMAH. Judah in the Shefelah (Josh. xv. 41), in the group with Lachish, etc. Lost.

NA'AMAN (*pleasantness*). 1. "Na'aman, the Syrian," Aramite warrior, cured of leprosy by Elisha (2 K. v.). See LEPROSY. This incident is referred to by Jesus (Luke iv. 27).—2. One of the family of Benjamin, who came down to Egypt with Jacob (Gen. xlvi. 21).

There is a Jewish tradition in Josephus (Ant. viii. 15, 5), which says that Naaman was the archer whose arrow struck Ahab with his mortal wound, and thus "gave deliverance to Syria." This feat gave the warrior a great place and favor at the court of king Benhadad and command of the army. He was also privy counselor to the king, and attended him to the Temple when he worshipped in state. In Judea his leprosy would have compelled him to seclusion, and kept him away from the king and all others, but the Syrians were not so cautious. It was Naaman who went in and told his master (lord, the king, in verse 4). His carrying away earth has been imitated many times in ancient and modern times. The Campo Santo at Pisa is filled with earth carried from Aceldama. Pilgrims to Mecca always bring away something: dirt, sand or stones. Elisha was made known in Damascus by this cure, and well received by Naaman's successor, Hazael.

NA'AMATHITE (Job ii. 11, etc.). Zophar, one of Job's friends, was from NAAMAH; but it is supposed that it must be looked for in Arabia, where the Temanite and Shuhite, his other two friends, lived. Lost.

NA'AMITES. The descendants of Na'aman 2, mentioned in Num. xxvi. 40.

NA'ARAH (*a girl*). Second wife of Ashur, a descendant of Judah (1 Chr. iv. 5, 6).

NA'ARAI. Son of Ezbai, one of David's "valiant men" (1 Chr. xi. 37).

NA'ARAN (*boyish*). An eastern limit of Ephraim (1 Chr. vii. 28). See GEZER). Naarath in Josh. xvi. 7. Perhaps Neara, from which Archelaus conducted water to irrigate the royal gardens at Jericho (Ant. xvii. 13, 1). It was between Ataroth and Jericho. There are large ruins at the foot of the hills and in the deep ravines a few miles north of Jericho, where there are also ruins; but no place has been pointed out as the site in question. *Wady Nauaimeh*, 3 miles N. of Jericho?

NAASHON or **NA'ASHON** (Heb. NAHSHON) (Ex. vi. 23).

NAAS'SON [(Gr. *Naasson*), (Matt. i. 4; Luke iii. 32).

NA'ATHUS. Of the family of Addi (1 Esd. ix. 31).

NA'AZUZ. The name of a tree, translated thorn, in Isaiah vii. 18, 19, lv. 13, a thorn tree.

NA'BAL (*fool*). A large owner of sheep and goats, near Carmel of Judah, descended from Caleb. He refused to supply provisions requested by David, through his young men, whom he insulted (1 Sam. xxv. 10, 11). His wife Abigail saved his life by appeasing the wrath of David. The excitement caused by the danger and rescue of Na'bal hastened his death, after which David married Abigail (1 Sam. xxv.). See ABIGAIL.

The history of Nabal is one of the few glimpses given of the private life of the Hebrews. Josephus says he was a Ziphite (Ant. vi. 13, 6), residing at Emmaus, south of Carmel in Judah. The vast flocks were pastured on the downs, and gathered yearly at shearing time, when there was feasting, and a joyous time (xxv. 2, 4, 36). David's ten messengers came to Nabal on one of these feast days, and were recognized by his shepherds as friends who had guarded them in the wilderness. They mentioned their services and David, and claimed a reward as for servants, but were denied by the churlish farmer. Josephus says he was not descended from Caleb, but was the son of a caleb, that is, a dog. The violence of his nature and manner on this occasion prevented his shepherds from telling him how David was, but his beautiful wife was ready to hear, and hastened to mend the mischief her hasty and obstinate husband had done. David had already vowed not to leave "a dog" even of the whole household of Nabal, when Abigail met him, and saluting him in the Eastern manner as a prince, explained to him in truly poetic phrases her husband's folly. David changed his mind, and Abigail returned, but finding her husband drunk, waited until next morning before telling him the news. When Nabal learned of the danger that had been only just averted by his wife's quick wit, his heart "became as a stone." Probably a stroke of paralysis followed, terminating in death in ten days (v. 37, 38). David never forgot Nabal's death but when the great general Abner was murdered he said, mournfully, "Died Abner as Nabal (a fool) died." The death of Nabal was a divine judgment on unrestrained passion and vice.

NA'BOTH (*fruit-produce*). A Jezreelite who was the owner of a vineyard coveted by king Ahab (see AHAB), near whose palace it was (1 K. xxi. 1, 2). Naboth declined to part with his land. Through the order of Jezebel, Ahab's wife, Naboth was publicly accused of blasphemy, conveyed beyond the walls and stoned to death with his children (2 K. ix. 26), the punishment for that crime (Lev. xxiv. 16; Num. xv. 30). Ahab then took possession. Elijah uttered the prophetic curse "In the place where the dogs licked the blood of Naboth, shall dogs lick thy blood even thine" (1 K. xxi.).

INDIAN IDOL.

The trial of Naboth was a fearful mockery of justice. He, as an Elder, was set "on high," that is, in the seat of honor, at the head of the divan among the rulers, and then false witnesses, hired for the business, swore away his life. The prophet denounced the crime, and retribution followed the judicial murder. The same crime was planned against Jesus, and carried out. The retribution in this case being a total loss of judicial power, which had been so grossly abused.

Tristram thinks the site of the vineyard can be identified on the rocky slope near the ruins of ancient Jezreel, where "not a shrub now clothes the bare hillside. A watch tower there would have given a view of the country for many miles over the route of Jehu" (*Land of Israel*, page 130).

NA'CHON'S. Threshing floor (2 Sam. vi. 6). Called also Chiden's (1 Chr. xiii. 9), and after the

sad event of Uzzah's death by the ark, it was named Perez Uzzah (perez, broken). (Ant. vii, 4, 2). Between Kirjath Jearim and Jerusalem.

NACHOR. NAHOR. 1. Mother of Abraham (Josh. xxiv. 2). Also spelled Nahor. The Hebrew ᴎ is a strong breathing, and is often written CH.—2. Grand father of Abraham (Luke iii. 34).

NA'DAB (*spontaneous*). 1. Eldest son of Aaron and Elisheba (Ex. vi. 23; Num. iii. 2).

Aaron, Nadab and Abihu, with seventy elders (Ex. xxiv. 1), were selected from the assembly of the people to worship "afar off," whilst Moses awaited God upon Mount Sinai. Nadab and his brother were afterwards destroyed by fire (Lev. x. 1) for burning in their censers fire not taken from that which perpetually burnt on the altar (Lev. vi. 13).—2. King Jeroboam's son (Jeroboam I), second king of Israel. He ascended the throne B. C. 954, reigned two years (1 K. xv. 25-31), and was slain at the siege of Gibbethon by his officer Baasha, who succeeded him, B. C. 953. (See ISRAEL.)—3. Son of Shammai (1 Chr. ii. 28), of the tribe of Judah.—4. Son of Gibeon (viii. 30, ix. 36), of the tribe of Benjamin.

ΑΡΟΥΚΑΝΘ ΝΟΣΜΕΝΔΕ
ΠΟ ΤΟ ΥΤΗ ΝΥΙΚΟΥΜΕΝ ΗΝΥΠΗΚΟ
Ο Ν Α ΠΑΣΑ ΝΘΙ ΝΟΙ ΝΟΜ ΩΙΑ ΕΤΩΙ
ΤΟ ΥΤΩΙ ΤΡΟ ΠΩΙ ΕΖΑΝΑ ΠΚΚΕΧΡΗΣ
ΘΑΙ ΤΗ ΝΕΛΛΑΔΑ ΣΥΝ ΕΛΟΝ ΤΑΙ

PAPYRUS, 1st CENTURY.

NADAB'ATHA (1 Macc. ix. 3; Ant. xiii. 1, 4). GABATHA. From which the children of Jambi were escorting a bride with great pomp and music, when they were attacked by Jonathan and Simon. On the east of Jordan, near *Es Salt!* Josephus says the bride was the daughter of an illustrious Arabian.

NAG'GE (Heb. NOGAH, *splendor*). An ancestor of Jesus Christ (Luke iii. 25), who lived in the time of Onias I.

NA'HALAL (*pasture*). In Zebulon (Josh. xxi. 35). Na'hallal (error in xix. 15). Na'halol (Judg. i. 30), *Malul*, 4 miles southwest of Nazareth, in the plain of Esdraelon.

NAHA'LIEL (*torrent of El*). One of the latest halting places; N. of the Arnon (Num. xxi. 19). Wady Encheyle, a branch of the Mojeb (Arnon). The word Encheyle is the Hebrew name Nahaliel reversed, or transposed. The identification of places by their names, even after the names have been changed by passing through several languages, is a work of patient research and thought, and was very successful in the case of Edward Robinson, who recovered several hundred localities in this way. There are many yet waiting for future research on the E. of Jordan.

NA'HAM (*consolation*). Brother of Hodiah, or Jehudijah, wife of Ezra (1 Chr. iv. 19).

NAHAMA'NI (*compassionate*). Returned with Zerubbabel and Jeshua from Babylon (Neh. vii. 7).

NA'HARAI (Heb. SNORER). Joab's armor-bearer (2 Sam. xxiii. 37).

NA'HASH (*serpent*). 1. King of the Ammonites (see AMMON). He treated the people of Jabesh-Gilead with the utmost cruelty, at which Saul attacked and destroyed the Ammonite force (1 Sam. xi. 1, 2-11). He retained the favor of David.—2. Mentioned only once (2 Sam. xvii. 16). The first husband of Jesse's wife; not Na'hash, the Ammonite.

NA'HATH (*rest*). 1. A duke, or sheikh, of Edom, eldest son of Reuel, the son of Esau (Gen. xxxvi. 13, 17; 1 Chr. i. 37).—2. A Kohathite Levite, son of Zophai (1 Chr. vi. 26).—3. A Levite in Hezekiah's reign; a collector of taxes, etc. (2 Chr. xxxi. 13).

NAH'BI (*hidden*). The son of Vophsi; a Naphtalite, one of the 12 spies (Num. xlii. 14).

NA'HOR (*snorting*, *snoring*). 1. Abraham's grand-father, the son of Serug (Gen. xi. 22-25). —2. Grand-son of Na'hor, called Na'hor, brother to Abraham. He married Milcah. Eight of his sons were by this wife (Gen. xxii. 20-24). Na'hor remained in the land of his birth.

GENEALOGY OF NAHOR'S DESCENDANTS TO JACOB.

	1. NAHOR.
1. Nahor.	2. Terah.
2. Terah.	3. Abraham.
"	4. Nahor.
"	5. Haran.
3. Abraham.	6. Isaac (mother)
4. Nahor.	7. Tebah. Reumah.
"	8. Gaham. "
"	9. Thahash. "
"	10. Maacah. "
"	11. Huz. Milcah.
"	12. Buz. "
"	13. Kemuel. "
"	14. Chesed. "
"	15. Hazo. "
"	16. Pildash. "
"	17. Jidlaph. "
"	18. Bethuel. "
11. Huz, Uz.	19. Job.
12. Buz.	20. Elihu.
13. Kemuel.	21. Aram. [dæans.
14. Chesed.	22. Chasidim or Chal-
18. Bethuel.	23. Laban.
"	24. Rebekah.
23. Laban.	25. Leah.
"	26. Rachel.
Isaac.	27. Esau. 24. Rebekah
	28. Jacob.

NAHOR, THE CITY OF (Gen. xxiv. 10).

NAH'SHON (*enchanter*). Also written Naason and Naashon; son of Amminadab, and prince of the children of Judah (1 Chr. ii. 10), at the numbering in the wilderness (Ex. vi. 23; Num. 1. 7, etc.). Elisheba, the wife of Aaron, was his sister. His son Salmon became the husband of Rahab after the fall of Jericho.

NA'HUM (*consolation*). See HISTORY OF THE BOOKS.

NAIL.—1. (T'FAR). A nail or claw of man or animal (Deut. xxi. 12; Dan. iv. 33, vii. 19). A point used in writing, as signets are engraves on gems or hard stones (Jer. xvii. 1). The captive wife was "to make herself neat," that is, to *stain* her nails (not *pare*), with the henna dye (Deut. xxi. 12). A nail (Is. xxii. 23-25, xxxiii. 20), a stake (xxxiii. 20). Tent peg (Judg. iv. 21, etc.). See JAEL—TENT. Tent pegs of wood and iron. Nails of the cross (John xx. 25, and Col. ii. 14).

NA'IN (*pleasant*). The scene of one of the greatest miracles of Jesus, the raising of the widow's son (Luke xii. 12). It is now a small village, of 20 huts, on a rocky slope, in the midst of extensive ruins of an ancient place, on the northwestern end of Little Hermon (*Jebel el Duhy*). There are sepulchral caves along the steep eastern approach from the plain, and also on the other side of the town (*Rob.*). It is but a few miles from Nazareth, in the vicinity of Endor and Shunem, places noted in the history, and its name remains unchanged from its ancient form. The custom of carrying the dead out of the villages, or cities, is still practiced in the East, as it was when Jesus met the procession coming out of Nain. And there is now on a hill side, about ten minutes walk from the village, the grave yard, with a few whitewashed grave stones, unfenced. The extent of the ruins of Nain indicate an ancient city of some extent, with a wall and gates. But now there is a painful

NAIOTH (*college buildings*). Where Samuel and his disciples lived (1 Sam. xix. 18, etc.). Where David fled for refuge from Saul. Samuel had a school here. Verse 20 is rendered by the Targum-Jonathan, "They saw the company of scribes singing praises, and Samuel teaching, standing over them." As Naioth was *in* Ramah (ver. 19), it was probably a dwelling used for a school in the town of Ramah. See 2 K. xxii. 14. Huldah lived in a college in Jerusalem.

NAME (Heb. SHEM). The root ONA, to know, has given rise to the Sanscrit *naman*, Greek *ōnōma*, Latin *nomen*, Gothic *nama*, and our *name*.

No monuments are more enduring than names. Sometimes they are the most ancient records of persons, places and things. They are fossils of thought. Bible names have almost always a meaning, which is often given by the writer for a purpose. The meaning of a name being known, we are able to get a better knowledge of persons and their history, especially if the name was given for some special reason or act. This work is very difficult because men's names are so constantly changing with the growth or decay of language, and the substitution of one language for another.

The Hebrews gave but one name to a child, except in peculiar cases (as Solomon, Jedidjah), or where it was necessary to add the father's or mother's name, if the mother was the more noted. There is but one David, but there are several named Jesus, as the Son of Sirach, etc. The ancient custom was more simple than the modern, which (among the Arabs) exalts a man's external affairs by giving him names and titles carrying terms of flattery and display. The custom of naming—simple, compound, or ornamental—indicates very nearly the age of the person so named. There were 3 kinds: 1. Simple. 2. Compound. 3. Derived. 1. Simple names are numerous, and quite plain in their meaning, as—ARIEH, lion; DEBORAH, bee; DAN, judge; TAMAR, palm-tree; JONAH, dove; DISHAN, gazelle. Diminutives were often used, as, Zebulon, (*my little dweller with me*), and Jeduthun (*little praiser*), a director of musical affairs in David's cabinet. 2. Compound names express more complete ideas than the simple, and are therefore more important in history. Abiezer, Abital, Abigail, Abraham, compounded of Ab, father, or maker. Abijail (*joymaker*, or *cheerful*), at first, probably, an epithet only, but afterward a name by consent and use. The Arabs have a habit of giving names in sport, or derision, which the Hebrews did not indulge in, as—Abul-Hussain, the father of the little castle, that is, a fox who lives in a hole; Abu-Ayuba, the father of Job, that is, the camel, because it is as patient as Job. A man is often called father of a place, village, or city, who was the settler, or builder, or only the ruler, of that place. See FATHER. The prefix AB was often joined to a term or name, to show dignity or character, as—ABNER, father of light, that is, a wise counsellor. Sometimes AB appears to mean brother, as, Achiram, brother of Ram (perhaps one who was accidentally fortunate). The word HUD, splendor, was compounded with Jehovah, as Jehudi, a Jewess (correctly Hajehudiah), that is, Jehovah's splendor (God's work). CHUR, free (Hur in Ex. xvii. 10), and ISH, a man, forms Asshur, a freeman. ISHOD, man of beauty.

The word, AM people, forms with many names of countries, cities, etc., names of the people, as distinguished from families, as AMMINADAB, that is he who belongs to the whole people; ITHREAM, the residue of the people; YORKOAM (1 Chr. ii. 44, Jorkoam), increaser of the people, at first a man's name, then the name of the place founded or enlarged by him.

Many compound names carry a religious sense with them, containing some divine name. These are found, in some cases, to contain a name and a verb, or a complete sentence; as NATHANAEL given by El (Theodore and Dorothea in Greek are on the same model). HOSHEA, help, with JAH becomes Jehoshua, God's help, or salvation. MELEK, king, with AB, father, becomes Abimelech, father king; with ZEDEK, righteousness, becomes Melchizedek, king of righteousness; ADONAI, lord; RAM, hight, Adonairam, lord of exaltation.

3. The names of men became names of women by a change of termination; as Meshullum, Meshullumeth; Haggai, Haggith; Dan, Dinah; Judah, Judith. (This does not account for the use of names of men which are used for women without change, and which were probably used as a kind of monument, being compound words, and incapable of regular feminine forms). Ai (imperfect form of Jah) with AMIT, truth, means truth of Jah; JEDID, darling, with Jah, Jedidiah, Jah's darling. Some names seem to have been used for both men and women, even the feminine forms, as Shelomith, feminine of Shelomo (Solomon), for a man (1 Chr. xxvi. 25). Many titles of men in office were feminine, as PEKAH, governor, KOHELETH, preacher. AB, father, becomes in the plural ABOTH (feminine) not ABIM (masculine). ZERUBBABEL (*scattered in Babylon*), was a hint of the man's history. Many names indicate the condition of the National history at the time they were given; as a time of religious elevation in Hodaiah, praise ye Jah; Elioenai, mine eyes look to El; Zephaniah, watcher of the Lord.

The pure Hebrew names Eleazar became Grecized into Lazarus; Joshua became Jason, and Jesus; Alcimus from Eleakim.

In the Old Testament there are many names which are derived from the heathen idols, as Bethaven, house of idols; Gurbaal, place of baal; Hadarazer, whose help is Hadad; and in the New Testament, as Apollonius, Phœbe, Artemas.

The Hebrews gave their children the names of many natural objects, as Tamar, a palm tree; Hadassah, myrtle; Zipporah, sparrow; and Zillah, shadow; Shimrath, vigilant; Tabitha, gazelle; Rachel, ewe; Shual, fox; Cheran, lamb. The right of naming belonged to the father, but was allowed to the mother in many cases. The time was usually at the day of circumcision, the 8th for boys, and for girls at any time during the first year. The boy often was called son of his father if he became noted, or to distinguish him from other relatives of the same name.

PLAN OF ANCIENT TOMB.

When a man had no sons he was the subject of his friends' sympathy who gave him an imaginary son, whose name was added to his. If a son became famous the father was honored by being called the father of such a one.

The name often indicated the character or office of the person, as Isaiah, Jah is helper. When God elects a man for a certain work he is said to call him by name, as Bezaleel, the shadow of God (Ex. xxxi. 1). Receiving a new name from God is an expression founded on the custom of giving chil-

dren or others new names when some act of theirs, or event in their history, or other cause, made them noted, as the change of Abram to Abraham; and means a new personal relation to God (Is. lxv. 15, lxii. 2; Rev. ii. 17, iii. 12).

NANE'A, THE TEMPLE OF. At Elymais, rich with the trophies of Alexander, and plundered by Antiochus Epiphanes (1 Macc. vi. 1-4; 2 Macc. i. 13-16).

NA'OMI (*my pleasantness*). Wife of Elimelech, mother-in-law of Ruth (Ruth i. 2, iii. 1, iv. 3). She buried her husband and sons, Mahlon and Chilion, in the land of Moab. She returned to Bethlehem with Ruth. Correctly, NOOMI.

family of Christians in Rome, alluded to by Paul in Rom. xvi. 11.

NARD. (See SPIKENARD).

NAS'BAS. Tobit's nephew, who, with Achiacharus, attended the wedding of Tobias (Tob. xi. 18).

NASITH. NEZIAH (1 Esd. v. 32).

NASOR, THE PLAIN OF. Near Kedesh Naphtali, the scene of a battle between Jonathan and Demetrius (1 Macc. xi. 67). HAZOR.

NA'THAN (*gift*). 1. Hebrew prophet in the reign of David and Solomon. In the consultation with David upon the building of the Temple (2 Sam. vii.

NAZARETH.

2, 3, 17) Nathan reproves David for his sin with Bath-sheba, and prophesies in the form of a parable of "the rich man and the ewe-lamb" (2 Sam. xii. 1-12). Nathan was the educator of Solomon (2 Sam. xii. 25). In the last days of David Nathan assisted the cause of Solomon. He assisted in the inauguration of Solomon (1 K. i. 8). He had a son, Zabud, who was the "king's friend." He wrote a Life of David (1 Chr. xxix. 29) and a Life of Solomon (2 Chr. ix. 29). The loss of his biography of David is a heavy one to history.—2. Son of David by Bath-sheba (1 Chr. iii. 5, xiv. 4, and 2 Sam. v. 14). He appears as one of the forefathers of Joseph in Christ's genealogy (Luke iii. 31).— 3. Related to one of David's "valiant men" (2 Sam. xxiii. 36; 1 Chr. xi. 38).—4. One of the chief men who returned from Babylon with Ezra on his second expedition (Ezr. viii. 16; 1 Esd. viii. 44).

NA'PHISH (*refreshment*). (1 Chr. v. 19). A tribe descended from the last but one of the sons of Ishmael; settled in the Hauran and Gilead; allies of Jetur (who was in Iturea). Traces of this tribe may be looked for in Arabia, for they were driven out by Reuben, Gad, and Manasseh. They were wealthy when dispossessed, having lost to the Israelites 50,000 camels, 250,000 sheep, and 2,000 asses. Ptolemy says the Agraei were a people of N. Arabia.

NAPH'ISI (1 Esd. v. 31). NEPHUSIM.

NAPH'TALI (NIPHTALI, *wrestled*). 5th son of Jacob, 2d-born of Bilhah (Gen. xxx. 8). He had 4 sons when Jacob went into Egypt (xlvi. 24). There is not a word said about him personally in the Scriptures. See EXODUS, TWELVE TRIBES.

NAPHTALI, MOUNT. The high land of the district occupied by the tribe (Josh. xx. 7).

NAPH'THAR (*a cleansing*). The name given to the substance said to have been found in the pit in which the sacred fire of the altar had been concealed at the destruction of the temple. This fable is related in 2 Macc. i. 19-36.

NAPH'TUHIM. Called on the Egyptian monuments Na-Petu, the people of (*Nine*) *bows*. The chief city of this nation (Naputa) is now in ruins, on the island of Meroë, on the Upper Nile, where there are found pyramids, temples (one of Osiris and Ammon), sphinxes, and many beautiful sculptures. In the British Museum are two lions, sculptured in red granite, fine works of art, brought from this ruined city.

NAPKIN. (See HANDKERCHIEF). As a wrapper to fold up money (Luke xix. 20). As a cloth bound round the head of a corpse (John xi. 44, xx. 7). As an article of dress; probably as a turban, or as the Bedawin *keffieh* (Acts xix. 12). Possibly the napkin was a cloth adapted to a variety of uses, such as described; also for a girdle; worn over the face, etc.

NARCIS'SUS (*the Narcissus plant*). One of a

NATHAN'AEL (*given of God*). Born at Cana of Galilee. One of the Twelve, under the name of Bartholomew (son of Talmai). (See BARTHOLOMEW). He was one of the seven Apostles to whom Jesus appeared after the resurrection at the Sea of Tiberias. When introduced to Jesus by Philip, Jesus said, "Behold an Israelite indeed, in whom there is no deceit," thus making his name almost a synonym for sincerity. Tradition says he preached in Arabia Felix, having Matthew's gospel, and was crucified in Armenia or Cilicia.

NATHANI'AS. Nathan, of the sons of Bani (1 Esd. ix. 34; Ezr. x. 39).

NA'THAN-ME'LECH (*placed by the king*). Steward in the court of Josiah (2 K. xxiii. 11).

NATION. Genesis x. gives the descendants of Noah. A record of primitive geography and ethnology of the utmost importance. By this record the geographical distribution of Noah's descendants can be ascertained, as also the origin of the earliest nations. The dispersion of these nations and the circumstances related to that important event, are recorded in Gen. xi. The date of this event of the dispersion can be fixed from the genealogy of Shem, here recorded. (See BABEL.)

Many nations and countries have been named after Shem, whose descendants wandered and divided into distinct tribes. This tendency is still a characteristic of the Arabs. See HAM. JAPHETH.

NA'UM. Son of Esli (Luke iii. 25).

NAVE (Heb. oav). The central part of a wheel.

NA'VE (Gr. Naué). Joshua's father NUN (Eccl. xlvi. 1)· so called in the Septuagint.

NAZARENE. An inhabitant of NAZARETH. Especially associated with the name of Christ and his followers, who were called Nazarenes (Acts xxiv. 5). It was used as a name of contempt to Christ's followers. In Christ's family making their home in Nazareth, the prophesy of Isaiah was fulfilled (Is. xi. 1; Jer. xxiii. 5), Christ being the young branch from the royal family of David.

NAZ'ARETH (*the branch*). First mentioned in Matt. ii. 23, or rather, in the order of time, in Luke i. 26, as the scene of the Annunciation to Mary of the birth and character of Jesus (v. 31–33). Before this event the place was unknown to history, but since then its name has become a household word through all the Christian world, equally reverenced with Bethlehem and Jerusalem.

A low, undulating ridge of hills encloses the green plain that lies like a lake, with Nazareth built on one of its shores. The valley runs nearly east and west, is about a mile long, and a quarter of a mile wide; the hills vary in height from 100 to 500 ft. above its level; the highest, Neby Ismail, being 1600 feet above the ocean. The soil is rich, and well cultivated, producing a great variety of fruit, grain, vegetables, and flowers, which ripen early and in rare perfection. Population about 4,000, nearly all Christians (Latin and Greeks), except a few Arabs, and not one Jew.

The parents of Jesus came here soon after their return from Egypt (Luke ii. 39); and after the visit to the Temple, when he was twelve years old, Jesus returned here with them (ii. 51); he grew up here to manhood (iv. 16); from here he went down to Jordan to be baptized by John (Mark i. 9; Matt. iii. 13); his first teaching in public was in its synagogue (xiii. 54); here he was first rejected (Luke iv. 29); and Jesus of Nazareth was a part of the inscription on the cross (John xix. 19).

The view from the top of Neby Ismail is very extensive, and includes many interesting Scripture localities, being one of the most noted in Palestine, combining the elements of the beautiful and the sublime. In the north are the white peaks of Lebanon, and Hermon towering high above them, because nearer. Eastward, the Hauran, Gilead, Tabor, Little Hermon, and Gilboa. South, the Plain of Esdraelon, the hills of Samaria; and west, Carmel and the Mediterranean. The villages in the view are Cana, Nain, Endor, Jezreel, Taanach, and many ruins not yet identified.

The rock of this whole region is a soft, white marl, easily crumbled; and there is probably not a house, or structure of any kind, nor even a loose stone, remaining of the time of Christ's residence there. Since the general features of hill and valley, fountains and water-courses, could not have greatly changed, we may accept the location of the "steep place," near the Maronite Church, and the Fountain of the Virgin, as historical. A great many other localities are pointed out by the residents as traditional sites of every event mentioned in the Gospels as having occurred there, but they

MAP OF NAZARETH.

have no other interest than in so far as they recall the gospel narrative.

NAZ'ARITE (Heb. NAZIR). Either a man or woman who, under ancient Hebrew law, bound himself or herself to abstain from wine and all products of the grape; to wear the hair long and uncut, and to observe purification in abstaining from contact with the dead. If they witnessed death or otherwise approached death, their consecration had to be entirely recommenced. The period of observance of this vow varied from eight days to a month, or even a life time. When this period had concluded, offerings were made, the hair was cut off and burnt, and the Nazarite was discharged from his vow (Num vi.; Amos ii. 11, 12). Paul assisted four Christian Jews in this ceremony (Acts xxi. 20–26).

NEAH (*the shaking*). Landmark on Zebulon's west border (Josh. xix. 13). *El Ain*, 3 miles N. W. of Nazareth.

NEAP'OLIS (*new city*). The first place visited by Paul in Macedonia (Acts xvi. 11). On a rocky

promontory, in a wide and beautiful bay, stands the Turkish village Kavala (5,000 inhab.), in the midst of the ruins of the ancient city. There was an aqueduct for bringing water from a distance of 12 miles; near the city, it passed a ravine over a double tier of arches, 80 feet above the brook below, in Roman style, hewn and cemented; fine sarcophagi, with inscriptions, of the age of Claudius, Ionic columns, and sculptured figures, besides foundations of ancient houses, etc., are witnesses of its ancient importance.

2. Shechem was also called Neapolis in Vespasian's time.

3. The bishops of Neapolis in Arabia were present at the councils of Chalcedon and Constantinople; a place now called Suleim, on Jebel Hauran (*Porter, Damascus*, ii. 85).

NEARI'AH (*servant of Jah*). 1. Son of Shemaiah (1 Chr. iii. 22, 23).—2. Son of Ishi, captain of 500 Simeonites (iv. 42).

NE'BAI (*fruit-bearer*). One who sealed the covenant (Neh. x. 19).

NEBAI'OTH. NEBA'JOTH. Ishmael's first-born (Gen. xxv. 13). Esau married Mahalath, the sister of Nebajoth (xxviii. 9). The country from the Euphrates to the Red Sea was called in Josephus' time Nabatene (Ant. i. 13, 4; Gen. xxv. 18). They were called by the Arabs *Nabat* (or *Nabet*), and were celebrated for their agriculture, astronomy, magic and medicine, accounts of which have been recently discovered in some ancient books of theirs, written from 2500 to 600 B. C., consisting of a book of agriculture, one of poisons, the works of Tenkeloosha, the Babylonian, and the Book of the Secrets of the Sun and Moon; all of which were translated in A. D. 904 by Ibn Washiyeh (*Kayse*). The rock-temples of Petra, in Edom, were the works of this people, who are thus proved to have been a highly cultivated race many ages before the Greeks.

NEBAL'LAT (*secret folly*). Benjamite town, after the Captivity (Neh. xi. 34). *Beit Nebala*, 4 miles N. E. of Lydda (*Rob.*).

NE'BAT (*look*). Father of JEROBOAM (1 K. xi. 26).

NE'BO, MOUNT. From which Moses took his first and last view of the Promised Land (Deut. xxxii. 49), and where he died and was buried in one of its ravines (xxxiv. 6). Located by Tristram (*Land of Israel*, 535) 3 miles S. W. of Heshbon; overlooking the mouth of the Jordan, over against Jericho, meeting every condition of the text.

NE'BO (*project*). Town east of Jordan, on the Mishor, in Gad (Num. xxxii. 3, 38); a ruin, 3 miles west of Heshbon, on the side of *Wady Heshban*.—2. In Benjamin, now called *Beit Nubah*, 12 miles N. W. of Jerusalem, in *Wady Mansur*. The Crusaders built the *Castle of Arnaldi* here (*William of Tyre*, xiv. 3).

NE'BO (*interpreter of the gods*). A Babylonish god. Nebo was the god of learning and letters among the Chaldæans, Babylonians and Assyrians (Is. xlvi. 1; Jer. xlviii. 1). Nebo was the Babylonian name of the planet Mercury. This word is in the formation of several names, such as Nebuchadnezzar, Nebuzaradan, Nebushasban, etc. The cut represents the statue of the god set up by Pul, king of Assyria, in the British Museum, London.

NEBUCHADNEZ'ZAR, or **NEBUCHADREZ'ZAR** (NEBO THE MIGHTY). The son of Nabopolassar, king of Chaldæa and founder of the Babylonian Empire. Nebuchadnez'zar, after having succeeded in recovering Carchemish, by defeating Necho, king of Egypt (Jer. xlvi. 2-12), and conquering Phœnicia, Palestine and Jerusalem, marched into Egypt, when he was informed of the death of his father. He hurried back, accompanied by his light troops, to secure his succession to the throne, which he ascended B. C. 604; the main army and captives (amongst whom were Daniel, Hananiah, Mishael and Azariah) following him by a longer route. These captives were of royal lineage, and the king had them educated in the language and learning of the Chaldæans, with a view to their employment in court (2 K. xxiv. 1; 2 Chr. xxxvi. 6; Dan. i. 1). Nebuchadnez'zar had left the conquered Jehoiakim, king of Judah, upon the throne as a tributary prince, but he soon after rebelled, probably anticipating support from Egypt (2 K. xxiv. 1). Phœnicia followed in the rebellion, and Nebuchadnez'zar, after having invested Tyre, advanced upon Jerusalem, which immediately submitted. He punished Jehoiakim with death, placing that king's son, Jehoiachin, upon the throne of Judah. This king soon after revolting, caused Nebuchadnez'zar for a third time to march to Jerusalem; he took Jehoiachin captive, together with ten thousand, amongst whom were Ezekiel the prophet, and Mordecai, the uncle of Esther (Esth. ii. 6). He also stripped the Temple and the treasury of riches, and placed the king's uncle, Zedekiah, upon the throne. After nine years, Zedekiah rebelled, the neighboring princes assisting him. The king of Babylon again marched to Judah, and after an obstinate siege of nearly a year, during which time he repelled an incursion of the Egyptians, he entered Jerusalem, seized Zedekiah, whose children he put to death before his eyes, and sent him, fettered, to Babylon, after having put out his eyes (2 K. xxiv. 25; 2 Chr. xxxvi.). Nebuchadnezzar raised his kingdom and city to the greatest splendor; the marvellous hanging gardens are ascribed to him, erected to please Amytis, his queen, by imitating the groves of her native country, Media. The ruins of Birs Nimroud attest the magnificence of his works; these are situated a few miles from the site of the city of Babylon. He died about B. C. 562, after reigning forty years.

NEBUSHAS'BAN (*adherent of Nebo*); an officer at the capture of Jerusalem. He was chief of the eunuchs (Jer. xxxix. 13).

NEBUZAR'ADAN (*favors*). Captain of the GUARD, an officer of high rank in the court of Nebuchadnezzar, especially engaged in the sieges of Jerusalem (1 K. xxv. 8-20; Jer. xxxix. 9, xl. 1, lii. 12, 30).

NECHO. PHARAOH 9 (2 Chr. xxxv. 20, 22).

NECH'OSHETH. Sometimes translated *brass*, but properly means *copper*—sometimes bronze. See METALS, p. 201. (Job xxviii. 2).

NECK. Used both literally (Gen. xxvii. 16) and figuratively (Luke xiv. 20). Burdens were borne on the neck (Gen. xxvii. 40). The neck was used figuratively for several ideas: To denote subjection, by placing the foot on it (Josh. x. 24); seizing a person by the neck securely (Job xvi. 12). To be stiff-necked was to be stubborn, rebellious.

NECO'DAN (1 Esd. v. 37).

NAZARETH.

NEC'ROMANCER (Deut. xviii. 11). DIVINATION.

NEDABI'AH (*whom Jah impels*). A son of Jeconiah (1 Chr. iii. 18).

NEEANI'AS. Son of Hachaliah (Ecclus. xlix. 13).

NEEDLE'S EYE. Supposed to mean a narrow door, or gateway, too low for a camel to pass through, standing. They are unloaded, and forced to creep through on their knees.

NE'GEB (*south*). The country S. of Beersheba. Its character is that of wide-rolling downs, green in winter, but bare in summer, affording pasturage, but not grain-crops.

NEG'INAH. (Heb.) A term by which all stringed-instruments are described (Ps. lxi.; Job xxx. 9) is the singular form of the next word.

NEG'INOTH. A general term for stringed-instruments: Ps. iv., vi., xlv., liv., lv. lxxvi., are addressed to leaders of stringed-instruments. See MUSIC, and MUSICAL INSTRUMENTS.

NEHEL'AMITE (*strong one*) **THE.** A false prophet (Jer. xxix. 24, 31, 32).

NEHEMIAH (*comforter of Jah*). His genealogy is not known, although he was perhaps of the tribe of Judah. He was the son of Hachaliah (Neh. i. 1). His brother was Hanani (Neh. vii. 2); most probably of royal descent and not of the priesthood as supposed from Neh. x. 1–8, but as a prince in Neh. ix. 38. His office was that of cup-bearer to King Artaxerxes Longimanus. At his own request he was appointed governor of Jerusalem about B. C. 444, when he relieved the people from the oppression of the Samaritans. In this good work he was assisted by Ezra (Neh. viii. 1, 9, 13, xii. 36). See HISTORY OF THE BOOKS.

NE'HILOTH (Heb. CHALAL). A term for perforated wind instruments of all kinds (1 Sam. x. 5).

NE'HUM (*comfort*). One who returned from captivity (Neh. vii. 7).

NEHUSH'TA (*brass*). Daughter of Elnathan (2 K. xxiv. 8).

NEHUSH'TAN (*brazen*), (Num. xxi. 8). The brazen serpent which Moses set up in the wilderness. It was destroyed by Hezekiah as it had become debased to the service of idolatry in the reign of Ahaz his father. Hezekiah gave the name Nehushtan to it as a term of derision, implying it to be mere brass (2 K. xviii. 4).

NE'IEL (*treasure of God*). Landmark of Asher, now *Mear*, on a lofty hight 10 ms. N. W. of Nazareth (Josh. xix. 27).

NE'KEB (*cavern*). On the N. border of Naphtali (Judg. iv. 11). Lost.

NE'KODA (*distinguished*). 1. The children of Nekoda who returned from captivity (Ezr. ii. 48). —2. The same who were unable to prove their descent from Israel (Ezr. ii. 60).

NEM'UEL (Heb. JEMUEL). 1. Son of Eliab (Num. xxvi. 9).—2. Son of Simeon (xxvi. 12).

NEM'UELITES, THE. Descendants of NEMUEL (Num. xxvi. 12).

NE'PHEG (*sprout*). 1. Son of Izhar (Ex. vi. 21).—2. Son of David (2 Sam. vi. 15).

NEPH'EW (Heb. NECHED), (*progeny*). Has various meanings, as in Judg. xii. 14, Job xviii. 19. In Gen. xxi. 23, son's son.

NE'PHI (NAPHTHAR), (2 Macc. i. 36).

NE'PHIS. Children of Nebo (Ezr. ii. 29).

CAMEL AND NEEDLE'S EYE.

NE'PHISH (NAPHISH), (1 Chr. v. 19).

NEPHISH'ESIM. Those who returned from captivity (Neh. vii. 52).

NEPH'THALI (Tob. i. 1, 2, 4, 5).

NEPH'THALIM (Tob. vii. 3).

NEPHTO'AH, THE WATER OF. Landmark between Judah and Benjamin (Josh. xv. 9). *Ain Lifta*, 2¾ miles N. W. of Jerusalem. Another fountain, *Ain Yalo*, in *Wady el Werd* (*roses*), is urged as the site by some, on account of the text in 1 Sam. x. 2.

NEPHU'SIM (*expansions*), (Ezr. ii. 50).

NER (*light*). Son of Jehiel (1 Chr. ix. 36).

NERD or **NARD.** See SPIKENARD.

NE'REUS. Name of an ancient sea-god. A Christian at Rome (Rom. xvi. 15).

NER'GAL (Heb.). An Assyrian deity (2 K. xvii. 30) represented in the Hellenic mythology by Mars. He presided over wars. In the monuments he is entitled "the storm ruler," "the king of battle," "the champion of the gods," "the god of the chase," etc. The allusion to Nergal in the Scriptures is in 2 K. xvii. 30, equivalent to the man-lion of Nineveh.

NER'GAL SHARE'ZER. 1. One of Nebuchadnezzar's military chiefs (Jer. xxix. 3).—2. The chief magi under the same king (Jer. xxxix. 3, 13) with the title Rab-Mag. Babylonian inscriptions suggest the identification of 2 with Neriglissar, who murdered Evil Merodach and became king of Babylon.

NE'RI. Son of Melchi (Luke iii. 27).

NERI'AH (*lamp of Jah*). Son of Maaseiah (Jer. xxxii. 12).

NERI'AS. NERIAH (Bar. i. 1).

NE'RO (*brave*). The Roman emperor (Lucius Domitius Ahenobardus) born A. D. 37. He was named Nero Claudius, etc., by his grand uncle Claudius, who had adopted him. Made emperor, A. D. 54. Accused of having burnt Rome, but Nero tortured and burnt Christians charging them

with the crime. Both Paul and Peter suffered martyrdom during his reign. He committed suicide A. D. 68, to avoid retribution. The Cæsar mentioned in Acts xxv. 8, xxvi. 32, xxviii. 19; Phil. iv. 22, is Nero; also Augustus in Acts xxv. 21, 25.

NEST (KEN). As in Job xxxix. 27; Matt. viii. 20: also as a dwelling as in Num. xxiv. 21. In Gen. vi. 14, *rooms* mean *nests* or *cribs*.

NET. The terms for net in the Bible are numerous, and refer to its application or construction. In the N. T. there appears *sagēnē*, denoting a large, hauling-net (Matt. xiii. 47); *amphiblestron*, a casting-net (Matt. iv. 20; Mark i. 16); and *diktuon*, a similar kind of net (Matt. iv. 20; Mark i. 18; Luke v. 2). Nets were used for hunting, as well as fishing. The Egyptians made their nets of flax, with wooden needles. In Egypt bird and animal nets were used, which last also appear on the Nineveh marbles. These nets were so constructed that the sides closed in upon the prey, or with movable frames. Net has frequently a figurative use, as in Ps. ix. 15, xxv. 15, xxxi. 4, as expressing God's vengeance, as in Ez. xii. 13; Hos. vii. 12.

NETHAN'EEL (*given of God*). 1. Son of Zuar (Num. i. 8).—2. Son of Jesse (1 Chr. ii. 14).—3. A priest in David's reign (xv. 24).—4. Father of Shemaiah (xxiv. 6).—5. Son of Obed-edom (xxvi. 4).—6. A prince of Judah (2 Chr. xvii. 7).—7. A chief Levite (xxxv. 9).—8. A priest of Pashur (Ezr. x. 22).—9. Another priest (Neh. xii. 21).—10. A Levite (ver. 36).

NETHANI'AH (*given of Jah*). 1. Son of Elishama (2 K. xxv. 23), of the royal family of Judah.—2. Son of Asaph, a chief in the course of the Temple-choir (1 Chr. xxv. 2, 12).—3. One of the Levites who taught the law in Judah (2 Chr. xvii. 8).—4. Father of Jehudi (Jer. xxxvi. 14).

NETH'INIM (*dedicated*). A body of men *given* to assist the Levites in the performance of the rites of the Temple (Ezr. vii. 24) as the Levites were given to Aaron (Num. ii. 9, viii. 19). The Nethinim performed the menial offices of the Temple, living near it. They assisted in rebuilding the Temple walls, etc., after the return from captivity.

NET'OPHAH (*a dropping*). Peopled after the return from captivity (Ezr. ii. 22). Two of David's captains were natives of this place (2 Sam. xxiii. 28). At the dedication of the wall built by Nehemiah, the singers were found residing in the *villages* of this people; so there were more than one town, perhaps a district, near Bethlehem. Seraiah (*warrior of Jehovah*), a native of this place, was an accomplice of Ishmael in the murder of Gedaliah (2 K. xxv. 23). Um Tuba, 2 ms. N. E. of Bethlehem. Beit Nettif, in the Wady Sumt, is mentioned in the Jewish traditions as famous for "oil of Netopha" (Rob. ii. 17).

NETOPH'ATHI (Neh. xii. 28).

NETO'PHATHITE (Heb. NETOPHATHI) THE. One from NETOPHAH (2 Sam. xxiii. 28, 29).

CHERUB.

NETTLE (Heb. CHARUL), (Job xxx. 7). A plant of rapid growth, and well known for its power of stinging. They have minute tubular hairs, which emit a poisonous fluid when pressed.

NEW MOON. Marked the commencement of each month (see MONTH), and was celebrated as a holyday. Offerings were made as ordained (Num. xxviii. 11, 15). All business was suspended (Amos viii. 5). The Day of the N. M. was recognized as a family festival with religious observances, although not especially ordained. It was proclaimed by the trumpet-sound (Ps. lxxxi. 3). After the establishment of Christianity the observance was discontinued.

NEW TESTAMENT. See HISTORY OF THE BOOKS.

NE'ZIAH (*illustrious*). Ancestor of Nethinim (Ezr. ii. 54).

NE'ZIB (Josh. xx. 43). Beit Nusib, in the low, hilly district between Beit Jibrin and Hebron. There are ruins of a building, 120×30 ft., and a tower 60 ft. sq., of ancient, massive masonry, besides broken columns.

NIB'HAZ (Heb. NABACH), (*to bark*). A deity of the Avites; the figure of a dog, or dog-headed man (2 K. xvii. 31). The Syrians worshiped the dog, and there was a colossal figure of one between Beirut and Tripolis, which has been lately destroyed.

NIB'SHAN (*light-soil*). A city on the W. shore of the Dead Sea (Josh. xv. 62). DESERT. 2. EN-GEDI.

NICA'NOR. 1. Son of Patroclus (2 Macc. viii. 9). A general under Antiochus Epiphanes and Demetrius I. He assisted in the first expedition of Lycias, B. C. 166 (1 Macc. iii. 38). He was defeated, but, after the death of Antiochus, Demetrius made him governor of Judæa (2 Macc. xiv. 12).

NICODE'MUS (NAKDIMON, *innocent of blood*). A Pharisee, ruler of the Jews, teacher of the law (John ii. 23, iii. 1, 10), a member of the Sanhedrin. He was probably wealthy, as his valuable tribute to the tomb of the Lord indicates. His timidity was shown in his night visit to the Great Teacher, where he received divine instruction, and a prediction of the crucifixion. When that prediction had been fulfilled and Joseph of Arimathea had begged for and was permitted by Pilate to take the body from the cross, Nicodemus assisted. Tradition says that he lived in intimacy with Gamaliel, and was buried near the grave of Stephen.

NICOLAI'TANS. A sect of heretics of the Apostolic period. They held it lawful to eat food sacrificed to idols; to join in idolatrous worship; and that God did not create the universe. They held their women in common. John's Gospel and also his Apocalypse opposes their teaching. (See HISTORY OF THE BOOKS). These doctrines have been supposed to have originated with the prophet Balaam. They are sometimes called Shualbites, from the Midianite Shualb, which is Balaam.

NIC'OLAS, NICH'OLAS, NICO'LAUS. One of the first seven deacons of the Church of Jerusalem (Acts vi. 5). He was a native of Antioch.

NICOP'OLIS (*city of victory*). Built by Augustus, in Epirus, on the site where his army encamped the night before the battle of Actium. The Temple of Neptune was placed on the spot occupied by his own tent. Paul requested Titus (iii. 12) to come to him from Crete, or from Dalmatia (2 Tim. iv. 10), to Nicopolis. He also urged Timothy in the same manner (v. 21). There are on the peninsula, N. W. of the Bay of Actium (*Gulf of Arta*), ruins of a temple, a theatre, walls, and other structures, on the hill and the low marshy plain; now deserted. It is possible that Paul was arrested here, and taken to Rome for his final trial (*Conybeare* and *Howson*).

NI'GER (*black*). A name given to SIMEON 6 (Acts xiii. 1).

NIGHT ((Heb. TO SINK; THE SINKING OF THE DAY). See CHRONOLOGY, p. 56.

NIGHT-HAWK (Heb. TACHMAS). In the enumeration of unclean animals in Lev. xi. 16, and in Deut. xiv. 15, this word appears. There is much controversy as to its meaning, whether the *nighthawk* or the *white owl*.

NILE. The Hebrew names of the river were SHICHOR (*black*); YEOR (*the river*); Sihor, in Jer. ii. 18. The Sanscrit *Nilah* means *dark blue*; and one of the upper branches of the river is now called the Blue Nile. The name Yeor is Egyptian, and is written AUR on the monuments. It is also called HAPEE MU (*the abyss*). Dr. Livingstone's late accounts show this to be the longest river in the world; rising in or beyond the lake Victoria Nyanza, south of the equator, and emptying into the Mediterranean at N. lat. 31°; its course running through 36 degrees, having been traced more than 2700 ms., while it is quite certain that it will be found to be 1000 ms. longer. (The Amazon extends through 30 degrees, and the Missouri and Mississippi together about 35 degrees). There are three chief branches: 1. The Blue (*Bahr el Azrak*) drains Abyssinia, and brings down the alluvial soil which fertilizes Egypt. 2. The White (*Bahr el Abyad*), joins the Blue at Khartoom, the capital of Soodan. 3. The Atbara (*black river*), rises also in Abyssinia, and joins the Nile at the north point of the Island of Meroë. There are no tributaries below the Atbara. The stream is interrupted by several cataracts formed by granite projected up through the sandstone of its bed. The first cataract is at the south boundary of Egypt (lat. 24°), the ancient Syene, now *Assouan*; the second, or Great Cataract, is in lat. 22°; the third in lat. 19° 45'; the fourth in lat. 18° 45'; and the fifth in 18° 20', 100 miles above the fourth. The river parts into several branches below the pyramids of Memphis and Cairo, and encloses the Delta. The ancients mention seven branches: 1. Pelusiac; 2. Tanitic; 3. Mendesian; Bucolic (Damietta); 5. Sebennytic; 6. Bolbytene (Rosetta); 7. Canopic (Is. xi. 15). The width, in its lower course, is from half a mile to a mile wide, where there are islands. The water is sweet, especially during the inundation, and quickly becomes clear by settling its sediment. As Egypt has no rain (Zech. xiv. 17–19), the river supplies water to the soil by its overflow. The annual rise is noticed at Khartoom in April, but is not visible in Lower Egypt before June, and continues until September. The prophet Amos refers to the inundation as a symbol of great power and utter desolation (viii. 8, ix. 5). Job was acquainted with the Nile floods, for the word that he uses in ch. xxviii., ver. 10, for *rivers*, is the plural of the name of the Nile, in the original. Jeremiah also uses it as a figure when speaking of Pharaoh Necho's army (xlvi.). Its waters abound in fish of many kinds (Num. xi. 5); but crocodiles (described minutely by Job (xli.), and mentioned by Ezekiel (xxix. 3), are becoming very scarce, and are only found in Upper Egypt. The monuments and the ancient writers give accounts of the banks of the Nile as being bordered with flags, reeds, and flowers, especially the lotus, and full of wild-fowls. Now the banks are nearly bare, as prophesied by Isaiah (xix. 6, 7). The papyrus, which was used for making paper, and for boats (which were remarkable for their swiftness—Is. xviii. 2), has entirely disappeared, except in the marshes of the Delta. Ezekiel compares Pharaoh to a crocodile (great dragon) in the Nile, fearing no one (xxix. 1–5; whale, in xxxii. 2). Moses was exposed on its waters in a boat of papyrus (bulrushes, Ex. ii.

NILE EMBLEM.

3). It is said traditionally that Jesus lived on its banks, near Heliopolis; and its name is associated with many other Bible characters, such as Absalom, Jacob, Joseph, Solomon (whose wife was a daughter of Pharaoh), besides the captive king of Judah, pictured on the walls of the temple at Karnac. See MEMPHIS.

NIM'RAH (*pure water*). In the "land of Jazer," afterward called Beth Nimrah (Num. xxxii. 3, 36); in the tribe of Gad. The name Nimrin (*panthers*) is found in several localities east of Jordan(*Port. r*). Two miles east of the Jordan, on the road from Jericho to Es Salt, are ruins near copious fountains (Is. xv. 6; Jer. xlviii. 34). Eusebius says it was a village north of Zoar. If our location of Nimrah is correct, Zoar must have been north of the Dead Sea.

NIM'ROD (*the extremely impious rebel*). Son of Cush (Gen. x. 8, 9). He established an empire in Shinar (Babylonia), the chief cities of which were Babel, Erech, Accad, and Calneh; and extended it northward over Assyria, including the cities Nineveh, Rehoboth, Calah, and Resen. There is no authentic account of his life. The tales of Ctesias, and others, except that in the Bible, are guesses or inventions; and of the great cities which he built very little has been known until within the last twenty-five years, when Layard exhumed the palaces, sculptures and inscriptions of *Nimroud*. See NINEVEH.

NIM'SHI (*drawn out*). Grandfather of Jehu, generally called the SON of Nimshi (1 K. xix. 16).

NIN'EVEH (*Nin-navah=Nin-town*). The ancient capital of Assyria. First mentioned in Gen. x. 11). The country was also called the land of Nimrod by Micah (v. 6). Balaam prophesied the captivity of Israel by Assyria (Num. xxiv. 22), and Asaph sings of their alliance with Moab (Ps. lxxxiii. 8). Jonah was sent to the city about 800 B. C., and Nahum devotes the whole of his book to "the burden of Nineveh," about 725 B. C. Isaiah says that Sennacherib resided in the city; and it was probably the scene of his death (Is. xxxvii. 37), while worshiping in the temple of Nisroch, his god. The last notice of it is by Zephaniah, B. C. 630 (ii. 13). Assyria is alluded to as having been destroyed, according to prophesy by Ezekiel (xxxi.), and Jeremiah omits it from his catalogue of all nations (xxv.). The city is not mentioned in the inscriptions of the Persian dynasty. Herodotus passed very near, if not over, the site of the city, about 200 years after its destruction, but does not mention it, except as having once been there. Xenophon, with his 10,000 Greeks, encamped near the site (B. C. 401), but does not mention its name (*Anab.* iii. 4, 7), although he describes the mounds as they appear now. Alexander marched over the very place, and won a great victory at Arbela, in sight of it, but his historians make no note of it. The Emperor Claudius planted a colony there, and restored the name Nineve. Tacitus calls it Ninos, when taken by Meherdates. On the coins of Trajan it is Ninus, and on those of Maximinus it is Niniva; Claudeopolis being added on both coins. Many relics of the Romans have been found; vases, sculptures, figures in bronze and marble, terra-cottas, and coins. The site was again deserted when Heraclius gained a victory over the Persians, A. D. 627.

The Arabs named their fort, on the east bank of the Tigris, *Ninawi* (A. D. 637). The accounts of its immense extent are various, and not very reliable. Diodorus Siculus says the dimensions were (according as we estimate his figures, from 32 to 60, or even) 74 miles in circuit. The walls were 100 feet high, and wide enough for three chariots to drive abreast; flanked by 1500 towers, each 200 feet high (accounts which have not yet been verified). Layard says: "If we take the four great mounds of Nimrud, Koyunjik, Khorsabad, and

Karamles, as the corners of a square, it will be found to agree pretty accurately with the 60 miles of Herodotus, which make the three days' journey of Jonah." Within this space there are many mounds, and remains of pottery, bricks, etc.

The name of Nineveh is found on the Egyptian monuments of the date of Thothmes III, about 1400 B. C.

The first notice in modern times of the ruins were by Mr. Rich, in 1820, who brought to London a few bricks, with inscriptions, some cylinders, gems, and other remains. Layard next visited them, in 1840; but Botta, a French consul at Mosul, found the first Assyrian monument, which was of value as a confirmation of Scripture. It was soon followed by a great variety of works of art, in 1844, at Khorsabad, the results of which exposition are in the Assyrian room at the Louvre, Paris. The great work of disentombing the remains of ancient Nineveh was performed by Layard, from 1845 to 1850.

BLACK OBELISK OF NIMROUD.

The accounts of Layard's discoveries are published in minute detail, filling volumes, and will repay the time spent in reading them; for, besides giving undoubted and truthful glimpses of antiquity, in almost every phase of society, they are as startling and exciting as the wildest romance, both in text and illustration. But far beyond these in value to us are their uses in confirmation of the Scriptures.

Place and Fresnel discovered, at Khorsabad, colossal, human-headed, winged bulls, which were in groups on each side of great doorways; besides other mythic figures. The most important inscription that has been brought to light, is that on two of the human-headed bulls from Koyunjik (now in the British Museum), giving an account of Sennacherib; his wars with Hezekiah, and the capture of Lachish, with pictures illustrating it (See LACHISH). Nearly equal in value is the Black Obelisk of Nimroud; a piece of black marble, 6 ft. 6 in. high, 1 ft. 6½ in. sq. at the top, and 2 ft. sq. at the bottom, the upper half covered with 5 panels of figures, with inscriptions between each panel, and also many lines below the lower one: altogether 210 lines. One side, only, is engraved here; the four may be seen in the work on "Nineveh and its Palaces," by Bonomi. The story may be inferred from the text in 2 K. xvii., xviii. The first panel, at the top, exhibits the king, attended by his eunuch, and a bearded officer (perhaps the returned conqueror); a captive kisses his foot, and two officers wait the king's orders. The image of Baal, and a circle enclosing a star (the sun?) are similar to those on the rocks at Nahr el Kelb. The same images, reversed in position, are in the second panel. One may mean Morning, and the other Evening; and both, with the figures in the other panels bringing and presenting tribute, indicate that the captives were so many, and the tribute so vast, that they consumed the whole day in their presentation. Some of the figures on the obelisk resemble those on the wall of the small temple of Kalabshe, who are enemies of Raamses II, and are understood to represent Jews in both cases. The inscription, as interpreted by Rawlinson, mentions the receiving by the king of tribute from the cities of Tyre, Sidon, and Gebal, in his 21st year; defeating the king of Hamath, and 12 other kings of the upper and lower country (Canaan, lower). Dr. Hincks reads the names of Jehu, king of Israel, and dates the obelisk 875 B. C. Dr. Grotefend reads the names of Tiglath Pileser, Pul, and Shalmanassar, and refers to the accounts in Isaiah (xx.), and Nahum (iii.).

Sargon's name was found in another inscription, with his title, Shalmaneser, and the account of the capture of Samaria (which in Assyrian is SAMARINA). He carried off 27,280 families, and placed colonies, in their stead, of people from Assyria (2 K. xviii.). The king of Egypt is called PIRHU (Pharaoh), and Heliopolis is RABEK (Ra—sun, bek—city). Ashdod, Jamnia, Hamath, Berœa, Damascus, Bambyce, and Charchemish, are mentioned among his captures. He is also styled the conqueror of remote Judæa. He had a statue and inscription in his honor on the island of Cyprus. The son of this king was Sennacherib, who built Koyunjik; and in the great palace there were found inscriptions in honor of his capture of Babylon from Merodach-Baladan (2 K. xx. 12; Is. xxxix. 1); and of Sidon, under King Luliya; and of his expedition into Judæa, in which occur the names KHAZAKIYAHU (Hezekiah), URSALIMA (Jerusalem), and YAHUDA (Jews). The king of Pelusium is mentioned. The tribute of Hezekiah, as recorded, consisted of 30 talents of gold, 300 talents of silver, the vessels and ornaments of the Temple, slaves, both boys and girls, maid-servants and men-servants—confirming the Scripture account (2 K. xviii. 13–16).

The tells or mounds (see Ezr. ii. 59; Ez. iii. 15; 2 K. xix. 12) which are scattered all over the region watered by the Euphrates and Tigris and their confluents, contain the remains of Assyrian, Babylonian, and Persian occupation. They vary in size from 50 to 150 feet high, and also much more in length, being from a few rods to several miles in extent. Those forming what is now called Nineveh are Koyunjik, which is 3,900 feet long by 1500 wide and 96 high; Neby Yunus (traditional tomb of Jonah), about 40 acres in extent; K'horsabad, 6,000 feet square; Selamiah, 410 acres; Nimrud, 1,000 acres; and in this group of mounds (called Nimroud) there are indications of more than 100 towers, at regular intervals. On the S. W. of this group there is a mound 2,100 feet by 1,200, with a cone at one corner (N. W.) 140 feet high.

A treasure-house of records, such as is alluded

NIN'EVITES. Inhabitants of Nineveh (Luke xi. 30).

NI'SON (Esth. xi. 2).

NIS ROCH (Heb.). The name of an idol of Nineveh (2 K. xix. 37).

NI TRE (Heb. NETHER). Used as a wash (Jer. ii. 22). This substance is not the same as our nitrate of potassa. Natron was and is much used by the Egyptians for washing clothes, for yeast and for soap; also as a cure for toothache mixed with vinegar. It is found in the soda lakes of Egypt, 50 miles W. of Cairo. The Natron lakes of Egypt were early occupied by hermits, who built large and fort-like monasteries, where, for ages, the study of the Christian religion was pursued, and its practice kept up, with the severest ritualistic forms. Their libraries were found, after several centuries of neglect, to contain valuable copies of the Gospels, homilies, and books of church services.

NOADI'AH (*with whom Jah converses*). 1. Son of Binnui (Ezr. viii. 33).—2. Noadiah the prophetess (Neh. vi. 14).

NO'AH (NOACH, *to rest*, or *give comfort*.) The second head of the human race, as Adam was the first. From his birth to the age of 500 years there is a blank in his history. Society in his day had become sadly corrupted by the custom of intermarriage of different races, especially of two distinct religious communities, called "The sons of God" (Elohim) and "The Sons of the Man" (Ha-Adam). There were also Nephilim, men of violence, who turned peaceable society upside down. The "Sons of God" (BENE-ELOHIM) were the descendants of Seth, and worshipers of God; the "Sons of the Man" were descendants of Cain, and probably idolaters. The union of the two families or races produced a mixed condition of religion, which could not be pure.

Another interpreter understands Bene Elohim to have been a race distinct from Adam's, and dating long before his creation, and therefore an inferior race, idolatrous and wicked, and therefore the name means "worshipers of false gods," as the Israelites are called children of God the Father. The daughters of men would then be of Adam's race. This supposition is against the received text in the first three chapters of Genesis. Another theory was long popular in the Church: that the "Sons of God" were angels, an intermediate race of spirits who have the power of assuming the human form. But as we have no evidence of any such appearance in our day it is very difficult to have faith in the supposition. If we were to receive the Book of Enoch as inspired, which claims a date of 1000 years before the Flood, we should have the record of a belief in such occurrences in that age, and some excuse for such a belief in our day. But that book is rejected by all Christians, except the Abyssinians.

The offspring of this mixture of races were men noted for strength and courage, Nephilim (giants in the A. V.), violent men. If the Nephilim of Canaan were descendants of those mentioned in Genesis (vi. 4), the fact is a strong evidence against the universality of the Deluge. (See GIANTS, DELUGE, GENESIS). Noah's Ark, and the Deluge are described in other places. The first act of Noah, after the Deluge, and the escape from the Ark, was to build an altar, and offer sacrifice to God, of every clean beast, and every clean fowl. New blessings and new laws are given to man, especially concerning human life. Noah's last act was the cursing of Ham, and the blessing of his other sons. This is believed to have been the origin of the *color* of the Negro (sons of Ham), and of the idolatrous tendencies of the Canaanites. When the sons of Israel (Shem) took possession of the country of Canaan, then Canaan became a servant to Shem; he became the slave of Japhet when Tyre and Carthage were taken by the Greeks and Romans (Japhet). For

DETAILS AT NOBAH.

Japhet to dwell in the tents of Shem, was when Japhet received the knowledge of the true God from Shem, that is, by the Hebrew Scriptures. Noah lived 350 years after the Deluge, and must have witnessed the confusion of tongues, and the dispersion from Babel. It is supposed that he had no other children than those named. See GENESIS, in the HISTORY OF THE BOOKS, for a notice of several traditions of Noah, and the Flood, in various countries.

NO'AH (*motion*). Daughter of ZELOPHEHAD (Num. xxvi. 33).

NO-A'MON (*populous No*). (Nahum iii. 8; Ez. xxx. 14, 15). Identical with Thebes. Multitude of No (Jer. xlvi. 25). See Thebes.

NOB (*high*). David fled from Saul and came to Nob (1 Sam. xxi. 1), which was near Anathoth (Neh. xi. 32). There are on a conical hill, 2¾ miles N. of Jerusalem, traces of a small, but very ancient city—cisterns hewn in the rock, large hewn stones, and ruins of a small tower, besides other indications. From the summit, Zion is in plain view (Is. x. 32).

NO'BAH (*a barking*). (See KENATH). Most of the chief towns of the Hauran have traces of the architectural magnificence that Rome lavished on her colonies. The tanks, bridges, and many houses are solidly built, and even at this late day nearly as good as new.

NO'BAH. An Israelite warrior (Num. xxxii. 42).

NO'BLEMAN. A man of high rank (John iv. 46, 49).

NOD (*flight*).

NO'DAB (*nobility*). The name of an Arab tribe (1 Chr. v. 19).

NO'E. The patriarch NOAH (Job iv. 12).

NO'EBA. NEKODA 1 (1 Esd. v. 31).

NO'GAH (*bright*). Son of David (1 Chr. iii. 7).

NO'HAH (*rest*). Son of Benjamin (1 Chr. viii. 2).

NON. NUN. Father of Joshua (1 Chr. vii. 27).

NOPH. Moph, Memphis. (Is. xix. 13). See MEMPHIS.

NO'PHAH (*blast*). Only mentioned in the fragment of an ode, composed by the Amorites after their capture of Heshbon from the Moabites (Num. xxi. 30), and quoted by Moses. A city between Heshbon and Medeba. Lost.

NORTH (Heb. ZAPHON; Gr. *borrhos*). As denoting the northern quarter (Gen. xiii. 14; Ex. xxvi. 20, 35; Luke xiii. 29); "Land of the North" (Jer.

iii. 18). Also expressed, relatively, to the direction of the hand.

NOSE (Heb. AF, *the organ of smell*), (Prov. xxx. 33). Figuratively, as "anger" in Gen. xxvii. 45, or "wrath," (Gen. xxxix. 19) suggested by hard breathing. Heb. APPAYIM (*two breathing holes*), is translated "nostrils" in Gen. ii. 70.

NOSE-JEWEL (Heb. NEZEM). A ring of metal—gold or silver—passed through the right nostril, worn for ornament by women in the East (Gen. xxiv. 22). It is usually from 1 to 3½ ins. in diameter. Beads, corals, and jewels, are strung upon it. ORNAMENTS. (See Cut, p. 82.)

NOVICE (Gr. *neophutos*). A new convert (1 Tim. iii. 6).

NUMBER. Hebraic numerals were denoted by letters. At a later period this was the mode of notation, as seen in the Maccabean coins. Certain numbers were used as figurative representations, and not actual quantities, such as, 7, 10, 40, 100, which represent completeness. 7 is thus used as "seven-fold" in Gen. iv. 24; seven times (meaning completely) in Lev. xxv. 24, and Ps. xii. 6; as also the general use of the number 7. 10 was a number of especial selection. The number 12 was specially mystical, and is found in many instances; as 12 months, 12 tribes, 12 loaves of showbread, 12 disciples or apostles. 40 was also very mystical; as 40 days of Moses; 40 years in the wilderness; 40 days and nights of Elijah in the wilderness, and of Jesus on the mount; 40 years each the life of several kings and judges. Seventy-fold, as in Gen. iv. 24, Matt. xviii. 22, etc. The mystic number 666, in Rev. xiii. 18, still remains the subject of controversy. One theory suggests the numerals to mean Lx., in Gr. *lateinos* (Lat. *latinus*), *beast*, or *kingdom*.

NUMBERING. See POPULATION.

NUMBERS. See HISTORY OF THE BOOKS.

NUMENIUS (*new moon*). Son of Antiochus. He was sent on an embassy to Rome and Sparta to renew the friendly connections with the Jews, B. C. 144 (1 Macc. xii. 16, 17). He was again sent, B. C. 144 (xiv. 24).

GREEK MS. A. D. 1000.—St. John i. 1, 2.

NUN (*a fish*). 1. Father of JOSHUA (Ex. xxxiii. 11).—2. The fourteenth letter of the Hebrew alphabet (Ps. cxix). WRITING.

NURSE. The position of the nurse when one was wanted, was one of much honor and importance (Gen. xxiv. 59). CHILD.

NUTS (*Botnim and Egoz*). Spoken of as among the good things of the land to be taken by Jacob's sons to propitiate the governor of Egypt. This nut was most likely the Pistachio. BOTNIM (Pistachio Town), a town of Gad (Josh. xiii. 26), probably derives its name therefrom. The word FOOZ occurs in Cant. vi. 11, and probably means walnut. One Arabic term (derived from the Persian) for walnut is *jooz*; another is *chusf*, which means *tall tree*. Walnuts were anciently very plenty around the Sea of Galilee. They are still cultivated near Sidon as an article of commerce.

NYMPHAS (*bridegroom*). A rich and devoted Christian in Laodicea. His house was used as a chapel (Col. iv. 15). Some ancient manuscripts say Nymphas was a woman, a view which is adopted by the Greek Church.

O

OAK. There are several Hebrew words which are rendered oak in the A. V., as EL, to be strong (Gen. xiv. 6); ELAH, terebinth (Is. vi. 13); ELON, oak (Gen. xii. 6); ILAN, strong tree (Dan. iv. 8); ALLAM, *an oak* (Josh. xxiv. 26); ALLON, evergreen oak (Hos. iv. 13). The most noted trees were Abraham's oak at Mamre, the oak at Shechem, of Deborah, Rebekah's nurse, of the wanderers. 1. EL (AEL), *to be strong* (Gen. xiv. 6); the plural of EL is ELIM, also ELOTH and ELATH. Elim is the name of the place where there were 70 palm trees, the word EL, instead of meaning oak, is used in that instance for grove, ELIM, groves (Ex. xv. 27). There was also a palm grove at Akabah. In Is. i. 29, ELIM means oaks, the same word in Is. lxi. 3, and Ez. xxxi. 14, means any thrifty, large tree.—2. ALAH, *the terebinth*. The most noted one was Abraham's Oak at Mamre, where the three angels appeared to him. It is now represented by an oak (Thomson thinks it was an oak and not the terebinth) of the species *Quercus-pseudo-coccifera*. (See cut on page 3).—3. ELON, *some kind of oak*. Translated plain in the A. V. and in the Targum.—4. ILAN, *strong tree* (Dan. iv., only), and possibly an oak.—5. ALLAM, *an oak* (Josh. xxiv. 26, only).—6. ALLON, *evergreen oak* (Hos. iv. 13), and also the Holly-leaved oak; the Hairy-cupped oak; the prickly-cupped; the Kermes, which furnishes the insect used in dyes (Is. i. 18, scarlet).

The oak forests of Bashan were noted in the earliest times (Is. ii. 13; Ez. xxvii. 6; Zech. xi. 2), and they are still extensive and contain several varieties of very fine trees. Besides these, there are others scattered all over the country, both in the hilly districts and on the mountains. Mount Carmel, Anti-Lebanon (west slopes), Lebanon (east slopes, and many ravines), and the Hill Country of Galilee and Judæa, are supplied with scrubby oaks 10 to 15 feet high, bearing acorns in great quantities, useful for bread. Where the ground is now stripped of trees of all kinds, its roots are often found and dug for fuel. The largest tree of this species is that near Hebron, called "Abraham's Oak," which is 23 feet in girth, and shades a space 90 feet across. The nut-gall bearing oak is plentiful in Galilee and Asia Minor.

The Valonia oak is valuable for its tannin, contained in the acorn cups. It is probable that this was the "Oak of Bashan" (Q. *ægilops*).

There are many storied oaks in Palestine. Rebekah's nurse, Deborah, was buried under one at Bethel (Gen. xxxv. 8); Saul and his sons, under another in Jabesh (1 Chr. x. 12). The national covenant was commemorated by a monument under an oak at Shechem, by Joshua (xxiv. 26); Jacob hid the stolen images under the same tree (Gen. xxxv. 4); Absalom was caught by his hair in one in Bashan; Gideon saw an angel under an oak in Ophrah (Judg. vi. 11), and many were the shelters of altars for both true and false worship. The Arabs now have a superstition that spirits, *jin* (called Jacob's daughters), live in oak trees, and they hang rags of all kinds on the branches as charms against them.

OATH. An appeal to Divine authority to ratify the truth of an assertion (Heb. vi. 16). Calling God to witness, as, "God do so to me, and more, also, if," etc. (Ruth i. 17; 1 Sam. ii. 17). Idolaters swore by their false gods. Many frivolous forms were used, as, "By the blood of Abel;" "By my head;" "By the Temple," etc. Jesus was asked by the high-priest to swear, "By the living God," to the truth of what he was teaching of himself (Matt. xxvi. 63). Jesus is believed to have prohibited profane, and careless, or false swearing—not telling the truth under oath. It appears that Jesus gave testimony on oath before the high-priest, and Paul did not teach against it (Gal. i. 20; 1 Cor. xv. 31;

2 Cor. i. 23). There would seem to be no use for oaths among genuine Christians, living in the presence of God, but they are useful in dealing with those who do not live a Christian life. When men everywhere, and at all times, prefer the truth to lies, then oaths may be dispensed with. The forms or actions in taking an oath, anciently, were :—1. Lifting up the hand (Gen. xiv. 22). 2. Putting the hand on the head of the accused (Lev. xxiv. 14). 3. Putting the hand under the thigh (Gen. xxiv. 2), by both parties (Jos.). 4. Standing before the altar, or looking towards Jerusalem (1 K. viii. 31). 5. Dividing a victim (as a lamb), and passing between the pieces (Gen. xv. 10). 6. Placing the hands on the Book of the Law (Ex. xxiii. 1). The crime of PERJURY was strongly condemned. It was taking the Lord's name in vain. If a man gave false witness, he received the punishment that he tried to inflict on another by his perjury (Ex. xx. 7; Lev. xix. 12). Women were not permitted to give evidence on oath (Deut. xix. 17). The Mohammedan swears on the open Koran; Mohammed swore "By the setting of the stars." Bedawin Arabs touch the middle tent-pole, and swear by the life of the owner. The Romans were strict with men under oath (authority in Matt. viii. 9; Acts xvi. 27, xxvii. 42).

OBADI'AH (*servant of Jah*), also written ABADIAS and ABDIAS. 1. Ancestor of some mentioned in the genealogies of Judah (1 Chr. iii. 21).—2. Son of Izrahiah (vii. 3).—3. Son of Azel (viii. 38, ix. 44).—4. Son of Shemaiah (ix. 16). ABDA 2 a musician in the Temple-choir (Neh. xii. 25).—5. A captain in David's army (1 Chr. xii. 9).—6. A prince who taught in Jehoshaphat's reign (2 Chr. xvii. 7).—7. Son of Jehiel (Ezr. viii. 9).—8. A priest who signed the covenant with Nehemiah (xi. 5).—9. One of the twelve prophets. See HISTORY OF THE BOOKS.—10. An officer of high rank in Ahab's palace (1 K. xviii. 3). During the fierce persecution of the prophets by Jezebel he concealed a hundred of them in caves and fed them with bread and water (vs. 4, 13).—11. Father of Ishmaiah (1 Chr. xxvii. 19).—12. A Levite, overseer of the workmen on the Temple (2 Chr. xxxiv. 12).

O'BAL (*bare district*). Son of Joktan (Gen. x. 28). EBAL.

OBDI'A (1 Esd. v. 38; Ezr. ii. 61).

O'BED (*serving*). 1. Son of Boaz and Ruth (Ruth iv. 17). The Book of Ruth gives an interesting account of his birth and the social and religious life of the Israelites at that time.—2. A descendant of Jarha (1 Chr. ii. 37, 38).—3. One of David's men (xi. 47).—4. Son of Shemaiah, firstborn of Obed-edom (xxvi. 7).—5. Father of Azariah. A captain (2 Chr. xxiii. 1).

O'BED-E'DOM (*serving Edom*). 1. A member of the family of Kohath (2 Sam. vi. 10, 11). After the death of Uzzah, the ark which was being taken to the city of David was carried into the house of Obed-edom, where it remained three months (1 Chr. xv. 25).—2. Son of Jeduthun (1 Chr. xvi. 38).—3. Treasurer of the Temple (2 Chr. xxv. 24).

O'BETH. EBED, the son of Jonathan (1 Esd. viii. 32).

O'BIL (*chief of the camels*). An Ishmaelite who had charge of a herd of camels (1 Chr. xxvii. 30).

O'BOTH (*bottles*). Encampment in Moab. Lost. (Num. xxi. 10).

OCHI'EL (1 Esd. i. 9).

O'CHIM. Heb. translated "doleful creatures" in Is. xiii. 21. Some creature uttering doleful screeches, perhaps an owl.

OCIDE'LUS. Error for Jozabad in 1 Esd. ix. 22 (Ezr. x. 22).

OCI'NA (Judith ii. 28). Name for Accho. (See William of Tyre).

OC'RAN (*afflicted*). Father of Pagiel (Num. i. 13).

O'DED (*erecting*). 1. Father of Azariah (2 Chr. xv. 1, 8).—2. A prophet who secured the release of the captives from Judah (xxviii. 9). This incident in the history of the Kingdom of Israel is in pleasant contrast to many others. A whole army were liberated, clothed and fed.

ODOL'LAM. ADULLAM. *Beit Ula.*

ODONAR'KES. Chief of a tribe slain by Jonathan (1 Macc. ix. 66).

OFFENCE. The Heb. MIT or CHEY (Eccl. x. 4), is translated sin (Lev. xix. 17; xx. 20, etc.), also fault in Gen. xli. 9. MICHSHOL (1 Sam. xv. 31; Is. viii. 14), "stumbling block," Gr. *skandalon* in Matt. xvi. 23; xviii. 7; Luke xvii. 1. To

BAAL.

eat with offence is to eat so as to be an occasion of sin in another (Rom. xiv. 20). "A temptation to sin," "perplexity," "danger," "that which produces disgust," etc.

OFFEND, TO (from Lat. *offendo*). Offence, as a breach of the law, is alluded to in Rom. v. 15, 17; as an offered excuse for sin in Matt. xv. 12; John vi. 61.

OFFERING. (See SACRIFICE).

OFFICER (Heb. NEZIR, SARIS, PEKAH, PEKUDAH, PAKID, RAB, SHOTER), and others, are terms conveying various meanings, from a commander of an army to a simple messenger of a court of justice (John vii. 32, 45, etc.). In Luke xii. 58, there appears *praktor* (*a doer*)—Revenue officers, (1 Macc. x. 41, xiii. 37). *Huperetes*, bailiff or some inferior officer (Matt. v. 25).

OG (*crooked*). King of BASHAN, ruler over sixty cities. He was one of the giant (violent, strong) race of Rephaim (Josh. xiii. 12). This race was probably Shemite in origin, dating earlier than the Canaanites. Og's conch (palanquin, Amos iii. 12), is described as of iron, 15 ft. 9 in. long, and 6 ft. wide (Deut. iii. 11). This would indicate Og's hight at 9 feet at least.

O'HAD (*union*). Son of Simeon (Gen. xlvi. 10).

O'HEL (*house*). Son of Zerubbabel (1 Chr. iii. 20). HASADIAH.

OIL. The Olive was the chief source of oil (See OLIVES). (Ez. xvi. 13). It was used in the preparation of meat offerings in the Temple (Lev. v. 11, vi. 21). The second pressing was used for lamps. Oil was an important article of merchandise (1 Chr. xxvii. 28; Ez. xxvii. 17). See OINTMENT. OLIVE.

OIL-TREE (Heb. 'EZ SHEMEN). A tree bearing fruit resembling that of the olive (Is. xli. 19). OLIVE.

OINTMENT (Heb. SHAMAN, *to be fat*; ROKAH, *to anoint;* MIRKAHATH, the vessel for holding the perfume, or ointment; MISHAH, *oil*. Ointment was a general term for perfumes, cosmetics, for substances used for medicinal, sacred, and ceremonial purposes. Olive oil formed the body of these ointments. A particular ointment was appointed for use in consecration (Ex. xxx. 23, 33, xxxi. 7, xxxvii. 29, xl. 9, 15), of myrrh, cassia, sweet cinnamon, sweet calamus and olive oil. With this, also, the furniture of the Tabernacle was anointed. Dead bodies were anointed with both ointment and oil. Christ refers to this in Matt. xxvi. 12; Mark xiv. 38; Luke xxiii. 56. It was largely used in medical

treatment, alluded to by Christ in curing the blind man (Is. i. 6; John ix. 6; Jer. viii. 22; Rev. iii. 18). As a cosmetic for the face, so common with the Greeks and Romans, it was also used by the Egyptians and Jews, and is now by the inhabitants of Palestine to this day. Allusion is made to the use of ointments in Ruth iii. 3; Eccl. vii. 1, ix. 8; Prov. xxvii. 9, 16; Matt. xxvi. 7; Luke vii. 42; Rev. xviii. 13.

OL'AMUS. Son of Bani (1 Esd. ix. 30).

OLD-GATE. A gate of JERUSALEM (Neh. iii. 6).

OLD TESTAMENT. See HISTORY OF THE BOOKS.

GREEK MS., A. D. 900.—John i. 1–3.

OL'IVE. (Heb. ZAYITH, or ZAIT). A tree from 15 to 30 ft. high, bearing berries, smooth, like an oval plum, violet color when ripe, having an oily pulp, and a hard, rough stone. The leaves are like the willow, and of a dull, olive green, on the smooth, upper surface, and silvery pale on the downy, under surface. The flowers are small and white. See cut, p. 37.

The body of the tree dies at the heart and stands up on several legs (see cut on page 114). The bark of old trees is very rough, like that on old willow trees. They live to a great age. (See GETHSEMANE). A sacred olive tree was kept in the court of the Temple of Pandrosus, on the Acropolis, Athens; and the allusion in Ps. lii. 8, would imply that they were grown in the Temple Court on Zion.

The best olive-oil is now raised where, before the Christian era, the tree was almost unknown, in Italy and Spain, and where millions depend on it for half their living. The trees are planted by cuttings. If the slip is from a wild olive it must be grafted from a good one. The Church is a cultured olive tree, and Gentilism a wild olive tree (Rom. xi. 16–24). The wild tree bears but very few berries, and scarcely any oil can be got from them.

Olive orchards are as common in the East around every village as apple orchards are in the United States. Anciently it was exported from Palestine to Egypt (Ez. xxvii. 17; Hos. xii. 1). Moses sings of "oil out of the flinty rock," in one of his odes (Deut. xxxii. 13), which indicates that then, as now, the best soil for the olive was the chalky marl, with flint, and just mould enough to cover the roots. The text may have alluded to the oil mills and presses, where the oil comes out of the rock, for the press vat is often hollowed out of a large rock.

The tree bears in its seventh year, and a good crop in its fifteenth, and continues to bear for several hundred years. The crop is yielded every other year, and a large tree will produce from ten to fifteen gallons of oil. The yield by the acre is about one hundred dollars.

It is their substitute for our butter and lard. Many dishes are cooked in olive oil. The lamp is supplied with it; and the second pressing (not so pure), is used in making soap. The orchards or groves are carefully guarded near harvest time, and the rulers announce the day for gathering the berries, which begins in October. The general harvest is in November. The trees are shaken, and beaten with poles, but a few always remain for the gleaning of the poor. The shaking of the olive tree is a cold, wet, laborious operation, as it occurs in the winter, when rain and cold winds, and frost are frequent.

OLIVES, MOUNT OF (HAR-HAZZATHIM, Zech. xiv. 4). "Before Jerusalem, on the east." Referred to as the "ascent of Olivet" in other places (2 Sam. xv. 30, etc.) in the Old Testament, and the various changes of the same in the New (Luke xix. 29; Acts i. 12). The first mention of the mount is at the time David fled over it, and the last is the triumphal progress of the Son of David over its slopes. The description, written, perhaps over 2,500 years ago, is now a good one. It is near Jerusalem—a ravine between them—olive-trees (Neh. viii. 15; Mark xi. 8), and gives a very distinct view of the Temple site and the city from its summit, where there is now a chapel (2 Sam. xv. 23, 32). Solomon built chapels for the worship of Ashtoreth, Chemosh, and Milcom, heathen divinities, on a part of Olivet called the "Mount of Corruption" (2 K. xxiii. 13), which some believe to be the highest summit, where the chapel of the Ascension now stands—the same spot that was held sacred by David.

Olivet is a ridge, 300 feet higher than the Temple site, and a mile long, north and south, divided into three or four summits, which are named—commencing at the north—1. Viri Galilæi, also Vineyard of the Sportsmen; 2. Ascension, by the Arabs Jebel et Tur; 3. Prophets; and 4, Offense, Arab Baten el Hawa, Belly of the Winds. During the middle ages the mount was dotted all over with chapels, or monuments of some kind, marking the localities selected as the sites of interesting events recorded in Scripture; among which are the tombs of the Virgin, Joachim, and Anna, near Gethsemane (in which are the Cave of Christ's Prayer and Agony, the rock on which the three disciples slept, and the place of the capture of Christ; spot on which the Virgin witnessed the stoning of Stephen; where her girdle dropped at the time of her Assumption; where Jesus wept over the city (Luke xix. 41); where Jesus first said the Lord's Prayer —(the Beatitudes were also pronounced here); where the woman taken in adultery was brought to him; Tombs of the Prophets (containing Haggai and Zechariah); cave in which the Apostles wrote the Creed; where Christ spoke of the judgment to come; Cave of St. Pelagia, and of Huldah, the prophetess; Place of the Ascension; where the Virgin was warned of her death by an angel; spot from which the Apostles witnessed the Ascension (viri Galilæi—men of Galilee); where the three Marys saw Jesus after his resurrection. All of these places on the side toward the city. On the slopes, south and east, the place of the barren fig-tree; Bethphage; Bethany (house of Lazarus, and the cave, or tomb); stone on which Christ sat when Mary and Martha saw him. Only three of these command our special attention—Gethsemane, the place of the Lamentation, and the place of Ascension. (See GETHSEMANE). Stanley says that the Lord's "triumphal entry" must have been on the road, not over the summit, but the longer and easier route round the south shoulder of the mount (between the summit called the Prophets and that called the Mt. of Corruption), which has the peculiarity of presenting two successive views of the city, just before and after passing a slight elevation in the path. Ezekiel mentions Olivet in his wonderful vision (xi. 23); and Zechariah says of the Messiah, "His feet shall stand in that day (of the destruction of Jerusalem) on the Mount of Olives" (xiv. 4).

Jesus stood somewhere on its brow when he predicted the overthrow of the city (Mark xiii. 1).

The whole mount is now called by the Jews Har-hammishkah, mount of corruption or destruction.

There are three paths leading from near Gethsemane to the top of Olivet, besides the road to

JERUSALEM FROM OLIVET.

... a ho. The first leads north of the central summit (Ascension) to the little village near the top (see map, p. 151). The second passes the Cave of Pelagia, in a direct course up the mount to the church and village. The third runs near the Tomb of the Prophets and ends at the same village. The fourth is the road to Bethany and Jericho, and passes between the Mt. of Offense and the Tomb of the Prophets. This is now, as it must have been anciently, the usual route for caravans and all large parties. Coming from Bethany you may get two views of the city: the first, of the southeast corner of the Temple site and Zion. The road then descends a slight declivity, and the city is hid behind a ridge of Olivet. A few rods further the path rises steeply up to a ledge of smooth rock, where the whole city is seen in one view. It is almost the only really authentic spot on Olivet or near Jerusalem that is not marked by a church, chapel or tower, and is the only one that is located without controversy (see view, p. 154).

OLYM'PAS (Gr. *given by heaven*). A disciple at Rome (Rom. xvi. 15). Tradition says he was of the 70, and died A. D. 69.

OLYM'PIUS. A title given to the Greek deity, Zeus (JUPITER), (2 Macc. vi. 2), from his residence on Mt. Olympus, in Greece.

OMAE'RUS. AMRAM, son of Bani (1 Esd. ix. 34).

O'MAR (*eloquent*). Son of Eliphaz (Gen. xxxvi. 11, 15). The name now found in the *Amir* tribe of Arabs, in Gilead.

O MEGA (Gr. Ō). The last letter of the Greek alphabet (Rev. i. 8, 11). Symbol of "the last," as A is of "the first."

O'MER (*handful*). See WEIGHTS and MEASURES.

OM'RI (*servant of Jah*). 1. "Captain of the host" to Elah, also the 6th king of Israel, a vigorous and unscrupulous ruler (1 K. xvi. 21), in Tirzah, he transferred his residence to the hill Shomron, (Samaria), which he bought of Shemer, where he reigned 6 years more.—2. Son of Becher (1 Chr. vii. 8).—3. Son of Judah, a descendant of Pharez (ix. 4).—4. Son of Michael (xxvi. 18).

ON (*power*). Son of Peleth. A chief who revolted against Moses (Num. xvi. 1).

ON. (*Heliopolis*). BETHSHEMESH (Jer. xliii. 13). Egyptian sacred name *ha-ra* (the *city of the sun*), and common name *an*. It was on the E. bank of the Nile, 20 miles N. E. of Memphis; once the capital of the district. Joseph's wife was a daughter of a priest of On (Gen. xli. 45). The site is now marked by low mounds, enclosing a space about ⅔ of a m. each way, where once stood the temple of the sun and the city, only a solitary obelisk (70 ft. high, and covered with hieroglyphics) being left of the former splendors of the place. The emperor Augustus carried a great many works of art, and an obelisk from this city to Rome; and Constantine adorned Constantinople from the same source. Tradition says that Joseph brought Mary and the infant Jesus to On, and points out a large fig-tree as the one under which they encamped.

O'NAM (*strong*). 1. Son of Shobal (Gen. xxxvi. 23).—2. Son of Jerahmeel (1 Chr. ii. 26, 28), by Atarah.

O'NAN. Son of Judah (Gen. xxxviii. 4). It was Onan's duty to marry his brother's widow, and perpetuate the race; but he took means to prevent the consequences of marriage. Jehovah was angry with him, and slew him as he had slain his brother (ver. 9).

ONE'SIMUS. A slave who had escaped from his master Philemon of Colosse, and had fled to Rome, where Paul converted him and recommended his forgiveness by his master in an epistle (Philemon). (See HISTORY OF THE BOOKS). Onesimus left Rome in the company of Tychicus, carrying the epistles to Philemon, to the Colossians, and Ephesians (Col. iv. 9). There is a tradition that Onesimus became Bishop of Berœa, where he is said to have been martyred.

ONESIPH'ORUS (*profit-bringing*). An Ephesian mentioned in 2 Tim. i. 16-18, who rendered Paul generous service during his second captivity in Rome, in acknowledging which, the apostle alludes

ON.

to the "house of Onesiphorus," and in 2 Tim. iv. 19, to "the household of Onesiphorus," which suggests that the family might have shared in rendering services to Paul.

ONIA'RES. An error in 1 Macc. xii. 20, for AREUS to ONIAS.

ONI'AS (Heb. ONIYAH, *strength of Jah*). The name of five high priests; two only are mentioned in the A. V., I and III.

JADDUA
JADDUA 1. ONIAS I - - - B. C. 330.
1. ONIAS 2. SIMON the Just.
2. SIMON 3. ONIAS II.
3. ONIAS 4. SIMON II.
4. SIMON 5. ONIAS III - - - B. C. 198.
" " 6. ONIAS IV (Menelaus).
5. ONIAS 7. ONIAS V.

Onias IV assumed the Greek name Menelaus to gain the favor of the Greek party. He had been reproved by his eldest brother, Onias III, for appropriating the sacred treasures, at which he murdered his brother through an assassin (Andronicus) about 171 B. C. (2 Macc. iii. 4).

ONI'AS, THE CITY OF. Where stood a temple built by Onias V, and the Jewish settlements in Egypt. The site of the city of Onias was in the district north of Heliopolis.

ONIONS (Heb. BETSALIM). A bulbous plant; a

favorite article of food with the Egyptians. They are very mild in Egypt, and grow to a large size.

O'NO (*strong*). Built by the sons of Elpaal. In Benjamin (1 Chr. viii. 12). 725 of the people of Lod, Hadid, and Ono returned from Babylon (Ezr. ii. 33). There was a plain near the city (Neh. vi. 2), where Nehemiah was invited (but he declined) five times to come to a village in it to meet Sanballat. *Beit Anna*, 4½ ms. N. of Lud.

ONY'CHA (Heb. SHEHELETH, or SHECHELETH). The origin of our word *shell*. The Hebrew word is only mentioned in Ex. xxx. 34, as an ingredient of the sacred perfume. This word has been variously rendered—As the horny lid closing the open part of a shell, a kind of mollusk. Gosse thinks it was some gum resin, as all marine animals, except fish with fins and scales, were unclean.

EAR-RING, NATURAL SIZE.

O'NYX (Heb. SHOHAM). See PRECIOUS STONES.

O'PHEL. A part of ancient Jerusalem, first mentioned as having its wall built "much" upon by Jotham (2 Chr. xxvii. 3). Manasseh enclosed it with a wall (xxxiii. 14). It was near the watergate (Neh. iii. 26), and a great corner-tower (v. 27). Josephus calls it Ophla (Ant. ix. 11, 2; B. J. ii. 17, 9). The prophet Micah (iv. 8) calls Ophel the daughter of Zion, which would indicate that Zion was the Temple-site, for Ophel is the hill S. of the S. wall of the Temple.—2. The Ophel of 2 K. v. 24, was the *residence* of the prophet Elisha, to which Gehazi returned after begging a present from Naaman, near Samaria.

O'PHIR (*dust—red dust?*). In the Himyarite language *ofir* is *red*, and the people of Mahra call their country red, and the Red Sea *Bahr Ofir*. Ophir was a region from which Solomon obtained gold in Tyrian ships, by the way of Eziongeber. It was in Arabia (Gen. x. 29), where several sons of Joktan settled, giving their names to regions or tribes. Sophir is the form of the name in the Septuagint and Josephus. The gold, silver, precious stones, ivory, apes, peacocks, and almug-wood are Indian articles, but may have been imported there. Jeremiah (x. 9) and Daniel (x. 5), say gold of *Uphaz*, probably meaning Ophir. On the shore of the Red Sea, in Arabia.

OPH'RAH (*a fawn*). Two places of this name. 1. In Benjamin (Josh. xviii. 23), 5 ms. E. of Bethel, now called *Et Taiyibeh* a small village on a conical hill, containing ancient ruins. Jesus retired to this obscure place, after the miracle of raising Lazarus, with his disciples (John xi. 54). (See cut on page 94). 2. In Manasseh, the native place of Gideon (Judg. vi. 11, viii. 27), and where he was buried. The prophet Micah calls it Aphrah (*dust*, i. 10).

OR. Used in the now obsolete sense of *ere* or *before* (Ps. xc. 2).

OR'ACLE (Heb. DEBIR). The inner sanctuary of the Temple (1 K. vi. 5, 16 ff.).

OR'ATOR (*a speaker*). The title given to TERTULLUS, the advocate of the Jews against Paul (Acts xxiv. 1). TRIAL.

OR'CHARD. See GARDEN. The East is naturally a country of orchards.—Of oranges, lemons, pomegranates, apples, olives, cherries, dates, apricots, figs, and other fruits. Nearly the whole support of a family can be had from the orchard. Trees are taxed very heavily, whether bearing or not, and from the time they are planted, which prevents enterprise.

ORDAIN. To order, constitute, appoint, found, or establish, as a priest or a deacon over a church. Heb. YASAD, founded in 1 Chr. ix. 22; 2. KUN, to establish (Ps. viii. 3); 3. MENAH, to set, or to number (Dan. v. 26; MENE in v. 25); 4. NATHAN to give (2 K. xxiii. 5); 5. AMAD, to raise up (Ex. ix. 16); 6. ARACA, to set in order (Ps. cxxxii. 17); 7. PAAL, work (Job xi. 8); 8. KUM, to confirm (Esth. ix. 27); 9. SUM, to appoint (1 Chr. xvii. 9); 10. SHAFATH, to set (Is. xxvi. 12); 11. ASAH, to make (1 K. xi. 31); 12. Greek, *diatasso*, to arrange (1 Cor. vii. 17); 13. *Kathistemi*, to place (Heb. v. 1); 14. *Kataskeuazo*, to prepare fully (Heb. ix. 6); 15. *Krino*, to separate (Acts xvi. 4), and "to judge" over 80 times; 16. *Horizo*, to bound, limit (Acts x. 42); 17. *Poieo*, to make (Mark iii. 14); 18. *Proorizo*, predetermine (1 Cor. ii. 17); 19. *Tasso*, to set in order (Acts xiii. 48); 20. *Tithemi*, to lay (John xv. 16); 21. *Cheirotoneo*, to stretch (Acts xiv. 23); 22. *Ginomai*, to begin to be (Acts i. 22), this word is repeated 700 times in the N. T.; 23. *Prographo*, to write before (Rom. xv. 4); 24. *Proctoimazo*, to appoint (Eph. iii. 3).

O'REB (*raven*). A chief of the Midianites who invaded Israel and was defeated by GIDEON. The disaster in which Oreb and Zeeb lost their lives (by the hands of Ephraimites), was one of the most awful on record. Two large rocks, near the scene, were named in memory of the event.

O'REB, THE ROCK (*the raven's crag*). (Judg. vii. 25; Is. x. 26). Not far from Bethshemesh, on the east (or west) side of Jordan. The Jews have a tradition that the prophet Elijah was fed by the people of Oreb (*ravens*). (See *Reland*).

O'REN (*pine*). Son of Jerahmeël (1 Chr. ii. 25).

OR'GAN. A musical instrument consisting of a combination of metal and reed pipes of different lengths and sizes. MUSICAL INSTRUMENTS.

ORI'ON. "God who made Arcturus, Orion and the Pleiades" (Job ix. 9; xxxviii. 31, 32; Amos v. 8). KESIL in Hebrew. Called the giant by the Arabs, which was Nimrod among the Chaldæans. Aben Ezra says Orion means the constellation now called Scorpion, or the bright star in it called Antares.

ORNAMENTS. The ancient monuments show that ornaments were used in great variety in ancient as well as modern times. Every rank uses

them, rich or poor, and as many as their means permit. If gold cannot be had, then silver, or brass, or tin, or glass, is used. Engraved gems were in use only by the most wealthy and educated. These bore besides the words or letters, figures of gods or mythical animals, or the portraits of relatives or friends (see PRECIOUS STONES). A few of the articles were: 1. NEZEM, ring; nose ring in Gen. xxiv. 22, 27.— 2. ZAMID, bracelet. —3. KELI, jewels.— 4. NEZEM-BEAZNOTH, rings in the ears.—5. CHOTHAM, seal, signet.— 6. PATHIL, string of beads (?). —7. TABBAATH, a signet ring (the badge of authority). —8. RABID, chain (of gold, Ez. xvi. 11).— 9. CHACH, buckle.—10. KUMAZ, tablets strung together, as hearts, diamonds, etc. (Ex. xxxv. 22).—11. MA-NOTH, looking-glasses. — 12. EZ'ADAH, chains (Num. xxxi. 20).—13. AGIL, circular ear-ring, solid. — 14. SAHARONIM, moonshaped little pieces, strung on a cord.—15. NETIFOTH, pendents (Judg. viii. 26).—16. TORIM, beads (rows), Cant. i. 10, 11, of gold or silver, or pearls.—17. CHAHUZIM, any perforated small articles.—18. ANAK, perhaps a hanging lock of hair, in Cant. iv. 9. — 19. CHALAIM, necklace (Cant. vii. 1). — 20. GELILOM, garland (v. 12). — 21. LIVYAH, wreath. — 22. AKASIM, tinkling ornaments (Is. iii. 23).—23. SHEBISIM, lace caps.—24. SHEROTH, bracelets made of twisted wires. — 25. REALOTH, spangles.—26. PEERIM, bonnets.—27. ZEADOTH, a chain to shorten the steps, worn on the legs.—28. KISSHURIM, girdle.—29. BOTTE-HANNEFESH, scent bottles.—30. LECASHIM, amulets used as earrings.—31. CHARI-TIM, purses (round, conical).—32. GILTONIM, a thin veil, gauze. Scarcely any new thing has been added in modern days. The ekoôra, a saucer-shaped ornament of metal, sewed to the top of the cap and ornamented with stones, or engraved, now used by the Arabs, was probably very ancient, as may be inferred from the "golden tower" of the Mishna. (See cut on p. 9).

OR NAN (*active*), ARAUNAH the Jebusite (1 Chr. xxi. 15, 18, 20, 25, 28).

OR'PAH (*forelock*). Wife of Chilion, son of Noomi. She accompanied her sister-in-law on the road to Bethlehem, but went back to her people and her gods (Ruth i. 4, 14).

ORTHO SIAS. Described by Pliny (v. 17) as near Tripolis, south of the river Eleutherus (which was the northern boundary of Phoenicia), in a strong pass; and a city of great importance, as commanding the route between Phoenicia and Syria. Tryphon fled there when besieged by Antiochus in Dora (1 Macc. xv. 37). The ruins are on the south bank of the *Nahr el Barid* (*cold river*).

OSE'A. Hoshea, king of Israel (2 Esd. xiii. 40).

OSE'AS. The prophet Hosea (2 Esd. i. 39).

OSE'E. The prophet Hosea (Rom. ix. 25).

OSHE'A. The original name of Joshua, son of Nun (Num. xiii. 8, 16).

OS'PRAY (Heb. OZNIYAH). An unclean bird. Very powerful; often weighing five pounds. It plunges under the water to catch fish. It belongs

OSTRICHES.

to the *Falconidæ*, or falcon family, and is found in Europe, North America, and occasionally in Egypt (Deut. xiv. 12).

OS'SIFRAGE (Heb. PERES), (*bone-breaker*). The Lammergeier. An unclean bird (Lev. xi. 13). It attacks the wild goat, young deer, sheep, calves, etc. It is found in the highest mountains of Europe, Asia and Africa, and is frequently seen in the sky flying alone. See EAGLE, page 92.

OS'TRICH (Heb. BATH HAYYA'ANAH, daughters of the wilderness—*female ostriches*, YA'ENIM, *ostriches*, and RANAN, *to wail*—sometimes rendered *peacocks*). The words are generally accepted to mean the ostrich. In Lam. iv. 3, appears the word YA'ENIM (plural) which rightly translates ostrich. NOTSEH, *feathers*, in Job. xxxix. 13. Several lay their eggs in the same nest, which is usually a hollow scooped in the sand, where (covered only by the sand, about a foot deep), the sun warms them during the day. A few eggs are left out of the nest, intended for food for the young brood. The supposed cruel habit of the bird is used as a type of the cruelty and indifference of the Hebrews (Lam. iv. 3; Job xxxix. 16). This supposition is an error, for the ostrich cares for, and defends its young, even risking its own life. The brood numbers 20 to 30, are gray when young, and can run at once. The old birds are black and white. The valued plumes are pure white. They are easily tamed, and will live among the goats and camels. The Arabs hang great numbers of the eggs in their mosques, and

also use them for cups, jars, etc. When chased they run in a circle, and can run a mile in about 2'. By running inside the circle, the horse gains on the ostrich, and comes up with him.

OTH'NI (*lion of Jah*). Son of Shemaiah (1 Chr. xxvi. 7). OTHNEN (*lion*).

OTH'NIEL (*lion of El*). Descendant of Kenaz, and brother of CALEB 1 (Josh. xv. 17). He is first mentioned as the captor of Kirjath-Sepher (Debir), near Hebron, where he won his wife (his niece Achsah), as a prize for leading the attack (Josh. xiv. 12-15; see ACHSAH). He is next called to be a judge (Judg. iii. 9), holding the office 40 years, or giving the nation rest in peace for that time.

OTHONI'AS. Error for Mattaniah (Ezr. x. 27), in 1 Esd. ix. 28.

OUCHES. Sockets in which the precious stones of the breast-place were set. (Nouches in Chaucer). (Ex. xxviii. 11, 13, xxxix. 6, etc.).

OV'EN (Heb. TANNUR). The ovens in the East are of two kinds. The stationary ones are found only in towns, where regular bakers are employed (Hos. vii. 4). The portable ones consist of a large jar made of clay, three feet high, larger at the bottom, with a hole for removing the ashes. Every house possesses such an article (Ex. viii. 3). It was heated with twigs, grass or wood (Matt. vi. 30), sometimes with dung, and the loaves were placed both inside and outside of it. FIRE.

OVERSEERS. A ministerial title, perhaps elder or bishop (Acts xx. 28).

OWL. Heb. 1. BATH HAYYA'ANAH (*daughters of the waste places*). (See OSTRICH). 2. YANSHUF or YANSHOF. The Ibis, an unclean bird, as in Lev. xi. 17 and Deut. xiv. 16. Probably not known in Palestine, but a native of Egypt. In Is. xxxiv. 11 it is mentioned in the desolation of Idumæa (Edom). 3. COS (*cup*), little owl (Lev. xi. 17, etc.). 4. KIPPOZ, the owl, which is common in the vicinity (and even in the city) of Jerusalem. LILITH, screech-owl, in Is. xxxiv. 14. The *lilith* was to the Hebrews what the *ghost* or *ghoul* is to the Arab, a "night-monster," and so they called the screech-owl by that name.

OWL.

OX. Heb. 1. BAKAR, horned cattle, of full age (Is. lv. 25).—2. FAR, BENBAKAR, calf.—3. SHOR, one of a drove of full grown cattle. TROR (the Chaldee form) in Ezr. vi. 9.—4. AGAL, calf of the first year; EGLAH, a heifer (Hos. x. 11), giving milk (Is. vii. 21), or plowing (Judg. xiv. 18).—5. AGIL, a bull two (7) years old (vi. 25).—6. ABARIM (*strong*) bulls.—7. TEO, wild bull (Is. li. 20); possibly the ORYX. Stall-fed cattle are alluded to in Prov. xv. 17, and 1 K. iv. 23. The cattle on the monuments are long-horned, short-horned, polled, or muley, besides the Abyssinian; and of every variety in color, as ours are. (See p. 10). The ox was the most important of all animals to the ancient Hebrews (as well as nearly all other nations). They were used for plowing (Deut. xxi. 10); threshing grain (Mic. iv. 13); for draught (1 Sam. vi. 7); to carry burdens (1 Chr. xii. 40), and riders; their flesh was eaten (1 K. i. 9); they were used for sacrifice, and the cow supplied milk, butter, tallow, hides, etc. The law contains many favorable clauses for its protection from misuse, abuse, starvation, and cruelty, and providing for its well-being, food and rest. The Hebrews did not castrate animals, but used them in their natural condition. Cattle grazing in distant pastures often became quite wild, as in Ps. xxii. 13. The present cattle in Palestine are small in size, and not good in quality. The buffalo is common now, and it was known anciently. The habits of this animal very nearly, if not entirely, answer the points in the text of Job xl. 15-24. They frequent the muddy pools, and the swift stream of Jordan, avoiding insects by keeping entirely under water, except their eyes and nose, under the covert of the reeds and willows. They are trained to the plow, and are much stronger than the ox.

O'ZEM (*strength*). 1. Son of Jesse (1 Chr. ii. 15).—2. Son of Jerahmeel (ii. 25).

OZI'AS. 1. Son of Micha, one of the governors of Bethulia (Judg. vi. 15).—2. Uzzi, ancestor of Ezra (2 Esd. ii. 2).—3. UZZIAH, king of Judah (Matt. i. 8, 9).

O'ZIEL. Ancestor of Judith (Jud. viii. 1). UZZIEL.

OZ'NI (*attentive*). Son of Gad (Num. xxvi. 16). EZBON.

OZ'NITES. Descendants of OZNI (Num. xxvi. 16).

OZO'RA. Nathan, Adaiah, Machnadebai, are corrupted into the sons of Ozora (1 Esd. ix. 34).

P

PA'ARAI (*open*). NAARAI, son of Ezbai (1 Chr. xi. 37).

PA'DAN (Heb. PODDAN, *a plain*). (Gen. xlviii. 7).

PA'DAN A'RAM. The family of the founder of the Jewish race settled here, with whom the descendants of Abraham married, as with an aristocratic people. (See HARAN.) *Padan* is Arabic for field, or ploughed land. The wife of the heir of the promise was sought here; and it was, probably, near Damascus, only a few days' journey from where Abraham was living, and not many weeks' (or months') travel, far away in Mesopotamia (Gen. xxxviii. xxxix).

PA'DON (*deliverance*). Ancestor of Nethinim, who returned from captivity (Ezr. ii. 44).

PAG'IEL (*event of El*). Son of Ocran (Num. i. 13).

PA'HATH-MOAB (*governor of Moab*). Head of one of the principal houses of the tribe of Judah. This title is obscure, but in 1 Chr. iv. 22 allusion is made to a family of Shilonites, of the tribe of Judah, who once had dominion in Moab. The family was of exalted rank, as is shown by its appearing fourth in the lists of both Ezr. ii. 6, and Neh. vii. 11. Among the lay princes PA'HATH-MOAB signs second (Neh. x. 14).

PA'I. A town in Edom (1 Chr. i. 50).

PAINTS. The only reference to paint is that of its universal use among women as a cosmetic to paint the eyes. (See EYE, p. 101).

PAL'ACE. The buildings, court-yards, etc., enclosed within the walls of a royal residence. The particular allusion to palace is that by the Herods, which was afterwards the residence of the Roman governor or praetor, hence it was called in Greek Pretorium. Christ was brought before the Roman procurator, Pontius Pilate, in this palace (Mark. xv. 16). The most celebrated palace mentioned in the Scriptures, is that of Solomon, a detailed description of which occurs in 1 K. vii. 1–12, and in Josephus (Ant. viii. 5, 1, 2). The Palace of Solomon was in the city on Mount Zion, opposite the Temple. It is estimated to have covered some 150,000 or 160,000 square feet. The first of the buildings upon entering, was "the House of the Forest of Lebanon." This was a hall so named from the cedars of Lebanon, worked into pillars and beams of which there were rows (1 K. vii. 2). The dimensions were 150 feet long by 75 feet in width and thirty high. This was the audience chamber. The next building of importance was the Hall of Judgment (1 K. vii. 7), 75 feet square. There was also a colonnade on "The Porch," 75 by 45 feet, used for reception and for the transaction of ordinary business.

There was further the inner court, with gardens and fountains, and accommodation for the harem officers of the court and guard.

PA'LAL (*judge*). Son of Uzai, who assisted at the Jerusalem walls (Neh. iii. 25).

PAL'ESTINE, PALESTI'NA. The translation of the Heb. PELESHETH, which is found only four times, and always in poetical passages in the O. T. (Ex. xv. 14; Is. xiv. 29, 31; Joel iii. 4). The same word is translated "Philistia" in Ps. lx. 8, lxxxiii. 7, lxxxvii. 4, cviii. 9. The two words were synonymous at the time our version was made, and Palestine in the Scriptures means only so much of the country as we now call Philistia.

On the Assyrian monuments there is a country described as PALAZTU on the West Sea, separate from Tyre, Damascus, Samaria and Edom. The Egyptians wrote it at Karnak PULUSATU. The Greeks called it Philistine Syria. Jerome (A. D. 400), also restricts the name to Philistia, and is followed by Procopius.

In our day the name is used of the whole country, including all that the Jews or Hebrews ever occupied.

It was originally called The Land of Canaan, low land (as compared to the high plateaus of Bashan and Gilead, Ps. cv. 11). The land of the Hebrews in Gen. xl. 15, only. The land of the Hittites in Josh. i. 4, and CHETU or CHITA on the Egyptian monuments.

The name HOLY LAND (TA-NETR) is as old as the Pharaoh Rameses II, and Thothmes III. The Phœnicians called their own country Holy Land, and the Egyptians may have borrowed the term, which argues that the idea of Holy Land belonged to the country before the Hebrews took possession, and is the most generally known now.

The Land of Israel (1 Sam. xiii. 19), land of Jah (Hos. ix. 3), the holy land (Zech. ii. 12), and the glorious land (Dan. xi. 41), were names in use during the monarchy.

There is no record of any division of the land, except the names of the several peoples inhabiting it, until the 12 tribes took possession, when the several divisions were known by the names of the tribes.

After the Captivity (if not before, 2 Chr. ix. 11), it was called Judæa, meaning the land of the Jews. The Romans divided it into Galilee, Samaria, Judæa, Perea, and gave names and limits to the surrounding country; as Phœnicia, Cœle-Syria, Lysania, Hauran, Edom, etc.

The land is about 140 ms. (Dan to Beersheba) long, and 40 ms. average width, between the Jordan valley and the West Sea; fenced in by this valley on the east, the Lebanon on the north, the desert on the south, and the Great Sea on the west. The whole of this district is high land, from 100 to 3000 feet above the sea level. The divisions are into Plain, Hill Country, Jordan Valley, and Mountains; each almost a strip from north to south, with a distinct history as well as structure.

1. The Plains lie along the shore of the Great Sea; are narrow at the north, and become wider southward, and are elevated from 100 to 500 feet; the surface sandy, rolling, with few forest trees, but many orchards, vines and shrubs, watered by brooks, fed by fountains. The great plain of Esdraelon cuts the country into two sections, between Galilee and Samaria. There are no safe harbors on the coast, and only a few such as they are, at Tripolis, Jebail, Beirut, Acre, Joppa. Tyre and Sidon have almost entirely lost their harbors with sand which comes across from the great Sahara desert, and is destroying all the harbors, and creeping inland in many places, as at Beirut, Askulan, and Gaza.

2. The Hill Country, on both sides of the Jordan is elevated from 1000 to 4000 feet, has a few isolated peaks, and many deep ravines. The torrents flow mostly in winter, and there are many fountains and wells, and two rivers, Kishon and Leontes.

Galilee is about 20 miles wide, undulating, with plains, and several mountain peaks, as Safed, Jermuk (4000), Hattin, Kaukab, Tabor and Gilboa, rugged and sharp, with forests of oak, terebinth, thorns, and fruit orchards. The whole region is carpeted with flowers in the rainy season. The dews of Hermon increase the length of the green season and continues its freshness long after the southern section is dried up. There are many brooks flowing the year round, numerous fountains, and few wells.

HEAD-DRESS.

Carmel rises from the sea, south of Esdraelon (see CARMEL), joins the hills of Samaria, which extend south through Judæa to the desert. (See EPHRAIM and SAMARIA). The hill-tops are rounder than those in Galilee, and well wooded. The noted peaks are Gerizim, Ebal, Samaria, Jedua, Haskin, Farsi and Kurn Surtabeh, none of which are very high. The noted valleys (or plains) are Mukhna, 6 miles long by one wide; Sanur, 2 miles; Kubatiyeh, 2½, and Dothan, 2½ miles. Orchards and groves of fruit are numerous, and the soil is excellent for raising grain.

The hills of Judæa are drier, with fewer fountains or permanent brooks, and the soil is poorer and less productive than Galilee or Samaria, which are nearer the mountains. There are few plains and no high peaks. The forests are few, shrubs many, and orchards and vineyards are cultivated extensively.

The country S. of Hebron and Beersheba is called the South (NEGEB). In the hot season it is dry and parched, hot and dusty, but the first rains bring up the grass, and start the fresh leaf on the trees, and all through the winter it is a delightfully fresh and green pasture. Very few orchards and vineyards; fountains are rare, and wells numerous, with no running brooks, all being winter-torrents. Very little grain is raised. See GILEAD, HAURAN. 3. The mountains are a continuation of Lebanon, on the W. of Jordan, and of Anti-Lebanon on the E., ending at Hebron and Kerak, nearly. The highest peaks in both ranges are N. of the Holy Land, on each side of the Leontes river. On Lebanon there are Dhor el Khodib (thôr el kôdib), 10,051 ft.; Sunnin,

8,500; Keniseh, 6,824; and Tomat Niha (*twin-peaks*) 6,500; on Anti-Lebanon, Mt. Hermon, 10,000: the range runs N. E., and varies in hight from 4,500 to 7000 ft. The peaks S. of Hermon are, Osha, country are limestone, having few fossils. Over that there is a white cretaceous deposit, full of fossils, flints, ammonites, echinites (cidaris, petrified olives), fish, and others. This deposit is most noticeable on the western slopes of Lebanon, and the eastern slopes of Anti-Lebanon. Geodes of chalcedony, from an oz. weight to a 100 lbs., are numerous in Galilee, besides jasper and agate. Soft, friable sandstone, is found in extensive beds in both ranges. Coal is found near Beirut, in thin veins, and of poor quality. Iron and copper mines were worked anciently (Deut. viii. 9, xxxiii. 25; Eusebius viii. 15, 17). There are two kinds of limestone, the lower, white, and the upper, creamy, with streaks. The great quarry under Jerusalem (cut on p. 162), affords both kinds. The white (Arabic *melekeh*) is chalky, and may be easily cut, and sawed into blocks; the dark (Ar. *mezzeh*) is much harder, and takes a fine polish. Many of the caves are in limestone, some of which, as those in the north, at Paneas, and on the Dog river, are immense fountains. Many are used for storing grain, etc., and some for dwellings. The chalk deposits are found on summits only, N. of Hebron, as at Olivet, Bethlehem, Carmel, etc.; S. of Hebron it is more abundant, and near the surface, especially on the E. side of the Arabah, where the Romans named one place *Gypsaria* (Chalk-town). Flints are very abundant in the chalk on the W. shore of the Dead Sea. Sandstone is the under-stratum, in two layers, or series: one dusky-red, twisted, full of caverns, and colored with iron and other minerals, the other is dark grey, compact, bearing fossils—the chief underlying rock of the whole region E.

MAP OF
PALESTINE
in the time of
CHRIST.
Circles 5 miles.
▲ Ancient ruins.

5000, near Es Salt (Ramoth Gilead); Nebo, 4,600, near Heshbon; and Zumla, E. of Gilead, about 4000 to 5000 ft. 4. The most remarkable feature of Palestine is the valley of the Jordan, the ancient Arabah (see ARABAH; DEAD SEA; JORDAN).

GEOLOGY. The great masses of rock under the

of Jordan. The chalk is of not so recent a deposit on the E. of Jordan, and is capped with a soft, friable sandstone, without fossils. The Abarim mountains are different, being sandstone, capped with chalk, bearing fossils. The red sandstone appears at Kerak. Both the sandstone and the limestone, on the E. are of an earlier age than those on the W. of Jordan. At Zurka Main, and at Wady Mojib, they form cliffs 400 ft. high. From Hermon to Kerak the whole region is limestone; 1000 ft. higher than Canaan, W. of Jordan.

EARTHQUAKES have been frequent, even in the historical period, the most noted, since that in the days of Uzziah, being those at Aleppo, in 1616–1812; Antioch, 1737; Laodicea, Beirut, Sidon, Tyre, Safed, and Tiberias, 1837. The principal sources of lava-streams on the E. of Jordan were at Phiala (so called), on Hermon, which is an extinct crater, now full of water; Tell Abu Tumeis; Kuleib; and El Hish, on Jebel Hauran, from which streams flowed over the whole district bounded by the Pharpar, the Jordan, and the Yarmuk. The Yarmuk was once dammed up by the stream from Phiala, and has made a new channel through the limestone beside the black basalt. There are many extinct craters in the Hauran (see TRACHONITIS, ARGOB). Lava and basalt have been traced eastward over the summits of Jebel Hauran (Alsadamum), but have not been followed beyond El Hish and Salcah. Basalt underlies Esdraelon, extending through the district bounded by Delata on the N. Tiberias on the E., Tabor on the S., and Turan and Sefuriyeh on the W. One centre of eruption was at Hattin—the most ancient—which sent out a stream of dark, iron-grey, solid, and massive basalt, towards the Sea of Galilee, forming cliffs near Tiberias, 500 ft. high, overlaying limestone; and another, more recent, from three craters near Safed, El Jish, Taiteba, and Delata, which poured out a dark brown and a reddish-grey lava—porous. The Arabah is a deep ditch, from Hermon to the Red Sea, with a dividing ridge (see AKRABBIM) just S. of the Dead Sea. The width is an average of 10 ms., and the surface is everywhere below the ocean level; being deepest at the Dead Sea, where it is 1312 ft. below in the wet, and 5 or 6 ft. lower in the dry season. Tertiary and alluvial deposits are found in the valley, along the whole course of the Jordan, and on both shores of the Dead Sea, at the mouths of the rivers. There are two terraces of chalky marl: the upper extending across from side to side, between the mountains, and the lower, 50 to 150 ft. below; forming a ditch in which the river has worn a still lower channel of 10 or 20 ft. deep. The whole plain is worn into rounded knolls, by water from the high land on both sides; most distinctly seen on the edges of the terraces.

The strata exposed are limestone, rolled boulders, pebbles of flint, sandstone, tufas, marl, chalky deposits, pure chalk, conglomerates, sand, gravel, clay and detritus. South of Massada there are tall, conical knolls, shaped like hay-stacks, with pointed tops.

The shores of the Dead Sea are cut down on all sides, through crystalline rocks, into ravines, 600 to 1200 feet deep, with traces of extinct waterfalls and other evidences of remote antiquity. At Wady Derejeh there are eight terraces of gravel, marking different beaches, one above another—the highest 14 feet above the present level. There is no evidence that the Dead Sea was ever connected with either the Mediterranean or the Red Sea; but it was at one time 350 feet higher than at present, if not 540, as we may learn from the chalky deposits at Wady Hasasah. The ocean level is marked very distinctly all around the sea, indicating that there has been no general disturbance since the present arrangement of strata was completed. See Mr. SEIR, MT. SINAI, RED SEA; also, CLIMATE, FLOWERS, TREES.

Mr. Tristam described 322 species of birds gathered by him and his party, and now safely deposited by him in a museum in London. Swimmers and waders were not well represented; 27 species are native to Palestine. He caught an ostrich in the Belka, east of the Dead Sea. (See the articles on the name of each bird). The whole country abounds in birds of every kind known in the temperate zone. Caged birds are found in almost every house.

Fish are caught in great plenty on the Great Sea and in Galilee; and one at least of its varieties is painted on the monuments in Egypt.

Reptiles are abundant, especially lizards, tortoises, geckos and chameleons. The common frog and tree-toad abound in wet places. Snakes are not very numerous, and none large. There are 3 species of scorpion. Mollusks are very numerous, in more than a hundred varieties. Butterflies are as numerous, in proportion, as the flowers.

TEMPLE OF DIANA.

PALESTI'NA (*Palestine*). (Heb. PELESHETH); (Ex. xv. 14; Is. xiv. 29; Joel iii. 4; in Ps. lx. 8. Philistia, which was a synonymous term at one time). Palestine in the Scripture means Philistia, only (which see)

PAL'LU (*distinguished*). Son of Reuben (Ex. vi. 14).

PAL'LUITES, THE. Descendants of Pallu (Num. xxvi. 5).

PALM'ERIST (*palm of Christ*). Castor-oil plant (Jon. iv. 6).

PALMER-WORM. A voracious, hairy caterpillar, which does great damage to fruit-trees, and other vegetation (Joel i. 4).

PALMO'NI ("*that certain*"). An expression used to designate a person without calling him by name (Dan. viii. 13).

PALM-TREE (Heb. TAMAR; Gr. *phoinix*). The variety most common in the East is the date-palm (*phœnix dactylifera*). The palm-tree was always associated with Palestine; the name Phœnix being probably derived from Phœnicia. The coins of Vespasian, commemorating the conquest of Jerusalem by Titus, represent a woman of Judæa, weeping under a palm-tree. The date-palm is endogenous (growing from the end); its average hight is about 70 ft. About 8 yrs. after being planted, it yields fruit, averaging about 100 lbs., and continues productive for 100 yrs. Dates take the place of bread to a large extent in the East, and all the other parts of the tree are used for building, fencing, roofs, mats, baskets, couches, bags, etc. There is a saying with the Arabs that "The palm-tree has 360 uses." Jericho, "The City of Palm-Trees" (Deut. xxxiv. 3; Judg. i. 16, iii. 13). The palm-groves of Jericho were always famous. See page 209.

HAZE'ZON-TAMAR (*the pruning of the palm-tree*). Is alluded to in Gen. xlv. 7, and in 2 Chr. xx. 2. TAMAR (*the palm*), in the vision of Ezekiel (Ez. xlvii. 19, xlviii. 28). BETHANY (*the house of dates*) suggests that there were palms in the district of the Mt. of Olives, whence the people "took branches of palm-trees and went forth to meet Him" (John xii. 13): "Dwelt under the palm-tree of Deborah" (Judg. iv. 5). Women were named after the palm-tree, as the wife of En, named TAMAR (Gen. xxxviii; also in 2 Sam. xiii. 1, and xiv. 27). Its form used in decoration in the Temple (2 Chr. iii. 5; 1 K. vi. 29, 32, 35, vii. 36), and in Ezekiel's vision (Ez. xl. 16, xli. 18). "The righteous shall flourish like the palm-tree" (Ps. xcii. 12). Its grace—the lofty and ever-green foliage, cresting the top of the tree, near to heaven—all suggest abundant illustration. The Jews commemorated victories by carrying palms (1 Macc. xiii. 51; Esd.

ii. 44-47), etc. Also, the glorified are mentioned in Rev. vii. 9, as "clothed with white robes, and palms in their hands. See DATES.

PAL'SY. (Gr. *paralusis, relaxation*). An abolition of function, whether of intellect, special sensation, or voluntary motion.

To destroy action or energy; *a disabling of the nerves* of a part of a body, afterward also *of the whole body* (Matt. iv. 24). The withered hand was an instance, cured by Jesus (Mark iii. 1).

PAL'TI (*deliverance of Jah*). Son of Raphu, a spy (Num. xiii. 9).

PAL'TIEL (*deliverance of God*), Son of Azzan and prince of Issachar (Num. xxiv. 26).

PAL'TITE (*descendants of Pelet, the*). One of David's men (2 Sam. xxiii. 26).

PAMPHY'LIA. A province of Asia (Minor), on the south coast, bordering the same sea as, and west of Cilicia (Acts xx. v. ii. 5). The sea is now called *Adalia*, from the ancient Attalia. The region was only 20 ms. wide, inland, between Taurus and the sea. Paul here first entered Asia, having just left Cyprus, landing at Perga (Acts xiii. 13), where John Mark left him and Barnabas. The language seems from Luke's account (Acts ii. 10), to have been corrupted to some local dialect. The region is now thinly peopled, with a few towns along the coast, in the midst of fine orchards, surrounded by fertile fields. Ruins here and there mark ancient sites.

PAN'NAG. Some kind of spice, or aromatic plant exported from Palestine at Tyre (Ezr. xxvii. 17). It may possibly have been a flavoring substance used in bread. The Syriac renders it millet.

PAPER-REEDS. PAPYRUS. "Paper reeds by the brooks" in Is. xix. 7, should read "meadows by the river" (Nile).

PANE'AS. (See CÆSAREA PHILIPPI.)

PA'PHOS. In Cyprus at the west end of the island (Salamis being at the east end and a road between); the seat of the Roman governor, Sergius Paulus, who "believed" after hearing Paul and Barnabas (Acts xiii. 12). Elymas (*magician, sorcerer*), was struck with blindness (for a season), as a punishment for deceiving people with his magic. They had a fine temple in honor of Aphrodite (Venus), who was worshiped, and was fabled to have risen from the sea at this place (Homer, Od. viii. 362). The temple was at a place now called *Kuklia*, some distance from the new town called *Baffa*.

COIN OF RHODES.

PAPY'RUS (*Reed*). (Heb. names: AGMON, GOME, AROTH, KANEH). A tall reed (3 to 6 ft., angular), with a broom-shape head, formerly lining the Nile banks, and growing elsewhere in marshes in Egypt and Palestine. Its lower part was used for food, after cooking. It is without leaves, and the pulp was used for making paper. Some ancient specimens of the papyrus (covered with writing and drawings), are to be found in the Abbott Museum, New York, (and in several museums in Europe). See page 106.

The several words translated reed in the A. A. are: 1. AGMON, *a rush.* In Job xl. 26, it is asked, "Canst thou put a rush through the nose of the crocodile?" as you do through the gills of a fish!— 2. GOME, *the papyrus, paper-reed;* translated rush and bulrush. The word occurs four times: when Moses was hid in a boat made of papyrus, in Ex. ii. 3; in the notice of the skiffs or canoes of the Ethiopians (Is. xviii. 2); and as a reed in Is. xxxv. 7, and in Job viii. 11. The stem is three inches thick at the base, and ten to sixteen feet long.

The Abyssinians use it for light boats. There were other similar plants of which boats were also made. See cut, Egyptians making a papyrus boat, on page 122.

The papyrus (paper) was made from the soft pulp, which is cellular, and could be sliced very thin. These slices were cut as long as the paper was to be wide, and were laid side by side, and other slips laid over the seams and gummed into place, until the whole was of the required size and thickness. The papyrus-reed grows in Syria, in the marsh of the Huleh (from which place Antigonus got it to make cordage for his ships), on Gennesaret, in Sicily, in Abyssinia, along the White Nile, and in Nubia.

There is another species in Palestine, growing near Caiffa, under Carmel. This has a top like an umbrella. The true papyrus hangs the top on one side, like a broom. See cut on page 106. The Arabs use both kinds for mats, roofs and walls for their huts.—3. AROTH (once only as paper-reeds in Is. xix. 7), green herbage, such as grows in wet, marshy places.—4. ACHU (flag in Job viii. 11, and meadow in Gen. xli. 2, 18). Some water-plant, eaten by cattle; perhaps the beautiful Flowering Rush, or it may be the Edible Rush.—5. SUF (flags in Ex. ii. 3, 5, where the boat containing Moses was laid; flags in Is. xix. 6, and reeds in Jonah ii. 5). Weeds. The Red Sea is called *Yam Suf*, by the Arabs—Sea of Weeds. Suf is a term for all marine vegetation.—6. KANEH, *a cane* (*stalk* of wheat or corn in Gen. xli. 5, 22; *branches* of a candlestick in Ex. xxv. 31; a measure equal to six cubits in Ez. xl. 5; and in anatomy, the name of the bone between the shoulder and the elbow in Job xxxi. 22).—7. Greek *kalamos*. Used for a reed growing, a measuring-rod (Rev. xi. 1, etc.), and a reed-pen (3 John 13).

There was a fragrant reed also, KENEH BOSEM (Ez xxx. 23), and KANEH HATTOB (Jer. vi. 20). The *Calamus aromaticus* is very fragrant, and is used for perfume in ointments. The lemon-grass is another aromatic reed or grass.

PAR'ABLE (Heb. MASHAL; Greek *parabole;* Latin *parabola*). A similitude, a comparison. See FABLE. The Hebrews used the term mashal (similitude) for the Proverbs (1 Sam. x. 12, xiv. 13), prophesy (Num. xxiii. 7), enigmas (Ps. lxxviii. 2), and narrative (Ez. xii. 22). The parable was used by the Hebrew teachers from the earliest times, and especially by Hillel, Shammai and other great Rabbis just before the Christian era. The parable is a low form of speech, adapted to the ignorance of the great mass of mankind. The Scribes had a kind of parable that was understood by the few only, and therefore it is said that the Sermon on the Mount was open and plain instruction, and "not as the Scribes." Jesus chose this form of teaching the people, who were spiritually blind and deaf (Matt. xiii. 13). The parable attracts, and if understood, is remembered, yet sometimes the meaning is lost. There were probably many spoken which were not recorded (ib. 34). The number is about 30 or 31.

The parables of Jesus are the most characteristic and beautiful portions of his teachings, full of interest to the youngest and instruction to the oldest, conveying, in delightful narratives, the profoundest truths relating to his kingdom, of which we become sensible in proportion as our views of religion rise into the spiritual and ideal. All outward things take on a fuller meaning and have a richer color and brighter light. The great object of Jesus was to manifest himself, and his parables do this by laying bare the hearts of men.

The interpretation of the parables belongs to the highest order of Biblical exegesis, requiring knowledge, spiritual discernment, taste and tact, and a well-balanced mind. There are no rules applicable to this work.

It may be noticed that there seems to be but one leading idea in each parable. The aim is ethical, and is not poetical, the story being told for the sake of the lesson.

It is extremely difficult to classify the parables. The chronological order is given as near as may be in the article JESUS. It does not appear that they were delivered in any order or sequence, but in answer to inquiries, or called forth by certain circumstances from time to time. In the following table only one reference is given; the others can be found in the article JESUS.

GROUP 1.—RELATING TO CHRIST'S KINGDOM.
1. Wicked Husbandmen (Matt. xxi. 33-44). The fate of those who abuse their privileges and refuse to enter the kingdom.
2. The Rich Fool (Luke xii. 16-21). The vanity of all worldly things without the kingdom.
3. The Marriage of the King's Son (Matt. xxii. 1-14). Danger of rejecting the invitations of the kingdom.
4. The Barren Fig-tree (Luke xiii. 6-9). Danger of delay.
5. The Great Supper (Luke xiv. 15-24). Outward privileges useless without a personal use of the means of salvation.
6. The Pearl of Great Price (Matt. xiii. 45, 46). The kingdom to be sought for alone.
7. The Hid Treasure (Matt. xiii. 44). Sacrifice for the kingdom when found.
8. The Rich Man and Lazarus (Luke xvi. 19-31). The kingdom in the estimate of God and of man.

GROUP 2.—CHRIST'S KINGDOM IN THE HEART.
9. The Sower (Matt. xiii. 3-8). Preparation of the heart.
10. The Seed Growing Secretly (Mark iv. 26-29). The kingdom grows in the heart silently and constantly.

GROUP 3.—MANIFESTATION OF THE KINGDOM.
14. The Two Debtors (Luke vii. 41-43). The kingdom appears in obedience springing from love.
15. The Good Samaritan (Luke x. 30-37). Aid in love, which knows no limits and spares no pains.
16. The Two Sons (Matt. xxi. 28). In the obedience of deeds not words.
17. The Unmerciful Servant (Matt. xviii. 23-35). In mercy and forgiveness without limit.
18. The Unjust Steward (Luke xvi. 1-9). In wise and energetic improvement of temporal advantages.
19. The Friend at Midnight (Luke xi. 5-8). In constant prayer.
20. The Unjust Judge (Luke xviii. 1-8). Persevering prayer.
21. The Pharisee and Publican (Luke xviii. 9-14). In humility and contrition.
22. The Laborers in the Vineyard (Matt. xx. 1-16). Unselfish rejoicing in the salvation of others.
23. The Lost Sheep (Matt. xvii).
24. The Lost Piece of Money (Luke xv. 8-10).
25. The Prodigal Son (Luke xv. 11-32).
 In acknowledging the wisdom and beauty of receiving sinners, and in a missionary spirit.
26. The Unprofitable Servant (Luke xvii. 7-10). Confessing all that we can do is nothing.
27. The Ten Virgins (Matt. xxv. 1-13). Preparation for the coming of the Lord.
28. The Talents (Matt. xxv. 14-30). Active preparation for the coming of the Lord.

GROUP 4.—THE CONSUMMATION OF THE KINGDOM.
29. The Pounds (Luke xix. 11-27). The final reckoning.
30. The Draw-net (Matt. xiii. 47-50). The final separation.

PA′RAH (*cow*). Five miles N. E. of Jerusalem. The name is continued in *Wady Farah* (*mouse*), the Arabs keeping the *sound* only of the ancient name, as they have done in many other cases. Dr. Barclay claims this wady for the ancient locality of ÆNON, where John was baptizing; for there is a large intermitting fountain there (John iii. 23; City of the Great King, 558). Khurbet Farah (*ruin of*) lies on the fork between Wady Tuwar and Wady Farah (Josh. xviii. 23).

PA′RAN (*place of caves*). Name of a mountain and a wilderness. The mountain is only mentioned in two poetical passages (Deut. xxxiii. 2; Hab. iii. 3). This name is preserved in Wady FARAN

WADY FARAN.

11. The Tares and the Wheat (Matt. xiii. 24-30). Difficulties in the way of the kingdom.
12. The Mustard-seed (Matt. xiii. 31, 32). Outward growth of the kingdom.
13. The Leaven in the Meal (Matt. xiii. 33). Inward growth.

(*faran*), in Sinai; and the mountain is probably that now called Serbal, one of the grandest in the region (*Bartlett*, Forty Days; *Stanley*). The wilderness is described minutely in the Scriptures; and had Palestine on the north, Arabah on the east, and Sinai on the south; corresponding to the

PAR'BAR (1 Chr. xxvi. 18). An open porch, or some structure on the west side of the Temple court.

PARCHED GROUND. In Is. xxxv. 7. Heb. SHARAB, should be read "mirage," a peculiar deceptive appearance of the heated air, by which you are led to think you see trees, houses, water, etc., at a distance.

GREEK PARTRIDGE.

PAR'LOR. The king's audience chamber (Judg. iii. 20–25).

PARMASH'TA (*superior*). Son of Haman (Esth. ix. 9).

PAR'MENAS (*abiding*). A deacon (Acts vi. 5).

PAR'NACH (*delicate*). Ancestor of Elizaphan (Num. xxxiv. 25).

PA'ROSH (*a flea*). 2,172 descendants of Parosh who returned from captivity (Ezr. ii. 3). Another 150 males accompanied Ezra (Ezr. viii. 3). They assisted in building the wall of Jerusalem (Neh. iii. 25), and sealed the covenant (x. 14).

PARSHAN'DATHA (*interpreter*). Eldest of Haman's sons, slain by the Jews (Esth ix. 7).

PART. (Heb. PELECH, *circuit or district*). Used in reference to Jerusalem, Beth-haccerem, Mizpah, Beth-zur and Keilah (Neh. iii. 9).

PARTHIA (Acts ii. 9). The Parthians here meant were Jews only, who were present at Jerusalem on the day of Pentecost. Originally it was a small mountainous district N. E. of Media, between Aria and Hyrcania, but afterward included a large district. The country is mountainous, climate pleasant, soil fertile, well watered by many small streams (which do not reach the seas, but are absorbed in the ground), and has many ruins of ancient cities, such as Ctesiphon, Akker-kuf, El Hammam and Takt-i-Bostan, some of the most remarkable Oriental remains, which are evidence of a former state of prosperity and wealth. It is now a part of Persia. The first known of this Scythian people is of the time of Darius Hystaspis; although it is supposed that Cyrus annexed their territory to his empire (B. C. 550). They were in Xerxes' great army in Greece. Alexander gave their country to Eumenes. The Parthian Empire began under Arsaces, B. C. 256, and extended from the Tigris to India, and from the Chorasmian desert to the Southern Ocean. It was the only power that opposed Rome with final success. The Roman general, Crassus, was defeated by them at Carrhæ (Harran). (*R. K. Porter*).

PAR'TRIDGE (KORE). The desert partridge, used as a simile by David when pursued by Saul (Sam. xxvi. 20), and as a simile of a man who reaps what he does not sow (Jer. xvii. 11). They are very prolific, laying 20 or more eggs. There are several species in Palestine. The word KORE may also include the black partridge of India and the sand grouse, which latter is very common in Syria.

PARU'AH (*blossoming*). Father of Jehoshaphat (1 K. iv. 17).

PARVA'IM. From whence gold was brought for the ornamentation of the Temple (2 Chr. iii. 6). The Sephar of Gen. x. 30, which was a mountain, and probably the same as Ophir. Others hold that Parvaim means Eastern, as the modern *Levant* does, and therefore say that the text means only eastern gold. Pliny mentions a Barbatia on the Tigris (vi. 32).

PA'SACH (*cut up*). Son of Japhlet (1 Chr. vii. 33).

PASDAM'MIM (*hand of confusion*). Ephes Dammim (1 Chr. xi. 13). Where a fierce conflict with the Philistines occurred. *Damun* is a ruin, 3 miles east of Socho, but it is not identified beyond dispute.

PASE'AH (*lame*). 1. Son of Eshton (1 Chr. iv. 12).—2. Ancestor of Nethinim, who returned from captivity (Ezr. ii. 49). PHASEAH.—3. Ancestor of the Jehoiada who assisted in repairs of the "old gate" (Neh. iii. 6).

PASH'UR (*prosperity*). 1. Son of Malchiah, one of the princes in the court (Jer. xxxviii. 1). The name of a family of priests of the house of Malchijah (Jer. xxi. 1).—2. Another priest, son of IMMER, and governor of the house of the Lord. He was opposed to Jeremiah in Jehoiakim's reign, and for this indignity his name was changed to MAGOR-MISSABIB (*terror on every side*), (xx. 1–6).—3. Father of GEDALIAH 4 (xxxviii. 1).

PAS'SAGE (Heb. EBER, MAABAR, MAEBARAH). A river ford or mountain pass (1 Sam. xiii. 23). See JORDAN.

PAS'SENGERS (Heb. OBERIM). Those who go right on their ways. "The valley of the passengers" means the valley where Gog's multitude were to be buried (Ez. xxxix. 11).

PASSION. Suffering of the Lord JESUS CHRIST on the cross (Acts i. 3).

PASS'OVER (Heb. PESACH; Greek *Pascha*). The first of the three great annual festivals of the Hebrews, held in Nisan, 14th to 21st. There are several distinct passages relating to the Passover in Exodus and Deuteronomy, where its original intention, the unleavened bread, the first-born sanctified, are mentioned, and the paschal lamb. In Ex. xxiii. 14–19, the paschal lamb is mentioned as My Sacrifice, and the feast is called "of unleavened bread." The redemption of the first-born is noticed in xxiv. 18–26. In Deut. xvi. 1–8, the command is given to keep the passover in Jerusalem. A lamb was roasted whole—not a bone of it to be broken—and eaten entirely, the same night, with bitter herbs; if not all eaten, the remnant to be burnt. The blood of the victim was to be sprinkled on the door-post.

The meaning was to commemorate the Exodus from Egypt, when the Lord passed over the first-born of the Hebrews and smote those of the Egyptians. The Rabbis affixed the penalty of whipping to any one who should not kill the paschal lamb in the Court of the Temple, and separated the people into three companies at that time to avoid confusion. During the killing trumpets were blown and the Hallel was sung by the Levites. See LORD'S SUPPER, AGAPE.

The position of sitting down to the meal or reclining was adopted by the Hebrews as a sign of their freedom, as though just out of Egypt.

The use of wine had no place in the original institution, but was sanctioned by Jesus both in the Passover and the Lord's Supper.

It has been debated whether the Lord ate the

Passover the last time on the same day as the Jews did or the evening before; but the frequent references to the event by all the Evangelists, without hesitation as to the time, leaves no doubt that it was eaten at the usual time. The Sadducees and Pharisees differed as to the proper day.

Jesus, the Christ, was himself the Paschal Lamb, the spiritual Passover, of whom the Hebrew rite was a type.

PAS'TOR (Heb. ROEH, *a shepherd*), (Jer. ii. 8); also applied to CHRIST, the Great "Shepherd" (Jer. xxvi. 31), and to the spiritual ministers of a church (Eph. iv. 11). BISHOP. ELDERS.

PAS'TURE. To those who had large flocks and herds, an abundance of pasturage and water were of great importance. ABRAHAM, ISAAC, and JACOB, moved from place to place in order to obtain these essentials. Palestine is well adapted to grazing. Figuratively it is applied to the spiritual wants of the people of God (Ps. xxiii. 2). PASTON.

PAT'ARA. The seaport of Xanthus, near the coast, in Lycia. It was devoted to the worship of Apollo (Hor. Odes, iii. 4, 64), and the coins of the district exhibit traces of the respect paid to the divinity. Some of the ruins—among which are a triple arch of a gate of the city, and a ruined theatre, baths, temples, etc.—indicate a once populous and important city; such as it probably was at the time of Paul's visit (Acts xxi. 1, 2), when it was an emporium of commerce between the east and west coasts of the Levant (see Livy, xxxvii. 16; Beaufort's *Karamania, Ionian Ant. of the Dilettanti Soc.*, and Fellows).

PATHE'US. PETHAHIAH, the Levite (1 Esd. ix. 23).

on a hill, to the S. is the monastery of "St. John the Divine" (built by Alexius Comnenus). In the library of this church are many ancient MSS., two of which contain an account of John after the Ascension. There are no forest-trees, but many flowering shrubs and plants. Walnut and fruit-trees are grown in orchards; and the wine is famous for its strength and flavor. Now called Patina, and Palmosa. Pop. 4,000. (See *Patmos and the Seven Churches*).

PAT'ROBAS. A Christian at Rome (Rom. xvi. 14).

PATRO'CLUS (*famous from his father*). Father of Nicanor (2 Macc. viii. 9).

PA'U (*bleating*). The capital of Hadar (Gen. xxxvi. 39).

PAUL (Heb. SAUL). He was a Benjamite, a native of Tarsus, Cilicia, and was born about A. D. 5, a free Roman citizen (by descent from his father). He had a sister (whose son is mentioned), and perhaps other sisters, some of whose names may possibly be those given by Paul in his Epistle to the Romans, as Andronicus, Junia, and Herodion. Tarsus was then the rival of Athens and Alexandria as a seat of learning, where Paul began that acquaintance with the classical writers which was continued when he went to Jerusalem as a pupil of Gamaliel, who was a strict Pharisee, and well known by his title of "The Glory of the Lord," and "Rabban" (Our Master). It seems to have been the intention of his parents to fit him for the rabbinical profession. It was the custom to teach every son a trade, and he was brought up to the making of tent-cloth (from goats' hair, called cilicia). These black tents are now

PATMOS.

PATH'ROS. A district in Egypt, and a Mizraite tribe.

PA'TRIARCH (Greek *patriarches*). Head of a family or tribe (Heb. vii. 4; Acts vii. 8, ii. 29). It is a title of many of the ancestors of the Hebrews, as David, Abraham, Noah.

They were the head of the religious faith and practice, as well as leader and judge in civil affairs, and represented God who is the great father of all men. When the Temple worship took the place of family worship the patriarch became a sheikh, and was no longer a priest.

The Arabs still keep up this form of government in civil affairs, but not in religious.

PAT'MOS (Rev. i. 9). A rocky island, S. of Samos—one of the Sporades, in the Icarian Sea, a part of the Ægean Sea—15 ms. around; divided almost in two by a narrow isthmus, on the E. side of which are the town and harbor, and near them,

used in Syria, and are mentioned by the ancient poets. While yet a young man he showed a great zeal for the law of Moses (Judaism), in consenting and assisting at the stoning of Stephen, by holding the cloaks of those who threw the stones. The main events of his life, as given by Luke, and by himself, are:—His conversion; labors at Antioch; the first missionary journey, in which he assumed the character of the Apostle to the Gentiles; the visit to Jerusalem, to settle the relation of the Gentile and Jewish converts; the introduction of the Gospel into Europe; the third missionary journey, during which time he wrote the four great Epistles; the arrest, imprisonment, voyage to Rome, and death. The chronology and details are given in the table below. Personally, Paul is almost unknown to us, unless we accept tradition and the statements of the ancients. The portrait given (p. 237) represents the idea that the artist formed

of him hundreds of years after his death, and it is only interesting to us as a relic of early Christian art. From the Gospels we learn that he was of a subtile, tenacious and versatile intellect; intolerant before, but, after his conversion, tolerant of the opinions of others; of a weak bodily presence, and a poor voice; but full of fresh ideas, and so thoroughly systematic and persistent as to deserve the name of the chief founder of the Christian Church.

Stephen is called the forerunner of Paul ("the blood of the first martyr, the seed of the greatest apostle"); and he was his anticipator in spirit and power, as may be seen in his defense before the Sanhedrin, wherein he gave a critically just and true summary of the Jewish Church—denouncing the local worship, and bringing out the spiritual element in its history. The substance of the whole speech, and its style, seems to have been thrown over Paul's spirit, like the mantle of the prophet.

His mission to Damascus was to arrest the disciples of Jesus there, and bring them to Jerusalem for trial and punishment, as apostates from the Jewish Church. On the way he was arrested by a miracle, converted by receiving knowledge of the truth; was consecrated by Ananias; and, after his recovery from the temporary blindness, began his work for the new cause, in the synagogue at Damascus, by preaching Jesus the Christ to the Jews, and Jesus the Son of God to the Gentiles.

His preaching naturally excited the rage of his late friends and employers, who regarded him as an apostate and a dangerous man, and aimed at his life; when he was obliged to escape from the city by night, his friends letting him down from a window in the wall in a basket. See DAMASCUS.

His return to Jerusalem (after three years' absence), as a disciple, only caused alarm to the brethren, who remembered his zeal against them, in the case of Stephen and as the highpriest's officer, until he was introduced as a believer by Barnabas. Being driven out of the city in a short time by the Jews, he returned by Cæsarea to Tarsus, from whence he was summoned by Barnabas to come to Antioch to help in the gospel work. On account of the famine, predicted by Agabus, Barnabas and Saul were sent to Jerusalem with a contribution for the poor there; and on their return, John Mark (nephew of Barnabas), accompanied them as an assistant.

It was on the first missionary journey, while they were in Cyprus, that his name was changed from Saul to Paul, which was the Greek form of the name,—as Jason is for Jesus, Pollio for Hillel, Alphæus for Clopas, etc.

Paul and Barnabas were again sent to Jerusalem, to have a decision made, by the apostles and elders, on the question of circumcision; when Peter declared the fact that God himself had set the seal of the gift of the Holy Ghost on the Gentile as well as on the Jew convert.

HEAD-DRESS.

Before setting out on his second missionary journey Paul separated from Barnabas, because he could not trust Mark, who had left them at a critical time on their first journey; so Paul took Silas instead of Barnabas, and Barnabas took Mark with him. The business of the next year was founding churches in Phrygia and Galatia, which he did with great success.

In a vision, the spirit of Jesus turned him back from Bithynia; and while at Troas, in the form of a man of Macedonia (in another vision), directed him to carry the gospel into Europe, in the memorable words, "Come over into Macedonia and help us."

The style of the narrative in Acts intimates, in the change from "they" to "we," that Luke, the writer went with Paul from Troas.

They preached from city to city for nearly a year, and passed on into Greece (to Athens). Here he set forth the gospel in the synagogue, the market-place, and, by invitation, in the venerable assembly of the Areopagus, where were gathered the most polished men of the foremost seat of learning in the world, who were acute, witty, shrewd, and most intensely scornful. He exposed the folly of their superstitions with exquisite tact and ability, and unfolded the character and claims of the "unknown God" whom they were already worshiping unintelligently. But he made very little impression on the popular religion, probably because his simple faith, having no splendid show of material accession, could not be expected to take the place of their highly poetical mythology, which was celebrated by the most magnificent displays of temples, vestments, processions, and sacrifices.

A year and a half in Corinth was spent in preaching and working at his trade, with better results than at Athens.

Again at Ephesus, he made so many friends that the idol-makers became alarmed for the business, and stirred up a tumult against Paul. They made small copies of the temple and image of Diana, which were used in private houses, or carried on journeys; and Paul declared that they were "no gods," but that Jesus the Christ was the only proper object of worship as the Son of God. See EPHESUS and SEVEN CHURCHES.

After another visit to Macedonia, Greece, and Illyria, he turned toward Jerusalem for the fifth and last time. On the way there occurred, at Miletus, one of the most affecting incidents in the whole story of his life. The elders of the church at Ephesus had come to Miletus to meet him. He was over sixty years of age, naturally feeble of body, always a hard worker, and it seemed probable that this was their last interview. He recalled his labors among them, assuring them that his single object had always been the preaching the gospel of Jesus; and referred to the dangers through which they all had passed, and those that the Holy Spirit had predicted were to come, and to his determination to press on, as though his life was in his hand, and entreated them to follow him for the sake of their Lord Jesus.

The visit to Jerusalem seemed to his friends at Cæsarea also to be dangerous; and Agabus, who had 17 years before proved himself a prophet, showed Paul that he would be put in bonds if he went up to the city.

The story cannot be told in better words than Luke uses, in the 21st and the following chapters of Acts. His enemies had determined on his destruction, and watched for an opportunity, and were finally compelled to invent an accusation on the pretext that Paul had taken some Greeks into the Temple, and thereby had broken the Law of Moses, and had polluted the Holy House. He was rescued from the furious mob of Jews by the Roman soldiers, and also protected on account of his Roman citizenship; but was for years kept in chains, without trial, with occasional examinations before the governor and the king (which, it is more than suspected, were for the purpose of extorting a bribe from Paul or his friends), and was finally sent to Rome, on his appeal to Cæsar. Luke's account of the voyage has been most severely criticised, and found to agree with the nature of the region, climate, winds, coasts, habits and superstitions of the people, and even the make of the ships at that age; and since its purpose was to follow the spiritual Paul chiefly, has been shown to

be one of the finest and truest records extant (see MELITA).

Of Paul's death almost nothing is known. Tradition affirms that he was beheaded at Rome, where a grave is now shown, which is honored with a monument.

His personal appearance had little to command admiration, or even respect. A small figure, a bald head, with weak eyes and a hooked nose, like some of the Jews of our day—and, added to these, feeble health—makes a whole that would excite, besides ridicule, only sympathy, until we become acquainted with the great soul and ardent spirit that was the tenant of this poor frame.

PAUL.
Engraved on copper an ideal portrait, found in a cemetery, dated 450. A. D.

He is one of the most wonderful characters known to history. Called to a peculiar work, he was most peculiarly adapted to that work from nature, education and circumstances, and most nobly did he succeed. His labor in establishing the Church in many cities and countries occupied nearly thirty years of constant application—in traveling, preaching, writing and working with his own hands at his trade; some of the time, even while a prisoner, chained to a guard, or in a cell, writing, when he was "ready to be offered," in his death at the age of nearly 70 years. See ROME.

He was a poor mechanic, and in the eyes of the Greeks and Romans was of an origin as hateful as that of the Jews, who are called the enemies of mankind; and, as his enemies said, he was of a bodily presence that was weak, and had a contemptible speech; yet he did more than any other man to set in motion those new ideas that were to lift mankind up out of the darkness of superstition, purify their minds from the errors of ages, open their hearts to the great truths of the oneness of God, and the brotherhood of men, and the value of a good and true life; enforcing these great truths by a life equally great, full of bravery, self-sacrifice, and self-denial, and which have gained power to crush and scatter the Paganism of the Greek and Roman world.

This work was not done without pain, and danger, and toil. From the very beginning he suffered hardship, risk of life from his former associates; continued in long journeys by sea and land; shipwreck; stoning by an infuriated mob; exposure to the fury of wild beasts in the amphitheatre; and finally loss of life by violence.

If privation, suffering, patience, and perseverance—warmed by zeal and tempered with wisdom and love, elevated and polished by scholarship and brilliant talents, inspired with the knowledge of the Divine Spirit, and all these qualities softened with a charming urbanity that was never laid aside—if all these rare endowments can build an enduring memorial in the earth, surely among the immortals in the memory of men will be found, along with the names of Adam, Moses, David, Solomon, and Jesus, the noble name of Paul the Apostle. Already his epistles are printed in a hundred and fifty languages; read by as many millions, and churches are dedicated to his name in every Christian city in the world.

TABLE OF EVENTS IN THE LIFE OF PAUL THE APOSTLE.

A. D.			
5 Born in Tarsus, in Cilicia	Acts	xxii.	3
A Roman citizen by birthright. A Pharisee	Phil.	iii.	5
By trade a tent-maker. (Goat's hair—Cilicia)	Acts	xviii.	3
20 At the school of Gamaliel, Jerusalem	"	xxii.	3
30 Assists in stoning Stephen	"	vii.	58
Makes havoc of the Church	"	viii.	4
36 Goes to Damascus to persecute the disciples	"	ix.	2
Baptized. Begins to preach Jesus the Crucified	"	ix.	18, 20
Journey into Arabia; return to Damascus	Gal.	i.	17, 18
38 Escape from Damascus in a basket (2 Cor. xi. 31)	Acts	ix.	25
Goes up to Jerusalem. Disciples afraid of him	"	"	26
Introduced by Barnabas; preach'd the Lord Jesus	"	"	27
39 Driven out of Jerusalem; goes to Tarsus	"	"	30
40 At Antioch. Preaches to the Gentiles	"	xi.	25
Disciples first called Christians in Antioch	"	"	26
Two Roman, three Jewish scourgings (2 Cor. xi. 24–26).			
42 Agabus prophesies a famine	"	"	28
44 Barnabas and Saul sent to Jerusalem with money	"	"	30
45 Joined by Mark, Barnabas' sister's son	"	xii.	25
46 Barnabas and Saul "separated" for the work	"	xiii.	2
FIRST MISSIONARY JOURNEY. Antioch to Seleucia	"	"	4
In Cyprus at Salamis. Paphos	"	"	8
Saul's name changed to Paul. Elymas blinded	"	"	9
Sailed from Paphos to Perga, in Pamphylia	"	"	13
Antioch in Pisidia. Discourse to the Jews	"	"	14
The Gospel preached to the Gentiles	"	"	46
Paul and Barnabas expelled from Pisidia	"	"	50
They come to Iconium	"	"	51
To Lystra. A cripple healed	"	xiv.	6
The people propose to sacrifice to them	"	"	13
Paul stoned, and supposed to be dead	"	"	19
He recovers, and they go to Derbe	"	"	20
Lystra, Iconium, and Antioch	"	"	21
Passed through Pisidia to Pamphylia	"	"	24
Preached in Perga, Attalia, and Antioch	"	xiv.	25, 26
48 End of the first missionary journey	"	"	27
50 Visit to Jerusalem with Barnabas and Titus (Gal. ii.).			
51 The Council at Jerusalem	"	xv.	
Barnabas and Silas sent with Paul to Antioch	"	"	22
Paul and Barnabas preach in Antioch	"	"	35
THE SECOND MISSION'Y JOURN'Y	"	"	36
Paul and Silas go through Syria and Cilicia	"	"	41

	A.D.		
Derbe. Lystra. Timothy called to help	"	xvi.	
Phrygia, Galatia, Mysia (Gal. i. 2)	"	"	6
52 Forbidden by the Spirit to go into Bithynia	"	"	7
Troas. Paul's vision, "Come over and help us"	"	"	9
Samothracia and Neapolis. Philippi	"	"	12
Lydia of Thyatira baptized	"	"	15
Slave girl cured of sorcery	"	"	18
Paul and Cyrus whipped and imprisoned	"	"	22
Delivered from prison	"	"	25
Amphipolis. Apollonia. Thessalonica	"	xvii.	
Jason persecuted on account of Paul and Silas	"	"	9
They go to Berea	"	"	10
Paul goes to Athens. Silas and Timothy remain	"	"	15
Discourse to the Greeks on Mars' Hill	"	"	22
Dionysius and Damaris believe	"	"	34
53 Corinth. Tent-making with Aquila and Priscilla	"	xviii.	1
Silas and Timothy join him at Corinth	"	"	5
The two epistles to the Thessalonians written.			
Crispus and many Corinthians believe	"	"	8
Paul before Gallio, the proconsul. Sosthenes beaten	"	"	13
54 On the way to Jerusalem. At Ephesus	"	"	18

SILOAM.

Cæsarea. Jerusalem. Antioch. (Dispute with Peter. Gal. ii.) Acts		xviii.	22
THIRD MISSIONARY JOURNEY. Galatia and Phrygia	"	"	23
Epistle to the Galatians written at Ephesus.			
Apollos instructed by Aquila and Priscilla	"	"	24

	A.D.		
56 Paul baptizes and gives the Holy Ghost	"	xix.	
Two years in the hall of Tyrannus	"	"	
Special miracles wrought by Paul	"	"	
Books of divination burned	"	"	19
Supposed visit to Corinth (2 Cor. xii. 14, xiii. 1).			
57 First Epistle to the Corinthians written at Ephesus.			
Plans another journey, and sends Timothy and Erastus	"	"	21
Great tumult raised by Demetrius in the theatre	"	"	23
Departs for Macedonia	"	xx.	1
Timothy joins Paul at Philippi (2 Cor. i. 1, xiii. 14).			
Second Epistle to the Corinthians sent by Titus.			
Travels through Macedonia as far as Illyria (Rom. xv. 19).			
58 Corinth. Epistle to the Romans.			
Luke joins Paul at Corinth	"	"	5
Troas. Eutychus killed by a fall, and restored	"	"	12
By land to Assos; by ship to Mitylene	"	"	14
Chios. Samos. Trogyllium. Miletus	"	"	17
Coos. Rhodes. Patara, past Cyprus to Tyre	"	xxi.	3
Urged not to go to Jerusalem	"	"	4
59 Ptolemais (Acre). Cæsarea, at Philip's house	"	"	8
Agabus prophesies Paul's danger at Jerusalem	"	"	11
Fifth and last visit to Jerusalem	"	"	17
Performs the Nazarite's vow in the Temple	"	"	26
The Jews arrest him in the Temple	"	"	30
Beaten by the Jews, rescued by the Romans	"	"	32
Bound with chains	"	"	33
Paul's defense, spoken in the Hebrew tongue	"	xxii.	1
Persecuted for his mission to the Gentiles	"	"	22
Saved by his Roman citizenship	"	"	27
Before the council. Ananias the high priest	"	xxiii.	1
The dispute between Pharisees and Sadducees	"	"	6
Vision of the Lord Jesus. Paul cheered	"	"	11
Conspiracy of the Jews to kill him	"	"	12
The plot exposed by his sister's son to Claudius Lysias	"	"	16
Paul sent under guard to Antipatris	"	"	31
Delivered to Felix at Cæsarea	"	"	35
Accused by Tertullus	"	xxiv.	1
Paul defends himself before Felix	"	"	10
Plot of the high priest to kill him (Festus)	"	xxv.	3
Paul before Festus	"	"	6, 7
Paul appeals to Cæsar	"	"	10
He is brought before Agrippa and Bernice	"	"	23
Defends himself before the king and queen	"	xxvi.	
60 Paul sent to Rome with other prisoners	"	xxvii.	
Sidon. Cyprus. Sea of Cilicia and Pamphylia	"	"	5
Myra in Lycia, Cnidus, Crete, Salome	"	"	7
Fair Havens, near Lasea	"	"	8

PAVILION 239 PELAIAH

	A. D.	
Aug.—Storm in Adria. Clauda	Acts xxvii.	14
The ship lightened by casting overboard the tackle	"	19
Vision of the angel by Paul	"	23
Prophesies the events of the voyage	"	26
All escaped safe to land. Ship wrecked	"	44
A viper fastens on Paul's hand. Malta	Acts xxviii.	3
The father of Publius healed by Paul	"	8
After three months they sail for Syracuse	"	11, 12
Rhegium, Puteoli, Appii Forum	"	13
Three Taverns	"	13-15
61 Rome. In his own house	"	16
He persuades the Jews	"	23
62 Writes to Philemon, Colossians, Ephesians and Philippians at Rome.		
63 Goes to Macedonia (Phil. ii. 24).		
Asia Minor (Phil. xx. ii.).		
64 Spain. Supposed visit (Rom. xv. 24).		
66 Asia Minor (1 Tim. i. 3).		
67 Writes First Epistle to Timothy from Macedonia.		
Epistle to Titus from Ephesus. Nicopolis.		
68 In prison at Rome. Writes Second Epistle to Timothy.		
Beheaded in May or June.		

VOTIVE OFFERING.

PAVIL′ION. A general term for an awning or tent. Three different words are thus translated in the Scriptures: "He shall hide me in his pavilion," in Ps. xxvii. The Heb. *soc* means a hut. In Jer. xliii. 10, Nebuchadnezzar is alluded to as "spreading his royal pavilion"—the word SHAFRUR or SHAFRIR is the one used—meaning bright, or rich tapestry, famed in Babylonian times.

PE (PE, *mouth*). The 17th letter of the Hebrew alphabet (Ps. cxix). WRITING.

PEACE (Heb. SHALOM, *soundness, health, welfare, prosperity*). "Peace be unto thee" (Judg. vi. 23; 1 K. ii. 33; Ps. xxxvii. 11, 37, etc.). Peace as the opposite of war: "And I will give peace in the land" (Lev. xxvi. 6; Judg. iv. 17, etc.). Peace, as friendship, in Ps. xxviii. 3, xli. 9. "Peace be unto you," was a common form of Eastern salutation (John xx. 19, 21, 26, etc.); "Your peace!" (Matt. x. 13). See SALUTATION.

PEACE-OFFERING (Heb. SHELEM); (Lev. iii.-vii. 11). There were three kinds: 1. Praise or thanksgiving. 2. Votive. 3. Voluntary or free-will offerings. The sacrifice was accompanied by an offering of "unleavened cakes mingled with oil, and unleavened wafers anointed with oil, or fine flour, fried" (Lev. vii. 12-13). From the peace-offering the fat was burned on the altar; the right shoulder of the animal sacrificed was given to the priest; the breast was a *wave-offering*. The rest was to be eaten by the offerer upon the day of offering. This was the characteristic of the peace-offering, suggesting, figuratively, peace with God. See OFFERING; SACRIFICE.

PEA′COCK (Heb. TUKIIM). Imported into Palestine through the Tarshish navies of King Solomon (1 K. x. 22; 2 Chr. ix. 21). The importation of peacocks is named with that of ivory and apes. The birds were probably brought from India or Ceylon, where there is reason to believe the navies visited. (See TARSHISH.) The Cingalese word (*tokei*) for peacock, bears a close resemblance to the Hebraic.

PEARL (Heb. GABISH). They are formed inside the shells of several species of *mollusca*, and consist of carbonate of lime and animal matter; are hard and smooth, and have a silvery-white lustre. Pearls were held among the most precious stones in the ancient world. Their beauty is due to Nature, alone, as they are not improved by Art. The "pearl of great price" is a fine specimen yielded by the pearl oyster, which is found in the Persian Gulf (Matt. xiii. 45, 46).

PED′AHEL (*God delivers*). Son of Ammihud (Num. xxxiv. 28).

PEDAH′ZUR (*God delivers*). Father of Gamaliel (Num. i. 10).

PEDAI′AH (*Jah delivers*). 1 Father of Zebudah (2 K. xxiii. 36).—2. Father of ZERUBBABEL, brother of SALATHIEL (1 Chr. iii. 17-19).—3. Descendant of Parosh (Neh. iii. 25).—4. A priest who assisted Ezra (viii. 4).—5. Ancestors of Sallu (xi. 7).—6. A treasurer (xiii. 13).—7. Father of Joel (1 Chr. xxvii. 20).

PEDIGREE. GENEALOGY (Num. i. 18).

PEEL, TO (Heb. MARAT). "Peeled" in Ez. xxix. 18, translates literally that the skin of the shoulder was *peeled* by the carrying of earth to form earth-works at the siege of Tyre. In Is. xviii. 2, 7, "a nation scattered and *peeled*" is variously rendered. Gesenius suggests "a people drawn out and smoothed."

PE′KAH (*open-eyed*). Son of Remaliah, captain of Pekahiah whom he assassinated, and succeeded to his throne B. C. 758, and thus became eighteenth king of Israel. He reigned twenty years, in the seventeenth of which he combined with Rezin, king of Damascus, against Ahaz, king of Judah, (2 K. xvi. and 2 Chr. xxviii.). (See prophecies of Isaiah, Is. vii.-ix). The result was the seizure of Damascus and all the lands east of the Jordan and north of Galilee, by Tiglath-Pileser king of Assyria. Pekah was killed by Hosea, son of Elah, who headed a conspiracy, and afterwards mounted the throne (2 K. xv. 25-38, xvi. 1-9). Assyrian inscriptions record the taking of Damascus by TIGLATH-PILESER.

PEKAHI′AH (*Jah has opened his eyes*). Son and successor of MENAHEM; was the seventeenth king of Israel. He reigned two years, and was killed by Pekah, his general, who succeeded him. His death took place B. C. 758 (2 K. xv. 22-25).

PE′KOD. A name given to the Chaldæans in Jer. l. 21 and Ez. xxiii. 23. The meaning of this word is uncertain; in one sense it would appear to be *to visit, to punish.* In another it means a *prefect* (officer).

PELAI′AH (*whom Jah distinguished*). 1. Son of Elioenai (1 Chr. iii. 24).—2. A Levite who as-

sisted Ezra (Neh. viii. 7), and also sealed the covenant (x. 10).

PELALI'AH (*whom Jah judges*). Son of Amzi, a priest (Neh. xi. 12).

PELATI'AH (*whom Jah delivers*). 1. Son of Hananiah (1 Chr. iii. 21).—2. A captain of the Simeonites (iv. 42).—3. One who sealed the covenant (Neh. x. 22).—4. Son of Benaiah (Ez. xi. 5-12, 13).

PE'LEG (*division*). Son of EBER; brother of JOKTAN (Gen. x. 25). CHRONOLOGY.

PE'LET (*deliverance*). 1. Son of Jahdai (1 Chr. ii. 47).—2. Son of AZMAVETH 3 (xii. 3).

PE'LETH (*swiftness*). 1. Father of On who joined in the Rebellion (Num. xvi. 1).—2. Son of Jonathan (1 Chr. ii. 33).

PEL'ETHITES (Heb. PELETHI, *courier*). Mentioned with the Cherethites: they were the body-guard of King David (2 Sam. viii. 18; xxii. 23). See CHERETHITES.

PELI'AS. BEDEIAH (1 Esd. ix. 34).

PEL'ICAN (Heb. KAATH, *to vomit*). The bird is supposed to be so named from its habit of emptying the pouch under the beak to feed its young. Cormorant, translated in Is. xxxiv. 11, and Zeph. ii. 14, means *pelican*. It is mentioned as among unclean birds in Lev. xi. 18, and Deut. xiv. 17. "A *pelican* in the wilderness" (Ps. cii. 6) as a sign of desolation for the solitary habits of the bird and its inhabiting desolated spots.

PEL'ONITE, THE. Two of David's strong men are called Pelonites; Helez and Ahijah (1 Chr. xi. 27, 36). "Mr. So-and-so."

PELU'SIUM. A city of EGYPT (Ez. xxx. 15).

PEN'IEL, PENUEL (*face of El—God*). (Gen. xxxii. 30). Where Jacob wrestled with a man, who changed Jacob's name to ISRAEL. Does not appear again until after 500 yrs. when Gideon, on his way from Succoth, on the Jordan, chasing Zeba and Zalmunna, being faint from want of food, asked the people of this place for bread for his soldiers, and was denied (Judg. viii. 8). He destroyed the tower of the city on his return (ver. 17). Jeroboam rebuilt the place (1 K. xii. 25). It has never been mentioned since, and is now lost.

PENIN'NAH (*coral*). Wife of ELKANAH (1 Sam. i. 2). HANNAH.

PEN'NY, PENNY-WORTH. Refer to MONEY. Gr. *denarion*; Roman *denarius*.

PEN'TATEUCH. See HISTORY OF THE BOOKS.
PEN'TECOST. See FESTIVALS.
PENU'EL. PENIEL.
PENU'EL. 1. Founder of GEDOR (1 Chr. iv. 4).—2. A chief, son of Shashak (viii. 25).

PE'OR (*the opening*). A mountain in Moab, from the top of which Balaam saw Israel encamped in the plain below (Num. xxiii. 28). There was a shrine, or holy high-place, on the summit, and the town of Beth Peor at its foot (Deut. iii. 29). Baal Peor was named from this mountain.—2. There is a *Beit Fughur*, 5 ms. S. W. of Bethlehem, in *Wady Hior*, which is included in the list of towns in Judah, in the Septuagint, as Phagor (Josh. xv. 59).

PERA'ZIM, MOUNT (*of divisions*). Isaiah refers to it in his warnings of the divine vengeance which was threatened (xxviii. 21). It must have been on some of the hights bordering the plain of Rephaim; and on its top a high place to Baal (Baal Perazim, 2 Sam. v. 20).

PERDI'TION. DAMNATION.

PE'RES (*a breach*), (Dan. v. 28). Phā'rez, a fragment.

PE'RESH (*dung*). Son of Machir (1 Chr. vii. 16).

PE'REZ. Son of Judah. The children of Perez were of importance for several centuries (1 Chr. xxvii. 3).

PEREZ-UZZAH (Uzzah—*broken*). (See NACHON'S threshing-floor).

PER'FECT. Ten different words are used. 1. Heb. CALIL, *perfect* in Ez. xvi. 14. *Perfection* in Lam. ii. 15. The verb CALAL translated "to perfect" (Ez. xxvii. 4).—2. Heb. SHALEM, "*perfect*" in Deut. xxv. 15; 1 Chr. xii. 38; "*perfected*" in 2 Chr. viii. 16; "*Whole*" in Deut. xxvii. 6; "*Just*" in Prov. xi. 1.—3. Heb. TACHLITH, *perfect* in Ps. cxxxix. 22; perfection in Job xi. 7.—4. Heb. TAM, perfect in Job i. 1, 8. "Upright" in Prov. xxix. 10.—5. Heb. TOM, translated *perfect* in Ps. ci. 2. "Full" (Job xxi. 23). 6. Heb. TAMIM, corresponding to 4 and 5 (Gen. v. 9; Lev. xxii. 21, etc.).—7. Gr. *akribos* (Luke i. 3). *Perfectly* in 1 Thess. v. 2; "*diligently*" in Matt. ii. 8.—8. Gr. *artios* (2 Tim. iii. 17). The verb *katartizo*, to make perfect (Heb. xiii. 21).—9. Gr. participle, *peplēromenos*.—10. Gr. *teleios*, Matt. v. 48. "Of full age" (Heb. v. 14). "Men" in 1 Cor. xiv. 20.

PERFUMES. Were used freely by the Orientals (Prov. xxvii. 9). The Hebrews made their perfumes from SPICES imported from Arabia, and from aromatic plants of their own country. Perfumes were used in the Temple-service in INCENSE and OINTMENT (Ex. xxx. 22-38). They were used in private life both on the person and on garments (Ps. xlv. 8), and beds (Prov. vii. 17). When a royal person went abroad "pillars of smoke" were thrown about his path (Cant. iii. 6). Perfume was not used in times of mourning (Is. iii. 24). See OINTMENT.

PER'GA. The ancient capital of Pamphylia, on the river Cestrus, 7 ms. from the sea. Diana (Artemis) was worshiped there, in a fine temple near the town. The coins of the city bear figures of Diana and the temple. Paul landed here from Paphos (Acts xiii. 13), and visited the city a second time on his return from the interior (xiv. 25). When Pamphylia was divided, Perga was made the capital of one section, and Side of the other. Called by the Turks *Eski-Kalessi*.

PERGA'MOS. In Mysia 3 ms. N. of the ancient Caicus. (See SEVEN CHURCHES).

PERI'DA (*kernel*). Ancestor of children of Solomon's servants who returned from captivity (Neh. vii. 57). PERUDA.

PER'IZZITE, THE (*rustic*). Ancient inhabitants of Canaan (Gen. xv. 20); of the six tribes (Canaanites, Hittites, Amorites, Perizzites, Hivites, and Jebusites), who inhabited the lands west of Jordan previous to the conquest of Joshua (Josh. xvii. 15). They were

PERGA.

PERSEP'OLIS. The capital of Persia, and partly burnt by Alexander, the temples—built of stone—only escaping. Antiochus Epiphanes attempted to capture and rob the temples, but was defeated (1 Macc. vi. 1, 2; 2 Macc. ix. 2). This city has been supposed to be identical with Passargadæ, the capital of Cyrus; but that city was 42 ms. N. of Persepolis, at a place now called *Murgaub*, where there is shown a tomb of Cyrus. The site of Persepolis is called Chehl-Minar (*forty pillars*, or *minarets*), from the remaining pillars of the palace built by Darius and Xerxes. Nanea (Diana, Artemis, Aphrodite), was the moon-goddess of the Persians, and had a temple in her honor, rich in gold shields, breastplates, and coverings of gold, and great treasures. The ruins of the palace now cover the platform, which

PERSEPOLIS.

is 350 by 380, and 30 ft. above the plain. A stairway of marble leading up to this platform is peculiar in having the rise only 3 or 4 inches for each step, with a tread of 14 inches, and the side-approaches decorated with sculpture. The ruins here show such parts of buildings as have entirely disappeared from the remains in Assyria, such as gates, columns, window-frames, staircases, etc., and giving a new style of column—very tall and slender. Pasargadæ was the ancient, and Persepolis the latter capital of Persia.

PER'SEUS. Son of Philip V and last king of Macedonia. He continued the war with Rome after his father's death (B. C. 179). He was defeated B. C. 168 and died at Alba (1 Macc. viii. 5). See cut on p. 203.

PER'SIA (*pure*). The province of Fars—Farsistan; is now not very large; and north of the Persian Gulf. The ancient empire extended north to Media, south to the Persian Gulf, east to Caramania, and west to Susiana; and in its greatest prosperity, from India to Egypt and Thrace (Ez. xxxviii. 5). The north country is mountainous, with very few valleys or plains, but very picturesque, and generally fertile, among which is the famous Shiraz of Arabian poetry. That part bordering the Gulf is sandy, like Arabia, and not very productive.

KING AND QUEEN OF PERSIA.

The original religion was simple; required temples, but neither altars, images, nor priests, and was based on a belief in the double nature of the infinite power, good and evil (Ormuzd and Ahriman), which was symbolized by light and darkness. Sacrifice was not practiced. Magianism and fire-worship mingled with, and almost superseded the ancient faith (Gomates, a Magian, became emperor, or Shah, B. C. 522), and the worship grew more and more complicated until the empire was destroyed. The Ahasuerus of Esther is probably Xerxes, the son of Darius, by Atossa, the daughter of Cyrus, the founder of the empire. The marriage with Esther is supposed to have taken place in the seventh year of his reign, the year after his flight from defeat in Greece. Artaxerxes, his son, is mentioned by Ezra (vii. 11-28) and Nehemiah (who was the king's cup-bearer, ii. 1-9) as friendly to the Jews; and he is the last but one of the Persian kings mentioned in Scripture. The last was Darius the Persian (Neh. xii. 22).

PER'SIAN (Heb. PARSI). The Persians were probably of the same race as the Medes, both of the Aryan root. Their mention only occurs in the later periods of biblical history. In Daniel, Esther, Nehemiah and Ezra, a very complete idea of the Persian court and administration is presented. The vizier or secretary of state was invested with great power as illustrated in the cases of Haman and Mordecai. (See MORDECAI.) The royal signet was the badge of this office. The remarkable influence which Esther and Mordecai exercised over Xerxes was the result of the noble qualities of mind and body, for which the Hebrew race was, and still is, conspicuous.

PER'SIS (Gr. *destroying*). A Christian woman at Rome (Rom. xvi. 12).

PERU'DA (*kernel*), (Ezr. ii. 55).

PES'TLE, PESTILS. MORTAR (2 Chr. xxvi. 14; Prov. xxvii. 22).

PE'TER. Originally SIMEON, or SIMON, *heard*. (Cephas, *a stone*—Peter, *a rock*). The son of Jonas, and a native of Bethsaida, in Galilee. He was married (his wife's name was Concordia?) at the time of his call to follow Jesus; and lived with his mother-in-law, at Capernaum. He was a fisherman, and was fishing with his father and brother, Andrew, when Jesus found him. Peter and his brother Andrew were, probably, disciples of John the Baptist. Peter, James, and John, only, of the twelve, were witnesses of the transfiguration and the agony in Gethsemane. It seems that Peter was more intimate than any of the other apostles with Jesus, for the tax-collector asked him if his Master paid tribute; and to him and John was given the duty of providing the lamb for the paschal supper, although Judas carried the purse. Peter walked on the Sea of Galilee, but his heart failed, and he cried for help. He frequently declared his faith in Jesus, although he was disappointed that the Christ was not the temporal prince that the Jews had looked for. He first refused to have Jesus wash his feet; but when he learned that it was a symbol, he wished to have his hands and head washed also. He boldly and vauntingly avowed his attachment to Jesus, and offered to lay down his life for Him, and then disgracefully denied Him the same day,

and wept bitterly when conscious of what he had done. Jesus forgave him, accepted his renewed professions, and gave him a new commission to work in his cause. After this time his character changed. Instead of a hasty zeal, he showed a sober dignity. He first proclaimed salvation through a crucified Saviour, and, when arrested with the others, boldly declared his faith and purpose before the Sanhedrin. He, by a miracle, punished with death two who tried an experiment on the omniscience of the Holy Ghost; and rebuked Simon the magician, at Samaria, who wished to buy the secret of working miracles. At Joppa he was taught, in a vision, that the ancient ritual distinctions of clean and unclean were abolished. Herod put him in prison, at Jerusalem, and he was released by an angel. He first advocated an exemption from the ceremonial law of Moses. Paul rebuked him for timidly dissembling on the question of the equality of the Jews and Gentiles, at Antioch. Here the Gospel history ends, and we have tradition only for the rest of his life, which says that he traveled (as Paul did) among the cities and churches to which his epistles are addressed, in Pontus, Galatia, Bithynia, Cappadocia, and Asia; that he visited Rome, and was made bishop of the church there, and suffered martyrdom under Nero, being crucified with his head downward.

PETHAHI'AH (*Jah sets free*). 1. A priest of the nineteenth course (1 Chr. xxiv. 16).—2. A Levite (Neh. ix. 5).—3. Son of Meshezabeel (xi. 24).

PE'THOR (*a table*). A town where Balaam resided (Num. xxii. 5).

PETHU'EL (*man of God*). Father of Joel the prophet (Joel i. 1).

PETRA (Gr. *rock*). The Greek translation of Sela, a celebrated Edomite city (Is. xvi. 1).

PEUL'THAI (*wages of Jah*). Son of Obed-edom (1 Chr. xxvi. 5).

PHAC'ARETH. Pochereth of Zebaim (1 Esd. v. 34).

PHAI'SUR. Pashur 1 (1 Esd. ix. 22).

PHALDAI'US. Pedaiah 4 (1 Esd. ix. 44).

PHALE'AS. Padon (1 Esd. v. 29).

PHA'LEC. Peleg (Luke iii. 35).

PHAL'LU. Pallu (Gen. xlvi. 9).

PHAL'TI. Palti, son of Laish, to whom Saul gave Michal (1 Sam. xxv. 44).

PHANU'EL. Father of Anna (Luke ii. 36).

PHAR'ACIM. Ancestor of servants of the Temple who returned from captivity (1 Esd. v. 31).

PHA'RAOH (Heb. PAR'ŌH, *the king;* from PHRA, *the sun*). The title of the kings of Egypt. The Egyptian king represents the sun-god. 1. The earliest mention of *Pharaoh* is in the history of Abraham (Gen. xii. 10-20); probably one of the shepherd-kings.—2. The *Pharaoh* of Joseph (Gen. xxxvii. 36).—3. The *Pharaoh* of the oppression, "who knew not Joseph."—4. The *Pharaoh* who enslaved the Israelites is supposed by some to have been Rameses II: by others, as of Assyrian descent, from Is. lii. 4. The Exodus is dated in his time. 5. *Pharaoh* the father-in-law of Mered (1 Chr. iv. 18).—6. *Pharaoh* the father-in-law of Hadad (1 K. xi. 18) (see HADAD); perhaps Osochor.—7. *Pharaoh* father-in-law of Solomon, PSUSENNES II (1 K. iii. 1).—8. *Pharaoh,* the ally of the Jews against Sennacherib (Is. xxxvi. 6)—9. PHARAOH-NECHO (Jer. xlvi. 2). This and the Pharaoh which follows are the only two mentioned with proper names. He appears to have been an enterprising king, and to have reigned 16 years. He opposed the Assyrians; defeating and fatally wounding Josiah, King of Judah (2 K. xxiii. 29, 30). See, also, 2 K. xxiii. 30-34; 2 Chr. xxxvi. 1-4. This battle lost to Pharaoh all his Asiatic dominions (2 K. xxiv. 7).—10 PHARAOH-HOPHRA (*son of the sun*) was the second successor of Necho, and mounted the throne B. C. 589. Several kings of Egypt are mentioned by their titles only, and it is important to give some account of them by way of distinction:

1. The Pharaoh of Abraham's time, according to the best authors, was of the line called Shepherd-Kings of the XVth Dynasty. The presents made to Abraham argue that Pharaoh was an owner of flocks and herds, and *camels,* which are not drawn on the monuments, or possessed by any other of Egypt's kings besides the Shepherd line, and were regarded by the people as hateful animals. See ABRAHAM.

2. In the history of Joseph there are many particulars of the Pharaoh who made him his minister of state. In the account of the death of Jacob, Joseph is made to address a petition to the Pharaoh, in such a manner as to give the impression that it was a successor of the one who had advanced him to honor. Some discoveries at Zoan, Egypt, lately made, have determined the historical question, that the Pharaohs of Joseph's time were shepherds, who had become Egyptianized, and built many monuments, which are known for several peculiarities. A strong argument is, the supposition that a native Egyptian king would not have elevated a Hebrew slave as he did Joseph. In our day, the Oriental rulers make viziers of barbers, or of any one who has the requisite ability, without regard to rank, condition, or religion.

3. The "new king which knew not Joseph," may have been a successor in the Shepherd line, but it is possible, if not probable, that he was of a new dynasty which did not favor the Hebrews. He set them harder tasks, building store cities; and attempted to diminish them by the use of midwives, but neither plan succeeded. This Pharaoh has been supposed to have been of the XVIIth dynasty, but it is difficult to determine the matter since the names of the whole line are unknown. His residence was at Avaris, in the sandy district, as we learn from the fact that Moses buried the body of the Egyptian that he killed, in the sand. The kings whose names are found in the Turin Papyrus bear names which are Egyptian translations of Assyrian titles.

4. The Pharaoh of the Exodus is described to us as impious and superstitious, vascillating between right and wrong. He seems to have expected the same works from his magicians as from Moses and Aaron. He was ready to promise, and as ready to break his promise, a course of conduct that only ended when he and his army were destroyed in the Red Sea. A recently deciphered record of Thothmes III, contains many names bordering the Hebrew territory, and mentions the battle of Megiddo. The Egyptians were either friendly at that time, or deemed it prudent to remember the Red Sea, and not attack the Hebrews. The first king of Egypt after the Exodus who did attack them was SHISHAK, a foreigner in that country, and not acquainted with the Jews. The friendly Egyptians had certain privileges under the law (Deut. xxiii. 7).

5. Bithiah a Pharaoh's daughter married a Hebrew, Mered, not long after the Exodus. Mered had a sister Miriam, perhaps named after the sister of Moses. It is supposed that this Pharaoh's daughter was taken in a foray from some caravan (1 Chr. iv. 18).

6. A Pharaoh gave shelter to Hadad and his followers, enemies of Solomon, assigning them land and provisions, and married his wife's sister to him (1 K. xi. 18-20). Hadad returned to Palestine after the death of David and Joab. It is not known which this one was, any nearer than that he was probably the predecessor of the one who gave his daughter to Solomon for a wife.

7. Solomon married a Pharaoh's daughter not later than the 11th year of his reign. This king has not been identified. He made a raid into Philistia, took a city (Gezer), and gave it for a present to his daughter, Solomon's wife. This alliance to Egypt was distinctly forbidden in the law, and produced fearful disasters, both spiritual and temporal.

Then after him came the Pharaohs Shishak, Zerah, and So. See SHISHAK, ZERAH and SO. Zerah (Userken), is called a Cushite (2 Chr. xiv. 9). These were not called Pharaohs because they were not Egyptians, and had foreign names.

8. The Pharaoh who opposed Sennacherib was Tirhakah of Cush, also called the king of Mizraim. The symbol of a broken reed used in the Scriptures suggests the title of the king of Upper Egypt, SU-TEN, *reed-king*, whose emblem was a bent reed. This Pharaoh was Sethos according to Herodotus, called Zet by Manetho.

9. The first Pharaoh whose proper name is given is Necho, on the monuments NEKU, who was of XXVIth dynasty, and reigned 16 years. His name is given to a part of the canal between the Nile and the Red Sea; and is credited with sending an expedition around Africa in ships; and a war against Assyria, in which he killed Josiah, king of Judah. In his account of this expedition, Herodotus calls Jerusalem Cadytis—almost the same in sound as its modern Arabic name El-Kuds (*the Holy*). Some suppose that Cadytis refers to Ketesh, on the Orontes, which was then the chief city in Syria. Necho at that time worshiped Apollo. On its return towards Egypt, at Circhemish, Nebuchadnezzar defeated his army. Necho probably not being with it. The Egyptian after that "came not again out of his land" towards Palestine (2 K. xxiv. 7).

11. Pharaoh Hophra was the second successor after Necho. He attacked Sidon, and fought a battle at sea with Tyre, and after losing an army in Cyrene, probably by Nebuchadnezzar, he was superseded by Amasis as Pharaoh, and he was strangled. He is supposed to have aided king Zedekiah in one of his wars (Jer. xxxvii. 5, 8). Ezekiel's prophesy, and the history of Herodotus agree as to the character of this Pharaoh, describing him as an arrogant crocodile (xxxix. 3). There is no other Pharaoh mentioned in the Scriptures after Hophra.

PHA'RAOH, WIFE OF. Named Tahpenes; wife of the 6th Pharaoh.

PHA'RAOH'S DAUGHTER. Three daughters of Pharaoh appear in the Scriptures: 1. As the discoverer of the infant Moses, daughter of 3d Pharaoh (Ex. ii. 5-10).—2. Daughter of 5th Pharaoh—named Bithiah; she was wife of Mered, an Israelite (1 Chr. iv. 18).—3. Daughter of 7th Pharaoh; married to Solomon (1 K. iii. 1, viii. 8, ix. 24). A house was built for her (1 K. vii. 8, ix. 24).

PHAR'ATHONI (1 Macc. ix. 50). In the S. of Judæa? Lost.

PHA'RES. Son of Judah (Matt. i. 3).

PHAREZ (*a breach*). 1. Twin son with ZERAH 1 of Judah. The first-born of the twin sons of Judah by his daughter-in-law Tamar (Gen. xxxviii. 29). 2. In the line of David. In Ruth iv. 12 occurs the passage—"Let thy house be like the house of *Pharez*, whom Tamar bare unto Judah!"—3. PHARAZITES (Num. xxvi. 60).

PHARI'RA (1 Esd. v. 33). PERUDA.

PHAR'ISEES (Heb. PERUSHIM). One of the three sects of Judaism in the time of Christ. The name means separated by special works. The sect included all Hebrews who separated themselves from every kind of Levitical impurity, following the Mosaic law of purity.

They are first noticed as a sect about 150 B. C., but their origin is not recorded.

Their influence was very great, ruling, beyond question, the Sanhedrin, and all Jewish society, except the slight opposition of the Sadducees, even overawing the civil courts; and as they had gathered to themselves all the worst features of Judaism in the time of Christ, and used this against any reform, and especially against the Messiah, it was needful that Jesus should protest against them; and the contest resulting from his protest grew fiercer and more relentless on the part of the Pharisees, ending only with the crucifixion.

The applicant for admission to the sect was required to promise in the presence of three members: 1. That he would not eat of anything which had not been tithed, nor if there was any doubt about it; and 2. That he would keep the law of purity in all matters, most especially in family affairs.

In this matter they made of the civil rule of tithes a religious obligation, and so set apart the tithe as a holy thing, and taught that the eating of a holy thing was a deadly sin; and that if the tithe was not taken out, set apart, and paid to the priest, the whole produce was unlawful for food.

The law of clean and unclean was also applied in the extreme.

Their doctrines and rules are the basis of the faith of the orthodox party of the Jews to this day. The Essenes were a kind of intensified Pharisees, and the Sadducees were never a large or influential sect.

The Pharisees made themselves the people's party by teaching that "God has given to all men alike the kingdom, the priesthood, and Holiness (2 Macc. ii. 17). They tried to realize that the Jews were *a people of priests, a holy nation*, by diligent study of the law, a preparation for the office and duties of Rabbi, and by arranging the concerns of life on the model of those who minister in holy things.

Their social meals were modeled after the paschal supper, with all its ablutions, blessings, and Levitical rules.

That Jesus did not overstate their peculiar defects their own account of themselves will show. The Talmud says:

"There are seven kinds of Pharisees:

1. Shechemites; who keep the law for what it will profit them.

2. Tumblers; always hanging down the head, and dragging the feet.

3. Bleeders; who to avoid looking at women shut their eyes and so bump their heads.

4. Mortars; wearing caps in the form of a mortar, covering the eyes from seeing impurities.

5. What-am-I-yet-to-doers; who as soon as one law is kept, ask what is next.

6. Fearers; who keep the law from fear of a judgment.

7. Lovers; who obey Jehovah because they love him with all the heart.

Surely this indicates that they were impartially divided among fanatics and worldly-minded hypocrites; and yet they had developed the ideas of a Messiah, of a kingdom of heaven, the immortality of the soul, the future life. Of them were the devout Simeon, who took the infant Jesus in his arms; and also Zacharias, and Gamaliel, and Saul of Tarsus, who never uttered a word against the sect.

Jesus described them as whited sepulchres, hidden graves, and in retaliation they were his most determined enemies.

The spirit of proselytism (Matt. xxiii. 15), which was so strong in the time of Christ, led the way for the spread of Christianity, as is plainly shown in Paul's life. Their peculiar doctrines also opened the minds of men for the new facts of the life and work of Jesus.

PHA ROSH (PAROSH, Ezr. viii. 3).

PHAR'PAR (*swift*). One of the two rivers mentioned by Naaman as rivers of Damascus, better than all the waters of Israel (2 K. v. 12). The Awaj is divided from the Barada (see ABANA) by the ridge of the Jebel Aswad, which is no where less than 8 ms. wide. It has two sources in the S. E. slopes of Hermon—one near the village of Arny, and the other near Beit Jenn, the two streams uniting below Sasa—and empties into the Hijaneh, the most southerly of the lakes E. of Damascus. There are nearly 50 villages in its course, containing about 18,000 people (Porter, *Five Years in Damascus*).

PHAR'ZITES, THE. Descendants of PHAREZ (Num. xxvi. 20).

PHAZE'AN. PASEAH 2 (Neh. vii. 51).

PHASE'LIS. In Lycia, near Pamphylia, on the coast. It was a city of importance in the 6th century B. C., but became a resort of pirates. It was a convenient port, on account of the lofty mountain Solyma (8,000 ft.), which was only 4 ms. back of the city, affording a landmark for sailors. Homer mentions the Solyma range in the Odyssey. The Romans broke up the pirates' stronghold, under Publius Servilius Isauricus, B. C. 75, and Pompey. The Romans required all their allies to deliver up to Simon, the high-priest, all Jewish exiles, naming this city among others (1 Macc. xv. 23).

PHAS'IRON. An Arab tribe (1 Macc. ix. 66).

PHAS'ARON. PASHUR (1 Esd. v. 25).

PHE'BE (*pure, bright*). (Goddess of the moon). A servant of the church at CENCHREÆ (Rom. xvi. 1, 2). DEACONESS.

PHE'NICE (*the date-palm*). Town on the S. coast of Crete, now called Lutro. Paul was on the way there from Fair Havens when the storm drove the vessel into Adria (Acts xxvii. 12). The White Mountains rise 9,000 ft. near the bay, which is a safe harbor in winter.

PHENI'CIANS. See PHŒNICIA.

PHER'ESITES. PERIZZITES (1 Esd. viii. 69).

PHIBE SETH (Ez. xxx. 17).

Epistle Paul recommends the granting pardon to Onesimus, who conveyed the Epistle, with those to the Colossians and Ephesians, from Rome to Colossæ. See Philemon i. 2, iv. 7, 19, etc., and Col. iv. 9, 17. See ONESIMUS. Philemon was probably a man of wealth, influence and liberality.

PHILE'MON, EPISTLE TO. See HISTORY OF THE BOOKS.

PHILE'TUS. An apostate Christian, who joined with HYMENŒUS and ALEXANDER (1 Tim. i. 20, and 2 Tim. ii. 18).

PHIL'IP (*fond of horses*). 1. Father of Alexander the Great (1 Macc. i. 1, vi. 2). King of Macedonia, B. C. 359-336.—2. Governor at Jerusalem (B. C. 170). He was very cruel toward the Jews (2 Macc. v. 22).—3. The foster-brother (ix. 29) of Antiochus Epiphanes, regent of Syria and guardian of Antiochus V (B. C. 164), son of the king (1 Macc. vi. 14, 15, 55, 56, 63).—4. Philip V, king of Macedonia, B. C. 220-179 (1 Macc. viii. 5).

PHIL'IP. One of the twelve apostles. A native of Bethsaida, in Galilee (John i. 44). He became a disciple of John the Baptist, and was the fourth of the twelve in the order of his call. He introduced Nathanael, who was afterwards called Bartholomew, the fifth apostle. Jesus asked Philip where bread (vi. 5) was to be found for feeding the 5000, and Philip did not even suspect the real source; nor did he seem to know the spiritual character of Jesus and his teaching much later, when he said to him, "Lord, show us the Father," (xiv. 8), and he had heard the voice from heaven, which was sent for the special instruction of such as were so slow to perceive the light—although he was at Cana when the water was made wine. He consulted with Andrew before gratifying the request of the Jews from Greece to see Jesus (out of curiosity only?) Philip was with the other apostles in that "upper room" (Acts i. 13) at Jerusalem, after the ascension, and on the day of Pentecost.

Tradition says he preached in Phrygia. There is no account of his death.

PHILIPPIANS, EPISTLE TO. See HISTORY OF THE BOOKS.

PHILIP, THE EVANGELIST. A resident (in the latter part of his life) of Cæsarea, where he had a wife and family, of whom four daughters are mentioned as singers. He was one of the SEVEN DEACONS of the Church in Judæa (Acts vi. 5, viii. 29). After Stephen was stoned he went to Samaria, where he baptized the magician Simon. From there he was sent by Peter to Gaza, and on the way (at Ain Karem?) he baptized the Ethiopian eunuch (Acts viii. 26-40). His tour extended from Azotus to Cæsarea, where he settled, and was visited by Paul, Agabus, and others (xxi. 8, 9). His death is not recorded.

PHILADELPHIA.

PHI'CHOL (*mighty*). Captain in the army of ABIMELECH (Gen. xxi. 22, 23).

PHILADEL'PHIA. In Lydia, near Phrygia. (See SEVEN CHURCHES). There is a village on the ancient site called *Allah Shehr*—"City of God."

PHILAR'CHES. The name of an office. Commander of the cavalry (2 Macc. viii. 32).

PHILE'MON (Gr. *affectionate*). A Christian, probably a native of Colossæ, to whom Paul addressed the Epistle. See HISTORY OF THE BOOKS. In this

PHILIP'PI. In Macedonia, 9 miles from the sea, on the banks of the deep, rapid stream Gangites (now *Angista*). Paul says: "On the Sabbath we went out of the city by the river side, where prayer was wont to be made" (Acts xvi. 13). The ancient walls can be traced along the course of the river; and there are remains of a gate leading to a bridge across the stream. Philippi was a Roman military colony, originally named Krenides (*springs*), or Datum; and the Jews were probably not permitted to worship inside of the walls.

A ridge, 1600 feet high, behind the city, divided a broad plain from the bay and town of Neapolis, in Thrace. The mines produced 1000 talents of gold a year, from which Philip's coins were made (see COIN, in MACEDONIA). The Via Egnatia passed through it. The ruins of the city are very extensive, but the place is not inhabited.

The famous battle which ended the Roman Republic, was fought on this plain, near Philippi, between armies led by Octavius Cæsar and Marc Antony on one side, and on the other by Brutus and Cassius, who were defeated with their republican forces (B. C. 42).

Paul visited the city a third time (Acts xx. 6), where he remained, in company with Silas, for some time. The church at Philippi was friendly to Paul, and sent him help frequently (Phil. iv. 10, 15, 18; 2 Cor. xi. 9; 1 Thess. ii. 2), for which, and their other kindnesses, he wrote them an Epistle from Rome.

PHILISTIA (*emigrant*). PALESTINE (Ps. xl. 8). A region extending from Joppa, 40 miles south, to Gerar, being 10 miles wide at the north and 20 at the south, and generally called SHEPHELAH in the Scriptures. The prophets describe the people as the Philistines from Caphtor (Amos ix. 7), the remnant of the maritime district (Jer. xlvii. 4); and Moses as the Caphtorim that came out of Caphtor (Deut. ii. 23) and drove out the Avim. This would require us to read Gen. x. 14, "and Caphtorim, whence came Philistim." (See CAPHTOR). The most reasonable supposition seems to be that Philistia was settled by emigrants from Egypt, dating from the time of Amenoph, B. C. 1970, up to the time of the Judges in Israel, B. C. 1200.

Since we have only ten or twelve words remaining out of their language, and these, it may be, affected by contact with the Hebrew forms, it is impossible to determine their origin as a race. They came after the Canaanites (Gen. x. 19), who once occupied as far as Gaza and Gerar. Abimelech was king of the Philistines in Abraham's time. Moses avoided them on account of their strength; and Joshua found a confederacy of five cities—Gaza, Gath, Askelon, Ashdod and Ekron—ruled by princes, with whom he did not go to war. The first victory over them is recorded of Shamgar, who killed 600 with an ox-goad. They carried off the sacred ark after the battle of Aphek, and only restored it in David's time, when their territory was added to the kingdom of Judah; and the great king made Ittai, a man of Gath, captain of his body-guard, who were Philistines (2 Sam. xv.). For the location of the chief city of Philistia see GATH.

Their religion was similar to that of Phœnicia—nature-worship. Their name for God was Elohim; but they had other special divinities, such as Dagon, Derketo, Baal Zebub, and Ashtoreth, whose images were carried with them on their campaigns, besides charms which they wore on their persons (2 Macc. xii. 40). Josephus speaks of a council of 500 rulers at Gaza (Ant. xiii. 13, 3). Baal was a union of human (the head) and fish-like forms. Oracles, priests, sorcerers, altars, temples, etc., were scattered all over the land.

PHILISTINES (Heb. PELESHETH, *wandering*). See PHILISTIA.

PHILOL'OGUS (*learned*). A Christian at Rome (Rom. xvi. 15).

PHILOS'OPHY. There was no Hebrew system of philosophy. The divine law furnished the rule, about which no speculation was needed. Facts built upon a species of divine philosophy, which led from God to man. The Greek philosophy led the mind from man up towards God. The philosophy of the Hebrews was developed in their national life; their books recording acts and not thoughts. The two books, Job and Ecclesiastes, have many philosophical thoughts. See HISTORY OF THE BOOKS.

The Kabbala, mystical and speculative philosophy, arose in the time of the Captivity, and flourished most during the decay of the nation, when it was subject to the influence of other people, especially the Greeks. The Kabbala in its two great divisions, "the chariot," which treated with the manifestation of God in Himself, and "the creation," with His manifestation in Nature. The influence of other philosophies resulted in the adopting the Persian idea of emanation, and of the Incarnation, afterwards a leading idea in the Christian Church. The books now known among Jews on these subjects do not claim an earlier date than A. D. 1000 to 1500, and are colored all through with Pantheism. There are diluted imitations of the teachings of Pythagoras; and are much affected with the mystery of numbers (see KABBALA). Numbers are used to express the idea of the Divine Wisdom, the universe being a harmonious thought of Divine Wisdom, which having been formed into letters becomes reflected into man's soul; and he represents the whole universe repeated in miniature. This mingling of many systems, without definite design, produced a school of interpreters of the supposed hidden meanings of Scripture texts, whose influence is still felt in some quarters of the Christian Church.

The Pharisees were Stoics in their philosophy (see PHARISEES). The Sadducees advocated human freedom in its purest and widest sense (see SADDUCEES). The Essenes taught a system of mystic asceticism (see ESSENES), which, with the other two sects, completed the cycle of doctrine.

Much interesting detail on these points may be found in the fourth book of Maccabees (see HIST. OF THE BOOKS).

In Proverbs there is a certain advance in the idea of wisdom as a philosophy, which was expanded in the WISDOM OF SOLOMON, and in ECCLESIASTICUS (see HISTORY OF THE BOOKS), in which there is an approach to the doctrine of the Word, the Divine Logos, which John stated so clearly and truthfully. Philo had treated the subject, but not plainly, and the Gnostics mystified it beyond all possibility of understanding beginning or end.

Ancient philosophy has been regarded as a kind of covenant between God and man, which stood to the pagan world as the Abrahamic covenant did to the Hebrews, and in a peculiar sense it was a preparation for Christianity, for which work the Greek philosophy was most fit.

Philosophy is a natural outgrowth of human thought in the west, as the promulgation of law is natural to the despotic character of the Oriental. Greek philosophy was based on simple reason, without reference to faith, which stood separate and distinct by itself. After the Christian Church was established, philosophy left Greece and renewed its vitality in Alexandria, Egypt (see ALEXANDRIA). But the grand questions of the creation, future life, and man's true relation to God were left unsettled by philosophy, and were only answered by the simple and sublime words of the Old Testament and the New.

The spirit of Christianity is independent of history and of persons, and concerns the immediate relation of the soul to God.

PHIN'EES. Gr. form of PHINEHAS. 1. PHINEHAS 1 (1 Esd. v. 5; viii. 2, 29).—2. PHINEHAS 2 (2 Esd. i. 2 a).—3. PHINEHAS 3 (1 Esd. viii. 63). —4. PASEAH 2 (v. 31).

PHINE'HAS (*mouth of brass*). 1. Son of ELEAZAR 1 (Ex. vi. 25) and grandson of Aaron (Ex. vi. 25). He was promised the priesthood in his family forever for his services during the plague in Egypt (Num. xxv. 7; 10-13).

PHŒ'BE. Referred to by Paul in Rom. xvi. 1, as "our sister which is a servant of the church at

Cenchreæ." She was probably the bearer of the Epistle to the Romans.

PHŒNIC'IA. Phœnice (*phoinix — palm tree*). Phoinos, *purple*, another derivation of the name. Phœnix, the son of Agenor, and brother of Cadmus, is also honored as the source. This was the Greek name, while the native name was KENAAN, as may be seen on a coin of Laodicea, of the time of Antiochus Epiphanes; and from them—the strongest race—the country was called by the Hebrews the Land of Canaan. The country extended from the Ladder of Tyre, or rather the Ras el Abyad (*White Cape*), to the *Nahr el Auly*, above Sidon, 28 miles; with a width at Sidon of two miles, and at Tyre of five; and was called by Josephus the great plain of Sidon (Ant. v. 3, 1). Sidon and Tyre were 20 miles apart. (See SIDON and TYRE). Sarepta was a colony of Sidon, 8 miles south; and Tyre was either a colony of Sidon or received the honor of a change of the chief rule to it, after the war with the Philistines, because it was a stronger place than Sidon. Perhaps, at this time, the island was fortified. There were also colonies in Cyprus, the Grecian Isles, Lybia, and in Spain. Phœnicia was extended, in later times, north to the island of Aradus, and Antaradus, the boundary being the river Eleutherus, making a

male and female powers; whose symbols were the sun, moon and planets (7), which has been said to have been the most complete and beautiful form of idolatry ever devised. This system always had an influence over the Hebrews, more or less in different ages, recommended to the simple, pastoral Jews by the wealth and polished manners of the commercial Phœnicians. Solomon paid his respect to King Hiram by making shrines to his gods on Olivet, and his successors permitted houses to be built near the Temple for idolatrous practices (2 K. xxiii. 7). The worst feature of the system was the sacrifice of children to the god Molech. The colonies of Phœnicia also inherited this dreadful superstition, and we read that when Carthage was besieged by Agathocles, there were offered as burnt sacrifices to the god Saturn (the planet), *at the public expense*, 200 boys of the aristocracy; and when they had gained a victory, the most beautiful captives were sacrificed in the same manner (Diod. xx. 14, 65). The worship of Astarte also tended to break down the restraints of virtue between the sexes, and to solemnize the most abominable practices. Twice were a large number of the priests of Baal destroyed by a reformer in Israel; by Elijah, who killed 450 on Mt. Carmel, and by Jehu, who gathered all the Baal worship-

SIDON.

coast of 120 miles. Beirut is now the chief, and almost the only port of this region. Gebal was anciently famous for its ship-builders, sailors (Ez. xxvii. 9), and workers in stone. Tripolis (now *Tarabulus*) was colonized in three distinct districts a few rods apart, each walled in and named after the cities from whence the emigrants came—Tyre, Sidon and Aradus. Aradus (Arvad, Gen. x. 18) was on a small island, colonized from Sidon. Massive ruins are still standing there. Carthage, in Africa, was its most famous colony. (For rivers, etc., see LEBANON.)

The language was Semitic (that is, from Shem), to which family belong the Arabic, Aramaic and the Hebrew, which are as nearly allied as are English and German. No other language was so widely spread, because of their mariners and colonists. The Greeks gave the honor of the invention of letters to the Phœnicians, having first received 16 letters from Cadmus (*eastern* or *olden*). (See ALPHABETS). The letters are supposed to have been originally rude pictures, in outline, of natural objects, as—Aleph, an ox's head; Beth, a house; Gimel, a camel (the hump-back); Daleth, the tent-door; Lamed, an ox-goad; Ajin, an eye; Caph, the back of the head; Reish, the head; and Tau, a cross. The Egyptian phonetic characters were made on the same principle. The names of the Greek letters which end in *a*, are Aramaic in form.

The religion was a nature-worship, recognizing

ers in Israel, and in true Oriental style gave each one a garment for the grand occasion, and then killed every one, and burned the images and destroyed the temple of Baal (2 K. x. 18-28). The Phœnicians believed in the development theory, that the first created beings were without intellect, and progressed from one stage to another up to man (Sanchoniathon). Melchisedec was of this race and faith, worshiping Elyon, called *their* most high god; but Abraham worshiped Jehovah, the Lord (Gen. xiv. 22).

The country has always had a great many tribes, each holding to its peculiar religion, and they now live together, but separate, without friendship or mutual trust, suspecting and hating every other faith but their own; and this want of common union is the great obstacle to their progress.

There is a hopeful future for this people, for which the American mission is preparing the way quickening a desire and taste for education among the young of all classes, and of every faith, and meeting these new demands with schools of the best grades, good books, and qualified, earnest teachers. The material progress of the country will follow the advance in its moral elevation, as is the case in all other lands. The population is stated by *Thompson* (Land and Book, i. 246) to be less than two millions, divided among Moslems, the rulers (800,000), Kurds (50,000), Nusariyeh (Arabs, 150,000), Yezidy and Gipsies (20,000),

Druses (100,000), Jews (25,000), Maronites (200,000), Greeks (150,000), Armenians (20,000), Jacobites (15,000), Romanists (80,000), and a few Protestants from England, Scotland and America, besides the roving tribes of Arabs who cannot be counted, or even estimated. The cities have a population of all classes, numbering in Tripoli 18,000, Beirut 50,000, Tyre 35,000, Acre 5,000, Khaifa 3,000, and Deir el Kamar, the Druse capital, 7,000; besides which there are a great number of small villages.

PHI'SON. PISON (Ecclus. xxiv. 25).

PHLE'GON (*burning*). A Christian at Rome (Rom. xvi. 14).

PHO'ROS. PAROSH (1 Esd. v. 9).

PHRY'GIA (*parched*). Asia Minor. Inland, S. of Bithynia and Galatia, W. of Cappadocia and Lycaonia, N. of Lycia and Pisidia, and E. of Caria, Lydia, and Mysia. The empire once included nearly all Asia Minor. The surface is level, with few ridges, and very productive of corn, fruit, wine, cattle, sheep, and horses. Laodicea, Hierapolis, and Colosse (and perhaps Antioch) were the chief cities, mentioned in the New Testament.

PHUD. PHUT (Judg. ii. 23).

PHU'RAH (*bough*). Servant of GIDEON on his visit to the camp of the Midianites (Judg. vii. 10, 11).

PHU'RIM. PURIM (Esth. xi. 1).

PHUT, PUT. Son of HAM (Gen. x. 6). For the country and people, see LEHABIM.

PHU'VAH (*mouth*). Son of Issachar (Gen. xlvi. 13). PUAH.

PHYGEL'LUS (*fugitive*). A Christian (2 Tim. i. 15), a native of Asia, who deserted Paul at Rome in a critical time.

PHYLAC'TERY (*safeguard*). FRONTLETS.

PHYSICIAN. MEDICINE.

PI-BES'ETH (Egyptian *bahest*). *Bubastis* is the Greek form. On the Pelusiac branch of the Nile. Called, also, Bubastite, and named from the goddess whom the Greeks identified with Artemis (Coptic *Pascht*). The city was built on an artificial elevation, raised by criminals (chiefly), from the mud taken from the canals leading from this place to Suez. Pascht was the goddess of fire, and had a grand temple in her honor, to which multitudes flocked yearly on pilgrimage. Herodotus describes the city very minutely (ii. 5-9). The only remains are a few stones of the finest red granite, and heaps of broken pottery, mud banks, etc. When Ezekiel prophesied its destruction it was in its period of greatest prosperity (xxx. 17).

PICTURE. Idolatrous representations, or images (Is. ii. 16).

PIECE OF GOLD (2 K. v. 5). See MONEY.

PIECE OF MONEY (Matt. xvii. 27). STATER.

PIECE OF SIL'VER. "The piece of money paid Judas is represented by the tetradrachm of Antiochus III, which was equal to a shekel. (See cut on page 13.) (Matt. xxv. 15). See MONEY.

PI'ETY (*L. pietas*). Dutiful conduct toward God, parents, etc., (1 Tim. v. 4).

PIG'EON. See DOVE.

PI-HAHI'ROTH (*mouth of the caverns*, or if Egyptian, *where sedge grows*). Near Suez, a camping-place during the Exodus (xiv. 2, 9). There is a place there now called *Ghuweibet el boos* (*the bed of reeds*).

PI'LATE, PON'TIUS. (L. *Pilatus*, probably from *pilum*, armed with a javelin. Pontius—probably of Gens Pontia a plebeian clan of Samnite origin) The sixth Roman procurator of Judæa, the successor of Valerius Gratus, under Tiberius Cæsar (Luke iii. 1). Tacitus writes "The author of that name (Christian) or sect was Christ, who was capitally punished in the reign of Tiberius by Pontius Pilate." The early fathers, Justin Martyr, Eusebius, Tertullian and others, say that Pilate sent to Rome an official report of the trial of Christ. Pilate oppressed the Jews, and violated the Roman law which respected the Jewish religion; of this there is the especial evidence of Josephus (Ant. xviii. 3, 1). He disregarded the law in having brought into Jerusalem effigies upon the ensigns, and by an attempt to force their introduction. Also in appropriating sacred money or treasure for the construction of an aqueduct (Luke xiii. 1). During the feasts the Roman governors resided in Jerusalem to preserve order. Thus at the feast of the Passover, Pilate was in Jerusalem in his official residence, Herod's palace. It was to the gates of this palace that the Jews brought Christ in the early morning, they not entering the house of a Gentile at the period of Passover (John xviii. 28). Pilate therefore came out to hear the indictment. (See JESUS.) Pilate assumed his office about A. D. 25. After ten years an appeal from the Samaritans (whom he had oppressed) to Vitellius, the President of Syria, caused him to be sent to Rome, to answer the charges brought against him. Tiberius died ere he reached Rome. It is generally held that he committed suicide from mortification.

PIL'DASH (*flame of fire*). Son of Nahor (Gen. xxii. 22).

PILE'HA (*a slice*). A chief who sealed the covenant (Neh. x. 24).

PIL'LAR (Heb. AMMUD; Gr. *stulos*). Pillars were an important feature in Oriental architecture: 1. *For monuments* (Gen. xxviii. 18). 2. *In building* (Judg. xvi. 25). 3. *As objects of idolatrous worship*

CARTHAGE, A COLONY OF PHŒNICIA.

(Deut. xii. 3). 4. Figuratively or symbolically (Ex. xxxiii. 9-10).

PILL'ED (*peeled*), (Gen. xxx. 37, 38). PEELED.

PIL'LON (Heb. CERIB, *braided*), (1 Sam. xix. 13, 16).—2. Heb. pl. CESATHOTH, *cushions* (Ez. xiii.

18, 20).—3. Heb. pl. MERAASHOTH, *under the head* (Gen. xxviii. 11, 18).—4. Gr. *proskephalaion*, a *cushion for the head* (Mark iv. 28).

PIL'TAI. The head of the priestly house of Modiah (Neh. xii. 17).

PINE, PINE'-TREE. 1. Heb. TIDHAR (Is. xli. 19). Several varieties of pine grew upon Mt. Lebanon. 2. SHEMEN (Neh. viii. 15), rendered "oil-tree." See CEDAR.

PIN'NACLE (Matt. iv. 5). Some high part of the Temple, or of the courts or wings belonging to it. Josephus says Herod built the royal gallery on the S. part, from the top of which, if any one looked down, he would become dizzy (Wars, v. 5, Ant. xv. 11, 5, xx. 9, 7). Late explorations have discovered the actual hight of the foundation wall to be about 150 ft., and the Temple buildings must have been 50 to 75 ft. more; making over 200 ft. (287 ft.—Barclay, *City of Great King*, 251). Eusebius says that James, brother of Jesus, was precipitated from this hight.

PI'NON (*darkness*). Founder of a tribe of Edom (Gen. xxxvi. 4).

PIPE (Heb. CHALIL). One of the simplest, but most prominent, of MUSICAL INSTRUMENTS.

PI'PER (Rev. xviii. 22). MUSIC.

PI'RA (1 Esd. v. 19). Repetition of CAPHIRA.

PI'RAM (*indomitable*). King of Jarmuth (Josh. x. 3, 27).

PIR'ATHON (*chief*). Where Abdon was buried, in the land of Ephraim (Judg. xii. 13, 15). Benaiah, one of David's captains, was from this city (2 Sam. xxiii. 30). Now called Ferata, 6 ms. S. W. of Shechem, in Wada Aly, near the foot of the mountain Shekh Abraham (Rob. iii. 134).

PIRA THONITE. Native of PIRATHON. 1. ABDON 1 (*the judge*), (Judg. xii. 13, 15).—2. BENAIAM 2 (2 Sam. xxiii. 30).

PIS'GAH (*to divide*—i. e., *isolated peak*). Mountain in Moab (Deut. iii. 17, xxxiv. 1; Josh. xii. xiii. 20). Although minutely described in the Scriptures, yet it has been difficult to locate. The present explanation of the matter is, that Abarim was the name of the range; Nebo one of the peaks; and Pisgah the top of Nebo. The passage would then read, "Moses went up to Mount Nebo, to the top of the hill." (See NEBO). The name Ras el Feshkah (the same as Pisgah) must have been transferred across the Dead Sea, as well as the name of the Jebel Mousa, S. E. of Bethany.

PISID'IA. In Asia Minor, S. of Phrygia, E. of Lydia, W. of Cilicia, and N. of Pamphylia. It is mountainous, but has many fertile plains and valleys. The scenery is wild and grand (some cliffs rising 1000 ft. over a foaming torrent); hightened by forests of oak, pine, and other trees, orchards of fruit-trees, and vineyards. Its people, in the time that Paul traveled through it, were warlike highlanders, and probably exposed the Apostle to the "perils of robbers" that he mentions. Antioch was in Pisidia, though on the border of Phrygia.

PI'SON (*overflowing*). River in Eden (Gen. ii. 11).

PIS'PAH (*spreading*). Son of Jether (1 Chr. vii. 38).

PIT. Used with a figurative as well as literal meaning. Heb. 1. SHEOL (Num. xvi. 30, 33), hollow.—2. SHAHATH (Ps. ix. 15), a pit dug into the earth.—3. BOR (Gen. xxxvii. 30, ff), a pit for water.

PITCH. A mineral pitch or asphalt. Heb. 1. ZEPHETH (Ex. ii. 3), liquid.—2. HEMAR, solid.—3. KOPER, in reference to its use in overlaying woodwork. Its nature is mentioned in Is. xxxiv. 9.

PITCH'ER (Heb. KAD, *barrel*). Water-jars with one or two handles, used by women for carrying water (Gen. xxiv. 15-20). They are carried on the head or shoulder. The Bedawin women use skin-bottles (Gen. xxi. 14).

PIT'DAH. One of the precious stones in the breast plate of the high priest (Ex. xxviii. 17). See PRECIOUS STONES.

PI'THOM. One of the store-cities built by the Israelites in Egypt, for the first oppressor (Ex. i. 11.) *Patumus* of Herodotus (ii. 158). Now called *Abbasch*, at the entrance of *Wady Fumilat*, on the line of the ancient canal to the Red Sea.

PI'THON. A descendant of Saul, son of Micah (1 Chr. viii. 35).

PLAGUES, THE, OF EGYPT. The so-called plagues of Egypt form the chief part of the miraculous side of the great deliverance of the Israelites from Egyptian bondage. These plagues will teach essentially the same lessons that the deliverance itself teaches. Indeed, the meaning of the deliverance from Egypt will be best learned from considering these miracles, which show it not to have been a mere symbolical act—shadowing or foreshadowing by this temporal deliverance from worldly bondage a spiritual redemption from spiritual oppression—but to have been itself a conflict with the powers of evil, deep and various, and a victory over them, and so a real redemption from the oppression of spiritual wickedness. The Jewish people were not only oppressed with sore bondage in brick and mortar, but their spirits were led captive under Egyptian idolatries; and the sight and circumstances of this deliverance shook them clear of these enslaving influences, though not completely. The so-called plagues are *ten* in number: 1. The turning of the waters of the Nile into blood (Ex. vii. 15). 2. Bringing up frogs from the river (Ex. viii. 1). 3. The gnats or mosquitoes (Ex. viii. 16). 4. Of flies (Ex. viii. 20). 5. The murrain of beasts (Ex. ix. 6). 6. The boils upon men and beasts (Ex. ix. 8). 7. Hail, etc. (Ex. ix. 13). 8. The locusts (Ex. x.). 9. The darkness (Ex. x. 21). 10. The destruction of the first-born of man and beast (Ex. xi.). The number *ten* is significant, ending, as it does, with the terrible blow struck direct from heaven—the full outpouring on Egypt of the divine wrath. See EXODUS, in HISTORY OF THE BOOKS.

PLAIN. Eight different Hebrew words are translated by this one word *plain*, in our version. 1. ABEL (*meadow*—see ABEL).—2. BIKA (*to cleave, a valley*). The valley between the two ranges of Lebanon is now called Buka. (See LEBANON). The same word is used to describe the plain on which the image was set up in the *plain* of Dura (Dan. iii.).—3. HAK-KIKKAR (*circar*), (*to move in a circle, as a coin or a loaf*), the plain around Jericho (Gen. xiii. 10).—4. HAM-MISHOR (*even place, plain*), in Deut. iii. 10, it refers to the region now called *El Belka*, the high level table-lands (of Moab) east of the Dead Sea.—5. HA-ARABAH (*dry region*), the peculiar name of the valley of the Jordan.—6. HA-SHEFELAH (*a low plain*), the name of the Plain of Philistia.—7. ELON (*oak*, or *grove of oaks*). The mistranslation loses much of the beauty and force of the original, as may be seen by correcting the reading in Gen. x. 6, to oak or grove of Moreh; and the same in Deut. xi. 30; in Gen. xiii. 18, to oak grove of Mamre; in Judg. iv. 11, to grove of the wanderers (Zanaim—wanderers), (where Bedawins pitch their tents?); in Judg. ix. 6, to the oak of the covenant, or monumental oak (The Charter Oak, Boston Elm, and Penn's treaty Elm, are instances in our country); in ver. 37, to grove of Meonenim (magicians); and in 1 Sam. x. 3, to oak or grove of Tabor.—8. EMEK, (*valley*), applied to the Plain of Esdraelon and other valleys or plains, as Achor, Ajalon, Baca, Berachah, Ledhrehob, Elah, Gibeon, Hebron, Jehoshaphat, Keziz, Rephaim, Shaveh, Siddim, and Succoth, besides the valley of "decision" in Joel iii. 14.

PLAIT'ING. Braiding the HAIR (1 Pet. iii. 3).

PLANES (Is. xliv. 13). Carving tools. HANDICRAFT.

PLANE'-TREE (Ecclus. xxiv. 14). CHESTNUT-TREE.

PLAN'ETS (2 K. xxiii. v.). ASTRONOMY.

PLAS'TER. 1. A house infected with LEPROSY was to be replastered (Lev. xiv. 42, 43, 48).—2. The law was to be engraved on Mount Ebal, on stones coated with plaster (Deut. xxvii. 2, 4).—3. (Dan. v. 5), the writing by the mystic hand was on the plaster of the wall.—4. A plaster of figs were applied to boils (Is. xxxviii. 21).

PLAT, TO (Gr. *pleko*). Interweaving (Matt. xxvii. 29).

PLE'IADES (Gr. *pleo, to sail*). A cluster of seven stars in the constellation Taurus. The sun enters Taurus about the middle of April; its appearance was a sign of Spring.

PLOW. See AGRICULTURE.

PLUMB'-LINE (Heb. ANAK). A line with a weight attached (Amos vii. 7, 8). HANDICRAFT.

PLUM'MET (Heb. MESHKELITH). Used in leveling (Is. xxvii. 17).

POCH'ERETH (*snaring*). The children of Pochereth were among those who returned from captivity (Ezr. ii. 57; Neh. vii. 59).

PO'ETRY. See PSALMS, in the HISTORY OF THE BOOKS.

POI'SON. References to poison in the Scripture are very rare and no death occurring through poison is recorded. The two Heb. words, 1. CHEMAH, feverish heat, 2. ROSH, applied to some poisonous herb. The crime of poisoning never prevailed among the Hebrews. It was studied as a science in the East, and common at Rome. There were many venomous snakes and insects in Palestine. The poison of snakes was used by the Scythians and Arabs to anoint their arrows; as also alluded to by Job (Job vi. 4). It is used figuratively in poetry for anger and hate (Ps. lviii. 4).

POLL. The head (Num. i. 2, 18).

POLL. To clip (2 Sam. xiv. 26). HAIR.

POLYG'AMY. See MARRIAGE.

POMEGRANATE.

POME'GRANATE. (Heb. RIMMON). A bush with dark green foliage and crimson flowers. The fruit is red when ripe and very juicy. The rind is used in the manufacture of leather. It is a native of Asia. The pillars in Solomon's Temple were adorned with carved figures of this fruit (1 K. vii. 18, 20). A fragment of the fruit with its pearly seeds imbedded in ruby liquid, is very beautiful. "Thy cheeks are like a piece of pomegranate" is the allusion of the poet to the line transparent tint (Ca. iv. 3).

POM'MELS (*little apples*), (2 Chr. iv. 12, 13). BOWL.

POND (Heb. AGAM). The ponds of Egypt (Ex. vii. 19) were doubtless water left by the inundation of the Nile. Ponds for fish are mentioned in Is. xix. 10.

PON'TIUS PI'LATE. PILATE.

PON'TUS. A district on the Black Sea (Acts. ii. 9, 10).

POOL. 1. Heb. AGAM, pond.—2. Heb. BERAKAH, blessing.—3. Heb. BEREKAH, a reservoir for water. These pools in many parts of Palestine and Syria are the only resource for water in a dry season (Is. xlii. 15). Those of Solomon, 3 miles S. W. of Bethlehem, and Bethesda in Jerusalem, are the most celebrated (Eccl. ii. 6). See JERUSALEM.

POOR. The poor received special favors from the law (Deut. xi. 7). 1. The right of GLEANING (Lev. xix. 9, 10). 2. Their portion from the produce of the land in the SABBATICAL YEAR (Ex. xxiii. 11). 3. Possession of land in the JUBILEE year (ver. 25, 30). 4. USURY and pledges (35, 37). 5. Permanent bondage forbidden (Deut. xv. 12, 15). 6. Portions of tithes (Deut. xiv. 28). 7. Their entertainments at feasts (xvi. 11, 14). 8. Payments of WAGES (Lev. xix. 13).

POP'LAR (Heb. LIBNEH). Poplar and storax trees are common in Palestine (Hos. iv. 13).

POR'ATHA (*favored*). Son of Haman (Esth. ix. 8).

PORCH. 1. ULAM, a vestibule, open in front and at the sides. Sometimes closed with awnings or curtains.—2. MISDRON, a corridor, connecting the principal rooms of the house (Matt. xvi. 71).

PORCIUS, FESTUS. FESTUS.

PORT (L. *Porta*). Gate (Neh. ii. 13).

POR'PHYRY (*purple*). A hard rock of various colors, greatly prized for its beauty when polished (Esth. i. 6). MARBLE.

POR'TER (SHOER, *a gate-keeper*), (1 Chr. ix. 21). LEVITES.

POSIDO'NIUS. An envoy sent to Judas (2 Macc. xiv. 19).

POST. The door-case of a door (Is. vi. 4). The posts of the Temple door were of olive-wood (1 K. vi. 33). 1. AJIL, door-case of a door (Ez. xl. 16). —2. AMMAR, *cubit*, a post (Is. vi. 4).—3. MEZUZAH, motion on a centre.—4. SAF, threshold (Ex. xxvi. 1).—5. RAZ, to run, posts (Esth. iii. 13); also guard; and a runner or carrier of messages in Job ix. 25.

Our word post means a fixed place—as a post, station, military or for travelers; also, the one who carries messages or travels by post (that is, with horses supplied at the post), and also the letter-carrier; and hence post-office.

POT. Is applied to many kinds of vessels, bowl, basin, cup, etc. 1. ASUK, an earthen jar, deep and without handles.—2. CHERES, an earthen jar, used for baking (Ez. iv. 9).—DUD, a kettle, used for cooking (1 Sam. ii. 14).—4. SIR, used for flesh (Ex. xvi. 3).—5. MAZREF, fining-pot (Prov. xxvi. 23. xxvii. 21).—6. GEBIYIM, bulging jars in Jer. xxxv. 5.

The water-pots of Cana were of stone or earthenware. They were also of precious metals for domestic or public use. The water-pot of the Samarian woman was either an earthen jar or a leather bottle. Pottery was a handicraft among the Hebrews, remains of which are found in the debris of the most ancient ruins.

POT'IPHAR (*belonging to the sun*). A captain of

the guard to whom Joseph was sold (Gen. xxxix. 1).

POTIPH'ERAH. A priest of On. Father of Asenath. Wife of Joseph (Gen. xli. 45, 50).

POT'SHERD (Heb. cheres). Earthen vessel or bottle. Anything mean and contemptible, or very dry (Is. xxx. 14, xlv. 9; Job. ii. 8).

POTTER'S FIELD. Bought by the priests with the bribe of 30 pieces given to Judas (Matt. xxvii. 7). ACELDAMA.

"THE GREAT CAMEO."
A Sardonyx, 13×11 inches; in five colored layers.

POTTERY. Was one of the most common and ancient of all manufactures. The clay, when wet, was trodden by the feet to form a paste, then placed on the wheel, and shaped by the hands. The wheel consisted of a wooden disc, placed on another larger one, and turned by the hand, or by a treadle (Is. xlv. 9). The vessel was then smoothed, and coated with a glaze, and burnt in a furnace (Is. xli. 25).

POUND. 1. (Heb. MANEH, *a weight*). See WEIGHTS AND MEASURES.—2. A piece of money (Luke xix. 12–27). MONEY. MANEH.

PRÆTO'RIUM. The head-quarters of the Roman governor. JUDGMENT-HALL.

PRAYER (Heb. TEHINNAH, *supplication*; TEFIL LAH, *to bow down*). To ask God for a blessing. Men have believed in all ages that the Divine Being hears prayer (Deut. iv. 29; 1 Chr. xxviii. 9, etc.), and answers it graciously (Ps. cxlv. 18, 19; 2 Chr. vii. 1) and willingly. Prayer is also called "seeking the Lord" (1 Chr. xvi. 10), intreating the face of the Lord (see FACE), pouring out the heart or soul before Him or before His face (Ps. lxii. 8; 1 Sam. i. 15), crying (1 K. viii. 28) or calling unto God, and a beseeching of God (Ps. iv. 16; Ex. xxxii. 11).

In the N. T. the approach of the soul unto God, with desire and request for help, is very distinctly stated in many passages (Matt. vi. 6, vii. 7; Luke x. 2; John xiv. 13; Eph. vi. 18; Phil. iv. 6; Col. iv. 2, 3, etc.). Nowhere in the Bible is there any word of explanation of the reason for prayer; the fact is dealt with as a fact, as plain as day and night.

The use of forms, in some cases, seems intended to secure the praise of men rather than of God (Matt. vi. 5). When the form is the most extensive and showy the true spirit is in danger of being lost.

The Lord's Prayer (Matt. vi. 9–13; Luke xi. 2–4) is the model for all Christian prayer.

Prayer is first distinctly mentioned in Abraham's time. Moses gave no special rules or laws for prayer, but we learn that it was considered as a privilege and a duty to which man's own nature prompted him. The altar was the place where prayer was believed to be most acceptable in the patriarchal age, and the tabernacle, under the Mosaic covenant (1 Sam. i. 10), which was changed for the Temple, was called "the house of prayer" (Is. lvi. 7). Those who could, prayed in the Temple; others at a distance turned their faces towards it—a custom which is still in practice. The Mohammedans also turn their faces towards the city of Mecca, which contains the holy house, the kaaba. See 1 K. viii. 30; 2 K. xix; 2 Chr. vii. 14; Dan. vi. 10; Jonah ii. 4; Zech. vii. 2; Luke ii. 37, xviii. 10; Acts xxii. 17. There is a certain power in outward symbols in helping men to realize the presence of God, in quickening their faith, and in carrying out the idea that sinful man can best approach his Maker by a sacrifice. These sentiments are as extensive as the human race. There are seven prayers recorded at their full length in the Scriptures (David, 2 Sam. vii. 19–29; Solomon, 2 Chr. vi.; Hezekiah, 2 K. xix.; Jeremiah, ch. xxxii.; Daniel, ch. ix. 3; Nehemiah, chs. i. ix.).

Nearly all of the prayers recorded in the O. T. were for temporal blessings—the Mosaic covenant promising no other; and many were intercessory, by priests or prophets, except, as may be learned from the Psalms, where there is shown a spirit of striving against sin and for help against temptation. The Hebrews prayed three times a day (Ps. lv. 17; Dan. vi. 10), and particular times or hours were thought to be more fit than others, when prayer was thought to be more acceptable (Ps. lxix. 13). Confession of sins to God was usual at the time of prayer as a part of the intercession.

In the Christian Church, Jesus the Christ takes the place of the temple and the altar and the priests and prophets in the old dispensation. He is the intercessor for His people, asking of God the Father blessings for His sake. The Christian form of prayer includes the Hebrew idea of intercession, pleading for benefits; and also adds the higher spiritual desires based on the idea of the brotherhood of all men (Matt. v. 44, ix. 38; 1 Tim. ii. 2, 8; 1 Col. iv. 13; Phil. iv. 6; James v. 14).

It is supposed that if certain rules are neglected in prayer that God will not answer prayer (Ps. lxvi. 18; Pet. xv. 29, xxviii. 9; James iv. 3; Is. i. 15), nor if one of God's commands is disobeyed (1 Sam. viii. 18), or the supplicant is proud and independent (Job xxxv. 12; Luke xviii. 20), or a hypocrite (Job xxvii. 9), or if he doubts, wavers, or is double-minded (James i. 6; Jer. xxix. 13; Mark xi. 24). Enmity in the heart and secret idolatry are also stumbling-blocks. For posture in prayer see ADORATION.

Prayer is the free utterance of the soul's wants to God the Father, asking benefits in the name of our Saviour, and interceding for the good of others also. Faith is quickened by prayer; and it may be said that prayer is an indication of the spiritual condition of the soul—it being to the soul what breath is to the body.

PREACH, TO. 1. (Heb. BASAR, *to bring glad tidings* (Ps. xl.).—2. KARA, *to call* (Gen. 1, 5).—3. Gr. *diangello, to announce fully* (Luke ix. 60).—4. Gr. *dialegomai, to discourse* (Acts xx. 7).—5. Gr. *euaggelizo, good news* (Luke iii. 18).—6. Gr. *kataggello, to publish* (Acts iv. 2).—7. *Kerusso, to proclaim* (Matt. iii. 1).—8. Gr. *laleo, to speak* (Mark ii. 2).—9. *Prokerusso, beforehand* (Acts iii. 20).—10. Gr. *Proeuaggelizomai, to announce glad tidings beforehand* (Gal. iii. 8).—11. *Parrhesiazo-*

mai, to be free, in speech or action (Acts ix. 27).—
12. Gr. *pleroo, to fulfil* (Rom. xv. 19).—13. Gr. *akoē, the hearing* (Heb. iv. 2).

PREACH'ER (Heb. KOHELETH). A public instructor of the Gospel (1 Tim. ii. 7).

PREACH'ING (Heb. KERIAH). Public discourse of the prophets (Matt. xii. 41).

PRE'CIOUS STONES. Alluded to very often in the Scriptures, and were known, used, and valued from the earliest times. Engraved gems worn in rings (Cant. v. 14), and used for private seals (Neh. x.), are mentioned in Genesis, and all through the Bible. The twelve stones of the high-priest's breast-plate were engraved with the name of one of the 12 tribes (Ex. xxviii. 17-21), and the whole when in their proper position on the breast of the high-priest were called Urim and Thummim (*light and perfection*).

The figurative uses of precious stones are very many, and highly poetical and important for instruction, and signify value, beauty, durability, excellence.

1. AD'AMANT (SHAMIR), the diamond, (Jer. xvii. 1; Ez. iii. 9; Zech. vii. 12), was known and used for its peculiar hardness in cutting other stones, and figuratively to describe the obduracy of the Israelites. The word is the same in all the texts, although rendered both diamond and adamant. The Greek *smiris* was a corundum, our emory.

2. AG'ATE (SHEBO), (Ex. xxviii. 19), the second stone in the high-priest's breastplate. Named from the river Achates, Sicily, where it was first found by the Greeks. It is a quartz in colored layers.

3. AM'ETHYST (AHLAMAH), 3d in the 3d row of the breastplate, and is alluded to in Rev. xxi. 20, as one of the stones of the heavenly Jerusalem.

4. BER'YL (TARSHISH) a yellow EMERALD. There is little or nothing to lead to any satisfactory conclusion as to its identity, except in Cant. v. 14. The streets of Jerusalem shall be paved with beryl (Rev. xxi. 20; Tob. xiii. 17).

5. CAR'BUNCLE. 1. (Heb. EKDAH,) bright, sparkling, gem.—2. (BAREKATH), the third stone in the first row of the breast-plate (Ex. xxviii. 17); also one of the treasures of the king (Ez. xxviii. 13). It is a precious stone of a deep red color, commonly called *garnet*.

6. CHAL'CEDONY, (Gr. *Chalkedon*), a precious stone (Rev. xxi. 19), resembling the agate; of various colors, but often light brown or blue, found in most parts of the world, named after Chalcedon.

7. CHRYS'OLITE (*golden stone*). A transparent precious stone, having the color of gold mixed with green. It has a fine lustre (Rev. xxi. 20). Many suppose it to be the topaz of the moderns.

8. CHRYSO'PRASUS. The tenth of those precious stones in the walls of the heavenly Jerusalem. Its color was golden green (Rev. xxi. 20).

9. CHRYS'OPRASE is the leek-green variety of agate.

10. EM'ERALD, (NOPHECH; Gr. *Smaragdos*). First in the second row on the breastplate of the high-priest (Ex. xxviii. 18). Used as a seal or signet (Ecclus. xxxii. 6), and spoken of as one of the foundations of Jerusalem (Rev. xxi. 19). It is of a fine green color, found anciently in Ethiopia, in modern times only in South America (Ex. xxviii. 18). It ranks next in value to the diamond.

11. JA'CINTH, (Gr. *huakinthos*), (*hyacinth*). A precious stone, of a dark purple color (Rev. xxi. 20). It loses its color when heated, and resembles the diamond.

12. O'NYX (SHOHAM, *a nail*). An agate colored like a finger nail (Ex. xxviii. 20; Gen. ii. 12).

13. RU'BY, (PENINIM). A red sapphire diamond, and more valuable than a diamond of the same weight (Is. liv. 12).

14. SAP'PHIRE (SAPPIR). Next in hardness and value to the diamond (Ex. xxviii. 18), of a blue

EGYPTIAN PRIESTS.

color and of various shades. Pliny described it as the lapis lazuli (Ultramarine), but that could not have been the kind in the breastplate.

15. SAR'DIUS, SARDINE (ODEM). Josephus says sardonyx (Ant. iii. 7, 6). Now called carnelian from its flesh color. The Hebrew name means red like flesh. The Sardius is a kind of flint, or chalcedony, and is valued more as it is deeper red. The name Sardius was given it at Sardis, where it was worked and engraved. It was in the high-priest's breastplate (Ex. xxviii. 17), and is alluded to by John in the Revelation (iv. 3).

16. SAR'DONYX (YAHALOM). A chalcedony with layers of several shades, much used in finger rings for the signet (Rev. xxi. 20). Rendered diamond in the A. V.

17. TO'PAZ (PITDAH, Gr. *topazion*). Second in the breastplate of the high-priest (Ex. xxviii. 17), and the ninth in the foundation of the heavenly Jerusalem (Rev. xxi. 20). Its color is wine yellow, of every degree of shade, from dark red, sometimes lilac, to pale grayish yellow, or celadon green. It was highly prized. Job says that wisdom is more valuable than the petdah of Cush (xxviii. 19). There is a topaz island in the Red Sea, where it is found. See SEAL, SIGNET RING.

ENGRA'VER, HARASH, (Ex. xxviii. 11). Print, to HAKAK, *to cut in* (Job xix. 23, 24).

PREPARA'TION, THE. (Mark xv. 42). PASS-OVER.

PRES'BYTERY (from Gr. meaning *old*, *elder*). A body of elders in the Christian Church (1 Tim. iv.). Also a body consisting of pastors, ruling elders, laymen, commissioned to represent the churches belonging to the presbytery. This work is subject to the revision of the synod.

PRESS (Joel iii. 13). WINE-PRESS.

PRETO'RIUM, or PRÆTO'RIUM (*leader*). The head-quarters of the Roman military governor. JUDGMENT-HALL (Mark xv. 16).

PREVENT, TO (Gr. *proevenio, to come before*). 1. (Heb. KADEM, *to anticipate*), (2 Sam. xxii. 6, 19). Gr. *prophthano, to precede* (1 Thess. iv. 15.)

PRICK (*goads*): "To kick against the pricks" (Acts ix. 5), should read, to kick against the goads; as an ox kicking against the goad in the hand of the driver.

PRIEST (Heb. KOHEN, *to foretell?* or *a mediator, a messenger*), Job xxxiii. 23). The word priest means one who presides over things relating to God, or, as Paul says, "Every high-priest taken from among men, is constituted on the behalf of men, with respect to their concerns with God, that he may present both gifts and sacrifices for sins" (Heb. v. 1). Adam is the first recorded priest; Noah was the

first after the deluge. It is probable that the patriarchs were priests, as in Job i. 5. The prophet differed from the priest in receiving supernatural communications of knowledge, of the past, present, and future. In the patriarchal system, the first-born male was the priest of the family, and succeeded his father. The Mosaic system substituted the tribe of Levi, instead of the first-born (Ex. xxviii.). The Hebrews were promised that, if they would keep the law of Moses, they should be "a peculiar treasure," "a kingdom of priests," "a holy nation" (Ex. xix. 5, 6). [For dress of the priest, see DRESS. See cuts of priests, on pps. 16, 69, 77, 131.] The age at which they were permitted to serve was not definitely fixed, as in the case of the Levites, but was, probably, at maturity—from 20 yrs. old. The support of the high-priest was, the tithe of 1-10th of the tithes assigned to the Levites (Num. xviii. 28; Neh. x. 38). The candidate for orders must prove his descent from Aaron; be free from bodily defects (Lev. xxi. 16-23); must not mourn outwardly; must marry only a young woman. They were to keep the sanctuary and altar (Num. xviii. 5); to keep the fire always burning on the altar (Lev. i. 7, vi. 13); to prepare the burnt offerings, and kill the passover (2 Chr. xxix. 34; Ezr. vi. 20); to do the work of a certain part of the sacrifices, generally (see OFFERING; SACRIFICE); to attend to the services of atonement; to blow the trumpets for all occasions; to prepare the ointment, or perfumed oil, and the water of separation; act as assessors in judicial matters; to assist in the work of organizing and encouraging the army; and to keep the books of the law (Deut. xx. 1-4, xxi. 5, xxxi. 9). They were permitted to eat, at the sanctuary, the flesh of the various offerings; and also to carry away—to be eaten in Jerusalem—certain parts of offerings; and had a right to the first-fruits of oil, wine, and grain, and certain parts of sacrifices (Deut. xviii); the price of redemption of man and of unclean beasts; restitutions, and all devoted things; the skins of the sacrificed animals (which was a very rich perquisite); donations; and might own land (1 K. ii. 26; Jer. xxxii. 7, 8). The total income is supposed to have been about 1-5th of the

EMMAUS.

entire national income (see Gen. xlvii. 24). The priesthood was a perpetual inheritance, transmitted from father to son. After the Captivity, those who could not prove their descent from Aaron lost their privileges as priests. The corruption of the priesthood, by making their office a means of amassing wealth, and intriguing, in politics, for political power, hastened the ruin of the Jewish nation. Christ is described in the N. T. as the first-born, the king, the anointed, a priest after the order of Melchizedek (Heb. vii., viii.). The priesthood in the Christian Church is a spiritual matter, deriving its powers and privileges from the Holy Spirit.

PRINCE. Governor of districts or local magistrates. JESUS CHRIST is "the PRINCE OF LIFE" (Acts iii. 15). SATAN "the prince of this world" (John xii. 31). PROVINCE.

PRIN'CESS (*noble lady*). "Queen" (Is. xlix. 23). Lady (Judg. v. 29).

PRINCIPALITY (*rulers*). The dominion of a PRINCE (Jer. xiii. 18).

PRINT, TO. (Heb. MATMAN, *to give*), (Gen. i. 29). See ENGRAVER; WRITING. "Printed," in Job xix. 23, should be "written" or "marked down."

PRIS'CA (*ancient*). PRISCILLA (2 Tim. iv. 19)

PRISCIL'LA. The wife of AQUILA (Rom. xvi. 3). The position, in several ancient MSS., of the name of Priscilla before that of her husband, indicates that she was the more active of the two in the Church, as appears in her teaching of Apollos. She is the type of the married servant of the Church, as Phebe is of the unmarried. Her assistance was asked by Timothy as of the utmost value in pointing out the actual wants and condition of the needy members of the Church.

PRIS'ON. Special places used as prisons were under the custody of a military officer (Gen. xl. 3). Private houses now sometimes used as places of confinement (Jer. xxxvii. 15). See PUNISHMENTS.

PRIS'ON-GATE. A gate of the JERUSALEM wall enclosing the Temple.

PROCH'ORUS (*leader of the chorus*). A Deacon (Acts vi. 5). DEACON.

PROCON'SUL. (Gr. *anthupatos, to be deputy*). A division of conquered provinces not requiring military rule, was governed by the Roman Senate by proconsuls, civil officers, and their districts were called proconsular. The term was usually one year. A coin of Ephesus gives the title ANTHUPATOS (Acts xix. 38). They did not have the power of life and death.

PROC'URATOR. Is the Latin name of the Roman ruler, translated GOVERNOR in the N. T. See PILATE. Gr. *êgemon*. They were similar in power to the proconsul, and were selected from among those who had been consuls or prætors, or senators. Their term of office depended on the will of the emperor. They wore a military dress and sword, and were attended by six lictors. They had the power of life and death. The head-quarters in Judæa were at Cæsarea, but held judicial wherever they were, as Pilate at Jerusalem. The high priest could be removed at will by him.

PROGEN'ITORS. Parents or ancestors (Gen. xlix. 26). GENEALOGY.

PROGNOSTICATORS, MONTHLY (Is. xlvii. 13). MAGICIANS.

PROPH'ET (Heb. NABI). Signifies an inspired person, an announcer of the words of another, not from his own influence and will (Ex. vii. 1, iv. 16); to foretell the future and secret events, and who revealed the will of God.

The O. T. prophets were special agents of Jehovah, raised up and sent, as occasion required, to incite to duty, to convict of sin, to call to repentance and reformation, to instruct kings and denounce against nations the judgments of God (2 K. xvii. 13). The prophets received their messages

from God in visions, trances and dreams (Num. xxiv. 2-16). The O. T. contains the inspired writings of sixteen of the Hebrew prophets, four of whom, Isaiah, Jeremiah, Ezekiel and Daniel, are called the greater, and the other twelve the minor prophets. Christ, of whom all the prophets bore witness (Luke xxiv. 27, 44), is THE PROPHET of His Church in all ages (Deut. xviii. 15), revealing to them by His inspired servants, by Himself and by His spirit all we know of God and immortality.

PTOLEMY I.

PROPH'ETESS (Heb. NEBIAH). A female PROPHET (Ex. xv. 20). MIRIAM; DEBORAH.
PROPITIA'TION. One who makes ATONEMENT (1 John ii. 2).
PRO'REX (*for the king*). Viceroy (2 K. i. 17).
PROS'ELYTE (Gr. *proselyti;* Heb. GERIM). This word is often used in the Septuagint as the rendering of the Heb. GEN, *a sojourner*, translated "a stranger" (Ex. xii. 48, xx.10, xxii. 21, etc.). The word from meaning "one who comes to," means, also, one "who comes over" from one faith to another. The law was liberal to strangers (GERIM), ordaining that they should be treated with forbearance and kindness (Ex. xxii. 21, xxiii. 9; Lev. xix. 33, 34). "The stranger that dwelleth with you shall be unto you as one born among you, and thou shalt love him as thyself, for ye were strangers," etc. The stranger or sojourner was ordered to be welcomed to the Passover Feast upon its observance of certain regulations (Ex. xii. 43, 45). The word in the sense of convert appears in the history and the writings of the prophets in Is. lvi. 3-8, "the sons of the stranger that join themselves to the Lord. The conquests of Alexander, the wars between Egypt and Syria, the struggle under Maccabees, and the occupation by Rome, brought the Jews into wide notice, and gave opportunities for proselytism. Such proselytes attended the Jewish worship and made pilgrimages to the feasts (Acts ii. 10). The admission into Judaism of a convert was by circumcision. Converts to Judaism were classed: 1. As love-proselytes. 2. Man-for-woman or woman-for-man proselytes; where the husband followed the wife's religion or the reverse. 3. Esther-proselytes, where conformity was assumed to escape danger (Esth. viii. 17). 4. King's-table-proselytes, converts for the hope of court favor—as under David and Solomon. 5. Lion-proselytes, converts in the fear of a divine judgment—as the Samaritans (2 K. xvii. 26). Proselytes became numerous during and immediately after Christ's period; many were converted in parts remote from Jerusalem (Acts ii. 10, viii. 27).
PROV'ERBS. See HISTORY OF THE BOOKS.
PROV'ENDER. Food for cattle (Gen. xxiv. 25). GRASS, CORN, HAY, etc.
PROV'IDENCE. Foresight (Acts xxiv. 2). GOD.
PROV'INCE. (Heb. MEDINAH). A small district ruled by a judge (1 K. xx. 14, 15, 19).
PROVIS'ION. Food. To lay up a supply of food, or what is desired (Rom. xiii. 14).
PRU'NING-HOOK (Is. xviii. 5). See KNIFE.
PSALM (Heb. MIZMOR, *a song of praise*), (1 Cor. xiv. 26). Music.

PSALMS, PSAL'TER. See HISTORY OF BOOKS.
PSAL'TERY (Heb. NEBEL). See MUSICAL INSTRUMENTS.
PTOL'EMAIS (*Ptolemy's city*). Acho, Acre (1 Macc. v. 15, 55, x. 1, 58, 60, xii. 48; Acts xxi. 7).
PTOL'EMEE. 1. Son of Dorymenes (1 Macc. iii. 38). He was active in the expedition which Lysias organized (1 Macc. iii. 38). He had great influence with Antiochus Epiphanes.—2. Son of Agesarchus, governor of Cyprus (2 Macc. viii. 8).—3. Son of Abubus, who married Simon's daughter. He was governor of the district of Jericho. He murdered Simon and two of his sons (1 Macc. xvi. 11).—4. Father of LYSIMACHUS I, the Greek translator of ESTHER (Esth. xi. 1) —5. PTOLEMY VI, PHILOMETOR (1 Macc. i. 18).—6. Son of DOSITHEUS (Esth. xi. 1). PTOLEMY.
PTOL'EMY. PTOL'OMEE, PTOL'EMEE (*the warlike*). The Greek title of the king of Egypt, as Pharaoh was the Egyptian title: first known to history in the time of Alexander, B. C. 323.

TABLE OF THE PTOLEMIES.

		1 Ptolemæus I. Soter. B. C. 323-285.
1 Ptol.	2 Ptol. II. Philadelphus. 285-247.
"	3 Arsinoe.
2 Ptol.	4 Ptol. III. Euergetes I. 247-222.
"	5 Berenice, married Antiochus II.
4 Ptol.	6 Ptol. IV. Philopator. 222-205.
"	7 Arsinoe. [Cleopatra)
7 Arsin.	8 Ptol. V. Epiphanes. 205-181; (m
8 P. &C.	9 Ptol. VI. Philometor. 181-146.
"	10 Ptol. VII. Euergetes II. Physcon
"	11 Cleopatra. [171-146-117.
11 Cleop.	12 Cleopatra (Alex. Balas her son).
"	13 Ptol. Eupator.
"	14 Cleopatra.
14 Cleop.	15 Ptol. VIII. Soter II. 117-81.

PTOLEMY I.—SOTER. Was the son of Lagus, a Macedonian, a natural son of Philip the King. Alexander made him a ruler in Egypt, where he

PTOLEMY II.

made a strong government. Daniel alludes to him (xi. 5), as one who should receive a part of Alexander's kingdom, by the title "King of the South." He treacherously captured Jerusalem on a Sabbath. Having carried many Jews to Alexandria, he gave them the full privileges of citizens in the new city. (See ALEXANDRIA).

PTOLEMY III.

PTOLEMY II.—PHILADELPHUS. Youngest son of Ptol. I, and was made king two years before his father's death. His daughter Berenice married Antiochus II: (see p. 18). This reign was a trying time for Judaism, and for the intellectual development of the ancient world (ALEXANDRIA). Philadelphus was a patron of art and science, and collected famous men and a large library. Daniel alludes to him in ch. xi.

PTOLEMY III.—EUER'GETES.—B.C. 247-222. Oldest son of Ptolemy Philadelphus, brother of Berenice (5). His sister's murder gave him an occasion for invading Syria (B. C. 246), alluded to in Dan. xi. 7. He recovered the images stolen out of Egypt by Cambyses, and brought home a vast treasure, earning the title of Benefactor (euergetes), and almost miraculously escaped from the threatened attacks of Seleucus (Dan. xi. 9), and developed the resources of his country.

PTOLEMY IV.—PHILOP'ATOR.—B. C. 222-205. He was a sensual and effeminate man, but energetic ruler. Daniel alludes to him (xi. 10-12). He offered sacrifices at Jerusalem in honor of his victories; but on attempting to enter the Holy of Holies he was struck with paralysis, for which he attempted to take revenge on the Alexandrian Jews, but was turned from his purpose by certain strange signs, which are differently reported by various historians. See APOCRYPHA. He was succeeded by

PTOLEMY V.—EPIPHANES.—B. C. 205-181. It was during this reign that ONIAS, the rightful

PTOLEMY IV.

high-priest, who had been driven away from Jerusalem, built a temple at Leontopolis. Daniel again pictures the actual condition of affairs in the words: "The robbers of the people exalted themselves to establish the vision" (xi. 14). "Many stood up against the king of the South" (Egypt); "so the king of the North (Antiochus) came and cast up a mount, and took the most fenced city" (Sidon), to which Scopas, the general of Ptolemy, had fled,

PTOLEMY V.

"and the arms of the South did not withstand" (Antiochus defeated the Egyptians at Paneas, B. C. 198—Dan. xi. 14, 15). The Romans then came in to make peace; "gave him (Ptolemy, his, Antiochus's, daughter) a young maiden" (as his wife, Dan. xi. 18), who did "not stand on his side," but supported her husband against her father.

PTOLEMY VI.

PTOLEMY VI.—PHILOMETER.—B. C. 181-146. Was son of Ptolemy V and Cleopatra, and was a child when his father was poisoned, the government being managed by his mother, who preserved peace with Syria until she died, B. C. 173. Antiochus Epiphanes invaded Egypt, but was forced to retreat by the Roman power. (See Dan. xi. 25-30). In this prophesy the ships of Chittim are the Romans. PTOLEMY EUERGETES II was ruler of Cyrene (1 Macc. xi. 18). Philometor is the last of the line mentioned in the Scriptures. In his reign the Jews were divided by the temple at Leontopolis. Onias, son of Onias III (see ONIAS), fled to Egypt from the political and priestly corruption at Jerusalem, and entered the service of the Ptolemy, with another Jew, Dositheus, and rose to supreme command, rendering important services to the Egyptian cause, in favor of Ptolemy Physcon against his brother. This service he made the basis of a demand for a ruined temple of Diana at Leontopolis, which he proposed to rebuild in imitation of the Temple at Jerusalem, quoting as divine authority Isaiah xix. 18. The building was made the same, but the furniture was different. Instead of the seven-branched candlestick there was a single lamp, suspended by a gold chain (Jos. Wars, vii. 10, 3). The altar and offerings were the same, and the service was by priests and Levites of clear descent. The building of the temple is dated about B. C. 149, but cannot be definitely fixed. Priests who had served in Egypt were forbidden to serve in Jerusalem, and the temple never had any great favor in Palestine, being looked upon as a kind of idolatrous shrine.

There were many Jews in Egypt (Jer. xliii. 6, 7), and Ptolemy Soter increased the number by policy and by force (Ant. xii. ii. 1), and they had great influence in Egypt (Ant. xii. 4); and one ARISTOBULUS is mentioned as the tutor (counselor) of the Ptolemy.

The Romans, in B. C. 71, plundered and closed the temple at Leontopolis (Jos. Wars, vii. 10).

PU'A. PUAH 2. Son of Issachar (Num. xxvi. 23).

PU'AH (*mouth*). 1. Father of Tola (Judg. x. 1).—2. Son of Issachar (1 Chr. vii. 1).—3 (*splendid*). One of the mid-wives whom Pharaoh ordered to kill the Hebrew male children (Ex. i. 15).

PUBAS'TUM (Ez. xxx. 17). PI'BESETH.

PUB'LICAN (Lat. *publicanus*; Gr. *telones*). Collectors of the Roman revenue. The publicans of the N. T. were regarded as traitors and classed with sinners (Matt. ix. 11), harlots (xxi. 31, 32), and with the heathen (xviii. 17). No money received from them was permitted to go into the alms-box. They were not allowed to sit in judgment or give testimony. Some of them were the earliest disciples of John the Baptist and of Christ (Luke xviii. 13).

PUB'LIUS (*public*). Governor of MELITA (Acts xxviii. 7, 8).

PU'DENS (*bashful*). A Christian friend of Timothy (2 Tim. iv. 21), at Rome. Martial, the Spanish poet, who lived at Rome about A. D. 66, mentions two or three friends, Pudens, Claudia, and Linus, who were the same as the friends of Paul and Timothy.

PU'HITES (*Jah is revelation*). Descendants of the family of Kirjath-Jearim.

PUL. Error for Phut or Put.

PUL (*king*). An Assyrian king, the first mentioned in Scripture. He made an expedition against MENAHEM, king of Israel. But we learn from the Assyrian monuments that Jehu had already paid tribute to Shalmanezer II, as recorded on the black obelisk. It is difficult, if not impossible, to identify Pul with any known Assyrian king. None of the monuments have a name at all like Pul. The monuments tell us that Tiglath-pileser took tribute of Menahem, and they say nothing of Pul. He may have been a usurper holding power in Western Assyria, and able to descend into Palestine; or a Babylonian, who grew to great command in those days. The period of Pul's invasion may

be thus fixed: Tiglath-pileser records that he took tribute from Menahem—a war which was carried on from his fourth to his eighth year, about B. C. 741 to 737.

Menahem reigned ten years, so that Pul's expedition could not be earlier than B. C. 751, or later than B. C. 745.

PUL'PIT (Heb. MIGDAL). An elevated stage, usually translated "tower" (Neh. viii. 4).

PULSE (Heb. ZEROHIM, ZERONIM, "to scatter, to sow"). A general name of peas, beans, and such kinds of garden sauce (Dan. i. 12, 16).

PUNISHMENTS. Were two fold, capital and secondary. 1. Stoning (Ex. xvii. 4). 2. Hanging (Num. xxv. 4). 3. Burning (Gen. xxxviii. 24). 4. By the sword (Ex. xix. 13). 5. Strangling (John xviii. 31). 6. Drowning (Matt. xviii. 6). 7. Sawing asunder (2 Sam. xii. 31). 8. Pounding in a mortar or beating to death (Prov. xxvii. 22). 9. Precipitation (2 Macc. vi. 10).

OF SECONDARY.—1. Retaliation (Ex. xxi. 24-25). 2. Compensation in money, or goods, or service (Ex. xxi. 18-36). 3. Stripes (Deut. xxv. 3). 4. Scourging (Judg. viii. 16).

PUNISHMENTS, for crime, or offense against the law, were inflicted directly on the person, or indirectly on his goods, or relatives. Capital punishment was instituted among the covenant people by Noah (Gen. ix. 5, 6), because murder was an offense against the image of God. The system of blood avenging was also set on foot by him, requiring the near relative to slay the murderer, even among near kinsmen. The patriarch of the family or tribe dispensed justice in the case (Gen. xxvi. 11, 29; xxxviii. 24). The mode was usually by stoning. Cutting off the head with the sword is not sanctioned in the Mosaic law, except that it might be a retaliation *in kind*, as in the case of Agag (1 Sam. xv. 33). Precipitation from a rock, or high place, was borrowed from other nations, as also cutting asunder (Dan. ii. 5; iii. 29; Luke xii. 46); and whipping or beating to death (Heb. x. 33). Casting into a den of lions is still practiced in Morocco. Moses permitted the hanging of the body on a tree after death, but it must be buried the same night (Deut. xxi. 22). Hanging alive was a Canaanite mode (2 Sam. xxi. 9). Stones were heaped over the body (buried or unburied), as a mark of contempt (Josh. vii. 25, 26), and "to make heaps" of a city was a peculiar ignominy (Is. xxv. 2; Jer. ix. 11), as also to burn a dead body, which was only permitted in two cases (Lev. xx. 14; xxi. 9). Crucifixion was practiced in the last days of the nation. Scourging (whipping on the bare back) was limited to 40 stripes (which were in later limited, by custom, to 39, lest by accident the number 40 be exceeded, 2 Cor. xl. 24). The soles of the feet were beaten with rods, or a lash, when the victim was lying on his face, and assistants held his feet in position (Lev. xix. 20; Deut. xxii. 18; xxv. 2, 3). Servants might be whipped (Ex. xxi. 20). Offenses against the rules of the church were punished by whipping (Matt. x. 17; Acts xxvi. 11) in the synagogue. The law of *retaliation* was regulated by rules,

so as to prevent mere revenge (Ex. xxi. 23-25; Lev. xxiv. 19-22), and a system of compensation was adopted (Ex. xxi.).

A false accuser suffered what he proposed to inflict wrongfully on another (Deut. xix. 19). Imprisonment was practiced for convenience rather than punishment (Lev. xxiv. 12). Debtors were shut up until they paid (Matt. xviii. 30); stocks were used (xiii. 27). See ANATHEMA. There is no direct reference to rewards or punishments in the future life in the Old Testament. See HADES.

PU'NITES, THE. Descendants of PUA, son of Issachar, (Num. xxvi. 23).

PU'NON (*darkness*). Identified with Pinon, the site of the copper-mines (Num. xxxiii. 42, 43), between Petra and Zoar. *Kalaat Phenan* is a ruined castle on a spur of Mt. Seir, and probably marks the ancient site.

PUR (*a lot*), (Esth. iii. 7). PURIM.

PURIFICATION (L. *making clean*). In all cases consisted by the use of waters—by ablution or sprinkling.

PU'RIM. The annual feast in memory of Esther. See HISTORY OF THE BOOKS.

PURSE. A BAG, in which the Hebrews carried their money when on a journey (Gen. xliii. 35); and merchants carried their weights (Deut. xxv. 13). The GIRDLE was used as a purse (Matt. x. 9).

PUT (1 Chr. i. 8). See PHUT.

PUTE'OLI. 8 ms. N. W. of Naples, on the shore; once called the Bay of Cumæ (see Virgil), and also Puteolanus. It was a famous watering-place, on account of its many warm springs. Ships landed cargoes of corn, and also passengers from the Levant, at this, the best harbor near Rome. The harbor was protected by a mole, the ruins of which are still to be seen. Scipio sailed from this port to Spain; Cicero had a villa in the vicinity, and Hadrian was buried near. Now called Puzzuoli.

PU'TIEL (*afflicted by God*). Daughter of Putiel, and mother of Phinehas (Ex. vi. 25).

PY'GARG. A clean animal (Deut. xiv. 5), of the antelope species.

PYTHON. A serpent slain by Apollo (Acts xvi.

PUTEOLI. PUZZUOLI.

16). DIVINATION. In the Greek and Roman mythology, Python was a huge serpent (darkness, or ignorance), which was born in the mud of Deucalion's Deluge, and killed near Delphi by Apollo (the sun or intelligence).

Q

QUAILS (Heb. SELAV). The quail is a bird of passage, about the size of a turtle-dove, and resembles the American partridge. They are plentiful near the shores of the Dead Sea, the Jordan, and in the deserts of Arabia. Its flight is very low, especially when fatigued, and it keeps

COIN OF HADRIAN.

close to the ground. They migrate in vast flocks, and at night, when they settle, they are so exhausted they may be captured by the hand (Ex. xvi. 13).

QUAR'RY (Heb. PESEL). In Judg. iii. 19, only, in 52 other places graven, or carved images. See IDOL—GEOLOGY IN PALESTINE.

QUAR'TUS (*four, fourth*). A disciple of Corinth (Rom. xvi. 23). Tradition says he became bishop of Berytus.

QUATER'NION (*four*). A guard of four soldiers, two were attached to the prisoner, and two kept watch outside the cell (Acts xii. 4).

QUEEN (Heb. MALCAH, *wife*), (Esth. i. 9). SHEGAL, consort (Neh. ii. 6), GEBIRAH, *powerful* (1 K. xv. 13). Queen is applied to the woman who exercises the highest authority; and this in the East, is not the wife but the mother of the master. The case of Esther is an exception.

QUEEN OF HEAV'EN (MELECHETH HASSHAMAYIM). See MOON and HERA.

QUICK. 1. (Heb. HAY or CHAY, *alive, living*) (Num. xvi. 30).—2. (Heb. MIHYAH or MICHYAH, *the quick*), (Lev. xiii. 10).—3. (Heb. HARIHO or HARICHO, *to breathe*), (Is. xi. 3). Gr. *zon*, "the quick and the dead " (Acts x. 42).

QUICK'EN, TO (Heb. HIYAH or CHIYAH, *to live*), to give spiritual or eternal LIFE (John vi. 63).

QUICK'SANDS (Gr. *surtis;* Lat. *syrtis*), (Acts xxvii. 17). The sand from the great desert of Sahara is carried by the wind into the sea, along the shore, where the sluggish currents in the Syrtis Minor and Syrtis Major (two great bays on the coast of Africa) allow it to settle and form quicksand—that is sand and water in such a state as to move with a current or be tossed into waves by a storm of wind—where a vessel is in great danger. This same sand, when carried by currents to the shore of Palestine, fills up the harbors there, and creeps up inland, destroying every green thing for miles, as at Gaza, Ascalon, Acre, Tyre, etc.

QUIN'TUS MEM'MIUS (Latin), (2 Macc. xi. 34). See MEM'MIUS, QUINTUS.

QUIV'ER. 1. Heb. TELI, *to hang* (Gen. xxvii. 3).—2. Heb. ASHPAH (Job xxxix. 23). A case or sheath for holding arrows. See ARMS.

R

RA'AMAH (*trembling*). Fourth son of Cush (Gen. x. 7). Settled on the Persian Gulf (probably where we find Sheba, on the island Bahreyn), and renowned in Ezekiel's time as trading with Tyre (Ez. xxvii. 22) in spices, precious stones and gold.

RAAMI'AH. A chief who returned from captivity (Neh. vii. 7).

RAAM'SES. RAMESES (Ex. i. 10).

RAB'BAH (*greatness*). Several places of this name. 1. (Deut. iii. 11). A very strong place east of Jordan; almost the only city of the Ammonites. This may have been the city of the Zuzims, in Ham (Gen. xiv. 5). The sarcophagus of the giant Og was here (Deut. iii. 11). The extensive ruins of Rabbah, now called *Ammon*, are found on both sides of a perennial stream, the banks and bed also being paved through the city, about 19 miles southeast of Es Salt, and 22 miles from the Jordan, in a long valley, a branch of the Wady Zerka. The theatre is very large and well preserved. Roman and Christian buildings are also found. Some of the columns are five feet in diameter. Ezekiel's prophesy is literally fulfilled, and the place has become a stable for camels and a couching place for flocks (xxv. 5). David took the city by his general, Joab, when Uriah the Hittite was killed (2 Sam. xi.). It was named Philadelphia by Ptolemy Philadelphus, B. C. 250. Coins of this city are extant, bearing the figure of Astarte. The Christian Church is still in excellent preservation.—2. The city of AR was also called Rabbath Moab.—3. A city of Judah (Josh. xv. 60). Lost.—4. In Josh. xi. 8, Zidon is called Zidon Rabbah, translated great Zidon.

RAB'BATH. Of the children of Ammon (Deut. iii. 11).

RAB'BI (*my master*). A title of respect which the Jews gave to their teachers and physicians, and especially to our Lord (Matt. xxiii. 7, 8). EDUCATION. SCRIBES.

RAB'BITH (*multitude*), (Josh. xix. 20). Issachar. Lost.

RABBO'NI (*great master*), (John xx. 16). RABBI.

RAB'MAG (*chief priest*). A title borne by the king, NERGAL-SHAREZER (Jer. xxxix. 3, 13).

RAB'SACES. RABSHAKEH (Ecclus. xlviii. 18).

RAB'SARIS. 1. An officer of the king of Assyria (2 K. xviii. 17).—2. A prince who was present at the capture of Jerusalem, B. C. 588 (Jer. xxxix. 3-13).

RAB'SHA-KEH (*chief cup-bearer*). An officer of the king of Assyria sent against Jerusalem (2 K. xviii., xix.).

RA'CA (Chal. *reyka, worthless*). A term of contempt used by the Jews in Christ's age (Matt. v. 22).

RACE. See GAMES.

RA'CHAB. RAHAB, the harlot (Matt. i. 5).

RA'CHAL (*traffic*), (1 Sam. xxx. 29). South, in Judah. "Haunted" by David. Lost.

RA'CHEL (*a ewe*). The youngest daughter of LABAN, wife of JACOB, mother of JOSEPH and BENJAMIN. The history of Rachel may be found in Gen. xxix., xxxiii., xxxv. See JACOB.

The so-called tomb of Rachel is about half a mile from Bethlehem, near the Jerusalem road.

RAD'DAI (*treading down*). Brother of David, and son of Jesse (1 Chr. ii. 14).

RA'GAU (Judg. i. 5, 15). RAGES? Mts. of R. 2. REU, in the line of CHRIST, (2 K. iii. 35).

RA'GES (Tob. i. 14, v. 5; Jud. i. 5). In Media, 5 ms. S. E. of the modern Teheran. Mentioned in the ancient inscriptions of Darius. The Zendavesta records that "the earliest settlement of the Aryans" in Media was in this city, and district of

the same name. It was near the celebrated Caspian Gates, which guarded the great highway between India, Bactria, etc., to Media. The ruins cover a space of 13,500 ft. long, by 10,500 ft. broad. The walls were of great thickness, and flanked by towers, and there are immense heaps of ruins. The modern city, Teheran, was built from the ancient ruins, which are now called Rhey.

RA'GUEL (*friend of God*). 1. A prince-priest of Midian, father of ZIPPORAH (Ex. ii. 18, 21).—2. A pious Jew, father of Sara (Tob. iii. 7, 15).

RA'HAB (*broad*). A woman of Jericho, who entertained the spies sent by JOSHUA, and was saved, with her family, when the city was destroyed (Josh. ii. 1-21). She became the wife of Salmon, a prince of Judah (Ruth iv. 21), and so a mother in the royal line of David and of Jesus.

RA'HAB (Ps. lxxxvii. 4). A poetical name for Egypt. The word in Hebrew means *fierceness*, *insolence*, *pride*.

RA'HAM (*womb*). Son of Shema (1 Chr. ii. 44).

RA'HEL (RACHEL), (Jer. xxxi. 15).

RAI'MENT. DRESS.

RAIN (Heb. MALKOSH, *violent rain*). The "early" and the "latter" rain of Palestine is mentioned in Deut. xi. 14. See CLIMATE.

RAIN'BOW (Heb. KESHETH), (Gen. ix. 13-16). The token of the COVENANT.

RAIS'ING FROM THE DEAD. RESURRECTION.

RAI'SIN. VINE.

RA'KEM. Son of Sheresh (1 Chr. vii. 16).

RAK'KATH (*shore*), (Josh. xix. 35). A fortified city in Naphtali, near Hammath and Chinnereth. There is a Kerak near the outlet of Jordan, from the sea of Galilee, which may mark the site.

RAK'KON (*thinness*), (Josh. xix. 46). Near Joppa. Me-jarkon? Lost.

RAM (*high*). 1. Son of Hezron (Ruth iv. 19).— 2. First born of Jehrahmeel (ii. 25, 27).—3. Son of Barachel (Job xxxii. 2).

RAM (Heb. AYIL). Male sheep (Ezr. vi. 9, 17).

RAM, BATTERING (CAR). See ARMS.

RA'MA (Matt. ii. 18). RAMAH (Jer. xxxi. 15). A city in Mt. Ephraim, or Benjamin. Matthew refers to the ancient massacre, and also at the same time to that of the innocents of Bethlehem. The name Ramah forms a part of several names, and means *high*. 1. In Benjamin (Josh. xviii. 25). Five miles N. of Jerusalem, near Geba. The palm tree of Deborah (Judg. iv. 5) was near it, in a valley toward Bethel. It is now a poor village in the midst of columns, hewn stones, and other ruins of antiquity. Cirama (1 Esd. v. 20).—2. In Mt. Ephraim (1 Sam. i. 1). The home of Elkanah, Samuel's father; the birthplace of Samuel, his home and official residence, the station of his altar, and where he was buried (xx. 1). Supposed by some to be the same as the first, in Benj.—3. (Josh. xix. 29). Boundary of Asher, 1 mile N. E. of Ras el Ain, two and a half S. E. of Tyre. There is another *Ramch*, 10 miles S. E. of Tyre. 4. In Naphtali (ib. v. 36), one of the fortified cities, 7 miles S. E. of Safed on the way to Acre, on a lofty hill commanding one of the finest views in Palestine. 5. RAMOTH GILEAD (2 K. viii. 29; 2 Chr. xxii. 6).—6. Ramleh (Neh. xi. 33), near Joppa.

RAMAH IN MOAB.

RA'MATH LEHI (Judg. xv. 17). Where Samson slew 1,000 men with a jawbone, and named the place *Wielding of the Jawbone*.

RA'MATH MIZ'PEH (*high place of the watchtower*), (Josh. xiii. 26). Boundary of Gad. Where Jacob and Laban set up a monument of stones. Lost. Dr. Eli Smith found many names of places on the east of Jordan, which, when more carefully examined and their sites explored, may result in settling many points of topography in that region now wholly uncertain. The Palestine Exploration has made several discoveries, and added much to our knowledge of this region, and are still at work.

RA'MATH OF THE SOUTH (Josh. xix. 8). In Simeon, in the extreme south. Baalath Beer? South Ramoth (1 Sam. xxx. 27), or Ramoth Negeb. Lost.

RAMATHA'IM ZOPHIM (*the double eminence*). (1 Sam. i. 1). Supposed to have been south of Jerusalem. The same as Ramah 2?

RAM'ATHEM. Error in 1 Macc. xi. 34, for RAMATHAIM.

RAM'ATHITE, THE. Native of RAMAH. Shimei had charge of the royal vineyards of King David (1 Chr. xxvii. 27).

RAM'ESES, RAAM'SES (Gen. xlvii. 11). The

land of Goshen. A city in the same land, enlarged and fortified by the Jews (Ex. i. 11, xii. 37). There were (and now are) other places of this name in Egypt. Abu Kesheyd, a modern village, has an antique monolith, on which is carved a group, Rameses II, between Tum and Ra.

RAM'IAH (*Jah hath s.t*). Son of Parosh (Ezr. x. 25).

RA'MOTH (*hights*), (1 Chr. vi. 73). Issachar. Jarmuth? Remoth?

RA'MOTH (*hights*). A layman (Ezr. x. 29).

RA'MOTH IN GILEAD (Deut. iv. 43; Josh. xx. 8). Now Es Salt. The site is on a high and picturesque hill, almost surrounded by deep ravines, and encompassed by mountains. Jebel Osha, the highest peak of Gilead, is only 2 ms. N. Vineyards and olive-groves beautify and enrich the place; the ruins are not extensive, being a square castle with towers, and a moat, on the hight, and a great number of tombs and grottos in the ravines.

RAM'S SKINS, DYED RED. Were presented by the Israelites, as offerings for the making of the Tabernacle (Ex. xxv. 5). They served for the inner coverings.

RAN'GES FOR POTS (Lev. xi. 35). Rack or bed for holding the egg-shaped-bottom earthern jars (pots), which will not stand alone.

RAN'SOM. 1. (Heb. kofer, *a cover*), (Ex. xxxi. 12).—2. (Heb. pidyon), (Ex. xxi. 30). Redemption. Gr. *lutron*, *a ransom* (Matt. xx. 28).

RA'PHA (*tall*). 1. A giant, and father of a family of tall men (2 Sam. xxi. 16, ff).—2. A descendant of Benjamin (1 Chr. viii. 2).—3. Son of Binea (1 Chr. viii. 37).

STORK.

RA'PHAEL (*the divine healer*). One of the 7 holy angels (Tob. xii. 15).

RAPH'AIM. Ancestor of Judith (Jud. viii. 1).

RA'PHON (1 Macc. i. 37). Raphana (?), one of the Decapolis. Er Rafe?

RA'PHU (*healed*). Father of Palti (Num. xiii. 9).

RAS'SUS, CHILDREN OF. A nation whose country was ravaged by Holofernes (Jud. ii. 23).

RATH'UMUS. The story-writer (1 Esd. ii. 16, 17, 25, 30).

RA'VEN (Heb. oreb). A bird similar to the crow, but larger. It feeds on dead bodies (Prov. xxx. 17). It drives away its young as soon as they can shift for themselves (Job xxxviii. 41). Elijah was fed by ravens (1 K. xvii. 6). The raven was sent from the Ark on the subsiding of the waters (Gen. viii. 7).

RA'ZIS (*destruction*). An elder of Jerusalem, who killed himself rather than fall into the hands of the wicked (2 Macc. xiv. 37-46). This is the only instance of a suicide in the whole range of Jewish history, unless the cases of Samson and Saul are so considered.

RA'ZOR. The razor was very little used by the Jews (Num. vi. 9, 18).

REAI'A. Son of Micah (1 Chr. v. 5).

REAI'AH (*whom Jah cares for*). 1. Son of Shobal (1 Chr. iv. 2).—2. Ancestor of Nethinim, who returned from captivity (Ezr. ii. 47).

RE'BA (*fourth part*). A king of the Midianites (Num. xxxi. 8).

REBEK'AH, Rebecca (*ensnarer*). Daughter of Bethuel (Gen. xxii. 23). Sister of Laban, married to Isaac. There is a beautiful and touching incident of "Rebekah at the well." This bright little picture, with its conclusion, comprises all the circumstances of a perfect marriage. The sanction of parents, the favor of God, the domestic habits of the wife, her beauty, kindness, modest consent, and her successful hold on her husband's love (even in the same tent with her mother-in-law). The account in Genesis gives many allusions to manners and customs, purely Oriental and strictly peculiar to the Hebrews as distinct from the people around them. The drawing of water at the well by women, the very mode of carrying the pitcher *on her shoulder* instead of on the head, as other people do; her manner of giving drink from the pitcher *on her hand*; her respectful request, "Drink, my lord," and finally her watering the camels in the trough—all are true in every particular, and of Hebrews only. The ornaments she wore, the hospitality offered and given, the marriage contract, journey to Canaan, the manner in which she met and saluted her betrothed husband, all indicate the minute truth and accuracy of the Bible text. Rebekah was buried in Machpelah, where she is still honored with a tomb near her husband's.

RE'CHAB (*horseman*). 1. Ancestor of Jehonadab (2 K. x. 15, 23).—2. Captain of bands in the service of Ishbosheth (2 Sam. iv. 2).—3. Father of Malchiah (Neh. iii. 14).

RE'CHABITES (*descendants of* Rechab). Ancestor of Jehonadab (1 Chr. ii. 55). See Jehonadab.

RE'CHAH (*side*). The founder of Ir-nahash (1 Chr. iv. 12).

RECORD'ER (Heb. mazcir). An officer of high rank of the privy council (2 Sam. viii. 16).

REDEEM'ER (Heb. goel). One who redeems a field by paying back what it had been sold for; this right belonged to the nearest kinsman (Lev. xxv. 25, 26); often applied to God as the redeemer of men, and especially Israel (Job xix. 25).

REDEEMER, JESUS, THE (Gal. iii. 13, iv. 5).

REDEMPTION. 1. Heb. geullah, the *redemption* or repurchase of a field (Lev. xxv. 24, 51, 52).—2. Heb. peduth, pidyom, pidyon, *ransom* (Num. iii. 49; Ps. xlix. 8). 3. Gr. *apolutrosis*, *letting off for a ransom* (2 K. xxi. 28). 4. Gr. *lutrosis*, *deliverance* (2 K. ii. 38).

RED HEIF'ER. Purification.

RED SEA (Num. xxi. 14). Called *the sea*, in Ex. xiv. 2, 9, 16, etc. The Gulf of Suez in the Exodus, and also the Gulf of Akabah later in the wandering. Called the *sea of suph* in Ex. x. 19, that is, the sea of *reeds*, or *flags*. A seaweed resembling *wool* (in whiteness) is thrown up in great quantities on the shores of the Red Sea (Diodorus iii. 19). The same word was used to name the weeds, or reeds, in which Moses was laid when an infant (Ex. ii. 3). It is thought the *papyrus* was meant. The Abyssinians now use papyrus boats.

It is supposed that "the tongue of the Egyptian

Sea," the head of the Suez Gulf, has dried up, as predicted by Isaiah (xi. 15, xix. 5), for a distance of 50 ms. The ancient head would have been at *Aboo Keshayd*, which has been identified with the ancient Hero. Necho's canal, which was wide enough for two triremes to row abreast (Herodotus ii. 158), once led from the gulf to the Nile, but it is now filled with sand. The Suez canal, just opened, leads to the Mediterranean. The sea is nearly 1400 ms. long by 100 to 200 ms. in its widest part. The deepest water is 6,324 feet, in lat. 22° 30'. It is filled with coral and other rocks and rocky islands for 40 or 50 ms. on each side, leaving a narrow and dangerous channel, which is narrowest opposite El Medeenah. The Suez Gulf is 130 ms. long and 18 wide. The Akabah Gulf is 100 ms. long by 15 wide. This is a continuation of the *Arabah*, and is bordered on both sides by steep and high mountains—Sinai on the west, and the spurs of Mt. Seir, Edom, on the east, from 3,000 to 6,000 feet high, the highest being to the south. The island of Graia, fortified by the crusaders, lies near the west shore, not far from the north end. The ruins of walls, castles, a church, etc., mostly of the middle ages, cover the whole rocky area. The straits at the south end of the sea are called Bab el Mandeb (*Gate of Tears*), from the many shipwrecks which have happened after passing them, either way

REED. See PAPYRUS.

REELAI'AH (*Jah makes tremble*). One who went with Zerubbabel (Ezr. ii. 2).

REE'LIUS (1 Esd. v. 8). BIGVAI.

REESAI'AS. RAAMIAH (1 Esd. v. 8).

REFI'NER (Heb. ZOREF. MEZAREF). Refining being the separation of the pure metal from the dross, by means of fire, suggested an apt subject for illustration, as in Is. i. 25; Zech. xiii. 9; Mal. iii. 2, 3. A full, figurative allusion to the refiner's process is in Jer. vi. 29, 30. See METALS.

REFUGE, CITIES OF. 6 out of the 48 Levitical cities were set apart as a refuge for any one who should accidentally kill another, to stay there until the death of the high-priest (Num. xxxv. 6, 13, 15; Josh. xx. 2, 7, 9). There were 3 on each side of Jordan. On the E. side were Bezer, Ramoth in Gilead, and Golan, and on the W. side were Kedesh in Galilee, Shechem, and Hebron. The right of asylum of many cities, in ancient classic nations, and of sanctuary in Christian countries (the privilege of many churches in the middle ages especially), are parallel, and show the wisdom of the law-makers, in providing a means of abating the evils of the system of blood-revenge, which are peculiarly Oriental, and very wasteful of human life. Moses abolished the custom of allowing money to be paid as a compensation for a human life, as was the case in Athens and many eastern countries, and is now among the Arabs. The cities are each described under their respective names.

RE'GEM (*friend*). Son of Jahdai (1 Chr. ii. 47).

RE'GEM ME'LECH (*friend of the king*). He, with Sherezer, was sent on behalf of some of the Captivity, to make inquiries at the Temple concerning fasting (Zech. vii. 2).

REGENERA'TION (*born again*). Birth into new spiritual life (John iii. 3), and thus becoming a new creature (2 Cor. v. 17), and being made partakers of the Divine Nature (2 Pet. i. 4) by means of the Holy Spirit (John iii. 4). "The washing of regeneration" alludes to the purifying by the Holy Spirit (Titus iii. 5). The especial work of the Holy Spirit in restoring man to the original image of God.

RE'GION. 1. (Heb. HEBEL, *a rope*), (Deut. iii. 4, 13). Once translated "the country of Argob" (iii. 14). Coast, in Zeph. ii. 5–7.—2. NOPHAH (*hight*). The region of Dor (1 K. iv. 11).—4. Gr. *klima*, climate (2 Cor. xi. 10).—4. Gr. *chora*, country (Matt. ii. 12).

RE'GION ROUND ABOUT, THE (Gr. *he perichoros*). The populous and flourishing country which contained JERICHO, in the Jordan valley, enclosed by the hills of *Quarantania* (Mark vi. 55).

REHABI'AH (*whom Jah enlarges*). Son of Eliezer (1 Chr. xxii. 17).

RE'HOB (*room*). 1. Father of Hadadezer, king of Zobah (2 Sam. viii. 3, 12).—2. A Levite, who sealed the covenant (Neh. x. 11).

RE'HOB. Several of this name. 1. The northern limit of the exploration of the spies (Num. xiii. 21). Toward Hamath. Dan was "by Beth-rehob," *Ruhaibeh*, 25 miles N. E. of Damascus, has been offered as the locality. Dr. Robinson favored *Hunin*, a village and castle west of Paneas.—2. In Asher (Josh. xix. 28), near Zidon.—3. Another in Asher, not identified.

REHOBO'AM (*he enlarges the people*). The son of Solomon, by the Ammonite princess Naamah (1 K. xiv. 21, 31), whom he succeeded. By neglecting his father's counselors he hastened the division of the tribes which had been restrained by the government of Solomon. Instead of forcing submission by military means, Rehoboam was advised by Shemaiah to fortify the cities against the Egyptians (2 Chr. xi. 6–10). But resistance was useless against Shishak, king of Egypt, who, after having forced the protecting line of fortresses, marched upon Jerusalem, and Rehoboam had to purchase his release by giving up the treasure accumulated by Solomon, including the golden shields. After this calamity he reigned peacefully. He was on the throne seventeen years.

REHO'BOTH (*room*). A well dug by Isaac (Gen. xxvi. 22). The wells Sitnah, Esek and Rehoboth were west or southwest of Beersheba. *Wady Ruhaibeh* is 20 miles S. W. of Beersheba, and is claimed as the place by Dr. Bonar (*Desert of Sinai*, 316).—2. Rehoboth by the River (Gen. xxxvi. 37). On the Euphrates, just below the Khabur, stands *Rahabah*, in the midst of extensive ancient ruins. —3. THE CITY. One of the four built by Nimrod. As the name means in our tongue, "to be wide," or "spacious," or "streets," the passage in Gen. x. 11, 12, may describe one city, Nineveh, which was spacious, and had several quarters, as Resen, Calah, altogether forming "a great city."

RE'HUM (*compassionate*). 1. One who returned from captivity (Ezr. ii. 2). NEHUM.—2. One of those who wrote to Artaxerxes to stop the rebuilding of the Temple (iv. 8, 9, 17, 23).—3. A Levite, who rebuilt the wall (Neh. iii. 17).—4. A chief who sealed the covenant (x. 25).—5. Head of a priestly house (xii. 3).

RE'I (*friendly*). A person mentioned as loyal to David, during the rebellion (1 K. i. 8).

REINS (Gr. *renes*, kidneys). 1. (Heb. KELAYOTH.) In ancient physiology the kidneys are believed to be the seat of desire, and are often coupled with the heart (Ps. vii. 9).—2. (Heb. MALATSAYIM, *loins*, Gen. xxxv. 11; Gr. *nephros*, Rev. ii. 23).

RE'KEM (Heb. *flower-garden*). 1. One of the kings of Midian (Num. xxxi. 8).—2. Son of Hebron (1 Chr. ii. 43, 44).

RE'KEM (Josh. xviii. 27). Ain Karem, W. of Jerusalem? See page 172.

REMALI'AH (*Jah decks*). Father of PEKAH, king of Israel (2 K. xv. 25, 37).

REM'ETH (*hight*), (Josh. xix. 21). Wezar (Ar. for *hight*), a ruin on a hill 5 ms. N. of Jenin, at the foot of Mt. Gilboa.

REM'MON (Josh. xix. 7). In Simeon. RIMMON.

REM'MON METH'OAR (Rimmon, *which reaches*), (Josh. xix. 13.) Zebulun, 6 miles N. of Nazareth.

REM'PHAN. An error for CHI'UN (in Acts vii. 43, from Amos v. 26). The Hebrew name of the Greek god Saturn. See IDOLATRY. Saturn was a king of Latium, and was, after his death, deified, and worshiped as the god of agriculture. (Gr. *sotor, planter*).

RENDING, RENT. DRESS; MOURNING.

REPENT'ANCE (Heb. NOHAM). (Hos. xiii. 14). (Gr. *metanoia, change of purpose*), (Heb. xii. 17).—(Gr. *ametameletos, unchangeable*), (Rom. xi. 29). A change of mind, with sorrow for something done, and a wish that it was undone (Matt. xxvii. 3). Esau found no repentance in his father (Heb. xii. 17). God is sometimes said to repent of something he had done (Gen. vi. 6). The true Gospel repentance is sorrow for sin (Matt. xiv. 17).

RE'PHAEL (*God heals*). Son of Shemaiah (1 Chr. xxvi. 7).

RE'PHAH (*riches*). Son of Ephraim (1 Chr. vii. 25).

REPHAI'AH (*whom Jah healed*). 1. His sons are among the descendants of Zerubbabel (1 Chr. iii. 21).—2. A Simeonite chief (iv. 42).—3. Son of Tola (vii. 4).—4. Son of Binea (ix. 43).—5. Son of Hur and ruler of the half-part of Jerusalem (Neh. iii. 9).

REPH'AIM (Heb. REPHAIM). See GIANTS.

REPH'AIM, THE VALLEY OF (*valley of the stretch-downgiants*). On the south of a hill which borders the valley of Hinnom, on the west. David made it famous on two (or three) distinct occasions (2 Sam. v. 18, 22; Is. xvii. 5). The very interesting incident related in 2 Sam. xxiii. 13-17, took place on one of these invasions of the Philistines. This valley (or plain) is flat, fertile, is shut in on all sides by rocky hill-tops and ridges, and ends to the west of the valley of Roses (*Wady el Werd*).

REPHI'DIM (*rests*, or *stays*), (Ex. xvii. 1, 8, xix. 2). Station of the Exodus, between Egypt and Sinai. The people murmured for water, and Moses smote the rock in Horeb "before the people;" and therefore if Horeb and Sinai be located at Jebel Safsafeh and its vicinity, then Rephidim would be in Wady es Sheikh. WANDERING.

REP'ROBATE (Heb. NIMAS, *worthless, rejected*), (Jer. vi. 30). Hardened in sin and unbelief (Rom. i. 28).

RE'SEN. The ruins called *Nimrud*, at Mosul, on the Euphrates, are understood to represent the ancient Calah, and those on the opposite side of the river are the remains of Nineveh; and there are remains between the two, at *Shamiyeh*, which answer to the locality of Resen.

RESH (Heb. REYSH). The twentieth letter of the Hebrew alphabet (Ps. cxix). WRITING.

RE'SHEPH (*flame*). Son of Ephraim (1 Chr. vii. 25).

RESURREC'TION, Gr. *anastasis*, uprising; *examstasis*, a rising up out of (Phil. iii. 11); *egersis*, waking up; "resurrection" in John xi. 25; and several other words, or derivatives, are rendered resurrection.

The idea is the rising again of the body from death, or its return to life in two senses; 1, of those who have been brought back to this life after death, as Lazarus, the widow's son of Nain, etc., and 2, of all true Christians, who will be raised in the future world.

This is one of the vital points in the Christian's creed. If there is no resurrection then there is no hope beyond this life. The Old Testament history prefigures the doctrine, in its records of several instances of restoration to life after death, as by Elijah (1 K. xvii. 21-24), and Elisha (2 K. iv. 20, 32-36). The vision of the dry bones may be accepted as touching on the general belief, though not a case of practical proof; the translations of Enoch and Elijah cannot argue resurrection, because death did not take place, and they are simply evidence of a continued existence after this life (Gen. v. 22; 2 K. ii.).

The Hebrews believed in an underworld, where the spirits or souls of all who had lived were still living and recognizable, which they called Hell, and did not restrict it to the modern meaning of that word, which is that it is the place of the wicked only. To the Hebrews it was the place where all souls went—or the condition that all souls were in after death and separation from the body (Ps. xvi. 10; fulfilled in Acts ii. 25-31, xiii. 35). In Isaiah (xxvi. 19), there is a direct statement of the belief as a prophecy of the restoration of the Jewish nation; as though he founded his argument on a well known and undoubted belief. Daniel (xii. 1-3), gives exactly the Christian idea of the final resurrection.

"Life and immortality" are "brought to light by the gospel." The New Testament idea is that it is (1) to be universal (John v. 28, 29; 2 Cor. v. 10; Rev. xx. 13), (2) and that souls will be recognizable; but whether the identity will be from physical or spiritual sources we are not instructed, unless Paul means that it will be spiritual in his argument to the Romans (vi. viii.) and to the Corinthians (1 Cor. xv. 44), where we may possibly see evidence of a belief in the rising of the identical shapes of our bodies of flesh, but changed into a spiritual substance. (3). The belief in a future life for the saints only and a second death for the impenitent is held by many, who find in the life and works of Jesus, and in Paul and John's teaching much to confirm this view. (4). It is the work of Jesus that has secured the resurrection and life of all who believe on Him, and His voice will call them from the tomb, who prayed, "Father, I will that they also, whom thou hast given me, may be with me where I am." (5). The time of the resurrection is not determined. There may be two, or rather two objects or ends to be answered: one being the actual life, which is believed to have been already given to several, whose names are mentioned in the Bible; and the other the great day of judgment. SECOND ADVENT.

The judgment comes after death, which is the end of the world for each soul, without regard to the whole human race. It does not follow that there will be no judgment until the last soul is born, lives, and dies, for it may be understood as an Orientalism, meaning the end of this life for each soul, what will happen to each soul and all souls, without exception (small and great), who must stand before the great white throne (white-pure—the only perfectly just tribunal).

Jesus "the author and finisher of our faith" was "the first fruits of them that slept," and His was the same body that was crucified, as He convinced Thomas by actual touch, but He did not instruct His disciples what to expect, so it remains a matter of faith for all His followers to expect to be like Him (1 John iii. 2).

RE'U (*friend*). Son of Peleg (Gen. xi. 18, 21).

REU'BEN (REU, *behold*, and BEN, *a son*). Eldest son of Jacob (Gen. xxix. 32), son of Leah. The tribe of Reuben was located, at their own request, on the E. side of Jordan, and against the wishes of Moses (Num. xxxii. 19). See 12 TRIBES.

REU'BENITE. Descendants of REUBEN (Num. xxvi. 7).

REU'EL (*friend of God*). 1. Son of Esau (Gen. xxxvi. 4, 10, 13, 17).—2. One of the names given to Moses' father-in-law (Ex. ii. 18).—3. Father of Eliasaph (Num. ii. 14).—4. Ancestor of Elah (1 Chr. ix. 8).

REU'MAH (*raised*). Second wife of Nahor (Gen. xxii. 24).

REVELATION. Gr. *apokalupsis*, *unveiling*, or *manifestation*, from God, by dream or vision (2 Cor. xii. 1, 7).

REVELATION OF ST. JOHN. See HISTORY OF THE BOOKS.

REVENGER OF BLOOD. AVENGER OF BLOOD is a name given to a man who had the right (and whose duty it was), of taking revenge on him who had killed one of his relations.

REZEPH (2 K. xix. 12; Is. xxxvii. 12). A day's march W. of the Euphrates, now called Rasapha. Another is mentioned as near Bagdad.

REZIA (*delight*). Son of Ulla, a chief (1 Chr. vii. 39).

REZIN (*friend*). 1. King of DAMASCUS who united with Pekah, king of Israel, to invade Judah, B. C. 742 (2 K. xv. 37).—2. Ancestor of Nethinim who returned from captivity (Neh. vii. 50).

REZON (*prince*). Son of Eliadah, and the founder of a small kingdom in Syria-Damascus, and a great annoyance to Solomon (1 K. xi. 23, 25).

RHEGIUM. In Italy, on the straits of Messina, opposite the city of Messina, in Sicily (Acts xxviii. 13).

RHESA. Father of Joanna in the genealogy of Jesus (Luke iii. 27). Supposed, by some, to be an error, the word meaning "prince," the title of Zerubbabel.

RHINOCEROS (Heb. REEM, *wild ox*). The word is always rendered unicorn. See UNICORN.

RHODA (*rose*). A maid, in the house of Mary, who announced Peter's arrival (Acts xii. 13).

RHODES. An island 120 miles long, by 36 wide, opposite the S. W. extremity of Asia Minor, celebrated from remote antiquity for commerce, navigation, literature and the arts; and during the middle ages as the residence of the Knights of St. John. Its maritime code was adopted by the Romans. The soil is fertile and the climate delightful. There are two cities: Rhodes (built 482 B. C.), which was celebrated by its having erected over the entrance to its harbor a brass statue of Apollo, 105 feet high (built by Chares of Lindus, B. C. 290, and thrown down by an earthquake, 224 B. C.); and Lindus and a number of villages. Population 30,000. Paul visited the island on his way to Jerusalem (Acts xxi. 1).

RHODOCUS. A Jew who betrayed his countrymen (2 Macc. xiii. 21).

RHODUS. RHODES (1 Macc. xv. 33).

RIBAI. Father of Ittai (2 Sam. xxiii. 29).

RIBAND. RIBBON (Heb. PATHIL, Num. xv. 38). See HEM, THREAD.

RIBLAH (*fertility*). In the land of Hamath (2 K. xxiii. 33), on the east side of Ain (Num. xxxiv. 11). Both places are located in the Orontes valley, 35 miles N. E. of Baalbek; Riblah lying on the banks of a mountain stream, in the midst of a vast and fertile plain. Mentioned as Diblath in Ez. vi. 14. At Riblah, Pharaoh Necho deposed king Jehoahaz (2 Chr. xxxvi.), and Nebuchadnezzar put out the eyes of Zedekiah after killing his sons (2 K. xxv. 7).

RIDDLE (Heb. HIDAH, *intricate*). Artifice (Dan. viii. 23); a proverb (Prov. i. 6); an oracle (Num. xii. 8); a PARABLE (Ez. xvii. 2); in general, any wise or intricate sentence (Hab. ii. 6). The queen of Sheba came to ask riddles of SOLOMON (1 K. x. 1). The ancients were fond of riddles. They were generally proposed in verse. The only mention of a riddle in the N. T. is in Rev. xiii. 16-18.

RIGHTEOUS (Heb. ZADDIK; sometimes YASHAR; Gr. *dikaios*). One who pursues the *right* course (Ex. ix. 27).

RIGHTEOUSNESS (Heb. ZEDEK, ZEDAKAH; Gr. *dikaioma*). Holiness, justice, rectitude, an attribute of God only (Job xxxvi. 3; Is. li. 5-8, John xvii. 25). The righteousness of Christ includes His spotless holiness and His perfect obedience to the law while on earth, and His suffering its penalty in our stead. "For the kingdom of God is not meat and drink; but righteousness, and peace, and joy in the Holy Ghost" (Rom. xiv. 17).

RIGHT HAND. Signifies power; the most efficient member of the body (Matt. v. 30). Figuratively the power of the Almighty (Ex. xv. 6; Ps. xxi. 8); the place of honor (Ps. xlv. 9; Matt. xxv. 34), of special benediction, paternal love, etc. It was raised in act of taking an oath, and of prayer (Gen. xiv. 22). The right hand means south in 1 Sam. xxiii. 19, as the left means north, as when facing east.

RIMMON (*pomegranate*). 1. Zebulites (1 Chr. vi. 77), belonging to the Levites, Merari family.— 2. Judah, in the extreme south, near Ziklag (Josh. xv. 32); afterward given to Simeon (xix. 7). Occupied after the return from Babylon (Neh. xi. 29). EN-RIMMON. UM-ER-RUMMANIM (*mother of pomegranates*), is a village and ruin 15 miles S. E. of Hebron. Between two hills (both covered with ruins), a mile south of the village, is a large fountain, the chief watering-place in the region.—3. THE ROCK RIMMON. A high rock or hill, 10 miles north of Jerusalem and 4 east of Bethel, on which is a modern village. The remnant of the tribe of Benjamin held this rock for four months against their enemies (Judg. xx. 47).—4. RIMMON-PAREZ (*breach*). The second station after Hazeroth, in the Exodus (Num. xxx. 19). Lost.

RIMMON. Father of Rechab (2 Sam. iv. 2, 5, 9).

RIMMON. Correctly RAMAM (*exalted*). The name of some idol under which the sun was represented (2 K. v. 18) in Damascus.

RINGS.

RING (TABBA'ATH, GALIL; Gr. *daktulios*). The ring, besides being an ornament, was used as a signet, or sign-manual, when its setting was engraved with some device, with or without the name of the owner, which was recognized as his personal emblem (Neh. x.). Such rings or seals were used by all persons in authority, and when stamped upon the parchment, or on a piece of wax or clay attached, stood instead of the name of the person agreeing to the compact. See SEAL. Several ancient rings have been preserved to the present, among which are the rings of Thothmes III, and of Pharaoh (Suphis): [cuts on pps. 84, 12.] The Scriptures mention several instances of their use in important business matters, as in Esth. iii. 10, where Ahasuerus gives Haman his ring as a badge of supreme authority over the army, and the treasury, for a certain purpose, and in 1 Macc. vi. 15, where Antiochus gave Philip his ring as a mark of his appointment as guardian to his son. It was worn on the right hand.

RINNAH (*shout*). Son of Shimon (1 Chr. iv. 20).

RIPHATH (Gen. x. 3; 1 Chr. i. 6). A northern people, descended from Gomer. We have several names derived from this source, as the Riphaean mts., the river Rhebas in Bithynia; the Ribibi, a people E. of the Caspian and the Riphaeans, the original Paphlagonians.

RIS'SAH (*worm*). Station in the wilderness (Num. xxxiii. 21). Lost.

RITH'MAH (*broom*, the shrub, *retem*). Desert station (ib. ver. 18). Lost.

RIVER. 7 distinct Hebrew words are translated by "river" in our version. By river we mean a large stream of water, flowing summer and winter, and we have names for smaller streams, as, stream, creek, brook, torrent, rill, rivulet, etc. There are such differences in the original Hebrew, which were overlooked in the translation, and it may be interesting to notice them: 1. AUBAL, YUBAL (Jer. xviii. 8; Dan. viii. 2, 3, 6), *tameth*, *fulness*. The word used for the deluge is from the same root, and is HAMMABUL (only in Genesis, and Ps. xxix. 10).—NAHAR (Gen ii. 10; Ex. vii. 19, etc.), *to flow*. This means a river, as we use the word. With the definite article HAN-NAHAR, (*the river*), the Euphrates is meant (Gen. xxxi. 21; 2 Sam. x. 16, etc.).—Incorrectly rendered "flood" in Josh. xxiv. 2, where the Euphrates is meant; and in Job xiv. 11, Ps. lxvi. 6, where the Red Sea, or the Jordan, is referred to. The Arab name of river is *nahr*; now used for all perennial streams.—3. *Nakhal*, (*to receive*), as, a water-course, therefore, a torrent-bed, common in Palestine, having water only in winter. This is translated "valley" in Gen. xxvi. 17, Num. xxi. 12; "brook," Deut. ii. 13, 2 K. xxiii. 6-12; "river" in Amos vi. 14; "streams" in Ps. lxxviii. 20; and, in all these cases *valley* is the true meaning. The modern term is WADY for such valleys as are dry in summer.—4. PELEG (*to flow*, or *division*): "River," in Ps. i. 3, Is. xxx. 25, Job xx. 17; "stream," in Ps. xlvi. 4; "divisions," in Judg. v. 15, 16. The word means, artificial streams for irrigation.—5. APHIK (*force* or *hold*, as, the bank of a river): "River" in Cant. v. 12, Ez. vi. 3, xxxi. 12, and "streams" in Ps. cxxvi. 4; in which last passage it refers to the dry water-courses of the Negeb, or South. In 2 Sam. xxii. 16 it is translated "channels," and also in Ps. xviii. 15.—6. YEOR, (the *Nile*), a word adopted into the Hebrew from the Egyptian language. This is the word used for the Nile in Genesis and Exodus, and is mistranslated "flood" in Amos viii. 8, ix. 5. RIVER OF EGYPT. Two terms were used in the original—differing, as will be seen—both of which are translated "river of Egypt." 1. NAHAR MITZRAIM (Gen. xv. 18), meaning *The Nile* (probably before the name YEOR was known to the Hebrews). —2. NAKHAL MITZRAIM (Num. xxxiv. 5), meaning the dry water-course of El Arish. The Nile is also called SHIHOR (Josh. xiii. 3, etc.). The importance of these corrections is felt, when it is seen that we are able to prove by them that the original Hebrew text was true in every one of its references to the peculiar features of the countries referred to, even in minute particulars.

RIZ'PAH (*a coal*). Second wife of King Saul, memorable for the touching example of maternal affection which she displayed in watching the dead bodies of her sons (2 Sam. iii. 7, xxi. 8, 10. 11).

ROADS. There were no roads, in ancient times, in the East, only narrow tracks, which we would call bridle-paths (1 Sam. xxvii. 10). See HIGHWAY.

ROB'BERY. Has ever been one of the principal employments of the Bedawin tribes of the East (Gen. xvi. 12). For an instance of a truly Bedawin character, see 1 Sam. xxvi. 6-12.

RO'BOAM. REHOBOAM (Ecclus. xlvii. 23).

ROCK (SELA, TSUR). Rocks were used for fortresses and strongholds. The word denotes a place of security, and, figuratively, a refuge, defense or protection (Ps. xviii. 2, 31, 46).

ROD (HOTER, MATTEH, MAKKEL, SHEBET; Gr. *rhabdos*). A branch or stick, such as may be used for a whip (Prov. xiv. 3); also a shepherd's staff (Ex. iv. 2 ff). The badge of authority of a ruler or king (Ps. cx. 2). An instrument for punishment or correction (Prov. x. 13).

ROD'ANIM (1 Chr. i. 7). DODANIM.

ROE. Roebuck (Heb. ZEBI, masc., ZEBIYAH, fem.). The Oriental antelope or gazelle. It is about two and a half feet in hight, of a reddish brown color, with white feet and belly, has long naked ears, and a short erect tail. The horns are black, about twelve inches long and bent like a lyre. It inhabits Barbary, Egypt, Arabia and Syria, and is about half the size of the fallow-deer. It goes in large flocks; is easily tamed, though very timid; its flesh is considered excellent food (Deut. xii. 15, 22).

RO'GEL (*fuller*) (1 K. i. 9). EN-ROGEL.

RO'GELIM (*feet*). The residence of Barzillai, the Gileadite (2 Sam. xvii. 27). East of Jordan. Lost.

ROH'GAH (*outcry*). A chief of the sons of Shamer (1 Chr. vii. 34).

ROI'MUS. REHUM 1 (1 Esd. v. 8).

ROLL (Heb. and Chal. MEGILLAH.) See WRITING.

ROMAM'TIE'ZER (*I have exalted his help*). Son of Heman, and chief in the twenty-fourth division (1 Chr. xxv. 4, 31).

RO'MAN. An inhabitant of Rome (John xi. 48); also one who had the rights of a citizen of Rome (Acts xvi. 37, 38).

ROMAN EMPIRE. Rome is first mentioned in 1 Macc. i. 10, in connection with Antiochus Epiphanes, who had been a hostage there, and was a "wicked root." Pompey made Syria a Roman province, B. C. 65, and took Jerusalem two years later (Ant. xiv. 2, 3, 4; Wars i. 6, 7). Herod was made the first king under Roman rule by Antony, B. C. 40, and was confirmed by Augustus, B. C. 30. The tribute paid to Cæsar (Julius) was a fourth part of their agricultural produce in addition to the tithes (Ant. xiv. 10, 6). After A. D. 6, Judæa was made a province of Syria at the request of the Jews, who were worn out by the cruelties of the Herods, with the capital at Cæsarea; Coponius was the first procurator, and Pilate was the fifth. Jesus was crucified during Pilate's reign (A. D. 25 to 35). The many complaints of the tyranny of Pilate caused him to be ordered to Rome for trial by Vitellius, president of Syria; but the Emperor Tiberius died before his arrival. (Ant. xviii. 4, 1-3). Justin Martyr, Tertullian, Eusebius and others say that Pilate made an official report to Tiberius of the crucifixion of Jesus; which account is also mentioned by Chrysostom. Eusebius says that Pilate killed himself, being "wearied with misfortunes,"—perhaps on account of remorse for his conduct in Jerusalem.

The Roman empire was but a narrow strip along the shores of the Mediterranean until Pompey added Asia Minor, Syria, and (Antony) Egypt; Cæsar conquered Gaul; the generals of Augustus, Spain, and from the Alps to the Danube. Its population in the time of Christ was 85 millions. Gibbon says it was 120 millions in the time of Claudius, who appointed Felix procurator (A. D. 52-60). Festus succeeded him, and heard Paul (Acts xxv., etc.). Vespasian was sent into Judæa in A. D. 67, with a large army. Nero died in 68, and Vespasian was elected emperor by the legions in Judæa. Titus was sent to conduct the war in Judæa by his father A. D. 70, when he took Jerusalem after a siege of four months. Julius Cæsar allowed the Jews to live after their own customs, even in Rome; which privileges were confirmed by Augustus, who also respected their Sabbath (Ant. xiv. 10, 11, 19), and exempted them from military service; but Tiberius and Claudius banished them from Rome, as Suetonius says, because they were continually raising disturbances under the impulse of Chrestus—*i. e.*, Christ.

All official acts were strictly carried out in the Latin language, even to the remotest limits of the empire, but the people were generally left to use their native tongue. Scholars and the wealthy classes spoke Greek besides Latin, and official edicts were translated into Greek. The inscription that Pilate put on the cross was written in Hebrew, Latin, and Greek, the usual custom—Hebrew for the common people, Latin the official language, and Greek the polite language. The prophets mention Rome as the fourth kingdom (Dan. ii. 40, vii. 7, 17, 19, xi. 30-40; and Deut. xxviii. 49-57°). The empire proper began with Augustus, at the battle of Actium, B. C. 31, when he became sole master, and ended by the abdication of Augustus, A. D. 476.

ROME. The City of Rome was founded B. C. 753, on 7 hills, 15 ms. from the mouth of the Tiber (Rev. xvii. 9). The modern city lies to the N. W. of the ancient site, on what was the Campus Martius (Field of Mars), a plain north of the

ROME, THE FORUM.

seven hills. It is only mentioned in Maccabees, Acts, Epistle to the Romans, and 2d Timothy. The Jews first settled in Rome after Pompey's conquests, when the Jewish king, Aristobulus, and his son were led in triumph. At the time of Paul's visit (after Augustus had "found the city of brick and left it of marble") the population was one million two hundred thousand (*Gibbon*)—one-half being slaves, and a large part of the freemen dependent on the rich, and living like paupers on public gratuities. Rome became the greatest repository of architecture, pictures, and sculptures that the world ever saw. The luxury, profligacy, and crime of this age is beyond the descriptive power of letters. It is believed that Paul lived here "two whole years," in his own hired house, bound by a chain to a soldier, according to the then custom of keeping certain prisoners (Acts xii. 6, xxviii. 16, 20, 30). Five of Paul's epistles were written at Rome, one of them just before his death, as is believed by beheading.

The localities made interesting by Paul at Rome are: the Appian Way, by which he approached the city; Cæsar's Court, or Palace (Phil. i. 13); and the Palatine Hill, on which was Cæsar's household (ib. iv. 22), and probably Paul's residence. It is also said, traditionally, that Peter and Paul were fellow-prisoners, for nine months, in the Mamertine prison, which is now shown under the church of S. Giuseppe dei Falegnami; and that they separated on their way to martyrdom at a spot on the Ostian road, now marked by a chapel; and the church of S. Paolo marks the site of Paul's martyrdom. The spot where Peter suffered is also covered by the church of S. Pietro in Montorio, on the Janiculum. A chapel on the Appian Way locates the beautiful legend of Jesus appearing to Peter as he was escaping from martyrdom, who, ashamed, returned and submitted to his fate (Ambrose). The bodies of the two apostles were first laid in the catacombs, and were finally buried, Paul on the Ostian road, and Peter in the church of St. Peter. The ruins of the Coliseum are still standing, as a memorial of those early nameless Christians who were exposed to the wild beasts in its arena, for the gratification of the people, who, while witnessing these awful sights, were sprinkled with perfumed water, which was conveyed about the building in secret pipes. Nearly two-thirds of the ancient site (within Aurelian's walls) are covered with ruins, and a few churches and convents, or open waste-places. In Pliny's time the circuit of the city was 20 ms.; it is now about 15 ms.

The first Christian church in Rome was built by Constantine, who gave his own palace on the Cælian hill as a site. St. Peter's on the Vatican hill was built next, A. D. 324—the first edifice built on the site—out of the ruins of the temples of Apollo and Mars, and stood 1200 years, being superseded by the present magnificent structure.

Rome is called Babylon (on account of the special hate of the Jews for the tyranny of its rulers), in Rev. xiv. 8, xvi. 19, xvii. 5, xviii. 2,—as the centre of heathenism, in contrast to Jerusalem, the centre of Judaism. It is supposed that the first Church in Rome consisted mainly of Gentiles. (See *Conybeare* and *Howson's* Life of St. Paul, *Gibbon*, *Draper's* Hist. Int. Devel. of Europe).

RO'MANS, EPISTLE TO THE. See HISTORY OF THE BOOKS.

ROOM (Heb. MAKOM). Place (Gen. xxiv. 23); KEN. Nest (vi. 14). Gr. *anogeon* or *anagion*. Any thing above ground; an upper room (Mark xiv. 15). Room is sometimes synonymous with seat or place (Luke xiv. 8, 59).

ROOT (Heb. SHORESH; Gr. *rhiza*). The part of a tree or plant under ground (Job viii. 17). In poetry persons and nations are often compared to a plant or tree (Is. v. 24); figuratively, the lowest part, bottom (Job xxviii. 9); metaphorically, descendant, offspring (Is. xi. 10).

ROSE. 1. Heb. CHABAZZELETH (Cant. ii. 1). I am the rose of Sharon. 2. Gr. *rhodon* (Wis. ii. 8). Roses are greatly prized in the East, for the rose-water, which is in much request. Several varieties are still found in Palestine. The "rose of Sharon" is sacredly associated with the heavenly bridegroom (Cant. ii. 1).

The Rose of Sharon is thought by some to have been the Cistus, Rock-rose, of which there are several varieties in Palestine, and is now chiefly found on the hills, and especially on Mount Carmel, where it almost covers whole districts, tinting entire hillsides, as seen from a distance, in April.

Others, as Tristram (*Nat. Hist.* 476), thinks it was the Sweet-scented Narcissus, a native of Palestine, growing on Sharon, and nearly all over the country. It is very fragrant, and an especial favorite of the people, who, men and women, carry

them for their perfume and fine color, vast numbers being sold in the bazaars.

Dr. Thomson suggested the Mallow, marsh-mallows, which grows into a stout bush, and bears thousands of beautiful flowers. Others again suggest the asphodel or the lily.

ROSH. In Ez. xxxviii. 2, 3, xxxix. 1, this name is translated "chief," and should read, "Magog, the prince of Rosh, Meshech, and Tubal." The Russ, or Russians, are also mentioned in the Koran. The country of the children of Rasses (Jud. ii. 23) was ravaged by Holofernes. Meshech is said to be the original Muscovy, and Rosh, the original Russia.

ROS'IN. The *resin* of turpentine after distillation. 1. In Ez. xxvii. 17, BALM.—2. In the Song of the Three Holy Children (23) the servants of the king are said to have "ceased not to make the oven hot with rosin (properly *neophtha*).

RU'BIES. See PRECIOUS STONES.

RUE (Gr. *peganon*, in Luke xi. 42, only). Is doubtless, the common garden-rue (*ruta graveolus*), having a strong odor and a bitter taste; a shrubby plant, about 2 ft. high, and used as a medicine. In the middle ages it was used by the priests to sprinkle holy water, and was called *herb of grace*.

RU'FUS (L. *red*). Son of Simon the Cyrenian, who carried the cross on which the Saviour was to be crucified (Mark xv. 21). He is supposed to be the same person whom Paul salutes in Rom. xvi. 13.

RUHA'MAH (*pitied*). See HOSEA in HISTORY OF THE BOOKS.

RU'MAH (*lofty*), (2 K. xxiii. 36). DUMAH (Josh. xv. 52).

RUSH (Heb. AGMON). See PAPYRUS.

RUST (Gr. *Brosis*, Matt. v. 19, 30). A destroying substance that attacks treasures of any kind long undisturbed. In James v. 3, "rust" is the translation of Gr. *ios*, the *tarnish* which spreads silver, rather than "rust."

RUTH. See HISTORY OF THE BOOKS.

RYE (KUSSEMETH), (Ex. ix. 32). Rye is not an Egyptian or Syrian grain, but rather a northern plant. It is closely allied to wheat, which it much resembles. The sheath is coarser, and rougher, and the beard long. It is of less value, and the flour is generally mixed with that of wheat. See HARVEST.

S

SABACTHA'NI (*hast thou forsaken me?*). A part of our Saviour's exclamation on the cross (Matt. xxvii. 46); the whole is taken from Ps. xx. 1, where it is used prophetically.

SAB'AOTH (ZEBOTH, *hosts or armies*), (Joel ii. 15; 2 Sam. vi. 2; Ps. xxiv. 10; Jas. v. 4).

SA'BAT. 1. Ancestor of sons of Solomon's servants, who returned from captivity (1 Esd. v. 34). —2. SEBAT (1 Macc. xvi. 14). MONTH.

SABATE'AS. SHABBETHAI (1 Esd. ix. 48).

SABATUS. ZABAD (1 Esd. ix. 28).

SAB'BAN. BINNUI 1 (1 Esd. viii. 63).

SAB'BATH (Heb. SHABBATH, *the* [*day of*] *rest*). The name given to the seventh day of the week under the old covenant. Division of time into weeks was the custom from the earliest recorded ages, among the rudest as well as the most cultivated people. (CHRONOLOGY.) It is the only ordinance besides marriage which dates from the Creation (Gen. ii. 3), and it is one of the subjects of the Decalogue (Ex. xxxiv. 21). In Leviticus the whole law is repeated (xxiii. 2, 3), and one of the finest of the Psalms was written in honor of the day (Ps. xcii.). The prophets also honor the Sabbath as a holy day (Is. lvi. 1, 2; Ez. xx. 12, xliv. 24, xlvi. 3).

The observance of the Sabbath indicated a prosperity of religion, and its neglect showed a decay of religion generally. The day of rest was a great boon to the laborer, and to animals (Ex. xxiii. 12), but the great importance of the institution was its spiritual and religious meaning, and as a sign of the holiness of God, and the holiness required of His people. Its deliberate violation was punished with death (Num. xv. 32-36).

The special rites and services appointed for the day show that it was to be spent in thoughts and exercises on the character and ways of God. The services of the sanctuary were peculiar to the day (Num. xxviii. 9; Lev. xxiv. 3-9); and the laws of Moses were read (Acts xv. 21), "teaching Jacob God's judgments and Israel His law" (Deut. xxxiii. 10).

Josephus alludes to the origin, design, and observance of the day in his discourse against Apion (ii. 18).

Jesus instructed His disciples, by His example as well as words, to keep the law of the Sabbath, and to works of kindness and mercy, and exercise of piety (Matt. xii. 1-13; Mark iii. 1-5; Luke iv. 16, vi. 9), and to keep the day in its true spirit, as a day of personal privilege and benevolent usefulness, for "the Sabbath was made for man, and not man for the Sabbath."

In Colossians ii. 16, Paul argues from the fact of the Sabbath having been superseded by the Lord's day.

SABBATH DAY'S JOURNEY. The distance between the tents and the ark in the camp, which was 2000 cubits. The common cubit of 18 inches would be 3000 feet, and the sacred cubit of 19.05 inches would be 4,762 feet. The English mile is 5,280 feet.

SABBATHE'US. Shabbethai, the Levite (1 Esd. ix. 14).

SABBE'US. SHEMAIAH 14 (1 Esd. ix. 32).

SABE'ANS. People of SEBA.

SA'BI. ZEBAIM (1 Esd. v. 34).

SAB'TAH. Third son of Cush (Gen. x. 7). Located in Arabia, along the southern coast. Pliny (vi. xxiii. 32) says the chief city of the region had 60 temples, and was the capital of king Elisarus.

SABTE'CAH. Fifth son of Cush (Gen. x. 7). Settled on the Persian Gulf, on the Persian shore.

SA'CAR (*reward*). 1. Father of Ahiam (1 Chr. xi. 35).—2. Fourth son of Obed-edom (xxvi. 4).

SACK'BUT (Chal. *sabbecha*). A musical instrument; a brass trumpet with a slide, like the modern trombone (Dan. xii. 7, 10, 15).

SACK'CLOTH (Heb. SAK; Gr. *sakkos*). A coarse stuff, of a dark color, often made of goats'-hair (Is. l. 3), and the coarse, black hair of the camel. In great calamities—in penitence, in trouble—the Jews wore sackcloth about their bodies (Gen. xxxvii. 34); The robe resembled a sack, and was confined by a girdle of the same material (2 Sam. iii. 31). In times of joy those who were clad in sackcloth took it off, and put on their usual clothing (Is. xxxii. 11). See DRESS.

SAC'RIFICE (Heb. MINCHAH, *to give;* KORBAN, *to approach;* ZEBACH, *to slaughter animals;* OLAH, *whole burnt-offering;* SHELEM, *peace-offering;* CHATTATH, *sin-offering;* ASHAM, *trespass-offering;* Gr. *thusia* (Matt. ix. 13); *doron*, *gift* (Matt. ii. 11); *eidolothuton, idol-sacrifice* (Acts xv. 29); *prosphora, offering* (Acts xxi. 26). The first recorded sacrifices were those of Cain and Abel (Minchah). Of Noah, after the flood (Gen. viii. 20); a burnt-offering (olah). The sacrifice of Isaac (Gen. xxii. 1-13), the only instance of human sacrifice, having been commanded by God as a test of faith, but not actually offered. In the burnt-offerings of Job (Job i. 5, xlii. 8), the offering was accompanied by repentance and prayer. The sacri-

fires of the Mosaic period commenced with the offering of the Passover (Ex. xxiv.). The law prescribed five kinds of sacrifices: the burnt-offering, the meat-offering (unbloody), the peace-offering (bloody), the sin-offering and the trespass-offering. In the consecration of Aaron and his sons (Lev. viii.), there was first a *sin-offering*, as an approach to God; next, a *burnt-offering*, typical of dedication to His service, and the *meat-offering* of thanksgiving; and further, a peace-offering for the congregation, which was accepted by the miraculous descent of fire upon the altar. This was ever afterwards the order of the sacrifices. The sacrifices regularly offered in the Temple were of burnt-offerings: first, the daily burnt-offerings (Ex. xxix. 38-42); second, the double burnt-offerings on the Sabbath (Num. xxviii. 9, 10); third, the burnt-offerings at the great feasts (Num. xxviii. 11, xxix. 39).

OF MEAT-OFFERINGS.—The daily meat-offerings accompanying the daily burnt-offerings (flour, oil and wine), (Ex. xxix. 40, 41); second, the shew-bread (twelve loaves, with frankincense), replaced every Sabbath (Lev. xxiv. 5-9); third, the special meat-offerings at the Sabbath—a great feast (Num. xxviii. and xxix.); fourth, *wave-offerings*—the first fruits of the Passover (Lev. xxiii. 10-14) and at Pentecost (xxiii. 17-20). *Peace-offerings* of the first fruits of the threshing-floor at the harvest-time (Num. xv. 20, 21).

OF SIN-OFFERINGS.—First, a *sin-offering* each new moon, of a kid (Num. xxviii. 15); second, *sin-offerings* at the Passover, Pentecost, Feast of Trumpets and Tabernacles (Num. xxviii. 22, 30, xxix.); third, the offering of the two goats (one the scape-goat) for the people, and of a bullock for the priest on the great day of ATONEMENT (Lev. xvi.). Incense was offered morning and evening (Ex. xxx. 7, 8), and on the Great Day of Atonement. There were also the individual offerings of the people. See PRIESTS.

SADAMI'AS. Shallum, ancestor of Ezra (2 Esd. i. 1).

SA'DAS. AZGAD (1 Esd. v. 13).

SADDE'US. IDDO (1 Esd. viii. 45).

SAD'DUC. Zadok, the high-priest (1 Esd. viii. 2).

SAD'DUCEES (named from ZADOK, the high-priest). A religious sect of the Jews at the time of Christ, who refused to accept that the oral law was the revelation of God to the Israelites, and believed exclusively in the written law. They joined with the Pharisees in asking for a sign from heaven (Matt. xvi. 1, 4, 6), but opposed their doctrines otherwise. The Sadducees never exercised the influence that the Pharisees did, and were more tolerant. They rejected the belief in a resurrection (Matt. xxii. 23), nor did they believe in future rewards and punishments. The high-priest, at the time of Christ, was of this sect, and the doctrine of the resurrection preached by Christ rendered the Sadducees especially bitter against him (Acts iv. 1, v. 17), but he did not censure the Sadducees as much as the Pharisees.

SA'DOC. 1. ZADOK 1 (2 Esd. i. 1).—2. A descendant of Zerubbabel in the genealogy of Jesus Christ (Matt. i. 14).

SAFFRON (Ar. *Zafran*, *yellow*. Heb. CARCOM). A small bluish flower, whose yellow stigma is pulled out and dried, having a peculiar aromatic and penetrating odor and a bitter taste. Used as a stimulant in medicine and highly valued in the East as a perfume (Cant. iv. 14).

SAINT (Heb. HASID, KADOSH. Gr. *Nagios*, *a holy one*), (Dan. viii. 13). A title by which the disciples were known. Originally including all members of the Church, afterward restricted to a few (Rom. i. 1; Acts ix. 32; 1 Thess. iii. 13).

SA'LA. SALAH (Luke iii. 35).

SA'LAH (*extension*), (Gen. x. 24). Father of Eber. Settled in N. Mesopotamia.

SAL'AMIS. City on the east end of the island of Cyprus. Visited by Paul and Barnabas on their first missionary journey (Acts xiii. 5). There were many Jews in Cyprus, attracted by the copper mines. The ancient city was near the modern *Famagosta*, by the river Pediæus, on a plain.

SALASAD'AI. ZURISHADAI (Jud. viii. 1).

SALA'THIEL or SHEALTIEL. Father of Zerubbabel (Ezr. iii. 2). One of the ancestors of Christ (Matt. i. 14; Luke iii. 27).

SAL'CAH (Deut. iii. 10; Josh. xiii. 11). A city on the extreme east limit of Bashan and Gad (1 Chr. v. 11). There was a district of the same name (Josh. xii. 5), belonging to Og. Now called *Sulkhad*, at the south end of Jebel Hauran. The great Euphrates desert begins near this city and extends to the Persian Gulf. About three miles in circuit. In it is a castle on a lofty (volcanic) hill, 400 feet high. An inscription on a gate is dated A. D. 246, and one on a tombstone, A. D. 196.

SA'LEM. SHALEM (*peace*). Jerome said Salem was 8 Roman miles from Scythopolis (Bethshean), and in his day contained the ruins of the palace of Melchizedek. Some have identified it with Jerusalem. The plain of Salem has the mountains Ebal and Gerizim, with Shechem, on its west end, and the hills on which Salem stands on its east end. In Psalm lxxvi. 2, Salem means Jerusalem.

SA'LIM (John iii. 23). Near Ænon. 6 miles south of Bethshean and 2 miles west of Jordan is a site of ruins on the *Tell Redghah*, with a Mohammedan tomb, called *Sheikh Salim*. The brook in *Wady Chusneh* runs close by, and a copious fountain gushes out near the tomb, while rivulets wind about in all directions. "Here is much water."

SAL'LAI (*basket maker*). 1. One who settled in Jerusalem after the Captivity (Neh. xi. 8).—2. Head of a course of priests who went with Zerubbabel (xii. 20).

SAL'LU (*weighed*). Son of Meshullam (1 Chr. ix. 7).

SALLU'MUS. SHALLUM 2 (1 Esd. ix. 25).

SAL'MA (*garment*), or SALMON (*clothed*). Son of Nashon, prince of Judah, the husband of Rahab (Matt. i. 4, 5).

SAL'MAH. SALMA (Ruth iv. 20).

SALMANA'SER. SHALMANESER (2 Esd. xiii. 40).

SALMANAS'SER. SHALMANESER (Hos. xi. 5).

SAL'MON (Judg. ix. 48). A hill near Shechem, on which Abimelech and his men cut down boughs with which they burnt the tower of Shechem. ZALMON. White as snow in Salmon (Ps. lxviii. 14).

SALMO'NE. The east point of the island of CRETE (Acts xxvii. 7).

SA'LOM. 1. SHALLUM, father of Hilkiah (Bar. i. 7).—2. SALU, father of Zimri (1 Macc. ii. 26).

SALO'ME (*pacific*). 1. Wife of ZEBEDEE, mother of the *Apostles* James and John. She was a most devout and faithful disciple (Matt. xx. 20; Acts xvi. 1).—2. Salome, the daughter of Herodias; she was the cause of John Baptist's death (Matt. xiv. 6; Mark xvi. 22). She was the wife of Philip, Tetrarch of Trachonitis, and afterwards married Aristobulus, king of Chalcis (Jos. Ant. xviii. 5, 4).

SALT (MELAH; Gr. *nats*). See SODOM.

SALT, CITY OF (Josh. xv. 62). In the wilderness, near Engedi and the Dead Sea. It may be the site is found in the modern *Nahr Malch*, which is near the *Wady Amrch*, which is believed to be *Gomorrah*. The *Valley of Salt*. Two memorable victories occurred here: that of David over the Edomites (2 Sam. viii. 13; Ps. lx.); and that of Amaziah over the same people (2 K. xiv. 7). The

site is lost. It has been located by some in the plain at the south end of the Dead Sea.

SA'LUM. 1. SHALLUM 8 (1 Esd. v. 28).—2. SHALLUM 6 (viii. 1).

SALUTA'TION (Heb. SHALOM LEKHA). Peace be with thee (John xx. 19). By this term is meant the friendly greeting, which, in ancient as in modern times, takes place between persons when meeting or parting; also when sending letters.

At parting the form was much the same as at meeting. "Go in peace (Judg. xviii. 6). The letter of an Arab will be nearly filled with salutations; and should he come in to tell you your house is on fire, he would first give and receive the compliments of the day before saying your house is on fire. Salutations are also given by kissing the hand, the forehead, cheek, the beard of a superior. The long, ceremonious greeting which occupied so much time, was deemed unfit for the use of the preachers of the gospel, and they were directed to salute no one by the way. It is not unusual for two ceremonious gentlemen to inquire carefully after every male relative, especially ancestors, of each other, several times over, at each meeting, smoking and sipping coffee during the one or two hours required for this very friendly (?) greeting. Custom does not permit inquiries after each others' female relatives, it being equal to a decided insult to even allude to another man's wife. If a man speaks of his wife he apologizes for the discourtesy.

SAMARITAN PRIEST.

SALVA'TION (Heb. YESHAH, YESHA; Gr. sotēria). Deliverance from temporal evils or earthly destruction (Ex. xiv. 13). GOD is figuratively called "salvation" (Ps. xxvii. 1). JESUS CHRIST has provided the salvation of the Gospel, and is preeminently "the SAVIOUR" (Matt. i. 21).

SAM'AEL. SALAMIEL (Jud. viii. 1).

SAMAI'AS. 1. Shemaiah 23 (1 Esd. i. 9).—2. Shemaiah 11 (viii. 39).—3. The "great Samaias," father of Ananias and Jonathas (Tob. v. 13).

SAMA'RIA (watch mountain). Six miles N. W. of Shechem, on a hill which is surrounded by a broad basin-shaped valley. Here OMRI built the capital of the kingdom of Israel, on the hill which he bought (B. C. 925) of SHEMER for two talents of silver (1 K. xvi. 24). The site is singularly beautiful, and is always admired by every visitor. Ahab built a temple to Baal, with images; and that part of the city was called "the city of the house of Baal" (1 K. xvi. 22), which was destroyed by Jehu (2 K. x. 25).

The Syrians besieged it in 901 B. C. (1 K. xx. 1), and in 892 B. C. (ib. vi. 24, vii. 20), and in both cases without success.

Shalmanezer, king of Assyria, took it after a siege of 3 years, B. C. 721 (2 K. xviii. 9, 10), and carried the people away to Assyria. Esarhaddon repeopled the country from Assyria, and these citizens were called Samaritans. Josephus describes it as a very strong city in the time of John Hyrcanus, who took it (B. C. 109), after a year's siege (Ant. xiii. 10, 2). After this time the Jews inhabited the city, until the age of Alexander Janneus, and until Pompey restored it to the descendants of the original inhabitants (probably the Syro-Macedonians).

Herod the Great rebuilt it with some splendor, and called it SEBASTE (Augustus), after his patron the Emperor Augustus. The wall was 20 stadia in circuit. A magnificent temple was dedicated to Cæsar. 6,000 veteran soldiers were colonized here, and a large district given them for their support (Ant. xv. 8, 5; B. J. i. 20, 3, etc.).

The remains of the ancient city are mostly colonnades of Herod's time, or older. There is a group of 16 in a recess near the bottom of the hill, another of 16 near the top, and a long line of columns running around the hill, on one side, on a broad terrace, of which 100 are now standing, and a great many others fallen. The whole hill is covered with rubbish, the remains of a large and well-built city.

The city is not mentioned in the New Testament, and it was commanded, "Into any city of the Samaritans enter ye not."

Septimius Severus planted a Roman colony there in the 3d century. Roman coins struck in the city are preserved of the ages extending from Nero to Geta. In A. D. 409 the Holy Land was divided into 3 districts, of which the country of Philistia, the northern part of Judæa and Samaria, formed Palestina Prima; with Cæsarea for its capital.

The bishop of Samaria was present at the Council of Nicea, A. D. 325, signing his name as Maximus Sebastenus.

The Mohammedans took Sebaste during their siege of Jerusalem.

The present village is called Sebustiyeh, and consists of a few houses scattered among the ruins of the past. The ruined church of St. John the Baptist bears traces of its former magnificence. A long avenue of columns, many fallen, still lines the upper terrace of the hill. The prophecies of Micah (i. 6), and Hosea (xiii. 16), are descriptive of its present condition.

SAMARIA, THE DISTRICT OF. Was so called before the city was named (1 K. xiii. 32), and included all the tribes who accepted Jeroboam as king, on both sides of the Jordan, and the royal residence was Shechem (1 K. xiii. 25). The name Samaritan became contracted, as the kingdom was divided from time to time. The first limitation was probably the losing of Simeon and Dan. The second, when Pul, king of Assyria (B. C. 771) carried away the Reubenites and Gadites, and the half tribe of Manasseh (1 Chr. v. 26); the third, when Galilee and Gilead were taken by the Assyrians (2 K. xv. 29); and the fourth, when just before the last king of Israel, Hoshea, was deposed, Asher, Issachar and Zebulon, and also Ephraim and Manasseh, sent men up to the Passover at Jerusalem (2 Chr. xxx. 1-26), in Hezekiah's reign. Thus, the kingdom which once extended from the sea to the desert of Syria, and from Bethel to Dan in the north, was divided, until only the city Samaria, with a few villages, remained to the name, and even these were wiped out by Shalmanezer (2 K.

xvii. 5-26), who placed other people there instead of the Jews (v. 24), B. C. 721.

These new-comers were idolaters, and brought their idols with them (2 K. xvii. 29), and although instructed by Jewish priests, never became pure worshipers of Israel's God. When Judah and Benjamin returned from the Captivity and began to build the Temple, the Samaritans asked permission to assist, and on being refused they petitioned the king of Assyria and had the work stopped (Ezr. iv.). From this time the "adversaries of Judah and Benjamin" became open enemies, and the feud grew year by year more bitter. In the year B. C. 409, Manasseh, a priest who was expelled from Jerusalem for an unlawful marriage, obtained permission from the Persian king to build a temple on Mt. Gerizim, and made a copy of the law, which was the 5 books of Moses only (called the Pentateuch), and they claimed for this copy the highest antiquity, even above any copy in possession of the Jews.

The Samaritans claimed from Alexander an exemption from taxes on the Sabbatical year, on the plea that they were Jews; but on examination their claim was found to be false. The woman of Samaria also claimed to be a descendant of Jacob, when talking with Jesus (John vi. 12).

The boundaries, according to Josephus, in the time of Christ were from Jenin to Acrabatta. (See MAP). The soil, productions, etc., are described under EPHRAIM and ISSACHAR.

SAM'ATUS. Son of Ozora (1 Esd. ix. 34).

SA'MECH (Heb. *fulcrum*, *support*). The 15th letter of the Hebrew alphabet (Ps. cxix.). WRITING.

SAMEI'US. SHEMAIAH 13 (1 Esd. ix. 21).

SAM GAR-NE BO (Jer. xxxix. 3). The whole name is SAMGAR-NEBO-SAMSECHIM, which is to say, The *Cupbearer*, Nebo-Sarsechim.

SA'MI. SHOBAI 1 (1 Esd. v. 28).

SAM'IS. SHIMEI 13 (1 Esd. ix. 34).

SAM'LAH (*a garment*). A king of Edom (Gen. xxxvi. 36, 37).

SAM'MUS. SHEMA (1 Esd. ix 43).

SA'MOS (*height*). An island opposite the boundary between Ionia and Caria. Paul anchored for a night at Trogyllium, in the narrow strait between Samos and Mycale. The ancient Greeks fought a naval battle against the Persians in this strait, B. C. 479. Herod the Great met Marcus Agrippa in Samos, and obtained many privileges for the Jews (Jos. Ant. xvi. 2, 2).

SAMOTHRA'CIA (Acts xvi. 11). Mentioned in Paul's first voyage. It is a lofty and conspicuous island, seen at a great distance, being visible from the shore at Troas (*Eothen*, p. 64; Homer, Il. xiii. 12, 13). Paul anchored for a night off the island. A strong current from the Dardanelles sets southward between the island and the mainland. The mysteries of the Cabeiri (pagan divinities) were practiced here.

SAMP SAMES. Now Samsun, on the coast of the Black Sea, between Trebizond and Sinope.

SAM'SON (Heb. SHIMSHON, *strong*). Son of MANOAH, in the tribe of DAN (Josh. xv. 33). The account of his birth, life, and exploits, is given in Judg. xiii. xvi. He was the strongest man, and celebrated for his fearless and wonderful acts, for his moral infirmities, and his tragical end. His sins brought him in great disgrace and misery (Heb. xi. 32).

SAM'UEL. See HISTORY OF THE BOOKS.

SANABAS'SAR. SHESHBAZZAR (1 Esd. ii. 12, 15).

SANABAS'SARUS. SHESHBAZZAR (1 Esd. vi. 18, 20).

SAN'ASIB. Ancestor of certain priests said to have returned with Zerubbabel (1 Esd. v. 24).

SANBAL'LAT. A Moabite of HORONAIM, but a resident of Samaria (Neh. ii. 10, 19), and a great enemy of the Jews. He was an officer in the service of Artaxerxes (Neh. iv. 2). See Nehemiah in the HISTORY OF THE BOOKS. His daughter married Manasseh, the high-priest, Eliashib's grandson, son of Joiada (Tobiah, a companion of his, had "allied" himself to Eliashib's family in the same manner—Neh. xiii. 4), on account of a settled policy of Sanballat, Tobiah and Geshem, who concerted together for the injury of the Jews. Nehemiah expelled Manasseh for marrying a Gentile wife. Sanballat attempted to entice Nehemiah from Jerusalem to some village near Ono (vi.), but the scheme failed, for the Tirshatha suspected mischief. Nothing further is related of Sanballat in the Scripture, and Josephus continues the history in rather a fabulous manner.

SANCTIFICA'TION. SANCTIFY (KADASH, *to sanctify*), (Gen. ii. 3); (Gr. *hagiazo*), (Matt. xxii. 17, 19). To be holy. In the O. T. it denotes the consecration of a person to God (Ex. xxxi. 13). To make holy, or to set apart for God (Gen. ii. 3; Ex. xix. 23). The tabernacle, altar, priests, etc., were solemnly set apart and sanctified for divine service (Lev. viii. 10-12). A day was set apart for fasting and prayer (Joel i. 14), and the Sabbath was so regarded (Deut. v. 12). In the N. T. the doctrine is the making truly and perfectly holy what was before defiled and sinful, and is a progressive work of divine grace upon the soul justified by the love of Christ. After a gradual cleansing from sin the sinner is presented "unspotted before the throne of God," which is the work of the Holy Spirit (John xiv. 26, xvii. 17). The ultimate sanctification of every believer in Christ is a covenant of mercy, purchased on the cross.

SAND (Heb. HOL; Gr. *ammos*), (Gen. xxii. 17, Job vi. 3). See SINAI. The sand of the desert of Petra and Sinai is very light, easily carried with the wind, and penetrates even the cases of a watch so as to stop the wheels. Some of it is a whitish yellow, hard and shining, and some is red.

SANDALS.

SANDAL (Heb. NA'AL; Gr. *sandalon*, little sandal), (Mark vi. 9). See DRESS.

SAN'HEDRIM, correct **SANHEDRIN.** Gr. *sunedrion*. "COUNCIL." See HISTORY OF THE BOOKS.

SAN'HERIB. SENNACHERIB (2 K. xviii. 13).

SANSAN'NAH (*palm branch*). One of the towns in the S. of Judah (Josh. xv. 31). Lost, unless *Simsim* is the site.

SAPH (*threshold*). Son of "the Giant" slain by Sibbechai (2 Sam. xxi. 18), called SIPPAI in 1 Chr. xx. 4.

SA'PHAT. SHEPHATIAH 2 (1 Esd. v. 9).

SAPHATI'AS. SHEPHATIAH 2 (1 Esd. viii. 34).

SA'PHETH. SHEPHATIAH 3 (1 Esd. v. 33).

SA'PHIR (*fair*). (Micah i. 11). In the hill country, 8 miles N. E. of Ascalon. Now called *Es Sawafir*.

SAPPHI'RA (*beautiful*). Wife of ANANIAS 10, and the participator in his guilt and punishment (Acts v. 1-10).

SAP'PHIRE. See PRECIOUS STONES.

SA'RA. 1. Sarah, wife of Abraham (Heb. xi.

11). See ABRAHAM.—2. SERAH. Daughter of Asher (Num. xxvi. 46).

SARABI'AS. SHEREBIAH (1 Esd. ix. 48).

SARAI'AS. 1. SERAIAH, the high-priest (1 Esd. v. 5).—2. SERAIA, father of Ezra (viii. 1).

SAR'AMEL. Where Simon Maccabeus was made high-priest (1 Macc. xiv. 28). It is not certain whether this word means a place or a title of honor.

SA'RAPH (*fiery*). Descendant of Shelah, the son of Judah (1 Chr. iv. 22).

SARCHED'ONUS (Gr. *sucherdonos*). ESAR-HADDON (Tob. i. 21).

SAR'DIUS. AZIZA (1 Esd. ix. 28).

SAR'DINE. See PRECIOUS STONES.

SAR'DIS. A city on a spur of the mountain range Tmolus, about 2 ms. from the river Hermus, the ancient residence of the kings of Lydia. Its original name, in the time of Omphale, was HYDE'. It was naturally, from its convenient position and the fertile region surrounding it, a commercial mart of importance. Chestnuts were first made an article of commerce here, and called Nuts of Sardis. Pliny says the art of dyeing wool was invented here, and Phrygia furnished the material from its vast flocks. The carpets of Sardis were very celebrated. The Spartans sent to Sardis for gold to cover the face of Apollo at Amyclæ. The sands of the Pactolus, a brook from Tmolus running near Sardis, furnished the gold. Sardis was a slave mart, in very early times, and here traders first became stationary, as distinguished from traveling merchants. It was taken by Antiochus the Great, B. C. 214, and afterward became subject to Pergamus.

CYBELE.

The city waned after the conquest of Alexander. The inscriptions remaining now visible are all of the Roman age, although there are remains of the earlier ages. The temple of Cybele still bears evidence to its former grandeur in its columns, two of which, with their capitals, "surpass any specimen of the Ionic in perfection of design and execution." There are remains of a theatre of 400 ft. diameter, and of a stadium of 1000 ft. The modern name is SERT KALESSI, and the river (Hermus) Wadis-tchai, which is about 180 ft. wide, 3 ft. deep, and muddy. In the time of Tiberius, the city, with 12 others, was destroyed by an earthquake, and suffered so much that its distress excited the compassion of its Roman rulers, who remitted its tax for 5 yrs. Mentioned in Rev. iii. 1-6. See SEVEN CHURCHES.

SAR'DITES, THE. Descendants of Sered, the son of Zebulun (Num. xxvi. 26).

SARDI'US. ODEM. Gr. *Sardios*. See PRECIOUS STONES.

SAR'DONYX. Gr. *Sardius and Onyx*. See PRECIOUS STONES.

SARE'A. An assistant secretary to Ezra (2 Esd. xiv. 24).

SAREP'TA. ZAREPHATH. E. of Sidon (Luke iv. 26).

SAR'GON (*king in fact*). One of the greatest Assyrian kings. He sent Tartan, his general, with an army against Ashdod, and took it. He built the palace at Nimroud. He was successor to Shalmanezer IV. The wars of Sargon were numerous, and he carried his victorious arms into many countries. A statue of Sargon, which is now in the Museum of Berlin, was discovered at Idalium, in Cyprus (Is. xx. 1, 4; 2 K. xvii. 9, 10).

SA'RID (Josh. xix. 10, 12). Zebulon, west of Chisloth Tabor. Lost.

SA'RON. The district in which Lydda stood (Acts ix. 25). The Sharon of the Old Testament.

SARO'THIC. One who returned from captivity; ancestor of sons of Solomon's servants (1 Esd. v. 34).

SAR SECHIM (*chief of the eunuchs*). A general in Nebuchadnezzar's army (Jer. xxxix. 3). RABSARIS.

SA'RUCH. SERUG (Luke iii. 35).

SATAN. See DEVIL.

SATHRABUZA'NES. SHETHAR-BOZNAI (1 Esd. vi. 3, 7, 27).

SA'TYR (Heb. SAIR; pl. SEIRIM). "Hairy" in Gen. xxvii. 11, 23; "rough" (Dan. viii. 21); "devils" (Lev. vii. 7); "shaggy animals" (Is. xiii. 21). It is frequently applied *he-goats* (Lev. iv. 21). Satyrs, in Greek mythology, were imaginary demons, half men and half goats, believed by the superstitious to haunt forests and groves.

SAUL (Heb. SHAUL, *asked for*). 1. Saul of Rehoboth by the river; one of the early kings of Edom (Gen. xxxvi. 37, 38); called SHAUL in 1 Chr. i. 48.—2. Saul, the son of Kish, of the tribe of Benjamin; he was the first king of Israel; anointed by Samuel privately (1 Sam. ix., x.). Afterwards Saul was elected in a solemn assembly at Mizpah by the determination of the miraculous lot. Saul was remarkably tall, and of a courageous disposition (1 Sam. ix. 2, x. 23). His immediate act upon his election, was to head an army and oppose the invasion of the Ammonites. He found them, led by their king, Nahash, at Bezek, and totally routed them (1 Sam. xi. 11). After this triumph Saul was publicly anointed at Gilgal by Samuel (1 Sam. xii.). From this period Saul's reign was marked by a series of transgressions: he assumed upon the priestly office and disregarded God's injunction by ordering the offering up of sacrifices (1 Sam. xiii. 9) during his contest with the Philistines. He rebelled against Jehovah in regard to the destruction of the Amalekites (1 Sam. xiv. 48). Saul behaved with the utmost cruelty to David—twice attempting his life (1 Sam. xviii. 10, 11, xix. 10). He committed a great atrocity in the murder of Ahimelech, the priest (1 Sam. xxii.), and of eighty-five other priests of the house of Eli, as well as the inhabitants of Nob. He forced David into opposition, who twice mercifully spared his life (1 Sam. xxiv. 3-7, xxvi.).

Saul committed a further offense in consulting the witch of Endor (1 Sam. xxviii. 7), although he had previously expelled all practicers of magical arts (xxviii. 3). At this interview he was warned that he and his sons would die the following day. On that day he met the Philistines in Gilboa, on the plain of Esdraelon, and after seeing the utter rout of his army and the death of his three sons (Jonathan of the number), he killed himself upon the battle-field. The bodies of Saul and his sons were exposed by the enemy upon the wall of Bethshan, but were secretly removed by the men of Jabesh-Gilead who in the remembrance of their former obligations to Saul (1 Sam. xi.), gave the bodies honorable burial. Their bones were afterwards removed by David to Zelah, and buried in the sepulchre of Kish. Saul was anointed B. C. 1791.

	KISH.
	1 Saul.
1 Saul,	2 Jonathan.
"	3 Ishui.
"	4 Malchi-Shua.
"	5 Abinadab.
"	6 Eshbaal.
"	7 Merab.
"	8 Michal, dau.
"	9 Armoni.
"	10 Mephibosheth.
2 Jonathan,	11 { Merib-baal / Mephibosheth. }
"	12 Micah.
12 Micah,	13 Pithon.
"	14 Melech.
"	15 Tahrea.
"	16 Ahaz.

SAV'ARAN. An error for Avaran, borne by Eleazar 9 (1 Macc. vi. 43).

SAVI'AS. Uzzi, ancestor of Ezra (1 Esd. viii. 2).

SA'VIOR or **SA'VIOUR.** See JESUS.

SAW (Heb. MEGERAH, MASSOR). Egyptian saws were single-handed, the teeth usually inclining toward the handle, instead of away from it like ours. In most cases they have bronze blades, attached to the handles by leather thongs, but some of those in the British Museum have their blades let into them like our knives. A double-handed iron saw has been found at Nimroud. Double-handed saws were used (1 K. vii. 9; 2 Sam. xii. 31).

SCALES. Heb. PELES, *a balance*, (Is. xl. 12); also weight (Prov. xvi. 11). See WEIGHTS and MEASURES.

SCAPE'-GOAT. See ATONEMENT.

SCAR'LET. COLORS.

SCEP'TRE (Heb. SHEBET, Gr. *skeptron*). ROD or STAFF. A rod or decorated staff, sometimes six feet long, borne by kings and magistrates as a symbol of authority (Gen. xlix. 10).

SCE'VA (*prepared*). A Jew at Ephesus and leader among the priests (Acts xix. 14, 16). His seven sons pretended to practice exorcism.

SCHIN (Heb. SHIN, *a tooth*). The twenty-first letter of the Hebrew alphabet (Ps. cxix.).

SCHISM (Gr. *schisma*). Division (1 Cor. i. 10; rent, Matt. ix. 16). A rent or fissure, used in the N. T. to denote a division in the Church, by contentions.

SCHOOL (Gr. *schole, leisure*), (Acts xix. 9). A place where a teacher and his disciples met and held discussions. See EDUCATION.

The Arab school is primitive—a room with a smooth floor (often the bare ground) and one or two windows (generally without glass or any protection), a board and piece of chalk for each boy, and one for the teacher. The teacher also has a Koran from which he reads. The pupils learn to write by imitating the writing of their teacher. They spell by reciting the names of the letters as (B) NOON, (a) ALIF, (g) GAMEL, NAG (a colt). The rules of the Church are carefully taught, also grammar. Very few go beyond this in the schools. Those who are destined to the Church are educated specially for that end; and study theology, rhetoric, numbers, and other branches. Some of the priests (ulema) are very well educated, and have a good knowledge of their own and the literature of other people. Robert Morris, LL. D., in 1868, found the Pasha of Damascus able to converse in French and English, and to quote long passages from such poets as Shakespeare, Milton, Byron, Longfellow, Bryant, and to give a sketch of our history as a people—in the United States. On geography he was not so well informed. The native maps are more amusing than instructive.

Every mosque must support one or more schools, according to its income. The best schools are now being conducted in a few places by the American missionaries; the principal one being the Seminary at Beirut. See PHŒNICIA.

SCI'ENCE (L. *scientia, knowledge*; Heb. MADDA; Gr. *gnosis*). In Dan. i. 4, and 1 Tim. vi. 20, the original means knowledge and not science.

In Wickliffe's Bible, in Luke i. 77, there is the sentence "science of health," instead of "knowledge of salvation," in the present edition. In Col. ii. 3, is "wisdom and science" for "wisdom and knowledge," as now written, and in 1 Tim. vi. 20, for science the old edition has "kunyinge" (cunning). See TIMOTHY, in HISTORY OF THE BOOKS.

SCOR'PION (Heb. AKRAB; Gr. *skorpios*). One of the largest and most malignant of all the insect tribes. It resembles the lobster. Those found in S. Europe seldom exceed 2 ins. in length, but, in tropical climates, they are 10 or 12. They live upon other insects, but kill and devour their own species also. When it is placed in danger, and sees no way of escape, it will sting itself to death. Their sting is very poisonous; it occasions great pain and inflammation, with alternate chills and burning. The scorpion of Judea when curled up resembles an egg; hence the comparison in Luke xi. 11, 12; Rev. ix. 3-10.

SCORPION.

SCOURG'ING. See PUNISHMENTS.

SCRIBE. See HISTORY OF THE BOOKS.

SCRIP (Heb. YALKUT—ZIKLON; Gr. *pera*). A bag or sack, in which travelers carried their food, or articles of convenience (1 K. xvii. 40; Matt. x. 10).

SCRIP'TURE. See HISTORY OF THE BOOKS.

SCROLL (Heb. SEPHER; Gr. *biblion*). MS. roll. See WRITING.

SCUR'VY. The diseases rendered "scab" and "scurvy," in Lev. xxi. 20, xxii. 22, and Deut. xxviii. 27, may be almost any skin-disease.

SCYTHE. See SICKLE (Jer. i. 16).

SCYTH'IAN (Col. iii. 11). Barbarians, living on the N. of the Black Sea and the Caspian. Herodotus (i. 103) says the Scythians made an incursion through Palestine, into Egypt, in the time of Josiah. This may account for the name *Scythopolis*, which may have been given by some of those people who settled at Bethshean.

SEA. This word is used in several ways: 1. Ocean (Gen. i. 10).—2. The Mediterranean Sea (Deut. xi. 24).—3. Any inland lake or sea (Ez. xlvii. 8).—4. Any great water-course, as the Nile or Euphrates (Is. xix. 5).

SALT SEA, THE. The most ancient name for the Dead Sea (Gen. xiv. 3; Num. xxxiv. 3; Deut. iii. 17; Josh. iii. 16). It is called the Sea of the Arabah (*plain*) in Deut. iii. 17, and the East Sea by Joel (ii. 20), Ezekiel (xlvii. 18), and by Zechariah (xiv. 8). In 2 Esd. (v. 7) it is called the Sodomitish Sea. Josephus calls it Lake Asphaltitis. The name Dead Sea was given by the Greeks (Pausanias, v. 7, and Galen, iv. 9); and by the Latins (Justin, xxxiv. 3). The Arabic name is Bahr Lut (*Sea of Lot*). The Dead Sea is the 3d of the lakes in the course of the Jordan, lying deepest in the valley at its S. end. It is 46 ms. long from N. to S., and 10 ms. wide, and its surface is 1317 ft. below the ocean level (Lynch). The depression was first noticed (in our day) in 1837. The great heat of the region carries off the water by evaporation. The Jordan flows into the N. end. 12 ms. (by the path) down the E. shore there enters the Zurka Main (the ancient Callirrhoë—the En Eglaim), and, 8 ms. further down the shore, the Mojib (Arnon); 10 ms. further, the Beni Hamad; 2 ms. beyond this, the Wady Kerak entering, by several channels, just above the peninsula; and just below it, in the lower bay of the lake, there are 10 or 12 streams, large and small; the largest being

the Wady el Jeib, which drains ⅔ds of the Arabah. On the W. side, the first large stream is the Kedron (Wady el Nar), 5 to 6 ms. from the N. end of the lake; 8 ms. further S. is Wady Khureitun; 5 ms. beyond is Wady Sudeir, at Ain Jidy (Engedi); 2 ms. from this, Wady Areyeh, which, near Hebron, is called Wady Dilbeh; and beyond, at intervals of 3 or 4 ms., are, Birket Halil (Khuberah), Wady Seiyal, and Wady en Nemriyeh, which last flows by the N. side of the rock Masada, and Wady Zuweirah, just N. of the salt mountain of Usdum. Besides these, there are a great number of smaller streams all around the sea, with or without names. There is no visible outlet. The sea is divided into 2 parts by the peninsula of Lisan (tongue, Heb. LASHEN), which is about 9 ms. long, from N. E. to S. W., 4 to 6 ms. wide, and joined to the E. shore by a neck 5 ms. wide. The channel of the sea is 3 to 5 ms. wide opposite the Lisan, and is said to be fordable at the time of the lowest water, in October. The water of the main basin is 1309 ft. deep in the deepest part, opposite Ain Terabeh. The S. bay (Josh. xv. 2) is very shallow, varying from 12 to 3 ft. Careful observations have found that 20 million cubic ft. of water are poured, daily, into the sea, while its evaporating capacity is 24 million in the hottest months, and less than 20 in the rainy season. (See Humboldt). It is believed that the level rises 10 to 15 ft. during the winter rains — falling again during the summer.

SEAL OF EGYPTIAN AND ASSYRIAN KINGS.

The mountains come close to the shore on both the east and west sides, and are quite uniform in hight throughout the whole length, the eastern range being much the higher, and more broken by ravines. The general color is brown or reddish brown on the east (being sandstone, red and yellow, with porphyry), and gray, with whitish tints, on the west side (being limestone over sandstone). The only vegetation is found around the springs, and in the wadies, where palms, tamarisks, mimosa, osiers, oleanders, and a variety of trees and shrubs, besides grain and flowers, form a grateful relief to the general desolation. A plateau divides the mountains on the east side, half way up, extending from the head of the sea south as far as the Zurka Main, which is visible, near sunset, from Jerusalem. The western side is divided into several strata, which are quite distinct; and there are three parallel beaches, one above the other — the highest, 50 feet above the water, extending from *Wady Zuweirah* north to *Ain Jidy*, nearly 20 miles. Above *Ain Jidy* there is but one beach (covered with angular bits of flint, not rounded gravel), which skirts the mountains, being widest at the mouths of the largest brooks, as at the Kidron (*Wady Nar*) and *Ain Terabeh*, where it is more than half a mile wide. Many of the headlands come down steep into the water, cutting the beach in two, and therefore cannot be passed, except by climbing. There is a line of driftwood bordering the beach and marking the high-water line, all around the sea, brought down by the Jordan and other streams, gray and bleached, and some of it of great antiquity. On the west shore of the south bay is the Salt Mountain of Sodom, called by the Arabs *Khasm Usdum*. (See GEOLOGY). There is an island in the sea, west of the Jordan, lying 300 feet from the shore at low water, circular and 400 feet in diameter. Stones and driftwood entirely cover the island. Some suppose the square stones found here are remains of ancient structures, because there are no similar stones on the shore. The plains at the north and south ends of the sea are flat, barren, stony, gently sloping up from the water, crusted with salt, soft and slimy to the foot, and destitute of vegetation, except a few reeds cluster round a spring. The eastern side of the south bay is an exception, where the vegetation, fed by copious streams of sweet water, is abundant, and with great variety of trees, plants, flowers and grasses.

The water of the sea is the heaviest known in all the world, being 12¼ lbs. to the gallon, distilled water weighing 9⅜ lbs. This weight is due to the mineral salts held in solution. Eggs float with one-third exposed above the surface. The color is like the ocean, a greenish blue. The Jordan may be traced for several miles by its muddy color, as it flows into the clear water of the sea.

The analysis of the water of the Dead Sea by many scientific men, gives generally the same result, with but little variation, which is, that there are salts of magnesia, soda, lime, potass, manganese, ammonia, aluminum and iron; and of these there are chlorides, sulphates and bromides. The quantity averages from 13 to 26 parts in 100, according to the season of the year and the part of the sea from which the sample was taken.

Except the absence of vegetation, the appearance of the sea is that of savage and beautiful wildness. The presence of many kinds of birds and wild fowl enlivens the scenes. All along the shores, wherever a brook flows in, there the canebrakes, trees and shrubs harbor partridges, snipe, ducks, doves, hawks, larks, quails, besides many kinds not yet named, or not identified, in great flocks. Frogs are also to be seen in the marshes (not the salt marshes) and hares in the thickets.

There has been no change in the size of the sea within the historic period; except the filling up of the south bay by silt from the rivers, and the destruction of the Cities of the Plain is believed to have been independent of the position or character of the sea, or the bed in which it lies. (See SODOM and GEOLOGY).

SEAL (Heb. HOTHAM; Gr. *sphragis*). The seal takes the place of our signature in the East. A name or device, well known as belonging to a certain person, was engraved on a seal of a ring, or on a small cylinder, and this was stamped on the papyrus, or parchment, with ink, or was pressed on a piece of clay, or wax, which was attached to the document. Many seals and cylinders of this kind have been found among the used by the ancient kings in signing or witnessing their treaties or decrees, and there is a piece of clay bearing the impression of both the Assyrian and Egyptian king's seals in the British Museum, deposited there by Layard, who found it in Assyria, and who thinks it the compact of Sabacho and of Sennacherib.

Doors of tombs, or houses, or treasuries, or any place that was to be guarded from intrusion, were closed, and a piece of clay stuck over the fastening, and this was impressed with the seal of the keeper or owner, so that the least meddling with the clay would break it (Job. xxxviii. 14). The ancient ruins in Assyria and Egypt. Seals were

modern Orientals carry a seal hung by a string, or chain to the neck, or on the finger ring.

Specimens of engraved seals and gems are found in great numbers in the museums of antiquities, some of which are most valuable as confirmations of history. One in Alnwick museum bears the name of Osirtasen I., 3900 B. C. See the ring of Tuothmes, and of Suphis, page 81. See seal of Haggai, p. 105, and Abraxas, p. 107.

SEA'MEN. See SHIP.
SEA MONSTERS. See DRAGON.
SEASON. CLIMATE.
SE'BA. First son of Cush (Gen. x. 7). A nation in Africa included in Cush, and leaving a name and power in Solomon's time (Ps. lxxii. 10). Located in the island Meroe, which lies at the junction of the white and blue branches of the Nile. The chief city (Meroe) had an oracle of Jupiter Ammon (or the ram-headed Nun), ruins of which are now visible, besides pyramids, and other indications of a great population. The great stature and beauty of this people was a theme of the ancients (Herod iii. 20, 114; Is. xliii. 3, xlv. 14; Ez. xxiii. 42). See Josephus, A. J. ii. 10, 2.

SEBAS'TE. SAMARIA 1. Sebaste means in Greek the same as Augustus in Latin, which is "venerable," a title of the Roman Emperors.

SE BAT. MONTH. SHEBET.

SECA'CAH. In the wilderness of Judah (Josh. xv. 61). Lost.

SECHENI'AS. 1. SHECHANIAH 2 (1 Esd. viii. 29). 2. SHECHANIAH 3 (viii. 32).

SE'CHU (*eminence*), (1 Sam. xix. 22). Famous for a great well or cistern. Supposed to be *Bir Nebulla* near *Neby Samuil*. Five ms. N. of Jerusalem.

SECUN'DUS (*second*). A disciple who went with Paul in some of his journeys (Acts xx. 4).

SEDECI'AS. 1. Father of Maasiah (Bar. i. 1), apparently identified with the false prophet in Jer. xxix. 21, 22.—2. Zedekiah, king of Judah (Bar. i. 8).

SEED. Often used figuratively in Scripture (Dan. ix. 1). The Mosaic Law would not permit a field to be sown with mingled seed of several kinds (Lev. xix. 19). The precious seed is often committed to the ground with many fears, but the harvest is a season of joy (Ps. cxxvi. 5, 6).

SEED-TIME. See SOWING.

SEER. One who sees into the future. PROPHET.

SEETHE. To boil (Ex. xvi. 23). To prepare food in hot liquor.

SE'GUB (*elevated*). 1. Youngest son of Hiel (1 K. xvi. 34).—2. Son of Hezron (1 Chr. 21, 22).

SEIR (*rugged*). MOUNT (Gen. xiv. 6), and LAND OF (Gen. xxxii. 3. xxxvi. 30). The mountain and district on the east side of the Arabah, from Akabah to the Dead Sea (Deut. ii. 1, 8). Seir, the Horite, inhabited the land (ib. 20). Called GEBALA (*mountain*) by Josephus; and the northern section, from Petra, is still called JEBAIL by the Arabs. Its north border was probably Mt. Halak (*naked*), a range of white cliffs which run across the Arabah 8 ms. south of the Dead Sea (Josh. xi. 17). Esau drove out the Horites who dwelt in rock-hewn dwellings (Deut. ii. 12), probably such as are seen now in Petra, and changed its name to EDOM. Ezekiel prophesied the desolation of Mt. Seir, which seems to have been fulfilled in the present condition of the country (Ez. xxxv.).—2. Seaн (Josh. xv. 10). In Judah, between Kirjath-Jearim and Beth Shemesh. The village of SARIS, on the ridge between *Wady Aly* and *W. Ghurab*, is

EGYPTIAN CHARIOT.

probably near the ancient site, which is rugged enough to bear the name.

SEI'RATH (Judg. iii. 26). In Mt. Ephraim, where Ehud gathered the army with which he destroyed the Moabites who were with Eglon, the fat king, whom he killed in his tent. Lost.

SE'LA. SELAH (*the rock*). Petra. See EDOM, SEIR.

SE'LA-HAM-MAH'LEKOTH (*the cliff of divisions*). In the wilderness of Maon. Where David escaped from Saul (1 Sam. xxiii. 28). Lost.

SE'LAH. Pause. This word occurs 72 times in the Psalms, and 3 times in Habbakuk, and has given much trouble to translators; but it is now thought to mean a musical pause; when the choir rested, while the instruments played an interlude.

SE'LED (*exultation*). Son of Nadab (1 Chr. ii. 30).

SELEMI'A. An assistant of Ezra (2 Esd. xiv. 24).

SELAMI'AS. SHELEMIAH 4 (1 Esd. ix. 34).

SELEU'CIA. The seaport of Antioch in Syria. On the sea, near the mouth of the river Orontes. Paul (and Barnabas) sailed from here on his first journey (Acts xiii. 4), and probably landed there on his return (xiv. 26). Named after the first Seleucus, who built the fort and made the harbor, and was buried here, B. C. 175. It was a free city in Paul's time (Pliny, v. 18). The remains of the ancient works are still sound, and in use, especially the two piers of the harbor called Paul and Barnabas.

SELEU'CUS IV, PHILOP'ATOR (*loving his father*). King of Asia (2 Mace. iii. 3), son and successor of ANTIOCHUS THE GREAT. After his father's death he ascended the throne. He was murdered after a reign of twelve years, B. C. 175,

by HELIODORUS (Dan. xi. 20). His son gained the crown in 162 B. C. (1 Macc. vii. 1; 2 Macc. xiv. 1).

SEM. SHEM the patriarch (Luke iii. 36).

SEMACHI'AH (*Jeh sustains*). Son of SHEMAIAH 9 (1 Chr. xxvi. 7).

SEM'EI. 1. SHIMEI 14 (1 Esd. ix. 32).—2. SHIMEI 16 (Esth. xi. 2).—3. Father of Mattathias, in the genealogy of Jesus (Luke iii. 26).

SEMEL'LIUS. SHIMSHAI (1 Esd. ii. 16, 17, 25, 30).

SE'MIS. SHIMEI 13 (1 Esd. ix. 23).

SEMIT'IC. SHEM. LANGUAGES. SHEMITIC.

SENA'AH (*thorny*). The "children of Senaah" were among the "people of Israel" who returned from captivity (Ezr. ii. 35; Neh. vii. 38).

SEN'ATE (Gr. *gerousia, the elders*), (Acts v. 21). ELDER.

SEN'EH (*thorn*), (1 Sam. xiv. 4). The south rock at the pass of Michmash, memorable in connection with the adventure of Jonathan and his armor-bearer.

SENIR' (*a coat of mail*). The Amorite name of Mt. HERMON (1 Chr. v. 23; Ez. xxvii. 5; Deut. iii. 9); should be written without the "h," and also in Cant. iv. 8.

SENNACH'ERIB (Heb. TSIN-AKKI-IRIB, *the moon increases, brothers*). King of Assyria. He mounted the throne B. C. 702. In the fourteenth year of Hezekiah he attacked the fenced cities of Judah, and took them (2 K. xviii. 13-16) after having successfully made various war expeditions. He attacked Babylon B. C. 699, and then made a second invasion into Palestine. Hezekiah had sought the protection of Egypt, upon which Sennacherib marched into Egypt and sent proposals to Hezekiah (2 K. ix. 7). Hezekiah not submitting, caused the king of Assyria to send him a threatening written message. Whilst Sennacherib was awaiting the result his camp received a divine visitation, by which, in one night, one hundred and eighty-five thousand of his men were destroyed (2 K. xviii. 13), at which the king fled to his capital. He reigned for twenty-two years. He appears to have been the first king who fixed the seat of government permanently at Nineveh, which he adorned. Of his closing life we read in 2 K. xix. 37; Is. xxxvii. 38. The monuments, palaces, etc., at Koyunjik, and Khorsabad, record his exploits, and refer to the Hebrew nation as fallen from its proud station in the time of David and Solomon. The vessels drawn on the walls as trophies are of fine design, and it seems probable that they were from the Temple. The bas-relief on the rocks at Nahrel Kelb (Dog River), N. of Beirut, shows the king in the midst of six other kings, with a long inscription, in wedge-shaped characters, recording his exploits in Syria and Phœnicia. There are, also, inscriptions in Persian, Greek, Latin, and Arabic. On the monuments the amount of the tribute (2 K. xviii. 13-16), is stated differently from the amount in Kings; giving 800 talents of silver for the 300 talents in Kings. The probability is, that 800 talents was the value of the whole tribute, including the gold. There is in the British Museum a clay impression from this king's seal. His attack on Lachish (see LACHISH) is, also, recorded in pictures and inscriptions. (See p. 175). The iii. iv. and v. chapters of Isaiah, are most wonderfully fulfilled on the Assyrian monuments; where Jews appear as doing the work of horses, drawing the king's chariot, or carts and boats, loaded with sculptures. See the BLACK OBELISK, p. 229.

SEN'UAH (properly HASSENUAH, *bristling*). Father of Judah (Neh. xi. 9), who was over the second city.

SEO'RIM (*barley*). Chief of the fourth course of priests in David's time (1 Chr. xiv. 8).

SE'PHAR (Gen. x. 30). A mount in the East. Now called ZAFAR, an ancient seaport town in Yemen, in the province of Hadramawt (*Hazarmaveth*), Arabia, between Oman and Mirbat, on the shore of the Indian Ocean, at the foot of a lofty mountain. Frankincense is only found on the mountain of Zafar. It was the capital of the Himyerite kings. There was a Christian church there in A. D. 343.

LEOPARD.

SEPHA'RAD (Obad. v. 20). Where the Jews of Jerusalem were held captive. Most probably IONIA is meant.

SEPHARVA'IM (2 K. xix. 13; Is. xxxvii. 13; 2 K. xvii. 24). A city of Assyria, from which people were brought to repeople Samaria. Now SIPPARA, on the Euphrates, above Babylon (Ptol. v. 18). A tradition affirms that Noah buried near this city the records of the antediluvian world. It was a great seat of learning. The sun was the chief

object of worship, and they burnt their children in the fire to Adrameleeh and Anameleeh, the male and female powers of the sun (2 K. xvii. 31), which pagan worship they carried with them to Samaria.

SEPHAR'VITES. People from SEPHARVAIM.

SEPH'ELA. Greek form of the Hebrew HAS SHEFELAH, the ancient name for the plains between the hills of Samaria and Judæa and the Mediterranean Sea. Its northern part is called SHARON (Deut. i. 7; Josh. ix. 1, and in many other passages). Between Ekron and Gaza there were 47 cities besides their villages. It is one of the most productive districts of Palestine, and yearly produces fine crops of grain and fruit. It was anciently the grain-producing district, and was the subject of constant contention between the Israelites and Philistines.

SEP'TUAGINT (L. *septuaginta, the seventy.*) The most ancient Greek version of the O. T. See HISTORY OF THE BOOKS. So named from the sacred idea attached to the number 70.

SEP'ULCHRE (*a burial-place or tomb*). See TOMB.

SE'RAH (*abundance*). Daughter of Asher (Gen. xlvi. 17).

SERAI'AH. The name of persons alluded to in the following passages: 2 Sam. viii. 17; 2 K. xxv. 18; Ezr. vii. 1; Jer. xxxvi. 26; xl. 8, li. 59. The last is termed "a quiet prince." He bore to the Jews a message from Jeremiah.

SER'APHIM (*burning ones*, or *angels of fire*). Two beings, each with 6 wings, seen by Isaiah in a vision (Is. vi. 2, 3).

SE'RED (*fear*). First-born of ZEBULUN, and ancestor of the SARDITES (Gen. xlvi. 14).

SER'GIUS PAU'LUS. Governor of the isle of Cyprus. He was converted under the teachings of Paul, A. D. 48 (Acts xiii. 7).

SER'JEANT (Gr. *rhabdouchos*, *a rod-holder*). An officer who attends on Roman magistrates of the higher class, and executes their orders (Acts xvi. 35, 38).

SE'RON. A general of Antiochus Epiphanes, defeated by Judas Maccabæus, B. C. 166 (1 Macc. iii., iv. 24).

SER'PENT (Heb. NAHASH, any serpent, but especially the cobra). The serpent is alluded to in many passages in the Bible, and nearly always for its typical qualities, or habits, as intensifying similar things in the human family. Satan is called "The Old Serpent" (Rev. xii. 9; 2 Cor. xi. 1). See ADDER, ZAHAL, TANNIN, SARAF; Gr. *herpeton, ophis*, EPHEH, (*hisser*). A poisonous snake, about a foot long, called, by the Arabs, *el effah* (Gr. *echidna*). The viper that fastened on Paul's hand, in Malta (Acts xxviii. 3), and was either the common viper (*pelias verus*), or the *vipera aspis*—both found in the island. The Scriptural allusions are: To its subtilty (Gen. iii. 1); wisdom (Matt. x. 16); poison (Ps. lviii. 4; Prov. xxiii. 32); its forked, sharp, tongue (Ps. cxl. 3; Job. xx. 16); the bite (Num. xxi. 9); sly concealment, in hedges (Eccl. x. 8), in holes (Amos v. 19); living in dry, sandy places (Deut. viii. 15); crawling (Prov. xxx. 19); their birth alive (Is. lix. 5—"cockatrice"). The art of taming, or charming, is of great antiquity, and is alluded to in the Psalms lviii. 5; Eccles. x. 11; Jer. viii. 17, and, perhaps, James iii. 7. The Orientals believe the serpent to have a large share of sagacity, and they cite various reasons for it. They have, in all ages, been used as emblems of cunning and craftiness. There are two erroneous notions

that are popular regarding the serpent before the Fall, which are: 1. That they moved in an erect attitude, and 2. That they fed on dust. There is no reason to believe that the animal has been changed in form or habit; but it was set apart as a form to be hated, and avoided, with fear and disgust. And the eating of dust is only an accident, following wherever an animal eats its food from the ground. The expression means to do any dirty or dishonorable act; or also to speak offensive words. The serpent has been worshiped by several nations —as Phœnicians, Hindus, Chinese—as a beneficent

HIPPOPOTAMUS

genius, of superior wisdom and power. The Egyptians used its form to represent KNEF, the author of all good, and also the god TYPHON, the author of all physical and moral evil; and in their symbolical alphabet the serpent stood for subtility, cunning, lust, sensual pleasure. The serpent coiled around a globe, winged, is a familiar emblem of eternity.

The Greeks used it as a sign of certain attributes in Ceres, Mercury, Æsculapius, in their best qualities, and in the terrible Furies, and the fearful monster, the Python, which was only destroyed by Apollo's arrows; and also as the legs of the impious giants who despise and blaspheme the power of heaven. See ABRAXAS GEM, p. 167.

In Hindo mythology Krishna (the good spirit) contends with a serpent, and finally crushes his head.

The *fiery* serpents of Num. xxi. 6, 8, were so named from the burning sensation caused by their bite, or it may possibly also refer to their brilliant color. There is a small black snake, spotted with

white, in the desert, whose bite is quickly fatal, causing great swelling of the body.

The Egyptians painted and sculptured monstrous serpents with wings, which may have been idealized from lizards.

BRAZEN SERPENT. The scene of the events was either Zalmonah or Punon; Zalmonah meaning the image's position, and Punon the origin of the material from which it was made, Punon the copper mines.

To some critics the brazen serpent is only the sign of the camp hospital—it really was the sign of the Great Physician. The serpent rod of Æsculapius was also a symbol of the supposed healing power of the god. It is difficult to account for the making of the image of the serpent, in the face of the 2d commandment; and yet it was probably made by the appointed artizan of the Tabernacle, Bezaleel or Aholiab. That it was a type of Christ does not explain how it acted as a healer at the time, because the faith in the Messiah never became a present reality, but was rather a future good to be expected. It has been interpreted as a symbol of wisdom, which left to itself leads the soul astray, but when guided by divine law, is the source of all healing, the serpent form would, in that light, be the symbol of health and deliverance.

The rod of Moses, that turned to a serpent, was a symbol to him of divine wisdom.

The brazen serpent was kept a long time after its proper work was done, and became an object of idolatry, in the reign of Hezekiah, who destroyed it (NEHUSHTAN).

The Church of St. Ambrose, Milan, has boasted of having the identical brazen image which Moses had made in the Wilderness, and which Hezekiah destroyed. It was probably the object of worship of some ancient serpent worshipers. OPHITES.

SMYRNA.

SERPENT CHARMING. From the earliest times in the East certain persons have exercised a remarkable power over poisonous snakes, and this is noticed in James iii. 7. The horned cerastes, and the hooded snakes are the kinds usually handled. They do not always take out the poison fangs. The secret of the power seems to be the simple courage and confidence of the men. They use shrill flutes and drums, which seem to attract the attention of the serpents.

SE´RUG (*branch*). Son of Reu, ancestor of Abraham (Gen. xi. 20-23). Jewish tradition says he was the first idolater (Josh. xxiv. 2).

SER´VANT. 1. Heb. ENOSH, "man" (1 Sam. xxiv. 7).—2. Heb. NAAR (Num. xxii. 22), boy, lad, young man (Gen. xiv. 24).—3. Heb. MESHA´RETH, *to wait on, serve* (Ex. xxxiii. 11).—4. Heb.

EBED; found in the O. T. 800 times, and usually rendered servant, sometimes man-servant (Gen. ix. 25-27). This word often denotes a man who dedicates himself voluntarily to the service of another. Thus, Joshua was the servant of Moses. The servants of God are those who are devoted to His service. The word usually means in the Bible a hired servant, or one whose service was the property of his master. The households of the early patriarchs contained many servants, who were treated with kindness, justice, and they were trusted and confided in (Gen. xiv. 11-16). They shared the religious privileges of the family (Gen. xvii. 9-13), and were not transferred to other masters.

SE SIS. SHASHAI (1 Esd. ix. 34).

SES´THEL. BEZALEEL, of the sons of Pahath-Moab (1 Esd. ix. 31).

SETH. First son of Adam after the death of Abel (Gen. iv. 25, 26).

SE´THUR (*hidden*). A spy and son of Michael (Num. xiii. 13).

SET´TLE (Heb. AZARAH), (Ez. xliii. 14). A port *settled* or sunk lower. Elsewhere "Court" in 2 Chr. iv. 9. Ledge in Fairbairn.

SEV´EN. See NUMBER.

SEVEN CHURCHES OF ASIA (Rev. i. 4). 1. Eph´esus was originally called Smyrna; and the orator Callinus, in an address to Jupiter, called the people Smyrnæans (Strabo xiv. 1, 4). Scattered over the site of Ephesus are now only heaps of shapeless ruins. The great Greek temples, in Athens, have come down to us so well preserved, although mutilated and ruined, that they are the admiration of the civilized world. But here, at the site of the temple which was the pride of all Asia, and one of the wonders of the world, we look in vain for even a relic of the multitude of columns; for they have been "removed," as well as the Christian Church. The most probable site is supposed to be that on which the artist stood to sketch for this picture, where the swamp fills the spaces among the piles of crumbling stones. The proudest title of an Ephesian was "a temple-sweeper" of the goddess Diana (NEOKOROS on the coins). The temple itself has been swept away. Its decay began in the 3d century, when Trajan sent the gates to Constantinople.

The Diana-worship was a mass of Oriental superstitions, weaving into itself magic, charms, amulets and the pretense of special miracles. The image of the tutelary divinity was of a great light, carved in ebony wood, representing a woman with a great many full breasts, ending below in a pedestal ornamented with figures of lions, cows and stags; the whole decorated with gold and silver. The head was turreted, like that of Cybele (see page 130); the moon was symbolized behind the head; on her bosom were the Zodiacal signs of the bulls, twins and crab, with two garlands below them of flowers and acorns. Her priests were women and eunuchs (*Melissai* and *Megabyzi*), with a high-priest (*Essen*). There were no bloody sacrifices. Its image was copied for use in private families, where it was more honored than any other, being carried into distant places. Games were celebrated at regular intervals in honor of the goddess, especially in May (the month of Diana), which attracted vast

crowds of pilgrims, and gathered wealth from many countries.

The theatre of Ephesus is the only relic that is preserved so as to be recognizable. It is one of the largest in the world, ranking with the Coliseum of Rome and the theatre of El Djem, in Africa.

In 1869, J. T. Wood found what is supposed to be the monument (or part of it) of the tomb of Luke, on which there is a cross and a bull finely chiseled.

About two miles N. of Ephesus, in Aiasluk, is the great mosque, which was once the Church of St. John (rebuilt, on its original site, by Justinian); a peculiar building, having in it many carved marble slabs, with Arabic inscriptions, and four monolith granite columns, each four feet in diameter, which are supposed to have been in Diana's temple. (See EPHESUS.)

2. SMYR'NA, the second of the "seven," is, unlike Ephesus, but once mentioned in the Scriptures; and yet that was an honorable position which was given it in the apocalyptic message (Rev. ii. 8–11). It rejoiced in the proud title, "The Ornament of Asia." The great prosperity of the ancient city was the result of its policy in following the fortunes and securing the favor of each conqueror, in turn, who overran Asia. This was the reason why they gave to Antiochus the title "God and Saviour," and to his mother that of "Venus of Victory," and worshiped Tiberius, and stamped the head of Mithridates on their coins, and erected temples in honor of deified Rome. But the peculiar worship of the city was of the god Bacchus, the mysteries of which were solemnized with great pomp. Apollo was also honored; and there is a colossal head, in marble, now near the western gate of the city, which once crowned a statue of the god. The walls of the buildings in the upper part of the city are filled with fragments of columns, cornices, entablatures, and even busts, some of which were portraits of men or the ideals of the gods, built in with the common stone as so much rough material. The Turks have mutilated the features of these busts because of their hatred of images. It has been well said that the Moslem horror of all representations of the human form as idolatrous, has destroyed more Grecian statues than are now known to exist. There are many remains of the beautiful tesselated pavements of the ancient temples generally built into walls as raw material. The citadel on the hight behind the town (Mt. Pagus), is built of the ruins of the ancient structure, whose massive foundations may still be traced. The theatre, in which Polycarp (who was bishop over the Church for seventy-four years), was burnt, was on the brow of the hill toward the sea; and it has almost entirely disappeared, except a few seats and the dens in which the wild beasts were kept. The ancient port was filled up by Taimour-Lang during his siege (A. D. 1400). The modern bay or harbor is about 33 ms. long, 15 ms. wide, and sheltered by high, steep, wooded hills on three sides; and the water is deep to the very shores, so that vessels may lie close to receive or discharge their cargoes. The "Two Brothers" (mountains near the head of the gulf) are 3,000 feet high, and are the weather-gauge of the vicinity, giving the signal by their whitecloud cap.

The city is famous for its ample supply of fruit, vegetables, and its excellent wine. The suburbs

THYATIRA.

are occupied by the summer residences of the merchants and the wealthy classes, whose fine gardens, shady groves, and fragrant orchards, are watered by many canals and branches of the river Meles. Population about 160,000; about one half of whom are Christians of the Greek rite. The mission here has succeeded in calling a studious attention to the Bible among both the Greeks and Armenians. 3 lines of railway have been built: 1 leading to Ephesus and Tralles (Aidin), 80 ms.; and another to Magnesia and Kassaba, 60 ms; and the third to the suburb of Bournabat, 6 ms., where there are many country-houses, which are also scattered along the sea-coast, N. W. and S. Not far from Smyrna, at Kara Bell, is the sculpture mentioned by Herodotus (ii. 106), cut in a panel in the limestone rock, perpendicular, and about 7 ft. high. It is an Egyptian figure, in profile, looking east, holding a spear in the left hand, and a bow in the right, with inscriptions in hieroglyphics near, and across the breast this one: "I conquered this country by the might of my arms." (See Daniel xi., and Van Lennep's *Asia Minor*.)

3. PER'GAMOS (correctly, Pergamum). This was the third Church addressed by the author of the Apocalypse; and it was commended for its fidelity

and firmness, in the midst of persecutions, in a city so eminently given to idolatry. It was the capital of a district of the same name, in Mysia, on the river Caicus, 20 ms. from the sea, and 60 from Smyrna. Its origin is lost in antiquity, dating beyond the Trojan war, when Pergamos, son of Pyrrhus, found King Arius here, and deposed him. The city was built on the lower slopes of two high and steep mountains. Eumenes founded the race of the Attalian kings of Pergamos, 200 yrs. B. C.; and his successors formed a large library, which rivaled the Alexandrian, besides making the city the equal of, or superior in importance to, all others in Asia Minor. Sheep and goat-skins were here first made into parchment (*pergamena*), and it is still the chief manufacture of the city. The library was removed to Alexandria by Cleopatra, to whom Antony gave the permission. The ruins of temples, a theatre, stadium, amphitheatre, and other buildings, are scattered over the ancient site. The great glory of the city was the grove Nicephorium—said to have been extremely beautiful—containing temples and statues of all the deities: Zeus, Athena (Minerva), Apollo, Æsculapius (its tutelary deity), Dionysius, and Aphrodite. Pergamos had no rival in splendor, being a union of a cathedral city, a university town, and a royal residence. The Roman Senate recognized the right of sanctuary in the Grove of Æsculapius, which (with the others) was irrigated by many canals from the Caicus, and made very luxuriant in shade and fruit trees. It is called *Neokora* (*New City*) on the coins. This was probably the "throne of Satan," referred to by John (Rev. ii. 13); the idea having arisen from the title of *Soter*, which was given to Æsculapius on account of the *serpent* being his chief emblem (found on several coins of Pergamos), and also because charms and magic were a part of the worship. Nearly all of the pagan temples, and Christian churches (some of which were remodeled temples), are heaped alike in ruins. Their columns, capitals, cornices, and sculptures, of fine marble, have been carried away to rebuild other places, or burned into lime for mortar, or lie in heaps waiting such an inglorious end. The church of St. John (anciently a temple) is roofless, but still standing; and that of St. Sophia is remodeled into a mosque. The Acropolis (see cut on page 22) was the site of the temple of Minerva, built on an artificial platform, raised like that of Solomon's at Jerusalem. Some of the beautiful white-marble columns of this temple measure 4 ft. in diameter, and 40 feet long, as they lie prostrate. Half-way down the hill was the palace of the Attalian kings, connected with the town by an aqueduct, which now crosses the river on its ancient and perfect masonry, the river Selinus passing under it through a double tunnel, 500 ft. long, each arch being 40 ft. wide and 20 high. Besides this work there are 5 ancient bridges. There are very perfect remains of theatres, and a vast Roman amphitheatre, in which Antipas was made the first martyr of Pergamos, followed by a long line. The present population of *Bergamah* is 30,000, only 4,000 of whom are Greek and Armenian Christians, the others being Moslems.

4. THYATIRA. On the river Lycus, N. E. of Smyrna 60 ms. It has been known as Pelopia, Semiramis, Euhippa, (Pliny), and is now called Ak Hissar (*white castle*). Apollo was worshiped under the name of Tyrimnas (a Macedonian king), also Artemis; and, besides these, there were several other gods. There was a curious worship of a certain Sambatha, a Chaldæan (or Jewish Sibyl; said to have been brought there by the Jews, and which is referred to in Rev. ii. 20, etc., under the name of Jezebel. Rome was also deified, as also Hadrian (see Coins, on pps. 29, 236), and other emperors.

SARDIS.

Games were celebrated in honor of Tyrimnas, Hercules, and of the ruling emperor. On the coins there are stamped the heads of Bacchus, Athene, Cybele, and the emperors. There are many remains of antiquity, such as marble sculptures, generally in fragments built into modern walls, or used as troughs or well-covers, and a church of St. John, which was originally a pagan temple, and is now a mosque, with a tall minaret. Inscriptions are found which give an account of many corporate societies of different trades—bakers, potters, weavers, robe makers, and dyers, of which last Antonius Claudius Alphenus was at one time the honored leader, and of which Lydia, whom Paul met in Philippi, was a member. The distant view of the city is very beautiful, but, inside of the limits, there is little order, and less neatness. 2,000 houses pay taxes, and 500 hovels are exempt, sheltering, altogether, about 15,000 people. The railway from Smyrna now reaches Magnesia (30 ms. distant), and is to be continued to Thyatira, and perhaps beyond.

5. SARDIS. The capital of the ancient Lydia (which Homer called Mæonia), once "The Queen of Asia," was the famous valley of the classic Hermus, 2 ms. S. of the river, at the foot of Mt. Tmolus, on the river Pactolus. Its first king of whom we have a record was Candaules (716 B. C.); and the last was the renowned Crœsus, who enriched himself and the city by the golden sands of the Pactolus. But the real wealth of the city was derived from its commerce and manufactures (see SARDIS, on page 248). The invention of the art of dyeing, and of the system of trading in shops, is credited to it. (See Coin, p. 125). Not many years ago there were 6, and there are still standing 2, of the pillars of the temple of Cybele (60 ft. high), which are the oldest Greek monuments in the world, having been set up about 300 yrs. after Solomon's temple; the other 4 were made into lime by the Turks. The eminent author Melito was bishop of Sardis, in the 2d century; and the oldest catalogue of the books of the O. T. by any Christian writer, that has come down to us, was by his hand. The Council of Sardis was convened in 347, from a rule of which the Pope of Rome claims

his earliest authority; which was, that in case a bishop was deposed by the council, he might appeal to the bishop of Rome. (4th canon.)

Julian the Apostate closed the churches and reopened the temples in Sardis in his endeavor to re-establish Pagan worship, A. D. 360.

The cemetery of the ancient kings of Lydia (of the dynasty of Crœsus) is on the top of a high plateau, 6 ms. north of Sardis, where there are mounds extending over a vast area. The monument of **Alyattes, the** father of Crœsus, so minutely described by **Herodotus** (i. 93), is still quite perfect. It is 3800 feet around and 1300 feet long, rising 300 feet above the plain. It has never been disturbed, and is supposed to contain many treasures valuable to the antiquary, illustrating the customs of a people whose civilization dates long before that of Greece, and second only to Egypt and Assyria.

Xerxes gathered his great army at Sardis when he marched to invade Greece by way of the Hellespont. Cyrus the Younger beautified the vicinity by making some fine gardens. Alexander left his general Pausanias here, and ordered the erection of a temple to Jupiter.

6. PHILADEL'PHIA was founded and named by Attalus Philadelphus, B. C. 140, as a mart for the great wine district, which is celebrated by Virgil. It is on the little river Cogamus, which joins the Hermus near Sardis, surrounded almost by an amphitheatre of hills, and bowered in orchards, in the midst of extensive gardens. The rock is basaltic, and streams of lava may be traced in several tracts, but covered by deep, black, rich soil. The great staple is opium, which is entirely monopolized by the government. Herodotus says the sugar-cane was anciently cultivated, and mentions a confection which was made of tamarisk and wheat, which is to-day the favorite sweetmeat of Philadelphia (called *halva*), after a continuance of over 2000 years. When Xerxes was on his way to Greece he rested under a great plane-tree near the city, and so much admired its beauty that he appointed a keeper for it, and adorned it with golden ornaments. Plane-trees still flourish here which surpass all others in the country.

Philadelphia was included in the message with Smyrna as deserving approbation and encouragement; and these two only out of the seven cities have continued to our day, and now possess a material prosperity somewhat equal to their ancient importance.

The present name is *Allah Sh-hr (city of God, or High town)*. The site is a hill, with four flat summits, from which the view is very fine. The valley of the Hermus is here one of the most beautiful and extensive in Asia. There are fifteen churches in use, and about twenty in ruins. Of the ancient cathedral of St. John, all that is left are a few massive pilasters, which are shown in the engraving, towering above the modern buildings, and these are built up from fragments of more ancient pagan temples.

There are 15,000 people, one-third of whom are Greek Christians, who have a bishop, enjoy the free exercise of their religion in church, in processions in the streets, in the use of church bells (nowhere else allowed in the interior of Asia Minor), and their chief glory is in the honorable mention of their church in the Revelation.

7. LAODICE'A, an ancient city on the Lycus, in the valley of the Meander, forty miles east of Ephesus. Its site was on seven hills, which were drained by two brooks, the Asopus and Caprus. The ruins are of a stadium, in very complete preservation, three theatres (one of which was 450 feet in diameter), bridges, aqueducts, and a gymnasium, which testify to its ancient wealth and importance. Its original name was Diospolis (the city of Jupiter), which was changed to Rhoas, under which title it became the largest city in Phrygia (Pliny). Antiochus II gave it the name of his wife Laodice.

The imagery in Rev. ii. 18, was suggested by the images of Apollo, the sun-god, on the coins. Sanbatha had a fane there also (see THYATIRA). The emperors were also deified, especially Hadrian.

It became the seat of an archbishop, and in its cathedral church were gathered several councils; in one of which, a system of supplying the villages or small societies in the interior with church services by itinerating presbyters, was adopted (somewhat similar to the Methodist plan now in use), under the direction of the bishop of Laodicea. Here also was adopted a rule "that Christians should not Judaize by resting on the seventh day, but to work on it as usual, and rest on the Lord's day as far as possible, like Christians."

The city was utterly destroyed A. D. 1230, since when it has lain in shapeless ruins, only visited for its marble and other materials.

The aqueduct (which supplied the city, and is now almost perfect), which conveyed water down one hill, across the plain, and up another, in *stone pipes*, proves the Romans to have been acquainted with the hydrostatic law of water finding its level. The stone pipes have a diameter of two feet, and are fitted into each other at the ends, and the calcareous deposit from the water has incrusted them, forming almost a continuous pipe without a visible joint.

The seats in the stadium have letters and numbers, their owners' or the keeper's marks.

A recent visitor found a number of workmen sawing up the richly sculptured entablature of the ancient theatre, having been busy there for six years, cutting up the marble. Near them was a colossal statue, sawn into several pieces. In this manner have disappeared, during the past twenty years, two agate pillars, 18 inches in diameter; a great number of composite richly sculptured columns, adorned with busts and heads in relief, and vases with wreaths of leaves and fruits, and statues and busts and architectural ornaments without number (the tribute the art-world pays to Mohammed).

COLOSSÆ is about ten miles east from Laodicea, near the village of *Chonas*, but is without any interesting ruins, although it was an important city in the time of the expedition of Xerxes. (See view on page 62). Hierapolis has lately afforded a fine proof of the truth of an account of Strabo (xiii. iv. 14), who speaks of a deadly vapor (carbonic acid gas?) which killed any animal that approached the place. The experiment was tried by Svoboda recently on two fowls, and resulted fatally to both in a few seconds.

SEV'EN STARS, THE. See ASTRONOMY.

SEV'ENEH. SYENE (Ez. xxix. 10).

SEV'ENTY, THE. 1. The seventy disciples of Jesus sent out (Luke x. 17).—2. Is also used to denote the Septuagint.

SEXTA'RIUS (Gr. *xestes*). Nearly one pint English (Mark vii. 4). WEIGHTS, etc.

SHAAL'ABBIN (Josh. xix. 42). Dan, near Ajalon, probably the same as SHA'ALBIM (*city of foxes*), (Judg. i.). Now *Eselin*, near *Sura*, (ZORAH). Eliahba was one of David's 37 heroes (2 Sam. xxiii. 32), and is called THE SHAALBONITE.

SHAAL'BONITE THE. One of David's 37 heroes (2 Sam. xxiii. 32), a native of Shaalbon.

SHA'APH (*division*). 1. Son of Jahdai (1 Chr. ii. 47).—2. Son of Caleb I (ii. 49).

SHAARA'IM (*two gateways*). Judah, in the Shefelah (Josh. xv. 36). On the way to Gath (1 Sam. xvii. 52), where the Philistines fled after Goliath's death, which was in the *Wady Sumt*.

SHAASH'GAZ (*beauty's servant*). Eunuch in charge of the women in Ahasuerus' Palace (Esth. ii. 14).

SHAB'BETHAI (*Sabbath-born*). 1. A Levite who assisted Ezra (Ezr. x. 15), and apparently the same who was with Jeshua (Neh. viii. 7).—2. A chief (xi. 16).

SHACHI'A (Heb. SHACHEYAH, *accusation*). Son of Shaharaim (1 Chr. viii. 10).

SHAD'DAI (Heb. SHADDAY). The Almighty. See JAH.

SHA'DRACH (*circuit of the sun*). The Chaldee name of Hananiah, one of the three friends of Daniel delivered from the burning furnace (Dan. i. 3). He was promoted to a high office after the appointment of Daniel as ruler of the province of Babylon. In refusing to worship the idols of Nebuchadnezzar, Shadrach, with Meshach and Abednego, were thrown into a furnace (Dan. iii.).

SHA'GE (*erring*). Father of Jonathan (1 Chr. xi. 34).

SHAHARA'IM (*the two dawns*). See 1 Chr. viii. 8. It has been proposed to remove the period from the end of verse 7, and read thus, "and Gera begat Uzza, Ahihud, and Shaharaim," etc.

SHAHAZI'MAH (*hights*). Issachar, between Tabor and the Jordan (Josh. xix. 22).

SHA'LEM (Gen. xxxiii. 18). The opinion seems to be that the text ought to read "Jacob came safe to the city of Shechem." If a proper name is meant, there is a place ready for it in the modern Salim. See JESON.

SHA'LIM, THE LAND OF. Benjamin. Between the "land of Shalisha," and the "land of Yemim," through which Saul passed on the way after his father's asses. Probably the land of Shual, 6 ms. north of Michmash (1 Sam. ix. 4).

SHAL'ISHA, THE LAND OF (1 Sam. ix. 4). Between Mt. Ephraim and the land of Shalim. Lost.

SHALLECH'ETH, THE GATE (*falling or casting down*). One of the gates of the house of Jehovah; now supposed to be the Bab. Silsileh, which enters the Haram wall 600 feet from the S. W. corner.

SHAL'LUM (*retribution*). 1. Son of Jabesh who killed Zachariah 1, king of Israel, and usurped his kingdom, B. C. 772 (2 K. xv. 10-15).—2. See JEHOAHAZ 2.—3. The husband of Huldah, the prophetess (2 K. xxii. 14). Others of this name are alluded to in Num. xxvi. 49; 1 Chr. ii. 40, ix. 17, 19, 31; Ezr. ii. 42, vii. 2, x. 24, 42; Neh. iii. 12, vii. 45.

SHAL'LUN. Son of Col-hozeh. He was ruler of a district and repaired the fountain-gate and the wall (Neh. iii. 15).

SHAL'MAI (*my thanks*). Ancestor of Nethinim, who returned from captivity (Ezr. ii. 46).

SHAL'MAN. Shalmaneser, king of Assyria (Hos. x. 14).

SHALMANE'SER (*reverential toward fire*). King of Assyria. He ascended the throne, B. C. 730 (2 K. xvii. 3). He compelled Hoshea to pay tribute two years, but when he joined with So, king of Egypt, in rebellion, the Assyrian came again and took Samaria after a siege of three years, and carried Hoshea captive beyond the Euphrates, ending the kingdom of Israel. See ISRAEL and the BLACK OBELISK, page 220. He conquered Phœnicia, except the island part of the city of Tyre, which he besieged for five years in vain.

SHA'MA (*hearing*). Son of Hothan of Aroer (1 Chr. xi. 44). An assistant of David.

SHAMARI'AH. Son of Rehoboam (2 Chr. xi. 19).

SHAM'BLES (Gr. *makellon*). A meat market, or place for the sale of provisions (1 Cor. x. 25).

SHA'MED (*persecution*). Son of Elpaal (1 Chr. viii. 12).

SHA'MER. 1. A Levite (1 Chr. vi. 46).—2. Son of Heber (vii. 34).

SHAM'GAR (*cup-bearer*). Son of Anath, third Judge of Israel. It is recorded that he killed 600 Philistines with an ox-goad (Judg. iii. 31, v. 6).

SHAM'HUTH (*waste*). Captain in David's army (1 Chr. xxvii. 8).

SHA'MIR (*a thorn*), (Josh. xv. 48). In the mts. of Judah, S. of Hebron, near Jattir. Lost.—2. In Mt. Ephraim, the residence and burial-place of Tola, the judge (Judg. x. 1, 2). Supposed to be SAMMUR, a ruin 10 ms. N. E. of Shechem, on the edge of the Jordan valley.

SHA'MIR (*tried*). Son of Micah (1 Chr. xxiv. 24).

SHAM'MA (*desolation*). Son of Zophar (1 Chr. vii. 37).

SHAM'MAH. 1. One of the 3 chiefs of David's 30 heroes (2 Sam. xxiii. 11-17).—2. Brother of David (1 Sam. xvi. 9). Others of this name are mentioned in Gen. xxxvi. 13; 2 Sam. xxiii. 25, 33; 1 Chr. xi. 27, xxvii. 8.

SHAM'MAI (*desolated*). 1. Son of Onam, and brother of Jada (1 Chr. ii. 28, 32).—2. Son of Rekem (1 Chr. ii. 44, 45).—3. Brother of Miriam and Ishbah (1 Chr. iv. 17).

SHAM'MOTH (*desolations*). One of David's men (1 Chr. xi. 27).

SHAMMU'A. 1. Son of Zaccur (Num. xiii. 4).—2. Son of David by Bath-sheba (1 Chr. xiv. 4).—3. Father of Abda (Neh. xi. 17).—4. One of the priestly family of Bilgah (xii. 18).

SHAMMU'AH. Son of David (2 Sam. v. 14).

SHAM'SHERAI. Son of Jeroham (1 Chr. viii. 26).

SHA'PHAM (*cold*). A Gadite of Bashan (1 Chr. v. 12).

SHA'PHAN (*coney*). 1. Secretary of King Josiah, son of Azaliah (2 K. xxii. 3).—2. Father of Ahikam (2 K. xxii. 12).

SHA'PHAT (*judge*). 1. Son of Hori (Num. xiii. 5).—2. Father of the prophet ELISHA (1 K. xix. 16, 19).—3. Son of Shemaiah, in the line of Judah (1 Chr. iii. 22.)—4. A Gadite (v. 12).—5. Son of Adlai (xxvii. 29). Keeper of David's oxen.

SHA'PHER, MT. (*mt. of pleasantness*), (Num. xxxiii. 23). A desert station. Lost.

SHA'RAI (*Jah frees him*). Son of Bani (Ezr. x. 40).

SHA'RAIM. SHAARAIM (Josh. xv. 36).

SHA'RAR (*twist*). Father of Ahiam (2 Sam. xxiii. 35). SACAR.

SHARE'ZER (*prince of fire*). Son and murderer of SENNACHERIB (2 K. xix. 37). ADRAMMELECH 2. 1. Son of Sennacherib, who assisted in killing his father (Is. xxxvii. 38).—2. A delegate sent to Jerusalem with Regemmelech and others soon after the return from captivity (Zech. vii. 2, viii. 19).

SHA'RON (Heb. HAS SHARON, *straight or even*). A broad, rich tract of land lying between the hills of Judæa and Samaria and the sea, and the northern part of the Shefelah. It was a place of pasture (1 Chr. xxvii. 29); beautiful as Carmel (Is. xxxv. 2). It was a simile for loveliness (Cant. ii. 1). The forest of Sharon was the scene of one of the most romantic exploits of Richard, the Crusader (*Michoval*, viii). (See GEOLOGY). The Sharon of 1 Chr. v. 16, is supposed to have been on the east side of Jordan, in Gilead, but it has not been identified.

SHA'RONITE, THE. One from SHARON. Shitrai had charge of the royal herds (1 Chr. xxvii. 29).

SHARU'HEN (Josh. xix. 16). Given to Simeon. Tell Sheriah, in the Wady Sheriah, 10 miles west of Beersheba, may be the site.

SHA'SHAI (*whitish*). Son of Bani (Ezr. x. 40).

SHA'SHAK (*eagerness*). Son of Beriah (1 Chr. viii. 14, 25).

SHA'UL. 1. Son of Simeon (Gen. xlvi. 10).—2. A king of Edom (i. 48, 49).—3. Son of Uzziah (vi. 24).

SHA'ULITES. Descendants of SHAUL 1 (Num. xxvi. 13).

SHA'VEH, THE VALLEY OF (Gen. xiv. 17). A place on Abraham's route from Damascus, when he rescued his brother Lot. Lost.

SHA'VEH KIRIATHA'IM. Valley of K. (Gen. xiv. 5). Residence of the Emim. On the E. of Jordan. Lost.

SHAV'SHA (corruption of SERAIAH). Secretary in David's time (1 Chr. xviii. 16).

SHAWM. A musical instrument, resembling the clarionet (Ps. cxviii. 7).

SHEAF. The offering of the Omer or sheaf was to be brought to the priest on the 16th of the month, and waved before the altar in acknowledgment of the fruitfulness of the season (Lev. xxiii. 5, 6, 10, 12).

SHE'AL (*an asking*). Son of Bani (Ezr. x. 29).

SHEAL'TIEL (*I have asked him of God*). Father of Zerubbabel (Ezr. iii. 2, 8).

SHEARI'AH (*whom Jah estimates*). Son of Azel (1 Chr. viii. 38).

SHEARING-HOUSE, THE (2 K. x. 12). Near Mt. Gilboa, now Beth Kad. Where Jehu killed 42 members of the royal family of Judah.

SHE'BA (Josh. xix. 2). Simeon, near Beersheba. Job (i. 15, vi. 19), with the robber habits that are peculiar to the Bedawin of our day.

SHE'BA (Josh. xix. 2). Simeon, near Beersheba. SHEMA.

SHE'BAH. Shibeah was the fourth well dug by Isaac's people (Gen. xxvi. 33). Abraham dug a well here also (Gen. xxi. 25-32). The name is one of the most ancient known, and is interpreted variously as "*seven,*" "an oath," "abundance," and as "a lion." BEERSHEBA.

SHEBAM' (Num. xxxii. 3). East of Jordan. Given to Reuben. It was "a land for cattle." SHIBMAH or SIBMAH.

SHEBANI'AH (*Jah has made grow*). 1. A Levite who sealed the covenant (Neh. x. 10; ix. 4, 5).—2. One of a priestly family who sealed the covenant (x. 4).—3. Another Levite who sealed the covenant (x. 12).—4. A priest (1 Chr. xv. 24).

SHEB'ARIM (*dividing*), (Josh. vii. 5). Near Ai. Lost.

SHE'BER (*breaking*). Son of CALEB 1 (1 Chr. ii. 48).

SHEB'NA (*youth*). A steward in king Hezekiah's palace (Is. xxii. 15).

SHEB'UEL (*captive of God*). 1. A descendant of

SHECHEM.

SHE'AR JA'SHUB (*the remnant shall return*). Son of ISAIAH (Is. vii. 3).

SHE'BA (*red*), (Gen. x. 7). 1. Grandson of Cush; 2. Tenth son of Joktan (ver. 28); 3. Grandson of Keturah (ib. xxv. 3). 1. The name of the kingdom in South Arabia, before Himyer took its place, a few years before Christ (24—Strabo). Here were the Sabæans of Diodorus (iii. 38, 46). A queen of Sheba visited Solomon (1 K. x.), attended by a great train, camels loaded with spices, gold, and precious stones. The chief cities were Seba, Uzal (now *Sana*), Sephar (now *Zafar*), and Mariaba (now *Marib*). This district had the chief riches, best country, and greatest numbers of all the four peoples of Arabia. The local history is authentic only as far back as the first century A.D. Their ancient religion was pagan.—2. Settled on the Persian Gulf. On the island of Bahreyn, in the Gulf, are the ruins of an ancient city called Seba. Its merchants are mentioned in Ezekiel xxvii. 22.—3. The sons of Keturah are charged by

Gershom (1 Chr. xxiii. 16).—2. Chief in the thirteenth course in the Temple-choir (xxv. 4).

SHECANI'AH. 1. Chief of the tenth course of priests in David's time (1 Chr. xxiv. 11).—2. One who distributed portions to priests in Hezekiah's reign (2 Chr. xxxi. 15).

SHECHANI'AH (*families with Jah*). Seven of this name are mentioned in 1 Chr. iii. 21, 22; Ezr. viii. 3, 5, x. 2; Neh. iii. 29, vi. 18, xii. 3.

SHECH'EM (*ridge*). SICHEM (Gen. xxxiii. 18). It is not certain whether the city was named from Shechem, the son of Hamor, or that he was named after the city. It is on the top of the ridge between the waters of the Jordan and the Mediterranean Sea, between Ebal and Gerizim (Judg. ix. 7). Called Sychar in John iv. 5, in the story of the meeting of Jesus and the woman of Samaria. Now Nablus (Neapolis, so named by Vespasian—Jos., B. J., iv. 8, 1). Also known as Mabortha (Pliny v. 13). The situation is a favored one, and excites

the admiration of all travelers, Dr. Clarke saying, that "there is nothing finer in all Palestine." The valley is sheltered by a high mountain on each side, and only about 1500 ft. wide, and elevated 1800 ft. above the sea. Water flows from the city E. and W. to the Jordan, and to the Mediterranean sea. The valley is full of gardens, orchards of all kinds of fruits, watered by fountains, and enlivened by the songs of birds. Abraham, on his first visit to the Land of Promise, pitched his tent under the oak of Moreh, at Shechem (Gen. xii. 6). Jacob bought a field of the children of Hamor (Gen. xxxiii. 19), where he dug a well, about a mile from the present town, and left it as a special patrimony to Joseph (Josh. xxiv. 32). Shechem was given to Ephraim (Josh. xx. 7), was assigned to the Le-

SHEEP-FOLD.

vites, and was made a City of Refuge (ib. xxi. 20, 21). The people assembled at Shechem to hear the law of Moses read, "half of them over against Mt. Ebal," the chief men and priests being around the ark in the midst (Josh. viii. 30-35); and again Joshua gathered all the tribes here just before his death (xxiv.), and delivered his last counsels. Abimelech raised a revolt in Shechem, and was made king (Judg. ix.); and Jotham denounced him and the men of Shechem in a parable, from the top of Gerizim (ver. 22), and after 3 yrs. he destroyed the city and the strong tower that was in the city, but lost his own life also (ver. 55). The 10 tribes made Jeroboam their king and Shechem their capital (1 K. xii. 20). When the people were carried away to Babylon the city was colonized from Assyria (2 K. xvii. 24), and again admitted strangers under Esar-haddon (Ezr. iv. 2). The present town of Nablus has about 5,000 people, living in stone houses of very ordinary style, except those of the wealthy sheikhs. There are no fine public buildings. There are not less than 80 springs of water in the valley. One of the largest, Ain Balata, rises in a chamber partly under ground, a few rods from Jacob's well. Olives, figs, almonds, walnuts, mulberries, pomegranates, oranges, apricots, and grapes, abound, besides vegetables of every sort. There are manufactories of wool, silk, and camel's-hair cloth, and especially of soap; and the district around it is rich in wool, grain and oil. As a confirmation of the truth and accuracy, even to minute detail, it is interesting to cite the words of the original Hebrew, describing this spot, on which Joseph's tomb stands, which are, CHELEAT HASSADE, meaning a *dead-level*; differing from SHEFELAH, (a *plain*), and EMEK (a *valley*), and this description is exactly correct—and besides, there is no other spot like it in all Palestine.

SHECH'INAH (*habitation*). Indwelling of God, is properly applied to visible manifestations of God's presence. Thus, Num. v. 3, *in the midst whereof I dwell* is rendered by the Targum "among whom my *shekinah* is dwelling." Difference of opinion exists as to whether there was any continuous visible manifestations of God's presence in the Holy of Holies over the *coppereth* or mercy-seat. Jewish authorities hold there was, and that this shekinah did not return to the second temple. Many Christian writers deny its continuous visibility even in the first.

SHED'EUR (*darting of fire*). Father of Elizur (Num. i. 5).

SHEEP. Heb. AYIL, a ram (Gen. xv. 9); KAR, a lamb; KEBES, a he-lamb (xxx. 40); fem. KIBSAH, ewe-lamb (Gen. xxi. 28); ZON, ZONA, ZONAH, a flock of small cattle (Gen. iv. 4); RAHEL, RACHEL, fem. "ewe" (Gen. xxxi. 38); SEH, one of a flock, i. e. sheep or goat (Gen. xxii. 7); TALEH, a lamb, young and tender.

Of the Syrian sheep there are two varieties: the Bedaween, which have long and thick tails, but differ in no other respect from the larger kinds of sheep among us. The others have very large and broad tails, with a small end which turns back upon itself; they are of a substance between fat and marrow, which is not eaten separately, but mixed with the lean meat in many of their dishes, and also used instead of butter. A common sheep of this sort, without the head, feet, skin, and entrails, weighs from 60 to 80 pounds, of which the tail itself is usually 10 or 15 (see cut on page 89), and when fattened, twice or thrice that weight.

The sheep or lamb was the common sacrifice under the Mosaic law (Ex. xxix. 22). The innocence, mildness, submission and patience, of the lamb, render it suitable for a sacrifice (John i. 29).

There are frequent allusions in Scripture to sheep, and its proneness to go astray (Is. liii. 6). It is gregarious, and dependent on the protection and guidance of its master. Its name is often given to the people of God (2 K. xxii. 17). Sheep and goats are still found in Syria, feeding together, as in ancient times (Gen. xxx. 35). The season of sheep-shearing was one of great joy and festivity (1 Sam. xxv. 2, 8, 36). The Bedawins are compelled to move from place to place as their flocks and herds consume the pasture, and the supply of water is the one great question. The noon is the time for watering the animals (Ps. xxiii. 1, 2), when the tribe, or the shepherds gather to talk over the news. Sheep-cotes or folds are generally open houses or enclosures, walled round (Num. xxxii. 16; 2 Sam. vii. 8).

SHEEP-MARKET, THE (John v. 2). Supposed to have been a GATE, and at present called St. Stephen's; and the great open ruined cistern near it is called the Pool of Bethesda.

SHEHARI'AH (*Jah seeks*). Son of Jeroham (1 Chr. viii. 26).

SHEK'EL. See MONEY.

SHE'LAH (*petition*). 1. Son of Judah 1 (Gen. xxxviii. 5, 11, 14, 26).—2. Heb. *missile*, *sprout*. Salah, son of Arphaxad (1 Chr. i. 18, 24).

SHE'LANITES, THE. Descendants of Shelah 1 (Num. xxvi. 20).

SHELEMI'AH. Nine of this name are alluded to in Ezr. x. 39; Neh. iii. 30, xiii. 13; Jer. xxxvii. 3, 13; 1 Chr. xxvi. 14; Ezr. x. 41; Jer. xxxvi. 14, 26).

SHEF'ELAH (see PHILISTIA). Low country; the plains below the hills of Judea.

SHEL'EPH (*partridge chick*). Second son of Joktan, and father of a tribe who settled in Yemen, in Arabia, where there is now a district called *Sulaf* (Gen. x. 36).

SHE'LESH (*tried*). Son of Helem (1 Chr. vii. 35).

SHEL´OMI (*pacific*). Father of Ahihud (Num. xxxiv. 27).

SHEL´OMITH (*love of peace*). 1. Daughter of Dibri (Lev. xxiv. 11).—2. Daughter of Zerubbabel (1 Chr. iii. 19). Five others of the name are mentioned in 1 Chr. xxiii. 18, xxvi. 25, 26, 28, xxiii. 9; Ezr. viii. 10; 2 Chr. xi. 20.

SHEL´OMOTH (1 Chr. xxiv. 22). SHELOMITH.

SHEL´UMIEL (*friend of God*). Son of Rurishaddai (Num. i. 6).

SHEM. Eldest son of Noah (Gen. v. 32), settled between Japheth and Ham, the country from the Mediterranean Sea to the Indian Ocean, and from Lydia to the Red Sea, including Syria (Aram), Chaldæa (Arphaxad), Assyria (Asshur), Persia (Elam), and Arabia (Joktan). A special blessing is promised Shem in Gen. ix. 27.

SHEM´A. In Judah (Josh. xv. 26). SHEBA. Given to Simeon.

SHE´MA. 1. Ancestor of Bela (1 Chr. v. 8).—2. Son of Elpaal (viii. 13).—3. One who assisted Ezra (Neh. viii. 4).

SHEMAI´AH (*Jah hears*). Twenty-five of this name are alluded to in 1 K. xii. 22; 2 Chr. xi. 2, xii. 5, 7, 15; 1 Chr. iii. 22; Neh. iii. 29, iv. 37, v. 4, ix. 14; Neh. xi. 15; 1 Chr. ix. 16, xv. 8, 11, xxiv. 6, xxvi. 4, 6, 7; 2 Chr. xxix. 14; Ezr. viii. 13, 16, x. 21, 31; Neh. vi. 10, x. 8, xii. 6, 18, 34, 35, 36, 42; Jer. xxix. 24, 32; 2 Chr. xvii. 8, xxxi. 15, xxxv. 9; Jer. xxvi. 20, xxxvi. 12.

SHEMAI´AH (*Jah hears*). 1. A prophet of Israel (1 K. xii. 22-24). He is said to have written a history of Rehoboam's reign.—2. A Levite, who made a registry of 24 priestly classes (1 Chr. xv. 8).—3. A false prophet among the exiles in Babylon, opposed to Jeremiah (xxix. 24).—4. A false prophet in the pay of Sanballat and Tobiah (Num. iii. 8; Neh. vi. 10). 21 others were of no particular note.

SHEMARI´AH (*Jah keeps*). 1. A warrior who assisted David (1 Chr. xii. 5).—2. A layman (Ezr. x. 32).—3. One of the family of Bani (x. 41).

SHEME´BER (*lofty flight*). King of Zeboim (Gen. xiv. 2).

SHE´MER (*preserved*). The owner of the hill on which the city of Samaria was built (1 K. xvi. 24).

SHEM´IDA (*form of wisdom*). Son of Gilead (Num. xxvi. 32).

SHEM´IDAH (1 Chr. vii. 19).

SHEM´IDAITES, THE. Descendants of Shemida (Num. xxvi. 32).

SHEM´IMITH. The name of a melody in Ps. vi. xii.

SHEMIR´AMOTH (*Heaven most high*). 1. One in David's choir (1 Chr. xv. 18, 20).—2. A Levite, teacher of the law (2 Chr. xvii. 8).

SHEMIT´IC. The Shemitic languages (see Gen. x. 21), are also called Aryan, and Syro-Arabic. The extent of this family of languages may be indicated by the boundaries—the highlands of Armenia on the north, the Tigris and its mountain ranges on the east, the Red Sea, Levant, and Asia Minor on the west—the south is limited by the ocean. The uniform climate of this vast region has tended to keep the people to their unvarying customs from age to age, whether in the cities, or in the country, or on the trackless waste.

TABLE OF THE SHEMITIC LANGUAGES.

Living.	Dead.	Classy.
Arabic and its dialects	Ethiopic	Arabic.
Amharic	Himyaritic.	
Hebrew	Biblical, Hebrew / Samaritan Pentateuch / Carthaginian / Phœnician } Inscrip'n	Hebraic.
Neo. Syriac	Chaldee, Masora, Targum / Biblical-Chaldee, Syriac / Peshito of 2d cent. A. D. / Cuneiform of Bab. & Nin.	Aramaic.

The Old Testament has traces of the changes in the languages of Palestine and Assyria, especially in the fragments of ancient poems, which contain many Aramaic words not used anywhere else in the Scriptures. The natural tendency of the Aryans has been, in all cases, to keep their language and customs free from any mixture from their neighbors; adopting very few words and very few habits from other people. Their language, religion, and manners were all unsocial, despotic, conservative; and what treasures they borrowed from the nations around them were not assimilated, but kept entire as when first found.

The peculiar character of these languages is that the original root words are nearly all of one syllable. The changes incident to growth have resulted in arranging the particles around the root words, or if making particles of these words, which become parts of the later form of words. There are no compound words—or very few. There are no logical arrangements, but the grouping of words which record facts, and carry forward the train of thought.

An instance:

"Who is this, the King of Glory?
Jehovah, strong and mighty;
Jehovah, mighty in battle.
Lift up your heads, ye gates,
And lift up, ye everlasting doors
That the King of Glory may come in.
Who, then, is He, the King of Glory?
Jehovah of hosts,
He is the King of Glory." (Pause).
.Ps. xxiv. 8-10

Here the mind is carried forward from one fact to another, in simple and sublime statement, without logic, except the irresistible logic of facts.

It appears to be beyond dispute, as can be proved from the ancient monuments, from tradition, and from dialects now spoken by their descendants, that a great Hamitic population must have over-spread Europe, Asia and Africa, speaking languages more or less dissimilar in their vocabulary, but having almost a common grammar and construction. These people civilized Phœnicia, Babylonia, South Arabia and Egypt, and prepared the way for the Hebrew race, or the Shemitic races, who came after and benefited by their works.

The materials for a history of the Hebrew language are as few as for a history of a rock. The language from Abraham's time to this has not changed in one essential feature or element, except to decay. Very few words have been dropped, and not many added, and the greater number of the additions date from the Captivity. The language shows historic progress from Moses (the Pentateuch) to the Captivity (Ezra and Malachi), always degenerating, and every adopted word can be selected, even in its Hebrew dress, as YAVAN, from the Sanscrit yuvajana, young emigrants, meaning the Greeks. From the Captivity, pure Hebrew was confined by custom to the priests and the sanctuary, from which use it was never again separated, and with the passing away of the Temple worship, has become a dead language. It was even dead in the time of Christ, for the Scriptures were at that time known only in the Aramæan. The present Jewish speech is a combination of words Hebraized and borrowed from every quarter of the world.

It is argued that the Hebrew could not have been the one original source of languages for its oldest names, as Adam, Eve, etc., are derivatives, and may have been translated from other languages by Moses.

The language is rich in different terms for the same object, as 9 for "trust in God;" 14 for "inquire or ask;" 24 for "keep the law."

The Phœnician was so closely allied to the He-

brew as to be used in common; and it was more widely distributed (by sailors and merchants) than any other ancient speech, and from this very cause it went to pieces, after having become overloaded by adopted words. (The English language is being overloaded by Latinisms in the same manner).

The successor to Aramaic is Syriac, dating from the 2d century, A. D., in which there is a wealth of foreign words, especially Greek. The Aramaic after a career of eleven centuries as the sacred language of the Israelites, has, according to a law which works the same in all cases, passed away.

The remains of the ancient languages of Assyria are almost entirely found in the wedge-shaped and arrow-head characters; and the history of the language can be traced, quite distinctly, from the age of clay tablets to those of bricks and alabaster. It appears that the Babylonian alphabet was constructed on the more ancient syllabic alphabet of the wedge-shaped period. Some few remains of this speech are found in Daniel (see HISTORY OF THE BOOKS), but the originals of the Apocryphal books are lost, while the Gemaras are not free from mixture with other tongues, and the Zohar is peculiar in describing Gnostic atheism in Aramaic forms of speech, and so adds little to our knowledge of the Aramaic idiom. The peculiar idioms are better preserved in the Masora. Not much additional can be found in the Samaritan, which was the vulgar Aramaic and Hebrew mingled after the sacred dialect became the language of the sanctuary and Holy Books.

The dialect of Galilee was local, largely influenced and mingled with foreign elements, confused by the indifferent use of certain letters, as soft k and hard k, b and p, d for t final. The sacred dialect had but little influence, and was so little known in the time of Ezra and Nehemiah (viii. 8), as to need interpretation when read in public.

Eastern Aramaic is the language of the Targums, and of the Pharisees; while the Western branch is the language of the New Testament, of the Christians of the first century. As the sacred dialect disappeared from the popular mind, the work of the scholars arose to importance, in such works as the Targums. The Talmud was the growth of the ages dating from the Captivity to A. D. 426, but there are few additions to our knowledge of the languages used in the work.

Of the Palmyrene dialect the only remains are the inscriptions dating from A. D. 49 to A. D. 250, which contain words borrowed from the Arabic, Greek, and Latin.

The sacred dialect became classic, and confined to books, after the fall of Jerusalem, the chief seat of its schools being at Edessa until A. D. 410, when it was removed to Nisibis. Since the 8th century it has declined in interest, and was but partly restored to favor by the facilities afforded by the discovery of printing. (See CANON.) Chaldaic paraphrases of the Scriptures have thrown much light on manners and customs, and on certain difficult passages of the O. T., especially those claimed by Christians to be prophesies of the Messiah, which are proved beyond a question, by the paraphrases, to have been so regarded by the Jews, in all ages, before the appearance of Jesus the Christ.

The sacred language of Ethiopia, the Jeez (Ghez), has been traced to its relation with Arabic and Aramaic, and it is probably a relic of Himyarite emigration. Cush was on both sides of the Red Sea (see HAM). The alphabet is very curious; every consonant contains an r, and the vowels are made by adding a sound to a consonant. This system requires 202 letters.

The Arabic language shows by internal evidence its great antiquity, and its local habitation from the beginning in Arabia. Palgrave says that in Central Arabia, where very little or no foreign influence has ever been felt, that the Arabic is spoken now in the same purity as when Mohammed wrote the Koran, 1200 years ago. It is said in a legend that the language was formed by the union of several dialects, of which the Koreish was the leading one, and in which the Koran was written.

Arabian historians describe a golden age of poetry just preceding Mohammed, in which poets contended with each other for national honors, in grand public assemblies. Poetry and romance were the chief objects of attention, held in greater honor than trade or labor. These poets were either skeptical or voluptuaries, and their writings, as we now have them, give no idea of what their religion was before Mohammed. The Koran contains evidences of a change in Arabic literature, in progress at the time it was written; the closing chapters appearing to have been written earliest in point of time.

The Arabic is especially rich in words and in grammatical forms, and in greater number and variety than any other language.

The language was, as we know it, first the speech of robbers and herdsmen, without religion, superstitious, uncultivated; and afterwards that of a cultivated, self-satisfied, luxurious, licentious people, whose philosophy was borrowed, and religion invented and dogmatized in the most offensive and tiresome manner.

Its chief value to the Bible student is the vast mass of words that it furnishes in illustration of obscure Hebrew words, by which many obscure passages have been explained.

The question of the antiquity of the art of writing is settled in favor of a much earlier age than that of Moses, for he regulates a certain use of the art in Lev. xix. 28, and it is not probable that the Hebrew alphabet and system of writing was invented during the sojourn in the Wilderness. The theory most favored now is that the Egyptians had the art many years before the Hebrews were a people, or even before Phoenicia had its alphabet.

The oldest alphabet that is known is the Phoenician, and the oldest monument of it is the MOABITE STONE, recently discovered (see page 173). Coins are next in order of antiquity, and those struck by the Maccabaeans are instances (see WRITING and MONEY).

The ancient relics exhibit the growth of the square Hebrew letter from age to age, having become settled in Ezra's time, and continuing without change from that to about 500 A. D. The letter became consecrated, and was preserved with superstitious care, especially after the fall of Jerusalem. The reverence of the Jews for their sacred writings would have been outraged by any attempt to introduce a system of interpretation different from the ancient one. To establish a uniform system was the object of the Masoretes (masters of tradition), by means of written vowels and accents, which dates from about the 6th century A. D. The Syriac adopted a similar system in the 1st or 2d century.

The ordinary Hebrew verb has 5 forms:

1. KAL. Simple form.

Causative.	Reflective.	Intensive.
2. HIPHIL.	3. NIPHAL.	4. PIEL.
Passive, HOPHAL.		Passive, PUAL.

5. HITHPAEL.

There are no moods. In the Arabic there are 15 forms in the verb, by which ideas of time, place and action are conveyed as well as by our system of moods.

Names are intensified by prefixtures, as Ha-Arabah, the Arabah. There are dual names, as horse, meaning both horse and mare, or two horses, and there is a third class, meaning many, as attudim, goats, zône, sheep, as a flock. A fourth class represent many different individuals without dis-

tinction, as sand does in ours (many grains forming sand); Elohim (Gods) God.

There are no compound words. The great extent of the verb supplies this defect in some degree, some of the verb-forms indicating color, condition, etc.

The Arabic alphabet contains all the Hebrew letters; but in some cases there is not an exact parallel. The arrangement of the two alphabets was once the same, as is proved by the numbers expressed by each letter; but the order is now different. The earliest form of the letter is what is now called Himyarite.

SHEM UEL. SAMUEL. 1. Son of Ammihud (Num. xxxiv. 20).—2. SAMUEL the prophet (1 Chr. vi. 33).—3. Son of Tola (vii. 2).

SHEN (1 Sam. vii. 12). Where Samuel set up the stone Ebenezer, between "the Mizpah and the Shen." Lost.

SHENA'ZAR (*fiery torch*). Son of SALATHIEL (1 Chr. iii. 18).

SHE'NIR (Deut. iii. 9; Cant. iv. 8). Senir, Mt. Hermon.

SHE OL (Heb. SHEOL, *hell*). See HADES.

SHEPH'AM (Num. xxxiv. 10, 11). On the E. boundary of the land. Lost.

SHEPHATHI'AH. Father of Meshullam 6 (1 Chr. ix. 8).

SHEPHATI'AH. The name of 7 distinguished Jews, alluded to in the following passages: 2 Sam. iii. 34; 1 Chr. xii. 5, xxvii. 16, 2 Chr. xxi. 2; Ezr. ii. 4; 7 vii; Neh. xi. 4; Jer. xxxviii. 1.

SHEP'HERD (Heb. ROEH, *shepherd, pastor*). (Gen. xlix. 4; Jer. ii. 8). The wandering character of life, and the dependence upon flocks, rendered the care of sheep amongst the most important duties of life, from the earliest time in the East. (See SHEEP). "Abel was a keeper of sheep" (Gen. iv. 2). The employment of shepherd was not only followed by the chiefs (Gen. xxx. 29), but by their sons and daughters as well (Gen. xxix. 6; Ex. ii. 19). Extensive flocks fed in the wilderness of Judah (1 Sam. xxv. 2); at Bethlehem (1 Sam. xvi. 11; Luke ii. 8); at Gedor (1 Chr. iv.). As the people became more settled, agriculture became more general, and the care of sheep less important. Figurative allusion is continually made, both in the O. and N. T.; Christ applying the expression to himself, and frequently using the term figuratively (Ps. xxiii.; Is. xl. 11, xlix. 9, 10; Jer. xxiii. 3, 4; John x. 12, 14, 16; 1 Pet. v. 4; Luke ii. 8). It is the habit of the shepherd, in the East, to walk before his flock, leading by his voice (John x. 4); the dog following in the rear of it (1 Chr. xxx. 1). In leading to and from the pasturage, the mothers are led by the shepherd (Gen. xxxiii. 13), who *also* carries the tender lambs (Is. xl. 11). Tents and towers were erected for the shepherd as a point of observation: such was the tower of Eden (Gen. xxxv. 21). Shepherds used the sling (1 Sam. xvii. 40), both for defence and amusement; they also played upon a flute. The towers are still found in nearly every little district in Palestine. The shepherd follows the same customs of care, and watching of the flock, to-day, as in ancient times. In pleasant weather sleeping near them, in the field, under some rude hut, or under a tent; leading them to drink, and helping the young lambs, or lame sheep, by carrying or lifting them out of dangerous places by his crook. The custom of giving names to the members of the flock is still in use; the flock recognizing the shepherd's voice, and answering to their names. The shepherd is also exposed to danger of his life, in the protection of his flock against robbers and wild beasts. Many shepherds make a heavy cloak of sheep-skin, with the wool on; and others use the coarse goat's-hair, or camel's-hair cloth.

SHE'PHI (*wearing away*). Son of Shobal (1 Chr. i. 40), also written

SHE'PHO (*smoothness*), (Gen. xxxvi. 23).

SHEPHU'PHAN (*serpent*). A son of Bela (1 Chr. viii. 5).

SHE'RAH (*kinswoman*). Daughter of Ephraim (1 Chr. vii. 24).

SHERD. POTSHERD, fragment of an earthern vessel (Job ii. 8).

SHEREBI'AH (*heat of Jah*). An assistant of Ezra (Neh. viii. 7, ix. 4, 5; Ezr. viii. 18, 24).

SHE'RESH (*root*). Son of Machir (1 Chr. vii. 16).

SHERE'ZER. A messenger sent to inquire about the fasting (Zech. vii. 2).

SHER'IFFS (Heb. TIFTAYE, *lawyers*). The name of certain high officials among the Babylonians.

SHE'SHACH (Jer. xxv. 26, li. 41). Supposed to be Babylon by some. Others say it means UR, the ancient capital of Babylonia, the city of Abraham.

SHE'SHAI (*whitish*). Son of Anak (Num. xiii. 22; Josh. xv. 14).

SHE'SHAN (*lily*). Descendant of Jerahmeel; father of AHLAI (1 Chr. ii. 31, 34, 35).

SHESHBAZ'ZAR (*fire-worshiper*). The Persian name given to ZERUBBABEL (Ezr. i. 8, 11).

SHETH. 1. SETH (1 Chr. i. 1).—2. The "Sons of Sheth" (Num. xxiv. 17).

SHE'THAR (*a star*). A prince of Persia and Media (Esth. i. 14).

SHETH'ARBOZ'NAI (*star of splendor*). A Persian officer of rank (Ezr. v. 3, 6).

SHE'VA. A corruption of SERAIAH. 1. Secretary of David (2 Sam. xx. 25).—2. Son of CALEB 1 (1 Chr. ii. 49).

SHEW-BREAD.

SHEW-BREAD (Heb. LEHEM, PANIM, *bread of the faces, of the presence of Jehovah*), (Ex. xxv. 30). On the north side in the holy place of the Tabernacle was the table of acacia wood, 3 feet 6 in. long, 1 foot 9 in. wide, and 2 feet 4 in. high; overlaid with gold; a rim and crown of gold encircling the top and another the bottom (Ex. xxv. 23–30). A figure of the table (removed by Titus from the Temple of Herod) is carved on the arch of Titus at Rome. Golden rings were attached to the corners of the table, through which poles could be passed for carrying it (as in the case of the ark). Upon it on every Sabbath were placed, in two piles, twelve freshly baked unleavened loaves of fine flour (typical of the twelve tribes), as an offering (Lev. xxiv. 7). See SACRIFICE. A golden pot filled with incense was placed on the top of each pile, and remained until the next Sabbath, when the incense was burned, the loaves were eaten by the priests in the Sanctuary, and twelve fresh ones laid for an offering (Lev. xxiv. 6, 7; 1 Chr. xxiii. 29). David, in extreme hunger, eat of the shew-bread (1 Sam. xxi. 4–6; Matt. xii. 4).

SHIB'BOLETH (*a stream*), (Judg. xii. 6). The

Hebrew word which the Gileadites made use of at the passage of the Jordan after their victory over the Ephraimites.

SHIB'MAH (Num. xxxii. 38). Shebam, east of Jordan.

SHIC'RON (Josh. xv. 11). Boundary of Judah, near Jabneel. Lost.

SHIGGAI'ON (Ps. vii. 1). Title of a melody.

SHI'HOR OF EGYPT (1 Chr. xiii. 5; Josh. xiii. 2, 3). *Wady el Arish*, Arabia Petræa. SHIHOR, the Nile. See SIHOR.

SHI'HOR LIBNATH (Josh. xix. 26). Boundary of Asher, below Mt. Carmel. Lost.

SHIL'HI (*armed*). Father of Azubah (1 K. xxii. 42).

SHIL'HIM (Josh. xv. 32). Judah. Perhaps the same as SHARUHEN, which was given to Simeon (xix. 6).

SHIL'LEM (*requital*). Son of Naphtali (Gen. xlvi. 24).

ANCIENT SHIPS.

SHIL'LEMITES, THE. Descendants of Shillem (Num. xxvi. 49).

SHILO'AH, THE WATERS OF (Jer. viii. 6). The prophet compares a quiet confidence in Jehovah with the waters of a brook, that "go softly," and contrasts this with the "waters of a river, strong and many, even the king of Assyria and all his glory; and he shall come up over all his channels, and go over all his banks." Supposed to refer to Siloam, near Jerusalem.

SHI'LOH (*rest*), (1 Sam. i. 24, iii. 21; Judg. xxi. 19). In Ephraim, north of Bethel, east of the road to Shechem, south of Lebonah. Now called *Seilun*. This was one of the earliest and most sacred of the Jews' sanctuaries. The ark was kept here (in a tent or tabernacle only), from the last days of Joshua (xviii. 1) to the time of Samuel (1 Sam. iv. 3). Here Joshua completed the division of the land among the tribes (xviii. 10, xix. 51). The Benjamites seized the "daughters of Shiloh," and preserved a tribe from extinction (Judg. xxi. 19), "at an annual feast of the Lord." Eli resided here as judge of Israel, and died of grief at the news that the ark of God was taken (1 Sam. iv. 11, 18). The story of Hannah, Samuel's mother, is an interesting incident, as illustrating the character and life of the Hebrews (1 Sam. i., etc.). Ahijah the prophet lived here when Jeroboam sent his wife to him to inquire what should become of their sick son (1 K. xiv.). The city was on a low hill, rising from an uneven plain surrounded by higher hills, except a narrow valley on the south. Very few, and not any important ruins are found here. An immense oak of great age grows among the ruins, and a few olive trees are scattered through the hollows The hills were once terraced and finely cultivated. A fine large fountain, half a mile away, flows out in a narrow vale, first into a pool, and then into a large reservoir, where flocks and herds are watered. There are rock-hewn sepulchres near, where perhaps some of Eli's "house" were laid.

SHILO'NI. Descendant of Shelah, the son of Judah (Neh. xi. 5).

SHI'LONITE, THE. Native of SHILOH (1 K. xi. 29).

SHI'LONITES, THE. Descendants of Judah, dwelling in Jerusalem (1 Chr. ix. 5).

SHIL'SHAH (*triad*). Son of Zophah (1 Chr. vii. 37).

SHIM'EA (*rumor*). 1. Son of David (1 Chr. iii. 5).—2. A Levite (vi. 30).—3. Ancestor of Asaph (vi. 39).—4. Brother of David (xx. 7).

SHIM'EAH. 1. Brother of David (2 Sam. xxi. 21).—2. A descendant of Jehiel (1 Chr. viii. 32).

SHIM'EAM (*fame*). Son of Mikloth (1 Chr. ix. 38).

SHIM'EATH. Mother of Jozachar (2 K. xii. 21).

SHIM'EATHITES (*descendants of Shimeath*). A family of scribes (1 Chr. ii. 55).

SHIM'EI. 1. A son of Gershom (Num. iii. 18).—2. Son of Gera; he insulted king David (2 Sam. xvi. 5-14).—3. An officer under David (1 K. i. 8). Others of this name are alluded to in the following passages: 1 K. iv. 18; 1 Chr. iii. 19, iv. 26-27, v. 4, vi. 42, xxv. 17, xxvii. 27; 2 Chr. xxix. 14, xxxi. 12, 13; Ezr. x. 23, x. 33, x. 38; Esth. ii. 5; 1 Chr. vi. 29, xxiii. 9.

SHIM'EON. A layman of the sons of Harim (Ezr. x. 31).

SHIM'HI. A Benjamite (1 Chr. viii. 21).

SHIM'I (Ex. vi. 17). SHIMEI.

SHIM'ITES, THE. Descendants of SHIMEI 1, the son of Gershom (Num. iii. 21).

SHIM'MA. Third son of Jesse (1 Chr. ii. 13).

SHI'MON (*desert*). The four sons of Shimon (1 Chr. iv. 20), are mentioned among the tribe of Judah.

SHIM'RATH (*watch*). Song of Shimhi (1 Chr. viii. 21).

SHIM'RI (*watchful*). Three of this name are mentioned in 1 Chr. iv, 37, xi. 45; 2 Chr. xxix. 13.

SHIM'RITH. Mother of Jehozabad (2 Chr. xxiv. 26).

SHIM'ROM. Son of Issachar (1 Chr. vii. 1).

SHIM'RON (*watch, guard*), (Josh. xix. 15). In Zebulon. Now *Simuniyeh*, west of Nazareth. The king of Shimron Meron was one of 31 vanquished by Joshua (xii. 20).

SHIM'RON. Fourth son of Issachar (Gen. xlvi. 13).

SHIM'RONITES, THE. The family of SHIMRON (Num xxvi. 21).

SHIM'SHAI (*sunny*). Secretary of Rehum (Ezr. iv. 8, 9, 17, 23).

SHI'NAB (*father's tooth*). King of ADMAH in Abraham's time (Gen. xiv. 2).

SHI'NAR, THE LAND OF (*country of the two rivers*), (Gen. xi. 2). Ancient name of Chaldæa and Babylonia. It is the Jewish name, and is not found in the native inscriptions. Abraham brought the name with him to Canaan.

SHIP (Heb. ONIYAH, SEFINAH; Gr. *ploion*). The fullest description of ships is in the narrative of Paul's voyage to Rome (Acts xxvii. xxviii.). Paul sailed first on an Adramyttian vessel from Cæsarea to Myra—a coasting ship of moderate size (Acts xxvii. 1-6), then in a large Alexandrian corn ship, in which he was wrecked on the coast of Malta (Acts xxvii. 6, xxviii. 1), and finally in a large Alexandrian corn ship, from Malta, by Syracuse, to Puteoli (xxviii. 11-13). The ship in which Paul was wrecked held 276 persons (Acts xxvii. 37), and was laden with wheat. From this it is estimated that such ships were between 500 and 1000 tons burden. Ships are often mentioned in the Old Testament, and figuratively in Job ix. 23; Ps. xlviii. 79, civ. 26, cvii. 23. Solomon built a fleet at EZION-GEBER (1 K. ix. 26). The fleet of Jehoshaphat, built in the same place, was destroyed (1 K. xxii. 48, 49; 2 Chr. xx. 36, 37). War ships are first alluded to in Dan. xi. 40. The ships' prows bore figure-heads or other insignia, called "sign" in Acts xxviii. 11.: "Whose sign was Castor and Pollux." When large, the ships were impelled by sails as well as oars, which were used alone in small craft. The sail was a large square one, attached to a long yard. The Gr. *artemon* mentioned in Acts xxvii. 40, was the foresail, useful in putting a large ship about. The anchors resembled those now in use. The ship in which Paul sailed had four anchors on board; they were anchored by the stern (Acts xxvii. 29). The ships were steered by two paddles at the stern, which are the rudders alluded to in the narrative of Paul's voyage. Anchoring by the stern necessitated the lashing up of these paddles to prevent interference. The build and rig of ancient ships caused a tendency in them to start their planks by their beams yielding; it was therefore necessary to provide under-girders or helps (Acts xxvii. 17) of chains or cables, to girth the frame of the ship in case of need. The ships also carried boats (Acts xxvii. 16, 32). The captains of these merchant ships were often the owners in part or whole. The steersman is called "the governor" in James iii. 4.

SHIPH'I (*abundant*). Father of Ziza, a prince in Hezekiah's time (1 Chr. iv. 37).

SHIPH'MITE, THE. One from Siphmoth (1 Chr. xxvii. 27).

SHIPH'RAH (*beauty*). One of two Hebrew women who disobeyed the command of Pharaoh (Ex. i. 15-21).

SHIPH'TAN (*judicial*). Father of Kemuel 2 (Num. xxxiv. 24).

SHI'SHA. Corruption of Seraiah, father of Elihoreph and Ahiah (1 K. iv. 3).

SHI'SHAK. A king of Egypt. He entered Judah, B. C. 971, and captured the strongest places in the country, and carried away the treasures. See EGYPT.

In the article on Egypt it is mentioned that Shishak invaded Judæa, and took several cities, and tribute from Rehoboam at Jerusalem, the account of which has lately been deciphered on the Egyptian monuments. Shishak's name is written SHESHONK, and he is said to have been an Ethiopian. He is shown as presenting to the gods of Thebes the prisoners taken by him in war, each name (of a king, or city, or nation) being in an oval shield. See page 84.

Here are some of the names as they stand on the walls of the great temple at Karnak. The first name recognized was Judæa. (see "king of Judah," page 84) by Champollion, which gave the clue to the others.

The names not yet identified are omitted. There were 133 in all.

	Egyptian.	*Hebrew.*
13.	Rebuta.	Rabbith?
14.	Taankau.	Taanach.
15.	Shenema-aa.	Shunem.
16.	Bat-shenraa.	Bethshan.
17.	Rehaboa.	Rehob.
18.	Hepurmaa.	Haphraim.
19.	Aterma.	Adoraim.
22.	Mahamua.	Mahanaim.
23.	Kebaana.	Gibeon.
24.	Bat-huaren.	Beth-horon.
25.	Katmet.	Kedemoth.
26.	Ayuren.	Ajalon.
27.	Maketau.	Megiddo.
28.	Ateera.	Edrei.
29.	Yuteh-mark.	Judæa.
31.	Haanena.	Anem?
32.	Aarana.	Eglon?
33.	Barma.	Bileam.
36.	Bat-narmet.	Alemeth.
37.	Kakaree.	Kikkar (Jordan).
38.	Shauka.	Shoco.
39.	Bat-tepu.	Beth Tappuah.
40.	Abaraa.	Abel?
56.	Atmaa.	Edom?
66.	An-aateman.	Azem, (great?)
68.	Pehakran.	Hagarites.
69.	Fetyushaa.	Letushim?
72.	Mersarama.	Salma?
73.	Shelperet.	Shephelah.
78.	Baalayt.	Nebaioth.
79.	Aatetmaa.	Tema.
83.	Kanaa.	Kenites?
84.	Penakbu.	Negeb.
85.	Atem-ketet-het.	Azem? (little?)
98.	Mertmam.	Duma?
103.	Heetban.	Abdeel?
107.	Harekma.	Rekem (Petra).
108.	Aaratan.	Eldaah.
109.	Rabat.	Rabbah?
110.	Aarataay.	Eldaa.
112.	Yurahma.	Jurahmeelites?
117.	Mertraaa.	Eddara.
119.	Mahkaa.	Maachah?
124.	Bataaat.	Beth-anoth?
127.	Keruaa.	Golan?

This record of the conquest is peculiar to Egypt, and entirely independent of the Jews, or any of the writers of the Bible, and is a confirmation of the historical truth of 2 K. xxiii. 29, etc., and 2 Chr. xxxv. 20, etc.

SHIT'RAI (*Jah is arbitrator*). A Sharonite who had charge of David's herds (1 Chr. xxvii. 29).

SHITTAH-TREE. SHIT'TIM. Understood as the acacia tree, of which there are three or four species in the East, especially used in the construction of the tabernacle, ark, table of shew-bread, altars, etc. (Ex. xxv., xxvi., xxxvi., xxxvii., xxxviii.). "I will plant in the wilderness the cedar, the shittah-tree, and the myrtle, and the oil tree" (Is. xli. 19). It was probably the only available wood in the wilderness. This tree yields the gum arabic of commerce, from incisions cut deeply in the bark. Probably the burning-bush of Moses (Ex. iii. 2), called SENEH, was the shittim (or acacia) tree. The last camping ground of Israel was on the plains of Shittim. The Arabs use the gum for food. The bark is very astringent, and used in tanning leather. The wood is very hard, close-grained, of a fine brown color, excellent for cabinet-work. It grows in dry places, where no other tree can live. It is not the *acacia* of this

SHITTIM

country, which is a kind of locust. Tristram mentions trees on the Dead Sea shore at Engedi and other places, which are four feet in diameter.

SHITTIM (*acacia trees*), (Num. xxxiii. 49). Abel Has Shittim (*meadow of the acacias*). In the Arboth Moab, by Jordan. Jericho (Num. xxii. 1, xxvi. 3). Under the cool shade of the acacia groves the Israelites were led into the worship of Baal Peor by the Midianites, which sin Moses, by command, avenged (xxxi. 1). Joshua sent spies to Jericho from here (ii. 1).

ACACIA OR SHITTAH-TREE.

SHI'ZA (*loved*). Father of Adina (1 Chr. xi. 42).

SHO'A. A proper name which occurs only in Ezr. xxiii. 23, and signifies officer and ruler.

SHO'BAB (*rebellious*). 1. Son of David (2 Sam. v. 14).—2. Son of CALEB 1 (ii. 18).

SHO'BACH (*pouring*). A General of HADAREZER (2 Sam. x. 15-18).

SHO'BAI (*taking captive*). One who returned from captivity (Ezr. ii. 42; Neh. vii. 45).

SHO'BAL (*flowing*). 1. Son of Seir (Gen. xxxvi. 20).—2. Son of Caleb (1 Chr. ii. 50).—3. Descendant of Judah (iv. 1, 2).

SHO'BEK (*forsaking*). A chief who sealed the covenant (Neh. x. 24).

SHO'BI. Son of NAHASH (2 Sam. xvii. 27).

SHO'CO (2 Chr. xi. 7). See SOCOH.

SHO'CHO (2 Chr. xxviii. 18). See SOCOH.

SHO'CHOH (1 Sam. xvii. 1). See SOCOH.

SHO'HAM (*onyx*). Son of Jaaziah (1 Chr. xxiv. 27).

SHO'MER (*a keeper*). 1. An Asherite (1 Chr. vii. 32).—2. Mother of Jehozabad (2 K. xii. 21).

SHO'PHACH. SHOBACH (1 Chr. xix. 16, 18).

SHO'PHAN (Num. xxxii. 35). East of Jordan; fortified. Lost.

SHOSHAN'NIM. Title of a melody (Ps. xlv., lxix.).

SHOSHAN'NIM E'DUTH. Name of a melody called *lilies of testimony* (Ps. lxxx.).

SHU'A (*riches*). 1. Father of Judah's wife (1 Chr. ii. 3).—2. Daughter of Heber (vii. 32).

SHUSHAN

SHU'AH (*pit*). 1. Son of ABRAHAM by KETURAH (Gen. xxv. 2).—2. A Descendant of Judah (iv. 11).—3. SHUA, father of Judah's wife (Gen. xxxviii. 2, 12).

SHU'AL (*a fox or jackal*). Son of Zophah, a chief (1 Chr. vii. 36).

SHU'AL, THE LAND OF (*jackal*), (1 Sam. xiii. 17). North of Michmash. Lost.

SHU'BAEL. 1. Son of GERSHOM (1 Chr. xxiv. 20).—2. Son of HEMAN (xxv. 20).

SHU'HAM (*pit-digger*). Son of Dan (Num. xxvi. 42).

SHU'HAMITES, THE. Descendants of SHUHAM, the son of Dan (Num. xxvi. 42, 43).

SHU'HITE. Descendant of SHUAH 1. This name is frequent in the Book of Job.

SHU'LAMITE, THE (*peaceful*). The name given to the bride in Cant. vi. 13.

SHU'MATHITES (*natives*). One of the 4 families who lived in Kirjath-Jearim (1 Chr. ii. 53).

SHU'NAMMITE, THE. Native of SHUNEM (2 K. iv. 1); applied to two persons: ABISHAG, the nurse of David (1 K. i. 3, 15), and the nameless hostess of Elisha (2 K. iv. 12, 25, 36).

SHU'NEM (*two resting-places*), (Josh. xix. 18). Issachar. Where the Philistines encamped before the battle of Gilboa (1 Sam. xxviii. 4). Here dwelt the good Shunammite, who welcomed Elisha the prophet, who oft passed by; and fitted up a little chamber for him (2 K. iv. 8), and was rewarded (ver. 36). This pleasant village was the native place of Abishag, David's attendant (1 K. i. 3), and possibly the heroine of Solomon's Song. The modern village is on the S. W. flank of Little Hermon, Jebel Duhy, 3 ms. from Jezreel, N., in full view of Mt. Carmel, and in the midst of the finest grain-fields in the land.

SHU'NI (*quiet*). Son of Gad (Gen. xlvi. 16).

SHU'NITES, THE. Descendants of SHUNI (Num. xxvi. 15).

SHU'PHAM (Heb. SHEPHUPHAM). SHUPPIM.

SHU'PHAMITES, THE. Descendants of SHUPHAM (Num. xxvi. 39).

SHUP'PIM (*serpents*). 1. He and HUPPIM, the children of Ir, are mentioned in 1 Chr. vii. 12.—2. A porter (xxvi. 16).

SHUR (*a wall*). (Gen. xvi. 7). Hagar sat by a fountain in the way to Shur, when the angel sent her back with a promise of a blessing. Abraham dwelt between Kadesh and Shur, in Gerar (xx. 1). Ishmael's descendants dwelt from Havilah unto Shur that is before Egypt (xxv. 18). Called, also, Etham (Ex. xv. 22; Num. xxxiii. 8).

SHU'SHAN (*lily*). Shushan the palace (Esth. i. 2). One of the most important towns in the whole East. Capital of ELAM, SUSIS, or SUSIANA. Inscriptions, dated 660 B.C., record the capture of the city by Asshur-bani-pal, giving, also, its plan. Daniel saw his vision of the ram and he-goat at Shushan the palace (Dan. viii. 2). Cyrus made it a Persian city, and its metropolis (Æschylus and Herodotus), although the building of the palace is credited to Darius. Alexander found there $50,-000,000, and all the regalia of the great king. After this, Susa was neglected for Babylon. Now called Sus, a vast ruin between the Eulæus and Shapur. E. and W. of the city, a few ms. were the rivers Coprates and Choaspes. The water of the Choaspes (now *Kerkhah*) was thought to be peculiarly healthful, and was the only water drank by the kings, at home or on journeys (Herod i. 188), and it is now prized above all other river-water by the people. The ruins cover a space 6,000 ft. E. to W. by 4,500 N. to S., being about 3 ms. in circuit. There are 4 artificial platforms. The smallest of these has an eminence 119 ft. high above the river,

facing the E., and made of sun-dried brick, gravel, and earth. One platform has a surface of 60 acres. The remains of the Great Palace have been examined, and a plan made out, including 72 columns, some bearing tri-lingual inscriptions, having the names of Artaxerxes, Darius, Xerxes, Hystaspes, and crediting the building to Darius; besides naming the gods Ormazd, Tanaites, and Mithra. The number of columns is the same as in the Great Hall of Xerxes at Persepolis. It stood on a square platform, 1000 ft. each way, 60 ft. above the plain; itself being 120 ft. to the top of the roof, making a

Bered is a change of Becher, and Tahath becomes Tahan. The true genealogy is:

1. Joseph.	1. Joseph.
2. Ephraim.	2. Ephraim.
3. Shuthelah.	3. Shuthelah.
4. Eran.	4. Eran (Laadan).
5. Ammihud.	5. Ammihud.
6. Elishama.	6. Elishama.
7. Nun.	7. Nun.
	8. Joshua.

The story in 1 Chr. vii. 20, 21; viii. 13, belongs

SIDON.

hight in all of about 180 ft. The appearance must have been truly grand, rising as it did to such a great hight, amidst lower structures, beautified with trees and shrubs, reflected in the river at its base. Esther plead in this palace for her people, and saved them.

SHU'SHAN E'DUTH. The title of a melody; it denotes "the lily of testimony" (Ps. lx.).

SHU'THALHITES, THE. Descendants of SHU-THELAH (Num. xxvi. 35).

SHU'THELAH (*noise*). Head of an Ephraimite family (Num. xxvi. 35), and ancestor of Joshua (1 Chr. vii. 20-27).

The text in 1 Chr. vii. 20, is an error from careless copying, probably. The names Eran, Laadan, Eleadah, Elead, are repeated from one original.

to the history of the country after the passage of Jordan; the *descent* upon the Shefelah (Gath, etc.) agreeing with the topography of Palestine. This is probably a marginal gloss of some ancient scribe which has been adopted into the text.

SI'A (*congregation*). Ancestor of a family of Nethinim, who returned from captivity (Neh. vii. 47).

SI'AHA (Ezr. ii. 44). SIA.

SIB'BECAI. The Hushathite (2 Sam. xxi. 18).

SIB'BECHAI (*thicket of Jah*). A captain in David's army for the eighth month of 24,000 men (1 Chr. xl. 29). He belonged to one of the principal families of Judah.

SIB'BOLETH. The Ephraimite word for SHIBBOLETH (Judg. xii. 6).

SIB'MAH (Josh. xiii. 19). East of Jordan, in Reuben. SHEBAM. Lost.

SIBRA'IM (Ez. xlvii. 16). A north boundary of the land. Lost.

SIC'CUTH (*a tabernacle* or *shrine*), (Amos v. 26).

SI'CHEM. SHECHEM.

SICK'LE (HERMESH, MAGGAL; Gr. *drepanon*). A curved knife for reaping; a reaping-hook or scythe (Deut. xvi. 9; Joel iii. 13).

SIC'YON (*market—weekly?*), (1 Macc. xv. 23). A later city built on the acropolis of an ancient city of the same name, near the eastern end of the Corinthian Gulf, about two miles from the sea, near a range of mountains, which were terraced, and rent with gorges. In the time of the Maccabees it was the most important Roman possession in Greece.

SID'DIM (*the vale of*), (Gen. xiv. 3, 8, 10). The Hebrew words *Emek hes Siddim* mean a plain cut up by stony channels. Located by some scholars at the north end of the Dead Sea.

As an *emek* it resembled Jezreel; and therefore a suitable place for the combat mentioned in the text (ver. 8); but having a number of pitch-pits, or, as Josephus says, Wells of Asphalt (Ant. i. 9), and who says the site is under the Dead Sea (Asphaltitis). More probably near it. See GEOLOGY and SEA.

If the Salt Mountain, Usdum (see SODOM) is a recent elevation, then the cities may have been in the plain at the S. end of the Dead Sea, which would then have been the Vale of Siddim.

SI'DE (1 Macc. xv. 23). A colony of Cumaeans on the coast of Pamphylia. The navy of Antiochus was made up of ships from Side and Aradus, Tyre and Sidon, and the fleet was stationed at Side on the eve of the battle with the fleet from Rhodes (Livy 37, 23). Its ruins indicate former wealth. The theater of the Roman time was one of the largest in Asia, seating 15,000. It was used as a fort in the middle ages. There was an AGORA (as at Athens), 180 ft. in diameter, surrounded by a double row of columns, and a pedestal for a statue in the centre, and a temple on the south side (mentioned by Strabo). The harbor was closed in, and was 1500 by 600 ft. in extent, with docks for unloading ships.

SI'DON (*fishing*). ZIDON (Phœnician *Tsidon*), (Gen. x. 15, 19). Great Zidon (Josh. xi. 8). Sidon (Matt. xi. 21; Mark iii. 8; Luke vi. 17). On the coast of the Mediterranean Sea, in the narrow Phœnician plain (2 miles), under the range of Lebanon, to which it once gave its own name (Jos. Ant. v. 3, 1). The city is built on the northern slope of a promontory that juts out into the sea, pointing S. W.; and the citadel is on the hight behind it. Zidon was the first-born of Canaan, and probably the city is an older one than Tyre, and the Phœnicians are (often) called Sidonians (never Tyrians) in Josh. xiii. 6; Judg. xviii. 7, etc. Skilled workmen were their special pride, not traders (1 K. v. 6). The prize given to the swiftest runner by Achilles was a large silver bowl, made at Sidon (Homer, Il. xxiii. 743). Menelaus gave Telemachus a most beautiful and valuable present, "a divine work, a bowl of silver with a gold rim, the work of Hephaestus, and a gift from king Phaedimus of Sidon" (Od. iv. 614). Homer mentions the beautifully embroidered robes of Andromache, brought from Sidon. Pliny mentions the glass factories (v. 17).

Under the Persians, Sidon attained to great wealth and importance. To live carelessly, after their manner, became a proverb (Judg. xviii. 7). The prize in a boat-race, witnessed by Xerxes at Abydos, was won by Sidonians; and when he reviewed his fleet he sat under a golden canopy in a Sidonian galley; and when he assembled his officers in state the king of the Sidonians sat in the first seat. It was almost utterly destroyed by the Persians, B. C. 351. Being rebuilt, it opened its gates to Alexander. The Jews never conquered the city, and so far failed of the promise. Strabo said there was the best opportunity for acquiring a knowledge of the sciences of arithmetic and astronomy, and of all other branches of philosophy. At this time Greek was probably the language of the best society.

It is the most northern city visited by Jesus, and is about 50 miles from Nazareth. Now called *Saide*. The whole neighborhood is one great garden, filled with every kind of fruit-bearing trees, nourished by streams from Lebanon. Its chief exports are silk, cotton and nutgalls. A missionstation of Americans are working among 5000 people.

There are many ancient sepulchres in the rocks at the base of the mountain east of Sidon, and sepulchral caves in the plain. In one of these caves, in 1855, was discovered one of the most beautiful and interesting Phœnician monuments in existence. It is a sarcophagus of black syenite, with a lid carved in human form, bandaged like a mummy, the face being bare. There is an inscription in Phœnician on the lid, and another on the head. The king of the Sidonians is mentioned in them, and it is said that his mother was a priestess of Ashtoreth. It is supposed to belong to the 11th century B. C. It is now in the Louvre, Paris. See p. 192.

SIEVE (Is. xxx. 28). "To sift as wheat" (Luke xxii. 31); figuratively, to agitate and prove by trials and afflictions.

SI'HON (*sweeping away*). King of the Amorites (Num. xxi. 21).

SIHOR (*black*). Correctly Shihor. The Nile. (Sanscrit, *Nilah*, dark-blue). The water of the Nile is dark with mud, like our Ohio or Mississippi. The Egyptian name was *Yeor*. (The name of Egypt was *Kem*, black). The present name in Arabic is *Bahr el Azrak, dark-blue river*. Shihor is the name of the brook of Egypt (*Wady el Arish*), which is mentioned as the south boundary of David's kingdom (1 Chr. xiii. 5; Josh. xiii. 2, 3). See NILE.

SI'LAS. Contraction of SILVANUS, one of the chief men among the first disciples at Jerusalem (Acts xv. 22). He is mentioned in 2 Cor. ii. 9, 1. 19; 1 Pet. x. 12; Acts xvi. 19, 25; Phil. iv. 10.

SILK (Heb. MESHI), (Ez. xvi. 10, 13). Silk in the time of the Ptolemies was sold for its weight in gold. It sometimes came in skeins, and was woven into a thin light gauze. It is not known how early or extensively the Jews used it (Rev. xviii. 12; Gen. xli. 42).

SIL'LA. Where Joash, the king, was killed (2 K. xii. 20). Lost.

SILO'AH (*dart*), SILOAM (*sent*), (Heb. SILOACH), (Neh. iii. 15). Arable, *Silwan*. One of the few undisputed localities around Jerusalem. The water was "sweet and abundant" in Josephus' day (B. J. v. 4, 1). It is in the Tyropœon valley, 200 ft. from the Kidron. There are no less than 40 natural springs within a circle of 10 miles around Jerusalem. The water flows out of a small artificial basin, under the cliff, into a reservoir 53 ft. long by 18 ft. wide and 19 ft. deep. It has been lately proved, by exploring, that the water flows from the Virgin's fountain to Siloam; and there is a remarkable ebb and flow, which varies in frequency with the season and supply of water (John ix. 7). The village of Siloam (*Silwan*) is not mentioned in Scripture, and is probably modern. It is poorly built, and occupies the site of Solomon's idol-shrines (1 K. xi. 7; 2 K. xxiii. 13).

SILOAM, TOWER IN. Mentioned by Jesus (Luke xiii. 4). Not located.

SILVER (Heb. KESEF, Chal. *kesaf*, Gr. *argurion*).

One of the precious metals, and the one used most as a coin among all nations. The ancient Hebrews weighed it out, instead of having coins. It is mentioned in Gen. xiii. 2, xx. 16, xxiii. 16, and Ex. xxvi. 19, 32; 1 Chr. xxix. 4. See MONEY.

SIL'VER-LINGS (*little silvers*). Pieces of silver or silver coins (Is. vii. 23).

SIMALCU E (Heb. MELECH, *king*). An Arabian chief who had charge of ANTIOCHUS VI (1 Macc. xi. 39).

SIM EON (*hearkening*). Second son of Jacob and Leah (Gen. xxix. 33).

The tribe of Simeon numbered six families (the head of one of which, Shaul, was a son of a Canaanite woman) when Jacob went down into Egypt (Gen. xlvi.), and at the Exode 59,300 men over 20, but only 22,000 at the last census by Moses.

POOL OF SILOAM.

In the wilderness Simeon was on the south side of the Tabernacle. The only great name of the tribe on record is that of the widow Judith, the heroine of the apocryphal Book of Judith, where she appears as an ideal type of piety, beauty, courage, and chastity. There were 18 cities, with their surroundings, given to Simeon out of the portion allotted to Judah, including the famous well of Beersheba, and one of which (Ziklag) became the private property of David, as a present from Achish the Philistine. A part of the tribe (500 men) took possession of a district in Mount Seir, where they were still living after the return from the Captivity (1 Chr. iv. 42, 43).

SI'MON. One of the twelve apostles. See PETER.

A name of frequent occurrence in Jewish history. 1. Son of MATTATHIAS 2, and one of the famous MACCABEES (1 Macc. ii. 65).—2. Son of Onias, the high-priest.—3. A governor of the Temple (2 Macc. iii. 4).—4. SIMON, THE BROTHER OF JESUS (Matt. xiii. 55; Mark vi. 3).—5. Simon, the Canaanite, one of the twelve apostles (Matt. x. 4), otherwise described as Simon Zelotes (Luke vi. 15).—6. Simon of Cyre'ne. A Hellenistic Jew (Acts ii. 10), born in Cyrene, Africa.—7. Simon the Leper. A resident at Bethany, who had been miraculously cured of leprosy by Jesus (Matt. xxvi. 6).—8. Simon Mag'gnus, a sorcerer or magician (Acts viii. 9).—10. A Pharisee (Luke vii. 40).—11. The Tanner, a disciple living at Joppa (Acts ix. 43).—12. Father of JUDAS ISCARIOT (John vi. 71). Simon Chosame'us, error of the scribe in combining the last letters of Malluch eh with the first part of Shemariah. SHIMEON and the three following names in Ezr. x. 31, 32, are thus written in 1 Esd. ix. 32.

SIM'RI. Son of Hosah (1 Chr. xxvi. 10).

SIN (*mire*). Pelusium (*pelos*, Greek for *mire*), in Egypt. Sin, the strength of Egypt (Ez. xxx. 15). Probably a fortified city. Pompey was murdered here by order of Ptolemy, B. C. 48.

SIN, WILDERNESS OF. See WILDERNESS OF WANDERING.

SIN'AI. Mountain and desert forming a part of the peninsula between the gulfs of Suez and Akabah. The district of Sinai is near the center of the triangular space between the two arms of the Red Sea. (See maps, pps. 54–55). This peninsula is formed of granite, with dykes of porphyry and greenstone, without a trace of volcanic rocks. It is separated from the limestone district of Et Tyh (see WILDERNESS OF THE WANDERING), by the narrow plain of Er Ramleh, a desert of red sand. There are 3 mountain groups: Serbal on the W., Sinai in the center, and Katerin S. of Sinai; all nearly bare of foliage, but peculiarly beautiful in colors the most varied. A belt of sand borders the shore of the two arms of the Red Sea. The granite is the same kind as the red sienite, found at Assouan, on the Nile, of which the temples in Egypt were built. In Sinai, itself, the base is of a coarser quality than the peak, which has more quartz. Mt. Katerin is nearly all porphyry. There is a difference of opinion as to which peak is the Sinai of Moses and the Law; some claiming Serbal with its ancient inscriptions (see WRITTEN VALLEY, p. —), and others Sufsafa, with its convent, pit, and chapel. Both answer some of the requirements of the text, but neither all of the points. See Ex-ODUS, WILDERNESS.

SINCERE' (Gr. *adolos, guileless, pure*, 1 Pet. ii. 2). Gr. *eilikrines*, judged of in sunlight (Phil. i. 10).

SIN'IM (Is. xlix. 12). The Chinese.

SIN'ITE (Gen. x. 17). The fortress of Sinna is mentioned by Strabo (xvi. 756) as in Mt. Lebanon. The ruins of Sini were known in the days of Jerome (Gen. loc. cit.).

SI'ON. A name of Mt. Hermon (Deut. iv. 48).

SIPH'MOTH (*bare-places*). Place in the S. of Judah, which David frequented during his wandering (1 Sam. xxx. 28). Site unknown.

SIP'PAL. Son of RAPHA, or "The Giant" (1 Chr. xx. 4).

SI'RACH. See HISTORY OF THE BOOKS.

SI'RAH (*a-going-off*) **THE WELL** (2 Sam. iii. 26), 1 m. out of Hebron.

SIRI'ON. The Sidonian name for Mt. Hermon (Deut. iii. 9; Ps. xxix. 6).

SIS'AMAI (*distinguished*). A descendant of Sheshan (1 Chr. ii. 40).

SIS'ERA (*battle-array*). 1. A general in the army of Jabin, king of Hazor (Judg. iv. 5).—2. One who returned from captivity (Ezr. ii. 53).

SISIN'NES. TATNAI (1 Esd. vi. 3).

SIS'TER (Heb. AHOTH, Gr. *adelphe*), used to denote one who is the daughter of the same parents (Gen. iv. 22), or the same parent (Lev. xviii. 9, 11); also, one of the same faith (Rom. xvi. 1).

SIT'NAH (*hatred*). The 2d of the two wells dug by Isaac (Gen. xxvi. 21). Site lost.

SI'VAN. MONTH.

DAVID AND JONATHAN. See pp. 70, 165.

SLAVE (Heb. ERED, Gr. *somata*). Servitude, under the Mosaic law, was more that of bondman than slave. In the patriarchal period the servitude was of two kinds; those slaves or servants born in the house, and those who were purchased or taken in war (Gen. xvii. 13). Those born in the house often enjoyed the utmost confidence and privilege. This was illustrated in the case of Abraham commissioning his servant to select a wife for Isaac. Servitude under the law was much restricted (Ex. xxi. 16; Deut. xxiv). Debt, or poverty, were causes for servitude (Lev. xxv. 39, 40); also, it was the penalty for theft (Ex. xxii. 1-14); the servitude ceasing when an equivalent of labor had been paid. All Hebrew bondmen were released in the year of Jubilee (Lev. xxv. 47-54). Foreign slaves were not so treated. They could become the property of the Hebrews, as captives of war (Deut. xx. 14), or by purchase from the dealers (Lev. xxv. 44). The slave-trade is mentioned as being carried on with Tyre by Javan (Greeks), Tubal and Meshech (Ez. xxvii. 13). Joseph was the first person recorded as having been sold into slavery (Gen. xxxvii. 27, 28). Slaves were employed upon menial work (Lev. xxv. 39) in the household, and in attendance upon the master. It was a duty of female slaves to grind corn (Ex. xi. 5; Job xxxi. 10; Is. xlvii. 2).

SLEEP. Slumber or repose of the body (Gen. xxviii. 11). Used to denote DEATH (Jer. li. 39), or spiritual torpor (Rom. xiii. 11).

SLIME. Heb. HEMAR, *asphaltos and bitumen* (Gen. xi. 3). Found on and near the Dead Sea. It is commonly found in a solid state, but when heated and used as a mortar, it becomes hard as the rocks it cements together.

SLING. An instrument much used before the invention of fire-arms (Judg. xx. 16; 1 Sam. xvii. 48-50).

SMITH. An artificer in brass, iron, etc.; first mentioned in Gen. iv. 22. See HANDICRAFT.

SMYR'NA (Rev. ii. 8-11). Designed by Alexander the Great, and built by his successors Antigonus and Lysimachus, near the site of the ancient city of the same name (which had been destroyed by the Lydians 400 years before). It stood at the head of a gulf of the Ægean Sea, by the mouth of the river Meles, having a range of mountains on three sides of it. Tiberius granted the city permission to erect a temple in honor of the Roman emperor and senate. John (Rev. ii. 9) probably referred to the pagan rites in his letter to the church in Smyrna. See SEVEN CHURCHES.

The only ancient ruins are on the mountains, south. On the summit is a ruined castle. So convenient has it been to carry away antiquities that Smyrna has been nearly stripped. Van Lennep, the missionary, found a great number of small articles in the dirt-heap of the ancient city; rings, seals, lamps, household gods, and many other articles, more or less broken (except the seals), and probably thrown away as rubbish, or lost. In the time of Strabo it was one of the most beautiful cities in all Asia (Minor). There were a library and museum, with grand porticoes, dedicated to Homer (claimed as a native); an Odeum, and a temple to the Olympian Zeus. The Olympian games were celebrated. Polycarp was martyred here, being condemned by the Jews also.

SNAIL (Heb. SHABLUL). In Lev. xi. 30 a sort of lizard; and in Ps. lviii. 8 the common slug or snail without a shell, which consumes away and dies by depositing a slime wherever it passes. 1. SHABLUL. The Septuagint says "melted wax" in Ps. liii. 9 (8 A. V.).—2. CHOMET. The name of an unclean animal in Lev. xi. 30. Perhaps a lizard or a chameleon.

SNARE (Heb. MOKESH, pah). A noose for catching birds (Job xl. 24).

SNOW (Heb. SHELEG; Chal. telag; Gr. chion). Is often alluded to for its whiteness Ex. iv. 6; Num. xii. 10; in Prov. xxv. 13, "as the cold of snow in time of harvest" alludes to its use in cool drinks for the reapers. The snow lies deep in the ravines of Lebanon until late in the summer. The summit of Hermon perpetually glistens with snow. Snow, as actually falling, is alluded to but twice (2 Sam. xxiii. 20; 1 Macc. xiii. 22). Job refers to its supposed cleansing effects when melted (ix. 30), and to the rapid melting under the rays of the sun (xxiv. 19), and floods following (vi. 16). In Ps. lxviii. 14, thick-falling snow is alluded to as a synonyme for a host flying from defeat, probably with white dresses or turbans. Snow lies deep on Lebanon and Hermon late in the summer, from whence it is carried to the cities for cooling drinks. It never leaves the highest peaks of Lebanon or Hermon. (See HERMON, CLIMATE).

SNUFFERS. (Heb. 1. MEZAMEROTH, forceps). Snuffers for lamps (1 K. vii. 50).—2. MELKAHAYIM (Ex. xxxvii. 23), tongs.

SO (Heb. SEVECH or SEVEC). A deity represented in the form of a crocodile. So, King of Egypt, made an alliance with Hosea, king of Israel, and promised him assistance, but was unable to prevent the king of Assyria from taking Samaria, B. C. 721 (2 K. xvii. 4). In the remains of Sennacherib's palace, recently disentombed, among the seals was found one of So, well known to students of Egyptian antiquities. See page 131.

SOAP (Heb. BORITH), (Jer. ii. 22). A term for any substance of *cleansing* qualities. The soap familiar to us was unknown to the Egyptians, and probably to the ancients generally. They used certain vegetables and their ashes for cleansing linen, etc. Numerous plants, yielding alkalies, exist in Palestine, which, when pounded, serve as a substitute for soap. The *gilloo* or "soap-plant" of Egypt is used in the manufacture of soap at Joppa.

SO'CHO (1 Chr. iv. 18). SOCOH.

SO'CHOH (*branches*), (1 K. iv. 10).

SO'COH. 1. (Josh. xv. 35). In the Shefelah, now called *Esh Shuweikah*, in *Wady Sumt*, 3½ ms. S. W. of Jerusalem.—2. (ib. xv. 48). Judah, in the hill region. Now called *Esh Shuweikah* in *Wady Khalil*, 10 ms. S. W. of Hebron (1 Chr. iv. 18).

SOD. The preterite of seethe, to burn or cook.

SO'DI (*confident of Jah*). Father of Gaddiel (Num. xiii. 10).

SOD'OM (*vineyard* or *burning*). One of the most ancient cities of Canaan, in the Jordan valley, the chief of the five cities (Gen. x. 19). The plain was once like a garden, and was chosen by Lot, when Abram chose Canaan (ib. xiii. 10). As the two patriarchs were standing on a hight between Bethel and Ai they could see Jericho and the Jordan plain (called KIKKAR in the Hebrew, a term peculiar to this district alone); while they could not see the south end of the Dead Sea. But opposed to this is the event of Abraham looking toward the plain, and seeing the smoke go up as from a furnace (xix. 28). And that from no hight near Hebron can the Jordan plain near Jericho be seen, while the south end of the Dead Sea and the Lisan are distinctly visible. There is a salt-mountain called Usdum (Sodom) on the S. W. shore of the Dead Sea, which may have inherited and preserved the name of the ancient city, but the site of that city is lost. See UZDUM.

SOD'OMITE (*one from Sodom*). One of those who practiced their peculiar religious rite (Deut. xxiii. 17; 1 K. xiv. 24).

SOLDER. That the ancient Hebrews were acquainted with the use of solder is evident from Is. xli. 7. Nothing is known as to the composition of the solder, but, probably, lead was one of the materials used.

SOL'DIER. See ARMOR. Soldiers are first men-

SOLOMON ON HIS THRONE.

tioned in 2 Chr. xxv. 13; and in Ezra (viii. 22), and Isaiah (xv. 4), and many times in the N. T. Paul alludes to fighting as a soldier (1 Cor. ix. 26), as also James (iv. 2), as well as nearly every writer in the Scriptures. The Christian's life is the life of a soldier, constantly in the armor of faith, fighting against evil.

SOL'OMON. In Hebrew, SHELOMOH (*the peaceful*). The youngest son of David and Bathsheba (1 Chr. iii. 5). He was educated under the care of Nathan, the prophet, in all that the priests, Levites, and prophets had to teach, and was named by him Jedidiah (*loved of Jah*), (2 Sam. xii. 25). He was only looked upon as the heir of the throne after Absalom's revolt and death; and only after Adonijah endeavored to seize the throne, Solomon was anointed by Nathan, and solemnly acknowledged as king, at the age of 19 or 20, 1015 B. C. (1

K. i. 5). David died soon after. From that time his history is nearly that of the nation. It is supposed by some that his personal appearance is the subject of the Shulamite's language in the Canticles (Cant. v. 10). His great wealth, which had been accumulated by David through many years, cannot be computed by our system, because the figures in the original accounts of the sum set apart for the Temple are uncertain, and vary in the two records: in 1 Chr. xxii. 14, the sum being stated at 100,000 talents of gold, and 1,000,000 of silver, and in chapter xxix. 4, at 3,000 talents of gold, and 7,000 of silver. The sources of this wealth were

M USE-TOIS.

many, for Solomon was a merchant as well as a monarch (2 Chr. viii. ix. 10). The exports were, wheat, barley, oil, wine, wool, silk, hides, fruit, and other articles. His ships (in care of or assisted by the Tyrians) navigated the Mediterranean and the Red Sea, and to the regions beyond; trading in gold, precious stones, ivory, apes, spice, and scented woods. Besides the ships, caravans of camels were, probably, used across the Syrian desert, and to the Red Sea and Egypt: which called for the building of Tadmor (Palmyra), and the fortifying of Thapsacus, on the Euphrates, and Eziongeber on the Red Sea.

The visit of the Queen of Sheba was one of the results of this commercial intercourse, and her very rich presents show the extreme value of their trade (1 K. x.).

Solomon's fame was established by the building of the great Temple at Jerusalem (1 K. vi.); but besides that he built his own palace, the queen's palace, the house of the forest of Lebanon, a grand porch, and the porch of judgment (law court). He had increased the walls of the city, and fortified Millo and other strongholds in different parts of the land (2 Chr. xxxii. 5, viii.).

In the work of building the Temple especial (and probably in all others) he employed slaves of whom the Jews held at that time no less than 153,000, who were, it may be, Hittites (2 Chr. ii. 17). In this he followed the example of the Pharaohs, as he did also in state ceremony and display.

As soon as Nathan and Zadok, his father's counselors, were dead, he began to lower the standard of religious purity, by building shrines to heathen gods, although two sons of Nathan and a son of Zadok were among his advisers (1 K. xi. 33). (See JERUSALEM). This grant of indulgence to his heathen wives might have had a political motive (iii. 16). It is quite probable that Solomon himself was a believer in, if not an actual practicer of, the soothsayer's or magician's arts, for which he has, from his time to the present, had a reputation everywhere in the East.

It is in accordance with Eastern royalty that Solomon sometimes acted as a judge in cases of oppression, as in the case of the two children; and it may be that his porch of judgment contained his stated council and judicial chamber.

His harem was established on a magnificent scale; and he made a grand display of the chief luxury of wealth, in the number of his women, and especially in marrying an Egyptian princess (xi.). By these practices, and the idolatries which his foreign wives led him into, he lost the hearts of the prophets, and lost for his posterity the rule of the ten tribes. The most of this evil is charged by some to the influence of his mother, Bathsheba, who was grand-daughter to Ahithophel, who was renowned through all Israel for worldly wisdom and political sagacity.

It is to be regretted that we have not more of the writings of Solomon, and also that we do not even know certainly what he wrote of the books that are now attributed to him. After the return from the Captivity, the Rabbis of the Great Synagogue made extracts from the well-known books of law, history, poetry, and proverbs, accepting and preserving only a small part. These represent in the Canticles the young man, passionate but pure; in the Proverbs, the middle-aged man, with a practical, prudential thought, searching into the depths of man's heart, resting all duty on the fear of God; and in the Preacher, the old man, who had become a moralist, having passed through the stages of a philosopher and of a mystic, now made confession of his "crime of sense," and he could only realize that weariness which sees all earthly things only as vanity of vanities.

The immense influence which Solomon produced, on his own and later ages, is seen in the fact that men have claimed his great name for even the noblest thoughts of other authors—as in the Book of Wisdom, and possibly in Ecclesiastes—and have woven an endless fabric of fantastic fables, Jewish, Arabian, and Christian. Spells and charms of his invention (of which the famous seal of Solomon is an example) are supposed to have a power over disease, and evil spirits, which he conquered and cast into the sea; and magicians have "swarmed" in the Old World, who mingled his name in their incantations. His wisdom interpreted the speech of birds and beasts; and he knew the hidden virtues (mystic) of plants. His magic ring revealed to him the past, the present, and the future. And

finally, all vast works, especially of architecture, of past time, whose history is lost, are credited to him.

The New Testament does not add to our knowledge of Solomon, but gives us his true measure as a man and a king, in a single sentence, which declares that in the humblest work of God, as a lily, there is a grace, and beauty, and purity, not equaled by all Solomon's glory (Matt. vi. 29).

SOL'OMON'S SER'VANTS, CHILDREN OF (Ezr. ii. 56, 58; Neh. vii. 57, 60). These appear in the lists of the exiles who returned from Captivity. They occupy almost the lowest places in those lists.

SOL'OMON'S SONG. See HISTORY OF THE BOOKS.

SOL'OMON, WISDOM OF. See HISTORY OF THE BOOKS.

SON (Heb. BEN; Gr. *huios*). A male child (Gen. xvii. 16, 19), or any remote descendant (Gen. xix. 5), or a son, by adoption (Gen. lxviii. 5), or by law (Ruth iv. 17), or education (1 Sam. iii. 6), or conversion (Tit. i. 4). And it also denotes a mental or moral resemblance (Judg. xix. 22). Men are sometimes called sons of God (Luke ii. 38) in a similar sense.

SON OF GOD. A peculiar appellation of Christ, expressing His eternal relationship to the Father (Ps. ii. 7). Christ always claimed to be the only begotten son of the Father (Matt. iv. 3, viii. 29, xxvii. 54); and the Jews rightly understood him as thus making himself equal with God (John v. 18, x. 30-33).

SON OF MAN. A title of Christ, assumed by Himself in His humiliation (John i. 51). It is applied to Him more than eighty times in the N. T. See HISTORY OF THE BOOKS.

SOP'ATOR (a contraction of SOSIPATOR). The son of Pyrrhus.

SOPH'ERETH (*scribe*). Ancestor of children of Solomon's servants, who returned from Captivity (Ezr. ii. 55).

SOPHONI'AS. ZEPHANIAH (2 Esd. i. 40).

SOUTH. Heb. DAROM, bright, sunny, region; NEGEB, dry, parched quarter; TEYMAN, on the right hand. "The South Country" is often used for the southern part of Judah (Gen. lxx. 1).

SOUTH RA'MOTH (*hights south*). One of the places David visited (1 Sam. xxx. 27).

SOW'ER. See AGRICULTURE.

SPAIN. The ancient name of both Spain and Portugal, and a Roman province in Paul's time, containing many Jews. It is not certain that Paul carried out his intention of visiting Spain (Rom. xx. 24, 28), since neither he nor any other writer of his time has left any evidence of such a visit.

SPAR'ROW (Heb. ZIPPOR; Gr. *strouthion*). (Ps. lxxxiv. 3; Matt. x. 29, 31). A small bird, with quill and tailfeathers brown; its body gray and black; resembling the small chirping-bird: it is bold and familiar in its habits. These birds are still numerous, troublesome, and cheap, in Jerusalem (Luke xii. 6).

SPAR'TA. A celebrated city of ancient GREECE, and the capital of Laconia. It was long the rival of ATHENS. Situated in a valley, on the Eurotas, 20 ms. from the sea. The remarkable correspondence related in 2 Macc. v. 9, probably had no foundation in history.

SO'REK (*noble vine*), **THE VALLEY OF.** Samson loved a woman in the valley of Sorek (Judg. xvi. 4). *Wady es Surar.*

SOSIP'ATER (*saving a father*). 1. A general of Judas Maccabaeus (2 Macc. xii. 19-24).—2. Kinsman of Paul (Rom. xvi. 21).

SOS'THENES. Chief of the synagogue at Corinth (Acts xviii. 17).

SOS'TRATUS (*saving an army*). A commander of the Syrian garrison, B. C. 172 (2 Macc. iv. 27, 29).

SO'TAI (*one who turns aside*). Ancestor of a family of Solomon's servants who returned from Captivity (Ezr. ii. 55).

SPARROWS.

SOUL. Heb. 1. NEDIBAH (Job xxx. 15), elevated and happy state.—2. NEPESH, more than 500 times (Gen. ii. 7, xii. 5, 13). The meanings are: *a.* breath (Job. xii. 13); *b.* vital spirit, soul (Gen. xxxv. 18); *c.* life (Ex. iv. 19); *d.* ghost (Job xl. 20); *e.* pleasure (Ps. cv. 22).—3. NESHAMAH, breath; also blast (2 Sam. ii. 16; Job iv. 9); "spirit," "inspiration."—4. Gr. *psucho* (Matt. x. 28), the vital breath, life; properly, the soul.

The ancients supposed the soul, or rather the animating principle of life, to reside in the breath. Hence the Hebrew and Greek words where they refer to man are translated "soul" and rendered "life" or "breath" (Gen. ii. 7). The immortality of the soul is a fundamental doctrine of revealed religion. The ancient patriarchs lived and died persuaded of this truth, and it was in the hope of another life that they received the promises (Gen. l. 33; Num. xxiii. 10). To save the souls of men, Christ gave himself freely to death.

SPEAR'MEN (Gr. *dexiolaboi*), those taking the right). 200 formed part of the escort which accompanied PAUL in his march from Jerusalem to Caesarea (Acts xxiii. 23).

SPICE, SPI'CERY, SPI'CES. 1. (Heb. BASAM, BESEM, Cant. v. 1). Sweet spices, incense, or spices; a general term to denote those aromatic substances which were used in the preparation of the anointing oil, the incense-offerings (Ex. xxv. 6, xxxi. 11).

SPI'DER (Heb. AKKABISH), (Job viii. 14; Is. lix. 5). Both passages allude to the fragile nature of the spider's web. They are found in every habitable portion of the globe, but are largest in warm climates.

SPIKE'NARD (Heb. NERD, Gr. *nardos*). A highly perfumed ointment, prepared from a plant in India growing in short spikes. Prized by the ancients,

and was a favorite perfume at their baths and banquets. It was very costly (John xii. 3).

SPIN'NING. Is mentioned in Ex. xxxv. 25, 26; Matt. vi. 28; Luke xii. 27. The distaff round which the flax or wool for spinning was wound, and spindle on which the yarn or thread was wound in spinning. The spindle was held in one hand, while the other was employed in drawing out the thread.

SPIRIT. See SOUL.

SPIKENARD.

SPIRIT, THE HOLY (Heb. NESHAMAH; L. *Spiritus*). The *Third person of the Trinity.* The *Spirit of God.* The character and influence of the Holy Spirit are chiefly shown in the N. T. That which was but imperfectly understood in patriarchal times became full of meaning to Christians. It is called the Holy Spirit of Jehovah in Ps. liii. 10, 11, the Good Spirit, Jehovah, in Ps. cxliii. 10. In the work of the creation the Holy Spirit is mentioned (Gen. i. 2). As the bestower and sustainer of life (Gen. ii. 7; Job xxvii. 3). From the epoch of Samuel, the work of the Spirit is manifest (1 Sam. x. 10, xvi. 14; 2 K. ii. 9; Neh. ix. 30; Is. xl. 27). In the N. T., both preceding and after the birth of Christ, the agency of the Holy Spirit was especially prominent in its manifestations. The presence of the Holy Spirit is constantly associated with the birth and life of Christ and the work of His disciples. The holy conception was of the Spirit (Matt. i. 18). The Holy Spirit openly appeared at Christ's baptism by John, and afterwards led Him into the wilderness (Luke iv. 1). In Christ's charge to the apostles are the words "For it is not ye that speak, but the Spirit of your Father which speaketh in you" (Matt. x. 20; also in John xiv. 16; Acts i. 8). It was probably to correct the prevailing ignorance upon this subject that Christ condemned the blasphemers of the Holy Ghost (Matt. xii. 31). From the date of the Ascension commenced what is termed the "Dispensation of the Spirit" (Eph. iv. 8; John vii. 39). Christ ordained that Christians should be baptized in the name of the Holy Ghost (Matt. xxviii. 19). The rite of "laying on of hands" in its relation to the Holy Spirit is referred to in Acts vi. 6, etc.

SPONGE (Gr. *sponggos*). Belong to the animal kingdom. They have, when living, an apparently homogeneous jelly filling their pores and covering their surface. They come mostly from the Mediterranean and Bahama Islands. The value of the sponge was known from very early times, and was probably used by the Hebrews (Matt. xxvii. 48; Mark xv. 36).

SPOON. (Heb. CAPH, *palm* or *hollow*), (Ex. xxv. 29).

STA'CHYS (*an ear of grain*). A disciple at Rome saluted by Paul (Rom. xvi. 9).

STAC'TE (Heb. NATAF). One of the sweet spices in the holy incense (Ex. xxx. 34). From the myrrh tree, the natural gum; myrrh being artificially produced by incisions. See MYRRH.

STARS (*Star of the Wise Men*). A general name for any of the heavenly bodies, except the Sun and Moon (Gen. i. 16). See ASTRONOMY.

STA'TER (*standard*). A piece of money. See MONEY.

STEEL. See METALS.

STEPH'ANAS (*crowned*). A convert of Corinth (1 Cor. i. 16, xvi. 15).

STE'PHEN (Syr. *Chelil*, a crown). The first Christian martyr; chief of the first seven deacons of the early Church of Jerusalem. He denounced the narrowness of Jewish worship (Acts vi. 13, 14). His continual attacks upon the Jewish ritual and worship caused his being charged with blasphemy before the Sanhedrim. In this tribunal the Pharisees were in the majority. In his defense he gave a critically just and true summary of the Jewish Church: denouncing the local worship, and bringing out clearly the spiritual element in its history; and he showed that in the previous Jewish history the presence of God was not limited to the Temple at Jerusalem; and that there was among the Jews, from the earliest, a spirit of intolerance. He addressed them with calmness (Acts vi. 15), but his words were received with anger. He was sentenced to death, and the sentence was at once executed, Saul of Tarsus (Paul) consenting and assisting (Acts vii. 58, viii. 1). He died with the greatest firmness (Acts vii. 60).

The gate now called St. Stephen, at Jerusalem, is on the east side of the city. In the time of the Crusades it was on the north side, at what is now called Damascus Gate, near the probable site of the crucifixion on the hillock, over the so-called cave of Jeremiah, near which it is also probable that Stephen was stoned.

STOCKS (Heb. MAHPEKETH). In which the body was placed in a bent position; SAD, when the feet alone were confined. They consisted of two beams, the upper one movable, with grooves between them large enough to receive the ankles of the prisoner. They were often erected in market-places, that the insults of the people might be added to the pain of confinement (Job xiii. 27; Jer. xx. 2).

STOICS. A sect of fatalistic heathen philosophers, so named from the Greek word *stoa*, "porch," or portico, because Zeno, its founder, held his school in a porch of the city, more than three centuries before Christ (Acts xvii. 18). See EPICURUS.

STOM'ACHER. An ornament or support to the breast. Heb. PETHIGIL, a sort of girdle (Is. iii. 24). See DRESS.

STONES. Were used for building (Mark xiii. 1). Some were very large. Also for pavements (2 K. xvi. 17). Large stones were used for closing the entrances of caves (Josh. x. 18). Flint stones sometimes served for a *knife* (Ex. iv. 25). Stones were used in slings as ammunition of war (1 Sam. xvii. 40, 49), as weights for scales (Deut. xxv. 13), and for mills (2 Sam. xi. 21). Large stones were set up to commemorate any remarkable event (Gen. xxviii. 18). Such stones were occasionally consecrated by ANOINTING (Gen. xxviii. 18). The heathens worshiped stones (Is. lvii. 6). See JERUSALEM.

STONES, PRECIOUS. See PRECIOUS STONES

STORE. A quantity (Gen. xxvi. 14).

STORK (Heb. HASIDAH, *kindness* or *mercy*). It has the beak and legs long and red; it feeds on field-mice, lizards, snakes, frogs, and insects. Its

STRAIN AT (Gr. *diulizo, strain out*). There can be little doubt that this obscure phrase is due to an error, and the true reading is "*strain out*" (Matt. xxiii. 24).

STRANGE WOMAN (Heb. ZONAH, KEDESHAH). Used for *foreign* in some passages, and as being the wife of another, or, at least, one who has no business with the person whom she tempts (Prov. ii. 16, 17). An adulteress.

STRANGER (Heb. GER, TOSHAB). A foreigner; one not an Israelite, living in the Promised Land. Explained by some to be all those not members of the Jewish Church; not the "foreigner" (Heb. NOCHRI) who was merely visiting the land as a traveler. The mixed multitude that went out of Egypt with the children of Israel (Ex. xii. 38); the original Canaanites, captives of war, fugitives, hired servants, etc., were all called foreigners. They equaled one-tenth of the whole population in Solomon's time (2 Chr. ii. 17). If the stranger was a bondman he had to be circumcised (Ex. xii. 44); and without this rite, if he were even independent, he could not be admitted to full privileges. The number of strangers who were slaves in Solomon's time were very great—probably 150,000.

STRAW (TEBEN). Both wheat and barley straw were used by the ancient Hebrews chiefly as fodder for their cattle (Gen. xxiv. 25). It was used by the Egyptians in making bricks (Ex. v. 7, 16). They reaped their corn close to the ear and cut the straw close to the ground. This was the straw that Pharaoh refused to give to the Israelites, and they were therefore compelled to gather STUBBLE (Heb. KASH), the short straw left standing (Is. v. 24).

STRAW, TO. To strew, to scatter (Ex. xxxii. 20).

STREAM OF EGYPT. See SIHOR, the RIVER OF EGYPT (Is. xxvii. 12).

STREET (Heb. HUZ, REHOB, SHUK; Gr. *plateia, rhume*). See JERUSALEM.

STRINGED INSTRUMENTS. See MUSICAL INSTRUMENTS.

STRIPES. PUNISHMENTS.

STRONG DRINK. DRINK.

STUBBLE (Heb. KASH). See STRAW.

SU'AH (*a sweeping*). Son of Zophah (1 Chr. vii. 36).

SU'BA. Ancestor of sons of Solomon's servants who returned from Captivity (1 Chr. vii. 36).

SU'BAI. SHALMAI (1 Esd. v. 30).

SUB'URBS (Heb. MIGRASH). A place where herds are driven to graze, *a pasture* (1 Chr. v. 16). Especially the open country round the Levitical cities (Lev. xxv. 34). According to the Talmud, and most English expositors, the space from the wall outward measured 1,500 feet (Num. xxx. v. 4), and was used as a common or suburb; and the space from without the city on the east side (ver. 5) was 3,000, and used for fields and vineyards.

SUC'COTH (*booths*), (Gen. xxxiii. 17). Where Jacob built booths (of reeds, long grass, branches of trees, etc.), and thus gave the place a name. *Sokut* is a ruin 10 miles S. of *Beisan*, on the W. bank of the Jordan, where there is a copious spring in a fertile plain. But this is on the wrong side of the Jordan, for it belonged to Gad (Josh. xiii. 27). The name may have been transferred across the river. Succoth was mentioned as being near the clay ground where the metal work for Solomon's Temple was cast.—2. A station of the Wandering (Ex. xii. 37). Site lost.

SUC'COTH-BENOTH. Occurs only in 2 K. xvii. 30. It represents the Chaldean goddess ZIRBANIT, the wife of MERODACH, who was especially worshiped at Babylon.

SU'CHATHITES (*descendants of a Suchah*). A family of Scribes at Jabez (1 Chr. ii. 5).

SUD. A river near Babylon, on whose banks the Jewish captives lived.

SUD. SIA or SIAHA (1 Esd. v. 29).

SU'DIAS. HODAVIAH 3 and HODEVAH (1 Esd. v. 26).

SU'ET. FAT (Heb. YEKEB). Press-fat (Joel ii. 24).

SUK'KIIM (Heb. SUKKIYIM, *dwelling in booths*). A nation mentioned (2 Chr. xii. 3), as supplying part of the army which came out of Egypt with Shishak.

SUM'MER. CLIMATE.

SUM'MER FRUIT (KAYIZ, *fruit-harvest*). Fruit, especially figs, as harvested in summer (2 Sam. xvi. 1, 2).

There are many summer fruits in Palestine, and scarcely a month where there are not-fruits of some kind to be had.

SUN (Heb. SHEMESH; Gr. *helios*). The great luminary of the day, which furnishes so many similitudes to the Hebrew poets, as well as those of all nations (Judg. v. 31; Prov. iv. 18; Luke i. 78, 79; John viii. 12). For the idolatrous worship of the sun, see BAAL. ANNAM'MELECH.

INTERIOR OF HOUSE.

SUN'DIAL (Is. xxxviii. 8). DIAL.

SUPERSTI'TION (Gr. *deisidaimonia, fear of the gods*). Excessive exactness or rigor in religious opinions or practice; extreme and unnecessary scruples in the observance of religious rites not commanded (Acts xxv. 19, xvii. 22).

SU'PHAH. Translated Red Sea in Num. xxi. 14. The modern name is Yam Suf. See RED SEA.

SUR. One of the places on the seacoast of Palestine (Judg. ii. 28).

SUR, THE GATE OF (2 K. xi. 6). A gate of the Temple, called also "the gate of the foundation" (2 Chr. xxiii. 5).

SURETISHIP. One who makes himself responsible for the safe appearance of another (Gen. xliv. 32; Prov. xx... 26), or the payment of his debts. Christ is the "surety of a better testament" (Heb. vii. 22).

SUSA. SHUSHAN (Esth. xi. 3).

SUSANCHITES, PEOPLE OF. SHUSHAN (Ezr. iv. 9).

SUSAN'NA (*a lily*). 1. The heroine of the Judgment of Daniel, or History of Susanna, in the Apocrypha.—2. One of the women who ministered to the Lord (Luke viii. 3).

SU'SI (*horseman*). Father of Gaddi (Num. xiii. 11).

SWAL'LOW (Heb. DEROR and AGUR, "swallow" "crane"). The well-known bird of passage, common in our country, Europe and the East (Is. xxxviii. 14).

SWAN. The translation of the Heb. TINSHEMETH in Lev. xi. 18, and Deut. xiv. 16. Some think it the purple hen or water fowl.

SWEARING. OATH.

SWEAT, BLOODY (Luke xxii. 44). A peculiar physical accompaniment of the agony in the garden.

SWEET. HONEY.

SWINE (Heb. HAZIR; Gr. *choiros, hus*). A well-known animal forbidden as food to the Hebrews, who held its flesh in such detestation that they would not pronounce its name (Lev. xi. 7; Deut. xiv. 8; Is. lxv. 4, lxvi. 3, 17; Matt. viii. 32; Luke v. 14, 16; 2 Pet. ii. 22; Matt. xvii. 6.).

KING OF EGYPT. (SEE PAGE 285.)

SYC'AMORE (Heb. SHIKMAH, Gr. *sukaminos*), (Luke xvii. 6). A tree of Egypt and Palestine, the fruit of which resembles the fig (1 K. x. 27). It grows to the size of a walnut tree, has wide-spreading branches, and affords a delightful shade, and is planted by the way-sides. Its leaves are heart-shaped, downy on the under side and fragrant. The fruit grows from the trunk itself on little sprigs, and in clusters like the grape. To make the fruit eatable, three or four days before gathering it is punctured with a sharp instrument (Amos vii. 14). The wood is very durable; Egyptian mummy-coffins made of it being still perfectly sound. These trees were held in great value (1 Chr. xxvii. 28), and it was one of Egypt's calamities that her sycamores were destroyed (Ps. lxxviii. 47). The sycamore of America and of England are very different from those of the Scriptures.

SYC'AMINE TREE (Gr. *sukaminos*). A species of the mulberry tree (*morus*). Both black and white mulberry trees are common in Syria and Palestine, and are largely cultivated for supplying food to the silk-worm (Luke xvii. 6).

SY'CHAR (*falsehood*), (John iv. 5). A city of Samaria. (See SHECHEM.) Named so from the false worship on Mt. Gerizim (John iv. 22; Hab. ii. 18).

SY'CHEM. See SHECHEM.

SY CHEMITE, THE. Inhabitants of Shechem (Jud. v. 16).

SYE'LUS. JEHIEL 3 (1 Esd. i. 8).

SYE'NE. Properly Sereneh (Ez xxix. 10, xxx. 6). From Migdol to Syene was a term for the whole extent of Egypt. Migdol was the last town in Egypt toward the E., and Syene was the last toward the S., and is now known by its ancient name. Its Egyptian name was SUN, which meant "to open," that is, the opening into Egypt from the south.

SYM'EON. SIMON (2 Pet. i. 1).

SYM'PHONY. A harmony of sounds (Dan. iii. 5).

SYN'AGOGUE. See HISTORY OF THE BOOKS.

SYN'TYCHE (*happy choice*). A woman, and a member of the Church of Philippi (Phil. iv. 2, 3).

SYR'ACUSE. On the E. coast of Sicily. A wealthy and populous place, when visited by Paul (Acts xxviii. 12). Taken by the Romans 200 yrs. B. C.

SYR'IA (from TSUR, Tyre); ARAM (*high*) in the Hebrew. Aram was the fifth son of Shem (Gen. x. 22). Called Aram in Num. xxiii. 7. The country he settled is called Aram or Syria, and extended from the Mediterranean Sea to the Tigris, and from Canaan to Mt. Taurus, and had 6 names for its different sections, for which see ARAM. The country is divided into long, narrow sections, from N. to S. 1. Plains next to the sea, extending from the Ladder of Tyre to the Taurus, including the plains of Phœnicia, of Seleucia, and of the Issus.—2. The range of mountains called the N. Amanus, and Bargylus, and in the S. Lebanon.—3. The valley between Lebanon and Anti-Lebanon, Cœle, or Hollow Syria.—4. The mountain range rising N. of Aleppo, and ending at Mt. Hermon.—5. The Syrian desert, extending to the Euphrates. The principal rivers are the Orontes, (El Asy, *the rebellious*), and the Litany. The source of the Orontes is a little N. of Baalbek, where, within a few miles, a stream from both Lebanon and Anti-Lebanon unite to form the stream, flowing N. E.: It passes through a lake, 6 ms. long by 2 wide, near Emesa (HUMS); a little below Hamath it receives a branch; being turned W. by the Amanus, it receives the Kara Su (*Black river*), flows by Antioch, and empties into the sea; having a course of 200 ms. The Litany rises from a small lake, 6 ms. S. W. of Baalbek, and runs S. until it is turned W. by the hills of Galilee, when it reaches the sea 5 ms. N. of Tyre, having run about 80 ms. There are many other small streams, as the Eleutherus, Lycus, Adonis, the rivers of Damascus (Abana and Pharpar), which are lost in marshy lakes, the Koweik, near Aleppo, terminating in a marsh, and the Sajur, a branch of the Euphrates. The lakes are: The Lake of Antioch; the Salt Lake, near Aleppo; Kades, on the Orontes; and the Bahr el Merj, near Damascus. The cities are: Antioch, Damascus (150,000); Apamea, Aleppo (70,000); Beirut (50,000); Hamath (30,000); (Num. xiii. 21); Hums (20,000); Tripoli (13,000); Seleucia, Tadmor, (Palmyra), and many others, mentioned in their places. Syria was settled by Canaanites and Aramæans, descendants of Ham. Damascus and Zobah were

MOUNT SINAI FROM THE PLAIN ERRAHAH.

the chief cities in David's time. Assyria made it a province, and Alexander conquered it (B. C. 323); and after him the Seleucid family governed it, one of them building Antioch, which was their only capital until 114 B. C. The Romans, under Pompey, captured it, B. C. 65. The Mohammedans succeeded the Romans A. D. 634, when, for 100 yrs. after, they made Damascus their capital.

SYR'IAC VER'SIONS. HISTORY OF THE BOOKS.

SYR'IA MA'ACHAH (1 Chr. xix. 6).

SYR'IAN. A native of Syria (Gen. xxv. 20).

SY'ROPHENI'CIAN. Is Phœnicia properly so-called, which was a part of Syria only when the Syrian kings governed Phœnicia. The Canaanitish woman is called a Syrophœnician (Mark vii. 26).

T

TA'ANACH (*sandy soil*), (Josh. xii. 21). An ancient city of Canaan, built on the end of a ridge which runs northward from the hills of Manasseh into the plains of Esdraëlon, at the base of which is the modern village of the same name (Ar. *Ta'annuk*). It was the headquarters of the army of Deborah and Barak, and Sisera's host was encamped between it and Megiddo (Judg. v. 19).

TA'ANATH-SHI'LOH (*approach to Shiloh*), (Josh. xvi. 6). Supposed to be Shiloh; Taanath being the Canaanite and Shiloh the Hebrew name of the same city.

TAB'AOTH. TABBAOTH (1 Esd. v. 29).

TAB'BAOTH (*rings*). Ancestor of a family of Nethinim, who returned from Captivity (Ezr. ii. 43).

TAB'BATH (Judg. vii. 22). In the Jordan valley, below and not far from Bethshean. It may be Tubakat Fahil (*Terrace of Fahil*).

TA'BEAL. The "son of Tabeal" was apparently a Syrian, whom the Syrians and Israelites intended to place on the throne (Is. vii. 6).

TA'BEEL (*God is good*). An officer of the Persian government (Ezr. iv. 7).

TABEL'LIUS. TABEEL (1 Esd. ii. 16).

TAB'ERAH (*burning*), (Num. xi. 3; Deut. ix. 22). In the Sinai district, but not identified.

TA'BERING. METHOFEFOTH, *a timbrel;* to beat with loud strokes upon such an instrument (Neh. ii. 7).

TAB'ERNACLE (*a tent*). See TEMPLE.

TAB'ERNACLES, THE FEAST OF. See FESTIVALS.

TAB'ITHA (*a gazelle*). Also called DORCAS, the name of a pious and charitable woman at Joppa, whom Peter raised from the dead (Acts ix. 36-42).

TA'BLE (Heb. LUAH, *a table* or *tablet*). Used especially of the tablets or slabs of stone on which were the TEN COMMANDMENTS (Ex. xxiv. 12). Also of other tablets for WRITING (Ex. xxx. 8). Heb. MESAB (Cant. i. 12), "at his table." Heb. SHULHAN, *a table spread with food* (Ex. xxv. 23 ff.); Gr. *kline*, *a bed* (Mark vii. 4); also, a *couch* for resting or reclining at MEALS (Matt. ix. 2, 6).

TAB'LETS. 1. Heb. BOTTEYHAN-NEFESH, *houses of the soul; perfume-boxes.*—2. Heb. CUMAZ (Ex. xxxv. 22), (*a globule of gold*, or, rather, *a string of gold*). Drops like beads were worn round the neck, or arm, by the Israelites in the desert.

TABOR, MT. (*hight*). (Josh. xix. 22). On the border of Issachar and Zebulon. It is of limestone, 1800 ft. high, rounded in form, and is studded with forests of oaks, pistachios, terebinths, mock-oranges, and other trees and bushes. Wolves, boars, lynxes, and other wild animals, besides reptiles, are found. It is now called *Jebel et Tur*, and is one of the most favorable points for beautiful and extensive views. The plain of Esdraëlon is seen, spread out like a carpet, between the hills of Samaria and those of Galilee, ending at Carmel, and in the season of early harvest (March and April) is diversified with the various colors of different fields in cultivation: some red from recent plowing—some yellow, white, or green, as the state of the crop may determine. The sea of Galilee and the Mediterranean are visible. The course of the Jordan can be traced for many miles. Lebanon and Hermon, with their snow-capped summits, and the hills of Galilee, including Hattin, the Mt. of Beatitudes, are on the N., and the countless hills and valleys of Bashan (*Hauran*), and Gilead, are to the E.; Little Hermon (Hill Mizar) and Gilboa to the S., while the mountains of Samaria fill up the view to the W., ending in the ridge of Carmel to the N. W., where we began. All around the top are foundations of a thick wall, built of large stones, some of which are beveled. There are ruins of towers and bastions. Toward the E. end of this enclosure are confused heaps of ruins of houses, churches, towers, and other buildings—some of hewn and others of beveled stones. One

TABLE.

tall, pointed arch is standing, called the Gate of the Wind. The ruins are of different ages, from remote antiquity, the time of Josephus, the Crusades, and still later days. The early Christians adopted the legend of the Transfiguration of the Saviour on this mountain (Rob. ii. 358), but this is now located on Hermon, near Paneas.

TABOR, THE PLAIN OF. (Heb. ELON, properly *The Oak of Tabor*). Only mentioned once (1 Sam. x. 3). This plain, or oak of Tabor, was evidently somewhere between Rachel's tomb and Bethel, probably not far from Jerusalem. But its locality cannot be ascertained.

TABRI'MON, properly **TAB'RIMMON** (*good is Rimmon*). Father of Ben-hadad I, King of Syria (1 K. xv. 18).

TACHE (Heb. KEREN, *hook*). The small hooks by which the curtains of the tabernacle were suspended to the rings from which it hung (Ex. xxvi. 6, 11, 33).

TACH'MONITE, THE. Error for Jashobeam the Hachmonite, "son of Hachmoni" (2 Sam. xxiii. 8).

TAD'MOR. PALMYRA. City of Palms (1 K. ix. 18). Built by Solomon on the route from Palestine to the Euphrates, about midway between Damas-

cus and the river; the whole distance being about 240 ms. The ruins are chiefly of Corinthian colonnades and temples, and, seen at a distance, are peculiarly imposing, and seem to surpass all others in their apparent vastness and general effect. None of Solomon's buildings have been identified, and the ruins are ascribed to works of the date of the 2d or 3d century of our era. (See Wood's *Palmyra*).

PALMYRA-TADMOR.

TA'HAN (*station*). Descendant of Ephraim (Num. xxvi. 35).

TA'HANITES, THE. Descendants of TAHAN (Num. xxvi. 35).

TAHAP'ANES. TAHPANHES.

TA'HATH (*below*). 1. Ancestor of Samuel and Heman (1 Chr. vi. 37).—2. Son of Bered (vii. 20).—3. Grandson of No. 2 (vii. 20).

TA'HATH (*lower*), (Num. xxxiii. 26). Desert station. Lost.

TAH'PANHES (*Daphne?*). An important town in Lower Egypt, in the land of Goshen, near Pelusium (Jer. xliii. 7). Located at *Tel Defenneh*, in the present Delta.

TAH'PENES. An Egyptian queen, wife of Pharaoh 6 (1 K. xi. 18-20).

TAHRE'A (*cunning*). Son of Micah (1 Chr. ix. 41).

TAH'TIM HOD'SHI, THE LAND OF (2 Sam. xxiv. 6). Lost. Supposed by some to be Harosheth (compare Judg. iv. 2).

TAL'ENT (Heb. KIKKAR; Gr. *talanton*). The greatest weight of the Hebrews. See MONEY, WEIGHTS AND MEASURES.

TALI'THA CU'MI. Two Syriac words, meaning *damsel arise* (Mark v. 41). The Chaldee or Aramaic paraphrase on Prov. ix. 3, signifies a girl. Gesenius says the same word means a lamb.

TAL'MAI (*furrowed*). 1. Son of ANAK (Num. xiii. 22).—2. Son of Ammihud, and king of Geshur (2 Sam. iii. 3).

TAL'MON (*oppressed*). Head of the porters for the camps of the sons of Levi (1 Chr. ix. 17).

TAL'MUD. Is the work which embodies the canonical and civil law of the Jews. It contains those rules, precepts and interpretations by which the Jewish people profess to be guided, in addition to the O. T., and includes not merely religion, but philosophy, medicine, jurisprudence, history and the various branches of practical duty. The Jews have been accustomed to divide their law into written and unwritten: the written contained in the Pentateuch, the unwritten handed down orally, until it was found necessary to write it. Some Jews have assigned the same antiquity to both, alleging that Moses received them on the Mount. *Midrashim*, or explanations of biblical topics, were of gradual growth. The system of interpretation which they exemplify and embody existed in the age of the so-called Sopherim (Scribes), who succeeded the prophets. The oldest Mishna is accredited to Hillel. It is divided into 6 orders or books, 63 treatises (MASSIKLOTH), and 525 chapters (PERAKIM). The first *Seder* treats of sowing, the productions of the earth, trees, and the uses of fruits, seeds, etc. The second *Seder* (MOED), the order of festivals. The third *Seder* (NASHIM) discusses the rights of men and women, marriage and divorce. The fourth *Seder* (NEZIKIN), consisting of ten treatises, with the losses and injuries which one person may bring upon another. The fifth (KODASHIM) treats of sacrifices, oblations, etc. The sixth (TAHAROTH) relates to purifications of vessels, household furniture, etc. Rabbinical Jews have always set a high value on the Talmud, often placing it above the old Mosaic law. Hence we find in the Masseceth Soferim the saying, "The Biblical text is like water, and the Mishna like wine, and the six orders like aromatic wine." In another passage, "The law is like salt, the Mishna like pepper, but the six orders like fine spices." Again, "The words of the Scribes are lovely, above the words of the law; for the words of the law are weighty and light, but the words of the scribes are all weighty." These extravagant praises of the oral traditions agree with the Saviour's words: "Making the word of God of none effect, through your tradition, which ye have believed" (Mark vii. 13).

The first complete edition of the Babylonian Talmud was published at Venice in 1520-1523, in 12 vols. folio. This is the celebrated Bomberg edition now so rare, but not accurate.

The Jerusalem Talmud was first published by Bomberg about 1522-23, at Venice, folio; and subsequently at Cracow, 1609, folio.

The entire Talmud has not been translated into any language. The Mishna appeared in Latin in Surenhusius's edition, Amsterdam, 1698-1703, fol.

TAL'SAS. ELASAH (1 Esd. ix. 22).

TA'MAH (*laughter*). Ancestor of Nethinim, who returned from Captivity (Neh. vii. 55).

TA'MAR (Heb. THAMAR, *palm-tree*). 1. Wife of Er and Onan, the two sons of Judah (Gen. xxxviii. 6-30). She practiced a deception upon Judah, in retaliation for his neglect to give her his third son, Shelah, for a husband.—2. Daughter of David, mother of Absalom. She was badly treated by her brother Amnon (2 Sam. xiii. 1-32).—3. Daughter of Absalom (2 Sam. xiv. 7). The mother of Maachah 3, queen of Judah (1 K. xv. 3).

TA'MAR (*palm-tree*). (Ez. xlvii. 19). A town S. of Hebron, now called Kurnub.

TAM'MUZ. A Syrian idol mentioned in Ez. viii. 14, where the women are represented as weeping for it. It is generally supposed that Tammuz was the same deity as the Phœnician Adonis. The fabled death and restoration of Adonis, supposed to symbolize the departure and return of the sun, were celebrated at the summer solstice with lamentations first, and then rejoicings and obscene revels.

TA'NACH. TAANACH (Josh. xxi. 25).

TAN'HUMETH (*comfort*). Father of Seraiah (2 K. xxv. 23).

TA'NIS. Zoan, in Egypt (Jud i. 10).

TA'PESTRY (Heb. MARBADDIM). Cloth for hangings and bed-covers, ornamented with needle-work (Prov. vii. 16).

TA'PHATH (*drops*). Daughter of Solomon (1 K. iv. 11).

TAP'PUAH (*apple-region*). Son of Hebron (1 Chr. ii. 43).

TA'PHON (1 Macc. ix. 50). Beth Tappuah, near Hebron.

TAR'SUS. Chief town of CILICIA; the birthplace of Paul the Apostle (Acts ix. 11, xxi. 39). It was an important city in the time of the Greek kings. Alexander conquered it; and it was under the rule

TARSUS.

TAP'PUAH (Josh. xv. 34). In the Shefelah, 12 ms. W. of Jerusalem.—2. EN-TAPPUAH (Josh. xvi. 8, xvii. 7, 8). On the boundary of the children of Joseph—a city and a district of the same name. Supposed to be S. W. of Shechem. Perhaps in Wady Falaik.

TA'RAH. Desert station. Lost.

TAR'ALAH (Josh. xviii. 27). City of Benjamin. Site lost.

TARE'A. TAHREA (1 Chr. viii. 35).

TARES. A noxious plant, of the grass family, supposed to mean the darnel. It grows among the wheat everywhere in Palestine, and bears a great resemblance to it while growing—so closely that, before they head out, the two plants can hardly be distinguished. The grains are found, 2 or 3 together, in 12 small husks, scattered on a rather long head. The Arabs do not separate the darnel from the wheat, unless by means of a fan or sieve, after threshing (Matt. xiii. 25-30). If left to mingle with the bread, it occasions dizziness, and often acts as an emetic.

TAR'GET. A small, round shield (1 Sam. xvii. 6).

TAR'GUM. A translation of the Scriptures in the Chaldee language. Of these, the *Targum* of Jonathan, and that of Onkelos, are held in most esteem by the Jews.

TARPE'LITES (Ezr. iv. 9). Supposed to refer to the people of Tripolis, Phœnicia.

TAR'SHISH (Gen. x. 4; Ps. lxxii. 10; Jonah i. 3, etc.). Probably Tartassus, in Spain (Strabo, iii. 148). There was a city and a river in Spain of the same name; perhaps the same river is now called Guadalquiver. The articles brought to Tyre from Tarshish, such as silver, iron, lead, and tin (Ez. xxvii. 12), were productions of Spain.—2. (2 Chr. ix. 21, xx. 36). From these passages it seems that there was another Tarshish, which was in the direction of the Red Sea, and probably in India, judging from the articles brought from there, which were gold, silver, ivory, apes, and peacocks (1 K. x. 22). India was the native land of the peacock (Cuvier, viii. 136).

of Antioch, and also that of the Ptolemies. Cæsar changed its name to Juliopolis. Augustus made it a free city. It was a celebrated seat of learning in the time of the early Roman emperors, and was compared by Strabo to Athens and Alexandria, and considered superior to them (xiv. 673). Among its famous citizens were Athenodorus, the tutor of Augustus, and Nestor, the tutor of Tiberius. Antony and Cleopatra met on the banks of the river Cydnus, which divides Tarsus in two.

TAR'TAK. An idol of the Avites of Samaria (2 K. xvii. 31).

TAR'TAN. An Assyrian general who went to Jerusalem (2 K. xviii. 17).

TAT'NAI (*gift*). A governor of Samaria who treated the Jews with great justice and moderation (Ezr. v. viii.), B. C. 519.

TAU (Heb. TAV, a mark or sign). The 23d letter of the Hebrew alphabet.

TAV'ERNS. Three Taverns. A station on the Appian road between Puteoli and Rome, where Paul met brethren when on his way from Jerusalem. The modern Cisteran is probably near the site of the ancient place, which was about 30 ms. from Rome.

TAX'ES. Every Jew was required to pay an annual tribute or poll-tax of half a shekel, about 25 cents, in acknowledgment of God's sovereignty, and for the support of the Temple service (Ex. xxx. 12-15; Matt. xvii. 25, 26). In the N. T. passages, tribute means the tax levied by the Romans (Matt. xxii. 16-22). Christ warned them to render to all men their dues (1 Cor. x. 31; 1 Pet. ii. 9, 13).

TAX'ING (Gr. *apographe*). The question about the truth of Luke's record of the taxing by the Emperor of Rome is quite surely settled in Luke's favor by the best critics (Luke ii. 1; Acts 5, 37).

TEACH'ER. One that imparts instruction, and communicates knowledge of religious truth or other things.

TEARS. Drops of water from the eye (2 K. xx. 5). The ancient Romans collected the tears of mourners for the dead, and preserved them in a bottle, of thin glass or simple pottery. They used to be placed in the sepulchres of the dead, in Rome and Palestine, where they are found in great numbers, on opening ancient tombs (Ps. lvi. 8).

TE'BAH (*slaughter*). Eldest son of NAHOR II (Gen. xxii. 24).

TEBALI'AH (*whom Jah has purified*). Third son of Hosah (1 Chr. xxvi. 11).

TE'BETH. The tenth month of the Hebrew sacred year, commencing with the new moon in January (Esth. ii. 16).

TEHAPH'NEHES. TAHPANHES.

TEHIN'NAH (*mercy*). Founder of IR-NAHASH, son of Eshton (1 Chr. iv. 12).

TEIL'-TREE. The lime-tree, or linden.

hill-country of upper and western Mesopotamia, near Haran, and inhabited by the children of Eden (2 K. xix. 12). The name indicates the site of a temple built in honor of Asshur. The Targums locate this place, with Resen (Gen. x. 12), on the Tigris, near Nineveh and Calah.

TEL'EM (*oppression*). Judah (Josh. xv. 24). S. of Hebron. Now called Dhallam.

TEL'EM. A porter of the Temple (Ezr. x. 24).

TEL-HARSA. Tel-Haresha (*hill of the wood*). (Ezr. ii. 59; Neh. vii. 61). In the low country of Babylonia, near the Persian Gulf.

TELL HUM has recently been proved to be the site of the ancient CAPERNAUM. The original building of the synagogue, as appears by an inspection of the ruins, was 74 feet 9 inches long by 56 feet 9 inches wide; longer between north and south, with entrances at the south end. Many finely cut capitals were found in the interior, buried in the rubbish; and also several of the pedestals in their proper places. Epiphanius says there was a Christian church there A. D. 600, some of the ruins of

TELL HUM, CAPERNAUM.

TEKO'A (*strikers*), (2 Chr. xi. 6). E. of Hebron; built by Ashur, son of Hezron (2 Chr. ii. 24). Residence of the wise woman who made peace between David and Absalom (2 Sam. xiv.). Ira, the Tekoite, was one of David's 30 "mighty men" (Ib. xxiii. 26). Rehoboam fortified it (2 Chr. xi. 6). Its people helped Nehemiah rebuild the walls of Jerusalem after the return from Babylon (Neh. iii. 5, 27). The prophet Amos was born here (Amos i., vii. 14). The modern name is Tekua, and it is a small village of Arab houses, on an elevated hill, from which there is an extensive view reaching to the mountains of Moab, Dead Sea, the hills around Jerusalem, and W. to Hebron, while toward the S. the mountains of Edom fill the horizon. There are ruins of walls of houses, cisterns, broken columns, and heaps of building-stones. Some of the stones have the peculiar Hebrew bevel, proving their antiquity. The ruins of Khureitun (possibly KERIOTH, the city of Judas) are near Tekua, on the brink of a frightful precipice.

TEKO'A. Son of Ashur, in the genealogies of Judah (1 Chr. ii. 24).

TELA'BIB (*hill Abib*). In Babylonia. (Ez. iii. 15). Lost.

TEL'AH (*breach*). A descendant of Ephraim, and ancestor of Joshua (1 Chr. vii. 25).

TEL'AIM (1 Sam. xv. 4). Saul gathered the people, and numbered them, at Telaim; and it is not certain whether a city of this name was meant, or that the numbering occurred at the time of the Passover, for the word is also translated "lambs of the Passover."

TELAS'SAR. Thelasar (*hill of Asshur*). In the

which are found near the synagogue. The plan of the synagogue was always peculiar, and different from that adopted by the Christians, or Pagans, or Mohammedans, so that there is no difficulty in determining the nature of certain ruins. This building may have been the one built by the centurion (Luke vii. 45), and that in which Jesus delivered the discourse recorded in John vi. One of the stones has a pot of manna sculptured on it.

At the north end of the town there are the remains of two very interesting tombs. One was built of limestone blocks, in a chamber cut from the basalt; and the other a building above ground, which had been whitewashed inside and out. (See Matt. xxii. 27).

TEL-ME'LAH (*hill of salt*). A city of the low district near the Persian Gulf. The city is called Thelme, by Ptolemy (v. 20).

TE'MA (*desert*), (Gen. xxv. 15; Is. xxi. 14.) A small town on the border of Syria, on the pilgrim route from Damascus to Mecca. It was once a stronghold.

TE'MAN (Gen. xxxvi. 11). A city or country named after one of the dukes of Edom, in the S. of the land of Edom. Eusebius and Jerome mention it as being 15 ms. from Petra.

TEM'ANI (Gen. xxxvi. 34). TEMANITE.

TEMAN'ITE. Descendant of TEMAN (1 Chr. i. 45). ELIFAZ, the Temanite, was Job's friend, and one of the wise men of Edom (Job ii. 11).

TEM'ENI (*lucky*). Son of Ashur (1 Chr. iv. 6).

TEM'PLE (Heb. 1. MISH'KAN, *dwelling*; an open, inclosed place, which can be dwelt in), (Ex. xxv. 9;

Lev. viii. 10, xvii. 13; Num. i. 50-53). It connects itself with the Jewish word SHECHINAH, as describing the dwelling-place of the Divine Glory.—2. OHEL, the tent, as a whole, or, perhaps, the covering, or roof only (Gen. iv. 20, ix. 21, etc.). This is used when applied to the Sacred Tent (Ex. xxvi. 9).—3. BAYITH, house (Ex. xxiii. 19).—4. KODESH, holy.—5. MIKDASH, sanctuary (Ex. xxv. 8); Heb. and

TEMPT TO, and TEMPTA'TION. These words denote the trying or putting one to the proof. (Heb. RAMAH MASSAH; Gr. *peirazo, ekpeirazo, peirasmos*, etc.). Designate the action of God or the course of His providence, or the earthly trial by which human character and feelings are brought out (Gen. xxii. 1). The Temptation may be used with reference to our first parents (Gen. iii.) or of the

TEMPLE.

Chal. 6. HEY'KAL, temple, palace (2 K. xxiv. 13; 1 Sam. i. 9).—7. MO'ED, place of meeting (Ex. xxix. 42).—8. HA'EDUTH, place of a fixed meeting (Num. ix. 15).—9. OHEL HA'EDUTH, tabernacle of testimony (Num. xvii. 7); so named from the two tables of testimony. The tabernacle was a tent-like structure, adapted to the roving life of the desert, and made more important than the ordinary tent, or even than the best tents of the wealthiest skeikhs, which are lined with silk, or fine linen, or woolen, and very showy in form and color.

Its form was twice the length of its width, 30 cubits (45 feet) long by 10 cubits (15 feet) wide, and the side-walls were 10 cubits (15 feet) high. It stood in an inclosed place, 50 cubits (75 feet) wide by 100 cubits (150 feet) long, 15 feet from the west end. (See the plan on the map of the TWELVE TRIBES). The Holy of Holies, at the west end, was a cube of 10 cubits each way, and in it was the mercy-seat, on the lid of the ark, the cherubim, the ark and the Book of the Law. The room in front was 20 cubits long by 10 wide, and called the Holy Place. In it were the table of shew-bread and the seven-branched candlestick and the altar of incense (Ex. xxv.). The tent had a ridge, forming a right-angle, over which the roof coverings of cloth and skins were thrown. These extended 5 cubits beyond the walls all round the tent, like wide, projecting eaves. There were three coverings to the sides; the inner of fine linen; the next of badger-skins; the outer of ram-skins dyed red; and besides these, the roof had one of goats' hair. It was made under the direction of Bezaleel and Aholiab. Its place was in the centre of the camp (see ENCAMPMENT), where it was set up on the first day of the second year of the Exodus (Ex. xl. 2). It was the place where man met with God (Num. xi. 24, 25). It was moved from its place (a moving Bethel) in the Wilderness and in Canaan until the Temple was built, or rather until it lost its glory, when the ark was captured by the Philistines (1 Sam. iv. 22; Ps. lxxviii. 60). The form and size of the tent were symbolical; and to the Hebrews, who believed in the mystical and occult powers of numbers, it was peculiarly sacred because of its peculiar structure. On its altar of incense no strange fire must ever be used.

Jesus (Matt. iv. 1-11) in which Satan was the Tempter.

TEMPT'ER. One who tempts or entices another to sin (Matt. iv. 3).

TEN COMMANDMENTS. See DECALOGUE.

TENT (Heb. OHEL). Dwelling in tents was very general in ancient times among Eastern nations (Gen. iv. 20). The patriarchs, the Israelites from Egypt, dwelt in tents until they obtained the Promised Land, and to some extent afterwards (Judg. vii. 8; Heb. xi. 9). The people of the East live much in the open air. But those most remarkable for this unsettled and wandering life are the Arabs, who still live in tents. This kind of dwelling is not confined to the Arabs, but is used throughout Asia. Tents were usually made of canvas stretched out, and resting on poles, with cords secured to pegs driven into the ground (Is. xxxiii. 20). The house of God, and heaven, are spoken of in Scripture as the tent or tabernacle of Jah (Ps. xv. 1). Says Lord Lindsay: "There is something very melancholy in our morning flittings. The tent-pins are plucked up, and in a few minutes a dozen holes, a heap or two of ashes, and the marks of the camels' knees in the sand, soon to be obliterated, are the only traces left of what has been for a while our home. Often we found ourselves shelterless before being fully dressed." What a type of the tent of our body!

Tents are of various colors; black (Ps. cxx. 5), red, yellow, and white. They are also of various shapes; some circular, others of an oblong figure like the bottom of a ship turned upside down. In Syria the tents are generally made of cloth of goats' hair (Ex. xxxv. 26). Those of the Arabs are of black goats' hair. The Egyptian and Moorish inhabitants of Askalon use white tents. An Arab sheikh will have a number of tents (Gen. xxxi. 33). Usually one tent suffices for a family, being divided, if large, into apartments by curtains.

TENT MAKERS (Acts xviii. 3).

TENTA'TION (Ex. xvii. 7). TEMPTATION.

TENTH. The tenth part of an ephah, probably the same as the Omer, about five pints (Lev. xxiii. 17).

TE'RAH (*station*). Son of Nahor, and father of

Abram (Gen. xi. 24-32). NAHOR 2, and HARAN 1, and through them the ancestor of the great families of the Israelites, Ishmaelites, Midianites, Moabites, and Ammonites. He dwelt in Ur, and was an idolater (Josh. xxiv. 2). He lived 205 years, and died in Haran (xi. 31, 32).

TER'APHIM. This word is rendered "images," "idolatry," or the like. Now understood to represent small images, used as household gods.

Rachel is said to have stolen her father's teraphim (Gen. xxxi. 19). Laban calls them his gods (ver. 30). In the history of Micah of Mount Ephraim the teraphim appeared as objects of worship, and as part of the furniture which he provided for what is called "his house of Gods" (Judg. xvii. 5). Jacob pointed to the teraphim, when he called upon his household to put away "the strange gods" that were among them (Gen. xxxv. 2); to them also Josiah referred (2 Chr. xxxiv. 7; 2 K. xxii. 24). They are named by Hosea among the articles of false worship, and are among the objects of superstitious regard with the king of Babylon (Ez. xxi. 21).

TE'RESH (*severe*). One of the eunuchs who was discovered in his plot to assassinate Ahasuerus (Esth. ii. 21)

TER'TIUS. A disciple who assisted Paul (Rom. xvi. 22).

TERTUL'LUS. A Roman orator, whom the Jews employed to bring forward their accusation against Paul (Acts xxiv. 1-2).

TES'TAMENT. See HISTORY OF THE BOOKS.

TES'TIMONY (Heb. EDAH, EDUTH, TEUDAH; Gr. *marturia, marturion*). Witness, evidence, proof (Matt. viii. 4; John iii. 32, 33, etc.). Applied also to the precepts, law, revelation of God (Ps. xix. 7), and especially to the TEN COMMANDMENTS, or DECALOGUE (Ex. xvi. 34).

TE'TA. HATIPA (1 Esd. v. 28).

TETH (Heb. TEYTH, *a serpent*). The ninth letter of the Hebrew alphabet (Ps. cxix.).

TET'RARCH. Governor of the fourth part of a country. 1. HEROD ANTIPAS (Matt. xiv. 11), who is distinguished as "Herod the tetrarch;" also the title of king is assigned to him (Matt. xiv. 9).—2. HEROD PHILIP II is called tetrarch of ITUREA (Luke iii. 1); LYSANIAS (iii. 1), tetrarch of ABILENE. This title was probably applied to petty tributary princes also.

THAD'DEUS (Heb. TADDAY, *courageous*). JUDE. JUDAS. Also called Lebbeus and Thaddeus (Matt. x.). One of the twelve. He is only mentioned as among those who could not see the spiritual kingdom of Jesus (John xiv. 22). Of his life, labors, and death, we know nothing. Tradition says he preached at Edessa, and died a martyr there (Mark iii. 18).

THA'HASH. BADGER. Son of NAHOR 2 by his second wife, Reumah (Gen. xxii. 24).

THA'MAH. Ancestor of a family of Nethinim (Ezr. ii. 53), who returned from Captivity.

THA'MAR. TAMAR 1 (Matt. i. 3).

THAM'NATHA. TIMNATH (1 Macc. ix. 50). Now called Tibneh, half way between Jerusalem and the Mediterranean.

THANK-OF'FERING. SACRIFICE.

THA'RA. TERAH (Luke iii. 34).

THAR'RA. TERESH (Esth. xii. 1).

THAR'SHISH. 1 (1 K. x. 22).—2. A Benjamite of the family of Bilhan (1 Chr. vii. 10).

THAS'SI (*debilitation*). The surname of Simon the son of Mattathias (1 Macc. ii. 3).

THE'ATER (Gr. *theatron*). The place where dramatic performances or other public spectacles are exhibited (Acts xix. 29). Theaters were often used among the Greeks for public assemblies and the transaction of public business. Criminals were sometimes exposed and punished in the theaters (1 Cor. iv. 9). See EPHESUS.

THEBES. A chief city of ancient Egypt, the capital and residence of the kings during the age of its highest splendor. There were three names, Zam, Pamen (*abode of Amon*), and Thebes. No-Ammon (*portion of Ammon*), is the name in the Scriptures (Jer. xlvi. 25; Nah. iii. 8; Ez. xxx. 14). Mentioned by Homer (Il. ix., 381). Its origin is lost in antiquity. In the 1st century, B. C., Diodorus describes it as having a circuit of 140 stadia; public edifices of vast size; magnificent temples; a great number of monuments; private houses, of 4 or 5 stories

TENT.

high; giving it a grandeur and beauty surpassing all other cities in the world (Diod. i. 45). Nearly 100 yrs. later, Strabo speaks of Thebes under the name of Diospolis, and says that "vestiges of its magnitude still exist, which extend 80 stadia in length. There are a great number of temples, many of which Cambyses mutilated." Pliny wrote of Thebes as "a hanging city;" that is, built on arches, having the river (Nile) flowing through the middle of it. The ruins of Thebes are now found in a valley of about 10 ms. in extent, on both sides of the Nile, which is here ¼ a m. wide, and the city was anciently about 2 ms. in extent from N. to S., and 4 ms. from E. to W. The quarters are called Karnak and Luxor on the E., and Koornah and Medinet Haboo on the W. side, in each of which localities there are ruins of great temples, with remains of avenues of sphynxes, and colossal figures, of 2 ms. in extent, leading from one to the other. (See Wilkinson and Mariette.) Almost every pillar, obelisk, and stone, tells its historic legend of Egypt's greatest monarchs. "To-day Thebes is but a nest of Arab hovels, amid crumbling columns, and drifting sands." (J. P. Thompson, D.D.)

THE'BEZ (*brightness*), (Judg. ix. 50.) A place 15 ms. N. E. of Shechem, now called Tubas, on a gentle hill, surrounded by large groves of olives, and well-cultivated fields (Rob. iii. 305). Abimelech was killed here by a piece of a millstone (2 Sam. xi. 21).

ARCH AT THESSALONICA.

THEC'OE (*the wilderness*). Thec'oe, the Greek form of TEKOA, which see.

THEFT. PUNISHMENTS.

THELA'SAR. TEL-ASSAR (2 K. xix. 12).

THELER'SAS. TEL-HARSA (1 Esd. v. 36).

THE MAN. TEMAN (Bar. iii. 22, 23).

THEOCA'NUS. TIKVAH.

THEOD'OTUS (*God-given*). An envoy, sent by Nicanor to Judas Maccabæus, about B. C. 162 (2 Macc. xiv. 19).

THEOPH'ILUS (*friend of God*). 1. The person to whom Luke inscribes his Gospel and the Acts of the Apostles (Luke i. 3.—2. A Jewish HIGH-PRIEST, A. D. 37-41; the son of ANNAS.

THEOPH'YLACT (*God-guarded*). A native of Constantinople, and Archbishop of Acris, A. D. 1077 (Mark vii. 3).

THE'RAS. AHAVA (1 Esd. viii. 41, 61).

THER'MELETH. TEL-MELAH (1 Esd. v. 36).

THESSALO'NIANS. People of THESSALONICA.

THESSALO'NIANS, FIRST AND SECOND EPISTLES TO THE. See HISTORY OF THE BOOKS.

THESSALONI'CA. Named after the sister of Alexander the Great. She was wife of Cassander, who rebuilt and enlarged the city. Its original name was Therma. In Macedonia, between the rivers of the Thermaic Gulf. It is still the most important town in European Turkey, after Constantinople, having a population of 70,000, about one-third of whom are Jews. It was the residence of Cicero at one time, and the headquarters of Pompey and his Senate, and was made a free city by Octavius Cæsar. In the 1st century A. D., the time of Paul's visit and his two Epistles to the Thessalonians, it was the most populous city in Macedonia. This was the chief station on the great Roman Road, the VIA EGNATIA, which led from Rome toward the whole country north of the seas, and therefore a most important centre for spreading the gospel. Its commerce was equal to Corinth and Ephesus. The first Christians of this city mentioned by name were Jason (Rom. xvi. 21), Demas (2 Tim. iv. 10), Gaius (Acts xix. 29), and Aristarchus and Secundus (Acts xx. 4). The truth and accuracy of the Scripture are confirmed in the mention of the fact of this being a free city and in giving the peculiar and correct term for the chief magistrate, who was called in Greek POLITARCH (Acts xvii. 6). This name is found nowhere else, and is preserved on an arch of the Imperial times, which spans the main street of the city (Aug. Beck. Insc. No. 1967). For several centuries after Christ this was called "The Orthodox City," and was the great center of Oriental Christianity.

THEU'DAS (*gift of God*). An insurgent Jew, mentioned by Gamaliel A. D. 33 (Acts v. 35-39), as of the preceding generation, and not to be confounded with a Theu'das of A. D. 44, mentioned by Josephus.

THIEVES, THE TWO (Gr. *lestai*, *robbery*). The men who appear in the history of the crucifixion (Matt. xxvii. 38, 44; Mark xv. 37, 42) were robbers, belonging to the lawless bands in Palestine. Against these brigands every Roman procurator had to wage war. They kept an armed police to encounter them (Luke xxii. 52).

THIMNA'THAH. Dan (Josh. xix. 43). Between Eglon and Ekron. The residence of Samson's wife. There must have been several towns of the same name. One is now known as Tibneh, ten miles south of Akir (Ekron).

THIS'BE. Naphtali (Tobit, i. 2). The birthplace of the prophet ELIJAH, THE TISHBITE (1 K. xvii. 1). The place has not been identified, but is looked for in the vicinity of Safed or Kadesh.

THISTLE, AND THORNS. There are nearly twenty Hebrew words which point to different

THESSALONICA.

kinds of prickly or thorny shrubs, and are variously rendered "thorns," "briers," "thistles," "brambles," etc. Thistles of various species are numerous in Palestine, and often of prodigious size, and in some parts the thorns and briers grow so luxuriantly that they must be burned off before the

plow can operate (Thess. ii. 5, 28). They were a symbol of desolation (Prov. xxiv. 31); and were often used as fuel (Is. xxxiii. 12); also for hedges (Hos. ii. 6).

THOM'AS (*a twin;* Gr. *Dydimus, a twin.* Lydia

THRASE'AS. Father of Appollonius 1 (2 Macc. iii. 5).

THRESH'OLD (Heb. MIFTAN, SAF). A door-sill, a piece of timber or stone under a door or entrance (Judg. xix. 27).

TIBERIAS.

was his twin-sister). A native of Galilee. It has been suggested that he was a twin-brother of Jesus, but there is no proof that he was any relation to him. He was slow to believe, weighing the difficulties of the case, of a desponding heart, but ardently attached to his Master. He was ready to go with Jesus into any danger, but was incredulous about the unknown future; and after the resurrection, he would and he could only believe after he had seen and felt the very wounds made by the nails and the spear. He was one of the seven apostles who saw Jesus at the Sea of Galilee, and met with the others in the "upper room" after the ascension. Tradition says he preached in Parthia, was a martyr, and was buried at Edessa. The church in Malabar claims him as its founder, and shows a tomb as his.

THRESH'OLDS, THE. (Heb. ASUPPEY) (Neh. xii. 25). The thresholds of the gates. Heb. ASUPPEY HASH-SHEARIM, the store-chambers of the gates.

THRONE (Heb. CISSE; Gr. *thronos*). Any elevated seat occupied by a person in authority as high-priest (1 Sam. i. 9); judge (Ps. cxxii. 5); or a military chief (Jer. i. 15). The use of a chair in a country where squatting and reclining were the usual postures was regarded as a symbol of dignity (2 K. iv. 10). Solomon's throne was approached by six steps (1 K. x. 19), and Jehovah's throne was high and lifted up (Is. vi. 1). The materials and workmanship were costly (1 K. x. 18-20). Heaven is called God's throne, and the earth his footstool (Is. lxvi. 1).

THUM'MIN. URIM AND THUMMIM.

THUN'DER (Heb. RAAM, Gr. *bronte*), and LIGHTNING are extremely rare, during the summer, in Palestine; hence it was selected by Samuel as an expression of the divine displeasure toward the Israelites (1 Sam. xii. 17). As a symbol of God's power and majesty, thunder is frequently referred to in Scripture (Ex. xix. 16).

THYATI'RA. See PATMOS, and the SEVEN CHURCHES.

THY'INE-WOOD. An aromatic, evergreen tree, resembling the cedar, and found in Barbary, growing to the hight of 15 to 25 ft. The wood was used in burning incense, and, under the name of citron-wood, was highly prized by the Romans for ornamental wood-work. The rezin, known as sandarach is, the product of this tree (Rev. xviii. 12).

TIBE'RIAS. A city on the W. shore of the Sea of Galilee (John vi. 23). Some have supposed that it was built on the ruins (or near) of an ancient city, Rakkath, or Chinneroth (see *Land and Book*). Josephus says that it was built over an ancient cemetery, and was, therefore, unclean. Jesus never visited Tiberias, and it is scarcely mentioned in the Gospels. It was the capital of Galilee from its origin to the time of Herod Agrippa II. Celebrated schools of learning flourished here for several centuries. The MISHNA was compiled here

THRONE.

THRA'CIA (2 Macc. xii. 35). Thrace anciently included the whole country north of Macedonia and the Black Sea. It is supposed that TIRAS, in Gen. x. 2, means Thrace. It is also supposed that Tiras was the ancestor of the Tyrsi or Tyrseni, the Etruscans of Italy.

RUINS OF THE SYNAGOGUE AT TELL CAPERNAUM.

by Rabbi Judah Hakkodesh, A. D. 190. That most important work, the MASORAH (*traditions*), originated here. By it has been preserved the vowel system and pronunciation of the Hebrew, and therefore the correct reading and understanding of the O. T. The Christians held it during the Crusades, and now it is under Turkish rule. Population about 4,000, ¼th being Jews. The Jews hold that 4 cities are holy, which are, Jerusalem, Hebron, Safed, and Tiberias. An earthquake, in 1837, nearly destroyed the city, and its effects are still seen, in walls tumbled down and houses in heaps.

TIBE'RIUS. The second emperor of Rome, successor of AUGUSTUS, A. D. 14-37. He was the son of Claudius Nero and Livia. He distinguished himself in various wars. At first he was moderate and just, but soon became infamous for his vices and crimes, and died A. D. 37, after a reign of 23 years. He is several times mentioned under the title of Cæsar (Luke xx. 22-25, xxiii. 22; John xix. 12). His subjects were commanded to worship his images. See cut on page 105. PENNY.

TIB'HATH (*slaughter*). A city of Hadarezer, king of Zobah (1 Chr. xviii.) On the eastern skirts of Anti-Lebanon.

TIB'NI (*building of Jah*). An unsuccessful competitor with Omri, the general, for the throne of Israel (1 K. xvi. 18-23).

TI'DAL (*fear*). "A king of nations," under CHEDORLAOMER (Gen. xiv. 1-16).

TIG'LATH-PILE'SER (*lord of the Tigris*). King of Assyria; was invited by Ahaz, king of Judah, to assist him against the kings of Assyria and Israel (2 K. xvi. 7-10). He exacted a heavy tribute, so as to distress him without helping him (2 Chr. xxviii. 20-21). He made captive many of the inhabitants of Israel, and placed them in his kingdom, B. C. 740 (1 Chr. vi. 26), thus fulfilling unconsciously the predictions of Is. vii. 17, viii. 4).

CENCHREA.

TIG'RIS (*arrow*). River of Mesopotamia. Called Hiddekel in Hebrew. Like the Euphrates, it has two sources; the principal one is near the high mountain-lake Golenjik, which lies in the great bend of the Euphrates, in lat. 38° 10', long. 39° 20', and only 2 or 3 ms. from that river. The course is generally S. E. to its junction with the Euphrates at Kurnah, having traversed 1150 ms. 1000 ms.

POTTER.

of its course can be navigated by rafts. The river rises rapidly in March, from the melting snow of the Niphates mountains, and reaches the highest point in May, often flooding the country around Baghdad. Low water occurs again in July. In autumn the flood is much less in hight than in spring. The river has been purposely obstructed by dams at several places by the Persians for the uses of irrigation. The Tigris is mentioned by Daniel (x.) as the Great River, the Hiddekel. It traversed ancient Armenia, Assyria, and separated Babylonia from Susiana. The water is yellowish, runs in a rapid current, and abounds in fish. The banks are fringed with groves of palms, pomegranates, and jungles of reeds, the haunts of wild beasts.

TIK'VAH (*expectation*). 1. Father of Shallum 2 (2 K. xxii. 14).—2. Father of Jahaziah (Ezr. x. 15).

TIK'VATH (*obedience*). Tikvah 1 (2 Chr. xxxiv. 22).

TILE. A broad and thin brick, usually made of fine clay, and hardened in the fire. Such tiles were very common in Euphrates and Tigris (Ez. iv. 1). At Nineveh Layard found a large chamber stored full of inscribed tiles, like a collection of historical archives (Ezr. vi. 1). They are about 1 foot square and 3 inches thick.

TIL'GATH-PILNE'SER. Tiglath-pileser (1 Chr. v. 6, 26).

TI'LON (*gift*). Son of Shimon (1 Chr. iv. 20).

TIM'BREL, TAB'RET. (Heb. TOF, Gen. xxxi. 27); TOFETH (Job xvii. 6). See MUSICAL INSTRUMENTS, and cut on page 106.

TIME. Beside the ordinary uses of this word, the Bible sometimes employs it to denote a year, as in Dan. iv. 16, or a prophetic year, consisting of 360 natural years, a day being taken for a year. Thus in Dan. vii. 25, xii. 7, the phrase "a time, times, and the dividing of a time," is supposed to mean 3½ prophetic years, or 1,260 natural years. This period is elsewhere paralleled by the expression "forty-two months," each month including 30 years (Rev. xi. 2, xii. 6, 14, xiii. 5).

TIME'US (*unclean*). Father of the blind Bartimeus (Mark x. 46).

TIM'NA (*one withheld*). 1. Second wife of Eliphaz, son of Esau (Gen. xxxvi. 12).—2. Son of Eliphaz (1 Chr. i. 36), a duke of Edom in the last list (1 Chr. i. 51).

TIM'NAH (*divide*). 1. In the north of Judah (Josh. xv. 10), near Bethshemesh. It may be identical with Timnatha of Samson, a city of Dan (xix. 43). There is a modern village called Tibneh 2 ms. W. of Ain Shems (Bethshemesh), which is believed to be on the site of the ancient city.—2. In the mountain district of Judah (Josh. xv. 57), south of Hebron.

TIM'NATH. TIMNAH. 1. (Gen. xxxviii. 12). Where Judah kept his flocks.—2. The residence of Samson's wife (Judg. xiv. 1, 2, 5). In Philistia. There were vineyards; but as a lion was found in one, the place must have been thinly inhabited.

BLESSING.

TIM'NATH-HERES. The city and burial-place of Joshua (Judg. ii. 9). Also called *Timnath-serah* (Josh. xix. 50). In Mt. Ephraim, on the north side of Mt. Gaash. The site is lost, and with it the tombs of Joshua and Caleb. Dr. Eli Smith offered the ruins of a place 15 to 20 ms. N. W. from Jerusalem as the site in question, where there are, in a higher hill opposite, sepulchres hewn out of the rock, equal in size and decoration to the tombs of the kings at Jerusalem.

TI'MON (*honorable*). One of the seven deacons (Acts vi. 1-6).

TIMO'THEUS (*honoring God*). 1. A captain of the Ammonites, who was defeated by Judas Maccabæus, B. C. 164 (1 Macc. v. 6, 11, 34-44).—2. A leader in the invasion of Nicanor, B. C. 166 (2 Macc. viii. 30); killed at Gazara (x. 24-27).—3. The latin for Timothy (Acts xvi. 1).

TIM'OTHY. Is first mentioned in Acts xvi. 1, where he is described as the son of a Greek, by a Jewish mother. The father's name is unknown; his mother's was Eunice, and his grandmother's Lois (2 Tim. i. 5). The family resided either at Derbe or Lystra, which is uncertain (Acts xvi. 2). He became a disciple of Paul during his first visit to Lystra, A. D. 48, and was his friend and companion in his journeys, and shared for a time his imprisonment at Rome (Heb. xiii. 23), and left by him at Ephesus to continue his work (1 Tim. i. 3, iii. 14). He possessed the confidence and affection of Paul (Acts xvi. 1, xvii. 14).

TIMOTHY, FIRST EPISTLE TO. See HISTORY OF THE BOOKS.

TIN (Heb. BEDIL). A well-known white metal, easily melted, and very malleable. It was used at an early period (Num. xxxi. 22), and brought by the Tyrians from Tarshish (Zech. xxvii. 12). It was used for plummets (Zech. iv. 10), and it was known to the Hebrew metal-workers as one of the inferior metals. Tin is not found in Palestine. There can be little doubt that the mines of Britain were the chief source of supply to the ancient world.

TIPH'SAH (*ford*), (1 K. iv. 24). The outpost, toward the Euphrates, of Solomon's kingdom (2 K. xv. 16). Probably Thapsacus of the Greeks and Romans, and situated in Northern Syria, where the route eastward crossed the Euphrates. It was a great and important town in the time of Xenophon. A ford and a bridge supplied passage for caravans and armies. At the modern town of Suriyeh, on the Euphrates, there are paved causeways, visible on both sides of the river, which are the remains of the approaches to the ancient bridge; and a long line of mounds, arranged like those of Nineveh, in the form of a parallelogram.

TI'RAS (*longing*). The seventh son of Japheth. Tyrrhenians (?), in Italy.

TIRATH'ITES, THE (*people of Tira*) [*gate*]. One of the 3 families of Scribes residing at Jabez (1 Chr. ii. 55).

TIRE (PEER). An ornamental HEAD-DRESS, worn on festive occasions (Ez. xxiv. 17, 23).

TIR'HAKAH (*exalted*). King of ETHIOPIA, or Cush, and of Egypt, and the opponent of SENNACHERIB (2 K. xix. 9). He was a powerful monarch, ruling both Upper and Lower Egypt, and extending his conquests far into Asia.

TIR'HANAH (*inclination*). Son of Caleb 1 (1 Chr. ii. 48).

TIR'IA (*fear*). Son of Jehaleleel (1 Chr. iv. 16).

TIRSHA'THA (*stern*). It is added as a title after the name NEHEMIAH (Neh. viii. 9, x. 1), and usually rendered governor.

TIR'ZAH (*delight*). Youngest daughter of ZELOPHEHAD (Num. xxvi. 33).

TIR'ZAH. City of Canaan (Josh. xii. 24). After the separation of Israel and Judah it was the residence of Jeroboam (1 K. xiv. 17), and of his successors, Baasha, Elah and Zimri. The royal sepulchres (xvi. 6) of the first four kings of Israel were here. Omri destroyed Zimri in his palace by fire, and soon afterward removed the capital to Samaria (Shomron). Its beautiful situation is mentioned in Canticles (vi. 4) as equal to that of Jerusalem. There is a modern village called Teliuzah, 4 or 5 mls. N. of Shechem, on a high hill, large and thriving, but without antiquities, which is supposed to be on the site of Tirzah.

TISH'BITE, THE (Heb. TISHBI). See THISBE.

TI'TANS (*avengers*). "The sons of Titans" stands parallel with giants.

TITHE (Heb. MA'ASER; Gr. *dekate, a tenth*). The proportion of a man's income devoted to sacred purposes (Gen. xiv. 20, xxviii. 22) prescribed by the Mosaic Law (Num. xxxi. 31). A twofold tithe was required of each Jewish citizen. The first consisted of one-tenth of the produce of his fields, trees, and herds, to be given to God (Lev. xxvii. 30-32). The Levites paid a tenth part of what they received to the priests (Num. xviii. 26-28). The second tithe required of each landholder one-tenth of the nine parts of his produce remaining after the first tithe, to be used at the Temple in entertaining the Levites (Deut. xii. 17-19, 22-29). Every third year a special provision was made for the poor, either out of this second

WINDOW ON THE WALL.

tithe or in addition to it (Deut. xiv. 28, 29). The system of tithes was renewed both before and after the Captivity (2 Chr. xxxi. 5, 6, 12); but they were not always regularly paid, and then the Divine blessing was withheld (Mal. iii. 8-12).

TI'TUS (Gr. *Titus*). A Christian teacher of Greek origin (Gal. ii. 3), the companion of Paul, who converted him (Tit. i. 4; 2 Cor. viii. 23). He was one of those sent upon a mission to Jerusalem from the Church of Antioch (Acts v. 2; Gal. ii. 1). He was thence sent to Corinth, where he labored successfully (2 Cor. viii. 6; xii. 18). In his mission to collect for the poor of Judæa, he conveyed the Second Epistle of Paul to the Corinthians (2 Cor. viii. 16, 17, 23). Eight or ten years later he was at Crete, superintending the churches of the island (Tit. i. 5); he here received the epistle inscribed to him by Paul, then at Ephesus (Tit. iii. 12). This epistle is supposed to have been written A. D. 65.

TOBI'JAH. 1. A Levite, sent to teach the Law in Judah (2 Chr. xvii. 8).—2. One who returned from Captivity (Zech. vi. 10, 14).

TO'BIT (*my goodness*). Father of Tobias 1 (Tob. i. 1).

TO'BIT. See HISTORY OF THE BOOKS.

TO'CHEN. In Simeon (1 Chr. iv. 32).

TOGAR'MAH. A part of Armenia, named after Togarmah, a brother of Ashkenaz and son of Gomer (Gen. x. 3).

TO'HA. Ancestor of Samuel the prophet (1 Sam. i. 1).

TO'I (*error*). King of Hamath, in Syria, sent his son to rejoice with David (2 Sam. viii. 9-11.

TO'LA (*a worm*). 1. Eldest son of Issachar (Gen. xlvi. 13).—2. Judge of Israel after Abimelech (Judg. x. 1, 2); son of Puah, the son of Dodo.

TO'LAD. Simeon (1 Chr. iv. 29). EL-TOLAD.

THE ANCIENT TOWER AT TIBERIAS.

Paul therein desires him to meet him at Nicopolis. It is supposed that Titus accompanied Paul on his last journey to Rome. He is alluded to in 2 Tim. iv. 10, as being in Dalmatia. See cut on page 71.

TI'ZITE (Heb. TITSI). One from TAVITS (*extension*). One of David's heroes (1 Chr. xi. 45).

TO'AH (*inclined*). A Levite; ancestor of Samuel and Heman (1 Chr. vi. 34).

TOB, THE LAND OF (*good*). Jephthah's refuge (Judg. xi. 3), and residence, until invited to return by the sheikhs of Gilead (v. 5). Tob was somewhere in the Hauran, but is not identified.

TOB'ADONI'JAH (*God is my Lord Jah*). A Levite sent to teach the Law to the people of Judah (2 Chr. xvii. 8).

TOBI'AH (*pleasing to Jah*). 1. The children of Tobiah were a family who returned from Captivity, but were unable to prove their connection with Israel (Ezr. ii. 60).—2. A servant who took part in the opposition of SANBALLAT (Neh. ii. 10, 19) to the rebuilding the Temple.

TOBI'AS. 1. Son of TOBIT.—2. Ancestor of Hyrcanus, who was a man of great wealth (2 Macc. iii. 11).

TO'BIE. The seat of a colony of Jews (1 Macc. v. 13). The same as Tob.

TOBI'EL (*goodness of God*). Father of Tobit, and grandfather of Tobias 1 (Tob. i. 1).

TO'LAITES, THE. Descendants of Tola, son of Issachar (Num. xxvi. 26).

TOL'BANES. TELEM, a porter in Ezra's time (1 Esd. ix. 25).

TONGS (Heb. MELKAHAYIM, MAAZAD). Tongs with which burning coals and stones were handled (Is. vi. 6).

TONGUE (Heb. LASHON; Gr. *glossa dialektos, dialect* or *speech*). Literally the organ in the mouth, used by animals for tasting, licking, etc.; and by mankind for articulation (Ex. xi. 7); also language, nation or people, having their own language (Josh. vii. 21).

TOMB. The most extensive tombs were arranged as in the plan, cut in the solid rock (see pages 208, 213), and had many little places for the bodies, which were laid in the *loculi* (*places*) in their dress, with the ordinary costume of the living, or graveclothes, as in some cases. See cut of TOMB, p. 122. The *loculus* (*one place*) was closed up by a stone, or several small stones, cemented into place; and the entrance to the tomb was securely closed by a heavy stone door, or by a roller (round like a millstone, without the center hole), and a door also.

Eleven of the kings of Judah were buried in the Sepulchre of the Kings, in the City of David (City of the King), of two of whom only is there any special record (2 Chr. xvi. 14, xxxii. 33). Two other kings of the line were buried in the City of

David, but not in the Sepulchre of the Kings (xxi. 20, xxiv. 25); and one king (Uzziah), was buried in the field because he was a leper (xxvi. 23).

The Sepulchres of the Kings were probably on Zion, but have not yet been discovered, although some think they must have been near the Temple on Mt. Moriah (which is also supposed to have been the ancient Zion). The Mohammedans refuse to allow any explorations there at present. Ahaz was buried in Jerusalem, and not in the Sepulchre of the Kings.

ORIENTAL WOMEN.

There is not one tomb which can be traced beyond the Roman era. The so-called Tomb of Zechariah, in Kidron, is not a tomb, being cut in the solid rock, and only one side finished. There is no chamber or opening of any kind. The so-called Tomb of Absalom is also solid, and not a tomb. The Zechariah is 18 ft. 6 inches square, by 20 high; and the Absalom is 21 ft. square, by 24 high to the cornice, above which is a structure of stones cemented, and in the form of a bell or trumpet-shaped dome, making the whole 60 feet high. There is a chamber inside, with two very narrow loculi. Just behind this is an excavation, called the Tomb of Jehoshaphat, the plan of which is not known.

The most remarkable tomb is that of the "Judges," which has nearly 60 loculi, in double rows, the upper having a shelf or ledge in front. The "Tombs of the Kings," so called, north of Jerusalem (see map JERUSALEM and ZION). This tomb is also called Herod's, and in it, a few years ago, there was discovered two sarcophagi, in the Roman style.

TONGUES, CONFUSION OF. The Jewish historians, who wrote the original records in Genesis, evidently intended to teach, in their two distinct accounts of the origin of the families of man, in which all are derived from a single family on the two occasions, Adam's and Noah's, that there was but one original pair, who were the first parents of the races of men, and also, that there was, originally, but one language, and that the Hebrew, or Aramaic, and that the great diversity of tongues was produced miraculously, at the building of the Tower of Babel, when the races were also distinctly separated from each other in color and feature. This appears to be the Scriptural view of the question; but it is received, now, with extreme caution by scholars. The whole question of the origin of language is beyond the possibility of proof, as to its history; and therefore theories about the origin of the substance of language cannot be sustained by historic facts. The Greeks held that reason was inward speech, and speech outward reason, and [both] independent of sound. The labors of scholars, during the present century, have resulted in a wonderful amount of interesting knowledge concerning the different languages of the world; arranging a large part of them into groups, or families, and showing, by a careful analysis, the affinities of many languages before this supposed to have nothing in common, as, Greek and Celtic, English and Sanscrit. The chain of historical evidence necessary to show any close connection between the great families of languages does not, at present, appear to be in existence. The original unity cannot be proved, and can only be supposed. Those who hold to a direct creation of distinct species of animals, trees, etc., see the same evidences of an original pair for each race of men, etc. It is asserted that there are certain "root-words," in all languages, from which the entire vocabulary is derived, by expansion or addition, and which are always of one syllable, of two or more letters (that is, a vowel-sound before or after, or between, two consonants). From these "roots" the languages are all formed in three modes: 1. By isolation. 2. By agglutination. 3. By inflection.

In the first group there is no such thing as grammar—that is, there is no difference between a noun (name) and a verb (a name and an action), and there are no adjectives, prepositions or pronouns. In the other two groups there are two kinds of "roots," one of which forms names, verbs, adjectives, and the other conjunctions, prepositions and particles. The terminations of names, verbs and adjectives are supplied by both kinds. An example is seen in the preposition of, which is traced to the German ab, the Greek apo, and the Sanscrit apa, the base of which was a.

The one-syllable form is not the only characteristic of the root of the Shemitic languages; there are many two-syllable forms also, if these are not single syllables joined by a consonant. Single syllables are found with two, three, and even four consonants. It is held by some scholars that the purely one-syllable languages have never advanced beyond their primitive condition. The answer to this is that these languages have developed in a way peculiar to themselves.

The most apparent differences between the two kinds of languages are, that the agglutinating kind preserves the original root unchanged, although combined, while the inflectional join the roots, so

as to lose the identity of the original roots. But it seems necessary that in all languages there should have been combination of roots—joining two or more simple words to make a more complete one—and also an isolation, when such compound words became familiar and useful, and were adopted for certain ideas or their uses, and so became stock words, of which every language has a number.

The ancient languages in America and Africa are distinct and peculiar, and can not be described in common with any in Asia or Europe. Their derivation is unknown, and there has not yet been traced any connection in root, structure or history with any other family.

An interesting inscription has been lately discovered in the East, which is interpreted by Dr. Oppert, in which it appears that the ancient Babylonians had a tradition of the confusion of tongues, preserved in the name Borsippa or Borsif, which means confusion in Chaldee. Borsippa is therefore Tongue-Tower, and was what is now called *Birs Nimroud* (see BABEL). Herodotus described the tower as dedicated to Jupiter Belus. The original name of the tower was BIT-ZI-DA, *spirit-house* (the same as *Sarukh, tower, temple*). Nebuchadnezzar named it the Seven Lights of the Earth (7 planets). In the inscription there is the sentence, "Since the remote time people avoided the tower—cause unknown."

TONGUES, GIFT OF. The gift of tongues was the special work of the Holy Spirit on the Day of Pentecost; and the power was used as soon as received. "They were all filled with the Holy Ghost, and began to speak with other tongues as the spirit gave them utterance." At that time there were Jews from many nations in Jerusalem, speaking foreign tongues, and they heard and understood, every one in his native language. This power fulfilled the promise implied in the command "Go and teach all nations." It gave the teachers of the new religion access to the heart, while the priest of the old dispensation addressed the eye. Judaism had been local; Christianity was to "go" into all the world. Those who used the gift of tongues were also made to understand them; for if not, then he could not have increased his own knowledge nor faith nor those of others. This gift was only for a short time. Even Paul did not long enjoy its benefits. It appears from the record that the gift on the Day of Pentecost fell on all alike, Apostles and hearers, men and women.

TOOTH (Heb. SHEN, Gr. *odous*), used mostly in respect to men and animals (Gen. xlix. 12). "Cleanness of teeth" indicates hunger and famine (Amos iv. 6); "gnashing of teeth" violent rage, anguish, or desperation (Ps. xxxv. 16); "tooth for tooth" was an instance of compensation (Ex. xxi. 24).

TO'PARCHY (Gr. *toparchia*). A district governed by a toparch, or governor (1 Macc. xi. 28).

TO'PAZ. See PRECIOUS STONES.

TO'PHEL. At the S. E. corner of the Dead Sea, now called Tufileh. It is in a most fertile valley, having many springs and rivulets flowing into the Ghor, and large plantations of fruit-trees. Figs are exported. Partridges (katta) are found in great numbers, and deer (steinbock) in herds of 40 or 50 together.

TO'PHETH (*tabret-grove*). S. E. of Jerusalem, in the Valley of Hinnom (Jer. vii. 31, xix. 2). A music-grove of the king; a part of the royal gardens. After the sacrifices to the idol Moloch, it became a place of abomination (vii. 32).

POOL OF SILOAM.

TOR'MAH (Heb. BETORMAH); "privily" Judg. ix. 31).

TORMENT'OR (Gr. *basanistes, a torturer, or prison-keeper*. Among the ancient Romans, a creditor might use certain legal tortures, as, a heavy chain, or of half-starvation, to extort from the debtor a confession of any concealed treasures (Matt. xviii. 34).

TOR'TOISE (Heb. ZAB). Various fresh-water tortoises, land-tortoises, and sea-tortoises, are found in Palestine and its neighborhood (Lev. xi. 29).

TO'U (TOI), (1 Chr. xviii. 9, 10).

TOW. 1. Heb. NE'ORETH; tow as shaken off from flax (Judg. xvi. 9.—2. PISHTAH, *a wick*, made of linen (Is. xliii. 17).

TOW'ER (Heb. MIGDAL, Gr. *purgos*). Towers were erected not only in the outer walls, and on the hights, within cities (Judg. ix. 47-49), but along the frontiers (Judg. ix. 17). A tower afforded refuge to the people in case of invasion (Prov. xviii. 10). They were built in vineyards for the watchmen, and on the hights, or along the side-hill, at convenient distances, so that the watchmen could see from one to another, and give signals of the approach of any danger, as of an enemy, or of wolves, bears, or other animals, destructive of the crops. Many of these are now in use all over the country. Some of them were very noted as Edar, Antonia, Migdol, Ophel, etc. The tower was a figure of God (Ps. lxi. 3), and of proud and powerful men (Is. ii. 15, xxx. 25).

TOWN. 1. Heb. BATH, *daughter;* in specifying small, dependent "towns" and "villages" (Josh. xv. 45, 47).—2. HAVVOTH, *villages,* properly places of *living* or dwelling (Josh. xiii. 30.—3. Heb. HAZER (Gen. xxv. 16), "court" or "village".—4. Heb. IR (Deut. iii. 5) translated "city" more than 1,000

times.—5. Heb. KIR, "wall" Josh. ii. 15).—6. PE-RAZOTH, *country regions, open country*, unwalled towns (Zech. ii. 4).—7. Gr. *kome*, a hamlet, country towns, without walls.—8. Gr. *komopolis*, a large village, without walls (Mark i. 38).

TOWN'-CLERK (Gr. *grammateus, a scribe, secretary—clerk*). The title of the magistrate at Ephesus who appeased the mob (Acts xix. 35), in the theater-tumult excited by Demetrius.

SANHEDRIN.

TRACHONI'TIS (*heap of stones*), (Luke iii. 1). The region also called ARGOB, GESHUR, and now EL-LEJAH, and is S. of Damascus, consisting of a plain and the W. slope of Jebel Hauran. On the N. border of this region are the extensive ruins of Mismiyeh, where there is an inscription on the door of a once beautiful temple, which contains the name of the ancient city, PHOCUS. On the E. are the ruins of Saccæa and Kenath, on the slope of Hauran. Josephus describes the inhabitants as having neither towns nor fields—dwelling in caves, and having cisterns of water and granaries; and the ground as almost a plain, covered with rugged rocks. See ARGOB, and GESHUR.

TRADI'TION (Gr. *paradosis, a precept, ordinance, instruction*). Applied, particularly, to the Oral Law of the Jews, or their doctrines, handed down from age to age (Matt. xv. 2, 3, 6). The Jews pay great regard to *tradition* in matters of religion, as do the Roman Catholics. Protestants reject the authority of *tradition* in sacred things, and rely, only, on the written word. *Traditions* may be good or bad—true or false (2 Thess. ii).

TRANCE (Heb. LOPAL, *falling*; Gr. *ekstasis*; Lat. *excessus*). The state in which a person has passed out of the usual order of its life, beyond the usual limits of consciousness and volition. The condition of seeming death. Loss of conscious perception. In medical terms, one form of catalepsy. A state in which there is a sudden suspension of thought, of sensibility, and of voluntary motion; or rather lost to all outward impressions, and absorbed in the imagination; sometimes the result of religious impressions. Some persons can throw themselves into the state of religious trance at will (ecstasy of adoration). Mohammed was of this nature, and in that condition he made his (visionary) journey to heaven. Balaam sees the vision of God, *falling*, but with opened eyes (Num. xxiv. 4). Saul also prophesied and fell down (1 Sam. xix. 24).

Jeremiah was described as one that is mad and maketh himself a prophet (Jer. xxix. 26). Ezekiel sits motionless for seven days in stupor (Ez. iii. 15). He also sees the visions of God, lifted up between the earth and the heaven (viii. 3). Peter saw in a trance the vision of tolerance (Acts x. xi.). Paul received in a trance the command to preach to the Gentiles (Acts xxii. 17-21). In another he heard unspeakable words (2 Cor. xii. 1-4). The prophets received their messages from God in visions, trances, and dreams (Num. xxiv. 2-16; Joel ii. 28; Acts x. 11; Rev. i. 10-20).

The prophet is also called a SEER (Num. xii. 6; Lam. ii. 9); and received the word of the Lord (1 Sam. iii. 21). The spiritual man (Hos. ix. 7), is another term. The name prophet (NABI) means *inspired person*, one whom God has qualified to impart consolation, light, and strength to others; a declarer and interpreter of the divine will respecting the past, the present, and the future. There are two elements in prophesy; the predicative and the moral. The moral or spiritual is always highest, although inseparable from the spoken word. Prophesy is the opposite of the miracle—miracles being evidences, signs, and prophesies being the word for edifying the church, comforting believers, and a sign to unbelievers, drawing their attention to Christ (1 Cor. xiv. 22). Miracles are addressed to unbelievers; prophesies to believers.

Three elements were essential: 1. Personal and direct communication from heaven. 2. The word to be consistent with the use of a supernatural agency. 3. And be delivered faithfully.

The Bible is a book of facts, and prophesy is based on history.

The *present* was (and is) the germ of the future, and a prophetic thread runs through the whole length of the history of the chosen people.

The theme entire was enunciated, at first, by Adam, Noah, Abraham and Moses; and was expanded as the world's history demanded. The first promise in the Garden of Eden contains, as in a seed, the whole of revelation and prophesy; and the growth of Christ's kingdom in the earth will restore the earth to the original state of Eden. All truly religious teaching is prophetical, as it always has been.

The line of prophets from Samuel to Malachi were the divinely accredited teachers of the Jewish people, and were supernaturally endowed with spiritual knowledge and genuine foresight to train them for the development of the future divine kingdom, and their succession during a period of 4000 years (Adam to Jesus), with their continual flow of divinations, perfect harmony of character, oneness of object, and sanctity of motive, is a greater mystery and miracle than any of their predictions. They were the witnesses for a divine kingdom among men, the commentators on its history, the exponents of its laws, and the heralds of its triumphs; directing the minds of the people to the person, the work, and the character of the King.

The Epistle to the Hebrews sets forth the doctrine that in person Jesus was joined to God in a mysterious union, and there are many references to the Old Testament in the New Testament throughout, touching on this theme, as in Malachi (iii. 1), quoted by Luke (vii. 27), where Jesus, in an allusion to himself, purposely changed the expression to avoid giving offense to the Jews; and also Psalms ex., alluded to in Matt. xxii. 42, 43, where his hearers distinctly understood him as making himself David's Son and Lord, in a spiritual sense, which was the same as God; and when he refers to the prophesy of Zechariah (xiii. 7), predicting his crucifixion (Matt. xxvi. 31).

The work of the Messiah was the foundation of his spiritual kingdom, the corner stone of the Church, as prophesied from the first, and especially promised to Abraham.

The prophesies prepared the minds of the Jews for the extinction of the national life at the appearance of the Messiah. The nation died that its spiritual life might be resurrected in the Gospel; a type of the experience of every disciple, prefiguring his entry upon a bright future when called away from this life. The polity and priesthood had served their end when it merged into the Church of Christ. In the new Church there is no local temple, no visible altar, no material offering, no sacrificing priesthood. It is a new earth and a new heaven. The whole world has now become a people of priests, where every soul may worship God in spirit and in truth (Ex. xix. 6).

TRANSFIGURA'TION. This event occurred in that period of the life of Christ between the temptation in the wilderness and the agony in Gethsemane. The incident is described in Matt. xvii. 1–9. It is supposed to have taken place on Mount Hermon, the highest of the Anti-Lebanon mountains. At the transfiguration Moses and Elijah appeared, representing the law and prophesy. The Apostles, Peter, James, and John, were the only witnesses (1 Pet. i. 16; John i. 14).

TREAS'URE (Heb. OZAR, HOZEN, MATMON; Chal. *ginzin*; Gr. *thesauros*), (Acts. viii. 27). Whatever is laid up in store—as provisions, gold, silver, etc. (Gen. xliii. 23).

TREASURE-CITIES (Ex. i. 11). Store-cities; that is, cities where were magazines or depôts of provision (Ezr. v. 17).

TREAS'URER (Heb. GIZBAR; Chal. *gedaberin*). One who has charge of royal treasures or a TREASURY (Ezr. i. 8).

TREAS'URY. 1. Heb. OZAR, *what is laid up;* a store or stock of produce or goods (Josh. vi. 19, 24).—2. Heb. GENAZIM, *treasure-chests* (Esth. iii. 9). —3. Heb. GANZACH, the *treasury* of the Temple (1 Chr. xxviii. 11), which, according to Rabbins, was in chests (called *trumpets*), into which the Jews cast their offerings (Matt. xii. 41). Kings used to store their possessions, and guard what they most valued (Ex. i. 11).

TREES. Were frequently used as types of kings or men of wealth and power (Ps. xxxvii. 35; Dan. iv. x.). The "tree of knowledge of good and evil" (Gen. ii. 9, 17). The "tree of life," a seal of eternal holiness and bliss if man had not sinned (Rev. xxii. 2). The principal trees mentioned in Scripture are algum, or almug (1 K. v. 6; 2 Chr. ii. 8, ix. 10, 11; Rev. xviii. 12); Almond (Gen. xliii. 11; Ex. xxv. 33, 34, xxxvii. 19, 20; Num. xvii. 8; Eccles. xii. 5; Jer. i. 11); aloes (Ps. xlv. 8; Prov. vii. 17; Cant. iv. 14; John xix. 39); apple (Deut. xxxii. 10; Prov. xxv. 11; Cant. ii. 3, 5; Joel i. 12; Zech. ii. 8); bay (Ps. i. 3, xxxvii. 35; Dan. iv. 4); box (Is. xli. 19; lx. 13; 2 Esd. xiv. 24); cedar (Lev. xiv. 4, 6, 49, 51, 52; and about 60 other passages in the O. T., besides many in which it is called the glory of Lebanon); chestnut (Gen. xxx. 37; Ez.

SCRIBES.

xxxi. 8); fig (Gen. iii. 7; and in many passages all through the Bible): fir (2 Sam. vi. 5; and 20 other places in the O. T.); holm (Sus. ver. 58); juniper (1 K. xix. 4, 5; Job. xxx. 4; Ps. cxx. 4, 5); mastich (Sus. ver. 54); mulberry (2 Sam. v. 23, 24; 1 Chr. 14; 1 Macc. vi. 34; Luke xvii. 6); myrtle (Neh. viii. 15; Is. xli. 19, lv. 13; Zech. i. 8, 10, 11); oak (Gen. xxxv. 4, 8; and many times in the O. T. Several times the original word for oak (ELON, etc.) is rendered *plain); oleaster,* wild olive (Rom. xi. 17, 24); olive (Gen. viii. 11, and all through the Bible, in nearly every book); palm (Ex. xv. 27, and in nearly every book also); pine (Neh. viii. 15; Is. xli. 19, lx. 13); pomegranate (Ex. xxviii. 33, 34, xxxix., and nearly every other book of the O. T.); shittah-tree, acacia (Ex. xxv. 10, 23, and many other passages in Num., Deut., Is., and Micah); sycamine (Luke xvii. 6); sycamore (1 K. x. 27, and several others); willow (Lev. xxiii. 40; Job xl. 22; Ps. cxxxvii. 2; Is. xv. 7, xliv. 4; Ez. xvii. 5).

TRIAL. See JESUS CHRIST, PROCURATOR, SANHEDRIN, etc. The trial of Jesus Christ before Pilate was for an offense punishable by Roman law with death (Luke xxiii. 2, 28; John xix. 12, 15). Paul and Stephen were tried before the high-priest and Jewish rulers (Acts v. 27, vi. 12, etc.); the *decemviri* ("magistrates," A. V.). The trials of Paul at Cæsarea were conducted under Roman law. In that one held before Felix, the plaintiffs employed an advocate. In the second trial Paul appealed to Cæsar, as a Roman citizen, and the procurator conferred with the council or assessor who sat on the judicial bench (Acts xxv. 12). A judicial court held sessions in Ephesus (Acts xix. 38).

TRIBE (Heb. MATTEH, SHEBEH, Gr. *phule*). A race, people, or nation (Ps. lxxiv. 2). Usually a division, or branch of a people, especially one of the great divisions of the Israelites (Ex. xxxi. 2, 6). The 12 tribes continued united as one state, one people, till after the death of Solomon, when they revolted. See TWELVE TRIBES.

TRIB'UTE (Heb. MECHES, MAS). See TAXES.

TRI'POLIS. Possibly the ancient KADYTIS. On the coast N. of (Beirut), Sidon, and Tyre. The river that runs from Lebanon through the city is called Kadisha. Demetrius Soter landed here (B. C. 161), and made it his head-quarters while conquering Syria (2 Macc. xiv. 1). Pop. 16,000.

TROAS.

TRO'AS. Alexander Troas, in Asia Minor (Mysia), opposite the island of Tenedos. It was one of the most important towns in Asia. Paul made two voyages from here to Macedonia. (See LIFE OF PAUL.) It was connected, by good roads, with cities on the coast and in the interior. Constantine had, before he gave a just preference to the situation of Byzantium, conceived the design of erecting the seat of empire on this celebrated spot, from which the Romans derived their fabulous origin.

TROGYL'LIUM. Samos is exactly opposite this point of land, which lies at the boundary between Ionia and Caria. The channel is narrow (about 1 m.), and the current rapid, southward. E. of the point there is now an anchorage, called St. Paul's Port. (Acts xx. 15). In this bay there was a great naval battle between the Greeks and Persians, B. C. 479.

TROOP (Heb. GEDUD). Is used, mostly, of light-armed troops engaged in plundering (Gen. xlix. 19). "Company," "band" (2 K. v. 2); "band of the rovers" (Hos. vi. 9).

TROPH'IMUS (*nourished*). A disciple of Paul, a Gentile, and an Ephesian by birth. He accompanied him in his journey to Jerusalem, A. D. 58 (Acts xx. 4). Paul left him sick at Miletus (2 Tim. iv. 20). He was the innocent cause of the tumult in which Paul was apprehended (Acts xxi. 27-29).

TRUM'PET. See MUSICAL INSTRUMENTS.

TRUM'PETS, FEAST OF (Num. xxix. 1). (See FESTIVALS).

TRYPHE'NA (*delicious*) and **TRYPHO'SA** (*living delicately*). Two women at Rome, saluted by Paul (Rom. xvi. 12); they were very useful and benevolent.

TRY'PHON (*reveler, glutton*). A usurper of the Syrian throne. His proper name was DIODOTUS (1 Macc. xiii.).

TUBAL (Heb. *to prepare*). Son of Japheth, who, with his brothers Javan and Meshech, traded in slaves and vessels of brass (Gen. x. 2; 1 Chr. i. 5). See SLAVES; also Ez. xxvii. 13).—2. Fifth son of Japheth. (See MESECH).

TUBAL-CAIN (Persian *tupal, iron;* Arabic *kain-smith*). Worker in metals. "A furbisher of every cutting instrument of copper and iron" (Gen. iv. 22). He was the son of Lamech. See METALS.

TUBIE'NI (Gr. *Toubienoi*). The Jews called Tubieni (2 Macc. xii. 17) those who were living in the towns of *Toubion*.

TUR'BANS (Dan. iii. 21). See HEAD-DRESS.

TUR'PENTINE-TREE (Gr. *tereminthos*). It is numbered among the choicest of trees, common in Palestine and the East. It grows to a large size. From incisions in the trunk a sort of balsam is said to flow, which constitutes a very pure and fragrant species of turpentine.

TUR'TLE-DOVE, or TURTLE (Heb. TOR). A name derived from the note of the bird. See DOVE. The migratory habits of this bird are alluded to in Cant. ii. 11, 12; Jer. viii. 7. It was allowed for a sin-offering by the poor (Lev. i. 14, v. 7; Matt. xxi. 22); also in purification, etc. (Lev. xii. 6-8). Before the giving of the law Abraham offered a turtle and a pigeon (Gen. xv. 9).

TWELVE, THE. The apostles of Jesus Christ, originally twelve in number (Matt. xxvi. 20, 47). See APOSTLE.

TYCH'ICUS (*fortunate*). A fellow-worker of Paul, accompanying him from Corinth to Jerusalem (Acts xx. 4). In Paul's first imprisonment he calls Tychicus "a beloved brother and a faithful minister and fellow-servant of the Lord" (Col. iv. 7, 8). With Onesimus, he was doubtlessly the bearer of the epistles to the Colossians, the Ephesians, and to Philemon.

TYPES (Gr. *tupoi, examples;* pl. of *tapos, type,* "print"), (John xx. 25); "figure" in Rom. iv. 15. Moses was to make the tabernacle according to type he had seen in the mount (Acts vii. 44).

TYRAN'NUS (*a tyrant*). The name of a person at Ephesus in whose school Paul taught the Gospel (Acts xix. 9).

TYRE (*rock*). Ar. *Sur;* Heb. ZOR. On a rocky peninsula which was formerly an island (Ez. xxvii. 25), before the siege of Alexander. There was probably a city on the mainland, opposite the island city; but which was the more ancient is not decided. One of the places was called Palætyrus (Old Tyre). Hercules was worshiped under the name of Melkarth, and the temple in his honor on the island was said by Arrian (ii. 16) to have been the most ancient in the world.

The people were called Sidonians (Judg. xviii. 7; Josh. xiii. 6; Ez. xxxii. 30); Tyre and Sidon

TYRE.

being inhabited by Phœnicians, and only 20 ms. apart (1 K. v. 6). Sidon (son of Canaan) is mentioned in the Pentateuch; Tyre is not (Gen. x. 15); it being mentioned first in Joshua (xix. 29), where it appears as a fortified city.

The Canaanites were not driven out of Tyre and Sidon, and other Phœnician cities (Judg. i. 31), as Moses directed, but the Jews lived among them. Hiram, king of Tyre, sent cedar-wood and workmen to build David a palace (2 Sam. v. 11); and afterward he also sent Hiram the widow's son, a Jew of the tribe of Naphtali, who cast the vessels of bronze for the temple, king Hiram furnishing the metal, besides also the cedar and fir trees; the Jews and Phœnicians working together. The friendship between the Jews and Phœnicians continued for at least a century, when King Ahab married a daughter of King Ethbaal of Sidon.

In the time of Joel (iii. 6–8) the Phœnicians sold Jewish children as slaves to the Greeks, and Joel threatened retaliation.

Carthage was planted as a colony of Tyre, 143 years after the building of Solomon's temple.

There is no record of a war between Jews and Phœnicians; and the reason why peace was so constant is, that Palestine furnished Phœnicia with grain, oil, grapes, and wine, besides cattle and sheep, as is the case now.

There was an altar in honor of Ashtoreth, the Tyrian goddess, "Queen of Heaven," built by Solomon on one of the summits of Olivet as a token of his friendship with Hiram, king of Tyre, which stood for 350 years, when it was destroyed by Josiah, only a few years before Jerusalem was taken by the Assyrians, under Nebuchadnezzar. Tyre was besieged for 13 years (B. C. 715) by the same king soon after, but it has never been settled whether he captured it or not. But Alexander did take the city after a siege of seven months (B. C. 332), when the island was connected to the mainland by a causeway built during the siege.

The dye called Tyrian purple was a source of great wealth. It was extracted from shell-fish found on the coast.

At the time of Christ, Tyre was equal in population to Jerusalem. Cassius, bishop of Tyre, attended the Council of Cæsarea. At the time of the Crusades (A. D. 1124) William was made archbishop, and his account of the city preserves the record of its wealth and strength. Glass and sugar are mentioned as articles of great value in trade. In June, 1291, Tyre was occupied by the Saracens (the Christians having abandoned it the night before), and from that day to this they have held it. It is now only a village of about 3,000 people; its strong walls have entirely disappeared, and the harbor is almost useless. The prophet Ezekiel (xxviii. 2) mentions the pride of Tyre—its boast that it was a god, and sat in the seat of God in the midst of the seas; and also describes its present desolation (xxvi. 3–5). The most complete fulfillment of his prophecies is felt in the silence and desolation of Tyre.

Almost the only relic of Tyre's great sea-wall, lies in the northern end of the island, and is a stone 17 ft. long, 6½ thick, and seems to lie in its original position, where it was placed 3000 yrs. ago. There are columns and floors of marble buried under rubbish or sunk in the sea, all over the site and along the sea border; and thousands of fine pieces of stone, wrought into columns, capitals, and panels, have been carried away to other cities—to Joppa, Acre, and Beirut. On the mainland are the ruins of the ancient Christian cathedral, 290 by 140, massive, and Byzantine in style. Paulinus was its bishop, and Eusebius wrote the consecra-

TYRE FROM THE NORTH.

tion oration, which is still extant, for its opening. The historian, William of Tyre, held a priestly rank here, and the crusaders their last religious service in Palestine. In its dust lie the remains of the emperor Barbarossa, and of Origen, the Bible scholar. See pages 137, 179.

TZAD'DI (Heb. ZADEY, *reaping-hook or scythe*). The 18th letter of the Hebrew alphabet (Ps. cxix.). WRITING.

TZI'DON. ZIDON (Gen. x. 15).

TZOR. TYRE (Josh. xix. 29).

U

U'CAL (Heb. *eaten up, consumed?*) Mentioned with the name of Ithiel in Prov. xxx. 1, who were disciples or sons of Aguz, the son of Takeh. The reference is obscure.

U'EL (Heb. *will of God*). Of the family of Bani; he married a foreign wife during the Captivity (Ezr. x. 34).

UK'NAZ (Heb. KENAZ, *even*), (1 Chr. iv. 15). Probably a word is omitted before kenaz.

ULA'I (Dan. viii. 2, 16). A river near Susa. Called Eulæus by the Greeks and Romans. The river has changed its course since ancient days, and now has two branches—the Kerkha and the Kuran, by which its waters reach the Tigris. The Persian kings drank the water of this river only, when at home or on a journey, believing it to be lighter, and more wholesome and pleasant to the taste, than any other.

U'LAM (Heb. *front*). 1. Descendant of Gilead, the grandson of Manasseh (1 Chr. vii. 17).—2. Descendant of Saul; a Benjamite, and the first-born of Eshek (1 Chr. viii. 39, 40).

UL'LA (Heb. *yoke*). An Asherite chief (1 Chr. vii. 39).

UM'MAH (*gathering*). Asher (Josh. xix. 30). The modern site is called Alma, and is on the high land of the Ladder of Tyre, 5 ms. from the cape Ras en Nakura, in the midst of many ruins as yet without names.

UNCIRCUMCIS'ION. See CIRCUMCISION.

UNCLEAN MEATS. See CLEAN.

UNCLEANNESS. See CLEAN.

UNICORN. (Heb. REEM, REEYM, REYM). The name of some wild animal, not fabulous or one-horned (Deut. xxxiii. 17,) as it may be correctly translated: "His glory is like the firstling of his bullock, and his horns are like the horns of

unicorn" (REEM). The unicorn is now believed to have been the Urus, an extinct species of Buffalo and not the rhinoceros. It is spoken of as a powerful and violent animal (Ps. xxii. 19, 21; Job xxxix. 9-12).

UNLEAVENED BREAD. See LEAVEN. PASSOVER.

UN'NI (Heb. *depressed*). 1. A musician and Levite doorkeeper (porter) in the time of David (1 Chr. xv. 18, 20).—2. A second Levite connected with the sacred office (Neh. xii. 9).

U'PHAZ (Jer. x. 9; Dan. x. 5). See OPHIR.

UR (Gen. xi. 28). The land of Haran, Ur of the Chaldees, from which Terah and Abraham came into the land of Canaan. Four localities are offered as the ancient site of Ur. 1. Now called Oorfah. The Greeks called it Edessa. The chief mosque is named Abraham's, and a pond in which some sacred fish are kept is called the Lake of Abraham the Beloved.—2. The second place is Warka, the Orchon of the Greeks, and Huruk in the Assyrian.—3. A place in eastern Mesopotamia, Ur, below Nineveh, on the Tigris.—4. Mugheir, or Om Mugheir (Mother of Bitumen), on the right bank of the Euphrates, 125 ms. from the sea. The ruins here are extensive and of the most ancient character, containing inscriptions. Once called Camarina. This was for ages the burial-place of the Assyrian kings.

UR. Father of Eliphal. One of David's strong men (1 Chr. xi. 35).

UR'BANE (L. *Urbanus, of the city, refined*). A disciple whom Paul saluted, in Rom. xvi. 9.

U'RI (Heb. *fiery*). 1. One of the tribe of Judah. Father of BEZALEEL 1, architect of the Tabernacle (Ex. xxxi. 2).—2. Father of Geber (1 K. iv. 19).—3. A doorkeeper in Ezra's time (Ezr. x. 24).

URI'AH (*flame of Jehovah*). 1. One of the "worthies" of king David; a captain in his army and a Hittite. He was the husband of Bathsheba, who became the object of David's criminal passion. When Uriah was commanding with the army before Rabbah, David directed Joab to place him in an exposed position in battle, where he was killed (2 Sam. xi. xxiii. 39). See DAVID, BATHSHEBA.—

BAZAAR.

2. A priest at the time of Ahaz, witness of Isaiah's prophesy concerning his son (Is. viii. 2). Probably Urijah (2 K. xvi. 18).—3. A priest of the family of Koz at the time of Ezra (Ezr. viii. 3). In Neh. iii. 4, 21, called Urijah.

URI'AS. 1. Husband of Bathsheba (Matt. i. 6). —2. URIJAH 3 (1 Esd. ix. 43).

U'RIEL (*fire of God*). The father of Michaiah, the mother of Abijah, king of Judah, according to 2. Chr. xiii. 2. Elsewhere the mother of Abijah appears as Maacah, the daughter of Absalom (1 K. xv. 2, 10, 13). Two Kohathites of the name of Uriel appear in 1 Chr. vi. 9, xv. 5-11.

URI'JAH (*flame of Jehovah*). 1. High-priest at the time of Ahaz. Without divine authority he had constructed and also made offerings upon an altar designed by Ahaz (2 K. xvi. 10-12). Notwithstanding the committal of this error, Urijah appears to have been a righteous man, and one of the "faithful witnesses" selected by Isaiah (Is. viii. 2) to attest his prophesy.—2. A prophet, son of Shemaiah; he uttered prophesies against Judea and Jerusalem in the time of Jehoiakim. He was menaced with death by the king, and fled to Egypt, but was delivered up by Pharaoh-Necho to Jehoiakim, who had him executed and dishonorably buried (Jer. xxvi. 20-21).

U'RIM AND THUM'MIM (Heb. *light and perfections*). The twelve precious stones, when in position in the breast-plate of the high-priest, were consulted as an oracle. They were worn when the high-priest entered the Holy of Holies (Ex. xxviii. 30). The ceremony of placing the engraved gems in their proper positions in the breast-plate was very solemn and imposing, for it typified the presence of the twelve tribes before the altar of Jehovah. See PRECIOUS STONES.

U'SURY (Heb. NESEK). Interest for money or property loaned. Usury is forbidden by the laws, although it was permitted for the Israelites to take usury from any one not a Jew. This was used as a means of ruining the Canaanites. After the return of the Jews from Captivity they were ordered by Nehemiah "to leave off usury" (Neh. v. 10, 11), and to restore what had been exacted. Christ denounced all methods of extortion: "Give to every man that asketh of thee; and of him that taketh away thy goods ask them not again." "Love ye your enemies, and do good, and lend, hoping for nothing again" (Luke vi. 30-35; Ps. xv. 5).

U'TA. Ancestor of certain Nethinim (1 Esd. v. 30).

U'THAI (*Jeh succors*). 1. Son of Ammihud (1 Chr. ix. 4).—2. Son of Bigvai, who returned from Captivity (Ezr. viii. 14).

U'THI. UTHAI 2 (1 Esd. viii. 40).

UZ. The land in which Job lived (Job i. 1), and evidently settled by a son of Aram, grandson of Shem (Gen. x. 23). Supposed to have been E. or S. E. of Palestine (Job i. 15, 17), in the vicinity of the Sabeans and the Chaldeans, and of Edom (Lam. iv. 21). The description of the people corresponds to that of the nomade tribes of Arabia Deserta.

U'ZAI (*strong*). Father of Palal, who assisted Nehemiah (Neh. iii. 25).

U'ZAL (*wanderer*), (Gen. x. 27; 1 Chr. i. 21; Ez. xxvii. 19). Javan. The capital city of Yemen,

Arabia; originally called Awzal, and now known as Sana. The city is better built than any other in Arabia, has many palaces, mosques, baths and khans, "resembling Damascus in the abundance of its trees or gardens, and the rippling of its waters."

UZ'ZA, GARDEN OF (2 K. xxi. 18, 26). Where Manasseh and his son Amon, kings of Judah, were buried. Supposed to have been in Jerusalem (2 Chr. xxxiii. 20). Lost.

UZ'ZA (*strength*). 1. A Benjamite of the sons of Ehud (1 Chr. viii. 7).—2. UZZAH (xiii. 7, 9–11). 3. One who returned from Captivity (Ezr. ii. 49). 4. A Levite, son of Shimei (1 Chr. vi. 29).

UZ'ZAH. Son of Abinadab, in whose house the Ark rested for twenty years, and who died while conducting the Ark from Kirjath-jearim (2 Sam. vi.; 1 Chr. xxiii.).

UZ'ZEN SHE'RAH (OZEN, *ears*), (1 Chr. vii. 24). Built by Sherah, a daughter of Ephraim, near the Beth horons. Now Beit Sira in Wady Suleiman, 13 miles N. W. of Jerusalem.

UZ'ZI. 1. Son of Bukki, and father of Zerahiah (1 Chr. vi. 5, 51).—2. Son of Tola (1 Chr. vi. 2, 3).—3. Son of Bela, a chief (vii. 7).—4. Ancestor of the Elah, settled at Jerusalem after the Captivity (ix. 8).—5. Son of Bani, and overseer of the Levites at Jerusalem (Neh. xi. 22).—6. A priest (xii. 19).—7. A priest who assisted Ezra (xii. 42), also No. 6.

UZZI'A, the ASHTERATHITE. One of David's men (1 Chr. xi. 44).

UZZIAH (*might of Jah*). 1. King of Judah; in some passages he is called AZARIAH. He began his reign at 16 yrs. of age, B. C. 806. This name was common among the Jews. He was afflicted with leprosy (2 Chr. xxvi. 16–23).—2. A Levite, ancestor of Samuel (1 Chr. vi. 24).—3. A priest of the sons of Harim (Ezr. x. 21).—4. Father of Athaiah (Neh. xi. 4):—5. Father of Jehonathan, one of David's overseers (1 Chr. xxvii. 25).

UZ'ZIEL (*might of God*). 1. The ancestor of the Uzzielites, the fourth son of Kohath, and one of the three families of the Kohathites (Ex. vi. 18, 22; Num. iii. 27).—2. Son of Ish; he was chief of an expedition against the remnants of the Amelekites left on Mount Seir (1 Sam. xiv. 48, xv. 7), he destroyed them and possessed their country (1 Chr. iv. 42, 43).—3. One of the goldsmiths who assisted in repairing the wall of Jerusalem (Neh. iii. 8).

V

VA'HEB (Heb. *a gift?*) An obscure word, translated "what he did." Only found in Num. xxi. 14. Probably a proper name of some place in Moab, on the Arnon.

VAIL. See DRESS.

VAIL OF THE TABERNACLE. See TEMPLE.

VA-JEZ'A-THA, or VAJ-E-ZA'THA (*white, pure*). One of Haman's ten sons killed in Shushan by the Jews (Esth. ix. 9).

VALE, VALLEY. Five Hebrew words are translated valley, each conveying a separate meaning. 1. BIKAH (*to cleave*), generally a broad, open valley, enclosed by mountains or otherwise. The plain of Shinar is thus named (Gen. xi. 2). Palestine a "land of hills and valleys" (Deut. xi. 11).—2. GAI and GE (*to flow together*). A narrow valley or ravine. "Doves of the valleys" alluding to the rocks bordering the glens in Palestine being the resort of doves (Ez. vii. 16). The word GE itself is used in combination with other words.—3. NAKHAL (*to receive*) signifies a torrent—bed, or a valley dry in summer but with a river or torrent flowing in winter. This word corresponds to the modern Arabic term for valley—*wady*. Used also to signify a brook. "My brethren have dealt deceitfully as a *brook*, as the stream of *brooks* they pass away" (Job vi. 15–17). Also used for *valley* and for *stream*, as in 1 Kings xvii. 3, 4.—4. ERNEH (*to be deep*), a low tract of land, surrounded by hills on high ground; as the wide "*valley* of Jezreel," lying between Gilboa and Moreh (Judg. vi. 35). Except in Josh. xix. 27, where the Hebrew word itself is used as Bath-EMEK, this word is translated valley or vale.—5. SHEPHELAH (*a low plain*). With the exception, in Josh. xi. 16, where "*the valley of the same*" is used without the article denoting it a proper name, the word Shephelah means the plain of Philistia. See PLAIN.

PRISON GATE.

VASH'NI. The eldest child of Samuel (1 Chr. vi. 28).

VASH'TI (*a beauty*). The queen of Persia, divorced by Ahasuerus, her husband, for refusing to appear unvailed before his reveling company (Esth. i.).

VAU (Heb. VAV, *a peg, nail, hook*). The 6th letter of the Hebrew alphabet (Ps. cxix). WRITING.

VER'SIONS, AN'CIENT, OF THE O. AND N. T. See HISTORY OF THE BOOKS.

VES'SEL. See CUP.

VI'AL (Heb. PACH, *a flask, bottle*), (1 Sam. x. 1). Gr. *phiale, a bowl, goblet*, broad and shallow (Rev. v. 8). Heb. MIZRAK, BASIN and BOWL.

VIL'LAGE. See CITY and TOWN.

VINE (Heb. GEFEN, SOREK). "The choicest vine" (Is. v. 2). NAZIR "vine undressed" (Lev. xxv. 5, 11). See VINEYARD.

VINE OF SODOM. "Their vine is the vine of Sodom" (Deut. xxxii. 32). This is generally supposed to allude to the apples of Sodom; but it is improbable, for a vine is distinctly mentioned. Probably it was used figuratively as in Ps. lxxx. 8, 14; Is. v. 2, 7. The enemies of Israel in this relation would be compared to the people of Sodom.

VINEYARDS, PLAIN OF THE (Judg. xi. 33). Beit el Kerm, 10 ms. N. of Kerak, on the ancient Roman road, where there are ruins of a temple.

VINEYARD. The vine, its fruit, the grape, and wine and vinegar produced from it, are frequently mentioned in the Scripture, as is natural from its being a native of the East (supposed to have originated in Marginia, S. of the Caspian Sea). It is

mentioned in the earliest histories of all people, and has always been highly valued. Moses, Homer, and Herodotus wrote about it; and before their day, the Egyptians pictured it, and methods of preparing its products for use, on their monuments. Various preparations from the vine are in use, among which are: The juice of the unripe grape, for acid; in some parts the unripe grapes are dried and powdered, forming a pleasant acid; grapes, both fresh and dried, as raisins; the juice of grapes fresh pressed is valued as a pleasant beverage, called *must*; this juice is also boiled down into bibs (*molasses*), used at the table; wine, alcohol, and vinegar are made by fermentation; cream-tartar is made from the lees; a fragrant oil is pressed from the seeds; the ashes from the twigs and stalk yield carbonate of potash. A fruitful vine is often used as an emblem of the Hebrew nation, and a period of security, repose, peace, and prosperity is figured by every one sitting under his own vine and fig-tree; and the drinking of wine was also used as a symbol of the highest spiritual blessings (Is. lv. 1, 2). In fearful contrast to this is the desolation of the house of Israel, figured by the neglected, trodden-down, wasted vineyard, by Isaiah (v. 1-7); and by the vine brought out of Egypt, by Asaph (Ps. lxxx. 8-16). The first notice of wine in the Scriptures is when Noah planted a vineyard (Gen. ix. 20, 21), and suffered (himself and his posterity) from excess in its use. The next is in the story of Lot (xix.). When Isaac blessed Jacob, he prayed the Lord to give him, among other things, plenty of corn and wine (xxvii. 28). Pharaoh's chief butler made *must* for his king (xl. 11). Moses mentions wine (frequently in his laws, and) as a drink-offering (Num. xv. 5, 7, 10; see, also, Judg. ix. 13); but it was forbidden to the priests during their service in the tabernacle (Lev. x. 9); and it is thought that Nadab and Abihu transgressed because of an excess in its use. During a vow the Nazarite was not to drink wine or vinegar, to eat grapes, or touch any product of the vine: (as carbonate of potash enters into some kinds of bread, he may have been restricted to unleavened bread. Num. vi. 3, 4). The people drank wine at their sacred festivals (Deut. xiv. 22-26). The Rechabites abstained from wine (and from living in houses) in obedience to the command of their ancestor. Wine was used in the ceremony of the Passover. There was a custom of giving medicated wine or vinegar to criminals who were condemned to death, to stupefy them, and thus lessen the pains of execution (Prov. xxi. 6, 7; Amos ii. 8), as in the case of the crucifixion, when the soldiers gave Jesus vinegar mixed with some drug, evidently with kind intentions (Matt. xxvii. 34; Mark xv. 23). Mixed wine is frequently mentioned. It was mixed with water (perhaps only to weaken it for common use, or it may be for deception (Is. v. 22), and with milk (Cant. v. 1), and with spices to increase its strength and flavor (Ps. lxxv. 8; Is. v. 22). The wine of Lebanon was peculiarly fine (Hosea xiv. 7), and had a grateful odor, and the Tyrians imported a famous quality from Helbon (Ezr. xxvii. 8). Wine (and other liquids) are kept in skins (bottles) made of goat-skins, or from the skins of other animals, especially of the ox for the largest, sewed and pitched, and stored, not generally in their houses, but in a wine-store, where it was fermented. Jesus sanctioned the use of wine, and made a supply at a marriage-feast (John ii.), and is charged with being a wine-bibber by his enemies, in contrast to John the Baptist, who abstained from both bread and wine (Luke vii. 33, 34). Paul advises Timothy to use *a little* wine for its expected relief from his "often infirmities" (1 Tim. iv. 23). The warnings against excess in its use as a beverage are frequent and severe in both the O. T. and the N. T. (Prov. xx. 1, xxiii. 29-35, xxxi. 4, 5; 1 Cor. vi. 10; Gal. v. 21). The wine-press was generally in the vineyard (Is. v. 2; Matt. xxi. 33), outside of the cities (Zech. xiv. 10; Rev. xiv. 20), where, in the vintage, they had a merry time treading the grapes (Judg. ix. 27; Is. xvi. 10; Jer. xxv. 30, xlviii. 33; Neh. xiii. 15; Is. lxiii. 2; Joel ii. 24), which custom furnished strong figures to the prophets of the judgments of the Lord upon Israel (Lam. i. 15; Joel iii. 13), and of his mercies and blessings also (Prov. iii. 10). The vineyards are generally planted on hill-sides, which are often terraced to the summit, far from the village, without hedge or fence, requiring constant watching. The strongest young men are set apart for this duty, and take their stand on the hill-tops or on towers; which custom Isaiah makes the subject of one of his finest figures of the prosperity of Zion (lii. 7, 8). The watchmen are stationed near each other (within sight and hearing of each other's voices), and have certain calls to use in case of danger, or in "publishing" peace and safety, now as in the olden time (*Land and Book*, ii. 412).

PETER IN PRISON.

VIN'EGAR (Heb. HOMEZ). See VINEYARD.

VI'OL. A stringed instrument of music, resembling the psaltery (Is. v. 12; Amos vi. 5). See MUSICAL INSTRUMENTS.

VI'OLET. COLORS.

VI'PER. SERPENT.

VIRGIN (Heb. BATHULIA, ALMAN; Lat. *virgo*,

young women), (Is. viii. 3, 4; Matt. i. 23; Prov. xxx. 19).

VIS'ION. A supernatural presentation of certain scenery or circumstances to the mind of a person either while awake or asleep (Is. vi.; Ez. i.; Dan. viii.; Acts xxvi. 13). See DREAM.

VOPH'SI (*my addition*). Father of Nahbi (Num. xiii. 14).

VOW (Heb. NEDER, *vow of devotion*; Heb. ESAR, *vow of abstinence*; and HEREM, *vow of destruction*). Vows, in general, are mentioned in Job xxii. 27, etc. (Gr. *euchē'ōmai, devoted*). The earliest vow mentioned is Jacob's (Gen. xxviii. 18-22, xxxi. 13). The law regulated the practice of vows. A man might devote to sacred uses possessions or persons, but not the first-born either of man or beast (Lev. xxvii. 26). Moses enacted several laws for the regulation and execution of vows (Deut. xxiii. 21, 23). The vows of minors were not binding without the consent of the head of the family (Num. xxx.). These self-imposed services were more in keeping with the ancient dispensation—in which outward sacrifices had so large a share—than with enlightened Christianity.

VUL'GATE, THE. See HISTORY OF THE BOOKS.

VUL'TURE (Heb. DAAH), (Lev. xi. 14); (Heb. DAYYAH), (Deut. xiv. 13); AYYAH (Job. xxviii. 7). A large bird, belonging to the genus *hawks*, and including a great many species. It is pronounced unclean by Moses (Lev. xi. 14; Deut. xiv. 13). The vulture has a naked or downy head, a bare neck, and long wings. It is a carrion-bird, and is remarkable for its powers of vision, and the great height at which it soars. It scents its prey from afar. Scarcely can an exhausted camel fall on its route, and die, before numbers of these filthy scavengers show themselves (Job, xxviii. 7).

W

WA'FER (Heb. RAKIK). A thin cake made of flour or leaf-like bread (Ex. xvi. 31), and used in various offerings, anointed with sweet oil.

WA'GES (Heb. MASKORETH, SACHAR; Gr. *misthos, opsōnia*). The law was very strict in requiring daily payment of wages (Lev. xix. 13). The employer who refused to give his laborers sufficient food was censured (Job xxiv. 11), and the withholding wages was denounced (Jer. xxii. 13). The rich oppressed the poor in the later times, and called down Malachi's denunciation (iii. 5).

WAG'ON (Heb. AGALAH). See CART.

WALL. 1. Walls, supporting terraces on side-hills, were made from the loose stones gathered on the side-hill, either with or without mortar. These walls, ruined or entire, are found all over the hill-country, and are especially noticeable at Bethlehem and Gibeah, N. W. of Jerusalem. This custom doubled the capacity of the hill-sides in its power of producing grain or supporting trees, for the soil was washed down by the heavy rains, if not terraced. Walls were built around sheepcotes, in the open country, for the protection of the flock at night, and many such are still to be seen in the desert S. of Palestine. See GEDOR.

The ancient walls of temples and forts were sometimes built of very large stones, laid in a channel cut in the solid rock (see JERUSALEM). The style of rebated faces of blocks in a wall (called also beviled) is the mark of great antiquity, and almost always of Phœnician origin. The Hebrews followed this style in the temple-wall, and in some parts of the city wall of Jerusalem,

WHIRLING DERVISHES.

as appears in the remains of the temple-wall at the wailing-place, and underground, lately examined by the Palestine Exploration, and at the Damascus Gate, David's Tower, etc. Many other specimens are found at Hebron, in the mosque over Machpelah, at Paneas, Tyre, etc.

The Assyrians often faced a wall of some coarse material (earth, loose stones, etc.) with slabs of marble, or bricks.

Walls of houses were made of dirt, clay, bricks (sunburnt or fire-kilned), and of stone, rough or dressed.

Where a common highway ran through a vineyard, it was often walled on both sides (Num. xxii. 24).

WAR. In war the custom of the Israelites resembled that of surrounding countries. See ARMY. Their first object in war was conquest; and then, when in Canaan, their defense against enemies. They consulted the Urim and Thummim, or the prophet, before going to war, or into battle. The Hebrews were almost always at war, with others or among themselves, generally on account of neglecting the true worship, when Jehovah punished the nation by the means of other people sent against them.

WASHING THE HANDS AND FEET. As no knives or forks were used at the table, washing of the hands before and after meals was necessary (Matt. xv. 2). Because of the dust and heat of the Eastern climate, washing the feet on entering a house was an act of respect to the company, and of refreshment to the traveler (Gen. xviii. 4). When done by the master of the house it was an especial mark of respect and honor to the guest.

WATCH. A division of the night. See CHRONOLOGY.

WATCH'ER. A figurative designation of heavenly things, apparently angels, as seen by Nebuchadnezzar in his dream (Dan. iv. 13, 17-23).

WATCH'MEN. Are of as early a date as cities, robbers, and wars (Ex. xiv. 24). Jerusalem and other cities had regular guards night and day (Cant. iii. 1-3, 5, 7). When danger is apprehended they are required to call to each other every few

minutes. They were stationed at the gate of a city and in the adjacent tower (2 Sam. xviii. 24-27); and their responsible office required great vigilance and fidelity (Jer. vi. 17).

WA'TER (Heb. MAYIM; Gr. *hudor*). To the ancient Hebrews water was of inestimable value (Ex. xv. 22). It is an emblem of the spiritual blessings or SALVATION, which God bestows upon his people (Is. lv. 1). See JERUSALEM.

WA'TER-GATE (Neh. xii. 37). A gate of Jerusalem.

WATER OF JEALOUSY. Holy water mixed with dust from the floor of the Tabernacle, given in the case where a wife was suspected by the husband, on whom had fallen "the spirit of jealousy;" described in Num. v. 11-31. In such a case an offering had to be brought by the husband (Lev. ii. 2).

WA'TER-POT (Gr. *hudria*). A large vessel of stone in which water is kept standing, also for carrying water (John ii. 6, 7).

WAVE'-OF'FERING (Heb. TENUFAH). The breast of every PEACE-OFFERING, the Passover sheaf, loaves and lambs at Pentecost, etc., were to be "waved" before the Lord, and were hence called wave-offerings (Ex. xxix. 24-28).

WAX (Heb. DONAG). Mentioned in scripture as easily melted by heat (Ps. xxii. 14; Ex. xxii. 24).

WAY (Heb. DERECH, Gr. *hodos*). A road, track, path or HIGHWAY (Gen. xvi. 7); in Acts ix. 2 applied to the Christian religion.

WEA'SEL (Heb. CHOLED). Is identical with the Arabic *chuld* and the Syriac *chuldo*, both words signifying a mole; and therefore that the unclean animal mentioned in Lev. xi. 29, is not a weasel but a kind of mole. Several varieties of weasels and moles are found in Palestine.

WEAV'ING. Was practiced by the ancients, and exhibited on the ancient monuments of Egypt (Gen. xli. 42). It was usually performed by women (2 K. xxiii. 7). The distaff, the shuttle, and the weaver's beam and pin are mentioned in Judg. xvi. 14; 1 Sam. xvii. 7; Job viii. 6.

WEEK (Heb. SHABUA). See CHRONOLOGY.

WEIGHTS AND MEASURES. The notices of weights and measures in the Bible are few and incomplete, and we have to supply the wanting information from other sources; chiefly from the systems of ancient nations, following the chain from Rome up through Greece, Egypt, and Phœnicia, to Babylon, the origin. The system was nearly uniform everywhere, but varied from one age to another. Layard found at Nineveh the weights used by the Babylonians, which were in the form of lions and of ducks, with rings for handles, of different sizes, in a certain system, the lightest weighing about 4 oz., the heaviest about 40 lbs.

TABLE OF SILVER COIN WEIGHTS—PROPORTIONS AND VALUES.

	Paris grs.	Prop.	lbs.	oz.	dwt.	grs.				
Gerah (*bean*)	13.7	60,000				13.7	1 Gerah	=		2½ cts.
Bekah (*divided*)	137	6,000			6	17	10 Gerahs	=	1 Bekah	= 25 "
Shekel (*weight*)	274	3,000			13	14	2 Bekahs	=	1 Shekel	= 50 "
Maneh (*talent*)	13,700	60	2	3	2	12	50 Shekels	=	1 Maneh	= 25 dolls.
Kikkar (*round*)	822,000	1	142	9	5	0	60 Manehs	=	1 Kikkar	= 1500 "

Gold was reckoned at 10, 12 or 13 times the value of silver in different ages.

COPPER COINS.				GREEK COINS.			ROMAN COINS.		
	Grains.	Value.							
Mite (lepton)	15 to 20	2 mills.		Lepton	=	2 mills.	As (farthing)		1½ cents.
½ of a shekel	81 " 88	3 "		Drachm	=	16 cents.	Quadrans		3¾ mills.
Quarter	125 " 132	5 "		Didrachm	=	32 "	Denarius (penny)		15 cents.
Half (bekah)	235 " 264	1 cent.		Stater (tetr)	=	64 "	Aureus (stater)		3 dollars.
Shekel	528	2 cents.		Mina (pound)		16 dollars.	Talent	961	"
Talent = 1500 shekels				Talent		960 "			

Silver was 60 to 80, and even once as high as 112 times the value of copper.

HEBREW COPPER COINS.			EGYPTIAN COPPER COINS.		
	Grains.	Value.		Grains.	
Gerah (1-20)	16 to 20	2 mills.	½ KeT	70	3 mills.
One-sixth	81 " 88	3 "	KeT	140	6 "
Zuzah (¼)	125 " 132	4 "	2 KeT	280	1 c. 2 "
Half (bekah)	235 " 264	8 "	5 KeT	700	3 c. 5 "
Shekel	528	1 c. 6 "	MeN (Maneh)	1400	7 c.
Talent = 1500 shekels = 25 dollars.					

The comparative weights of the talents of different nations may be seen in this table, each number standing for 1000 grains:

Hebrew gold,	1 320	Babylonian silver,	959	Egyptian silver,	840
" silver,	660	" lesser "	479	Æginetan "	660
" copper,	792	Persian gold,	400	Attic	500

MEASURES OF LENGTH.

The names are derived from members of the human body—the CUBIT, the length of the forearm from the elbow point to the third finger-tip, was the unit, a name and custom derived from Egypt, and recorded on the monuments. There is no record of the unit in the Bible, Josephus, nor in any ancient Hebrew building.

TABLE OF MEASURES OF LENGTH (Egyptian).

	Paris lines.	Inches.		Paris lines.	Inches.				
Cubit (*sacred*)	234.33	19.05	Cubit (*common*)	204.8	18	4 Fingers	=	1 Palm.
Span	117,166	9.52	Span	102.4	9	3 Palms	=	1 Span.
Palm (*wide*)	39.55	3.17	Palm	34.13	3	2 Spans	=	1 Cubit.
Finger "	9.76	0.79	Finger	8.53	¾	6 Cubits	=	1 Reed.

Land was measured by the cubit and reed, but never computed by square-measure, for they had no unit such as our acre.

MEASURES OF DISTANCE.

The ordinary day's journey for *one person*, was 30 ms.; for *a company*, 10. The Sabbath-day's journey was measured by the distance fixed between the tents and the ark in the wilderness, which was 2,000 cubits (*Smith's Dict.;* Kitto), which was also the limit outside of the Levitical cities. The moderns reckon by hours' travel, which vary from 4 to 2½ ms., as the length of the hour varies with the length of the day in summer and winter.*

MEASURES OF CAPACITY (Josephus).

There were two sets—one for dry, another for liquid things—both having a unit of the same value, the bath and the ephah (Ex. xlv. 11).

TABLE OF DRY AND LIQUID MEASURES.

								Equal to, in gallons, according to	
								JOSEPHUS.	RABBINS.
Homer								86.6	44.2
Bath of Ephah	10	1						8.6	4.4
Seah	30	3	1					2.8	1.4
Hin	60	6	2	1				1.4	0.7
Gomer	100	10	3½	1⅗	1			0.8	0.4
Cab	180	18	6	3	1 4-5	1		0.4	0.2
Log	720	72	24	12	7 1-5	4	1	0.1	0.6

The common cubit of 18 in. would give 3,000 ft. The sacred cubit of 19.05 in. would give 4,762 ft. An English mile is 5,280 ft.

* Kitto, Sabbath-day's journey, v. iii., p. 722; Smith, do., v. iii., p. 1073.

WELL (Heb. BEER). The necessity and demand for water in a hot climate has rendered it a possession of the greatest importance (Judg. i. 15; Gen. xxi. 30, 31). So that, in war, the wells were often filled in by the enemy (2 K. iii. 19). Wells in Palestine have generally to be sunk through limestone; sometimes they are descended by steps (Gen. xxiv. 16). A curb or low parapet-wall encircles their mouths; sometimes they were furnished with stone covers (Ex. xxi. 33). Christ sat on the curb of the well when he conversed with the woman of Samaria (John iv. 6). The water was hoisted by a rope attached to a bucket, water-skin, or stone jar (Gen. xxiv. 14-20; John iv. 11). Also a wheel was used upon which was slung an endless belt, on which jars to hold the water were attached at intervals. The well-swing was of ancient use, being a beam balanced upon a pivot, with a rope and bucket at one end and a stone balance-weight at the other. Women were usually employed to fetch water. Many places are named in relation to wells, such as Beersheba, Beer-Elim, Rehoboth, etc.

WEN (Heb. YABBAL, *flowing*), (Lev. xxii. 22). A tumor which is movable, pulpy, and often elastic to the touch.

WENCH. Maid-servant (2 Sam. xvii. 17, only).

WEST (Heb. YAM (*sea*). MAARAB (Is. xlv. 6). MAARABAH. The place where the sun sets. Gr. *dusme*, the *setting* of the sun, the quarter of the heavens or earth which lies toward the setting sun, or opposite the east (Gen. xii. 8).

EAST (Heb. KEDEM, KADIM, KIDMAH, KADMON, KADMONI, *before*, or *in front of*, a person), (Job xxiii. 8, 9). Heb. MIZRAH, the place of the *sun's rising* (Ps. ciii. 12).

NORTH (Heb. ZAFON, Gr. *borrhas*). That quarter of the heavens or earth, or that direction which is at the left hand of a person who faces the east (Gen. xiii. 14).

SOUTH (Heb. DAROM, *bright, sunny*. TEYMAN. What is on the right hand of a person facing the east (Gen. xii. 9).

WHALE (Heb. TAN or TANNIN, *sea-monster, dragon*). "Even the sea-monsters (TANNIN) draw out the breast, they give suck to their young ones" (Lam. iv. 3). Here the whale is evidently alluded to. Probably the fish swallowed Jonah was some large kind of shark, or a fish especially provided (John i. 17; Gen. i. 21; Matt. xii. 40).

WHEAT (Heb. DAGAN, RIFOTH, CHITTAH). In the account of Jacob's sojourn with Laban occurs the first mention of wheat (Gen. xxx. 14). Egypt was celebrated for wheat; of the bearded and also of the seven-eared kind (Gen. xli. 22), known now as mummy-wheat, from being found encased in the mummies: if such grain be planted it will yield. Wheat was plentiful in Syria and Palestine (Ps. lxxxi. 16, cxlvii. 14, etc.). The common kind would produce sometimes one hundred grains in the ear (Matt. xiii. 8). The wheat was planted in the winter, and reaping commenced towards the end of April, in May, and in June. See AGRICULTURE. HARVEST.

WINDOW.

WHIRLWIND (Heb. SUFAH), (Job. xxvii. 9). Storm (Job xxi. 18); SA'AR, tempest (Ps. lv. 8). A violent wind or hurricane. Sometimes the desert storms lift vast quantities of dry, hot sand into the air, darkening the sun at noon-day, and burying several feet deep any object in their course, even a whole caravan, with thousands of animals and travelers (Job i. 19). The Arabs name this sand-cloud "Efreet," *the bad one*. Houses, trees, and even great rocks, are moved by these terrible wind storms, which are sudden in coming, and are soon over.

WHITE (*purity*), (Is. i. 18). See COLORS.

WID'OW (Heb. ALMANAH; Gr. *chera*). The Mosaic dispensation made no provision for the maintenance of widows. They were left dependant upon their friends, especially the first-born or eldest son, whose birth-right or extra share of the property imposed such a duty upon him. The widow was commended to the care of the community (Ex. xxii. 22). The widow, when left childless, was to marry the brother of her deceased husband (Deut.

xxv. 5, 6). The high-priest was forbidden to marry a widow (Lev. xxi. 14). Poor widows were cared for, among others, in the early Church (Acts vi.; James i. 27).

WIL'DERNESS. 1. SIN. See EXODUS. 2. Of the Wandering. The district over which the Israelites wandered between the two visits to KADESH, for about 38 years is not certainly known. The probability is that it was what is now called Et Tyh, the *Wandering*. See PARAN. It is a high, limestone plateau, affording good pasture in the rainy season, and is not a desert at any time except in a few isolated patches. It may be divided into the sandy plain along the sea shore, the wadies (dry river vallies), and the high table-land. There are mountain peaks. The shore of the Mediteranean is bordered by a low sandy plain, grassy where watered, which extends, in the Wady El Arish and its branches, far inland, and is full of hills and shifting sand. The only really barren waste, like the Nefood, or the Dahna (*red waste*), of Arabia, occurs only here and there, where the springs have dried up from the loss of trees, and sand has been brought by the winds. Above the plain rise low table-lands, covered with a hard, white soil, which on the more elevated plateaus is displaced in places by gravel. Everywhere there are dry, treeless water-courses, green with herbage where there are trees and plants, and evidences of a greater extent in the past. The remains of large trunks of trees scattered over this region indicate a more copious rain-fall, and the existence of groves, if not of forests, in some past age. Evidences of a former state of cultivation are found in stone walls all over the district, and, wherever there is water, flowers, herbs, grasses, and groves of acacia, tamarisk, and other trees. This region is now capable of supporting immense flocks and herds, and, under more favorable conditions of forest and rain, might have given support to the tribes of Israel for ages, independent of any miraculous supply. There are very few names even now, in the district, and none which can be traced to the time of the Exodus. See SINAI, GEOLOGY.

WILDERNESS OF THE WANDERING. See WANDERING IN THE WILDERNESS AND EXODUS.

WIL'LOWS (Heb. ARABIM). Were used for making booths at the Feast of Tabernacles (Job xl. 22), also giving shade to BEHEMOTH (Is. xliv. 4); a common tree which grows in marshy places (Job xl. 22); with a leaf much like the olive (Lev. xxiii. 40). The "weeping willow" memorable in connection with the mourning Hebrew captives (Ps. cxxxvii. 2), is a native of Babylonia. The "Brook of the Willows," (Heb. NAHAL), (Is. xv. 7), on the S. border of Moab, flows into the S. E. extremity of the Dead Sea (Num. xxi. 19). NAHALIEL.

WILLS. Two instances are recorded in the O. T. under the Law, of testamentary disposition. 1. Effected in the case of Ahithophel (2 Sam. xvii. 23). 2. Recommended in the case of Hezekiah (2 K. xx. 1; Is. xxxviii. 1).

WIM'PLE (Heb. MITPAHATH). A mantle or shawl (Ruth iii. 15; Is. iii. 22).

WIND (Heb. RUAH or RUACH). Wind from the North, South, East, and West, was expressed as of the "four quarters" or "four winds" (Ez. xxxvii. 9; Dan. viii. 8; Matt. xxiv. 31). The cold wind of the N. is appealed to in Cant. iv. 16. The N. W. wind lasts from the autumnal equinox to the beginning of November, and the N. wind from June to the equinox. As the E. wind passes over the sandy wastes of the Arabian desert before arriving in Palestine, it was called the "wind of the wilderness" (Job i. 19; Jer. xiii. 24). The S. wind after passing over the Arabian peninsula acquires great heat (Job xxxvii. 17; Luke xii. 55). The W. and S. W. winds reach Palestine in a humid state acquired from the Mediterranean. The sea of Genesaret was subject to squalls of wind (Mark iv. 37; Luke viii. 23). The wind spoken of, figuratively, as in Jer. xviii. 17, typical of the waste of war; as transitory, in Job vii. 7; Ps. lxxviii. 39, etc. It represented the operations of the Holy Spirit in John iii. 8; Acts ii. 2.

WINDOW (Heb. HALLON or CHALLON). The windows were apertures closed in with lattice-work, called in Heb. ARUBBAH (Eccl. xii. 3). Although there were windows looking into the street

GRACE AT THE TABLE.

In the rainy season, furnishing good pastures but no tillage. The highest plateau is covered with a light, rich soil, with a few springs and wells, and brooks which are permanent for a mile or two only, they, for the most part, opened into the inner court (Judg. v. 28; Prov. vii. 6). See HOUSE.

WINE. The word wine is the translation of ten Hebrew and two Greek words. 1. Heb. YAYIN,

that which yields wine, in Micah vi. 15.—2. TI-ROSU, vintage-fruit (Micah vi. 15), new wine.—3. ASIS, grape-juice (Cant. viii. 2).—4. SOBE, or SOVE, boiled *must*, syrup (wine in Is. i. 22; literally, thy SOBE circumcised with water).—5. MEMER, pure red wine (Deut. xxxii. 14), or HAMAR (Ez. vi. 9, vii. 22), the pure blood of the grape, red wine in Is. xxvii. 2 (Ps. lxxv. 8, meaning desirable vineyard?).—6. MIMSACH, mixed wine; MIMSACH, mixed wine (Prov. xxiii. 30).—7. MESECH, mixture (mingled her wine, in Prov. ix. 2; wine is red, in Ps. lxxv. 8).—8. MEZEG, spiced wine, in Cant. viii. 2; liquor, in vii. 2.—9. SHEKAR, strong drink (strong wine in Num. xxviii. 7; "SHEKAR shall be bitter to them that drink it," in Is. xxiv. 9). Occurs 21 times in the N. T. (Arabic, *sukkar*, sugar).—10. HEMEZ, vinegar; vinegar (HOMEZ, in Num. vi. 3); (homez of yayin, and homez of shekar). Thine sour wine (Ruth ii. 14); as the *posca* (Greek), which the Roman soldiers gave to Jesus on the cross (John xix. 29, 30, etc.); ASHISHAH, a cake of dried raisins; flagons of wine, in 2 Sam. vi. 19; Cant. ii. 5, etc.; SHEMARIM, wine-lees.—1. Greek, *posca*.—2. *gleukos*, new wine in Acts. ii. 13, now called *must*. —3. *oinos*. Put young wine (*oinos neos*) into new skins (bottles in Matt. ix. 17); not to ferment, as that would burst the *bottles* or skins, new or old, but into new ones, to avoid the refuse of the old wine, which may be sour.

WINE-PRESS, THE (PURAH, GATH). Is of the highest antiquity, and is drawn on the walls of the Egyptian temples and tombs. Remains of wine-vats are found in many parts of Palestine, cut in the solid rock. Some were very large, as that in which Gideon threshed (Judg. vi. 11). Wine has always been in use, and the Scriptures only condemn its excessive use. Corn, wine, and oil are special gifts of Providence. It was the usual drink-offering (Ex. xxix. 40) to be presented among the first-fruits (Lev. xxiii. 13). The priests were prohibited from the use of wine and strong drink before service in the Temple (Lev. x. 9), and the Nazarite during his vow (Num. vi. 3). The wine-cup was handed round four times during the Paschal Feast, especially after the Captivity. Jesus speaks of the wine used as the *fruit* of the vine (Matt. xxvi. 29). Wine is generally mixed with water (warm; see Justin Martyr, *Apol.* i. 65). Those holding office in the Church were not to be given to wine (1 Tim. iii. 3), or to much wine (iii. 8), or a slave to much wine (Titus ii. 3). Paul once recommends its use (to Timothy, 1 Tim. v. 23).

WIT, TO. To know (Gen. xxiv. 21; 2 Cor. viii. 1).

WITH, WITHES (Heb. YETHARIM), (Judg. xvi. 7-9), a *cord* or *rope*. A *with* or *withe* is, probably, a flexible twig for binding.

WISDOM OF SOLOMON, THE. See HISTORY OF THE BOOKS.

WITNESS. The law was very careful to provide and enforce evidence for all its infractions and all transactions bearing on them (Num. xv. 30, 40). Two witnesses, at least, are required to establish any charge (xxxv. 30). A false witness was punished. Women and slaves were not admitted to bear testimony (Josh. iv. 8).

In the N. T. the original notion of a witness is in the special form of one who attests his belief in the Gospel by personal suffering (Acts xxii. 20).

WOLF (Heb. ZEEB; Gr. *lukos*). A fierce and rapacious animal (Gen. xlix. 27) which prowls at night (Jer. v. 6), and especially destructive to sheep (Matt. x. 16; Luke x. 3). They were very plentiful in Palestine, but are now much less common. It closely resembles the dog. They are cruel but cowardly animals, swift of foot and strong enough to carry off a sheep at full speed, and is now, as of old, the dread of the shepherds of Palestine. They secrete themselves till dark among the rocks, then leap into the fold and seize their victim by stealth. The wolf first tears out the entrails and devours the heart, liver and lungs before the muscular parts. His bite is vigorous and deadly; his mode of attack is by short, rapid snaps. A single wolf is far more destructive than a whole pack of jackals. The Syrian wolf is of lighter color than that of Europe, and larger and stronger.

TAMARISK.

WOMAN, WOMEN (Heb. ISHSHAH, *female;* Gr. *gune, theleia, female*), (Rom. i. 26, 27). Is mentioned in the Scriptures as the beloved and honored companion and helpmeet of man (Gen. xxii. 23, 24). In the East women have always lived in seclusion, not appearing in public unless closely vailed, not seeing the men who visit their husbands and brothers, nor even taking their meals with the men of their own family. They were chiefly engaged in domestic duties (Prov. xxxi.). The poor gleaned the remnants of the harvest (Gen. xxix. 9, xxiv. 15-20). Oriental women are never regarded or treated as equals by the men. This is seen on all occasions. They pronounce women to be weak and inferior in the most absolute terms. Even in polite society the gentlemen must be served first. So the husband and brothers sit down and eat, and the wife, mother, and sisters wait and take what is left. If they accompany their female relatives anywhere, they walk before, and the women follow at a respectful distance. It is very common to see small boys lord it over their mothers and sisters in the most insolent manner; and they are encouraged to do so by the father. They literally use the rod upon them. Instances are not rare in which the husband kills the wife outright, and no legal notice is taken of the murder. She is confined closely, watched with jealousy, and everything valuable is kept under lock and

key; necessarily so, they say, for the wife will not hesitate to rob her husband if she gets an opportunity. The Arabs have a word—"*ajellack*"—by which they preface the mention of anything indelicate or unclean. Thus, ajellack, a donkey, or a dog, or my shoes; so, when compelled to speak of their women, they say "ajellack, my woman," or simply, "the woman is so and so." These and similar customs enable us to understand why it is that acquaintance before marriage is ordinarily out of the question. It is considered quite immodest for an unmarried lady to manifest any special regard for her future husband. The birth of a son is always a joyful event in a family; but that of a daughter is often looked upon as a calamity. If the first wife has no children the husband marries another or takes a slave. The whole system is productive of evil, and that only, to the individual, the family, and the community.

WOOL (Heb. ZEMER; Chal. *amar*; Gr. *erion*). Wool was an article of the highest value among the Jews (Lev. xiii. 47). The "fleece" (Heb. GEZ, GIZZAH), is mentioned in Deut. xviii. 4. The wool of Damascus was highly prized in Tyre (Ez. xxvii. 18). Wool is an image of purity (Is. i. 18; Dan. vii. 9). Garments made of woolen and linen were prohibited by the law; the cloth bore a peculiar name (Heb. SHAATNEZ), "thou shalt not wear a garment of divers sorts" (Deut. xxii. 11). Josephus (iv. 9, §11), says the reason for the law against wearing a garment woven of linen and wool was that such were worn by priests alone.

WORD (Heb. EMER, OMER, IMRAH, DABAR, MILLAH, etc.; Gr. *logos* and *rema*. "Word" is applied to the Lord JESUS CHRIST. See HISTORY OF THE BOOKS.

WORLD (Heb. EREZ), (Is. xxiii. 17). Earth. Heb. HEDEL, *place of rest, region of the dead*. Heb. HELED, *this world*. Heb. OLAM (Ps. lxxiii. 12), "world without end." Heb. TEBEL, the earth fertile and inhabited. Gr. *aion, eternal* (Matt. xii. 32). See ALEXANDRIA.

O. and N. T. as a symbol of the gnawing pain of eternal punishment (Is. lxvi. 24; Mark ix. 44, etc.).

WORM'WOOD (Heb. LAANAH; Gr. *apsinthos*). A bitter plant, a symbol of whatever is nauseous and destructive (Deut. xxix. 18; Jer. ix. 15). Different species are found in Palestine. It was used by the Romans as a stomachic infusion in wine.

PALIMPSEST. SEVERUS, WRITTEN OVER LUKE XX. 9, 10.

Diffused in alcohol, it is now used to an alarming extent in France and Switzerland. The Jews put it in their wines, probably for tonic purposes. The word occurs frequently in the Bible, and generally in a metaphorical sense (Amos v. 7).

WOR'SHIP, WOR'SHIPER. See ADORATION.

WORTH. Used as now to indicate value or equality in value (Gen. xxiii. 9, 15; Ez. xxx. 2).

WOT, TO. To know; to have knowledge (Gen. xxi. 26). WRITING.

WRITING (Heb. KATHAB, *to write*; SEFER, *a book*; SOFER, *a writer*). The Phœnician was the most ancient alphabet that is known to us. The Egyptian writing may have been more ancient, but that was not alphabetic, being both ideographic and phonetic. Pliny (vii. 56) says the Syrians (Phœnicians) invented writing, but gives the Assyrians credit for great antiquity in the use of the art. The discovery of the Moabite Stone (see p. 175) proves the origin of the Greek letters to have been Phœnician; and it is probable that the Hebrews used the alphabet in common with the Phœnicians, as may be inferred from their names; as Aleph, *ox*; Gimel, *camel*.

TABLE OF DERIVATION OF ALPHABETS.
1 Phœnician.
2 Greek (ancient), Persian (anc.), Numidian, Hebrew (anc.), Aramæan (anc.).
3 From Greek, Etruscan, Umbrian, Oscan, Samnite, Celtiberian, Roman, Runic; Later Greek, Coptic, Gothic, Slavonian.
4 From Persian, Sassanid, Zend, Pehlvi, Armenian."
5 From Aramæan, Palmyrene, Hebrew square, Estrangelo, Nestorian, Sabian, Cufic, Nischi, Peshito, Miguric or Old Turkish.
6 From Hebrew, Samaritan.

HARLEIAN. JOHN I. 1, 2.

WORM (Heb. SAS), (Is. ll. 8, only). Evidently denotes the caterpillar of the clothes-moth. Heb. RIMMAH and TOLEAH are used in various passages together, and more generally for the maggots or caterpillars of insects than for the earth-worm (Ex. xvi. 20-24). The worm is also named in the

The English is the first pure alphabet, without double-letters.
The Hebrew alphabet has 22 letters. (See their names in the TABLE OF ALPHABETS). The arrangement of the letters is after the order as given in Psalm cxix. The meaning of each name as far as known is: 1. ALEPH, an ox; 2. BETH, a house; the Ethiopic is like a round-top tent; 3. GIMEL, a camel, the Greek gamma—some say the camel's hump; 4. DALETH, a door, that is, a tent-door, a triangle; Greek delta; 5. HE, no name; Greek E, and also Phœnician turned round; 6. VAU (*vow*), a hook, or tent-peg, the Greek upsilon; 7. ZAIN (*zajin*), sword, ancient Greek *san*; 8. CHETH, a

ALPHABETS.

NISCHI ARABIC		ETHIOPIC			ARMENIAN		COPTIC		
Elif	ا	Hoi	U	ha	Ա ա	Aip	Ⲁ	ⲁ	Alpha
Be	ب	Lawi	Λ	la	Բ բ	Pjent	Ⲃ	ⲃ	Vida
Te	ت	Haut	ሐ	ha	Գ գ	Kim	Ⲅ	ⲅ	Gamma
The	ث	Mai	ም	ma	Դ դ	Ta	Ⲇ	ⲇ	Dalda
Gjim	ج	Saut	ሠ	sa	Ե ե	Jetsch	Ⲉ	ⲉ	Ei
Hha	ح	Res	ረ	ra	Զ զ	Za	Ⲍ	ⲍ	Zida
Kha	خ	Sat	ሰ	sa	Է է	E.	Ⲏ	ⲏ	Hida
Dal	د	Schaat	ሸ	scha	Ը ը	Jeth	Ⲑ	ⲑ	Thida
Dsal	ذ	Kaf	ቀ	ka	Թ թ	Tho	Ⲓ	ⲓ	Jauda
Re	ر	Beth	ቡ	ba	Ժ ժ	She	Ⲕ	ⲕ	Kabba
Ze	ز	Thawi	ተ	tha	Ի ի	Ini	Ⲗ	ⲗ	Laula
Sin	س	Tjawi	ጠ	tja	Լ լ	Liun	Ⲙ	ⲙ	Mi
Schin	ش	Harm	ኀ	cha	Խ խ	Che	Ⲛ	ⲛ	Ni
Sad	ص	Nahas	ነ	na	Ծ ծ	Dsa	Ⲝ	ⲝ	Exi
Ddad	ض	Gnahas	ኘ	gna	Կ կ	Gjen	Ⲟ	ⲟ	O
Ta	ط	Alph	አ	a	Հ հ	Hho	Ⲡ	ⲡ	Pi
Tza	ظ	Kaf	ከ	ka	Ձ ձ	Tsa	Ⲣ	ⲣ	Ro
Ain	ع	Chaf	ኸ	cha	Ղ ղ	Ghad	Ⲥ	ⲥ	Sima
Ghain	غ	Wawe	ወ	wa	Ճ ճ	Dshe	Ⲧ	ⲧ	Dau
Fe	ف	Ain	ዐ	a	Մ մ	Mjen	Ⲩ	ⲩ	He
Kaf	ق	Zai	ዘ	za	Յ յ	Hi	Ⲫ	ⲫ	Phi
Kef	ك	Jai	የ	ja	Ն ն	No	Ⲭ	ⲭ	Chi
Lam	ل	Janam	ደ	ja	Շ շ	Sha	Ⲯ	ⲯ	Ebsi
Mim	م	Dent	ዸ	da	Ո ո	Wo	Ⲱ	ⲱ	O
Nun	ن	Djent	ጀ	dju	Չ չ	Tsha	Ϥ	ϥ	Fei
He	ه	Geml	ገ	ga	Պ պ	Be	Ϫ	ϫ	Giangia
Wau	و	Tait	ጠ	ta	Ջ ջ	Dshe	Ϭ	ϭ	Scima
		Tschait	ጨ	tscha	Ռ ռ	Rra	Ϣ	ϣ	Scai
		Pait	ጰ	pa	Ս ս	Sa	Ϩ	ϩ	Hori
		Tzadai	ጸ	tza	Վ վ	Wjev	Ϧ	ϧ	Chef
		Zappa	ፀ	tza	Տ տ	Diun	Ϯ	ϯ	Dei hgam
Je	ي	Af	ፈ	fa	Ր ր	Re	Ⲉ	ⲁ	So
		Psa	ፐ	pa					

ā, ŏ, ĭ, ō, ū, ȳ, *long*; ă, ŏ, ĭ, ŏ, ŭ, ў, *short*; câre, fär, lăst, fąll, whạt; thêre, vĕil, tẽrm; pîque, fįrm; dōne, fŏr, dọ, wǫlf, fōod, fŏŏt.

ALPHABETS.

fence, Greek ETA; 9. TET (*teth*), a snake, or basket, Greek *thēta*; 10. YOD, a hand, the Phœnician and Samaritan yod has a hint of fingers; 11. CAPH, the hollow of the hand, Greek *kappa*; 12. LAMED, *sigma*; 16. AIN (*ajin*), an eye, O in Phœnician; 17. PE, a mouth, Greek *pi*; 18. ZADE, a fish-hook, Greek *zeta*; 19. KOF, back of the head (some say ear, others a pole, or eye of a needle); the old

NAME	PHŒNICIAN	HEBREW on Coins	SAMARITAN	ARAMAIC on Egyptian Monuments	PALMYRENE	SQUARE HEBREW	RABBINIC	SYRIAC PESHITO
Aleph	✡ ✡	✡	א	א ג	אאג	א	ñ	ܐ
Beth	9 9	9 9	ב	ע	ﬠ	ב	ב	ܒ
Gimel	7 7	1 1	ג		ג	ג	ג	ܓ
Daleth	4 9	9 4	ד	ד	ﬠ	ד	ל	ܕ
He	ヨ	ヨ	ה	ה	ה	ה	ה	ܗ
Waw	7 7	×	ו	ח ח	ח ח	ו	ו	ܘ
Zajin	Z		ע	ן	I	ז	ז	ܙ
Cheth	日 日	日	ש	ח	ה	ח	ח	ܚ
Teth	⊙		ט	ט	G	ט	ט	ܛ
Jod	m m	z	m	ג	> ▷	י	י	ܝ
Caph	7 7 4	ד	ד	ד	כ כ	כ, Final ך	כ Final ך	ܟ
Lamed	L L 4	ל	ז	ﬞ	ﬠ	ל	ל	ܠ
Mem	ɣ 4 4	ל	ﬡ	א א	כ	מ, Final ם	מ, Final ם	ܡ
Nun	ן ן	ן	ן	ן ן	ﬖ	נ, Final ן	נ, Final ן	ܢ
Samech	ﬣ ﬣ		ﬢ	ﬤ	ﬡﬡ	ס	ס	ܣ
Ajin	O O	U	▽	ﬞ	ﬠ	ע	ע	ܥ
Phe	ן	ד	ל	ן	ﬠ ﬡ	פ Final ף	פ Final ף	ܦ
Zade	⅓ ⅓	⋙	ﬠ		ﬢ	צ Final ץ	צ, Final ץ	ܨ
Koph	ף ף	ף ף	ﬤ	P ן	ﬠ	ק	ק	ܩ
Resch	9 4	9 4	ב	4 4	ﬤﬠ	ר	ר	ܪ
Sin						ש		
Schin	ʎ ʎ ʎ	W ᴗ	ﬡ	V	V	ש	ש	ܫ
Taw	ꜩ ꜩ	× ᴛ	✕	ꜩ ꜩ	ꜩ	ת	ת	ܬ

ox-goad, Greek *lambda*; the ancient Phœnician was curved like the modern Arabic; 13. MEM, water, or a trident and symbol of the sea; Greek *mu*; 14. NUN, a fish, Greek *nu*; 15. SAMECH, a prop, Greek Hebrew P became the Greek *kappa*, and the Roman Q; 20. RESH, the head, Greek *ro*; 21. SHIN and SIN, a tooth, Greek *sigma*; 22. TAU, a mark, or sign, perhaps a cross ✕, Greek *tau*.

fûrl, rgde, pṳsh; e, i, o, silent; ç as s; ch as sh; ċ, ch as k; ġ as j; ġ as in get; ẓ as z; g as gz; ŋ as in linger, link; ṭh as in thine.

WRITING 325 TRANSLATION

The form of five of the Hebrew letters was changed when the letters were final (at the end of the word), a system which was useful when sentences were written without spaces between the words; for instance IWASGLADWHENTHEYSAID UNTOMELETUSGOUPTOTHEHOUSEOFTHELORD (Ps. cxxii. 1). This writing without division into words is a more close following of speech, which is a continuous flow of sound, the mind separating the words, or ideas. The Moabite Stone (page 94) is an instance from antiquity. The spaces there show where the stone has been broken or defaced, and letters lost.

Abbreviations were common both in books, and on coins, and also in inscriptions on the monuments, as ISR for ISRAEL, YAH for JEHOVAH.

Numbers were indicated by letters and figures. Figures are found on the Phœnician coins, and monuments in Palmyra, and Egypt. The Greeks also used letters in writing numbers. Differences in certain statements of numbers can be explained in this way; the scribe, or copyist mistaking a c for a o, c being 700, and o being 7,000.

The signs used by the Babylonian writers differed from those of Tiberias, and were nearly all above the letters. The present system is uniform everywhere and dates from about A. D. 1030.

Accents were also marked, for the purpose of noting the tone-syllable (directing the reader in the synagogue), and the chief words in the sentence. There were peculiar styles of recitation for each class of books, the law, prophets, and poets, which are still in use. The metrical chants have been lost. See MUSIC.

The materials which have come down to us from antiquity are, stone, bricks, papyrus, vellum, parchment. Embossed leather is still preserved, bearing the names and date of the Pharaohs 3,300 years ago. Papyrus is alluded to in 3 Macc. iv. 20, and 2 John 12 (Gr. *zartēs*, *chartēs*); and in Josephus (Ant. iii. 11, 6, xii. 2, 10); and parchment in 2 Tim. iv. 13 (Gr. *membrana*). Skins of clean animals only could be used for the Scriptures; as KELEF (skin of the hairy side), for the tophillim, phylacteries; diksostos (Heb. DIKS), for the mezuzoth; and gĕvil (of undivided skin, dressed). The ink (DEYO, Gr. *melan*, black), was of lampblack wet with gall-juice, sometimes diluted with vitriol. The inkstand (KESETH HASSOFER), was carried in a case (KALMARIN), with pens, knife, etc., by a strap over the shoulder, or fastened at the girdle.

WRITING MATERIALS.

The rolls were written in columns (DELA­THOTH), (one, two, or three, according to the width of the roll), with a margin above of 3 fingers, below of 4, and between the columns of an inch. The columns are about 2 fingers wide in the Herculaneum rolls; and others there are 3 in. (4 fingers).

The case in which the rolls were kept were called KEREK or KARKA.

Tablets of wood covered with wax were used for ordinary writing not intended for keeping a long time. On these the letters were impressed with a stylus (Job xix. 24), sometimes of iron (Ps. xlv. 2). For engraving on stone the point called CHE­RET (Ex. xxxii. 4; Is. viii. 1), and ZIPPOREN (Jer. xvii. 1), were used.

A reed pen (3 John 13; 3 Macc. iv. 20), was used on parchment and papyrus.

The oldest monument in alphabetical writing is the Moabite Stone (p. 173), which is dated as early as 900 B. C., if it does not belong to David's time (1025 B. C.). The ancient Phœnician monuments, dating later than the Moabite stone, are counted by hundreds.

No vowel points are found on the coins, in the Palmyrene inscriptions, or on the Phœnician monuments. It is probable that the vowel-points were first written by Ezra. The Arabic is the first in point of time to show the use of vowel-points, dating before A. D. 650. The present Arabic system of writing dates from about A. D. 930.

Some scholars contend that the vowel-points were not in use before A. D. 550.

In the 8th century A. D., Moses the Punctator, followed by his son Judah the Corrector, used the

και ω τασουρακον
ται εηχρο νων γ. κρονωσφορησθη
αυτοιω εντη ερημω. καυθλων
ιδ ονλιβμω ον λιχαν αι αι κατε
κληρονομιασντολινλιωαινοη
ιω σ κεδοντιτεραχοσιοισζηθνητικον
ται.

A. D. 1044. ACTS XIII. 18-20.

points for the first time that is recorded, to assist his pupils.

TRANSLATION OF THE INSCRIPTION ON THE MOABITE STONE (p. 173).

1 I am Mesa, son of Chamos-nadab, the king of Moab (son of) Yabnis.
2 My father ruled over Moab (** years), and I have
3 reigned after my father. And I have built this high-place of sacrifice in Karkha, and platform for Chamos **.
4 (I call myself) Mesa, because he (Chamos) has saved me from (all who fought against Moab).
5 (Omri) the king of Israel joined (Moab's) haters, and oppressed Moab (many days). Chamos was angry.
6 The king's son succeeded him, and Moab was oppressed very sore.
7 ** And I saw him and his house (temple ?). Israel was dispersed for ever. Omri took
8 Medeba, and remained there, and built forty **.
9 Chamos is our god. To him I built Baal Meon (walls and mounds), and sacrificed.
10 I took Kirjathaim, and men of Gad dwelt in the land from the days of their fathers.
11 The king of Israel built Kirjathaim. I fought against and took it, and
12 killed all the people that were in the city (as a sacrifice) to Chamos, god of Moab,
13 *** before the face of Chamos, in Kirjathaim; then I made prisoners the (old) men and the ****
14 * of the youth (morning). Chamos said: Go rule over Israel.
15 I went by night, and fought with him from the *** of the dawn to mid-day. I ***
16 **** entirely *****
17 **** who is for Astar Chamos ***
18 ** Jahveh (Jehovah) ** before the face of Chamos and the king of Israel (came to)
19 Yahas, and dwelt there (until?) my combat with him, and Chamos drove him from ****.
20 I took of Moab two hundred men in all, and I made them go up to Yahas, and I ******* (to annex it to)
21 **** on Dibon. It is I who built the esplanade(?) to the walls of Yearim(?) and the walls of
22 *** And it is I who have built its gates, and it is I who have built its fortress, and it is ***

23 I who have built Bet-Moloch, and it is I who have made the two ****
24 ** Kir and there were no wells in the interior of Kir on its esplanade. And I said to all the people
25 Make every man a well in his house. It is I who have offered the holocaust on the esplanade(?) in
26 ** Israel. It is I who have built Aroër(?) and it is I who have made the road of Arnon.
27 It is I who have built Bet-Bamoth, which was destroyed(?) It is I who have built Bosor, which ***
28 *** Dibon, of the military chiefs, because all Dibon was subject, and I have
29 *** with the cities which I have added to the earth, and it is I who have built ***
30 *** Bet-Diblathaim and Bet-Baal Meon, and I have erected there the ***
31 *** the land. Horonaim, where resided **
32 ** Chamos said to me ** Fight at Horonaim, and I
33 ** Chamos ** on **
34 **

Some pieces of the broken stone have been lost.

Translation of the inscriptions on the sarcophagus which was found at Sidon:

ON THE BODY.

1. In the month of Bul, year 14 of my reigning, I king Ashmanezer king of the Sidonians
2. Son of King Tabinth, king of the Sidonians; spake King Ashmanezer king of the Sidonians, saying: I have been stolen away
3. before my time—a son of the flood of days. The whilom great is dumb—the Son of God is dead. And I rest in this grave, even in thy tomb,
4. in the place which I have built. My adjuration to all the ruling powers, and all men. Let no one open this resting-place, and
5. not search with us for treasure, for there is no treasure with us, and *let him not bear away the couch of my rest*, and not trouble
6. us on this resting-place by disturbing the couch of my slumbers. Even if people should persuade thee, do not listen to their speech. For all the ruling powers and
7. all men who should open the tomb of this my rest, or any man who should *carry away the couch of my rest*, or any man who trouble me or
8. this my couch, unto them there shall be no rest with the departed; they shall not be buried in a grave, and there shall be to them neither son nor seed
9. in their stead, and the holy gods will send over them a mighty king who will rule over them, and
10. cut them off with their dynasty. If any human being should open this resting-place, and any man should carry away
11. this tomb—be he of royal seed or a man of the people; there shall be unto them, neither root below nor fruit above, nor honor among the living under the sun * * *

X—Y

XAN'THICUS. One of the Macedonian months (Neh. NISAN). MONTH.

YARN (Heb. MIKVEH, MIKVE). An error in 2 Chr. i. 16. The king's merchants from Coa took the horses from Coa at a price.

YEAR. CHRONOLOGY.

YELLOW. COLORS.

YOKE (Heb. MOT "bar"), (Nahum i. 13); MOTAH, "bands" (Ez. xxx. 18); Heb. ZEMED, a pair of oxen, so termed as being yoked together (1 Sam. xi. 7). A symbol of subjection and servitude (1 K. 12, 4). See AGRICULTURE.

YOKE-FELLOW (Gr. *suzugos*). A fellow-laborer (Phil. iv. 3).

Z

ZAAN'AIM, THE PLAIN OF, or probably the OAK OF. A sacred tree by Heber's tent, when Sisera took refuge in it (Judg. iv. 11). Near Kedesh Naphtali. Lost.

ZAAN'AN. In the Shefelah. ZENAN.

ZA'AVAN (*unquiet*). Son of Ezer (Gen. xxxvi. 27), a chief.

ZA'BAD (*whom God gave*). 1. Son of Nathan, son of Attai (1 Chr. ii. 31-37). He was one of David's men.—2. An Ephraimite (1 Chr. vii. 21).—3. Son of the Ammonitess Shimeath, and an assassin of King Joash (2 Chr. xxiv. 26).—4. The name of three Israelites in Ezra's time (Ezr. x. 27).—5. The second, one of the sons of Hashum (x. 33).—6. The third, one of the sons of Nebo (x. 43).

ZABADAI'AS. ZABAD 6. (1 Esd. ix. 35).

ZABADE'ANS (1 Macc. xii. 31). The modern *Zebdany* is a village, in a plain of the same name, high up on Anti-Lebanon, watered by the Barada. Pop. 3,000. Kefr Zabad is a small village near.

ZAB'BAL. A corruption of ZACCAI. 1. Son of Bebai (Ezr. x. 28).—2. Father of the BARUCH, who assisted Nehemiah (Neh. iii. 20).

ZAB'BUD. Son of Bigvai, and companion of Ezra (Ezr. viii. 14).

ZABDE'US. ZEBADIAH 6 (1 Esd. ix. 2).

ZAB'DI (*gift of Jah*). 1. Son of Zerah, and ancestor of Achan (Josh. vii. 1, 17).—2. Son of Shimhi (1 Chr. viii. 19).—3. David's officer over the wine-cellars (xxvii. 27), called the *shiphmite*.—4. Son of Asaph (Neh. xi. 17).

ZAB'DIEL (*gift of God*). 1. Father of JASHOBEAM (1 Chr. xxvii. 2).—2. An overseer, son of Haggedolim (Neh. xi. 14).—3. An Arabian chieftain who put ALEXANDER BALAS to death (1 Macc. xi. 17).

ZA'BUD (*given*). Son of NATHAN 1 (1 K. iv. 5) and confidential friend of Solomon.

ZAB'ULON. Gr. form of ZEBULUN (Matt. iv. 13).

ZAC'CAI (*pure*). Ancestor of 760 who returned from Captivity (Ezr. ii. 9; Neh. vii. 14).

ZACCHE'US (Heb. ZACCAI). 1. An officer of Judas Maccabeus (2 Macc. x. 19).—2. A tax-gatherer at Jericho, who climbed up into a sycamore tree to see Jesus as He passed through that place (Luke xix. 1-10). He was son of Abraham, i. e., a Jew.

ZAC'CHUR. One of the family of Mishma (1 Chr. iv. 26).

ZAC'CUR (*mindful*). There are six of this name of no particular note.

ZACHARI'AH. 1. King of Israel who succeeded his father B. C. 773 (2 K. x. 30).—2. Father of Abi (2 K. xviii. 2).

ZACHARI'AS. 1. Father of John the Baptist (Luke i. 5, etc.). There are 10 others, but of no particular account.

ZA'CHER (*remembrance*). Son of Jehiel (1 Chr. viii. 31).

THE GENEALOGY OF ZADOK.

1 Chr. vi. 3-14.	ix. 11.	Ezr. vii. 15.
1. Aaron.		1. Aaron.
2. Eleazar.		2. Eleazar.
3. Phinehas.		3. Phinehas.
4. Abishua.		4. Abishua.
5. Bukki.		5. Bukki.
6. Uzzi.		6. Uzzi.
7. Zerahiah.		7. Zerahiah.
8. Meraioth.		8. Meraioth.
9. Amariah.		
10. Ahitub.		
11. Zadok.		
12. Ahimaaz.		
13. Azariah.		
14. Johanan.		
15. Azariah.	15. Azariah.	
16. Amariah.	16. Amariah.	
17. Ahitub.	17. Ahitub.	
	Meraioth.	
18. Zadok.		18. Zadok.
19. Shallum (Meshullam).		19. Shallum.
20. Hilkiah.		20. Hilkiah.
21. Azariah.		21. Azariah.
22. Seraiah.		22. Seraiah.
23. Jehozadak.		* * *
		Ezra.

ZAD'OK (*righteous*). Son of AHITUB 2, and father of Ahimaaz, high-priest of the Jews (1 Chr. xxix. 3, xii. 28). Others of this name are mentioned in 2 K. xv. 35; 1 Chr. vi. 12; Ezr. vii. 2; Neh. iii. 4, xii. 13. Zadok was called the father of all faithful priests after his time (Ez. xl. 46, etc.).

ZA'HAM (*loathing*). Son of Rehoboam (2 Chr. xi. 19).

ZA'IN (*a weapon*). The seventh letter of the Hebrew alphabet (Ps. cxix.). WRITING.

ZA'IR (2 K. viii. 21). South of Kerek. Lost.

ZA'LAPH (*wound*). Father of Hanun (Neh. iii. 30).

ZAL'MON, MOUNT. Near Shechem (Judg. ix. 48).

ZALMO'NAH. Desert-station (Num. xxxiii. 41). Supposed to be Maan, a few ms. E. of Petra.

ZALMUN'NA (*shelter is denied him*). One of the two kings of *Midian* slain by GIDEON (Judg. viii. 5-21).

ZAM'BIS. AMARIAH 5 (1 Esd. ix. 34).

ZAM'BRI. ZIMRI 1 (1 Macc. ii. 26).

ZA'MOTH. ZATTU (1 Esd. ix. 28).

ZAMZUM'MIM (*noisy people*). A race of giants (Gen. xiv. 5). They were exterminated by the Ammonites (Deut. ii. 20, 21).

ZANO'AH. Two towns in Judah. 1. (Josh. xv. 34), in the Shefelah, now called Zanua, in Wady Ismail. Peopled after the return from Babylon (Neh. xi. 30).—2. (Josh. xv. 56), in the mountain district, 10 ms. S. of Hebron.

ZAPH'NATH-PA-A-NE'AH (Heb. ZAFENATH PA ANEAH). A name given by Pharaoh to JOSEPH 1 (Gen. xli. 45), meaning preserver of the age.

Egyptian titles of princes of high rank, in that age, were generally SUTEN-SA, Pharaoh's superintendent of buildings (or of public works); Other titles were descriptive, as MERKETU, superintendent of buildings (or of public works); Some appear to have been nicknames, as MA, the shepherd (one of the Pharaohs); PE-MAY, the cat; S-NUFRE, good king; S-NUFRE ANKHEE, good worker; PET-AMEN-APT, belonging to Amen of Thebes; SHAFRA-SHA, Shafra rules; and AMEN-EM-HA, Amen in the front.

The original Egyptian name of Joseph has not yet been found on the monuments, where, indeed, but very few records of the age in which he lived have been found. It is expected that further discoveries will bring such records to light. The skilful suggestion of Mr. Poole gives Egyptian words PSENT-ANKHEE, meaning delight lives.

ZA'PHON (*northward*), (Josh. xiii. 27). On the E. side of Jordan. Lost.

ZA'RA. ZERAH 1 (Matt. i. 3).

ZARA'CES. Brother of Jehoiakim (1 Esd. i. 38).

ZA'RAH. ZERAH 1 (Gen. xxxviii. 30).

ZARAI'AS. 1. ZERAHIAH 1 (1 Esd. viii. 2).—2. ZERAHIAH 2 (viii. 31).—3. ZEBADIAH 5 (viii. 34).

ZA'REAH. ZORAH (Neh. xi. 29).

YA'REATHITES, THE. Inhabitants of ZAREAH (1 Chr. ii. 53).

ZA'RED, THE VALLEY OF. Zered.

ZARE'PHATH. Sarepta, near Sidon (Ant. viii. 13, 2). The residence of the prophet Elijah. The miracle of the widow's cruse of oil was wrought here by Elijah (1 K. xvii. 9, 10; Luke iv. 26). There are remains of columns and slabs, and the Roman road is quite perfect here.

ZAR'ETAN. ZARTHAN (Josh. iii. 16). Supposed to be Kurn Surtabeh, N. of Jericho, in the Ghor.

ZA'RETH-SHA'HAR (Josh. xiii. 19). Reuben.

ANTIOCH.

Sara, near the Dead Sea, at the mouth of Wady Zerka Main.

ZAR'HITES, THE (*descendants of Zerah*). 1. A branch of the tribe of Judah (Num. xxvi. 20).—2. A family of Simeonites (Num. xxvi. 13).

ZART'ANAH (1 K. iv. 12). Near Bethshean. Zarthan?

ZAR'THAN. 1. Near Succoth (1 K. vii. 45).—2. The same as Zaretan in Josh. iii. 16.—3. In the upper part of the Jordan valley, near Bethshean.—4. Zeredathah, Zererah, Zererath, Zererathah.

ZATH'OE. Error for ZATTU in 1 Esd. viii. 32.

ZATHU'I. ZALTU (1 Esd. vi. 12).

ZAT'THU. ZALTU (Neh. x. 14).

ZAT'TU (*a sprout*). Ancestor of a family of laymen of Israel, who returned from captivity (Ezr. ii. 8; Neh. vii. 13).

ZA'VAN. ZAAVAN (1 Chr. i. 42).

ZA'ZA (*projection*). Son of Jonathan (1 Chr. ii. 33).

ZEAL (Heb. KINAH, Gr. *zelos*). May include warmth of feeling and vehemence of action, according to the good or bad motive, or the wisdom or folly, of the actor. Thus the zeal of Jehu (2 K. x. 16), of Saul (Phil. iii. 6), of the Israelites (Rom. x. 2), etc.

ZEBADI'AH (*Jah gave*). 9 of these persons mentioned, but none noted (1 Chr. viii. 15, viii. 17, xii. 7, xxvii. 7; Ezr. viii. 8, x. 20; 1 Chr. xxvi. 2; 2 Chr. xvii. 8, xix. 11.)

ZE'BAH (*sacrifice*). A king of MIDIAN, killed with ZALMUNNA (Judg. viii. 5–21).

ZEBA'IM (*antelopes*). The children of Pochereth, of Zeboim, are mentioned among those of Solomon's who returned from Captivity (Ezr. ii. 57; Neh. vii. 59).

PHILIP AND THE EUNUCH.

ZEB'EDEE. The husband of Salome and father of James and John the apostles (Matt. iv. 21, xxvii. 56).

ZEBI'NA (*bought*). Son of Zebo (Ezr. x. 43).

ZEBO'IM (Gen. x. 19). One of the five cities of the plain. Shemeber was its king (xiv. 2). Lost.

ZEBO'IM, THE VALLEY OF (*ravine of the hyenas*), (1 Sam. xiii. 18). E. of Michmash.

ZEBU'DAH. Daughter of Pedaiah, wife of Josiah and mother of King Jehoiakim (2 K. xxiii. 36).

ZE'BUL (*habitation*). Governor of the Shechem (Judg. ix. 28).

ZEBU'LONITE. A member of the tribe of ZEBULUN (Judg. xii. 11, 12).

ZEB'ULUN (*dwelling*). 10th son of JACOB; 6th son of LEAH (Gen. xxx. 20, xxxv. 23). His tribe was respected for numbers (Num. i. 30, xxvi. 26). His posterity is often mentioned with Issachar, his nearest brother (Deut. xxxiii. 18). See TWELVE TRIBES.

ZEB'ULUNITES, THE. People of the tribe of ZEBULUN (Num. xxvi. 27 only).

ZECHARI'AH (*whom Jah remembers*). 1. The 11th in order of the 12 minor prophets. See HISTORY OF THE BOOKS.—2. Son of Shelemiah (1 Chr. ix. 21).—3. Son of Jehiel (ix. 37).—4. A Levite (xv. 18, 20).—5. A prince of Judah (2 Chr. xvii. 7).—6. Son of the high-priest Jehoiada (xxiv. 20).

22 others of this name are mentioned, but are of no particular account.

ZE'DAD (Num. xxxiv. 8; Ez. xlvii. 15). On the N. border of the land as promised by Moses. Passed through by the prophet Ezekiel on his way to Assyria as a captive. Sadud is on the N. end of Anti-Libanus, 50 ms. N. E. of Baalbek.

ZEDEKI'AH (*justice of Jah*) 1. The last king of Judah and Jerusalem. Son of JOSIAH and Hamutal (2 K. xxiv. 17, 19). His history is given in 2 K. xxv. 7, etc. Jer. xxxix. 1-7, lii. 1-11; and 2 Chr. xxxvi. 10, etc., also in Jer. xxi., xxiv., xxvii., xxix., xxxii., xxiv., xxxvii.—2. A false prophet, exposed by Micaiah (2 K. xxii. 11-37).—3. Another false prophet denounced by Jeremiah (Jer. xxix. 21, 22)—4. Son of Hananiah, a prince of Judah (Jer. xxxvi. 12).

ZE'EB (*the wolf*), (Judg. vii. 25, viii. 3; Ps. lxxxiii. 11). One of the two princes (sheikhs) of Midian defeated by Gideon and the 300. He was killed at a winepress which was near the fords of Jordan, and his name given to the place.

ZE'LAH. In Benjamin (Josh. xviii. 28). Here was the residence and the family tomb of Kish, the father of Saul (2 Sam. xxi. 14), where Saul and Jonathan, and the two sons and five grandsons of Saul were buried. Probably Saul's residence before he was made king. Lost.

ZE'LEK (*fissure*). One of David's men (2 Sam. xxiii. 37).

ZELOPH'EHAD (*firstborn*). Son of Hepher, son of Gilead (Josh. xvii. 3). He came out of Egypt with Moses, but died in the wilderness, leaving five daughters and no sons, which led to the establishment of a law that in such cases the daughters should inherit their father's patrimony, but they were not to marry out of their tribe (Num. xxvi. 33, xxvii. 1-11).

ZELO'TES. An epithet given to Simon 5 to distinguish him from Simon Peter (Luke vi. 15).

ZEL'ZAH (1 Sam. x. 2). Benjamin, near Rachel's sepulchre. Mentioned by Samuel the prophet, after anointing Saul king. Lost.

ZEMARA'IM (Josh. xviii. 22). Benjamin. Near Bethel, to the East. Es Sumrah is 4 ms. N. of Jericho, and is probably the place. There was also a Mount Zemaraim (2 Chr. xiii. 4), which has not been identified, and may possibly mean the same locality. The Zemarite's tribe were sons of Canaan (Gen. x. 18), and belonged to this district, given to Benjamin.

ZEMI'RA (*song*). Son of Becher (1 Chr. vii. 8).

ZE'NAN (*flocks*), (Josh. xv. 37). Judah, in the Shefelah. The same as Zaanan (Micah i. 11). Placed by some travellers 2½ ms. S. E. of Mareshah, and now called Zanabra.

ZE'NAS (*given by Zeus*). A lawyer and a friend of Paul (Titus iii. 13).

ZEPHANI'AH. 1. A Kohathite, in the 7th generation from Levi (1 Chr. vi. 36).—2. A priest. He

was among the captives slain by the king of Babylon (2 K. xxv. 18-21).—3. A prophet of the tribe of Simeon (2 Chr. xxiv. 3; Zeph. i. 4, 5).

ZE'PHATH (Judg. i. 17). A Canaanite city destroyed by Judah and Simeon, and its name changed to Hormah. Located in the pass Es Sufa, S. of the Dead Sea.

ZE'PHATHAH, THE VALLEY OF (2 Chr. xiv. 10). Near Mareshah, probably *Tell es Safieh*. Where Asa fought Zerah the Ethiopian and his host, and pursued them unto Gerar.

ZE'PHI. ZEPHO (1 Chr. i. 36).

ZE'PHO (*watch-tower*). Son of Eliphaz (Gen. xxxvi. 11), also a duke ver. 15.

ZE'PHON. Son of Gad (Num. xxvi. 15).

ZE'PHONITES, THE. A family of the tribe of Gad, descended from ZEPHON (Num. xxvi. 15).

ZER (Josh. xix. 35). Fortified town in Naphtali, S. W. of the lake of Gennesareth. May possibly be Hattin.

ZE'RAH (*a rising of light*). 1. Son of Reuel, and grandson of Esau (Gen. xxxvi. 13, 17).—2. Son of Judah and Tamar (Gen. xxxviii. 30); called Zara in Matt. i. 3.—3. Son of Simeon (Num. xxvi. 13); called Zohar in Gen. xlvi. 10.—4. Son of Iddo (1 Chr. vi. 21, 41).—5. A Cushite king who invaded Judah (2 Chr. xiv. 9-13); he was defeated by Asa.

ZERAHI'AH (*Jah caused to be born*). 1. Son of Uzzi, and ancestor of Ezra the scribe (1 Chr. vi. 6, 51). —2. Father of Elihoenai (Ezr. viii. 4).

ZE'RED, THE BROOK OF (*brook of willows*), (Deut. ii. 14). Now called Wady el Ahsy, and running into the S. E. corner of the Dead Sea. Here the wanderings of the Israelites ended; or it may be they continued to the time of the death of Moses.

ZER'EDA (*cooling*), (1 K. xi. 26). In Ephraim. The native city of Jeroboam, the first king of the kingdom of Israel, formed by the ten tribes that revolted. It was fortified for Solomon. The site has not been found, but is supposed by some to be the same as Tir'zah; and by others, Zeredatha.

ZERED'ATHA (2 Chr. iv. 17). Called *Zarthan* (1 K. vii. 46). The vessels for Solomon's temple were cast in the clay-ground between Succoth and this place, in the plain of Jordan. The finest clay is found on the banks of the Jordan, near Succoth, and is carried away for use in casting brass.

ZER'ERATH (Judg. vii. 22). In the Jordan valley. Zeredatha.

ZE'RESH (*gold*). Wife of HAMAN (Esth. vi. 10, 14).

ZE'RETH (*splendor*). Son of Ashur (1 Chr. iv. 7).

ZE'RI. IZRI, son of Jeduthun (1.Chr. xxv. 3).

ZE'ROR (*a bundle*). Ancestor of Kish, the father of Saul (1 Sam. ix. 1).

ZERU'AH (*leprous*). Mother of JEROBOAM 1 (1 K. xi. 26).

ZERUBB'ABEL (*sown in Babylon*). In N. T. and Apocrypha.

ZERU'IAH (*cleft*). Sister of David and mother of his famous generals Joab, Abishai, and Asahel (1 Chr. ii. 16).

ZE'THAM. Son or grandson of Laadan (1 Chr. xxiii. 8).

ZE'THAN (*olive tree*). Son of Bilhan (1 Chr. vii. 10).

ZE THAR (*star*). One of the seven chamberlains of Ahasuerus (Esth. i. 10).

ZI'A (*motion*). A Gadite who dwelt in Bashan (1 Chr. v. 13).

ZI'BA (*statue*). A servant in Saul's house (2 Sam. ix. 2-12, xvi. 1-4, xix. 17, 29).

ZIB'EON (*dyed*). Father of ANAH (Gen. xxxvi. 2).

ZIBI'A (*roe*). Son of Shaharaim by his wife Hodesh (1 Chr. viii. 9).

ZIBI'AH (*roe*). Mother of King JOASH 1 (2 K. xii. 1).

ZICH'RI (*renowned*). 1. Son of Izhar the son of Kohath (Ex. vi. 21).—2. Son of Shimhi (1 Chr. viii. 19).—3. Son of Shashak (viii. 23).—4. Son of Jeroham (viii. 7).—5. Son of Asaph (ix. 15). 7 others of this name are mentioned in the following

WOMEN AT THE WELL.

passages: 1 Chr. xxvi. 25, xxvii. 16; 2 Chr. xvii. 16, xxiii. 1, xxviii. 7; Neh. xi. 9, xii. 17.

ZID'DIM (*the sides*). A town of Naphtali (Josh. xix. 35).

ZIDKI'JAH. ZEDEKIAH, one who sealed the Covenant (Neh. x. 1).

ZI'DON. See SIDON.

ZIF (*blooming*). MONTH.

ZI'HA (*dry*). 1. Ancestor of a family who returned from Captivity (Ezr. ii. 43).—2. Chief of the Nethinim in Ophel (xi. 21).

ZIK'LAG (Josh. xv. 31). Judah in the Negeb. It was the private property of David, and at one time his residence (1 Sam. xxx.). Supposed to be the site now called *Asluj*.

ZIL'LAH (*shade*). Wife of LAMECH 1 (Gen. iv. 19, 22, 23), the mother of Tubal-Cain and Naamah 1.

ZIL'PAH (*a dropping*). The maid of LEAH, who became the second wife of Jacob and mother of Gad and Asher (Gen. xxix. 24, xxx. 9–13).

ZIL'THAI (*shadow of Jah*). 1. A chief, son of Shimhi (1 Chr. viii. 20).—2. A captain who joined David (xii. 20).

ZIM'MAH (*mischief*). 1. Son of Jahath (1 Chr. vi. 20).—2. Son of Shimei, and grandson of Jahath (vi. 42).—3. Father of Joah (2 Chr. xxix. 12).

ZIM'RAN, (*sung*). Eldest son of ABRAHAM by KETURAH (Gen. xxv. 2).

ZIM'RI (*celebrated in song*). 1. A prince of the tribe of Simeon, slain by Phinehas (Num. xxv. 14). —2. A general of half the cavalry of Elah, king of Israel. He rebelled against his master, killed him, usurped his kingdom, and cut off the whole family, not sparing any of his relatives or friends. He reigned but seven days; for the army of Israel made their general, Omri, king, and took the city of Tirzah. Zimri burned himself in the palace, with all its riches (1 K. xvi. 1–20; 2 K. ix. 31). Others of this name are mentioned in 1 Chr. ii. 6; viii. 33–36.

AT LYSTRA.

ZI'NA. Zizah (1 Chr. iii. 10).

ZIN (*coldness*), **THE WILDERNESS OF.** A district between the Arabah and the Desert of Paran, or Tyh mountains, and consisting of three terraces, sloping toward the Dead Sea, by the *Wady Fikreh*. KADESH was in this. Josephus speaks of a hill called Sin, where Miriam was buried. This hill may be what is now *Mod-rah*, isolated, conical, and standing a little S. of Wady Fikreh.

ZI'OR. Judah (Josh. xv. 54), 6 ms. N. E. of Hebron. Now *Sair*.

ZIPH (*mouthful*). 1. Judah, in the Negeb (Josh. xv. 24). Lost.—2. Judah, between Carmel and Juttah (Josh. xv. 55), about 3 ms. S. of Hebron. Some of David's greatest perils and most successful escapes belong to this district (1 Sam. xxiii. 14, 15, 24, xxvi. 2). Also called the Wilderness of Ziph. Rehoboam fortified Ziph (2 Chr. xi. 8).

ZIPH. Son of Jehaleleel (1 Chr. iv. 16).

ZI'PHAH. ZIPH (1 Chr. iv. 16).

ZIPH'IM, THE. Inhabitant of ZIPH 2 (title of Ps. liv).

ZIPH'ITES, THE. ZIPHIM (1 Sam. xxiii. 19).

ZIPH'ION (*a looking out*). Son of Gad (Gen. xlvi. 16).

ZIPH'RON (*sweet odor*). (Num. xxxiv. 9). In the N. boundary of the land. Now *Sudud*, near *Kurietein* (HATSAR ENAN).

ZIP'POR (*sparrow*). Father of BALAK, king of Moab (Num. xxii. 2, 4, 10, 16).

ZIP'PORAH. Daughter of JETHRO, wife of MOSES, and mother of GERSHOM 1 and ELIEZER 2 (Ex. ii. 21, iv. 25, xviii. 2).

ZITH'RI (*protection of Jah*). Son of Uzziel (Ex. vi. 22).

ZIZ, THE PASS OF (2 Chr. xx. 16). Pass of Ain Jidy.

ZI'ZA (*abundance*). 1. A Simeonite chief (1 Chr. iv. 37).—2. Son of Rehoboam (2 Chr. xi. 20).

ZI'ZAH. ZIZA. Second son of Shimei (1 Chr. xxiii. 11).

ZO'AN (*departure*). Tanis, Egypt, on the E. bank of the Tanitic branch of the Nile. It was an important post on the E. of the country, and chief town of a large district of pasture-lands. Called by the Egyptians HA-AWAR, and fortified by SALATIS, the first shepherd king, who stationed here 240,000 men as a protection against the Assyrians. Hebron was built 7 years before Zoan (Num. xiii. 22). There was a great temple here, dedicated to SET (Baal), embellished by Rameses II. The Pharaohs dwelt here, both in the time of Joseph and of the Exodus (Ps. lxxxviii. 12, 43). Mentioned by Isaiah, xix, 13, xxx. 4, 14. The ruins of the temple area show its size, 1250 by 1500 ft., and its remains prove its ancient grandeur. There were 10 or 12 obelisks, all now fallen; the stone for which was originally brought from Syene. The inscriptions and figures are of the age of the shepherd kings.

ZO'AR (*little*), (Gen. xiv. 2, 8). One of the oldest cities of Canaan. First called BELA. When the cities of the plain were destroyed, Zoar was spared as a refuge for Lot (ib. xix. 22, 30). Zoar was seen by Moses from the top of Pisgah (Deut. xxxiv. 3). Following Josephus (Ant. i. 11, § 4), the Crusaders, and later travelers, Zoar was on the LISAN, a promontory on the E. side of the Dead Sea, and now seen in extensive ruins in the lower end of Wady Kerak. Palms once flourished here so abundantly as to give it the name of City of Palms (William of Tyre, xxii. 30). Some have supposed Zoar to have been much nearer Jericho, and on the E. of Jordan, in the *Wady Seir*, near Nimrin.

ZO'BA. In Syria; a kingdom in the time of Saul, David, and Solomon. Its cities were Hamath Zobah (2 Chr. viii. 3); Betah (2 Sam. viii. 8); Tibhath (1 Chr. xviii. 8), which is probably Taibeh, near Aleppo; and Berothai. Hadadezer, king of Zobah, was conquered by David.

ZOBE'BAH (*slow-moving*). Son of Coz, of the tribe of Judah (1 Chr. iv. 8).

ZO'HAR (*whiteness*). 1. Father of Ephron, the Hittite (Gen. xxiii. 8).—2. Son of Simeon (Gen. xlvi. 10).

ZOHEL'ETH (*serpent*), **THE STONE.** By En Rogel (1 K. i. 9). Supposed to refer to the Virgin's Fountain, or a stone near it.

ZO'HETH (*strong*). Son of Ishi (1 Chr. iv. 20).

ZO'PHAH (*a cruse*). Son of Helem or Hotham, the son of Heber (1 Chr. vii. 35, 36).

SERPENT.

ZO'PHAI. ZUPH, son of Elkanah (1 Chr. vi. 26).

ZO'PHAR. ZIPPOR, one of the three friends of Job (Job. ii. 11).

ZO'PHIM (*watchers*), (Num. xxiii. 14). A cultivated field near the top of Pisgah, from which Baalam had his second view of Israel's camp. Perhaps the ruins of *Main*, at the foot of *Jebul Attarus*, surrounded as they are by a fertile plain, mark the site of Zophim.

ZO'RAH (*hornets*), (Josh. xix. 45). Dan, in the Shefelah. The residence of Manoah, and the birthplace of Samson (Judg. xii. 25, xvi. 31), who was buried between Zorah and Eshtaol. It was fortified by Rehoboam (2 Chr. xi. 19), and occupied after the return from Captivity (Heb. xi. 29). Now called *Surah*, on a sharp, conical hill, on the N. side of *Wady Ghurab*. There is a large spring here, "a noble fountain," walled up with large square stones, and gushing over with fine water.

ZO'RATHITES, THE. People of ZORAH (1 Chr. iv. 2).

ZO'REAH. ZORAH (Josh. xv. 33).

ZO'RITES, THE. Are named in the genealogies of Judah (1 Chr. ii. 54).

ZOROBA'BEL. ZERUBBABEL (1 Esd. iv. 13, v. 5–70).

ZOROBA'BEL. The head of the tribe of Judah at the return from the Babylonish CAPTIVITY in the first year of Cyrus. His exact parentage is obscure, from his being called the son of SHEALTIEL or SALATHIEL (Ezr. iii. 2, 8, v. 2, etc.). Cyrus entrusted him with the sacred vessels of the temple, with which he returned to Jerusalem (Ezr. i. 11). He laid the foundations of the temple (Ezr. iii. 8-9), and restored the worship of the Lord, and the usual sacrifices. He refused to permit the Samaritans to assist in rebuilding the Temple (Ezr. iv. 2). In the genealogy of Jesus (Matt. i. 12; Luke iii. 27), he is called the son, and in 1 Chr. iii. 19 the nephew, of SALATHIEL. He was head of the nation and foremost among them.

ZU'AR (*smallness*). Father of Nethaneel, a chief of Issachar (Num. i. 8, ii. 5).

ZUPH. Ancestor of Elkanah and Samuel (1 Sam. i. 1).

ZUPH, THE LAND OF (*honey*), (1 Sam. ix. 5) Not far from the tomb of Rachel, in Judah. *Soba*, 7 ms. W. of Jerusalem.

ZUR (*a rock*). 1. Father of Cozbi (Num. xxv. 15), one of the five princes of Midian (xxxi. 8).—2. Son of Jehiel the founder of Gibeon (1 Chr. viii. 30, ix. 36).

ZURISHAD'DAI (*my rock is the Almighty*). Father of Shelumiel (Num. i. 6, ii. 12.

ZU'ZIM, THE (*strong people*). An ancient people, subdued by Chedorlaomer and his allies (Gen. xiv. 5).

MAP OF EXODUS.

CONCORDANCE
TO THE
OLD AND NEW TESTAMENTS.

TO THE READER.—1. This Concordance doth not pretend to comprehend any more than any other larger ones, but to contain the principal substance of them all in little room. 2. By observing one or more principal words of any remembered text, and what are the first three letters of them, and searching under answerable words in the Concordance, the sentence will be found. 3. The original words, whether nouns or verbs, are marked in CAPITAL letters, and those derived from them come after in *Italics*. 4. Where words are found in many places, the plural is distinguished from the singular, and the parts of verbs ending in *-ed*, *-est*, *-eth*, from their original. But when the examples are few, no such distinction is made, but may be easily observed. 5. The concordant words, except the first, are marked by the first letter, *a*, *b*, &c.; and the mark — stands for several words marked in *Italics*; divine persons are noted by answerable capitals. 6. Even other words, especially names of divine persons, are often marked by one or more of their first letters, **that the sense of the line might be more complete.**
JOHN BROWN.

ABA

A BASE, make low, &c.
Job 40. 11. every one proud *a.*
Isa. 31. 4. lion will not *a.* himself
Ezek. 21. 26. exalt him that is low and *a.* him that is high
Psal. 18. 27. those that walk in pride he is able to *a.*
Matt. 23. 12. whosoever shall exalt himself shall be *a*based
Phil. 4. 12. how to be *a.* and how to
2 Cor. 11. 7. offence in *a*basing myself
ABATED, waters were, Gen. 8. 3.
Gen. 8. 11. so Noah knew that the waters were *a.*
Lev. 27. 18. it shall be *a.* from thy estimation
Deut. 34. 7. his eye was not dim, nor his natural force *a.*
Judg. 8. 3. then their anger was *a.* towards him
ABBA, father, Mark 14. 36. Rom. 8. 15. Gal. 4. 6.
ABHOR, greatly hate and loathe
Lev. 26. 11. my soul shall not *a.* you
15. if your soul *a.* my judgments
30. my soul shall *a.* you
44. neither will I *a.* them
Deut. 7. 26. utterly *a.* it
a. 7. not *a.* Edomite
1 Sam. 27. 12. hath made his people to *a.* him
Job 30. 10. they *a.* me, they flee
42. 6. I *a.* myself and repent
Ps. 5. 6. Lord will *a.* the bloody
119. 163. I hate and *a.* lying
Jer. 14. 21. do not *a.* us for thy name's sake
Amos 5. 10. they *a.* him that speaketh
6. 8. I *a.* the excellency of Jacob
Mic. 3. 9. ye that *a.* judgment
Rom. 12. 9. *a.* that which is evil
Ex. 5. 21. made our savour *ab*horred
Rev. 26. 43. their soul *a.* my statutes
Deut. 32. 19. when the Lord saw it he *a.*
1 Sam. 2. 17. men *a.* the offering of the Lord
Job 19. 19. all my inward friends *a.* me
Ps. 22. 24. nor *a.* affliction of afflicted
78. 59. wroth and greatly *a.* Israel
89. 38. hath cast off and *a.* anointed
106. 40. *a.* his own inheritance
Prov. 22. 14. *a.* of the Lord shall fall
Lam. 2. 7. Lord hath *a.* his sanctuary
Zech. 11. 8. made thy beauty to be *a.*
1 cap. 2. 22. thou that *abhorrest* idols
Zech. 11. 8. their soul *abhorred* me
Job 33. 20. his life *a.* bread
Ps. 10. 3. covetous whom the Lord *a.*
36. 4. he *a.* not evil
107. 18. their soul *a.* all manner of meat
Isa. 49. 7. him whom the nation *a.*
Ch. 31. he *a.* *abhorring* to all flesh
ABIDE, continue, bear
Gen. 19. 2. *a.* ye every man in his place
Num. 35. 25. *a.* in it unto the death of the high priest
2 Sam. 11. 11. ark and Israel *a.* in tents
Ps. 1. 1. who shall *a.* in thy tabernacle
61. 4. I will *a.* in thy tabernacle
7. he shall *a.* before God for ever
91. 1. shall *a.* under the shadow of the Almighty
Prov. 7. 11. her feet *a.* not in her house
19. 23. that hath it shall *a.* satisfied
Hos. 3. 3. shall *a.* for me many days
4. *a.* Israel *a.* without a king
Joel 2. 11. day of the Lord is great and very terrible; who can *a.* it
Mal. 3. 2. who may *a.* the day of his coming
Matt. 10. 11. there *a.* till ye go thence
Luke 19. 5. to-day I must *a.* at thy house
John 12. 46. should not *a.* in darkness

ABO

14. 16. Comforter that he may *a.*
15. 4. *a.* in me and I in you,
10. ye shall *a.* in my love, *a.* in his
Acts 20. 23. afflictions *a.* me
1 Cor. 3. 14. if any man's work *a.*
7. it is good for them if they *a.* even as I
20. let every man *a.* in the same calling wherein he was called
24. is called therein *a.* with God
Phil. 1. 24. to *a.* in the flesh is needful
25. know that I shall *a.* with you
1 John 2. 24. let that therefore *a.* in you
27. 28. ye shall *a.* in him
Ps. 49. 12. man in honour *abideth* not
55. 19. even he that *a.* of old
125. 1. as mount Zion which *a.*
Eccl. 1. 4. the earth *a.* for ever
John 3. 36. wrath of God *a.* on him
8. 35. servant *a.* not but the Son *a.* ever
12. 24. except it die it *a.* alone
34. Christ *a.* for ever
15. 5. *a.* in me brings forth fruit
1 Cor. 13. 13. now *a.* faith, hope
2 Tim. 2. 13. yet he *a.* faithful
1 Pet. 1. 23. word of God *a.* for ever
1 John 3. 6. whoso *a.* in him sinneth not
24. hereby we know he *a.* in us
John 5. 38. not his word *abiding* in you
1 John 3. 15. no murderer hath eternal life *a.*
John 14. 23. make our *abode* with him
ABILITY, in strength, wealth, &c.
Lev. 27. 8. Ezra 2. 69. Neh. 5. 8. Dan 1. 4.
Matt. 25. 15. to every man according to his *a.* Acts 11. 29.
1 Pet. 4. 11. as of the *a.* God giveth
ABJECTS, base sort, Ps. 35. 15.
ABLE, man, such as Sardinia, Ex. 18. 21.
Lev. 14. 22. such as he is *a.* to get
Deut. 16. 17. every man give as he is *a.*
2 Chron. 20. 6. none is *a.* to withstand
Ezek. 46. 11. as he is *a.* to give
Isa. 5. 17. our God is *a.* to deliver us
4. 37. walk in pride he is *a.* to abase
Matt. 3. 9. God is *a.* of these stones to raise us children, Luke 3. 8.
9. 28. believe ye that I am *a.* to do this
10. 28. are not *a.* to kill the soul
19. 12. *a.* to receive it let him
20. 22. are ye *a.* to drink of cup
Mark 4. 33. as they were *a.* to hear
John 10. 29. no man *a.* to pluck you out of my hands
Rom. 4. 21. promised he is *a.* to perform
14. 4. God is *a.* to make him stand
1 Cor. 3. 2. neither yet now are ye *a.*
10. 13. tempted above that ye are *a.*
2 Cor. 9. 8. *a.* to make all grace abound
Eph. 3. 20. *a.* to do exceeding abundantly
Phil. 3. 21. *a.* subdue all to himself
2 Tim. 1. 12. *a.* to keep that committed to him
3. 15. Scriptures *a.* to make thee wise
Heb. 2. 18. *a.* to succour the tempted
5. 7. *a.* to save him from death
Heb. 7. 25. *a.* to save to the uttermost
13. 19. *a.* to raise him from dead
James 1. 21. *a.* to save your souls
4. 12. *a.* to save and to destroy
Jude 24. *a.* to keep you from falling
ABOLISHED, made to cease
Isa. 2. 18. idols he shall utterly abolish
51. 6. righteousness not be *a.*
Ezek. 6. 6. your works may be *a.*
2 Cor. 3. 13. to the end of that *a.*
Eph. 2. 15. having *a.* in his flesh
2 Tim. 1. 10. Jesus Christ who hath *a.* death
ABOMINABLE, very hateful, Lev. 7. 21. & 11. 43. & 18. 30. Isa. 14. 19. & 65. 4.

ABS

Jer. 16. 18.
1 Chron. 21. 6. king's word was *a.* to Joab
Job 15. 16. how much more *a.* is man
Ps. 14. 1. have done *a.* works, 53. 1.
Jer. 44. 4. do not this *a.* thing that I hate
Ezek. 16. 52. hast committed more *a.* than they
Nah. 3. 6. I will cast *a.* filth on thee
Tit. 1. 16. in works deny him being *a.*
1 Pet. 4. 3. walked in *a.* idolatries
Rev. 21. 8. unbelieving and *a.* shall have their part in the lake
ABOMINATION, what is very filthy, hateful, and loathsome, as sin, Isa. 66. 3. Idols, Ez. 8. 28.
Prov. 6. 16. seven things are an *a.* to the Lord
17. a false balance is *a.* to the Lord
24. they of froward heart are *a.* to the Lord
12. 22. lying lips are *a.* to the Lord
15. 8. the sacrifice of the wicked is an *a.*
26. the thoughts of the wicked are an *a.*
16. 5. proud in heart is an *a.* to the Lord, 3. 32.
20. 23. divers weights are an *a.* to the Lord
28. 9. his prayer shall be *a.*
29. 27. unjust man is *a.* to the just
Isa. 1. 13. incense to me *a.* to me
Dan. 11. 31. *a.* that maketh desolate, 12. 11. Matt. 24. 15. Mark 13. 14. *a.* of desolation
Luke 16. 15. is *a.* in the sight of God
Rev. 21. 27. whatsoever worketh *a.*
2 Kings 23. 24. *abominations* of the heathen
Ezra 9. 14. join with the people of these *a.*
Prov. 26. 25. seven *a.* in his heart
Jer. 7. 10. delivered to do all these *a.*
Ezek. 16. 2. cause Jerusalem to know her *a.* 20. 4. & 23. 36.
11. 13. hath done all these *a.* shall surely die
Dan. 9. 27. for the overspreading of *a.*
Rev. 17. 5. mother of harlots and *a.*
ABOVE, higher, heaven, Ex. 20. 4.
John 3. 31. cometh from *a.* is *a.* all
8. 23. I am from *a.* ye are from
19. 11. power given thee from *a.*
Gal. 4. 26. Jerusalem, which is *a.* is free
Eph. 4. 6. one God who is *a.* all
Col. 3. 1. seek things which are *a.*
2. set your affections on things *a.*
Jas. 1. 17. every perfect gift is from *a.*
3. 15. 17. wisdom from *a.* is pure
ABOUND, become very full, large blessings
Prov. 8. 24. Rom. 3. 7.
Matt. 24. 12. because iniquity shall *a.*
Rom. 5. 20. offence might *a.*, but where sin *a.* grace did much more *a.*
6. 1. shall we continue in sin that grace may *a.*
2 Cor. 9. 8. able to make all grace *a.*, that ye may *a.* in every good work
Phil. 1. 9. that your love may *a.* more
4. 12. I know how to be abased and how to *a.*
17. fruit that may *a.* to your account
18. I have all and *a.*
1 Thess. 3. 12. the Lord make you *a.* in love
2 Pet. 1. 8. if these things be in you and *a.*
Col. 2. 7. *a.* therein with thanksgiving
1 Cor. 15. 58. always *abounding*
ABSENT one from another, Gen. 31. 49.

1

ACC

2 Cor. 10, 1.
1 Cor. 5, 3. as a. in body but present
2 Cor. 5, 6. in body we are a. from the Lord
8. willing rather to be a. from the body
9. that whether present or a.
10, 1. being a. am bold toward you
Col. 2, 5. though I be a. in the flesh
ABSTAIN from ideals, Acts 15, 20.
1 Thes, 4, 3. a. from fornication
5, 22. a. from all appearance of evil
1 Tim.4, 3. commanding to a. from meats
1 Pet. 2, 11. a. from fleshly lusts
Abstain for from meat, Acts 27, 21.
ABUNDANCE, great fulness, and plenty, Job 22, 11, & 38, 34. Deut. 33, 19.
1 Chron, 29, 3, 4, 14, 15.
Deut. 12, 47. for the a. of all things
Eccl. 5, 10. he that loveth a. with increase
12. a. of the rich will not suffer him to sleep
Isa. 66, 11. delighted with a. of her glory
Matt. 12, 34. out of a. of the heart the mouth speaketh, Luke 6, 45.
13, 12. shall have more a. 25, 29.
Mark 12, 44. they did cast in of their a.
Luke 12, 15. life consisteth not in a.
2 Cor. 8, 2. a. of their joy abounded
12, 7. through a. of revelations
ABUNDANT in goodness and truth
Ex. 34, 6. 2 Cor, 4, 15, & 9, 12.
2 Cor. 11, 23. in labours more a.
1 Tim. 1, 14. grace of Lord exceeding a.
1 Pet. 1, 3. hast a. mercy hath begotten us
Job 12, 6. God bringeth abundantly
Ps. 36, 8. shall be a. satisfied with fatness
Song 5, 1. yea drink a. O beloved
Isa. 55, 7. he will a. pardon
John 10, 10. might have life more a.
1 Cor. 15, 10. laboured more a. than all
Eph. 3, 20. able to do exceeding a.
Tit. 3, 6. shed on us a. through Jesus
2 Pet. 1, 11. entrance shall be ministered unto you more a.
ABUSE not my power, 1 Cor. 9, 18.
1 Cor 7, 31. use the world as not *abusing* it
ACCEPT, receive kindly in favour, Gen. 32, 20. Acts 24, 5.
Lev. 26, 41. a. punishment of iniquity, 43.
Deut. 33, 11. a. work of his hands
Isa. 24, 23. Lord thy God a. thee
Job 13, 8. will ye a. his person, 10.
32, 21. let me not a. any man's person
42, 8. servant Job, him will I a.
Ps. 119, 108. a. free-will-offerings of my mouth, O Lord
Prov. 18, 5. it is not good to a. the person of the wicked
Ezek. 43, 27. I will a. you, saith the Lord
Mal. 1, 13. should I a. this of your hand
Gen. 4, 7. shalt thou not be *accepted*
19, 21. a. thee concerning this thing
Lev. 1, 4. shall be a. for atonement
Luke 4, 24. no prophet a. in his own country
Acts 10, 35. worketh righteousness is a.
2 Cor. 8, 9. we may be a. of him
6, 2. heard thee in a time a.
8, 12. is a. according that a man hath
Eph. 1, 6. made us a. in the beloved
Luke 20, 21. neither *acceptest* the person
Job 34, 19. him that *accepteth* not the persons of princes
Eccl. 9, 7. God now a. thy works
Hos. 8, 13. Lord a. them not
Gal. 2, 6. God a. no man's person
Heb. 11, 35. not *accepting* deliverance
Acceptable day of the Lord, Isa. 58, 5.
Ps. 19, 14. let the meditation of my heart be a.
Eccl. 12, 10. sought out a. words
Isa. 49, 8. in an a. time I heard thee
61, 2. to proclaim the a. year of the Lord, Luke 4, 19.
Dan. 4, 27. let my counsel be a.
Rom. 12, 1. sacrifice holy a. to God
2. know good and a. will of God
Eph. 5, 10. proving what is a. to the Lord
Phil. 4, 18. sacrifice a. well-pleasing
1 Pet. 2, 5. a. to God by Jesus Christ
Heb. 12, 28. serve God acceptably with fear
1 Tim. 1, 15. worthy of all *acceptation*
ACCESS, admission through Christ, Rom. 5, 2. Eph. 2, 18. & 3, 12.
ACCOMPLISH, perform fully, finish, Lev. 22, 21. Job 14, 6.
Ps. 64, 6. a. a diligent search
Isa. 53, 11. it shall a. that I please
Ezek. 6, 12. thus will I a. my fury
Dan. 9, 2. would a. seventy years
Luke 9, 31. decease he should a. at Jerusalem
2 Chron. 36, 22. word might be *accomplished*
Prov. 13, 19. desire a. is sweet to soul
Isa. 40, 2. her warfare is a. her sin
Luke 12, 50. how am I straitened till it
John 19, 28. all things were now a.
1 Pet. 5, 9. same afflictions are a. in your brethren

2

ADD

Heb. 9, 6. *accomplishing* service of God
ACCORD, hearty agreement, Acts 1, 14. & 2, 1, 46, & 4, 24, & 15, 25.
Phil. 2, 2. of one a. of one mind
ACCOUNT, reckoning, esteem
Job 33, 13. giveth not a. of his matters
Ps. 144, 3. that thou makest a. of him
Eccl. 7, 27. one by one to find out the a.
Matt. 12, 36. give a. in the day of judgment
18, 23. would take a. of his servants
Luke 16, 2. give a. of thy stewardship
Rom. 14, 12. give a. of himself to God
Heb. 4, 17. fruit that may abound to your a.
Heb. 13, 17. as they that must give a.
1 Pet. 4, 5. shall give a. to him that is ready to judge the quick and
Ps. 22, 30. *accounted* to the Lord for a generation
Isa. 2, 22. wherein is he to be a. of
Luke 20, 35. shall be a. worthy to obtain that world
21, 36. a. worthy to escape
22, 24. which should be a. greatest
Gal. 3, 6. a. to him for righteousness
Heb. 11, 19. a. God able to raise
Accursed, devoted to ruin
Deut. 21, 23. hanged is a. of God
Josh. 6, 18. keep yourselves from the a. thing
Isa. 65, 20. sinner a hundred years old shall be a.
Rom. 9, 3. wish myself a. from Christ
1 Cor. 12, 3. no man by Spirit calls Jesus a.
Gal. 1, 8, 9. preach other gospel be a.
ACCUSATION, Ezra 4, 6. Matt. 27, 37.
Luke 6, 7. & 19, 8. John 18, 29. Acts 25, 18.
1 Tim. 5, 19. against an elder receive not an a.
2 Pet. 2, 11. bring not railing a. Jude 9.
ACCUSE, charge with crimes
Prov. 30, 10. a. not servant to master
Luke 3, 14. neither a. any falsely
John 5, 45. that I will a. you to the Father
1 Pet. 3, 16. that falsely a. your good conversation in Christ
Tit. 1, 6. not *accused* of riot
Rev. 12, 10. a. them before our God *accuser* of brethren is cast down
Acts 23, 30. have a. face to face
2 Tim. 3, 3. false a. Tit. 2, 3.
John 5, 45. there is one that *accuseth*
Rom. 2, 15. thoughts *accusing* or excusing
ACCUSTOMED, Jer. 13, 23.
ACKNOWLEDGE, own, confess
Deut. 33, 9. neither did he a. his brethren
Ps. 51, 3. I a. my transgression
Prov. 3, 6. in all thy ways a. him
Isa. 61, 11. ye that see a. even as my might
63, 16. though Israel a. us not
Jer. 3, 13. only a. thine iniquity
14, 20. we a. our wickedness
Hos. 5, 15. until they a. their offence
1 Cor 16, 18. a. them that are such
Ps. 32, 5. I a. my sin
1 John 2, 23. that *acknowledgeth* the Son
2 Tim. 2, 25. *acknowledging* the truth
Tit. 1, 1. a. of the truth which is after godliness
Col. 2, 2. in the *acknowledgment* of the mystery of God
ACQUAINT thyself with him Job 22, 21.
Ps. 139, 3. *acquainted* with my ways
Isa. 53, 3. a. with grief
Acquaintance, familiar friends or companions, Job 19, 13. & 42, 11. Ps. 31, 11. & 55, 13. & 88, 8, 18.
ACQUIT, hold innocent, Job 10, 14.
Nah. 1, 3. will not at all a. the wicked
ACTS of the Lord, Deut. 11, 3, 7.
Judg. 5, 11. rehearse righteous a. of the Lord
1 Sam. 12, 7. reason of all righteous a. of the Lord
Ps. 103, 2. utter mighty a. of Lord
145, 6. speak of thy mighty a. 4.
150, 2. *praise* him for his mighty a.
Isa. 28, 21. his a. his strange a.
John 8, 4. taken in adultery in very a.
ACTIONS weighed, 1 Sam. 2, 3.
ACTIVITY, men of, Gen. 47, 6.
ADAMANT, Ezek. 3, 9. Zech. 7, 12.
ADD fifth part, Lev. 5, 16. & 6, 5. & 27, 13, 15, 19, 27, 31.
Deut. 4, 2. shall not a. unto the word 29, 19. a. drunkenness to thirst
1 Kings 12, 11. I will a. to your yoke
Ps. 69, 27. a. iniquity to their iniquity
Prov. 30, 6. a. not unto his words
Isa. 30, 1. that they may a. sin to sin
Matt. 6, 27. can a. one cubit, Luke 12, 25.
Phil. 1, 16. to a. affliction to my bonds
2 Pet. 1, 5. a. to your faith, virtue
Gen. 22, 18. if any man a. unto these things, God shall a. unto him
Deut. 5, 22. he *added* no more
1 Sam. 12, 19. a. unto all our sins this evil
Jer. 36, 32. were a. many like words
45, 3. a grief to my sorrow
Matt. 6, 33. all these things shall be a. unto you, Luke 12, 31.

ADV

Acts 2, 41. same day were a. about three thousand souls
47. Lord a. to the church such as should be saved
5, 14. believers were the more a. to the Lord
11, 24. much people was a. to the Lord
Gal. 3, 19. the law was a. because of transgression
Prov. 10, 22. *addeth* no sorrow with
ADDER, poisonous serpent, Gen. 49, 17.
Ps. 58, 4. & 91, 13. & 140, 3. Prov. 23, 32.
Isa. 14, 29.
ADDICTED, given up, 1 Cor. 16, 15.
ADJURE, to charge under pain of God's curse, 1 Kings 22, 16. 2 Chron. 18, 15. Matt. 26, 63. Mark 5, 7. Acts 19, 13. Josh. 6, 26. 1 Sam. 14, 24.
ADMINISTRATION, 1 Cor. 12, 5. 2 Cor. 9, 12, & 8, 19, 20. *administered*
ADMIRATION, high esteem, Jude 16. or wonder and amazement, Rev. 17, 6.
2 Thess. 1, 10. *admired* in them that believe
ADMONISH, warn, reprove
Rom. 15, 14. able to a. one another
1 Thess. 5, 12. over you and a. you
2 Thess. 3, 15. a. him as a brother
Eccl. 12, 12. by these be *admonished*
4, 13. foolish king who will no more be a.
Jer. 42, 19. know that I have a. you
Acts 27, 9. Paul a. them
Heb. 8, 5. as Moses was a. of God
Col. 3, 16. *admonishing* one another in psalms and hymns
1 Cor. 10, 11. are written for our *admonition*
Eph. 6, 4. bring them up in the a. of the Lord
Tit. 3, 10. after first and second a. reject
ADOPTION, putting among God's children, Jer. 3, 19. 2 Cor. 6, 18.
Rom. 8, 15. received spirit of a.
23. a. redemption of our body
9, 4. to whom pertaineth the a.
Gal. 4, 5. might receive a. of sons
Eph. 1, 5. unto a. of children
ADORN, deck out, Isa. 61, 10. Jer. 31, 4.
Tit. 2, 10. a. the doctrine of God our Saviour
Jer. 31, 4. *adorned* with thy tabrets
Luke 21, 5. a. with goodly stones and gifts.
1 Pet. 3, 5. holy women a. themselves
Rev. 21, 2. as a bride a. for her husband
Isa. 61, 10. as a bride *adorneth* herself
1 Pet. 3, 3. whose *adorning* let it not
1 Tim. 2, 9. women a. themselves in modest apparel
ADVANTAGE hath Jew, Rom. 3, 1.
2 Cor. 2, 11. lest Satan get an a.
Jude 6, 23. what is a man *advantaged*
ADVERSARY, opposer, enemy
Ex. 23, 22. I will be a. to thy a.
1 Kings 5, 4. is neither a. nor evil occurrent
Job 31, 35. my a. had written a book
Matt. 5, 25. agree with thine a.
Luke 18, 3. avenge me of mine a.
1 Tim. 5, 14. give no occasion to a.
1 Pet. 5, 8. your a. the devil as a roaring lion
1 Sam. 2, 10. *adversaries* of the Lord broken
Lam. 1, 5. her a. are the chief
Luke 21, 15. all your a. not be able
1 Cor. 16, 9. and there are many a.
Phil. 1, 28. nothing terrified by your a.
Heb. 10, 27. shall devour the a.
ADVERSITY, affliction, misery
2 Sam. 4, 9. redeem my soul from all a.
Ps. 10, 6. I shall never be in a.
35, 15. in my a. they rejoiced
94, 13. give rest from days of a.
Prov. 17, 17. brother is born for a.
24, 10. if thou faint in the day of a.
Eccl. 7, 14. in the day of a. consider
Isa. 30, 20. give you the bread of a.
2 Chron. 15, 6. God did vex with all a.
Ps. 31, 7. hast known my soul in a.
1 Sam. 10, 19. saved you out of all a.
ADVICE, Judg. 19, 30. 1 Sam. 25, 33. 2 Sam. 19, 43. Prov. 20, 18.
ADULTERER, put to death, Lev. 20, 10.
Job 24, 15. eye of a. waits for twilight
Isa. 57, 3. seed of a. and whore
Jer. 23, 10. land is full of *adulterers*
9, 2. Hos. 7, 4. be all a.
Mal. 3, 5. I will be a swift witness against a.
1 Cor. 6, 9. neither a. shall inherit the kingdom of God
Heb. 13, 4. whoremongers and a. God will judge
James 4, 4. ye a. and *adulteresses*
Prov. 6, 26. *adulteress* will hunt for life
32. committeth *adultery* lacks understanding
Matt. 5, 28. committeth a. in his heart
2 Pet. 2, 14. having eyes full of a.
Matt. 15, 19. out of the heart proceed *adulteries*, fornications, Mark 7, 21.
Prov. 30, 20. way of *adulterous* woman
Matt. 12, 39. a. generation seeketh a sign. 16, 4. Mark 8, 38.
ADVOCATE with Father, 1 John 2, 1.

DEA — DEC — DEL

DAVID, for Christ. Ps. 89. 3. Jer. 30. 9.
Ezek. 34. 23, 24. & 37. 24, 25. Hos. 3. 5.
Isa. 55. 3.

DAY, time 1. 5. & 32. 28.
Ps. 19. 2, d. unto d. uttereth speech
84. 10. a d. in thy courts is better
118. 24. this is the d. which the Lord
Prov. 27. 1. what d. may bring forth
Amos 5. 3. put far away evil d.
Zech. 4. 10. despised the d. of small
Matt. 6. 34. sufficient to d. is the evil thereof
25. 13. know neither the d. nor hour
John 8. 56. rejoiced to see my d.
1 Cor. 3. 13. the d. shall declare it
Phil. 1. 6. till d. of Jesus Christ, 2. 16.
2 Thess. 2. 2. 1 Cor. 1. 8
Thess. 5. 5. children of the d.
Matt. 10. 15. day of judgment, 11. 22, 24. & 12. 36. Mark 6. 11. 2 Pet. 2. 9. & 3. 7. 1 John 4. 17.
Isa. 2. 12. day of the Lord 13. 6. 9. &
34. 8. Jer. 46. 10. Lam. 2. 22. Ezek. 30.
3. Joel 1. 15. & 2. 1, 31. & 3. 14. Amos
5. 18. Oba. 15. Zeph. 1. 8, 18. & 2. 2, 3.
Zech. 1. 7. & 14. 1. Mal. 4. 5. 1 Cor. 5.
5. Rev 1. 10. 2 Cor. 1. 14. 1 Thess. 5.
2. 2 Pet. 3. 10
Ps. 20. 1. Lord hear thee in the *day of trouble*
50 15. call on me in—91. 15.
59 16. my defence and refuge in—
77 2. in—I sought the Lord
86 7. in—call on thee
Isa. 37. 3. it is a—and rebuke
Nah. 1. 7. Lord is good, a strong hold in—

Hab. 3. 16. I might rest in—
Zeph. 1. 15. a—and distress, desolation
Job 8. 9. days on earth as a shadow
14. 1. of few d. and full of trouble
32. 7. d. should speak, and multitude
Ps. 90. 12. teach us to number our d.
Prov. 8. 16. length of d. is in her right hand
Eccl. 7. 10. former d. better than these
11. 8. remember d. of darkness, many
12. 1. while evil d. come not
Jer. 2. 32. forgotten me d. without
Matt. 24. 22. except those d. be shortened
tial, 4. 10. observe d. months, and years
Eph. 5. 16. because the d. are evil
1 Pet. 3. 10. would see good d.
Gen. 49. 1. *last days*, Isa. 2. 2. Mic. 4. 1.
Acts 2. 17. Jas. 5. 3. 1 Heb. 1. 2. James 5. 3. 2 Pet. 3. 3.
Num. 24. 14. *latter days*, Deut. 31. 29.
Jer. 23. 20. & 30. 24. Dan. 10. 14. Hos. 3. 5.

Job 10. 20. *my days*, 17. 1, 11.
7. 6.—are swifter than a shuttle
16. 1 loathe it—are vanity
9. 25.—are swifter than a post
Ps. 39. 4. know measure of—
6. made—as a handbreadth
102. 3.—are consumed like smoke
11.—are like a shadow, 23 and are shortened
Isa. 39. 8. *peace and truth in—*
Jer. 20. 18.—are consumed with
Ps. 61. 8. daily perform my vows
84. 10. d. loads us with benefits
Prov. 8. 34. watching d. at my gates
Isa. 58. 2. seek me d. and delight in
Acts 2. 47. added to church d.—saved
Heb. 3. 13. exhort one another d.
Job 9. 33. *days-man*, or umpire
38. 12. *day-spring*, Luke 1. 78.
2 Pet. 1. 19. *day-star* arise in your hearts

DEACON, Phil. 1. 1. 1 Tim. 3. 8, 10, 12, 13.

DEAD, Gen. 20. 3. & 23. 3.
Num. 16. 48. stood between d. and living
1 Sam. 24. 14. after a d. dog after
Ps. 88. 10. shall d. of praise, 115. 17.
Eccl. 9. 5. the d. know not any thing
10. 1. d. flies *cause the ointment to stink*
Matt. 8. 22. let the d. bury their d.
22. 32. not God of d. but of living
Luke 8. 52. the maid is not d. but
John 5. 25. d. shall hear the voice of the Son of God
— 11. 25. though he were d. yet shall he live
Rom. 6. 2. d. with Christ, 11. d. to sin
Gal. 2. 19. I through law am d. to law
Eph. 2. 1. who were d. in trespasses
Col. 2. 13. being d. in your sins
3. ye are d. and your life hid with Christ
1 Thess. 4. 16. d. in Christ shall rise first
2 Tim. 2. 11. d. with him, we shall live
Heb. 11. 4. being d. yet speaketh
Rev. 14. 13. blessed are d.—in Lord
Ps. 17. 9. deadly, James 3. 8. Rev. 13. 3.

DEATH, Gen. 21. 16. Ex. 10. 17.
Num. 23. 10. let me die the d. of the righteous
Deut. 30. 15. set before you life and d.
Ps. 6. 5. in d. no remembrance of thee
13. 3. deliver word from d. 116. 8.
48. 20. to Lord belong issues from d.
73. 4. have no bands in their d.
89. 48. liveth and—d. and not see d.
116. 15. precious—is d. of saints
118. 18. not given me over to d.

Prov. 2. 18. her house inclines to d.
8. 36. they that hate me, love d.
18. 21. d. and life in power of tongue
Eccl. 7. 26. more bitter than d. the
8. 8. hath no power in day of d.
Isa. 25. 8. swallow up d. in victory
28. 15. made covenant with d.
38. 18. d. cannot celebrate thee
Jer. 8. 3. d. chosen rather than life
21. 8. way of life, way of d.
Ezek. 18. 32. no pleasure in d. 33. 11.
Hos. 13. 14. I will be thy plagues
Matt. 16. 28. not taste of d. Luke 9. 27.
26. 38. sorrowful even unto d.
John 5. 24. passed from d. to life, 1 John 3. 14.
8. 51. shall never see d.
12. 33. what d. he should die, 21. 19.
Acts 2. 24. loosed the pains of d.
Rom. 5. 12. sin entered, and d. by sin
6. 3. baptized into his d.
4. buried by baptism into d.
5. planted in the likeness of his d.
6. 9. d. hath no more dominion over
21. end of those things is d.
23. the wages of sin is d. but gift of God
7. 5. bring forth fruit unto d.
8. 2. free from law of sin, and d.
6. to be carnally minded is d.
38. d. nor life shall separate from
1 Cor. 3. 22. or life, or d. or things present
11. 26. ye show Lord's d. till he come
15. 21. by man came d. by man
26. d. is swallowed up in victory
55. O d. where is thy sting
56. sting of d. is sin, and strength
2 Cor. 1. 9. had the sentence of d. in ourselves
10. deliver from so great a d.
2. 16. we are savour of d. unto d.
4. 11. delivered to d. for Jesus' sake
12. d. worketh in us, but life in you
Phil. 2. 8. obedient to d. the d. of the cross
Heb. 2. 9. tasted d. for every man
15. through fear of d. are subject to
11. 5. should not see d. Luke 2. 26.
James 1. 15. sin finished brings d.
5. 20. save a soul from d. and hide
1 Pet. 3. 18. put to d. in the flesh
1 John 5. 16. there is a sin unto d.
17. there is a sin unto d. I do not say
Rev. 1. 18. I have the keys of hell and d.
2. 10. be faithful unto d. and I will
12. 11. loved not their lives unto d.
20. 6. second d. hath no power
21. 4. there shall be no more d. nor sorrow

DEAF, Ex. 4. 11. Ps. 38. 13. Isa. 42. 18, 4. 35. 5. Mic. 7. 16.
Lev. 19. 14. shalt not curse the d.
Isa. 42. 18. hear, ye d. and look, ye blind
19. who is d. as my messenger
43. 8. d. people that have ears
Matt. 11. 5. d. hear, dead are raised

DEBATE, Prov. 25. 9. Isa. 27. 8. & 58. 4.
Rom. 1. 29. 2 Cor. 12. 20.

DEBT, Rom. 4. 4. Matt. 6. 12, 18, 27.
Ezek. 18. 7. d. debtor, Gal. 5. 3. Rom. 1. 14. & 8. 12. & 15. 27. Luke 7. 41. Matt. 6. 12.

DECEASE, Luke 9. 31. 2 Pet. 1. 15.

DECEIT, Jer. 5. 27. & 9. 6, 8.
Ps. 72. 14. redeem their souls from d.
101. 7. worketh d. shall not dwell
Prov. 20. 17. bread of d. is sweet
Isa. 53. 9. any d. in his mouth
Jer. 8. 5. they hold fast d. and refuse
Col. 2. 8. spoil you through vain d.
Ps. 35. 20. deceitful, 109. 2. Prov. 11. 18. & 14. 25. & 23. 3. & 27. 6.
Jer. 5. 6. utter bloody and d. man
8. 23. d. men shall not live half
9. 8. turn like a d. bow, Hos. 7. 16.
12. 3. from d. tongue, 52. 4. Mic. 6. 12. Zeph. 1. 13.
Prov. 31. 30. favour is d. and beauty vain
Jer. 17. 9. heart is d. above all things
Eph. 4. 22. according to d. lusts
Ps. 5. 6. deceitfulness of riches
Jer. 14. d. dreadfully, Jer. 48. 10. Job 13. 7. 2 Cor. 4.

DECEIVE, 2 Kings 4. 28. & 18. 29.
Prov. 24. 28. d. not with thy lips
Matt. 24. 4. take heed that no man d. you
24. if possible d. the very elect
1 Cor. 3. 18. let no man d. himself
6. 9. be not deceived, Rev. 12. 9.
Gal. 6. 3. when he is nothing, d. himself
James 1. 26. d. his own heart, 22.
DECENTLY, 1 Cor. 14. 40.

DECLARE, Gen. 41. 24. Isa. 42. 9.
Ps. 22. 22. I will d. thy name unto

38. 18. I will d. my iniquity and
50. 16. what to do to d. my statutes
78. 6. ms. d. them to their children
145. 4. shall d. thy mighty acts
Isa. 3. 9. they d. their sin as Sodom
41. 22. let them d. former things
Mic. 3. 8. d. to Jacob his transgression
Acts 17. 23. we worship, him d. I unto
20. 17. not shunned to d. all counsel
Rom. 3. 25. to d. his righteousness
Heb. 11. 14. say such things d. plainly
1 John 1. 3. seen and is and d. we
— 5. d. declared—Son of God with power
2 Cor. 3. 3. manifestly d. to be the epistle of Christ
Acts 4. 13. d. to man what his thoughts
1 Cor. 2. 1. d. to you testimony of God

DECLINE, Ps. 119. 51, 157.
DECREE, Ezra 6. 13, 17. & 6. 1, 12.
Ps. 2. 7. I will declare the d.
Prov. 8. 15. princes of justice
Zeph. 2. 2. before d. bring forth
Isa. 10. 22. decreed, 1 Cor. 7. 37.

DEDICATE, Deut. 20. 5. 2 Sam. 8. 11.
1 Chron. 26. 20, 26, 27. Ezek. 44. 29.
Num. 7. 84. dedication, Ezra 6. 16, 17.
Neh. 12. 17. John 10. 22.

DEEP, Gen. 44. 15. Judg. 19. 30.
Rom. 10. 18. obedient in word and d.
Col. 3. 17. whatsoever ye do in word or d.
1 John 3. 18. love in d. and in truth
Neh. 17. 14. wipe not out my good deeds
Ps. 28. 4. give them according to their d. Jer. 25. 14. Rom. 2. 6. 2 Cor. 5. 10.
John 3. 19. because their d. were evil
8. 41. do the d. of your father
Rom. 3. 20. by d. of law no flesh be justified
2 John 11. partaker of his evil d.
Jude 15. of all their ungodly d.

DEEP, Gen. 1. 2. Job 38. 30.
Ps. 36. 6. thy judgments are a great d.
42. 7. d. calleth unto d. at the noise
1 Cor. 2. 10. yea d. things of God
2 Cor. 11. 25. I have been in the d.
Isa. 31. 6. deeply revolted
Hos. 9. 9. d. corrupted themselves
Mark 8. 12. sighed d. in spirit
DEFAME, 1 Cor. 4. 13. Jer. 20. 10.
DEFENCE, 2 Chron 11. 5. Isa. 19. 6.
Num. 14. 9. their d. is departed
Job 22. 25. Almighty shall be thy d.
Ps. 7. 10. my d. is of God who saveth
59. 9. God is my d. 16, 17. & 62. 2, 6. & 89. 18. & 94. 22.
Eccl. 7. 12. wisdom is a d. money is a d.
Isa. 4. 5. on all the glory shall be d.
33. 16. place of d. the munitions
DEFER, Eccl. 5. 4. Isa. 48. 9. Dan. 9. 24.
Prov. 13. 12. & 19. 11.

DEFILE, Lev. 11. 44. & 15. 31.
Song 5. 3. how shall I d. them
Dan. 1. 8. would not d. himself
Matt. 15. 18. they d. the man, 20.
1 Cor. 3. 17. if any d. temple of God
Ezek. 22. 8. earth is d. under inhabitants
Tit. 1. 15. are d. and unbelieving, their mind and conscience is d.
Heb. 12. 15. thereby many be d.
Rev. 3. 4. have not d. their garments
14. 4. are not d. with women
22. 27. any thing that defileth
DEFRAUD, Lev. 19. 13. Mark 10. 19.
1 Cor. 6. 7, 8. & 7. 5. 1 Thess. 4. 6. 1 Sam. 12. 3, 4. 2 Cor. 7.
DELAY, Ex. 22. 29. & 32. 1.
Ps. 119. 60. I delayed not to keep thy commandments
Matt. 24. 48. my lord delayeth his coming
Luke 12. 45.

DELICATE, Deut. 28. 56. Isa. 47. 1. Jer. 6. 2. Mic. 1. 16. Jer. 51. 34.
1 Sam. 15. 32. *delicately*, Prov. 29. 21.
DELIGHT, Gen. 34. 19. Num. 14. 8.
Deut. 10. 15. Lord had d. in fathers
1 Sam. 15. 22. hath the Lord as great d. in burnt offerings
Job 22. 26. have thy d. in Almighty
27. 10. will he d. himself in Almighty
Ps. 1. 2. his d. is in the law of God
16. 3. saints in whom is all my d.
37. 4. d. thyself in Lord, he will give
40. 8. I d. to do thy will, O my God
94. 19. thy comforts d. my soul
119. 24. thy testimonies are my d. 174.
Prov. 11. 20. upright are his d. 12. 22.
15. 8. prayer of upright is his d.
Song 2. 3. under shadow with great d.
Isa. 58. 2. let not your soul d. itself in fatness
14. d. to honourable d. of holy of the Lord, honourable
Rom. 7. 22. I d. in the law of God after inward
Ps. 112. 1. delighteth greatly in his commandments
Prov. 3. 12. son in whom he d.
Isa. 42. 1. elect in whom my soul d.
62. 4. Hephzibah, Lord d. in thee
Mic. 7. 18. because he d. in mercy
Ps. 119. 92. thy law hath been my delights, Eccl. 2. 8.
Prov. 8. 31. my d. with sons of men
Song 7. 6. how pleasant, O love, for d.
Mal. 3. 12. for ye shall be a delightsome

19

ENE

Dan. 8. 19. at the time appointed *e.* shall be
12. 8. what shall be the *e.* of these
13. go thy way till the *e.* be
Hab. 2. 3. at the *e.* it shall speak and not tarry
Matt. 13. 39. harvest is *e.* of world
24. 3. what sign of the *e.* of world
6. but *e.* is not yet, Luke 21. 9.
Rom. 6. 21. *e.* of these things is death
22. ye have the *e.* everlasting life
10. 4. Christ is *e.* of law for righteousness
Rom. 14. 9. to this *e.* Christ both died and rose
1 Tim. 1. 5. *e.* of commandment is charity
Heb. 6. 8. whose *e.* is to be burned
16. oath—make an *e.* of all strife
13. 7. considering the *e.* of their conversation
James 5. 11. seen the *e.* of the Lord
1 Pet. 1. 9. receiving the *e.* of your faith
4. 7. *e.* of all things is at hand
17. *e.* of those that obey not gospel
Rev. 21. 6. beginning and *e.* 22. 13. & 1. 8. 1 Sam. 3. 12.
Jer. 4. 27. make a full end. 5. 10, 18. & 30. 11. Ezek. 11. 13.
Num. 23. 10. last end, Jer. 12. 4. Lam. 1. 9. & 4. 18. Dan. 8. 19. & 9. 24.
Deut. 8. 16. latter end, 32. 20. Job 42. 12. Prov. 19. 20. 2 Pet. 2. 20.
Ps. 119. 33. unto the end, Isa. 6. 26. Matt. 24. 13. & 28. 20. John 13. 1. 1 Cor. 1. 8. Heb. 3. 6, 14. & 6. 11. Rev. 2. 26.
1 Tim. 1. 4. endless, Heb. 7. 16.
Ps. 22. 27. all the ends of the world remember
65. 5. confidence of all *e.* of earth
67. 7. all *e.* of earth shall fear him
98. 3. all *e.* of the earth have seen salvation
Prov. 17. 24. eyes of fool in *e.* of the earth
Isa. 45. 22. be ye saved, all *e.* of the earth
52. 10. all *e.* of the earth shall see salvation
Zech. 9. 10. his dominion to *e.* of the earth
Acts 13. 47. for salvation to the *e.* of the earth
1 Cor. 10. 11. on whom *e.* of world are come
ENDOWED, Gen. 30. 20. 2 Chron. 2. 12, 13. Luke 24. 49. James 3. 13.
ENDURE, Job 8. 15. & 31. 23.
Gen. 33. 14. as children are able to *e.*
Ps. 30. 5. weeping may *e.* for a night
132. 26. they perish, but thou shalt *e.*
Prov. 27. 24. doth crown *e.* to every generation
Ezek. 22. 14. can thy heart *e.* ye hands
Mark 4. 17. no root, and so *e.* but for a while
13. 13. that shall *e.* unto end shall
2 Tim. 2. 3. *e.* hardness as a soldier
10. 1. *e.* all things for elect's sake
4. 3. they will not *e.* sound doctrine
5. watch thou, *e.* afflictions, do
Heb. 12. 7. if ye *e.* chastening
James 5. 11. we count happy who *e.*
Ps. 81. 15. should have *endured* for ever
Rom. 9. 22. *e.* with much long suffering
2 Tim. 3. 11. what persecutions I *e.*
Heb. 6. 15. had patiently *e.* he obtained
10. 32. ye *e.* a great fight of afflictions
11. 27. he *e.* as seeing him who is invisible
12. 2. *e.* cross, 3. *e.* contradiction
Ps. 30. 5. his anger *endureth* but a moment
52. 1. the goodness of God, continually
100. 5. his truth *e.* to all generations
145. 13. thy dominion *e.* throughout all
Matt. 10. 22. that *e.* to end, shall be saved, 24. 13. Mark 13. 13.
John 6. 27. meat which *e.* unto life
1 Cor. 13. 7. charity *e.* all things
James 1. 12. blessed that *e.* temptation
Ps. 9. 7. *endure* for ever, the Lord, 102. 12, 26. & 104. 31. his name, 72. 17. his word, 10. 29. 30.
1 Chron. 16. 34, 41. *endureth* for ever, his mercy, 2 Chron. 5. 13. & 7. 3, 6. & 20. 21. Ezra 3. 11. Ps. 106. 1. & 107. 1. & 118. 1, 2, 3, 4, 29. & 136. 1—26. & 138. 8. Jer. 33. 11.
Ps. 111. 3. his righteousness—112. 39. 10. his praise—117. 2. truth of the Lord—
119. 160. every one of thy judgments—135. 13. thy name—
1 Pet. 1. 25. word of Lord—
Ps. 19. 9. fear of Lord enduring for ever
Heb. 10. 34. in heaven *e.* substance
ENEMY, Ex. 15. 6, 9. Ps. 7. 5.
Ex. 23. 22. I will be an *e.* to thy enemies
Deut. 32. 27. I feared wrath of the *e.*
1 Sam. 24. 19. find his *e.* will he let
Job 33. 10. counteth me for his *e.*
Ps. 7. 5. let *e.* persecute my soul
8. 2. mightest still the *e.* and the avenger
Prov. 27. 6. kisses of *e.* are deceitful
Isa. 60. 19. he turned to be their *e.*
1 Cor. 15. 26. the last *e.* destroyed is death

ENT

Gal. 4. 16. am I become your *e.*
2 Thes. 3. 15. count him not as *e.*
James 4. 4. friend of world, *e.* of God
1 Kings 21. 20. mine *enemy,* Ps. 7, 4. Mic. 7. 8, 10. Job 16. 9. Lam. 2. 22.
Ex. 23. 4. thy enemy, Prov. 25. 21. Rom. 12. 20. Matt. 5. 43.
Mic. 7. 6. man's enemies are men of
Rom. 5. 10. if when *e.* we were reconciled
1 Cor. 15. 25. put all *e.* under his feet
Phil. 3. 18. *e.* to the cross of Christ
Col. 1. 21. *e.* in your minds by wicked
2 Thess. 3. 17. his enemies, Ps. 68. 1, 21, & 112. 8. & 132. 18. Prov. 16. 7. Isa. 59. 18. & 66. 6. Heb. 10. 13.
Deut. 32. 41. my enemies, Ps. 18. 17, 48. & 23. 5. & 119. 98. & 139. 22. & 143. 12. Isa. 1. 24. Luke 19. 27.
Num. 32. 21. our enemies, Luke 1. 71, 74.
Ex. 23. 22. thy enemies, Num. 10. 35. Deut. 28. 48, 53, 55, 57. & 33. 29. Judg. 5. 31. Ps. 21. 8. & 92. 9. & 110. 1. Matt. 22. 44. Heb. 1. 13.
Gen. 3. 15. I will put enmity between
Rom. 8. 7. carnal mind is *e.* against God
Eph. 2. 15. abolished *e.* 16. slain *e.*
ENGAGETH his heart, Jer. 30. 21.
ENJOIN, Philem. 8. Esth. 9. 31. Job 36. 23. Heb. 9. 20.
ENJOY, Num. 36. 8. Deut. 28. 41.
Lev. 26. 34. land *e.* her sabbaths, 43.
Acts 24. 2. we *e.* great quietness
1 Tim. 6. 17. giveth richly all things to *e.*
Heb. 11. 25. *e.* pleasures of sin for
ENLARGE, Ex. 34. 24. Mic. 1. 16.
Gen. 9. 27. God shall *e.* Japheth
Deut. 33. 20. blessed be he that *e.* Gad
Ps. 4. 1. thou hast *enlarged* me in distress
25. 17. troubles of my heart are *e.*
119. 32. when thou shalt *e.* my heart
Isa. 5. 14. hell hath *e.* herself
54. 2. *e.* the place of thy tent
60. 5. thy heart shall fear, and be *e.*
Hab. 2. 5. *e.* his desires as hell
2 Cor. 6. 11. our heart is *e.* 13.
Esth. 4. 14. enlargement
ENLIGHTEN darkness, Ps. 18. 28.
Eph. 1. 18. understanding being enlightened
Ps. 19. 8. commandment is pure, enlightening the eyes
Heb. 6. 4. impossible for those once *e.*
EXHORT, 1 Thess. Gen. 33. 9, 11.
Gen. 45. 28. it is Joseph is alive
Ex. 36. 5. bring more than *e.*
2 Sam. 24. 16. said to angel, it is *e.*
1 Kings 19. 4. it is *e.* take away
Prov. 30. 15, 16. say not, it is *e.*
Hos. 4. 10. eat, and not *e.* Hag. 1. 6.
Matt. 10. 25. it is *e.* for disciple
Mark 14. 41. it is *e.* the hour is come
Luke 3. 17. bread *e.* and to spare
22. 38. *e.* *e.* in his temple
24. 34. returned and *e.* early after God
Eccl. 7. 10. thou dost not *e.* wisely
Isa. 21. 12. if ye will *e.* ye
Ezek. 36. 37. this I will be *enquired* of by the house of Israel
Zeph. 1. 6. have not *e.* for him
Matt. 2. 7. Herod *e.* of them diligently
1 Pet. 1. 10. of which salvation prophets have *e.*
Judg. 20. 27. *enquired of the Lord.* 1 Sam. 23. 2, 4. & 30. 8. 2 Sam. 2. 1. & 5. 19, 23. & 21. 1. Jer. 21. 2.
Prov. 20. 25. after vows make *enquiry*
ENRICHED, 1 Cor. 1. 5. 2 Cor. 9. 11.
Ps. 65. 9. thou greatly *e.* it with the river of God
ENSAMPLE, 1 Cor. 10. 11. Phil. 3. 17. 1 Thess. 1. 7. 2 Thess. 3. 9. 1 Pet. 5. 3. 2 Pet. 2. 6.
ENSIGN, Isa. 5. 26. Zech. 9. 16.
Isa. 11. 10. stand for *e.* to people, 12.
Ps. 74. 4. set up their *e.* for signs
ENTER, Gen. 12. 11. Num. 4. 23. Judg. 18. 9. Dan. 11. 17, 40, 41.
Job 22. 4. will he *e.* into judgment, 34. 23.
Ps. 100. 4. *e.* into his gates with
118. 20. gate into which the righteous shall *e.*
Isa. 2. 10. *e.* into rock and hide
26. 2. open, righteous nation may *e.*
20. *e.* into thy chambers, and shut
57. 2. he shall *e.* into peace
Mark 3. 20. in no case *e.* into the kingdom of
6. 6. when thou prayest, *e.* closet
7. 13. *e.* at strait gate, Luke 13. 24.
21. shall *e.* into kingdom of heaven
18. 8. better to *e.* into life, halt
19. 23. rich man hardly *e.* into the kingdom
24. than for rich man to *e.* into the kingdom of heaven, Mark 10. 25. Luke 18. 25.
25. 21. *e.* thou into joy of Lord
Mark 14. 38. watch and pray, lest ye *e.* into temptation, Luke 22. 46.
Luke 13. 24. seek to *e.* but not able
24. 26. suffered and *e.* into his glory
John 3. 4. can he *e.* the second time
5. he cannot *e.* into the kingdom of

ERR

10. 9. by me if any man *e.* in
Acts 14. 22. through much tribulation *e.* kingdom of God
Heb. 4. 3. believed, do *e.* into rest
10. 19. *e.* into holiest by blood of Jesus
Rev. 15. 8. no man able to *e.* into temple
21. 27. *e.* into it, any thing defileth
Rev. 22. 14. *e.* through gates into city
Ps. 143. 2. *enter not into judgment.*
Prov. 4. 14. *e.* not into path of wicked
23. 10. *e.* not into the fields of the fatherless
Matt. 26. 41. that ye *e.* not into temptation
Ps. 119. 130. *entrance,* 2 Pet. 1. 11.
Luke 11. 52. ye *entered* not yourselves
John 4. 38. ye *e.* into their labours
10. 1. that *e.* not by door, but
Rom. 5. 12. sin *e.* into the world
20. the law *e.* that offence might abound
Heb. 4. 6. *e.* not in because of unbelief
10. that is *e.* into his rest, he *e.*
Matt. 23. 13. *entering,* Luke 11. 52. Mark 4. 19. & 7. 15. 1 Thes. 1. 9. Heb. 4. 1.
ENTERTAIN strangers, Heb. 13. 2.
ENTICE, Ex. 22. 16. Deut. 13. 6. 2 Chron. 18. 19, 20, 21. Prov. 1. 10.
Job 31. 27. *enticed,* James 1. 14.
1 Cor. 2. 4. *enticing words,* Col. 2. 4.
ENVY sheweth silly one, Job 5. 2.
Prov. 3. 31. *e.* not the oppressor
14. 30. *e.* is the rottenness of bones
23. 17. let not thy heart *e.* sinners
Eccl. 9. 6. their *e.* is perished
Isa. 11. 13. *e.* of Ephraim shall depart, not *e.* Judah
26. 11. shall be ashamed for their *e.*
Ezek. 35. 11. do according to thine *e.*
Matt. 27. 18. for *e.* they delivered
Acts 7. 9. moved with *e.* 17. 5.
13. 45. Jews filled with *e.* spake
Rom. 1. 29. full of *e.* murder
Phil. 1. 15. preach Christ of *e.*
1 Tim. 6. 4. whereof cometh *e.*
Tit. 3. 3. living in *e.* hateful and hating
James 4. 5. spirit in us lusteth to *e.*
1 Pet. 2. 1. laying aside all *e.*
Gen. 26. 14. Philistines *envied* him
30. 1. Rachel *e.* her sister
37. 11. his brethren *e.* him
Ps. 106. 16. they *e.* Moses in camp
Eccl. 4. 4. man is *e.* of his neighbour
Num. 11. 29. *enviest* thou for my sake
1 Cor. 13. 4. charity *envieth* not
Rom. 13. 13. not in strife and *envying*
1 Cor. 3. 3. there is among you *e.*
2 Cor. 12. 20. debates, *e.* wraths
Gal. 5. 26. *e.* one another
James 3. 14. ye have bitter *e.* and
16. where *e.* is, there is confusion
Gal. 5. 21. *envyings,* murders
Ps. 37. 1. *envious,* 73. 3. Prov. 24. 1. 19.
EPHOD, Ex. 29. 2. Judg. 8. 27. & 17. 5. 1 Sam. 2. 18, & 21. 9. & 23. 9. & 30. 7. 2 Sam. 6. 14. Hos. 3. 4.
EPISTLE, Acts 15. 30. & 23. 33. Rom. 16. 22. 1 Cor. 5. 9. 2 Cor. 7. 8. Col. 4. 16. 1 Thes. 5. 27. 2 Thes. 2. 15. & 3. 14, 17. 2 Pet. 3. 1.
2 Cor. 3. 2. *e.* written in our hearts
3. ye are declared the *e.* of Christ
EQUITY, Ps. 98. 9. Ps. 17. 2. & 65. 18. Prov. 26. 7. Lam. 2. 13.
Isa. 40. 25. to whom shall I be *e.*
46. 5. to whom will ye make me *e.*
Ezek. 18. 25. way of Lord is not *e.*
29. & 33. 17, 20. their way is not *e.*
Matt. 20. 12. made them *e.* to us
Luke 20. 36. *e.* to the angels
John 5. 18. making himself *e.* with God
Phil. 2. 6. no robbery to be *e.* with God
Col. 4. 1. give that which is just and *e.*
Rev. 21. 16. length, breadth, and height *e.*
Gal. 1. 14. *equals,* Ps. 55. 13.
2 Cor. 8. 14. *equality*
Ps. 99. 4. dost establish *equity*
72. 2. judge poor with *e.* 98. 9.
Prov. 1. 3. receive instruction of *e.*
2. 9. understand judgment and *e.*
17. 26. to strike princes for *e.*
Eccl. 2. 21. whose labour is in *e.*
Isa. 11. 4. reprove with *e.* for
59. 14. truth is fallen, and *e.* cannot enter
Mic. 3. 9. that pervert all *e.*
Mal. 2. 6. walked with me in *e.*
ERR, 2 Chron. 33. 9. Isa. 19. 14.
119. 21. do *e.* from thy commandments
Prov. 14. 22. do they not *e.* that devise ill
19. 27. instruction that causeth to *e.*
Isa. 3. 12. lead—cause to *e.* 9. 16.
28. 7. bridle causing them to *e.*
35. 8. way faring men shall not *e.*
63. 17. why made us to *e.* from thy
Jer. 23. 13. prophet caused to *e.* by lies
32.
Hosea 4. 12. of whoredom caused them to *e.*
Amos 2. 4. lies caused them to *e.*
Mic. 3. 5. prophets make my people to *e.*
Matt. 22. 29. ye *e.* not knowing the Scriptures
James 1. 16. do not *e.* my brethren
5. 19. if any of you *e.* from truth

FRU

1 Pet. 3. 14. may be f. of him in *peace*
Matt. 7. 25. *founded on a rock*, Ps. 24.
2. Prov. 10. *Isa.* 14. 32.
Ps. 11. 3. if the *foundato*'ns be destroyed
Job 4. 19. whose f. is in the dust
Prov. 10. 25. righteous is an everlasting —
Isa. 28. 16. I lay in Zion a sure f.
Rom. 15. 20. lest I build upon another man's —
1 Cor. 3. 10. laid f. 12. build on this f.
Eph. 2. 20. built on f. of the prophets
1 Tim. 6. 19. for a good f. for time
2 Tim. 2. 19. the f. of God stands sure
Heb. 11. 10. a city which hath f.
Rev. 21. 14. the city hath twelve f.
Matt. 13. 35. *foundation of the world*,
25, 34. John 17. 24. Eph. 1. 4. 1 Pet.
1. 20. Rev. 13. 8. & 17. 8. Ps. 104. 5.
Prov. 8. 29. Isa. 51. 13, 16.
FOUNTAIN, Gen. 7. 11. Deut. 8. 7.
Deut. 33. 28. f. of Jacob on a land
Ps. 36. 9. with thee is f. of life
vs. 26. bless the Lord from f. of Israel
Prov. 5. 18. let thy f. be blessed
13. 14. law of wise is a f. of life
14. 27. fear of Lord is a f. of life
Eccl. 12. 6. pitcher broken at the f.
Song 4. 12. f. sealed, 15. f. of gardens
Jer. 2. 13. Lord f. of living waters, 17. 13. that my eyes were a f. of tears
Joel 3. 18. a f. out of the house of the Lord
Zech. 13. 1. be a f. opened for the house of
Rev. 21. 6. give of f. of life, freely, 22. 17.
FOXES, Judg. 15. 4. Ps. 63. 10. Song
2. 15. Lam. 5. 18. Ezek. 13. 4. Matt.
8. 20. Luke 13. 32.
FRAGMENTS, Matt. 14. 20. Mark 6. 43. & 8. 19, 20. John 6. 12, 13.
FRAIL I am, Ps. 39. 4.
FRAME, Ps. 50. 19. & 94. 20. & 103. 14. Isa. 29. 16. Jer. 18. 11. Eph. 2. 21.
Heb. 11. 3.
FREE, Ex. 21. 2. Lev. 19. 20.
2 Chron. 29. 31. as many as were of a f. heart
Ps. 51. 12. uphold with thy f. Spirit
vs. 5. f. among the dead, like slain
John 8. 32. truth shall make you f.
36. if Son make f. shall be f. indeed
Rom. 5. 15. so also is f. gift, 16. 18.
6. 7. f. from sin, 18. 22. f. from righte- ousness, 20.
7. 3. f. from law, 8. 2. f. from the law of sin
1 Cor. 7. 22. the Lord's f. man, Christ's servant
Gal. 3. 28. neither bond nor f. Col. 3. 11.
5. 1. Christ hath made us f. not
2 Thes. 3. 1. the word may have f. course
1 Pet. 2. 16. as f. and not using liberty
Hos. 14. 4. I will love them *freely*
Matt. 10. 8. f. ye have received, f. give
Rom. 3. 24. justified f. by his grace
8. 32. with him f. give us all things
1 Cor. 2. 12. things f. given us of God
Rev. 21. 6. of fountain of life f. 22. 17.
FRET not, 1. 7, 8. Prov. 24. 19.
Prov. 19. 3. his heart f. against the Lord
Ezek. 16. 43. hast *fretted* me in all
FRIEND, Jer. 6. 21. Hos. 3. 1.
Ex. 33. 11. to Moses as a man to his f.
Deut. 13. 6. f. which is as his own soul
2 Sam. 16. 17. is this kindness to thy f.
2 Chron. 20. 7. Abraham thy f. Isa. 41. 8. James 2. 23.
Job 6. 14. pity should be shewed from his f.
Prov. 17. 17. f. loveth at all times
18. 24. a f. that sticks closer than a brother
27. 10. own f. and father's f. forsake not
Song 5. 16. this is my beloved and f.
Mic. 7. 5. trust ye not in a f. put not confidence in a guide
John 15. 13. lay down his life for his f.
15. 14. ye are my f. if I5 called you f.
James 4. 4. f. of the world is enemy of God, *friendship* of the world, *enmity* with God
Prov. 22. 24. make no f. with an angry man
Prov. 18. 24. hath f. must show himself *friendly*
FROWARD, Job 5. 13. 1 Pet. 2. 18.
Deut. 32. 20. a very f. generation
Ps. 18. 26. with f. will show thyself f.
101. 4. f. heart shall depart from
Prov. 4. 24. f. mouth, 6. 12. & 8. 13.
10. 31. f. tongue, 11. 20. f. heart, 17. 20.
3. 32. the f. is abomination to the Lord
Isa. 57. 17. went on *frowardly*
Prov. 6. 14. *frowardness* is in him
FRUIT, Gen. 4. 3. Lev. 19. 24.
Gen. 30. 2. withheld f. of the womb,
Ps. 127. 3.
2 Kings 19. 30. bear f. upward, Isa. 37. 31.
Ps. 92. 14. shall bring forth f. in old age
127. 3. f. of womb is his reward
Prov. 11. 30. f. of righteous is a tree of life
Song 2. 3. his f. was sweet to taste
4. 15. *pleasant* f. 7. 13. f. of valley, 6. 11.
Isa. 3. 10. at the f. of their doings
27. 9. all the f. to take away sin

GAI

57. 19. create f. of the lips, peace
Hos. 10. 1. empty vine brings f. to himself
14. 8. from me is thy f. found
Mic. 6. 7. f. of my body for sin of my soul
Matt. 7. 17. good tree brings forth good f. 21. 19.
12. 33. f. good; tree known by his f. 26. 29. not drink of f. of vine till
Luke 1. 42. blessed is the f. of thy womb
John 4. 36. gathers f. to eternal life
15. 2. branch beareth not f. he taketh away; every branch beareth f. he purgeth it, to bring forth more f.
Rom. 6. 21. what f. had, 22. f. to holiness
Gal. 5. 22. f. of Spirit is love, joy
Eph. 5. 9. f. of Spirit is in all goodness
Phil. 4. 17. desire f. that may abound
Heb. 12. 11. peaceable f. of righteousness
13. 15. sacrifices of praise f. of our
James 3. 18. f. of righteousness is sown in
Rev. 22. 2. yielded f. every month
Matt. 3. 8. bring forth fruits meet for repentance
7. 16. small know them by their f.
2 Cor. 9. 10. increase the f. of righteousness
Phil. 1. 11. filled with the f. of righteousness
James 3. 17. full of good f. without hypocrisy
FRUSTRATE, Isa. 44. 25. Gal. 2. 21.
FULL, Gen. 15. 16. Ex. 16. 3. 8.
Deut. 34. 9. Joshua f. of the spirit of wisdom
Ruth 1. 21. I went out f. and returned again empty
1 Sam. 2. 5. that were f. have hired
Job 5. 26. come to grave in f. age
14. 1. of few days and f. of trouble
Ps. 17. 14. they are f. of children
Prov. 27. 7. f. soul loath the honey-comb
30. 9. lest I be f. and deny thee
Luke 4. 1. Jesus being f. of the Holy Ghost
6. 25. wo to you that are f. for
John 1. 14. of God f. of grace and
1 Cor. 4. 8. now ye are f. now ye are
Phil. 4. 12. know both to be f. and
Col. 2. 2. *riches* of f. assurance
2 Tim. 4. 5. *proof* of thy ministry
Heb. 6. 11. diligence to f. assurance
10. 22. draw near in f. assurance
Gen. 29. 27. *fulfil*, Ex. 23. 26.
Ps. 145. 19. f. the desire of them
Matt. 3. 15. it becometh us to f. all righteousness
5. 17. not to destroy the law, but f.
Acts 13. 22. who shall f. all my will
Luke 21. 24. till times of Gentiles be f.
Gal. 5. 14. law is f. in one word
16. shall not f. lust of the flesh
6. 2. bear burden and so f. law of Christ
Eph. 2. 3. f. the desires of flesh and mind
Phil. 2. 2. f. ye my joy, that ye be
Col. 4. 17. ministry, in the Lord, that thou f.
2 Thes. 1. 11. f. all the good pleasure
James 2. 8. if ye f. the royal law
Rev. 17. 17. put in their hearts to f.
Acts 26. 16. in thy *presence* is f. of joy
John 1. 16. of his f. have we received
Rom. 11. 25. till f. of the Gentiles be come
15. 29. f. of blessing of the Gospel
Gal. 4. 4. when the f. of time was come
Eph. 1. 10. *dispensation* of f. of times
23. f. of him that filleth all in all
3. 19. ye may be filled with the f. of God
4. 13. perfect man to the stature of f. of Christ
Col. 1. 19. in him should all f. dwell
2. 9. in him dwells all the f. of the Godhead
FURNACE, Deut. 4. 20. Jer. 11. 4. Ps. 12. 6. Isa. 31. 9. & 48. 10. Dan. 3. 6, 11.
Matt. 13. 42, 50. Rev. 1. 15.
FURNISHED, Deut. 15. 14. Prov. 9. 2.
2 Tim. 3. 17. thoroughly f. to all good works
FURY is not in me, Isa. 27. 4.
59. 18. *repay* f. to his adversaries
Jer. 6. 11. I am full of f. of the Lord
10. 25. pour out thy f. on heathen
Prov. 22. 24. with *furious* man not

G.

GABRIEL, Dan. 8. 16. & 9. 21. Luke 1. 19, 26.
GAIN, Prov. 3. 14. Job 22. 3.
Job 27. 8. hope of hypocrite though he hath g.
Isa. 33. 15. despiseth the g. of oppressions
Phil. 1. 21. to live is Christ, to die is g.
3. 7. what were g. to me I counted loss
1 Tim. 6. 5. *supposing* g. is godliness
6. godliness with contentment is great g.
Matt. 16. 26. if he should g. whole
1 Cor. 9. 19. servant to all, that I might g.
18. 15. thou hast *gained* thy brother
Luke 19. 16. thy pound hath g. ten
Tit. 1. 7. *require greedy* g.
Acts 19. 29. *gainsaying*, Rom. 10. 21. g.

GEN

people
Jude 11. perished in the g. of Core
GALL, Job 16. 13. & 20. 14, 25.
Deut. 29. 18. the root bears g. and wormwood
32. 32. their grapes are grapes of g.
Ps. 69. 21. gave me g. for drink, Matt. 27. 34.
Jer. 8. 14. given us water of g. 9. 15.
Lam. 3. 19. remembering the wormwood and g. 5.
Acts 8. 23. thou art in the g. of bitterness and
GAP, to stand in, Ezek. 22. 30.
GARDEN, Gen. 2. 15. & 3. 23. 13. 10.
Song 4. 12. a g. enclosed is my sister
16. blow on my g. 5. 1. & 6. 2. 11.
Jer. 31. 12. soul as a watered g. Isa. 58. 11.
GARMENT, Josh. 7. 21. Ezra 9. 3.
Job 13. 17. how thy garments are warm
Ps. 22. 18. parted my g. among them
Isa. 9. 5. battle with g. rolled in blood
59. 17. put on g. of vengeance
61. 3. g. of praise for the spirit of heaviness
Joel 2. 13. rend your hearts and not g.
Matt. 21. 8. spread their g. in way
Acts 9. 39. showing g. Dorcas made
James 5. 2. your g. are motheaten
Rev. 3. 4. have not defiled their g. 16. 15. watcheth and keepeth his g.
GATE, Gen. 19. 1. & 34. 20, 24.
Gen. 22. 17. possess g. of his *enemies*
28. 17. this is the house of God, and the g. of heaven
Job 29. 7. I went to g. prepared
Ps. 118. 20. this g. of the Lord into
Matt. 7. 13. enter strait g. Luke 13. 24.
Heb. 13. 12. suffered without the g.
Ps. 9. 13. lift up your heads, o g. 9. Isa. 26. 2.
87. 2. Lord loveth g. of Zion
100. 4. enter his g. with thanksgiving
118. 19. open for me g. of righteousness
Isa. 38. 10. to go to g. of the grave
Matt. 16. 18. g. of hell shall not prevail
GATHER thee from all nations, Deut. 30. 3. Neh. 1. 9. Jer. 29. 14.
Ps. 26. 9. g. not my soul with sinners
Ezek. 3. 15. g. them that are sorrowful
Matt. 3. 12. g. his wheat into garner
7. 16. do men g. grapes of thorns
Eph. 1. 10. to g. in one all things
Ex. 16. 18. 21. he that *gathered* much, had nothing over; g. little, no lack, 2 Cor. 8. 15.
Matt. 23. 37. g. thy children as hen g.
John 4. 36. g. fruit unto eternal life
GAVE, Gen. 14. 20. Ex. 11. 3.
Job 1. 21. Lord g. and Lord taketh away
Ps. 81. 12. I g. them up unto their hearts' lust
Eccl. 12. 7. spirit return to God that g. it
Isa. 42. 24. who g. Jacob for a spoil
John 1. 12. he g. power to become sons
3. 16. God g. his only begotten Son
1 Cor. 3. 6. God g. the increase
2 Cor. 8. 5. first g. themselves to Lord
Gal. 1. 4. who g. himself for our sins
2. 20. g. himself for me, Tit. 2. 14.
Eph. 4. 8. g. gifts unto men, 11. g. some apostles
1 Tim. 2. 6. g. himself a ransom for all
Ps. 21. 4. asked life, thou *gavest* it
John 17. 6. men thou g. me, 22. glory thou g. me, 6. the men thou g. me, 12. & 18. 9. which thou g. me, lost none
GENEALOGIES, 1 Tim. 1. 4. Tit. 3. 9.
GENERATION, Gen. 2. 4. & 6. 9.
Deut. 32. 5. they are a perverse and crooked g.
20. a very froward g. in whom
Ps. 14. 5. God is in the g. of the righteous
22. 30. *accounted* to Lord for a g.
24. 6. this is g. of them that seek
102. 18. written for the g. to come
112. 2. g. of upright shall be blessed
145. 4. one g. shall praise thy works
Isa. 53. 8. who declare his g. Acts 8. 33.
Matt. 3. 7. g. of vipers, 12. 34. & 23. 33.
Luke 16. 8. g. wiser than the children of light
Acts 13. 36. had served his g. according
1 Pet. 2. 9. chosen g. to whom praises
Ps. 33. 11. thoughts to all *generations*
45. 17. name to be remembered in all g.
72. 5. fear thee throughout all g.
79. 13. show forth thy praise in all g.
85. 5. draw out thy anger to all g.
89. 4. build thy throne to all g.
90. 1. our dwelling place in all g.
102. 12. thy truth endureth to all g.
102. 24. thy years are throuout all g.
119. 90. thy faithfulness is to all g.
145. 13. thy dominion endureth to all g.
Col. 1. 26. the mystery hid from ages and
GENTILES, Gen. 10. 5. Jer. 4. 7.
Isa. 11. 10. to it shall the g. seek
42. 6. a light of the g. 49. 6. Luke 2. 32. Acts 13. 47.
60. 3. g. shall come to thy light
60. 5. g. shall see thy righteousness
Matt. 6. 32. after these things do the g. seek

HUS

Isa. 57, 15. of contrite and h. spirit to revive the spirit of h. and heart
James 4, 6. giveth grace to the h. 1 Pet. 5, 5.
Ex. 10, 3. thou refuse to h. thyself
Deut. 8, 2. to h. thee, and to prove, 3, 16.
2 Chron. 7, 14. shall h. themselves and pray
34, 27. because didst h. thyself before God
Prov. 6, 3. h. thyself, and make sure thy friend
Jer. 13, 18. h. yourselves, sit down
Matt. 18, 4. whoso h. himself shall be exalted, 23, 12. Luke 14, 11. & 18, 4.
2 Cor. 12, 21. my God will h. me among you
James 4, 10. h. yourselves in sight of the Lord
1 Pet. 5, 6. h. yourselves therefore
Lev. 26, 41. if uncircumcised hearts be humbled
2 Kings 22, 19. hast h. thy self before the Lord
2 Chron. 12, 6. princes and kings h. themselves
12. be h. himself, 32, 26. & 33, 12.
33, 12, 23. h. not himself before the Lord, 36, 12.
Ps. 35, 13. I h. my soul with fasting
113, 6. Lord who h. himself to behold
Isa. 2, 11. lofty looks shall be h. 9, 17. & 5, 15. mighty man shall be h. and eyes of the lofty shall be h.
10, 33. high and haughty shall be h.
Jer. 44, 10. are not h. unto this day
Lam. 3, 20. my soul is h. in me
Dan. 5, 22. hast not h. thy heart
Phil. 2, 8. h. himself and became obedient
Deut. 21, 14. humbled her, 22, 24, 29. Ezek. 22, 10, 11.
Col. 3, 12. put on humbleness of
Mic. 6, 8. walk humbly with thy God
Prov. 22, 4. by humility are riches and honour, 15, 33. & 18, 12.
Acts 20, 19. serving Lord with all h.
Col. 2, 18. in a voluntary h. 23.
1 Pet. 5, 5. be clothed with h.
HUNGER, Ex. 16, 3. Deut. 28, 48.
Ps. 34, 10. young lions suffer h.
Prov. 19, 15. idle soul shall suffer h.
Jer. 42, 14. no war nor have h. of
Lam. 4, 9. sword better than slain with h.
Deut. 8, 3. suffered thee to h.
Isa. 49, 10. shall not h. nor thirst, Rev. 7, 16.
Matt. 5, 6. blessed are they that h.
Luke 6, 21. blessed are ye that h. now
25 woe you that are full, for ye shall h.
John 6, 35. that cometh to me shall never h.
Rom. 12, 20. If thine enemy h. feed
1 Cor. 4, 11. we both h. and thirst
11, 34. if any man h. let him eat at
Ps. 107, 9. fill the hungry with goodness
146, 7. God giveth food to the h.
Prov. 25, 21. if enemy be h. give him
27, 7. to the h. every bitter thing is sweet
Isa. 58, 7. is it not to deal thy bread to the h.
10. if thou draw out thy soul to h.
65, 13. shall eat; but ye shall be h.
Ezek. 18, 7. hath given his bread to the h. 16.
Luke 1, 53. filled the h. with good
Phil. 4, 12. how to be full and to be h.
HUNT, 1 Sam. 26, 20. Job 38, 39
Ps. 140, 11. evil doth h. the violent
Prov. 6, 26. adulteress will h. for precious
12, 27. slothful roasts not what he took in h.
Ezek. 13, 18. ye h. the souls of my people
Job 10, 16. thou huntest me as a fierce lion
HURT, Gen. 4, 23. & 26, 29.
Josh. 24, 20. will turn and do you h.
Ps. 15, 4. sweareth to his h. and
Eccl. 5, 13. riches kept for owners to their h.
Jer. 8, 11. healed h. of the daughter, 8, 11, 21.
Rev. 2, 11. shall not be h. of second death
6, 6. h. not the oil and wine, 7, 3. & 9, 4.
Ears 4, 15. hurtful, Ps. 144, 10.
1 Tim. 6, 9. fall into foolish and h. lusts
HUSBAND, Gen. 3, 6, 16. & 29, 32.
Ex. 4, 25. bloody h. art thou to me, 26.
Isa. 54, 5. thy Maker is thy h. Lord of hosts
Jer. 31, 32. though I was a h. to them
Mark 10, 12. if a woman put away her h.
John 4, 17. I have no h.
18. and five h.
1 Cor. 7, 14. unbelieving h. is sanctified by
34 careth how she may please h.
14, 35. let them ask h. at home
2 Cor. 11, 2. espoused you to one h.
Eph. 5, 22. wives submit to your h.
23. the h. is the head of wife, 24.
25. h. love your wives, as Christ, Col. 3, 19.

JEW

Eph. 5, 33. the wife see that she reverence her h.
Col. 3, 18. wives submit to your h.
1 Pet. 3, 1. subject to their own h.
7. ye h. dwell with them, according to knowledge
HUSBANDMAN, my Father is, John 15, 1.
1 Tim. 2, 6, h. that laboureth must be
James 5, 7. h. waiteth for precious fruits
1 Cor. 3, 9. ye are God's husbandry
HYMN, Matt. 26, 30. Eph. 5, 19. Col. 3, 16.
HYPOCRISY, Isa. 32, 6. Matt. 23, 28.
Mark 12, 15. Luke 12, 1. 1 Tim. 4, 2.
James 3, 17. 1 Pet. 2, 1.
Matt. 7, 5. hypocrite, Luke 6, 42. & 13, 15.
Matt. 24, 51. appoint him portion with h.
Job 20, 5. joy of h. is but for a moment
27, 8. what is the hope of the h.
36, 13. h. in heart heap up wrath
Isa. 9, 17. every one is a h. and evil
33, 14. fearfulness hath surprised h.
Matt. 6, 2. hypocrites, 16. & 15, 7. & 16, 3. & 23, 13, 14, 15, 23.
Job 8, 13. the h. hope shall perish
15, 34. congregation of h. shall be desolate

I. & J.

IDLE, they be, Ex. 5, 8, 17
Prov. 19, 15. an i. soul sh/all suffer
Matt. 12, 36. every i. word give
20, 3. standing i. 6. why stand ye i.
Luke 24, 11. words seemed as i. tales
1 Tim. 5, 13. they learn to be i. not only i.
Prov. 31, 27. idleness, Eccl 10, 18. Ezek. 10, 49.
IDOL, 2 Chron. 15, 16. & 33, 7.
Isa. 66, 3. as if he blessed an i.
Zech. 11, 17. who to the i. shepherd
1 Cor. 8, 4. an i. is nothing in world
Ps. 96, 5. gods of nations are idols
Isa. 2, 8. land is full of i. they worship them
Jer. 50, 38. they are mad upon i.
Hos. 4, 17. Ephraim is joined to i.
Acts 15, 20. abstain from pollutions of i.
Rom. 2, 22. thou that abhorrest i.
1 Cor. 8, 1. touching things offered to i.
2 Cor. 6, 16. agreement hath temple of God with i.
1 John 5, 21. keep yourselves from i.
Rev. 2, 14. eat things sacrificed to i.
9, 20. worship devils and i. of gold
1 Cor. 5, 10, 11. idolater, 6, 9. & 10, 7.
Eph. 5, 5. Rev. 21, 8. & 22, 15.
1 Sam. 15, 23. stubbornness as iniquity and idolatry
Acts 17, 16. city wholly given to i.
1 Cor. 10, 14. dearly beloved, flee i.
Gal. 5, 20. i. witchcraft, hatred
Col. 3, 5. covetousness, which is i.
1 Pet. 4, 3. walked in abominable idolatries
JEALOUS God, I am a, Ex. 20, 5. & 34, 14. Deut. 5, 9. & 6, 15. Josh. 24, 19.
1 Kings 19, 10. I have been very j. for the Lord, 14.
Ezek. 39, 25. be j. for my holy name
Joel 2, 18. will Lord be j. for land
Nah. 1, 2. God is j. and the Lord revengeth
Zech. 1, 14. I am j. for Jerusalem, 8, 2.
2 Cor. 11, 2. over you with godly jealousy
Deut. 29, 20. Lord's j. shall smoke against man
32, 16. provoked him to j. with strange gods, 21. 1 Kings 14, 22. Ps. 78, 58.
79, 5. shall thy j. burn like fire
Prov. 6, 34. j. is the rage of a man
Song 8, 6. j. is cruel as the grave
Rom. 10, 19. provoke them to j. 11, 11.
1 Cor. 10, 22. do we provoke Lord to j.
JEHOVAH, Ex. 6, 3. Ps. 83, 18. Isa. 12, 2. & 26, 4. when 22, 14. Ex. 17, 15. Je'vv, 6, 24. it is about 2000 times translated Lord, in capitals
JERUSALEM, for the church, Isa. 24, 23. & 62, 1. & 66, 10, 13. Jer. 3, 17. Joel 2, 32. & 3, 16, 17. Zech. 12, 10. & 8, 22. Gal. 4, 25, 26. Heb. 12, 22. Rev. 3, 12. & 21, 2.
JESHURUN, i. e. Israel, Deut. 32, 15. & 33, 5, 26. Isa. 44, 2.
JESUS, or Joshua, Acts 7, 45. Heb. 4, 8
JESUS the Saviour of men, Matt. 1, 21. & 2, 1. & 8, 29. & 14, 1. & 27, 37.
1 Cor. 12, 3. 2 Cor. 4, 5. Eph. 4, 21.
Heb. 2, 9. & 12, 2. Rev. 22, 16. and in about 650 other places
JEWS first, and also Greeks, Rom. 1, 16. & 2, 9, 10, 28. not a J. which is one outwardly; but is a J. which is one inwardly, 29.
Rom. 10, 12. no difference between J. and Greek
1 Cor. 9, 20. to J. I became as a J. to gain J.
Gal. 3, 28. neither J. nor Greek, Col. 3, 11.
Rev. 2, 9. say they are J. and are not

INC

JEWELS, I make up my, Mal. 3, 17.
IGNORANCE, sin through, Lev. 4, 2, 13, 22, 27. Num. 15, 24, 28. Acts 3, 15.
Acts 17, 30. the times of this i. God winked at
Eph. 4, 18. alienated through i. in them
Ps. 73, 22. so foolish was I and ignorant
Isa. 63, 16. though Abraham be i. of us
Rom. 10, 3. being i. of God's righteousness
1 Cor. 14, 38. if any man be i. let him be i.
Heb. 5, 2. who can have compassion on
Acts 17, 23. ignorantly, 1 Tim. 1, 13.
ILLUMINATED, Heb. 10, 32.
IMAGE, Lev. 26, 1. Dan. 2, 31.
Gen. 1, 26. & 9, 6. Col. 3, 10.
Gen. 5, 3. Adam begat a son after his i.
Ps. 73, 20. Lord, thou shalt despise their i.
Matt. 22, 20. whose i. is this, Luke 20, 21.
Rom. 8, 29. conformed to i. of son
1 Cor. 15, 49. have borne the i. of the earthly we shall also bear i. of the heavenly
4, 4. Christ who is the i. of God, Col. 1, 15.
2 Cor. 3, 18. into same i. from glory to
Heb. 1, 3. express i. of his person
Rev. 13, 14. make an i. to the beast
15. 23, 24. break down images, 34, 13.
10, 4. & 17. Acts 4, 23.
IMAGINE, Ps. 2, 1. Nah. 1, 9. Zec. 7, 10. & 8, 17. Acts 4, 25.
Gen. 6, 5. every imagination of the thoughts was evil, 8, 21. Deut 29, 19.
Prov. 6, 18. Lam. 3, 60, 61. Rom. 1, ... 2 Cor. 10, 5.
IMMEDIATELY, Mark 4, 15. Acts 12, 23.
IMMORTAL, invisible, 1 Tim. 4, 17.
Rom. 2, 7. seek for immortality
1 Cor. 15, 53. this mortal must put on i.
1 Tim. 6, 16. who only hath i. in light
2 Tim. 1, 10. brought i. to light by the gospel
IMMUTABLE, Heb. 6, 17, 18.
IMPART, Luke 3, 11. Rom. 1, 11. 1 Thess. 2, 8.
IMPENITENT heart, Rom. 2, 5.
IMPERIOUS whorish woman, Ezek. 16, 30.
IMPORTUNITY, Luke 11, 8.
IMPOSSIBLE, Matt. 17, 20. & 19, 26.
Luke 1, 37. with thee nothing is i.
17, 1. it is i. but offences will come
Heb. 6, 4. it is i. for those once enlightened
18. in two things it is i. for God to lie
11, 6. without faith it is i. to please
IMPOTENT, Prov. 7, 13. Ezek. 2, 4.
IMPUTE, 1 Sam. 22, 15. Lev. 7, 18. &
Ps. 32, 2. to whom Lord i. not iniquity
Rom. 4, 6, i. righteousness without
8. blessed to whom Lord will not i.
11. righteousness might be i. to them
22. i. to him for righteousness, 24.
5, 13. sin is not i. when there is no law.
2 Cor. 5, 19. not i. their trespasses
James 2, 23. i. to him for righteousness
IN Christ, Acts 24, 20. Rom. 12, 5. 1 Cor. 1, 2, 30, & 3, 1. & 15, 18, 22. 2 Cor. 1, 21. & 2, 14. & 3, 14. & 5, 17, 19. & 12, 2. Gal. 1, 22. Eph. 1, 1, 3, 10, 12, 20. & 2, 6, 10, 13. Phil. 1, 1, 13. & 2, 1, 5. & 3, 14. Col. 1, 2, 4
1 Thess. 1, 1. in God, 4, 16. John 9, 21. Col. 3, 3.
Gen. 15, 16. iniquity of Lord, Ps. 4, 5. & 31, & 34, 7. & 35, 23. & 44, 77. Isa. 45, 17, 24, 25. Jer. 3, 20. Zech. 12, 5. 1 Cor. 1, 31. & 4, 17. & 7, 22, 39. Eph. 2, 21. & 6, 10. Phil. 4, 4. Col. 3, 18. & 4, 7, 17. 1 Thess. 5, 12. Philem. 16, 20. Rev. 14, 13.
INCHANTMENT, Lev. 19, 26. Num. 23, 23. Eccl. 10, 11. Isa. 47, 9.
INCLINE heart, Josh. 24, 23. Judg. 9, 3. 1 Kings 8, 58. Ps. 119, 36, 112. &
141, 4.
Ps. 78, 1. incline, 49, 4, 4. & 116, 2. Prov. 2, 2. & 5, 13. Jer. 7, 24, 26, & 11, 8. & 17, 23. & 25, 4. & 34, 14. & 35, 15. & 44, 5. Isa. 55, 3.
INCLOSED, Ps. 17, 10. & 22, 16. Song 4, 12. & 8, 9. Lam. 3, 9.
INCONTINENT, 1 Cor. 7, 5. 2 Tim. 3, 3.
INCORRUPTIBLE God, Rom. 1, 23.
1 Cor. 9, 25. to obtain an i. crown, 15, 52. dead shall be raised i.
1 Pet. 1, 4. begotten to inheritance i. 23. born not of corruptible seed, but of i.
1 Cor. 15, 42, 50, 53, 54. incorruption
INCREASE, Lev. 19, 25. & 25, 7.
Lev. 25, 36. take no usury nor i. 37.
Num. 32, 14. risen up an i. of sinful
Deut. 16, 15. bless thee in all thine i.
Ps. 67, 6. earth yield her i. 85, 12.
Isa. 9, 7. of the i. of his government
Ezek. 18, 8. neither taken any i. 13, 17.
1 Cor. 3, 6. I planted; but God gave the i. 7.
Col. 2, 19. increaseth with i. of God

40

MED

Rev. 19. 7. the m. of the Lamb is come, 9
Jer. 2. 14. I am m. to you, saith Lord
Luke 14. 20. I have m. a wife, and
17. 27. they drank, m. and given in m.
Isa. 62. 5. as a man m. a virgin; thy sons m.
Cor. 7. 9. better to m. than to burn
1 Tim. 4. 3. forbidding to m. and
5. 14. that younger women m. and
MARROW, to bones, Prov. 3. 8. Job 21. 24.
Ps. 63. 5. soul is satisfied as with m.
Isa. 25. 6. feast of fat things full of m.
Heb. 4. 12. dividing asunder joints and m.
MARTYR, Acts 22. 20. Rev. 2. 13. & 17. 6.
MARVEL not, Eccl. 5. 8. John 5. 28. Acts 3. 12. 1 John 3. 13.
Ps. 48. 5. they *marvelled*, Matt. 8. 27. & 9. 8. 33. & 21. 20. & 22. 22. Luke 1. 63. Acts 2. 7. & 4. 13.
Matt. 8. 13. Jesus m. Mark 6. 6.
Job 5. 9. doeth *marvellous* things
10. 16. showed thyself m. against
Ps. 17. 7. show me thy m. kindness, 31. 21.
98. 1. done m. things, Mic. 7. 15.
118. 23. it is m. in our eyes, Matt. 21. 42.
1 Pet. 2. 9. called from darkness into m. light
1 Chron. 16. 12. remember his m. works, Ps. 105. 5. & 9. 1.
Ps. 139. 14. m. are thy works, Rev. 15. 3.
MASTER, Isa. 24. 2. Mal. 1. 6. & 2. 12. Matt. 23. 10. one is your M even Christ.
Mark 10. 17. good M. what shall I do
John 3. 10. art thou a m. in Israel
13. 13. ye call me M. and say well
14. if I your M. have washed your feet
Rom. 14. 4. to his own m. he stands
Eccl. 12. 11. *masters* of assemblies
Matt. 6. 24. no man can serve two m.
Matt. 23. 10. neither be ye called m. James 3. 1.
Col. 4. 1. m. give your servants, Eph. 6. 9.
1 Cor. 3. 10. I as a *master builder*
MATTER, Ex. 18. 22. & 23. 7. 1 Sam. 10. 16. Job 19. 28. & 32. 18. Ps. 45. 1. Prov. 7. 28. 2 Cor. 9. 5.
Acts 8. 21. part nor lot in this m.
Job 33. 13. account of any of his *matters*
Ps. 131. 1. exercise myself in great m.
Matt. 23. 23. omitted the weightier m.
1 Pet. 4. 15. a busybody in other men's m.
MEAN, what, Ex. 12. 26. Deut. 6. 20. 24. Josh. 4. 6. 21. Ezek. 17. 12. Acts 17. 20. & 21. 13. Ezek. 37. 18. Jonah 1. 6.
Gen. 50. 20. ye thought ill; God meant it good
Ps. 39. 7. by any *means*, Jer. 5. 31. 1 Cor. 9. 22. Phil. 3. 11. 1 Thess. 3. 11.
MEASURE, Lev. 19. 35. Deut. 25. 15. Job 11. 9. the m. is longer than earth
Ps. 39. 4. make me know the m. of my days
Isa. 27. 8. in m. when it shooteth
Jer. 30. 11. correct thee in m. 46. 28.
Matt. 7. 2. with what m. ye mete
23. 32. fill up the m. of your fathers
John 3. 34. giveth not Spirit by m.
Rom. 12. 3. gives to every man m.
2 Cor. 1. 8. were pressed out of m.
12. 7. lest I should be exalted above m.
Eph. 4. 7. according to m. of the gift of Christ
13. to the m. of fulness of Christ
Rev. 11. 1. m. the temple of God
MEAT, Job 6. 7. Ps. 42. 3. & 69. 21.
Ps. 104. 27. give m. in due season, 145. 15.
111. 5. giveth m. to them that fear him
Prov. 6. 8. provided m. in summer, 30. 25.
Hos. 11. 4. I laid m. unto them
Hab. 1. 16. portion is fat and m. plenteous
3. 17. the fields shall yield no m.
Hag. 2. 12. his skirt touch m. shall it
Mal. 1. 12. that say his m. is contemptible
Matt. 6. 25. is not life more than m.
10. 10. workman worthy of his m.
John 4. 32. I have m. to eat ye know not of
34. my m. is to do the will of my Father
6. 27. labour not for m. that perisheth
55. my flesh is m. indeed
Rom. 14. 15. destroy not him with thy m.
17. kingdom of God is not m. and drink
1 Cor. 6. 13. m. for belly, belly for m.
8. 8. m. commendeth us not to God
10. 3. did all eat same spiritual m.
MEDDLE, 2 Kings 14. 10. Prov. 17. 14. & 20. 3. 19. & 24. 21. & 26. 17.

MEM

MEDIATOR, is not m. of one, Gal. 3. 20. Gal. 6. 19. ordained by angels in the hand of a m.
1 Tim. 2. 5. one m. between God and
Heb. 8. 6. he is the m. of a better covenant
9. 15. m. of New Testament
12. 24. m. of new covenant
MEDICINE, Prov. 17. 22. Jer. 30. 13. & 46. 11. Ezek. 47. 12.
MEDITATE, Isaac went to, Gen. 24. 63. Josh. 1. 8. m. in thy law day and night, Ps. 1. 2. & 119. 15. 23. 48. 78. 148.
Ps. 63. 6. m. on thee in the night
77. 12. I will m. of thy works, 143. 5.
Isa. 33. 18. thy heart shall m. terror
Luke 21. 14. not m. before what to answer
1 Tim. 4. 15. m. upon these things
Ps. 5. 1. consider my *meditation*
19. 14. let the m. of my heart be acceptable
49. 3. m. of my heart shall be of understanding
104. 34. my m. of him shall be sweet
119. 97. thy law is my m. all the day
99. thy testimonies are my m.
MEEK, Moses was very, Num. 12. 3.
Ps. 22. 26. the m. shall eat and be satisfied
25. 9. m. will he guide in judgment
37. 11. m. shall inherit the earth
76. 9. Lord rose to save all m. of
147. 6. the Lord lifteth up the m.
149. 4. he will beautify the m. with salvation
Isa. 11. 4. reprove for m. of the earth
29. 19. m. shall increase their joy
61. 1. preach good tidings to m.
Amos 2. 7. that turn aside way of m.
Zeph. 2. 3. seek the Lord all m. of the earth
Matt. 5. 5. blessed are m. for they shall inherit the earth
11. 29. I am m. and lowly in heart
21. 5. thy king cometh m. sitting
1 Pet. 3. 4. ornament of m. and quiet
Zeph. 2. 3. seek righteousness, seek *meekness*
Ps. 45. 4. ride prosperously because of m.
1 Cor. 4. 21. come in the spirit of m.
2 Cor. 10. 1. I beseech you by the m. of Christ
Gal. 5. 23. faith, m. against such is no law
6. 1. restore him in spirit of m.
Eph. 4. 2. walk with all lowliness and m.
Col. 3. 12. put on m. longsuffering
1 Tim. 6. 11. follow after faith, love, m.
2 Tim. 2. 25. in m. instructing those
Tit. 3. 2. showing all m. to all men
James 1. 21. receive with m. ingrafted
3. 13. show his works with m. of wisdom
1 Pet. 3. 15. of hope in you with m.
MEET, help, for him, Gen. 2. 18.
Job 34. 31. it is m. to be said to God
Matt. 3. 8. fruits m. for repentance, Acts 26. 20.
1 Cor. 15. 9. not m. to be called an apostle
Col. 1. 12. m. to be partakers of the inheritance
2 Tim. 2. 21. vessel m. for the master's use
Heb. 6. 7. m. for them by whom dressed
Prov. 22. 2. rich and poor m. together
Isa. 47. 3. I will not m. thee as a man
64. 5. thou m. him that rejoiceth
Hos. 13. 8. I will m. them as a bear
Amos 4. 12. prepare to m. thy God
1 Thess. 4. 17. caught up to m. Lord
MELODY in heart to the Lord, Eph. 5. 19.
MEMBER, body not one, 1 Cor. 12. 14.
James 3. 5. tongue is a little m. and
Ps. 139. 16. and in thy book all my *members*
Matt. 5. 29. one of thy m. perish
Rom. 6. 13. yield your m. as instruments
7. 23. I see another law in my m.
12. 5. every one m. one of another
1 Cor. 6. 15. your bodies are m. of Christ
12. 12. the body is one, and hath many m.
Eph. 4. 25. we are m. one of another
5. 30. m. of his body, his flesh and
Col. 3. 5. mortify your m. on earth
MEMORY cut off, Ps. 109. 15.
Ps. 145. 7. utter the m. of thy great goodness
Prov. 10. 7. m. of the just is blessed
Eccl. 9. 5. m. of them is forgotten
Isa. 26. 11. made their m. to perish
1 Cor. 15. 2. if ye keep in m. what I
Ex. 3. 15. my *memorial* to all generations
13. 9. be for m. between thine eyes
17. 14. write this for a m. in book
Ps. 135. 13. thy m. through all generations
Hos. 12. 5. Lord of hosts; the Lord is his m.

MER

Matt. 26. 13. be told for a m. of her
Acts 10. 4. come up for a m. before God
MEN, Gen. 32. 28. & 42. 11.
Ps. 9. 20. know themselves to be but m.
17. 14. m. of thy hand; m. of this world
62. 9. m. of low degree are vanity; m. of high degree are a lie
82. 7. ye shall die like m. and fall
Eccl. 12. 3. strong m. shall bow
Isa. 31. 3. Egyptians are m. not God, Ezek. 28. 2.
46. 8. remember this; show your selves m.
Hos. 6. 7. they like m. transgressed
Rom. 1. 27. m. with m. working
Eph. 6. 6. menpleasers, Col. 3. 22. 1 Thess. 2. 4.
MENSTRUOUS, Isa. 30. 22. Lam. 1. 17. Ezek. 18. 6. neither come near a m. woman
MENTION, Ex. 23. 13. Job 28. 18.
Ps. 87. 10. I will make m. of thy righteousness
Isa. 26. 13. by thee only make m. of
62. 6. ye that make m. of the Lord
Rom. 1. 9. make m. of you in my prayers. Eph. 1. 16. 1 Thess. 1. 2. Philem. 4.
MERCHANT, Hos. 12. 7. Matt. 13. 45.
Isa. 23. 18. *merchandise* be holiness, Matt. 22. 5. John 2. 16. 2 Pet. 2. 3.
MERCY, Gen. 19. 19. & 39. 21.
Ex. 34. 7. keep m. for thousands, Deut. 7. 9. 1 Kings 8. 23. Neh. 1. 5. & 9. 32. Dan. 9. 4.
Num. 14. 18. Lord is of great m.
Ps. 23. 6. goodness and m. shall follow me
25. 10. all paths of Lord are m. 33. 18. fear him and hope in his m. 147. 11.
52. 8. I trust in the m. of God for
57. 3. God shall send forth his m. 10. 20. not turned away his m.
86. 5. plenteous in m. to all, 103. 8.
101. 1. I will sing of m. and
103. 11. great is his m. to them that fear him
17. m. of the Lord is from everlasting to everlasting
106. 1. his m. endureth for ever, 107. 1. & 118. 1. & 136. 1—26. 1 Chron. 16. 34. 41. 2 Chron. 5. 13. & 7. 3. 6. & 20. 21. Ezra 3. 11. Jer. 33. 11.
Prov. 16. 6. by m. and truth, iniquity is purged
20. 28. m. and truth preserve the king
Isa. 27. 11. he that made them will not have m.
Hos. 6. 6. I desired m. and not sacrifice 10. 12. reap in m. 12. 6. keep m.
14. 3. in thee fatherless findeth m.
Jonah 2. 8. they forsake their own m.
Mic. 6. 8. what doth God require, but to love m.
7. 18. delights in m.
20. m. to Abraham
Hab. 3. 2. in wrath remember m.
Luke 1. 50. his m. is on them that fear
78. through tender m. of our God
Rom. 9. 23. on vessels of m. prepared unto glory
15. m. on whom he will have m.
11. 31. through your m. they obtain m.
15. 9. may glorify God for his m.
2 Cor. 4. 1. as we have received m. we faint not
1 Tim. 1. 13. I obtained m. because I did it ignorantly. 2. grace, m. and peace, Tit. 1. 4. 2 John 3. Jude 2.
2 Tim. 1. 18. grant may find m. in
Tit. 3. 5. according to his m. saved
James 2. 13. shall have judgment without m. that showed no m. and m. rejoiceth against judgment
Heb. 4. 16. we may obtain m. and
James 3. 17. full of m. and good
5. 11. Lord is pitiful and of tender m.
Jude 21. looking for the m. of our Lord Jesus Christ
Gen. 32. 10. not worthy of the least of thy *mercies*
1 Chron. 21. 13. great are his m.
Ps. 69. 13. in multitude of thy m. 16.
Isa. 55. 3. the sure m. of David, Acts 13. 34.
Lam. 3. 22. of Lord's m. we are not consumed
Dan. 9. 9. to the Lord belong m. and
Rom. 12. 1. I beseech you by the m. of God
2 Cor. 1. 3. Father of m. and God of
Col. 3. 12. put on bowels of m.
Ps. 25. 6. *tender mercies*, 40. 11. & 51. 1. & 77. 9. & 79. 8. & 103. 4. & 119. 77. 156. & 145. 9.
Prov. 12. 10.—of wicked are cruel
Gen. 19. 19. thy *mercy*, Num. 14. 19. Neh. 13. 22. Ps. 5. 7. & 6. 4. & 13. 5. & 25. 7. & 31. 7. 16. & 33. 22. & 36. 5. & 44. 26. & 85. 7. & 86. 13. & 90. 14. & 94. 18. & 108. 4. & 57. 10. & 119. 64. & 143. 12.
Ex. 15. 13. Lord that *merciful* and gracious, 2 Chron. 30. 9. Neh. 9. 17. 31. Ps. 103. 8. Joel 2. 13. Jonah 4. 2.

NUR　　　　　　　OCC　　　　　　　OIN

O.

PEA

Phil. 4. 7. peace of God which p. all understanding
1 John. 2. 17. world p. away and lusts
PASSION, Acts 1. 3. & 14. 15.
PASSOVER, Ex. 12. 11. Deut. 16. 2.
Josh. 5. 11. 2 Chron. 30. 15. & 35. 1, 11.
Heb. 11. 28.
1 Cor. 5. 7. Christ our p. is sacrificed
PASTORS, Jer. 3. 15. & 17. 16. Eph. 4. 11.
Ps. 74. 1. sheep of thy pasture, 79. 13. & 95. 7. & 23. 2. & 100. 3. Isa. 30. 23. & 49. 9. Ezek. 34. 14, 18. John 10. 9.
PATH, Num. 22. 24. Job 28. 7.
Ps. 16. 11. will show me p. of life
27. 11. lead me in a plain p.
119. 35. go in p. of thy commandments.
139. 3. compasseth my p. and lying down
Prov. 4. 18. p. of the just is as the shining light
26. ponder the p. of thy feet
5. 6. lest thou ponder the p. of life
Isa. 26. 7. thou dost weigh p. of just
Ps. 17. 4. keep me from paths of the destroyer
5. Lord up my goings in thy p.
25. 4. show thy ways; teach me p.
10. all p. of the Lord are mercy
65. 11. all thy p. drop fatness
Prov. 3. 17. all her p. are peace
Isa. 59. 7. destruction are in their p.
8. they have made them crooked p.
Jer. 6. 16. ask for old p. the good
Hos. 2. 6. shall not find her p.
Matt. 3. 3. make his p. straight, Isa. 40. 3.
Heb. 12. 13. make straight p. for feet
PATIENCE with me, Matt. 18. 26, 29.
Luke 8. 15. bring forth fruit with p.
21. 19. in your p. possess your souls
Rom. 5. 3. tribulation worketh p. and experience
8. 25. we do with p. wait for it
15. 4. that we through p. might have hope
5. God of p. grant you to be like minded
2 Cor. 6. 4. as ministers of God, in p.
12. 12. wrought among you in all p.
Col. 1. 11. strengthened unto all p.
1 Thes. 1. 3. p. of hope in our Lord
2 Thes. 3. 4. for your p. and faith
1 Tim. 6. 11. follow after p. meekness
2 Tim. 3. 10. my doctrine, charity, p.
Tit. 2. 2. sound in faith, charity, p.
Heb. 6. 12. through p. inherit the promises
10. 36. have need of p. that after
12. 1. run with p. race set before us
James 1. 3. trying of your faith worketh p.
4. let p. have her perfect work
5. 7. long p. for it till he receive
10. prophets for an example of p.
11. ye have heard of the p. of Job
2 Pet. 1. 6. to temperance p. to p. godliness
Rev. 1. 9. brother in the p. of Jesus
2. 2. I know thy p. 19. hast p. 3.
13, 19. here is p. of saints. 14. 12.
Eccl. 7. 8. the patient in spirit better than the proud
Rom. 2. 7. by p. continuance in well doing
12. 12. p. in tribulation, instant in
1 Thes. 5. 14. be p. toward all men
2 Thes. 3. 5. p. waiting for Christ
1 Tim. 3. 3. not greedy of lucre but p.
2 Tim. 2. 24. gentle, apt to teach, p.
James 5. 7. p. unto coming of Lord
8. be ye also p. establish your
Ps. 37. 7. wait patiently for the Lord, 40. 1.
Heb. 6. 15. after he had p. endured
1 Pet. 2. 20. ye be buffeted, take it p.
PATRIARCH, Acts 2. 29. & 7. 5. Heb. 7. 4.
PATRIMONY, his, Deut. 18. 8.
PATTERN, 1 Tim. 1. 16. Tit. 2. 7. Ezek. 43. 10. Heb. 8. 5. & 9. 23.
PAVILION, Ps. 27. 5. & 31. 20. & 18. 11.
1 Kings 20, 12, 16. Jer. 43. 10.
PAY, Matt. 18. 28. Ps. 37. 21.
PEACE, Lev. 26. 6. Num. 6. 26.
Job 22. 21. acquaint thyself with God, and be at p.
Ps. 34. 14. seek p. and pursue it
37. 37. the end of that man is p.
85. 8. he will speak p. unto people
10. righteousness and p. kissed
119. 165. great p. have they that love
120. 6. hateth p. 7. I am for p.
122. 6. pray for p. of Jerusalem
125. 5. p. shall be upon Israel, 128. 6.
Prov. 16. 7. his enemies to be at p.
Isa. 9. 6. everlasting Father, Prince of p.
26. 3. keep him in perfect p.
27. 5. that he may make p. with me, and he shall make p. with me
32. 17. make p. and create evil
48. 18. had thy p. been as a river
22. there is no p. to the wicked, 57. 21.
57. 2. enter into p. shall rest in beds
19. p. p. to him that is far off

54

PER

20. 8. way of p. they know not, Rom 3. 17.
Isa. 62. 17. will make thy officers p.
66. 12. I will extend p. to her like a river
Jer. 6. 14. saying p. p. when there is no p. 8. 11. Ezek. 13. 10. 2 Kings 9. 19, 22.
Jer. 8. 15. looked for p. but no good come
29. 7. seek p. of the city, for in the p. thereof ye shall have p.
11. thoughts of p. and not of evil
Mic. 5. 5. this man shall be the p.
Zech. 8. 19. love the truth and p.
Matt. 10. 34. I came not to send p.
Mark 9. 50. have p. one with another
Luke 1. 79. guide our feet in the way of p.
2. 14. on earth p. good will towards
19. 42. things that belong to thy p.
John 14. 27. p. I leave; my p. I give
16. 33. in me ye might have p.
Rom. 5. 1. we have p. with God through Jesus Christ
8. 6. spiritually minded is life and p
14. 17. kingdom of God is righteousness
15. 13. fill you with all p. and joy
1 Cor. 7. 15. God hath called us to p.
2 Cor. 13. 11. live in p. and the God of p. shall
Gal. 5. 22. fruit of Spirit is love, p.
Eph. 2. 14. he is our p. 15. making p.
4. 3. unity of Spirit in bond of p.
6. 15. the p. of God, Col. 3. 15.
1 Thes. 5. 13. at p. among yourselves
Heb. 12. 14. follow p. with all men
James 3. 18. sown in p. of them that make p.
1 Pet. 3. 11. let him seek p. and ensue
2 Pet. 3. 14. found of him in p.
1 Tim. 2. 2. lead a peaceable life in all godliness
Heb. 12. 11. yielding p. fruit of righteousness
James 3. 17. is first pure, then p.
Rom. 12. 18. live peaceably with all
Matt. 5. 9. blessed are the peacemakers
PEARL of great price, Matt. 13. 46.
1 Tim. 2. 9. gold, or p. or costly array
Rev. 21. 21. gates were twelve p.
PECULIAR treasure, Ex. 19. 5. Ps. 135. 4.
Tit. 2. 8. p. treasure of promises
Deut. 14. 2. p. people, 26. 18. Tit. 2. 14
1 Pet. 2. 9.
PEN of iron, Job 19. 24. Jer. 17. 1.
Ps. 45. 1. tongue is as the p. of a ready writer
PENURY, Prov. 14. 23. Luke 21. 4.
PEOPLE, Gen. 27. 29. Ex. 6. 7.
Ps. 144. 15. happy is the p. whose God is the Lord
Isa. 1. 4. sinful nation, a p. laden with iniquity
10. 6. against the p. of my wrath
27. 11. a p. of no understanding
54. 5. upon the p. of my curse
Hos. 4. 9. like p. like priest
1 Pet. 2. 10. in time past were not p.
Ps. 73. 10. his people return hither
100. 3. we are called sheep of his
Matt. 1. 21. Jesus shall save—from their sins
Rom. 11. 2. God hath not cast away—
Ps. 50. 7. hear, O my people, and I will speak
Isa. 1. 3.—would not hearken, 8. 13.
Isa. 29. 25. blessed be Egypt—and
26. 20. come—enter into thy chambers
65. 3. surely they are—that will not lie
Jer. 30. 22. ye shall be—and I will be your God, 31. 33. & 24. 7. & 32. 38. Ezek. 11. 20. & 36. 28. & 37. 27. Zech. 2. 11. & 8. 8. & 13. 19. 2 Cor. 6. 16.
Hos. 1. 9. ye are mine, 10. say to them which were not—thou art—
Heb. 11. 25. p. of God, 1 Pet. 2. 10.
PERCEIVE, Deut. 29. 4. 1 John 3. 16.
PERDITION, John 17. 12. Phil. 1. 28.
2 Thes. 2. 3. 1 Tim. 6. 9. Heb. 10. 39.
2 Pet. 3. 7. Rev. 17. 8, 11.
PERFECT, Deut. 18. 13. Ps. 18. 32.
Gen. 6. 9. Noah was a just man and p.
17. 1. walk before me, and be p.
Deut. 18. 13. shalt be p. with God
32. 4. his work is p. is just and right
2 Sam. 22. 31. his way is p. Ps. 18. 30
Job 1. 1. man was p. and upright, 8. & 2. 3.
Ps. 19. 7. law of the Lord is p. converting the soul
37. 37. mark the p. man and behold the upright
Ezek. 16. 14. it was p. through my comeliness
Matt. 5. 48. p. as your Father is p.
19. 21. if thou wilt be p. go and sell all
1 Cor. 2. 6. wisdom among them that are p.
2 Cor. 12. 9. strength is made p. in weakness

PER

13. 11. be p. be of good comfort
Eph. 4. 13. to a p. man unto the measure of stature of Christ
Phil. 3. 12. not as though I were already p.
15. as many as be p. thus minded
Col. 1. 28. present every man p. in Christ Jesus
4. 12. may stand p. and complete
2 Tim. 3. 17. man of God may be p.
Heb. 2. 10. captain of salvation p.
7. 19. the law made nothing p.
12. 23. spirits of just men made p.
13. 21. make you p. in every good
James 1. 4. be p. and entire
17. p. gift
1 Pet. 5. 10. make you p. establish
1 John 4. 18. p. love casteth out fear
Rev. 3. 2. not found thy works p.
2 Cor. 7. 1. perfecting holiness in fear
Eph. 4. 12. for the p. of the saints
Job 11. 7. find out the Almighty to perfection
Ps. 119. 96. have seen end of all p.
Luke 8. 14. bring no fruit to p.
2 Cor. 13. 9. we wish, even your p.
Heb. 6. 1. let us go on unto p.
Col. 3. 14. charity the bond of perfectness
PERFORM, Gen. 26. 3. Ruth 3. 13.
Job 5. 12. hands cannot p. their enterprise
Ps. 119. 106. I have sworn and I will p. it
112. inclined my heart to p. thy statutes
Isa. 9. 7. zeal of Lord of hosts will p.
44. 28. shall p. all my pleasure
Mic. 7. 20. he will p. truth to Jacob
Rom. 4. 21. promised, was able to p.
7. 18. how to p. that which is good
Phil. 1. 6. he will p. it unto day of Jesus Christ
1 Kings 8. 20. Lord hath performed his word
Neh. 9. 8. hast p. thy words
Isa. 10. 12. Lord hath p. his whole work
Jer. 51. 29. every purpose of Lord shall be p.
Ps. 57. 2. God that performeth all things
Isa. 44. 26. p. counsel of messengers
PERILOUS times, 2 Tim. 3. 1.
PERISH, Gen. 41. 36. Lev. 26. 38.
Num. 17. 12. we die, we p. we all p.
Esth. 4. 16. I will go in, if I p. I p.
Ps. 2. 12. ye p. from the way, when 119. 92. have p. in my affliction
Prov. 29. 18. where no vision is, the people p.
Matt. 8. 25. Lord save us, or we p. Luke 8. 24.
John 3. 15. believeth should not p. 10. 10. 28. I give eternal life, they shall never p.
1 Cor. 8. 11. through thy knowledge the weak p.
2 Pet. 3. 9. not willing that any p.
PERMIT, if Lord, 1 Cor. 16. 7. Heb. 6. 3.
1 Cor. 7. 6. by permission, not of commandment
PERNICIOUS ways, 2 Pet. 2. 2.
PERPETUAL, Jer. 50. 5. & 51. 39, 57.
PERPLEXED, 2 Cor. 4. 8. Isa. 22. 5.
PERSECUTE me, Ps. 7. 1. & 31. 15.
Job 19. 22. why p. me as God, 28.
Ps. 10. 2. wicked doth p. the poor
35. 6. let angel of the Lord p. them
71. 11. p. and take him; is none to 83. 15. p. them with thy tempest
2 Thes. 3. 66. p. and destroy them in
Matt. 5. 11. blessed are ye when men p. you
44. pray for them that p. you
Luke 21. 12. they p. you in this city
Rom. 12. 14. bless them which p.
Ps. 109. 16. persecuted the poor and
119. 161. princes p. me without cause
143. 3. the enemy hath p. my soul
John 15. 20. if they p. me they will p. you
Acts 9. 4. why p. thou me, 22.
22. 4. I p. this way to death, 5, 8.
26. 11. I p. them to strange cities, 16.
1 Cor. 4. 12. being p. we suffer it
15. 9. because I p. the church of
2 Cor. 4. 9. p. but not forsaken, cast
Gal. 1. 13. beyond measure I p. the church of God
4. 29. p. him born after the Spirit
1 Thes. 2. 15. have p. us and please not God
1 Tim. 1. 13. who was before a persecutor
2 Tim. 3. 12. live godly, shall suffer persecution
PERSEVERANCE, watching, Eph. 6. 18.
PERSON, Lev. 19. 15.
Mal. 1. 8. will he accept thy p.
Matt. 22. 16. regardest not p. of men
Acts 10. 34. God is no respecter of p.
Deut. 10. 16. ibid. 2. 6. Eph. 6. 9. Col. 3. 25. 1 Pet. 3. 17.
Heb. 1. 3. express image of his p.
12. 16. fornicator or profane p. as

WAR

6. 4. w. in newness of life
8. 1. w. not after the flesh, 4.
2 Cor. 5. 7. we w. by faith, not sight
10. 3. though w. in flesh, not war after the flesh
Gal. 5. 16. as many as w. according to this rule
Eph. 2. 10. ordained that we w. in
4. 1. w. worthy of the vocation
5. 15. w. circumspectly, not as
Phil. 3. 17. mark them who w. so as
Col. 1. 10. that ye might w. worthy
1 Thes. 2. 12. ye would w. worthy of
4. 1. how ought ye to w. and please
1 John 1. 7. if we w. in the light
2. 6. ought so to w. as he walked
3 John 4. to hear that my children w. in truth, 3.
Rev. 3. 4. shall w. with me in white
16. 15. lest he w. naked and see his
21. 24. nations shall w. in light of
John 12. 35. w. in light while ye have
Rom. 13. 13. let us w. honestly as in
Gal. 5. 16. w. in Spirit, and not fulfil
25. if we live in Spirit, let us w. in
Eph. 5. 2. w. in love as Christ loved
w. as children of light
Phil. 3. 16. let us w. by the same rule
Col. 2. 6. as ye received Christ, so w.
4. 5. w. in wisdom, redeeming the
Gen. 6. 9. Noah walked with God
5. 22. Enoch w. with God, 24.
Ps. 55. 14. we w. unto the house of God in company
81. 12. w. in their own counsels
13. O that Israel had w. in my
Isa. 9. 2. people that w. in darkness
2 Cor. 10. 2. as if we w. according to the flesh
12. 18. w. we not in same spirit
Gal. 2. 14. saw that they w. not uprightly
Eph. 2. 2. in time past ye w. Col. 3. 7
1 Pet. 4. 3. we w. in lasciviousness
Isa. 43. 2. when thou walkest through the fire
Rom. 14. 15. w. thou not charitably
Ps. 15. 2. he that walketh uprightly
32. 6. every man so w. in a vain show
Prov. 10. 9. he that w. uprightly, w. surely
13. 20. w. with wise men shall be
Isa. 50. 10. w. in darkness, and hath
Jer. 10. 23. not in man that w. to direct his steps
Mic. 2. 7. do good to him that w. uprightly
2 Thes. 3. 6. w. about seeking whom he may devour
Rev. 2. 1. w. in midst of the seven golden candlesticks
Gen. 3. 8. voice of Lord walking in
Ps. 67. 2. w. in his own uprightness
Jer. 6. 28. revolters w. with slanders
Mic. 2. 11. if man w. in falsehood do
Luke 1. 6. w. in all commandments
Acts 3. 31. w. in the fear of the Lord
2 Cor. 4. 2. not w. in craftiness
1 Pet. 5. 3. w. after their own lusts, Jude 18.
2 John 4. thy children w. in truth
WALL, Ps. 62. 3. Prov. 18. 11. Song 2. 9. & 8. 9, 10. Isa. 26. 1. & 60. 18.
WANDER, Num. 14. 33. Ps. 119. 10. Lam. 4. 14. wandered, Heb. 11. 37.
Prov. 21. 16. wandereth, 27. 8.
1 Tim. 5. 13. wandering, Jude 13.
Ps. 56. 8. tellest my wanderings
WANT, Deut. 28. 48. Job 31. 19.
Ps. 23. 1. the Lord is my shepherd, I shall not w.
34. 9. no w. to them that fear him
Prov. 6. 11. thy w. come as an armed man, 24. 34.
2 Cor. 8. 14. a supply for your w.
Phil. 4. 11. w. speak in respect of w.
James 1. 4. perfect and entire, wanting
WANTONNESS, Rom. 13. 13. 2 Pet. 2. 18.
WAR, Ex. 13. 17. & 17. 16. Ps. 27. 3.
Job 10. 17. changes and w. are against
Ps. 18. 34. teacheth my hands to w. 144. 1.
120. 7. I am for peace, they for w.
Prov. 20. 18. with good advice make w.
Eccl. 8. 8. is no discharge in this w.
Isa. 2. 4. not learn to w. any more, Mic. 4. 3.
Mic. 3. 5. prepare w. against him
2 Cor. 10. 3. we do not w. after flesh
1 Tim. 1. 18. mightest w. a good warfare
1 Pet. 2. 11. fleshly lusts which w.
Rev. 11. 7. beast shall make w.
12. 7. there was w. in heaven
17. 14. these make w. with Lamb
19. 11. in righteousness judge and make w.
Num. 21. 14. in the book of the wars of the Lord
Ps. 46. 9. he maketh w. to cease
Matt. 24. 6. hear of w. and rumours of w.
James 4. 1. whence come w. and
2 Tim. 2. 4. no man that warreth
Isa. 31. 5. warring, Rom. 7. 23.
WARFARE, Isa. 40. 2. 1 Cor. 9. 7.

WAT

2 Cor. 10. 4. 1 Tim. 1. 18.
WARN, 2 Chron. 19. 10. Acts 20. 22.
Ezek. 3. 19. if thou w. the wicked
33. 3. blow the trumpet and w. the people, 9.
Acts 20. 31. I ceased not to w. every one night and day
1 Cor. 4. 14. my beloved sons I w.
1 Thes. 5. 14. w. them that are unruly
Ps. 19. 11. by them is thy servant warned
Matt. 3. 7. who hath w. you to flee
Heb. 11. 7. Noah being w. of God
Jer. 6. 10. to whom I give warning
Col. 1. 28. teaching every man, w.
Ezek. 6. 27. & 14. 15, 16.
Job 9. 30. if I w. myself in snow
Ps. 26. 6. w. my hands in innocency
51. 2. w. me thoroughly from iniquity
7. w. me and I shall be whiter than
58. 10. he shall w. his feet in blood
Isa. 1. 16. w. you, make you clean
Jer. 2. 22. thou w. thee with nitre
4. 14. w. thy heart from wickedness
Luke 7. 8. to w. his feet with tears
John 13. 8. began to w. disciples' feet
5. I w. thee not, thou hast no part
10. needeth not save to w. his feet
14. ought to w. one another's feet
Acts 22. 16. be baptized and w. away
Job 29. 6. when I washed my steps
Song 5. 3. I have w. my feet
Isa. 4. 4. w. away the filth of the daughter of Zion
Ezek. 16. 4. neither wast thou w. in
16. 9. I thoroughly w. away blood
1 Cor. 6. 11. w. are w. justified
Rev. 1. 5. w. us from sins in his blood
7. 14. w. robes, and made white in
Eph. 5. 26. washing, Tit. 3. 5.
WASTE, Ps. 80. 13. Matt. 26, 8.
Luke 15. 11. wasted, 30. 1 Tim. 1. 13.
Job 14. 10. wasteth, Prov. 19. 26.
Prov. 18. 9. waster, Isa. 54. 16.
Isa. 59. 7. wasting and destruction, 60. 18.
WATCH, Neh. 4. 9. Job 7. 12.
Job 14. 15. dost thou not w. over sin
Ps. 102. 7. I w. and am as a sparrow
130. 6. they that w. for morning
141. 3. set a w. before my mouth
Jer. 44. 27. w. over them for evil
Matt. 24. 42. w. for ye know not, 25. 13.
26. 41. w. and pray that ye enter
Mark 13. 34. take heed, w. and, 37.
1 Cor. 16. 13. w. ye, stand fast in the
Col. 4. 2. in the same with thanksgiving
1 Thes. 5. 6. let us w. and be sober
2 Tim. 4. 5. w. thou in all things
Heb. 13. 17. they w. for your souls
1 Pet. 4. 7. be sober, w. unto prayer
Rev. 3. 3. if thou shalt not w. I will
20. 16. familiars so for my hasting
Matt. 24. 43. he would have w.
Ps. 37. 32. the wicked w. the
Ezek. 7. 6. the end is come; it w. for
Rev. 16. 15. blessed is he that w. and
Dan. 4. 13. a watcher and holy one, 17. 23.
Ps. 63. 6. watches, 119. 148. Lam. 2. 19.
Rev. 3. 2. be watchful
Prov. 8. 34. watching daily at gates
Luke 12. 37. blessed whom the Lord shall find so
Eph. 6. 18. w. with all perseverance
2 Cor. 6. 5. in watchings, 11. 27.
Isa. 21. 11. watchman, Isa. 5. 17. & 55. 7.
Song 3. 3. watchmen, 5. 7. Isa. 52. 8. & 56. 10. & 62. 6. Jer. 31. 6.
WATER, Gen. 49. 4. Ex. 12. 9. & 17. 6.
2 Sam. 14. 14. we are as w. spilt on the ground
Job 15. 16. drinketh iniquity like w.
Ps. 22. 14. I am poured out like w.
Isa. 12. 3. draw w. out of the wells of salvation
27. 3. I will w. it every moment
30. 20. give you w. of affliction
44. 17. when poor seek w. and find
44. 3. pour w. on him that is thirsty
58. 11. shall be like a spring of w.
Lam. 1. 16. mine eye runneth down with w. 3. 48.
Ezek. 36. 25. sprinkle clean w. on
Amos 5. 11. nor a thirst for w.
Matt. 3. 11. I baptize you with w.
10. 42. cup of cold w. in name of
Luke 16. 24. dip tip of his finger in w.
John 3. 5. except a man be born of w.
23. baptized because there was much w. there
4. 11. shall be in him a well of w.
7. 38. flow rivers of living w.
19. 34. came thereout blood and w.
Acts 8. 38. both went down into w.
10. 47. can any forbid w. that these
Eph. 5. 26. cleanse it with the washing of w.
1 John 5. 6. he that came by w. and
6. three bear witness, spirit, w. and
Jude 12. clouds they are without w.
Rev. 7. 17. lead them to living fountains of w.
21. 6. fountain of w. of life, 22. 1.
22. 17. take the w. of life freely

WAY

Ps. 23. 2. leadeth me beside the still waters
89. 1. w. are come into my soul, 2.
124. 4. w. had overwhelmed us, 5.
Prov. 5. 15. drink w. out of thine own cistern, and running w. out of thine own well
9. 17. stolen w. are sweet
Eccl. 11. 1. cast thy bread upon w.
Song 4. 15. a well of living w.
Isa. 32. 20. blessed are ye that sow beside all w.
33. 16. bread given him; his w.
35. 6. in wilderness shall w. break out, I give w. in the wilderness
54. 9. this is as w. of Noah unto me
55. 1. come ye to w. buy and eat
58. 11. whose w. fail not
Jer. 2. 13. fountain of living w. 17. 13.
9. 1. O that my head were w.
Hab. 2. 14. as w. cover the sea, Isa. 11. 9.
Zech. 14. 8. living w. shall go out from Jerusalem, Ezek. 47. 1.
Rev. 1. 15. his voice as the sound of many w. 14. 2. & 19. 6.
Prov. 11. 25. he that watereth shall be watered
Isa. 58. 11. be like a w. garden, Jer. 31. 12.
1 Cor. 3. 6. I planted, Apollos w. 7.
Ps. 42. 7. noise of thy waterspouts
WAVERING, Heb. 10. 23. James 1. 6.
WAX, Ex. 32. 10, 11, 22. Ps. 22. 14. & 68. 2. & 97. 5. Matt. 24. 12. Luke 12. 33. 1 Tim. 5. 13. 2 Tim. 3. 13.
WAY, Ex. 13. 21. & 23. 20. & 32. 8.
1 Sam. 12. 23. teach you good and right w.
1 Kings 2. 2. I go w. of all the earth
Ezra 8. 21. seek of him a right w.
Ps. 1. 6. the Lord knoweth the w. of the righteous
2. 12. lest ye perish from the w.
Ps. 49. 13. this their w. is their folly
67. 2. that thy w. may be known
78. 50. made a w. to his anger
119. 30. I have chosen w. of truth
32. run w. of thy commandments
104. I hate every false w.
Prov. 2. 8. Lord preserveth the w. of his saints
10. 29. w. of the Lord is strength
14. 12. a w. that seemeth right
15. 9. w. of wicked is abomination
5. w. of life is above to the wise
Eccl. 11. 5. thou knowest not what is the w. of the spirit
Isa. 26. 7. w. of just is uprightness, 8.
30. 21. this is the w. walk ye in it
35. 8. a high w. and a w. called the w. of holiness
40. 3. prepare the w. of the Lord, Luke 3. 4.
Isa. 43. 19. make a w. in the wilderness, 19.
59. 8. w. of peace they know not
Jer. 6. 16. where is a good w. and
10. 23. w. of man is not in himself
21. 8. set before you the w. of life and the w. of death
32. 39. give them one heart and w.
50. 5. shall ask the w. to Zion
Amos 2. 7. turn aside w. of the meek
Mal. 3. 1. and he shall prepare the w. before me
Matt. 7. 13. broad is w. to destruction
14. narrow is w. that leadeth to life
22. 16. teachest w. of God in truth
John 1. 23. straight the w. of Lord
14. 4. w. ye know, 6. I am the w.
Acts 16. 17. which show unto us the w. of salvation
18. 25. instructed in w. of Lord, 26.
1 Cor. 10. 13. make a w. to escape
12. 31. show you more excellent w.
2 Pet. 2. 2. the w. of truth be evil
1 Kings 8. 32. bring his way on his head
Job 15. 9. righteous shall hold on—
Ps. 18. 30. as for God—is perfect
17. 23. delight in—and keep—
119. 9. shall a young man cleanse—
Prov. 14. 8. prudent to understand—
16. 9. man's heart deviseth—
Isa. 55. 7. let the wicked forsake—
Ps. 78. 8. teach sinners in thy way
139. 24. lead me—everlasting
Isa. 26. 8. in the—of thy judgments we waited
Matt. 5. 25. agree with adversary—
21. 32. John came—of righteousness
Luke 1. 79. guide our feet—of peace
Ps. 84. 5. in whose heart are—of God
Prov. 3. 17. w. are w. of pleasantness
4. 21. w. of man are before Lord
16. 2. w. of man are clean in his
Prov. 16. 7. when a man's w. please
Jer. 7. 3. amend your w. and doings
Lam. 1. 4. the w. of Zion do mourn
3. 4. let us search and try our w.
Deut. 32. 4. his ways, Ps. 145. 17. Isa. 2. 3. Mic. 4. 2. Rom. 11. 33.
Ps. 119. 5. my ways, 15, 26, 59, 168 & 8. & 49. 11.
Prov. 14. 14. own ways, Isa. 53. 6. & 58.

WRI

tow, the remainder of w. shalt thou restrain
Prov. 16. 14. w. of a king is as messengers of death
Isa. 54. 8. in a little w. I hid my face
Hab. 3. 2. in w. remember mercy
Matt. 3. 7. flee from w. to come
Rom. 2. 5. treasure up w. against the day of w.
5. 9. saved from w. through him
12. 19. give place unto w.
13. 5. not only for w. but conscience
Eph. 2. 3. by nature children of w.
4. 26. let not the sun go down on your w.
1 Thes. 1. 10. delivered from the w.
2. 16. w. is come on them to the uttermost
5. 9. not appointed us to w. but to obtain salvation
1 Tim. 2. 8. holy hands without w.
Heb. 11. 27. not fearing w. of king
James 1. 19. slow to speak, slow to w.
20. w. of man worketh not righteousness of God
Rev. 6. 16. from w. of the Lamb
Rev. 12. 12. having great w. because
14. 8. wine of w. of her fornication, 18. 3.
Ezra 8. 22. his wrath, Ps. 2. 5, 12. & 78. 38. Jer. 7. 29. & 10. 10. Rev. 6. 17.
Num. 25. 11. my wrath, Ps. 95. 11. Isa. 10. 6. & 60. 10. Ezek. 7. 14. Hos. 5. 10.
Ps. 38. 1. thy wrath, 85. 3. & 88. 7, 16. & 89. 46. & 90. 9, 11. & 102. 10. 89. 50. wroth, Isa. 54. 9. & 57. 17.
WREST, Ex. 23. 2. 2 Pet. 3. 16.
WRESTLE, Gen. 32. 24, 25. Eph. 6. 12.
WRETCHED, Rom. 7. 24. Rev. 3. 17.
WRINKLE, Job 16. 8. Eph. 5. 27.
WRITE, Ex. 34. 1. 27. Deut. 27. 3. Isa. 3. 8. Jer. 30. 2. Hab. 2. 2.
Deut. 6. 9. w. them upon the posts
Prov. 3. 3. w. them on the table of thine heart, 7. 3.
Jer. 31. 33. I will w. it in their heart
Ps. 69. 28. not be written with the
102. 18. be w. for the generation
Prov. 22. 20. have not I w. to thee
Eccl. 12. 10. that which was w.
Dan. 12. 1. shall be found w. in book
Cor. 10. 11. w. for our admonitions

YOK

2 Cor. 3. 2. epistle w. in our hearts
3. w. not with ink but Spirit of the
Heb. 12. 23. are w. in heaven, Luke 10. 20.
WRONG, Ps. 105. 14. Jer. 22. 3, 13. Matt. 20. 13. I do thee no w. doist
1 Cor. 6. 7. why not rather take w. 8.
Col. 3. 25. that doeth w. shall receive
2 Cor. 7. 2. wronged, Philem. 18.
Prov. 8. 36. wrongeth his own soul
WROUGHT, 1 Sam. 6. 6. & 14. 45.
Ps. 139. 15. curiously w. in lowest parts of the earth
Isa. 26. 12. w. all our works in us
Ezek. 20. 9. I w. for my name's sake, 22.
John 3. 21. his works are w. in God
Rom. 7. 8. w. in me all manner of concupiscence
2 Cor. 5. 5. that hath w. us for the selfsame thing is God
Eph. 1. 20. which he w. in Christ
1 Pet. 4. 3. have w. will of Gentiles

Y.

YEA, yea, nay, nay, Matt. 5. 37.
2 Cor. 1. 18. y. and nay
20. y. and amen
YEAR, acceptable, Isa. 61. 2. Luke 4. 19.
Isa. 63. 4. y. of my redeemed is come
Jer. 11. 23. y. of visitation, 23. 12. & 48. 44.
Job 10. 5. thy years as man's days
15. 20. number of y. is hidden from
Ps. 90. 4. a thousand y. in thy sight
2 Pet. 3. 8. a thousand y. as one day
Rev. 20. 2. bound him a thousand y.
YESTERDAY, Job 8. 9. Hab. 13. 8.
YIELD yourselves. 2 Chron. 30. 8.
Ps. 67. 6. land y. her increase, 85. 12.
Rom. 6. 13. nor y. members instruments of unrighteousness
16. yielded members servants, 19.
Heb. 12. 11. yieldeth peaceable fruit
YOKE, Deut. 28. 48. 1 Kings 12. 4.
Isa. 9. 4. broken the y. of his burden
14. 27. the y. shall be destroyed
Lam. 1. 11. y. of my transgression
3. 27. that he bear y. in his youth
Matt. 11. 29. take my y. upon you
3. my y. is easy and burden light

ZIO

Gal. 5. 1. y. of bondage, Acts 15. 10.
2 Cor. 6. 14. be not unequally yoked
YOU only have I known, Amos 3. 2.
Luke 10. 16. heareth y.
13. 28. and y. yourselves thrust out
2 Cor. 12. 14. I seek not yours but y.
Eph. 2. 1. y. hath he quickened
Col. 1. 21. y. that were sometime
Luke 6. 20. y. is the kingdom of God
1 Cor. 3. 22. all are y. and ye are Christ's, 23.
YOUNG, I have been, Ps. 37. 25.
Isa. 40. 11. gently lead those with y.
1 Tim. 5. 1. entreat the younger men as brethren
14. I will that y. women marry
1 Pet. 5. 5. ye y. submit to elder
1 Kings 18. 12. the Lord from my y.
Job 13. 26. possess iniquities of my y.
Ps. 25. 7. sins of my y.
103. 5. thy y. is renewed as eagle's
Eccl. 11. 9. O young man, in thy y.
10. childhood and y. are vanity
Jer. 2. 2. the kindness of thy y.
1 Tim. 4. 12. man despise thy y.
Prov. 7. 7. youths, Isa. 40. 30.
2 Tim. 2. 22. flee youthful lusts

Z.

ZEAL for Lord, 2 Kings 10. 16.
Ps. 69. 9. the z. of thine house hath
119. 139. my z. hath consumed me
Isa. 9. 7. z. of the Lord will perform
59. 17. I was clad with z. as a cloak
63. 15. where is thy z. and strength
Rom. 10. 2. they have a z. for God
2 Cor. 7. 11. z. yea, what revenge
Phil. 3. 6. concerning z. persecuting
Num. 25. 13. was jealous for his God
Acts 22. 3. I was z. towards God
Tit. 2. 14. people z. of good works
Rev. 3. 19. therefore be z. and repent
Gal. 4. 18. good to be zealously affected in a good thing
ZION, 2 Sam. 5. 7. 1 Kings 8. 1. for Jerusalem, temple or church, 2 Kings 19. 31. Ps. 2. 6. & 9. 11. & 14. 7. & 48. 2, 11, 12. & 146. 10. & 147. 12. Isa. 1. 27. & 2. 3. & 60. 14. & 62. 1. and in about seventy other places.

www.ingramcontent.com/pod-product-compliance
Lightning Source LLC
Chambersburg PA
CBHW021233300426
44111CB00007B/534